Advanced Research and Trends in New Technologies, Software, Human-Computer Interaction, and Communicability

Francisco V. Cipolla-Ficarra
ALAIPO - AINCI, Spain and Italy

A volume in the Advances in Human and Social Aspects of Technology (AHSAT) Book Series

Managing Director: Lindsay Johnston
Production Manager: Jennifer Yoder
Development Editor: Christine Smith
Acquisitions Editor: Kayla Wolfe
Typesetter: Lisandro Gonzalez
Cover Design: Jason Mull

Published in the United States of America by
Information Science Reference (an imprint of IGI Global)
701 E. Chocolate Avenue
Hershey PA 17033
Tel: 717-533-8845
Fax: 717-533-8661
E-mail: cust@igi-global.com
Web site: http://www.igi-global.com

Library of Congress Cataloging-in-Publication Data

Advanced research and trends in new technologies, software, human-computer interaction, and communicability / Francisco V. Cipolla-Ficarra, editor.
pages cm
Includes bibliographical references and index.
ISBN 978-1-4666-4490-8 (hardcover) -- ISBN 978-1-4666-4491-5 (ebook) -- ISBN 978-1-4666-4492-2 (print & perpetual access) 1. Social networks. 2. Electronic commerce. 3. Internet--Social aspects. I. Cipolla-Ficarra, Francisco V. (Francisco Vicente), 1963- editor of compilation.
HM741.A344 2014
302.3--dc23

2013032110

This book is published in the IGI Global book series Advances in Human and Social Aspects of Technology (AHSAT) (ISSN: 2328-1316; eISSN: 2328-1324)

British Cataloguing in Publication Data
A Cataloguing in Publication record for this book is available from the British Library.

All work contributed to this book is new, previously-unpublished material. The views expressed in this book are those of the authors, but not necessarily of the publisher.

For electronic access to this publication, please contact: eresources@igi-global.com.

Advances in Human and Social Aspects of Technology (AHSAT) Book Series

Ashish Dwivedi
The University of Hull, UK

ISSN: 2328-1316
EISSN: 2328-1324

Mission

In recent years, the societal impact of technology has been noted as we become increasingly more connected and are presented with more digital tools and devices. With the popularity of digital devices such as cell phones and tablets, it is crucial to consider the implications of our digital dependence and the presence of technology in our everyday lives.

The **Advances in Human and Social Aspects of Technology (AHSAT) Book Series** seeks to explore the ways in which society and human beings have been affected by technology and how the technological revolution has changed the way we conduct our lives as well as our behavior. The AHSAT book series aims to publish the most cutting-edge research on human behavior and interaction with technology and the ways in which the digital age is changing society.

Coverage

- Activism & ICTs
- Computer-Mediated Communication
- Cultural Influence of ICTs
- Cyber Behavior
- End-User Computing
- Gender & Technology
- Human-Computer Interaction
- Information Ethics
- Public Access to ICTs
- Technoself

IGI Global is currently accepting manuscripts for publication within this series. To submit a proposal for a volume in this series, please contact our Acquisition Editors at Acquisitions@igi-global.com or visit: http://www.igi-global.com/publish/.

The Advances in Human and Social Aspects of Technology (AHSAT) Book Series (ISSN 2328-1316) is published by IGI Global, 701 E. Chocolate Avenue, Hershey, PA 17033-1240, USA, www.igi-global.com. This series is composed of titles available for purchase individually; each title is edited to be contextually exclusive from any other title within the series. For pricing and ordering information please visit http://www.igi-global.com/book-series/advances-human-social-aspects-technology/37145. Postmaster: Send all address changes to above address.

Titles in this Series

For a list of additional titles in this series, please visit: www.igi-global.com

Emerging Research and Trends in Interactivity and the Human-Computer Interface
Katherine Blashki (Noroff University College, Norway) and Pedro Isaias (Portuguese Open University, Portugal)
Information Science Reference • copyright 2014 • 580pp • H/C (ISBN: 9781466646230) • US $175.00 (our price)

Creating Personal, Social, and Urban Awareness through Pervasive Computing
Bin Guo (Northwestern Polytechnical University, China) Daniele Riboni (University of Milano, Italy) and Peizhao Hu (NICTA, Australia)
Information Science Reference • copyright 2014 • 440pp • H/C (ISBN: 9781466646957) • US $175.00 (our price)

User Behavior in Ubiquitous Online Environments
Jean-Eric Pelet (KMCMS, IDRAC International School of Management, University of Nantes, France) and Panagiota Papadopoulou (University of Athens, Greece)
Information Science Reference • copyright 2014 • 325pp • H/C (ISBN: 9781466645660) • US $175.00 (our price)

Innovative Methods and Technologies for Electronic Discourse Analysis
Hwee Ling Lim (The Petroleum Institute-Abu Dhabi, UAE) and Fay Sudweeks (Murdoch University, Australia)
Information Science Reference • copyright 2014 • 546pp • H/C (ISBN: 9781466644267) • US $175.00 (our price)

Advanced Research and Trends in New Technologies, Software, Human-Computer Interaction, and Communicability
Francisco Vicente Cipolla-Ficarra (ALAIPO – AINCI, Spain and Italy)
Information Science Reference • copyright 2014 • 361pp • H/C (ISBN: 9781466644908) • US $175.00 (our price)

New Media Influence on Social and Political Change in Africa
Anthony A. Olorunnisola (Pennsylvania State University, USA) and Aziz Douai (University of Ontario Institute of Technology, Canada)
Information Science Reference • copyright 2013 • 373pp • H/C (ISBN: 9781466641976) • US $175.00 (our price)

Cases on Usability Engineering Design and Development of Digital Products
Miguel A. Garcia-Ruiz (Algoma University, Canada)
Information Science Reference • copyright 2013 • 470pp • H/C (ISBN: 9781466640467) • US $175.00 (our price)

Human Rights and Information Communication Technologies Trends and Consequences of Use
John Lannon (University of Limerick, Ireland) and Edward Halpin (Leeds Metropolitan University, UK)
Information Science Reference • copyright 2013 • 324pp • H/C (ISBN: 9781466619180) • US $175.00 (our price)

Collaboration and the Semantic Web Social Networks, Knowledge Networks, and Knowledge Resources
Stefan Brüggemann (Astrium Space Transportation, Germany) and Claudia d'Amato (University of Bari, Italy)
Information Science Reference • copyright 2012 • 387pp • H/C (ISBN: 9781466608948) • US $175.00 (our price)

www.igi-global.com

701 E. Chocolate Ave., Hershey, PA 17033
Order online at www.igi-global.com or call 717-533-8845 x100
To place a standing order for titles released in this series, contact: cust@igi-global.com
Mon-Fri 8:00 am - 5:00 pm (est) or fax 24 hours a day 717-533-8661

Editorial Advisory Board

Table of Contents

Detailed Table of Contents

Preface xxxii

Acknowledgment xxxix

Chapter 1
Software and Emerging Technologies for Education, Culture, Entertainment, and Commerce 1
Francisco V. Cipolla-Ficarra, ALAIPO – AINCI, Spain and Italy

In the chapter, the author makes a first description of a set of topics that have been interrelated for a long time among themselves but have acquired special attention in the context of the scientific research of the new millennium. The author resorts to a set of techniques of the social sciences (rhetoric) to decipher some of the main problems through which these interrelations are going in the South of Europe, for instance, education and work imposed by a perennial parochialism, showing some solutions that may constitute future lines of research.

Chapter 2
A Practical Setup for Projection-Based Augmented Maps 13
Filippo Bergamasco, Dipartimento di Scienze Ambientali, Informatica e Statistica, Università Ca'Foscari di Venezia, Italy
Andrea Albarelli, Dipartimento di Scienze Ambientali, Informatica e Statistica, Università Ca'Foscari di Venezia, Italy
Andrea Torsello, Dipartimento di Scienze Ambientali, Informatica e Statistica, Università Ca'Foscari di Venezia, Italy

In the chapter, the authors introduce a novel projected augmented reality setup where the user can explore geographically located information by moving a passive physical inspection tool over a printed map. A simple yet effective calibration procedure has been developed to let the system locate and project images on the tool simulating an active tablet-like device. After a detailed explanation of the inner working of the system, they show an example application in which a high resolution aerial view of Venice is superimposed to an old lithography of the same area through the inspection tool that acts like a simulated magnifying glass.

Chapter 3
A Study on Emotion Releasing Effect with Music and Color 23
Chih-Fang Huang, Department of Information Communications, Kainan University, Taiwan
Chih-Hsiang Liang, Department of Information Communication, Yuan Ze University, Taiwan
En-Ju Lin, Department of Musicology, Heidelberg University, Germany

The chapter presents an innovative way for the music emotion model to introduce the possible emotional response during music listening, including music structure, listener's background, and surroundings. The related research for human physical and psychological influence by the automatically generated electronic sound will be discussed with the emotion releasing effect of music. Various emotional responses derived by various colors are applied to the music emotion model to break the limitation of the existing music forms and to develop the possible music color synesthesia applied to all aspects. Two experiments of color and music emotion synesthesia for both musicians and non-musicians showed a consistent result that the music and color integrated system can reinforce the releasing emotion with the proposed synesthesia system, regardless of the musical background of the listeners.

Chapter 4
An Algorithm for Occlusion-Free Texture Mapping from Oriented Images 32
Mattia Previtali, Department of Building Environmental Science and Technology, Politecnico di Milano, Italy
Marco Scaioni, Tongji University - College of Surveying and Geo-Informatics, Center for Spatial Information Science and Sustainable Development Applicatoins, Shanghai, P.R. China
Luigi Barazzetti, Department of Building Environmental Science and Technology, Politecnico di Milano, Italy
Raffaella Brumana, Department of Building Environmental Science and Technology, Politecnico di Milano, Italy
Daniela Oreni, Department of Building Environmental Science and Technology, Politecnico di Milano, Italy

In the chapter, the authors present a new methodology able to reconstruct the original texture of 3D objects to obtain a photorealist visualization. A series of geometric and radiometric problems are taken into account. In particular, possible self-occlusions are considered in order to prevent wrong mapping situations. In case the object is textured using different images, the transition between an image to another one should be sufficiently smooth in order to prevent a sharp color change due to a difference in both color and brightness. The final aim is the creation of realistic, detailed, and accurate models with a correct correspondence between the geometric part and its visual appearance: the final model must represent the material and its real color.

Chapter 5
Anti-Models for Universitary Education: Analysis of the Catalans Cases in Information and Communication Technologies.. 43
Francisco V. Cipolla-Ficarra, ALAIPO – AINCI, Spain and Italy
Valeria M. Ficarra, ALAIPO – AINCI, Spain and Italy

The authors highlight the conformation and functional maintenance of educational antimodels in the field of computer science and multimedia. The current work presents a table of heuristic evaluation under the acronym EEE: Evaluation of the Excellence in Education, that is, detecting the failings in the alleged education of university excellence. It has been developed through a many years' experience in the Catalan universities with some extensions in the Lombardy system.

Chapter 6
Application of Verification Techniques to Security: Model Checking Insider Attacks 61
Florian Kammüller, DTU Copenhagen, Denmark
Christian W. Probst, Middlesex University, UK
Franco Raimondi, Middlesex University, UK

The authors examined one of the aspects of great interest for the support of security of real-world systems with mechanized verification techniques, for example, model checking. An interesting summed-up state of the art has been included by the authors. There is also an interesting bibliography, which may be looked at by those interested in broadening the concepts that the authors present in the research work.

Chapter 7
Banking Online: Design for a New Credibility 71
Francisco V. Cipolla-Ficarra, ALAIPO – AINCI, Spain and Italy
Jaqueline Alma, Electronic Arts – Vancouver, Canada

In the research, the authors analyze the loss of credibility of online banking information. They indicate the financial risks for the consumer of banking services through the bogus or non-veridical contents of online publicity. In this sense, the first results of an evaluation of European bank Websites highlighting the main failings in the usability and communicability of said Websites are presented.

Chapter 8
Building Recommendation Service with Social Networks and Semantic Databases 83
Sašo Karakatič, Institute of Informatics (FERI), University of Maribor, Slovenia
Vili Podgorelec, Institute of Informatics (FERI), University of Maribor, Slovenia
Marjan Heričko, Institute of Informatics (FERI), University of Maribor, Slovenia

In the work, the authors research the integration of social networks and semantic databases. The work consists of an overview of popular social networks with API and looks into one of the popular semantic Internet databases, Freebase. The authors describe in detail how a working hybrid recommendation service can be built with the integration of the popular Facebook social network and previously mentioned semantic database. The main focus of the detailed description is on the machine learning algorithm based on the "k nearest neighbors" classification algorithm. The authors give detailed information of how the algorithm is used to find the recommendation for specific users based on the users' preferences. Finally, the service that recommends movies, music, literature, and games is presented.

Chapter 9
Cloud-Assisted Services for Mobile Applications: CLASS-MA.. 93
Domen Verber, Institute of Informatics (FERI), University of Maribor, Slovenia

In the chapter, the author discusses mobile applications that are assisted with services provided by the Cloud. This combines the two most pervasive topics within information technology today: Cloud computing and mobile computing. The chapter describes the challenges and opportunities offered by these technologies and the issues arising during their implementation. Some representative Cloud services for mobile applications are offered as part of an on-going CLASS research project.

Chapter 10
Context-Aware Mobile System for Public Bus Transportation 102
Mitja Krajnc, Institute of Informatics (FERI), University of Maribor, Slovenia
Vili Podgorelec, Institute of Informatics (FERI), University of Maribor, Slovenia
Marjan Heričko, Institute of Informatics (FERI), University of Maribor, Slovenia

In the chapter, the authors present a convergence of smartphones and context data into a smart mobile application for the public bus transportation. Their goal was to enhance user experience through adaptation of information shown to the user. Contextual awareness was identified as a suitable basis for such adaptation. Furthermore, they have identified constraints for mobile applications, and in order to overcome them, they have designed a system where smartphones are used only to present information and collect context data. All data processing is executed remotely on a Web server. The completed mobile system collects the user's location, identity, and current time. Together with his history, the goal of the system is to predict the appropriate bus lane and identify the closest bus station.

Chapter 11
Educational Social Networks as a Means for Better Social Cohesion in Education 112
Vili Podgorelec, Institute of Informatics (FERI), University of Maribor, Slovenia
Maša Dobrina, Institute of Informatics (FERI), University of Maribor, Slovenia

In the chapter, the authors study and analyze the contribution of social networks to the enhanced sense of community in educational environments. In their work, the authors discuss if social networks are effective in decreasing social and psychological distance in (online) education and in contributing to the benefits of social cohesion in education. Their research focused on how social relations in the classroom are portrayed on the Internet in social networks and how it affects success in education. In this regard, a study has been performed in which the survey data from 151 university students has been thoroughly analyzed and the results and conclusions are presented in a detailed way.

Chapter 12
Semantic Web Services-Based Knowledge Management Framework 121
Vili Podgorelec, Institute of Informatics (FERI), University of Maribor, Slovenia
Boštjan Grašič, Institute of Informatics (FERI), University of Maribor, Slovenia

In the chapter, the authors study the possibilities, strengths, and weaknesses of new information technologies, especially Semantic Web technologies, for enabling holistic knowledge management in organizations. By analyzing modern information systems, the authors have found a gap between technology and needs that arise in organizations and argue that knowledge, not IT, provides competitive advantage for organizations, while the role of IT should be to help to identify opportunities, follow, and support changes. In this manner, the authors provide a knowledge management framework, based on Semantic Web technologies and service-oriented architecture, for holistic knowledge management and integration with modern IT architecture that enables business agility. As the framework is based on accepted industry standards, there is a good support for underlying infrastructure technologies.

Chapter 13
Universality and Communicability in Computer Animation 131
Francisco V. Cipolla-Ficarra, ALAIPO – AINCI, Spain and Italy
Miguel Cipolla-Ficarra, ALAIPO – AINCI, Spain and Italy

The evaluation of the content and the realism of computer graphics, video, audio, etc., in the 2D and 3D computer animations is the main issue of the chapter. Its authors examine a universe of study aimed at the infantile and/or adult audience. The obtained results serve to stress the positive and negative elements when those audiovisual productions are aimed at the infantile and/or adult public, as it can be seen in the learned lessons section and the conclusion. Those results may serve as a guide to the designers of 2D and 3D animations, irrespective of the age of the targeted audience of those computer-animated contents, whether in the classical or current interactive multimedia systems.

Chapter 14
Learning by Means of an Interactive Multimodal Environment 143
Serena Zanolla, Department of Mathematics and Computer Science, University of Udine, Italy
Sergio Canazza, Department of Information Engineering, University of Padova, Italy
Antonio Rodà, Department of Information Engineering, University of Padova, Italy
Gian Luca Foresti, Department of Mathematics and Computer Science, University of Udine, Italy

The Stanza Logo-Motoria (SLM), a technological system used in real educational contexts in order to teach pupils by implementing a multimodal and interactive learning experience, is presented. In particular, by means of the SLM, it is possible to actualize an Interactive Multimodal Environment in which whatever happens depends on the learner's actions. The SLM takes a broad empty space and, using video tracking techniques, fills the environment with sound events and images; the user's presence inside the "interactive space" triggers the playback of the audio/visual content. The authors also describe in detail Resonant Memory, the first application for the Stanza Logo-Motoria, and the positive partial results of a preliminary study, which was conducted using the system as a listening tool in English as a Second Language (ESL) classes.

Chapter 15
Learning Computer Vision through the Development of a Camera-Trackable Game Controller 154
Andrea Albarelli, Dipartimento di Scienze Ambientali, Informatica e Statistica, Università Ca' Foscari di Venezia, Italy
Filippo Bergamasco, Dipartimento di Scienze Ambientali, Informatica e Statistica, Università Ca' Foscari di Venezia, Italy
Andrea Torsello, Dipartimento di Scienze Ambientali, Informatica e Statistica, Università Ca' Foscari di Venezia, Italy

The authors explore how some basic computer vision concepts can be effectively taught to prospective students who have little or no previous background in programming and strongly diversified knowledge with respect to mathematics. In the chapter, a detailed description of the setup for the laboratory lecture is presented along with the outline of the lessons that gently guides the students to the development of a vision-based game controller similar to the interfaces currently adopted in modern game consoles.

In the chapter, the author illustrates the contribution of projective geometry and automated matching techniques to several photographic applications: high dynamic range, multi-focus, and panoramic photography. Although very different, the processing algorithm relies on a similar workflow, where a set of projective transformations is used to align different images. All these products can be created in an almost fully automated way, allowing expert operators or normal tourists to overcome some drawbacks of single shots. After a brief review of the most common 2D transformations, it will be demonstrated that a homography can be successfully used to register images and create HDR, multi-focus, and panoramic images.

In the chapter, the authors discuss different perspectives around inclusion and accessibility in higher education through the analysis of a conducted strategy at the University Teaching Department, University of Costa Rica. The chosen case portrays a set of actions, goals, and measures necessary to overcome challenges in a given learning context. Furthermore, one of the elements implemented—a game activity—is taken up to understand the relevance that falls between any didactical domain in its connection with the pedagogical sphere at universities. In this chapter, the authors claim there are decisive elements in play at such structures, every time we aim for meaningful learning within large groups of individuals.

The chapter presents a Music Emotion Classification (MEC) method referring to the music cognition of mind with the categorized emotion result mapping music parameters. The synthesized meta-level algorithmic music based on the analysis result from the previous research, with the proposed Emotion Map System (EMS) mapped into the innovated Wu Xing Emotion Map System (WXEMS) indicates the emotion situation based on the X-Y coordinate movement in the WXEMS plane. The MEC result shown in the EMS/WXEMS trajectory controls the algorithmic music variation with the proposed mapping rules, and the generative music will vary smoothly according to the correspondent WXEMS data changed with any emotion transition. The methodology of the WXEMS for the generative music can be applied to automated background music for game and multimedia.

Chapter 19
Prediction of Change-Prone Classes Using Machine Learning and Statistical Techniques 193
LinRuchika Malhotra, Deptament of Software Engineering, Delhi Technological University, India
Ankita Jain Bansal, Deptament of Software Engineering, Delhi Technological University, India

The authors work on predicting the quality attribute (change proneness) in the early phases of the software development life cycle. This would lead to efficient and effective utilization of resources (time, money, and manpower). Besides this, developers get an insight about the design of the software by correctly predicting the change-prone classes. The authors have worked on two versions of an open source software, Frinika (a complete music workstation software). The classes, which are common to both the versions, are extracted and analyzed. Various object-oriented metrics are calculated for these common classes, and their relationship with change proneness has been determined. Then, using the significant metrics, various machine learning and statistical models are constructed to predict change proneness. The study shows that the machine-learning methods are more efficient than regression techniques. Among the machine-learning methods, boosting technique (i.e., Logitboost) outperformed all the other models.

Chapter 20
Storyboard and Computer Animation for Children: Communicability Evaluation 203
Francisco V. Cipolla-Ficarra, ALAIPO – AINCI, Spain and Italy
Alejandra Quiroga, Universidad Nacional de La Pampa, Argentina
Jim Carré, University of The Netherlands Antilles, Curaçao

The chapter presents the results of a heuristic evaluation of the main components of the narration and communicability in computer-made animations, which are based on literary works. It analyzed the animated series in 3D and with international diffusion, "The Little Prince." It reveals some of the keys of graphic computer science and storyboards that help hold the attention of a variegated public, whose ages range from children to adults.

Chapter 21
New Generation of Artificial Intelligence for Real-Time Strategy Games 220
Damijan Novak, Institute of Informatics (FERI), University of Maribor, Slovenia
Domen Verber, Institute of Informatics (FERI), University of Maribor, Slovenia

In the chapter, the authors present and compare different open-source real-time strategy game development tools, and they also propose an enhanced combat artificial intelligence algorithm. First, the role of AI in computer games is explained. Next, the focus of the work is to summarize the biggest challenges of AI in computer games. After the open source RTS development tools are presented, a detailed description of the evaluation function and strategies for advanced players are discussed. At the end, implementation of the game AI bot, "Omar Bradley," is presented.

Chapter 22
Static Graphics for Dynamic Information 230
Francisco V. Cipolla-Ficarra, ALAIPO – AINCI, Spain and Italy
Jacqueline Alma, Electronic Arts – Vancouver, Canada

The authors reveal the validity of the main aspects of traditional design in paper support for the static graphic information online when it refers to economic and/or financial information, as well as its derivations in the social context. The corpus of the analysis is the result of several decades of compilation of graphic information in the mass media focused on the graphic evolution of this information. The conclusions of the publicity banners on the online pages of economic and financial information are also presented. The research work presents results of experiments made in a human-computer interaction lab.

Chapter 23
Mashing-Up Weather Networks Data to Support Hydro-Meteorological Research 245
Tatiana Bedrina, CIMA Research Foundation, Savona, Italy
Antonio Parodi, CIMA Research Foundation, Savona, Italy
Andrea Clematis, Institute of Applied Mathematics and Information Technology, National Research Council, Genoa, Italy
Alfonso Quarati, Institute of Applied Mathematics and Information Technology, National Research Council, Genoa, Italy

In the chapter, the authors present the use of Internet technologies for the collection and visualization of geoscentific data. The work aimed at the designing of a Web mashup for the aggregation of meteorological variables published online. In addition, the authors analyze conflict resolution and thoroughly describe the details for an easy implementation of hydro-meteorological data. A series of experiments have been carried out, and the results are presented.

Chapter 24
Negative Exponent Fraction: A Strategy for a New Virtual Image into the Financial Sector 255
Francisco V. Cipolla-Ficarra, ALAIPO – AINCI, Spain and Italy

The chapter releases the results of the analysis, applying semiotics, in the online corporative communication strategies, to which are resorting the financial, banking institutions, etc. in Spanish and Italian networks, to keep and/or attract new clients to those institutions. Simultaneously, it is seen how currently the quality attributes related to transparency, credibility, and/or veracity of the online information is equal to zero in many banking and/or financial Websites. Finally, the authors present failings in the interactive design categories related to the universality of the contents.

Chapter 25
Co-Designing Novel Interior Design Services that Utilise Augmented Reality: A Case Study 269
Tiina Kymäläinen, VTT Technical Research Centre of Finland – Tampere, Finland
Sanni Siltanen, VTT Technical Research Centre of Finland – Espoo, Finland

In the chapter, the authors present a case study that aimed at developing interior design concepts and service ecosystem descriptions that exploited Augmented Reality (AR), 3D models, and user-generated content. The concepts and systems were co-designed with designers, bloggers, and serious amateurs in the field of interior design. The chapter describes the co-design process with critical users and illustrates the possibilities and challenges of a chosen key technology, augmented reality, for interior design.

Chapter 26
Art, Future, and New Technologies: Research or Business? 280
Francisco V. Cipolla-Ficarra, ALAIPO – AINCI, Spain and Italy
Valeria M. Ficarra, ALAIPO – AINCI, Spain and Italy

Through an evaluation technique called CASTE (Computer Art, Software, and Technology Evaluation), the authors show how the human factors not only contaminate scientific knowledge in the universities and research centres of the Iberian Peninsula but also the neutral diffusion of said knowledge. The work investigates the resources used through the social communication media online, for instance, for the international expansion of computer art and the new technologies used for its realization through the opacity of the online contents. A set of rhetoric questions make up the base of the obtained results.

Chapter 27
Reality-Based 3D Modelling from Images and Laser Scans: Combining Accuracy and Automation 294
Luigi Barazzetti, Department of Building Environmental Science and Technology, Politecnico di Milano, Italy
Marco Scaioni, Tongji University - College of Surveying and Geo-Informatics, Center for Spatial Information Science and Sustainable Development Applicatoins, Shanghai, P.R. China

In the chapter, the authors illustrate modern instruments and techniques for 3D modeling of complex objects. Different examples and real case studies are taken into consideration, starting from cultural heritage documentation and preservation up to architectural, geological, and structural applications. Several instruments (total station, GNSS, cameras, and laser scanners) and procedures for data integration, orientation, and registration are discussed along with the achievable information and its intrinsic accuracy. The aim of this work was to prove how the combined use of photogrammetric and computer vision techniques coupled with modern sensors for data acquisition and algorithms for data processing is a powerful tool to obtain accurate, detailed, reliable, precise, and complete 3D reconstructions.

Chapter 28
Differences between Role of Strong Ties and Weak Ties in Information Diffusion on Social Network Sites 307
Sanaz Kavianpour, Advanced Informatics School, Universiti Teknologi Malaysia, Kuala Lumpur, Malaysia
Zuraini Ismail, Advanced Informatics School, Universiti Teknologi Malaysia, Kuala Lumpur, Malaysia
Bharanidharan Shanmugam, Advanced Informatics School, Universiti Teknologi Malaysia, Kuala Lumpur, Malaysia

The authors present information propagation through social network sites and describe the factors that have a significant role in information diffusion. The results illustrate that among all the significant factors, users play an important role in information diffusion; in addition, their controlling from different aspects like the number and the strength can be used in order to manage the received information to rebroadcast or block it. Then a comparison of the number, influence, and the probability of information dissemination by strong ties and weak ties is made in order to compare the role of ties in spreading information and evaluating the strength of ties. The comparison results show that although strong ties have an important role, the likelihood of information diffusion by weak ties is higher.

Chapter 29
Degree of Similarity of Web Applications 312
Doru Anastasiu Popescu, Faculty of Mathematics and Computer Science, University of Pitesti, Romania
Dragos Nicolae, National College "Radu Greceanu" – Slatina, Romania

In the chapter, the authors present a method of measuring the similarity between two Web applications. The Web applications used in this chapter use HTML constructive elements. This method is based on a new formula for determining similarity of Web pages relative to a Web application, and it does not take into account a number of fixed tags, a TG set. After introducing the basic concepts necessary to calculate the similarity between two Web pages, there is an example and an algorithm together with some results obtained by its implementation in Java. TG sets used to test the program written in Java are increasingly larger in order to view their importance in measuring the similarity of two Web applications built using HTML tags.

Chapter 30
Museum Information and Communicability Evaluation 319
Francisco V. Cipolla-Ficarra, ALAIPO – AINCI, Spain and Italy
Alejandra Quiroga, Universidad Nacional de La Pampa, Argentina
Jim Carré, University of The Netherlands Antilles, Curaçao
Jacqueline Alma, Electronic Arts – Vancouver, Canada
Miguel Cipolla-Ficarra, ALAIPO – AINCI, Spain and Italy

The authors of the chapter show the results of a diachronic analysis of the interactive design of the off-line multimedia systems (commercial and with international distribution), from 1990 until 2012, whose contents are related to European museums. They present a methodology called "abc" for the presentation of the interactive information related to cultural heritage, such as painting and sculpture. In the current research work and through linguistics and semiotics aimed at the main notions of the hypertext, the multimedia and hypermedia establishes a "escamotage" to speed up the evaluation tasks with regard to the different categories that make up the interactive design.

Chapter 31
Rough Set Analysis and Short-Medium Term Tourist Services Demand Forecasting 341
Emilio Celotto, Department of Management, Ca' Foscari University of Venice, Italy
Andrea Ellero, Department of Management, Ca' Foscari University of Venice, Italy
Paola Ferretti, Department of Economics and SSE, Ca' Foscari University of Venice, Italy

The authors apply Rough Sets Theory to analyze Italian tourist behaviour. The study uses a set of statistical surveys on households, life conditions, incomes, consumptions, travels, and holidays. Data, which are provided by GfK Eurisko, concern social, cultural, and behavioural trends in Italy. Interesting relations, in terms of decision rules, between consumer behaviours and tourism consumption are detected. For example, they find that people who read books, go to the cinema, or have other cultural interests most likely also go on vacation. This kind of information could then be used, as the authors claim, in order to find some "sentry variables" for tourism consumption.

Chapter 32
The Promotion of European Tourism in the Emerging Countries: Pyramidal Marketing 350
Francisco V. Cipolla-Ficarra, ALAIPO – AINCI, Spain and Italy
Alejandra Quiroga, Universidad Nacional de La Pampa, Argentina
Valeria M. Ficarra, ALAIPO – AINCI, Spain and Italy

The authors present a set of strategies of the European pyramidal marketing to appeal to potential tourists from emerging countries through the use of commercial software such as the presentations made with PowerPoint. The universe of study, the results obtained with different types of users, and the lessons learned have served to elaborate the conclusions, where the interrelation of the widely diffused software among the users of the emerging countries with the human and social factors from the Old World is made apparent, that is, European users who use the electronic mail to promote tourism, through the pyramid system.

Chapter 33
"Cozinha da Madeira": A Sustainable Tourism Service Concept for Madeira Island 364
Valentina Nisi, Madeira-ITI, University of Madeira – Funchal, Portugal
Nuno Nunes, Carnegie Mellon University, USA
Kanarak Isarankura, Carnegie Mellon University, USA
Jodi Forlizzi, Madeira-ITI, University of Madeira – Funchal, Portugal

The chapter shows how we can leverage tourism, cultural and natural heritage, etc. in order to promote sustainable services and experiences. Through a collection of examples, a perfect amalgam between new technologies and avant-garde perspectives can be seen in order to approach complex issues such as international tourism on European island.

Chapter 34
Story Objects: An Interactive Installation to Excavate Immigrant History and Identity through Evocative Everyday Objects 377
Andreas Kratky, Institute for Multimedia Literacy, University of Southern California, USA
Daphne Ho, School of Cinematic Arts, University of Southern California, USA

The authors present a method of using computer-based interactive media to foster the intergenerational communication in immigrant families. The authors characterize the reasons and effects of the communication problems for the acculturation process and the chances of immigrants to integrate into a new cultural setting. They devise an installation joining psychological factors, storytelling, and a tangible interface linking familiar food objects through RFID technology to a computer system. The text explains the conceptual considerations and the design process of the installation explaining how it was targeted to be relevant for different immigrant groups. The system was exhibited and tested with a diverse immigrant audience to obtain first results on its effectiveness.

Chapter 35
Teaching Human–Computer Interaction in the Capital of Culture 388
Damjan Obal, Institute of Informatics (FERI), University of Maribor, Slovenia
Domen Verber, Institute of Informatics (FERI), University of Maribor, Slovenia

In the chapter, the authors illustrate the process of teaching HCI to Media Communication students at the University of Maribor in Slovenia. They describe how they modified the Double Diamond design process and combined it with their own EPUI (Explore-Participate-Understand-Integrate) methodology for integrating all key stakeholders in the design process.

Chapter 36
Design and Behaviour Computer Animation for Children 401
Francisco V. Cipolla-Ficarra, ALAIPO – AINCI, Spain and Italy
Jacqueline Alma, Electronic Arts – Vancouver, Canada
Jim Carré, University of The Netherlands Antilles, Curaçao
Miguel Cipolla-Ficarra, ALAIPO – AINCI, Spain and Italy

The authors present a set of experiments carried out to establish the basic criteria of the high quality inside computer graphics and the behaviour computer animation. The conformation of the universe of study is related to the child audience with didactical purposes. The authors explain in detail the stages of the evaluative process since the selections of the computer-made 3D animations aimed at the traditional audiovisual communication until the obtained results. This process examines the main elements of the triad design, communicability, and pedagogy.

Chapter 37
Generic Textile Structure Editor 413
Georges Győry, Birkbeck, University of London, UK

The author describes the SAWU104 textile editor (freeware, downloadable from CNET). This can be used to document non-rectilinear textiles like lace, sprang, netting, tricot, etc. or for knot diagrams. It can visualise the underlying structure of the textiles (as opposed to photographic images showing one face of it). Its original use is to document efficiently museum pieces and show the techniques applied in their construction, allowing a weaver to reproduce them. This chapter describes its (linked) data structure, graphical user interface, set of operators, and gives some non-trivial examples of use.

Chapter 38
Bi-Manual 3D Painting: An Interaction Paradigm for Augmented Reality Live Performance 423
Alexis Clay, ESTIA, Bidart, France
Jean-Christophe Lombardo, INRIA, Sophia Antipolis, France
Nadine Couture, LaBRI/ESTIA, Bidart, France
Julien Conan, ESTIA, Bidart, France

The authors explore how manual interactions could be achieved in a CAVE. ISIVR is the 3D engine being developed at INRIA (Sophia Antipolis, France), which focuses on augmented reality and device implementation. It provides a cluster, position tracking, and multi-display. In a second part, they develop a mobile prototype composed of MVN motion capture suit and 5DT Datagloves at ESTIA (Bidart, France). It can track the whole skeleton of a professional dancer on stage and display visual augmentations to a large audience at the same time. Both prototypes are being used to explore manual interactions and improve user interactions with virtual matter.

Chapter 39
Towards a Cyber-Destructors Assessment Method 431
Francisco V. Cipolla-Ficarra, ALAIPO – AINCI, Spain and Italy
Alejandra Quiroga, Universidad Nacional de La Pampa, Argentina
Jacqueline Alma, Electronic Arts – Vancouver, Canada

The authors present the modus operandi of cyberdestructors. The method of analysis is the result of the intersection of formal and factual sciences, which allow the attacks to be detected online through the social networks by pressure groups although they act in an anonymous and individual way. The study presents the confirmation of the attacks groups and the psychological/psychiatric profile of their members and the Internet resources they use to carry out their destructive actions. Finally, the first patterns of behavior and negative values detected among the cyberdestroyers are summed up.

Chapter 40
(Re)Engineering Cultural Heritage Contexts using Creative Human Computer Interaction Techniques and Mixed Reality Methodologies 441
Carl Smith, Learning Technology Research Institute, London Metropolitan University, UK

The author presents the current state of location-based technology including Mobile Augmented Reality (MAR) and Global Positioning Systems (GPS). The focus will be on its application for use within cultural heritage as an educational and outreach tool. A wide range of examples allows one to quickly confront the uses of these Information and Communication Technologies (ICT). The conclusions are a series of future lines of research, which open new fields of research for all those interested in the issues.

Chapter 41
Knowledge and Background of the Multimedia Culture: A Study of the Spatio-Temporal Context in Claymation and Computer Animation for Children and Adults.. 452
Francisco V. Cipolla-Ficarra, ALAIPO – AINCI, Spain and Italy
Miguel Cipolla-Ficarra, ALAIPO – AINCI, Spain and Italy
Jacqueline Alma, Electronic Arts – Vancouver, Canada

The authors present the importance of multimedia culture, developed by the users of the interactive systems, across time, with the goal of increasing the quality of the contents in mobile multimedia phones. The study made and the results reached allow one to see the existence of common areas, in the union of the users of the interactive systems, irrespective of their age and the experience accumulated in the use of computers. The chapter presents a comparative work between digital animation (2D and 3D) and analog (claymation).

The authors present the results obtained within the framework of the research project that consists of the design of a basic model from an e-culture system that can promote and disseminate world cultures. Culture as a complex phenomenon is studied from the Systemic Paradigm, which is optimized by the transdisciplinary features that allows the concurrence of other complementary perspectives. The methodic process consists of the systemic modelling process and the retroprospective methodology that involves the use of models and scenarios. Through analogy simulation, using the technique of syntegration for the processing of empirical evidence, the validation of an operative model is presented. The results confirm the selected features of a local culture and generate a more general and comprehensive model, which could be of value to other cultures.

Scientific knowledge derived from the field of ICTs, such as marketing, is the central topic of the chapter. Its authors make known the main human factors that increase the digital divide and university parochialism. Through the rhetoric, it can be seen how the scientific knowledge stemming from the context of the ICTs are not neutral. The chapter presents a set of real examples online where that scientific-technologic knowledge is treated like a marketing object, mainly in the field of the scientific publications. Lastly, the authors indicate the need to establish a new language style to tackle the negative human factors in the era of the expansion of communication.

The authors present the research, development, and findings of a communication technology developed to enable older adults living in retirement communities to share public events. The project draws reference from the fields of industrial design, universal design, and computer science to design a technology for residents at a retirement community. Residents were included in the design process by evaluating designed technologies. Their project demonstrates the relevance of designing simple yet innovative technologies that meet the needs of older adults.

The authors present a different way to combine two big technologies that give a great opportunity to handicapped people. They discuss the increase of handicapped people and show a solution to this problem. In this prototype, the authors developed a software that interprets the signals given by the Mindwave sensor, and through an Arduino board, it communicates with a computer with a hardware prototype. They have accomplished the first objectives successfully and plan to do some clinical trials and a friendly interface in the software.

The author presents a detailed study of video games evolution. A group of examples allows one to have a 360° vision of the subjects presented, for intance, software, multimedia interactive systems, interface, communicability, etc. The author also makes an interesting and detailed diachronic analysis about edutainment and the SimCity video game. The conclusions and implications of the developed work allow us to point out new roads for future investigations in the context of graphic design applied to video games.

The authors present a solution to the problem of task scheduling based on genetic algorithms to distribute tasks more efficiently on a computational grid. This algorithm was implemented in GridSim, a simulated grid computing with features and attributes of a real grid. Problems in the nature of task allocation, evolutionary algorithms, in general, have been shown to be more efficient, with the best solutions achieved in a more timely manner than the exact algorithms.

Chapter 48
Web Divide and Paper Unite: Towards a Model of the Local Tourist Information for All 536
Francisco V. Cipolla-Ficarra, ALAIPO – AINCI, Spain and Italy
Miguel Cipolla-Ficarra, ALAIPO – AINCI, Spain and Italy
Jacqueline Alma, Electronic Arts – Vancouver, Canada
Alejandra Quiroga, Universidad Nacional de La Pampa, Argentina

The authors present the first results of joining criteria and quality attributes that must have the information systems related to local tourism, irrespective of the digital support being interactive or analog. The work includes two decades of compilation of touristic information between Europe and America, in analog and digital support. The results with multimedia users are also presented, analyzing the quality attributes, orientation, and accessibility. In them, two categories of design have been considered: presentation and content. In the learned lessons, the research lines aimed at the touristic promotion and the conclusions may serve as foundation for future works related to the presented topic.

Chapter 49
Generic Model of a Multi-Agent System to Assist Ubiquitous Learning 544
Elena B. Durán, Departamento de Informática, Facultad de Ciencias Exactas y Tecnologías, Universidad Nacional de Santiago del Estero, Argentina
Margarita M. Álvarez, Departamento de Informática, Facultad de Ciencias Exactas y Tecnologías, Universidad Nacional de Santiago del Estero, Argentina
Silvina I. Únzaga, Departamento de Informática, Facultad de Ciencias Exactas y Tecnologías, Universidad Nacional de Santiago del Estero, Argentina

The authors present the importance of software agent and ontology technologies in ubiquitous learning systems in the context of Web engineering. A review of works about ontology and agent technology applied in ubiquitous learning is given. After that, model-based development approach is presented and the generic model of an application to support ubiquitous learning obtained with this approach is shown in detail. The authors also find the ontology model for the multi-agent system with the description of all ontologies and the description of the multi-agent system architecture. Finally, the main advantages of the proposed generic model are cited.

Chapter 50
MLW and Bilingualism: Case Study and Critical Evaluation 555
Daniela López De Luise, CIIS Lab – Buenos Aires, Argentina
Débora Hisgen, CIIS Lab – Buenos Aires, Argentina

Language has been studied for many years and for many reasons. Understanding the inner process and its long-term consequences is very hard. From the computational linguistic point of view, most of the approaches include processes to help automatically manage textual information for different purposes. This chapter comes from an alternate perspective: to get deep insight into the linguistic reasoning. Understanding this process enables computers to replicate sentence generation by native speakers with good approximation. As a consequence, it allows other disciplines to analyze closely related phenomena, for instance autism verbal behavior, bilingualism effects, culture influence in language usage, etc. The theory presented in this chapter depicts a step-by-step recipe for building a model, using a processing inspired by traditional wavelets concepts.

The inherent complexity of the groupware systems entails a great effort in design and development, due to its multidisciplinary measure and its technical complexity. The interface of the user of a groupware constitutes a key element for usability, tending to improve the quality of the group work in coordination, communication, collaboration, etc. From different fields of computer science (human-computer interaction, computer supported cooperative work, user centered design, and software engineering), others have proposed methodologies, models of processing, and tools that facilitate and improve different aspects involved in the development of the user interface for cooperative environments. However, the analyzed proposals have not succeeded in totally covering the development process of a groupware system where interactive aspects are integrated with the cooperatives both in the interface and in the application itself. In this work, the authors analyzes the methodological proposals to different development issues, trying to detect the strengths and weaknesses of each and identify the relevant aspects which have not been tackled yet in any of the fields dedicated to the interface development of the user of this kind of system.

This chapter is a continuation of other works that make apparent attacks online tending to the destruction of multidisciplinary teamwork, international events, etc. in southern Europe. The human factors that are enumerated in the chapter refer to veridical situations, where the use of simple ASCII files may cause irreparable damage due to the legal immunity of their authors. The goal of the current work is to detect the interrelations existing between university education and its commerce.

Preface

Emerging technologies, such as social networks and interactive Web applications, have played a vital role in the way we communicate. These technologies are fundamental in reducing the digital gaps among users. *Advanced Research and Trends in New Technologies, Software, Human-Computer Interaction, and Communicability* presents scientific, theoretical, and practical insight on the software and technology of social networks and the factors that boost communicability. By highlighting different disciplines in the computer and social sciences, this reference is essential for practitioners, researchers, and scholars invested in the current studies, as well as for future generations in the field of ICT (Information and Communication Technology).

However, the technological advance must not make us lose sight of other social and human factors, which may interfere negatively with the development of the sciences for the common good of all mankind. There are values and essential principles that must be defended more than ever in the new millennium, where technology switches from evolution to revolution in seconds, everyday, in myriad research and development labs. These values constitute the safeguard of the peoples who historically have contributed to improving the quality of life of their denizens.

One of the key words in the constitution of the nations of the American continent is freedom. That notion interpreted in those lands is synonymous with equality as one can see reflected in the stanzas of many of their national anthems. It is a word that not only shelters all the deeds of millions of inhabitants from Alaska to Tierra del Fuego but also grants a special dignity to all those born in the New World. Freedom and equality are two mainstays, which again are connected to a third keyword, fraternity. The origins of this notion—fraternity—are already latent in the Declaration of the Rights of Man and of the Citizen (*Déclaration des droits de l'homme et du citoyen, French Revolution 1789*). In the 20th century, another keyword would follow, solidarity. These four words are the cardinal points of a very special weathercock: Dignity, whose north is freedom and which guides all the inhabitants of the Americas on a daily basis. When one of their members is unfairly attacked, automatically those four winds are activated which go through the American continent. A proof of all of this is the current book, aimed at the latest theoretical and practical breakthroughs of the formal and factual sciences (Bunge, 2001).

The compilation of the current educational and scientific material is the fruit of the solidarity showed by a group of people located in a very special avenue, Chocolate, in Hershey (Pennsylvania), USA, in the face of the unfair attacks of the everlasting and immune parochialism of the Old Continent. A parochialism immune to the change of millennia, especially when it comes to the triad "education/research/industry-trade" as will be shown further on. From that city with a very famous sweets factory, our call for help was not only attended to, but in a timely way masterful solutions have been found thanks to an exceptional human team who lead their actions according to the four cardinal points mentioned above. To each one of those members my infinite gratitude, and also the whole space that surrounds our planet.

In our days, McLuhan's global village is going through a dilemma between expansion and those who are opposed to it, through patterns of behavior typical of the dungeons in the Middle Ages. In other words, on the one hand we have a free, horizontal, and democratic expansion, which supports the access to the multimedia online information and the diffusion of knowledge without any distinction between the users of the different interactive systems, and regardless of the geographical place where they are located. On the other hand—and in total opposition—are all those groups that reject the age of the expansion of communicability, through myriad destructive strategies. Their actions, which weaken the interaction between users and new technologies, boost the digital divide and generate a set of educational antimodels. The latter are exported to the emerging countries.

It is important to bear in mind that education, together with healthcare, are the essential cornerstones of all developed societies from an economic point of view. Those values are threatened by the destructive actions of those groups, and we can read about their consequences daily in the press of the countries of the South of Europe: Universities that do not have a sufficient academic-scientific level, a high number of unemployed, generations of young people who do not study or work, massive migration of the young, with and without a university degree, and a long etcetera.

In short, the actions and the patterns of behavior of those small groups establish an evident parallelism with those denizens of the Garduña (n.d.), whose origins go back to 1412 in Toledo (Spain). However, in the second decade of the new millennium they are destroying our fundamental cornerstones for a correct intersection of the formal and factual sciences. It is enough for them to put a simple post online on a corrupt Website in summer to destroy non-profit associations, professor groups, scientific publishing houses, etc., actions that are totally unpunished in the rest of the scientific community. This immunity is due to the fear of denouncing those unworthy and destructive actions that contradict the main principles of the epistemology of the sciences.

The motivations of those patterns of behavior in an academic context are variegated: the immutable relationship master-slave or superior race-inferior race, in those lands where the origin of the people or their surnames have not evolved a jot since the Middle Ages, regarding as slaves all those who do not belong to the local Garduña, imposing wild mercantilism in the educational and scientific sector, taking hold of the professional personality of their work colleagues, fostering stalking, mobbing, academic bullying, etc., behavior patterns that are totally opposed to the original ideas of Marshal McLuhan.

The odus operandi of certain characters of the academic sector who fluctuate between the real and the virtual of the new technologies are exceptionally described by Tomas Maldonado (1992). Now those characters of the Garduña, without being real experts in said technologies, not only manage to survive the passing of time, but they even expand due to the European subventions they get. Subventions that allow them to interrelate among themselves, through pseudo-scientific projects. The use of the term "pseudo" is due to the fact that in reality they are mere rehashes of other works made outside the European borders or plagiarized or carried out by "slaves of the lower race." All those who do not belong to the local, national, or international Garduña, or who do not accept those nefarious modus operandi, be it for ethical reasons or professional motives, are automatically classified as enemies, who must be destroyed. Some examples are described in several sections of the current book. In short, those examples will show how directly and indirectly, a myriad local, regional, national, European subventions, etc., have served, serve, and will serve to boost the owners of the Figure 1. The control of the authorities is equal to zero in these cases.

Figure 1. The financial crisis of Southern Europe has made apparent a series of failings in the educational system and in the university structures, which are periodically commented on in the media that make up McLuhan's global village. For example, in A: "Those with a recent degree who neither work nor study rise to 69%" (www.elpais.es), and B: "No Spanish campus reaches the 200 first places in the ranking of Shangai" (www.elpais.es).

EL PAÍS — PORTADA | INTERNACIONAL

SOCIEDAD (A)

VIDA & ARTES · EDUCACIÓN · SALUD · CIENCIA · MEDIO AMBIENTE · IGUALDAD · CONSUMO

ESTÁ PASANDO · TJUE · AEPD · Internet · Femen · Becas · Educación · Recortes

Los recién titulados que ni estudian ni trabajan suben un 69%

- Casi dos millones de jóvenes han dejado los libros y no encuentran empleo, según la OCDE
- Los que ya tienen titulación y no han salido al mercado laboral suben un 69%

J. A. AUNIÓN | Madrid | 25 JUN 2013 - 11:50 CET

Archivado en: Paro juvenil · Crisis económica · OCDE · Estudiantes · Jóvenes · Recesión económica · Comunidad educativa · Desempleo · Juventud · Coyuntura económica · Empleo · España · Educación

Una oficina de empleo de Valladolid. / NACHO GALLEGO (EFE)

EL PAÍS — PORTADA | INTERNACIONAL

SOCIEDAD (B)

VIDA & ARTES · EDUCACIÓN · SALUD · CIENCIA · MEDIO AMBIENTE · IGUALDAD · CONSUMO

ESTÁ PASANDO · Universidad · Sanidad · OMS · Investigación médica · Cáncer

Ningún campus español alcanza los 200 primeros en el 'ranking' de Shanghái

- Hay 10 universidades españolas entre las 500 mejores del mundo, una menos que en 2012
- El sistema sale mejor parado en las clasificaciones por áreas de conocimiento

J. A. AUNIÓN | Madrid | 15 AGO 2013 - 14:12 CET

Archivado en: Clasificación · Universidad Harvard · Recortes presupuestarios · Universidad · Educación superior · Sistema educativo · Investigación científica · Educación · Finanzas públicas · Ciencia

Ceremonia de graduación en la Universidad de Harvard (EE UU).

Efficient control should exclude all those who systematically receive money and mothball the projects, without ever following the future lines of research promised at the time the proposals were submitted to get financial funds; it should detect the professors or researchers who cannot research in an autonomous way and whose works are all co-authorships; it should inspect those universities where favoritism turns the students into professors disguised as administration staff; it should eliminate the outsourcing to third parties to carry out the approved project; it should prevent the interference of the industrial or entrepreneurial world with the academic formation of masters, training courses, continuous training, etc.; it should prohibit that the business associations or industrial syndicates from being the spokesmen or the prime guidelines for the signature of agreements with foreign universities, etc. This latter point is very serious because the interference of the industrial world in the formation of the engineering, graduate degrees, Masters, PhDs, etc. violates the freedom that the public universities in Europe are intended to have. In addition, when these industries—for the purpose of increasing their financial profits in a geometric or exponential way—decide to transfer their manufacturing activities outside the province or region where they are located, they destroy the homes of thousands and thousands of workers, workers who have been trained exclusively for the activities of those industries or firms and therefore have an extremely specialized or vertical training. Those workers lack the skills that would allow them a fast adaptation to the new requirements of the global market, which are obtained through academic programmes where the theory and the practice are well balanced and up to date with the ICTs. Unfortunately, many programmes do not have a comprehensive view of the real world. For example, we can see in Figure 2, section A: "Work, 64% percent of Italian students are ready to migrate. Where to? France, Swiss, and UK" (www.ilsole24ore.com); section B: "In the second semester of 2013 unemployment is 12%, and among the young it raises to 39.5%" (www.ilsole24ore.com), and section C: "Temporal evolution of the total number of Spanish unemployed, since 2005 until 2013, whose total surpasses the 6 million of the active population in Spain (6,202,700), and the 58.43% are long term unemployed. In the low right angle of the graphic can be seen that the 43.32% have a PhD, and 48.82% have a higher education (university degree) but without a PhD" (www.elpais.es).

The next set of rhetorical questions shows how the law of silence coming from the Garduña prevails, leaving us with questions without logical answers: How is access to lifelong posts for university teaching possible for individuals who do not have academic training nor any experience in the topics they must teach or who openly manifest xenophobia? How is it possible that the university endogamy goes beyond family links making up an endless semiosis of friendships of the relatives? How is it possible that there are meteorite students in public, private, and hybrid universities who in less than a decade accumulate six diplomas with various degrees including PhDs without having any affinity to their matter, and holding at the same time high ranking jobs in private businesses? How is it possible that a university grants PhDs in four years to people who cannot even speak the official language of the state? How is it possible that the director of a Doctoral thesis never helps her/his students or publishes jointly

Figure 2. The super specialization of the short European degrees has drastically contributed to increasing the number of the unemployed, with partial or poor university training in the face of the real challenges of the global market in the new millennium

Scopri l'offerta PROVA GRATIS!

Milano 9° (cambia)

24 ORE

ITALIA & MONDO

Martedì • 02 Aprile 2013 • Aggiornato alle 19:42

HOME | ITALIA & MONDO | NORME & TRIBUTI | FINANZA & MERCATI | IMPRESA & TERRITORI | NOVA24 TECH | PLUS24 RISPARMIO | COMMENTI INCHIESTE

Italia Europa USA Americhe Medio Oriente e Africa Asia e Oceania Sport L'agenda

Notizie › Italia

Lavoro, il 64% dei giovani italiani pronti ad andare via. Dove? Francia, Svizzera e Inghilterra

(A)

con una videoanalisi di Serena Uccello Cronologia articolo 02 aprile 2013 Commenti (7)

Tweet 47 Consiglia 505 Invia Accedi a My24

Il 64% dei giovani italiani sarebbe propenso ad andare a vivere lontano, il 37% ha inviato il suo curriculum all'estero e sarebbe pronto a trasferirsi, il 25% è disposto ad essere sottopagato. Come cercano lavoro? Il primo alleato è Internet, ma gli annunci sul giornale resistono ancora. E la legge Fornero? Un disastro per il 57,6% degli intervistati. Questi alcuni dei risultati emersi dal sondaggio del Centro di ricerche sociali sul lavoro e le nuove forme di occupazione "Work in Progress".

Il sondaggio, costruito attraverso la raccolta di dati con metodo "cawi" (computer-assisted web interviewing), ha coinvolto 800 giovani tra i 18 e i 35 anni, per il 66% con una laurea di secondo livello, ed e' stato realizzato in collaborazione con FondItalia, Fondo paritetico per la formazione continua, e seguito dai media partner Labitalia e "Walk on Job".

Abbonati subito! 24 ORE BUSINESS CLASS

Milano 28° (cambia)

24 ORE

IMPRESA & TERRITORI

Venerdì • 30 Agosto 2013 • Aggiornato alle 16:50

HOME | ITALIA & MONDO | NORME & TRIBUTI | FINANZA & MERCATI | IMPRESA & TERRITORI | NOVA24 TECH | PLUS24 RISPARMIO | COMMENT INCHIESTE

Industria Reti&utility Made in Lavoro Mondo&mercati Regole&incentivi Rapporti24 Agricoltura Finanz

Impresa & Territori ▸ Industria

Nel secondo trimestre disoccupazione al 12%, quella giovanile risale al 39,5%

(B)

30 agosto 2013 Commenti (11)

Tweet 19 Consiglia 84

Il tasso di disoccupazione nel secondo trimestre 2013 è pari al 12%, in crescita di 1,5 punti percentuali rispetto a un anno prima. Il numero dei disoccupati, pari a 3.075.000, è in ulteriore aumento su base tendenziale (13,7%, pari a +370.000 unità). Lo comunica l'Istat (dati grezzi). Per gli uomini l'indicatore passa dal 9,8% all'attuale 11,5% e per le donne dall'11,4% al 12,8%. Il tasso di disoccupazione giovanile è pari al 39,5% a luglio. Aumenta di 0,4% punti rispetto al mese precedente e di 4,3 punti sul 2012. Nel secondo trimestre tra i 15-24enni il tasso sale al 37,3% (+3,4 punti), con un picco del 51% per le giovani donne del Mezzogiorno.

a work with reference to the thesis that allegedly she/he is directing? How is it possible that PhDs are given when the candidate has individual scientific publications in associations or high-level publishers? How is it possible that the EU subsidizes publishers that invoice millions of Euros, training the future scoundrels and terrorists of the sciences? How is it possible that the national and international smearing campaigns of professional mudslinging are not only unpunished in front of the law, but they are accepted as normal in the local and international scientific community? How is it possible that from the private sector they try to rule in an authoritarian way the activities of scientific diffusion in the public field and vice versa? How is it possible that the stalking, mobbing, academic, and scientific bullying is extolled and covered by associations of international prestige in the sectors of communication, electronics, computer science, etc.? How is it possible that corrupt local associations since their origins are protected by prestigious international associations of the ICTs sector? How is it possible that individuals with a high academic training have such unworthy behavior in the new millennium but they are awarded by local and/or international scientific community? Obviously, this listing could be widely expanded. So far a brief sample of what is called the "Garduña factor" has been presented in the education of the ICTs, the ways of structuring the educational sector of a state, the transfer of the technology from the university to the businesses and industries and vice versa, research and development, distribution of financial resources, etc. In short, we have been showing the negative influences in the advancement of the sciences.

However, all those scientific dysfunctions can generate positive aspects such as the set of selected works for a whole year in several international conferences, workshops, and symposia: Software and Emerging Technologies for Education, Culture, Entertaiment, and Commerce (SETECEC 2012) and Advances in New Technologies, Interactive Interfaces and Communicability (ADNTIIC 2012), Human-Computer Interaction, Tourism, and Cultural Heritage (HCITOCH 2012), Communicability, Computer Graphics, and Innovative Design for Interactive Systems (CCGIDIS 2012). The research presentations and papers of those events make up the current academic-scientific book. This book does not contain 100% of the submitted works. The partiality of the set is due to the attack received in the summer vacations of 2012 from Heidelberg, Trento, Milano, Barcelona, Valencia, Madrid, Mallorca, Lerida, etc. (Figure 3) through the Dbworld (n.d.) Website – ACM SIGMOD, among other communication media.

Now, aside from this explanation, each of these international events has been respected; they have been grouped into different sections, and obviously, among them there are several common denominators, such as: software, quality metrics, heuristic evaluation, the use of avant-garde hardware, the design of online and offline multimedia interactive systems, interfaces, communicability, education, human-computer interaction, computer graphics, computer animation, cultural and natural heritage, tourism, Web 2.0, Web 3.0, etc. Some of these topics are repeated in different international events making up a kind of isotopy, although all of them are directly and indirectly related to computer science, quality of communication, design, human-computer interaction, multimedia, telecommunications, robotics, and the social sciences.

In the first section, there are those research works of First International Conference on Software and Emerging Technologies for Education, Culture, Entertaiment, and Commerce (SETECEC 2012) in Venice, Italy, whose main and secondary topics are aimed at education, entertainment, trade, mobile multimedia, and the social networks, among others. Each one of them has been outstanding not only for the originality of the proposals but also for a high degree of compatibility with the goal of the current conference. A conference that over time we hope may constitute a kind of compass for all those interested in going deeper into each one of the cardinal issues of the event.

Figure 3. Garduña factor for online attacks

WEB ATTACKS
"Urbi et Orbi"
Springer in Dbworld
University of Trento (DISI), Polytechnic of Milano (DEI), USI Lugano (Dept. of Communication), Our Lady of the Assumption Catholic University (DEI), University of Modena and Reggio Emilia (DISMI), University of Bergamo (Dept. of Human and Social Sciences), Pompeu Fabra University (Dept. of ICT, ex IUA), Autonomous University of Barcelona (Dept. of Audiovisual Communication and Advertising), University of the Balearic Islands (EPS - Dept. Computer Science and Mathematics), University of Lerida (IPO), University Polytechnical of Valencia (Dept. of Communications), University of Carlos III (DEI), Polytechnic University of Catalonia (LSI)
... etc.

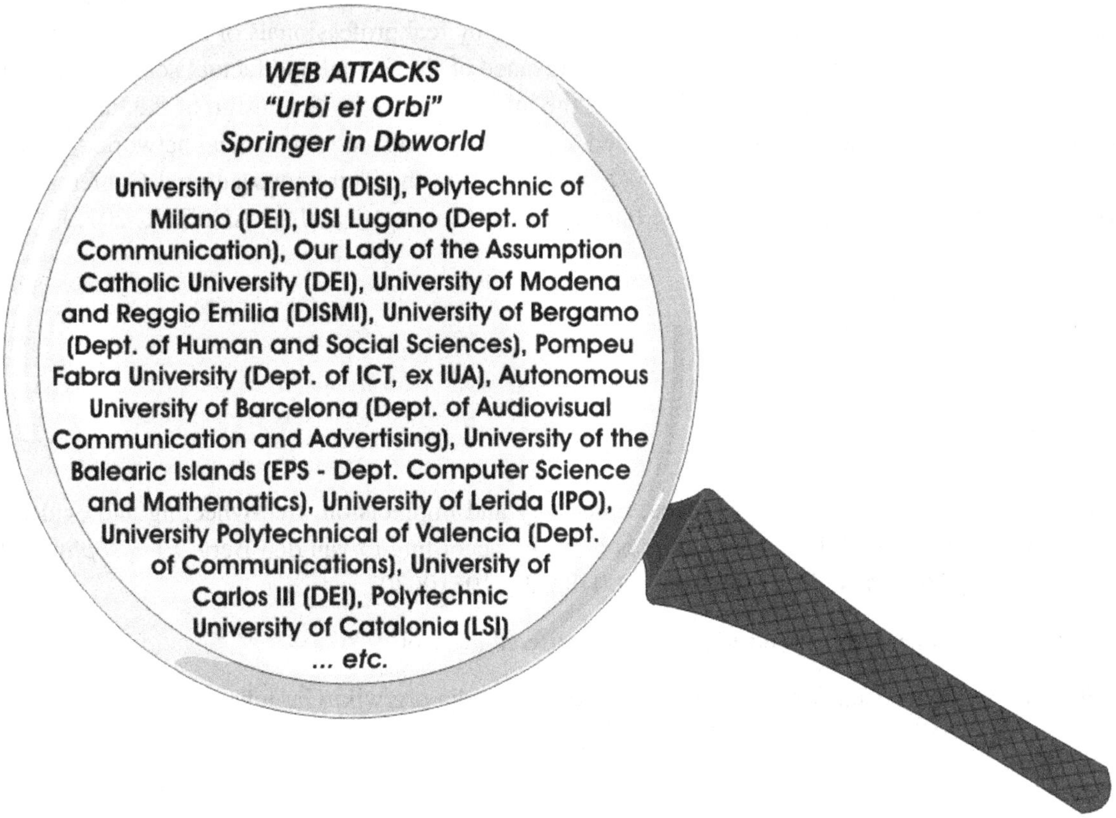

The second section groups the favorably evaluated proposals in the oral presentation, including the splendid demonstrations in some cases of the second edition of the International Symposium on Communicability, Computer Graphics, and Innovative Design for Interactive Systems (CCGIDIS 2012) (Valle d'Aosta, Italy). Said demonstrations refer to the kernel of communicability, the latest breakthroughs of computer graphics, and the trends in interactive design, whether for the traditional or for the new interactive devices related to multimedia, virtual reality, mixed reality, augmented reality, etc. This new edition of the international event has allowed the consolidation of some lines of research of the previous event and incorporated a few new ones to the topics list in keeping with technological evolution.

The third International Workshop on Human-Computer Interaction, Tourism, and Cultural Heritage (HCITOCH 2012) (Venice, Italy) constitutes the origin of our experience in organizing international gatherings. In this event, the human-computer interaction, cultural heritage, and tourism triad has been bolstered by a second goal, the definition of strategies. Strategies keen on a future where creativity is the backbone of computer science, qualitative design, and communicability. These goals have been reached once again through the selection made of all the works that we have received and of which only 33% have been approved very satisfactorily. This means that the workshop is highly selective and measures up to our average of approval in each one of the events, which is between 25% and 37%. The opening of the event in Venice deserves a special mention in the current section. Once again, it was made by Professor Dr. Kim Henry Veltman (Virtual Maastricht McLuhan Institute, The Netherlands), whom we thank again for his admirable and masterful lesson from the pedagogical point of view and the contents presented under the title "Beyond an Internet of Things."

The fourth section denotes how from Argentina a constantly increasing amount of research and development works are submitted by myriad professors, students, and local and international researchers. Over time, it can be seen how the new generations guided by real professionals of university pedagogy have set on their rails again the locomotive of the advance of the formal and factual sciences. Starting from the latest advances in the new technologies, the intersections with the design of the interface and the communicability of the contents are analyzed, contents specialized in the social networks, the Web 3.0, tourism, health, e-commerce, and 2D, 3D, xD design, in the Third International Conference on Advances in New Technologies, Interactive Interfaces, and Communicability (ADNTIIC 2012).

Francisco V. Cipolla-Ficarra
ALAIPO – AINCI, Spain and Italy

REFERENCES

Bunge, M. (2001). Systems and emergence, rationality and imprecision, free-wheeling and evidence, science and ideology: Social science and its philosophy according to van den Berg. *Philosophy of the Social Sciences*, *31*(3), 404–423. doi:10.1177/004839310103100307

Dbworld. (n.d.). Retrieved from http://research.cs.wise.edu/dbworld

Garduña. (n.d.). *Wikipedia*. Retrieved from http://en.wikipedia.org/wiki/Garduña

Maldonado, T. (1992). *Lo real y lo virtual*. Barcelona: Gedisa.

Acknowledgment

I would like to thank the following people for their helpful comments and assistance on the present book: Maria Ficarra, Christine Smith, Joel Gamon, Carlos Albert, and Miguel C. Ficarra.

Francisco V. Cipolla-Ficarra
ALAIPO – AINCI, Spain and Italy
September 2013

Chapter 1
Software and Emerging Technologies for Education, Culture, Entertainment, and Commerce

Francisco V. Cipolla-Ficarra
ALAIPO – AINCI, Spain and Italy

ABSTRACT

In the current work the bidirectional relationships exisitng between education, culture, entertainment, and trade are presented. A state-of-the-art of the main components is made through of the rhetoric questions. One resorts to rhetorics as a communicative technique to detect not only the keys of the present but also the new horizon for the new technologies of information and interactive communication, whether it is in the immediate future or long term. Finally, in the set of rhetoric questions, some analyze knowledge and/or experiences over two decades in the field of computer science and the interactive multimedia systems in some cities of the Mediterranean in the European continent.

INTRODUCTION

The rhetoric question is without any doubt one of the instruments that have served for centuries to pave new roads in scientific research, irrespective of whether they were formal or factual sciences. Although it is a question that is asked without waiting for an answer, it admits two modalities of presentation: the "interrogation", with answers of the binary kind, that is, yes or no, and the "quaesitum" if the answer answer has to be more precise. Obviously we are inside the context of the speech. That is, its transversal character of several disciplines of the sciences allows it to analyze and systemize whether it is the procedures and techniques of the use of language.

DOI: 10.4018/978-1-4666-4490-8.ch001

Some procedures and techniques which have been perfected along the centuries since their inception in classical Greece, placing its use for the first time in the current Sicilian city of Syracuse – 485 B.C (Kennedy, 1994). It was there where was esteemed the eloquence or the art of speaking well in a rather judiciary than literary context (at the time, some members of the democratic people would try to get back lands which had been unfairly taken away from them by the tyrant authorities, resorting to oratory for such an end). Consequently, the public and free word is always related to rhetoric. Not for nothing, many of the advances inside software engineering, computer sciences, systems, are born from rhetoric questions. However, we can't forget that persuasive aspect of the language as those used by the ancient inhabitants of Syracuse (Kennedy, 1994; Aristotles, 2004). Theoretically (the historical sources still are split on the issue) in the year 450 B.C. Corax of Syracuse elaborated a communication system to speak in front of the audience. Later on, Tisias, a disciple of Corax, would spread it from Syracuse to Athens (Kennedy, 1994; Aristotles, 2004). The truth is that the rhetoric would already be used by the Greek traders. A modality which abuses the use of rhetoric in our days is the use of percentages when discussing the Internet. That is, there is an exaggerate use of the commercial language in the face of the sciences and the disciplines that make it up. Some examples are the hours that the users stay connected from the home, the office, the multimedia phone devices, etc. the potential number of students who will be wired from the elementary schools in the emerging countries in a present lapse of time, the use of certain software or hardware for the communications among businesses, etc. In few words, percentage figures whose sources of information are of doubtful validity or scientific truthfulness but which keep a great persuasive effect in the new millennium to the public who listens to those percentage values.

Now in the face of the reality of those examples, currently there are in agreement to the semiotics notions of Umberto Eco, "apocalyptic and integrated" (Eco, 1996), that is, those who have a positive view and a negative one in the face of such reality. The positive view stems from those professionals coming from sciences diametrically opposed to the disciplines on which they work scientifically, resort to the notions of interdisciplinarity, transdisciplinarity, etc. so that everything merges in a new set of sciences, instead of looking for the common elements among them that is, discover the intersection areas. The reason for this behaviour in the field of the education, culture, entertainment and commerce is due to the obtainment of profits with the minimal effort and in the least possible time. Here is how our quartet interrelates with the ethical and aesthetical aspect which can be found from the first treatises of the rhetoric written by Aristotle in his work "Rhetorics" and completed in the "Rhetoric to Aleander", written by Anaximenes of Lampsacus (Kennedy, 1994; Lucaites, 1998), The former is more practical in regard to the aspects of eloquent speech, whereas the latter is more philosophical (Matsen, 1990; Enos, 2010). That is, it is aimed at the theoretical aspects.

DUALITY BETWEEN THEORY AND PRACTICE

The current biunivocal duality should be constant and balanced in the sciences related to the new technologies inside the context of the ICTs (information and communication technologies). However, the balance is broken out of financial or commercial reasons which make that everything that turns around computer science must be profitable in the least possible time, including education. An education which does not take into consideration whether it is public, private or mixed.

The public study centres do not have enough resources to buy the latest technological breakthroughs in hardware and/or software for their practice labs. Fortunately inside the context of the free software it has been possible to partly solve this problem which many scientists place in the emerging countries. Paradoxically now it is the common denominator in the emerged countries, but which oscillate in the come and go of the economy and the global finances. Also in the hardware sector important breakthroughs have taken place with such projects as "one laptop for child" OLPC). However, we have even in these cases yet another dychotomic contradiction, since in many cases in the emerging countries in Latin America these projects are managed directly or indirectly by private or religious universities, as is the case of Paraguay, Uruguay, Chile, etc. That is, universities which have financial resources for the purchase of the latest commercial breakthroughs of software and hardware but are waiting for the subsidies of the states, local or regional institutions to equip the ICTs labs, for instance. It is striking in some places in Europe that once these labs have been set in motion, generally with international staff with garbage contracts (as it was said in the Spain of the 90s), the theoretical issues are left aside and they go directly to the practical issues. These changes are related to the guidelines of an inexperienced local staff with lifelong jobs but who have as a dogma the demonstration that theories do not work. The immediate goal is to cover the technology and knowledge transfer towards the entrepreneurial or industrial sector. Now in Spain, for instance, in less than a decade the consequences of this imbalance show themselves. First it is the figures of highly skilled experts in commercial or canned software, but with degrees in multimedia engineering, degrees in audiovisual, software engineering, computer science and systems engineering, bachelors in maths, industrial engineers, physics bachelors, telecommunications engineers, etc. In few words, they are the local and nice alleged experts, those who have broken the balance between the theory and the practice in the universities in which they give their lifelong services. Their persuasive arguments, linked to the ethos of rhetoric inspired confidence towards their superiors and the rest of members of these academic centres, even though they were decisions totally against the epistemology of the sciences for the post of higher or university teaching. In the second place, it is also they who daily redraw the borders between the educational and the commercial issues, since they manage the studies as if they were businesses with a view to a profit in the short term. It is there where are to be found the main heads of the current educational antimodels, as they exist in the cities of Southern Europe, such as Barcelona, Palma of Mallorca, Valencia, Madrid, Zaragoza, Girona, Lleida among others and with the purpose of exporting educational antimodels in the emerging countries under the heading of educational excellence or high quality studies with practices in labs equipped with the latest breakthroughs of the commercial (not scientific) sector (Nöth, 1995; Cipolla-Ficarra, 2010a). Finally, they are also those to blame for the Neets (not in education, employment or training). In short, the first argument of rhetoric (ethos) of an affectionate and moral character in the private and/or religious institutions are sources of educational antimodels. The consequences can be seen in the digital gap which daily widens among the population of allegedly emerged communities in the EU, for instance.

The other two arguments, pathos and logos, complete the triad of rhetoric (Lucaites, 1998; Enos, 2010). The pathos is the one used recurrently from the private or hybrid university institutions. These two words refer to the public educational reality managed as a private body due to the prevailing parochialism in mountainous regions such as the Pyrenees or the Alps. In other words, they belong to the group of private universities even if officially they are public. In these educational structures they resort to the affective aspect to catch and keep the students considered as mere clients, who monthly pay a fee for their studies and who after a given period will get the title. Regardless of whether they have the competence, the ability and the knowledge that are reflected in these titles: specialization courses, masters, PhDs, post-doctorate, etc. The arguments of the pathos and the logo can be found in the corporate publicity of these teaching centres, allegedly elite or excellence. The latter argument of the rhetoric triad, such as the logo, can be seen on how the arguments are focused on the subject and message itself of the speech. Here is where dialectic prevails. A dialectic which allows the persuasive enunciators to modify the balances between theory and practice inside the curricula of the subjects related to the new technologies, for instance (Cipolla-Ficarra, 2010a). All of this ends up in the figures of the news which can be read in the news of the digital papers.

A dialectic which also includes an implicit dual phenomenon in education as if finding a job came first to studying, or before to study and then find a job. We find the earliest relationship in many private educational models in Southern Europe since the 90s. The second relationship has been a model for centuries in many Latin universities and which has been exported to America, lasting for centuries until the end of the 20th century. It was from this moment on that little by little has been introduced a very negative antimodel for the coming generations who first try to get a steady or even lifelong job and then get academic titles in a record time. The European educational legislation has adapted to these requirements which have an influence on the macroeconomic data of a community such as can be the total number of the active population with college studies. However, nobody has analyzed the quality of the training to face crisis of the working system which concern the social structure.

CULTURAL FACTORS VS. HUMAN FACTORS

There are several mechanisms of the social sciences to measure the quality of the training, such as the surveys, the questionnaires, etc. In each one of them should be considered the cultural factors which lead certain communities in the field to have available professionals or specialists in the ICTs sector, computer science, multimedia, etc. who have a horizontal knowledge with a 360 degrees vision. A frequent reality until the last century in some exceptional public universities on the other side of the Atlantic. The 360 degrees vision is reached by inserting in the computer science curricula, for instance, subjects belonging to the social sciences which allow the future professionals to adapt better to the changes that entails the dazzlingly fast advance of the software and the hardware, electronics, telecommunications, etc. However, in the coast of the Mediterranean have been followed the Nordic European models or from the north of the American continent, where the vertical view prevails or specialized in depth in few fields of scientific knowledge. For instance, in the era of the quality of software in the 90s some researchers of the sector of software engineering declared the need of introducing psychologists or anthropologists in the teams of analysis and programming of computer systems.

In the context of the computer animations in the Mediterranean there was a clear-cut split between the artists or fine arts bachelors and the programmers. This binary position in knowledge, that is, vertical or horizontal, leads us to the order of the parts which make up the culture of a community and how the community reacts in the face of the novelties which are presented through the technology transfer between the university and the industry (or vice versa).

Setting a parallelism with the rhetoric that order may be naturalis or artificialis. "Naturalis" is the order that respects the nature itself of the speech without intentioned alterations or that which follows the tradition (Kennedy, 1994; Aristotles, 2004; Enos, 2010). For instance, dividing the work teams in relation to the college titles, nationalities, age, etc. Here is one of the reasons why the audiovisual entertainment industry in computer animations in the decade of the 90s is inferior in Spain if compared to France. However, the results obtained in the quality-quantity equation between the west coast of the USA widely surpasses the French standard. Whereas the "artificialis", in contrast, alters the usual order of the parts. A 360 degrees horizontal vision should prevail in the context of the education for the new technologies. In this sense, the generation of our specialist in communicability is the result of the intersection of the factual and formal sciences. If the verticalist context of knowledge had prevailed, we would not be going through the era of the expansion of communicability (Cipolla-Ficarra, 2010a), thanks to the microcomputing devices and the mobile multimedia communication, just to mention two components of the progress in the multimedia communications. Evidently considering an intersection of the sciences instead of the union entails a series of difficulties which are to be framed in the human factors of the computer sector, the telecommunications, the audiovisual, industrial engineering, the fine arts, etc. if we are talking about the multimedia.

Human factors which are very well disguised with the rhetoric applied to the new technologies, especially when one resorts to the deliberative genre –*genus deliberativum* (Kennedy, 1994; Aristotles, 2004; Enos, 2010). It is a genre used for the generation of antimodels and which suits the strategy used by the dynamic persuader to advise or dissuade in terms of usefulness. The topic of the deliberative speeches is how to face in the future a given issue (Nöth, 1995). Obviously, the new technologies as a rule are oriented to the future, excepting a diachronic vision on history or the evolution of said technologies. The other two genres that make up this triad in the rhetoric are the demonstrative genre (genus demonstrativum) and the judicial genre –*genus iudiciale* (Kennedy, 1994; Aristotles, 2004; Matsen, 1990). The demonstrative is ambivalent, because it used for both praise and insult, and refers to the past. For instance, events are presented in front of an audience who have not witnessed them, but they must approve of them or disapprove. In some way this reference to the past is linked to the origins of rhetoric itself. To such extent that the latest genre is the so called judiciary, when once again there are only two alternatives, accusation and defense. The same as the design of interactive systems, the only way that exists to prove the mistakes made due to the human factors is the passing of time, which allows a diachronic analysis. Human factors which in some communities in the European Mediterranean basin have seen how the term "multimedia" had a strong mercantilist connotation in the 90s (Cipolla-Ficarra, 2010a). Later on, the same happened with the momentum of the internet and the online videogames, virtual reality, virtual firms, the current social networks, etc. Human factors which have generated strong virtual bubbles (many of them formed and provoked inside the college cloisters) thus seriously damaging the scientific aspect of avant-garde issues technologically speaking. However, this negative behavior, focused on the public and private universities for the continuous technological development, linked to the strength of rhetoric have contributed to a great extent in the current European Mediterranean societies to the current digital gap, which will increase with the passing of time. This last statement is due to the experience in the digital and/or interactive entertainment sector since 1990-2010 in these communities of Southern Europe (Cipolla-Ficarra, 2010a; Cipolla-Ficarra, 2010b; Cipolla-Ficarra, et al., 2011a; Cipolla-Ficarra, Nicol & Cipolla-Ficarra, 2010).

ENTERTAINMENT: THE CONVERGENCE OF RESOURCES

The crisis of the multimedia sector in the late 90s was originated by the bad use of the term that was made from the academic sector and in the fledgling offline and online interactive systems industry, the bursting of the virtual firms dedicated to e-commerce, in cities like Barcelona, Bilbao,

Madrid, Valencia, Palma of Mallorca, etc. with mentors who belonged to the audio-visual environment, architecture, electronics, mathematics, graphic computing, the fine arts, etc. made them focus their attention on the only sector that kept on growing: entertainment. Glances turned especially to the PC videogame industry Later on for the consoles, and the early models of mobile phones multimedia systems. The key to the expansion of this sector lay in the model of society that was taking shape at the end of the past and the beginning of the new millennium, that is, users of interactive systems with leisure time at their disposal, since the working days had to be cut, following some models like the French case.

Besides, from the point of view of interactive design, the graphic arts were switching their production from the analogical support to the digital one (Dubberly, 2011). Consequently, many professionals gave contents to those interactive products for entertainment in variegated work teams (Furtado, et al., 2011). It was so how those interactive contents where stories were told had a great acceptance among users of all ages. Stories where rhetoric constantly appeared in the content starting with the kids, what is now called the digital generation.

Since an early age they followed the narrative through computers with interactive tales. Some classical examples of great quality from each one of the design categories are Kiyeko (Ubisoft, 1995), The Interactive Alphabet (Corel, 1995a) and Nikolai's Trains (Corel, 1995b). In them we found in the speakers the genres of rhetoric locution (genera elocutionis), that is, the stylistic modalities which depend on the intersection of the elocution qualities grouped in three sets: the plain style (gens humile), which is typical when the purpose is teaching, the medium style (genus medium) whose purpose is entertaining that who listens to the tale and lastly the sublime style (genus sublime) which has its mission to move and it is there where we find the high level of the locution quality.

Whereas from the traditional graphic arts they accelerated the adaptation process to the digital supports, some members of the public, private and chartered academic world saw in the entertainment industry an interesting source of revenue.

Obviously, deeds that were diametrically opposed to the precepts of the great masters of Greek rhetoric like Isocrates (Kennedy, 1994). He thought that rhetoric was a plan of the integral education of the individual which served to create model citizens with his teaching system. Others in the private, public and hybrid universities have seen, see and will see mere clients who consume goods and services related to the ICTs. The entertainment sector, whether its aims are show business or education, is not excluded from this reality.

RHETORIC MISCELLANEOUS IN THE EDUCATION, CULTURE, ENTERTAINMENT AND TRADE QUARTET

Next we have the great set of rhetoric questions related to computer science, education, the human factors, the social factors, cultural heritage, the value of trade, the use of leisure time with the new technologies, etc. These questions are of a binary kind, which entails theoretically two kinds of answers, yes or no.

However, in some cases they will be accompanied by some brief comments, where the interested reader can enlarge the motivations of these answers in the following bibliographical references (Cipolla-Ficarra, et al., 2011a; Cipolla-Ficarra, 2011b; Cipolla-Ficarra, et al., 2010c). The reason of not inserting answers only of affirmative or negative options especially inside a rhetoric context, is due to the fact that the new generations of users of interactive systems in the different eras or stages of communicability must know well the past of the sector of the ICTs so that the human and social factors that have distorted it do not repeat themselves in the future.

Is it true that the bigger the financial investment in a R+D lab is, the greater is the educational excellence of the university where the said lab is installed? Apparently the answer should be yes, however it is not so in 100% of the analyzed cases. The error was, is and will be in the endogamy of the human team who make up these labs or universities. These are communities used to "leopardism" (cronyism) that is, changing everything so that nothing changes. Next a first listing of rhetoric questions which will be enlarged in future works:

- Is there a replacement of the academic heads who have bred the Neet generation and so many unemployed in Europe? Regrettably not. There couldn't possibly be because of the lifelong perks they have enjoyed, enjoy and will enjoy those bosses through the formula of lifelong tenure.
- Do the educational antimodels in university teaching perish with time and are they not exportable to other countries? They do not perish and they continue their expansion due to the international agreements among universities. The expansion area is related to the language of the contents and the cultural aspects or the idiosyncrasy of the nations that accept to implement foreign structures and cultural systems which do not work properly even in the countries where these antimodels originated.
- Is academic stalking born in the educational structures which generate the antimodels? In principle the answer is yes, and it is more intense in the institutions where the religious factor prevails. In the new technologies it is a human factor that becomes a social factor when it is exerted during decades. As a rule, the precept which governs these abnormal behavior is "nobody can do anything to us".
- Is educational authoritarianism inside the technological avant-garde of the ICts due to economic reasons? Yes, because it is an important source of revenue for institutions who regard the students as mere clients.
- Is publicity rhetoric used by those who generate national and international educational antimodels such as the practice of academic stalking? Yes, since the greater the corporative publicity is, the smaller is the educational quality, and also the alleged educational excellence aimed at the new technologies.
- Are the new technologies applied to the cultural contents a constant source of losses of financial resources? Contrarily to what many forecast with the first virtual visits to the collections of the museums or travelling exhibits, thanks to the multimedia systems of the 90s, the visits to the museums had an exponential momentum in the end of the last century and beginning of the new millennium.
- Is there still a confrontation between the promotion of cultural and natural heritage? Yes, but it should be overcome with the new technologies of mobile multimedia, especially for the users of the digital generation. In Europe should be esteemed the nature that surrounds the cities with museums and in America the historic past which surrounds the imposing natural landscapes.
- Will the online and offline multimedia systems aimed at entertainment keep on being a synthesis of the technological avant-garde of the interactive design? Yes, because they stand for the convergence of the most varied areas of the formal and factual sciences which range from the computer animations, the video, the ergonom-

ics of the devices, the interconnection of human beings under communicability, etc.
- Is there the chance that entertainment prevails over education in the interactive contents? Yes, because following Piaget's precepts, the learning process should be an entertainment in each one of the disciplines that make up human knowledge.
- Is traditional reading the element that may eradicate the information seen in the examples of the figures 1 and 2 related to the current quartet? Yes, because it has been the engine of the great scientific and technological breakthroughs. The great inventors of universal history, the discoverers, the computer technicians, the communicability specialists, the usability engineers, etc. have spent many hours reading. The current problem is that plenty of reduced digital information generates the mosaic culture that Moles predicted, that is, a lack of depth in the issues and the scant 360 degrees vision of the reality that surrounds us.

LESSONS LEARNED

Rhetoric was born in the face of an act of injustice. However, how many deeds of injustice have suffered those who have gone through universities where the profit issue was more important or swelling the numbers of the macro statistics of the ministries of education and culture. The European university reforms of the last decade in Southern Europe have not prevented the high percentages which affect the future of the new generations, although they were born in a digital and interactive environment. The equation of getting the biggest financial profit in the least possible time has prevailed over the reality of investing in the middle and long term in culture and in excellence education. The current technological means would allow to reach educational excellence for the whole of mankind. However, it is not feasible in the short term.

The problem lies in the fact that the educational structures have systems where the perennial human factors do not allow those qualitative changes. The philosophy of the sciences has been sidelined by the commercial factors. Perhaps it is time to go back to certain origins with valid tools to formulate rhetoric questions but with the sight set on the common wellbeing of the global society. A good use of the social networks should bear that premise as guide. However, in the second decade of the new century, one starts to see the same mistakes made with the social communication media in the first half of the 20th century. That is, the appearance of new forms of vertical structures in the spread of knowledge, with purposes alien to the common good. Besides, in many cases they are hard to detect because of the digital character of the current information, making up really destructive power castes, hidden in the net. Consequently, it is necessary to go back to the analysis of the digital contents, regardless whether these are dynamic or static, resorting to the instruments of linguistics and/or semiotics, for instance.

It is important to consider some mechanism which leaves a trail of the changes that are introduced in the online information by those pressure groups usually belonging to the non-secular education. Also an international online database can be generated so that the students can look up the qualitative educational parameters before registering in any kind and/or level of educational institution in Southern Europe.

CONCLUSION

Although the core of a computer program and from a logical point of view lies in answering to questions with binary options, that is, the classic if…then… of the BASIC (Beginner's All purpose Symbolic Instruction Code) which would then be completed with another option…else, that is, if… then…else. These bifurcations make apparent that the human being constantly and unconsciously makes a huge series of decisions in each one of

Figure 1. The total of the neet generation has increased with the global crisis and will affect the use of the new interactive systems since the digital gap in the population of the European Community increases, for instance, between the north and the south of Europe. According to official data, there are 800.000 people in Spain who neither study nor work and whose ages range between 18 and 24 years, that is, the age of college studies. El País (www.elpais.es) 12.16.2011.

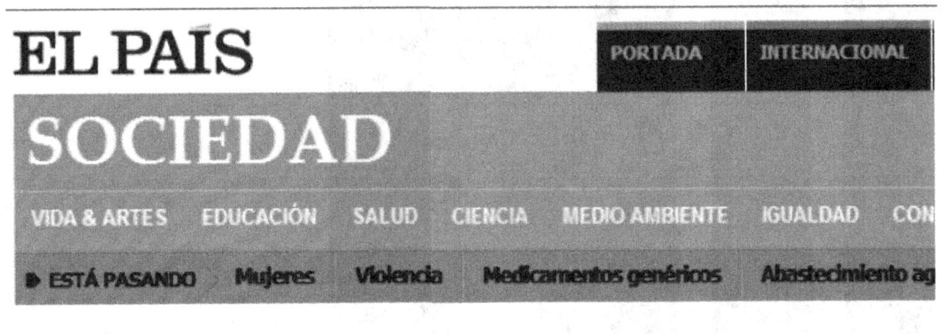

EL PAÍS

PORTADA | INTERNACIONAL

SOCIEDAD

VIDA & ARTES | EDUCACIÓN | SALUD | CIENCIA | MEDIO AMBIENTE | IGUALDAD | CON

ESTÁ PASANDO | Mujeres | Violencia | Medicamentos genéricos | Abastecimiento ag

EDUCACIÓN

La crisis eleva al 22% los jóvenes que ni estudian ni trabajan

- España tiene el quinto porcentaje más alto de la UE, tras crecer 8,6 puntos en tres años
- El problema crece en toda Europa por el paro y la falta de alternativas
- Generación 'ni-ni': ni estudia, ni trabaja

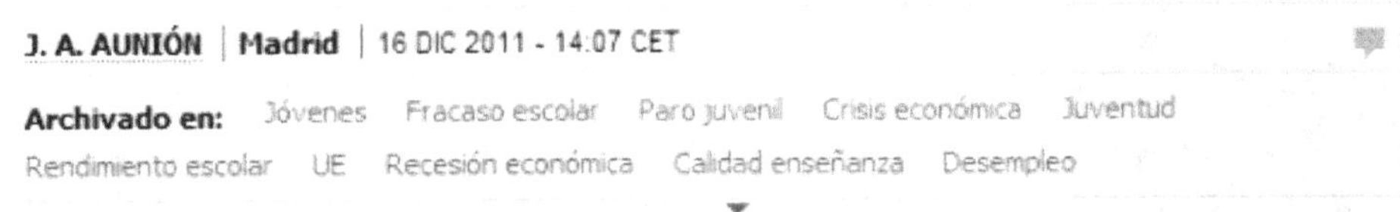

J. A. AUNIÓN | Madrid | 16 DIC 2011 - 14:07 CET

Archivado en: Jóvenes Fracaso escolar Paro juvenil Crisis económica Juventud Rendimiento escolar UE Recesión económica Calidad enseñanza Desempleo

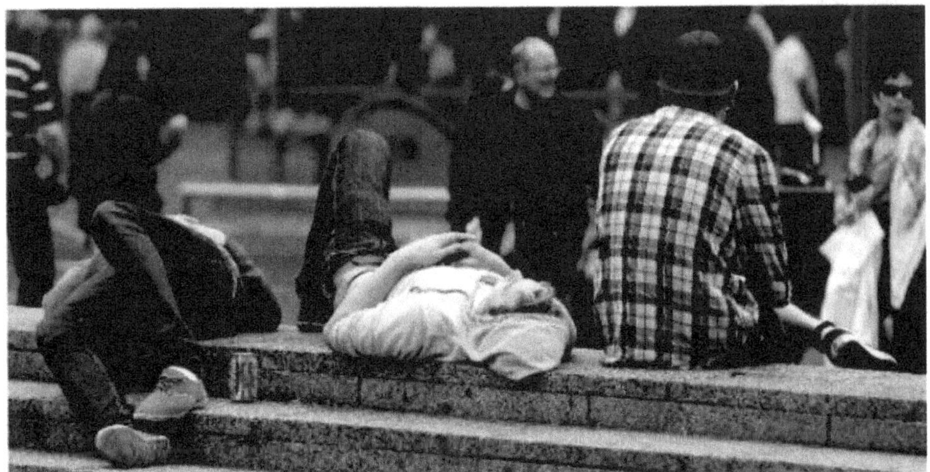

Unos jóvenes descansan en una plaza de Barcelona. / TEJEDERAS

Recomendar 1.089

La crisis está dejando descolgados a muchísimos jóvenes. En España 800.000 ciudadanos entre 18 y 24 años ni estudia ni trabaja.

Figure 2. The unemployed in communities which historically have been the avant-garde of design and industry are a clear example of how the use and abuse of the rhetorical techniques has eaten away the technological and working place future of millions of potential users of new technologies

Figure 3. Best examples of the interactive design of the 90s, for the off-line multimedia systems, whose content was aimed at the children audience

the days of his/her life. Since 1964 when the first BASIC program started to function, the goal was to simplify the learning of computer programming, not only to the students, but also to the professors who didn't come from the science environment.

In some way there were to be found the cornerstones of the quartet of components treated in the current work, and which keep among themselves a bidirectional relationship. The interrelations between the users and the last generation new interactive systems in the current social networks lead to the need of revaluing the rhetoric studies about manipulation and persuasion. Deeds and effects which are currently seen in the content of many messages. Interactive contents were rhetoric has been boosted in an exponential way due to the briefness and instantaneousness of the online multimedia contents and the pressure groups which attempt against the democratization and the veracity of digital information.

REFERENCES

Aristotle, . (2004). *Rethoric*. New York: Dover Publications.

Cipolla-Ficarra, F. (2010a). *Quality and communicability for interactive hypermedia systems: Concepts and practices for design*. Hershey, PA: IGI Global. doi:10.4018/978-1-61520-763-3

Cipolla-Ficarra, F. (2010b). *Persuasion online and communicability: The destruction of credibiltiy in the virtual community and cognitive models*. New York: Nova Publishers.

Cipolla-Ficarra, F. et al. (2010c). *Advances in new technologies interactive interfaces and communicability*. Heidelberg, Germany: Springer.

Cipolla-Ficarra, F. et al. (2011a). *Human-computer interaction, tourism and cultural heritage*. Heidelberg, Germany: Springer. doi:10.1007/978-3-642-18348-5

Cipolla-Ficarra, F., et al. (2011b). Handbook of advance in dynamic and static media for interactive systems: Communicability, computer science and design. Bergamo, Italy: Blue Herons Ed.s.

Cipolla-Ficarra, F., Nicol, E., & Cipolla-Ficarra, M. (2010). Vademecum for innovation through knowledge transfer: Continuous training in universities, enterprises and industries. In *Proceedings of International Conference on Innovation through Knowledge Transfer, Innovation KT 2010*. Heidelberg, Germany: Springer.

Corel. (1995a). *The interactive alphabet CD-ROM*. Ottawa, Canada: Corel.

Corel. (1995b). *Nikolai's trains CD-ROM*. Ottawa, Canada: Corel.

Dubberly, H. (2011). Extending negroponte's model of convergence. *Interaction*, *18*(5), 74–79. doi:10.1145/2008176.2008193

Eco, U. (1996). *A theory of semiotics*. Bloomington, IN: Indiana University Press.

Enos, T. (2010). *Encyclopedia of rhetoric and composition: Communication from ancient times to the information age*. New York: Routledge.

Furtado, A. et al. (2011). Improving digital game development with software product lines. *IEEE Software*, *28*(5), 30–37. doi:10.1109/MS.2011.101

Kennedy, G. (1994). *A new history of classical rethoric*. Princeton, NJ: Princeton University Press.

Lucaites, J. (1998). *Contemporary rhetorical theory: A reader*. New York: The Guilford Press.

Matsen, P. (1990). *Readings from classical rhetoric*. Carbondale, IL: Southern Illinois University Press.

Nöth, W. (1995). *Handbook of semiotics*. Bloomington, IN: Indiana University Press.

Ubisoft. (1995). *Kiyeko and the lost night CD-ROM*. Paris: Ubisoft.

Chapter 2
A Practical Setup for Projection-Based Augmented Maps

Filippo Bergamasco
Dipartimento di Scienze Ambientali, Informatica e Statistica, Università Ca' Foscari di Venezia, Italy

Andrea Albarelli
Dipartimento di Scienze Ambientali, Informatica e Statistica, Università Ca' Foscari di Venezia, Italy

Andrea Torsello
Dipartimento di Scienze Ambientali, Informatica e Statistica, Università Ca' Foscari di Venezia, Italy

ABSTRACT

Projected Augmented Reality is a human-computer interaction scenario where synthetic data, rather than being rendered on a display, are directly projected on the real world. Differening from screen-based approaches, which only require the pose of the camera with respect to the world, this setup poses the additional hurdle of knowing the relative pose between capturing and projecting devices. In this chapter, the authors propose a thorough solution that addresses both camera and projector calibration using a simple fiducial marker design. Specifically, they introduce a novel Augmented Maps setup where the user can explore geographically located information by moving a physical inspection tool over a printed map. Since the tool presents both a projection surface and a 3D-localizable marker, it can be used to display suitable information about the area that it covers. The proposed setup has been evaluated in terms of accuracy of the calibration and ease of use declared by the users.

INTRODUCTION

The landscape of Augmented Reality systems proposed in literature is very varied and includes a wide range of different techniques. However, most setups are built upon three fundamental blocks: a positioning system, a display device and an interaction model (Feng, Been-Lirn Duh & Billinghurst, 2008)

The positioning system is often composed of a camera and a set of artificial or natural markers. Within this kind of setup the camera is used

DOI: 10.4018/978-1-4666-4490-8.ch002

to acquire images of the markers and computer vision algorithms are applied to them in order to find the pose of the imaging system with respect to the world (Lowe, 1991; Davis, & DeMenthon, 1995; Lan & Zhong-Dan, 1999). All these pose recovery techniques require the determination of a number of correspondence between features on the scene and their images on the projective plane. In principle such correspondences can be recovered from naturally occurring features in the image such as interesting point on a planar surface (Simon, Fitzgibbon, & Zisserman, 2000)., ellipses (Qian, Haiyuan, & Toshikazu, 2004), straight lines (Elqursh, & Egammal, 2011) or even the user's hand (Lee, & Höllerer, 2009). In practice, for many real-world applications, this approach is not always feasible, since robust features cannot be guaranteed to exist in the scene, and even when found, their accuracy strongly depends on scene-dependant factor such as illumination, contrast or texture. To overcome these limitations, a number of artificial markers have been proposed over the last two decades. The goal of a fiducial marker design is to introduce elements in the scene that are easy to detect and that can be located with good accuracy. Some approaches rely on the invariance of conics such as concentric discs (Gartell, Hoff, & Sklair, 1991) or regularly arranged circles (Cho, Lee, & Neumann, 1998; Claus, & Fitzgibbon, 2005). In fact, under a generic projective transformation, circles always appear as ellipses, that are shapes easy to find and whose centers can be inferred with high precision. Other approaches exploit the invariance of straight lines, usually arranged to build high-contrast square boxes, that can be recognized by means of image-based recognition (Wagner, Reitmayr, Mulloni, Drummond, & Schmalstieg, 2010). or decoding of the marker content (Fiala, 2010).

The display device can be a screen, a head-mounted display, a portable device or even the real world, as some approaches adopt projection techniques to overlay information to real objects. Head-mounted displays can be used in conjunction with front cameras and trackers to offer an immersive experience to the user. By contrast, augmented environments can be displayed and navigated through desktop interfaces. Both approaches have been shown to have advantages and disadvantages (Sousa-Santos, et al., 2009). A popular intermediate solution between dedicated helmets and desktop navigation is represented by adopting portable devices such as mobile phones or tablet (Wagner, Reitmayr, Mulloni, Drummond, & Schmalstieg, 2010). This latter approach is very practical since these devices are becoming ubiquitous and come equipped with high resolution cameras and screens.

Finally, interaction models include both traditional computer-based controls and body mounted sensors or even more complex physical haptics. Recent approaches include wearable gestural interfaces (Mistry, Maes, & Chang, 2009), tangible interfaces (Pittarello, & Stecca, 2011) and virtual mirrors (Bichlmeier, Heining, Feuerstein & Navab, 2009).

In this chapter we develop a setup for projection-based augmented maps that is based on a projective-invariant marker design which is used for four different purposes: the detection of the physical controller moved by the user, the localization in the 3D space of the display surface and, finally, the calibration of both the camera and the projector. In the following sections the system will be described in depth and the calibration procedure will be defined. The concept of augmented maps is not new per se, in fact this concept has already been explored using both head-mounted (Bobrich & Otto, 2002) and projected displays (Reitmayr, Eade, & Drummond, 2005. Nevertheless, in the following sections we will introduce two novel contributions: an interaction model that involves the use of the exploration device in the entire 3D space, and a camera-projector calibration pipeline that does not require initial guesses about intrinsic or extrinsic parameters, is semi-automated and very simple to implement.

DESCRIPTION OF THE SYSTEM AND USER INTERACTION

A schematic representation of the setup can be seen in Figure 1. From a technical standpoint the system is made up of a digital projector, a camera, a board where the map of interest is physically printed and a navigation device. The projector and the camera are rigidly mounted on a stand and are both oriented toward the table so that their frustum covers the entire area of interest. A calibration procedure is performed to obtain an accurate estimate of the intrinsic parameters for both devices (i.e. their focal length, principal point and radial distortion) and of their relative orientation. The navigation device is basically a rectangular rigid board that exhibits a white matte projection area and a frame that contains the fiducial marker to track. This marker is continuously captured by the camera and its location in 3D space is estimated at each frame.

Since the rigid transform that binds the camera to the projector is known and the projector frustum itself corresponds to the map area, all the parameters are available to reconstruct the position of the navigation device with respect to the map and to the projector and thus to display on the matte area some contextual data related to the location observed by the user. The geometrical relation between the projector and the navigation device is used to rectify the displayed image so that it appears exactly as if it was formed on the screen of an active device. By printing different markers, more than one navigation device can be used simultaneously, thus allowing many users to operate on the table. Finally, since the marker position

Figure 1. Representation of the proposed setup

is determined in 3D, additional functions such as zooming can be controlled through the vertical position of the device.

FIDUCIAL MARKERS DESIGN

For our setup we decided to use a novel type of fiducial markers described in (Bergamasco, Albarelli, & Torsello, 2011) that exploit projective invariants to allow simple, fast and accurate pose estimation.

These tags are composed by a series of 12 dots arranged in a rectangle (Figure 3), with 2 dots per side and corner dots shared between each side. The relative distance of each dot is crafted to exploit the cross-ratio invariance among projective transformations. Given a constant α, a whole class of tags can be generated by ensuring that:

$$cr_{ij} = cr_{ik} = \alpha cr_{jh} = \alpha cr_{kh}$$

The well known instability of cross-ratio with respect to noise is partially compensated by the internal redundancy of their design and allow us to use up to about ten tags simultaneously in a practical scenario without sacrifice detection reliability. On the other hand, unlike other marker types available in literature, the ellipse-based design ensure great accuracy in pose estimation and the usage of projective invariants remove any rectification step usually involved in the recognition stage.

Pi-Tags exhibits several features particularly attractive for our purposes:

1. The marker interior is empty and so is the ideal choice to be used as a virtual screen to project multimedia content to the user.
2. The aspect ratio of the tag can be freely modified as it doesn't influence the cross-ratio constraint. This is particularly useful if the marker is used as a frame around a picture or other type of artistic content that cannot be modified.
3. The good pose estimation accuracy allows a steady projection without flickering or similar artifacts that may heavily hinder the user experience.
4. The tradeoff between the size of the dots and their relative distance from the camera can be adjusted to fit the individual application needing. If the hardware setup requires a camera far away and/or with low resolution the dot size can be increased without any modification even on tag descriptors.
5. Marker design is simple and not invasive against the content presented to the user.

They can be effectively used also for calibration purposes.

CALIBRATION PROCEDURE

To project multimedia content onto the physical marker plane we need to estimate the projector projection matrix P:

$$P = K_p[R_p \mid T_p]$$

where:

$$K_p = \begin{bmatrix} fx_p & 0 & cx_p \\ 0 & fy_p & cy_p \\ 0 & 0 & 1 \end{bmatrix}$$

are projector intrinsic parameters, and $[R_p|T_p]$ is the relative pose of the projector with respect to the marker, or the extrinsic parameters. Once the matrix P has been estimated, a 3D point p_w lying on the marker plane can be projected by transforming its 3D coordinates to $[\, x_w \, y_{w\,0} \,]^T$ projector image-space pixel coordinates $[\, u_p \, v_p \,]^T$ with the following equation:

$$\begin{bmatrix} u_p \\ v_p \\ 1 \end{bmatrix} = P \begin{bmatrix} x_w \\ y_w \\ 0 \\ 1 \end{bmatrix} = Pp_w$$

Unfortunately, the projector cannot estimate the relative pose $[R_p|T_p]$ by itself because it is a pure output device. To provide that data, a camera is placed nearby ensuring that the viewing frustum of the projector is contained in the viewing frustum of the camera. As long as the relative position between the camera and projector remains unchanged, $[R_p|T_p]$ can be estimated in terms of the camera pose $[R_c|T_c]$ obtained via fiducial markers in the following way:

$$\begin{bmatrix} R_p & T_p \\ \vec{0} & 1 \end{bmatrix} = \begin{bmatrix} R_{cp} & T_{cp} \\ \vec{0} & 1 \end{bmatrix} \begin{bmatrix} R_c & T_c \\ \vec{0} & 1 \end{bmatrix}$$

Where $[R_{cp}|T_{cp}]$ is the rigid motion that maps from camera coordinate system to projector coordinate system. The first step of the calibration procedure is the estimation of the camera intrinsic parameters and radial distortion. This step is achieved by creating a map between a large set of known 3D points, viewed from different positions, and their respective projection onto camera image plane. To build this mapping we created a planar calibration target with 6 pi-tags disposed at known position (Figure 3, right). This is done in order to capture a larger number of points for each shot, but, in principle, even a single marker could be used. The detection code of Pi-Tags allows to identify each dot on the calibration target and establish the correspondence between the 3D position of the dot (defined in the calibration target model) and its 2D projection on camera image (computed by the detector).

After the creation of this mapping, a non-linear optimization algorithm is used via OpenCV *calibrateCamera* function (Bradski, A., & Kaehler, A., 2008) to obtain the camera intrinsics:

$$K_c = \begin{bmatrix} fx_c & 0 & cx_c \\ 0 & fy_c & cy_c \\ 0 & 0 & 1 \end{bmatrix}$$

The estimation of K_p and $[R_{cp}|T_{cp}]$ is also performed from a set of known 3D-2D correspondences but, because the projector cannot "see" the markers and retrieve 3D positions of dots in the calibration target, an alternative method is used to provide this mapping.

A big square Pi-Tag marker is printed on a planar surface and placed under the camera/projector frustum (Figure 4). Once the tag is placed, a snapshot is taken by the camera and used for background subtraction. This allow us to project a dot (of similar size of marker's ones) with the projector by randomizing its 2D position in projector plane, and detect its center with no ambiguity using the camera. If the camera detects that the projected dot lies inside the marker, the 3D position of the dot can be recovered because the marker plane position is known with respect to the camera via Pi-Tag pose estimator.

The whole process can be summarized as follows:

1. A planar surface with a Pi-Tag marker is placed randomly under camera/projector frustum, and a snapshot is taken;
2. A dot $p_p = [\, u_p \, v_p \,]^T$ is projected randomly by the projector. Via background subtraction

the camera can identify the dot projected and determine its 2D position $p_c = [\, u_c\ v_c\,]^T$ in the camera image plane;

3. If the 2D position of the dot lies inside the marker, its 3D position $p_w = [\, x_w\ y_w\ z_w\,]^T$ (in camera world) can be recovered as the intersection of the line from the camera center of projection 0 and the point

$$\left[\frac{u_c - cx_c}{fx_c} \quad \frac{v_c - cy_c}{fy_c} \quad 1\right]^T$$

and the marker plane, computed using Pi-Tag pose estimator;

4. Steps 2 and 3 are repeated to collect hundreds of 3D-2D correspondences (p_w, p_p) from this point of view;
5. Steps 1 to 4 are repeated to collect correspondences between different point of views. For our purposes, about half a dozen of different point of views is usually enough;
6. OpenCV *calibrateCamera* function is used to estimate K_p and the rigid motion $[R_{cpi}|T_{cpi}]$ between the randomly-projected 3D points in camera world from each point of view and the projector. As final $[R_{cp}|T_{cp}]$ we simply choose the rigid motion with respect to the first point of view $[R_{cp0}|T_{cp0}]$ but different strategies may be used.

Only the first step requires human intervention instead of points 2 and 3 that needs to be iterated thoroughly to collect a large set of correspondences.

Even if the process is automatic, steps 2 and 3 may require a very long time depending by the probability that the random dot p_p will lie inside the marker at each iteration. To speed up the calibration procedure, for each point of view, after at least 4 projections lying inside the marker, an homography H can be computed that maps points from camera image plane to projector image plane. With the homography H, each point p_p can be randomized directly lying inside the marker thus eliminating the waste of time required to guess the correct set of positions.

In our setup we are able to collect more than 10 correspondences per second, for an average calibration time of less than 15 minutes.

EXPERIMENTAL EVALUATION

The described setup has been implemented in our laboratory for experimental purposes. To this end we chose to use as the base map the well-known lithography made by Jacopo De' Barberi in 1500 that represents an aerial view of the island of Venice (Boorsch, 1993) – see Figure 2. The data projected over this aerial view was a current satellite map of Venice obtained by downloading single tiles

Figure 2. Actual setup and examples of usage by moving the controller in space

Figure 3. Example of the Pi-Tag design and of the multi-tag calibration pattern adopted

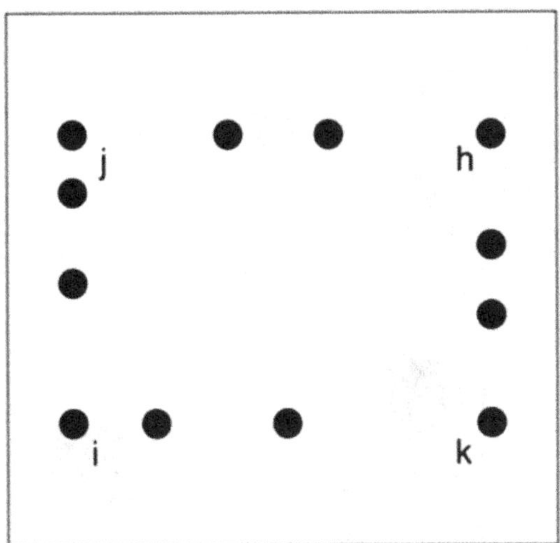

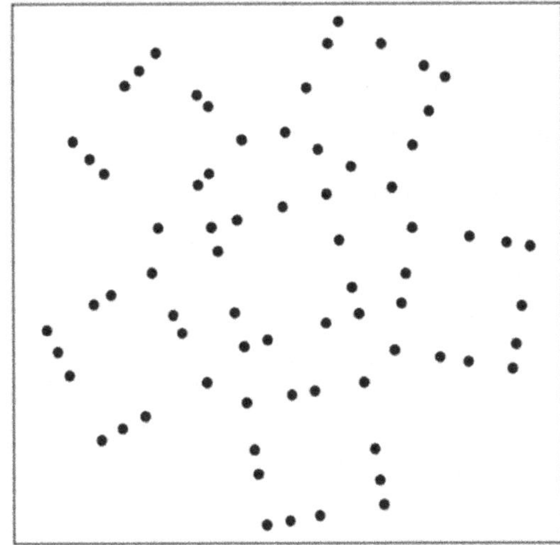

Figure 4. Geometric relation between the entities involved in the calibration procedure

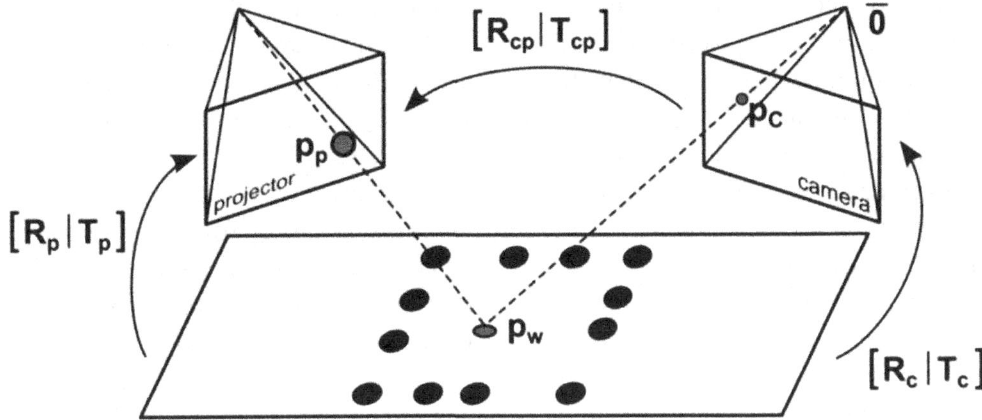

from Google Maps and by composing them in a complete view subject to a slight geometrical deformation. This transformation was needed to correctly overlay the data to the partially incorrect projective view provided by De' Barberi. The user interaction happens by moving an inspection tool printed on a PVC sheet. The user can move the tool over the original lithography and see through the inspection device the current photorealistic appearance of the same area together with optional toponomastic. By moving the target vertically the view is zoomed in a similar fashion to what would happen using a magnifying glass.

CALIBRATION ACCURACY

To create a quantitative evaluation of calibration accuracy obtainable with our setup we crafted a target with an embedded square figure surrounded by a 1-mm-spaced line grid (Figure 5, right). Specifically, a projector was placed 1500 mm above the table with a one-megapixel camera positioned 50mm on the right. A 240x240 mm calibration target was used. We tested the calibration procedure varying the number of dots (3D-2D correspondences) and point of views (positions of planar target with respect to the camera).

Figure 5. Accuracy of the calibration with respect to the number of dots projected and the different point of view presented to the camera

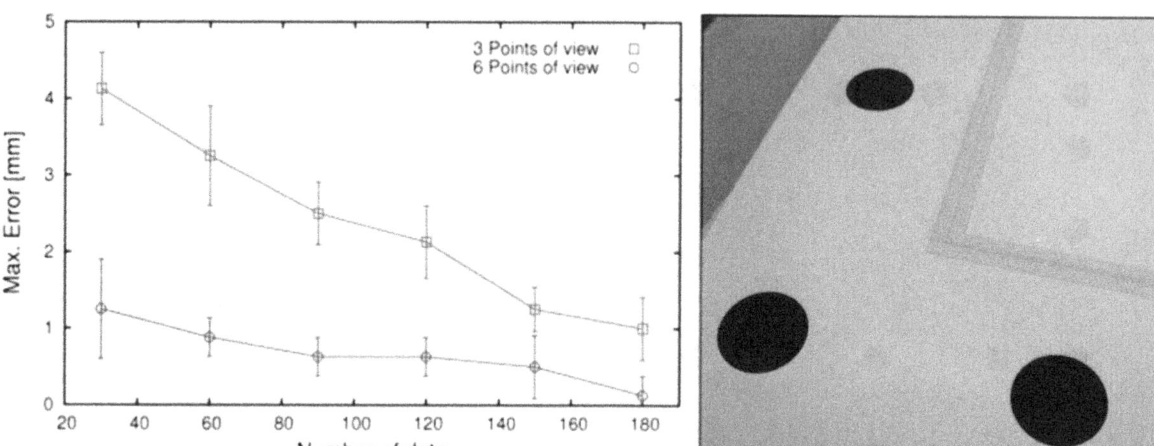

After each calibration procedure, a virtual square is projected onto the real square printed on the target to measure the displacement of each side with respect to the model and evaluate the maximum error in millimeters. The measure is repeated for different positions inside the projector frustum to compute the average error and its standard deviation. As shown in Figure 5 (left), the error decreases as the number of dot rises, being significantly lower when 6 points of view are presented. For any practical purposes, a calibration performed with a hundred of dots divided into 6 points of view is sufficient to obtain an average error less than 1 millimeter, getting an almost perfect projection on the inspection tool.

USER EXPERIENCE

Our augmented map of Venice was presented in the Ca' Foscari exhibition hall to about 50 individuals to analyze the overall user satisfaction. About all users were able to successfully interact with the system without assistance nor previously-given instructions. The overall satisfaction level was pretty high, after a period of testing vast majority of candidates were fascinated by the ease of use and novelty of the interaction model.

Two main drawbacks were reported by the users. The first was the slight latency detected especially while the inspection tool is moved quickly on the map. This is due to the fact that the internal buffer of the projector introduces an unavoidable latency from the time since a frame is sent to the projector and the time in which the frame is actually projected. The second drawback is that the augmented map cannot be projected successfully if the dots on the inspection tool are covered. In our setup this problem is partially reduced with a software-based tracker that interpolates the predicted tool position in between the frames where it is unseen. To address this issue more in depth, as a future work, we will experiment new types of fiducial markers resilient to severe occlusions.

CONCLUSION

We described a practical setup for projection-based augmented maps, based on a novel type of fiducial markers that allows to project multimedia content in their interior without sacrificing detection reliability nor pose estimation accuracy. The system is used to project virtual contents on a physical inspection tool depending on its position above a printed map, making it an effective augmented reality device for museum exhibitions, interactive learning etc. Since tracking can be easily performed in the whole 3D space, zooming or other inspection function can be implemented by taking advantage of vertical movements.

We also outlined a semi-automatic calibration procedure that uses the same fiducial marker components to precisely estimate the geometric relations between the camera and projector to allow an accurate display of contents regardless of the actual pose of the inspection tool, as presented in the experimental section.

REFERENCES

Bergamasco, F., Albarelli, A., & Torsello, A. (2011). Image-space marker detection and recognition using projective invariants. In *Proceedings of International Conference on 3D Imaging, Modeling, Processing, Visualization and Transmission.* Hangzhou, China: IEEE.

Bichlmeier, C., Heining, S. M., Feuerstein, M., & Navab, N. (2009). The virtual mirror: A new interaction paradigm for augmented reality environments. *IEEE Transactions on Medical Imaging*, *28*(9), 1498–1510. doi:10.1109/TMI.2009.2018622 PMID:19336291

Bobrich, J., & Otto, S. (2002). Augmented maps. *Geospatial Theory. Processing and Applications*, *34*(4), 891–923.

Boorsch, S. (1993). *Six centuries of master prints.* New York: Cincinnati Art Museum.

Bradski, A., & Kaehler, A. (2008). *Learning OpenCV: Computer vision with the OpenCV library*. Sebastopol, CA: O'Reilly Media Inc.

Cho, Y., Lee, J., & Neumann, U. (1998). A multi-ring color fiducial system and a rule-based detection method for scalable fiducial-tracking augmented reality. In *Proceedings of International Workshop on Augmented Reality*. IEEE.

Claus, D., & Fitzgibbon, A. (2005). Reliable automatic calibration of a marker-based position tracking system. In *Proceedings of IEEE Workshop on Applications of Computer Vision*, (pp. 300-305). IEEE.

Davis, L., & DeMenthon, D. (1995). Model-based object pose in 25 lines of code. *International Journal of Computer Vision*, *15*, 123–141. doi:10.1007/BF01450852

Elqursh, A., & Egammal, A. (2011). Line-based relative pose estimation. In *Proceedings of IEEE Conference on Computer Vision and Pattern Recognition (CVPR 2011).* Providence, RI: IEEE.

Feng, Z., Been-Lirn Duh, H., & Billinghurst, M. (2008). Trends in augmented reality tracking, interaction and display: A review of ten years of ISMAR. In *Proceedings of the 7th IEEE/ACM International Symposium on Mixed and Augmented Reality*. Washington, DC: IEEE/ACM.

Fiala, M. (2010). Designing highly reliable fiducial markers. *IEEE Transactions on Pattern Analysis and Machine Intelligence*, *22*, 1066–1077. PMID:20489233

Gartell, L., Hoff, E., & Sklair, C. (1991). Robust image features: Concentric contrasting circles and their image extraction. In *Proceedings of Cooperative Intelligent Robotics in Space*. Washington, DC: IEEE.

Lan, L., & Zhong-Dan. (1999). Linear n-point camera pose determination. *IEEE Transactions on Pattern Analysis and Machine Intelligence*, *21*(8), 774–780. doi:10.1109/34.784291

Lee, T., & Höllerer, T. (2009). Multithreaded hybrid feature tracking for markerless augmented reality. *IEEE Transactions on Visualization and Computer Graphics*, *15*(3), 355–368. doi:10.1109/TVCG.2008.190 PMID:19282544

Lowe, D. (1991). Fitting parameterized three-dimensional models to images. *IEEE Transactions on Pattern Analysis and Machine Intelligence*, *13*(5), 441–450. doi:10.1109/34.134043

Mistry, P., Maes, P., & Chang, L. (2009). WUW - Wear ur world: A wearable gestural interface. In *Proceedings of the 27th International Conference on Human Factors in Computing Systems*. Boston: IEEE.

Pittarello, F., & Stecca, R. (2011). Mapping physical objects to digital functions: A tangible interface for querying and navigating a multimedia database. In *Proceedings of 22nd International Workshop on Database and Expert Systems Applications*. Washington, DC: IEEE.

Qian, C., Haiyuan, W., & Toshikazu, W. (2004). Camera calibration with two arbitrary coplanar circles. In *Proceedings of European Conference on Computer Vision (ECCV 2004)*. ECCV.

Reitmayr, G., Eade, E., & Drummond, T. (2005). Localisation and interaction for augmented maps. In *Proceedings of IEEE International Symposium on Mixed and Augmented Reality*. Vienna, Austria: IEEE.

Simon, G., Fitzgibbon, A., & Zisserman, A. (2000). Markerless tracking using planar structures in the scene. In *Proceedings of International Symposium on Augmented Reality*, (pp. 120-128). IEEE.

Sousa-Santos, B. et al. (2009). Head-mounted display versus desktop for 3D navigation in virtual reality: A user study. *Multimedia Tools and Applications*, *41*(1), 161–181. doi:10.1007/s11042-008-0223-2

Wagner, D., Reitmayr, G., Mulloni, A., Drummond, T., & Schmalstieg, D. (2010). Real time detection and tracking for augmented reality on mobile phones. *IEEE Transactions on Visualization and Computer Graphics*, *16*(3), 355–368. doi:10.1109/TVCG.2009.99 PMID:20224132

Chapter 3
A Study on Emotion Releasing Effect with Music and Color

Chih-Fang Huang
Department of Information Communications, Kainan University, Taiwan

Chih-Hsiang Liang
Department of Information Communication, Yuan Ze University, Taiwan

En-Ju Lin
Department of Musicology, Heidelberg University, Germany

ABSTRACT

Music is considered a remedy for the body body, psychological therapy, and a mental release. During World War Two, health medical professionals held concerts to appease the wounded soldiers' emotions and to initiate the research and discussion of music and emotion applied to various fields in academia. This chapter attempts to use the music emotion model as the media to introduce the possible emotional response during music listening via music structure, listener's background, and surroundings, to do the research for human physical and psychological influence by automatic generated electronic sound, and to discuss the emotional releasie effect of music. This chapter also discusses various emotional responses derived by various colors applied to the music emotion model to break the limitation of the existing music forms and to develop the possible music color synesthesia applied to all aspects, in order to lay the foundation for next generation users.

INTRODUCTION

Music is shown to influence on emotion based on various research fields, while color has similar effect to emotion. The research of Oxford University by the psychological Professor Charles Spence indicates that we have the capability to hear shape and size, and even can taste sound; all of the people have synesthesia response in various degrees, and some people have stronger response, therefore a sensory stimulation can induce another sensory neurologically (Calvert, Spence & Stein, 2004; Spence, Senkowski, & Röder, 2009).

The late 19th century Russian composer Alexander Scriabin thought that synesthesia exists between the circle of fifths of music tonality and color frequency circle with a mapping relationship (Galeyev & Vanechkina, 2001). Music emotion

DOI: 10.4018/978-1-4666-4490-8.ch003

model can arouse listener's emotional response via the music structure and fundamental features, listener's background (expertise, preference, personality, mood, etc.), ambient environment events (Gabrielsson, 2001; Gabrielsson & Lindstrom, 2001) therefore the proposed system will generate a music color synesthetic model based on algorithmic composition (Cope, 1992; Cope, 2004; Winsor, 1992) and color model (Fairchild, 2005; Shevell, 2003) to investigate the possibility to use it to release our emotion.

MUSIC AND EMOTION PERCEPTION

Music can arouse strong emotional experiences. In the early stage, Hevner (Hevner, 1936) has proposed 8 categorized emotion terms including solemn, sad, longing, calm, humorous, joyous, agitated, majestic, etc., as shown in Figure 1, to present the music meaning with various emotions implicitly.

Music and Emotion

There are several music features which can make human perceive including pitch, dynamic, timbre, etc., however the features that can arouse emotion including pitch, tempo, loudness, tonality, articulation, and harmony. Among these features, tonality and loudness has greater relation with emotion other than other music features, as shown in Figure 2.

Energy Music Theory

In 1989 Thayer proposed a 2-Dimension emotion plane (Thayer, 1989) using Energy and Stress to

Figure 1. Hevner's adjective circle for emotion

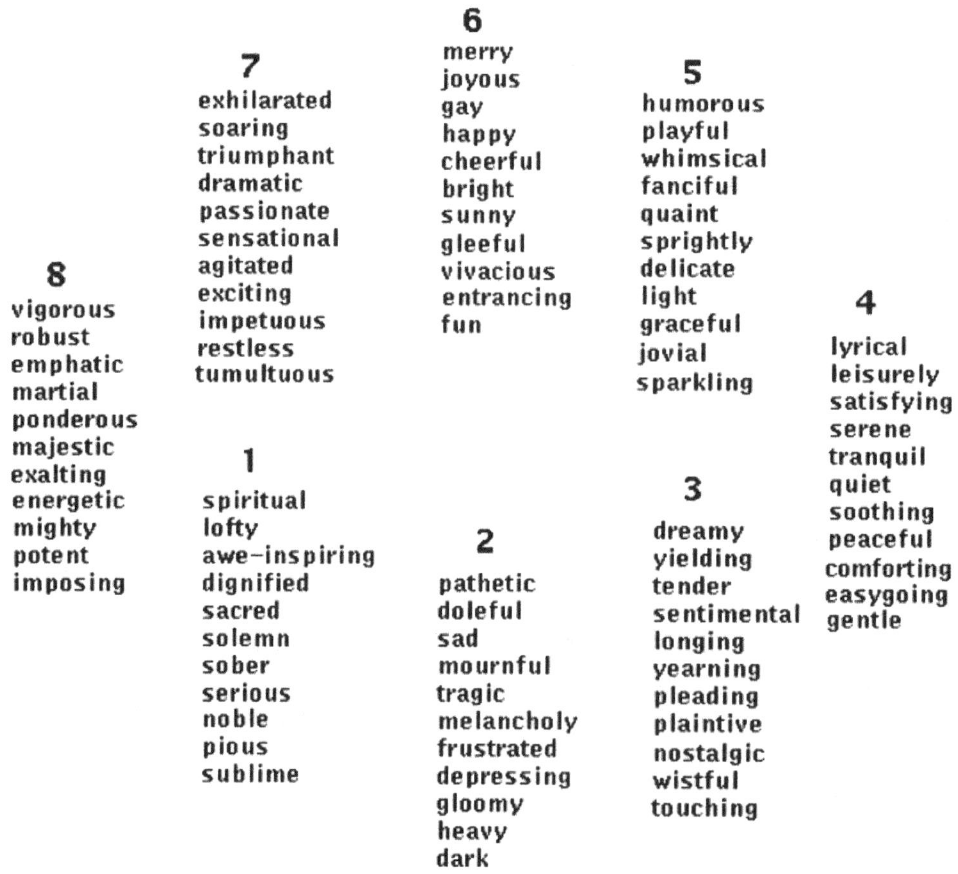

6
merry
joyous
gay
happy
cheerful
bright
sunny
gleeful
vivacious
entrancing
fun

7
exhilarated
soaring
triumphant
dramatic
passionate
sensational
agitated
exciting
impetuous
restless
tumultuous

5
humorous
playful
whimsical
fanciful
quaint
sprightly
delicate
light
graceful
jovial
sparkling

8
vigorous
robust
emphatic
martial
ponderous
majestic
exalting
energetic
mighty
potent
imposing

4
lyrical
leisurely
satisfying
serene
tranquil
quiet
soothing
peaceful
comforting
easygoing
gentle

1
spiritual
lofty
awe-inspiring
dignified
sacred
solemn
sober
serious
noble
pious
sublime

3
dreamy
yielding
tender
sentimental
longing
yearning
pleading
plaintive
nostalgic
wistful
touching

2
pathetic
doleful
sad
mournful
tragic
melancholy
frustrated
depressing
gloomy
heavy
dark

Figure 2. Music features to compose emotion music

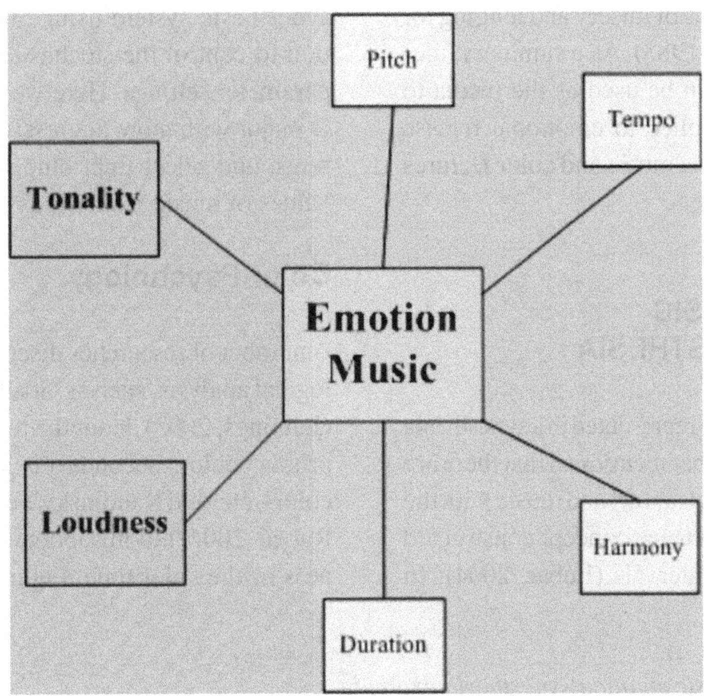

categorize emotion. Energy can be represented by Energetic and Calm for the emotional tension quantity, while Stress is represented by Happy and Anxious for the positive and negative emotions, as shown in Figure 3.

Figure 3. Thayer's 2-dimension emotion plane

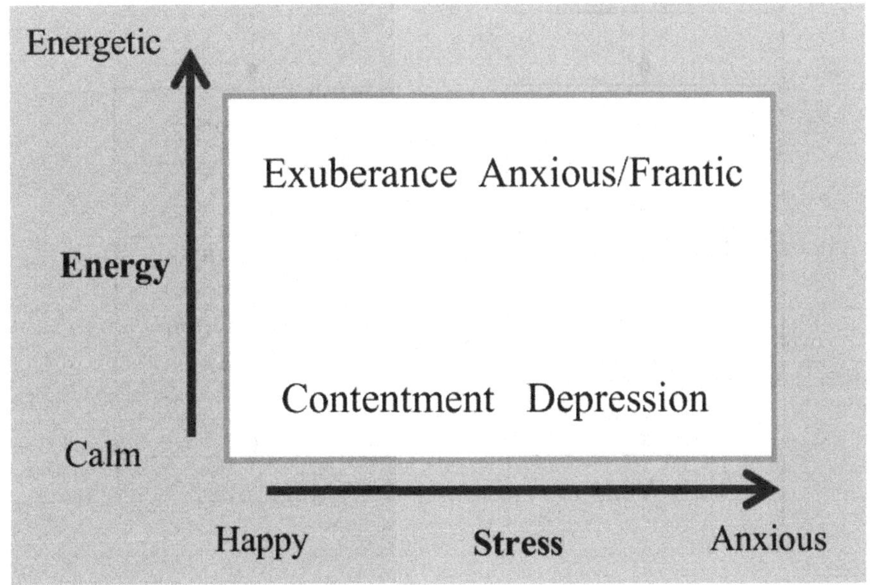

In 18th and 19th centuries, people thought musical keys can be related to various emotions. For instance, A major is "innocent love, satisfaction with one's state of affairs; hope of seeing one's beloved again when parting; youthful cheerfulness and trust in God", and f minor is "deep depression, funereal lament, groans of misery and longing for the grave" (Schubart, 1983). As a summary, music emotion model can be used as the media to discuss the music applied to emotional release effect, based on various music and color features controlled by computer.

COLOR AND MUSIC EMOTION SYNESTHESIA

Color and music can be represented in a synesthesia way with emotion. Lubar mentioned that there are correlations between visual art and music with the consonance and dissonance concept constructed by music and color intervals (Lubar, 2004). In this chapter we propose a color-music emotion synesthesia system using algorithmic composition to control the stochastic music with proper parameter settings. Here we use light yellow for D major with more aggressive music feature settings, and select light blue with less aggressive values of music features, as shown in Figure 4.

Color Psychology

A number of researches discuss the color psychological analysis, such as Goethe's "Color Wheel" (Jennings, 2003) about the relationships between primary colors, secondary colors, complementary colors, etc, and Kandinsky's color studies (Ball, & Ruben, 2004) talking about the warmth and coldness of the color tone. Figure 5 shows Goethe's

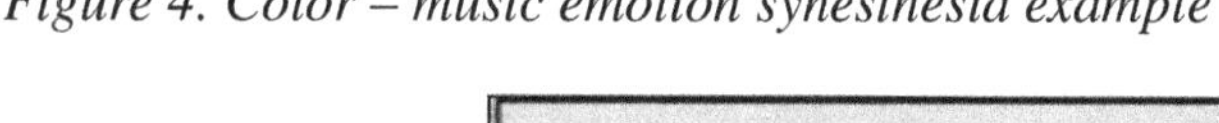

Figure 4. Color – music emotion synesthesia example

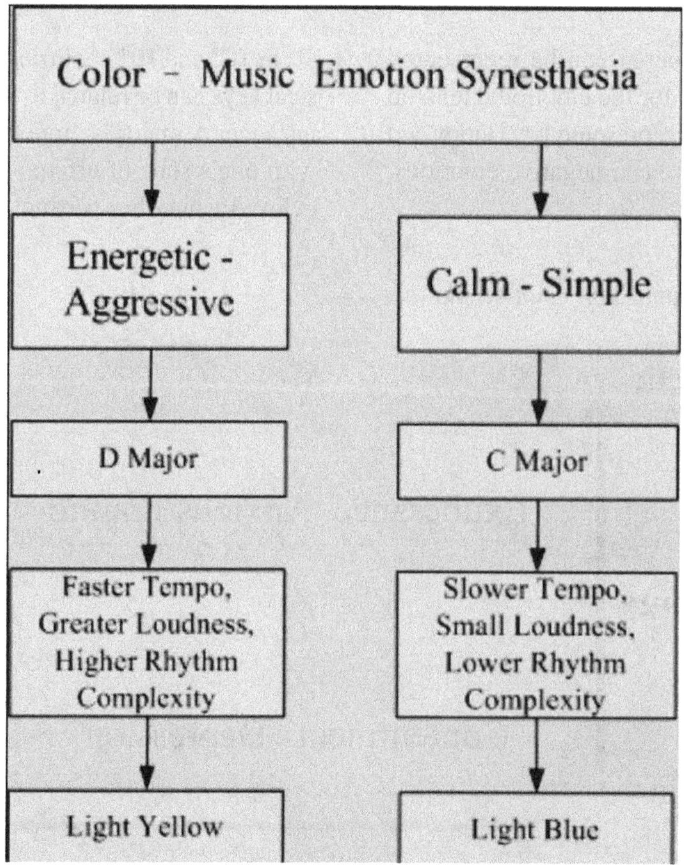

Figure 5. Goethe's color wheel

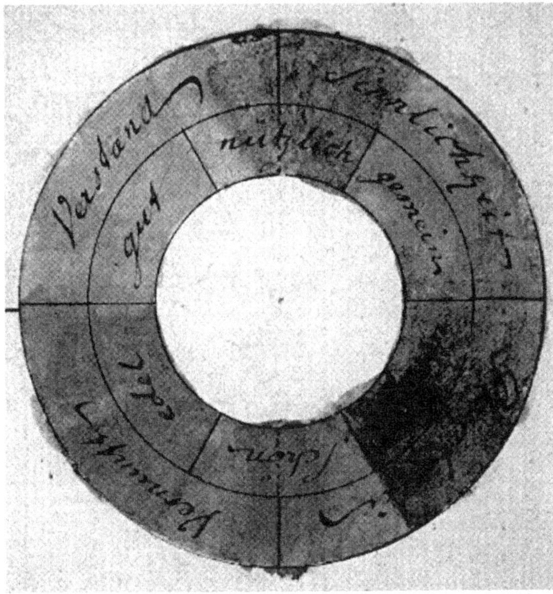

Color Wheel, with red, orange, yellow, green, blue, and purple for both spiritual and artistic concepts. These theories can be used for emotion based color recommendation psychologically for the proposed system.

Color and Emotion

Based on the above theories and concepts, especially from Goethe's theory, it is supposed that each color can provide a specific mood for people. For instance, yellow is correlated to positive, energetic, and aggressive, while blue is correspondent to less aggressive emotion, such as melancholic or calm, therefore the proposed music –color synthesthia system can incorporate the idea as the fundamental theory.

THE MUSIC: COLOR SYNESTHESIA IMPLEMENTATION WITH COMPUTER MUSIC

The automated music composition GIBAMC (Graphic Interface Based Automated Music Composition) is developed for this research, to correlate the music with color image, to investigate who much synesthesia for both musicians and nonmusicians. As the above described, C major and D major is selected with light blue and light yellow patterns designed, respectively. There are 10 subjects aged from 21 to 30, to listen to the simple work composed by the computer with the designed images.

Experiment #1

C major is selected for Experiment 1, for its simplicity, calamity, and purity. Music parameters such as tempo, loudness, and rhythm complexity is reduced to fit this situation, while a computer generated image pattern is designed in a comfortable, safe, and calm color, the light blue, to attain the goal of alleviated emotion. Figure 6 shows the automated music composition system in C major, Figure 7 shows the output score, and the designed light blue image pattern is shown in Figure 8.

Experiment #2

D major is selected for Experiment 2, for its passion, aggressiveness, and complexity. Music parameters such as tempo, loudness, and rhythm complexity is raised to fit this situation, while a computer generated image pattern is designed in an aggressive, exorbitant, and passionate color, the light yellow, to attain the goal of excited emotion. Figure 9 shows the automated music composition system in D major, Figure 10 shows the output score, and the designed light yellow image pattern is shown in Figure 11.

According to the above experiment setup, the questionnaire result is shown in Table. 1, and the music – color synesthesia can be constructed for both musicians and non-musicians. That means music and color integrated system can reinforce the releasing emotion with the proposed synesthesia system, regardless of the music background of the listeners.

Figure 6. Automated music composition system – C major HCI

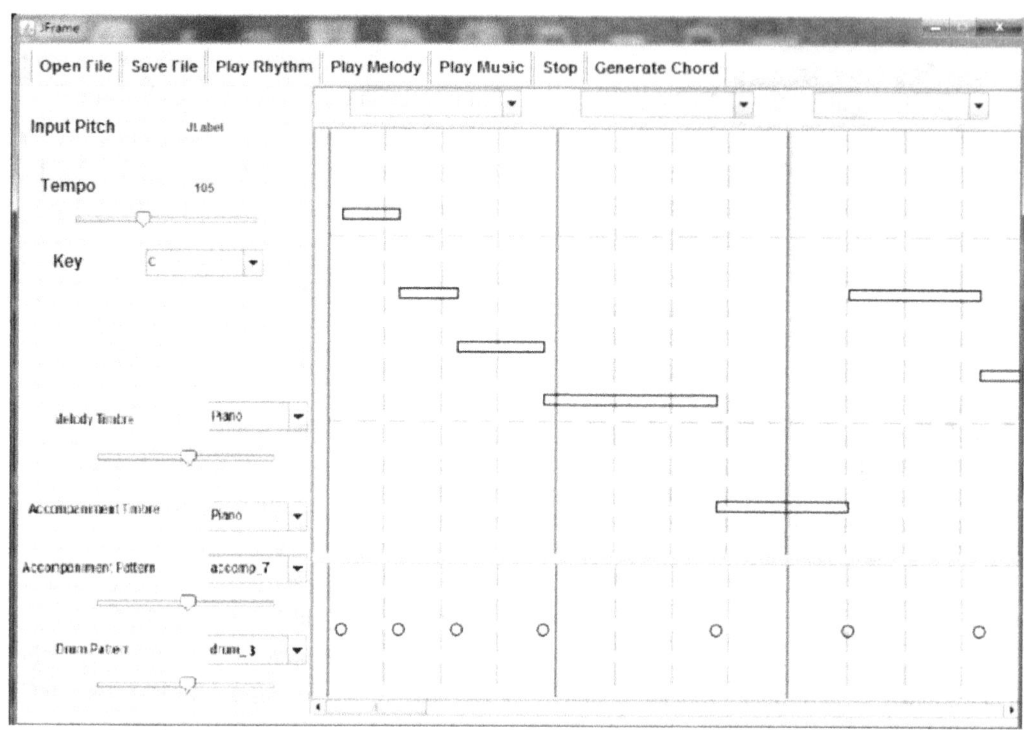

Figure 7. Automated music composition system – C major score output

Figure 8. Light blue image pattern

CONCLUSION

According to the above mentioned releasing emotion of the synesthesia discussion using the automated music composition system with color, the music - color synesthesia discussion since late 19th century has been developed progressively and applied into various fields with the invention of modern technology. In the future, it can be used for human-man-interface (HMI) or human-computer-interface (HCI) design, to emphasize the interactivity and real-time featres for automated computer music, to integrate with the emotion based interface for the innovated multimedia system between human and music with diversity hopefully.

Figure 9. Automated music composition system – D major HCI

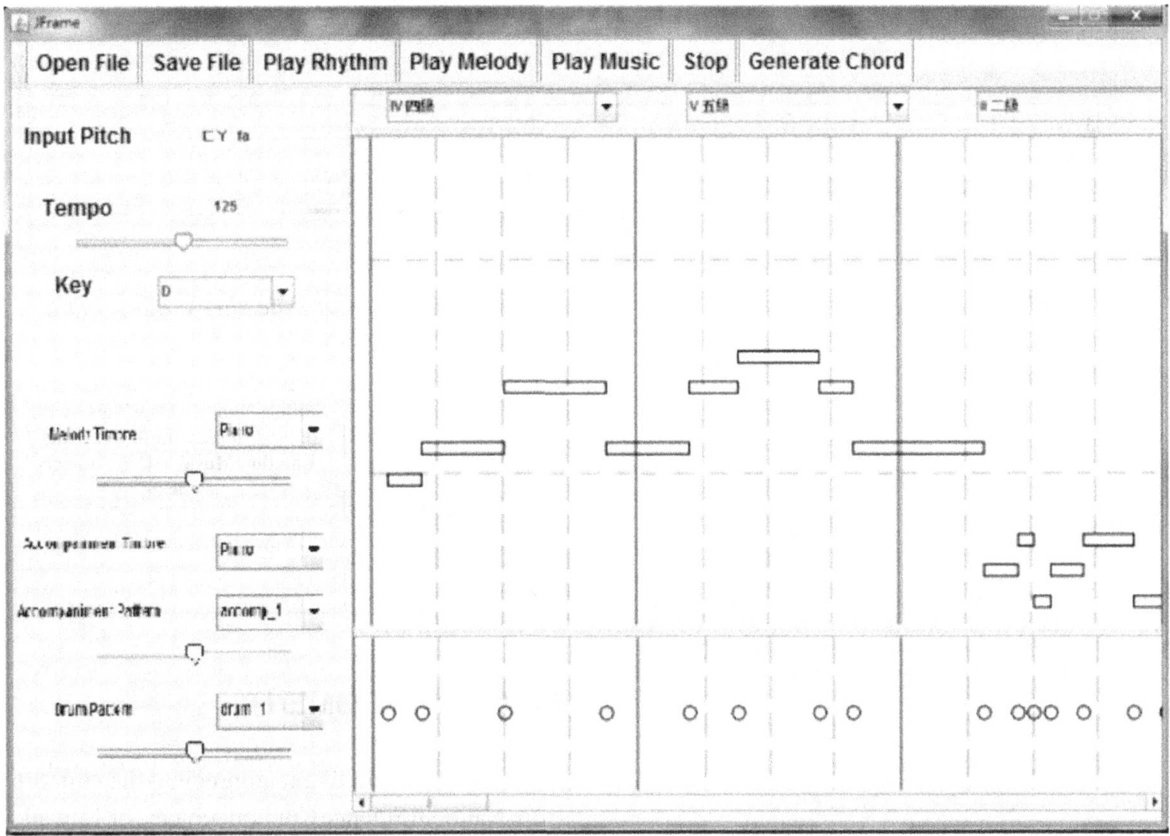

Figure 10. Automated music composition system – D major score output

Figure 11. Light yellow image pattern

Table 1. Music –color synesthesia questionnaire result

	Total Subject Number	Subject Number Who Agree with the Reinforcement of Releasing Emotion Music + Color Image Pattern
Musicians	5	4
Non-musicians	5	5

ACKNOWLEDGMENT

The authors would like to appreciate the support from National Science Council projects of Taiwan: NSC99-2410-H-155 -035 -MY2.

REFERENCES

Ball, P., & Ruben, M. (2004). Mario Ruben color theory in science and art: Ostwald and the Bauhaus. *Angewandte Chemie*, *43*(37), 4842–4847. doi:10.1002/anie.200430086 PMID:15317016

Calvert, G., Spence, C., & Stein, B. (2004). *The handbook of multisensory processes*. Cambridge, MA: MIT Press.

Cope, D. (1992). Computer modeling of musical intelligence in experiments in musical intelligence. *Computer Music Journal*, *16*(2), 69–83. doi:10.2307/3680717

Cope, D. (2004). *Virtual music: Computer synthesis of musical style*. Cambridge, MA: MIT Press.

Fairchild, D. (2005). Color appearance models. In *Imaging Science and Technology* (Vol. 3). Hoboken, NJ: John Wiley and Sons.

Gabrielsson, A. (2001). Emotions in strong experiences with music. In *Music and emotion: Theory and research*. Oxford, UK: Oxford University Press.

Gabrielsson, A., & Lindstrom, E. (2001). The influence of musical structure on emotional expression. In *Music and Emotion: Theory and Research*. Oxford, UK: Oxford University Press.

Galeyev, B., & Vanechkina, I. (2001). Was scriabin a synesthete? *Leonardo*, *34*(4), 357–362. doi:10.1162/00240940152549357

Hevner, K. (1936). Experimental studies of the elements of expression in music. *The American Journal of Psychology*, *48*, 246–268. doi:10.2307/1415746

Jennings, S. (2003). *Artist's color manual: The complete guide to working with color*. New York: Chronicle Books.

Lubar, K. (2004). Color music. *Leonardo Journal*, *37*(2), 127–132. doi:10.1162/0024094041139283

Schubart, C. (1983). Ideen zu einer Aesthetik der Tonkunst (1806). In *A History of Key Characteristics in the 18th and Early 19th Centuries*. UMI Research Press.

Shevell, S. (2003). *The science of color*. Amsterdam: Elsevier.

Spence, C., Senkowski, D., & Röder, B. (2009). Crossmodal processing. *Experimental Brain Research*, *198*(2-3), 107–111. doi:10.1007/s00221-009-1973-4 PMID:19690844

Thayer, E. (1989). *The biopsychology of mood and arousal*. New York: Oxford University Press.

Winsor, P. (1992). *Automated music composition*. University of North Texas Press.

Chapter 4
An Algorithm for Occlusion-Free Texture Mapping from Oriented Images

Mattia Previtali
Department of Building Environmental Science and Technology, Politecnico di Milano, Italy

Luigi Barazzetti
Department of Building Environmental Science and Technology, Politecnico di Milano, Italy

Marco Scaioni
Tongji University - College of Surveying and Geo-Informatics, Center for Spatial Information Science and Sustainable Development Applications, Shanghai, P.R. China

Raffaella Brumana
Department of Building Environmental Science and Technology, Politecnico di Milano, Italy

Daniela Oreni
Department of Building Environmental Science and Technology, Politecnico di Milano, Italy

ABSTRACT

The possibility of deriving digital reconstructions of real objects has given new emphasis to numerous research domains. The growing interest in accurate and detailed models has also increased the request of realistic visualizations and data management methods. The aim of this work is the implementation of an algorithm able to map digitaled images on 3D polygonal models of terrestrial objects. In particular, the authors focus on two different aspects: the geometric issues during the texture mapping phase with convergent images (e.g. self-occlusions) and the color brightness correction when multiple images are used to process the same portion of the mesh.

INTRODUCTION

Nowadays different instruments and techniques allow expert operators to obtain accurate 3D models of complex objects. This has had an impact on the customer's expectations, which have increased making realistic reconstructions important in many research domains (e.g. cultural heritage documentation and preservation, virtual reality, game and movie industry, reverse engineering, etc.).

Modern data acquisition and processing techniques are mainly based on strategies which use *active* or *passive* sensors. The former relies on the use of range-based systems that emit a signal

DOI: 10.4018/978-1-4666-4490-8.ch004

and detect its reflection (typical examples of such expensive instruments are laser scanning and structured light technology). The latter employs sets of digital images that are processed to obtain a tridimensional reconstruction of the scene. Basically, both methods have pro and contra and their combined use is often mandatory for real applications.

Images and laser scans are today exploited in both Computer Vision (Hartley & Zisserman, 2004). and Photogrammetry (Kraus, 2007), whose researchers have developed methods for data processing based on different algorithms and methods. Although the goal (in this case a digital reconstruction) is basically the same, the attention is paid to particular requisites such as automation, accuracy, and completeness: in a few words, the final result could be very different.

In this chapter we focus on the last step of the data processing pipeline, that is called *texture-mapping* and relies on the assignment of original color to the model. We therefore assume that a 3D digital model of the object (represented by a mesh) is already available, whereas the color information must be applied using a set of oriented images. This means that mesh and images are already registered in a common reference system.

The final aim is the creation of realistic, detailed, and accurate models with a correct correspondence between the geometric part and its visual appearance: the final model must represent the material and its real color.

The literature reports several examples of applications where a realistic 3D model was needed (e.g. –Guidi, et al., 2009; Pesci, Bonali, Galli, & Boschi, 2011). The market offers some packages (e.g. 3D Studio Max, Geomagic Studio, PhotoModeler Scanner, ShapeTexture, etc.) that are clearly based on different algorithmic implementations, even though they can be often used only as "black boxes". The scientific literature tried to solve for the texture mapping problem by different geometric and radiometric strategies (Rocchini, Cignoni, & Montani, 1999) developed a complete pipeline divided into several steps (vertex-to-image binding, patch growing, patch boundary smoothing, texture patches packing) where multiple views are stitched on the mesh and partially fused to generate a single textured model (El-Hakim, Gonzo, Picard, Girardi & Simoni, 2003) considers the problem of multiple image overlap for the same triangles. Their approach generates larger groups of triangles mapped from the same image and eliminates isolated texture mappings. Then, two procedures are run to compensate for radiometric differences. The first one is an iterative procedure based on a least squares adjustment which minimizes gray-value differences at both local and global levels. The second method, that is more like and alternative to the previous one, performs image blending (Lensch, Heidrich & Seidel, 2000; Niem & Broszio, 1995) through a weighted average of the textures of different images. However, this could lead to blurred results: if there are small triangles, blending cannot be sufficient to reduce the color transition. On the other hand, if the triangles are too large a blurring effect can occur. Alternative approaches for color correction are instead based on corresponding points [9-10] extracted from overlapping areas, where the aim is the analytic estimation of the color brightness variation.

In (Akca et al., 2007) the problem of self-occlusions was overcome by projecting the mesh in the image space and by verifying the intersection of different triangles. As their application was carried out with oriented images with a similar camera-object distance, the choice of the master image was performed by using the angle between the normal vector of the triangle and the viewing direction (Hanush, 2010) proposed a complete texture-mapping approach where different geometric (visibility analysis, triangle to image assignment) and radiometric issues (brightness and vignetting correction, overexposed regions, shadow removal) were analyzed. Moreover, the method is also able to produce true-orthophotos.

The idea behind this chapter is an automated texture mapping algorithm of 3D objects able to obtain realist results. We assume that both 3D mesh and images are already available and registered in the same reference frame and we exploit only the texture mapping phase. Here, a series of geometric and radiometric problems should be considered. In particular, concerning the geometric aspect, possible self-occlusions should be taken into account in order to prevent wrong mapping situations, e.g. when an image is used to texture a triangle oriented in the opposite direction with respect to the image viewpoint. In the case the object is textured using different images the transition between an image to another one should be sufficiently smooth in order to prevent a sharp color change due to a difference in both color and brightness.

Our work uses some of the methods previously described and introduces several novelties. Different algorithmic issues were taken into consideration, starting from the size of the datasets (point clouds composed of many million points and high resolution digital imagery) up to the complete automation of the procedure. As automatic methods (like that here illustrated) tend to produce gross errors, the procedure is also quite robust against these effects.

The chapter is organized in this way: paragraph 2 presents the implemented methodology and the main critical aspects of a tridimensional texture mapping approach. Paragraph 3 illustrates some real cases where objects were previously surveyed with photogrammetric techniques.

THE PROPOSED METHOD FOR TEXTURE MAPPING

The implemented procedure for texture-mapping of 3D objects can be split into two steps where both geometric and radiometric parts are analyzed independently. However, although these phases could be partially parallelized, information extracted from geometric analysis is the starting point for the following radiometric correction.

Image to Triangle Assignment: Visibility Analysis

Starting from a mesh that describes the surface of the object a simple texture mapping algorithm is essentially based on the automatic back-projection of all vertices (object space) to the image space by using an appropriate mathematical model. However, in the case of complex 3D situations this approach could produce inadequate results because of occluded areas, i.e. faces that are not visible from a fixed viewpoint (Figure 1). The final result could be the correct texturing of the first face and the wrong texture mapping of the remaining "aligned" faces.

For this reason, the polygonal mesh must incorporate not only the connection of the sparse original points, but also the orientation of each triangle in order to determine an initial mesh-to-image visibility. We define this more advanced geometric object as *oriented mesh.*

Visibility analysis is intended as a procedure which identifies all areas "invisible" in the images. As mentioned before, the data to be textured are mesh structures with oriented triangles. This means that the vertex order of every triangle should be (e.g. counterclockwise) structured to correctly define the front and back faces. In addition, the oriented images should be distortion free, i.e. images distortion should be eliminated with a proper correction model (Remondino & Fraser, 2006). Given an image I_j and a mesh of triangles $T_{1...N}$ a reduction of triangles to be tested can be done by using a cascaded approach where results are progressively refined. First of all, a *view frustum culling* (Figure 2) is run in order to label all triangles outside the camera view. This can be carried out by back-projecting the vertices of the

Figure 1. Example of wrong texturing due to simple back projection

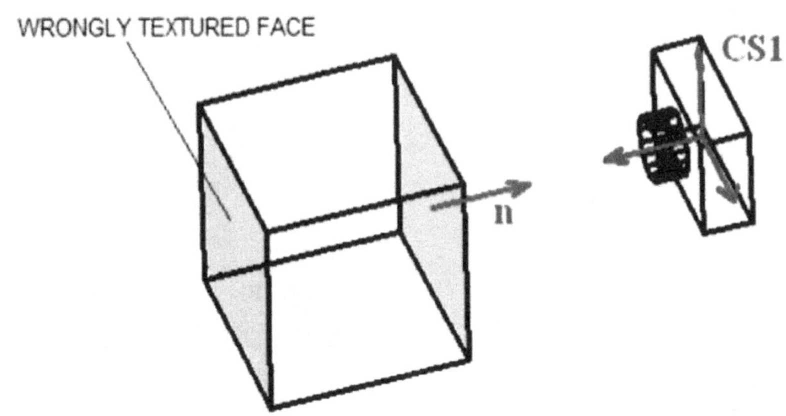

Figure 2. The view frustum culling principle: red triangles are not textured by the image

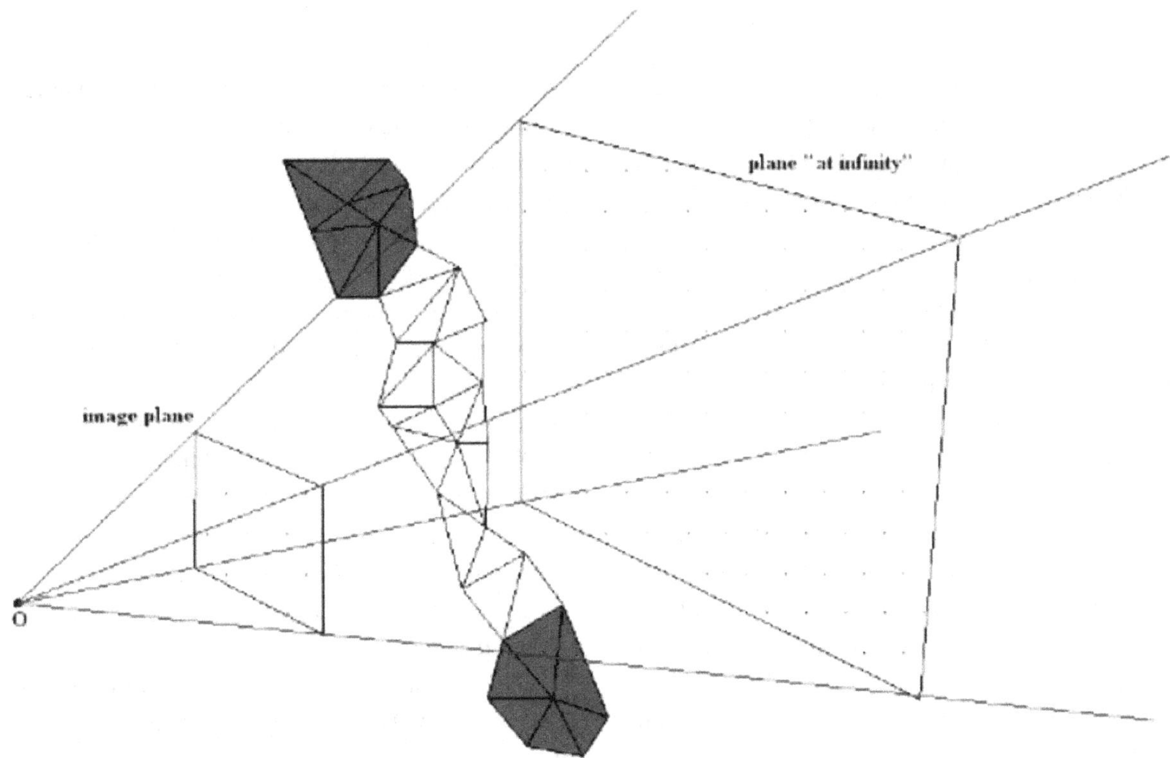

triangles $T_{1...N}$ on the image I_j: if the vertices of the triangle T_i fall outside the image boundaries the triangle can be labeled as invisible.

A further reduction of triangles can be obtained by using a *back-facing culling* (Figure 3). Given the triangle normals $N_{1...N}$ and the camera position j it is possible to define the vector normal to the image plane n_j. If the angle between the face normal N_i and the viewing direction of the camera n_j is larger than 90° the triangle is geometrically invisible, otherwise the triangle is potentially visible.

Figure 3. Back-facing culling principle: only the blue face of the cube is considered as potentially visible from the camera station

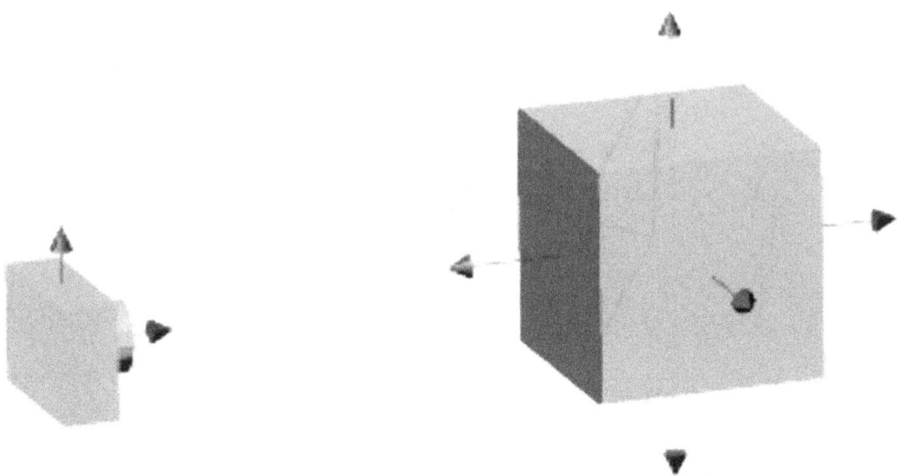

According to these considerations and depending on the structure of the dataset, the number of the triangles to be processed in the next phases can be significantly reduced. However, self-occluded areas are still present and could degrade the quality of the model. This is due to the fact that the previous steps do not consider the collinearity principle that is the real relationship behind the image formation process.

Given a reference triangle T_1, a testing triangle T_i, and the viewpoint j we have three possibilities: a face is visible, occluded, or partially occluded. However, at the end of our visibility analysis, triangles are labeled only as visible or invisible, as we assume that the triangle T_1 is occluded (say invisible) in the case of both full and partial occlusion.

Following that, two triangles are reprojected on the image space using the interior and exterior orientation parameters of the image to understand their reciprocal positions (Figure 4). Then, the distance between the vertices of the triangles is calculated in order to solve for the case of potential occlusions. The triangle far from the projection center is occluded, while the other is the occluding one. Lastly, after testing the triangle T_1 with all the triangles T_i it is possible to understand if there is an occlusion and, if the triangle is visible, texture mapping can be performed.

The process can be repeated for all the available images, obtaining a computation complexity O^2. This is a fundamental drawback for meshes with several triangles (millions) even with the triangle reduction obtained by running the view frustum and back-facing algorithms (although these steps can be speeded up by reducing the number of testing triangles). Indeed, in most cases, we need to test triangles that reprojected in the image are often quite far from the reference one, obtaining a series of not occluded results. On the other hand, we are more interested in the case of possible overlapping between the reprojected triangles.

The risk of intersection is higher for triangles that reprojected in the image are close to the reference one. These triangles are the most important to be tested. Practically, we limit the intersection test only to a certain amount of nearest neighborhoods. Their number depends on the quality of the geometric model and on the image scale. However, in all our practical cases this was not a limiting factor. The use of a reasonable number of neighborhoods to be tested does not affect the final result significantly.

Figure 4. The visibility analysis principle: (a) the two triangles do not occlude each other and no triangle intersection exists in the image space; (b) the red triangle occludes the blue one (they intersect in the image plane)

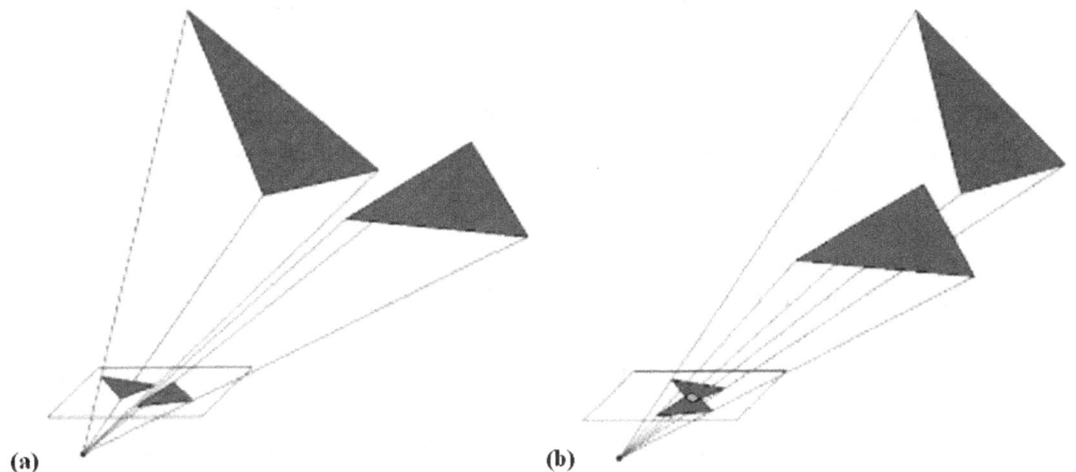

Radiometric Correction

After the visibility analysis the radiometric correction reduces the color brightness difference due to multiple images (Figure 5). The radiometric correction is not performed in the traditional RGB space but in the L*a*b* color space (ISO 1164A), where the L* channel represents the lightness of the color (L*=0=black, L*=100=diffuse white), the a* and b*channels define the color plane. The a* axis is positioned along the red/magenta and green direction (a*<0=green, a*>0=magenta), the b*axis is positioned along the yellow and blue direction (b*<0=blue, b*>0=yellow).

The color brightness correction is based on corresponding points detected in different images with the ATiPE algorithm (Barazzetti, Remondino & Scaioni, 2010). This is due to the fact

Figure 5. Color/brightness correction for a synthetic dataset made up of two images

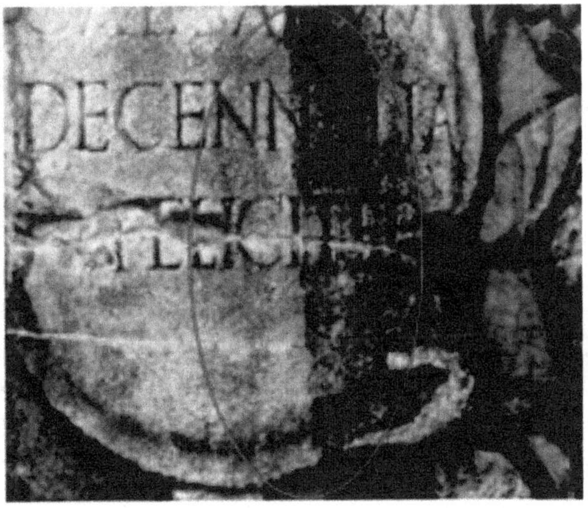

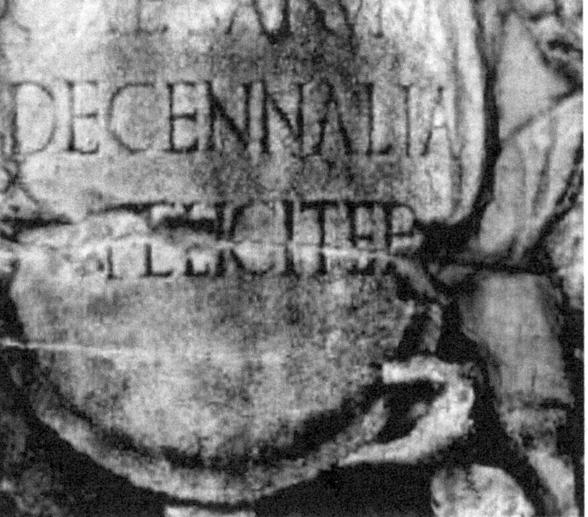

that in the L*a*b* space a brightness correction is carried out by adjusting the L* channel, whereas a color correction can be obtained with the analysis of a* and b* channels. These independent corrections are not possible in the case of the RGB space.

The correction uses one image as reference and the remaining ones are adjusted. The choice of the master image is not trivial: multiple factors (e.g. material, exposition, light, degradation, etc.) must be taken into consideration. The number of factors of this last step is too long to be exhaustively listed here. However, the expert operator should know very well all these issues, starting from white balancing up to brightness illumination.

Generally, two images present brightness differences that can be modeled as a function z=f(x,y), where z is the radiometric difference and x,y pixel coordinates. The use of corresponding points allows one to estimate a discrete color brightness difference function. If the number of common point is sufficient, sparse values can be interpolated in order to obtain f(x,y). Three key factors have a significant influence on the results: the corresponding point density and accuracy, and the interpolation method. The point density is the fundamental parameter to obtain a good approximation of the function f(x,y). It is therefore necessary to extract a large number of common points to obtain a pointwise evaluation of f(x,y). For this reason a manual measurement of corresponding points between the images, with only some tenth of points, is not the best choice. The image point accuracy plays a fundamental role in order to correctly evaluate the function f(x,y). Feature-based operators like SIFT (Lowe, 1999) that are implemented in ATiPE, are generally robust and accurate.

The last step concerns the interpolation method: our test with a Kriging-based interpolation Cressie (1991) provided satisfactory results. Generally, the grid spacing of the interpolated function f(x,y) is equal to the pixel size of the image and its extent in the image space is limited to the area covered by common points. In the case the number of corresponding points is very poor (e.g. due to low-textured areas or manual measurements) a color brightness correction based on the estimation of f(x,y) may not be reliable. A simple global color brightness, where the correction of color and brightness is constant over the whole image, revealed to be quite effective.

FINDINGS

In this paragraph some applications of the proposed approach are presented. The first dataset is a digital model of a small marble sculpture in the Church of S. Maria Maggiore (Bg, Italy). The geometric model was obtained through a photogrammetric process based on the data processing of calibrated images. The dense matching algorithm MGCM+ (Previtali, Barazzetti, Scaioni, & Yixiang, 2011) was used to reconstruct a mesh describing the surface of the object. The final digital model consists of about two million triangles. 12 images were acquired without using particular illumination systems in order to reconstruct the object geometry and to texture its surface: the natural sunlight was exploited (Figure 6).

Because of this choice and the material of the statue (white marble) there are significant radiometric problems. Due to many self-occlusions of some parts of the object (images are taken around the object exploiting a field of view wider than 180°), a visibility analysis is mandatory to prevent errors.

The color/brightness differences between the images are clearly visible in the final textured model without a radiometric correction. Corresponding points extracted in the orientation phase were used to reduce this effect (Figure 7), as previously explained. In particular, as the aim was a realistic result, a simple brightness correction (L* channel) was not sufficient due to irregular

Figure 6. Camera poses and 3D points after image orientation (left): it is quite evident that the algorithm must be able to work in 3D. Shaded and textured 3D models (right).

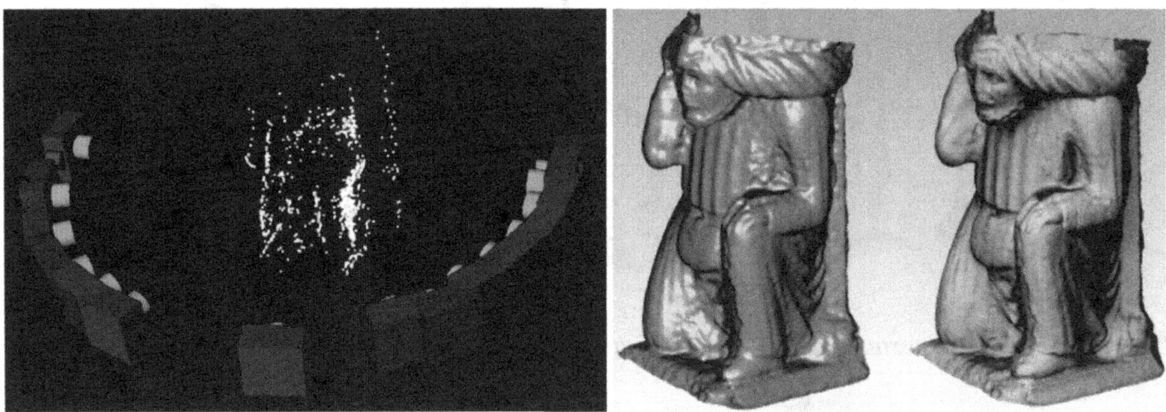

Figure 7. Color/brightness correction: (a) original images and (b) results obtained by using the method for radiometric image fusion

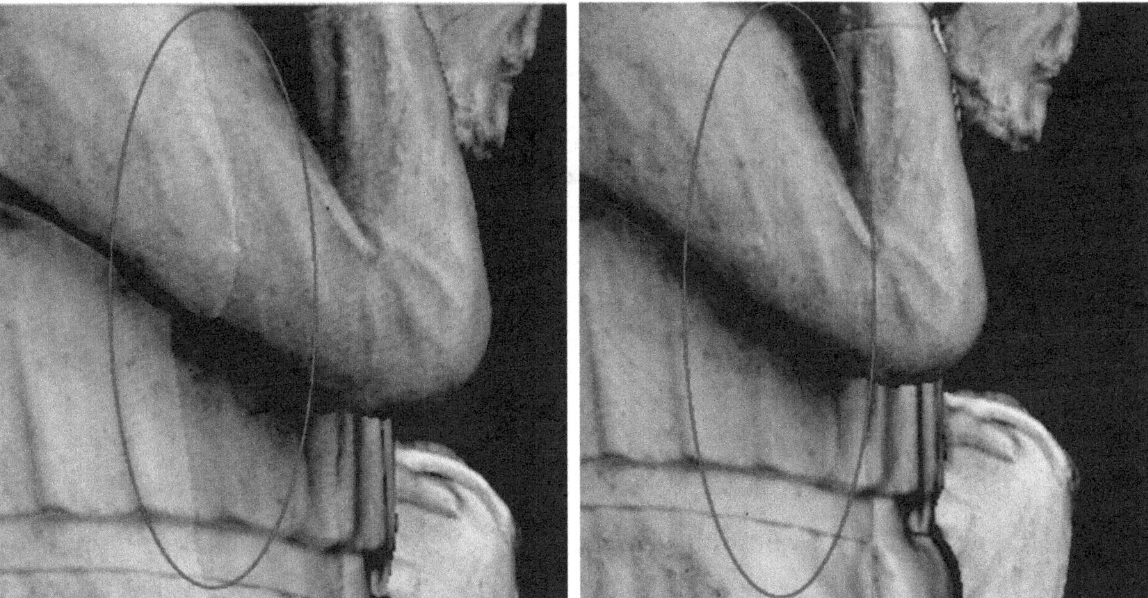

marble reflections: the correction of the color was mandatory, involving both a* and b* channels.

The second dataset is a digital model of a lion sculpture always located in Bergamo –Bg, Italy (Figure 8). The geometric model was obtained using the photogrammetric system ATiPE and the previously cited dense image matching algorithm. 22 images with uniform color variations were acquired in order to generate the textured model. Obviously, the complex geometry of the lion required a preliminary visibility analysis to remove self-occlusion problems.

The last dataset (Figure 9) is a digital model of a lion, which is a part of the Contarini Fountain in Piazza Vecchia (Bg, Italy). The geometric model was obtained through image matching us-

Figure 8. Shaded and textured 3D models of the lion

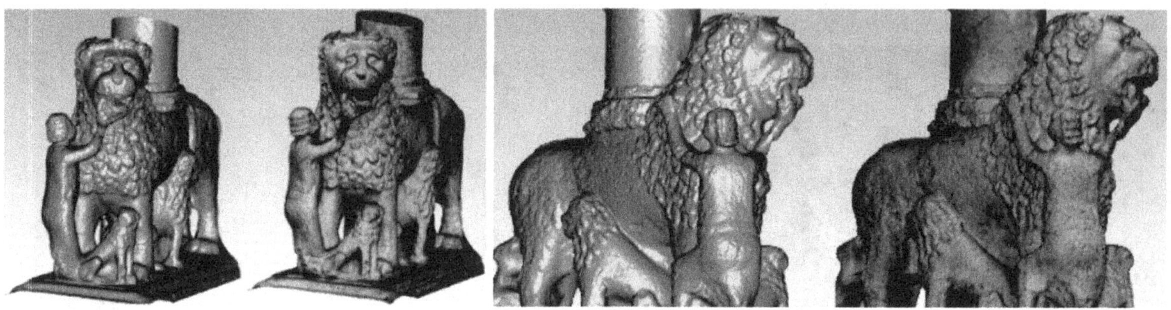

Figure 9. Shaded and textured model of a decoration of the Contarini Fountain

ing 18 images taken with a low-cost camera. The sculpture is a made of marble and a particular care was paid to the radiometric correction in order to obtain a uniform model. Visibility analysis was carried out for each image considering 300 neighboring triangles. This choice was motivated by the level of detail of the mesh and, after our experiments, demonstrated to be an appropriate choice in terms of CPU time: doubling the number of tested triangles increased the computational time without providing significant improvements of the final result.

CONCLUSION AND FUTURE WORK

This work aimed at developing an automated and robust technique for texture mapping of terrestrial objects. It combines geometric and radiometric strategies in order to remove most problems of these kind of applications: multiple texturing of self-occluded faces and color discontinuities in overlapping areas.

As things stand now, the operator has to manually set several thresholds (e.g. the number of triangles around the considered face) that are then assumed constant for the whole object. A final visual inspection represents the final check to establish the realist effect obtained.

Future developments concern the implementation of auto-adaptative algorithms able to modify the input parameters according to the investigated portion of the mesh. For instance, the number of neighboring triangles, their size, or the local behavior of the surface normals will be considered in a forthcoming version. Other parameters, which express the image-to-mesh connection (not only the viewing direction), like the camera-object distance and the pixel size projected on the mesh, will be also investigated.

Although in this chapter the objects are mainly statues and decorations, we are planning an extension to more complicated architectural scenes reconstructed with polygonal models.

REFERENCES

Agathos, A., & Fisher, R. (2003). Colour texture fusion of multiple range images. In *Proceedings of Fourth International Conference on 3-D Digital Imaging and Modeling (3DIM'03),* (pp. 139-146). 3DIM.

Akca, D., et al. (2007). Performance evaluation of a coded structured light system for cultural heritage applications. In *Proceedings of Society of Photo-Optical Instrumentation Engineers (SPIE) Conference*. SPIE.

Bannai, N., Agathos, A., & Fisher, R. (2004). Fusing multiple color images for texturing models. In *Proceedings of 2nd International Symposium on 3D Data Processing, Visualization and Transmission (3DPVT'04),* (pp. 558-565). 3DPVT.

Barazzetti, L., Remondino, F., & Scaioni, M. (2010). Orientation and 3D modelling from markerless terrestrial images: Combining accuracy with automation. *The Photogrammetric Record*, *25*(132), 356–381. doi:10.1111/j.1477-9730.2010.00599.x

Cressie, N. (1991). *Statistics for spatial data*. New York: John Wiley and Sons, Inc.

El-Hakim, S., Gonzo, L., Picard, M., Girardi, S., & Simoni, A. (2003). Visualisation of frescoed surface: Buonconsiglio castle, aquila tower, cycle of months. In *Proceedings of International Workshop on Visualisation and Animation of Reality-Based 3D Models*. IEEE.

Guidi, G. et al. (2009). A multi-resolution methodology for the 3D modeling of large and complex archeological areas. *International Journal of Architectural Computing*, *7*(1), 39–55. doi:10.1260/147807709788549439

Hanush, T. (2010). *Texture mapping and true orthophoto generation of 3D objects.* (PhD thesis). Swiss Federal Institute of Technology (ETH), Zurich, Switzerland.

Hartley, R., & Zisserman, A. (2004). *Multiple view geometry in computer vision*. Cambridge, UK: Cambridge University Press. doi:10.1017/CBO9780511811685

Kraus, K. (2007). *Photogrammetry: Geometry from images and laser scans*. Walter de Gruyter. doi:10.1515/9783110892871

Lensch, H., Heidrich, W., & Seidel, H. (2000). Automated texture registration and stitching for real world models. In *Proceedings of 8th Pacific Conference on Computer Graphics and Applications*, (pp. 317-326). IEEE.

Lowe, D. (1999). Object recognition from local scale-invariant features. In *Proceedings of International Conference on Computer Vision*. IEEE.

Niem, W., & Broszio, H. (1995). Mapping texture from multiple camera views onto 3D-object models for computer animation. In *Proceedings of International Workshop on Stereoscopic and Three Dimensional Imaging*, (pp. 99-105). IEEE.

Pesci, A., Bonali, E., Galli, C., & Boschi, E. (2011). Laser scanning and digital imaging for the investigation of an ancient building: Palazzo d'Accursio study case (Bologna, Italy). *Journal of Cultural Heritage*.

Previtali, M., Barazzetti, L., Scaioni, M., & Yixiang, T. (2011). An automatic multi-image procedure for accurate 3D object reconstruction. In *Proceedings of 4th International Congress on Image and Signal Processing*. IEEE.

Remondino, F., & Fraser, C. (2006). Digital camera calibration methods: Considerations and comparisons. *International Archives of Photogrammetry. Remote Sensing and Spatial Information Sciences*, *36*(5), 266–272.

Rocchini, C., Cignoni, P., & Montani, C. (1999). Multiple texture stitching and blending on 3D objects. In *Proceedings of Eurographics Rendering Workshop*. IEEE.

Chapter 5
Anti-Models for Universitary Education:
Analysis of the Catalans Cases in Information and Communication Technologies

Francisco V. Cipolla-Ficarra
ALAIPO – AINCI, Spain and Italy

Valeria M. Ficarra
ALAIPO – AINCI, Spain and Italy

ABSTRACT

In this work of heuristic evaluation, the authors present the state-of-the-art and the results of an analysis of university educational systems to detect anti-models, which have increased the number of the unemployed in the active population of Southern Europe, especially in Catalunya (Spain). The results of this analysis have allowed the authors to carry out a first table of heuristic evaluation called Evaluation of the Excellence in Education (EEE). The table serves to detect the quality of the academic offer in computer science and multimedia. The authors also present a set of strategies stemming from semiotics and the categories of interactive design to detect the lack of credibility of online information through the analysis of the online textual and visual context.

INTRODUCTION

When two societies with developed economies inside the European Union (EU) have the unemployment rates indicated in Figure 1 or Neet (not in education, employment, or training) in Figure 2. It means that one of the cornerstones of those states such as education has failed irrespective of whether we are talking of public or private education. When talking about developed economies it is understood that the ICT (information and communication technology) are present in almost

DOI: 10.4018/978-1-4666-4490-8.ch005

Figure 1. Unemployment in Spain, digital newspaper: El País –10.20.2011 (www.elpais.es)

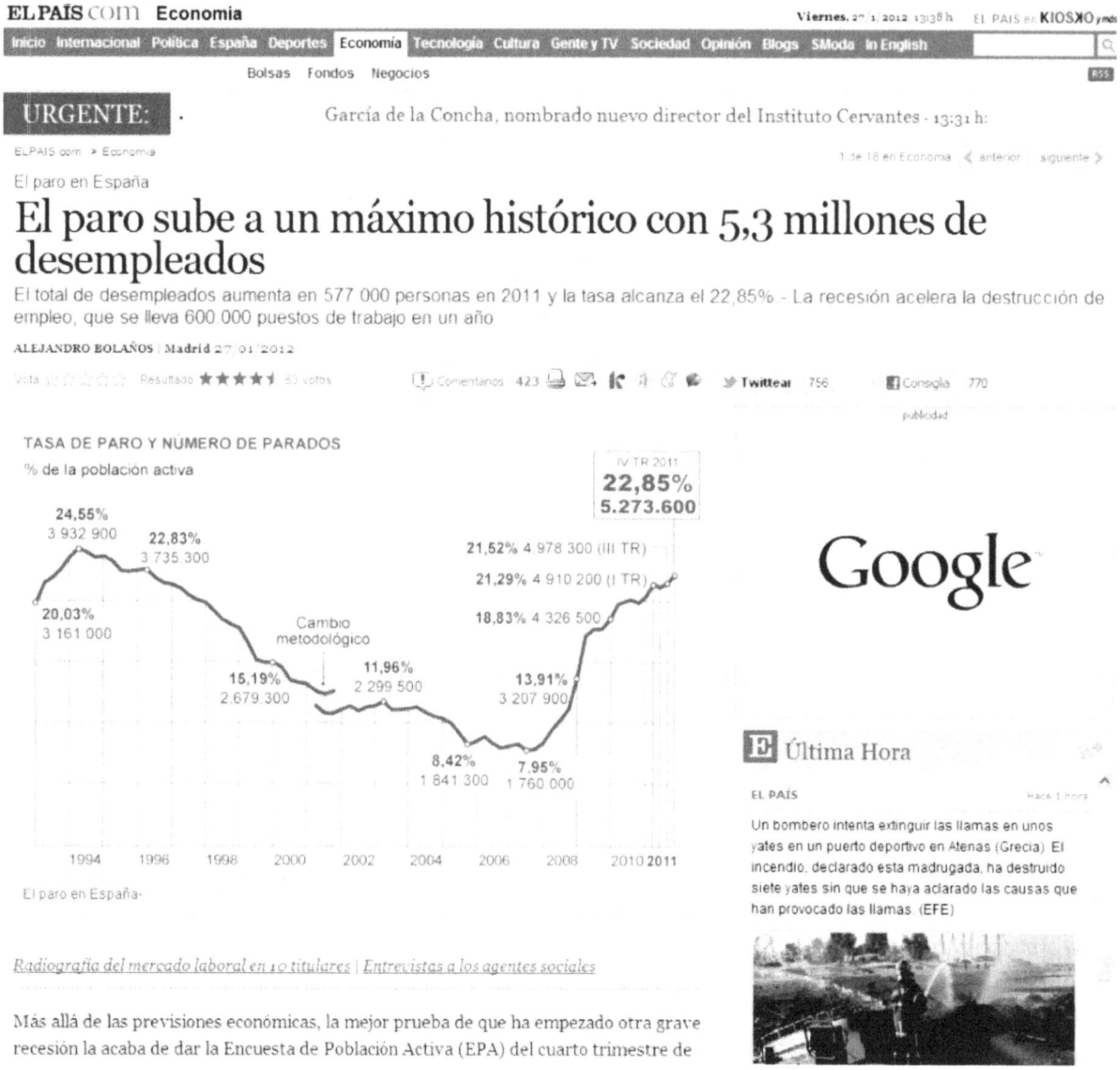

100% of the goods and services which are generated by these societies daily. The failures in the educational environment result from the structure and the system that every state has and has not converged on a common model inside the EU. It suffices to consider the homologation of the university diplomas and/or engineering degrees made beyond the European borders or inside some member states, when there is talk of PhDs or masters. Although some aspects related to the mobility of the students, professors, researchers, etc., or scholarships have been facilitated by the educational system.

However, the conformation of the university structures, public or private, remain unchanged in the new millennium thus generating educational anti-models but which are sold by the marketing as educational excellence, especially in the private universities or where prevails what Saussure called from a linguistic point of view

Figure 2. Neet (not in education, employment, or training) in Spain, digital newspaper: El País –12.18,2011 (www.elpais.es)

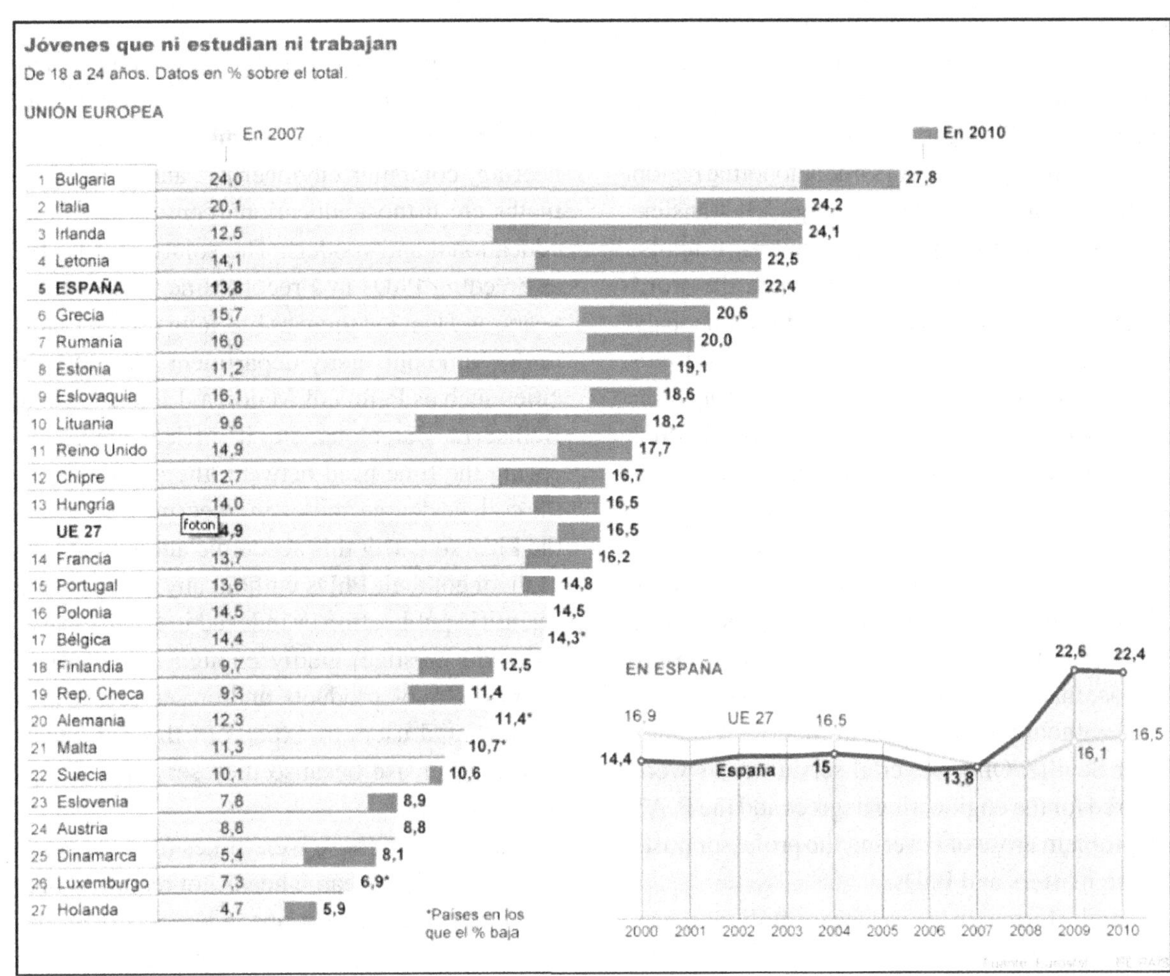

parochialism (Saussure, 1983; Cipolla-Ficarra, 2010a; Cipolla-Ficarra, 2010b). When we talk about university structures we mean the human structure and the organization chart of said structure.

The current work will start to describe the bad conformation of organizational charts in certain universities, especially in those where Catalan is spoken and some of its derivations such as Majorca, Valencia dialects and others until generating the current educational anti-models which affect the sector of ICT and the future generations. Later on we reveal the strategies followed to compile the table of heuristic evaluation of educational excellence, coupled with examples, which may be looked up online for their verification. Finally are presented results achieved with communicability evaluators in the universe of study with their matching conclusions and future lines of research.

THE LOUSY CONFORMATION OF THE UNIVERSITY ORGANIZATIONAL CHARTS

The conformation of the university organizational charts of the European Mediterranean basin in the 90s constitutes an antimodel with endless interrelations, that is, not only in the academic environment but in the nefarious consequences for the future generations of professionals and potential users of the new technologies aimed at the online and offline interactive systems, for instance (Cipolla-Ficarra, 2010b). The appearance of a myriad universities in a same autonomic region as they are called in Spain led to quickly transferring the professors from high schools, schools, academies, etc. which had associated the word "technical" to the universities. Simultaneously were raised the local linguistic barriers to put a brake to the university globalization phenomenon in cities such as Barcelona or Palma of Majorca among others located in Southern Europe. That is, the public civil servants (including the university professors in this category) in Madrid could not work in Barcelona because they didn't speak Catalan perfectly in the university classrooms, whereas in the inverse sense that was possible. That is, that a Catalan-speaking professor could work without any problems in Madrid, Valladolid or Seville. Once the civil servant posts were covered for the engineering degrees and the B.A., the problem arose of covering the professor posts for the masters and PhDs.

For the former in the private institutions it was not necessary to have any title to teach seminars or mini-courses inside them. An example regarding this were the masters related with multimedia engineering in the Universitat Ramon Llull (late 90s and early 21st century) where the owners of small computer animation firms or the members of the technical offices of the autonomic government (Generalitat de Catalunya) competed in the same themes, with the professors and collaborators of the alleged elitist universities and the educational excellence, which worked under "garbage" contracts (Spanish name of the contracts which didn't guarantee working stability). Obviously, the direction of those masters was in charge of the local professors inexperienced but endorsed by a strong campaign of commercial marketing in private education and in continuous training, especially in the avant-garde sector of the new technologies.

With regard to the PhDs, in principle, it may be more complex, but it wasn't at all for certain departments of the audiovisual, software engineering, computer engineering, and systems or maths, etc. in those educational centres generating educational anti-models. The solution consisted in breeding PhDs in a record time, two or three years, and leaving them as life-long civil servants in the same university department. Currently in cities such as Palma of Majorca, Lleida, Girona, Bellaterra, Barcelona, etc. it suffices with comparing the time used between the attainment of the college degree and/or engineering degree and the PhD. to detect this academic anomaly. Many of them got their PhDs without any international scientific publication or indexed in the databases of world prestige. Oddly enough, some patent in the USA of products and/or services which the potential users or experts of the ICT sector would never use because they served to widen the digital gap.

Remarkably, those were times (decade of the 90s) where the research heads got record figures in 100% subsidized European projects (Cipolla-Ficarra, et al., 2011). That is, that these PhDs had plenty economic funds to present works in the scientific congresses, workshops, etc. Exceptionally, if they did, we find articles with works of two or three folios, with over 10 authors. All of them in the same sector of scientific knowledge of which they wanted the lifelong working post, once their doctoral thesis was presented.

The exception to this reality was made up by the foreign students who not only had to pay the registration fees of the courses, but also the photocopies of the scientific articles from the library, the corrections of the translations of the articles or chapters, the inscription to the scientific congresses, the trip and the stay at the moment of submitting the scientific works, etc. Of course then those works merged in the production of the department generating of European anti-models to get new European subsidies and foster the training of professionals or meteorite doctors such as can be seen in Figure 3 (Cipolla-Ficarra, F. et al., 2011) and web 2.0 version in the appendix:

Now in view of the described reality (a small sample truthful and verifiable which for reasons of space in the current work and privacy of the agents generators of anti-models we can't enlarge) emerges a big question which includes several questions: How can these deviations be detected and quantified to avoid them and find solutions in regard to the future generations aimed at the new technologies? The answer is simple: resort to a communicability expert (Cipolla-Ficarra, F., 2010a), who using techniques and methods from the formal and factual sciences can draw exactly and quickly a map of the sites which do not meet the educational excellence they preach through the traditional mass media or from the last technological generation.

In the 90s it was the usability engineers who used the resources of the social sciences under the caption of heuristic techniques but did not detect the deviations that were generated from the new environments of the disciplines related to the technological avant-garde, usability engineering included. They spoke of the union of the methods and techniques but in reality it was intersections of knowledge and experiences, resorting to real professionals who count on a 360 degrees training such as is the case of the communicability experts.

INSTRUMENTS OF INTERACTIVE DESIGN FOR THE SEARCH OF EDUCATIONAL QUALITY

If we consider the design of an interactive system made up by several categories such as are content, presentation, navigation, structure, panchronism, connectability, etc. we can use some resources of the social sciences which have been applied with

Figure 3. The Catalan educational anti-model. The comets students have in less than a decade two degrees, a master and a PhD without scientific publications in none of those sectors, occupying high offices in firms of the editorial sector, multimedia, tourism, information, etc.

success in several projects of interactive systems of educational, commercial, industrial character etc. such as is semiotics. In the first place we can analyze the genesis of the hypermedia systems, that is, the hypertext. An analysis of the textual content allows us to establish several communication aspects which reveal the philosophy of the academic environment. In this sense, it is interesting to analyze the research heads of the different units and faculties inside a certain geographical environment.

The analysis can be made on the whole universe of study or a sample of it through random selection techniques of the samples, such as a draw. In this case we apply the notions stemming from statistics. For instance, in our universe of study we have analyzed the following text of a university located very close to the Catalan Pyrenees, whose name we do not insert because of privacy reasons, we hide the personal data and we have inserted letters coupled with numbers for the analysis of the text. Next the translated text of a curriculum online:

For the research stretch which comprises the years 2004-2010 I submit the set of magazine articles indexed inside the JCR (Journal Citation Report) which add up to 33,19 as an added impact factor (I do not count the impact of the LNCS/LNA1 (A1) although in my case they are not proceedings from congresses but publications per selection of articles, which would add the impact of 1,61), usually as first author or director of the thesis of the main author. It is a high impact in comparison with the area of knowledge where I develop my research. (A 2). Besides, I've got 121 quotes in the 2004-2010 period which is a high figure again if we compare it with my area of knowledge (ratio of 3,0 quotes per magazine article inside the ISI system, above the 1,1 quotes per article of the collective of Spanish researchers in the same areas of research, and also superior to the 1,5 quotes per article of the same collective at world level). (A3). My research in technology of intelligent agents is applicable to a high number of areas as is reflected in the variety of my transfer projects (A4). The 4 patents in the USA and Spain and 1 university spin-off (Strategic Attention Management created in 2007) show the degree of applicability of my research which has been supported in part by a wide set of research projects (25) and transfer in competitive calls at national and European level (A5). According to the searcher Scholar Google (on 26 April 2010) I have 703 quotes and a h-index=11. In regard to the magazines inside the Elsevier system, through the scopus http//www.scopus.com I've got 189 quotes (A6). In all the calculations have been excluded the self-references (I've used the CM http//scholar-agent software to remove the self-quotes). For an analysis of all my publications I have a tool at public disposal in http//scholar-agent/ which gathers them all, counts the quotes, discounts the self-quotes, and calculates a few useful indicators such as the H-index both with and without quotes, and the A and G indexes. Uses the Google Scholar searcher which is becoming a referent for the most approximate measure of the impact in the engineering areas, although it still has difficulties in having access to different databases in important associations (A7).

For the mini analysis that has been made we have used Veron's (Veron, 2004) concepts about speech, power and power of speech. Veron claims that the notion of speech designs every phenomenon of space and time manifestation of meaning, whatever is the support of said meaning, so it is not confined to the significant matter of the language in itself. The sense always manifests itself as coated in a matter, under the shape of product. As such, it always sends back to a social production work: the social production of the sense. Now the analytical concept of power of a speech can only manifest itself under the shape of an effect, that is, under the shape of another production of meaning. In other words, the power of a "A" speech is a "B" speech which manifest itself as an effect of the former.

Any speech which is produced in a given social context has and exercises a certain power. That's to say, it causes a certain effect. In the case of the selected text we can see in A1 the use of a first person who from a dominant position appeals to the use of statistics to say he/she is above the potential readers of that online information. However, he/she hides financial information in the paragraph we analyze, such as are the 3.653.860,80 euros received in subsidies for his/her researches between 2004-2010 without considering the 6.065.439,74 euros which go from the period 2009-2013. Supposedly in that Catalan city, seeing the budget that is handled by a single researcher in a public university, the unemployment of the ICT professionals ought to be equal to zero. However, it is not. Of course those figures are the ones he/she publishes online and which theoretically amount to the 100% the university declares to the tax revenue service. In A2 and through these scores there is a rebate of his/her domineering position, by not considering other elements which allegedly increase his/her scientific power. Here is already apparent the possessive aspect of the enunciator by using the first possessive adjective "my".

In A3 appears the social aspect, that is, in third place upon receiving from others an acknowledgement from his Spanish and foreign colleagues. In A4 there is an explicit elimination of his collaborators, assistants, employees, etc. because apparently he works by himself/herself in those projects which go above several million euros in less than a decade. In A5 appears the relationship between the university and the community where it is inserted by talking about the transfer of technologies. That is, the profits towards the community from which he gets the financial resources appears in the fifth place. In this section he also mentions the case of the patents in the USA and Spain as the creation of a spin-off firm (as a rule it is a project born as an extension from a former project, or even more from a firm originated from another through the separation of a department of the firm to become a firm in itself). In A6 there is again a favour towards the reader since allegedly he/she doesn't resort to statistic instruments which might increase the domination on the other people. That is, he/she presents an unbalanced relationship, since the bigger the knowledge, the lesser the power.

Finally in A7 he/she reveals the free access tools, from which he gets the statistic data which boost and strengthen his/her domineering position. As always the language used is the first person. Very briefly has been described the domineering position using a part of Greimas' action model (Nöth, 1995) that is, the competence to four modal objects: want-to-do, must-do, can-do and know-to-do. Want-to-do and must-do are virtualizing modal objects: can-do and know-to-do are actual modal objects. Although the modal objects present a canonical organization, there is always a manipulation aimed at the receiver of the textual content. It is that know-to-do which leads in many cases to situations of possession or ownership of objects, when in fact there is a teamwork of people but which is synthetically presented under the caption "my projects". Now the situation which is more striking from a point of view of the social psychology, for instance, is when the talk is about the possession of people (Cipolla-Ficarra, 2010b). A typical phenomenon in the Lombardian academic environment when they go as far as repeatedly saying "my student" (Cipolla-Ficarra, 2010b) when in fact the student has sometimes been a student of another professor, but they eagerly want to pick up the other people's fruits as if they were their own.

The goal of the dynamic persuader is to falsely increase for himself/herself the know-can relationship. The effect caused by introducing all those aggrandizement data, coupled with big figures of the received subsidies and with a reality described in the Figure 1 is very negative. Of course it is a model imported from the other side of the

Atlantic, even the Pacific Ocean, if we compare it with the Californian universities, for instance. Once again the originality in the university sector and the R&D in Southern Europe to present some kind of information online is equal to zero. Now simultaneously to the category design content for the attainment of data in the construction of the EEE table is the navigation as is the ease or not to access to certain type of online information in the university websites such as the university contests to take posts of professors, aids, etc. whose detailed data can be looked up in (Cipolla-Ficarra, F., 2008a). In the presentation or layout category have been analyzed the dynamic and static images used, with a semiotic analysis thereof. Some examples which explain that analysis are in the following bibliographical references for those interested in (Cipolla-Ficarra, 2001; Cipolla-Ficarra, 2008; Cipolla-Ficarra, 2011; Mitrovic, Martin & Suraweera, 2007).

BEYOND DESIGN: A SYNCHRONIC AND DIACHRONIC ANALYSIS

Educational excellence also requires a synchronic and diachronic analysis following both notions from Saussure's point of view (Saussure, 1983). For instance, if we consider the members of a panel in a doctoral thesis, we can find an interesting source to evaluate the educational quality of a university centre. In the following image obtained from an online database of Spanish doctoral theses (www.tesis.com.es), we see that in the profile there are fields of the register without data, such as the department in which it was made.

Later on and following the listing of the members of the panel, whose surnames have been left out because of privacy reasons, we see that the dean takes charge of the war strategy, the leadership, etc, that is, clearly persuasion issues, even though he has a maths degree. On his side the director of the panel is a priest with a great influence in the regional government (one of the alleged European economic engines, Catalonia) and decides which scientific policies have to be followed in certain fields of the new technologies, for instance, the human-computer interaction can only be accepted if the studies or research is aimed at people with disabilities in the late 1990s. As secretary a young man with a "mobile identity" since his anagraphic data such as his second surname will change in relation to the linguistic decrees of the birthplace. That is, sometimes he writes it with "ñ" and other times with "ny". Without any doubt, one of the situations of great qualitative loss towards the university institution, because the seriousness about the personal data of the professors who make up that educational centre is equal to zero, without considering the radical nationalistic aspect. (pejorative sense of the term). As last vocal (member) we find a graduate in fine arts, professor of the subject of architectonical graphic expression.

However, he/she has several variegated titles which denote parochialism to obtain them and entail the absolute decay of the Catalan-Mallorca educational system since with a 5 minutes long computer animation he/she has got an European master not to mention his/her PhD in computer science and maths. An academic title which allows him/her to paint murals in the bars of Mallorca or make commercial statues for wine cellars in his/her spare time.

A documental compilation allows us to develop the following diagram of the personal relations and professional "doctors" who have settled down thanks to the described parochialism. Schematically: Doctor-to-be → member of the panel of the future comet doctor and generator of the university educational anti-model. → Comet who follows her/his fast course in the working market and reaches a high office of the autonomous government in the sector of the new technologies, information and tourism. → The comet and the payback of favours: → (a) artistic member and "expert" in "maths and computer science" → Great clients of the tourism sector for publicity

Figure 4. Parochialism for a doctoral thesis in Barcelona, Catalunya (Spain)

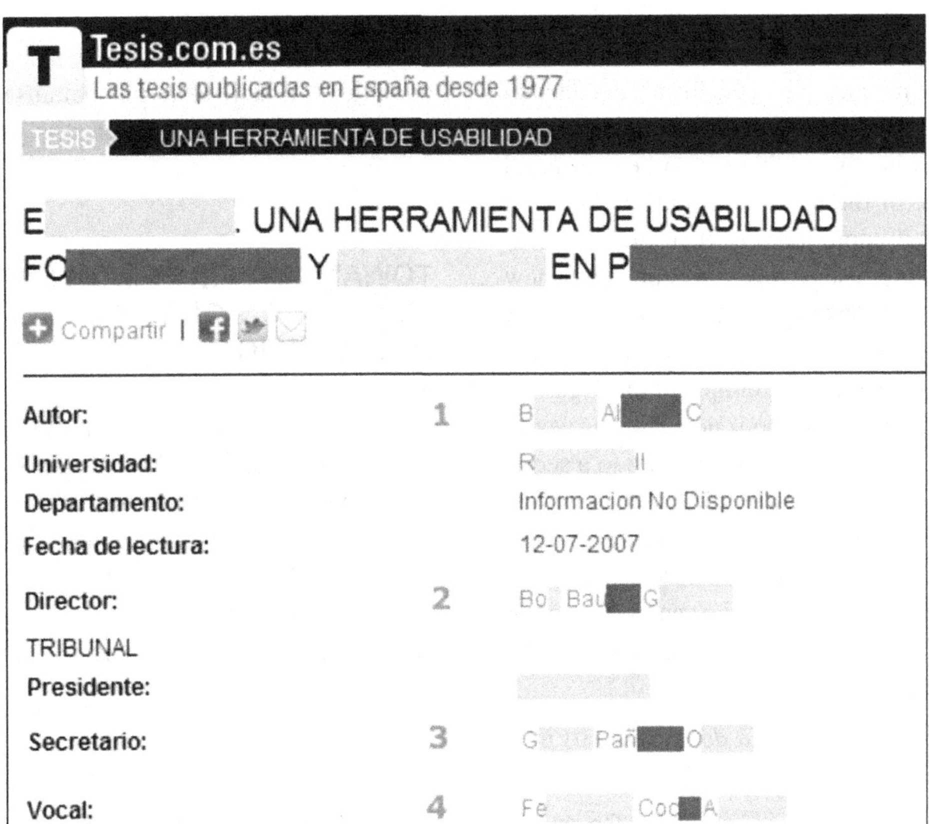

campaigns and generator of commercial image (b) entrepreneurial member → clients for the purchase of the electronic invoicing system for the hospitality and tourism sector. This member links to the cycle the first agent of the personal relationships since it was she/he who endorsed her/him as candidate doctor, that is, gives her/him all the tools to reach the titles without any problem, even in the panel of the defence of the developed work.

All this analysis is feasible in semiotics and the documentary recompilation (Veron, 2004). The documents are facts or traces of something that has happened, moreover, as witnesses they give information whether it is in the format of data or figures, thus being a very useful material for research inside the social sciences (Nöth, 1995). As an element of knowledge or source of information they can be used for the consultation or evidence. The documental recompilation becomes so an instrument or technique of social research. The purpose is to obtain data and information. Now both notions are usually used indistinctly in some computer science contexts. In our work the information is the result of a process, which starts with the data, and in turn the information may become a data of a new process.

In the documental recompilation these data and information may start from the text, the statistics, graphics or other media of audiovisual communication, susceptible of being used inside the purposes of a specific research. That is, regardless of the kind of support of the dynamic media or the static media of information or data.

Now there is no style guidelines which indicates to the compiler which documents to compile and which not. Obviously a communicability expert will have a training or experience which allows to bridge these limitations since he or she is the result of the intersection of the formal and factual sciences. Both for this expert as for those who are not, the important thing is to bear in mind the purpose of the research to judge whether it is useful and appropriate to that purpose. Following this premise one can save time, give new hypothesis, establish correlations and construct the right instruments for the research that is being made. In the case of the example of the Figure 5, evidently neither in Facebook nor Linkedin would we find this kind of data which relate to a series of individuals prompted by clearly mercantilist and non-academic purposes. Besides, a problem of social research may be transferred to a set of rhetoric questions, a hypothesis can be verified or checked in different ways, for instance with intelligent tutors (Cipolla-Ficarra, 2008b). Therefore, if an idea from which the research or a hypothesis is born can be formulated in such a way that the compiled available material contains in itself the answer, the use of this material is possible and adequate.

TOWARDS A FIRST TABLE FOR EVALUATION OF THE EXCELLENCE IN EDUCATION

Now the great rhetoric question is how to generate a table of evaluation of the excellent education in the second decade of the new millennium, with low costs and a high quality in the final results?

First of all it is necessary to count with a new type of professional in the age of expansion of communicability who represents the interaction

Figure 5. Interrelation for a doctoral thesis in Barcelona, Catalunya (Spain)

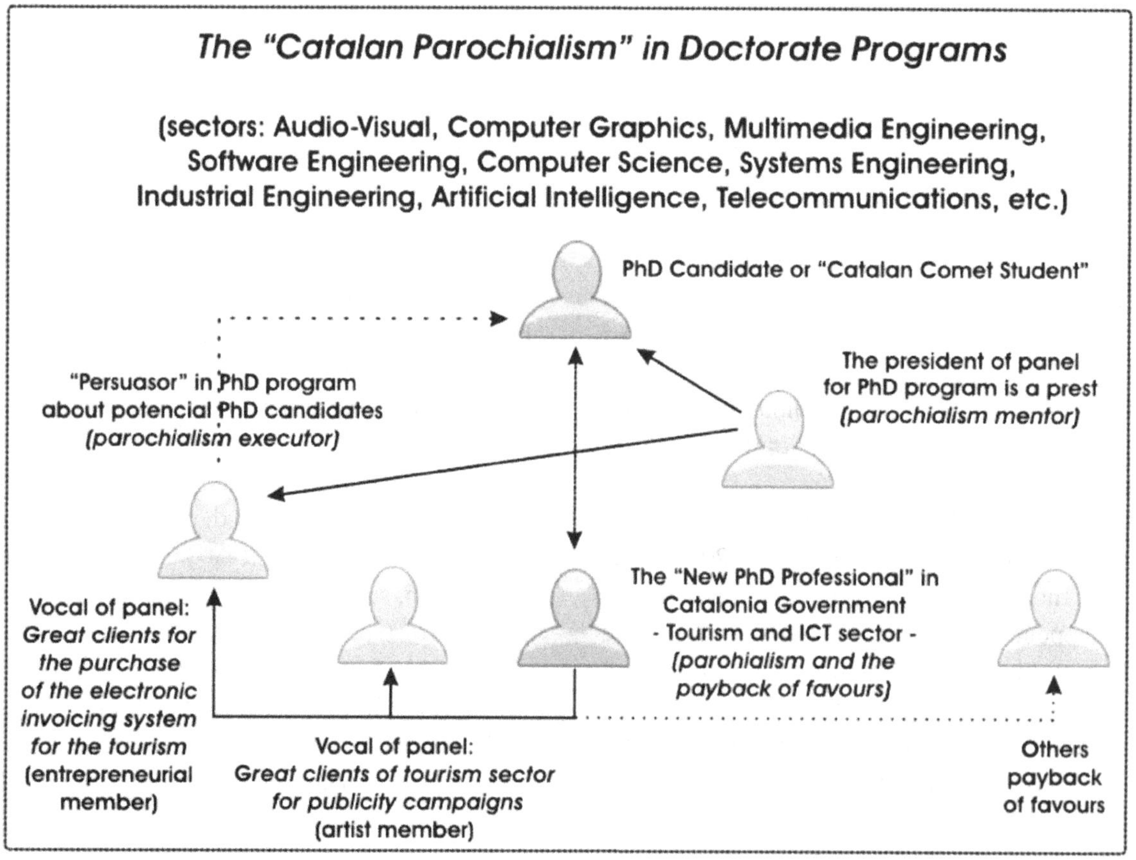

Figure 6. Digital and analogical information/data (photography, texts, numbers, flow diagram, etc.) for a not ethical behaviour (financial corruption) into snobbish business and law school in Barcelona, Catalunya (Spain). Digital newspaper: El País (www.elpais.es –02.28.2012).

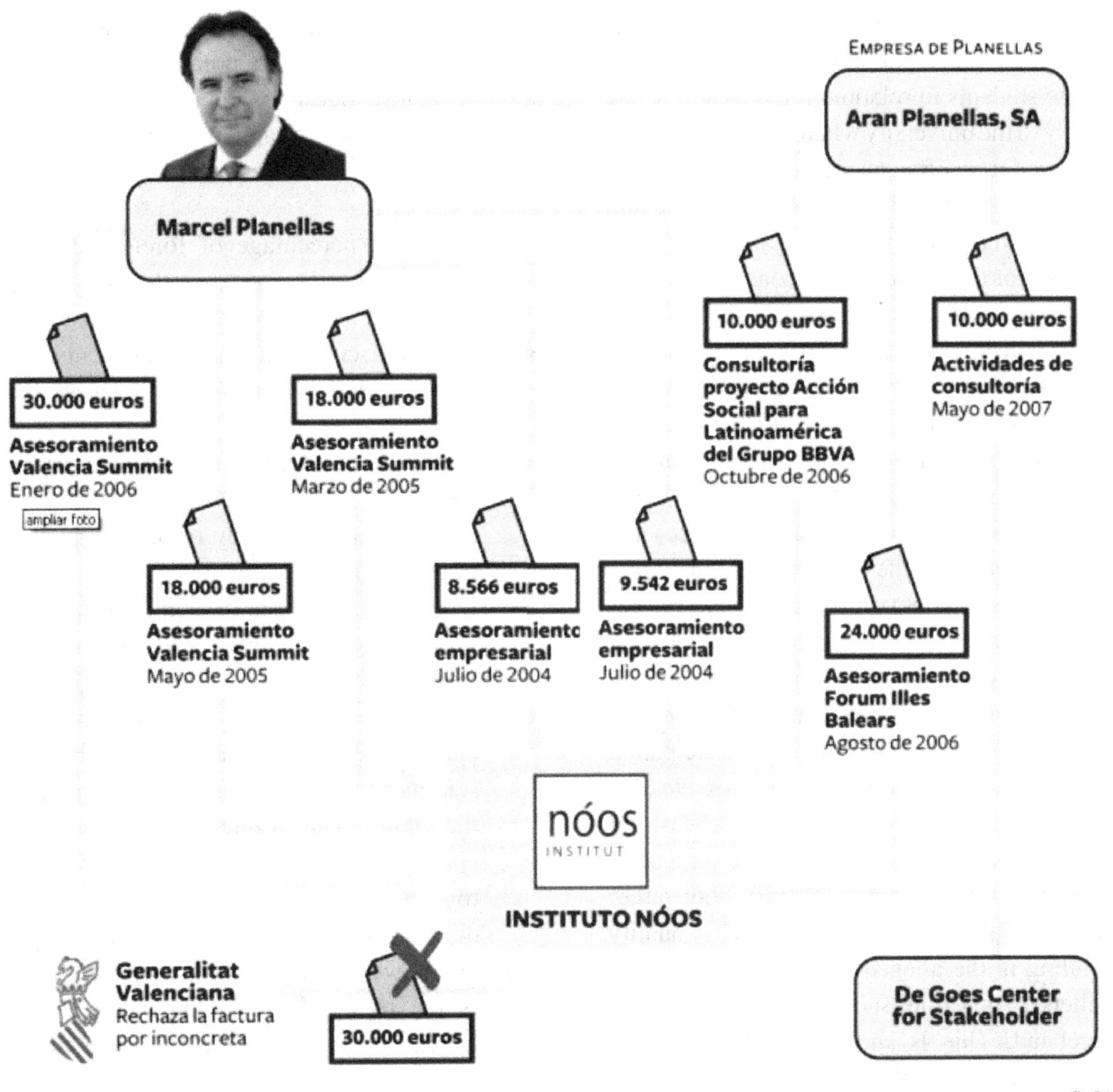

of the formal and factual sciences. In the second place, counting on a wide and verified truthful information at ready disposal to carry out the inferences operations in the face of certain situations. Third, it is necessary to plump for heuristic evaluation techniques which do not require great investments such as can be direct observation and the use of statistics, in the case of working with samples from the universe of study. For instance, a communicability expert may focus on the study of certain aspects of educational excellence in keeping with the existing technology in a given period of time and the access the students have had to said technology, and also the degree of knowledge, competences and skills they have acquired in the process. Obviously, in some realities in Southern Europe we are not surprised to find colleges where millions of euros in equipments have been invested, but only has access to its use the elite students in relation to the fees they pay monthly to the university where they are studying a multimedia or software engineering. Therefore, if the universe of study has been fractioned and there are several experts working simultaneously at the end of their studies and conclusions, they may serve as controllers of the results obtained by their colleagues. It is a way to cut down costs in labs and equipments, for instance. Fourth, give the greatest possible publicity to the obtained results, thus avoiding the commercial channels. Logically we are talking of the scientific channels, but regrettably the financial resources and pressure groups in the mass media, including the current social networks, that the said centres of alleged educational excellence have at their disposal are so big that they can afford to buy not only the scientific channels, but also the human team they have. For instance, in the participation in congresses, workshops, symposiums, etc., the inclusion of awards with heavy sums of cash for all those who present research works is a clear sign that this event is not scientific, but rather commercial and serves to conceal the low quality prevailing in the alleged centres of educational excellence As a rule, such awards are assigned beforehand. This is another of the strategies used by the educational commercial marketing in Southern Europe. Fifth, in the last example we have already seen the importance of the context where these centres for educational excellence are located. The human and social factor which is developed in certain environments and temporal spaces have an influence on the concentration or dispersion of the educational quality in a country (Cipolla-Ficarra, 2010a; Reed, Gannon & Larus, 2012). The same as with the analysis of the content of a text, what is intended is to know the latent motivations, not in a speech, but in a society so that its educational centres have excellence or not.

Considering these five points, we proceed to a set of rhetoric questions to build our first table of heuristic assessment and of a binary type (two feasible answers to every question; yes or no).

- Does the percentage of foreign teachers and/or researchers surpass the 50% of the staff?
- Have the curricula, the departments, the labs, etc. been developed by local or foreign staff?
- Is the use of other languages which are not the local freely allowed or is it imposed implicitly or contractually to the whole staff of the excellence centre?
- Do the local and the foreign staff have the same working conditions in the hiring of their services?
- Are those "illustrious visitors" who take part in the master classes, specialization seminars, etc. exclusive of the centre or do they participate in other places inside the national territory, that is, do they respond to a sort of war in disguise among centres of educational excellence in order to split up the war loot?
- Is the technology and knowledge transfer free inside the market or is it manipulated by the authorities of the centre of excellence?
- Are the equipments of the labs from different brands or do they belong to a few software or hardware brands?
- Do the providers of computer goods and services participate directly or indirectly in

the extracurricular activities, for instance, science fairs, "open days", tenders, congresses, etc.?

- Is there freedom to choose the subjects of projects, theses, etc?
- Are the subjects of research which do not respond to the mercantilist or scientific expectations of the centre of excellence excluded together with those students who propose them?
- Do the authorities who are neutral to the academic sector determine the excellence of the education centre?
- Is there an excessive use of the phrase "centre of educational excellence"?
- Is the access to the centre unimpeded and free of charge for all?

Although the questions may seem trivial, they aren't, because through the analysis of the content of the university portals and also the reformulation of these questions in questionnaires which have been distributed over two decades among professors and students.

We present the first heuristic results in the following graphic and with the following set of attributes created starting from our studies which should gather the excellence education centers since 1990 to our day (in brackets the acronyms that sum up these quality attributes, equality of labor conditions among natives and foreigners [EQL], free public education [FPE], balance between theory and practice [BTP], control of educational quality and external auditing of the presented results [CEQ], national and international mobility of the students [NIM], professors and researchers for continuous improvement [PRC], independence from brands for academic activities [IBA], freedom in the choice of subjects and topics of final projects [FCS], masters and PhDs, emancipation from the influence of the emeritus or lifelong professors [EIE], biannual update of the syllabus in the field of ICTs and its derivations [BUS].

Evidently, the obtained results in this figure strengthen the situation put forward in the Figures 1 and 2 in Southern Europe.

LESSONS LEARNED AND FUTURE WORKS

The digital and analog information since the 90s down to our days denotes the scarce credibility of the curricula which make up the university guidelines. A classical example of the guide is the Figure 8. Guides from public universities which during the whole decade of the 90s did not explain to the potential student not only the difficulties to succeed in the examinations but also the human factors in certain university cloisters being far-away from the scientific principles because of political or nationalistic reasons. A situation which remains nowadays even in online information, for instance in the lack of complete access to the subjects of the courses, masters, doctorates, etc. with their matching bibliography, practices, etc. in those departments of Catalan universities which are related directly and/or indirectly with the new technologies, such as, Software Engineering or Artificial Intelligence or School of Industrial Engineering of Barcelona (Polytechnic University of Catalonia –UPC), Information and Communication Technologies (Pompeu Fabra University –UPF), Audio-visual Communication and Advertising (Autonomous University of Barcelona –UAB), Computer Science and Applied Mathematics (University of Girona –UdG), Mathematics and Computer Science (University of the Balearic Islands –UIB), etc. This reality can be verified by visiting the respective websites. In this sense, any result presented by these

Figure 7. First results of the studies made since 1990 until the present days in the Catalan universities

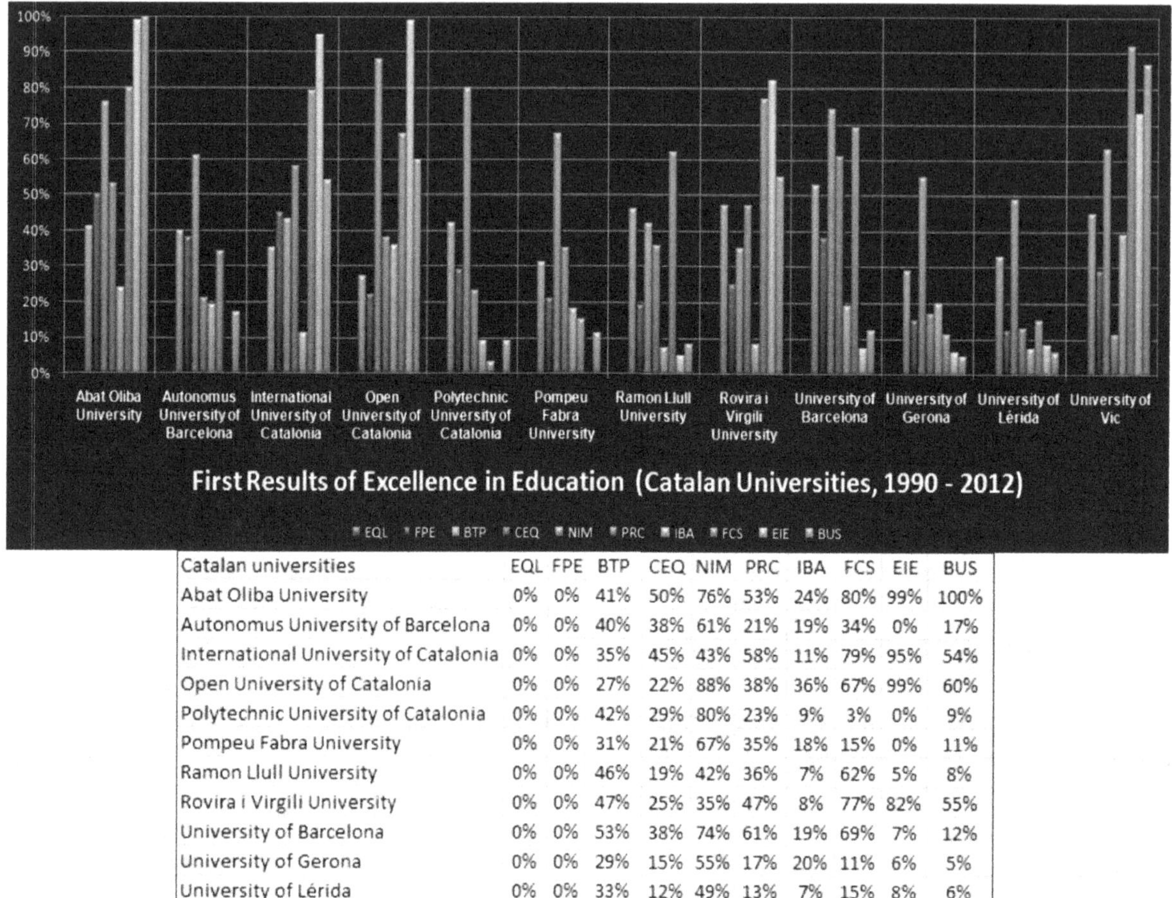

Catalan universities	EQL	FPE	BTP	CEQ	NIM	PRC	IBA	FCS	EIE	BUS
Abat Oliba University	0%	0%	41%	50%	76%	53%	24%	80%	99%	100%
Autonomus University of Barcelona	0%	0%	40%	38%	61%	21%	19%	34%	0%	17%
International University of Catalonia	0%	0%	35%	45%	43%	58%	11%	79%	95%	54%
Open University of Catalonia	0%	0%	27%	22%	88%	38%	36%	67%	99%	60%
Polytechnic University of Catalonia	0%	0%	42%	29%	80%	23%	9%	3%	0%	9%
Pompeu Fabra University	0%	0%	31%	21%	67%	35%	18%	15%	0%	11%
Ramon Llull University	0%	0%	46%	19%	42%	36%	7%	62%	5%	8%
Rovira i Virgili University	0%	0%	47%	25%	35%	47%	8%	77%	82%	55%
University of Barcelona	0%	0%	53%	38%	74%	61%	19%	69%	7%	12%
University of Gerona	0%	0%	29%	15%	55%	17%	20%	11%	6%	5%
University of Lérida	0%	0%	33%	12%	49%	13%	7%	15%	8%	6%
University of Vic	0%	0%	45%	29%	63%	11%	39%	92%	73%	87%

departments contradicts one of the principles of science: the universality of the results and the people constituting the human team to reach them. For good reason we can say in the context of the formal sciences, the more international the R&D labs are, the better the results (a verification of the reasons might be warranted in the next works).

The same should happen with the public and private universities. However, the radicalization factor in the mono-nationality gets stronger in the private field and with high financial resources in Barcelona, for instance. In the public sector it is a mere make-up operation on the websites to seize potential "customers-students" from other places from the same state or the rest of the world. The instruments stemming from the analysis of content of the social sciences and adapted to the new digital contents make it possible to reach superior levels of veracity of the academic information, especially that which is promoted under the label of "educational excellence" in Southern Europe. In future works we will widen the table analyzing each one of the quality attributes in metrics applied to the interaction design allow to detect the portals where the least persuasive information is offered for the potential students, professors and researchers of the Catalan educational centers. In order to verify the right functioning of those qualitative metrics will be applied to the Lombardian portals, for instance.

Figure 8. Software engineering master guide (1997) in Polytechnic University of Catalonia –UPC (Barcelona, Spain) for local and international students but only one language: "Catalan" (no Spanish or English, for instance). Evidently, the lessons for international students in Catalan language but the Catalan was not an official language in European Union (decade of the 90s).

CONCLUSION

The quality of the software offers a wide set of instruments to measure the quality of the last generation interactive systems. However, it is necessary to boost it with another complementary set of instruments of the social sciences, when the treated field is education and which is supposed to reach excellence.

In that direction, semiotics applied to the interactive design of offline and online systems has yielded excellent results in the last two decades, without need of making an engineer study of it. Semiotics, linked to linguistics, direct observation, the analysis of content, the experiences and/or knowledge of a communicability expert, among other components, can easily detect the presence or absence of educational excellence.

In the current work have been set the foundations to quantify the quality of the educational excellence in the face of the social results stemming from the current failures (for instance, the high rate of unemployed college students and the Neet generation) in one of the cornerstones of any thriving or emerging community such as college education, especially in the dynamic sector of the ICTs.

Now in view of the human and/or social factors such as those detected in the current universe of study, little or nothing can be done from the scientific perspective. In those Mediterranean communities those factors will slow down the correct advance of the ICTs.

REFERENCES

Cipolla-Ficarra, F. (2001). Communication evaluation in multimedia: Metrics and methodology. In *Proceedings of Human-Computer International* (Vol. 3). Mahwah, NJ: LEA.

Cipolla-Ficarra, F. (2008a). Eyes: A virtual assistant for analysis of the transparency and accessibility in university portal. In *Proceedings of International Conference on Applied Human Factors and Ergonomics*. Las Vegas, NV: AEI.

Cipolla-Ficarra, F. (2008b). Dyadic for quality in hypermedia systems. In *Proceedings of Applied Human Factors and Ergonomics*. Las Vegas, NV: AEI.

Cipolla-Ficarra, F. (2010a). *Quality and communicability for interactive hypermedia systems: Concepts and practices for design*. Hershey, PA: IGI Global. doi:10.4018/978-1-61520-763-3

Cipolla-Ficarra, F. (2010b). *Persuasion online and communicability: The destruction of credibiltiy in the virtual community and cognitive models*. New York: Nova Publishers.

Cipolla-Ficarra, F., et al. (2011). Handbook of advance in dynamic and static media for interactive systems: Communicability, computer science and design. Bergamo, Italy: Blue Herons Ed.s.

Cipolla-Ficarra, F., et al. (2011). Handbook of computational informatics, social factors and new information technologies: Hypermedia perspectives and avant-garde experiencies in the era of communicability expansion. Bergamo, Italy: Blue Herons Ed.s.

Mitrovic, A., Martin, B., & Suraweera, P. (2007). Intelligent tutors for all: The constraint based approach. *IEEE Intelligent Systems*, *22*(4), 38–45. doi:10.1109/MIS.2007.74

Nöth, W. (1995). *Handbook of semiotics*. Bloomington, IN: Indiana University Press.

Reed, D., Gannon, D., & Larus, J. (2012). Imagining the future: Thoughts on computing. *IEEE Computer*, *45*(1), 25–30. doi:10.1109/MC.2011.327

Saussure, F. (1983). *Course in general lingistics*. New York: McGraw-Hill.

Veron, E. (2004). *La semiosis social: Fragmentos de una teoría de la discursividad*. Barcelona, Spain: Gedisa.

APPENDIX

Figure 9. Anti-models for universitary education –Catalan parochialism and the phenomenon comet in Web 2.0

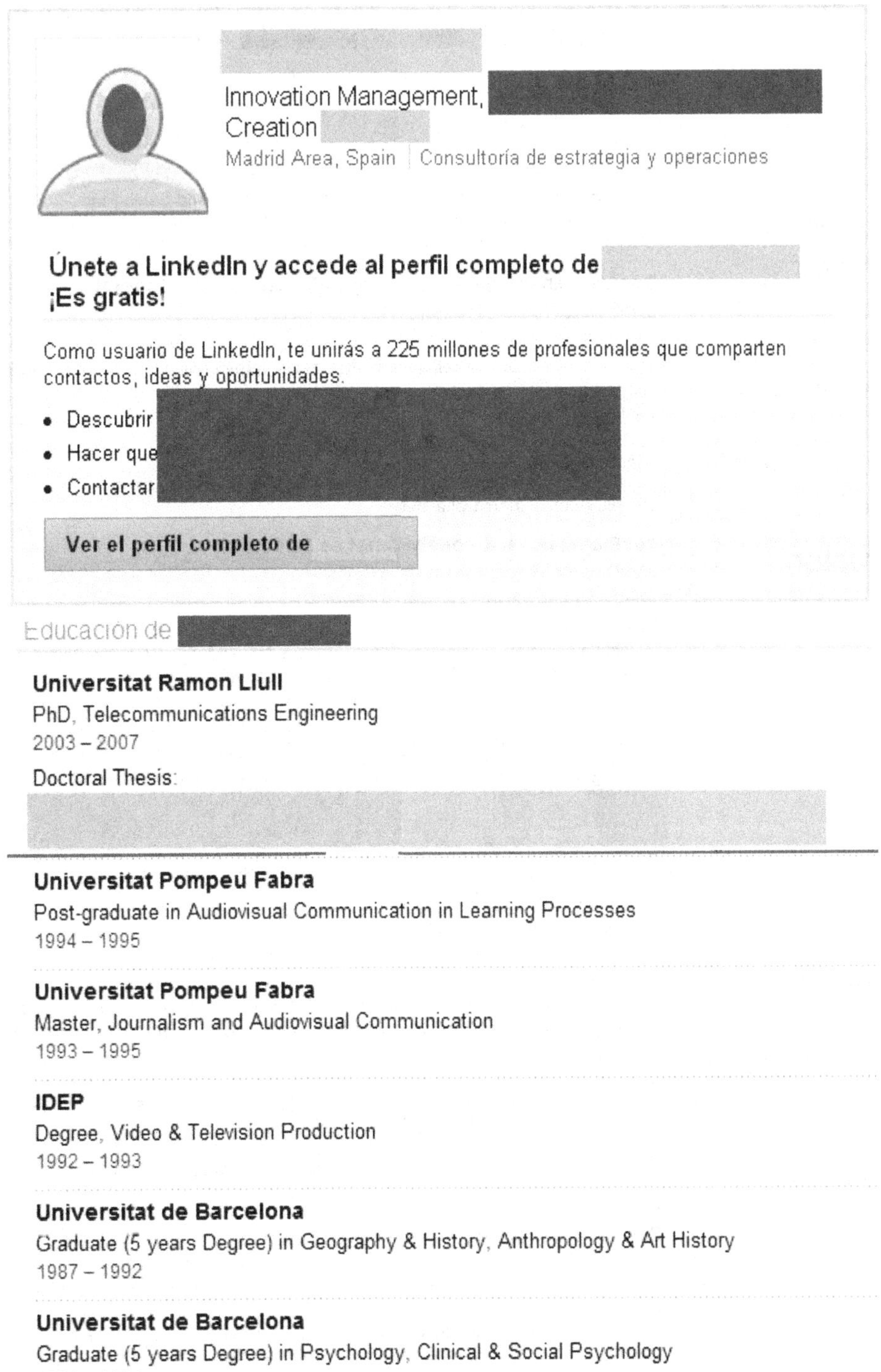

Innovation Management,
Creation
Madrid Area, Spain | Consultoría de estrategia y operaciones
Únete a LinkedIn y accede al perfil completo de
¡Es gratis!
Como usuario de LinkedIn, te unirás a 225 millones de profesionales que comparten contactos, ideas y oportunidades.
Descubrir
Hacer que
Contactar
Ver el perfil completo de
Educación de
Universitat Ramon Llull
PhD, Telecommunications Engineering
2003 – 2007
Doctoral Thesis:
Universitat Pompeu Fabra
Post-graduate in Audiovisual Communication in Learning Processes
1994 – 1995
Universitat Pompeu Fabra
Master, Journalism and Audiovisual Communication
1993 – 1995
IDEP
Degree, Video & Television Production
1992 – 1993
Universitat de Barcelona
Graduate (5 years Degree) in Geography & History, Anthropology & Art History
1987 – 1992
Universitat de Barcelona
Graduate (5 years Degree) in Psychology, Clinical & Social Psychology
1986 – 1991

Figure 10. Interrelations between the phenomenon meteorite-comet in jobs (director, manager, etc.) and the anti-models for universitary education (figures 3, 4, 5 and 9) in Catalonia –Spain

2005

Director

User Lab Director
User Lab. Innovation Park. University.
2003 – May 2005 (2 years)

In 2003 User Lab in Spain (First Prize IGC Innovation Awards 2005

Deputy Managing Director

Responsibilities:
- Creating and implementing Business Plan, Marketing and Sales Plan.
- Putting together in-house team, external contributor network and creating infrastructures.
- Research and Education Plan.

Deputy Managing Director of geoPlaneta (Grupo Planeta)
geoPlaneta (Grupo Planeta)
2002 – 2002 (less than a year)

geoPlaneta positioned itself as a market leader in the creation and commercialization of touristic contents for multichannel distribution (books, Internet, mobile devices and interactive TV -Quiero TV-).

Responsibilities:
- Marketing Plan, Online Communication & Business Development.
- Public Administration Channel.

Director

geoPlaneta.com & LonelyPlanet.es Director
geoPlaneta (Grupo Planeta)
2000 – 2002 (2 years)

Responsibilities:
- Creating and managing portals for PC, mobile and interactive television (first portal devoted to travel designed for TV). Managing geoPlaneta.com and LonelyPlanet.es virtual communities
- B2C unit: commercialization with travel agencies and advertising.

Manager

Projects Coordinator

Electronic Edition Manager
geoPlaneta (Grupo Planeta)
1998 – 2000 (2 years)

Responsibilities:
- Creating tourist content database in digital format for geoPlaneta: producing style guides, coordinating network of international authors and correspondents in Spain, editing and producing.

- Creating the Corporate Style Guide for online, mobile and printed materials and managing the design team and Design Thinking processes.

- Creating and launching portal for geoPlaneta.com and LonelyPlanet.es.

1998

Internet Projects Coordinator
Planeta Corporación (Grupo Planeta)
Privately Held; 10,001+ employees; Publicaciones industry
1997 – 1998 (1 year)

Responsibilities:
Coordinating viability studies for the launch of geoPlaneta (Dv. Librerías and AESA), BOL (Bertelsman and Dv. Librerías) and for all Grupo Planeta websites.

Chapter 6
Application of Verification Techniques to Security: Model Checking Insider Attacks

Florian Kammüller
DTU Copenhagen, Denmark

Christian W. Probst
Middlesex University, UK

Franco Raimondi
Middlesex University, UK

ABSTRACT

In this chapter, the authors give a short overview of the state of the art of formal verification techniques to the engineering of safe and secure systems. The main focus is on the support of security of real-world systems with mechanized verification techniques, in particular model checking. Based on prior experience with safety analysis—in particular the TWIN elevator (ThyssenKrupp) case study—the current case study ventures into the rising field of social engineering attacks on security. This main focus and original contribution of this chapter considers the security analysis of an insider attack illustrating the benefits of model checking with belief logics and actor system modeling.

INTRODUCTION

The high density of our population today requires efficient use of any resources like energy and space. The use of IT system in all but few domains of everyday life is a reality we have all learned to accept. In this symbiotic new lifestyle, safety and security of technical systems are of utmost importance. Safety can be informally defined as the protection of humans and goods from malfunctioning of technical systems, for examples trains, airplanes, or nuclear reactors. Security on the other side can be understood as the protection of computer systems from malicious humans.

DOI: 10.4018/978-1-4666-4490-8.ch006

In order to guarantee safety and security, application of standards is today common practice. Safety standards are widely applicable and often already include explicit use of formal techniques, whereas for security the use of formal specification and verification is still beyond the reach of everyday industrial practice. The most widely accepted global security standard, the Common Criteria –CC (Bundesamt fuer Sicherheit in der Informationsgesellschaft BSI, 2005). demands in its highest levels, above and including EAL5, the use of formal techniques and even completely mechanized formal proofs of properties in EAL7. However, apart from big enterprises – Microsoft's Windows 2003 has a CC-EAL4 accreditation – the application of CC is beyond the reach of everyday practice for small and medium size enterprises; reaching the highest levels seems even out of reach for large companies.

Systematic application of formal modeling for a mechanized verification is never independent from the nature of the system we investigate. System characteristics, like safety or security sensitivity, time dependent behavior, interaction patterns, and complexity issues of relevant control parts must be taken into account when deciding on the selection of a formalism for rigorous modeling and a method for automated analysis. This chapter makes a case for model checking (Clarke, Grumberg & Peled, 1999). of safety and security sensitive systems. Past experiments have shown that model checking is perfectly capable of proving *safety-critical* systems. For example, the elevator system Twin of ThyssenKrupp has been successfully modeled and all safety requirements have been verified using the SMV model checker [KP07]. This is particularly interesting as the Twin system operates two cabins in one elevator shaft; one driving above the other with collisions in principle possible as illustrated by the admissible routes in Figure 1.

The case study thus proves the capabilities of model checking in industrial scenarios. It is an example of a typical state-based, reactive system. Therefore, it is not very difficult to encode it in the standard model checker SMV (McMillan, 1992; McMillan, 1995). once the right abstraction of the system specification and the safety requirements is found.

More recently, research efforts started increasing to repeat the same success story in the domain of security. However, as has early on been recognized classical security properties, e.g. confidentiality, are fundamentally different properties from safety properties. Whereas a safety property can be expressed as a predicate over a single path composed of state transitions, confidentiality quantifies over a set of paths: intuitively, confidentiality of a system means that all observable

Figure 1. Safe routes of upper (U) and lower (L) cabin are shaded (Kammüller, F. & Preibusch, S., 2007)

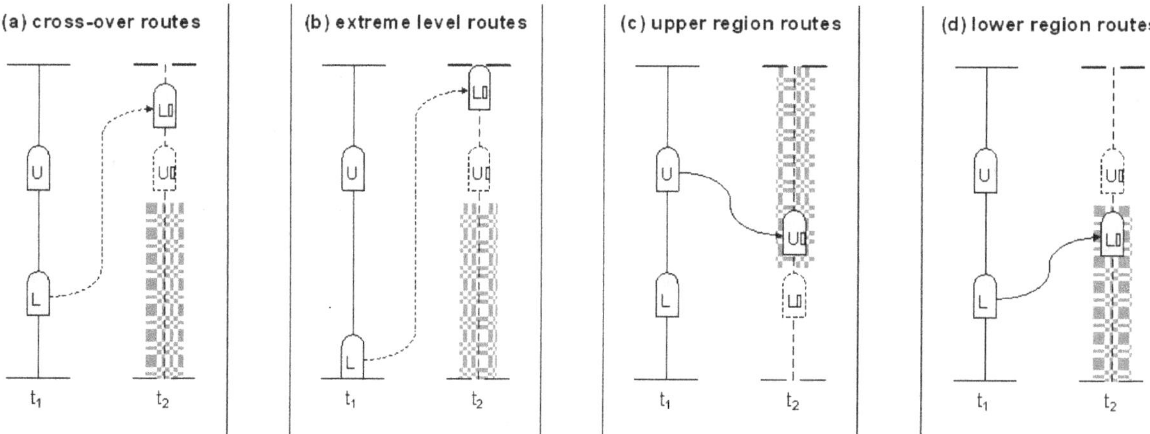

behaviors (sets of state transitions) remain the same if secret parts behave differently. This has been the *status quo* for security of information flows in programs and other systems. Nowadays, the need is felt to lift security analysis from a too thorough and too narrow interpretation of systems as programs in order to cope with real world attacks. Simple benchmark examples, like the insider attack done by a janitor show that *social engineering attacks* are the major challenge for security. The challenge for a formal analysis is here to come up with models that allow expressing enough detail of the environment to cover security relevant facts while staying small enough to make such models amenable to a rigorous analysis. The multitude of factors from physical, logical, and interaction domains that influence the security of a system produce complex models and thus necessitate the support with automated analysis tools.

In previous work, Probst and colleagues have shown that formal actor modeling makes such rich models accessible to static analysis techniques. While this previous work relies on classical static analysis as known from compiler techniques, we take the model checking approach further that we have successfully applied to safety applications like the Twin case study. Model checking is easier to apply: instead of writing a dedicated static analysis program, a formal model is simply implemented in the input language of the model checker and properties corresponding to the required safety or security predicates may be expressed and checked in a push button style on the implemented formal model. The difficulty lies in choosing the appropriate model checker and finding the right level of abstraction in modeling. So far, security seemed out of reach for model checking because of the aforementioned inherent complexity of security predicates as sets of traces. For the Janitor benchmark and the corresponding security requirements we propose the use of a novel model checker, the Mcmas (Lomuscio, Qu & Raimondi, 2009). system, which is based on belief logic, so-called epistemic logic (Zalta et al., 2006). Making human beliefs explicit part of the model, we examine whether the complexity problem of security properties can be coped with.

The contribution of this chapter is the application of belief logic model checking to the classic benchmark of the Janitor insider attack. After giving a short introduction to insider attacks (Section 2.1) and the state of the art of their analysis on the Janitor example (Section 2.2), we introduce belief model checking with the Mcmas system (Section 3.1) showing how it naturally enables a simple modeling of the Janitor model and what properties can be proved (Section 3.2). We finally compare and contrast our approach to previous work and give a short outlook (Section 4).

INSIDER ATTACKS

Probst, Hansen, and Nielsen start their influential paper by the highly motivating sentences "By definition an insider has better access, is more trusted, and has better information about internal procedures, high-value targets, and potential weak spots in the security, than an outsider. Consequently, an insider attack has the potential to cause significant, even catastrophic, damage to the targeted organization" (Probst, Hansen & Nielson, 2006).

Insider Attacks

Insider attacks are naturally much harder to recognize and to deal with than outsider attacks. Recent interest from both the scientific community as well as intelligence services has focused on them (Shaw, Ruby & Post 1998) emphasis is on insider attack detection but mostly reduced to the threat itself, i.e. its modeling and assessment. This roughly corresponds to techniques addressed by intrusion detection systems.

This section introduces a more general notion of insider attacks based on previous work.

Bishop (Bishop, 2005; Bishop, 2009). gives an overview of different definitions of insider threats. The RAND report (Anderson & Brackney,

2005) defines the problem as "malevolent actions by an already trusted person with access to sensitive information and information systems", and the insider is defined as "someone with access, privilege, or knowledge of information systems and services". Bishop then recalls Patzakis definition (Patzakis, 2003) of the insider as "anyone operating inside the security perimeter". Using the idea of a security perimeter (Gollmann, 1999; Gollmann, 2008) clarifies the situation: insider attacks differ from attacks launched from the outside of the perimeter, for example denial-of-service (DoS) attacks. In a DoS attack the attacker is usually placed outside the security perimeter (simply because if he were an insider he could much easier do harm). Based on the literature overview, Bishop gives a definition of insider and insider threat that seems to be acknowledged in the field (Probst, Hansen & Nielson, 2006). and is thus also recited here.

Definition 1: (Insider, Insider threat). An insider with respect to rules R is a user who may take an action that would violate some set of rules R in the security policy, were the user not trusted. The insider is trusted to take the action only when appropriate, as determined by the insider's discretion. The insider threat is the threat that an insider may abuse his discretion by taking actions that would violate the security policy when such actions are not warranted.

A convincing example for an insider threat is the janitor example that is going to be presented next.

The Janitor Example

The Janitor example (see Figure 2) is particularly challenging for formal modeling as it spans the whole spectrum of security: logical components of a computer system, like accessibility of data are at the core, but they are embedded in a real world scenario comprising the physical architecture of a building and its organizational security policies, like room access, that are supported by cypher locks, and the network architecture, like the physical link between computers and printers in the various rooms. The challenge of modeling such an example lies in finding an appropriate level of abstraction that enables dealing with sufficient context information to express threats as well as protection goals while staying sufficiently simple capturing just the essence so that the result will still be a decidable problem within the reach of static analysis or modelchecking. We therefore consider it as a "benchmark".

We start from the existing work by Probst and his collaborators. Probst, Hansen, and Nielsen (Probst, Hansen & Nielson, 2006). first develop a formal language to enable system descriptions of real-world scenarios. Their high-level models can be systematically mapped to acKlaim, a process algebra supporting access control. The process algebra acKlaim, has been designed for formal analysis of actor based systems and is here used to study and analyze properties of the modeled systems. The analysis identifies who may perform which actions, at which locations, and has access to which data. The goal of this analysis is to "compute a superset of audit result as a preventive measure, i.e. before an incident occurs" (Probst, Hansen & Nielson, 2006).

Now in our approach, we aim at a comparative case study of modeling and analysis using easily adaptable model checking techniques. The only small drawback in the previous work (Probst, Hansen & Nielson, 2006) is that a tailor-made implementation of a static analysis program had to be programmed in order to perform the insider analysis. By using a model checking approach that readily supports actors and beliefs, we think that we can do the same or similar analysis but saving a lot of effort in the construction of the analysis model. Besides illustrating the usability of Mcmas model checking, this may further indi-

Figure 2. The Janitor example (Probst,, Hansen. & Nielson, 2006): the user can print confidential files via the network connection. The cypher lock over the door of the user office only admits the user thus excluding the Janitor from logical access. But the cypher lock of the server room admits the Janitor to empty the waste bin. Thus, he can pick up that print out if the user prints it.

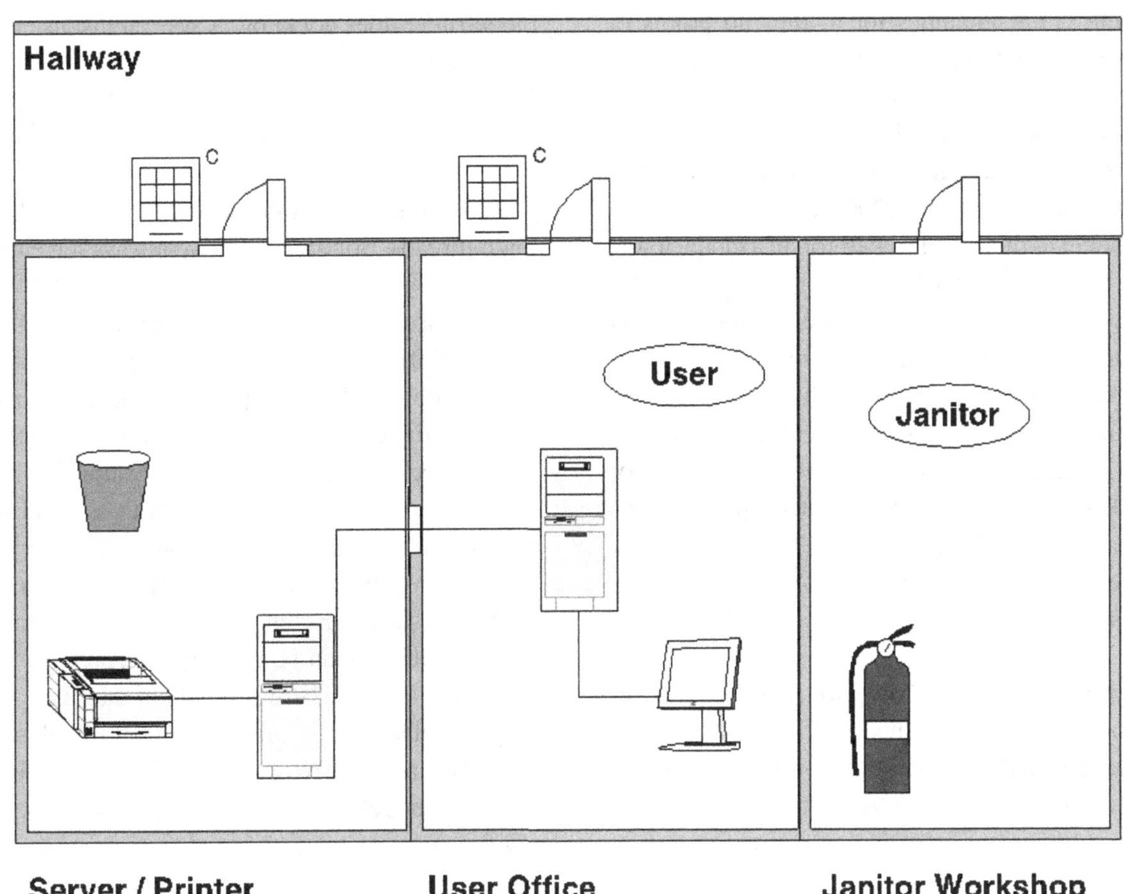

cate that our approach may be fruitfully applied in the more general context of formal analysis of human behavior.

BELIEF LOGIC MODEL CHECKING OF THE JANITOR BENCHMARK

We present next the major contribution of this keynote chapter: how the insider attack problem can be modeled and analyzed using model checking. We do so by explaining the application of Mcmas model checking to the Janitor benchmark.

MCMAs Modelchecking

In the early days of authentication protocol development, the BAN logic was one of the first logical attempts to use a systematic logic-based attempts on the analysis of authentication and key exchange protocols. This belief logic already used the idea of establishing "knowledge" of the principals involved in the setup of an online communication serving the analysis of the communication steps, i.e. the protocol: to establish whether it reaches the desired goal of authentication the logical goal in BAN is to prove by logical inference that both principals "believe" in the authenticity of each other and moreover whether they believe that the other believes in it (Burrows, Abadi & Needham, 1990). As a logic, the BAN logic is rather ad hoc. There is no semantics for it; thus no proofs of soundness or completeness are possible. However, it encapsulates very good engineering practice in a set of formal inductive rules. Besides, logical foundations for belief logic exist. So-called epistemic logics (Zalta et al., 2006). feature knowledge or belief as their modal operator. In a modal logic, the "world" is modeled as a directed graph over states; formulas true in a model must hold in all states of that graph. In epistemic logic, there is additionally a set of *agents* whose knowledge is defined by the propositions of each state. States are called possible worlds. The modal operator *K* (knows) and *B* (believes) quantify propositions over agents. For example,

```
M,w⊢ K(A,p)
```

Mcmas is now a belief logic model checker (Lomuscio, Qu & Raimondi, 2009). Although its principal modal operators are from epistemic logic, the model checker MCMAS (http://www-lai.doc.ic.ac.uk/mcmas), contains an expressive subset of CTL* augmented with epistemic logic. Thus, temporal properties may be specified together with properties containing statements about beliefs (K operator). As an example, consider the expression of the following statement: if the intruder knows that he has access to Bob's files, then he will find the keys B uses for communication with A.

```
AF(K(Intruder, keysB) -> K(Intruder,
keyAB));
```

The main advantage that immediately calls for using Mcmas as a tool to analyze insider attacks, like the Janitor example, is the inherent existence of *actors*. Since expression of real-world scenarios, like the Janitor, has as its core element *human behavior,* actors are almost indispensible for the modeling these scenarios adequately. Important for security, which mostly deals with absence of knowledge (secrecy), we can also express the lack of knowledge formally. To write down that the intruder does not know X we can just use the following formula.

```
AG(!K(Intruder, X));
```

In a combination of classical CTL and belief logic it reads "for all worlds we always have the intruder does not know X".

From a security engineering perspective (Anderson, 2001). Mcmas also has the great advantage of all model checkers: if a property, like the above given examples, is violated in the model then the model checker generates a counterexample. This counterexample is a possible path to a world in which the respective predicate is false. For security applications, the succession of steps leading into such a possible world in which the desired property is violated, can be directly interpreted into a possible attack. There is no doubt that this is a very useful feature for practical security analysis. It enables an iterative approach for engineering security models and checking given security requirements on them.

Modeling and Analysis of Janitor in Mcmas

As a simple application of the Mcmas model checker, we can directly consider our model of the Janitor problem since it is very straightforward and we have reduced it to the main features necessary for the security analysis. A Mcmas model consists of a set of agent definitions. The one for the user is given in Algorithm 1 and described subsequently.

The above agent definition of Mcmas introduces the agent user whose internal state variables model all necessary state variables for the representation of the Janitor benchmark in the Vars section given as initial and current position. Locations of the agents are inlined into the agent

Algorithm 1.

```
Agent User
Vars:
   initialposition: { hall }; -- The initial state is in the hall
                                 -- all moves are spelled out
   currentposition: { hall,pc,server }; -- The current position
      -- the data is modeled flatly as a boolean flag
   print_secretfile: boolean;
end Vars
  Actions = { print, move, move1, move2 };
Protocol:
  currentposition = pc or currentposition = server: {move};
  currentposition = hall: {move1,move2};
  currentposition = pc: {print};
end Protocol
Evolution:
   currentposition = pc if (currentposition = hall and Action = move1);
   currentposition = server if
                      (currentposition = hall and Action = move2);
   currentposition = hall if
       ((currentposition=pc or currentposition=server) and Action=move);
end Evolution
end Agent
```

definition as values hall, pc, server for the rooms. The changes of location of the agent user are modeled simply by the two actions move1 and move2 representing the change between the rooms. Actions are defined in Mcmas in a Protocol section; here it defines the possible trajectories of the user depending on his current position.

For simplicity and clarity of the exposition we completely abstract from the cipher locks and implement the different security policies (user can enter room2, janitor not) by their respective moving possibilities.

The agent Janitor is very similar to user but with the restriction that he cannot move into the user's office. The behavior specification of the model is given by the definition of the Evolution part in the two agent definitions. The security attack is encoded in the Janitor agent by the predicate has_secretfile which summarizes the actions the Janitor has to take in order to pick up the print out of the secret data by the user. This main security risk is expressed in the following Evaluation section of our Mcmas model.

```
Evaluation
  -- the attack
 janitor_succeeds if Janitor.has_se-
cretfile = true;
end Evaluation
```

Based on this model definition, the actual security analysis with Mcmas is simply done by stating the security attack as the following simple temporal property; the checking is performed in fully automated fashion.

```
EF(janitor_succeeds);
```

Algorithm 2.

```
Agent Janitor
Vars:
  initialposition: { janitor };
currentposition: { hall, server, janitor };
   -- the data is modelled flatly as a boolean flags
has_secretfile: boolean;
end Vars
Actions = { pickfromwaste, move, movej, movep };
Protocol:
currentposition = janitor or currentposition = server: {move};
currentposition = hall: {movej,movep};
end Protocol
Evolution:
currentposition=server if (currentposition=hall and Action=movep);
currentposition=janitor if (currentposition=hall and Action=movej);
currentposition=hall if
               ((currentposition=server or currentposition=janitor)
                and Action=move);
has_secretfile = true if
               (currentposition = server and User.Action = print);
end Evolution
end Agent
```

This result shows that in the current model – with the cipher lock configured such that the Janitor can go into the printer room to empty the waste bin – there exists a path in which he succeeds to lay his hand on the confidential file. If we adapt the model accordingly such that the Janitor cannot enter the printer room or the user never prints a secret file, a positive guarantee can be proved, like the following.

```
AG(! janitor_succeeds)
```

CONCLUSION

In this chapter, we have given an introduction to the application of model checking techniques to systems that are sensitive to safety and security. For safety, we provided an impression of the state of the art by briefly summarizing the results of a previous real-world case study of the safety-critical Twin elevator application (Kammüller & Preibusch, 2007) to show the feasibility of the model checking approach. Concentrating on the security aspects, we have introduced insider attacks. Based on previous work (Probst, Hansen & Nielson, 2006) that shows that real-world scenarios, like the Janitor benchmark, can be quite naturally expressed with actor formalisms, we have given a practical illustration: using the epistemic logic model checker Mcmas we formally modeled and analyzed the Janitor benchmark example exhibiting formally the security attack.

The analysis demonstration has been reduced for reasons of brevity and clarity to a very simplistic model omitting many aspects that could be potentially interesting for a more detailed analysis of this scenario. Although model checking always necessitates reduction of the model to avoid the state explosion problem, we did not reach the limits of Mcmas with this tiny application. In other words, for future exploration of security model checking, a richer model is feasible. It is remarkable that the use of knowledge operators of the belief logic was not necessary to express the central security goal. This seems to suggest that the beliefs are not as central to actor modeling as are the actors and their internal states. This observation could be further verified by using pure active object languages, e.g. (Henrio, Kammüller & Lutz, 2011). for further experimentation with modeling real-world scenarios.

In comparison to the role model for this experiment (Probst, Hansen & Nielson, 2006) our model appears to be almost trivial. The two layered approach of an abstract actor language for the description of the model, the translation to acKlaim, and the rich, many-faceted expression of actors and their locations of our precursor is clearly much more expressive than our simple model. The tailor-made static analysis program designed for this also exhibits some security analysis goals that are beyond what we can express in logic. However, we find that the relative ease of modeling the benchmark and the then trivial push button checking are compelling arguments for our approach as compared to static analysis.

The wider meaning of the presented project is to show that off-the-shelf analysis techniques, like model checking, are to some extent useful for formal modeling and analysis of real-world applications. For the future, we desire to generalize this into a methodology for formal methods for the modeling and analysis of human behavior.

REFERENCES

Anderson, R. (2001). *Security engineering – A guide to building dependable distributed systems*. Indianapolis, IN: Wiley.

Anderson, R., & Brackney, R. (2005). *Understanding the insider threat*. Santa Monica, CA: RAND Corporation.

Bishop, M. (2005). The insider problem revisited. In *Proceedings of New Security Paradigms Workshop 2005*. New York: ACM Press.

Bishop, M. (2009). *Introduction to computer security*. Boston: Addison Wesley.

Bundesamt fuer Sicherheit in der Informationsgesellschaft (BSI). (2005). *Common criteria for information technology security evaluation, part 3*. Retrieved from http://www.bsi.de/cc/ccpart3v2_3.pdf

Burrows, M., Abadi, M., & Needham, R. (1990). A logic of authentication. *ACM Transactions on Computer Systems*, *8*, 18–36. doi:10.1145/77648.77649

Clarke, E., Grumberg, O., & Peled, D. (1999). *Model checking*. Cambridge, MA: The MIT Press.

Gollmann, D. (1999). Insider fraud. In *Security Protocols (LNCS)* (Vol. 1550, pp. 213–219). Heidelberg, Germany: Springer. doi:10.1007/3-540-49135-X_29

Gollmann, D. (2008). *Computer security*. New York: McGraw Hill.

Henrio, L., Kammüller, F., & Lutz, B. (2011). Aspfun: A typed functional active object calculus. *Science of Computer Programming*.

Kammüller, F., & Preibusch, S. (2007). An industrial application of symbolic model checking – The TWIN-elevator case study. *Computer Science Research and Development*, *22*(2), 95–108.

Lomuscio, A., Qu, H., & Raimondi, F. (2009). *MCMAS: A model checker for the verification of multi-agent systems. Computer Aided Verification, (LNCS)*. Heidelberg, Germany: Springer.

McMillan, K. (1992). *Symbolic model checking –An approach to the state explosion problem*. (PhD Dissertation). School of Computer Science, Carnegie Mellon University, Pittsburgh, PA.

McMillan, K. (1995). *Symbolic model checking*. Boston: Kluwer Academic Publishers.

Patzakis, J. (2003). *New incident response best practices: Patch and proceed is no longer acceptable incident response procedure* (White Paper). Pasadena, CA: Guidance Software.

Probst, C., Hansen, R., & Nielson, F. (2006). Where can an insider attack? In *Proceedings of Formal Aspects of Security and Trust (LNCS)* (Vol. 4691). Heidelberg, Germany: Springer.

Shaw, E., Ruby, K., & Post, J. (1998). The insider threat to information systems. *Security Awareness Bulletin, 2*(98).

Zalta, E. et al. (2006). *Stanford encyclopedia of philosophy: Epistemic logic*. Stanford, CA: Stanford University.

Chapter 7
Banking Online:
Design for a New Credibility

Francisco V. Cipolla-Ficarra
ALAIPO – AINCI, Spain and Italy

Jaqueline Alma
Electronic Arts – Vancouver, Canada

ABSTRACT

The authors present the first results of a communicability evaluation of a set of online banking systems aimed at the new credibility of those institutions. They evaluate the strategies of interactive design, focusing on the presentation of the information on the interface. Finally, the first group of human factors is established which has affected negatively the veracity of banking information in Southern Europe in the last five years.

INTRODUCTION

One of the key elements of the institutional image of the banking bodies has been trust factor towards intangible services related to money and finances (Karat, Brodie & Karat, 2006). Now this flux of information must be available electronically to its clients, 24/7 in every day of the week. Allegedly it is a premise that is guaranteed from the banking publicity to the clientele, but in reality it is not so. The financial institutions have information processes in real time and others in batch processing – in execution of a series of programmes (also called "jobs") on a computer without manual intervention. This is a widespread reality in this kind of institutions, since the mid 20th century. The public in general doesn't know this reality, which is a source of constant complaints (previous to the global financial crisis), whether it is with the remote services or in the banking seats themselves. Consequently, there are processes which are carried out immediately such as the data consultation of the banking headquarters, such as the IBAN code (International Bank Account Number), SWIFT (Society for Worldwide Interbank Financial Telecommunication), etc.,

DOI: 10.4018/978-1-4666-4490-8.ch007

and others which require a whole series of previous verifications such as the transfer of currency inside and outside a state. From the point of view of communicability we can establish two kinds of factors, underlying and apparent. The underlying ones are the characteristics intrinsic to the information system, such as the information in real time or in batch, whereas the apparent are those which obey to the design factors of the computer programmes (Cipolla-Ficarra, 2005). For instance, it is not normal that an experienced or inexperienced user must resort to the Google or Yahoo searcher to find quickly the IBAN or SWIFT code of the banking institution he/she is member.

The issues related to the way of operating from the computer science point of view have joined a myriad human factors of the banking staff towards their clients. The latter have practically lost their trust towards these institutions, without distinguishing whether the problems stem from the computer systems or the human factors (Cipolla-Ficarra, et al., 2011). When we talk about human factors we mean those excellent clients who have never had red numbers in their accounts and who operated in the banking offices or electronically. These clients interrelated with these institutions without any kind of inconveniences, but who have been swindled by the disingenuous publicity of the banking institutions, that is, the lack of clarity in the marketing information. In our group of adult and inexperienced users in computer science, that knowledge of the banking staff has been termed as sadism in 97% of the analyzed cases.

The current work is structured in the following way: state of the art and strategies followed for the selection of the universe of study and the users, elaboration of the instruments for the measurement of communicability, veracity and credibility of the banking information, interaction with the banking systems, compiling of the results, learned lessons, future lines of work and conclusions. The examples that are commented in the current work over the banking experiences refer to the period 2008-2012 are truthful 100% belong to cities of Southern Europe, and have been extracted from our universe of study. These have been included to contextualize the data and the presented conclusions.

THE UNIVERSE OF STUDY: BANKS AND CLIENTS

Our universe of study is made up by adult people, whose ages oscillate between 40-60 years, clients of banking institutions in Southern Europe. All of them have 15 years of seniority of having bank accounts in the same institution. Some of them have access to the online banking systems, but their knowledge of computer science is elementary. They use the computer for the search of information in Google, Yahoo, etc. and the reception/emission of messages mainly. The analyzed banking institutions have their local headquarters in Catalonia and Lombardy mainly although some of the examples that we will address belong to international financial groups. With these institutions our group of users interact virtually from the workplace and/or the home and in the daily life. The emotional aspects deriving from scarcely transparent business practices have been quantified through the use of techniques stemming from the social sciences and statistics (Cipolla-Ficarra, et al., 2011). Some examples of these emotional variables are the result of financial prosperity and the deceitful publicity to get the excellent clients into debt are: the former Caixa in Barcelona, now CaixaBank, in the face of the closure of a small firm due to the global financial crisis does not allow the quick transformation of the debt into a personal debt. In contrast, they have chosen to demand the whole payment of the debt, increasing in 50% the overall amount of the debt, to end after several months of disputes in a personal credit to be paid back in several years. Another example is a Lombardian institution that dedicates itself to issuing double personal loans, which are managed externally from the bank, with pensioners who cash € 600 per month and whose monthly fees surpass 50% of their revenue due to the double charge of interests in the amount of the loan. In the face of these two small examples, the credibility towards those banks and the rest of the financial system is equal to zero for those customers. If we add to this the technological issues of not-functioning, such as the typical phrases in Latin America before making a payment with cards in a shop, hotel or even inside the banks themselves, "there is no system", we can find even worse situations in Europe, as it can be seen in the following example of the Figure 1, where the operations with the Iberian Peninsula are thwarted and the message of "non-existent" nation appears, as is the case of Spain inside the German banking circuit. Obviously, the "there is no system", is a lesser evil as compared to the "non-existent nation".

The example of "non-existent nation" with which not only it is not possible to make Internet banking operations from the south of the Mediterranean, makes apparent once again the real prejudices towards the clients, who must make the operations on the bank counter, pay fees and see how the batch process slows down the financial operations. Oddly enough, the call center does not inform over the exact date in which the service will be reactivated, nor are there dysfunction messages in the website. That is, that the credibility and the communicability of the online banking

Figure 1. Message of non-existent nation "Spain" (*) from an online service in Italy

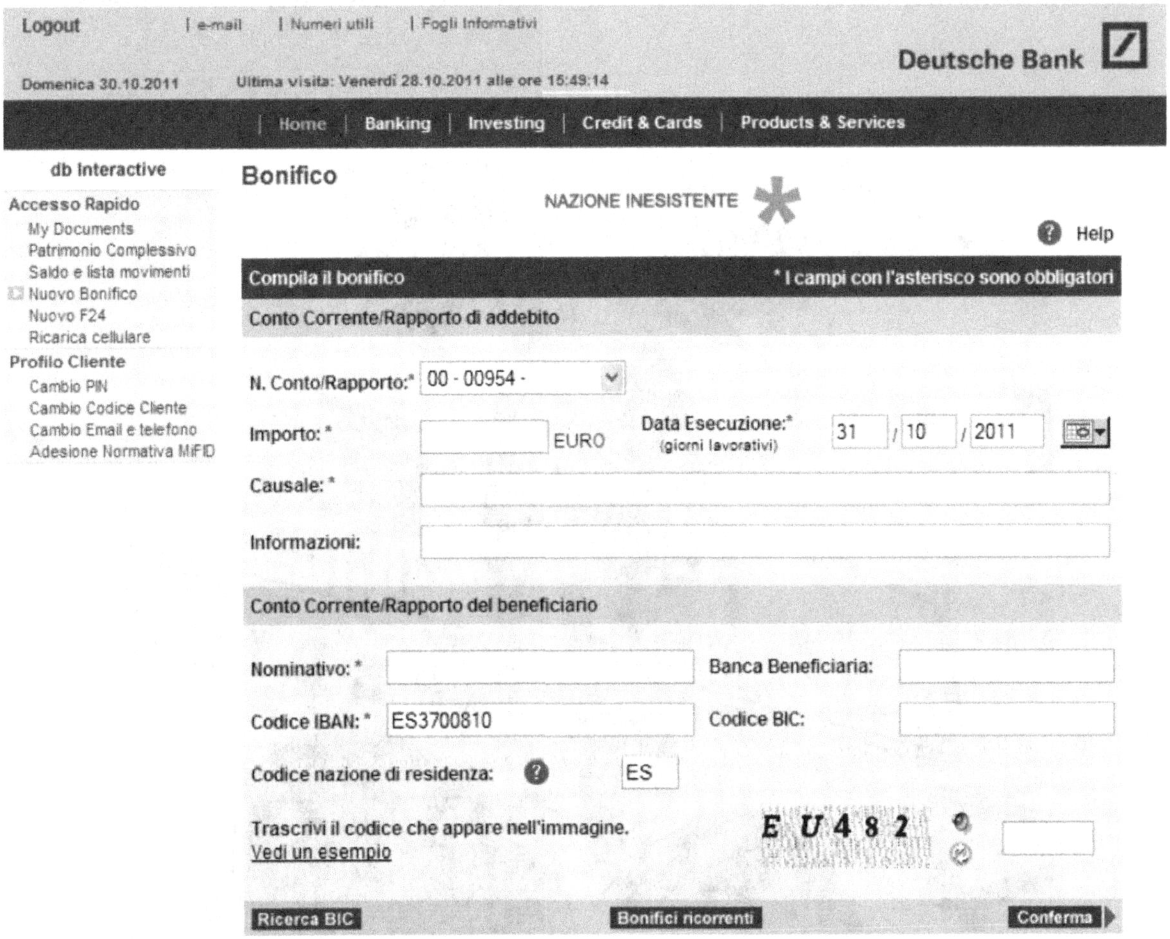

information is equal to zero. Of course the banking institutions between 2008-2012 in Southern Europe have carried out a series of make-up operations in their real or virtual structures, such as placing statues of the "angel" at the entrance (Figure 2), similar to victory or freedom by many sculptors, organizing paintings exhibits, theoretically aiding the disabled, fostering museums of the sciences, etc. of course the opinion gathered in our universe of study indicates that some of these institutions are parochial, antiglobalization, uncouth, among other variables related to the human and/or social factors (Cipolla-Ficarra, et al., 2011). These real values will be downplayed to the utmost through the publicity rhetoric of the banking and/or financial institutions. These are persuasive publicity campaigns, which have taken avail of almost every media of both digital and analogical communication in order to foster consumerism. Where they practically forced their clients to run into debt with personal credits, mortgages for cars, houses, etc. All of this happened in the period 2000-2007 in countries like Spain and Portugal. Since the 90 down to the early 21st century has had one of the widest ATMs networks on the European continent, with which the phenomenon of wild consumerism in an exponential way.

ANALOGICAL AND DIGITAL INSTITUTIONAL COMMUNICABILITY

The analogical institutional communicability of the financial institutions right now only admits a single way of evaluation; the quality of the paper they use in their brochures, postcards, catalogues of artistic samples, calendars, notebooks, etc.

Figure 2. Digital newspaper –L'eco di Bergamo, 03.25.2012 (www.ecodibergamo.it)

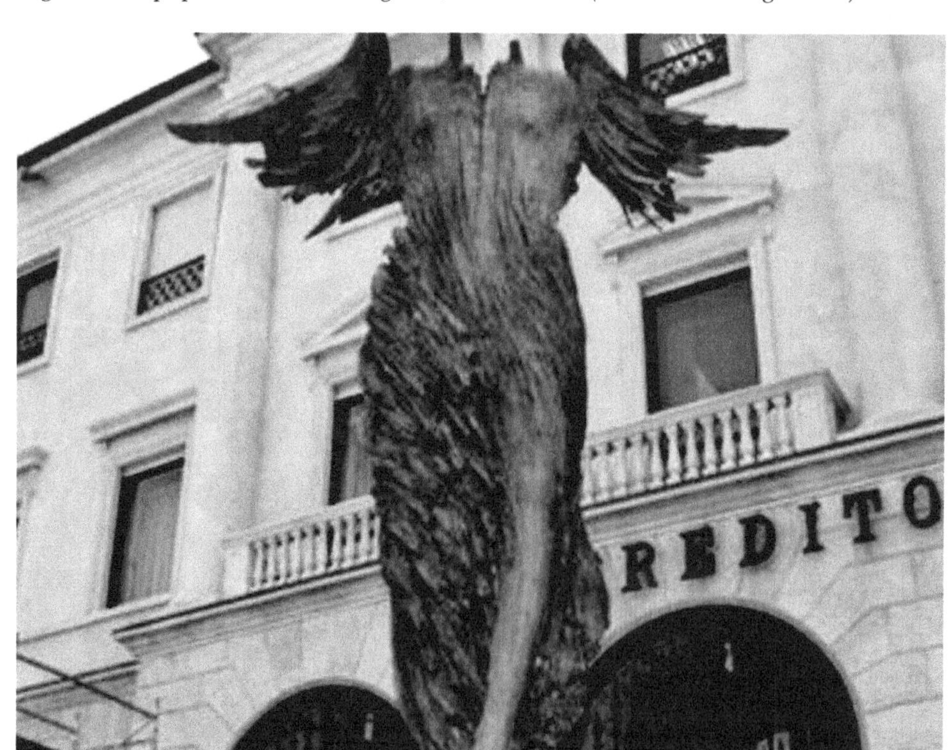

Products produced in Asian countries but designed in Europe make apparent that the bridge between average and small clients with the great, middle-size and small credit institutions has been destroyed. From a linguistic point of view, these institutions try to get back or keep their customers with notions such as "partner", "members of the same group", "safety", "future", etc., that is, as elements which belong to a same set who must work for the sake of the future. However, these are obsolete communicational forms in view of the human factors, backed by the computer systems, for instance, the reduction of the limits in the credit cards or the increase of the control mechanisms to carry out long distance operations through the use of the internet.

Examining the home pages of the banking and financial systems through a set of quality attributes and metrics developed in the mid 90s and perfected in the current millennium, such as isomorphism, richness and accesibility (Cipolla-Ficarra, 1997), which the interested reader can look up in the following bibliographical references (Cipolla-Ficarra, 1998; Cipolla-Ficarra, 2012). In our first work we will focus on two of the categories of interactive design such as are the presentation of the information and the content, applying the following table which was the basis of the set of quality attributes and metrics (Cipolla-Ficarra, 1998; Cipolla-Ficarra & Cipolla-Ficarra, 2008). The analyzed websites belong to the following banking institutions: Banca di Roma (Italy), Banca Nazionale del Lavoro (Italy), Banca Popolare (Italy), Banco Bilbao-Viscaya (Spain), Bankinter (Spain), CaixaBank (Spain), Citibank (Spain), Lloyds Bank (Italy), Sabadell-Atlantico (Spain), and Unicredit (Italy). All of them with headquarters in Spain and Italy. Evidently the visual factor of the websites (Alison et al., 1995; Gage, 2000; Brown, et al., 2002) of the Figures 3 and 4 makes apparent the existence of isotopy lines through the following colors: primary (red, blue, yellow), secondary (light blue, orange) and neuter (black and white). However, inside them can be seen the strengthening of the phenomenon called Argentinization of the colors and which are presented in the following flag with their matching values.

Although in a portal we have a drawing made by Joan Mirò such as the star of the current CaixaBank (Figure 3), the three colors are not so present in the intranet environments for the customers. In that environment it can be seen how the red is used few times, compared with the light blue, white and yellow. The former colours, light blue with white background of the websites, are currently fashionable even in the Spanish digital press such as can be the portals of El País (www.elpais.es) El mundo (www.elmundo.es), La Vanguardia (www.lavanguardia.es) that is, they have also chosen the Argentinization of their portals. In some way the portals of the banking institutions also try to establish chromatic links with the daily information of the digital press. Next the results of the communicability from the point of view of presentation and the contents of the online information (minimum value 0, maximum value 10).

SAFETY AND DESIGN

Without any doubt, this is an environment where the safety issue occupies a first place. Aside from all the mechanisms of computer safety applied to the current financial services and that they can be improved to avoid fraud, we focus on the ease of access the users have in our universe of study, without resorting to avant-garde technologies such as can be voice recognition, the iris of the eye, fingerprints, etc. As a rule, for the customers there are two or three keys before having access to their confidential information, such as can be the bank balances and/on movements of their bank accounts or credit cards. Now whereas in Spain with only four digits one can have access to the bank account through an ATM, in Italy it is necessary to type five digits to access the bank account.

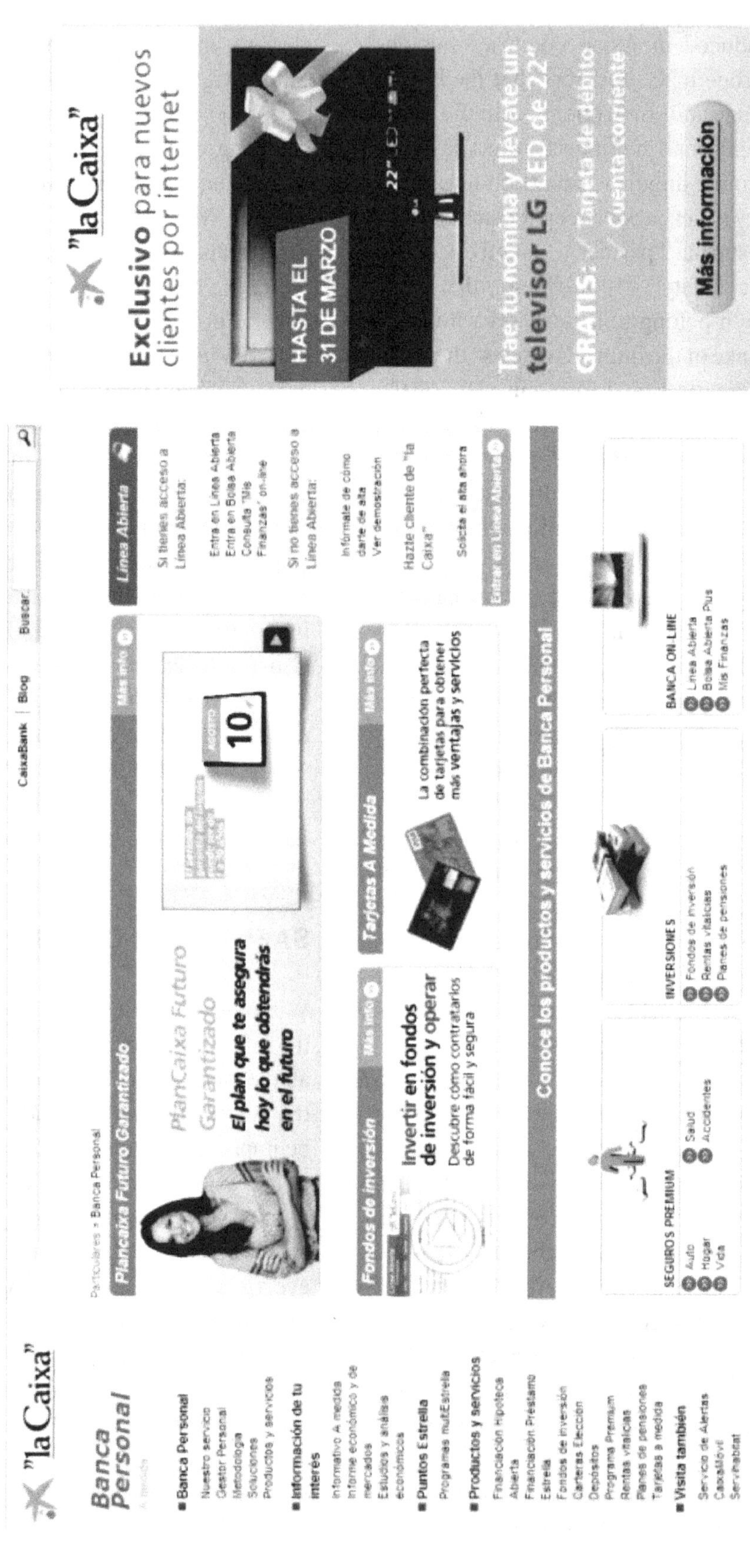

Figure 3. The Argentinization of the design: logo and banner in digital newspaper (www.elpais.es, www.elmundo.es, and www.lavanguardia.es, for example)

Figure 4. Argentinization of the design (www.bancsabadell.com)

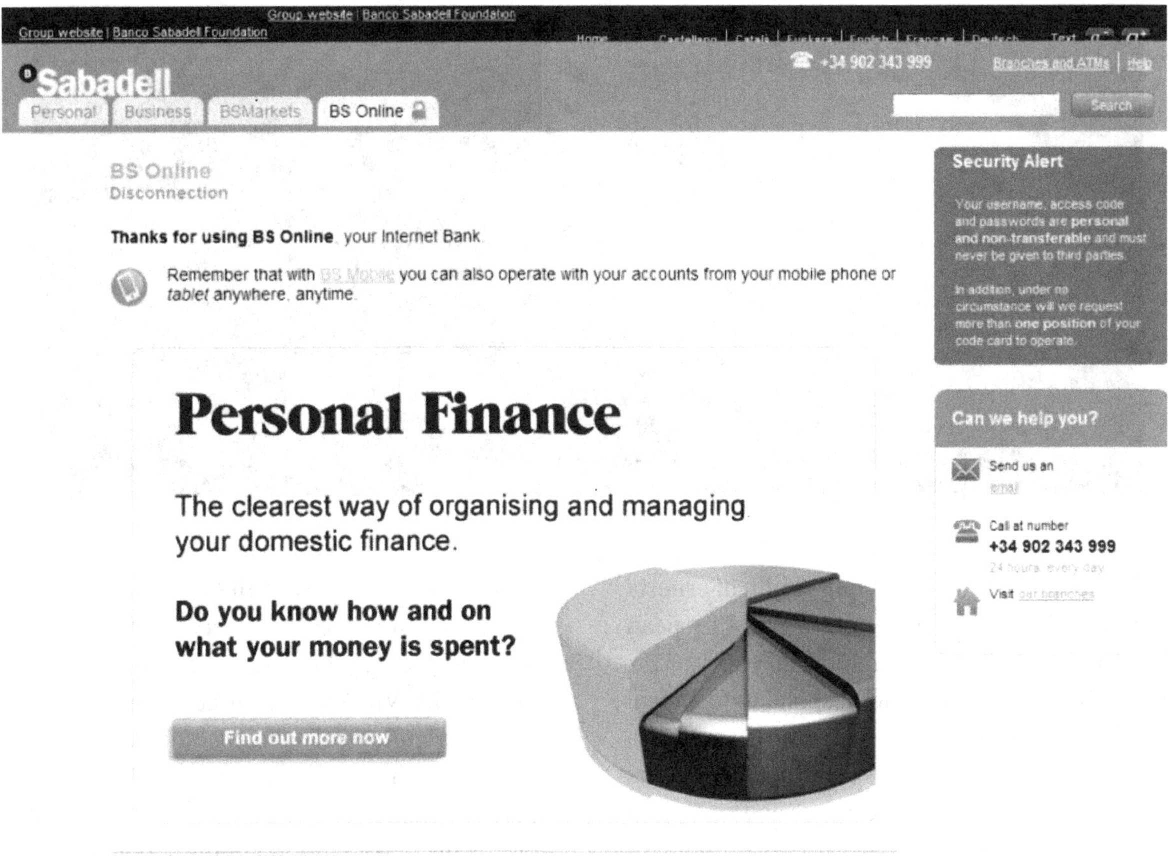

Figure 5. Flag of Argentina –colours and the different codes used in regard to the support that is used, The colors of this flag in a direct or indirect way are present in the banking websites

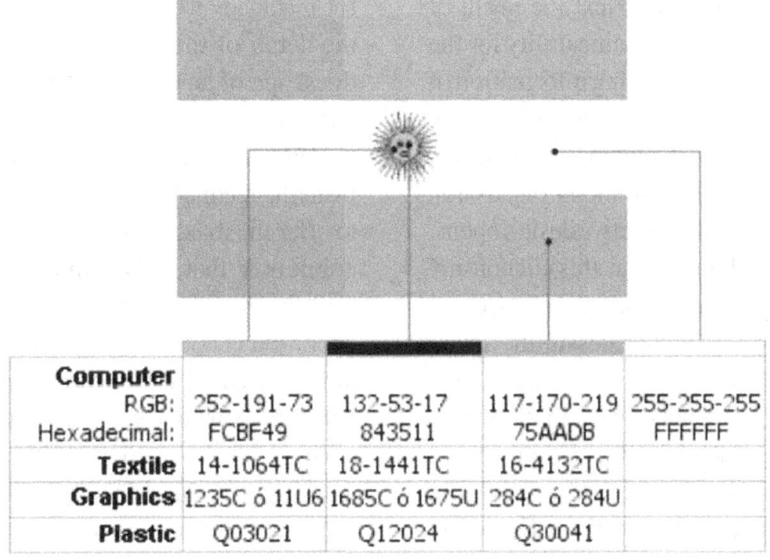

Computer RGB:	252-191-73	132-53-17	117-170-219	255-255-255
Hexadecimal:	FCBF49	843511	75AADB	FFFFFF
Textile	14-1064TC	18-1441TC	16-4132TC	
Graphics	1235C ó 11U6	1685C ó 1675U	284C ó 284U	
Plastic	Q03021	Q12024	Q30041	

Figure 6. Results of the main components of the free access online interfaces

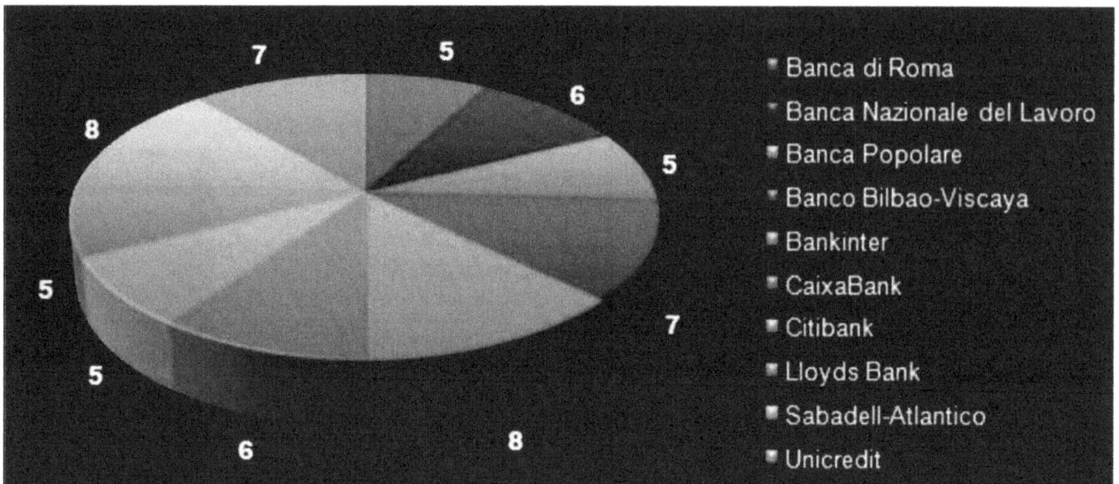

Here we have a first lack of uniformity of criteria of the banking systems inside a same European region, which have a common currency. This lack of uniformity does not respond to technical issues, but are rather political. Now these criteria create certain habits among the potential users who when they reach certain ages and/or certain educational levels do not grasp easily the logic of these differences. Nor is it easy to them the fact of having to introduce the components of a password in the shape of bidirectional coordinates (x e y), for instance, the firsr component of the key and below the second component. Next the result of the analysis made on the communicability for the ease of access to the online banking information of credit cards of the group that made up our universe of study (minimum value 0, maximum value 10).

Of course here the dichotomous discussion between online safety and interactive design opens. However, the ideal thing is that this dichotomy could merge in a single reality where safety, communicability, usability and accessibility were present.

From a topological point of view in the access websites to the confidential information we can claim that 100% of the cases are to be found in the upper/central area of the interface. Evidently it is a cultural issue of the Western world, and it obeys to the principles of the "divine or perfect proportion", in which the spectator focuses her vision on a rectangular or square figure and which Leonardo Da Vinci already used in his paintings.

The chronological factor also affects these two components that we are analyzing (safety and design), especially at the moment of finding out the movements of the bank accounts in the matching detail of the made operations. Whereas in some online systems it is possible to have access to the historical information in others it isn't, since there is a calendar which sets a limit towards the past, for instance, 30, 60, 90, 180, etc. days. Besides, the detail of the operation may be presented in the shape of an enclosed file of the pdf kind or a .txt file with synthetized information.

Once again we are in the face of a reality where from the technological point of view it is feasible to offer the maximum possible information to the online user, that is, the remote customer. However, said alternative is not active in all the banks. This operation is not provided in some financial institutions because it is a way to generate additional revenue, for instance, by cashing a commission for asking all the movements of the account in a year.

Although these institutions do not take into account the waste of time that it means for the customer, who is forced to visit the banking of-

Figure 7. The financial institution best valued by the users is Bankinter. The worst valued is Banca Populare.

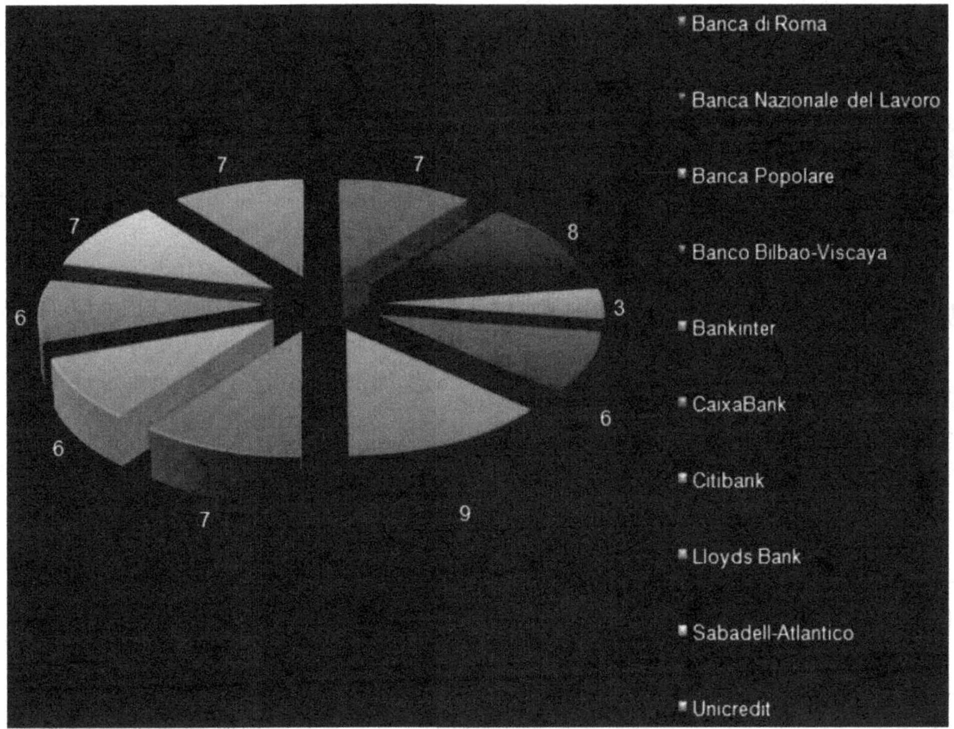

fice, since they are personal requests and are made in the counter of the bank. Here is another real situation which accumulates to the human factors as source of possible conflicts, especially for the users experienced in the use of computer systems but who are forced to go to the banks.

In the evaluation with users (20 in all) we have established a series of tasks to be carried out by them once they have reached the reserved or confidential areas. Some of these operations were doable and others not. In an affirmative case, the number of options that were chosen to reach the goal were counted (keyboard and mouse pulses). The same happened with those actions impossible to do in some websites. The tasks and their matching codifications arc the following:

- T1 = Knowing the balance;
- T2 = The last 20 movements;
- T3 = Having access to the detail to each one of those movements;
- T4 = Having access to a banking movement from 180 days back;
- T5 = Having access to the information linked to a movement of 6 months back;
- T6 = having access to the IBAN of the account.

The names of the banking institutions have been eliminated in the following graphic of results (confidential reasons).

The degree of difficulty to access wanted information is very high in the area of study that is made, if we compare the average of the results obtained by the evaluator who has carried out the set of tasks that the users had to perform.

- T 1= 3 options (here is calculated the total, that is, those made both from the keyboard and the mouse which are equivalent to an input or an enter or a click).
- T 2= 2 steps.

Figure 8. Total of operations carried out from the keyboard or with the mouse to have access to confidential information in the online service of some financial institutions which operate in Southern Europe

- T 5= In the cases when it is feasible to reach the average is 5, in other financial websites this task is impossible to make.
- T 7= it is not possible to carry out that operation.

RESULTS, LESSONS LEARNED AND FUTURE WORKS

Next the evaluation of the users accessing = confidential information is presented, that is, both the banking intranet, extranet and Internet information. This evaluation has been grouped in relation to the analyzed banking institutions:

- Banca di Roma (Italy)
- Banca Nazionale del Lavoro (Italy)
- Banca Popolare (Italy)
- Banco Bilbao-Viscaya (Spain)
- Bankinter (Spain)
- CaixaBank (Spain)
- Citibank (Spain)
- Lloyds Bank (Italy)
- Sabadell-Atlantico (Spain)
- Unicredit (Italy)

The lessons learned from the current work can be summed up in three large areas. In the first

Figure 9. The loss of credibility of the information and trust in the computerized services of the banking and/or financial institutions. Minimum value 0, maximum value 10.

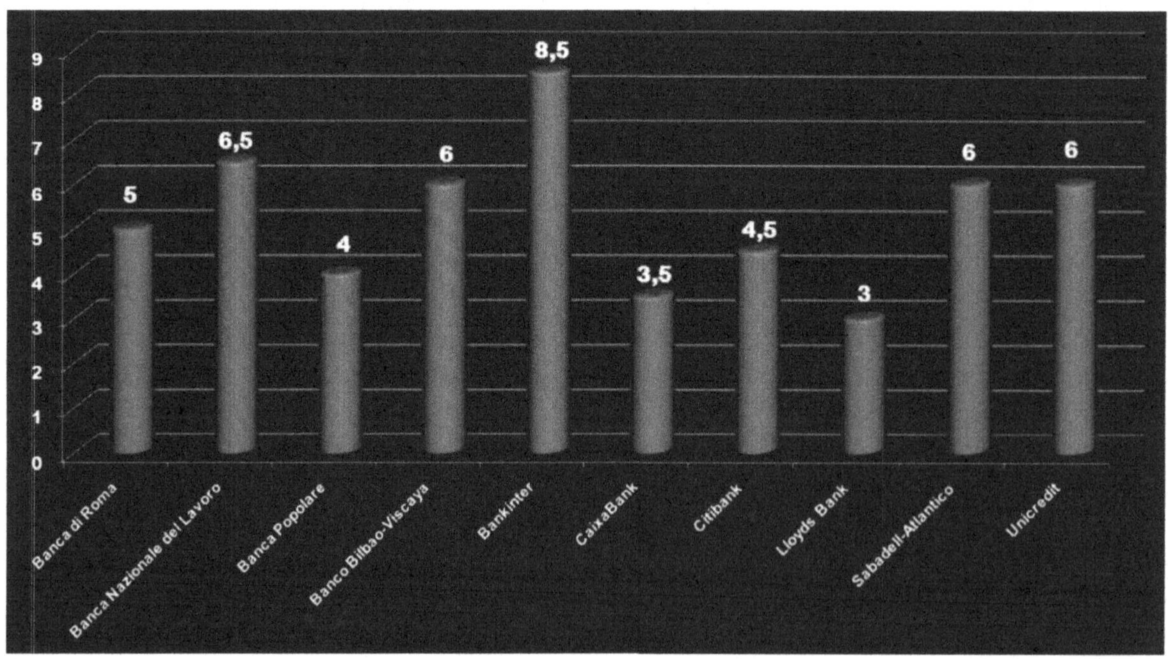

place, the results obtained make apparent that the interactive design of the online systems for banking institutions will not be able to give back the confidence and credibility of the information from those institutions to their clients or Internet users in all countries and regions south of Europe. Besides, the make-up operations which some financial institutions have made such as the change of name, linked to the pseudo interest towards the art, the sciences, the social assistance, grants, etc., can do little or nothing to solve the communicability problem between their websites and the references towards the real world, whether in relation to emulation or simulation situations of the reality of some interactive services of a high level of safety but of little informative transparency towards the clients or inexperienced users in the use of computers. Second, from the point of view of the online communicability of the banks there is a process to emulate the digital newspapers. This statement stems from the studies of the design categories belonging to the presentation of data in the interfaces as well as the way to distribute the contents on the screens of computers or mobile phones. However, the banks and the digital newspapers have plumped for the Argentinization of the interactive design, starting by the use of colours, and the topological distribution of the contents on the homepage, comparing them with the portals of banks and newspapers in France, for instance. Finally the human factors linked to the global economic context from 2008 to 2012 slow down the technological advances in the issue of safety which could be implemented in the online banking transactions. Besides, there is a rejection towards those institutions with which the digital gap between clients and banking services will increase in the next years. A way of cutting it down would be to increase the operations in real time and reducing those which are made in the batch modality. In future works we will enhance the number of users in the experiments in keeping with the goal that the clients have at the moment of having access to the banking services and inserting motley categories of users, for instance, trade clerks, industrial workers, university students, freelance professionals, researchers. We will also include banking entities from the north of Europe to contrast them with the south of Europe.

CONCLUSION

The negative human/social factors should be radically eliminated in the banks. Instead of carrying out operations of institutional make-up such as the sudden interest towards culture, nature, education, which do not help to restore a truthful and reliable interrelation between users and financial interactive systems. The institutional image of many financial entities with the global crisis has been totally destroyed in the credibility of millions of small and middle customers in the south of Europe. This is an image that was based on the absolute trust of the excellent clients or inexperienced users in computers. However, many of them have been swindled by the institutional communication. For instance, through the deceitful publicity design which has circulated in both a digital and an analog format. Those responsible for that mess have not reacted to the global crisis and keep on making portals where the "copy and paste" of foreign models prevails. See as an example the Argentinization factor of design. Perhaps the use of that fashion of the interactive design responds to the fact that the scandals occur always very far from where the banking institutions are located for which the interfaces for the computer systems are created. In the Spanish ATMs we have so far seen a minimalist design to facilitate the operations to millions of users for decades but little or nothing remains from that quality from the point of view of communicability in the current online systems. The online banking portals today not only have communicability errors, but also usability errors.

Theoretically the usability problems in the interactive design should be overcome in the current era of communicability expansion.

REFERENCES

Alison, F. et al. (1995). *Colours of life*. Torino, Italy: La Stampa.

Brown, D. et al. (2002). Evaluating web page color and layout adaptations. *IEEE MultiMedia*, *9*(1), 86–89. doi:10.1109/93.978356

Cipolla-Ficarra, F. (1997). Evaluation of multimedia components. In *Proceedings of IEEE Multimedia Systems*. IEEE.

Cipolla-Ficarra, F. (1998). MEHEM: A methodology for heuristic evaluation in multimedia. In *Proceedings of 7th Symposium on Analysis, Design and Evaluation of Man-Machine Systems – Human Interface*. Kyoto, Japan: Elsevier.

Cipolla-Ficarra, F. (2005). Synchronism and diachronism into evolution of the interfaces for quality communication in multimedia systems. In *Proceedings of HCI International 2005*. Las Vegas, NV: HCI.

Cipolla-Ficarra, F. (2012). New horizons in creative open software, multimedia, human factors and software engineering. Bergamo, Italy: Blue Herons Ed.s.

Cipolla-Ficarra, F., et al. (2011). Handbook of computational informatics, social factors and new information technologies: Hypermedia perspectives and avant-garde experiencies in the era of communicability expansion. Bergamo, Italy: Blue Herons Ed.s.

Cipolla-Ficarra, F., & Cipolla-Ficarra, M. (2008). HECHE: Heuristic evaluation of colours in homepage. In *Proceedings of Applied Human Factors and Ergonomics*. Las Vegas, NV: AIE.

Gage, J. (2000). *Color and meaning: Art, science, and symbolism*. Berkeley, CA: University of California Press.

Karat, C., Brodie, C., & Karat, J. (2006). Usable privacy and security for personal information management. *Communications of the ACM*, *49*(1), 56–57. doi:10.1145/1107458.1107491

Chapter 8
Building Recommendation Service with Social Networks and Semantic Databases

Sašo Karakatič
Institute of Informatics (FERI), University of Maribor, Slovenia

Vili Podgorelec
Institute of Informatics (FERI), University of Maribor, Slovenia

Marjan Heričko
Institute of Informatics (FERI), University of Maribor, Slovenia

ABSTRACT

In this chapter, it is shown how useful user services can be created through the integration of social networks and semantic databases. The authors developed a recommendation service in a form of a Web-based application, where a user's interests are imported from social network Facebook and linked with additional data from open semantic database Freebase. Based on a custom implementation of k-nearest neighbors algorithm, the developed method is able to find recommendations based on users' interests enriched with semantic information. The resulting list of found recommendations is then shown to the user in some basic categories like movies, music, games, books, and others.

INTRODUCTION

Online social networks are very popular and still gain popularity among web users. One of the leading online social networks, Facebook, is gaining users consistently year by year – at the beginning of 2012 it already has over 800 million users (Facebook Statistics, 2012). It enables its users to present themselves in an online profile, accumulate "friends" who can post comments on each other's pages, and view each other's profiles. Facebook members can also join virtual groups based on common interests, see what classes they have in common, and learn each others' hobbies,

DOI: 10.4018/978-1-4666-4490-8.ch008

interests, musical tastes, and romantic relationship status through the profiles (Ellison, Steinfield & Lampe, 2007).

All this information about users and their inter-connections, stored within the online social network system, have a great potential for discovering possibly usable patterns of a specific user and/or a group of users (Kleinberg, 2007). One of Facebook's most interesting features, which represent user's interests, is the possibility of "liking" things – a user can tag some entity with "like" if he/her likes it, what means that the user has some interest in the entity. The user's interest zone enables one to perform many personalized operations, such as targeted advertising, which improves the efficiency of the operation for a specific user.

We also decided to make use of the users' interests, stored within the Facebook's user profiles, and developed a prototype application, which is able of recommending possibly interesting entities (like movies, music, games or books) to a specific user. The developed recommendation searching algorithm, used to generate a list of possibly interesting entities, is based on the identification of other users sharing similar interests with the specific user. When a set of such users is identified, it is searched for the most common entities they are interested in and which are not already present within the specific user's profile. However, the problem here is that the users' profiles themselves do not contain enough information for accurate recommendations. In this manner, we decided to enrich the information, available from the social network users' profiles with the information from open semantic databases.

Semantic databases are basically knowledge bases, where all the data stored in them is semantically annotated. With the provision of semantic tags the meaning of the data becomes explicit, what allows some form of automatic processing of such data based on its meaning. In this way, the semantic data represents knowledge suitable for machine processing (Hull & King, 1987). As there are some open semantic databases publicly available, like DBpedia or Freebase, which offer public APIs for third party applications to use their semantic knowledge, a recent trend in intelligent applications is to use this knowledge for the improvement of their features (Auer, Bizer, Kobilarov & Lehmann, 2007).

Based on these propositions, a question that we would like to answer in this chapter is whether it is possible to create a relevant recommendation service by linking the two worlds, the social networks and open semantic databases. For this purpose, we developed and tested a prototype web application that provides recommendations upon several entities like movies, music, games, books, for a specific user based on his/her Facebook profile and knowledge obtained from a Freebase.

RECOMMENDATION SERVICE

The idea of predicting and recommending things to users based on their personal interest is not new. Similar commercial services already exist but are primarily aimed at recommending movies or music. One of them is Jinni[1], which searches for movie recommendations, based on user's profile created from semantic tags of liked movies. Another one is Pandora Radio[2] online music service and works on a similar concept. User can respond with positive or negative feedback for each song that is played and Pandora then compiles playlist based on those feedbacks. Worth of mention is also service Last.fm[3], where music recommendations are found through comparing user's likes, similar basic step as is in our prototype service.

Few researches have been performed, like the one on service FilmTrust, which examines semantic web-based social networks, augmented with trust, to create predictive movie recommendations (Golbeck & Hendler, 2006). There are few other papers on recommendation services, to start with Recommendz, which is based on user ratings feedback about different aspect of an entity, like plot in the movie (Garden & Dudek, 2005) and another two research papers about movie recommendations, one for service called MovieLens (Herlocker, Konstan & Riedl, 2000) and another web based service Film-Conseil (Perny & Zucker, 2001). They explore recommendation techniques, but none of them is simultaneously directly connected to social network and backed up with some sort of semantics, like our prototype.

Figure 1 shows an overview of how our service works, starting with fetching user information, particular user's likes or interests from his/hers Facebook profile. There are a few useful information gathered here – a name of the interest and its category. Information about category is important in order to categorize particular like in our service that is then used to more detailed queries later on with Freebase API. Sure, we can get a few more information from Facebook about likes, but the most of it are not of useful for our service and the ones we could use are not always provided. For this reason we decided to we get additional data exclusively from the Freebase semantic knowledge base.

The next step is to check whether our database already contains any of the gathered interests. For all new interests we get additional information from Freebase through its public API. From the results, we parse important data based on the category of the interest. Then this information is added to the interest in a form of a tag. If a tag already exists in our database, there's no need to create it, so just a relation is added.

Let us look at the described process on an example of a movie. Here we look for genre, plot, producers, directors, actors, characters and other

Figure 1. The recommendation service conceptual outline

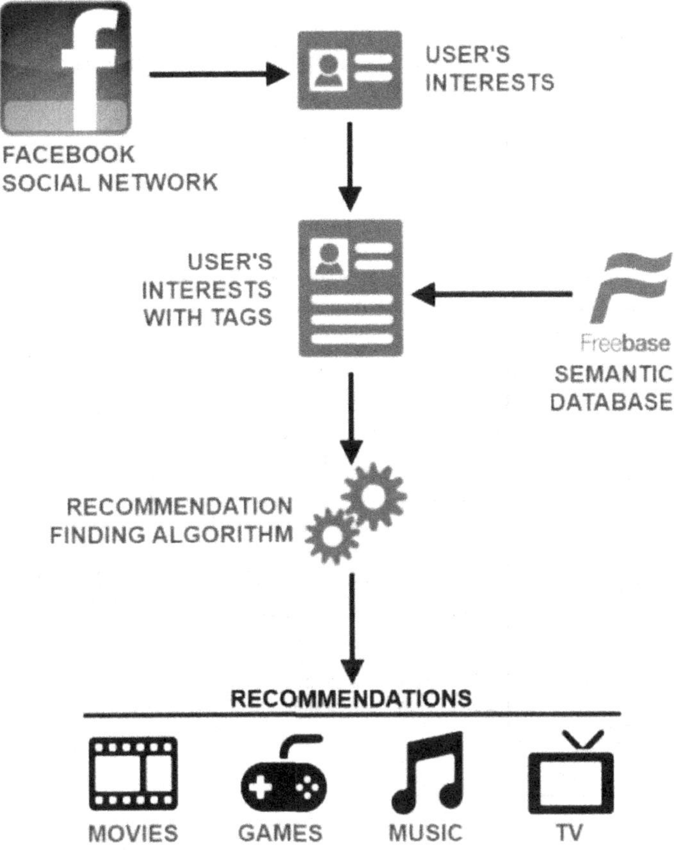

relevant information. We then get the information about picture and brief description from Freebase.

When all the gathered data is saved in a form of tags of a particular interest, recommendation finding algorithm can start. Algorithm is shown in details later on, for now let's just say that the results of the algorithm are the lists of recommendations shown on a web page to the user.

Importing Users Interests from Facebook

To begin using our recommendation service prototype user has to link it with the Facebook profile. This eliminates the need for conventional user registration and filling in interests. Facebook API is open to third party applications and we make use of that by reading important user information and importing its likes.

User login consists of three steps (the whole process is shown in Figure 2), where user has to intervene only on two occasions. Facebook authentication API is used for this process and it uses OAuth 2.0 open standard authentication protocol (Facebook Authentication, 2012). The first step is user authentication, where user inputs its username and password for Facebook. This operation is done entirely on Facebook, so there are no privacy concerns. If the user has already authenticated with a running browser session, this step is skipped. When user authentication completes, the user has to authorize our service, which means that user grants an approval that service can make specific actions. Our service demands access to basic user information and user's likes. After authorization, browser is redirected to the service homepage with additional parameter – authorization code.

The final step is the authentication of our service where no user intervention is needed here. Service authentication is made through a request to the specific URL with parameter containing

Figure 2. The interaction between our service, Facebook API, and Freebase API

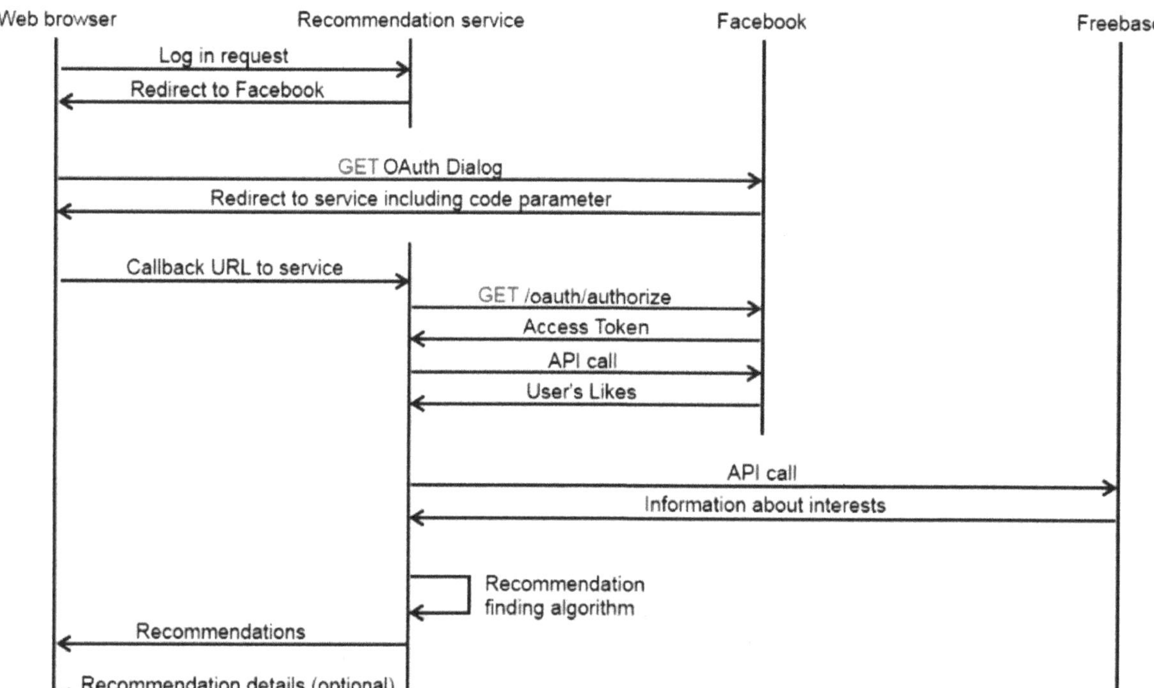

application's secret code and user authorization code fetched from previous step to which Facebook responds with access token and time until its expiration (in seconds).

The whole authentication process is now finished and the data, for which service was authorized, can now be read. Initially user basic information is read with call to

```
http://graph.facebook.com/{user-
nameORuserID}
```

The service can now check if user already exists in the database, and update its information, or create new user. Now the final two Facebook calls are made, reading user's likes and fetching users profile picture, using Graph API. To get likes a simple call to URI

```
http://graph.facebook.com/{user-
nameORuserID}/likes
```

```
http://graph.facebook.com/{user-
nameORuserID}/picture
```

At the end of this process all likes and basic user information is saved to our database. Before we can begin with finding relevant recommendations, we have to enrich interests first.

Enriching Data with Freebase

By now Facebook likes and user information have already been imported to our database and we could start finding recommendations just by comparing likes between users, but for more relevant and non-repetitive recommendations, likes/interests have to be enriched with additional information. We gather this additional information from the open knowledge database Freebase.

Freebase is a semantic database developed by a software company Metaweb and is available for commercial and non-commercial use through its open API, frequent database dumps or RDF endpoint (Freebase Wiki, 2012). At the time of writing it contained dataset with over 23 million topics (Freebase Data, 2012), most of which was and still is added by automatic harvesters through number of sources like Wikipedia, UN Stats, Stanford University and many others. A large part of data is also contributed by its community members.

Because we don't get enough data for successful recommendation from the Facebook's "Likes" data, the additional information is fetched from the Freebase's knowledge base. Using Freebase API for reading data is relatively simple; just a request to URI below needs to be made. Additional parameter is added – query or queries, which depends on whether we are querying multiple topics in one call or not.

```
http://www.googleapis.com/freebase/
v1/mqlread
```

Proprietary MQL[4] language, a derivate of more known SPARQL[5] language and in JSON format, is used to query for data. Each query is its own object with unique name. Basic properties in these objects are type, which selects category of the topic, and name, both known from the Facebook imported data. Additional properties are also added – in example for a book, plot, characters, author and other relevant properties. Their value is either null or an empty array.

The result is also in JSON format with four values. Two of them are about result status (code and status), one is description of result status and the other is a unique identification of status. The third value is a transaction identification number and the fourth one is a container for the result of a query. Each query result is its own object and all nulled properties and empty arrays are filled with data from knowledge base. A simple JSON parser may be used to extract the information.

Each gathered information is parsed and created in our database, unless it already exists. They are stored as "tags" about interests. Again, if we use the movie example used earlier, the information gathered, like actors, plot theme, producers, directors and others, are tags of our movie interest.

Every query call to Freebase API needs parameter with applications API key, except for applications and services that make less than 100,000 read calls per day have no need for authentication (Freebase Terms of Service, 2012). Otherwise there's a need to register an application to get an API key, which is added to all requests as a parameter.

Another part of Freebase API is used, the image service. Most of the topics in Freebase knowledge base have an image and it may be used in third party applications. Images are returned for a GET request to URI below.

```
http://usercontent.googleapis.com/
freebase/v1/image/en/
```

Unique identification key of the topic, returned in previous MQL reading, is added at the end of URI. Additional options include specifying maximum height or width and enabling padding and are added as parameters.

Our recommendation service also uses Text Service API. This Freebase service returns short description about a specific topic. For this purpose a call to URI below is made, again with an unique identification of the topic added at the end.

```
https://www.googleapis.com/freebase/
v1/text/en/
```

So far we gathered user's interest from its Facebook likes, enriched them with short description, title picture and additional information through the tags from the Freebase, so by now there is enough information so that the searching for recommendations can begin.

Recommendation Finding Algorithm

When user's interests have been filled with tag-like additional information, the recommendation finding algorithm can begin. This algorithm is based on k-nearest neighbor algorithm, which is a classification algorithm. Theory says that there are m object which are classified to one of the n classes. New object is then compared to all others and the distance between them is calculated. The distance is some kind of measurable difference between the objects. Then we take k closest objects to this specific one. The last step is to count which class dominates in this set of k-nearest objects. New object is then classified as the type of this dominant class (Seidl & Kriegel, 1998).

We recreate this process to some extent so that our algorithm also compares all objects (users) to one another, where the distance between them is defined by the amount of similar tags (more similar tags, closer are objects). No classification is made, but the nearest users are shortlisted and eventually they vote for recommendations.

The first step is to create a user's interest profile, if one doesn't already have it (if the user is using this service for the first time or his/her interests have been updated). User's tags are counted and added to the list, so that the list contains the tags and number of occurrences of the tags within the user's interests. Two such examples can be seen on Figure 3 – two user tag lists are shown.

Next step is to find the nearest neighbors. To evaluate the distance between users, their tag lists are compared. For every common tag, points are added to the connection between them. Amount of points added is equal to smaller occurrence in one of the lists of two compared users. Again, in example below, two users have two tags in common. First tag "A" is linked to user X four times, and 3 times to user Y through their interests. If compared, they get 3 common points for this tag. They also have tag "C" in common, so same the process is repeated here – except they get 1 point for it. That totals in 4 points of common tags.

Comparing could be done on all types of interests or it could be done on only a specific category of interest, which means that, if we are searching for book recommendations for specific

Figure 3. Finding similarities between two users – common tags

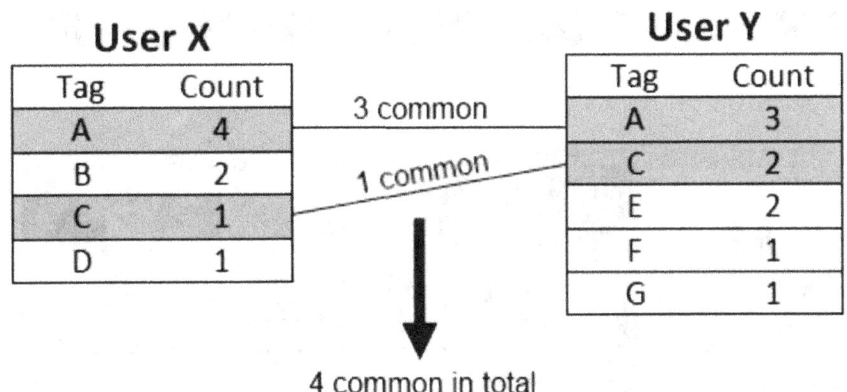

users, tag profiles are only made of tags associated with books. So selected nearest neighbors are category specific.

Every user in the database is compared to our specific user and common points are awarded, then users are sorted by these common points and the users with most points are nearest neighbors. We limited the size of nearest neighbor shortlist to 25, because the testing showed that additional neighbors produced no significant difference in the results. Nearest neighbors then vote for recommendations – each votes for its own interests. A list of interests, sorted by votes, is created.

Implementation

The service was implemented in the form of web application using JavaServer Faces. It can be deployed on any Java application server using any database. Prototype was deployed on Glassfish 3.1 and the database used was MySQL 5.5. Figure 4 shows a screenshot of the application.

RESULTS

The service was tested both on random data – for time efficiency of algorithm and response time of used APIs – as well as on real users to evaluate the relevance of the recommendations.

Hardware setup for testing was a PC with Intel Core2 CPU E6300 1.86 GHz, Gigabyte Tech 956P-S3 motherboard, 3GB DDR2 RAM, HDD with 7200 RPM and 8MB buffer and graphics card GeForce 7600 GT. Average internet speed before starting test 19.91 Mb/s download and 28.68 Mb/s upload.

The initial step was to create an algorithm for generating random data. Generated users had 50 interests on average (minimum 40 and maximum 60). First we tested an algorithm for seeking nearest neighbors. The datasets were 100, 500 and 1000 users large. As expected and as results in Table 1 show, the algorithm performance is proportional to the number of users in the database.

Next we tested an algorithm for finding recommendations, when nearest neighbors are already selected. Again, the performance is proportional to the number of nearest neighbors. Interest count or any other parameter had no effect on the performance. The results are shown in Table 2.

The next step was to test the response time of used APIs. Freebase API was called 702 times in this test and the results are show in Table 3. For Facebook we were separately measuring response time for authentication and Graph API data reading.

The service prototype was also tested on a small group of people – 51 users. Goal of this was to determine the relevance of found recommenda-

Figure 4. Web application screenshot: recommendations page with 8 most recommended movies

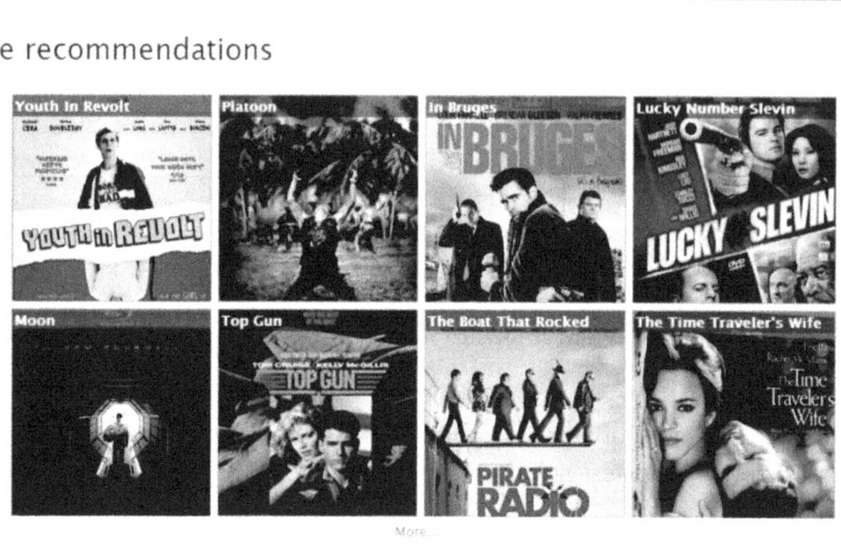

Table 1. Algorithm performance on finding nearest neighbors

User count	100	500	1000
Average time (ms)	8,514.25	41,550.49	84,065.71

Table 2. Algorithm performance on finding recommendations

Nearest neighbor count	10	25	50	100
Average time (ms)	1.22	3.47	6.35	12.2

tions. Despite the small number of participants, feedback was positive. Because of the nature of recommendation finding algorithm, the bigger the user base – better are the results, more relevant are the recommendations. Therefore even better results are expected with more participants. Testing on a larger scale is yet to be done.

Table 3. Response times of Facebook and Freebase APIs

API	Freebase	Facebook Authentication	Graph API Reading
Call count	702	250	250
Min time (ms)	183.1	566.5	268.0
Max time (ms)	594.9	1,027.3	503.8
Average time (ms)	213.3	951.2	336.2
Standard deviation (ms)	57.2	104.3	59.2

DISCUSSION AND CONCLUSION

As stated in the introduction the goal of this research was to test whether recommendation service can be made with combining social networks and semantic knowledge base. For this purpose we designed and developed a prototype service, which recommendations were relevant according to the feedback of the users.

Testing showed that Facebook API takes relatively long to respond, but this could easily be avoided using Ajax on web application. Testing also showed that implemented algorithm's time efficiency is not very good, but this problem can be solved by running algorithm on predefined times and not with every recommendation lookup.

Another solution for time inefficiency is implementing eager learning algorithm as opposed to lazy learning k-nearest neighbors. Our recommendation finding algorithm is based on k-nearest neighbors algorithm, which is by itself lazy or more specifically, instance based learning algorithm. Eager learning algorithm would perform explicit generalizations of users and compare new users to these generalizations.

As stated, the performance could be drastically improved with the proposed improvements, if application would grow beyond the prototype level. The conclusion is that combining data from social networks and semantic knowledge base resulted in a relevant recommendation finding service. The service performed excellent with finding relevant and non-repetitive recommendations based on users' interests. Binding social networks with semantic database was a success and algorithm performed exceptionally well.

REFERENCES

Auer, S., Bizer, C., Kobilarov, G., & Lehmann, J. (2007). *Dbpedia: A nucleus for a web of open data*. The Semantic Web. doi:10.1007/978-3-540-76298-0_52

Ellison, N., Steinfield, C., & Lampe, C. (2007). The benefits of facebook friends: Social capital and college students' use of online social network sites. *Journal of Computer-Mediated Communication*, *12*, 1143–1168. doi:10.1111/j.1083-6101.2007.00367.x

Facebook Authentication. (2012). Retrieved from http://developers.facebook.com/docs/authentication/

Facebook for Developers. (2012). Retrieved from http://developers.facebook.com/docs/core-concepts/

Facebook Statistics. (2012). Retrieved from http://www.facebook.com/press/info.php?statistics

Freebase Data. (2012). Retrieved from http://wiki.freebase.com/wiki/Freebase_data/

Freebase Terms of Service. (2012). Retrieved from http://wiki.freebase.com/wiki/Terms_of_Service/

Freebase Wiki. (2012). Retrieved from http://wiki.freebase.com/wiki/

Garden, M., & Dudek, G. (2005). Semantic feedback for hybrid recommendations in Recommendz. In *Proceedings of International Conference on e-Technology, e-Commerce and e-Service (EEE'05)*. New York: IEEE Press.

Golbeck, J., & Hendler, J. (2006). Filmtrust: Movie recommendations using trust in web-based social networks. In *Proceedings of IEEE Consumer Communications and Networking*, (pp. 282-286). IEEE.

Herlocker, J., Konstan, J., & Riedl, J. (2000). Explaining collaborative filtering recommendations. In *Proceedings of the 2000 ACM Conference on Computer Supported Cooperative Work*, (pp. 241-250). ACM.

Hull, R., & King, R. (1987). Semantic database modeling: survey, applications, and research issues. *ACM Computing Surveys*, *19*, 201–260. doi:10.1145/45072.45073

Kleinberg, J. (2007). Challenges in mining social network data: Processes, privacy, and paradoxes. In *Proceedings of Conference on Knowledge Discovery and Data Mining*. IEEE.

Perny, P., & Zucker, J. (2001). Preference-based search and machine learning for collaborative filtering: The film-conseil movie recommender system. *Revue I*, *1*, 1–40.

Seidl, T., & Kriegel, H. (1998). Optimal multi-step k-nearest neighbor search. *SIGMOD Record*, 154–165. doi:10.1145/276305.276319

ENDNOTES

1 http://www.jinni.com/

2 http://www.pandora.com/

3 http://www.last.fm/

4 MQL - Metaweb Query Language

5 SPARQL - SPARQL Protocol and RDF Query Language

Chapter 9
Cloud-Assisted Services for Mobile Applications: CLASS-MA

Domen Verber
Institute of Informatics (FERI), University of Maribor, Slovenia

ABSTRACT

This chapter discusses those mobile applications that are assisted with services provided by the cloud. This combines the two most pervasive topics within information technology today: cloud computing and mobile computing. This chapter describes the challenges and opportunities offered by these technologies and the issues arising during their implementation. Some representative cloud services for mobile applications are offered as part of an on-going CLASS research project.

INTRODUCTION

Unquestionably, over recent years, mobile computing and cloud computing have been the buzzwords within information technology (Adelstein, Gupta, Richard & Schwiebert, 2004; Sosinsky, 2011). Computers have become increasingly smaller and blend-in with the other devices around us. Consequently, mobile computers, in the forms of smart phones or tablet PCs, are becoming bestsellers and the fastest growing market for technical products. The same computer evolution has led to the emergence of large computer centers, the clouds, which offer a wide-variety of services to both companies and individual users. Nevertheless, there are differences in the usages of these technologies. Most applications for mobile computers today are designed for exclusive use on mobile devices. On the other hand, cloud computing represents the replacements of those computer servers and computer clusters utilized by a large number of clients. The majority of services they offer are designed for desktop computers. Is it possible to merge these two technologies together within a single solution, namely mobile computing in 'the clouds'? The answer is obviously 'yes'. This

DOI: 10.4018/978-1-4666-4490-8.ch009

chapter attempts to demonstrate the possibilities of using cloud-computing services for mobile devices and mobile applications.

The work presented was part of the research project KC CLASS (CLoud Assisted ServiceS), funded by the Slovenian Ministry of Higher Education, Science, and Technology (KC Class, 2012). The main aim was to develop services and products within the field of cloud computing. This article relates to the work-package WP2: Platform as a service (PaaS) and, especially, support for mobile computing in the clouds.

Mobile Computing

Mobile devices and mobile applications are different from those on personal computers in several respects. The most obvious difference is the user interface. Due to the smaller sizes of mobile devices, the sizes of the displays have been significantly reduced; there is no room for large keyboards, mouses, and the like. For that reason, mobile devices depend on the other kinds of interaction technologies such as touch, voice control, device orientation and tilt, etc (Hoober & Berkman, 2011). Similarly, due to its limited size, the mobile device cannot be connected to massive secondary storage devices, thus reducing the total amount of internally accessible information. Another distinctiveness of the mobile device is its limited energy-supply. Its processing capabilities and memory capacity have to be sacrificed, and have to be significantly smaller than on desktop computers, where the power supply is not an issue. For the same reason, rich and high-resolution graphics, 3D graphic accelerators, etc., are usually limited to desktop applications. In view of their mobility, many mobile applications utilize the known locations of their users. Therefore, such devices are often equipped with global-positioning systems (GPS), electronic compasses, accelerometers, etc. Desktop computers are stationary and usually do not benefit from such services.

These dissimilarities also create differences in the usages of both kinds of devices. PCs are frequently used for business, at work, for research, for education, etc. Such support on mobile devices is usually limited. The main purposes of mobile applications are communication, entertainment and delivering different kinds of information.

Cloud Computing

By using cloud computing, companies and individuals, in part or entirely, transfer their IT infrastructures to powerful host servers – the clouds. The motivation for this is the reduced costs of obtaining and maintaining the hardware, lower costs for IT staff, etc. Of course, the usage of cloud resources and services is not free. Solution providers in the clouds charge for the use of disk and processing capabilities.

Because of the abundance of computing and storage resources, the clouds can be dynamically adapted to the actual loads for individual users. When the workload is small, only part of a single server would be utilized. With the higher demands, data processing can take place over several servers simultaneously. Such a model also greatly increases reliability in case of hardware failure. Cloud computing introduces a new model for developing software applications. Generally, there are three levels of cloud resource utilization, as portrayed in Figure 1.

- **Infrastructure as a Service – IaaS:** In this model, the cloud provides the bare-bone servers. It is the user's responsibility to maintain the operating system, the system's software, and the applications. Ideally, the solutions in CLASS-MA should be independent of the underlying hardware infrastructure.
- **Platform as a Service – PaaS:** In this case, the operating system, the system's software and other supporting software are

Figure 1. Different levels of cloud resource utilization

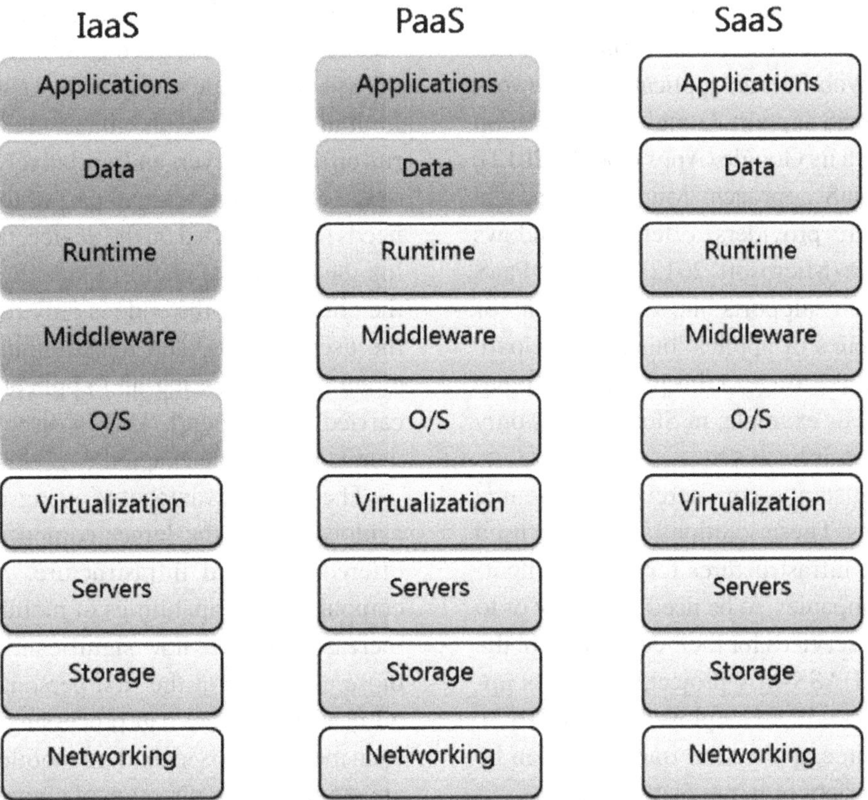

already installed on the server in the cloud. The cloud providers implement a rich programming environment that allows for the industrious development of applications in the cloud. The application framework provides a set of services for security, administration, user's authentication, structured and non-structured data storage, etc. Such application frameworks are also the primary focus of the CLASS-MA research presented in this chapter. The services of CLASS-MA are written specifically for supporting mobile applications. They are aware of the limitations of mobile devices and adjust dynamically to the capabilities of the client. Such services should be used regardless of the type of operating system and the model of the mobile device. In order to achieve this using a stateless model of the operations, a profile of the mobile device is sent with every service call. In a full- state model, it is established only once during the login phase. The device profile includes information on the resolution and color depth of the display, the available processing resources, the required bandwidth for data transmission, and the like.

- **Software as a Service – SaaS:** In this model, the cloud provides full outsourcing solutions for companies and end-users. It allows for remote application execution using Internet technologies. The role of the CLASS-MA in this case is to provide support for the development of rich mobile application in the cloud.

There are several providers who offer their versions of cloud computing, whether in the form of process resources, data storage, or on-line applications. Amongst the first was Amazon with its Amazon EC2 IaaS solution (Amazon, 2012). The Amazon Web-Service application framework provides for PaaS support. Google followed soon afterwards with its Google (Apps Google, 2012). It uses the SaaS approach. Microsoft, one the largest software providers, offers its Windows Azure platform (Microsoft, 2012). This is a PaaS solution, which supports the development of different varieties of applications for the cloud. Unfortunately, the usage of this platform is somehow limited. For example, in Slovenia it is only indirectly accessible, as yet.

There are also non-commercial, open-source cloud solutions. These solutions are usually used to provide the infrastructures for cloud computing within companies, to be used internally or to provide cloud services for their customers. In the case of the CLASS-MA project, the JBoss application server will be employed (Jboss, 2012). This open-source application framework can be used with a variety of target platforms.

Opportunities and Challenges for Using Mobile Computing with the Clouds

The first advantage of using cloud computing for mobile applications is the possibility of using its larger storage capabilities. This is already extensively exploited within existing mobile applications. There are several benefits from this. Firstly, the amount of memory resources on mobile devices is limited. Instead of keeping the data, images, and videos on the devices themselves, they are transferred to large disk-units within cloud. Secondly, many users today utilize more than one device and/or personal computers. By isolating the data storage from the client, the same data can be accessed and used from anywhere. Thirdly, data within cloud can be shared between several users.

A typical mobile application can only be run on a specific target platform (i.e., on devices with certain operating systems' versions). Programming languages and programming environments are too different between platforms for allowing the use of only one source code. Using cloud, this limitation can be overcome as the application is run on remote servers and is relatively independent of the client. Only a small part of the application needs to be installed on the device, thereby reducing the amount of platform-specific code. As for the client's part, the code is only responsible for the user interface and for communication with cloud. All processing and application logic are carried out in cloud. This is discussed in more details later in the chapter.

The third advantage of using clouds is the exploitation of the larger computing resources offered by cloud infrastructure. Although the computational capabilities of mobile devices are increasing and are now significantly higher than those available for the first personal computers, the need for complex data processing has increased even more. Trends in modern mobile applications are moving in the direction of complex voice and image processing. An example of such an application is Siri, which runs on the Apples's iOS (Apple, 2012). This application uses a natural language user interface to answer questions, make recommendations, etc. The voice commands of the user are stored within a compressed data package, which is sent to the server for processing. Other examples of such applications are face and object recognition regarding photographs from video feeds, etc. In all these cases, the application in the cloud can utilize tens or hundreds of processing units and provide instant responses. In this way, complex applications can be used even with less powerful and, therefore, less expensive devices.

There are also some disadvantages to using cloud computing for mobile devices. The main potential drawback of this approach would be the requirement to maintain a broadband Internet connection between the device and the cloud. In addition to the technological aspect and the necessities of modern communication infrastructure, there is also the financial aspect. Mobile operators charge for each transferred byte. For native mobile applications that run only on a mobile device, such communication is minimal or is unrequired. One solution to this problem is to utilize the cheaper communication channels when available (e.g., the open WiFi network infrastructure). Secondly, the amount of data transferred can be reduced using proper compression techniques. A further solution would be to use those intelligent software agents that operate in cloud on behalf of the user and perform certain operations independently in off-line mode. Communication with users takes place only occasionally. Although this sounds quite futuristic, there is a lot of research involved in this, and regarding similar problems (Fischer & Müller, 2011).

Other disadvantages of using cloud computing relate to safety, security, and the availability of cloud computing infrastructures. However, these problems are indirectly related to the usage of mobile applications and, with continuous development, their relevance will diminish (Fischer & Müller, 2011; Jnasen & Grance, 2011).

CLOUD SERVICES FOR MOBILE APPLICATIONS

The cloud-supported services for mobile applications can be observed from different points of view. Such services must manage various mobile devices, regardless of their capabilities and the operating system they use. They must be easy to develop, possibly independently of the cloud provider. Finally, they must be beneficial for the variety of mobile applications.

Main Features of Cloud Services for Mobile Applications

In general, there is no difference between cloud services for mobile and for desktop applications. Service written for the mobile devices can be equally well-used on the personal computers. However, such services must be are aware of the limitations of mobile devices and adjust dynamically to the capabilities of the client. This can be dealt with in several ways.

Firstly, the cloud service can adapt itself to the specific profile of the client's device. In order to achieve this, the client must provide device profile information. The device profile includes information on the resolution and color-depth of the display, the available processing resources, the required bandwidth for data transmission, and the like. Using a stateless model of the operations, a profile of the mobile device is sent with every service call. In a full-state model, it is established only once, during the login phase.

Secondly, an additional application layer can be implemented that transparently transforms the generic results of the service into a form suitable for specific devices. The benefit of this approach is that existing cloud services can be used with any mobile device. Furthermore, the same middleware layer can be used with all services. For example, a high-resolution image, generated by the main service for high-end clients, can be transparently converted into an image with a resolution suitable for a specific mobile device. In extreme case, such a layer may virtualize the client in the cloud, behaving similarly to remote desktop services. The display content of the virtual mobile client is rendered in the memory of the cloud service. These images are periodically sent to the mobile device.

Development of Cloud Services for Mobile Applications

The services for mobile applications are built as any other cloud services or cloud applications. In practice, this usually involves the creation of one or more virtual servers, which run the applications and/or provide some services to the clients.

The development process usually consists of constructing the code on the host environment, where cloud infrastructure is just simulated. Later, the code is deployed on the cloud. However, at first this code is executed in isolated context to allow for testing and debugging. At the end, the services are promoted to the production level and are consumed by the mobile applications.

From the developer's point of view, the main problem at this stage is the lack of a common application infrastructure. Each major cloud provider implements its own application framework, the programming language and programming libraries are predefined, etc. Therefore, today, it is impossible to deploy the same solution to different PaaS providers. For each target platform, the implementations of some services must be done from the beginning. This problem is somehow mitigated by using open-source solutions like JBoss. This application-server can be hosted on several different operating systems. It is even possible to install it on existing commercial IaaS products. Nonetheless, the JBoss application server is far from perfect. It lacks proper development tools, the developer's support, technical documentation, and the like. It is also bound to the Java programming language, which limits the available developer's base.

Development of Mobile Applications with Cloud-Assisted Services

More commonly, the services in the cloud are accessed from native mobile applications. Most development tools for mobile devices also provide applicative programming interfaces (APIs) for the services in cloud. Usually, this is a slightly trimmed set of components for desktop applications. Their advantage is that they hide the details when accessing the services in cloud. The programmer can include them in the application like any other components. In most cases, they utilize the processing and data storage resources of cloud. Most frequently, the clients have access to cloud resources via full web-service protocol (SOAP) or REST protocol.

An example of such an API is the Windows Azure Toolkit for Windows Phone 7 (Windows Azure, 2012). This set of components facilitates working with Windows Azure cloud using Windows Phone 7 devices. Similarly, a slightly richer solution is offered by Amazon for its own version of cloud-services (AWS-Amazon, 2012).

The main problem with such interfaces is that they depend on particular versions of the cloud solution. A different component needs to be used for each version. In the CLASS project, an attempt will be made to implement those universal interfaces that are independent of the provider.

HTML5 as a Universal Pilatform for Mobile Applications in the Cloud

All the software tools described above have the disadvantage of being limited to a specific target platform. Those software developers who would like to support a wide-range of users need to develop applications for different platforms and different versions of operating systems. Different platforms use different programming languages, different sets of programming libraries, etc.

Mobile applications within cloud can also be carried out independently in the form of Web programs, running on Web servers. In this case, communication with the user is performed using a Web browser. The Web applications can still exploit some services, the processing and storage capabilities of cloud by accessing them directly on the server side.

Modern Web applications are based on the HTML5 standard (W3, 2012), and, the accompanied, CSS3 standard. HTML5 is capable of producing dynamic, interactive Web applications that include support for graphics, multimedia, location-based services, and the like. Virtually all modern mobile devices support these standards and provide a rich user-experience (Mikkonen & Taivalsaari, 2011). As an advantage, it can be equally used for desktop clients. Cascading-style sheets (CSS) separate the visual aspects of the web pages from their contents. The newest version of these, CSS3, provides for many attractive extensions such as opacity, text-overflow, etc. The more interesting parts of CSS3 for mobile devices are media types and media queries. The media types are used to define how the content of a web page will be rendered on specific media, such as screen, paper, or hand-held devices. A media query consists of a media type and at least one expression that limits the 'style sheets' scope by using media features, such as width, height, and colour. This is similar to the device profiles described previously. Media queries allow the presentation of content to be tailored to a specific range of output devices without having to change the content itself.

However, there are some difficulties when using such Web solutions. Both HTML5 and CSS3 have been available for some time, but they are still being partially development and still in the process of final standardization. Furthermore, Web applications depend heavily on the browser. Only some browsers implement all the functionalities of HTML5. Several functionalities may not be implemented by some browsers at all. Additionally, a lot of programming code is still run on the client by means of JavaScript code. Therefore, an effective JavaScript interpreter is required for good user experience.

SOME PROTOTYPICAL CLOUD SERVICES FOR MOBILE APPLICATIONS

One of the aims when studying the CLASS protect was the implementation of those services within cloud that would be beneficial for mobile application. During the research, some archetypical services were selected that could also serve as guidance for the development of further ones. All services would be implemented in such a way that they would be independent of the cloud provider, and from the device used for the client.

- **Services for Structured and Non-Structured Data Storage:** The amount of data that can be stored on mobile devices is limited. To overcome this, a service is desirable that would allow for the storage of different kinds of data within cloud. Files, photos, videos, etc. are usually stored in a non-structured manner. On the other hand, the information can be organized in such a way that facilitates faster querying and retrieval. Such data is usually stored in databases therefore an interface should be implemented for accessing and managing remote databases.
- **Geolocation Services:** A frequent usage of mobile devices is for obtaining different information based on the current location of the client. Therefore, a geolocation service should provide information about events and objects around the device, based on the preferences of the user. Such a service would initiate several information requests in parallel with different information providers. The results would be evaluated based on user preferences, the distance from the current location, etc. Only after that would the information be transferred to the client in a unified format.
- **Image and Voice Processing:** Most mobile devices today are equipped with a camera. However, the processing capabilities of mobile devices are generally too limited for complex image editing and processing. Therefore, appropriate services would be beneficial for uploading an image, processing it somehow, and then sending the result back to the client. Initially, different image-editing operations should be implemented. Furthermore, more complex processing should be implemented, such as

biometric identification from the pictures, etc. This would allow for the integration of biometrics within mobile solutions, the usage of ambient intelligence, and the like. Similarly, to facilitate services like Siri, voice-processing services should be implemented. For superior support, in addition to signal-processing, more complex methodologies need to be implemented, like natural language understanding, machine learning, evidential and probabilistic reasoning, knowledge representation, etc.

- **Multimedia Data Compression and Transformation:** Data transfers to and from mobile devices can be expensive. The amount of data in the transmission of multimedia content is particularly high. In order to reduce it, a special service would be implemented that would allow for the real-time compression of video feeds, images, and other kinds of media. The compression could be implemented by one of several traditional compressing techniques. With additional services, the high-definition multimedia formats can be transformed into the resolution by hand on mobile devices. These services would act like middleware or filters between different peers. They could be used transparently with other services, regardless of the data source. Data compression/decompression can be used with all data transfer between the cloud and client. The concept of such services is portrayed in Figure 2.

Figure 2. Concept of media transformation and data compression

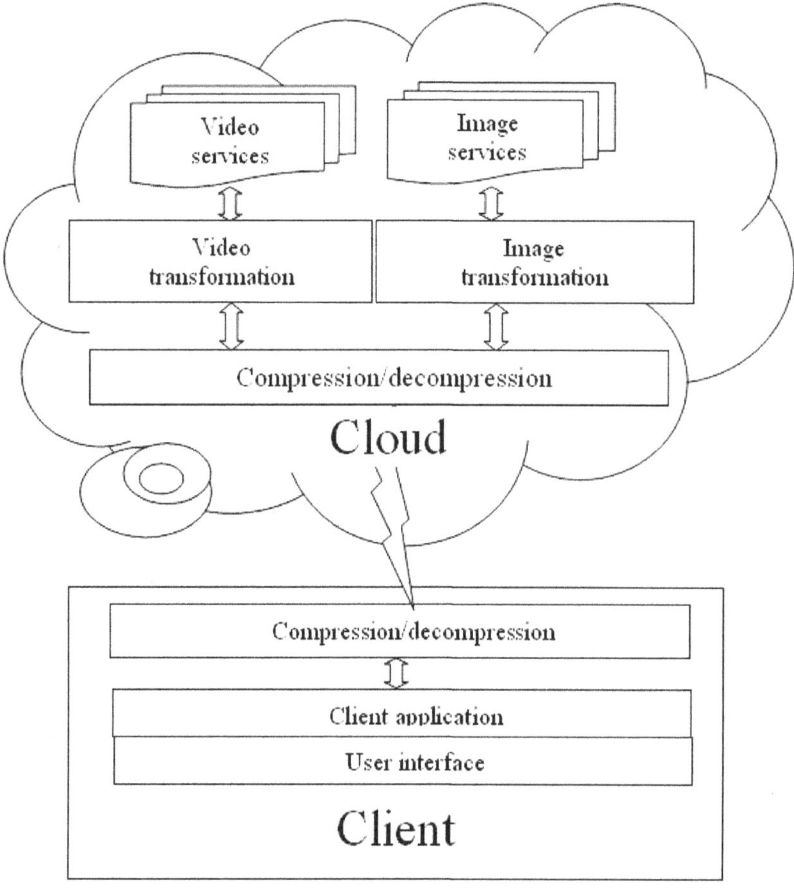

CONCLUSION

Cloud computing and mobile computing are both results of the natural evolution of computer devices, and they will evolve and merge in the future even more.

Centrally, there are many benefits of using cloud services within mobile applications. Although certain aspects of the application developments for the cloud are not yet fully matured, a lot of effort is being put into it by the cloud providers, the programmers, the researchers, and the like. Almost certainly, in the near future, we will connect other kinds of devices to the cloud: household appliances, medical devices, automobiles and transport infrastructure, etc. In the more distant future, all the clouds and the devices will be converged into a united cloud.

In the next phase of the CLASS-MA project, prototypical cloud services will be implemented on different platforms and used with services from other partners, so as to support the development of richer mobile applications.

REFERENCES

Adelstein, F., Gupta, S., Richard, G., & Schwiebert, L. (2004). *Fundamentals of mobile and pervasive computing*. New York: McGraw Hill.

Amazon. (2012). Retrieved from aws.amazon.com/ec2

Apple. (2012). Retrieved from www.apple.com/iphone/features/siri.html

AWS-Amazon. (2012). Retrieved from aws.amazon.com/sdkforandroid

Fischer, K., & Müller, J. (2011). Inter-organizational Interoperability through integration of multiagent, web service, and semantic web technologies. In *Proceedings of Agent-Based Technologies and Application for Enterprise Interoperability* (pp. 55–75). Toronto, Canada: IEEE.

Google. (2012). Retrieved from www.google.com/apps

Hoober, S., & Berkman, E. (2011). *Designing mobile interfaces*. Sebastopol, CA: O'Reilly.

Jboss. (2012). Retrieved from www.jboss.org

Jnasen, W., & Grance, T. (2011). *NIST SP 800-144 guidelines on security and privacy in public cloud computing*. Washington, DC: NIST.

KC Class. (2012). Retrieved from www.kc-class.eu

Microsoft. (2012). Retrieved from www.microsoft.com/windowsazure

Mikkonen, T., & Taivalsaari, A. (2011). Reports of the web's death are greatly exaggerated. *IEEE Computer*, *44*(5), 30–36. doi:10.1109/MC.2011.127

Sosinsky, B. (2011). *Cloud computing bible*. Hoboken, NJ: Wiley.

W3. (2012). Retrieved from www.w3.org/TR/html5

Windows Azure. (2012). Retrieved from watoolkitwp7.codeplex.com

Winkler, V. (2011). *Securing the cloud: Cloud computer security techniques and tactics*. Amsterdam: Elsevier.

Chapter 10
Context-Aware Mobile System for Public Bus Transportation

Mitja Krajnc
Institute of Informatics (FERI), University of Maribor, Slovenia

Vili Podgorelec
Institute of Informatics (FERI), University of Maribor, Slovenia

Marjan Heričko
Institute of Informatics (FERI), University of Maribor, Slovenia

ABSTRACT

The spread of smartphones in recent years announced an era of smarter and advanced mobile applications that not only show information but also adapt themselves to users' surroundings. In this chapter, the authors present a context-aware mobile system in public bus transportation domain based on Windows Phone platform. The principal objective of this system is using users' location, identity, and timeframe as context data to tailor shown information according to users' needs. Together with users' previous actions, the system predicts intended activity in the form of presenting users with preferred bus lines in the current context. The developed system shows how context-awareness and activity prediction can be combined to create mobile applications that do not require a lot of user interaction but still offer detailed information about specific domains.

INTRODUCTION

Out of 440.5 million mobile devices sold in the third quarter of year 2011, 115 million were smartphones, meaning that one of four buyers bought a smartphone (Gartner, 2011). Modern smartphones boast with powerful embedded sensors and thousands of applications that suit needs of various people. With the help of sensors in mobile devices the environment in which mobile device is used can be determined, making it an ideal platform for creating context-aware solutions (Lane, et al., 2010). To understand what context-aware applications are, the term context should

DOI: 10.4018/978-1-4666-4490-8.ch010

be explained first. There are several definitions that define this term, each of them being slightly different from another, but the one most relevant to our field of research is definition from Dey and Abowd (Abowd, et al., 1999). They have defined context as "any information that can be used to characterize the situation of an entity. An entity is a person, place, or object that is considered relevant to the interaction between a user and an application, including the user and applications themselves." This means any piece of information that can be used to enlighten the situation of participant's interactions is context.

Furthermore Dey and Abowd (Abowd, et al., 1999) elaborated that some context types are more important than others in practice. These so called primary context types are location, identity, activity and time. Based on these primary context types, secondary context types for same entity can be identified. For example, given person's location (e.g., getting location from mobile device's Global Positioning System (GPS)) other entities in vicinity of our person can be determined. Such categorization of context types is a two-tiered system, where primary context types are on the first tier and second tier consists of all other context types, which share same characteristic and are attributed to the entity with primary context. Such categorization can help developers to choose how they will incorporate context in their applications.

With knowing what exactly context is we can now think about how to incorporate context in context-aware mobile applications. Context awareness is not something new; it was already mentioned in 1994 by Schilt and Theimer (Schilit & Theimer, 1994). They described context-aware computing as software, which exhibits ability "to adapt according to its location of use, the collection of nearby people and objects, as well as the changes to those objects over time." As mentioned before the knowledge about mobile device's environment can be obtained through its sensors, thus making them the core of context-aware application.

Three of the four primary context types can be fairly easily determined with today's smartphone features (Lane, et al., 2010). Location is determined with use of the location service, which uses embedded GPS receiver, Wi-Fi networks and cellular network to locate mobile device (Brownworth, 2012) Identity can be determined with use of devices International Mobile Equipment Identity (IMEI) or any other identification method such as username and password. Since every mobile device has internal clock, determining time is just getting accurate reading from that clock. Last primary context type, activity, is hardest to determine using smartphone features. Using combination of different sensors that individually cannot represent activity itself, but they may result in better characterization of activity context (Gellersen, Schmidt & Beigl, 2002). Example: location is somewhere outdoors, user is sitting but is doing specific motion pattern of legs and absolute position is changing. Sensor data of the given situation can be related to a situation when user is cycling. The other possibility of determining user's activity is based on knowing what application the user is using.

Taking all this into consideration our goal was to develop a context-aware mobile application in the domain of public bus transportation which would use three of the primary context types (location, time and identity) to adapt information shown to user, and the fourth one (activity or intended activity) will be predicted based on the past actions of a specific user.

PUBLIC BUS TRANSPORTATION APPLICATIONS

Traditionally users of public bus transportation used to go to bus stops to check the arrival and departure times of their desired bus line. One of first important changes to this process was with the spread of the Internet. Bus companies used web pages to put complete bus timetables online. Later with the spread of GPS devices, process changed again and users are now able to track busses in real-time over the Internet or at special displays located on major bus stops (Shalaik & Winstanley, 2011). Such real-time tracking applications can be divided into two categories: information systems that only show where buses are located in real-time and intelligent systems that also predict the time of arrival at desired bus stop. Even though this advancements already proved to be quite a step up from traditional ways users checked time tables, problem still lies in user's mobility which offers good entry point for smartphones.

Mobility is a key factor why various mobile applications in this domain have already been developed. They vary from simple applications which only show basic bus timetables, to more complex location-aware and real-time applications. In our research we especially focused on two applications.

Shalaik and Winstanley (Shalaik & Winstanley, 2011) worked on real-time transit application system for bus transportation in BlackPool based on OpenStreetMap and Android mobile platform. Based upon user's location and desired destination, application returns appropriate bus, its last known position and prediction of arrival time at closest bus stop.

Mobile Public Transportation Information Service (Chang, Hsu, & Huang, 2005). which was developed on National Taiwan Ocean University is a map-based location-aware mobile transport information service. It allows user to get information about the nearest bus stop of the desired bus line or get nearest bus stop and bus line, which will take user to the chosen destination.

CONTEXT-AWARE BUS TRACKING APPLICATION

Customers of the public bus transportation in Maribor currently have two ways of checking the timetables: either on the company's webpage or at the appropriate bus stop. Also the timetables can be purchased in printed version. This led us to the development of a context-aware mobile application, which would adapt itself to user's needs. To achieve our goal we decided to use location, time and identity as our primary context types.

To further characterize situation in which our application is used, a user is allowed to pick a time interval and a radius. Both the time interval and the radius are used to determine which bus stops are of special interest of user and are shown in the application. The time interval is used to determine maximum still acceptable time span from current time in which a bus must arrive to a bus station, while radius is used to determine area where the desired bus stops must be located. This makes the time interval and the radius secondary context types.

System Architecture

To provide a user with up to date information without constantly updating application we created a system that consists of three parts: mobile application, web service and database. Web service is used to connect mobile application with database and to process all context data collected on mobile application. Such system architecture also ensures smaller and resource lighter mobile application.

In our system mobile application is used as a client that forwards context data to the web service on web server. The context data to be forwarded is collected from user input (time interval, radius), embedded GPS receiver (location) and common mobile device features (identity). Only context data, which is not forwarded to web service, is time. Current time is determined on web server itself. Web server then processes gained data and executes queries on Entity-Relationship database. If needed, an additional query results filtering occurs before returning it to the mobile application. Such architecture allows us to execute all important calculations on the web server. Only required context data and filtered end results are sent between the web server and the mobile application. The architecture of our system is presented on Figure 1.

Mobile Application

Designing mobile application is very different from designing PC application. Spatial, abstract and hardware constraints of the mobile device interface have to be taken into the consideration [9]. The most important constraint we have to consider is screen size and screen type which can differ from one mobile operating system to another. We decided to develop an application upon Windows Phone Operating System (OS). That means screen size available for our application is 800 X 480 pixels and that application should be operated using a touch screen (MSDN, 2012a). With all this in mind our user interface has to use controls, which are suitable for such screen size and touch input. Application was created using Silverlight for Windows Phone, which already includes special designed controls for Windows Phone OS. Even with use of special designed controls, interface tailoring is used to maintain user interface simplicity. Based upon Breadth-First Principle (Niu, Li, Meng, Sun & Dong, 2006) the core of our application is divided in three connected functionalities; each of them showing new information based on previous user's input and available context data.

First functionality makes use of user's location, chosen radius, time interval and the current time in order to identify bus stops in desired area, which will have at least one bus arriving in chosen time span. As stated before the current time is determined on the web server. Location is collected from the embedded GPS receiver and the user input is required for determining radius and time interval. Time interval is set in application settings, while radius is chosen with the help of Bing Map Control. We connected map zoom level

Figure 1. System architecture consisting of mobile application, web service and database

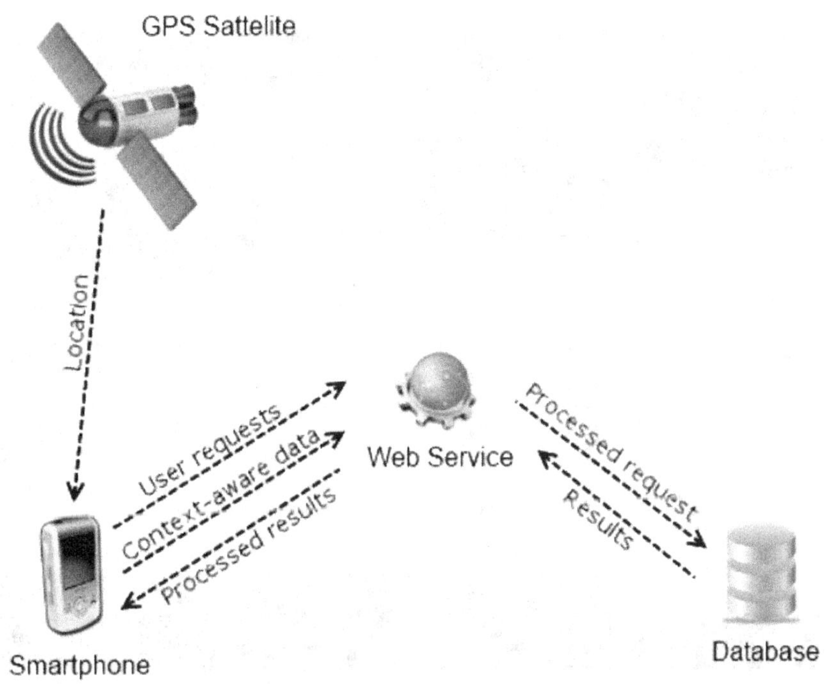

with radius, so that zooming in our out on map also changes radius. This means that desired bus stop area will be almost identical to area shown on map. Although user's identity is not needed in this functionality it is also sent to web service for purposes of second functionality. User's identity is determined with help of unique device ID. Figure 2 (left) shows identified bus stops, which are presented as bus shaped pushpins on Bing Map control.

Based upon presented bus stops, second functionality allows user to choose bus stop with the desire to obtain bus lines, which have bus arriving on this bus stop in the determined time span. Name of chosen bus stop is then presented to user at the bottom of the map. With the help of user's identity web service analyzes user's previous actions and context data forwarded to web service in first functionality. If there is any preferred bus line obtained through analysis, then such line is highlighted on user interface. Each presented bus line contains unique id, which is used in last functionality to show exact route and timetable. During testing, different options on how to dynamically position obtained bus lines onto user interface, we found positioning bus lines vertically alongside map is obstructing view on map too much. That led us to horizontal positioning of scrolling bus lines list on upper part of map. Scrolling bus lines list with appropriate bus lines is shown on Figure 2 (center).

With all appropriate bus lines presented to user, third functionality allows user to obtain exact route and timetables of specific bus line. This is done with selecting desired bus line on scrolling list. Selected bus line is then highlighted on scrolling list with additional information about direction of bus line presented right underneath. Unique bus line id is used to retrieve direction, timetables and exact route from web service. Time of arrival on chosen bus stop is shown on bottom of screen right under bus stop name. Due to limitations of displaying exact bus line path, bus line is represented with pushpins containing

Figure 2. Mobile application showing appropriate bus stops on map (left), chosen bus stop with available bus lines (center) and chosen bus line with time of arrival on chosen bus stop (right)

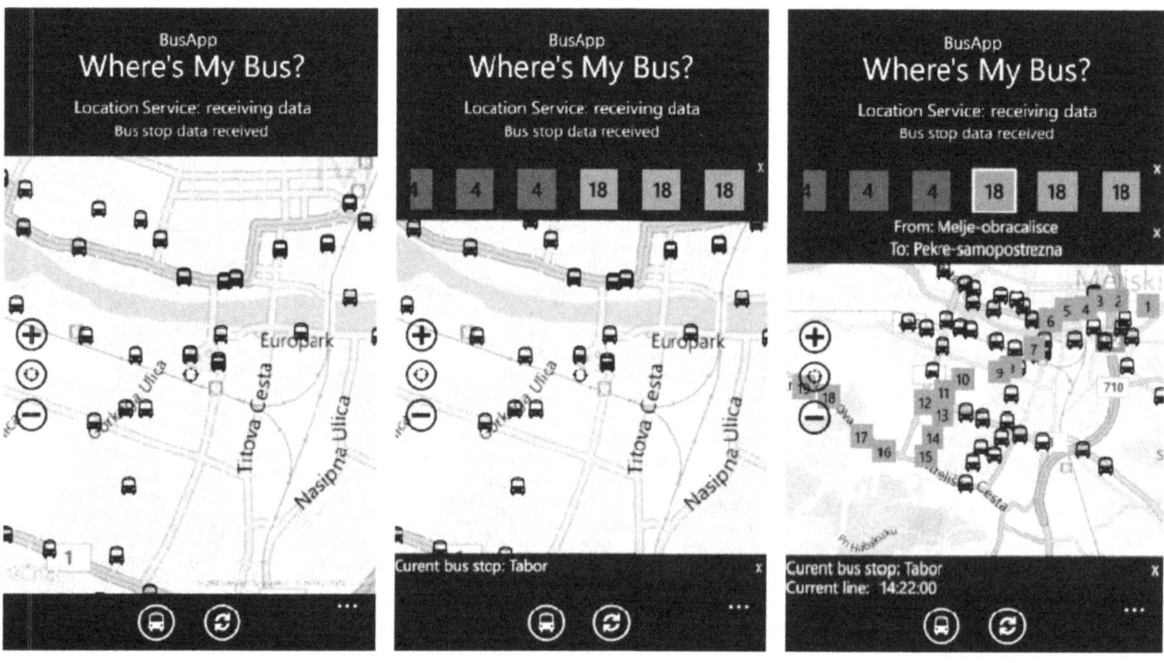

sequenced numbers for every bus stop on selected route. Presentation of exact bus line route with time of arrival on chosen bus stop can be seen on Figure 2 (right).

Web Service

Choosing Windows Phone as mobile operating system gave us the possibility to create web service in several different technologies. Since we control the data and web server, Windows Communication Foundation (WCF) services are the easiest way to expose a web service to Silverlight (MSDN, 2012b). Everything that web service exposes in WCF is determined by service contract, which defines groups of operations. Operations required in our system need to use request/reply pattern, which allows correlated response according to client's request (MSDN, 2012c). Defining operation with such pattern is done with the use of operation contract signature. Since core of our mobile application is composed of three functionalities, web service exposes three consumable operations signed as operation contracts:

- GetAllStops receives user's latitude, longitude, desired radius and time interval. Latitude, longitude and radius determine area, while time interval and current server time determine time frame for requested bus stops. Based on this data, operation returns all appropriate bus stops.
- GetLinesOnBusStop returns appropriate bus lines based on received bus stop id and time interval. Time interval is used to redetermine time frame, which may change since user's last actions.
- GetStopsOfLine receives id of desired bus line, which is used to return exact timetable and path of specified bus line.

Service contract with operation contracts for all three consumable operations can be seen on Figure 3. Consuming web service operations on

Figure 3. Web service with consumable operations

```
[ServiceContract]

public interface IServiceBusLines

{

[OperationContract]

List<AppropriateNearbyStops_Result> GetAllStops(string
deviceID, double? latitude, double? longitude, double?
radius, int interval);

[OperationContract]

List<AppropriateBusLines_Result>
GetLinesOnBusStop(string deviceID, int? id, int
interval);



[OperationContract]

List<BusStopTimetable> GetStopsOfLine(int? id);

}
```

mobile application is then realized with the help of Simple Object Access Protocol (SOAP) and Web Service Description Language (WSDL).

Database

Average timetable for single bus line in Maribor's public transportation system usually consists of over 20 bus stops along the route and 100 departure and arrival times per bus stop. It is essential, that such amount of data is properly stored and quickly accessed when web service needs to return specific data. As stated earlier, we decided to use Entity-Relationship database. Database itself is implemented using SQL Server 2008 R2, which is one of several database systems that allow developers to create stored procedures and user-defined functions. Among several benefits that we gain by using store procedures the two most important ones are: enhanced security for application and reduced network traffic (MSDN, 2012d). Similar to stored procedures, user-defined functions also decrease network traffic and allow faster execution, compared to using normal Structured Query Language (SQL) statements (MSDN, 2012e). We used user-defined function to calculate distance between user's location and bus stops using the atan2 Haversine formula, which is seen on Figure 4.

The connection between web service and database is done with Entity Framework. Together with stored procedures, this ensures us using higher level of abstraction when dealing with data, which has to be retrieved from the database. Interaction between database, web service and user is presented in sequence diagram in Figure 5.

Toward Intelligent Mobile Application: Predicting User's Activity

As already discussed, one of the very important features of mobile applications is the ability of adapting to the user's situation, commonly referred to as context awareness. It has been shown that an appropriate infrastructure should enable wide deployment of context-aware applications, where some of the main technical challenges to realize such an infrastructure are reasoning to infer higher-level and better quality context information, efficient exchange and distributed processing of context information in dynamic and pervasive environments (van Sinderen, et al., 2006). While the second challenge has already been addressed above, our approach to reasoning to infer higher-level and better quality context information is addressed in this section.

Agility, time-efficiency and non-optimal environment are inherent attributes of using mobile applications. In this manner, adapting application context to the needs of a specific user is of great importance. One of the most obvious ways to provide this user personalization is through the adaptation of user interface, which then provides individualized, just-in-time assistance to users by recording user interface events and frequencies, organizing them into episodes, and automatically deriving patterns; it also builds, maintains, and makes suggestions based on user profiles (Liu, Wong & Hui, 2003).

As the identity of a mobile user who is using a remote service from his/her device is automatically determined based on the device ID, we stored the

Figure 4. The atan2 Haversine formula

$$a = sin^2\left(\frac{\Delta lat}{2}\right) + cos(lat_1) \times \cos(lat_2) \times sin^2\left(\frac{\Delta long}{2}\right)$$

$$c = 2 \times atan2(\sqrt{a}, \sqrt{(a-1)})$$

$$d = R \times c, \qquad R = 6.371\ km$$

Figure 5. Three stepped interaction between user and mobile application

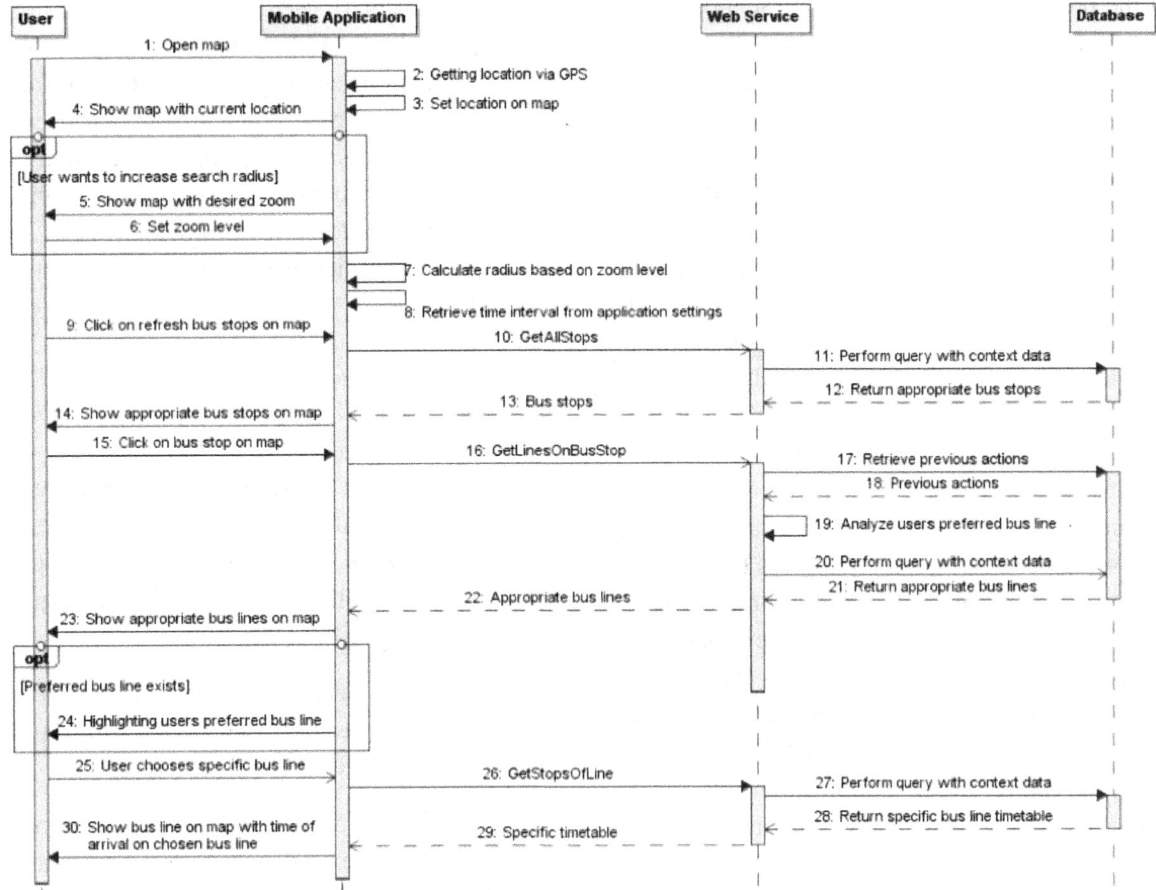

actions of each user in our database. An action comprises of data about a single bus drive – a bus stop where the user enters a bus, a bus line, time of departure, a bus stop where the user leaves the bus, and the arrival time. Based on this information, the preferred bus line for a specific user can be determined in a quite straight-forward manner. Our proposition here is that the basic patterns of bus rides of a specific user are quite obvious – the most frequent bus rides for a specific user usually take place at approximately same time (for example going to work or school and back home) and between the same (or nearby) bus stops, with the bus line operating these bus stops. We used this proposition to adapt the behavior of our mobile application based on the predicted activity of a user – which bus line the user would probably want to use. Based on this prediction the display and user controls are adapted appropriately.

In this manner, from all the stored bus rides of a specific user, those rides are identified first where the departure time is similar to the current time. Second, within these identified bus rides it is searched for those where the route and direction of the bus ride coincide with the user's current location. If any of the found route represents a user's driving pattern with an appropriate level of support and confidence (the route is frequently used by the user within a given timeframe), then the bus line operating on such route is identified as a user's preferred bus line. In such a case, the bus line is highlighted to the user and the user interface automatically adapts to show the nearest bus stops of the preferred bus line. How this adaptation is processed within our mobile application can be seen on Figure 5 (steps 17-19 and 24).

DISCUSSION AND CONCLUSION

As stated in introduction, we wanted to create context-aware mobile application, which would use identity, location and time with the help of activity to adapt itself to user's needs. Creating such application with regards to mobile device constraints took some specific design and implementation guidelines. Together with all data and business logic moved into separate database and web service, Silverlight for Windows Phone was used to overcome mobile device constraints. Such division not only allowed efficient development, but also creating application that uses less system resources and allows user to be up to date with any timetable change without the need to update it.

Furthermore dividing application into three connected functionalities and using Breadth-First principle turned out to be a quick and natural way of working with application and getting more detailed context based information about public bus transportation system.

With presented application we have shown that user's location, identity, time and activity as primary context types together with desired radius and time interval as secondary context types are a viable choice for context-aware application in public bus transportation domain. Adapting shown information with the use of context-awareness directly translated onto little user interaction required, which means user-friendlier application. Analyzing user's previous actions and predicting activity in the form of highlighting preferred bus line meant that user could easily recognize frequently used bus line in determined context. This means that adding this ability resulted in even further expansion of user-experience. Increasing used context data would allow even more accurate and detailed information given to user. Therefore as a future improvement of our application, user's speed and heading would be perfect addition to current secondary context types. Combined with real-time bus tracking this would allow us to calculate and predict user's possibility to catch the desired bus.

REFERENCES

Abowd, G. et al. (1999). Towards a better understanding of context and context-awareness. In *Handheld and Ubiquitous Computing* (pp. 304–307). Heidelberg, Germany: Springer. doi:10.1007/3-540-48157-5_29

Brownworth, A. (2012). *How location services work on mobile devices*. Retrieved from http://anders.com/cms/389

Chang, S., Hsu, G., & Huang, S. (2005). Location-aware mobile transportation information service. In *Proceedings of 2nd International Conference on Mobile Technology, Applications and Systems*. IEEE.

Gartner Inc. (2011). *Gartner says sales of mobile devices grew 5.6 percent in third quarter of 2011, smartphone sales increased 42 percent*. Retrieved from http://www.gartner.com/it/page.jsp?id=1848514

Gellersen, H., Schmidt, A., & Beigl, M. (2002). Multi-sensor context-awareness in mobile devices and smart artifacts. In *Multi-Sensor Context-Awareness in Mobile Devices and Smart Artifacts* (pp. 341–351). Dordrecht, The Netherlands: Kluwer Academic Publishers.

Lane, N. et al. (2010). A survey of mobile phone sensing. *IEEE Communications*, *48*, 140–150. doi:10.1109/MCOM.2010.5560598

Liu, J., Wong, C., & Hui, K. (2003). An adaptive user interface based on personalized learning. *IEEE Intelligent Systems*, *18*, 52–57. doi:10.1109/MIS.2003.1193657

MSDN. (2012a). *MSDN: Chapter 2 - Designing applications for Windows phone 7*. Retrieved from http://msdn.microsoft.com/en-us/library/gg490770.aspx

MSDN. (2012b). *Networking and web services*. Retrieved from http://msdn.microsoft.com/en-us/library/cc645029(v=VS.95).aspx

MSDN. (2012c). *Designing service contracts*. Retrieved from http://msdn.microsoft.com/en-us/library/ms733070.aspx

MSDN. (2012d). *Stored procedure basics*. Retrieved from http://msdn.microsoft.com/en-us/library/ms191436.aspx

MSDN. (2012e). *User-defined function basics*. Retrieved from http://msdn.microsoft.com/en-us/library/ms191007.aspx

Niu, Y., Li, X., Meng, X., Sun, J., & Dong, H. (2006). A constraint-based user interface design method for mobile computing devices. In *Proceedings of 1st International Sympsium on Pervasive Computing and Applications*. IEEE. doi:10.1109/SPCA.2006.297595

Schilit, B., & Theimer, M. (1994). Disseminating active map information to mobile hosts. *IEEE Network*, *8*, 22–32. doi:10.1109/65.313011

Shalaik, B., & Winstanley, A. (2011). Delivering real-time bus tracking information on mobile devices. In *Future Information Technology* (pp. 139–147). Heidelberg, Germany: Springer. doi:10.1007/978-3-642-22309-9_17

van Sinderen, et al. (2006). Supporting context-aware mobile applications: An infrastructure approach. *IEEE Communications, 44*, 96-104.

Chapter 11
Educational Social Networks as a Means for Better Social Cohesion in Education

Vili Podgorelec
Institute of Informatics (FERI), University of Maribor, Slovenia

Maša Dobrina
Institute of Informatics (FERI), University of Maribor, Slovenia

ABSTRACT

In the chapter, the authors argue whether social networks can contribute to the enhanced sense of community in an educational environment. Several studies show that the creation of a proper social environment with proper social integration has important positive effects on the students' success in learning environments. In the chapter, the results of the study performed at the University of Maribor are presented, which show that social networks can enhance social cohesion, improve communication between members, and contribute to goal achievement of a social group.

INTRODUCTION

There is no doubt that social networks have changed the way we communicate today, and in this chapter we discuss if they are effective in decreasing social and psychological distance in (on-line) education and in contributing to the benefits of social cohesion in education. Our research focused on how social relations in the classroom are portrayed on the Internet in social networks and how does it affect success in education.

Several distance education models are presently in use, such as broadcast television, video and audio teleconferencing, and asynchronous learning networks –ALNs (Rovai, 2002). Learners use computers and communications technologies

DOI: 10.4018/978-1-4666-4490-8.ch011

in ALNs to work with remote learning resources, including online content, as well as instructors, and other learners, but without the requirement to be online at the same time. Arguably, the most common ALN communication tool is the World Wide Web used in conjunction with e-learning software such as Blackboard or WebCT, providing student and instructor electronic access to course materials, grades, activities, and communication options such as discussion boards, email, and chat rooms (Rovai, 2002). But there is still no holistic approach to building social cohesion between students in online courses, at least no software uses the benefits of building social cohesion over an educational social network with the possibility for the learner to design his or her own educational profile.

Studies show that dropout rates are often 10 to 20 percentage points higher in distance education courses than in traditional courses, although there are significant variations among institutions (Carr, 2000). The physical separation of students in programs offered at a distance may also contribute to higher dropout rates. Such separation has a tendency to reduce the sense of community, giving rise to feelings of disconnection (Kerka, 1996), isolation, distraction, and lack of personal attention (Besser & Donahue, 1996) which could affect student persistence in distance education courses or programs. Tinto (Tinto, 1993) emphasized the importance of community in reducing dropouts when he theorized that students will increase their levels of satisfaction and the likelihood of persisting in a college program if they feel involved and develop relationships with other members of the learning community. The importance of community is supported by empirical research. Wehlage, Rutter and Smith (Wehlage, Rutter & Smith, 1989) found that traditional schools with exemplary dropout-prevention programs devoted considerable attention to overcoming the barriers that prevented students from connecting with the school and to developing a sense of belonging, membership, and engagement. The key finding of their report is that effective schools provide students with a supportive community. In a study of adult learners in a worksite GED program, Vann and Hinton (Vann & Hinton, 1994). found that 84 percent of completers belonged to class cliques, whereas 70 percent of dropouts were socially isolated. As a final example, Ashar and Skenes (Ashar & Skenes, 1993) found in a higher education business program that by creating a social environment that motivated adult learners to persist, social integration had a significant positive effect on retention. They found that learning needs alone appeared strong enough to attract adults to the program, but not to retain them.

This chapter discusses whether social networks can contribute to the enhanced sense of community in a learning, educational environment.

EXTENDING ONLINE COLLABORATION WITH EDUCATIONAL SOCIAL NETWORK

Within the field of education social networks can enhance social cohesion, improve communication between members and contribute to goal achievement of a social group (in our case group of students with the common goal of similar interests in the field of study and successful conclusion of an educational course). We believe that engaging in an educational social network would be a positive addition to all other forms of online collaboration because it would contribute to social cohesion between students, encourage innovation, and enhance the effectiveness of learning and searching for information, linked to education. The other side of benefits would be also for the outside student social groups as research and development sections to be more easily linked to research in education.

The Study

Participants of this study were drawn from the Faculty of Electrical Engineering and Computer

Science (University of Maribor) from all of the study specializations available (mostly from Media Communication, Computer Science and Informatics students) and from all years of study, the majority currently being involved in second and third year of studies, so the survey sample is biased with participants that should be information literate and involved in various aspects of new communication technologies. The results for this article were drawn from the section measuring attitudes towards the use of social networks, communication style over the internet and social cohesion in a classroom setting. The whole survey also measured the use of the Faculty's website, learning style, assignment preferences, use of virtual agents and educational networks. We collected a total of 151 complete responses.

On the collected data we first performed EDA (Exploratory Data Analysis). We calculated the mean, standard deviation and normality tests to determine whether the data is normally distributed. Since the survey consisted mostly of nominal and ordinal data (Likert scale), none of the questions were normally distributed, so we had to use nonparametric tests to determine the correlation among variables.

In testing nominal versus ordinal correlations we used the Chi Square statistic (χ^2) and in testing ordinal versus ordinal correlation we conducted the Kendall tau –b test (τ). The Chi Square statistic shows only the correlation but not the direction and strength of the relationship. The Kendall tau is asymmetric PRE (Proportional Reduction of Error) measure of association for ranked data in a square table (equal number of rows and columns) and uses the difference between concordant and discordant pairs as the basis for assessing whether an association exists and to determine its direction (Argyrous, G., 2005).

Social Cohesion

D. W. McMillan and D. M. Chavis (Koh & Kim, 2003) note that community consists of four elements concerning people involved:

- **A Sense of Belonging:** A sense that they belong to the community.
- **The Impact:** A feeling that they can add something, contribute to the changes in the community.
- **Fulfillment of Needs:** A sense of fulfillment, an expectation that the re-sources which are available in the community, will meet their individual needs and desires.
- **Emotional Ties:** The belief that community members have and share a similar history, time, space and experiences.

A sense of belonging was measured with the degree of consent with the statement "I feel I belong to my class."

The impact was measured with the degree of consent with the statement "I can affect the decisions concerning my class."

In our study Fulfillment of needs was interpreted as study success as our setting is a classroom and the purpose of this community is study success, graduation. It was measured with the degree of consent with the statement "I study successfully and within the expected time period."

Our survey did not measure emotional ties, as we wanted to explore how students would accept the implementation of social networks, specialized for education in order to contribute to build social ties, or to enhance social ties from real life relationships, as is more often the case.

Communication Style Over the Internet

We have measured communication style over the internet with the usage frequency (daily, once a week, a couple of times per month or never) of a specific communication tool (email, discussion boards, chat rooms, instant messaging programs, writing a blog, own web page for communicating ones activities and social networks). Our research shows that the majority of students use email (82%) and social networks (75%) daily. Half of them also use daily instant messaging programs

Table1. Social cohesion statements. Students evaluated the degree of consent with the statements (from 1 to 5, 1 being "I do not agree at all" and 5 being "I fully agree").

	Mean	Std. Dev.
I study successfully and within the expected time period.	3,80	1,365
I feel equal to other students on the Faculty.	3,71	1,125
I like educational activities in small groups.	3,67	1,246
I feel I belong to my class.	3,22	1,151
I can affect the decisions concerning my class.	2,89	1,051

like Skype or Messenger. Near 20% of students use discussion boards and chat rooms daily. Only 2% write their own blogs and 3,4% have their own web site where they communicate their activities. 10% of students are involved in 3 or more social networks, 23% in 2, but most of them are a member of only one social network. Almost 80% of students check their profiles everyday, 13% do that two to three times a week, and the ones that check their profile less than that are scarce.

Attitudes Towards Social Networks and Computer Mediated Communication

We measured attitudes toward social networks with Likart scales, the degree of consent with statements about use of internet, computer mediated communication and social networks.

The level of agreement was highest with the statement that students would miss social networks if they did not exist anymore. The second statement with the highest degree of consent was that communication via social networks is genuine and that they are in fact more relaxed and sincere when communicating via social networks. Students did not agree in a high degree with the statement

Table 2. Attitudes towards social networks and computer mediated communication. Students evaluated the degree of consent with the statements (from 1 to 5, 1 being "I do not agree at all" and 5 being "I fully agree").

	Mean	Std. Dev.
If social networks would not exist anymore, I would miss them.	2,73	1,311
Communication over social networks with my friends is genuine.	2,43	1,120
I am more relaxed and sincere in computer mediated communication.	2,16	1,178
When communicating over social networks I feel I belong to my groups.	1,94	0,972
I feel lost because of all the available social networks.	1,83	1,189
Communication over social networks is safe and private.	1,79	0,945

that they feel lost because of the numerous social networks available and they also did not agree that the use of social networks is safe and private.

The Use and Integration of a Social Network for Education

Most of the students (89%) responded that they would use a social network that would have the possibilities of customization of communication styles that would merge the information resources for education, leisure time activities outside the faculty, employment, and socialization with study mates. Little fewer students (64, 7%) responded that they would integrate the existing social network profile with the one specialized for education.

The question was measured with two possible answers, yes or no, missing values were coded as the answer of the students which did not know how to respond, or could not make up their minds.

Respondents had to evaluate (positively or negatively) how an implementation of an educational social network would affect communication among different groups of people (students, interest groups, student clubs, research institutions, faculty administration, professors, potential employers and student service offices) again on a Likert scale from 1 to 5.

Results show that the general effect of implementing a social educational network would be most beneficial to the communication among students, although the net results are positive (mean is higher than 3 – the neutral effect) in all groups of suggested people. The second most beneficial communication impact due to the social network for education would be, according to our survey, among students and interest groups, followed by students clubs, research institutions, faculty administration, professors, employers and the least for student service offices.

Table 3. Effects of an educational social network on different groups of people. On the scale of 1 to 5 asses how an implementation of a social network for education would affect the following groups of people, involved in education (1 means the most negative effect, 5 means the most positive effect).

	MEAN	STD. DEV.
Among students.	3,99	1,180
Among interest groups and students.	3,60	1,141
Among student clubs and students.	3,48	1,172
Among research institutions and students.	3,48	1,081
Among faculty administration and students.	3,45	0,960
Among professors and students.	3,40	0,992
Among employers and students.	3,32	1,168
Among student service offices and students.	3,16	1,203

RESULTS (HYPOTHESIS TESTING)

H1: Social Cohesion Affects Study Success

We have measured the indicators with the Likert scale which is ordinal, hence we used Kendall tau-b coefficient. The test shows that we can reject the null hypothesis and confirm the relationship in all indicators that measured the social situation in the classroom with study success in a positive manner. A significance (p) lower or equal to 0.05 rejects the null hypothesis of independence and confirms the hypothesis of correlation between variables. We computed the Tau-b coefficient for all the measures for social cohesion in relation to the variable asserting study success.

- "I feel equal to other students on the Faculty." vs. "I study successfully and within the expected time period." τ (N = 141) = 0.373, p = 0.000; correlation is significant at the 0.01 level (2-tailed test).
- "I like educational activities in small groups." vs. "I study successfully and within the expected time period." τ (N = 142) = 0.198, p = 0.005; correlation is significant at the 0.01 level (2-tailed test).
- "I can affect the decisions concerning my class" vs. "I study successfully and within the expected time period". τ (N = 137) = 0.221, p = 0.002; correlation is significant at the 0.01 level (2-tailed test).
- "I feel I belong to my class" vs. "I study successfully and within the expected time period". τ (N = 138) = 0.235, p = 0.001; correlation is significant at the 0.01 level (2-tailed test).

H2: Communication Style (Usability Preferences) Over the Internet Affects Study Success

After we examined the rest of the indicators that significantly affected study success, the results show correlation with the following elements of online communication:

- "I quickly find my way around the Faculty's web page" vs. "I study successfully and within the expected time period." τ (N = 143) = 0.202, p = 0.040; correlation is significant at the 0.01 level (2-tailed test).
- "Due to frequent social network use I communicate less over email messages" vs. "I study successfully and within the expected time period." τ (N = 118) = -0.201, p = 0.009; correlation is significant at the 0.01 level (2-tailed test).

The connection is negative, which means that there is less consent with the statement that use of social networks affects less communication over e-mail messages.

- "Importance of the possibility of setting which Rich Site Summary feeds are interesting on web pages" vs. "I study successfully and within the expected time period." τ (N = 144) = -0.222, p = 0.001; correlation is significant at the 0.01 level (2-tailed test).
- "Importance of the possibility of customizing content display settings on web pages" vs. "I study successfully and within the expected time period." τ (N = 142) = -0.147, p =0.034; correlation is significant at the 0.05 level (2-tailed test).
- "Frequency of use of own web page for communicating activities and news" vs. "I study successfully and within the expected time period". τ (N = 145) = 0.159, p = 0.033; correlation is significant at the 0.05 level (2-tailed test).

H3: Communication Style Over the Internet Affects the Willingness to Use an Educational Social Network

When computing contingency tables, Pearson's Chi square and Pearson's r coefficient, we confirmed a relationship between the frequent use of chat rooms and social networks, but there is no significant relationship among respondents who frequently use discussion boards, web pages and software for instant communication and writers of blogs.

- "Frequent use of chat rooms" and "Would you use an educational social network (with possibilities of customizing your communication style, shared course materials, off campus activities, employment and socializing with school mates)?" χ^2 (3, N =124) = 10.256, p = 0.017. After we confirmed a significant correlation, we further computed the Pearson's r coefficient to determine the direction and strength of the relationship. The relationship is slightly negative and not strong; r (N = 124) = -0.257, p = 0.004; correlation is significant at the 0.01 level (2-tailed test).
- "Frequent use of social networks (Facebook, Twitter)" and "Would you use an educational social network (with possibilities of customizing your communication style, shared course materials, off campus activities, employment and socializing with school mates)?" χ^2 (3, N =127) = 19.214, p = 0.000. We also computed Pearson's correlation coefficient and also

obtained a slightly negative correlation; r (N = 124) = -0.355, p = 0.000; correlation is significant at the 0.01 level (2-tailed test).

H4: Communication Style Over the Internet Affects Willingness to Integrate the Social Network Profile with the One Social Network for Education

We found a significant correlation only with a variable measuring frequent of use of social networks, and also a nearly significant correlation with variables measuring frequent use of chat rooms and writing a blog.

- "Frequent use of social networks (Facebook, Twitter) and "If it were possible to integrate the profile in an existing social network, would you synchronize it with the social profile intended for education?" χ^2 (3, N =119) = 38.140, p = 0.000.
- "Frequent use of chat rooms" and "If it were possible to integrate the profile in an existing social network, would you synchronize it with the social profile intended for education?" χ^2 (3, N =116) = 7.354, p = 0.061.
- "Frequency of writing a blog" and "If it were possible to integrate the profile in an existing social network, would you synchronize it with the social profile intended for education?" χ^2 (2, N =117) = 5.282, p = 0.071.

We then divided the answers in two groups, one group being the ones, that have answered positively (that want to use an educational social network) and the ones that answered negatively.

- "If it were possible to integrate the profile in an existing social network, would you synchronize it with the social profile intended for education?" and "Yes, I would use an educational social network (with possibilities of customizing your communication style, shared course materials, off campus activities, employment and socializing with school mates)?" χ^2 (1) = 28.167, p = 0.000

The results show that the ones who are willing to use an educational social network would also integrate their profiles.

H5: Attitudes Towards Social Networks Affect the Willingness to Use an Educational Social Network

- "I am more relaxed and sincere in computer mediated communication" and "Would you use an educational social network (with possibilities of customizing your communication style, shared course materials, off campus activities, employment and socializing with school mates)?" χ^2 (4, N =106) = 14.747, p = 0.005
- "Communication over social networks with my friends is genuine." and "Yes, I would use an educational social network (with possibilities of customizing your communication style, shared course materials, off campus activities, employment and socializing with school mates)?" χ^2 (4) = 25.667, p = 0.000
- "When communicating over social networks I feel I belong to my groups." and "Yes, I would use an educational social network (with possibilities of customizing your communication style, shared course materials, off campus activities, employment and socializing with school mates)?" χ^2 (4) = 53.447, p = 0.000

DISCUSSION

The measurement of success is performed by self-evaluation which tends to be more positive in comparison to reality. We could measure student success in terms of grades and yearly progress to a higher college year, but we decided we wanted to see how they feel about their success and maybe they were more intuitive when asserting other Likert scales. In addition, this kind of measurement gives a weighted value of success depending on one's individual ambitions and self-satisfaction.

The social cohesion measures in the classroom clearly indicated that students do not feel that they belong to their class and that they do not have a large impact on decisions concerning their class. However, our research confirmed the results from previous studies of social cohesion positively affecting study success.

According to our research, study success is also correlated with students that find their way around the faculty web site, students that demonstrate a higher value for RSS feeds, more interactive customization settings on a web site and communicate more frequently via their own web sites, which is also a sign of information literacy and the ability to navigate the internet in search for information. Successful students also responded that the use of social networks does not affect the flow of email messages, indicating that they are not limited by use of social networks and are open to all means of communication over internet and use them accordingly to their communication style.

Our research shows that the use of social networks and chat rooms is negatively correlated with the potential use of an educational social network, but since the majority of students responded positively to the question if they would use a social network, dedicated to education, this could also indicate that also the ones that do not use social networks find such an idea appealing. The students that responded positively to the use of an educational social network also responded that they would integrate the profiles as did the ones that frequently use social networks.

We have also confirmed that the attitudes towards social networks and computer mediated communication affect the willingness to use an educational social network. Although not all our measures confirmed the correlation, the statements that access the feelings of sincerity, genuine communication and sense of belonging confirmed the willingness to use an educational social network.

Students also responded that the most beneficial impact of a social network for education would be to the communication among students, and not so with professors, which indicates that they wish to have more social ties with their peers than with higher authorities of the faculty. This also indicates that an educational social network would be an effective gap filler for diminished social cohesion in online education.

CONCLUSION

On the field of education social networks can enhance social cohesion, improve communication between members and contribute to goal achievement of a social group (in our case group of students with the common goal of similar interests in the field of study and successful conclusion of an educational course). Because of the biased sample of students of the Faculty of electrical engineering and computer science we more likely obtained opinions that favor the use of new technologies, so we think further research in this area should include designing a comparative study for non-technical students that are less likely to embrace the idea of building social cohesion over an educational social network. The objective should be finally to put together a holistic and reasonable (but also customizable to different communication preferences at the same time) set of communication tools for social cohesion in online education. But altogether our study pointed out that social cohesion (over the internet) is important for study success and students demonstrated that they would want to use an educational social network as a part of their daily communication style over the internet mostly because of the possibility of socializing with their school mates. Much of daily communication has moved from personal, physical to online and computer mediated communication and educational social encounters should follow the overall communication style of the information generation. Our measures of communication style over the internet show that students use various tools of communication via internet daily and that there is a need to adapt and enhance the learning experience by communicating and socializing over networks.

REFERENCES

Argyrous, G. (2005). *Statistics for research with guide to SPSS*. Thousand Oaks, CA: SAGE Publications Ltd.

Ashar, H., & Skenes, R. (1993). Can Tinto's student departure model be applied to non-traditional students? *Adult Education Quarterly*, *43*(2), 90–100. doi:10.1177/0741713693043002003

Besser, H., & Donahue, S. (1996). Introduction and overview: Perspectives on distance independent education. *Journal of the American Society for Information Science American Society for Information Science*, *47*(11), 801–804. doi:10.1002/(SICI)1097-4571(199611)47:11<801::AID-ASI1>3.0.CO;2-6

Carr, S. (2000). As distance education comes of age, the challenge is keeping the students. *The Chronicle of Higher Education*, *46*(23), A39–A41.

Kerka, S. (1996). *Distance learning, the internet, and the world wide web*. ERIC Digest.

Koh, J., & Kim, Y. (2003). Sense of virtual community: a conceptual framework and empirical validation. *International Journal of Electronic Commerce*, *8*(2), 76.

Rovai, A. (2002). Building sense of community at a distance. *International Review of Research in Open and Distance Learning*, *3*(1).

Tinto, V. (1993). *Leaving college: Rethinking the causes and cures of student attrition*. Chicago: University of Chicago Press.

Vann, B., & Hinton, B. (1994). Workplace social networks and their relationship to student retention in on-site GED programs. *Human Resource Development Quarterly*, *5*(2), 141–151. doi:10.1002/hrdq.3920050205

Wehlage, G., Rutter, R., & Smith, G. (1989). *Reducing the risk: Schools as communities of support*. New York: The Falmer Press.

Chapter 12
Semantic Web Services-Based Knowledge Management Framework

Vili Podgorelec
Institute of Informatics (FERI), University of Maribor, Slovenia

Boštjan Grašič
Institute of Informatics (FERI), University of Maribor, Slovenia

ABSTRACT

In this chapter, a Semantic Web services-based knowledge management framework that enables holistic knowledge management in organizations is presented. As the economy is becoming one single global marketplace, where the best offer wins, organizations have to search for competitive advantage within themselves. With the growing awareness that key potentials of an organization lie within its people and their knowledge, efficient knowledge management is becoming one of key focuses in organizational activities. The proposed knowledge management framework is based on Semantic Web technologies and service-oriented architecture, supporting the operational business processes as well as knowledge-based management of services in service-oriented architecture.

INTRODUCTION

In modern global economy it is very hard for organizations to retain competitive edge over competitors. To be able to succeed in this highly competitive environment, organizations have to find value added in themselves and transform that to the market. Many authors are discovering, that organizations' greatest asset are their employees and knowledge they possess (Bergeron, 2003). In this manner knowledge management is becoming one of core processes in daily life of modern enterprises. Information technology can provide means to better acquire, organize and use knowledge in organizations.

By analyzing modern information systems, we have found a gap between technology and needs that arise in organizations (Zack, McKeen & Singh,

DOI: 10.4018/978-1-4666-4490-8.ch012

2009). It is not uncommon, that technology is being push factor for changes in organizations. While this is positive in some situations, it often has negative impact over time. The danger is that information technology could become the purpose for itself and it would not support business processes and business opportunities in a way that maximizes organizations' success and effectiveness (Zack, McKeen & Singh, 2009).

We argue that knowledge, not information technology, provides competitive advantage for organizations. In this manner, knowledge should be the driver for changes in organizations. The role of information technology should be to help to identify opportunities, follow and support changes. In this chapter we provide a framework for holistic knowledge management and integration it with modern IT architecture that enables business agility.

We identified two types of knowledge that appear in organizations:

1. Organizational knowledge
2. Operational knowledge

The former is knowledge about the organization itself, its structure and processes, while the latter is knowledge that is used for operational work in the organization. In this manner organizational knowledge is used by management, whose goal is to enable that business processes are able to run optimally, while the role of operational knowledge is to support optimal execution of the business processes.

The other very important element in modern organizations is information technology (IT). The role of IT is in many organizations limited just to support operational knowledge. In our opinion it is at least equally important the support for organizational knowledge. This enables managers to manage IT in such way, that technology supports business processes at the highest rate possible. According to that, management also has to have knowledge about IT implementation in the organization as also about dependency between IT implementation and business processes. We shall call this type of knowledge IT support knowledge.

In this chapter we present a framework that is suitable to capture both organizational and operational knowledge as also IT support knowledge. The framework is built upon semantic web technologies (SWT) that use semantic networks for knowledge representation (Davis, Shrobe & Szolovits, 1993). Because its flexibility and expressiveness, it is possible to model, bind and manage knowledge from different domains.

The framework we present also builds on concepts from service oriented architecture (SOA) that empowers organizational agility by providing flexible and robust architecture (Erl, 2005). By semantically annotating services in a SOA environment, we are able to incorporate knowledge about services in organizational semantic network (Akkiraju, 2006). That way, all three identified types of knowledge are represented in the semantic network. This integrated organization knowledge enables knowledge driven change, while service orientation provides better support for implementing these changes in the organization.

There is some related work done in both functional parts of our framework. Huang and Diao studied ontology based enterprise knowledge integration (Huang & Diao, 2008). The framework that we present in this chapter extends the described architecture by using service orientation concepts (Akkiraju, 2006). There is some related work done also in the field of incorporating semantics into SOA. Most notable are SESA (Anicic, et al., 2007). and METEOR-S (Rajasekaran, Miller, Verma & Sheth, 2005). The main difference to our approach is that they are targeted at open world environment, trying to provide automated discovery and mediation of web service, while our approach is targeted at closed world environment, where mediation is modeled in ontology. Other significant difference is that SESA uses WSMO for implementing SWS, while our approach uses SAWSDL.

The organization of the chapter is as follows. In section 2 we briefly present semantic web technologies and outline semantic web driven knowledge management system (KMS) architecture. In section 3, we present basic characteristics of service oriented architecture and introduce semantic web services. In section 4 we propose a knowledge management framework that is based on semantic web technologies and incorporates service orientation principles using semantic web services. Section 5 provides information about related work and conclusion.

SEMANTIC WEB ENABLED KNOWLEDGE MANAGEMENT SYSTEM

We already pointed out the importance of knowledge in contemporary environment. Our framework supports proactive management of knowledge. That way, the technology should support following activities/processes:

1. Knowledge creation/acquisition,
2. Knowledge modification,
3. Knowledge use,
4. Knowledge archiving,
5. Information transfer,
6. Knowledge translation/repurposing,
7. Knowledge access,
8. Knowledge disposal (Bergeron, 2003).

According to (Bergeron, 2003) it is not sufficient just to store information and capture knowledge. If the users can't use acquired knowledge it is not useful. Therefore it is significant, that users are able to access the knowledge, depending on their role in the organization, besides that, they should also make use of it. Knowledge is not eternal, it is subject to change over time. In this manner KMS must also allow knowledge modification, translation and even disposal of knowledge in case it becomes obsolete.

Technologies used for KMS have to meet two criteria:

1. They have to be suitable for knowledge representation, and
2. They have also to be flexible enough to support knowledge management processes, as discussed above.

Relational databases (RDB) fall short in both criteria. They are not expressive enough for knowledge representation and they are also not flexible enough for all KMS use cases (Lo & Choobineh, 1999).

In (Davis, Shrobe & Szolovits, 1993) authors define knowledge representation (KR) as a set of five roles, KR plays in. They argue that KR is a surrogate for the real world. In this manner KR technologies serve as a medium of human expression to describe the world or a particular domain. On top of the representation role, KR technologies have to support intelligent reasoning and also provide a platform for efficient computation, so that reasoning based on represented knowledge can take place.

There are several technologies suitable for KR, some of them are first order logic, rule based systems, frames and semantic networks (Davis, Shrobe & Szolovits, 1993). We propose use of semantic networks, which rely on ontologies for knowledge conceptualization. Ontologies are formal specification of a shared conceptualization (Borst, 1997). Modern ontology languages like OWL provide modeling of concepts, connections between concepts and restrictions. Most modern ontology languages are based on description or frame logic.

Semantic Web Technologies

Semantic web is a set of technologies, tools and recommendations proposed by World Wide Web consortium (W3C), that follow the vision of semantic web. The vision of semantic web is in evolution from web of documents (as we know the world wide web today) into semantic web (SW). In SW, computers would have an awareness of the meaning of the information and computer agents would be able to find and process information based on their meaning (Berners-Lee, Hendler & Lassila, 2001).

Semantic web technologies (SWT) provide technologies to achieve this vision. They form layered architecture that is shown on Figure 1. Core technologies that SWT are built upon are Unicode, URI and XML. This foundation enables SWT to be platform and programming language independent. Upon XML is RDF (RDF) layer. RDF (Resource Description Framework) is a XML based language for describing resources. On top of RDF is ontology layer. There exist many languages for modeling ontologies. The most used ontology language for semantic web used today is OWL (OWL) and is based on description logic. On top of ontology layer is logic layer. This layer provides similar features as first order logic. Candidate language for implementing this layer is SWRL. Trust and proof layers don't have any significant research work. The role of these two layers is to provide proof for the reasoning that took place and to provide means, that we can trust the provided information.

Using Semantic Web Technologies for Knowledge Management Purposes

Semantic web technologies enable description of resources, ontologies and rules in such way, that resources/data can be linked with concepts

Figure 1. The layers of semantic web technologies

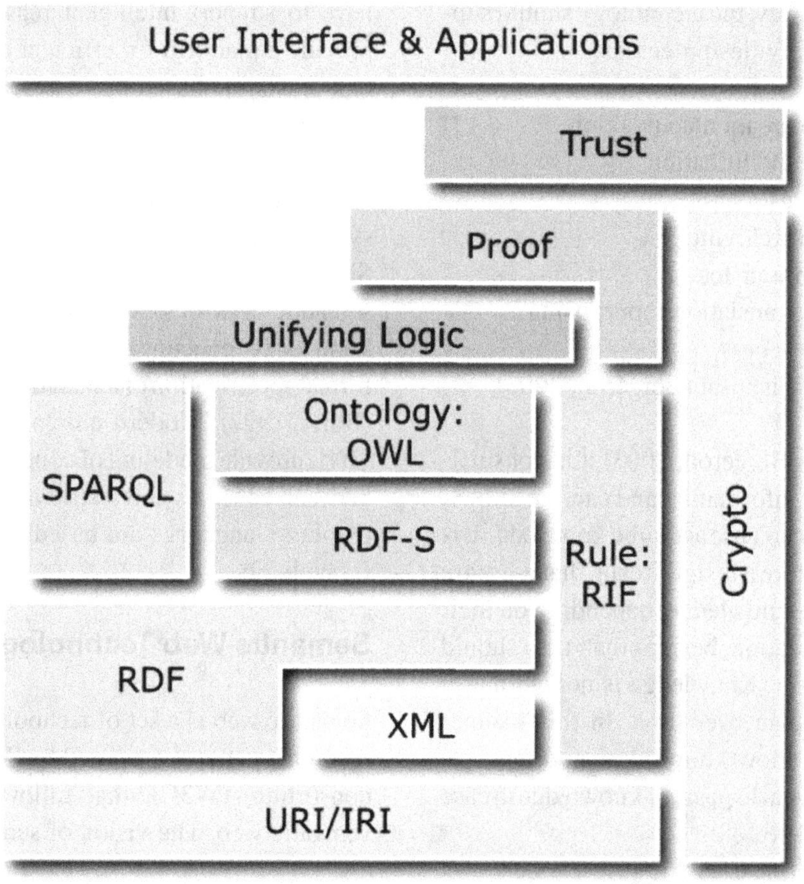

defined in ontologies. Further the same data can be processed by an inference engine either by defying rules in a rule language or by relationships and restrictions defined in ontology. These abilities make SWT useful for KR purposes.

There was already some previous research work done on the use of SWT for KR and KM. In (Garcia-Sanchez, et al. 2006) authors have built ontology driven employment web portal, where they captured knowledge in employment ontology. In (Trastour, Bartolini & Preist, 2003) authors have studied B2B interaction on semantic web platform, while (Huang & Diao, 2008) studied ontology based enterprise knowledge integration, which is a similar approach to the one presented in this chapter.

In our previous work we have built a knowledge driven customer relationship management system (oCRM) using SWT (Grasic & Podgorelec, 2008). The system was used for supporting customer support process for an IT company by providing knowledge about previous support for a particular client and about the client itself. The prototype seamlessly integrates data from various data sources (email, RDB, ERP) and is also able to reason on it. We implemented rule based logic by using concepts defined in ontology. The system is able to reason about supporter experience and to propose the most suitable supporter for the support request that is received by email.

For implementation we used three fundamental layers of the SWT stack – RDF, ontology and logic layer. We conceptualized knowledge in an ontology using OWL language. RDF is being used as data interchange language, while logic was defined as a set of rules using SWRL language. Rules were constructed based on the concepts in the OWL ontology. The architecture of the developed prototype is shown on Figure 2.

By using SWT, we were able to represent knowledge that is used in user support process. We were able to integrate data from different sources by using RDF as data interchange format and description logic for integration process.

Figure 2. The layers of semantic web technologies

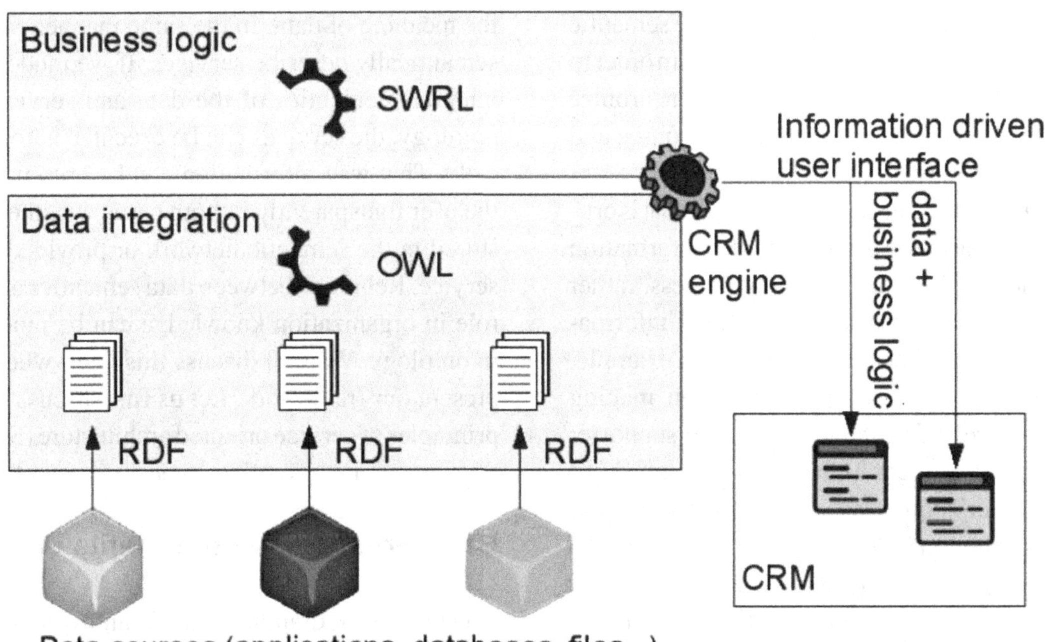

Because of the flexibility and expressiveness of SWT, this architecture can be used for implementing KMS for particularly any application domain.

INCORPORATING SERVICE ORIENTED ARCHITECTURE (SOA) CONCEPTS INTO KNOWLEDGE MANAGEMENT SYSTEM

Though SWT are very suitable for integration purposes, we identified some shortcomings in this approach. SWT are very flexible and we can transform practically any machine readable data into RDF and then process it based on the ontology. To be able to integrate data, we have to import it into the semantic network first. When the intention is not to reason on integrated data, but rather just to integrate it, there are other more suitable methods for data integration.

Because of the fact, that we have to import the data into the semantic network to be able to integrate it, there arise two main problems: (1) the size of the semantic network can grow at a very fast rate, because of this there can be performance issues and (2) by importing data into the semantic network, we basically replicate the data. In order to have accurate information, we have to synchronize the data between the originating data source and the semantic network.

In a KMS, we can have information, that is crucial for the reasoning process and also information that is not used for the reasoning process, rather it is used just for providing additional information to the user. Let us show this on a example. Suppose we want to support decision making process of selecting the most suitable supporter for a support request. To be able to reason about the supporter's competences, we need information about his previous experiences and education. To be able to propose a suitable supporter, we need information about the nature of the problem and competences of all the supporters.

Let us suppose that this information is sufficient for successful supporter selection. To be able to propose a supporter, we have to import this information into semantic network. While this information is sufficient for the reasoning process, the user, that uses KMS may have needs for additional information like contact information of the support requester, previous invoices for this particular client etc. Usually this information is already stored in some other information system and synchronization can result in high development costs and larger amount of processing.

Therefore we propose use of services to provide information that is not essential to reasoning process. That way we don't need to import a large amount of data into the semantic network. Instead of that, the data is being requested when the need for it arises. If we return to our example, when the knowledge system proposes a particular supporter, if the user has need to contact the customer (support requester), the service that provides customer contact information can be automatically executed and the user can be seamlessly presented with contact information.

Because the proposed KMS is based on semantic technologies, the data is described semantically. This means that, computers have an awareness of the meaning of data. In the same manner we can semantically describe services. If we model and integrate semantics of the data and services in ontology, the services can be executed automatically. That way information can be presented to the user transparently in both cases, whether it is stored in the semantic network or provided by a service. Relations between data semantics and its role in organization knowledge can be modeled in ontology. We will discuss this later, when we present our framework. Let us first discuss basic principles of service oriented architecture (SOA), that we are incorporating in our framework.

Base Principles and Benefits of SOA

Service oriented architecture is an evolutionary step from enterprise application integration (EAI). Main purpose and goal of both EAI and SOA is integration of information between several different information systems. EAI creates tight connections between different information systems in such way, that each information system imports data from other information systems. While this is fairly natural way of integration of information, it is often connected with high maintenance efforts and low level of reuse and flexibility.

Opposite to tightly coupled EAI, SOA introduces loosely coupled, distributed and flexible architecture. SOA introduces concepts of services. While EAI creates connections between each pair of applications, applications in SOA environment expose their data and also functionality in form of platform and program language independent services. Applications that need information or other applications functionality only have to query the service. By also exposing functionality greater level of reuse can be achieved.

According to [4] the key aspects of SOA are:

1. **Loose Coupling:** Services maintain a relationship that minimizes dependencies and only requires that they retain an awareness of each other;
2. **Service Contract:** A communications agreement, as defined collectively by one or more service descriptions and related documents;
3. **Autonomy:** Services have control over the logic they encapsulate;
4. **Abstraction:** Beyond what is described in the service contract, services hide logic from the outside world;
5. **Reusability:** Logic is divided into services with the intention of promoting reuse;
6. **Composability:** Collections of services can be coordinated and assembled to form composite services;
7. **Statelessness:** Services minimize retaining information specific to an activity, and
8. **Discoverability:** Services are designed to be outwardly descriptive so that they can be found and assessed via available discovery mechanisms.

SOA is basically a concept and is independent on the implementation technologies. When the term service oriented architecture is used, it mostly meant in a context of web services. In this manner, Erl defines contemporary SOA as SOA that is built around web service technologies (Erl, 2005). When we use the term SOA in this chapter, we actually mean contemporary SOA as defined by (Erl, 2005).

Using Semantic Web Services in SOA

Web service technologies mainly provide standards for functional and also non-functional description, e.g. quality of service, security, authorization. While they provide very good technical platform, they lack in providing semantics to the services. This results is worse than expected discovery, reuse and composition of web services. To overcome these issues, semantic web services (Erl, 2005) were introduced.

Semantic web services (SWS) combine concepts from semantic web and web services. As Grosof pointed out (Grosof, 2003) semantic web services can be understood in two ways: as (1) semantic [web services] and as (2) [semantic web] services. The former concept relies more on WS and is used for knowledge based service descriptions (discovery, execution, composition of WS), while the latter concentrates more on SW concepts and is used mainly for knowledge and information integration (refer to example provided in the beginning of this section). In our framework we use SWS in both contexts, as S[WS] for capturing IT support knowledge and supporting representation of organizational knowledge and as [SW]S for supporting representation of operational knowledge (classic KMS).

There are several approaches for implementing SWS, the most common are: WSMO, OWL-S and SAWSDL. There are slight differences in basic concepts, mainly because of two different aspects of SWS, we discussed earlier. WSMO and OWL-S follow [SW]S concept, while SAWSDL follows S[WS] concept. WSMO and OWL-S define their own ontologies and methods for service description, while SAWSDL uses accepted industry standards for description of services (WSDL, WS-* recommendations, BPEL) and links them with concepts defined in an ontology by annotating WSDL document. For more detail overview of SWS technologies, please refer to (Akkiraju, 2006).

In our framework, we use SAWSDL for defining SWS, mainly for these reasons: (1) they build on top of accepted industry standards for WS and are therefore fully compatible with current WS, (2) because they extend current description technologies, services can be deployed on well supported WS infrastructure, (3) organizations that already implemented SOA by using WS, can easily extend their current implementation with our framework, (4) semantic web services that are used in our framework, can normally be used in other non-semantic applications as plain WS (5) by just semantically annotating current WS, they can be modeled in our framework, providing knowledge based management of services.

INTEGRATION OF SEMANTICS ENABLED SOA INTO SEMANTIC WEB ENABLED KNOWLEDGE MANAGEMENT SYSTEM

Framework that we propose in this chapter builds on top of concepts we discussed above. We adopted concepts from semantic web and service orientation for building holistic KMS. We can define our framework in two functional parts. One functional part supports operational knowledge management, while the other functional part supports organizational and IT support knowledge management (as already discussed in introduction). The former functionality is used for supporting operative business processes, while the latter functional part is used for supporting management business processes.

Although our framework provides single knowledge base, we are going to describe our framework by separating it into two functional parts, we mentioned above. The functional part that supports operational knowledge is very similar to the architecture we described in section 2 and is shown on Figure 2. We propose using OWL ontologies for knowledge conceptualization and logic rules (SWRL) for additional reasoning. In this manner knowledge from particularly any domain can be represented. Data interchange is done in two ways. The information that is needed for reasoning purposes is transformed by agents into RDF format and then imported into the semantic network.

Information that is not essential for reasoning purposes is being provided by semantic web services. Because SWS provide semantic descriptions of the information they return, they can be modeled in an ontology. The role of the engine is to identify, which data is provided by RDF and which by SWS. If particular data is provided by SWS, engine executes SWS and seamlessly provides information to the user. This process is transparent to the user. Schema that captures both functional parts of the proposed framework is shown in Figure 3.

Second functional part is supporting organization wide information integration by using service oriented architecture. Standard web services provide mostly technical description and weak semantics. When the number of services increases, managing them can become a difficult job and one can quickly loose oversight over services. Our framework enables semantic description of web services and modeling them in ontology. That way better discovery and reuse of services can be achieved.

Main activities targeted by second functional part of our framework are: (1) enabling optimal

Figure 3. Proposed knowledge management framework

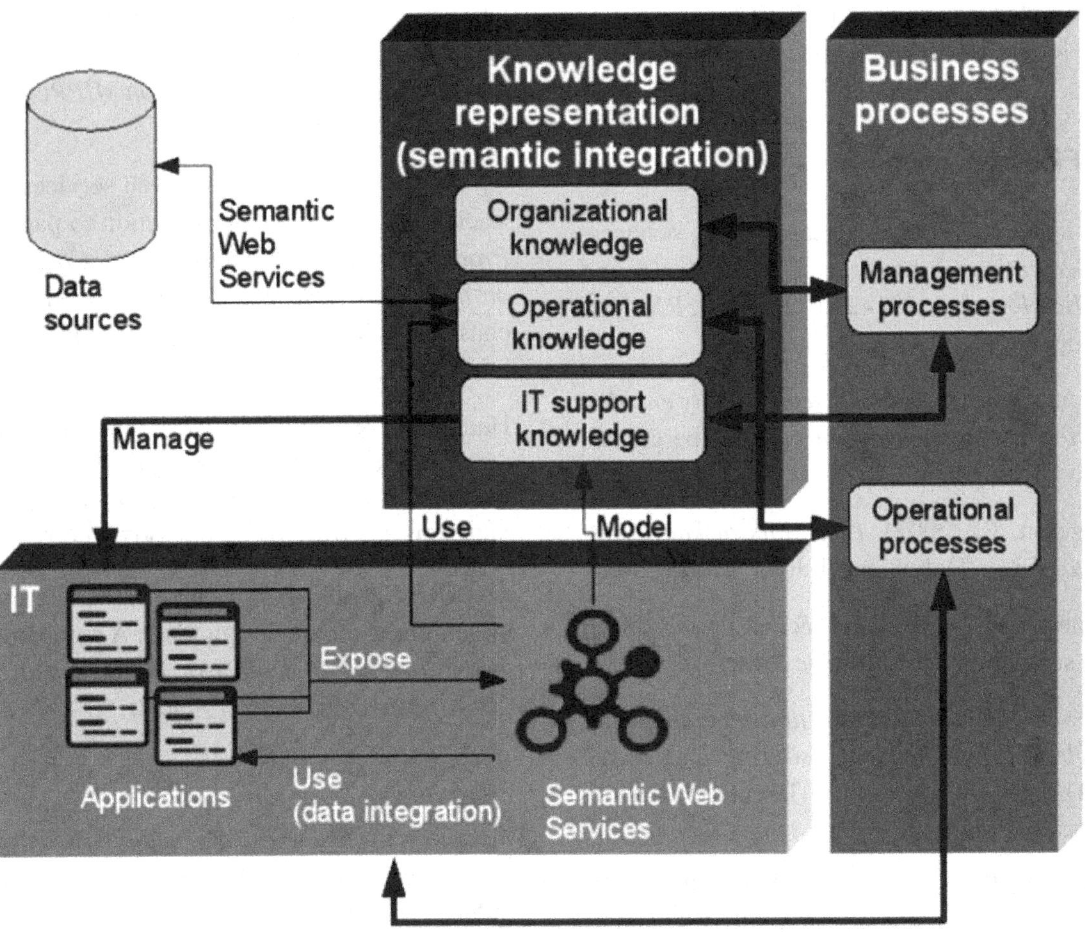

IT support for operational business processes, by having an overview over business processes, IT structure and services and (2) supporting management of services by providing semantic descriptions of services.

SWT enable us to model all three aspects of knowledge in organizations (operational, organizational and IT support knowledge) by using ontologies and to represent it in a single organization-wide knowledge base. The same services are used in both functional parts. Services developed for providing information to the operational knowledge management part can be used in other applications, which are not semantics enabled, and vice versa.

CONCLUSION

The framework we presented in this chapter provides intelligent knowledge management system for supporting operational processes and uses service oriented architecture for information integration. On the other hand, our framework also provides knowledge based management of service oriented architecture, which can increase discovery and reuse of service in service oriented architecture.

Proposed framework builds upon current industry standard technologies for implementing service oriented architecture; therefore it is adaptable in new and already established SOA environments. Because our framework is based on accepted industry standards, there is good support for underlying infrastructure technologies.

REFERENCES

Akkiraju, R. (2006). Semantic web services. In *Semantic web services – Theory, tools, and applications* (pp. 191–216). Hershey, PA: Idea Group.

Anicic, D. et al. (2007). *A semantically enabled service oriented architecture*. Heidelberg, Germany: Springer.

Bergeron, B. (2003). *Essentials of knowledge management*. Hoboken, NJ: John Wiley & Sons.

Berners-Lee, T., Hendler, J., & Lassila, O. (2001). The semantic web. *Scientific American*, 29–37.

Borst, W. (1997). *Construction of engineering ontologies for knowledge sharing and reuse*. (PhD thesis). University of Twente, Enschede, The Netherlands.

Davis, R., Shrobe, H., & Szolovits, P. (1993). Whait is a knowledge representation? *AI Magazine*, *14*, 17–33.

Erl, T. (2005). *Service-oriented architecture: concepts, technology, and design*. Upper Saddle River, NJ: Prentice Hall/Pearson PTR.

Garcia-Sanchez, F. et al. (2006). An ontology-based intelligent system for recruitment. *Expert Systems with Applications*, *31*, 236–248. doi:10.1016/j.eswa.2005.09.023

Grasic, B., & Podgorelec, V. (2008). Customer relationship management system architecture based on semantic web technologies. In *Proceedings of the 31st International Convention MIPRO 2008*, (pp. 204-209). MIPRO.

Grosof, B. (2003). Semantic web services: Obstacles and attractions, introduction to panel. In *Proceedings of 12th International Conference on the World Wide Web*. Retrieved from http://ebusiness.mit.edu/bgrosof/paps/talk-sws-panel-intro-www2003.pdf

Huang, N., & Diao, S. (2008). Ontology-based enterprise knowledge integration. *Robotics and Computer-integrated Manufacturing*, *24*(4), 562–571. doi:10.1016/j.rcim.2007.07.007

Lo, W., & Choobineh, J. (1999). Knowledge-based systems as database design tools: A comparative study. *Journal of Database Management*, *10*, 26–40. doi:10.4018/jdm.1999070103

Rajasekaran, P., Miller, J., Verma, K., & Sheth, A. (2005). *Enhancing web services description and discovery to facilitate composition*. Heidelberg, Germany: Springer. doi:10.1007/978-3-540-30581-1_6

Trastour, D., Bartolini, C., & Preist, C. (2003). Semantic web support for the B2B e-commerce pre-contractual lifecycle. *Computer Networks*, *42*, 661–673. doi:10.1016/S1389-1286(03)00229-9

Zack, M., McKeen, J., & Singh, S. (2009). Knowledge management and organizational performance: An exploratory analysis. *Journal of Knowledge Management*, *13*(6), 392–409. doi:10.1108/13673270910997088

Chapter 13
Universality and Communicability in Computer Animation

Francisco V. Cipolla-Ficarra
ALAIPO – AINCI, Spain and Italy

Miguel Cipolla-Ficarra
ALAIPO – AINCI, Spain and Italy

ABSTRACT

The current chapter presents the results of the heuristic evaluation of the landscape and digital contexts in computer animations where there is a combination of 2D and 3D images. In addition, a series of strategies is presented to be followed at the moment of generating computer animations to cut down the production costs at the stage of inserting the digital characters in an environment and a context. Finally, the isotopyes are shown that exists in the landscape to reach universality and communicability of the message without resorting to the oral or written word.

INTRODUCTION

One of the main goals of communicability in computer animation is reaching the universality of the message with low costs and a high artistic quality. In this sense the combination of techniques and methods stemming from 2D and 3D animation have yielded excellent artistic results, especially in the movie sector, with films such as Mary Poppins or Roger Rabbit, to mention two examples. Evidently, in the first example there is no use of computers as in the second film. However, the world diffusion of both films has consolidated with the passing of years, until being considered as a "cult classic" film by millions of people along the years. The combination of these forms of animation, real images combined with computer generated images, has been growing in the first decade of the new millennium, due to the reduction of the cost of hardware: digital picture

DOI: 10.4018/978-1-4666-4490-8.ch013

cameras, 3D scanner, digital video camera, etc. (Baskinger, 2008; Laurel, 2004; Kerlow, 2009).

The landscape and the digital contexts inside which is developed the narration of the main actors may be totally real, unreal and mixed or hybrid (Laurel, 2004). We focus on this latter case in the current research, taking as analysis the 78 episodes of the television series "Minuscule" (www.minuscule.tv). Our universe of study are all the episodes with a duration of 383 minutes. In it can be seen the different stories developed from the members of a small-sized animal kingdom. This entertaining animated series is sure to capture every children and adult imagination (Reeves & Nass, 1996; Veltman, 2006). as it follows the day-to-day life of a range of charming and adorable insects. In each 3 to 5 minute episode, the insects interact with each other in ways that mimic comical human behaviour. The audio is a combination of genuine insect and ambient recordings, with added synthesized buzzings generated from sound effects such as cars, helicopters, and aircraft engines. In each episode 'insect-like' words and sound effects replace normal dialogue.

As a rule, these three dimensional insects are incorporated into real landscapes or a digital context of an excellent visual quality (Cipolla-Ficarra, Cipolla-Ficarra, & Harder, 2008). Aside from the creative factor which takes us closer to the real world through an emulation or simulation of reality (both terms are not synonymous), currently and thanks to the 3D and 2D commercial software, a great variety of techniques can be used to make the animations easier to create and faster to render with which the production costs are cut (Schweppe, 2011). However, it is necessary to join to this cost-time equation the quality of the communication (Vicente, 2003) and the universality of the message.

CONTEXT FOR COMPUTER ANIMATION

At the moment of elaborating contexts for the unreal bidimensional or three-dimensional characters or real characters, it is necessary to consider the environments as scenarios where the main and secondary characters act in keeping with a script or storyboard and a set of norms and rules pre-established beforehand (Laurel, 2004; Rosenbloom, 1999; Cipolla-Ficarra, 2008). Inside

Figure 1. Minuscule TV episodes. Among the more commonly recurring insect characters are ants, grasshoppers, flies, ladybugs, spiders, and snails. Other occasional insect characters include bees, butterflies, caterpillars, cicadas, dung beetles, dragonflies, mosquitoes, and wasps.

these rules is the creative factor which is not necessarily synonymous with artistic originality. On the contrary, sometimes we can come across with contexts or scenarios where characters move which are rehashes of other works of classical cinematographic animation in black and white. These operations of copying and sticking from the illustrators destroy the originality of an animated production, since its cornerstone is always the analogical support, that is, paper (Cipolla-Ficarra & Cipolla-Ficarra, 2009). The interactive design and its derivations in both the dynamic and static means are no exception to this rule.

Artistic direction means who decides inside an audio-visual production, including computer animations, the look that a film will have. When we talk of look, we mean the colours, the type of lightning, the textures, the components or objects, basic and accessory inside the scenes, etc. (Kerlow, 2009; Schweppe, et al., 2011 & Lok, 2004). Obviously, the design styles turn out to be one of the main tasks inside the artistic direction which must establish the highest number of isotopyes inside the different scenes which make up animation in order to reach a great communicability in the least possible time.

Each one of the elements which nake up the scene must keep among themselves the maximum coherence in order to generate these isotopy lines (Cipolla-Ficarra, Cipolla-Ficarra & Harder, 2008; Lok, 2004). For instance, if the characters for a children audience are in a happy place, one can combine white light, warm colours, rounded shapes of the objects. An excellent example in this sense is the 3D animation series "Chuggington Trains" (www.ludorum.com). Even the integration of the trains with the environment is perfect given the excellent degree of realism that we find in the plants, the sky, the special effects, (the water steam in the old locomotives, the twinkle of sparks in the braking of the wheels, etc.), the animals, etc. In contrast, if the goal is to achieve a sinister and dark space, we can use dark textures, soft lights and seedy furniture, cobwebs, etc, In few words, the elements of the scenes contribute to the mood that must transmit the direct and indirect messages of the main and secondary characters. The components of the scenarios can be created one by one if they have to gather a set of special characteristics as can be the animation of the inanimate objects in daily life, or rather we can resort to the 2D or 3D bookshops either of free access or not.

The issue of the colour and the textures is very important to create these lines of the sense that is seen through the isootopies (Cipolla-Ficarra, 2008). The first component, colour, is very wide to be analyzed and has been approached from several points of view in the globalization of interactive design. The interested reader may go deeper into these issues in the following bibliographical references (Styliaras, Koukopoulos & Lazarinis, 2011; Cipolla-Ficarra, et al. 2011).

With regard to the textures, these can help to the interpretation of the characters. For instance, placing a texture of real tissue on a shirt one can considerably increase the realism of the message it transmits, in contrast to the use of plastic textures, as it can be seen in a myriad computer animations (Cipolla-Ficarra & Cipolla-Ficarra, 2009). whether it is for the small screen, that is, television, or the big screen, cinema . Some examples where have not been taken into account the textile realism of the clothes are in the following films and TV series: Pocoyo, Zumbers, Toy Story, etc. In contrast we have an excellent example of the use of woollen textures, in the 3D characters of the children series "The Adventures of Piggley Winks" (www.jakers.co.uk). Also here the natural environment and the landscape of rural Ireland has been considered from a realistic perspective by including 2D elements of digital photography such as can be the sky and the clouds, the textures of bushy vegetation where secondary characters move, such as the sheep of the farm, etc.

However, the integration of the 2D and the 3D of the textures of the context with nature does not have a 100% quality if it is considered from a synchronic perspective in the second decade of the new millennium (Cipolla-Ficarra & Cipolla-Ficarra, 2009). In these cases, in which is used the technique of direct observation for the evaluation, the diachronic aspect can be left out since the series was made in the first decade of the new millennium.

A visual strategy so that the characters and the environment don't get out of kilter, is using colours that complement each other but which are far away from each other in the colour scale. Not for nothing, in the series for children created with computer animations, the characters usually have warm colours (red, yellow, orange, etc.) and their context cold colours (the green of vegetation and the blue of the sky or the sea, for instance). This is a simplified solution valid for the first works of animation of the last century, so called short films. Currently it is necessary to go deeper into the colour issue and the textures before applying them to the characters. Fortunately, the new productions of computer animations as those centres who devote themselves to serious non-mercantilist teaching lead the future professionals to work with colours in the pre-production stage, generating a script or storyboard of the prevailing colours along the animation. It is a simple and economic method to obtain an excellent communicability in computer animations.

The same as the 2D and 3D object bookshops, there are bookshops of textures. As a rule the textures are bitmap images stemming from digital photography or scanner, but they can also stem from vectorial images (Figures 2 and 3).

Figure 2. The image of a bitmap file of a real tissue which may be taken to an electronic loom for its real production (dobbycad™, www.tex-cad.com)

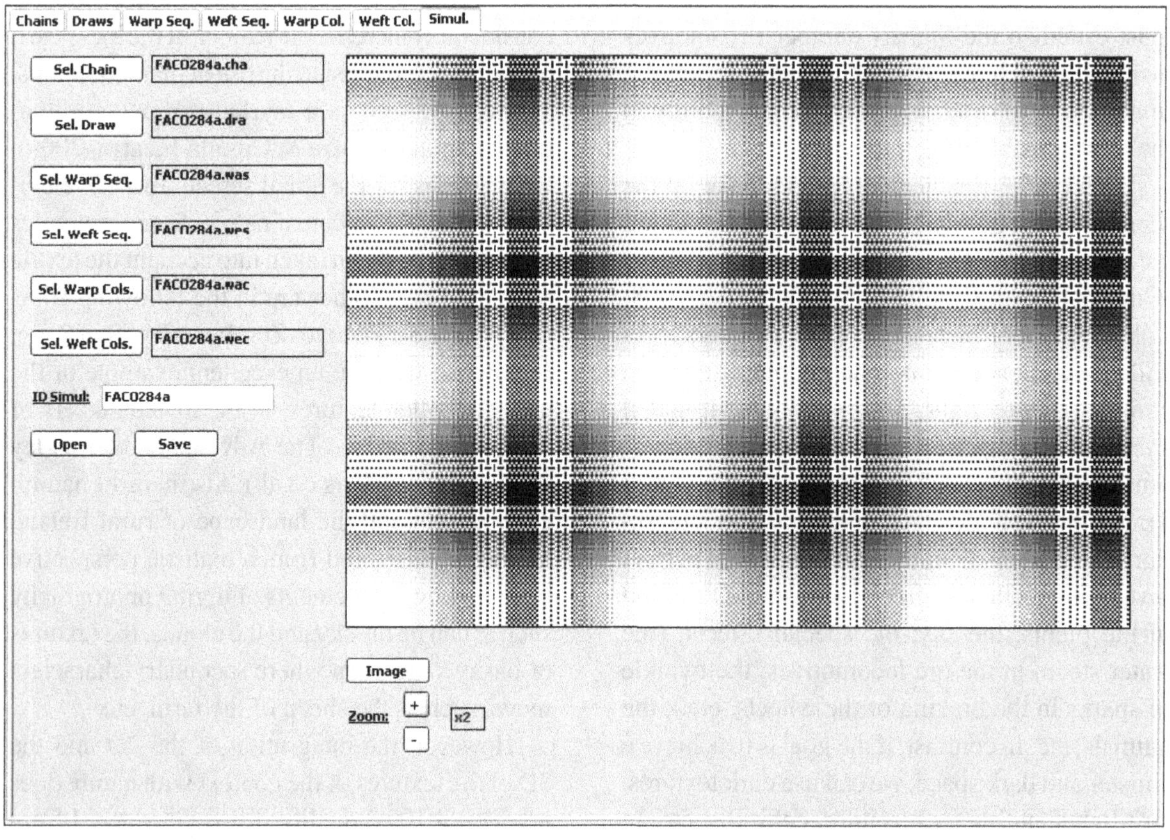

Figure 3. The image of a texture where the combinations of colours and shapes generate a visual illusion which can annoy the viewer if it is applied as texture on the clothes of the characters, for instance

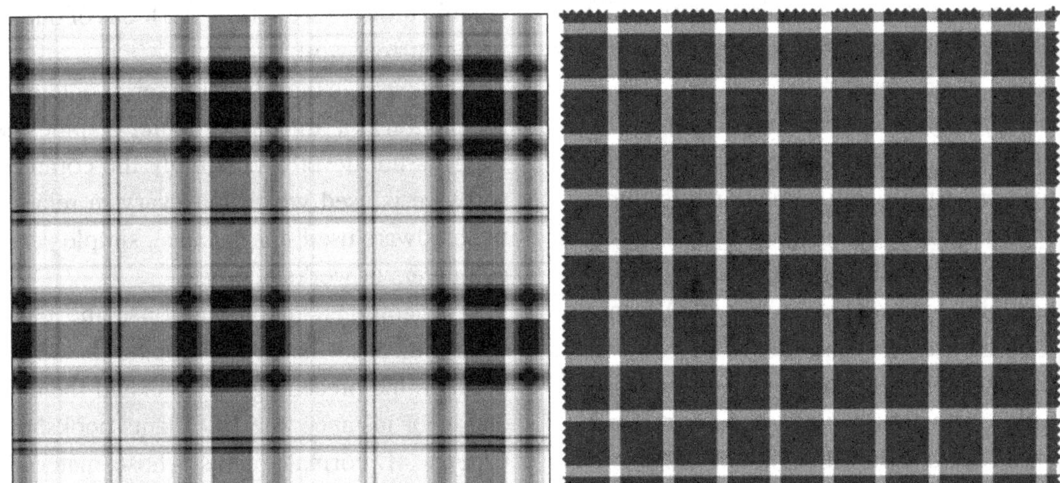

Evidently, images which can be modified (brilliance, colour, contrast, etc.) with self-edition programmes, before their use in animations. These modifications increase the chances of realism and/or communicability.

HUMAN AND TECHNICAL STRATEGIES FOR SKY, LAND AND PLANTS

A simple way used in the modelling of a sky is to insert images of real photographs inside a semisphere or dome (Kerlow, 2009). The ideal thing is that the sky has clouds. In this regard there are places of our planet where the different kinds of clouds (cumulus, stratus, cirrus, etc) are generated in a fast way and an interesting digital file of said clouds can be made up.

Once this sky with clouds is placed inside the semisphere, the digital photograph which becomes a texture will appear to the eye of the observer as a sky, regardless of where the camera is pointing. It is important that this sky texture doesn't accept shadows from the characters and/or objects of the scenes.

Another way to increase realism and avoid shadows is a directional light which shines on the whole dome, always looking for an agreeable and homogeneous lightening. Currently the commercial programmes of international diffusion include a wide range of algorithms to create atmospheric effects to increase the realism of the elements which make up the sky. Now this smesphere must join the ground. A way to do it without prompting a sudden cut in the horizon is through a foggy special effect. Another way is inserting mountains, buildings, rivers, trees, etc. which allows to break the horizontality between the semisphere and the land.

Also on land surface one can resort to deformation algorithms such as can be the fractals so that new vortexes are randomly introduced in each one of the rectangles or mosaics that make up the ground. These vortexes are at different heights to gain in realism in the horizontality of the scenes. Evidently, here it is also possible to resort to digital photography to introduce textures of the new world.

The mountains as elements for the break-up of the horizontal plane are very easy to generate because they are cones with noise effects on the surfaces. Then transformation forces can be applied such as a greater or lower escalation in the horizontal and/or vertical plane, with which variety is gained, once they are aligned in the background of the image.

One of the key elements of graphic computing has been the incorporation of physicists into R&D teams to improve the reality simulation algorithms. Although the human factors in some realities of Southern Europe finally generated caliphs ghettos with their platforms and ivory towers (Vicente, 2003; Cipolla-Ficarra, et al., 2011).

The opposite is at the other side of the North Atlantic, the formation of motley teams in research would yield better results than in the Old World, especially between 1990-2010. They "do there and here we explain what they do" (Ficarra, 1993). sentence by one of the members of the Eurographics (www.eg.org) sums up the scientific reality of the old continent.

The great exception is the good use of the inventions in international commercial computer graphics which we have in the French audiovisual industry (i.e., Minuscule).

This poor reality in results of computer graphics development is not due to the lack of financial resources (a sector which has enjoyed, enjoys and will enjoy good health because of the European subventions in Spain or Portugal, for instance) but rather the ultra nationalistic endogamic factor in the making of the teams of research and development (Cipolla-Ficarra, et al., 2011; Cipolla-Ficarra, Nicol & Cipolla-Ficarra, 2010). A reality which is light years away in the American continent, for instance.

Aside from the human factors, physics has given to the natural context a field of research to improve the generation of computer images in 2D and 3D where the human eye can't distinguish whether the images have been taken with a video camera or were made with the computer (Mayo, 2007; Prusinkiewicz, 2000). In this excellent combination we are setting the focus of our study in the current work.

Obviously in the television series or television production as a rule the computer graphics (software) is not developed, simply the commercial software is used which may vary in relation to the hardware used, for instance, simple personal computers or workstations.

The commercial products use the physical environment as media to compare the advances between the preceding versions and the current ones. For instance, the HQ Plants bookshops in Cinema 4D format, plants whose materials or textures ready for Advanced Reader functions and VRay linked to the 2 Side Material (www.vrayforc4d.net). Another example of combination of bookshops and commercial software may be the vegetation stemming from XFrog (www.xfrog.com) incorporated in Maya (usa.autodesk.com/maya) and the Oceania bookshop (www.xfrog.com) with the Maya rendering.

In few words, the investment in commercial software is minimal compared with the high need of creativity in the animated scripts of our universe of study.

However, in several fields of the university graphic computing of Southern Europe still persists the philosophy mentioned earlier: "do there and here we explain what they do" (Ficarra, 1993).

In Figure 4, we present the results of the communicability and the universality of the analyzed episodes of Minuscule (list of 78 French titles in the Appendix). The minimal value is 0 and the maximum is 10 (puntuation).

We have also incorporated the creative factor, dividing it between the adult and children audience (Figure 5). The first value in horizontal bar (blue) is the result of the adult audience. The

Figure 4. Universability and communicability

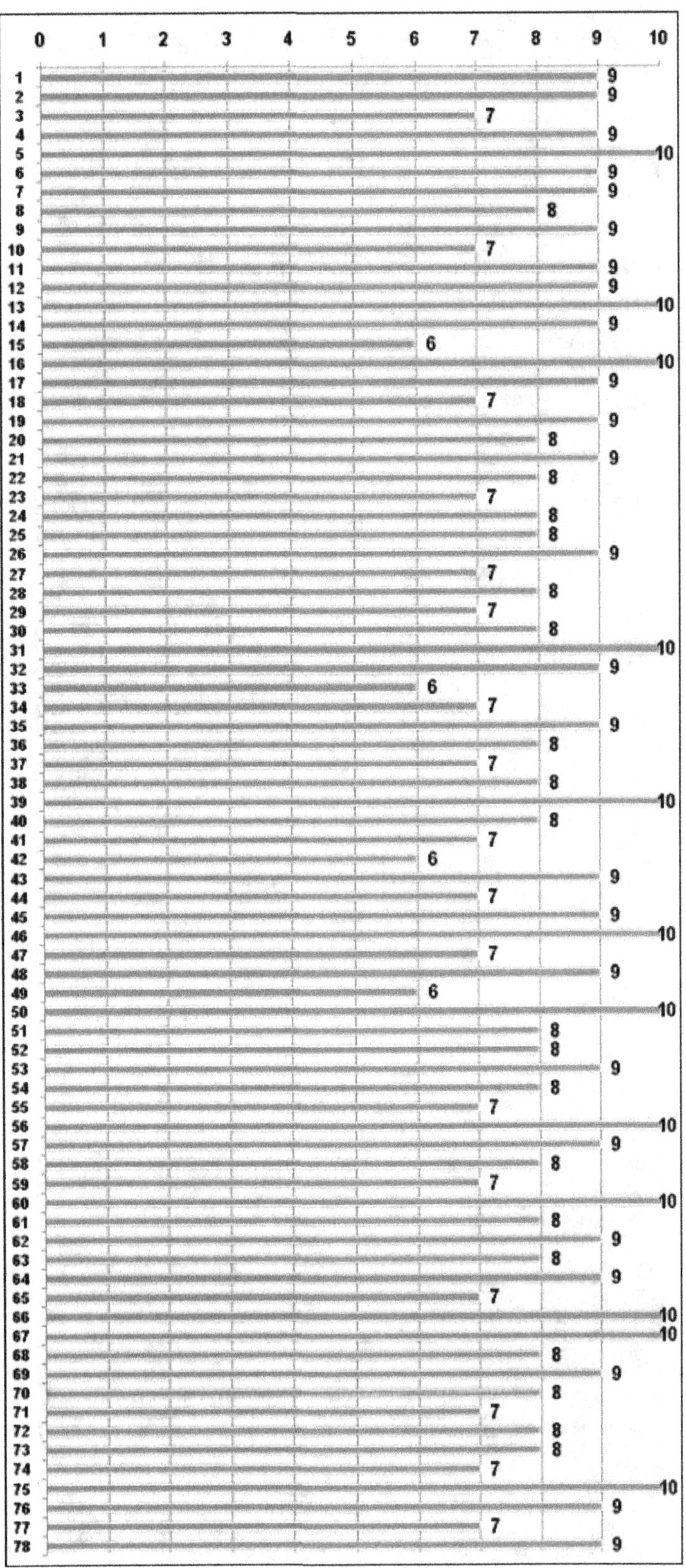

Figure 5. Creativity factor for adult and children

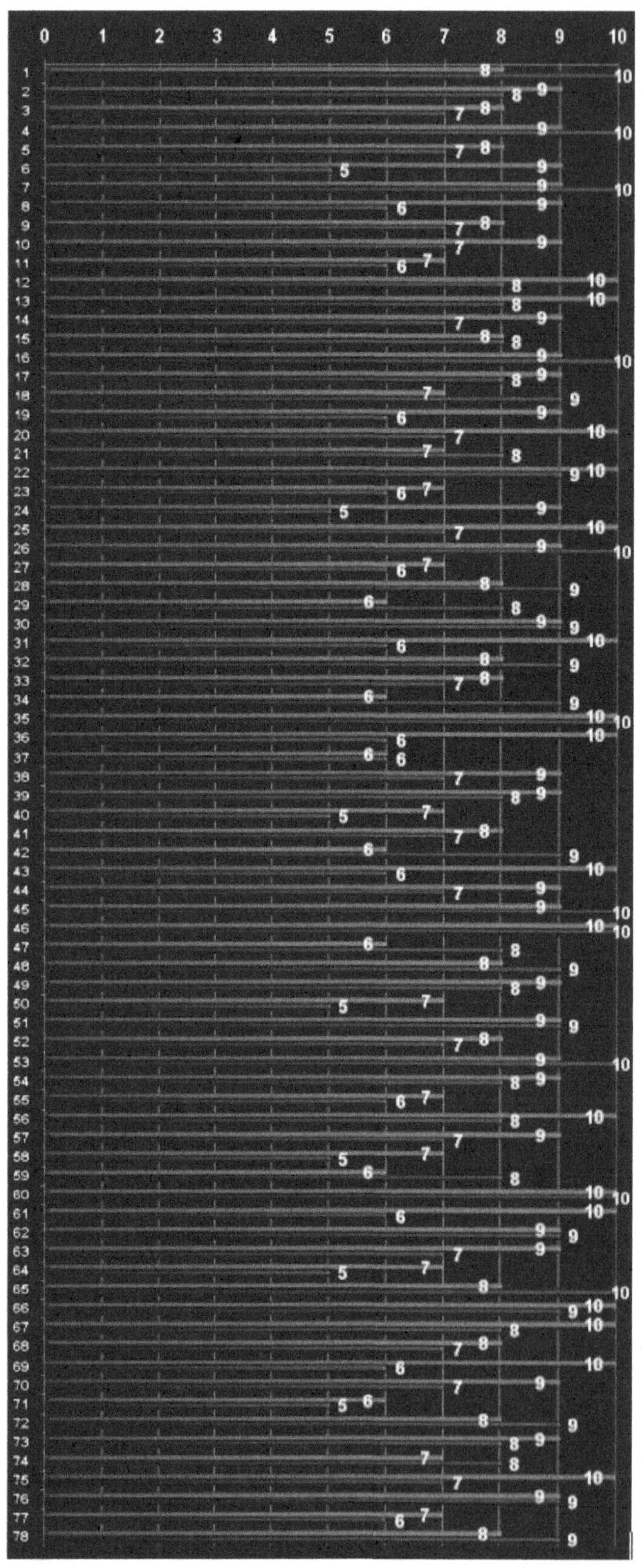

second number in horizontal bar (red) is the result of the children audience. All the episodes analysed are in numerical order –left column.

LESSONS LEARNED AND FUTURE WORKS

The tracing of isotopies is essential to reach the maximum of communicability and universality of the messages that are based only on the static or moving images, without resorting to audio. The audio, in this kind of work which responds to the factors of physics or the nature (the buzzing of a gnat, the noise of the big flies which constantly crash against the mirrors, etc.) linked to the natural registration of the singing of the birds, water passing through the stones in a stream, the sea waves hitting the stones of the coast, etc., serve to strengthen the veracity effects of the image, even if it was computer generated. Now the problem that has always arisen are the original or creative scripts or storyboards, whether it is in productions of computer animations such as short films, the episodes of a TV series of the full-length films of the big screen in the movies. This is the Achilles tendon in many artists in the European Mediterranean who devote themselves to the combination of 2D and 3D. Besides, the "copy and paste" without mentioning the sources is something "natural", inside and outside certain universities, because there isn't in some communities a legislation which thoroughly tutors the authors. In the case there was, it is simply not applied. That is, negative human factors which damage the production of 2D and 3D animation with a universal scope. Fortunately, our universe of study has been an excellent exception to this reality. In future works we want to analyze the humoristic factor and its influence on communicability, working with this same set of episodes among the different audiences, adults (housewives, salesmen in small towns, teachers, students of primary, secondary and university level) inside a same region and the children audience or with a pre-school age but belonging to several continents.

CONCLUSION

The universe of study and the reached results show that the level of quality is optimal in some European computer animation works of the new millennium, upon evaluating landscape and digital contexts. The speed of acceptance or rejection of the characters is also related to the context. The greater quality we have in the components of the graphics computing of the context, the least is the rejection 2D and/or 3D characters, even though they have defects in the modeling or the animation of the movements. The high current quality in the 2D and/or 3D animation productions is due to the reduction of the cost of the commercial software and the hardware. Now the reduction factor of the production costs of computer animations has been relegated by creativity. That is, creativity is one of the main goals to reach, since the techniques and production methods for users of personal computers have boosted domestic but professional spread of images in movement. However, creativity must be linked to communicability and the universality of the message. Creativity that does not always arise in the environments of public and private studies, but rather in the constant experimentations of the motley professionals of the digital images and above all of observation. Direct observation still remains one of the most important techniques, not only for heuristic evaluation, but also for the examination or analysis of communicability and creativity, when there is a combination of real images (video or photography, for instance) and those in 2D and 3D from the computer. In this sense, the expert in communicability for this combination of images must have a wide background of knowledge and/or experience of the formal and factual sciences, especially those which stem from computer graphics, computer animations, photography, video, cinema, television, radio, literature among others. Although the new technological horizons for the images that simulate or emulate reality are important, and legislative tutoring of creativity is also important. If creativity disappears, communicability and universality will also disappear in this kind of audiovisual products that we have analyzed.

REFERENCES

Baskinger, M. (2008). Pencils before pixels: A primer in hand-generated sketiching. *Interaction*, *15*(2), 28–36. doi:10.1145/1340961.1340969

Cipolla-Ficarra, F. (2008). Communicability design and evaluation in cultural and ecological multimedia systems. In *Proceedings of ACM Multimedia '08*. New York: ACM Press.

Cipolla-Ficarra, F., et al. (2011). Handbook of computational informatics, social factors and new information technologies: Hypermedia perspectives and avant-garde experiencies in the era of communicability expansion. Bergamo, Italy: Blue Herons Ed.s.

Cipolla-Ficarra, F., & Cipolla-Ficarra, M. (2009). *Computer animation and communicability in multimedia system: A trichotomy evaluation. studies in computational intelligence*. Heidelberg, Germany: Springer.

Cipolla-Ficarra, F., Cipolla-Ficarra, M., & Harder, T. (2008). Realism and cultural layout in tourism and video games multimedia systems. In *Proceedings of 1st ACM International Workshop on Communicability, Design and Evaluation in Cultural and Ecological Multimedia System*. New York: ACM Press.

Cipolla-Ficarra, F., Nicol, E., & Cipolla-Ficarra, M. (2010). Research and development: Business into transfer information and communication technology. In *Proceedings of First International Conference on Advances in New Technologies, Interactive Interfaces and Communicability – ADNTIIC 2010* (LNCS), (Vol. 6616, pp. 44-61). Berlin: Springer.

Ficarra, F. (1993). Eurographics. *PressGraph-Imaging*, *3*, 22–30.

Kerlow, I. (2009). *The art of 3D computer animation and effects*. New York: John Wiley.

Laurel, B. (2004). Narrative construction as play. *Interaction*, *11*(5), 75–76. doi:10.1145/1015530.1015568

Lok, B. (2004). Toward the merging of real and virtual spaces. *Communications of the ACM*, *47*(8), 49–53. doi:10.1145/1012037.1012061

Mayo, M. (2007). Games for science and engineering education. *Communications of the ACM*, *50*(7), 30–35. doi:10.1145/1272516.1272536

Prusinkiewicz, P. (2000). Simulation modeling of plants and plant ecosystems. *Communications of the ACM*, *43*(7), 84–93. doi:10.1145/341852.341867

Reeves, B., & Nass, C. (1996). *The media equation: How people treat computers, television, and new media like real people and places*. Cambridge, UK: Cambridge University Press.

Rosenbloom, A. (1999). Toward an image indistiguishable from reality. *Communications of the ACM*, *42*(8), 28–30. doi:10.1145/310930.310960

Schweppe, M. et al. (2011). Adapting a virtual world for theatrical performance. *IEEE Computer*, *44*(12), 33–38. doi:10.1109/MC.2011.354

Styliaras, G., Koukopoulos, D., & Lazarinis, F. (2011). *Handbook of research on technologies and cultural heritage: Applications and environments*. Hershey, PA: IGI Global.

Veltman, K. (2006). *Undestanding new media: Augmented knowledge and culture*. Alberta, Canada: University of Calgary Press.

Vicente, K. (2003). *The human factor*. New York: Routledge.

APPENDIX

Table 1. Minuscule – episodes assessed (in French)

1. La coccinelle	21. Libellules	41. La bonne graine	60. À tes souhaits
2. Catapulte	22. Cigale do Brazil	42. La chenille et le ruisseau	61. Mon beau Sapin
3. Bouse de là	23. Hoquet	43. Un radiateur pour deux	62. Top départ
4. Deux chenilles	24. Tomate cerise	44. Patrouille de bzzz	63. Mouche bizarre
5. Les Fourmis	25. Sans coquille	45. Le chant des cigales	64. Torpedo
6. Prisonnière	26. Bananes	46. Petit trouillard	65. Toiles d'intérieur
7. Rêve d'escargot	27. Les vers sont dans la pomme	47. Escargot qui roule n'amasse pas mousse	66. L'union fait la force
8. Love story	28. Le convoi	48. L'attaque de la sucette rose	67. Un après-midi de moustique
9. Grasse matinée	29. Bouse au carré	49. L'heure de la sieste	68. Grosse mouche bleue
10. Top guêpe	30. Fourmis à la noix	50. Moche	69. Pot de colle
11. La nouille	31. Hyperactive	51. Petit repas entre mouches	70. La conserve
12. Le pont de la rivière Bzzz	32. Le moustique	52. Narcisso	71. Nuit blanche
13. Zzzeplin	33. Salade	53. Coccinelles	72. Mouche folle
14. Une bonne éducation	34. Il pleut il mouille c'est la fête à l'escargouille	54. Le Totem	73. Poule mouillée
15. Rêve de chenille	35. A fond la caisse	55. L'évasion	74. La horde sauvage
16. Chewing gum	36. Pique nique	56. Tenace	75. Halloween parano
17. Un monde de brutes	37. Une nuit dehors	57. Pas de chance	76. Hop
18. Coup de vent	38. Tire au flanc	58. King size camembert	77. Fourmi rose
19. Silence	39. Ventilo	59. Chenille des villes papillon des champs	78. C'est noël
20. La fourmilière infernale	40. La chenille qui voulait voir la mer		

Chapter 14
Learning by Means of an Interactive Multimodal Environment

Serena Zanolla
Department of Mathematics and Computer Science, University of Udine, Italy

Antonio Rodà
Department of Information Engineering, University of Padova, Italy

Sergio Canazza
Department of Information Engineering, University of Padova, Italy

Gian Luca Foresti
Department of Mathematics and Computer Science, University of Udine, Italy

ABSTRACT

This chapter presents the Stanza Logo-Motoria, an Interactive Multimodal Environment (IME) for learning, which the authors have been developing and experimenting with since 2009 in several educational institutions. The aim of this chapter is a) to describe the activities carried out by the Resonant Memory, the first application for the Stanza Logo-Motoria, b) to illustrate the validation protocol of the system used as a listening tool for learning English as a Second Language (ESL), and finally, c) to document the positive partial results that demonstrate the improvement in ESL oral comprehension in pupils using the Stanza Logo-Motoria. The authors have also found that this environment can offer pupils: a) a truly interactive multimodal learning experience, b) a social opportunity for learning among children, and c) an intrinsically motivating experience.

INTRODUCTION

Although the verbal mode of instruction has long dominated education, our research has focused on Interactive Multimodal Environments (IMEs), especially those that combine auditory and pictorial representations of knowledge, because pupils' understanding can be enhanced by the addition of non-verbal knowledge representations to verbal explanations (Moreno & Mayer, 2007). The following are just a few examples of IMEs which, in recent years, have been developed in order to implement new modalities of learning in physical spaces.

DOI: 10.4018/978-1-4666-4490-8.ch014

SOUND=SPACE (Almeida, et al., 2008) was one of the first examples of using an IME with children. It is an interactive multi-user musical environment in which users (in particular groups with special needs) influence the sound production by moving in an empty space surveyed by an ultrasonic echolocation system.

In the area of education and entertainment, Krueger explored the full-body interaction in a room-sized space (Krueger, Gionfriddo & Hinrichsen, 1985). His applications (specifically Videoplace) have been used in the educational field as shared workspaces, scientific exploration for children, and physical therapy.

The interactive physical spaces were further explored by Davenport and Friedlander (Davenport & Friedlander, 1995) who developed the Wheel of Life which was an interactive world situated in a real space; the space contained a narrative which might be actualized by the actions of the visitor moving through it. The room used light, sound, video, and computer displays.

Another important perceptually-based and interactive story environment was the KidsRoom (Bobick, et al., 1999) which re-created a special bedroom for children. Two of the bedroom walls resembled the real walls; the other two were large video projection screens where images were back-projected. Six computers controlled the room, coloured lights on the ceiling, and four loudspeakers. Four video cameras and one microphone were installed. The goal of this system was to stimulate a child's imagination by using images and sound in order to transform the space into a fantasy world.

Finally, it is very interesting to mention the Hazard Room Game (Fails, et al., 2005) a game implemented both in desktop and physical environments, that focused on teaching children about environmental health hazards. The main goal of this project was to investigate, in direct comparison, the desktop and physical educational environments in the domain of young children's learning. The final results (obtained by means of qualitative and quantitative measurements) proved the advantages for physical environments over desktop environments.

In this chapter we will describe the Stanza Logo-Motoria (Camurri, et al., 2010) an IME for learning, which is used - as an alternative/additional tool for teaching - in several educational institutions, where we are performing a lot of interactive activities for schoolchildren and conducting an experimentation (which we will fully explain in the paragraph entitled "Validation Protocol of the Stanza Logo-Motoria"). With the Stanza Logo-Motoria it is possible to actualize an IME in which, whatever happens depends on the learner's actions (Moreno & Mayer, 2007). This system, which we will describe in the paragraph entitled "The Stanza Logo-Motoria", takes a broad empty space and, using video tracking techniques, fills the environment with sound events and images; the user's presence inside the "interactive space" triggers the playback of the audio/visual content.

Unlike the IMEs that we have briefly illustrated above, the Stanza Logo-Motoria uses standard hardware and input/output conventional peripheral devices such as a webcam, two loudspeakers and a video projector. The easy implementation of the system and the low cost of both the hardware and the software allow the use of the system on the part of public schools with real classes of schoolchildren. The modular software architecture enables users to adapt the environment to different educational contexts, for example, learning a second language, studying History, or improving their spatial ability. In the following paragraphs we will explain why, when, and how we use the Stanza Logo-Motoria in an educational environment such as the primary school (Figure 1).

Learning Needs for Interactivity

The school staff often faces cases of learning difficulties, problematic relationships, and school failures, experiencing a sense of helplessness since

Figure 1. Learning in the Stanza Logo-Motoria

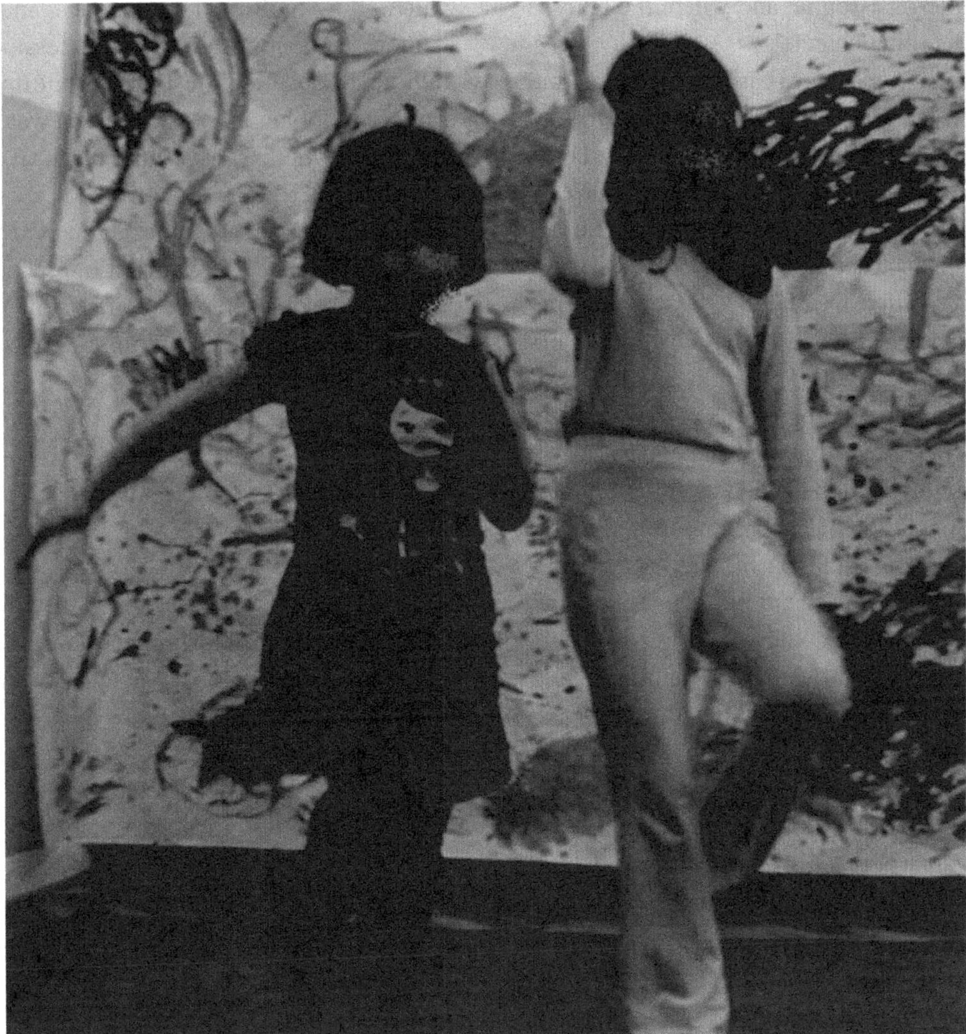

the traditional methodology of teaching scarcely provides specific criteria on how to deal with these issues. Nowadays there is the awareness that teaching has to be more student-centered and learning does not automatically occur when information is presented to a child. In order to better deal with the real needs of the pupils, innovative didactic approaches are required.

Technology can help teachers by offering a wide range of tools, such as computers, interactive whiteboards, wireless tablets, whose level of interactivity depends on how much children participate in the activities. Although these experiences can supply creative learning/teaching possibilities, they lack an important element: the physical environment. A critical part of a child's early cognitive development is in interaction with the physical world, within a social and cultural environment (Vygotsky, 1986). The enactive approach (Bruner, 1966; Marturana & Varela, 1980; Holton, 2010) attests that much knowledge comes through action within an environment and it is constructed on motor skills; enactive knowledge is based on motor skills: the representations are gained "by doing" and "doing" is the tool for learning (Bruner, 1968). This idea can help schoolteachers to face the specific learning difficulties of pupils, given that teaching is considered as a co-construction in which the active participation of the learner is essential and where the body is used as a learning channel.

Learning is not a mere transfer of information, whereas in learning processes the fundamental condition is the involvement of the learner's body. Educators, considering "embodiment", have to take the lead in using new enactive and embodied tools for instruction (Holton, 2010). Today, cognitive growth can occur also by means of the interaction between basic human capabilities and new technologies that are used as amplifiers of these capabilities (Bruner, 1968). Consequently the technological learning environments, which do not support the use of body and gesture, can limit what and how children learn. Therefore computer-based learning environments that do not support sensory-motor actions cannot facilitate learning (Roth & Lawless, 2001).

The Stanza Logo-Motoria (Zanolla, et al., 2011a) answers the need of interactivity by offering learners an IME in which gestures and the movement of the body in space trigger the audio/visual contents. In this environment the listener is a participant, whose goal is to extract meaning and respond at the same time, such as in real life where the input is more various and "interactional".

Learning Needs for Multimodality

According to the theory of multiple intelligences (Gardner, 1983) the traditional teaching methods, often based only on logical-mathematical and linguistic intelligences, disregard whoever uses other cognitive abilities more (spatial, bodily-kinaesthetic, visual). This theory validates teachers' everyday experience since students think and learn in many different ways, and leads educators to use a multimodal methodological approach which means that schoolchildren, for instance, are presented with a verbal representation of the content and the corresponding visual representation. The pedagogical implications of this theory include the organization of teaching strategies, which allow multimodal dynamics, and the use of more authentic methods of assessment than traditional educational testing. Despite this theory, primary schoolchildren encounter fewer learning situations where senses and physical, spatial, and visual activities are involved. By offering verbal and non-verbal information synchronized in time and space, the Stanza Logo-Motoria has a mixed-modality presentation of content that is very efficient since it exploits the existence of visual and auditory channels.

THE STANZA LOGO-MOTORIA

The System

The Stanza Logo-Motoria (Zanolla, et al., 2011b) is a room (classroom, gym, stage) where a webcam, positioned in the centre of the ceiling, is used to acquire the movement of the body in space and gestures; the image stream is processed by a software patch developed in the EyesWeb XMI environment and a number of low-level features are extracted, e.g., the position of the user in the room and the contraction index (Camurri, Mazzarino & Volpe, 2004). Space analysis starts from the trajectory followed by each user in the interactive space.

The overall system architecture of the Stanza Logo-Motoria (Figure 2) consists of two major components described below.

1. The "input and processing component" which receives the video stream captured by the webcam observing the space; this component is responsible for processing video data (e.g. denoising and background subtraction techniques to extract the user's silhouette) and the motion feature extraction which enables the:
    a. Analysis of input data in order to get information about how the user occupies

Figure 2. The system architecture of the Stanza Logo-Motoria

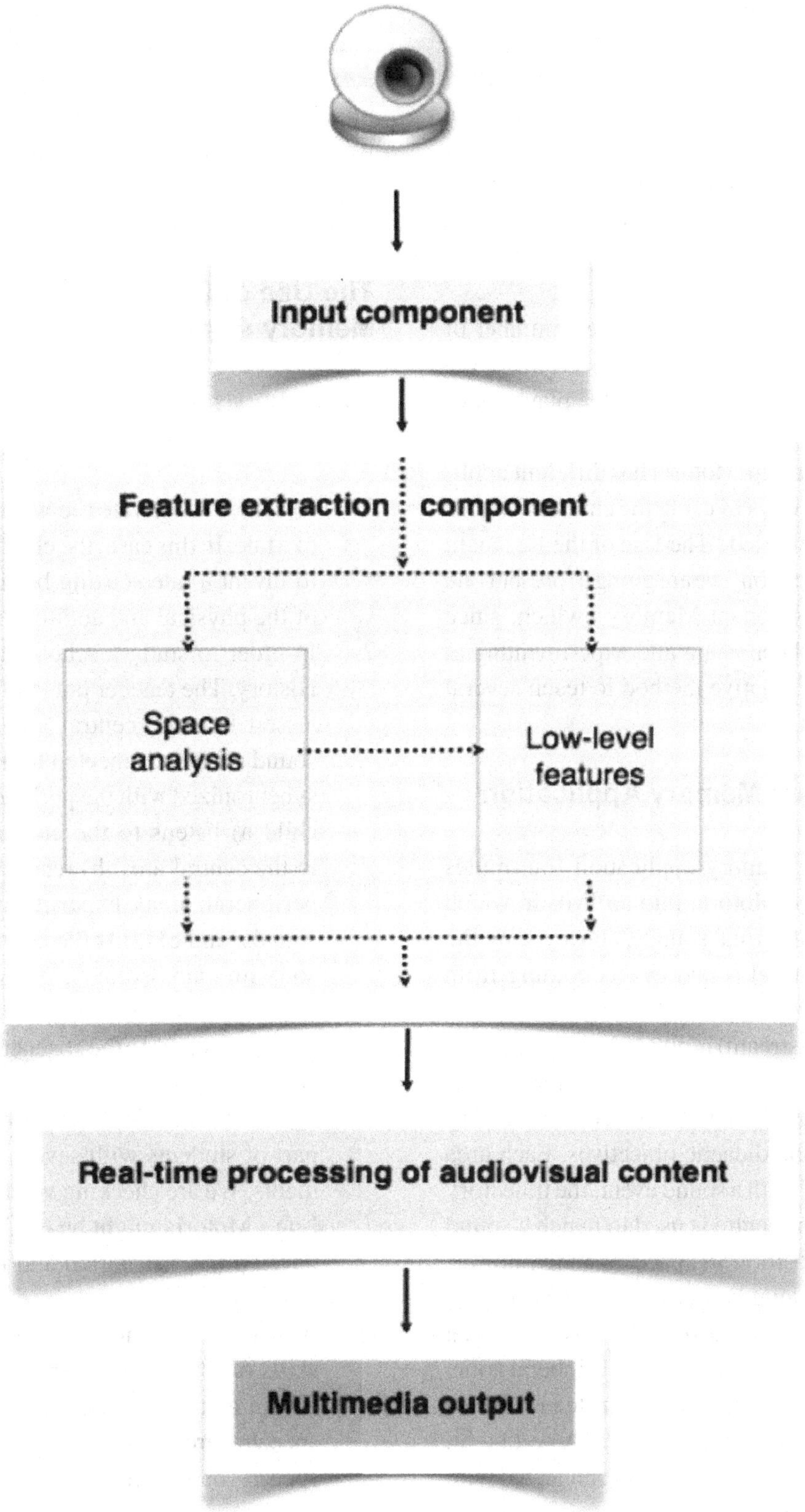

Input component

Feature extraction component

Space analysis

Low-level features

Real-time processing of audiovisual content

Multimedia output

the space (e.g. where he/she goes; how long he/she remains in a given area);
    b. Analysis of gesture features.
2. The "real-time processing of audio/visual content component" which is responsible for the real-time control and processing of audio/video material, and depends on the features extracted in the feature extraction stage.

This system allows us to define a number of regions within the space and synchronizes the user's occupation of a zone with the playback of the audio content.

The Stanza Logo-Motoria has different applications, that is, ways of using the environment; in the paragraph entitled "The Use of the Resonant Memory Application" we are going to present one of these –the Resonant Memory– which, since 2009, we have been using and experimenting at school as an alternative method to teach several school subjects.

The Resonant Memory Application

The Resonant Memory application transmutes the Stanza Logo-Motoria into an IME in which there is a mix of virtual sounds, conveyed by the system, and natural sound events coming from the real environment. The space captured by the webcam (video stream) is divided into nine areas: eight of these are peripheral, whereas the ninth is central, however the number of areas may vary depending on the didactic objectives. Each area is synchronized with a sound event: the trajectory of the user's barycentre is used to match a sound to a specific position in space. Usually, noises, environmental sounds, and music are associated with peripheral zones and are reproduced when the child reaches and occupies a peripheral zone. The central area is synchronized instead with the audio reproduction of the content to be taught, which contains the elements to be connected with sound events positioned in the various peripheral areas. A child explores the "resonant space" in which he/she can freely move without using sensors and, listening to the auditory content, enjoys searching for the sounds heard beforehand; in this way he/she creates in real time the soundtrack of the lesson. In the next paragraph we are going to explain how we use this application.

The Use of the Resonant Memory Application

Currently, schoolteachers use the Resonant Memory application to manage lessons as follows:

1. As a tool to activate the written production of a tale. In this case, the child is encouraged to invent a tale starting by the exploration of the physical and auditory space.
2. In order to study a school subject such as History. The teacher puts the content of the lesson into the central area, whereas the sound events, connected to the content, are synchronized with the peripheral areas. The child a) listens to the content reproduced in the central area, b) reaches the different peripheral areas experimenting with the sounds, and c) "fills the content of the lesson with sound events". This study modality is particularly indicated for children with dyslexia thanks to the absence of the writing code.
3. As a tool to develop the spatial ability on the part of students with severe visual impairments. We are checking whether the Stanza Logo-Motoria might be used as a means to develop the orientation and mobility skills of blind people.
4. As a method to improve the communication skills of foreign children who are learning Italian as their Second Language: various speech exercises might be planned where the speech sounds are not familiar to the child

because they do not belong to the phonemic repertoire of their mother tongue.

5. As a listening tool for ESL (English as a Second Language) lessons. The Resonant Memory application equips schoolchildren with the ability to deal with real-life listening where the input is very fast, and the listener is under pressure to extract the gist of what is being said.

On the basis of the last activity (ESL), we have designed and conducted an educational experimentation, following a validation protocol, which will be described in detail in the next paragraph.

VALIDATION PROTOCOL OF THE STANZA LOGO-MOTORIA

From February to June 2011, we completed the first stage of the experimentation (the second is running) of the Stanza Logo-Motoria in Resonant Memory modality. We are following a quasi-experimental design between-subjects (Campbel & Stanley, 1963) with two comparable classes: two Third Classes (Figure 3). We intend to verify (experimental hypothesis) if pupils who use the Stanza Logo-Motoria as a listening tool for learning ESL improve significantly in word recognition and language comprehension more than those who listen by means of a CD player and two loudspeakers in the language laboratory. The quasi-experimental design requires a pre-test and a post-test to establish group equivalence either for the treated (experimental) and the comparison (control) group. The use of the Stanza Logo-Motoria as a listening tool - in Resonant Memory modality – is the independent variable, whereas the significant improvement of listening comprehension ability in learning ESL is the dependent variable.

During the first stage of the experimentation, the teacher had four consecutive hours one day a week during which she taught the experimental group in the Stanza Logo-Motoria for two hours, followed by another two-hour lesson with the control group in the language laboratory.

The content of the lesson was the same for both classes, but the listening methodology was different: the control group did listening by using the

Figure 3. The validation protocol of the Resonant Memory application

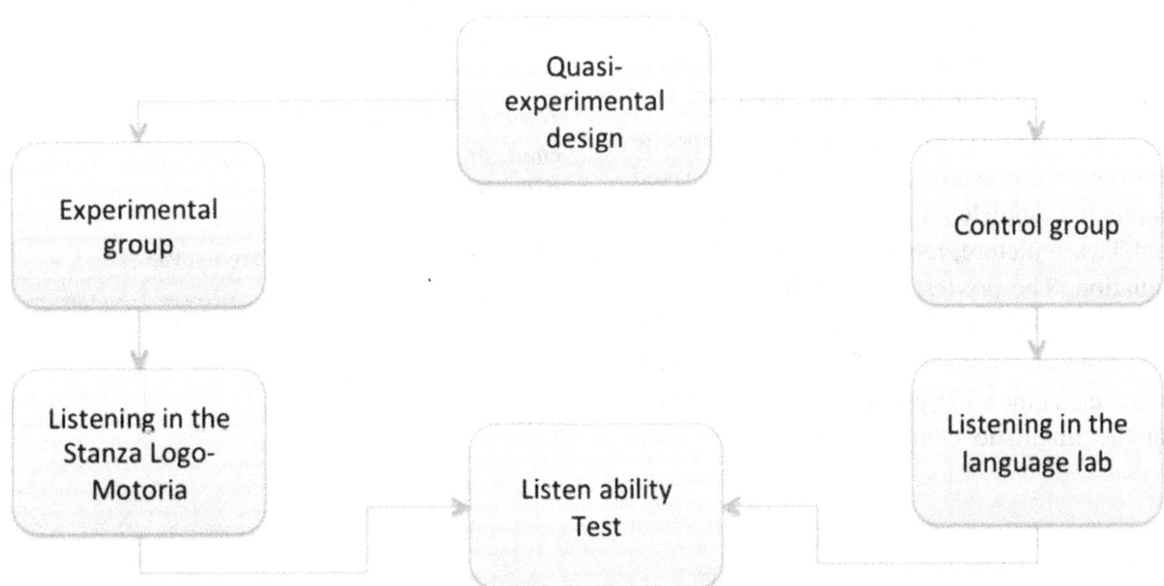

CD player and two loudspeakers in the language laboratory; the experimental group did listening by using the Stanza Logo-Motoria.

In ESL lessons, by means of the Stanza Logo-Motoria, children explore the eight peripheral areas and memorize the spatial coordinates of sound events; then, entering the central area, they activate the audio file of a story in English. Children must listen carefully in order to quickly comprehend the content and trigger at the right time - by entering the peripheral areas - the sound suggested by the story. Sometimes, in one or more peripheral zones, we include several sequences of the story without nouns, adjectives or verbs that the child must insert by saying them aloud.

Testing

We compared the baseline situation and the final one (listening and comprehension skills) of the schoolchildren, in order to check whether the hypothesis verified the forecast, that is, those who use the Stanza Logo-Motoria make more progress, thanks to the experimental factor (the innovation introduced), than those who do not use it. Moreover, before the experiment, we conducted a pilot study in order to point out the faults of the test procedure (Cottini, 2002).

We administered a pre- and post-listening test to both classes in order to evaluate listening skills and comprehension. The same test was used in both instances, and was a composite test combining words and dialogue. We asked pupils to complete a task, which was to Listen and Tick a picture, representing an object or a situation. The pre-test was administered prior to the experimental treatment (February); the post-test was administered after the experimental treatment (June). The pre-test content was based on the linguistic competences acquired until that moment; the post-test content was based on the linguistic competences acquired during the experimentation.

For each test, test-takers had to listen to an audio file three times, look at a number of pictures on a worksheet and choose the one that best described the listening. For every correct answer the child gained one point. The assessment was performed in the English laboratory by means of an audio system with two loudspeakers. The children wrote down their answers.

Results

Firstly, we calculated the number of every child's correct answers; secondly, we calculated the average score of the class on every test. The mean of the experimental group increased by 12%: from 79% (Pre-test) to 91% (Post-test). The mean of the control group increased by 1%: from 80% (Pre-test) to 81% (Post-test).

Then we adopted a statistical method of control, the Fisher Test, in order to identify the probability that the difference between the data obtained is solely due to changes introduced by the independent variable and not by random factors difficult to identify (Cottini, 2002). In order to calculate the p-value by means of the Fisher test we used the values below (Table 1).

Table 1. Number of pupils who improved, worsened, or maintained the level of competence in listening skills

Pupils		Pre-Test/Post-Test		
		Increase	**Decrease**	**No-Change**
Experimental group	15	6	1	8
Control group	14	4	6	4

The Fisher Test showed that the differences between the experimental group and the control group are statistically significant: in fact, the p-value, which is the probability of having the null hypothesis, was less than 0.05.

DISCUSSION

The experiment is continuing in the current school year in order to have more data to analyse: 4 classes are now involved (two Third classes and two Fourth classes), for a total of 70 children. The first stage of the experimentation has allowed us to collect early results which we have presented in this chapter. These results are confirming the experimental hypothesis: in the Stanza Logo-Motoria, learners are more likely to comprehend and remember what they are listening to than pupils using the language laboratory. By exposing them to this experiential, explorative and authentic model of learning, schoolchildren may be encouraged to shift from passive to active learning modes and thus become more successful learners. Meanwhile, teachers can furnish them with an appealing didactic context for understanding the real world, where sounds, noises, segments of spoken language and complete sentences are used to enhance their motor-auditory experiences. Segments of speech and sentences become part of the pupils' language knowledge since they are used to carry out a task, so speaking English becomes spontaneous, fun and natural. The high concentration in listening and the body movement in space ensure effective learning.

On the basis of the results above, we would also say that in the Stanza Logo-Motoria the arrangement of sounds in space captures the pupils' attention and allows them to spatially organize the knowledge acquired. Even after some time, children are able to recall the exact contents learnt during a particular session. From the analysis of video recording, together with the teachers we observed that this method of teaching increases the motivation to listen and consequently to learn new words and phrases.

CONCLUSION

The early results of the experimentation that we have shown in this chapter truly convince us that this can be the beginning of a path, which could introduce the IME in schools. The Stanza Logo-Motoria can offer an alternative and/or additional tool to traditional ways of teaching that often do not adapt to the individual learning ability. In real-time the system analyses the full-body movements and gestures of the children within a "sensorized" environment and maps them onto real-time manipulation and processing of audio-visual content. In this way, teachers might convey content by means of an alternative method and/or to verify the level of knowledge in children who better express their capabilities using their visual, spatial, or bodily intelligence.

The Stanza Logo-Motoria has sparked a lot of interest in many educational institutions because of its standard hardware and simple strategies of mapping. The system is suitable for the school environment thanks to its easy implementation; moreover, teachers are directly involved in the design of activities. In fact the use of the Stanza at school has shown that, by using the same basic scheme, it has been possible to develop, in collaboration with teachers, a great deal of educational projects involving several school subjects.

The Stanza Logo-Motoria in general is an innovative way of teaching, which:

1. Should not replace the teacher, on the contrary, this kind of technology is a resource, which offers greater access to knowledge and interaction with others and the environment;
2. Allows teachers and schoolchildren to discover the enactive approach of learning;

3. Helps schoolteachers to deal with specific learning difficulties. In actual fact, these children need to learn by means of alternative methodologies and tools often specifically designed for them.

ACKNOWLEDGMENT

The authors would like to thank Antonio Camurri, Gualtiero Volpe, Corrado Canepa, and Paolo Coletta (InfoMus Lab, University of Genova, Italy) who contributed to this work. We are grateful for their collaboration during the preliminary development of the Stanza Logo-Motoria.

REFERENCES

Almeida, A., et al. (2008). SOUND=SPACE opera. In *Proceedings of 7th International Conference on Disability Virtual Reality and Associated Technologies with ArtAbilitation*, (pp. 347-354). IEEE.

Bobick, A. et al. (1999). The KidsRoom: A perceptually-based interactive and immersive story environment. *Presence (Cambridge, Mass.)*, *8*(4), 367–391. doi:10.1162/105474699566297

Bruner, J. (1966). *Toward a theory of instruction*. Cambridge, MA: Belknap Press of Harvard University Press.

Bruner, J. (1968). *Processes of cognitive growth: Infancy*. Worcester, MA: Clark University Press.

Campbel, D., & Stanley, J. (1963). *Experimental and quasi-experimental designs for research*. Chicago: Rand McNally and Co.

Camurri, A., et al. (2010). The Stanza Logo-Motoria: An interactive environment for learning and communication. *Proceedings of SMC Conference, 51*(8).

Camurri, A., Mazzarino, B., & Volpe, G. (2004). Analysis of expressive gestures: The eyesweb expressive gesture processing library. [LNAI]. *Proceedings of Gesture-Based Communication in Human-Computer Interaction, 2915*, 460–467. doi:10.1007/978-3-540-24598-8_42

Cottini, L. (2002). *Fare ricerca nella scuola dell'autonomia*. Milano, Italy: Mursia.

Davenport, G., & Friedlander, G. (1995). Interactive transformational environments: Wheel of life. In E. Barrett, & M. Redmond (Eds.), *Contextual media: Multimedia and interpretation* (pp. 1–25). Cambridge, MA: MIT Press.

Fails, J. A., et al. (2005). Child's play: A comparison of desktop and physical interactive environments. In *Proceedings of the 2005 Conference on Interaction Design and Children (IDC '05)*. New York: ACM Press.

Gardner, H. (1983). *Frames of mind: The theory of multiple intelligences*. New York: Basic Books.

Holton, D. (2010). Constructivism + embodied cognition = enactivism: Theoretical and practical implications for conceptual change. In *Proceedings of AERA 2010 Conference*. AERA.

Krueger, M., Gionfriddo, T., & Hinrichsen, K. (1985). Videoplace –An artificial reality. In *Human factors in computing systems*. New York: ACM Press.

Marturana, H., & Varela, F. (1980). *Autopoiesis and cognition: The realization of the living*. Boston: Kluwer. doi:10.1007/978-94-009-8947-4

Moreno, R., & Mayer, R. (2007). Interactive multimodal learning environments. *Educational Psychology Review*, 309–326. doi:10.1007/s10648-007-9047-2

Roth, W., & Lawless, D. (2001). Computer modeling and biological learning. *Journal of Educational Technology & Society*, *4*(1), 13–25.

Vygotsky, L. (1986). *Thought and language*. Cambridge, MA: MIT Press.

Zanolla, S., et al. (2011a). When sound teaches. In *Proceedings of 8th Sound and Music Computing Conference,* (pp. 64-69). IEEE.

Zanolla, S., et al. (2011b). Teaching by means of a technologically augmented environment: The Stanza Logo-Motoria. In *Proceedings of INTETAIN2011 Conference*. Genova, Italy: INTETAIN.

Chapter 15
Learning Computer Vision through the Development of a Camera-Trackable Game Controller

Andrea Albarelli
Dipartimento di Scienze Ambientali, Informatica e Statistica, Università Ca' Foscari di Venezia, Italy

Filippo Bergamasco
Dipartimento di Scienze Ambientali, Informatica e Statistica, Università Ca' Foscari di Venezia, Italy

Andrea Torsello
Dipartimento di Scienze Ambientali, Informatica e Statistica, Università Ca' Foscari di Venezia, Italy

ABSTRACT

The trade-off between the available classroom time and the complexity of the proposed task is central to the design of any Computer Science laboratory lecture. Special care must be taken to build up an experimental setup that allows the students to get the most significant information from the experience without getting lost in the details. This is especially true when teaching Computer Vision concepts to prospective students that own little or no previous background in programming and a strongly diversified knowledge with respect to mathematics. In this chapter, the authors describe a setup for a laboratory lecture that has been administered through several years to prospective students of the Computer Science course at the University of Venice. The goal is to teach basic concepts such as color spaces or image transforms through a rewarding task, which is the development of a vision-based game controller similar in spirit to the recent human-machine interfaces adopted by the current generation of game consoles.

INTRODUCTION

The laboratory is a tool of paramount importance in science education for several reasons. Experimentation and hands-on activities allow students to connect theoretical facts with their effects. Moreover, challenges and intellectual rewards coming from such activities help in providing motivation for further studying. However, the design of good laboratory experiences is not an easy task (Hofstein, A., & Lunetta, V., 2004). The quandary between the conceptual complexity of

DOI: 10.4018/978-1-4666-4490-8.ch015

the activities to be offered and the limited scope of an experimental session is even more noticeable when dealing with advanced subjects such as Computer Vision (Bebis, G., Egbert, D., & Shah, M., 2003; Maxwell, B., 2001) or even Image Processing (Roman, D., Fisher, M., & Cubillo, J., 1998; Greenberg, R., 1998). In fact, these topics tend to be taught in graduated courses (Pridmore, T., & Hales, W., 1995) still, given the increasing importance of vision algorithms in the industry, they begin to be introduced also at undergraduate level (Sarkar, S., & Goldgof, D., 1998; Egbert, D., Bebis, G., McIntosh, M., LaTouttette, N., & Mitra, A., 2003; Hoover, A., 2003) or even during the high school (Greenberg, R., Raphael, J., Keller, J., & Tobias, S., 1998). In this paper we describe a laboratory setup that has been designed to be useful in teaching some basic Computer Vision concepts to high school students that are keen to join the undergraduate Computer Science course at the University of Venice. These prospective students exhibited a wide range of different knowledge backgrounds, since some of them have attended humanities studies, whilst others were more at ease with mathematics and physics.

For this reason it has been necessary to assume no previous programming skills and a very limited set of mathematical tools. To this end, we designed a laboratory session that includes about an hour of theoretical foundations and four hours of lightweight programming activity. The theoretical session introduces two concepts that will be central in the following experience: the YUV colorspace and the Hough Transform. They are both introduced with a minimal level of technicality and using very simple math notations. The programming session is performed within a custom environment that allows to write the body of the required functions directly without the need to know details such as how the images are acquired or how the methods are called. The functions have to be written with a subset of the Java syntax, that has proved to be simple to understand and suitable for this kind of laboratory lectures (Moscariello, S., Kasturi, R., & Camps, O., 1997). Before starting the programming activity itself, each student was supplied with a one-sheet handbook of the needed Java syntax and with some general instructions about the use of the integrated editor. The overall lab experience, which will be explained in detail in the following sections, imply the use of a simple game controller cut-out (see Figure 1) made out of a PVC sheet that must be recognized from an image with the help of the color of the band printed on it. Once the recognition happens, the orientation of the band must be determined and used to control a little game.

Figure 1. Shots of the vision-based controller and of the main panel of the educational application

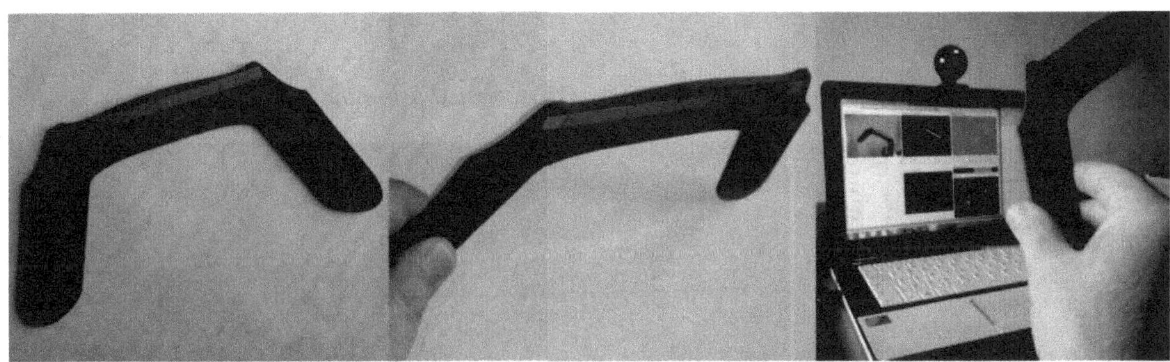

DESIGN OF THE CONTROLLER AND OF THE RECOGNITION PIPELINE

To keep the experience as simple as possible we avoided the use of recognition techniques involving the search for a specific shape. In fact, we designed a controller that contains a very specific cue: a colored magenta stripe with two small green squares at its ends. The stripe and the squares will be segmented from the rest of the image by exploiting their chroma value. The resulting masks will be further analyzed respectively to find the orientation of the controller and to determine if the buttons are pressed. The orientation will be detected through the localization of a maximum in the Hough space, while the buttons status will be assessed by checking the presence or absence of green masked pixels on the right and on the left of the stripe. These of course might not be the best practice from a Computer Vision standpoint, but they are simple enough to be implemented during a short laboratory session and they exhibit a satisfactory level of complexity with respect to the targeted students.

Chroma-Based Segmentation in the YUV Space

Since the detection of the controller should be invariant to changes in global illumination and gradients, the use of a colorspace that separates luminance and chroma should be preferred. We adopted the YUV color model (Wharton, W., & Howorth, D., 1971) that separates the pixel information in one luminance channel (Y) and two chroma channel (U and V). The values in the chroma channels do not depend on illumination, rather, they localize the exact color shade over the U/V plane (see Figure 3). In such plane the coordinates range from -0.5 to 0.5, the white light is locate at the origin, and at the four corners respectively the colors magenta, orange, green and blue can be found. The choice of magenta and green as distinctive colors for the controller is made specifically to allows for the maximum separability, since they are at the opposite positions in the U/V plane. To perform the segmentation of the stripe and the buttons, the students have been instructed about the principles of the YUV format and have been supplied with two matrices of floating point values (of Java type double) named respectively uData and vData, the location on the plane of the sought color (as a pair of double values named respectively u and v) and a radius of tolerance (as a double r). Their task was to build the body of a function that fills a Boolean matrix accordingly with the fact that a given pixel was or was not within the given tolerance from the sought point on the U/V plane. As described in Sec. 3, students were not required to write the whole method, since the signature was already available and they just needed to write the for loop needed to implement the segmentation. In Figure 2 we show the masking process performed on an

Figure 2. Original image and magenta and green masks extracted using the YUV colorspace

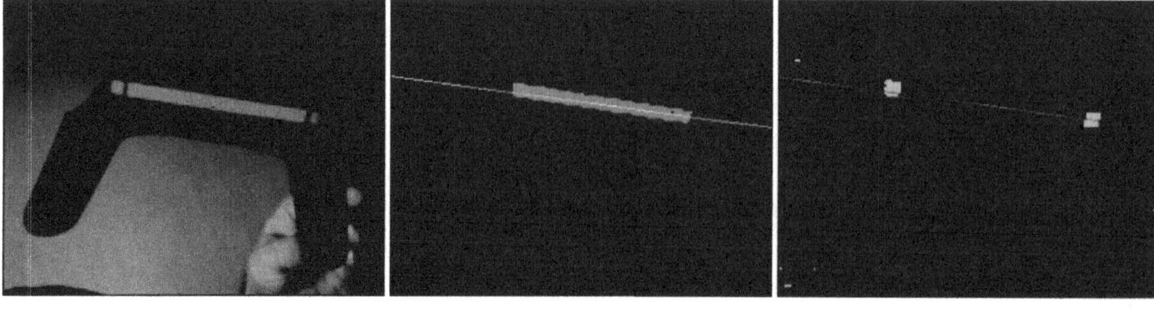

Figure 3. The U/V plane

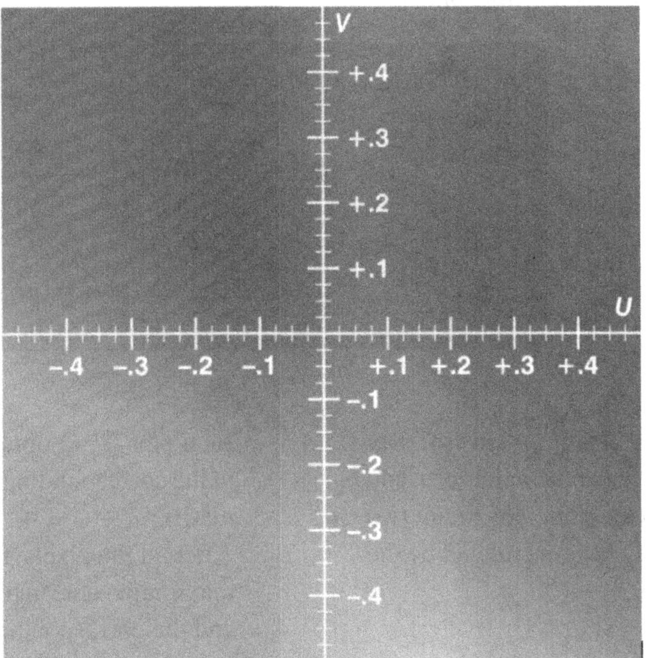

image grabbed by a webcam for both the stripe and the buttons by setting the target values for the colors respectively at (0.5,0.5) and (-0.5,-0.5) and the radius of tolerance to 0.5.

Controller Localization and Orientation Detection

Once the color segmentation has happened, the stripe can be localized and its orientation determined. This could be done, for instance, by applying a least square method to the points in the magenta mask. However this could lead to wrong results if a large number of structured outliers are present in the segmentation (which could easily happen if the student wears a purple outfit). Instead, we chose to take a different approach, which is also easier to understand with no previous knowledge other than basic Euclidean geometry of the straight line. This approach is the Hough Transform (Duda, R., & Hart, P., 1972). which casts the problem of finding the straight line that justifies a set of observations in the Euclidean plane to the problem of finding the maximum of a voting function in the so called 'Hough Space'. The main idea of the approach is to parameterize the straight line with its distance from the origin (r) and the angle that the line going through the origin and perpendicular to it forms with the x-axis (θ) (see Figure 4).

Using this parameterization the equation of the line (for non-vertical lines) becomes:

$$y = \left(-\frac{\cos\theta}{\sin\theta}\right)x + \left(\frac{r}{\sin\theta}\right) \quad (1)$$

which, in turn, can be generalized in the equation:

$$r = x\cos\theta + y\sin\theta \quad (2)$$

that must be true for each point belonging to the line.

Any pixel that results from the segmentation of the stripe potentially belongs to the phenomenon that produced such segmentation. Since the

Figure 4. Parameterization of the straight line used for the Hough Transform, mask for a stripe and respective representation in the Hough Space

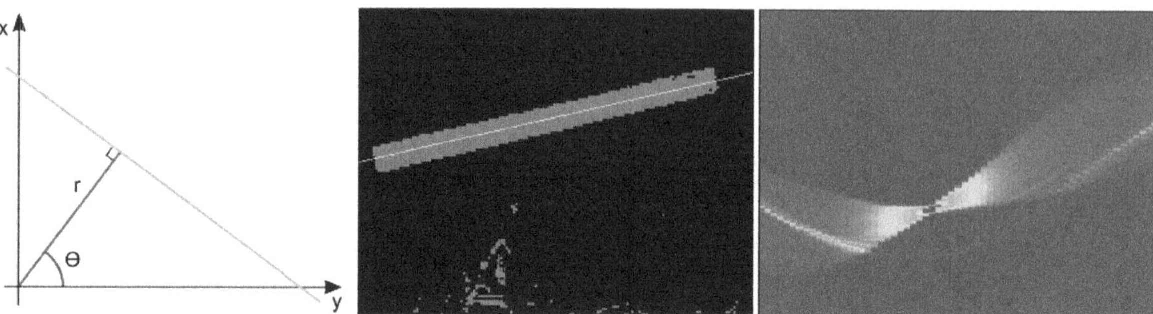

coordinates (x_0, y_0) of the point are known, they must verify Equation 2 for some value of r and θ. A single point is not enough to constraint two parameters, however they become related by the following equation:

$$r = x_0 \cos\theta + y_0 \sin\theta \qquad (3)$$

Equation 3 can be used to draw a curve in the θ/r plane, which is called the *Hough Space*. If all the pixels in the mask were aligned perfectly, all the curves in the Hough Space would pass through the same point, whose coordinates identify the correct solution for r and θ. Of course, the pixels coming from the segmentation cannot be perfectly aligned for several reasons: to begin with, the stripe is a rectangle rather than a monodimensional line, discretization errors are present and, finally, spurious pixel could be produced by background objects or any other source of noise. In practice, the selection of the parameterization associated to the mask id performed by mean of a discretized set of voting bins with the following steps:

1. A discrete step is chosen for both θ and r. This step is used to build an accumulator matrix of floating point values;
2. For each one of the pixels found in the mask Equation 3 is calculated for values of θ ranging from 0 to π with the chosen step. For each pair (θ, r) obtained a vote is inserted in the corresponding bin of the accumulator matrix;
3. After all the pixels have been processed the maximum value in the accumulator is found and the corresponding value for θ and r are retained.

In the last column of Figure 4 the accumulator populated with the votes coming from the segmentation shown in the middle column is displayed. The values have been colored with a chromatic scale that ranges from blue (lower values) to red (higher values). It should be noted that, while the maximum is well defined, a spurious set of curves has been produced by the erroneous pixels in the bottom half of the mask. Additionally, the choice of the step values for the accumulator has effects on the accuracy in the determination of the correct parameterization. In Figure 5 we show the difference in the accumulator for different granularities applied to the same scene. At a high accumulator resolution the maximum is well localized, whereas at a more coarse granularity the aliasing effect due to the binning hinders the result.

To perform this operation the students have been supplied with the Boolean matrix produced with the previous function, a pre-allocated accumulator matrix of floating point values named accumulator and the step amount for both for and

Figure 5. Different levels of accuracy of the accumulator at various step granularity

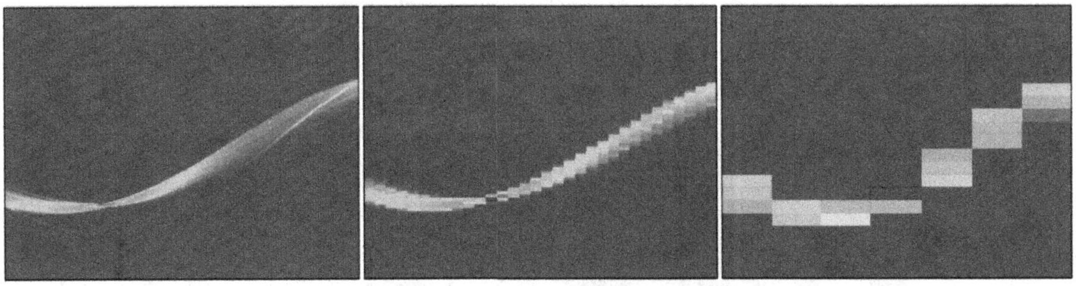

r. Their task was to fill the accumulator with the appropriate for loop. The educational value of the experience lies both in understanding the process (which involves an unusual transform between spaces) and in playing with the step parameters to grasp the effect of binning on voting.

Check of the Button Status

This last step is optional and has been included in the laboratory experience in order to allow the students with higher skills or previous programming experience to perform an additional challenge (and avoid them becoming bored). The student is supplied with two Boolean arrays that contain the projection of the magenta and green segmentations along the line corresponding to the extracted orientation of the controller and the function written should fill a two place Boolean array with the status of the two buttons. Again, a method signature is already loaded in the system and the user only needs to fill in the body of such method, however no suggestion is given about how to proceed with the implementation. A reasonable solution is to find the barycenter of the magenta stripe and check for the presence of green pixels respectively on the left and on the right.

A PRACTICAL SANDBOX TO SIMPLIFY THE COMPLEXITY

In principle, the proposed pipeline could be implemented from scratch, but this would require a lot of effort and skills, which is inappropriate considering both the target audience and the available time. Moreover, tasks such as image acquisition are notoriously cumbersome, as they require to fiddle with system specific APIs. To this end, we deployed a custom environment that takes care of most of the details and lets the students concentrate on the implementation of the algorithm and on the experimentation with the effect of the different parameters. In Figure 6 we show the main panel of the development environment. In the first column the webcam preview is available. Here a streaming video of the frames captured is displayed together with the controls offered by the camera driver. This allows the student to modify these parameters and learn how they affect the appearance of the acquired frame and the whole pipeline. Specifically, by changing the exposure control, students can learn about the trade-off between brightness and blurring for a dynamic scene, brightness and contrast controls give some insight about dynamic ranges, finally the saturation

Figure 6. The custom development environment implemented for the laboratory lecture (some text is in Italian language in order for it to be understandable by the target audience)

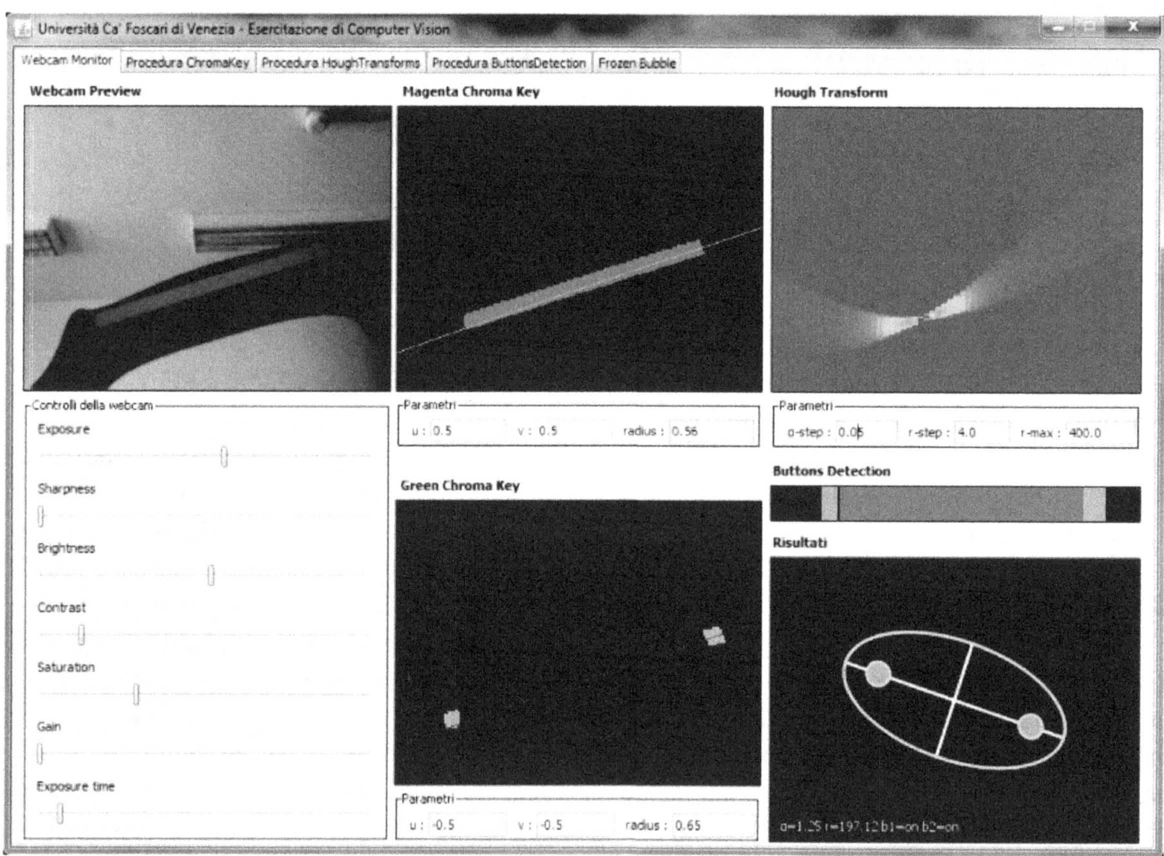

control is directly related to the intensity of the color channels and thus to the sensitivity of the detection step. In the remaining part of the panel the input parameters and the output of the different methods implemented are shown. Finally, the tool exhibits a set of three tabs that contain the editors that will be used to write the actual code and a last tab that allows to play a small game (Frozen Bubble) using the controller.

Acquiring Images from Camera and Running Custom Code on them

The acquisition of the stream coming from the webcam is done automatically by the custom environment by mean of the DSJ library. Since this library is a wrapper between Java and DirectShow, the implemented system can be used only within the Windows operating system. While this is quite a limitation, by adopting this solution all the webcams supported by Windows drivers can be used seamlessly. Each frame acquired is converted in the YUV format and supplied to the user-defined method as three matrices of floating point values. In addition to those matrices also other parameters need to be passed: those parameters are specified by the user in the text boxes shown in Figure 6, automatically converted to floating point and then properly supplied to the custom code written by the student. The output produced by each method is also displayed on the panel in an easily readable form. In detail, the masks produced by the chroma key filter are shown as binary images in the central column, respectively for the magenta and the green segmentation. The accumulator in the Hough Space is rendered as a color coded image at the top of the last column. Here are also shown the binary masks passed to the buttons detection method and a box that reports in a schematic representation the orientation of the controller and the status of the buttons as obtained by the Hough Transform processing function.

Writing, Compiling and Loading Code

The programming activity itself happens by writing the body of three Java methods into three specialized editor panes accessible through tabs on the main window. Each editor comes with the method signature already written, as well as with some lines of comments that explain the role of each parameter (see Figure 7). The methods to be completed are meant respectively to perform the color segmentation of the image, the estimation of the controller orientation and of the status of the buttons. Each time that the student needs to test the code written he can compile it by clicking on a button on the interface, that will trigger the compilation (using Java introspection). If the compilation fails the errors obtained are displayed to the user, otherwise the newly created method is loaded by the class loader, inserted in the running pipeline and called for each acquired frame with the parameters specified in the main panel. At this stage any runtime error is also presented to the user as well as any text that is printed on the standard output. Since the system must protect the pipeline from infinite loops that might happen in the user code, before compilation the methods body are modified at the source level and a safety watchdog variable is inserted as an additional exit condition into each for or while loop.

RECEPTION BY THE STUDENTS

The laboratory lecture described has been given to 206 prospective students over the last academic year. The effectiveness of the lecture and its appreciation by the students have been evaluated by submitting to them a multiple choice test and a

Figure 7. The editor panel used to fill in the methods body

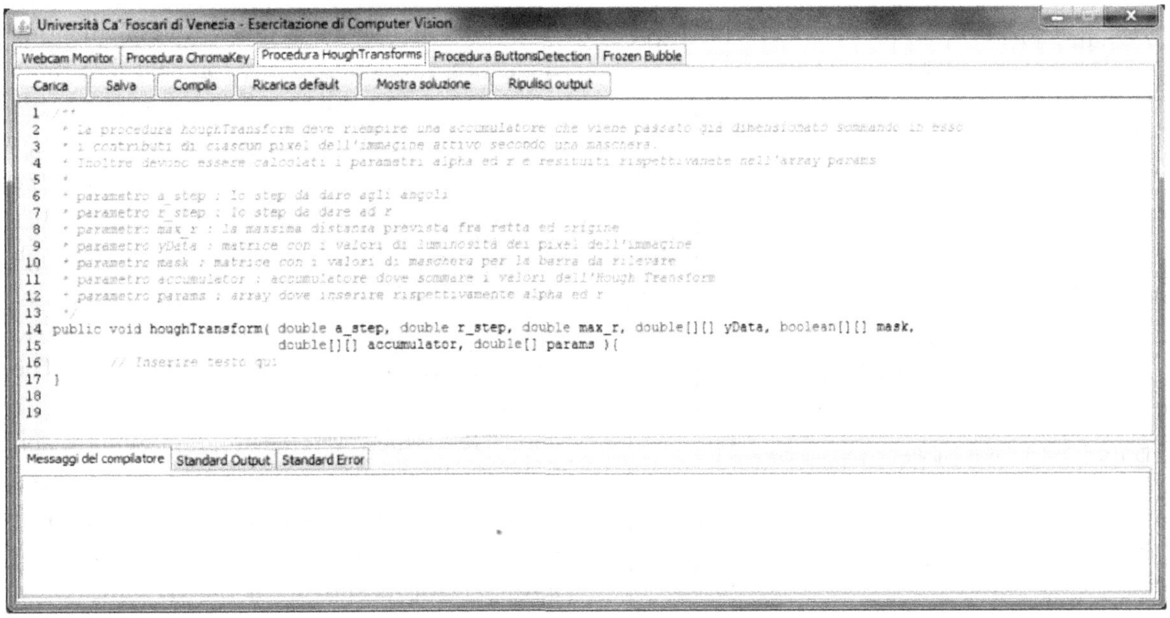

Università Ca' Foscari di Venezia - Esercitazione di Computer Vision

Webcam Monitor | Procedura ChromaKey | Procedura HoughTransforms | Procedura ButtonsDetection | Frozen Bubble

Carica | Salva | Compila | Ricarica default | Mostra soluzione | Ripulisci output

```
/**
 * La procedura houghTransform deve riempire una accumulatore che viene passato già dimensionato sommando in esso
 * i contributi di ciascun pixel dell'immagine attivo secondo una maschera.
 * Inoltre devono essere calcolati i parametri alpha ed r e resituiti rispettivanete nell'array params
 *
 * parametro a_step : lo step da dare agli angoli
 * parametro r_step : lo step da dare ad r
 * parametro max_r : la massima distanza prevista fra retta ed origine
 * parametro yData : matrice con i valori di luminosità dei pixel dell'immagine
 * parametro mask : matrice con i valori di maschera per la barra da rilevare
 * parametro accumulator : accumulatore dove sommare i valori dell'Hough Transform
 * parametro params : array dove inserire rispettivamente alpha ed r
 */
public void houghTransform( double a_step, double r_step, double max_r, double[][] yData, boolean[][] mask,
                            double[][] accumulator, double[] params ){
        // Inserire testo qui
}
```

Messaggi del compilatore | Standard Output | Standard Error

survey right after the programming session. The survey asked to express the degree of satisfaction with respect to five different aspects of the experience, each level of appreciation goes from a minimum to 1 to a maximum of 5. The results obtained are shown in Table 1.

Overall we can see that all the scores were rather good and that the outcome of the experience slightly exceeded the expectations.

The test contained 10 yes/no questions about the topics introduced in the theoretical session and further developed with the programming activity. The results of the test have been as shown in Table 2.

While about a half of the students got wrong the more theoretical questions (which unfortunately coincides with maximum entropy), the results indicate a good understanding of most new concepts introduced during the lecture. This is also true with respect to the awareness of the influence of the parameters over the detection process.

Table 2.

Question	% Correct
Several different color spaces exist and no one perfectly fits all the application scenarios	82.5
In the YUV color space white and blue are more distinguishable colors than green and magenta	85.0
The Y channel in the YUV color space is associated to the amount of yellow in a pixel	80.0
Images acquired by a digital camera are organized in a regular rectangular grid	82.5
To find lines in an image a parameterization based on intercept and slope has been used	50.0
A point in the Euclidean space can be related to a straight line in the Hough space	45.0
The angular resolution of the accumulator has effect on the estimation of the angular position of the controller	75.0
The distance from the camera (as long as the controller is visible) has an heavy influence on the accuracy of the detection	67.5
The presence of magenta or green objects in the scene prevents the operation of the system	70.0
It is useful to accumulate in the Hough space values that are proportional to the luminance channel	72.5

CONCLUSION AND FUTURE WORK

In this paper we presented a setup for a laboratory lecture aimed at teaching some basic Computer Vision concepts. The main goal was to mold an overall design of the experience that allows to fully enjoy the activity with no previous programming knowledge and after receiving a minimal set of theoretical insights from the lecturer. This has been done by implementing a custom development environment that takes care of acquiring images from a webcam and invoking the methods implemented by the students. The topic of choice for the lecture was the detection of a specially crafted game controller through chroma-based segmentation and Hough Transform. The experience has been proposed to about two hundred students and has shown to be generally well received and stimulating. The results obtained by the students with a multiple choice test issued after the programming session have demonstrated a good understanding of the new concepts introduced. In the future, additional laboratory experience could be designed taking advantage of recently available 3D sensors.

Table 1.

Question	Avg. Score
How much were you interested in the laboratory session before participating to it ?	4.22
The lecture was clear enough and the covered topics were easy to understand ?	4.39
Are you satisfied with the organization of the laboratory and the tools supplied to perform the required tasks ?	4.33
Do you think that the experience allowed you to acquire some new skills ?	4.42
Rate the overall experience	4.65

REFERENCES

Bebis, G., Egbert, D., & Shah, M. (2003). Review of computer vision education. *IEEE Transactions on Education, 46*(1), 2–21. doi:10.1109/TE.2002.808280

Duda, R., & Hart, P. (1972). Use of the Hough transformation to detect lines and curves in pictures. *Communications of the ACM, 15*(1), 11–15. doi:10.1145/361237.361242

Egbert, D., Bebis, G., McIntosh, M., LaTouttette, N., & Mitra, A. (2003). Computer vision research as a teaching tool in CS1. In *Proceedings of Frontiers in Education* (pp. 17–22). IEEE.

Greenberg, R. (1998). Image processing for teaching: Transforming a scientific research tool into an educational technology. *Journal of Computers in Mathematics and Science Teaching, 17*(2), 149–160.

Greenberg, R., Raphael, J., Keller, J., & Tobias, S. (1998). Teaching high school science using image processing: A case study of implementation of computer technology. *Journal of Research in Science Teaching, 35*(3), 297–327. doi:10.1002/(SICI)1098-2736(199803)35:3<297::AID-TEA4>3.0.CO;2-M

Hofstein, A., & Lunetta, V. (2004). The laboratory in science education: Foundations for the twenty-first century. *Science Education, 88*(1), 28–54. doi:10.1002/sce.10106

Hoover, A. (2003). Computer vision in undergraduate education: modern embedded computing. *IEEE Transactions on Education, 46*(2), 235–240. doi:10.1109/TE.2002.808264

Maxwell, B. (2001). A survey of computer vision education and text resources. *International Journal of Pattern Recognition and Artificial Intelligence, 15*(5), 757–773. doi:10.1142/S0218001401001131

Moscariello, S., Kasturi, R., & Camps, O. (1997). Image processing and computer vision instruction using Java. In *Proceedings of IEEE Workshop on Undergraduate Education and Image Computation*. IEEE.

Pridmore, T., & Hales, W. (1995). Understanding images: An approach to the university teaching of computer vision. *Engineering Science and Education Journal, 4*(4), 161–166. doi:10.1049/esej:19950406

Roman, D., Fisher, M., & Cubillo, J. (1998). Digital image processing-an object-oriented approach. *IEEE Transactions on Education, 41*(4), 331–333. doi:10.1109/13.728270

Sarkar, S., & Goldgof, D. (1998). Integrating image computation in undergraduate level data structures education. *International Journal of Pattern Recognition and Artificial Intelligence, 12*, 1071–1080. doi:10.1142/S0218001498000609

Wharton, W., & Howorth, D. (1971). *Principles of television reception*. London: Pitman Publishing.

Chapter 16
Multi-Photo Fusion through Projective Geometry

Luigi Barazzetti
Department of Building Environmental Science and Technology, Politecnico di Milano, Italy

ABSTRACT

Multiple images of the same object can be registered and fused after identifying a proper mathematical model. This chapter illustrates the contribution of projective geometry and automated matching techniques to several photographic applications: high dynamic range, multi-focus, and panoramic photography. The method relies on the estimation of a set of planar transformations that make the data consistent. This provides pixel correspondence and allows the photographer to obtain new digital products in an almost fully automated way.

INTRODUCTION

Image registration allows merging multiple shots acquired with digital cameras. Nowadays, most digital and film-based photographs can be indented as central perspectives in space. The geometric process behind the creation of a photo requires the alignment between the (i) perspective centre of the camera, the (ii) object point and its (iii) projection on the image plane. Most cameras follow this condition (called *collinearity principle*) and are therefore termed *pinhole cameras* (Hartley & Zisserman, 2004). For the sake of completeness, it is important to remember that there are other camera models. For instance, a standard SRL camera with a fisheye lens is no longer a pinhole camera, whereas pushbroom sensors are often employed in the field of aerial and satellite photogrammetry. In some cases, special line-based panoramic cameras are used in terrestrial applications (Luhmann & Tecklenburg, 2002).

Digital pinhole cameras are today very popular because they are simple, quick and reliable recording tools. The market seems to be growing

DOI: 10.4018/978-1-4666-4490-8.ch016

(the global digital camera shipment was about 130 million unites in 2009, 141 million units in 2010, and it is expected to reach 145 million units in 2011 (Global and China Digital Still Camera –DSC, 2011). and the development of digital camera technology provides sensors with high radiometric and geometric resolutions and good storage capacity. Data can be easily shared, modified, enhanced, and copied. If photography has been a chemical process for over 150 years, nowadays films, chemicals or dark rooms are a thing of the past.

As most consumer cameras produce pinhole images, this chapter focuses on this particular kind of data, although the collinearity principle is satisfied only in the case of ideal cameras. A real camera equipped with real lenses produced distorted images because of the effect of lens distortion. This effect is strongly reduced if the camera is calibrated (Remondino & Fraser, 2006). meaning that distortion coefficients are known and a new distortion-free image can be created.

One of the most remarkable advantages of digital data is the opportunity to run processing algorithms able to modify, enhance, and register multiple shots. In this chapter three products obtainable with pinhole cameras are illustrated and discussed. They include High Dynamic Range (HDR) images (Debevec & Malik, 1997). multi-focus images (Haeberli, 1994). and panoramas (Brown & Lowe, 2003). Although very different, the processing algorithm relies on a similar workflow, where a set of projective transformations is used to align different images. All these products can be created in an almost fully automated way, allowing expert operators or normal tourists to overcome some drawbacks of single shots. After a brief review of the most common 2D transformations, it will be demonstrated that a homography (Liebowitz & Zisserman, 1998) can be successfully used to register images and create HDR, multi-focus, and panoramic images.

IMAGE REGISTRATION THROUGH PROJECTIVE TRANSFORMATIONS

Projective geometry allows us to deal with geometric transformations and offers more powerful methods than conventional Euclidean geometry. For instance, in Euclidean geometry any two distinct points in a plane define a line. On the other hand, any two distinct lines define a point, unless the lines are parallel. Projective geometry overcomes this limitation in a symmetric way: *any two distinct points determine a unique line* and *any two distinct lines intersect at a point.* When we consider the image formation process by means of a pinhole camera, it is quite evident that Euclidean geometry is not sufficient. Properties like lengths, angles, areas, and parallelism are not preserved during the imaging process: parallel lines may intersect.

We get to projective geometry by taking Euclidean geometry and adding an extra dimension. A point in an n-dimensional Euclidean space is represented as a point in an $(n+1)$-dimensional projective space. Suppose we have a point $(x, y)^T$ in the Euclidean space, the *homogenous coordinates* of a point can be obtained by adding an extra coordinate to the pair as $(\lambda x, \lambda y, \lambda)^T$. We say that this 3-vector is the same point in homogeneous coordinates (for any non-zero value λ). An arbitrary homogeneous vector $\mathbf{x} = (x_1, x_2, x_3)^T$ represents the point $\mathbf{x} = (x_1 / x_3, x_2 / x_3)^T$ in $\mathbf{R}^2$.

As a line in the plane is represented by the equation $ax + by + c = 0$, a similar notation can be used to identify a line through a vector $\mathbf{l} = (a, b, c)^T$.

A point $\mathbf{x} = (x_1, x_2, x_3)^T$ lies on the line $\mathbf{l} = (a, b, c)^T$ if and only if $ax + by + c = 0$. This may be written in terms of a vector product as $\mathbf{x}^T \mathbf{l} = 0$. The intersection of two lines $\mathbf{l} = (a, b, c)^T$ and $\mathbf{l}' = (a', b', c')^T$ is the point $\mathbf{x} = \mathbf{l} \times \mathbf{l}'$. As can be easily seen, the role of points and lines can be interchanged: $\mathbf{x}^T \mathbf{l} = 0$ implies $\mathbf{l}^T \mathbf{x} = 0$. This observation indicates the presence of a *duality* between points and lines in the projective plane.

Euclidean geometry is a subgroup of projective geometry. In general, we can define a hierarchy of transformations, that includes two geometries between Euclidean and projective: similarity and affine.

Homogenous coordinates allows one to represent planar transformations with an elegant and compact notation. Let's start with an Euclidean transformation that, as previously mentioned, preserves angles, distances, and areas. *Isometry* is a simple transformation made up of a rotation and a translation. Using inhomogeneous coordinates, we may write:

$$\mathbf{x}' = \begin{bmatrix} x' \\ y' \\ 1 \end{bmatrix} = \begin{bmatrix} r_1 & r_2 & t_x \\ r_3 & r_4 & t_y \\ 0 & 0 & 1 \end{bmatrix} \begin{bmatrix} x \\ y \\ 1 \end{bmatrix} = \begin{bmatrix} \mathbf{R} & \mathbf{t} \\ \mathbf{0}^{\mathrm{T}} & 1 \end{bmatrix} \begin{bmatrix} x \\ y \\ 1 \end{bmatrix} = \mathbf{H}_I \mathbf{x} \tag{1}$$

where $\mathbf{R}$ is a 2×2 rotation matrix and $\mathbf{t} = [t_x, t_y]^{\mathrm{T}}$ a translation vector. Following a hierarchical approach, the transformation can be easily modified to take into consideration an isotropic scale factor λ. This new model is called *similarity* and has the following form:

$$\mathbf{x}' = \begin{bmatrix} x' \\ y' \\ 1 \end{bmatrix} = \begin{bmatrix} \lambda\mathbf{R} & \mathbf{t} \\ \mathbf{0}^{\mathrm{T}} & 1 \end{bmatrix} \begin{bmatrix} x \\ y \\ 1 \end{bmatrix} = \mathbf{H}_S \mathbf{x}. \tag{2}$$

A further step concerns *affine* transformations, that have 6 DoF and may be expressed by the following mathematical formulation:

$$\mathbf{x}' = \begin{bmatrix} x' \\ y' \\ 1 \end{bmatrix} = \begin{bmatrix} a_1 & a_2 & t_x \\ a_3 & a_4 & t_y \\ 0 & 0 & 1 \end{bmatrix} \begin{bmatrix} x \\ y \\ 1 \end{bmatrix} = \begin{bmatrix} \mathbf{A} & \mathbf{t} \\ \mathbf{0}^{\mathrm{T}} & 1 \end{bmatrix} \begin{bmatrix} x \\ y \\ 1 \end{bmatrix} = \mathbf{H}_A \mathbf{x} \tag{3}$$

where $\mathbf{A}$ is a non-singular matrix. The invariants are parallelism, ratios of lines of parallel lines segments, and ratios of areas, whereas it is quite evident that length ratios and angles are not preserved.

Finally, we may write the equations of the most general case. A planar projective transformation (or *homography*) is represented by a 3×3 matrix:

$$\mathbf{x}' = \begin{bmatrix} x' \\ y' \\ 1 \end{bmatrix} = \begin{bmatrix} h_1 & h_2 & h_3 \\ h_4 & h_5 & h_6 \\ h_7 & h_8 & h_9 \end{bmatrix} \begin{bmatrix} x \\ y \\ 1 \end{bmatrix} = \mathbf{H}\mathbf{x} \tag{4}$$

where $\mathbf{H}$ is a non-singular matrix and has 8 degrees of freedom. Given four collinear points A, B, C and D, the cross ratio $Cr = d(\mathrm{A,B})\, d(\mathrm{B,C}) / [d(\mathrm{A,D})\, d(\mathrm{B,D})]$ is invariant under projective transformations.

It is well-known that $\mathbf{H}$ expresses a mathematical relationship between a planar object and a distortion-free image. In other words, if $\mathbf{H}$ is known metric properties can be recovered from images. The estimation of $\mathbf{H}$ is usually carried out with a set of point to point correspondences $\mathbf{x}' \leftrightarrow \mathbf{x}$ (at least four). Alternative methods were presented in (Lourakis, 2009; Sugimoto, 2000), among others. Figure 1 shows the rectification result of a painting (*Le Repas chez Simon* le Pharisien, By Paolo Veronese, Versailles, Musee Nation du Chateau) with the package presented in (Barazzetti, 2011). In the next section, a set of homographic transformations will be used to register different images. As mentioned, the aim of this work is the recovery of image alignment in order to create HDR, multi-focus, and panoramic images.

AUTOMATIC DIGITAL IMAGE REGISTRATION

Homography is a mapping suitable for the creation of different kind of photographic products. Shown in the following sections are some applications where a set of corresponding points between two (or more) images are used to estimate different homographic transformations.

Figure 1. Rectification of a painting (Le Repas chez Simon le Pharisien) aimed at recovering metric properties. The rectifying homography was estimated with the approach described in (Barazzetti, L, 2011) that uses geometric quantities (vanishing line) and camera calibration parameters.

The extraction of corresponding points relies on different automatic operators. SIFT (Scale Invariant Feature Transform), undoubtedly, is the most used operator for image matching (Lowe, 2004) as it is highly distinctive and relatively quick if a kd-tree search (Arya, Mount, Netenyahu, Silverman & Wu, 1998) is run. Although very robust, SIFT can produce mismatches (outliers) that should be identified and removed. For this reason, a robust estimator, e.g., RANSAC (Rousseeuw & Leroy, 1987). becomes indispensable to discard wrong correspondences. This kind of check is usually performed by exploiting geometrical constraints that are here represented by homographic transformations.

HDR Photography

High Dynamic Range (HDR) photography allows one to capture the full dynamic range of light in real scenes. A camera can be intended as a tool that performs a discretization of the photographed scene that involves both spatial domain (i.e. the number of pixels) and radiometric resolution (i.e. number of bits per pixel). A colour image is a discrete function $c = f(x, y)$ where light information is associated to each pixel location (x, y). For a digital camera, c includes three channels (R, G, B) corresponding to red, green and blue components. Photographic cameras should capture a sufficient dynamic range (the ratio between the maximum and minimum pixel values) in order to simulate human vision.

However, the human visual system is highly sensitive to wavelengths in the visible spectrum and can deal with changes in brightness in order to preserve the original colour of the scene. Moreover, the eye has optimal adaptation mechanisms that allow one to see real scenes with dynamic ranges exceeding 4-5 orders of magnitude (Qiu, Guan, Duan & Chen, 2006). A common digital camera acquires only Low Dynamic Range (LDR) images and cannot represent the full dynamic range of light.

To overcome this limitation of the sensor, a set of multiple LDR images taken at different exposures can be used. HDR algorithms rely on pixel correspondences and therefore the camera should be mounted on a tripod to ensure that all images will align correctly. In addition, the scene should be as static as possible. In the case of hand-held shots, a preliminary geometric transformation is needed to register bracketed images and remove small misalignments.

The main problem is the choice of an appropriate mapping during the resampling phase. The proposed solution is based on a homography as it is a rigorous mapping between images acquired after rotating the camera around its perspective centre. Under this assumption, we assume that the image perspective centre is fixed, while we presuppose rotations could occur.

A pair of images taken with a rotating camera will differ by the numerical values of rotation matrices. Without loss of generality, we can write the following relationships between corresponding image points of pinhole images:

$$\mathbf{x}' = \mathbf{KRK}^{-1}\mathbf{x} = \mathbf{Hx} \tag{5}$$

where $\mathbf{K} = \text{diag}\,(f, f, 1)$ is the calibration matrix (Hartley & Zisserman, 2004) and the rotation matrices are **I** and **R**, respectively. This method can be extended in order to register a set of bracketed images, as proposed in (Qiu, Guan, Duan & Chen, 2006). The method is also quite robust to small translations of the camera centre.

The final result of a standard data processing pipeline is a sequence of homographies ($\mathbf{H}_{2,1}$, $\mathbf{H}_{3,2}$, …, $\mathbf{H}_{n,n-1}$) that are sequentially used to resample all images. The central image i of the sequence (sorted following the exposure values) is taken as reference and, assuming a relationship (5) between consecutive images, any other is processed using the following criteria:

$$\begin{aligned} \mathbf{x}_i &= \mathbf{H}^{-1}_{i+1,i}\mathbf{H}^{-1}_{i+2,i+1}\cdots\mathbf{H}^{-1}_{j,j-1}\mathbf{x}_j && \text{if} \quad i < j \\ \mathbf{x}_i &= \mathbf{H}_{i,i-1}\mathbf{H}_{i-1,i-2}\cdots\mathbf{H}_{j+1,j}\mathbf{x}_j && \text{if} \quad i < j \end{aligned} \tag{6}$$

An example is shown in Figure 2. The main entrance of the basilica of San Pietro al Monte (Civate, Italy) was captured with 5 bracketed images. A strong rotation of the camera during image acquisition is quite evident (Figure 2 top-left), while after the homography-based alignment with corresponding points (middle-left) images are consistent (bottom-left). The final HDR image is shown on the right.

Multi-Focus Imaging

Limited Depth of Field (DoF) is a fundamental problem in different disciplines. (e.g. photography and microscopy). DoF can be defined as the range of distances in an image over which the image is acceptably sharp and therefore refers to the zone in front of and behind a focused subject.

Although in some applications blurred images are acceptable (e.g. a sharp subject and a

Figure 2. The HDR mosaic of the Basilica of San Pietro al Monte in Civate (Italy)

fuzzy background could give more impact) the opportunity to have a sharp image and gather all the information contained in the scene is surely of primary importance. Obviously, the term "sharp" is just a visual quantification of image quality. To understand better the concept of "sharpness" we must consider the image formation process.

The image sharpness can be described with the circle of confusion (CoC). A lens placed at a given distance from the image plane will create point-like images only for point subjects at one given distance. For a point subject at any other distance, its image will be an optical spot (circle of confusion) caused by a cone of light rays from a lens not coming to a perfect focus when imaging a point source.

The depth of field is the area where the circle of confusion is not perceptible to the human eye. Although the DoF depends on several factors, aperture and focal distance are the most important. After setting the value of the circle of confusion (e.g. for a 35 mm camera a good choice is 0.03 mm), near and far limits of DoF can be estimated with simple mathematical relationships or with some free tools available on the Internet (e.g. http://www.dofmaster.com/dofjs.html).

In some cases, it is impossible to acquire an image where all areas appear sharp due to an excessive variation in depth. To overcome this limitation multiple shots with different focus points can be acquired and merged to obtain a sharp image. This field of research is termed multi-focus registration (Li, Manjunath & Mitra, 1995).

The key idea is a subdivision of source images into decompositions that are then integrated to obtain a composite reconstruction. Then the sharp image is created with an inverse multi-resolution transform (Li, Kwok & Wang, 2002). It is not the intention here to develop the mathematical solutions to this problem, since the number of papers dealing with this topic is too great to be listed exhaustively here. However, a pre-alignment of original images is recommended before running multi-focus registration algorithms. Also in this case more images can be registered with a sequence of homographic transformations. An example generated from 10 images is shown in Figure 3.

Panoramas –or panoramic images, Figure 4 (Brown & Lowe, 2003) can be easily created from several photos taken with a rotating camera. These images are then stitched and mapped with different projections (rectilinear, spherical, cylindrical, Vedutismo, etc.). Several commercial packages are currently available (Realviz Stitcher, PTgui, Autopano, etc.) for the automatic creation of panoramic images. Panoramic photography is also used for visualization on virtual tours and interactive explorations of multiple scenes and objects. Some links on the images allow the user to navigate the virtual scene.

Panoramas can be created by using a mathematical formulation based on projective geometry. Indeed, extending Equation 5, the transformation between two pinhole images i and j acquired by a rotating camera is a homography (Brown & Lowe, 2007).

$$\mathbf{H}_{ij} = \mathbf{K}\mathbf{R}_i\mathbf{R}_j^{\mathrm{T}}\mathbf{K}^{-1} \tag{7}$$

During the stitching process, the radial distortion is generally compensated, and enhancement procedures can reduce the radiometric differences between consecutive images. A gain compensation is applied to reduce the intensity difference between overlapping images, then a multi-blending algorithm (Burt & Adelson, 1983). removes the remaining image edges avoiding blurring of high frequency details.

Rectilinear panoramas (Figure 4a) are pinhole images that simulates a new virtual sensor. Obviously, deformations become inacceptable for large vertical and horizontal angles. Cylindrical panoramas (Figure 4b) have an horizontal field of view of 360° and a vertical of up to 180°. However,

Figure 3. Some of the images used to create the final multi-focus mosaic with their order in the original sequence

(3)

(6)

(10)

(final multi-focus)

the distortion towards the vertical limits (zenith and nadir) becomes inacceptable for practical applications, and a vertical limit is normally set to 100°-120°. Figure 4b shows the result when the limit is set to 140°.

To reduce these deformations, the Mercator projection (Figure 4b - 360°×130°) is usually employed. In this case a higher vertical field of view is guaranteed, without loosing the main geometric properties of the cylindrical projection. The equirectangular projection (Figure 4d) provides a field of view of 360°×180°. Spherical panoramas are created with this projection, where the horizontal and vertical lines are transformed into straight lines, while the other lines become curved.

Other interesting projections (e.g. rectilinear, Vedutismo, circular, stereographic, transverse cylindrical, ...) have different fields of view and are useful to depict particular scenes.

CONCLUSION

This chapter presented the role of projective transformations in modern digital photography, with a particular emphasis on HDR, multi-focus, and panoramic images. The registration algorithm behind each product relies on a planar homography (or a set of 2D homographic transformations), that are determined from a set of corresponding

Figure 4. It is normal to use these projections to obtain in panoramic photography: (a) rectilinear, (b) cylindrical, (c) Mercator, (d) equi-rectangular

points and robust estimation techniques. Indeed, automated matching procedures often produce gross errors and the usage of robust estimators becomes mandatory.

In all cases, pixel correspondence is the primary element for successive processing stages and a homography demonstrated to be an extremely efficient mapping. The method is also quite robust against small translations of the camera centre, especially when the hypothesis of rotating camera is no longer respected.

The rapid diffusion of such products is particularly interesting. In some cases, users can take advantage of these procedures without charge (e.g. Microsoft Photosynth generates panoramic images), where data can be automatically processed, visualized and shared. The market is growing fast and many algorithms for data processing are already available on the Internet.

REFERENCES

Arya, S., Mount, D., Netenyahu, N., Silverman, R., & Wu, A. (1998). An optimal algorithm for approximate nearest neighbour searching fixed dimensions. *Journal of the ACM*, *45*(6), 891–923. doi:10.1145/293347.293348

Barazzetti, L. (2011). Metric rectification via parallelograms. In *Proceedings of SPIE Optics+Photonics*, (Vol. 8085, pp. 23-26). Munich, Germany: SPIE.

Brown, M., & Lowe, D. (2003). Recognizing panoramas. In *Proceedings of International Conference on Computer Vision,* (Vol. 2, pp. 1218-1225). IEEE.

Brown, M., & Lowe, D. (2007). Automatic panoramic image stitching using invariant features. *International Journal of Computer Vision*, *74*(1), 59–73. doi:10.1007/s11263-006-0002-3

Burt, P., & Adelson, E. (1983). A multi-resolution spline with application to image mosaics. *ACM Transactions on Graphics*, *2*(4), 217–236. doi:10.1145/245.247

Debevec, P., & Malik, J. (1997). Recovering high dynamic range radiance maps from photographs. In *Proceedings of Siggraph*. New York: ACM Press. doi:10.1145/258734.258884

Global and China Digital Still Camera (DSC). (2011). *Industry report*. Retrieved from http://www.reportlinker.com

Haeberli, P. (1994). *A multifocus method for controlling depth of field*. GRAFICA Obscura.

Hartley, R., & Zisserman, A. (2004). *Multiple view geometry in computer vision*. Cambridge, UK: Cambridge University Press. doi:10.1017/CBO9780511811685

Li, H., Manjunath, B., & Mitra, S. (1995). Multisensor image fusion using the wavelet transform. *Graphical Models Image Processing*, *57*(3), 235–245. doi:10.1006/gmip.1995.1022

Li, S., Kwok, J., & Wang, Y. (2002). Multifocus image fusion using artificial neural networks. *Pattern Recognition Letters*, *23*, 985–997. doi:10.1016/S0167-8655(02)00029-6

Liebowitz, D., & Zisserman, A. (1998). Metric rectification for perspective images of planes. In *Proceedings of the IEEE Computer Society Conference on Computer Vision and Pattern Recognition*. IEEE.

Lourakis, M. (2009). Plane metric rectification from a single view of multiple coplanar circles. In *Proceedings of 16th IEEE International Conference on Image Processing (ICIP)*. IEEE.

Lowe, D. (2004). Distinctive image features from scale-invariant keypoints. *International Journal of Computer Vision*, *10*(56), 181–207.

Luhmann, T., & Tecklenburg, W. (2002). Bundle orientation and 3-D object reconstruction from multiple-station panoramic imagery. *International Archives of Photogrammetry, Remote Sensing & Spatial. Information Sciences*, *34*, 181–186.

Qiu, G., Guan, J., Duan, J., & Chen, M. (2006). Tone mapping for HDR image using optimization – A new closed form solution. In *Proceedings of ICPR 2006*. ICPR.

Remondino, F., & Fraser, C. (2006). Digital camera calibration methods: Considerations and comparisons. *International Archives of Photogrammetry. Remote Sensing and Spatial Information Sciences*, *36*(5), 266–272.

Rousseeuw, P., & Leroy, A. (1987). *Robust regression and outlier detection*. New York: John Wiley. doi:10.1002/0471725382

Sugimoto, A. (2000). A linear algorithm for computing the homography from conics in correspondence. *Journal of Mathematical Imaging and Vision*, *13*, 115–130. doi:10.1023/A:1026571913893

Chapter 17
Special Educational Needs Workshop Online:
Play Activity – Homework in the Jungle

Danny Barrantes
University Teaching Department, University of Costa Rica, Costa Rica

Maurizia D´Antoni
University Teaching Department, University of Costa Rica, Costa Rica

ABSTRACT

This chapter describes an educational setup experience implemented at the Department of University Teaching at University of Costa Rica. Its relevance lies upon the process and implementation of a didactic strategy based on a digital exercise, its mediation, and the resulting learning scenario that enhances and promotes accessibility and inclusion as a crucial discussion in higher education. A game activity involving a board game is one of the activities included, and its purpose aims to encourage changes in teachers' attitudes through creativity. It is relevant to foster appropriate curriculum arrangements and support measures as required, ensuring effective learning resulting in positive outcomes in higher education and wellbeing of students and staff. It is important to develop sector-wide technology facilities and staff development to enable colleges to provide an education capable of speaking everybody's language.

INTRODUCTION

Education and universities currently face great challenges in terms of setting themselves as spaces that conceive humans as integral social beings. The interest, of course, lies in the need to read a context that surrounds students in each of their disciplinary cultures, so that they can be aware of a world that moves easily between standards and trends; being this an unsafe understanding because of its very nature that opens up exclusively to that and those who meet the standards.

Therefore, our current educational thinking and subsequent educational development, which

DOI: 10.4018/978-1-4666-4490-8.ch017

is shaped in the various teaching strategies, must build learning processes that mediate interactions with "tools that promote learning, sociality, community, autonomous and creative intercourse among people, and the interaction of people with their environment," (Kahn & Kellner, 2007) a big concern that is held in the foundation of this present experience.

The Department of University Teaching (from now on referred to as DEDUN) belongs to the Teaching Training School in the Faculty of Education, at University of Costa Rica (UCR). This University strives to provide an environment free from any form of discrimination and, therefore, it is committed to non-discriminative and inclusive teaching practices, as for a deep interest and concern about diversity and inclusion, reflected on UCR´s policies that beyond any speech or ethical standing, are official and mandatory into the diverse development and processes in the different realms of our institution (Barrantes, et. al., 2011).

Article number 3 on the University of Costa Rica Constitution expresses the following: The purpose of the University of Costa Rica is to attain the changes society needs to accomplish the common good, through a policy aimed at achieving true social justice, integral development, full freedom and full independence of our people (Consejo Universitario, 2001). At the UCR, DEDUN is the department responsible for training and updating professors on issues related to teaching, education or inclusive education.

Moreover, in accordance with the enactment of Law 7600, the University aims to generate a teacher training process to address the issue of disability, as it is apparent from the University Senate agreement N. 4919, 2004, article N. 8 (Consejo Universitario, 2001). "To request the Department of University Teaching, Teacher Training School of the University of Costa Rica to include in the University Teaching course contents related to the implementation of the provisions of Act 7600 of Equal Opportunities for people with disabilities in Costa Rica (Consejo Universitario, 2004)".

"University teaching" is a 15 week course that is intended for in-service UCR´s professors from all the different disciplines that involve teaching. It promotes a critical and reflective approach to educational practices in the university classroom. Its nature and intention is introductory, so attendees can analyze different frameworks that exist in university teaching regarding different disciplines, every time a professor is planning and constructing educational scenarios.

There are two versions of the course: (1) blended: 50% online and 50% stationary meetings- and (2) an online version (Figure 1). In both cases, there is a department committee that defines the materials to be used as well as the order of topics and various logistical and administrative details. Thus, many of the materials are designed with the expressed intent of digital use, in order to promote interaction with teachers through the institutional spaces available, such as Mediation Virtual[1] and DEDUN webpage.

Within the range of different didactic material used, there is a special interest to develop customized teaching elements, this after given learning styles that come up in different combinations, specific to the diverse population who attend this course every semester.

This fact matches what Bolter remarks "HCI (Human-Computer Interaction) researchers critique existing and developing computer systems. Their critiques may be severe, but their purpose is to enable these systems to respond more effectively to the needs of those who use them. HCI aligns itself with social sciences in using qualitative and quantitative methods to come up with the principles of good design. In its practical intent, however, HCI more closely resembles the theoretical aspects of the industrial or fine arts such as graphic design." (Bolter, 2004). This could be one of the main variables to discuss since from its technical and didactical understanding, the priority to fulfill one's need remains as the major goal.

It is interesting that Illich's claim seems to be right when we talk about education and standard-

Figure 1. On-line interface for University Teaching Course

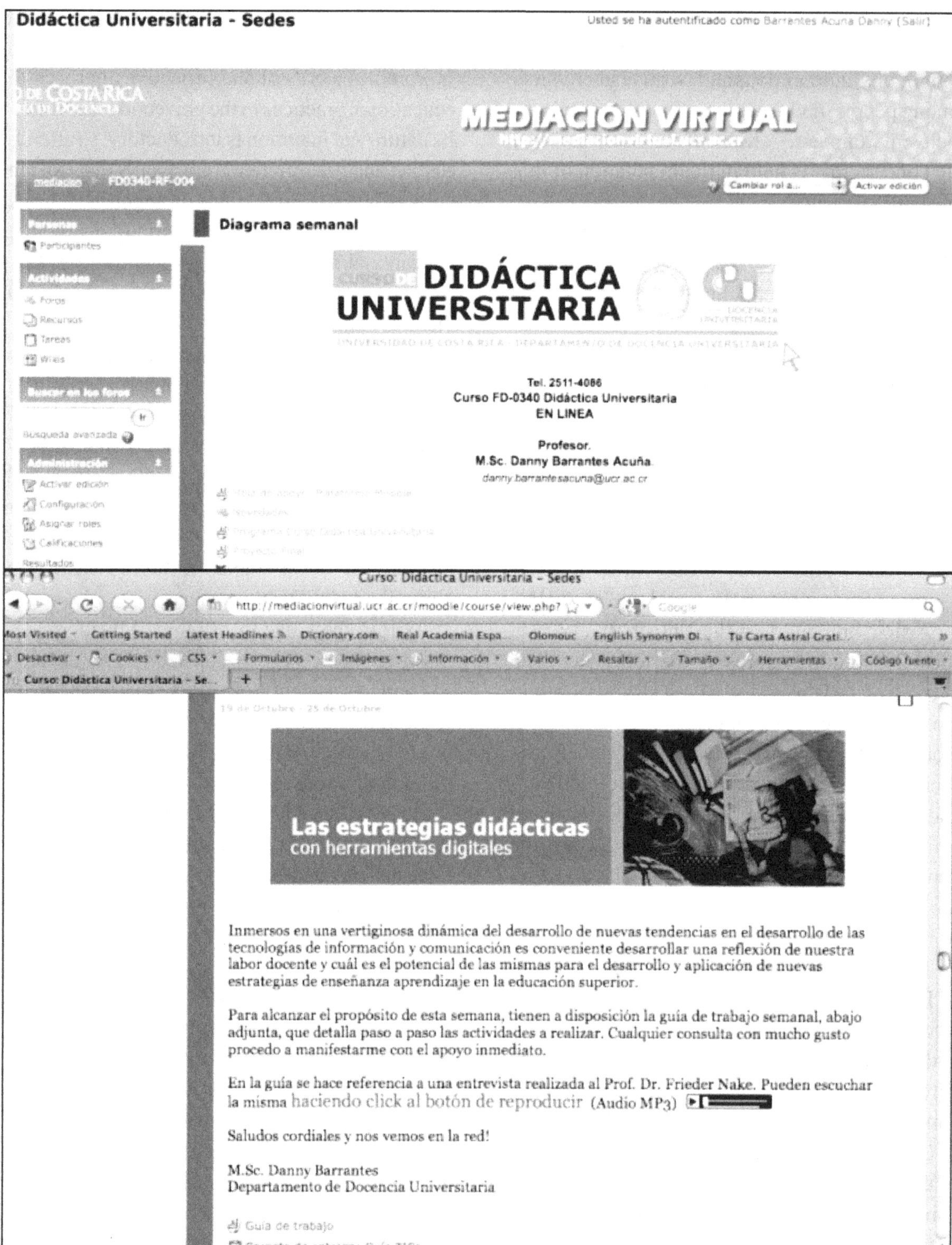

ization. "The individual's autonomy is intolerably reduced by a society that defines the maximum satisfaction of the maximum number as the largest consumption of industrial goods." (Illich, 1973). It is not trivial to conceive what a didactic strategy and its variables aim to: respond to students' needs, their learning style, their special educational needs, their own acknowledgment of a role, the kind of message and learning scenarios. All of the above flow side by side with any implementation, no matter if it is a book, a software application, a digital medium or an interactive exercise. Deleuze, quoted by Gere, points out that "the machine is always social before technical. There is always a social machine which selects or assigns the technical elements used." (Gere, 2008). Moreover, the UCR not only cares about students' special needs; the institution is very concerned about its workers' necessities and committed to their updated training. Under this understanding, we can point that the importance of the social function of the machine always exceeds its technical function.

ON OUR GOALS

One of the Department of University Teaching tasks is to train teachers to deal with special needs issues and curricular adjustments, being curricular adaptation one of our concerns in a college environment. This discussion normally takes place at a meeting during the course. However, there was an expressed need to design a follow up strategy, capable to enhance further discussions and possible debate lines.

We agree that educational technology is normally driven towards technological tools and software that have been created to support learning and teaching processes. Nevertheless, we have witnessed that there is an important distance between those learning spaces that are custom designed –including technical implications- and those where professors play a user role, without having any possibility to match their original intention during an implementation stage. Technology and digital gadgets should not be the ultimate goals by themselves, but pertinent means that match a given reality within a formative space. It is, however, mandatory to conceive any of such manifestations after a pedagogical process that holds didactics and its implementation lines coordinated.

Close to the previous idea, we have noticed that recently many universities have undertaken initiatives to promote inclusiveness. By *inclusiveness* in colleges we understand the inclusion in the student body of a full range of individuals with various barriers or with a special approach to learning.

Moreover, we intend to provide appropriate curriculum arrangements and support measures as required to ensure effective learning, resulting in positive outcomes.

Initially general policies about inclusion in our University have focused on meeting the requirements of disability legislation, and had, wisely but insufficiently, centered on how to meet student needs more effectively and consistently rather than on mere compliance.

Now we are aiming to promote pedagogical equity (González, 2003) by encouraging a formative activity at the University, which focuses on each individual's needs rather than on homogenized teaching methods.

THE BOARD GAME

In this study, educational technology is mainly viewed as a creative support to promote motivation and creativity in higher education teachers to reach the goal of inclusiveness. The high rate of utilization of educational technologies in special education reflects that students with individual needs have the potential skill to learn or take advantage of technology in general.

As for the strategy, we decided to develop an online module to accompany the discussions and debates that would take place during stationary meetings. We thought of having a mixed exercise capable of allowing community interaction as well as personal examination. This background fits perfectly with a game board called "The jungle test," that was a random activity developed during stationary sessions. The game presents a paradoxical situation in an elementary school with the forest animals, where the teacher assigns tasks to the different animals indiscriminately. Don't we all do it sometimes, too? Looking at us from outside, assigning absurd tasks to different animals can help to observe our actions in the classroom and the development of educational relationship, sometimes involving lack of respect towards the students.

Additionally, it can help us to "solve" seemingly absurd situations creatively. The awareness of being creative enough to unravel apparently hopeless situations gives teachers the opportunity to face the limitations of their daily work, and offers them the possibility to "include" people even in activities that may have not been designed to be inclusive.

The board game is originally inspired by a picture attributed to George H. Reavis, which shows a row of animals, allegedly students, queuing in front of a traditional desktop, at which an equally traditional teacher sits. What is not traditional is the environment: all the students are jungle animals while their teacher is human.

The reflection to be made with the players is related to how people have different skills and diverse curricular adaptations needs.

The suggestion we wish to share is that all humans have different talents and skills and can perform most tasks, with or without disabilities, whether they come from different or similar cultural background, if we, as teachers, "scaffold" them properly.

The desire and willingness to "include" must be present during the process, and the awareness that there is not only a single "good" way of doing things, increased. Inclusion is a concept that must guide us to improvement through creativity; however, instead we sometimes *fossilize* using methods, materials, or contents that could actually be changed to benefit everyone, students and teachers.

Unfortunately, like these animals in the jungle, our students are sometimes asked to perform impossible tasks only to fit into the traditional way, without taking into account that such performance can be possible using their own individual skills.

The curricular plan that this School of the jungle imposes on its students may be foolish (for example to ask the snake to fly), while the ultimate goal that different activities contain can often match the other skills each student/animal can count on.

The animals solving the test apparently face tasks "beyond" their means; however, what is wrong is the way in which the teacher requires them to do so.

After analyzing all the previous contents and variables, we decided to develop this game as a digital strategy, in a simple way though, to enhance more discussions among the students, this after previous debate. The implementation process consisted of three different stages.

Aesthetics and Design

During this phase, we had to analyze all necessary elements and their contextual understanding within the game, as for referencing it in terms of near-reality of the participants. A series of preliminary sketches (Figure 2) was made to decide an appropriate illustration style, taking into account criteria such as gestures, focusing on playful, innovative ideas. Once defined, the work was completed with the design of an interface suitable for both digital and printed media.

Prototype

After having a final draft of the game, a first paper interface version, there was a series of tests around its validation in terms of its logical application and

Figure 2. Preliminary sketches used for the final version of the board game

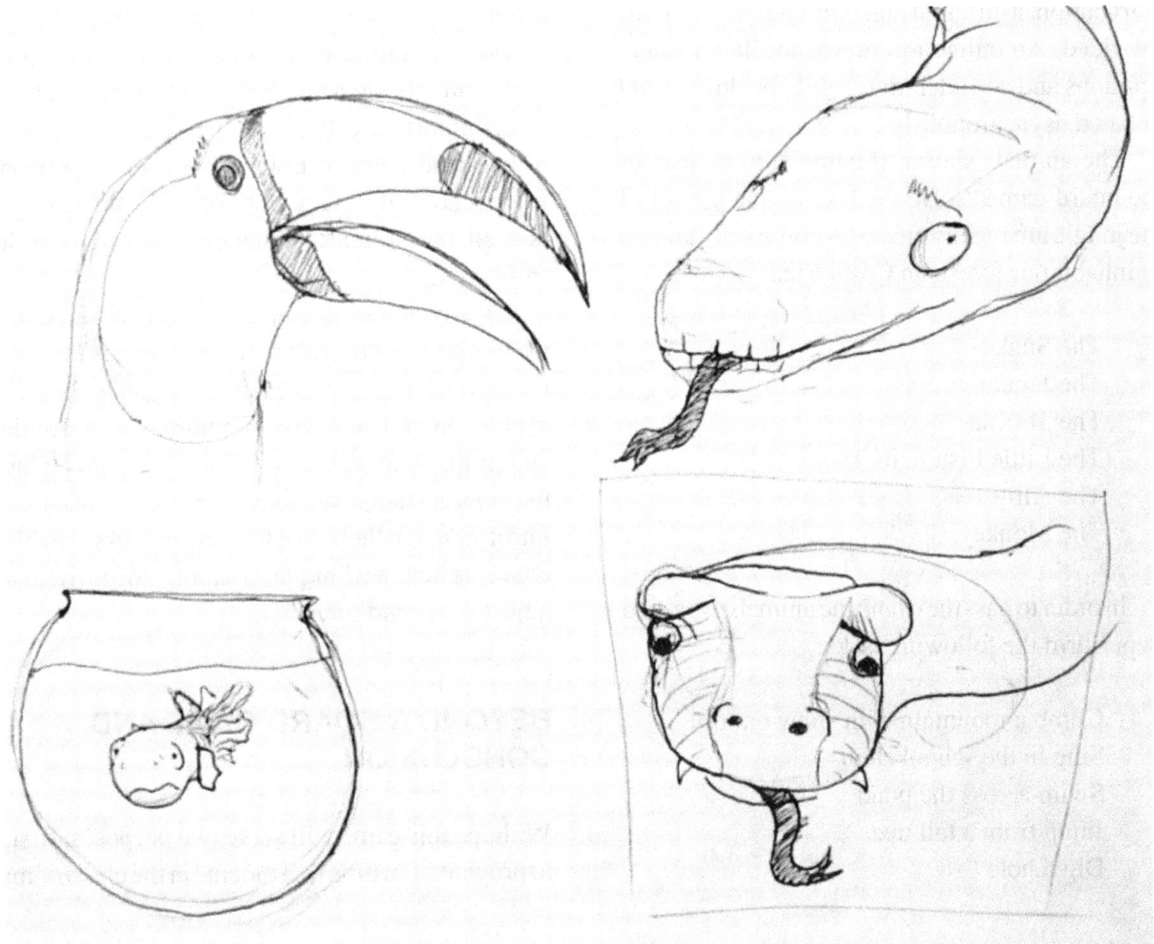

interaction. There were at least three groups of five members that after a number of tryouts, offered feedback with ideas, suggestions and possibilities in the use of the didactic materials.

Subsequently, a series of adjustments was made dealing with proportion of shapes, colors and order of elements.

Implementation

A first formal implementation of the game took place during the first semester of 2010, specifically during the 14th week. It consisted primarily of a traditional classroom meeting of the University Teaching course, intended as the starting point to make everyone aware about the issue. This session featured special guests who debated from their diverse perspectives about the role of the University in facing the challenges awaiting us in a public institution and a globalized society.

After the stationary session, participants were invited to enter the virtual university platform (Mediación Virtual, 2011) where they were able to find a class module for digital interaction. To serve this purpose, a flash application of the game (El examen de la selva, 2011) was developed and included. To get the expected effect of randomness, it was necessary to add an action script code; this feature allowed the application to execute random animations and, consequently, combinations of animals and tasks. As the student pressed the start button, a different outcome and question was provided. An online forum was available where opinions and considerations could be thrown and debated asynchronously.

The animals chosen (Figure 3) to be part of the board game "solve the test" in the school of the jungle are mainly creatures commonly known to inhabit our forests in Costa Rica:

- The Snake
- The Jaguar
- The Toucan
- The Little Fish in its Tank
- The Alligator
- The Monkey

In order to pass the exam, the animals are asked to perform the following tasks:

- Climb a mountain with snow on top
- Sing in the school choir
- Swim across the pond
- Jump from a tall tree
- Dig a hole

As you can see, all these tasks could sound ordinary at some point and even vital for our little friends in their natural environment. However, what animals are actually asked to perform, and more importantly, the way their teacher requires it, can lead them to failure and even expulsion from school. It is very important for the teacher and all the animals to understand and benefit from creativity.

Clearly, the objective is to guide professionals working in education not only to be flexible, but also to think and debate core points such as evaluation and subjectivity, and let them decide and promote an educational paradigm involving the appropriate strategies. Teachers must take into account in their own training process suitable concepts and techniques relating to curricular adjustments and inclusion.

BEYOND A BOARD GAME AND CONCLUSION

We hope this game will serve two purposes: first, to provide a fun time for students in the classroom;

Figure 3. Graphical outcome

Figure 4. Current interface

second, as an amusing way to become aware of absurd moments that sometimes we, the teachers, create in the classroom. It also aims to motivate our own creativity, once we identify ourselves with small animals whose skills the teacher intends to homogenize.

Moreover, this exercise would be plain and senseless if not complemented by reading, as well as by proper mediation throughout discussion of real cases of students from the University of Costa Rica, whose identity or location has been appropriately modified. These students have had some problems relating to inclusion or curricular adjustments and their cases became meaningful when they asked the university authorities for help to face and overcome their difficulties.

"Solving" the exercise of the proposed "cases" in the same way leads to a comparison with the game of "Homework in the jungle." It is usually very easy to build a bridge between the "absurd" jungle situation, which requires a creative solution in a game and fiction atmosphere, and the case-study where the teachers attending the workshop are told the situations are real, although the identities are disguised. The exercise helps them change from a fictional situation to one in which they can picture themselves, their students or colleagues in a very realistic scenario.

The workshop or course where the board game can be used includes reading the laws and regulations of both the country and the university about special educational needs. Adapting the curriculum involves, among other aspects, differentiating instruction so that the students are provided with a variety of ways to process information and diverse chances to demonstrate what they have learned, while teachers are given the appropriate tools in order to find out the different ways student construct knowledge.

REFERENCES

Barrantes, D. et al. (2011). *Nuevos formatos para la función universitaria*. San José: Editorial de la Universidad de Costa Rica.

Bolter, J. (2004). Theory and practice in new media studies. In *Digital Media revisited: theoretical and conceptual innovations in digital domains*. Cambridge, MA: MIT Press.

Consejo Universitario. (2001). *Reglamento de régimen académico estudiantil. San Pedro, Ciudad Universitaria Rodrigo Facio: Unidad de Información. Centro de Información y Servicios Técnicos*. San José: Universidad de Costa Rica.

Consejo Universitario. (2004). *Acta de la sesión no. 4919*. San José: Universidad de Costa Rica. Retrieved from http://cu.ucr.ac.cr/actas/2004/4919.pdf

El Examen de la Selva. (2011). Retrieved from http://docenciauniversitaria.ucr.ac.cr/juego/juego.html

Gere, C. (2008). *Digital culture*. London: Reaktion Books.

González, A. (2003). Una pedagogía de la diversidad y de la equidad: propuestas para una nueva relación profesor– alumno. *Ethos Educativo*, *27*, 55–65.

Higbee, J. (2003). *Curriculum transformation and disability: Implementing universal design in higher education*. Minneapolis, MN: University of Minnesota.

Illich, I. (1973). *Tools for conviviality*. London: Calder & Boyars.

Kahn, R., & Kellner, D. (2007). Technology, politics and the reconstruction of education. *Policy Futures in Education*, *5*(4), 439. doi:10.2304/pfie.2007.5.4.431

Mediación Virtual. (2011). Retrieved from http://mediacionvirtual.ucr.ac.cr

ENDNOTES

1 *Mediación virtual* is a Learning Management System (Moodle)

Chapter 18
Using Emotion Map System to Implement the Generative Chinese Style Music with Wu Xing Theory

Chih-Fang Huang
Department of Information Communications, Kainan University, Taiwan

En-Ju Lin
Department of Musicology, Heidelberg University, Germany

ABSTRACT

Wu Xing is an ancient mysterious Chinese philosophy applied to many fields. The Music Emotion Classification (MEC) refers to the music cognition of mind with the categorized emotion result mapping to music parameters. Many researchers focused the topic on the MEC with theory and experiment development in the past decades. This chapter mainly discusses the possibility to synthesize the meta-level algorithmic music based on the analysis result from the previous research, with the proposed Emotion Map System (EMS) mapped into the innovated Wu Xing Emotion Map System (WXEMS), which indicates the emotion situation based on the X-Y coordinate movement in the WXEMS plane. The MEC result shown in the EMS/WXEMS trajectory controls the algorithmic music variation with the proposed mapping rules. In addition, the generative music varies smoothly according to the correspondent WXEMS data changed with any emotion transition, which can apply the technology into the generative background music in Chinese style using the proposed Wu Xing Automated Music System (WXAMS).

INTRODUCTION

There are lots of research literatures show the relationship between music and emotion. Chinese Wu Xing (Fung, 1983; Wolfram, 1965) which means five elements, including metal, wood, water, fire, and earth, respectively, provides an abstract and mysterious philosophy applied for various fields including Chinese medicine, Cosmology or so-called Feng Shui, military strategy, and music, to pursuit the harmony in human and nature. In this chapter the music emotion classification (MEC)

DOI: 10.4018/978-1-4666-4490-8.ch018

will be discussed, and correlated to Wu Xing theory, in order to generate background music in Chinese style automatically.

Some of the music emotion researches retrieved the data from the speech, facial expression, and physiological signal (Healey, 2000; Picard, Vyzas & Healey, 2001; Haag, Goronzy, Schaich & Williams, 2004; Nasoz, Alvarez, Lisetti & Finkelstein, 2003), which are not sufficiently acceptable for the realistic application. The research by Johannes Wagner, Jonghwa Kim, Elisabeth André (Chen, 1996) shows a successful emotion recognition system including data analysis and classification for collecting physiological signals indifferent affective states for music and emotion with biosensors. Therefore we adopt and categorize the four emotions including "joy", "anger", "sadness", and "pleasure" to the well-know 2-D emotion model into the 4-quadrature plane, according to Johannes Wagner's expression. The horizontal axis (X-axis) with position and negative directions represents the "positive emotion" and "negative emotion" respectively, while the vertical axis (Y-axis) in positive and negative directions represents the "high arousal / energetic" and "low arousal / calm" emotions respectively. Figure 1 shows our proposed 2-D Emotional Model for the generative music with the "Emotion Trajectory" controlled by user, with proper emotion-music features mapping into our proposed "emotion map system" (EMS) to generate music automatically (Huang, 2011).

WU XING MUSIC THEORY

The proposed Wu Xing generative music is based on the fundamental Chinese Wu Xing philosophy (Fung, 1983; Wolfram, 1965; Rossi, Caretto & Scheid, 2007), and the properties metal, wood, water, fire, and earth construct this system as a universe. Chinese pentatonic scale will be discussed to map the Wu Xing emotion data correlated to the MEC system.

Wu Xing Cycles

There are five phases as the interactions between two of the Wu Xing elements. There are two main Wu Xing cycles including Generating Cycle to represent the constructive process, and Overcoming Cycle to present the deconstructive process (Rossi, Caretto & Scheid, 2007) as shown in Figure 2.

Furthermore many related literatures show the result based on the similar system to perform the MEC with more detailed analysis to obtain the four difference music emotion styles with the characteristics of all of the music parameters. Among all research papers, Livingstone and Brown's "Dynamic Response: Real-Time Adaptation for Music Emotion" divides the quadrature form into a more detailed octal form, with a 2DES –2 Dimensional Emotion Space (Wagner, Kim & André, 2005). As shown in Figure 3, our proposed Wu Xing Emotion Map System (WXEMS) is based on the mapping according to the octal rules and the Wu Xing emotion theory (Rossi, Caretto & Scheid, 2007) which summarizes every music parameter data with its priority of the importance mapped from the Wu Xing emotion state located in the correspondent coordinate area, according to the related literatures. The (X, Y) mapping data can be retrieved based on the EMS, to realize the music synthesis in real time with the Wu Xing emotional data change.

This research is mainly based on the classified result in (Haag, Goronzy, Schaich & Williams, 2004) to extract the most important mapping relationships between music parameters and emotion states, to implement the EMS / WXEMS with our selected mapping data, in order to find the possibility to compose emotion-based music in real time with smooth change.

MUSIC PARAMETER DISCUSSION

Based on (Haag, Goronzy, Schaich & Williams, 2004) we summarize and extract all of the music

Figure 1. The 2-D Emotional Map System (EMS) in a 4-quadrature plane

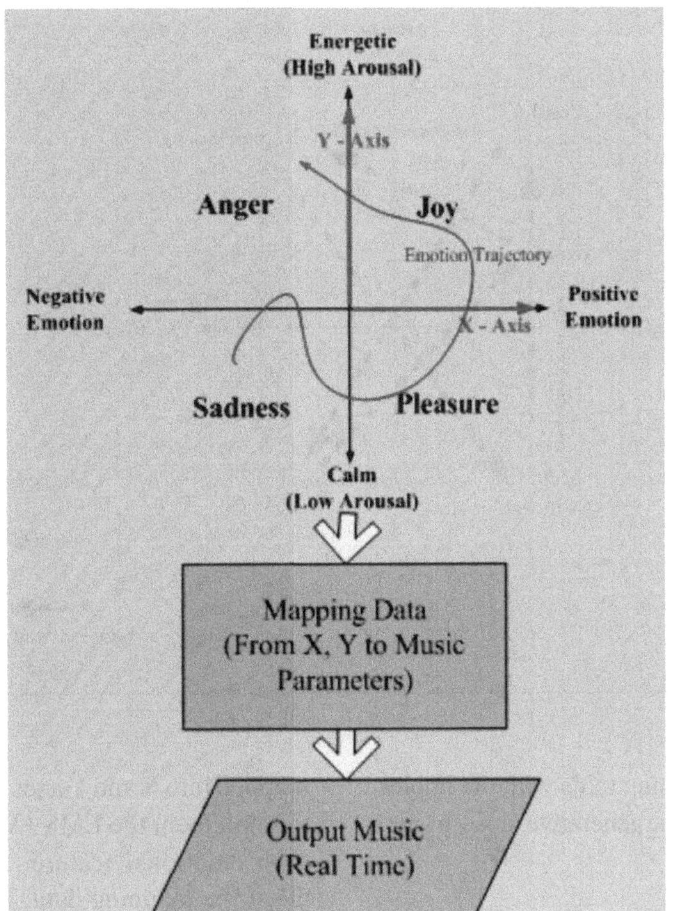

Figure 2. Wu Xing cycles

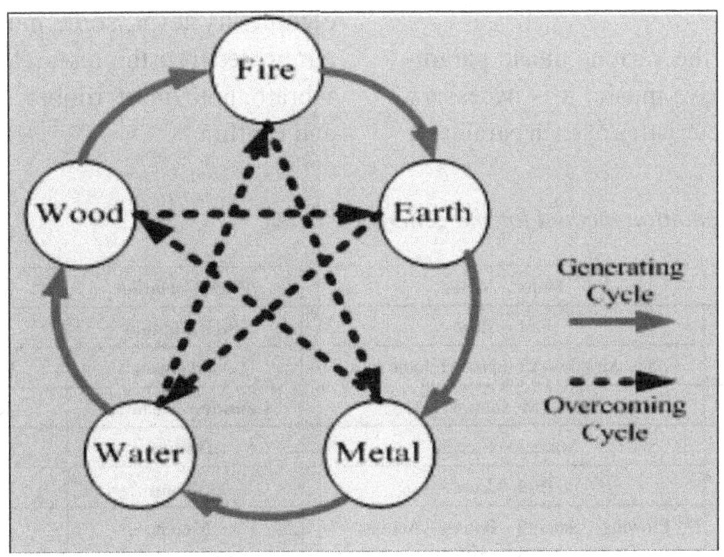

Figure 3. The Proposed Wu Xing Emotion Map System (WXEMS)

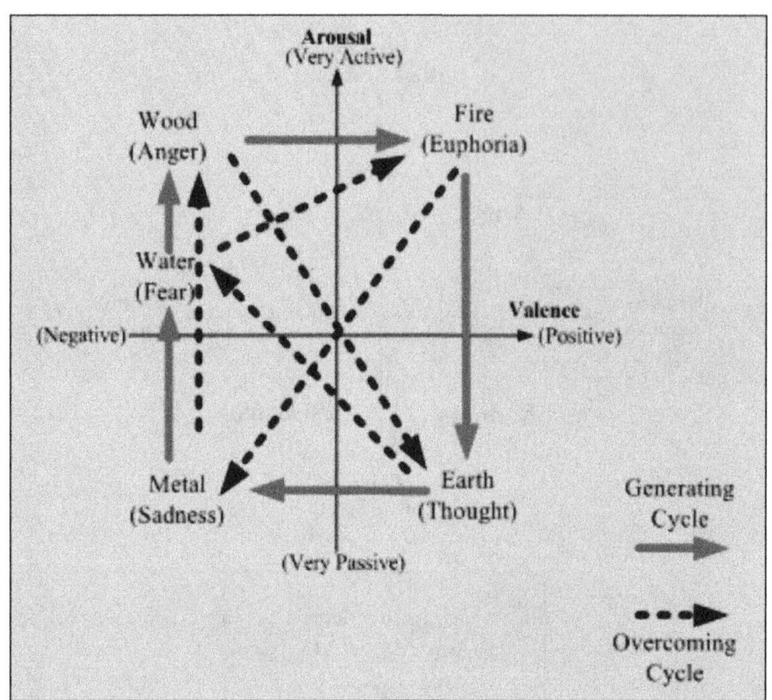

parameters into a mapping table with the implementation method for the generative music usage, as shown in Table 1:

MUSIC PARAMETER WITH X-Y MAPPING FOR EMS/WXEMS

Prior to implement the various music parameters for the generative music, it is necessary to observe the characteristics of each parameter mapped into X and Y axes, and then we can start to implement the EMS / WXEMS mapping for each emotional feature. After we summarize all of the mapping data, we find out that most of the music parameters own their significant features which are ready for use with EMS / WXEMS X-Y mapping. In order to reduce the complexity level, some music parameters are eliminated from this research, including tonality, vibrato, note onset, timbre, loudness variation, and rhythm.

Table 1. The implementation method for the generative music

Mode	Major – Minor	**Pitch Variation**	Large – Small
Tempo	Fast – Slow	**Pitch Contour**	Up – Down
Harmony	Simple -- Complex Melodic	**Note Onset**	Rapid - Slow - Sharp
Loudness	Soft – Medium -Loud	**Loudness Variation**	Rapid - Few - Small
Articulation	Staccato – Legato	**Timbre**	Few - Many – Sharp
Pitch	High – Low	**Vibrato**	Fast - Deep – Intense
Rhythm	Flowing – Smooth – Rough – Activity – Complex – Firm	**Meter**	Triple – Duple
Pitch Range	High – Low	**Tonality**	Tonal - Atonal – Chromatic

Coordinate Mapping

X Axis Data

With the increment of the X-axis value, the mode will be maintained in the tendency of the major, the articulation will be controlled with more staccato, and the harmony will be simpler. On the contrary, if the X-axis data value is decremented to the negative direction, then the mode, articulation, and harmony will be kept in more possibility of minor, legato, and complex, respectively.

Y Axis Data

If the data value in the Y-axis increased, then the tempo, loudness, pitch, and meter will go faster, louder, higher, and in more triplex. On the contrary these music parameters will be slower, less loud, lower, and in more duple, respectively.

The Implementation of Each Music Parameter

Mode

In this chapter "mode" refers to the variance between major and minor which is well defined in the literatures of the western music theory. However how to smoothly perform the modulation between major and minor without the abrupt change is one of our research topics. We propose to use the modulation in parallel keys between major and minor to solve this problem, where we use Chinese Gong mode as the major key, and Chinese Yu mode as the minor key (Livingstone & Brown, 2005). An example of the parallel keys is specified in Figures 4 and 5 which specifies two scales in the scores to implement for our proposed WXAMS:

The only difference between the major scale and the harmonic scale is the 3rd note and the 6th note, which can be manipulated with the probability control to guide the "trending" for major and minor keys. With using this point, when the data value of X coordinate is big enough, then the major key can be generated. When the X value is decreased, then the appearance rate of E-nature (3rd note of the major key) and A-nature (6th note of the major key) is lowered, and the E-flat (3rd note of the minor key) and B-flat (7th note of the minor key) begins to show up after the X value is across the X axis to the negative.

In addition to the music scale, the harmonic progression can be used to implement the concept of smooth transition between the parallel keys. In

Figure 4. C-Gong Mode Scale as the Major Key

Figure 5. C-Yu Mode Scale as the Minor Key

the case of C major and c minor, there are some methods can be used to perform the smooth modulation transition as follows:

1. The median (note E or E^b) for the harmonization of the C major tonic triad chord I (C-E-G) and c minor tonic triad chord I (C-E^b-G) can be controlled with the probability to perform the smooth modulation with transition in the EMS.
2. The submediant (note A or A^b) probability control as the subdominant chords IV (major) or iv (minor) is useful for the EMS / WXEMS smooth transition.
3. When the data value shown in the X axis or Y axis, then the "open fifth" chord (Notes C and G only) will be implemented without the median note.
4. Note that either major or minor key shares the exact same chord V (G-B-D) which will make no difference during the parallel key modulation.

The algorithmic composition will use the sieve theory and Markov chain (Winsor, 1992; Huang, Lu & Chou, 2008).

Tempo

The tempo value will vary with the increment of the y value. Here we define the maximum and minimum values as follows:

$$Tempo_{\max} = 120BPM \,|_{y=y_{\max}} \quad (1)$$

$$Tempo_{\min} = 40BPM \,|_{y=y_{\min}} \quad (2)$$

The data value between y_{max} and y_{min} will be proportionally increased or decreased.

Harmony

The chord progression will vary with the x value, and the fundamental chords including I, IV, and V will be generated accompanied with the melodic line. The more complicated altered chords are currently not discussed in this chapter.

Loudness

The music dynamic (loudness) will vary with the y value, and the boundary condition is defined as follows:

$$Loudness_{\max} = 110 \,|_{y=y_{\max}} \quad (3)$$

$$Loudness_{\min} = 50 \,|_{y=y_{\min}} \quad (4)$$

The loudness will be increased or decreased with 10 for every grid movement. Note that all of the loudness values are based on the MIDI "velocity".

Articulation

The "staccato" will become more significant when the x value is increased, to generate a short duration sound with the higher dynamic. In contrary if the x value is getting smaller, then the not duration will be longer with the lower dynamic, to produce the "legato".

Pitch, Pitch Range, and Pitch Variation

These three pitch related music parameters will vary with the Y-axis value, therefore the central point of Y axis, the origin of the Y-Y plan, is defined as the middle C, which is the MIDI note name 60. Therefore the pitch range is defined as the following equations within 4 octaves:

$$Pitch_{center} = 60 \,|_{y=y_0} \quad (5)$$

$$Pitch_{\max} = 84 \,|_{y=y_{\max}} \quad (6)$$

$$Pitch_{\min} = 36 \,|_{y=y_{\min}} \quad (7)$$

After that pitch range and pitch variation are implemented as the following rules:

$$Pitch_{variation} = k_1 \times y \quad (8)$$

where k_1 is a constant.

Furthermore we define the boundary condition for pitch range and pitch variation as follows:

$$Pitch_{variation} \leq 12 \mid y = y_{\min} \text{ and } Pitch_{range} \leq 4 \quad (9)$$

$$Pitch_{variation} \leq 36 \mid y = y_{\max} \text{ and } Pitch_{range} \leq 12 \quad (10)$$

Equation 9 means that the pitch variation will be generated within an octave and the pitch interval can not exceed major third when y is the minimum. Equation 10 refers to the limit that the pitch variation can be generated within three octaves and the pitch interval should be within an octave when y is the maximum.

Meter

Meter (Metre) is also mapped with Y axis. When y is greater, then the meter is with a higher probability of triple time, which makes the music more vigorous. When y is getting smaller, then the generative music is going more with the compound meter, which generates the music in a stable way.

$$\Pr(Meter_{triple}) = k_2 \times y \quad (11)$$

$$\Pr(Meter_{compound}) = 1 - \Pr(Meter_{triple}) \quad (12)$$

where Pr is the probability of the triple time (or compound meter) show-up rate, and k_2 is a constant.

RESULT

Based on the above mentioned methodology including all of possible music parameters implementation and the features mapping with Wu Xing emotion, the "Emotion Trajectory" shown in WXEMS which represents the emotion data varying with time will generate the emotion music in real time. The system flow chart for the WXEMS implementation with Wu Xing Automated Music System (WXAMS) is finally proved successfully as shown in Figure 6, using the real-time automated music program, Max/MSP (Bowe, R., 1992) and the Program GUI is shown as Figure 7.

CONCLUSION

There are lots of literatures discussing the music cognitive psychology, in an attempt to relate the specific music parameters to some certain emotion features, including the research methods from the questionnaire interview to the brain wave measurement, trying to obtain the result which can map human emotion to music. Here we confine the music into the tonal music in Chinese style with Wu Xing concept, and use of the most significant come out from the previous research to conclude

Figure 6. Wu Xing Automated Music System (WXAMS) Implementation

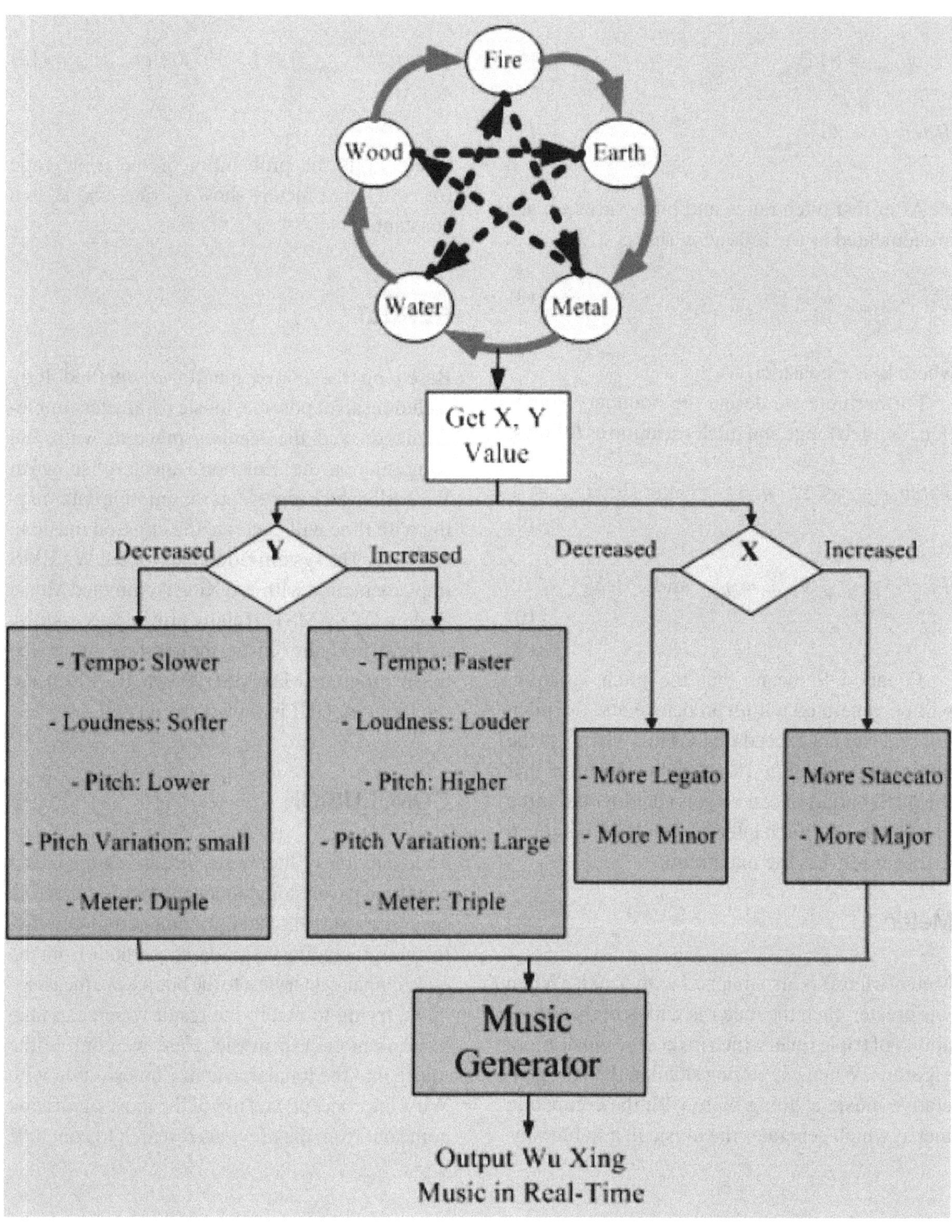

Figure 7. Algorithmic Composition GUI with WXEMS Using Max/MSP Program

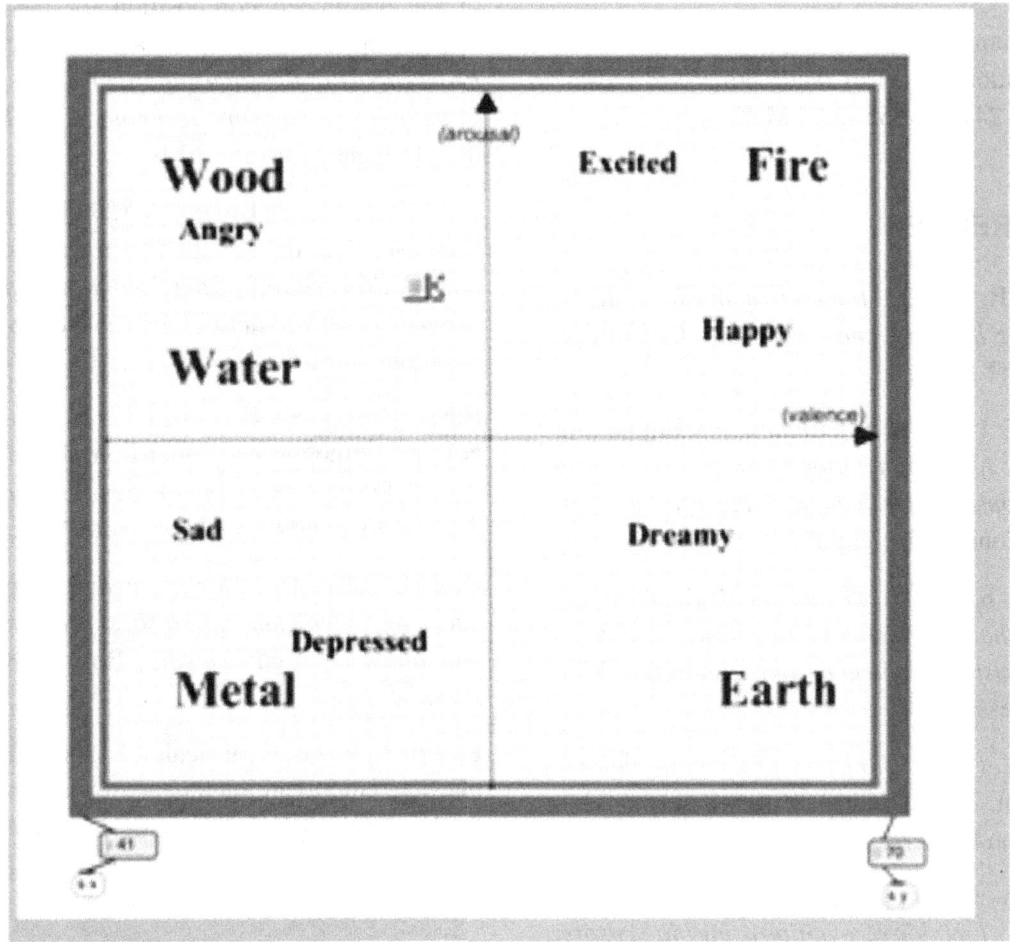

the statistic data with the implementation of the algorithmic composition to map various emotion-related music parameters to the emotion energy map distribution. Hence the real-time generative music according to the emotion coordinate is composed with the innovative WXEMS. The methodology of the WXEMS for the generative music can be applied to many fields, such as the generative game music (Huang, 2009), converting the scenarios into the classified emotion data, and mapping them to the background music automatically. Some other applications might include the generative background music to support the music production for multimedia, presentation, and film, etc. (Collins, 2008; Paul, 2007). This research emphasizes a smooth way to perform the transition among emotion music parameters, which can make the generative background music fluently. In addition the generative music is based on the real time automated technique, which will compose and play different music with more fun. There are more applications for the WXAMS, therefore it can be implemented with more mature software techniques to provide an efficient and economic way for the future music industry such as music therapy and multimedia music generation, etc.

ACKNOWLEDGMENT

The authors would like to appreciate the support from National Science Council projects of Taiwan: NSC99-2410-H-155 -035 -MY2.

REFERENCES

Bowe, R. (1992). *Interactive music systems: Machine listening and composing*. Cambridge, MA: MIT Press.

Chen, C. (1996). *Early Chinese work in natural science: A re-examination of the physics of motion, acoustics, astronomy and scientific thoughts*. Hong Kong: University Press.

Collins, K. (2008). *Game sound: An introduction to the history, theory, and practice of video game music and sound design*. Cambridge, MA: MIT Press.

Fung, Y. (1983). *A history of Chinese philosophy* (Vol. 2). (D. Bodde, Trans.). Princeton, NJ: Princeton University Press.

Haag, A., Goronzy, S., Schaich, P., & Williams, J. (2004). *Emotion recognition using bio-sensors: First step towards an automatic system, affective dialogue systems*. Tutorial and Research Workshop, Kloster Irsee.

Healey, J. (2000). *Wearable and automotive systems for affect recognition from physiology*. (PhD thesis). MIT, Cambridge, MA.

Huang, C. (2009). The study of the automated music composition for games. In *Proceedings of Conference on Digital Game-Based Learning*. Hong Kong: IEEE.

Huang, C. (2011). A novel automated way to generate content-based background music using algorithmic composition. *International Journal of Sound. Music and Technology*, *1*(1), 11–16.

Huang, C., Lu, H., & Chou, Y. (2008). The study of the automated composition for the music in Taiwanese Hakka Mountain song style. In *Proceedings of the International Conference on Computer and Network Technologies in Education*. Hsinchu, Taiwan: IEEE.

Livingstone, S., & Brown, A. (2005). Dynamic response: Real-time adaptation for music emotion. In *Proceedings of the Second Australasian Conference on Interactive Entertainment*. Sydney, Australia: Australasia.

Nasoz, F., Alvarez, K., Lisetti, C., & Finkelstein, N. (2003). Emotion recognition from physiological signals for presence technologies. *International Journal of Cognition, Technology and Work, 6*(10).

Paul, H. (2007). *Music for new media: Composing music for video games, web sites, presentations, and other interactive media*. Boston: Berklee Press.

Picard, R., Vyzas, E., & Healey, J. (2001). Toward machine emotional intelligence: Analysis of affective physiological state. *IEEE Transactions on Pattern Analysis and Machine Intelligence, 23*(10), 1175–1191. doi:10.1109/34.954607

Rossi, E., Caretto, L., & Scheid, V. (2007). *Shen: Psycho-emotional aspects of Chinese medicine*. Church Livingstone.

Wagner, J., Kim, J., & André. (2005). From physiological signals to emotions: Implementing and comparing selected methods for feature extraction and classification. In *Proceedings of IEEE International Conference on Multimedia & Expo*. IEEE.

Winsor, P. (1992). *Automated music composition*. University of North Texas Press.

Wolfram, E. (1965). Chinese regional stereotypes. *Asian Survey*, *5*(12), 596–608. doi:10.2307/2642652

Chapter 19
Prediction of Change-Prone Classes Using Machine Learning and Statistical Techniques

LinRuchika Malhotra
Deptament of Software Engineering, Delhi Technological University, India

Ankita Jain Bansal
Deptament of Software Engineering, Delhi Technological University, India

ABSTRACT

For software development, availability of resources is limited, thereby necessitating efficient and effective utilization of resources. This can be achieved through prediction of key attributes, which affect software quality such as fault proneness, change proneness, effort, maintainability, etc. The primary aim of this chapter is to investigate the relationship between object-oriented metrics and change proneness. Predicting the classes that are prone to changes can help in maintenance and testing. Developers can focus on the classes that are more change prone by appropriately allocating resources. This will help in reducing costs associated with software maintenance activities. The authors have constructed models to predict change proneness using various machine-learning methods and one statistical method. They have evaluated and compared the performance of these methods. The proposed models are validated using open source software, Frinika, and the results are evaluated using Receiver Operating Characteristic (ROC) analysis. The study shows that machine-learning methods are more efficient than regression techniques. Among the machine-learning methods, boosting technique (i.e. Logitboost) outperformed all the other models. Thus, the authors conclude that the developed models can be used to predict the change proneness of classes, leading to improved software quality.

INTRODUCTION

A number of studies have empirically validated the relationship between object oriented metrics and important external attributes such as reliability, effort, fault proneness, change proneness, etc. (Aggarwal, Singh, Kaur & Malhotra, 2009; Singh, Kaur & Malhotra, 2010; Gyimothy, Ferenc & Siket, 2005; Bieman, Andrews & Yang, 2003; Tsantalis, Chatzigeorgiou & Stephanides, 2005; Li & Henry, 1993; Briand, Wust & Lounis, 2001). This has been done to determine whether object

DOI: 10.4018/978-1-4666-4490-8.ch019

oriented metrics are useful quality indicators. In this chapter, we have investigated the relationship between object oriented metrics and change proneness. Every software undergoes number of changes throughout its life period - to improve functionality, to fix bugs, to add new features etc. Additionally, requirements of the user may change with time, leading to further changes in the software. This may result in various versions of a software. But making changes in a particular version of the software is not an easy task and requires large amount of resources in terms of money, time, and manpower. This is because software typically consists of a large number of classes. It might be possible that a single change in a class is propagated to other classes, which in turn will lead to change in the classes affected by the change. As a result, significant percentage of the classes may need to be changed. It has been studied that the largest percentage of the software development effort is spent on rework and maintenance. Thus, it would be highly beneficial if we get to know the classes which are prone to changes. This will help developers as they can concentrate on these change prone classes and make a more flexible software by modifying the classes which are more prone to changes. Developers can take focused preventive actions which will help to reduce the maintenance costs and improve quality. Also, developers can allocate resources more judiciously. Besides these advantages, we also get insight about the design of the software by correctly predicting the change prone classes, e.g., if a change in a particular class has a large impact on some other class, then we can conclude there is high coupling between the two classes and thus to improve the design, coupling must be reduced.

The aim of this chapter is to establish a relationship between object oriented metrics (Li, Henry, Kafura & Schulman, 1995; Chidamber & Kemerer, 1994; Lorenz & Kidd, 1994) and change proneness using various machine learning techniques i.e. adaboost, logitboost, naivebayes, bayesnet and J48, and one traditional statistical method i.e. logistic regression. We have also compared the performance of the machine learning techniques and statistical method. The empirical validation is carried out on an open source software, Frinika, written in java language. Two versions of the software are taken and analyzed for changes. The results are evaluated using Receiver operating characteristic curve (ROC) curve by measuring area under the curve (AUC).

The rest of the chapter is organized as follows: Section 2 reviews the related work focusing on the key points in the domain. Section 3 explains the independent and dependent variables used in our study and various evaluation measures used. Section 4 discusses the research methodology used to develop the model. Section 5 summarizes the results and finally the work is concluded in section 6.

LITERATURE REVIEW

A software undergoes number of changes to enhance its functionality. Various researchers have devised techniques to identify change prone classes. The paper (Bieman, Andrews & Yang, 2003) has identified change prone classes and then distinguished between the local change proneness and change proneness that occur due to interactions with other classes. The paper (Tsantalis, Chatzigeorgiou & Stephanides, 2005) has devised a technique to find the probability that each class will change in future generation. In other words, they have found the probability of change in a class A which is affected by another change prone class B. Similar type of work was done by A.R. Sharafat et al. (Sharafat & Tavildari, 2007). They have calculated three probabilities for each class: P_{ic} (internal change probability), a_{ji} (propagation probability) and P_{is} (total probability of change). Besides these probabilities, one more history based time normalized probability is calculated, referred to as P_{ih} . Finally, the authors have combined P_{ih} and P_{is} to predict whether or not each class will change in future generation. There are various change prone models based on source code. But Han et al. (Han, Jeon, Bae & Hong, 2008). have predicted the change prone classes at the earlier phases of software development before implementing the code. They have predicted change proneness in UML 2.0 design models. To predict the change proneness from design models, authors have calculated behavioral dependency measure (BDM), which is based on interactions between objects. Zhou et al. (Zhou, Leung & Xu, 2009) have used size metrics i.e. SLOC (source lines of code), NMIMP (number of methods implemented in a class) and NumPara (sum of the parameters of these methods) to find the confounding effect of class size on the relationship between object oriented metrics (cohesion, coupling and inheritance) and change proneness. SLOC is available during or after the implementation, whereas NMIMP and NumPara are available during the high level design phase. F.Khomh et al. (Khomh, Penta & Gueheneue, 2009). have found the effect of code smells (poor implementation) on change proneness. They concluded that the classes with code smells are more change prone than classes without code smells. D. Posnet et al. (Posnett, Bird & Devanbu, 2009) have studied the effect of design patterns on change proneness and have identified certain pattern roles that seem to be less change prone than others.

RESEARCH BACKGROUND

Independent Variables

We have used object oriented metrics as independent variables listed below:

- **Coupling between Object Classes (CBO):** Number of classes whose attributes is used by the given class plus those that use the attributes or methods of the given class.
- **Number of Children (NOC):** Number of direct children of a class in a hierarchy.
- **Number of Methods per Class (NOM):** Number of methods defined in the class.
- **Number of Attributes per Class (NOA):** Number of attributes/variables defined in a class.
- **Number of Instance Method (NIM):** Number of Instance Methods.
- **Number of Instance Variable (NIV):** It measures relations of a class with other objects of the program.
- **Number of Local Methods (NLM):** Number of local (not inherited) methods.
- **Response for a Class (RFC):** Number of methods in the class including the methods that are called by class's methods.
- **Number of Local Default Visibility Methods (NLDM):** Number of local default visibility methods.
- **Number of Private Methods (NPRM):** Number of local (not inherited) private methods.
- **Number of Protected Methods (NPROM):** Number of local protected methods.
- **Number of Public Methods (NPM):** Number of local(not inherited) public methods.
- **Number of Lines (NL):** Number of all lines.
- **Blank Lines of Code (BLOC):** Number of blank lines of code.
- **Lines of Code (LOC):** Number of lines that contain source code.
- **Lines of Declarative Code (LDC):** Number of lines containing declarative source code.
- **Lines of Executable Code (LEC):** Number of lines containing executable source code.
- **Lines of Comment (LC):** Number of lines containing comment.

- **Statement Count (SC):** Number of declarative and executable statements.
- **Depth of Inheritance (DIT):** Maximum number of steps from the class node to the root of the tree.
- **Lack of Cohesion (LCOM):** For each data field in a class, the percentage of the methods in the class using that data field; the percentages are averaged then subtracted from 100%.
- **Weighted Methods Per Class (WMC):** Count of sum of complexities of all methods in a class.

Dependent Variable

The dependent variable used in our study is change proneness. Change proneness can be defined as the probability of occurrence of change in a class. Change in a class can occur due to either internal changes within the class or the changes propagated from other classes. Internal changes can be found from the source code of the software and it includes any modification of methods, LOC, attributes etc. In this study, we are dealing only with internal changes. To measure the internal changes, we have used the number of lines of code added, deleted and modified in the recent version with respect to the previous version.

Correlation Based Feature Selection

It is very important to have a set of good features in order to have a good classification model. A feature is said to be 'good' if the features i.e. the independent variables are highly correlated with the dependent variable, but are not related with each other. Reducing the number of independent variables is termed as 'data dimensionality reduction'. For this purpose, we have used CFS (correlation based feature selection) provided in WEKA tool (Weka, 2013). CFS evaluated the best of a subset of variables by considering the individual predictive ability of each feature along with the degree of redundancy between them (Malhotra, & Jain, 2011). The best predictors out of independent variables in the data are selected (Hall, 2000; Malhotra, Kaur & Singh, 2010).

Performance Measures

In this study, we have found the relationship between object oriented metrics and change proneness by predicting various models. We have used various machine learning methods and one statistical method for this purpose. Out of various models predicted, we must conclude one of the models as the best model which can be used by researchers and practitioners in future. Various measures which we have considered to evaluate the performance of these models are explained below:

1. **Sensitivity and Specificity:** They measure the correctness of the model. Sensitivity measures the correctness of prediction of change prone classes, i.e. percentage of classes that are correctly predicted to be change prone. Specificity measures the percentage of classes that are correctly predicted not to be change prone. For a good model, both sensitivity and specificity should be high.
2. **Accuracy/Precision:** It is defined as the ratio of the number of classes (including both change and not change prone) that are predicted correctly to the total number of classes.
3. **Receiver Operating Characteristic Curve (ROC):** ROC curve also measures the performance of the model. The ROC curve is defined as the plot of sensitivity on the y-axis and (1-specificty) on the x-axis. ROC curve helps to select the optimal cut-off point –point that maximizes both sensitivity and specificity (Emam & Melo, 1999; Singh, Kaur & Malhotra, 2010).
4. **K-Cross Validation:** There are various validation methods available. The validation method used in our study is K-cross valida-

tion (value of K is taken as 10) in which the dataset is divided into K approximately equal partitions (Stone, M., 1974). One partition at a time is used for testing the model and the remaining K-1 partitions are used for training the model. This is repeated for all the K partitions.

RESEARCH METHODOLOGY

Empirical Data Collection

In this section, we have described the dataset used for the analysis. The software we studied was open source software written in java, namely Frinika. Frinika is complete music workstation software for Linux, Windows, Mac OSXtiger and other operating systems running java. The source code of this software is available at http://sourceforge.net. We studied the change in the classes of two versions, i.e. version 0.2.0 and version 0.6.0. Version 0.2.0 was released on 04-07-2006 and version 0.6.0 was released on 22-10-2009. Version 0.2.0 consists of 49532 lines of code (SLOC) and 539 classes, while version 0.6.0 consists of 113,093 lines of code (SLOC) and 1273 classes. We found that the number of classes which are present in both the versions are 248. Out of 248 classes, 126 classes are found to be change prone, while 122 classes are not change prone.

Descriptive Statistics

We calculated statistics of various independent variables including the minimum and the maximum values (range), mean (mean), median (med.) and standard deviation (SD) for all the metrics. Some of the important observations are as follows:

1. The lines of code are measured in terms of LOC. The maximum value of LOC is 1538.
2. The mean value of DIT is quite low, indicating that the software has less number of children and inheritance is not used much in the system.
3. The mean value of coupling is reasonably high indicating that there is high interaction between classes.

Methods Used

- **The Statistical Method (Logistic Regression):** Logistic regression is used to predict the dependent variable from a set of independent variables (a detailed description is given by (Basili, Briand & Melo, 1996; Hosmer & Lemeshow, 1989). It is used when the outcome variable is binary or dichotomous.
- **J48:** Decision tree learning uses a decision tree as a predictive model that predicts the value of a target variable based on several input variables. There are various decision tree algorithms such as ID3, C4.5, CHAID, MARS etc. J48 implements Quinlan's C4.5 algorithm for generating a pruned or unpruned C4.5 decision tree. J48 builds trees from a set of labeled training data using the concept of information entropy. To make the decision, the attribute with the highest information gain is used. The splitting procedure continues until all the instances in a subset belong to the same class.
- **Boosting:** Boosting is one of the machine learning algorithms for performing supervised learning. It is an effective method for improving the accuracy of any given learning algorithm by combining the simple

rules to from an ensemble such that performance of the single ensemble member is improved, i.e. 'boosted'. There are various boosting algorithms available such as LPboost, Logitboost, Adaboost etc. The main difference between various boosting algorithms is their method of weighting training data points and hypothesis. We have used logitboost and adaboost for the purpose of analysis. The most popular algorithm among all is the adaboost, introduced in 1995 by Freud and Schapire (Freund & Schapire, 1999). Adaboost tweeks the subsequent classifiers built by using the instances misclassified by previous classifiers. Adaboost calls a given weak or base learning algorithm in a series of rounds t=1…, T. Initially all the weights are set equal and on each round, weights of incorrectly classified examples are increased and weights of correctly classified examples are decreased so that weak learner focuses on hard examples in the training set (Freund & Schapire, 1999).

- **Bayes Net and Naïve Bayes:** A Bayesian network or Bayes net represents a set of random variables and their conditional dependencies via directed acyclic graph (DAG). For example, a Bayesian network can be used to represent probabilistic relationships between diseases and symptoms. Naïve Bayes is another probabilistic classifier. It is based on Bayes' theorem. Naïve Bayes model doesn't use Bayesian probability or any Bayesian methods. One of the advantages of naïve Bayes classifier is that it requires very less training data to estimate the parameter necessary for classification.

RESULTS ANALYSIS

An open source software written in java, namely Frinika is used to bring out the results. After applying CFS to the selected dataset, 22 independent variables are reduced to 4 independent variables, i.e. CBO, RFC, BLOC, and LDC.

The validation technique used is K-cross validation with the value of K as 10. Table 1 summarizes the results of 10-cross validation. The values of sensitivity, specificity, precision, area under the curve and cut-off point of each of the model is shown in the Table 1. To find the optimal cut-off point, ROC is used which is a plot between sensitivity and (1-specificity).We aim to have high values of sensitivity, specificity, precision, and AUC to classify the predicted model as the 'good' model. The ROC curve for all the models is shown in Figure 1. We can observe that the highest AUC i.e. 0.774 is shown by logitboost. Logitboost also shows the highest values of sensitivity, specificity and precision among all the other models. Decision tree algorithm, J48 has

Table 1. Validation results

S.No.	Method Used	Sensitivity	Specificity	Precision	Area Under Curve	Cut-Off Point
1	Adaboost	69.0%	64.8%	66.93%	0.728	0.434
2.	Bayesnet	66.7%	62.3%	64.53%	0.701	0.424
3.	Logitboost	72.2%	71.3%	71.75%	0.774	0.481
4.	J48	69.8%	70.5%	70.14%	0.697	0.671
5.	Naivebayes	65.1%	64.8%	64.95%	0.672	0.100
6.	Logistic Regression	66.7%	65.6%	66.15%	0.737	0.457

Figure 1. ROC curves

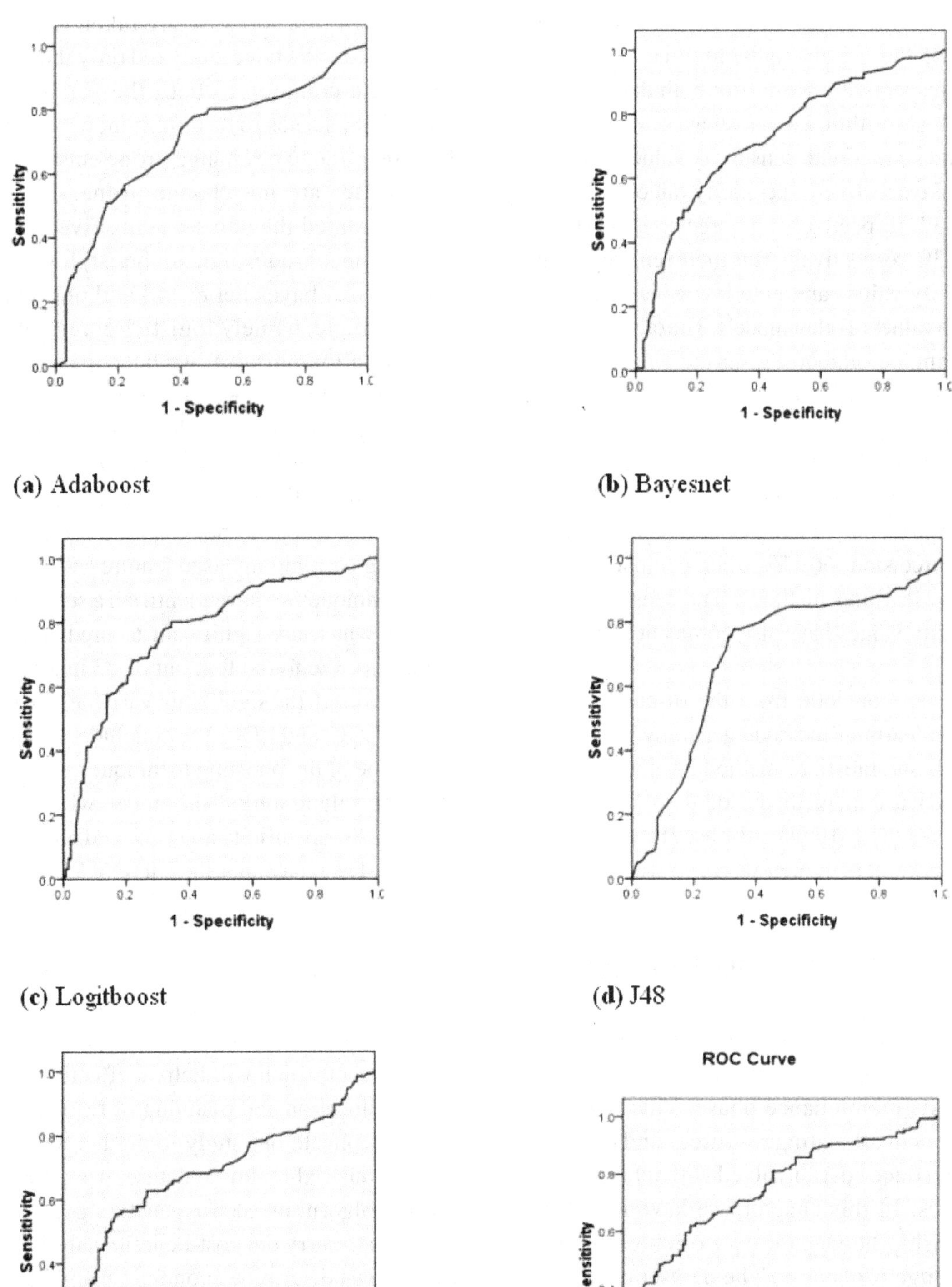

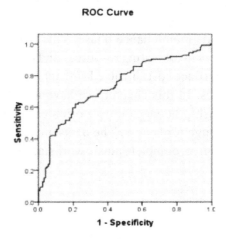

also shown good results with AUC as 0.697 and accuracy 70.4%. The sensitivity and specificity values of J48 are also quite high i.e. 67.8% and 70.5% respectively. Results of both the Bayesian network algorithm, i.e. naivebayes and bayesnet are quite similar with sensitivity values as 64.8% & 66.7% respectively, specificity values as 64.95% & 64.53% respectively and precision as 64.95% & 64.53% respectively. But their sensitivity and specificity values are quite low when compared with the values of other models. The other boosting algorithm, i.e. adaboost gives quite high AUC of 0.728 but low precision value of 66.93%.

Besides these machine learning techniques, we have used one statistical method, i.e. logistic regression. We can observe that AUC of logistic regression is comparable to adaboost. But it shows lowest precision, 66.15% when compared to the machine learning methods. The sensitivity and specificity values have also come out to be quite low.

We can conclude from the discussion, that machine learning methods generally give better values than statistical method. Among various machine learning methods, logitboost has shown the best results and thus can be used by researchers and practitioners in their work.

CONCLUSION AND FUTURE WORK

Predicting the change in the future versions of the software has become very important during its maintenance phase. This will help managers in allocating resources and thus will help to reduce costs involved with maintenance activities. In this chapter, we have found the relationship between object oriented metrics and change proneness. The dataset used is an open source, complete music workstation software, written in java, namely 'Frinika'. Two versions of this software are taken to analyze the changes. We have analyzed only the classes which are common to both the versions. We found 248 classes to be common, out of which 126 are found to be change prone classes while 122 classes are not change prone. Then, we have validated the dataset using five machine learning techniques, i.e. adaboost, logitboost, naïve bayes, bayes net & J48 and one statistical technique, namely logistic regression. For the validation purpose, we have used K-cross validation method (K=10). We used receiver operating characteristic (ROC) curve for finding the optimal cut-off point and compared the area under the ROC curve. Higher the area under the curve, the better is the model.

Using correlation based feature subselection, CFS technique; we have identified a subset of the metrics which are significant to predict change proneness. We found that out of 22 independent variables used, the significant variables are CBO, RFC, BLOC, and LDC. We concluded that logitboost, one of the boosting techniques, has shown the best results among all the models with sensitivity as 72.2%, specificity as 71.3% and precision as 71.75%. The area under the curve of logitboost is also quite high, i.e. 0.774. In general, we observed that machine learning methods outperformed statistical method.

The predicted results can be used by researchers and practitioners in early stages of software development which will help in effective and efficient allocation and planning of resources. We plan to replicate our study to predict models on larger industrial real time dataset using machine learning algorithms such as genetic algorithm. We also plan to carry out cost-benefit analysis which will help us determine economic viability of the predicted models.

REFERENCES

Aggarwal, K., Singh, Y., Kaur, A., & Malhotra, R. (2009). Empirical analysis for investigating the effect of object-oriented metrics on fault proneness: A replicated case study. *Software Process Improvement and Practice*, *16*(1), 39–62. doi:10.1002/spip.389

Basili, V., Briand, L., & Melo, W. (1996). A validation of object-oriented design metrics as quality indicators. *IEEE Transactions on Software Engineering*, *22*(10), 751–761. doi:10.1109/32.544352

Bieman, J., Andrews, A., & Yang, H. (2003). Understanding change-proneness in OO software through visualization. In *Proceedings of 11th IEEE IWPC*. IEEE.

Briand, L., Wust, J., & Lounis, H. (2001). Replicated case studies for investigating quality factors in object oriented designs. *Empirical Software Engineering: An International Journal*, *6*, 11–58. doi:10.1023/A:1009815306478

Chidamber, S., & Kemerer, C. (1994). A metrics suite for object oriented design. *IEEE Transactions on Software Engineering*, *20*(6), 476–493. doi:10.1109/32.295895

Emam, K, & Melo, W. (1999). The prediction of faulty classes using object-oriented design metrics. *Technical report: NRC 43609*.

Freund, Y., & Schapire, R. (1999). A short introduction to boosting. *Journal of Japanese Society for Artificial Intelligence*, *14*(5), 771–780.

Gyimothy, T., Ferenc, R., & Siket, I. (2005). Empirical validation of object-oriented metrics on open source software for fault prediction. *IEEE Transactions on Software Engineering*, *31*(10), 897–910. doi:10.1109/TSE.2005.112

Hall, M. (2000). Correlation-based feature selection for discrete and numeric class machine learning. In *Proceedings of the 17th International Conference on Machine Learning*, (pp. 359-366). IEEE.

Han, A., Jeon, S., Bae, D., & Hong, J. (2008). Behavioural dependency measurement for change proneness prediction in UML 2.0 design models. In *Proceedings of Computer Software and Applications 32nd Annual IEEE International*. IEEE. doi:10.1109/COMPSAC.2008.80

Henderson-Sellers, B. (1996). *Object oriented metrics: Measures of complexity*. Englewood Cliffs, NJ: Prentice Hall.

Hosmer, D., & Lemeshow, S. (1989). *Applied logistic regression*. New York: Wiley.

Khomh, F., Penta, M., & Gueheneue, Y. (2009). An exploratory study of the impact of code smells on software change-proneness. In *Proceedings of 16th Working Conference on Reverse Engineering*. IEEE.

Li, W., & Henry, S. (1993). Object oriented metrics that predict maintainability. *Journal of Systems and Software*, *23*, 111–122. doi:10.1016/0164-1212(93)90077-B

Li, W., Henry, S., Kafura, D., & Schulman, R. (1995). Measuring object –oriented design. *Journal of Object Oriented Programming*, *8*(4), 48–55.

Lorenz, M., & Kidd, J. (1994). *Object-oriented software metrics*. Englewood Cliffs, NJ: Prentice Hall Object-Oriented Series.

Malhotra, R., & Jain, A. (2011). Software effort prediction using statistical and machine learning methods. *IJACSA*, *2*(1).

Malhotra, R., Kaur, A., & Singh, Y. (2010). Application of machine learning methods for software effort prediction. *ACM SIGSOFT Software Engineering Notes, 35*.

Posnett, D., Bird, C., & Devanbu, P. (2009). An empirical study on the influence of pattern roles on change –proneness. *Empirical Software Engineering*, *16*, 396–423. doi:10.1007/s10664-010-9148-2

Sharafat, A., & Tavildari, L. (2007). A probabilistic approach to predict changes in object-oriented software systems. In *Proceedings of 11th European Conference on Software Maintenance and Reengineering*. IEEE.

Singh, Y., Kaur, A., & Malhotra, R. (2010). Empirical validation of object-oriented metrics for predicting fault proneness models. *Software Quality Journal*, *18*(1), 3–35. doi:10.1007/s11219-009-9079-6

Stone, M. (1974). Cross-validatory choice and assessment of statistical predictions. *Journal of the Royal Statistical Society. Series A (General)*, *36*, 111–147.

Tsantalis, N., Chatzigeorgiou, A., & Stephanides, G. (2005). Predicting the probability of change in object oriented systems. *IEEE Transactions on Software Engineering*, *31*(7), 601–614. doi:10.1109/TSE.2005.83

Weka. (2013). Retrieved from http://www.cs.waikato.ac.nz/ml/weka/

Zhou, Y., Leung, H., & Xu, B. (2009). Examining the potentially confounding effect of class size on the associations between object oriented metrics and change proneness. *IEEE Transactions on Software Engineering*, *35*(5), 607–623. doi:10.1109/TSE.2009.32

Chapter 20
Storyboard and Computer Animation for Children: Communicability Evaluation

Francisco V. Cipolla-Ficarra
ALAIPO – AINCI, Spain and Italy

Alejandra Quiroga
Universidad Nacional de La Pampa, Argentina

Jim Carré
University of The Netherlands Antilles, Curaçao

ABSTRACT

The authors present the key elements of the storyboard and computer graphics that must be contained in the computer animations that are broadcast as miniseries and are based on world-known literary works. The first analyses are established to set a differentiation between the contents aimed at the adult and the child audience. Finally, the authors make known the necessary strategies of storytelling applied to computer animation, bearing in mind the time and production cost factor.

INTRODUCTION

Computer graphics constantly improves its algorithms, so that the distance between the real and the virtual is every time less, even disappearing in the artistic context such as can be computer animations or scientific visualization in some exceptional cases (Terzopoulos, 1999; Roble, & Zafar, 2009; Minnery & Fine, 2009; Scharver, et al., 2004; Lu & Zhang, 1998). In the first case, the set of variables to consider are more, because there is a story to be told and the technical errors can even become a part of that story, even going unnoticed to the human eye. Whereas in the second, scientific visualization, errors practically shouldn't exist, especially in the case of medicine, for instance. An error in the representation of reality of the human organism (shape, color, lightning, etc.) may entail that a mistaken technique is used when extirpating a tumor, for instance.

DOI: 10.4018/978-1-4666-4490-8.ch020

Now the stories that are told through computer animation may be based on a literary work or not. Using a literary work has the advantage that part of the audience know beforehand the plot, the characters, the geographical context, etc. However, with the dysfunction of literary texts in the last decades, mainly due to the momentum of other reading devices of digital contents, the lack of interest in the traditional reading of classical works of world literature in paper support (Carr, 2010) the university rules stemming from the Bologna plan (Cipolla-Ficarra, et al., 2011). These are new educational rules which in some public or private universities of the EU prevent a professor from inserting over 80 pages of a same book as mandatory or complimentary reading, especially in Faculty of Educational Studies or foreign literature in Lombardy (Cipolla-Ficarra, et al., 2012). The extreme case may be the nullity of books in the university context of the audiovisual in some Catalan universities, for instance (Cipolla-Ficarra & Ficarra, 2012). In other words, reading has decreased considerably among the new generations and potential users of interactive mobile multimedia, for instance.

We can also find situations where the real television miniseries turn into computer animations. Here we also have another advantage for the understanding of a story, because the characteristics of the main characters are known beforehand, the main and secondary issues of the miniseries, the temporal context in which the events take place, etc. However, the new generations haven't grown up in front of the television screen, but rather the computer screen.

Besides, until the late 20th century the television miniseries were not broadcast on line because of technical reasons (speed of the internet connection), or the cost of the phone services for Internet access. Consequently, in the great cities, we have adult users of interactive systems who have a greater cultural background in reading and audiovisual, compared with children, teenagers and youth who have been in an endo-culturation and trans-culturation process (Styliaras, Koukopoulos & Lazarinis, 2011) different to those existing at the beginning of the new millennium.

Those who since an early age are interacting with computers and wired to the internet are more open to receiving positively the computer generated stories and which are not based on formerly existing stories. It is they who will take more into account the computer graphics aspects (mainly the special effects) in the development of the plot, compared to the adults. The latter will try to establish parallelisms between the development of the script of the animation and the version of the book or the television miniseries, for instance. The special effects for children and/or young people is linked to the consumption of hours in front of a videogame as compared to an adult user.

In this work we focus on the study of a chapter of the television series "The Little Prince" (Figure 1), which is based on an audiovisual adaptation of the book by Antoine de Saint-Exupéry. In it we consider the main aspects of the narrative script. For instance, which are the narrative mechanisms to correctly develop other stories in parallel with the purpose of boosting the attention of the viewer in the computer animations. Also will be presented the techniques and methods used from the point of view of graphic computing (static and animated) coupled with an heuristic assessment of the interactive design. We will focus in the current work on the layout category and in particular in scenes illumination. The episode we will analyze is "B782, the Planet of the Giant" of the series which is made up of 52 episodes of 26 minutes each. A summary of that chapter or episode (in this work, both notions are used as synonymous) can be seen in the current link: www.lepetitprince.com. The chapter has been randomly chosen through a previous draw.

Figure 1. The Little Prince –3D character (www.lepetitprince.com)

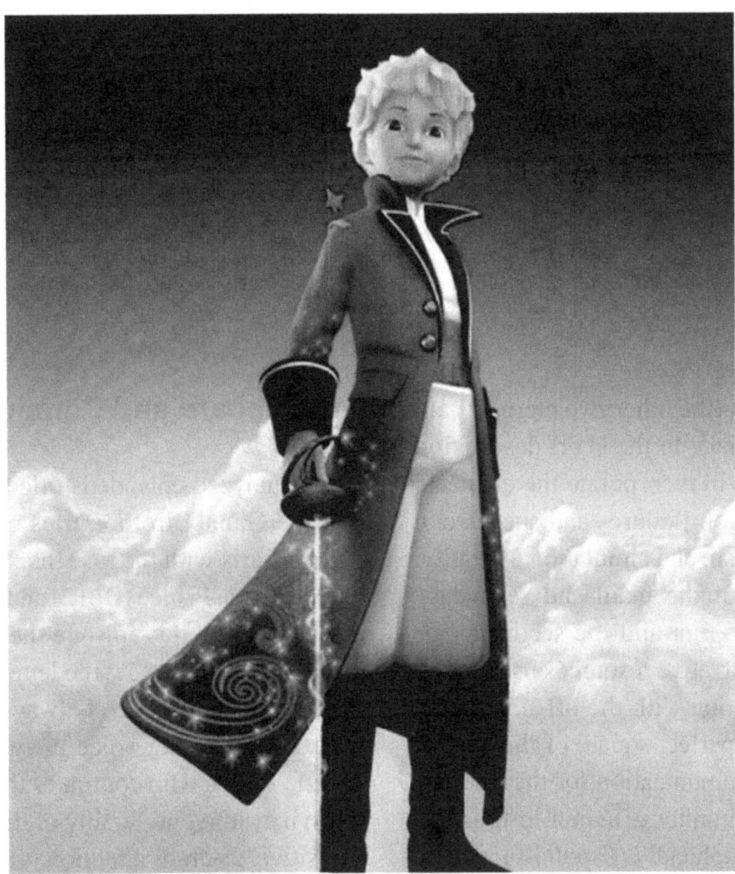

NARRATION AND QUALITY CRITERIA FOR INTERNATIONAL ANIMATIONS

Stories have been and still remain in many places of the planet a way to safeguard the local traditions. Oral communication is the most economic instrument which a community has to such a purpose. Not for nothing in many cultures –whose geographical access still remains very complicated, the oral media of communication still are very successful, such as can be the famous whistles in the La Gomera island, in the Canary islands archipelago, Spain. There survives a funny language which arises the interest of historians, linguists and neurophysiologists, the so-called Gomero whistle. Linguistics has taken care of the sounds at the moment of communicating among human beings, and it is through it that we can differentiate between dialects and languages, for instance. Many tales and stories have been picked from local dialects and have been translated into the prevailing language, and from this the universality of the content has taken place. One of the advantages of visual communication through computer animations is the possibility of communicating messages to millions of people without using words, only sounds and onomatopoeias. Achieving this goal in stories which are not based on previous literary texts is one of the keys in the success of a computer-made commercial or non-commercial product. It is a qualitative element of communicability which is directly related to the universality and the simplicity, inside the quality criteria of a

Figure 2. Four components of qualities interrelated for an excellent computer animation

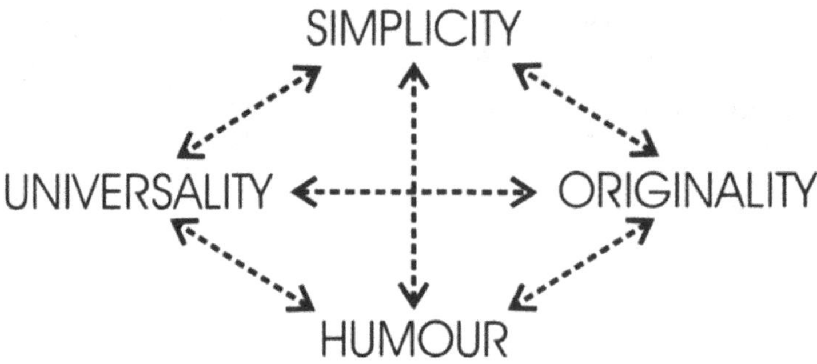

computer animation (the other two elements are originality and humor). In the short description of the episode we will incorporate the elements of graphic information (failures and successes), special effects, realism and simulation of reality, the characteristics of the main and secondary characters, the main plot and the secondary or parallel plots, the narrative resources used in the story, and their relation with the off-line multimedia systems, the perfect square of the quality attributes in the communication for the international animations: simplicity, humor, originality and universality. Graphically (Cipolla-Ficarra & Cipolla-Ficarra, 2009):

Storyboard and Computer Animation

The analyzed episode is titled "B782, the Planet of the Giant". In the series of episodes each of them starts with the rose that lives in the asteroid of the Little Prince (B612) and gets a letter from it (Figure 3). In this episode she sees a fleeting star and her wish is to get the letter which happens in an immediate way. As always she starts to read the letter and her voice merges with that of the Little Prince who continues the story. The use of two narrators, preferably of different sex, is very positive to draw attention and was a technique used in the early off-line multimedia systems for

Figure 3. The rose that lives in the asteroid of the Little Prince –B612 (www.lepetitprince.com)

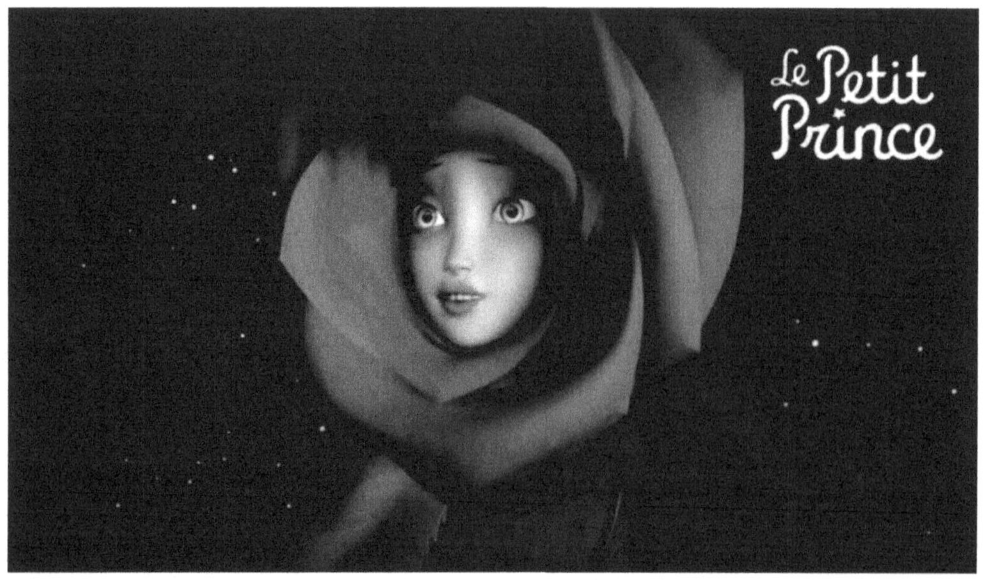

the children audience in the 90s. Later on the action goes on in the small plane of the Little Prince who is flying with the fox (friend). Here there is a direct reference to the author of the book "The Little Prince" that is, Antoine de Saint-Exupéry (aviator and French writer of the last century). The fox represents the sidekick inside the tale who constantly helps the main character to reach the main goal, that is, release the planets from the enemy forces. These forces are depicted in the shape of a snake (main antagonist) and black clouds (called black ideas, which help the main antagonist) which constantly change shape. In the Figures 1, 3, 4 are the main characters. The parallelism between the literary text and computer animation from the point of view of the main characters is practically exact. Although from the literary point of view the book is meant for a children audience due to the simplicity of the writing and the story told, in fact the book is a metaphor in which are treated issues for an adult reader, such as the meaning of life, friendship and love. In this regard we want to point out that in the current work we split the audience in the following way in relation to age: child (4), junior (12-17) adult (18-64) and senior (65).

In this sense, computer animation may prompt the attention of the children audience through the special effects such as the blowing away of the protagonists-antagonists or the metamorphosis of objects by the Little Prince, but the metaphors of the tale are related with an adult audience, little or nothing can these special effects do so that the children understand 100% of the tale. A strategy followed in these cases is to develop several parallel stories to the main one, where the main characters of the series and their antagonists intermix in the narrative, with new characters. We call this strategy "union of resorts". A graphic representation is in figure 5. The resorts represent an infinite semiosis (Colapietro, 1993) with the shape of the Archimedes spiral. That is, a bend that is generated by the combination of two uniform movements: a rectilinear one and a rotational one simultaneously. This shape and those movements make the tales of the Little Prince that we are

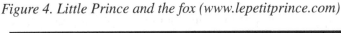

Figure 4. Little Prince and the fox (www.lepetitprince.com)

Figure 5. The resorts A, B, C and D represent an infinite semiosis with the shape of the Archimedes spiral

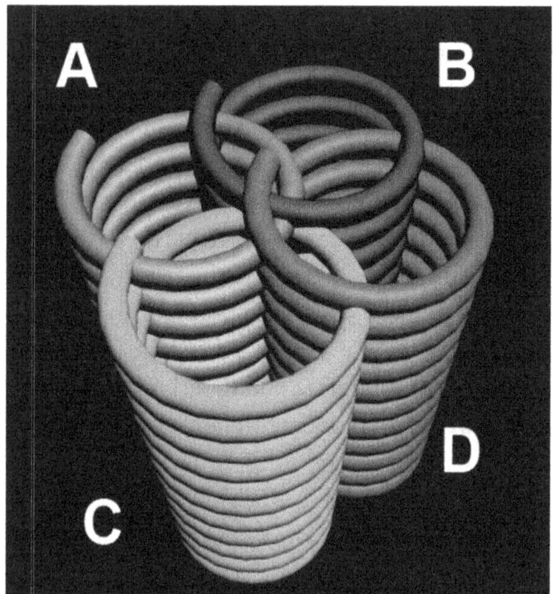

analyzing adequate to draw the attention and increase the motivation in following the stories.

Along the episode it can be seen how the lineal storytelling whose classical representation lies in Figure 5 resorts to the flashback so that the characters get to know what has happened previously. This resource recurs in each one of the episodes of the series.

Once they arrive to the planet where the antagonists are present (black clouds surround the planet) and metaphorically going into it through a door whose location they must find out and open it, the protagonists start to interact with the context (exploration) and with its inhabitants. In our case the planet is a giant of stone who is ill because its controller doesn't do his job due to the influence of the snake.

The first task of the addressee is to recompose the human figure since in the first minutes of the animation the close-ups or details prevail. In order to lengthen those takes, the main characters will fall from the heights because of the geographical unevenness of the surface. It is moment when they resort to special effects such as the metamorphose, for instance. In principle it is a green planet because there is exuberant vegetation, but the contradictions start, first the salty water in the middle of the mountains. Here can be seen an excellent transparence effect, since the swimming fishes can be seen (Figure 6). There also the hens that behave as if they were woodpeckers and then go after the fox.

Through the behavior of the elements of nature this call to attention is also constantly boosted. The issue of communication is always present in this series through the letters and everything related to the post service. Following some flying mailboxes the main characters will meet Natura and her students (Figure 7). Both she and the rest of the inhabitants have objects from the flora which make up their body, that is, flower petals, roots, leaves, etc. Evidently these resources generate from the environment in the surface and also the very structure of the planet itself with its links or isotopies. That is, common lines of sense irrespective of whether the characters are over or below the surface of the planet. For instance, from the chromatic point of view the warm colors prevail over the cold ones, specially green over light blue.

These resources are inside the set of elements that make up the identity of the characters. One of the processes to be followed to reach said identity could include the following steps:

- Choosing carefully one or two attributes which start to define the identity of the character.
- Stress everything that the children, junior and/or adult audience associates with the character in order to develop that identity thoroughly.
- Finally, creating a solid context to build the character.

Now the attributes in themselves do not give the characters the necessary variety and interest.

Figure 6. An excellent transparence effect (www.lepetitprince.com)

Figure 7. Natura and her students (www.lepetitprince.com)

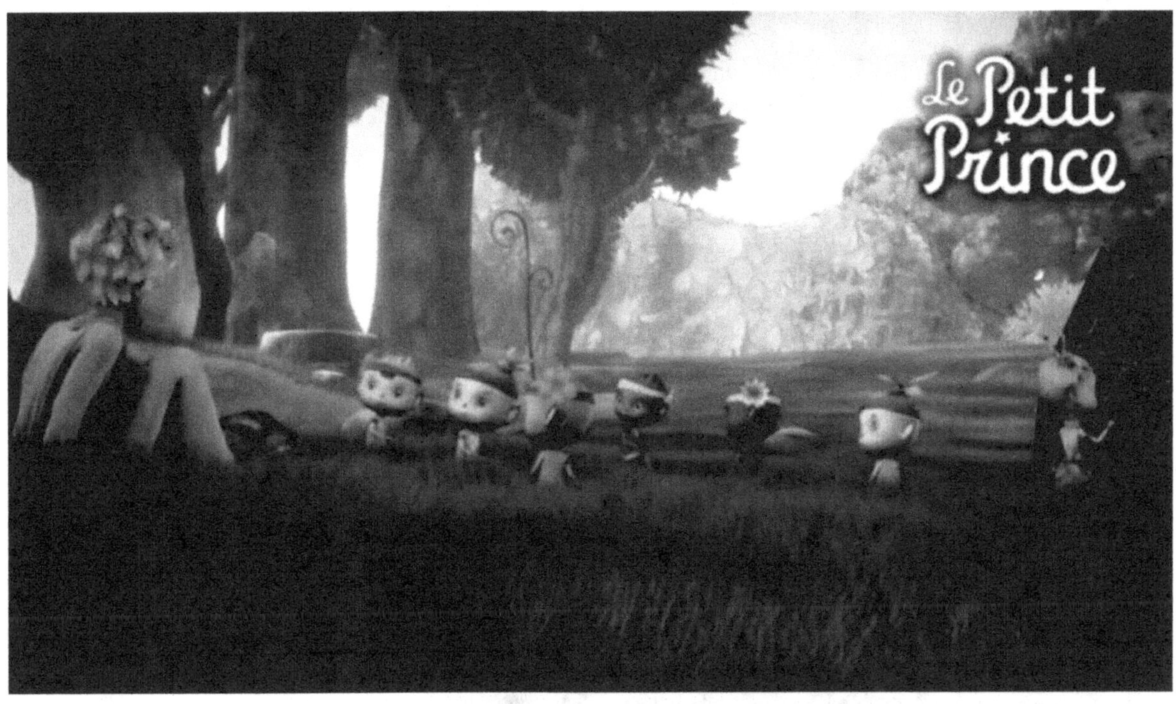

The audience need to project associations on the characters. In other words, join a quality. When this association takes place, it is what technically is called "halo effect". In the commercial publicity that effect leads the consumer to buy another product. When it is applied to the creation of non-human characters, for instance, said effect boosts the feeling of identity between the audience and the characters.

Narration: Structure

In the telling of a story with analogical or digital support, oral or audiovisual, among others, the main components are narration, the characters, the actions, space and time (Garrant, 2006). In our example of analysis the narration is in the first person. The narrator, called internal narrator, participates as main character or witness. When the narrator is at the same time the main character, we speak of an autobiofraphical story. Let's remember that the rose reads a letter at the start, that is, it is an example of the so-called autobiographical tales. If the author tells his/her own life, it is a real autobiography.

This realism is boosted in animation with the following components (Bendazzi, 1999; Rosebush, 1992; Barrier, 2003) vegetation, clouds, rocks, etc. The characters of the computer animated series are joined to the main characters of the planet called bodies, and they are: the Giant (planet–Figures 8 and 9), Natura (teacher–Figure 10), Talamus (who carries out the maintenance operations of the planet), Corbis (charged with reporting the dysfunctions of the planet, that is, the Giant –Figure 11), his wife Auricula and children. Supporting characters, the mailboxes and the flying hens, grouped in the main and the secondary. They appear ordered in time in relation to whether they are indispensable or not in the story that is being told.

With regard to the locution, it is important to bear in mind tthose who lend their voices to the animated characters. This factor increases its

Figure 8. The left hand (www.lepetitprince.com)

Figure 9. The face (www.lepetitprince.com)

Figure 10. Natura and Corbis (www.lepetitprince.com)

Figure 11. Narration: Freytag's triangle

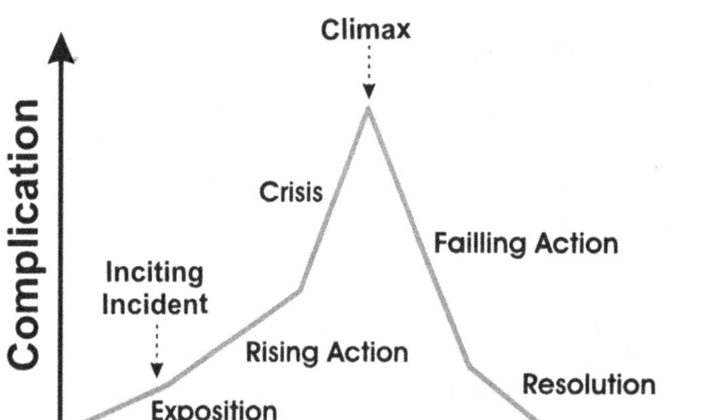

influence in those series dubbed from the original language to the place where they are broadcast, the programming, for instance, from English to Italian. That is, sometimes a same person can lend her voice to different animated characters (both male and female) thus creating some disorientation in the identification of the characters in a children's audience.

The narrator may tell the facts as they have started from beginning to end, or change the order of the events jumping in time towards the past or towards the future. According to this, we may distinguish several ways of temporal ordination.

The Lineal Development

The tale presents the events in a chronological order, from the most past to the most recent. The traditional tales, orally transmitted, for instance, usually present this organization. Generally, a way of graphic representation is what follows (Garrant, 2006):

- **Anticipation:** It is a rupture of the temporal order that consists in anticipating events and announcing facts that will take place later. In the case of the miniseries it is a way to join the two parts that make up the episode where the narrator gives back the main role to the rose that is in its asteroid.
- **Retrospection:** It is another break of the temporal order which consists in going back in time (give a jump backwards) to tell facts previous to the moment in which the story takes place. In the computer animated miniseries, they mix all these temporal styles.

All these resources are present in each of the episodes which make up the computer animated series. This is a key of the success of the series among the public audience, that is, the balanced combination along the minutes of the actions that are developed, thus fostering the understanding of the main story. In contrast, for the children, it would be necessary to follow a lineal plot, without temporal interruptions, that is, the flash-forward and the flash-back. Here is one of the reasons why children lose the notion of sequential continuity of the actions developed by the characters.

Protagonists

The protagonists are the main characters of the narration. Their presence is indispensable for the development of the story. The secondary characters accompany the main characters. They complete the action or are witnesses of what happens. According to their importance in the development of the tasks, the characters may be main or secondary. Among the former the protagonist stands out, who carries the weight of the action, and the antagonist, who opposes him. According to the degree of psychological depth with which they are presented, the characters may be flat or rounded. The flat characters do not change along the work and respond to a previous behavior pattern. The characters of the traditional tales, for instance, are usually built as flat characters who frequently embody a virtue, a flaw or a quality. The rounded characters, in contrast, possess individual features and evolve along the story, they are beings of psychological depth who end up looking like real people. The most important characters of the narrative literary texts belong to this kind.

- **Space:** It is the room where the narration takes place. It can be single or multiple. To some authors, the space of the narration may have a great importance. In the episode analyzed it is, since the whole space is unique, but is presented as multiple because we are talking of the body of a giant in the shape of a planet. The planet B782.
- **Time:** The actions take place for a given lapse of time, they may last little or a long time. The time in which take place the events must also be identified; the past, the present, the future or an indeterminate time. In the studied episode and following practically the rest of the episodes of the series, the action takes place in two days, because generally they refer to evening or nightfall, night and day. The handling of the elements of the passing of time is another of the key elements of the success of the series.

RESULTS OF THE MAIN NARRATIVE COMPONENTS AIMED AT THE CHILDREN AND THE ADULT AUDIENCES

Next we have the following graphic where are presented the results of a three-dimensional computer animaton for audiovisual TV series –theoretically is for a children audience. However, from the point of view of the structure of the tale and the systematic behavior of each of the main categories of the design it is not. These first components have been ordered in a table where the notions of computer graphics, computer animation, design, semiotics, literary theory, social psychology and social media. In principle these early components may appear trivial, but behind each one of them there is an intersection of these notions. The episode has been evaluated in an individual way by three communicability specialists, whether it is in the original language, that is, French, Italian and Spanish. We present the middle" or "typical" rounded value of a data set. The minimal value of the score is 0 and the top is 10.

The main elements of the story make apparent that these episodes do not allow a complete 100% comprehension by the children audience and by the junior audience. Although the special effects may strike the attention of the youngest, such as the generation of objects or animals through the notebook of the Little Prince (umbrellas that play the role of parachutes, boats which are hooked to the clouds to fly like an aerostatic balloon, paper elephants to fight against the antagonists, etc.) transformation and/or metamorphosis of the dress of the Little Prince with his light sword to fight the black ideas, shiny lights, dissolution or blurring of the antagonists, etc. the adult audience may see how the reflected shadow effects of the characters on the floor and other objects do not follow the same direction (see boat with the French color flag in Figure 13).

Figure 12. Communicability and narrative components evaluation

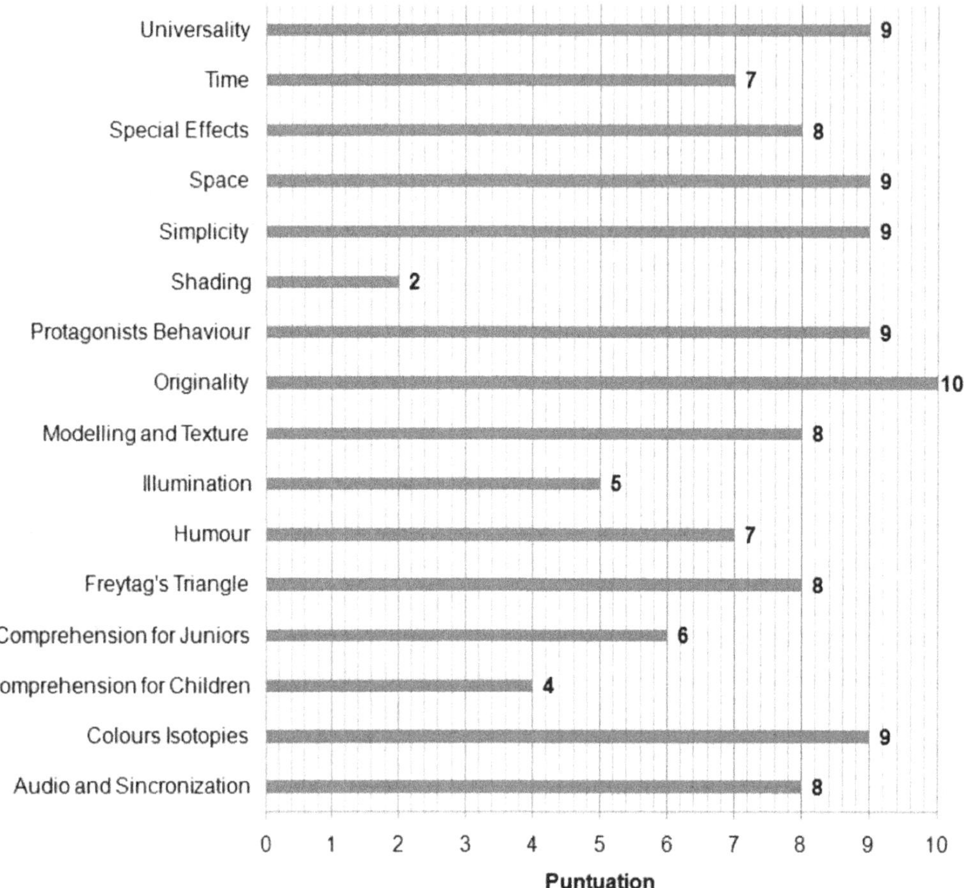

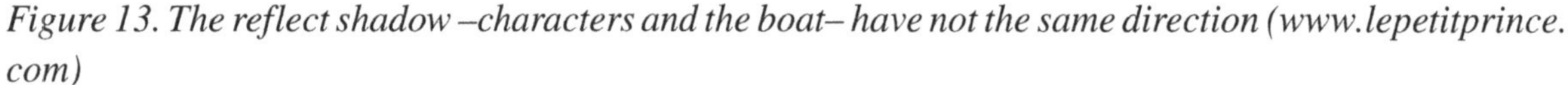

Figure 13. The reflect shadow –characters and the boat– have not the same direction (www.lepetitprince.com)

This technical flaw of the directional and overall lightening in the scenes that emulate daylight, for instance, practically remains the same in all the episodes of the series. Evidently the eyes of the children audience do not notice this, and the same may happen with the teenagers, but not so to a computer animations expert. Now this failing may also go unnoticed among many adults due to the great creativity which the current miniseries has, for instance, in the creations of the characters and their dresses, the nature that surrounds them, the central issue of the safeguard of the Earth, in this case epitomized in a giant. There are also the excellent isotrophies lines between the colors and the shapes of the static and animated components of each one of the scenes, such as can be the thoracic cavity of the Giant where his sick heart beats. The heart and love, whether it is in a metaphoric or real sense, are related to all the characters. That is, a content with a well structured plot, main and secondary goals to be reached perfectly divided, the excellent way of telling, the masterly combination of voiceover narrators, female (pink) and male (Little Prince) successful special effects, since they accomplish the function of boosting the tale, the avant-garde designs of objects and characters, among other components of the episode boost the link between the attention and motivation for the audience to stay in front of the computer and/or television screen.

LESSONS LEARNED

The strategy of the union of resorts in the narrative tale, broadening each one of the components of the storytelling which go from the characters to the scenery, allows to obtain a universal content of great creative quality. A creativity which enables it to overcome certain technical challenges of animation such as the handling of shadows due to the choice of different kinds of lightening in a scene. Creativity which also surpasses the degree of realism which certain complements of dress should have, such as the textile clothes or the hair of the Little Prince, for instance. However, the degree of realism in the scenes where the characters interact with nature are well achieved. It is through creativity that the production costs may be surpassed in computer animations, since having a realism where 100% of the real world is emulated entails extending for a very long time the production process, and besides the cost. Obviously creativity is not synonymous with the audiovisual, multimedia design, industrial engineering, etc. In these cases it is important to count on a staff where each of its members represents the intersection of the formal and the factual sciences. Even nowadays in the computer animation producers in countries like Germany, Spain, Portugal and Italy we have the groups of the creators and the programmers, split from each other, and generating constant trouble because of the human factors and not technical of computer animation. In these realities, the production costs of an episode like this analyzed are higher. In the future we will widen the analysis, from a prospect of visual communication as a publicity product, analyzing all the chapters of the miniseries. We will also analyze all the creative and design factors which boost acceptability in a junior audience.

CONCLUSION

In the analyzed episode we can see an excellent work in the creation of the characters who meet most of the four quality criteria of computer animation: originality, simplicity, hunor and universality. Although its authors have had as basis a literary text of international circulation, which makes it easier to focus the main characters, they have had to resort to these four cardinal points, since we are in the age of communicability expansion, regardless of the multimedia technological support used. Now the social communication media such as television should make clear that it is not a children series, but rather for teenagers, since the kind of narration used in the storytelling makes them not understand very well the content. From the point of view of computer animation can be seen the balanced use of special effects. That is, that its age has been left behind, in contrast to increasing the quality of the storyboard, for instance. Storyboards which were poor from the point of view of the main elements of the story, as it happened in the late 20th century or early 21st. This statement stems from the few productions we have analyzed, but which were made in Spain and Italy, and counting with a higher budget than the Little Prince. In few words, in the analysis of the current episode of the Little Prince, the creativity in 2D, 3D, etc. productions is sometimes inversely proportional to the financial resources.

REFERENCES

Barrier, M. (2003). *Hollywood cartoons: American animation in its golden age*. Oxford, UK: Oxford University Press.

Bendazzi, G. (1999). *Cartoons: One hundred years of cinema animation*. Bloomington, IN: Indiana University Press.

Carr, N. (2010). *The shallows: What the internet is doing to our brains*. New York: W.W. Norton & Company.

Cipolla-Ficarra, F., et al. (2011). Computational informatics, social factors and new information technologies: Hypermedia perspectives and avant-garde experiences in the era of communicability expansion. Bergamo, Italy: Blue Herons Ed.s.

Cipolla-Ficarra, F., et al. (2012). New horizons in creative open software, multimedia, human factors and software engineering. Bergamo, Italy: Blue Herons Ed.s.

Cipolla-Ficarra, F., & Cipolla-Ficarra, M. (2009). Computer animation and communicability in multimedia system and services: A trichotomy evaluation. In *Proceedings of New Directions in Intelligent Interactive Multimedia*. Heidelberg, Germany: Springer. doi:10.1007/978-3-642-02937-0_10

Cipolla-Ficarra, F., & Ficarra, V. (2012). Anti-models for universitary education: Analysis of the Catalans cases in information and communication technologies. In *Proceedings of First International on Software and Emerging Technologies for Education, Culture, Entertaiment, and Commerce: New Directions in Multimedia Mobile Computing, Social Networks, Human-Computer Interaction and Communicability (SETECEC 2012)*. Hershey, PA: IGI Global.

Colapietro, V. (1993). *Semiotics*. New York: Paragon House.

Garrant, T. (2006). *Writing for multimedia and the web: A practical guide to content development for interactive media*. Boston: Focal Press.

Lu, R., & Zhang, S. (1998). *Automatic generation of computer animation*. Berlin: Springer-Verlag.

Minnery, B., & Fine, M. (2009). Neuroscience and the future of human-computer interaction. *Interaction*, *14*(2), 70–75. doi:10.1145/1487632.1487649

Roble, D., & Zafar, N. (2009). Don't trust your eyes: Cutting-edge visual effects. *IEEE Computer*, *42*(7), 35–41. doi:10.1109/MC.2009.222

Rosebush, J. (1992). *Historical computer animation*. New York: ACM.

Scharver, C. et al. (2004). Designing cranial implants in a haptic augmented reality environment. *Communications of the ACM*, *47*(8), 32–39. doi:10.1145/1012037.1012059

Styliaras, G., Koukopoulos, D., & Lazarinis, F. (2011). *Handbook of research on technologies and cultural heritage: Applications and environments*. Hershey, PA: IGI Global.

Terzopoulos, D. (1999). Artificial life for computer graphics. *Communications of the ACM*, *42*(8), 32–43. doi:10.1145/310930.310966

APPENDIX

Figure 14. The realism in the water is excelent (www.lepetitprince.com)

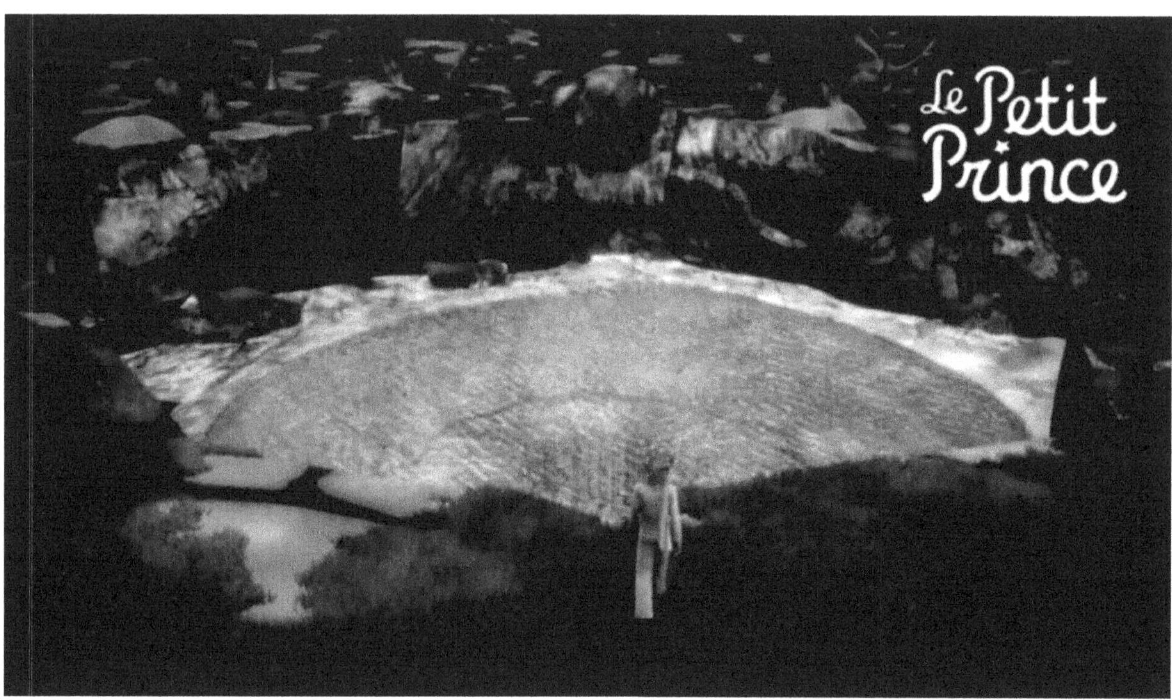

Figure 15. The special efects are simple and original (www.lepetitprince.com)

Figure 16. The umbrella that play the role of parachutes (www.lepetitprince.com)

Figure 17. The boat –with French flag color, is hooked to the clouds to fly like an aerostatic balloon (www.lepetitprince.com)

Chapter 21
New Generation of Artificial Intelligence for Real-Time Strategy Games

Damijan Novak
Institute of Informatics (FERI), University of Maribor, Slovenia

Domen Verber
Institute of Informatics (FERI), University of Maribor, Slovenia

ABSTRACT

Artificial intelligence in computer games is still well behind academic artificial intelligence research. The computer power and memory resources have increased exponentially over the last few years and improved game artificial intelligence should not hinder the performance of the game anymore. Improvements of game artificial intelligence are necessary because an appropriate artificial intelligence for the more advanced players does not exist today. This chapter discusses artificial intelligence for real-time strategy computer games, which are ideal test beds for research on movement, tactic, and strategy. Open-source real-time strategy game development tools are presented and compared, and an enhanced combat artificial intelligence algorithm is proposed.

MOTIVATION

What is Artificial Intelligence?

The exact definition of artificial intelligence is unclear. Most often artificial intelligence (AI) is defined as that branch of computer science, concerned with making computers behave like intelligent beings.

AI is not usually used as stand-alone. Instead, it adds knowledge and reasoning to existing applications and databases. Such applications look much friendlier and smarter to the user. In real-world applications with AI support (e.g., medicine diagnostic systems, theorem proving, data classification, etc.) the AI portion is significant and may consume much of the processing power. The use of AI in such applications has been widely

DOI: 10.4018/978-1-4666-4490-8.ch021

supported by the academic community for at least the last 30 years. On the other hand, AI regarding computer games, if used at all, represents only a small portion of the application. The methods and techniques of AI in computer games are usually much more primitive, and the amount of academic research on this topic is very limited.

The arcade and console games usually hardly incorporate any AI algorithms. They rely on a set of simple rules. The computer games that are more complex games (e.g., real time strategy games, role-playing games, etc.) usually do incorporate some kind of AI. However, the capabilities of such AIs are very basic. The AI is usually represented as a set of scripts. Each script contains a list of conditions and a sequence of action that should occur when some condition is met.

Such a kind of AI is not good enough, especially for the more experienced players. The behaviour of the opponent is predictable, the moves are repeatable, the characters are not "smart", etc.

The exceptions to this are board games (e.g., chess, checkers, go, etc.). In these kinds of games, the number of possible moves, at each stage during the play, is rather limited. With fast computer, it is possible to analyse millions of these moves (and the responses to them), so that the best next-move can be identified.

One of the main goals of the research presented in this chapter is the incorporation of AI techniques used by board-games, and other complex AI methodologies in other game genres, especially in real-time strategy (RTS) games.

How Can We Make AI Both Challenging and Interesting for the Players?

AI algorithms can be developed, for simple computer games, which can beat even the most experienced players. However, no one would want to play such a game. The opposite is also true. No one would enjoy playing a game where the opponent is inferior to you. In an ideal situation, the player should be on the same level or only slightly better than his/her opponent is. If this can be achieved, the player will have fun and the game would gain replay value. In order to achieve this goal, the AI should detect the skill of the player and, if possible, their tactics. Based on this information, the AI should adapt its behaviour to balance the player's skills. In situations where the computer program is confronted with another computer application, the AI should employ all its skills.

ROLE OF AI IN COMPUTER GAMES

AI in computer games can be employed in different ways.

Most often, the AI in games is used as an opponent for the human player. In board games and RTS games, AI defines the moves of the other party or parties. In role-playing and similar games, the adversary would be in the form of another human or creature that must be defeated.

In some games, AI can help the player. For example, a player's character can be part of a group where other members are controlled by AI. In this case, AI must support the player's moves. In other scenarios, AI can be assigned by the player to take care of some aspect of the game or to make suggestions to the player. It can also be used as a tutor for the novice during the early stages of the game.

The game may also include so-called non-playing characters or NPC's. The NPC's make the world richer and more populous, making the connection of the player with the game greater. Some NPC's may also be part of the game story. Such characters are also under the control of AI.

AI implementation for advisors and the NPC's would require some sort of verbal interaction between the player and AI. Proper implementation of such an interaction is very difficult to achieve and it is an undergoing study research. However, in current games, the interaction is usually implemented as a set of possible questions and associated responses.

Another important role of AI would be for games where the world of the game is generated randomly at the beginning of the game. The artificially generated terrain should be consistent and plausible. The key objects should be put on the map that is accessible for all participants. Such AI algorithms are implemented separately and are used only at the beginning of the game.

AI GAME ENGINES

Development of AI in Games

When developers were working on a new game in the past, they waited until the very last development stages before AI was implemented into the game. For many of the published games it cannot even be said they had an AI engine, because in some games AI code was so simple, that it blended in with the rest of the code. So there was a common practice that AI code was just part of game's engine or in some cases even part of graphic engine.

Nowadays games have gained a lot of complexity. So a game has to be split in 6 different modules, with each module having its own characteristics that can be represented by a model. But games come in many different genres and even two games inside the same genre can be very distinct one from another. That's what makes the modeling characteristics of a module very difficult. Once having a model of a module, that module can usually be used for all sorts of games, with only small modifications. E.g. a sound module –3D sound of a firing gun can be used in many first person shooters, real-time strategy games, roleplaying games etc.

AI is the most difficult part of a game engine to model. Because each game has its own environment, it has different characters with different behaviour, their own story telling and different player expectations of how an AI should behave. So, there is no easy way of implementing an AI for a new game, where the correct model would be chosen, used in conjunction with other modules of a game engine and the end result would be balanced, fun, and a worthy AI opponent.

Simplifying AI Development with Unified Structure of the AI Engine

Developing a new AI engine is hard, but not impossible. A simplified parallel can be made between all the games, since all the games use at least one of the following tehniques: moving, decision making and strategy – Figure 1. (Millington & Funge, 2009)

The structure of an AI engine can be used as a basic foundation for building AI's for every game there is. There is no need to use all three tehniques for each game, since some games are very simple and they only use moving parts of the AI engine, with no need for decision making or strategy (like the game Tetris). Whilst games such as Pac-man use movement with simple decision making, games such as Chess use only strategic level, and recent state-of-the-art games such as Crysis use all three tehniques.

Detailed Structure of the AI Engine

Movement: using the concept of movement different movement algorithms are refferded to where the reaction of a move is triggered based on a decision or on a request that the character needs to be moved, movement algorithm ensures that when a request for movement is given, a computer-guided character is moved according to the character's properties and whilst obiding with the rules of a virtual world.

Decision making: is a process where knowledge of a virtual world is used when performing action's (if the need arises), which would have an impact on that virtual world. Decision making is hidden from the outside observer (opposite to the

Figure 1. AI structure

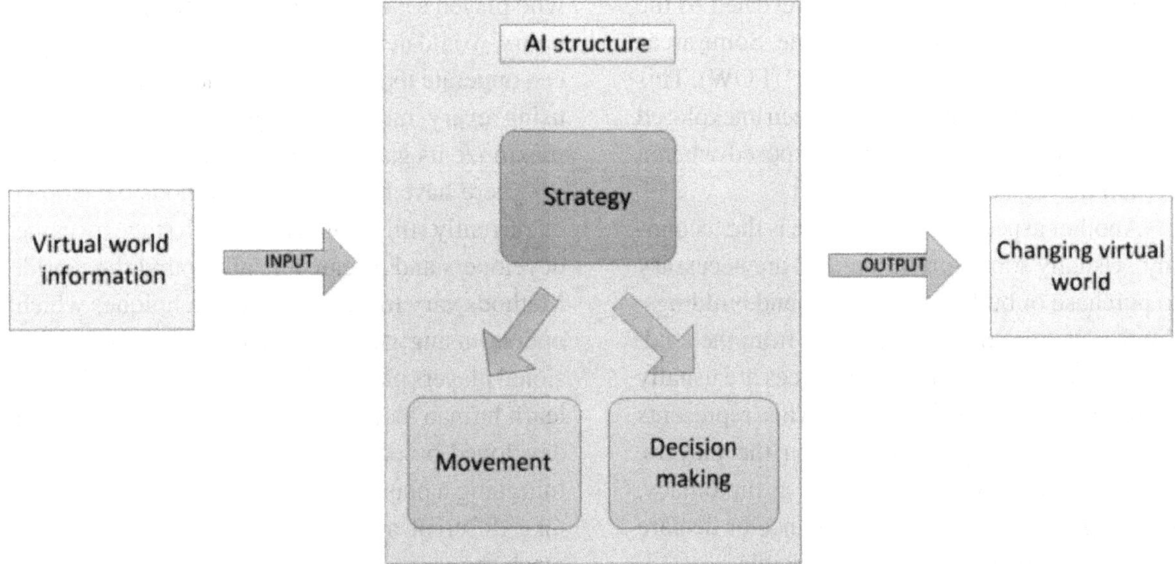

movement, where the move can be clearly seen), because the observer does not necessarily know that an action has taken place, nor does it have full information as to why the action was carried out. Nevertheless decision making is a very important part of AI if we want to give the game a deeper meaning.

Strategy: is the direction that a general (which can be NPC or a human player) takes through actions that influence the environment, in order to achieve her/his vision, over a longer period of time. If reffering to movement and decision making as lower level AI tehniques, then the strategy is on a higher level (usually using movement and decision making as tools to achieve its vision). For some games (or genres) strategy can be easier to implement than with others. e. g. strategy for sports games can be developed and implemented a lot faster because inspiration can be drawn from real teams and based on real actors, whilst RTS games do not have direct counterparts in the real world.

AI in RTS Games

Real-time strategy games are a sub-genre of strategy computer games, which are based on classical board games such as chess or tic-tac-toe. In strategy (computer) games, a player tries to gain the advantage over one or more opponents by a series of moves. The players perform in turns. During each turn, the players make their moves, and then the outcome is evaluated. In RTS games, the turns progress automatically over short-time intervals, which create the illusion of playing in real-time.

RTS games include several aspects of playing that must be managed by the player and the AI. RTS games are more commonly the simulations of war games. Each opponent is in possession of some sort of weapon units with different attacking and defending capabilities. An unit can be stationary (e.g. a cannon turret or a pillbox) or manoeuvrable (e.g. a contingent of marines, a tank, or a ship). In addition to combat units, RTS games may include different kinds of buildings and structures. Some buildings are used for constructing new combat units or other buildings, some buildings provide the 'energy', whilst the other structures serve for a fortification.

A war campaign is usually set on some fictitious land that consists of different types of terrain. Only a part of the map is usually shown on the player's screen. Traditionally, there is also a 'mini-map' that shows a minimised version of the whole world. Not all the land is revealed to the players at the beginning of the game. Some areas are hidden in so-called 'fog-of-war' (FOW). This is the area of land that, as yet, has been unexplored by the player. A new terrain is exposed when a certain player's unit is placed on it.

Another aspect of an RTS game is the 'economy'. Usually some sort of 'credits' are necessary to purchase or build the new units and buildings. Some resources must be gathered from the land, to earn these credits. These resources are usually scarce and must be harvested. This represents another point of conflict between the players. Other aspects of RTS games, such as diplomacy, where one peer may form an alliance or declare war with another peers, is also possible.

For the success at an RTS game, all these aspects must be properly considered and balanced. This article focuses on the attacking aspects of RTS games, with other features left on one side for future research.

CHALLENGES OF AI IN COMPUTER GAMES

How to Achieve a Balanced Game?

In the introductory chapter (1. Motivation / 1.2 How can we make AI both challenging and interesting for the players), some of the ideas have already been presented, how to make a game, that will have higher repetitive value. If we ask ourselves a question at this point, is a challenging and interesting AI opponent a balanced opponent? The best approximation to the answer would be that, whilst this can be true for some cases, it is not true for all of them. Because the AI opponent can use player's weaknesses in a smart way, it can operate hundred's of units in real time, it can make very clever and interesting attacks, it can be very difficult for a player to get through its defences that make the opponent very challenging, so overall the opponent is too good. So good, that a player who played a game for hundreds and hundreds of hours, would never be as good as the NPC, which can opperate its army with surgical precision and using every millisecond of game play-time to maximize its game performance.

There have been various methods developed or currently still are in the research stage by game developers and researchers all around the world. Methods vary from data mining tehniques which operate using game-replay data of how professional players play games, neural networks which learn human tactics whilst gaming, AI's that are developed based on human behaviour, AI's that mimicing a player etc. As can be seen, tehniques take different approaches, but they all want to reach the same goal, to get as close as possible with AI performance to the human performances whilst playing games. The best AI is the AI that is challenging and a worthy opponent for the whole durration of a game, and then in the end loses it to the player for less than a »nickel«.

How to Detect the Skills of the Gamer?

Several techniques can be employed in order to allow the AI to adapt to the skill of the player. Firstly, the skill may be pre-set in advance at the beginning of the game. e. g. the player choses the level of difficulty by himself/herself. In addition, if the game-play consists of several stages, the difficulties of consecutive stages would progress steadily. These approaches require no AI involvement.

Secondly, and much more challenging, the skill and tactics of the opponent would be determined by the AI itself. Several measurement metrics can be employed for the overall skill of the player. Some of them are:

1. **Duration of the Game play:** Prolonged play of the game would probably increase the experience of the player. Therefore, the

difficulty of the game must be increased steadily. However, this metric requires that the player can be identified. When the same console or computer is used by several players, this is not the case unless some kind of identification of the player is employed (e.g., by registration at the beginning of the play).

2. **The Frequency of the Keys Pressed:** If the game is controlled through the keypad interface or similar device, the intervals between two successive commands could be measured. It is expected that the more experienced player will have a higher frequency of using commands. However, the player may be skilled by using the console, whilst this is not the same for the game.
3. **The Time Required to Finish a Particular Stage in the Game:** It is expected that in multistage games, the experienced players will finish the level faster.
4. **The Time (or Number of Moves) for Destroying a Specific Target:** When a target is attacked, it usually requires more than one move to be destroyed. An experienced player would employ proper kind of units and perhaps deploy several units at the same time to destroy the target more quickly. However, because some randomness is always used during the resolution of the attacks, the observed times should not be compared directly.

Even more challenging would be to determine the tactics of the opponent.

By observing the position of the player's mobile units over time, the AI can determine the general speed and the direction of the opponent. For this, each unit is associated with the direction vector. Those units with similar direction vectors and in close proximity can be considered as a group. The direction vector of a group is defined by the averaging all direction vectors of units in the group. By observing these direction vectors and considering the strengths of the units within a group, the intention of the opponent can be deduced. For example, the direction vector may point to some of the key objects managed by the AI. Then it is most likely that the selected object will be the target of attack. However, such a deduction is not straightforward. The characteristics of the terrain may prevent a direct approach to the target. Therefore, the topology and other obstacles must be considered during opponent evaluation.

In the case where the AI's opponent is another computer program, adaptation of the opponent's skills is not required or even wise, because a computer program cannot be frustrated or bored. In this case, the AI must employ all of its capabilities. Nevertheless, determination of an opponent's tactics and plans may be crucial for the winning of the game.

OPEN SOURCE RTS DEVELOPMENT TOOLS

There are many open source RTS development tools in existence today. To name just a few: Stratagus, ORTS, Spring, 0 A. D., Glest, Globulation 2, Seven kingdoms and many more. Because there are many options when selecting a framework, these discussions are concentrated on three of the development tools that are mostly used in research articles. Our selection was Stratagus, ORTS and Spring.

Stratagus

Stratagus is a free cross-platform RTS game engine which started as a Warcraft II clone in 1998. But since then it has come a long way and now offers a high variety of games. Its most complete game is currently Wargus which is, as the name suggests, a very good clone of the Warcraft II game.

Stratagus engine is based on Lua which is their primary scripting language. So a developer can easily access all features of the engine, without modifying the original source, unless he chooses to do so, by adding a new feature (currently not supported by the engine). Stratagus is a 2D engine based on a set of pictures in a .png format to show animation, which is an old technology compared to the 3D engines currently in existence. Nevertheless it is an engine that is as close to a commercial RTS game as possible (http://en.wikipedia.org/wiki/Stratagus –13.5.2012).

AI calculations are not performed in real-time because AI is given time slices every game cycle, in between rendering graphics and calculating all the game state details (Rørmark, 2009).

ORTS

ORTS engine is a free open source RTS 3D engine based on client-server architecture in comparison to the commercial RTS engines which are peer-to-peer oriented. Using client-server architecture, developers aim at a hack-free environment, because the server represents the game engine with only visible parts of game's state sent to the client.

AI code is local to each client, and AI algorithms are programmed directly by upgrading the source-code of the client. Game environment is described in the form of scripts. Because ORTS was developed to serve as a test-bed for researchers it cointains only low-level AI logic. Leaving all the aspects of designing an AI to the developer (pathfinding, planing ect).

Spring

Spring is a free open source cross-platform versatile 3D engine which was originally developed to bring the popular game Total Annihilation back to life. During the years it did not only achieve the official goal, but overgrew it entirely and is now a powerful game engine with very realistic graphics –reflective bump mapped water and realistic weapon trajectories, deformable terrain, etc. (Rørmark, 2009).

Using Lua for scripting game-specific code makes nearly every aspect of the engine customisable, from GUI, to unit AI and pathfinding (http://springrts.com/wiki/About–9.5.2012). Developers of new AI's have plenty of API's to use, with basic AI templates already implemented, which leaves more time for developing tactical and strategical parts of the AI.

Our Choice

Our choice for developing an advanced AI is the Spring engine, because it is most developer-friendly, it has the biggest community with many game modes already developed for it, and most importantly with many AI's to test and compare our new AI with. Which means faster searching to the solution of a problem, if a problem arises. The engine also supports many programming languages (Java, Lua, C, C++, with Python during testing phases) to program AI's with, in the comparison to ORTS, which only supports C++.

OMAR BRADLEY: AI WAR GENERAL

Evaluation Function

In each move in an RTS game, a player may move some units or initiate an attack by combat units on the enemy units or buildings. The goals are usually to destroy the enemy units and structures, and to diminish the building and resource gathering capabilities of the enemy. When one unit attacks others, the attacking and defensive capabilities of the units are evaluated. There is usually a baseline as to how much damage can be done or how much damage can be inflicted on certain types of units. However, some kind of randomness in both precision and strength is also introduced for a better playing experience. During each turn, a player may also start resource harvesting, and initiate the building of new units and structures, etc.

To determine the best move, the AI must evaluate the current situation on the game field. To achieve this, some sort of evaluation function is required. On the basic level, the evaluation function evaluates a single unit or an object based on different criteria. The result of the evaluation function can be a scalar or a vector. In the first case, each object is given some value that determines its importance or strength. In the second case, different capabilities of the object are evaluated separately (e.g., attacking and defending capabilities). Some of those parameters are required by the game engine to determine the outcomes of individual combats (e.g. the toughness of armour, the strength of attack, etc.). Other ones can be used strictly for the purpose of AI.

The parameters that determine the weight of the unit or buildings are its defence and attack powers, moving speed, manoeuvrability (e.g., on what terrain the unit can move), importance within a current game-story, etc. During play, several units can converge into groups. The strength of a group is determined by a weighted sum of the strengths of each individual unit in the group. Furthermore, the groups may eventually converge into armies and the strength of the army is defined by the strengths of its groups.

Strategies for Advanced Players

This chapter believes that the main keys to building a worthy adversary for the more experienced players are cooperation between the units, and a deduction of opponent intentions.

Firstly, instead of controlling each unit separately, groups of units should be formed, pursuing some common goal. By this, the chances of achieving victory over a stronger opponent are much greater. At what point units should start to merge into groups depends on the skill of the player and the general settings. The units in a group are chosen according to theirs specialities as a way to obtain balance and a versatile entity. For example, a group may consist of some strong offensive and some strong defensive parts, the units with an extended field of view (e.g., units equipped with the radar), the repairing unit, etc. Furthermore, if necessary, the groups may merge into armies. The groups in an army would pursue some common goal. However, to achieve this goal, each group may perform different actions.

Secondly, if the intent of the opponent is known, then the AI can easily prepare contra measures. For example, if the AI can determine there is a single goal for the attack, the defences around this object can be strengthened. When AI detects an attack on several objects simultaneously, it should also appropriately spread the defences. For advanced players, AI may decide to sacrifice some targets and focus a counter attack on the opponent's units and buildings.

Yet, managing of groups is the most important part of the attacking part of AI. Which move needs to take place is determined by an evaluation function, but that is not the only requirement for an attack to succeed. Groups must be orchestrated through the use of grouping, fixing, merging and disbanding. Grouping and disbanding are in charge for combining/separating units into a group or from a group. Fixing of a group is needed after a group has been involved in an attack with an opponent and has suffered sufficient damage. Merging is used if there is a large force approaching and the separated groups would be unable to deal with it. So an army is formed by combining groups together.

Spring Implementation of Omar Bradley

The implementation of an AI in a Spring engine has already started (Spring was described in a chapter 4), by following the vision of strategies for advanced players, yet the development is still in its early stages.

During the initialisation function (which is part of Java Null AI template for Spring), shown in Figure 2, three main classes were initialised: MainAIObject, BuildManager and UnitControl.

MainAIObject is in charge of holding all the necessary game states, BuildManager is in charge of building units (buildings and dynamic units) and UnitControl is holding the implementations of strategies already presented in the previous chapter.

One of the internal classes in UnitControl is a WaitingLine that holds a queue with all the actions that its units are required to do. Example of the code inside UnitControl is shown in Figure 3.

CONCLUSION

The current state-of-the-art of AI in RTS and similar computer games is inadequate and very little has been done over the past 20 years to improve the situation. In the meantime academic AI research is having a new renaissance. Therefore, there are many opportunities for combining them both. The computer power and memory resources have increased exponentially over the last few years and improved AI should not hinder the performance of the game. Nevertheless, AI should not become omnipotent over the player. Instead, it should adapt to the skill of the player and let him/her win from time to time. An appropriate AI for the more advanced players does not exist today. By integrating the collaboration and opponent

Figure 2. Init function

```
public int init(int skirmishAIId, OOAICallback callback)
{
        mainAIObjects = new MainAIObjects(skirmishAIId, callback);
        buildManager = new BuildManager(mainAIObjects);
        unitControl = new UnitControl();
        return mainAIObjects.getRet();
}
```

Figure 3. Internal class of UnitControl

```
private class WaitingLine
{
    private Queue<WaitingObject> line = new LinkedList<WaitingObject>();

    public void addToLine(Unit unit, String action)
    {
        WaitingObject waitingObject = new WaitingObject(unit, action);
        line.add(waitingObject);
    }
}
```

tactic's predictions, the AI may become a worthily adversary for such gamers. The advances in AI in computer games can also contribute to better real-life applications.

A lot of advanced programming environment is available today for developing and testing AI in games. Most of them are open-source and have integrated powerful game-engines. A developer can easily use a plug-in approach: only the modules of interest can be replaced and tested, the rest can be left to predefined behaviour.

Last, but not least, at the end of the day, you can have plenty of fun developing your own AI.

REFERENCE

Millington, I., & Funge, J. (2009). *Artificial intelligence for games*. Burlington, VT: Morgan Kaufmann.

Rørmark, R. (2009). *Thanatos – A learning RTS game AI*. (Master Thesis). University of Oslo, Oslo, Norway.

Chapter 22
Static Graphics for Dynamic Information

Francisco V. Cipolla-Ficarra
ALAIPO – AINCI, Spain and Italy

Jacqueline Alma
Electronic Arts – Vancouver, Canada

ABSTRACT

The authors present the first results of the heuristic analysis of the static graphics in the digital newspapers for senior users. They examine the main systems of static graphics. A parallelism is drawn between the current static graphic information and the function of the banners in the quality attributes to boost the motivation of those users in the face of the economic news online in the digital papers.

INTRODUCTION

In the current era of the expansion of communicability (Cipolla-Ficarra, 2010) digital information in the online newspapers is focused on economics, especially that to be found in the home page. Many of the data which are presented in it have an ordination, tabulation and elaboration which require a systematic presentation of it. Traditionally this process may be visually depicted through written representation, semi-tabular representation, tabular representation and graphic representation. In the 20th century the tabular representation has taking a predominant place in the text and graphic representation has acquired a greater importance in visual information with the switch of the use of the computer (Cipolla-Ficarra & Cipolla-Ficarra, 2009) as a professional "instrument" (1960-1970) to a personal computer (1980-2000). The new multimedia devices such as the tablet PC are leaving behind the use of the PC in the new generations. However, in our universe of study and in the current work we focus on the classical sense of the term "personal computer" of the 80s and 90s for seniors users. We divide the users in the following way in relation to age: child (4), junior (12-17) adult (18-64) and senior (65).

In 1741 the Dane Achersen used for the first time tablets for the data (Ander-egg, 1986). That is, he incorporated in the shape of a text the

DOI: 10.4018/978-1-4666-4490-8.ch022

compiled statistic data. Currently in the digital online information there is still a valid modality, that is, writing a text and inside said text to overlap whole figures, in decimals, percentages, etc. For example, in Figure 1, "the public debt of the Balearic community is 4,479 billion euros and is equivalent to 16.7% of the Spanish GDP –Gross Domestic Product".

In the semi-tabular modality the data inside the text are used in the shape of columns to stress total figures and percentages, for instance. In the Figure 1 the graphic information on the growth of the Spanish debt could be expressed in the following way, if each of the autonomous communities was presented:

Total in billions of euros, name of the autonomic region, the relationship with GDP, that is,

- **42,000 billion:** Catalonia, 21%
- **20,832billion:** Valence, 20.2%
- **4,479 billion:** Balearic Islands, 16.7%, etc.

In the tabular representation, the numeric data are ordered in files and columns so that the numeric

Figure 1. Public debt of Spain by autonomic communities. Newspaper online: El País (www.elpais.es –06.15.2012)

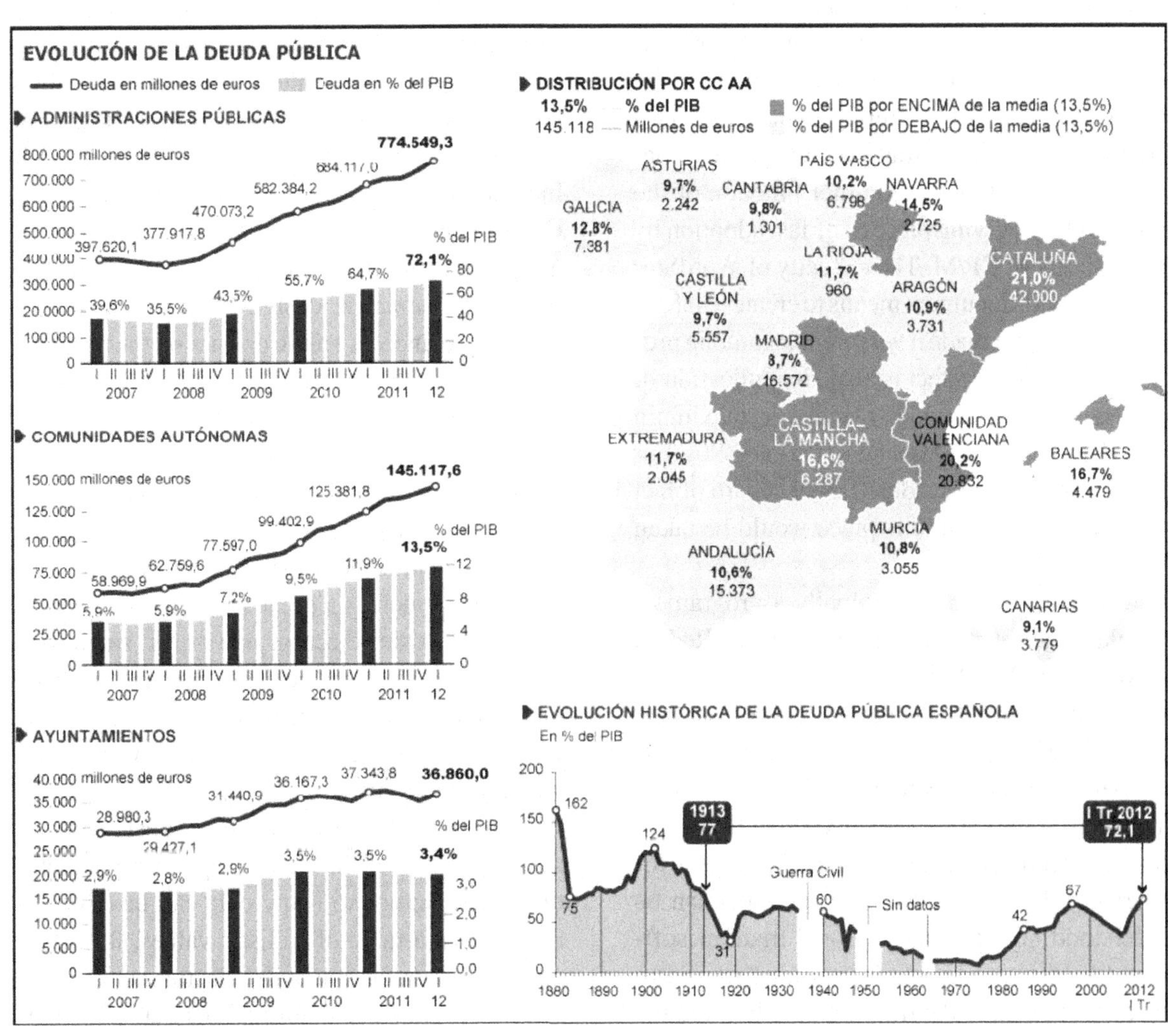

expression appears in a specific way, short and easy to interpret. In this regard the diffusion of the professional computer in the offices, specially in 1980, it is due not only that the traditional typewriters could be replaced (commercial programs like WordStar or WordPerfect) but mainly the generation of tablets and their graphic representation with commercial programs. Such as Lotus 1-2-3 (Power, D., 2002).

STATIC GRAPHICS, COMMERCIAL SOFTWARE AND NEWSPAPERS

The WordStar was the last processor of commercial texts for the operative system CP/M (Reddy, 1996). The 3.0 version of WordStar for DOS was launched in April of 1982. The version for DOS was very similar to the original and although the IBM PC (Bride, 2011) offered support for cursor and function keys, the traditional WordStar Diamond was maintained and other function of the type Ctrl+Key giving place to its fast adoption by the old users of CP/M. The capacity of WordStar of using a non-document means to create text files without a format made it very popular among programmers. WordPerfect is also an application of processing of texts, which reached its maximum popularity in the late 80s and in the early 90s. For many years it was considered the standard of fact in its sector. Later on this place would be taken by Microsoft Word.

Microsoft marketed originally a program of calculation sheet called Multiplan in 1982 (Reddy, 1996; Bride, 2011), which was very popular in the CP/M systems, but in the MS-DOS systems it lost popularity versus the Lotus 1-2-3. The Lotus company lost speed by taking 1-2-3 to Windows and this to some extent helped Microsoft to reach the position of the main software developers for Interface). In this short historical vision can be understood how the international trade of software for office tasks which was later moved to the home thanks to the Internet have boosted the circulation of statistic data, for instance, which can be presented in a classical way or not, to the user of PC interactive systems or to the new mobile multimedia systems.

In the 20th century the popular press and television took avail of the graphics as an auxiliary means to depict the statistic data to a wide audience (Reeves & Nass, 1996). People who in many occasions were totally ignorant of the issues that were introduced for the first time. It is true, though, that the statistic graphics depict in an attractive and expressive way the compiled data, since these are released only once, the whole of the information, in a concrete way, especially when the context is abstract. An example may be the current issues of macro economics for a wider audience in Southern Europe, inexperienced in these issues.

However, in the interfaces of some online newspapers, it is possible to find that the global information of a macro economic issue is split into parts. The fractioning of content gives to the user the impression of being in the face of a dynamic graphic information. This strategy of online interactive design can be seen when a user may glance an online dossier on the negative economic results, as it can be seen in Figure 2. In this sense it is also a communicability strategy, that is, to split negative information emulating in this way a real dossier, where the user may go forwards or backwards, in each one of the pages of the content. Placing all that information in a single page such as a great static graphic, would generate a wide rejection nowadays, since they contain the logos of the main Spanish banking institutions. Dynamism boosts at least a short interaction in each of the pages to have a global vision of the issue in hand.

Now this strategy allows to eradicate some of the limitations of the static graphics representation, such as: not so many data can be depicted as a box or a table of statistic values, it doesn't allow the appreciation of details, the exact values can't be seen, since deformations may be gener-

Figure 2. The emulation of the dossier allows a bidirectional navigation of the text by the user. Newspaper online: El País (www.elpais.es –06.06.2012).

ated by the scales used, etc. In other words, we have negative and positive aspects in the method of the static graphics. Aspects which were also recognized by the Scott William Playfair regarded as the inventor of four types of diagrams or graphics in the late 18th century and early 19th (Ander-egg, 1986) and which currently are incorporated into the office automation programs with a worldwide commercial circulation such as the Excel: line graph and bar chart of economics, and circle graph, used to show part-whole relations. Playfair said that the advantage of the proposed method is not giving a more accurate expression of the figures, but give a more simple and permanent idea of the gradual process and of amounts comparable in different periods, presenting to sight a figure or a graphic, whose proportions match the amounts that are trying to be depicted.

The programmers of the first applications of office automation such as the version of MS

(Microsoft) Excel for PC (1987) were aimed at the then novel graphic environment (Campell-Kelly & Aspray, 2004). The analysts and programmers knew that they had to guide themselves by the principles of traditional or classical graphic representation, that is, the fundaments of mathematic and statistic order. These fundaments or principles may be summed up in the following way: graphic representations in the plane (rectangular coordinates, angular, triangular, etc.), space representations (stereograms and level curves), cartographic representations (cartograms) space representations (pictograms and outlines) among others. Briefly a small description of those which have been used more frequently in the printed media, that is, the analogical newspapers or in paper support in Southern Europe are: broken line (Figure 4), cartography (Figure 1), circles, lineal (Figure 1), rectangular bars (Figure 2) and stacked bar chart (Figure 3).

GRAPHIC REPRESENTATIONS: EVOLUTION

The early graphic representations in the plane of the rectangular coordinates were presented by Renée Descartes in 1637 in his book Geometry (Descartes, 2010). Currently they have different names such as Cartesian coordinates, orthogonal system, etc. With the passing of time, it is necessary to put the values of the independent variables in the axis of the abscissa, and in the axis of the ordinates, the values of the independent variable. Finally, it is important to stress that in the graphic representation the first quadrant is used, since the work is with positive values.

In the graphic of Figure 5, the use of the metaphor of a thermometer stands as an interesting novelty in the financial-economic environment, with the arrows that go up and down, accompanied with the flags of the countries to which they refer. Although it can be attractive at first sight, it hasn't been correctly interpreted in our universe of study, because the zero of the coordinates is not represented. That is, the data must still be financially balanced, for instance, when they refer to the rates of interest and the premium risk of the foreign debt of some countries in the EU with regard to Germany.

Another of the graphic representations in the plane are the polar coordinates. In the interactive graphic design environment are the sectors or "portions" that make up a "circular cake". In this system the position of any point of the plane will be determined by the distance from the central point or "0", known as pole, through a vector radio which has the same function as the axis of the ordinates of the orthogonal system and because of the opening to the polar angle (alfa) which measures the distribution of the phenomenon. The radio vector turns around point 0 forming different angles "portions of the circular cake", in regard to its basic position, known as polar axis. Traditionally these types of graphics were used to depict phenomena which evolved in time with a variable rhythm. Now the circular diagrams are applied advantageously in the depiction of a set and in different components.

There are five types of traditional circular depiction: sectors, concentric circles, tangent areas, spiral graphics, and polar coordinates. For instance, the circular diagram of sectors or cake is a split circle in which the fact of considering it In its whole, that is, the equivalent of 360° of the circumference and each one of the classes or groups, will have a sector with a central angle, matching the percentage which must be distributed. Now so far have been enumerated some of the mathematic graphic representations. This set of graphics (circular) are complemented with the sets of the graphics of points, lineal graphics, surface graphics, stereometrics. There are also the graphics of non-mathematic basis, such as the cartograms (they depict figures on the maps), the pictograms (they consist in figures or isotypes which depict a phenomenon which is explained by the very nature of the figure, for instance, a

Figure 3. Stacked bar chart

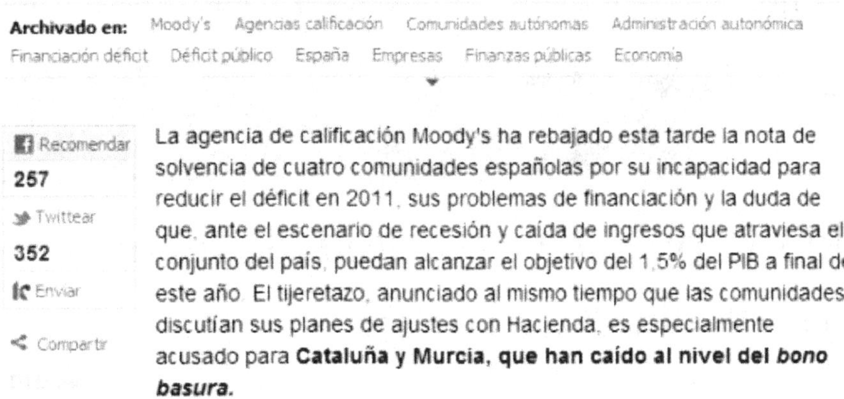

Moody's rebaja a Cataluña y Murcia a 'bono basura' por sus problemas de déficit

- La agencia reduce la nota de solvencia de cuatro regiones en plena tormenta en los mercados
- La Comunidad Valenciana y Castilla-La Mancha ya estaban consideradas de alto riesgo

ÁLVARO ROMERO | **Madrid** | 17 MAY 2012 - 19:15 CET 109

Archivado en: Moody's Agencias calificación Comunidades autónomas Administración autonómica Financiación déficit Déficit público España Empresas Finanzas públicas Economía

Recomendar 257
Twittear 352
Enviar
Compartir
Imprimir

La agencia de calificación Moody's ha rebajado esta tarde la nota de solvencia de cuatro comunidades españolas por su incapacidad para reducir el déficit en 2011, sus problemas de financiación y la duda de que, ante el escenario de recesión y caída de ingresos que atraviesa el conjunto del país, puedan alcanzar el objetivo del 1,5% del PIB a final de este año. El tijeretazo, anunciado al mismo tiempo que las comunidades discutían sus planes de ajustes con Hacienda, es especialmente acusado para **Cataluña y Murcia, que han caído al nivel del *bono basura*.**

Con la entrada de estas dos regiones por debajo del nivel considerado como una inversión aceptable ya son cuatro las autonomías restringidas a los especuladores, según se desprende de la descripción que hace Moody's de sus calificaciones. En concreto, la nota de **Andalucía baja en dos escalones, de A3 a Baa2, y la de Extremadura cae en uno, de A3 a Baa1**, lo que equivale a un aprobado muy raspado, pero todavía por encima de ser consideradas de alto riesgo. De las que han caído en bono basura Murcia ve su calificación recortada en dos escalones, con lo que pasa de Baa2 a Ba1, mientras Cataluña cede uno y se queda con una nota de Ba1.

GRADO DE CALIDAD		Moody's	S&P y Fitch
Inversión	Óptima	Aaa	AAA
	Alta	Aa1	AA+
		Aa2	AA
		Aa3	AA-
	Buena	A1	A+
		A2	A
		A3	A-
	Satisfactoria	Baa1	BBB+
		Baa2	BBB
		Baa3	BBB-
Especulación (*bono basura*)	Cuestionable	Ba1	BB+
		Ba2	BB

Escalas de calificación que usan las

Por su parte, **Valencia y Castilla-La Mancha, también dentro del paraguas del bono basura**, también estaban en revisión y se quedan como estaban con una calificación de Ba2 y Ba3, respectivamente. El argumento para ello es que, aunque cuentan con una posición financiera débil, el Estado garantizará su liquidez a cambio de un mayor control sobre sus cuentas para evitar una quiebra que sería inevitable sin el apoyo de la Administración central.

Además, la agencia ha dejado a todas estas autonomías en perspectiva negativa, lo que indica que hay más posibilidades de que registren un

Figure 4. Broken line or dashed line

EL PAÍS

PORTADA | INTERNACIONAL | PO

ECONOMÍA

ECONOMÍA EMPRESAS MERCADOS BOLSA FINANZAS PERSONALES VIVIENDA TECNOLO

▶ ESTÁ PASANDO | Rescate de España | Ayudas a la banca | Prima de riesgo | Telefonía m

DIRECTO

Suecia, 0 - Inglaterra, 1. Un gran cabezazo de Carroll adelan con Ucrania en la última jornada, y pone a la selección escandina

La deuda pública española alcanza su mayor nivel desde ¡1913!

- El endeudamiento español no superaba el 70% del PIB desde hace 99 años
- El mayor nivel registrado por el FMI es el 162% de 1880, posterior a una crisis bancaria

MIGUEL JIMÉNEZ | Madrid | 15 JUN 2012 - 13:26 CET 37

Archivado en: Crisis económica Crisis deuda europea FMI Recesión económica Deuda pública Coyuntura económica Crisis financiera Financiación déficit Déficit público Historia contemporánea

EVOLUCIÓN HISTÓRICA DE LA DEUDA PÚBLICA ESPAÑOLA

En % del PIB

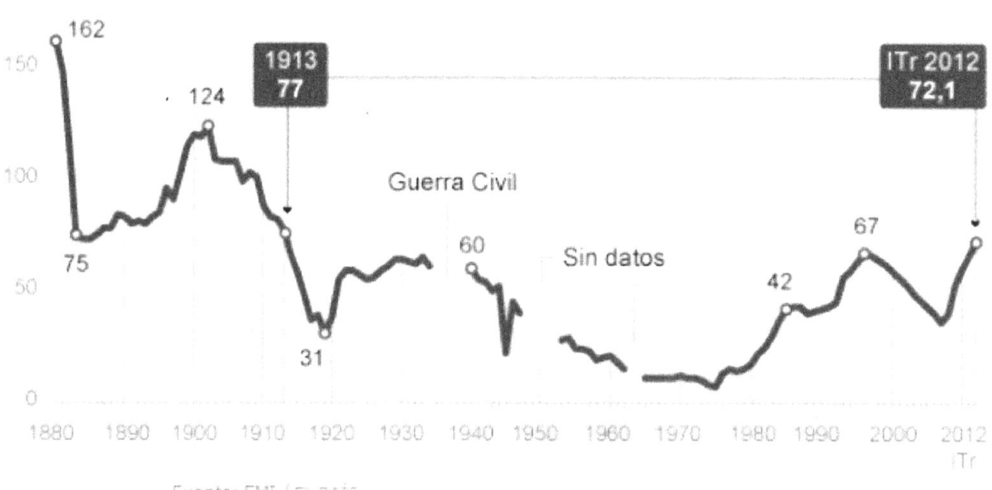

Figure 5. A modern representation of the passing of the time and the paying of interests through the notion of the thermometer, but it lacks basic information in the structure for the representation of the data. Newspaper online: El País (www.elpais.es –06.21.2012).

EL PAÍS

PORTADA | INTERNACIONAL | POLÍTICA | ECONOMÍA | CULTURA | SOCIEDAD | DEPORTES

ECONOMÍA

ECONOMÍA EMPRESAS MERCADOS BOLSA FINANZAS PERSONALES VIVIENDA TECNOLOGÍA OPINIÓN/ANÁLISIS BLOGS LA CRISIS TITULARES

ESTÁ PASANDO Banca La crisis de Bankia BCE Prima de riesgo Déficit público Crisis de deuda Indemnizaciones polémicas MÁS TEMAS »

La prima de riesgo repunta a un nuevo máximo pese a los mensajes de Bruselas

- El diferencial alcanza los 540 puntos básicos, nivel más alto desde 1995
- El BCE rechaza la capitalización de Bankia con deuda
- EN DIRECTO Evolución en directo de los mercados

ISABEL LAFONT | Madrid | 30 MAY 2012 - 17:17 CET 2138

Archivado en: Prima de riesgo IBEX 35 Comisión Europea BCE Bankia Indices bursátiles Financiación déficit Organización partidos UE Déficit público Bolsa Organizaciones internacionales

EL TERMÓMETRO DE LA CRISIS

En la zona euro, la prima de riesgo es el diferencial entre el tipo de interés del bono a diez años de cada país con el título alemán al mismo plazo en el mercado secundario. Para las finanzas públicas de un país es determinante a qué tipo de interés se endeuda: **cuanto más alto, más coste**

cow for cattle, a boat for the port, etc.) and the special graphics (Gantt, are used to depict the facts in relation to the passing of time, for instance, the work scheduled and the work really done; the level curves, for instance, the reference to topography to depict points of equal height or level, etc.)

In our universe of study we only use the graphics of mathematic base of a lineal type, surface diagrams (rectangular and circular), and of non-mathematic base such as the cartograms or cartographics. Now in the analysis of the online information of the digital papers it has been detected that due to the range of modalities that graphic representation has acquired, the statistic information does not obey the mathematic rules, nor logical, but rather artistic. In the second decade of the 20th century rules were drawn for the graphic representation in the Western culture countries and which the interested reader can look up in a summary in annex #1.

CONFORMATION OF THE UNIVERSE OF STUDY, ASSESSMENT AND RESULTS

The universe of study is made up by 20 adult users, whose ages range from 65 to 70 years of age. Half of them have previous experience in the use of computers and the other 50% not. They are people without physical or mental disabilities. All of them are or have been newspaper reads in paper support. Besides, half of them read daily the digital online version. In our work, we have assigned a number to each newspaper of national circulation in Spain and which has a free access online digital version. Later on, these numbers correspond to a ball inside a drum. Through a random draw the Spanish newspaper "El País" has been chosen for the analysis. From that moment on, daily have been stored the main pages of financial news where there were graphics (15 January 2012 – 15 June 2012).

The graphics have been printed in color in two dimensions: the real one of the digital publication and in A4. It has also been generated a file with the images of the graphics in their original environment, that is, accompanied by the rest of the components of the page of the digital paper: texts, pictures, drawings, etc. These images have made up a PowerPoint file. The techniques of heuristic evaluation used were direct observation by two communicability specialists and the questionnaire (Cipolla-Ficarra & Cipolla-Ficarra, 2009; Nielsen & Mack, 1994; Cipolla-Ficarra, Nicol & Cipolla-Ficarra, 2010) inside communicability lab.

In the questionnaire was requested information about the numeric data of the main information that the graphics transmitted, for instance, the autonomous community that less public debt had, those communities which were below the Spanish average of indebtedness, the banks or savings banks that more money would need from the public financial aid, the main and/or secondary colors of the logos of the institutions to which the financial information is related, etc. The answers of the questionnaires were ring-fenced or binary, that is, yes or no, with the possibility of writing which was the best and the worst of all the images, giving grounds for the answer. The total of questions was ten.

The first quality of attribute that was evaluated was visual prediction. That is, the skill that have the people who daily consume information in paper support and/or digital to anticipate the meaning of a structure of components –in our case isolated graphics or accompanied by texts or other images whether they are static (in paper support) or dynamic (in Internet), previously analyzed a structure or a similar operation but in different situations. The term "operation" refers to the interaction with interactive systems.

The motivation was the other attribute of quality that was evaluated in the users. That is, since the categories of layout design and content inside the set of structural resources boost the interests towards the contents that are presented. The motivation strives to focus the attention of the reader and/or user on the need of keeping on interacting with the content. The attention on the screen of the online interactive system, for instance. That is, it must be sustained so that the user keeps an attitude of permanent expectation in regard to the system. These are the visual resources, which prompt very good results in the attention and acceptance towards the system, especially when there is no previous experience in computer science by the user. In this case, we focus on the publicity banners, whether they are dynamic or static, which went with the economic and/or financial information. In both cases these criteria were turned into quality metrics, through the use of the updated MECEM (Metrics for the Communications Evaluation in Multimedia). The interested readers may find detailed information of each one of the steps in the following bibliographical references (Cipolla-Ficarra, 2001; Cipolla-Ficarra, 2011). The tests were made in an individual way, resorting to the computer for the users experienced in their use, the presentation of the images in analogical support (paper) and digital (PowerPoint), next the obtained results:

Figure 6. The results of the heuristic evaluation of the visual prediction (E = Users experts in the use of computers; NE = Non experts in the use of PCs)

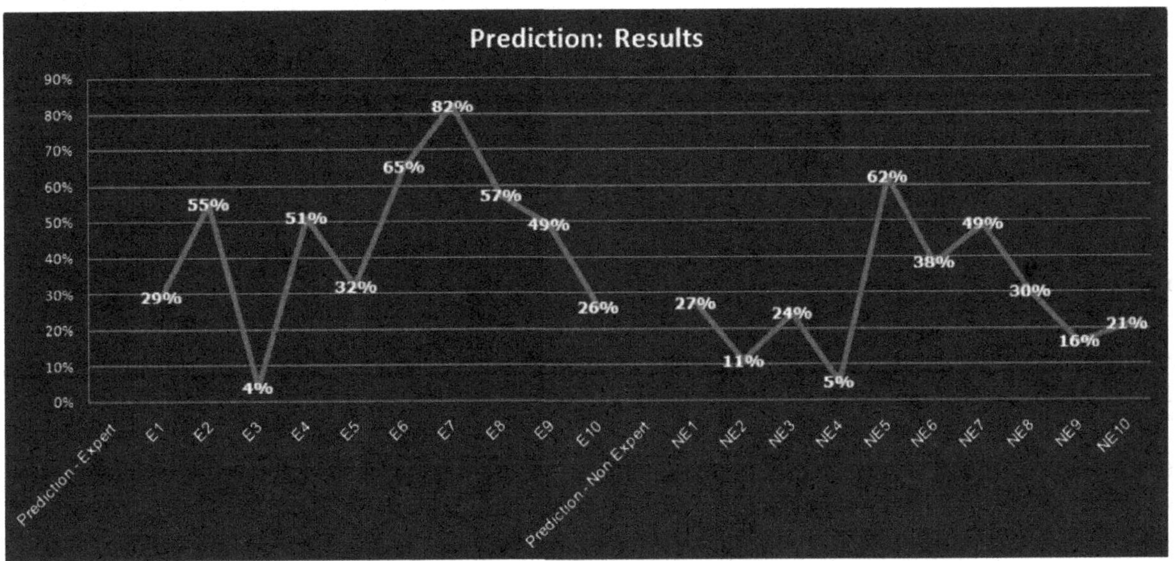

Figure 7. The results of the heuristic evaluation of the motivation (E = Users experts in the use of computers; NE = Non experts in the use of PCs)

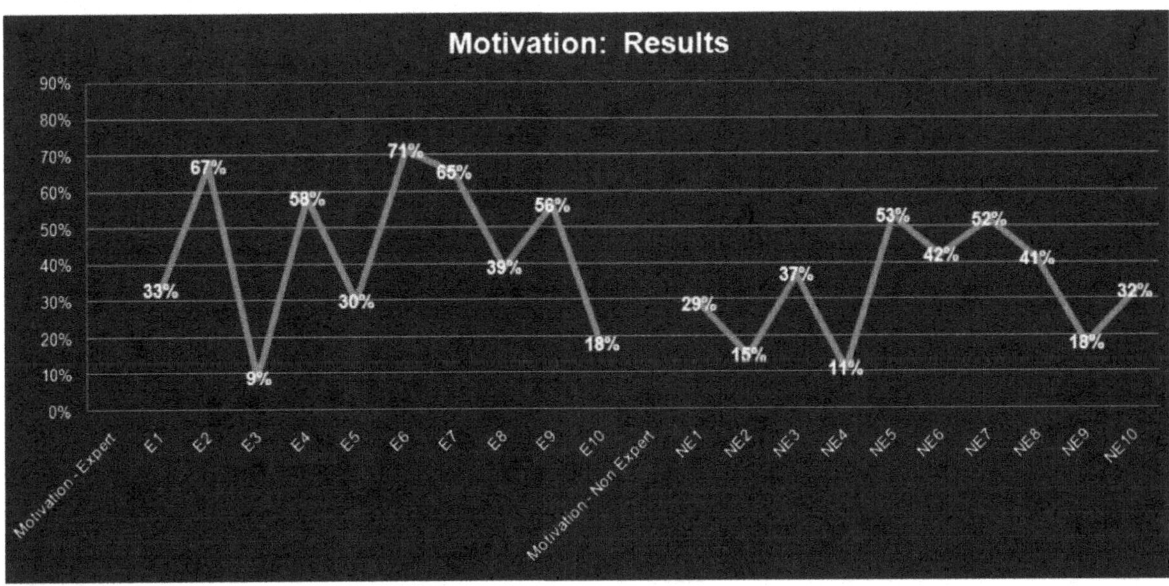

The visual prediction and the motivation between experienced users and non-experienced in the use of the computers is more or less similar. The dimension of the figures (widened or not) haven't seriously affected the final result of the interpretation of the economic-financial information.

The best graphic information that both groups of participants in the tests have in their majority selected meets the requirements listed in the Appendix. That is, irrespective of the digital or analogical support, the representation of the "traditional" or "classical" graphic information for the financial and/or economic context hasn't changed in the last century.

The visual prediction and the motivation between experienced users and non-experienced in the use of the computers is very similar. The dimension of the figures (widened or not) haven't seriously affected the final result of the interpretation of the economic-financial information. The best graphic information that both groups of participants in the tests have in their majority selected meets the requirements listed in annex #1. That is, irrespective of the digital or analogical support, the representation of the "traditional" or "classical" graphic information for the financial and/or economic context hasn't changed in the last century.

In contrast we have Figure 8, where unanimously all the users have considered that image as the worst. This evaluation is not due to the graphic information in itself but the publicity banner which is to be found in the upper part of the home page of the digital edition of the paper "El País". It is a commercial banner about travels (tourism) which goes with a negative news, in the upper right angle (that of the greatest attention in the screens) by the side of a publicity where there is an old destroyed car. That is, to take tourism or leisure trips when the economy of a country is very negative, as it is stressed by the idea of the broken car. All agreed that it was of very poor taste the drawing that is used where appears a strange character of green color, with wheels as feet, and with a funnel in his head. The connotation of the funnel is very negative in the context of the Southern Europe peninsula, since it means madness.

LESSONS LEARNED

These early results make apparent the importance of the simplicity of the static graphics to explain very current issues, although the addressee is inexperienced in the context. Besides, it confirms the evolution and the transfer of experiences and knowledge of the traditional graphic arts to the off-line multimedia systems in the 90s and online in the late 90s in Southern Europe, for instance. To such extent that the patterns of the start on graphics and statistics of the last century are still in force nowadays. Now in the context of interactive design and especially digital newspapers the insertion of publicity may trigger an absolute rejection to the best of graphics. That is, the static graphic is linked and interrelates with the remaining components of the page. Starting from 15th of June we have started to gather pages from other newspapers: English, French, Portuguese and Italian to enlarge our universe of study. This compilation will last until mid-December complementing the information of the Spanish newspapers. We have also decided to work with university students who use a PC tablet in the reading of digital papers and adults who read the digital papers in the personal computers. We have also incorporated to the universe of study the dynamic or animated graphics in 2D and 3D.

CONCLUSION

The human being seizes the messages in the interaction with the off-line multimedia systems in the following way: 20% through hearing, 40% through sight and 80% in-between what sees and listens. Now keeping the motivation in the face of unseen contents for the great part of the addressees

Figure 8. The best graphic and/or economic information of the universe of study. Newspaper online: El País (www.elpais.es –01.27.2012).

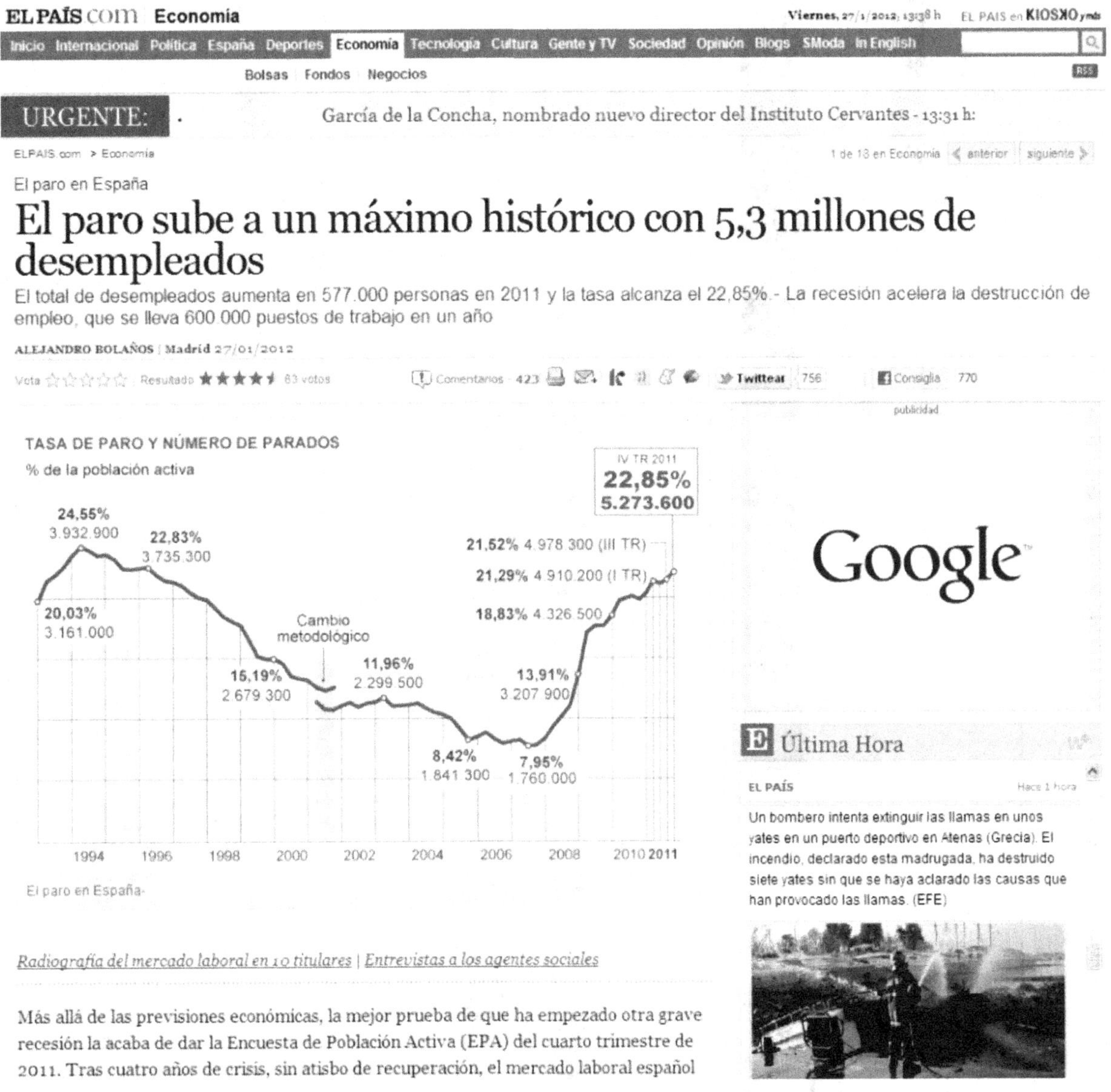

EL PAÍS com Economía

Viernes, 27/1/2012, 13:38 h EL PAÍS en KIOSKO y más

Inicio Internacional Política España Deportes Economía Tecnología Cultura Gente y TV Sociedad Opinión Blogs SModa In English

Bolsas Fondos Negocios

URGENTE: · García de la Concha, nombrado nuevo director del Instituto Cervantes - 13:31 h:

ELPAIS.com > Economía

1 de 18 en Economía anterior siguiente

El paro en España

El paro sube a un máximo histórico con 5,3 millones de desempleados

El total de desempleados aumenta en 577.000 personas en 2011 y la tasa alcanza el 22,85%.- La recesión acelera la destrucción de empleo, que se lleva 600.000 puestos de trabajo en un año

ALEJANDRO BOLAÑOS | Madrid 27/01/2012

Vota Resultado 63 votos Comentarios 423 Twittear 756 Consiglia 770

publicidad

Radiografía del mercado laboral en 10 titulares | Entrevistas a los agentes sociales

Más allá de las previsiones económicas, la mejor prueba de que ha empezado otra grave recesión la acaba de dar la Encuesta de Población Activa (EPA) del cuarto trimestre de 2011. Tras cuatro años de crisis, sin atisbo de recuperación, el mercado laboral español

Última Hora

EL PAÍS Hace 1 hora

Un bombero intenta extinguir las llamas en unos yates en un puerto deportivo en Atenas (Grecia). El incendio, declarado esta madrugada, ha destruido siete yates sin que se haya aclarado las causas que han provocado las llamas. (EFE)

such as can be macro economic information is not an easy task. However, the use of the graphics is very positive especially for those people who have a wide cultural background and who have been training along the years. In a special way through the social mass media, such as the press, television and radio, for instance. Interactive design resorts to the traditional knowledge of the statistic graphics with or without a mathematic basis. It is important that in the studies of human-computer interaction elderly people are taken into account, without physical or intellectual disabilities. Currently many of them are making economic and/or financial decisions in an autonomous and independent way. Finally, we think it is negative to introduce publicity on-line in the homepage of the digital papers, especially when there are economic and/or financial news which affect the

Figure 9. The worst economic/financial information due to the banner (in the upper right angle). Newspaper online: El País (www.elpais.es –05.28.2012).

lunes, 28 mayo 2012 | Actualizado 12:28 CET | Hemeroteca

Iniciar sesión | Registrarse

EL PAÍS

INTERNACIONAL | POLÍTICA | ECONOMÍA | CULTURA | SOCIEDAD | DEPORTES

ESTÁ PASANDO | Crisis de Bankia | Etarras detenidos | Liberación FARC | Palmarés en Cannes | Matanza Siria | Filtraciones en el Vaticano | MÁS TEMAS »

LA CRISIS DE BANKIA »

La prima de riesgo bate récords y Bankia se desploma en la Bolsa

- Los valores de la entidad se hunden hasta un 30% tras hacerse público que necesitará 19.000 millones adicionales

ISABEL LAFONT / MIGUEL JIMÉNEZ | Madrid

Las dudas sobre el plan de saneamiento de la entidad, cifrado en 19.000 millones de euros, empujan a la prima de riesgo por encima de 513 puntos, máximo histórico. Las acciones del banco vuelven al parqué a 1,15 euros frente a los 1,57 del cierre del pasado jueves, antes de suspender la cotización

- El rescate de Bankia pone la prima de riesgo en máximos
- EN DIRECTO Sigue la evolución de los mercados
- EN DIRECTO Consulta la cotización de Bankia
- 'Los disfraces de la mentira', por I. GABILONDO
- 'Alguna vez pudimos creer...', por SOLEDAD GALLEGO

OPINIÓN »

Fiasco en Facebook

EDITORIAL

Los bancos de inversión sobrevaloraron el precio de salida a Bolsa y dañaron a los inversores

SÍGUENOS EN

EL PAÍS KIOSKOymás

future in the short and long term of a community. This kind of information ought to be treated more seriously and using graphics in the following order of precedence: lineal, rectangular bars, circles and cartography.

REFERENCES

Ander-Egg, E. (1986). *Techniques of social investigation* (21st ed.). Buenos Aires, Argentina: Hvmanitas.

Bride, E. (2011). The IBM personal computer: A software-driven market. *IEEE Computer*, *44*(8), 34–39. doi:10.1109/MC.2011.193

Campell-Kelly, M., & Aspray, W. (2004). *Computer: A history of information machine*. New York: Basic Books.

Cipolla-Ficarra, F. (2001). *Communication evaluation in multimedia –Metrics and methodoloty*. Mahwah, NJ: LEA.

Cipolla-Ficarra, F. (2010). *Quality and communicability for interactive hypermedia systems: Concepts and practices for design*. Hershey, PA: IGI Global. doi:10.4018/978-1-61520-763-3

Cipolla-Ficarra, F. (2011). Usability engineering versus social sciences: An analysis of the main mistakes. In Advances in Dynamic and Static Media for Interactive Systems: Communicability, Computer Science and Design. Bergamo, Italy: Blue Herons Ed.s.

Cipolla-Ficarra, F., & Cipolla-Ficarra, M. (2009). Computer animation and communicability in multimedia system and services: A trichotomy evaluation. In *Proceedings of New Directions in Intelligent Interactive Multimedia*. Heidelberg, Germany: Springer. doi:10.1007/978-3-642-02937-0_10

Cipolla-Ficarra, F., Nicol, E., & Cipolla-Ficarra, M. (2010). Computer graphics and mass media: Communicability analysis. In *Proceedings of Advances in New Technologies, Interactive Interfaces and Communicability*. Heidelberg, Germany: Springer.

Descartes, R. (2010). *The geometry of Rene Descartes*. Whitefish, WI: Kessinger Publishing.

Nielsen, J., & Mack, R. (1994). *Usabilty inspection methods*. New York: John Wiley.

Power, D. (2002). *A brief history of spreadsheets*. Retrieved from http://dssresources.com/history/sshistory.html, version 3.6

Reddy, R. (1996). The challenge of artificial intelligence. *IEEE Computer*, *29*(10), 86–98. doi:10.1109/2.539726

Reeves, B., & Nass, C. (1996). *The media equation: How people treat computers, television, and new media like real people and places*. Cambridge, UK: Cambridge University Press.

APPENDIX

- The general disposition of a diagram must advance from left to right.
- It is convenient to depict the amounts through lineal magnitudes, curves and bars, since the surfaces and the volumes may lead to mistaken interpretations.
- Whenever possible, the vertical scale of the curve must be selected in such a way that the line of zero appears in the diagram. The visual impression is incorrect in case there is no such line.
- The zero line must be differentiated through a thicker drawing than the lines that depict the coordinates.
- When the curves depict percentages, it is advisable to stress the 100% line or any other used as basis of comparison.
- If the scale of a diagram is related to dates and the depicted period is not a complete unit, it is better to show the first and the last coordinate, since the diagram does not depict the beginning or the end of time.
- No more coordinate lines (frames) must be drawn than those necessary to help the reading of the graphic.
- The curves of a diagram must be thicker than the lines of the coordinates (frames).
- In the curves representing a series of observations, it is advisable, whenever possible, to indicate clearly in the diagram all the points that are depicted by the separate observations.
- The numbers indicating the scale of a diagram must be placed to the left of the lower part along the respective axes.
- It is advisable to include in the diagram the numeric data or formula represented.
- If the numeric data are not included in the diagram, it is advisable to give them in the form of a table accompanying said diagram.
- All the titles and figures of the diagram must be placed in such a way that they are easy to read starting from the lower horizontal or from the left margin, and as far as possible, the captions, signs etc. must be placed in a horizontal way and exceptionally in a vertical way.
- If a diagram requires the drawing of two or more curves, this must be of different color or of a different type of line. The crossing of lines must be avoided in order to prevent confusion.

Chapter 23
Mashing-Up Weather Networks Data to Support Hydro-Meteorological Research

Tatiana Bedrina
CIMA Research Foundation, Savona, Italy

Andrea Clematis
Institute of Applied Mathematics and Information Technology, National Research Council, Genoa, Italy

Antonio Parodi
CIMA Research Foundation, Savona, Italy

Alfonso Quarati
Institute of Applied Mathematics and Information Technology, National Research Council, Genoa, Italy

ABSTRACT

The use of Web technologies for the collection and visualization of geoscentific data has significantly increased the availability of free sensor data over the Internet. This work aims at designing a Web mashup for the aggregation of meteorological variables (precipitation, humidity, pressure, etc.) published on the Web by several weather networks and the rendering of query results through a graphic interface in a homogeneous way. The mashup approach is particularly suitable to provide an easy to develop and quickly deployed application capable to support HM scientists in their everyday activity. As a significant case study of the adoption of the tool, the authors consider the severe flash-flood event that occurred in fall 2011 in the Liguria region, Italy. To this end, they base their analysis on the aggregated rainfall data observed by an official and a personal weather network.

INTRODUCTION

Hydro-Meteorological (HM) science has made significant progress over the last decade. Although new modeling tools and methodologies for collecting and analyzing observational data are now nationally and internationally available, large quantity and complexity of datasets and formats create a significant obstacle in operating with data. Observational data, HM models and the necessary ICT (Information and Communications Technology) infrastructures are not always

DOI: 10.4018/978-1-4666-4490-8.ch023

available at the same time. Indeed they are often unevenly distributed between different research institutes, HM services and operational agencies.

To be fruitfully exploited huge datasets, whether from remote sensing instruments such as radar networks, or from ground-based observational sensors, need to be easily available. Availability implies easy to locate, easy to obtain the necessary permissions for use, and the presence of appropriate tools to handle the different formats and meta-data associated with different data types (Parodi, et al., 2011). Furthermore, HM scientists are constantly requiring support from ICT technologies and seeking for global certified management tools to deal with extreme HM events such as heavy precipitation and floods. For these reasons the design, development and deployment of user-friendly interfaces aiming to abstract HMR services provision from the underlying e-Infrastructure complexities and specific implementations, became of paramount importance to Earth scientists. The use of Web technologies for the collection and visualization of geoscentific data has significantly increased the availability of free sensor data over the Internet. It is therefore essential, from an HM scientist point of view, the deployment of ICT initiatives and tools enabling rapid data retrieving from different web sources, as well as the development of functionalities able to aggregate, homogenize, and visualize these datasets.

The chapter introduces a mashup application aimed to collect hydro-meteorological data spread in the Web by different sources. We describe some technical issue involving the access and retrieving of meteorological information through Web service technology. Then we discuss the rearranging of these heterogeneous data according to a common format (WaterML) and their visualization through a graphic tool Google Map. To give an overview of the intended use of our tool, we present a case study related to a severe flash-flood event recently occurred over the city of Genoa, Italy.

Section 2 presents motivations that address our work along with some related work. Section 3 gives some technical insight of our mashup aimed to visualize precipitation data provided by multiple weather networks. Section 4 briefly discusses the potential of our tool dealing with a real case scenario. Section 5 gathers conclusions.

IT SOLUTIONS TO HMR NEEDS

In 2010, as a major activity of the DRHIMS project (http://www.drihms.eu), a series of web polls in the HMR and ICT communities were conducted aimed at better understanding the existing gap between HMR requirements and ICT offer. The HMR polls registered a total amount of 182 answers and the ICT near 100. Amongst the main observations, the analysis of the questionnaires[1] revealed data-related issues such as: interoperability (models, formats, metadata, etc.); availability; extensiveness (amount and size of data). This is well testified, for example by the answers to one of the "hot topic" HMR questions: "Rank (in a 5 point scale) the importance to have easy access to data in formats that are easy to handle". The average result (4.28) testifies the degree of awareness between HM researchers, about the need of tools to tackle data access issues. Moreover, the analysis also pointed out the lack of commonly accepted tools for interchanging and merging scientific data from different sources and of common libraries for processing and visualizing scientific data and metadata. From this survey clearly emerged the urgency to develop IT initiatives and tools enabling rapid data discovery from different sources, from satellites to Personal Weather Stations (PWS), their collection and the development of functionalities to homogenize, compare and visualize these datasets.

In the last years have appeared a number of applications and projects to retrieve and visualize vast amounts of Earth science data from remote sensing observations and models. "The Live Linked Open Sensor Database" (Le Phuoc, et al., 2010) is an on-going project to provide a live database of semantically enriched sensor data, where each sensor reading is extended by adding proper metadata. In (Keiichirou, Toshiyuki, & Hiroyuki, 2008) authors described a tool that supplies transparent access to online meteorological databases where users are allowed to deal with online meteorological data as if they were stored in their own local file systems.

The diffusion of Web services technologies, a mix of data format, communication protocols and programming techniques (e.g. SOAP, RPC, REST, Ajax, Json, etc.), along with new software engineering paradigms like SOA, gave impulse to the development of a huge amount of applications (services) delivered through and accessed via the Web. The use of Web technologies to explore geo-scientific data is now well-established (Amagasa, Kitagawa & Komano, 2007) as well as it is often more frequent to find HM datasets, originated by public or private sources freely exposed, via Web services API. These data are usually provided as weather services such as in the case of NOOA (NOAA's National Weather Service, 2012), Weather Underground (Weather Underground, 2012), WeatherBug (Weather Bug, 2012), YahooWeather (Yahoo Weather, 2012). Again, what often lacks is the ability to manipulate, aggregate and re-arrange this heterogeneous information in some flexible way according to continuously changing HM scientists' need.

The concept of "mash up" has recently become very popular in many fields (Chow, 2007). Mashup stands for a methodology that permits the combination of data and/or programs published by external online sources into an integrated environment, by frequently using Application Programming Interfaces –

APIs (Wikipedia: The free Encyclopedia, 2012). In other words, a mashup application implies the fast integration of data gathered from several places on the Web, their re-elaboration and the visualization through a single interface.

For this reason mashup seems a promising methodology to respond to the various data-related activities into which HM researchers are daily involved (e.g. finding and retrieving high volume data; learning formats and developing readers; extracting parameters; performing filtering and mask; developing analysis and visualization tools). The system discussed in (Williams, Cornford, Bastin, Jones & Parker, 2011) wraps Weather Underground data to provide user access through an interoperable interface. The system also provides a mechanism for estimating the uncertainty and bias of the Weather Underground data providing users with more detailed information. In (Wang, Bishop & Stock, 2009) the author uses some mashup mechanism to allow users to explore existing spatial data and hypothetical future scenarios in a real-time 3D environment. Data included, i.e. weather conditions and real-time traffic, are visualized in real-time to enhance the reality of emergency training scenarios.Mashups are characterized by both advantages (e.g. reuse of existing services and data, no extensive IT skills required, rapid development, cost-efficiency) than disadvantages (e.g. dependability issues and QoS, no security mechanism). However, from the HM researcher point of view, for example, his alternation between the so-called *primary* and *ancillary* tasks, see (Parodi, et al., 2011), pp. 30-31, if looking at the most desiderate operations (merging heterogeneous data and light map visualization), it is clear that, a well-designed mashup may represent an almost ideal solution. Particularly interesting is the ability to reuse existing data and services, by means of a quickly developed application, without requiring great IT skills (as in the case of the majority of HM scientists). In this situation, the kind of pursued functionalities are only marginally affected by the typical disadvantages of mashups. Probably most critical is the frequent unavailability of a clear and uniform interface to access and visualized HM data.

MASHING-UP MULTI-SOURCES WEATHER DATA

The mashup application presented in this work is designed in order to harvest weather data from several weather networks, each managing thousands of Weather Stations (WS). The mashup then integrates, converts (into an interoperable standard) and uniformly visualizes the retrieved data, thus to provide such kind of usable information as envisaged by the results of the previously mentioned DRIHMS polls. Our application is build up using functionalities offered by GoogleMap API, plus the specific query APIs supplied by the included weather networks. All these tools are glued together by pHp and javascript code running respectively at server and client side.

Visualizing Georeferenced Data

To support HM scientists in their auxiliary role as scene-providers towards Civil Protection, the multi-sources mashed data are rendered by means of the Google Map visualization tool. The Google Maps Javascript (version 3) API[2] provides a number of utilities for manipulating and adding content to maps. The map in our mashup is populated with the georeferenced data retrieved by the weather sites. The majority of weather sites generally supply two types of query: one returning a set of stations for a given location and another

Figure 1. Google map visualization of current observation from Weather Underground and Weather Bug weather stations on north Italy

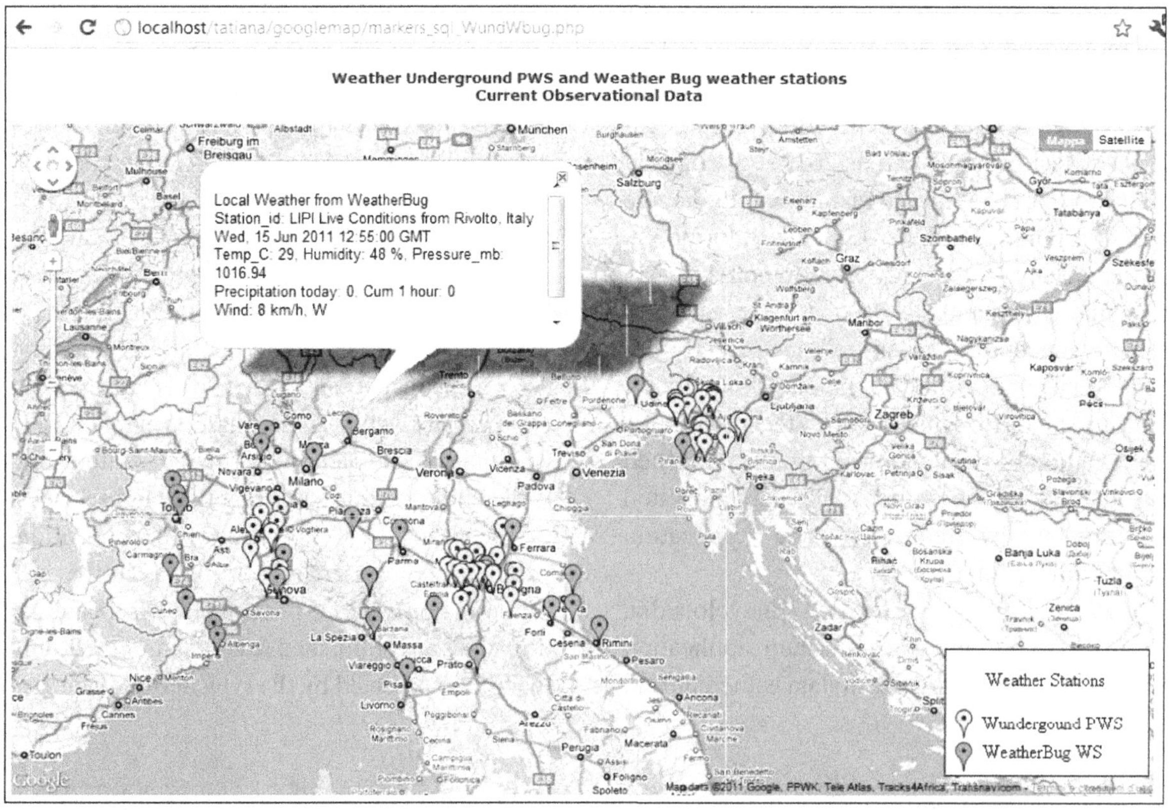

that, given some station identifier, retrieves the current observations recorded by the sensors of that station during a certain period.

Our mashup application follows this two-steps approach thus to provide a rapid rendering of the real presence of weather stations for a given region, leaving the user to decide which station(s) to query. This separation, however, did not avert more comprehensive query mechanisms capable to extract weather data from a pool of stations. In the case of operation involving set of points (for example an interpolation function), the previous second steps may be trivially modified by implementing some sort of loop that retrieve all the observed data from the stations in the set and visualizes the results (e.g. in the form of numerical precipitation per site) in one shot.

According to this query pattern a user selects on the map the location of the specific region whose precipitation data he/she is interested in and the mashup application proceeds with the retrieving of the results (i.e. the identifiers of the WS located in that area) by seeking the data from the set of target weather sites. As a result a set of geo-referenced points, each accounting for an observation station is highlighted on the map which is centered on the specified location. Each point is a clickable object (i.e. the Google Maps marker object) though which a set of information about the weather station is returned. By interacting with a marker the meteorological parameters, registered at that station, are retrieved by querying the weather sites for that specific station code and shown to the user as depicted in Figure. 1.

Collecting Weather Data

As an initial designing decision, thus to quickly develop a useful proof of concept, we focused on the use of Web sources that provide HM information free of charge, without posing any technical or access policy constraint. Due to these requirements, and given the quite large number of WS they managed, we have chosen two hydro-meteorological data provider namely Weather Underground and Weather Bug. These websites provide free (for educational and non-commercial use) data-feed APIs enabling the usage of their products and services. The supplied APIs could be used with almost any program language, as long as it provides constructs to embed the API calls in HTTP requests. At the heart of the sensor networks managed by Wunderground (Weather Underground, 2012), and Weather Bug (Weather Bug, 2012), are mainly the personal or professional-grade weather stations, each handling the weather sensors that track down a set of meteorological variables.

Both website provides a set of URLs construction schemas intended to submit specific queries according to the pattern discussed in Section 3.1. The response messages are then returned in XML or RSS feed format (in the case of Weather Bug). Through these URL-schemas it is possible to send requests to the weather services in order to:

- Search the city, country name or city code in the website database.
- Retrieve stations lists containing the weather stations identification numbers for the city or area of the interest, latitude/longitude pairs in degrees, ZIP code.
- Get the current weather conditions at several public (e.g. airport, government) or personal weather station.

The Weather Underground network consists of more than 13.000 airports and personal weather stations spread around the world. An example of a request for retrieve the Weather Underground stations located in the area of Genoa is the following:

```
http://api.wunderground.com/
auto/wui/geo/GeoLookupXML/index.
xml?query=Genoa,Italy
```

As a response, the Weather Underground service returns an XML file containing: city, country names, latitude/longitude pair and a list of codes, each identifying an airport or a personal weather station registered on the site for the specified area. Through these identification codes it is possible to construct a request for retrieving the current weather conditions at a specific weather station. As an example, the following is the URL requesting the current weather conditions at the personal weather station, with identification code ID equal to IGENOVAG3:

```
http://api.wunder-
ground.com/weatherstation/
WXCurrentObXMLasp?ID=IGENOVAG3
```

Every station query returns both static information about the selected station and dynamic information about weather conditions. The former are station-related data such as the Weather Underground website credit, location, latitude/longitude position, etc. The latter comprehends a set of current observational weather variables: observation time, precipitation, temperature, relative humidity, wind speed/direction, etc. The observations data are updated every few seconds depending on the station adjustment. The variables are represented both in metric and British system of units. The number of observed weather variables may vary from station to station, depending on the capacity of the sensors equipping each weather station.

Weather Bug is a brand of Earth Networks, which operates a net of professional-grade weather stations in more than 35,000 locations around the world, located at over citizens, educational, government, emergency management and recreational facilities, and personal weather stations –mainly in U.S. (Weather Bug, 2012).

Weather Bug provides a wide number of API URLs, to access the stations list for an area of interest and provide near real-time current observational data from each weather station. The stations list for a given region is retrieved by alternatively specifying in the 'SearchString' of the submitting URL: a city code; 'lat&long' – geographical coordinates in degrees; or 'zipCode' – ZIP code (for U.S. only). Each URL construct must contain the field ACode, an alphanumerical constant code that is assigned once the user registered on the Weather Bug website. As for Weather Underground, each weather station could be queried for local live weather conditions, by specifying the station identification number 'stationid'. By means of the 'unittype' parameter, it is possible to select the unit type returned. An example of query to retrieve weather conditions registered at station 'LIMJ' is the following:

```
http://api.wxbug.net/getLiveWeath-
erRSS.aspx?ACode=apiCode&stationid=LI
MJ&unittype=0
```

Data Format Interoperability

Not surprisingly the meteorological parameters returned by each weather network have completely different structure and field names. The first two columns of Table 1 give a clear idea of this fact by showing the different representations of the quite 'trivial' *observation time* parameter according to Weather Underground and Weather Bug. Either than make code development harder, these differences raise some interoperability issues, such as for example the possibility to easily re-expose this data towards third party Web Services. Moreover, the increasing numbers of web sources that could be further added to our mashup solution (such as those envisaged in Section 4), make more compelling the necessity to adopt some common data format to uniformly describe the parameters returned by each single website. To tackle this issue we leveraged on a common format, namely Water Markup Language (WaterML) an XML-based language aimed to describe weather collected information (Valentine & Zaslavsky, 2009). WaterML2.0 scheme is designed by the Consortium of Universities for the Advancement of Hydrologic Science (CUAHSI) and at present is an OGC (Open Geospatial Consortium) standard[3]. WaterML2.0 scheme is designed to be an aggregate scheme for hydrologic time series data from different sources and for representation of hydrologic data and metadata. Right column of Table 1 outlines the normative representation of the time parameter according to WaterML 2.0.

THE 4/11/2011 FLASH-FLOOD EVENT IN GENOA

To exemplify the usefulness of our mashup solution we briefly discuss its possible application in a real scenario where, to achieve a more exhaustive picture of an atmospheric disaster, both institutional and not-institutional weather networks have been considered. To this end, we carried out an analysis on the flash-flood event that occurred in Genoa city, on the northwest coastline of the Mediterranean Sea, on November 4th, 2011. In that date, about 450 mm of rain depth – nearly a third of the average annual rainfall (Frei & Schar, 1998) – came down in six hours. Six people were killed, hundreds of shops were flooded, and streets piled with cars (Figure 2). The area affected by the flash-flood event mainly interested basin of

Table 1. Different encoding of the observation time data

Weather Underground	Weather Bug	WaterML 2.0
<observation_time_rfc822> Wed, 22 Feb 2012 22:04:51 +0100 </observation_time_rfc822>	<aws:year number="2012"/> <aws:month number="2" text="February" abbrv="Feb"/> <aws:day number="22" text="Wednesday" abbrv="Wed"/> <aws:hour number="11" hour-24="23"/> <aws:minute number="20"/> <aws:second number="00"/> <aws:am-pm abbrv="PM"/>	<wml2:point> <wml2:MeasurementTVP> <wml2:time> 2011-11-17T00:00:00+11:00 </wml2:time> <wml2:value> 2.0 </wml2:value> </wml2:MeasurementTVP> </wml2:point>

Figure 2. Flash flood in Genoa on 4/11/2011

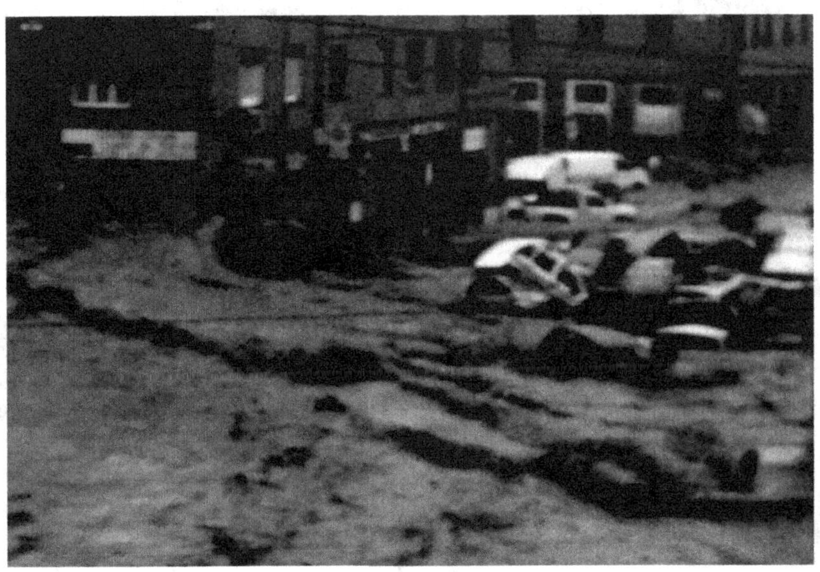

the Bisagno torrent and one of its affluents the Ferregiano creek, with basin area about 3,75 km^2 and having its terminal portion (about 800 m) passing through the cement pipe under the street coverage. To have an outlook of the precipitation in that area we examined the observations supplied by the two nearest stations (namely 'Vicomorasso' e 'Gavette') of the official Italian Civil Protection Department (ICPD) network and by one PWS (namely 'Quezzi') managed by the Meteorology Association of Liguria – LIMET[4] .

The 'Quezzi' PWS located in the Fereggiano sub-basin, registered the maximum observed rainfall depth of the event: about 450 mm of precipitation from 09:00 till 14:00 UTC and about 550 mm during the 24 hours. The maximum rainfall depth registered in one hour, from 11:00 till 12:00 UTC, by the same station, was more than 150mm. By using the data of this station, the peak flow value in the Fereggiano creek was estimated about 180 m^3/s, which is more than three times the discharge that the final underground segment is able to manage. Water depth at the street exceeded, in some places 1 m, and velocities were up to a few ms-1. To have a more complete overview of situation in the flood-affected area we also considered the precipitation data supplied by the two nearby ICPD stations. Indeed, as shown by the radar image in Figure 3, even if these two stations were not located at the centre of the overflowed area them, together with the 'Quezzi' PWS, allowed to gain a deeper understand of the magnitude and scope of the flood event. This fact enforce us in believing that a mashup approach as the one presented in this chapter could represent a valuable support to HM scientists for its ability to mix-up weather data supplied by heterogeneous providers.

Figure 3. The Radar National Mosaic map of radar reflectivity CAPPI at altitude 2000 m, 12UTC 04th November, 2011, ICPD 'Vicomorasso' e 'Gavette' stations (red markers), LIMET PWS 'Quezzi' (blue marker)

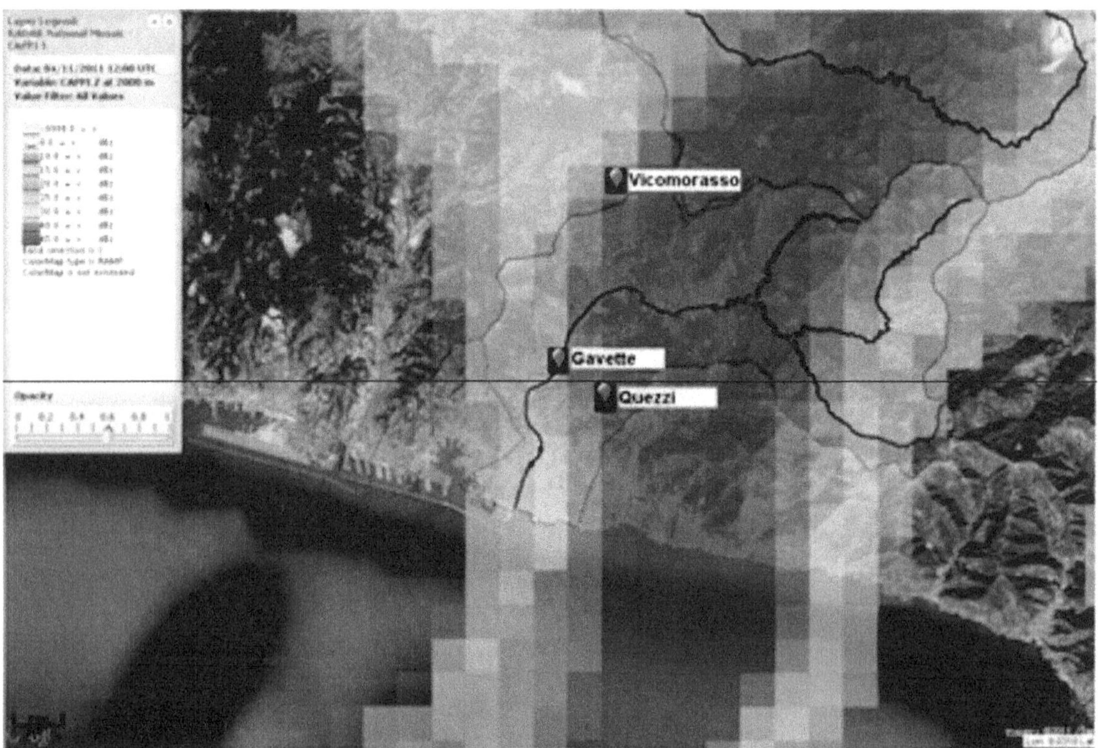

CONCLUSION

The present chapter describes some innovative IT approaches aimed to respond to the increasing HMR demand of suitable and easy-to-use tools able to retrieve and access meteorological data, generated by different sources/countries and stored in multiple formats. The adoption of mashup techniques to visualize weather data in a homogenized form is an initial step towards multisource data integration.

As discussed in Sections 4, the availability of free, close-to-reality, real-time weather data, provided by semi-professional weather networks, represented a great opportunity to increase the density of the institutional weather network. Indeed by comparing the maps visualizing the data supplied by both kinds of stations, we acknowledged the validity of a mashup approach which allows grasping all the available data at once in a more comprehensive way. Moving forward, our future target is to improve the application functionalities by the development of tools to support quality data control, basic statistical assessment and analysis of current weather and history time series.

ACKNOWLEDGMENT

The present work was partially funded by the DRIHM Project (Distributed Research Infrastructure for Hydro-Meteorology) - G.A. n° 283568 - co-Funded by the EC under 7th Framework Programme.

REFERENCES

Amagasa, T., Kitagawa, H., & Komano, T. (2007). Constructing a web service system for large-scale meteorological grid data. In *Proceedings of 3rd IEEE International Conf. on e-Science and Grid Computing*, (pp. 118-124). IEEE.

Chow, S. (2007). *PHP web 2.0 mashup projects*. Birmingham, AL: Packt Publishing.

Foster, I. (2002). The grid: A new infrastructure for 21st century. *Science Physics Today*, *55*(2), 42–47. doi:10.1063/1.1461327

Frei, C., & Schar, C. (1998). A precipitation climatology of the Alps from high-resolution rain-gauge observations. *International Journal of Climatology*, *18*, 873–900. doi:10.1002/(SICI)1097-0088(19980630)18:8<873::AID-JOC255>3.0.CO;2-9

Keiichirou, U., Toshiyuki, A., & Hiroyuki, K. (2008). A FUSE-based tool for accessing meteorological data in remote servers, scientific and statistical database management. *Lecture Notes in Computer Science*, 592–597.

Le Phuoc, D., Parreira, J. X., Hausenblas, M., Han, Y., & Hauswirth, M. (2010). Live linked open sensor database. In *Proceedings of 6th International Conference on SemanticSystems*. I-SEMANTICS.

Mashup. (2012). *Wikipedia*. Retrieved from http://en.wikipedia.org/wiki/Mashup_(web_application_hybrid)

NOAA's National Weather Service. (2012). Retrieved from http://www.nws.noaa.gov/observations.php

Parodi, A., et al. (2011). *DRIHMS: The white paper*. Retrieved from http://www.drihms.eu/publications/material/White%20Papers%20Drihms_final.pdf

Valentine, D., & Zaslavsky, I. (2009). *CUAHSI universities allied for water research, CUAHSI WaterML 1.0 specification, WaterML 1.0 schema description*. San Diego, CA: University of California at San Diego.

Wang, P., Bishop, I. D., & Stock, C. (2009). Real-time data visualization in collaborative virtual environments for emergency response. In *Proceedings of the Surveying & Spatial Sciences Institute Biennial International Conference*. Adelaide, Australia: Surveying & Spatial Sciences Institute.

Weather Bug. (2012). Retrieved from http://en.wikipedia.org/wiki/ Surface_weather_observation

Weather Underground. (2012). Retrieved from http://www.wunderground.com/

Williams, M., Cornford, D., Bastin, L., Jones, R., & Parker, C. (2011). Automatic processing, quality assurance and serving of real-time weather data. *Computers & Geosciences*, *37*, 353–362. doi:10.1016/j.cageo.2010.05.010

Yahoo Weather. (2012). Retrieved from http://weather.yahoo.com/

ENDNOTES

1 http://www.drihms.eu/publications/material/Deliverable_D2.2_revised_DRIHMS.pdf

2 https://developers.google.com/maps/documentation/javascript/reference

3 http://www.opengeospatial.org/projects/groups/waterml2.0swg

4 http://www.centrometeoligure.it

Chapter 24
Negative Exponent Fraction: A Strategy for a New Virtual Image into the Financial Sector

Francisco V. Cipolla-Ficarra
ALAIPO – AINCI, Spain and Italy

ABSTRACT

The authors present the mathematic strategy of the negative potency in the constitution of the new symbolic and corporative image of online banking and financing institutions. The current work focuses on the digital static images and semiotics applied to the contents for the homepage of the banking, financing, and newspaper portals. Also presented are online examples of those institutions that increase the loss of reliability in real or virtual customers.

INTRODUCTION

As a rule, in the educational field of the subject of mathematics for the young teenagers, the operations of addition and second degree multiplications are easier than the divisions among fractional numbers, for instance. The last two decades of the 19th century, the multimedia systems off-line and on-line, have reduced considerably those problems in the classrooms or at least make more entertaining the mathematics since an early age. Some excellent multimedia systems off-line from the point of view of the design categories, such as: layout, content, structure, navigation, etc. are Peter and the numbers (Ubisoft, 1994) or Pingu and friends (BBC, 1997). Now the exponentiation is a mathematic operation between two terms called: base a and exponent n. It is written $(a)^n$ and is usually read as "elevated to n". An elevated number to a negative exponent, is equal to the inverse of the same expression but with a positive exponent, whose classical representation is which follows:

$$a^{-n} = a^{0-n} - \frac{a^0}{a^n} = \frac{1}{a^n}$$

DOI: 10.4018/978-1-4666-4490-8.ch024

Now starting from the last years of the first decade of the new millennium and down to our days, this has been the strategy followed by the financial institutions in the face of the global economic crisis in Southern Europe, for instance. The examples in the current work belong to banking/financial institutions whose headquarters and/or branches are in Catalonia and Lombardy. The use of the terms financial institution and banking institution are treated here as synonymous, although from a financial point of view they are different. The reason for this balance on the level of significance is due to the banking institutions being included in banking institutions, post service, etc. and it is they who offer their services to the customers. The problem is that many real customers do not understand these differences with the real world, and then they come across the differences in the computer context, for instance. This is due to the fact that they try to be a subset inside the corporative image of other institutions of greater prestige or trust. That is, they interact from a virtual and commercial image which has been generated along the centuries by real institutions (Post Service) but which currently are not related to the service of lending money to its small customers, for instance. Simultaneously, they constantly try to invert the levels of significance and the signification of the images, in the spiral of the infinite semiosis defined by Greimas using real symbols from daily life. That is, symbols of great popularity in the local, provincial, national or international community. Consequently we are in a phenomenon of homogenization of the real and virtual image with those financial institutions which act from the intersection of the following sets:

In Figure 1, it can be seen how there is implicit a first operation of negative potency of the recently created financial institutions, that is, when they are placed at the same level of those which have a long time record such as can be the Post Service.

Now, the transmission of knowledge is exclusively made through signs, especially linguistic. The acquisition of know-do takes place through the manipulation of signs. With the semiotics can be considered the breaking down of the contents (according to their nature: qualities, facts or concepts), their way of presentation (resorting more or less systematically and programmatically to iconic signs such as diagrams) or indicial (such as photographs), their way of control, etc. This is the reason why we resort to semiotics.

In view of the rhetoric question: "Is semiotics a science or a philosophy?". We regard as appropriate the answer given by Claude Marty and Robert Marty when they claim that by introducing a well-defined and clearly limited theoretical object we can talk if not of a science, at least of a

Figure 1. Public or private or mixed institutions aimed at the banking activities (banks and saving banks), public service institutions, (for instance, Post Service), financial institutions

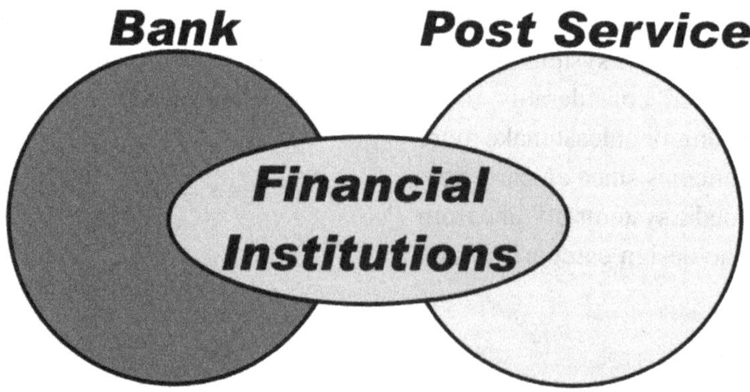

scientific attitude, and introducing the necessary explanations (Marty & Marty, 1992). Umberto Eco identifies general semiotics and philosophy of language (Nöth, 1995), doubting these can be signification and/or representation phenomena in the way physics or electronics are treated. In other words, in semiotic there is an epistemological break between science and philosophy. In the current work, we resort to semiotics like other disciplines, techniques and methods of analysis, stemming among others from software engineering (quality), usability engineering, user centered design, publicity, linguistics, sociology and marketing.

We start with an example of access to the online banking service, where a great part of the users can reject the service due to the use of a promotional video with polemical characters. Then we present the essential aspects on the use of color in the interface of the banking institution. Later on is analyzed the role of the image from a publicity point of view and the effects on the recipients, for instance. Also is considered the triad among interactive design, human values and financial values, to underscore the scarce transparency of online information, through the strategy of inverting reality as if we were in front of a negative exponent fraction. Finally there are the learned lessons and the future lines of research.

BANK AND FINANCIAL MARKETING ONLINE

In the interactive design, and more precisely in the category of the layout, the designer must make a series of decisions on the technological aspect in relation to what it communicates, whether it is to the current customers online as those who are regarded as potential customers (Cipolla-Ficarra, 2010). That is, there is a code in relation to the content that is going to be communicated, and the cultural aspects of those addressees (Styliaras, Koukopoulos & Lazarinis, 2011). Addressees who interact frequently or not with the banking or financing portals.

The designer will have to decide the kind of images to use (Kerlow, 2000), such as: digital pictures, computer static images, or the photogram of a computer animation, a realistic drawing (see Figure 7, in the Appendix), a caricature, the use of graphics or outlines (a very frequent resource since we are talking of financial institutions), drawings, etc. For instance, a Catalan bank plumps for black and white photography with an anchorman of programs of low cultural level in the "garbage television" of private property (Spanish name of the TV programs with a cultural level equal to zero) of private property.

However, that anchorman is very popular or high audience shares. Obviously this choice will draw a kind of young and adult potential internet users, but not so many elderly people who do not accept that cultural level but who are not either a wide majority in the use of the new technologies, such as Internet or the mobile phones.

The image is essentially a shape. In an image in black and white we can to infer the color of things, that is, the shape and the chiaroscuro and the volume which suggests. Black and white is the color of essential things. Undoubtedly, the picture of an autumn landscape in the mountains is more realistic when it shows its colors, similar to those which we perceive by observing that landscape directly. When the color has an iconic function, it increases the realistic or veracity sensation of the image (Cipolla-Ficarra, 2008). Whereas shape always remains intelligible on its own right, color can grant it a greater strength of veracity, or it may also add splendor to the image. In view of a graphic composition (image), static, whether it is in paper or digital support, the investment in voluntary time by the recipient increases with the interest the message arises, the originality, the sensuality of the images, the visual attention, the aesthetic pleasure, the psychological implication and the usefulness of the information content.

In the Figure 2 also takes place the phenomenon known as "Argentinization" of the interface because of the colors that prevail: that is, yellow and red. The interested reader may go deeper into this phenomenon in the following bibliographical reference (Cipolla-Ficarra, 2012).

LAYOUT ONLINE: STATIC IMAGE

Now each one of these types of images, its treatment in the layout (color, brightness, contrast, size, etc. and all the resources stemming from visual rhetoric) will offer different expressive results. The main goal of the interactive designer is to use to the utmost those results so that the communication has two attributes of quality such as

Figure 2. Catalan banking online with a video about the relations the customers with the bank. An anchorman of TV programs of low cultural level in the Spanish "garbage television".

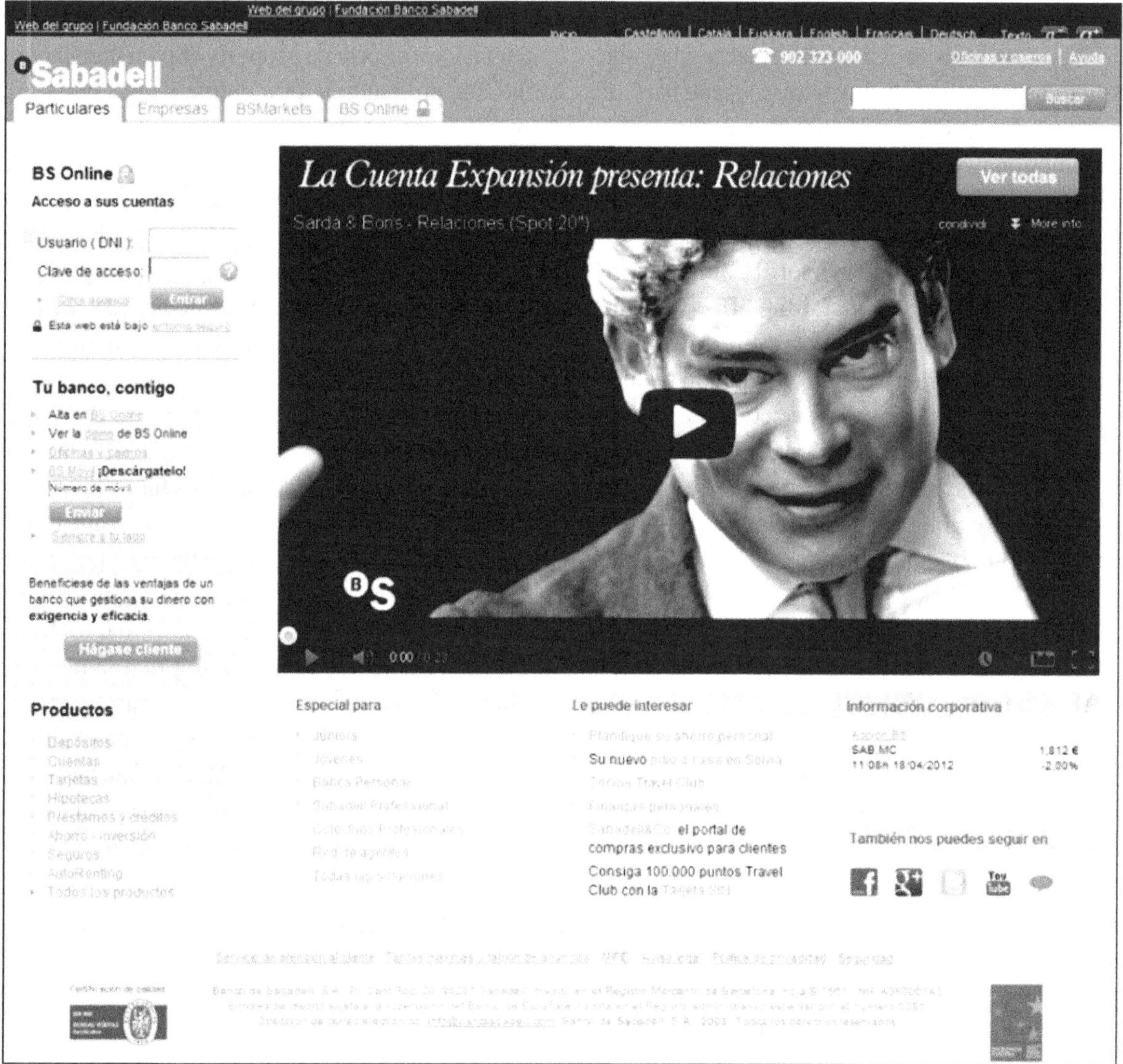

accuracy and acceptance by the highest number of users or recipients of interactive systems. In this sense, image has its own way of being perceived, because it is a static representation, since the visible environment is not anchored or fixed as in an image, but it is dynamic and affects the global sensorial (not only visual) perception of the human being. This function of representation of image denotes the fragment of reality, since the fixed image on a surface –i.e., the computer screen, tablet PC, a television screen, a display advertising, etc.–, is a static representation of a fragment of the environment. In the opposite sense, the direct perception of reality is dynamic and multisensorial. That is, that the human being does not perceive reality as static fragments, but as a continuum.

A continuity which is the constant shifting in the visual field. Now this condition of fragmentation of the reality entails that reality has been fragmented in the image. The choice of the fragment which is interesting entails a task for the interactive designer in two directions: the first, a special position, that is, the point of view or the composition of the scene (a topic deeply treated by Leonardo Da Vinci, for instance (Tosone & Frost, 2006). The second, it is creative, where there is an interrelation between aesthetics, visual culture and expressivity. What every interactive designer or expert in static images does in static images (digital or analogical) is an indirect task on reality: reshaping through images. The problem for the interactive designer of banking or financial products arises when the reality to which he refers goes through one of the greatest crisis in the history of humankind. A time in which even comics are used to denounce it, as can be seen in the following figure:

In the portal of Figure 4, we see the use of a virtual character (3D computer animation) who is covered with turf, with which he is included inside the ecological ensemble. However, in the Figure 3 there is an invitation to reflect on climatic change comparing it with the premium risk of the Spanish sovereign debt and in the second, totally false money lending services are offered because for example, the customers hit by the current crisis can't unify their debts and enjoy the alleged financial benefits. Besides, this financial firm places in a disguised way on the website its membership to the French banking group BNP Paribas (use of small letters in the left upper angle).

Achieving balance between the social tragedy stemming from the banks and other financial institutions with the current crisis, on the one hand; and on the other hand, the greater increase of profits for the summit of the population pyramid, is not an easy task. The complexity is due to the recipient of the message. A recipient who in an online publicity campaign, for instance,

Figure 3. A comic strip which generally deals with ecology issues. In this example. It approaches the financial issues in a tragic-comical way by comparing the rise of average temperature along time with the data from the Spanish stock market. Newspaper online: El Pais (www.elpais.es –06.21.2012).

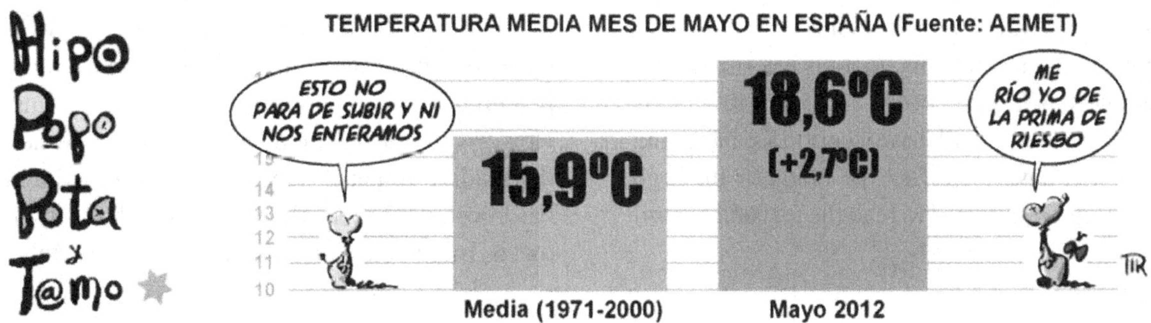

Figure 4. False information online with the alleged liberty to change the amount of the monthly fees (www.findomestic.it –06.01.2012)

recognizes that reality but depicted through the iconic forms. Besides, perceives those attributes which are not in the reality such as can be originality, expressivity, surprise, visual impact, etc. In other words, the main elements to which a designer or advertising creative resorts.

In this regard, the interested reader may consult the pioneering works, carried out by Georges Péninou and Henry Joannis (Péninou, 1972; Joannis, 1965). Some figures from their research works with regard to publicity in the traditional mass media show in Péninou that the ads where the text prevails are less usual. (35%) than those in which image prevails. Joannis has similar percentages as a result of his research: 40% of the target audience will have seen the advertising, 35% will have identified the brand or the logo, 10% will have started to read the text and 5% will have read it completely.

INTERACTIVE DESIGN, HUMAN VALUES AND FINANCIAL VALUES

Now, the look of the text is essential in the field of the interactive information, especially if a historic description is made of the interactive systems which had their origin in the hypertext. Later on the static and dynamic images were incorporated in the multimedia and hypermedia systems. Until the support of the information was off-line for the multimedia systems, such as the CD-Rom or the DVD of the 90s, for instance. Until that moment a great part of the reading was made in paper support, especially the new generations of potential users of mobile multimedia systems. However, with the momentum of the internet, the reading in paper support has decreased and has boosted "the mosaic culture" (Moles, 1971). that is, fragmented knowledge as Abraham Moles claims, united among themselves with links. In other words, the notions of link and node of the hypertext. However, the adult and senior audience still read in paper support. One of the reasons why the paper consumption has continuing growing since the appearance of the multimedia systems off-line and on-line in the 90s.

According to Joannis, there were three reasons why in visual communication an image can take a second place inside the composition of the message, however currently we see how also the "negative exponent fraction".

1. When the sender wants to be "serious", As a rule, the newspapers opened their first page with headlines in arial, and on the whole page, when there were negative news, natural disasters, for instance. However, with the passing of time, when dealing with financial news, this formula has fallen out of use, especially when the purpose of the digital newspaper is to increase profits, even with financial news which damage the whole community (Figure 5). The term "The cry" of the upper banner boost the title "Rescue to Spain". That is, another indirect example in the composition of this information page where in a willing or unwilling way has been generated the "negative-exponent fraction" strategy.

Figure 5. The sports factor overcomes the negative value of the financial news (financial rescue of Spain by the European Central Bank). Newspaper online: El Pais (www.elpais.es –06.09.2012).

El grito...

Actualizado 21:21 CET

EL PAÍS

INTERNACIONAL | POLÍTICA | ECONOMÍA | CULTURA | SOCIEDAD | DEPORTES

▸ ESTÁ PASANDO Rescate financiero Informe FMI Matanza en Siria Eurocopa Caso Urdangarin Demanda contra Dívar MÁS TEMAS »

CRISIS FINANCIERA »

RESCATE A ESPAÑA

- El Eurogrupo vigilará "de cerca y de forma regular" que España mantenga las constantes macroeconómicas y el cumplimiento del déficit
- El Gobierno español acepta la ayuda para la banca que le ofrece Europa de hasta 100.000 millones de euros
- Guindos mantiene que se trata de un préstamo en condiciones muy favorables que implicará contraprestaciones únicamente para la banca

España ha dado esta tarde el paso para recibir el rescate que le permitirá sanear su deteriorado sistema financiero. En una teleconferencia, Europa ha ofrecido al Ejecutivo de Mariano Rajoy hasta 100.000 millones de euros de ayuda. A cambio, el Eurogrupo mantendrá una vigilancia constante de las cuentas macroeconómicas de España y de sus esfuerzos para el cumplimiento del déficit

GRÁFICO

Falta 1 día

IBERDROLA

OPINIÓN »

Esta vez, Europa está de verdad al borde del precipicio

¿Qué pasará con sus ahorros, impuestos y créditos?

Las claves sobre el impacto del programa de asistencia financiera en la economía y cómo afectará a partir de ahora al ciudadano de a pie

Guindos: "Hablo yo porque soy miembro del Eurogrupo y Rajoy no"

El ministro anuncia que España pedirá ayuda para la banca, las condiciones impuestas por el Eurogrupo se limitarán al sector financiero, asegura

SÍGUENOS EN

2. When the social morality prevents illustrating the subject that is being advertised. We also see here in the digital version of the paper, in view of negative financial news, how the financial and real estate businesses resort to eroticism, surpassing even their own standards, with clearly mercantilist or financial purposes (Figure 8 in Appendix).
3. When the exceptional interest of the product or the publicity proposal makes it certain to draw attention to a simple textual statement. In the case of Figure 9 (Appendix), the whole campaign is based on a single word ("idealista" *–idealist*) which refers to the portal in which it is publicized (www.idealista.com).

Evidently the "moral factor" of the image falls into the background, when the main goal is provocation. A provocation which is generally born, grows and develops in the financial environments related to certain cultural or religious factors, which are based on the premise. "They can't do anything to us". The ideal thing is that the image takes a second place in the banking and/or financial information, when the content of the message is essentially informative and must contain the objective and quantitative data such as the hiring conditions of contracting credit cards, loans to consumption, mortgages, etc. (Figures 4 and 6). However, since 2005 down to our days it has been seen how the opacity of the financial and banking services prevail (for instance, in the

Figure 6. This online website (www.compass.it –06.01.2012) acquires a very negative sense in some Portuguese-speaking countries such as Brazil

cashing of fees and interests of the services which are offered to the clients) through the deceitful images. Images which have served to boost the wild European consumption frenzy. Those responsible for activating these publicity campaigns have remained virtually unscathed in the global crisis. In this sense, the theory of communication, semiotics, linguistics, sociology, etc., can only indicate the strategies that the information manipulators have used. Manipulators who boost the negative human factors through microcomputing, multimedia, telecommunications, the social networking, the digital terrestrial television (DTT), etc. The goal is widening to the utmost the financial bubbles in the Internet, in the least possible time, with the least possible costs, and without any responsibility in regard to the damage done to the population pyramid base.

Symbols

Symbol is one of the most overburdened terms in the field of the humanities. In its broadest sense, symbol is a synonym of sign. For instance, a sign based on convention or established usage (Nöth, 1995). But this word refers to various other types of signs as well. For Ferdinand de Saussure, a symbol is a sign in which the correlation between signifier and signified is, in some measure, motived–that is, nonarbitrary. In Charles Pierce's elaborate classification of signs, a symbol is almost the opposite of this. Pierce defines symbol as part of trichotomy: icon, index, symbol (Nöth, 1995). The trichotomy is based on the relationship between the sign vehicle and its object. If a sign vehicle is related to its object by virtue of a resemblance to that object (for instance, a map to its territory), it is an icon. If it is related to its object by virtue of an actual or physical connection (for instance, the direction of the weathervane to the direction of the wind being indicated by the vane), it is an index. If it is related to its object by virtue of a habit or convention (for instance a single red rose as the symbol of affection), it is a symbol. In other words, can be grouped into three categories: symbol as a conventional sign, symbol as a connotational sign and symbol as a kina of iconic sign. In the latter two definitions, the symbol is a key concept of aesthetics and cultural studies. However, the use of icons as symbols is very important, especially when we are transiting in the era of expansion of communicability (Cipolla-Ficarra, 2010).

In the Figure 6, we see how a young hand is used to make the letter "o" in the expression "round figure". Now the sign of drawing a circle with the thumb and the index finger and show it to another person may mean that things are ok., they can't be better and that we are in a good mood because of it. In Brazil, however, this gesture has the same meaning as the spread middle finger in many countries with an Anglosaxon or Latin culture in Europe. Besides, the use of the compass as a logo leads to other negative connotations such as loggias or sects.

From the point of view of communicability, we can see that in this interface there is a correct use in the text-image ratio (it takes a second place), giving more room to the textual financial information, such as the interest rate, the monthly rates, etc. here we also have the "negative exponent fraction" strategy or effect, due to the bad use of symbols or the connotations they may have because of cultural factors (Fernandes, 1996; Light, 2004; Chen, 2011).

LESSONS LEARNED

In the presented examples we have seen how the whole financial and/or economic information is not presented in a transparent, serious and professional way to the users of the online multimedia systems which allow the reading and interaction with online information. In spite of the international financial crisis of the last years, and without precedents in the history of humankind, it is necessary to resort to the strategy of the inversion of information, that is, as if information were a negative exponent fraction. This makes apparent the failure of the financial and banking institutions in generating a new virtual image online, although the use of new technologies can be seen, and also the social networks, for instance, to contact with their potential customers, offering them the chance of having access to the calculation of the personal loans.

Now in the era of communicability expansion the current users have had contact with the computers since a very early age in the great cities. They have quickly overcome the notions of the use of the computer and which had to be studied in the usability engineering in the 90s because of working reasons, mainly. Currently the mobile multimedia microcomputing systems need communicability experts so that the contents respect the main attributes of veracity and seriousness of economic information especially when the context of the sector is negative due to the financial damage caused to millions of users of interactive systems all around the world. In future works we will enlarge the examples of the banking and financial portals where the cultural factors of the interfaces are not considered, focusing on the presentation of the symbolic-iconic presentation.

CONCLUSION

Semiotics and heuristic analysis of the communicability experts have indicated the triviality of the treatment of economic and/or financial information in the financial, banking portals and the digital editions of certain newspapers. Real and virtual institutions located in Spain and Italy which have made apparent that the new technologies on their own can't eradicate the human factors which destroy online credibility. The alleged image of solidity of the Italian financial institutions which operate from the banking institutions, for instance, linked to the image of Spanish modernity, through the use of the latest technologies for the management of their online services, is practically equal to zero. As it also is the veracity and the understandability of the online information, especially in issues related to the fees and interests which are applied for their services to the current and potential customers. Consequently, the textual information in the hiring of services must be read under the strategy of negative exponent fraction.

REFERENCES

BBC. (1997). *Pingu and friends.* [CD-ROM]. London: BBC.

Chen, H. (2011). Social intelligence and cultural awareness. *IEEE Intelligent Systems*, *26*(4), 80–91. doi:10.1109/MIS.2011.21

Cipolla-Ficarra, F. (2008). HECHE: Heuristic evaluation of colours in homepage. In *Proceedings of Applied Human Factors and Ergonomics*. Las Vegas, NV: AEI.

Cipolla-Ficarra, F. (2010). *Quality and communicability for interactive hypermedia systems: Concepts and practices for design*. Hershey, PA: IGI Global. doi:10.4018/978-1-61520-763-3

Cipolla-Ficarra, F. (2012). The argentinization of the user centered design. In *Proceedings of 2nd International Conference on Advances in New Technologies, Interactive Interfaces and Communicability*. Heidelberg, Germany: Springer.

Fernandes, T. (1996). *Global interface design: A guide to designing international user interfaces*. Boston: Academic Press.

Joannis, H. (1965). *De l'étude de motivation à la création publicitaire et à la promotion des ventes*. Paris: Dunod.

Kerlow, I. (2000). *The art of 3D computer animation and imaging*. New York: John Wiley.

Light, A. (2004). Audience design: Interacting with networked media. *Interaction*, *11*(2), 60–63. doi:10.1145/971258.971279

Marty, C., & Marty, R. (1992). 99 *réponses sur la sémiotique*. Montpellier, France: Réseau académique de Montpellier, CRDP/CDDP.

Moles, A. (1971). *Art et ordinateur*. Paris: Casterman.

Nöth, W. (1995). *Handbook of semiotics*. Bloomington, IN: Indiana University Press.

Péninou, G. (1972). *Intelligence de la publicité*. Paris: Robert Laffont.

Styliaras, G., Koukopoulos, D., & Lazarinis, F. (2011). *Handbook of research on technologies and cultural heritage: Applications and environments*. Hershey, PA: IGI Global.

Tosone, A., & Frost, C. (2006). Leonardo da Vinci: The complete works. Cincinnati, OH: Davis & Charlie F+W Publications.

Ubisoft. (1994). *Peter and the numbers*. [CD-ROM]. Paris: Ubisoft.

APPENDIX

Figure 7. An excellent example of how painting can simulate photography. In other words, this picture is not a photo. Author: Iman Maleki (www.imanmaleki.com).

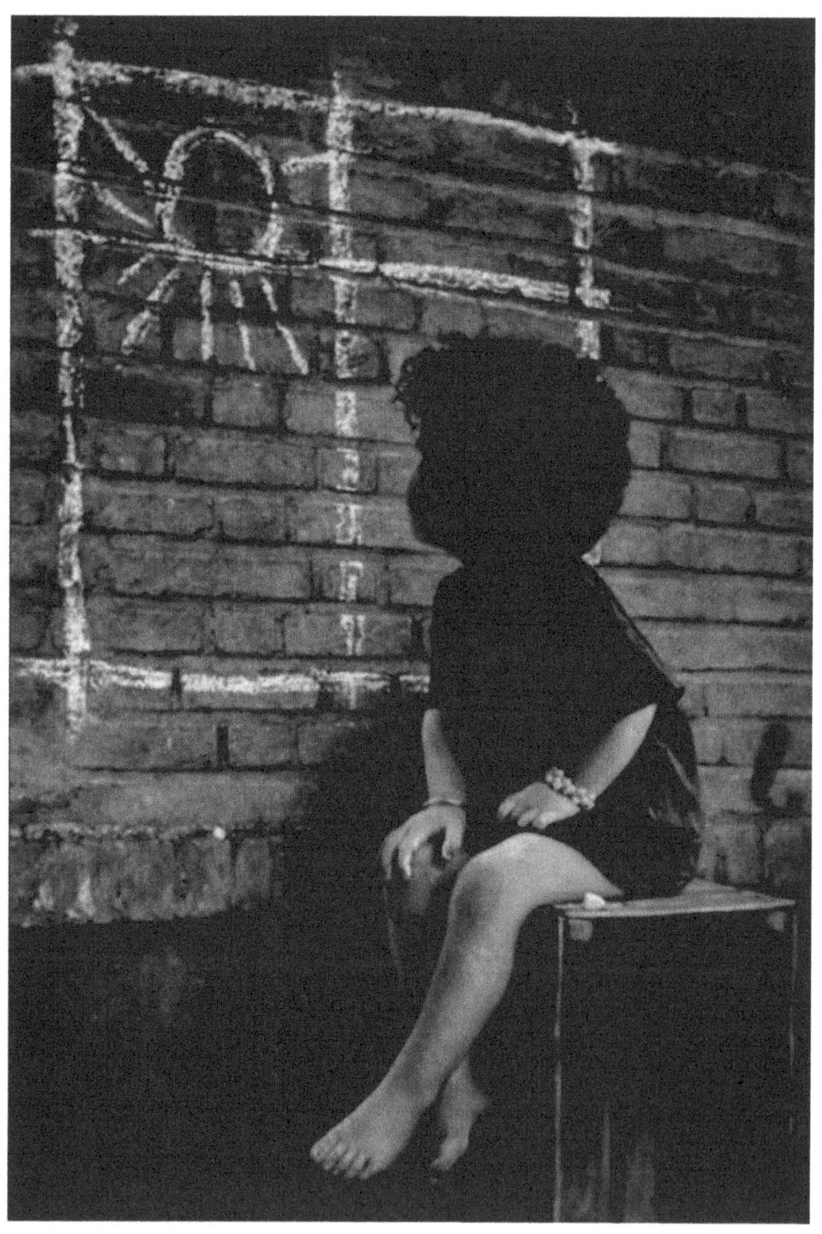

Figure 8. The three news of economics with regard to the euro in the left area are accompanied with a photo news on a same-sex marriage on the right with a publicity banner where the name of the portal stands written with letters typical of the dot matrix printer or impact matrix printer. However, the content of the banner surpasses the limit of eroticism in some pictures that make it up. Digital newspaper: El País (www.elpais.com –06.22.2012).

viernes 22 junio 2012 | Actualizado 12:54 CET Hemeroteca

Iniciar sesión | Registrarse

EL PAÍS

INTERNACIONAL | POLÍTICA | ECONOMÍA | CULTURA | SOCIEDAD | DEPORTES

ESTÁ PASANDO FMI Crisis del euro Asalto en Kabul Eurocopa Elecciones México 2012 Miami Heat Dimisión Divar MÁS TEMAS »

ENTREVISTA DIGITAL

Charla en directo con José Manuel Gómez Benítez. El vocal del CGPJ que denunció a Carlos Divar está contestando a las preguntas de los lectores »

LA CRISIS FINANCIERA »

El FMI critica con dureza a Alemania por su gestión de la crisis del euro

CLAUDI PÉREZ | Luxemburgo 593

El Fondo apuesta por recapitalizar directamente a los bancos débiles, "sin pasar por los Gobiernos", para romper el círculo vicioso entre la deuda soberana y la deuda bancaria

EL BLOG DE PAUL KRUGMAN

'La historia de éxito no tan exitosa de Estonia'

EDITORIAL: 'El primer paso'

La Bolsa española sube mientras los mercados mundiales caen

ISABEL LAFONT | Madrid 27

El Ibex sube más 1%, al contrario que las europeas, que bajan tras el empeoramiento del clima empresarial en Alemania

EN DIRECTO Sigue la evolución de los mercados

CUMBRE EN ROMA DE LOS CUATRO GRANDES DE LA UE

Mario Monti: "Europa debe arrinconar su lentitud"

PABLO ORDAZ | Roma 47

El primer ministro italiano defiende más rapidez para salvar la eurozona, en una entrevista con medios internacionales

TRIBUNA

'Bomberos, arquitectos y...', por J. I. TORREBLANCA

La RAE admite 'Matrimonio' para la unión de personas del mismo sexo

Una nueva revisión del Diccionario incluye 1.697 modificaciones. Hay numerosas palabras del mundo digital. Por WINSTON MANRIQUE

idealista.com

el portal inmobiliario líder

OPINIÓN »

Máxima transparencia

EDITORIAL

El Poder Judicial tiene que trabajar sin opacidades y no volver al modelo corporativo

SÍGUENOS EN

EL PAÍS KIOSKOymás

openbank

Financia tus ideas

INTERNACIONAL

Europa

Estados Unidos

América Latina

Oriente Próximo

Asia

África

Corresponsales

ESPAÑA

Andalucía

Cataluña

Comunidad Valenciana

Galicia

Madrid

País Vasco

Más comunidades

Figure 9. One of the least erotic static pictures that make up the set in banner format. This ad has also been broadcast in the public and private Spanish television. These provoking images, joined to to the image of the photo news, rip practically of all importance or seriousness to the textual and financial/ economic information of the left area. Digital newspaper: El País (www.elpais.com –06.22.2012).

Actualizado 12:54 CET

Iniciar sesión | Registrarse

EL PAÍS

INTERNACIONAL | POLÍTICA | ECONOMÍA | CULTURA | SOCIEDAD | DEPORTES

ESTÁ PASANDO | FMI | Crisis del euro | Asalto en Kabul | Eurocopa | Elecciones México 2012 | Miami Heat | Dimisión Divar | MÁS TEMAS »

ENTREVISTA DIGITAL

Charla en directo con José Manuel Gómez Benítez. El vocal del CGPJ que denunció a Carlos Divar está contestando a las preguntas de los lectores »

LA CRISIS FINANCIERA »

El FMI critica con dureza a Alemania por su gestión de la crisis del euro

El Fondo apuesta por recapitalizar directamente a los bancos débiles, "sin pasar por los Gobiernos", para romper el círculo vicioso entre la deuda soberana y la deuda bancaria

La Bolsa española sube mientras los mercados mundiales caen

El Ibex sube más 1%, al contrario que las europeas, que bajan tras el empeoramiento del clima empresarial en Alemania

CUMBRE EN ROMA DE LOS CUATRO GRANDES DE LA UE

Mario Monti: "Europa debe arrinconar su lentitud"

El primer ministro italiano defiende más rapidez para salvar la eurozona, en una entrevista con medios internacionales

La RAE admite 'Matrimonio' para la unión de personas del mismo sexo

Una nueva revisión del Diccionario incluye 1.697 modificaciones. Hay numerosas palabras del mundo digital. Por WINSTON MANRIQUE

OPINIÓN »

Máxima transparencia

El Poder Judicial tiene que trabajar sin opacidades y no volver al modelo corporativo

SÍGUENOS EN

EL PAÍS KIOSKO y más

openbank

Financia tus ideas

INTERNACIONAL
Europa
Estados Unidos
América Latina
Oriente Próximo
Asia
África
Corresponsales

ESPAÑA
Andalucía
Cataluña
Comunidad Valenciana
Galicia
Madrid
País Vasco
Más comunidades

POLÍTICA

Chapter 25
Co-Designing Novel Interior Design Services that Utilise Augmented Reality:
A Case Study

Tiina Kymäläinen
VTT Technical Research Centre of Finland – Tampere, Finland

Sanni Siltanen
VTT Technical Research Centre of Finland – Espoo, Finland

ABSTRACT

In this chapter, the authors describe a co-design process and the implementation requirements of an interactive interior design service system. To gain design information for the system, they study two focus groups composed of designers, bloggers, and serious amateurs in the field of interior design – the estimated critical users of the forthcoming service system. The framework for the co-design study is twofold. The design aim is to study users' innovation capability in the early phase of a complex process by utilising co-sketching as a means of obtaining a user model of the interactive system. The technological aim is to create interior design concepts that exploit Augmented Reality (AR), 3D models, and user-generated content within the system framework. This chapter reports the design process and results of the co-design sessions; furthermore, it presents requirements for the system, use cases utilising AR technology, plus consideration and evaluation of the AR functionalities.

INTRODUCTION

The case study was part of research that aimed at studying the use of new technologies and applications – social media services, augmented reality (AR) features and location awareness – in the field of advertising, and find new revenue models for media. This chapter presents a case study which aimed at understanding the needs and requirements of the design service providers. Research was carried out by co-designing interactive user-centred interior design system concepts

DOI: 10.4018/978-1-4666-4490-8.ch025

that utilised AR features. Co-design focus group sessions were arranged with interior designers and design bloggers – the anticipated critical users of the interior design system.

The participants of the study had taken part in a preliminary online survey, and were therefore all familiar with the background of the system concept. Participants received further information relating to the concept in the focus group sessions, first viewing scenarios that described possible ways of comprising interior 3D and AR services. Participants were then presented with some information from the preliminary online survey, including the key elements and materials thought by most respondents to be critical for the service. This was followed by a short presentation by the facilitators of the AR technology and existing AR applications.

In the co-design phase, the focus group participants co-sketched the system concepts. Sketching proved to be a practical method in this context, as the participants were able to produce dissectible results. Participants provided valuable design information during the discussions – in the form of use cases – concerning the promising ways of utilising AR technology in the service concept.

KEY TECHNOLOGY: AUGMENTED REALITY

Augmented reality is defined as an interactive real-time system that combines real and virtual elements in 3D (Azuma, et al., 2001). Virtual reality (VR) consists only of virtual elements. Diminished reality is a system where objects are removed from the real environment, and mediated reality refers to a system where real environment is altered virtually (Mann, 2002). Mixed reality (MR) is a concept that covers all possible combinations of real and virtual elements, from reality to total virtuality (Milgram, Takemura, Utsumi & Kishino, 1994). From the user's point of view, the functionalities of a system are more important than the technology categorisation. "The basis in all the discussions was an AR system in which real images are augmented with

Figure 1. With a mobile AR application the user can see virtual designs in the real environment

virtual objects. However, in sessions the discussion was open to all forms of combination and alteration of real and virtual elements, including all the above-mentioned technologies –we used the term AR for simplicity, though."

Augmented reality provides a practical visualisation method for purposes where there is a need to enhance the user's perception. Interior design, in particular, is an application field where the combination of real and virtual benefits the user (Siltanen, 2012). Web-based AR applications – in not requiring installation or downloading – are consumer friendly and can be integrated with social media and web stores. Also, recent mobile devices are equipped with reasonable-sized displays and have a network connection for accessing the Internet. Based on these facts, we selected a web-based AR interior design service as a starting point for the co-design discussions, and presumed that users could augment digital images and operate the system by using a PC or mobile device.

USER-DRIVEN INNOVATION

Methods

The co-design process falls under the methodological frame of participatory design, which generally aims at democratising design so that the people to be affected by the systems should also be able to participate in and influence the design process (Schuler & Namioka, 1993). Participants may be involved in the process by means such as focus groups, scenarios and early phase concept design (Morgan, 1998; Carroll, 2009; Greenbaum & Kyng, 1991) methods which were adapted to this study. Focus group interview is an interview method in which a small group, with similar background, discusses the topics disseminated by the facilitator (Morgan, 1998) –in this study, the similarity was the participants' interest in interior design. Because of their experience, the participants were seen as critical users (Cassim & Dong, 2003) of the future service.

The co-design process was pragmatically conducted by utilising sketching as a co-design method, to provide means for users to produce design outcomes of a complex design service system (Buxton, 2007). The sketching method appeared to be a flexible way of prioritising design issues, and considered suitable for these particular focus group participants. The hypothesis was that sketches would offer support in obtaining a user model of the overall system (Kymäläinen, 2010).

Set-Up of the Co-Design Session

The project group had identified a definition statement of the service concept for the focus groups: 'Novel web-based service concepts that exploited 3D and AR technologies, which may be used virtually when creating interior and renovation designs'. The statement described the system and its core requirements in brief, and was meant to provide focus for the participants' concept ideas. Because the focus group participants were seen as service providers, the emphasis of the co-design session was on the service ecosystem of the concept.

At first, participants were encouraged to identify their role in the service system. It was decided mutually in the sessions that each participant would define her role as an ambiguous designer. Participants were then divided into pairs, and each pair encouraged to produce a sketch of the ecosystem in the form of a flowchart. The descriptions were expected to include: 1) all necessary stakeholders and elements of the system (products, services, technologies); 2) how all stakeholders and elements were connected to the ecosystem, and finally 3) which were the most important stakeholders and elements (using a tree-level scale).

The participants were encouraged to think about the application through discussed scenarios, and to exploit the information from the online survey and demonstrated applications. In the sketching phase, participants were provided with sketching tools: paper, pens, cardboards etc. Other materials, such as used e.g. in IDEO's tech box (Kelley & Littman, 2001): colour patterns, pieces of wallpaper, images of furniture etc. were available for inspiration and reference purposes.

Following the sketching phase the focus group participants shared their ideas with others. After presentations, participants improved each other's ideas by paying attention to the application definition statement, scenarios, and, most importantly, personal interest.

Participants

The preliminary online survey data was collected from ordinary consumers (250 respondents) and serious interior design amateurs (36 respondents). The following two focus groups were composed of volunteers from the latter respondents, who were mostly interior designers or serious interior design amateurs: students and bloggers in the field of interior design. The two groups consisting of 3–4 participants, with 1–2 project participants in each group, and one evaluator leading the two-hour co-design session. The first focus group session was arranged in May 2011 at VTT Technical Research Centre of Finland, Espoo, and the second at Alma Mediapartners' facilities at Tampere, Finland. The interviewees were 27–49 years of age, all females.

RESULTS

Participants provided detailed information on the qualities of the service during the introduction, while sketching the ecosystems and, finally, when considering the AR features for the service. The following presents the results of the discussions, the ecosystem sketches and the participants' AR use cases with detailed considerations.

Comments Relating to Scenarios

Pre-made scenarios were first presented, discussed and evaluated in the focus group sessions. The preference of serious interior designers for using very simple design tools in the presented cases was emphasised by the participants, who stressed that usability would be the crucial factor for their interest in using the system. Participants assumed that the real, accurate sizes of the apartment, rooms and furniture were the most critical individual features of the service system. Besides size, the most important qualities for the products, furniture and representative 3D models were stated to be style and colour. It was considered reasonable, however, for colour to be merely suggestive – e.g. fair, mid-dark or dark – to give an impression of the overall design. Participants thought that placing old, existing furniture in the design was even more important than buying new furniture via the service.

It was stated very clearly that a design process often begins by placing existing furniture – an ancestral cupboard or piano, for example – in place, with this piece or artefact defining the overall design plan. However, participants speculated that there might not be any party interested in providing such a service. If the service were to concentrate exclusively on selling new furniture, this would mean all major furniture providers having all their products available in the service system.

Concerning the sharing of design ideas through social media, participants remarked that if they were providing services themselves they would prefer to share their ideas with other interior designers, design enthusiastic people or customers. Designers suspected that general users of the service would also prefer at least semi-professional feedback on their design plans. The participants who were design amateurs were pleased by the idea of the scenario – presenting a home decoration contest (see Figure 2) – perceiving that the special knowledge and expertise of interior designers and design amateurs could be fully utilised through the contest. Sharing design plans with a wider audience – or with friends and family – were seen as irrelevant.

Figure 2. Example of a Scenario: Interior design contest for design bloggers

Comments Relating to Example AR Applications

Participants subsequently saw three example applications that were benchmarked by the research group. The applications provided 3D and AR functionalities for creating interior designs. Participants were given an oral description of the benefits that were the criteria for selecting these specific applications.

Participants provided detailed evaluation of the presented applications. The most important statements related to the visual appearances: the aesthetics. Participants emphasised that the 3D environments and models needed to be attractive and realistic. The realism brought to interior scenes by the showing of lights and shadows and textures in detail, for example, would make them more convincing. It was also seen as advantageous to induce the user/designer to feel that decorating rooms and creating plans was "leisure activity" – that it was fun to spend time in this way and to explore the service. The design competitions for interior designers in the example applications seemed to lack purpose: there were too many of them with no reward. In addition, the most important priority was stated to be the overall costs of the products and services. The existing services, however, only showed prices for single articles.

Sketches of the Service Ecosystem

After the introduction phase, participants created system concepts in pairs and presented them to each other. Figure 4 presents an example of a concept made by one of the pairs. The pair explained that the ambiguous *designer* and the service tool were identical (as it is the designer who uses the tool). The first task was to feed the background information and facts into the system, e.g. the floor plans. The sketch contained a two-way arrow – at this point the information either exists or has to be created. The main service providers in the cooperation were interior decorating stores (for wallpapers, floor and wall materials) and furnishing companies. The existing furniture was equally important – *"the past life, which does not vanish when a new home comes along"*. Service providers were the second priority: the individual

Figure 3. An interior application that utilised AR technology by VividWorks Ltd (http://www.vividworks.fi/vivdplatform)

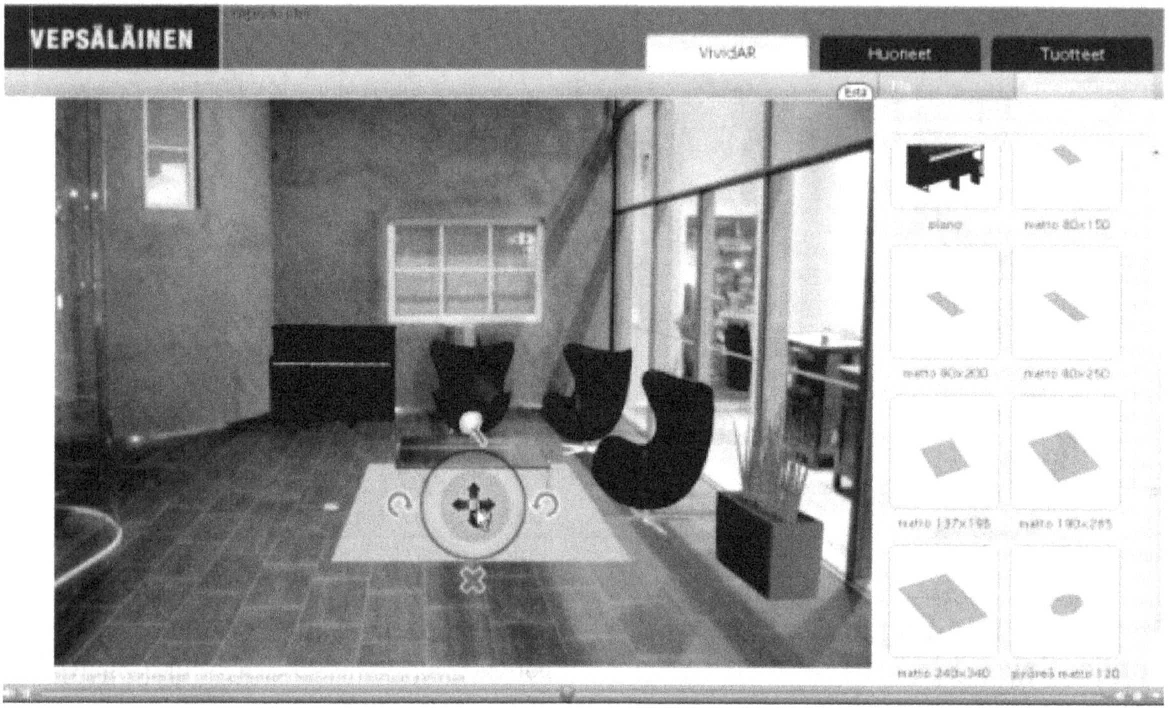

Figure 4. Example of a sketched service ecosystem

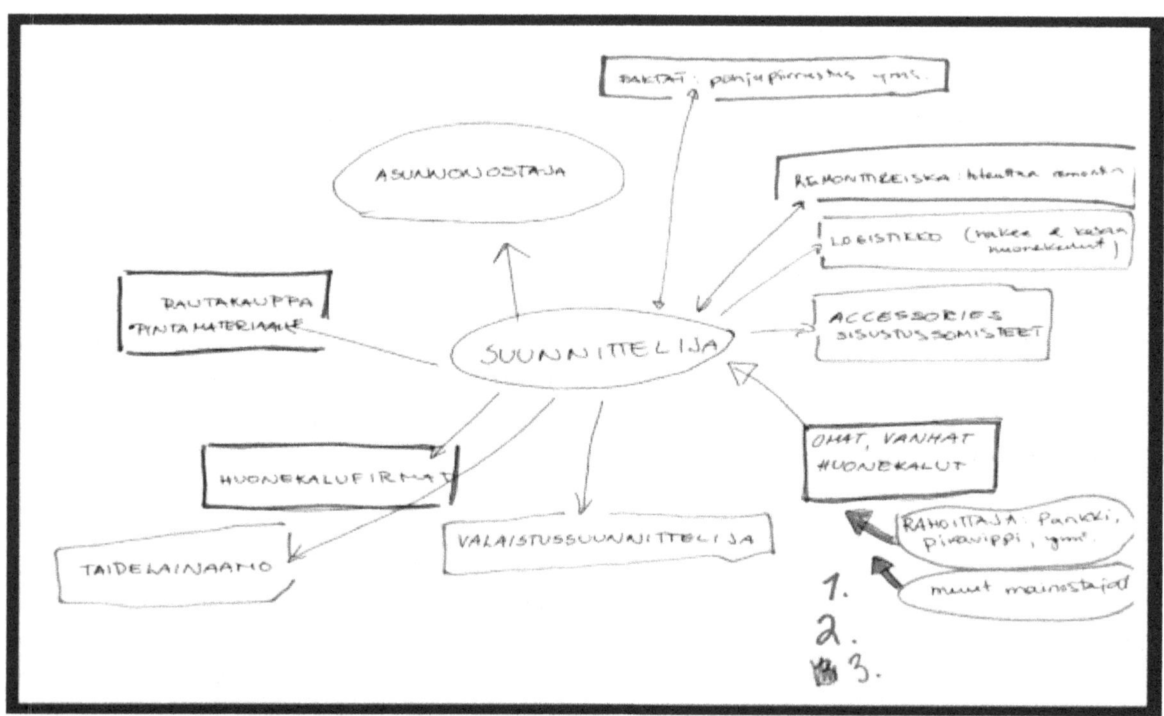

designers who offer their services, or could be accessed through the service. A third priority was logistics; those who put all thc pieces together and provide complete light decoration services, for example. This was followed by accessories, e.g. lighting providers and art suppliers. The sketch also described the chronology of events.

Table 1 presents the results of the service ecosystem sketches, and the conclusions of the co-sketching session. Participants were encouraged to determine the importance of the factors using a tree-level scale. For the most important factors, participants used numbering, a different colour, or a stronger line, and confirmed and explained the importance of the services after sketching the content. As the table shows, participants thought that the new furniture and interior decoration providers were key factors in the service. The participants perceived themselves in the co-design situation as designers, but while creating concepts all mentioned the importance of the customer relationship. Also, all mentioned the other designers – competitors or designers with different expertise. The participants highlighted some new providers to be included in the service: kitchen-, window- and carpet providers,

Table 1. Results of the service ecosystem sketches. If all pairs (groups 1–4) thought a service was most important, the service received 12 points. If only one mentioned it, and did not value it highly, the service received only one point.

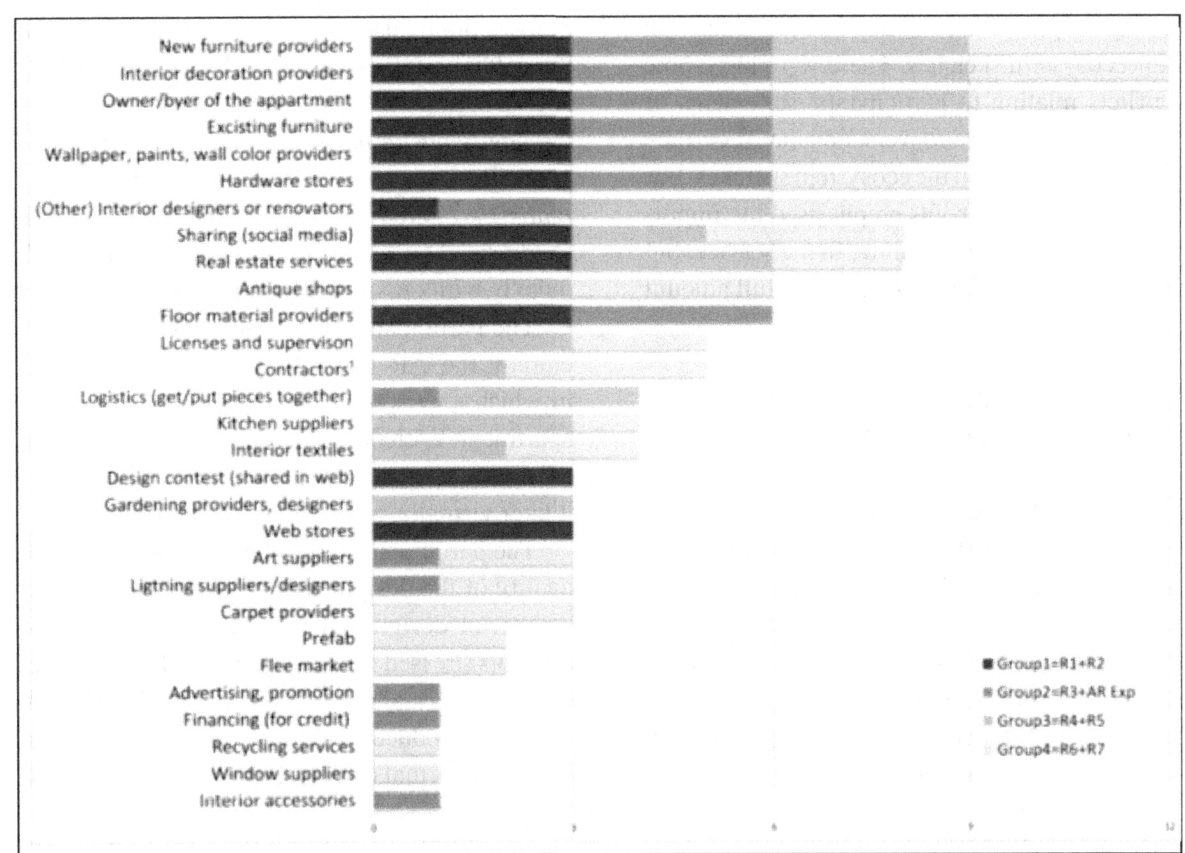

[1]Contractors = e.g. HPAC-planning, electricity, masons.

antique shops, flea markets, art suppliers, gardening-, lighting- and 3D-model designers of existing furniture. From this viewpoint the service was seen as a cluster for smaller providers.

With a service dealing with novel ideas, participants emphasised that the price of furniture, material and accessories would constitute the essential feature of the concept. It was therefore considered important that the total cost of the new furniture and design alterations should be clearly visible. One group remarked that the customer could apply for a loan from a credit provider if it were possible to refer to an estimate provided by the service.

Because of the qualitative nature of the information was qualitative there was some overlapping with the service providers presented in the table. Some participants, for example, mentioned hardware stores, but described them later as interior decoration providers, and placed both of them in their ecosystem sketches. There were also some conflicts relating to participants' statements of preference during the conversations, and how they were implemented in the ecosystem sketches. For example, all participants emphasised the importance of old, existing furniture in the service, but this nonetheless failed to receive the full amount of points in the analysis.

Ideas for Augmented Reality in Interior Design System

After sketching the service ecosystem concepts, the focus group participants thought more thoroughly about the AR features of the interior design service. Three topics were highlighted above others in the discussions: realistic lighting, number and variety of furniture models available (including 3D reconstruction of existing furniture), and search functionalities.

Based on their experience, participants emphasised how the lighting conditions affected the overall feeling and atmosphere of a space – and how difficult it was to explain for the customers. By using the AR technology, they saw an opportunity to visualise lighting effects: e.g. an ideal system would show the space in realistic lighting in the evening, morning, winter or summer, or according to the position of the windows. This would show the virtual apartment in a more realistic light: *"All dark corners during winter days, and harsh light during spring"*. Besides the ambient lighting, participants pointed out that it would also be useful to be able to model and visualise the lighting effects of different light sources e.g. to demonstrate the accurate size of selected spotlights.

Designers explained further that they constantly experienced situations in which they had no tools to communicate with the customers e.g. about the colours of the walls. One designer described such a situation: *"The effect of black walls are unimaginable for most customers, as white walls are still so common, but the atmosphere could really be altered by simply changing one wall to black."* This situation could be demonstrated quickly with on-site AR or VR technology.

The participants created use cases that could employ the AR technology, presenting a case in which a person was interested in a particular apartment. With this type of use the person could take pictures of the physical apartment and furnish it later virtually, at home, using the AR service.

The participants raised the issue of the visual quality of the design, which is highly important in interior design planning processes. The participants stressed the importance of the rendering quality of virtual objects: the application should be able to produce realistic materials and lighting effects on virtual objects. Participants stated that they would not engage AR features in the service unless the quality correlated sufficiently with the real environment.

Another important issue was that the availability of virtual models should not restrict the inspiration of a design. If the designer has e.g. an antique furniture model in mind, it should be possible to add it to the interior design plan or at least to represent it using an almost equivalent model. The same need applies to existing furniture; the user should be able to add virtual counterparts of the furniture easily into the design. This means that the 3D-object library should be large, and should contain generic objects whose colour, size and materials could easily be changed. Alternatively, designers should easily be able to create their own models e.g. based on images of an item of furniture. The service should also contain smaller objects, such as curtains, plants and flowers, paintings, posters and photo frames. Participants hoped for a sophisticated database search that enables search by colour, style and size. Typical situations were described as e.g. "I need a chair of this size..." *or* "I want a reddish couch...".

REFLECTION: TECHNOLOGICAL FEASIBILITY CONCERNING AR

Concerning the remarks on the AR functionalities, it was said that virtual lights and shadows affect not only the visual quality perceived by the user, but also the realism of the augmentation. In other words, virtual objects seem to hang in the air if they are not attached to the floor with virtual shadows. Virtual lighting, similar to real lighting, embeds the virtual furniture as part of the environment. It is also possible to adjust virtual lights easily, according to real light sources, with user interaction in interior design application (Siltanen & Woodward, 2006).

Photorealistic rendering, i.e. the production of photo-like 3D graphics, is computationally demanding, similarly in applications where live video feed is augmented. However, still images are well suited to interior design applications (Siltanen & Woodward, 2006) and therefore computation time is not an issue. It is possible to measure the real lighting conditions of the environment, adapt the virtual object to it, and produce adaptive photorealistic AR (Aittala, 2010).

The participants expressed a need for a large object library that supports creativity, together with sophisticated search functionalities. The challenge of a model library lies in economics: how to create a business model that supports the creation and sharing of 3D models. We may assume that if an interior design service has a sufficient number of users, the creation of a large number of 3D models would be viable.

CONCLUSION

Since the focus group participants' expertise was high, they were able to create several new, aesthetic ideas for the interior design system concepts. AR technology was mostly speculated upon by offering examples of existing AR features, yet the participants were able to provide valuable feedback: AR use cases, and the fact that the evaluations of the feasibilities were based on the experience of interior designers.

The sketching approach for empowering a co-design process proved to be a flexible and productive method of involving users in the innovation conception phase, and for perceiving a user model of an interactive design system. Table 1 – the results of the service ecosystem sketches – presents certain evidence that it is also conceivable to analyse users' models. Moreover, because of the ecosystem descriptions, the highlighted issues were discussed more thoroughly in the focus groups. In exploiting sketching as a means of involving users in the interaction design processes, the key finding was that during the co-design session the sketches remained in the custody of the participants: even if the conversation and new information led opinions and ideas along different courses, participants expressed their judgements by referring to their sketches.

After studying the most important requirements of the critical users for the AR technology, it can be said that most ideas could easily be implemented in an interior design service system. When it comes to participants' needs for modelling existing furniture, however, it may take some time before practical solutions are available; current solutions for 3D reconstruction (i.e. construction of a three-dimensional model of an object from several two-dimensional views) require too much involvement and knowledge from the user. Research is nevertheless moving towards rapid 3D reconstruction on mobile devices (Hartl, et. al, 2011). In future interior design services, the user is expected to scan the interior environment effortlessly with a mobile device, and even obtain modelling of an existing item of furniture.

Focus group user evaluations and co-design sessions provided adequately new information for further design and development of interactive interior design services that utilise AR technology. The focus group participants, whom we anticipated to be the critical users of the service, in turn described the users of the service as: interior designers, interior architects, various decorators, model creators, lighting consultants, electrical consultants, small or large furniture companies (or individuals), decoration- and renovation providers.

ACKNOWLEDGMENT

The research study was carried out within the Adfeed project which is supported by TEKES as part of the next Media programme of TIVIT (Finnish Strategic Centre for Science, Technology and Innovation in the field of ICT). Minni Kanerva provided the illustrations for Figures 1-2.

Figure 5. Focus group participants creating novel interior design service concepts

REFERENCES

Aittala, M. (2010). Inverse lighting and photorealistic rendering for augmented reality. *The Visual Computer*, *26*(6), 669–678. doi:10.1007/s00371-010-0501-7

Azuma, R., Baillot, Y., Behringer, R., Feiner, S., Julier, S., & MacIntyre, B. (2001). Recent advances in augmented reality. *IEEE Computer Graphics and Applications*, *21*(6), 34–47. doi:10.1109/38.963459

Buxton, W. (2007). *Sketching user experiences: Getting the design right and the right design*. San Francisco, CA: Morgan Kaufmann.

Carroll, J. (2009). *Making use: Scenario-based design of human-computer interactions*. Cambridge, MA: MIT Press.

Cassim, J., & Dong, H. (2003). Critical users in design innovation. In *Inclusive Design: Design for the Whole Population*. London: Springer-Verlag. doi:10.1007/978-1-4471-0001-0_32

Greenbaum, J., & Kyng, M. (1991). *Design at work: Cooperative design of computer systems*. Hoboken, NJ: Lawrence Erlbaum Associates.

Hartl, A., Gruber, L., Arth, C., Hauswiesner, S., & Schmalstieg, D. (2011). Rapid reconstruction of small objects on mobile phones. In *Proceedings of IEEE Computer Society Conference*, (pp. 20-27). IEEE.

Kelley, T., & Littman, J. (2001). *The art of innovation: Lessons in creativity from ideo*. New York: Doubleday.

Mann, S. (2002). Mediated reality with implementations for everyday life. *Presence (Cambridge, Mass.)*.

Milgram, P., Takemura, H., Utsumi, A., & Kishino, F. (1994). Augmented reality: A class of displays on the reality-virtuality continuum. In *Proceedings of the SPIE Conference on Telemanipulator and Telepresence Technologies*, (pp. 282-292). SPIE.

Morgan, D. (1998). *The focus group guidebook*. Thousand Oaks, CA: Sage Publications.

Schuler, D., & Namioka, A. (1993). *Participatory design: Principles and practices*. Hillsdale, NJ: Lawrence Erlbaum Associates.

Siltanen, S. (2012). Theory and applications of marker-based augmented reality. *VTT Science, 3*.

Siltanen, S., & Woodward, C. (2006). Augmented Interiors with digital camera images. In *Proceedings of Seventh Australasian User Interface Conference (AUIC2006)*. ACS.

Chapter 26
Art, Future, and New Technologies: Research or Business?

Francisco V. Cipolla-Ficarra
ALAIPO – AINCI, Spain and Italy

Valeria M. Ficarra
ALAIPO – AINCI, Spain and Italy

ABSTRACT

The authors present the first results of a heuristic evaluation of online content and the social networks that allows the detection of the manipulators of the mass media communication, the universities, and the research centers in the Iberian Peninsula. They present the strategies used in a technique of heuristic evaluation called CASTE – Computer Art, Software, and Technology Evaluation. Finally, a first graphic is presented that shows the results of applying CASTE and the manipulating extension in other territories of the disguised research business in art and new technologies.

INTRODUCTION

Science, technology and art have always converged in an intersection, although in the history of humankind it was thought that it was not so. In this sense, it is impossible to think the impressionists as separate from the research on light and optics, for instance. Here is one of the reasons why it is necessary to make a short historic review of the evolution of science. The Greeks in the fifth century B.C. granted science a bidirectional relation, which is made up by a theoretical part and a practical one (McClellan & Dorn, 2006). However, they developed the theoretical aspect. That is, in that time and in that geographical context, reason prevailed to probe into the causes of the phenomena and consequently their effects. Now in the Arabic context the advance of the other component takes place, since it was they who looked for the practical and useful aspect of knowledge. Of course, along

DOI: 10.4018/978-1-4666-4490-8.ch026

the centuries the obtained data accumulated. It is so how the first libraries were made, which stored human wisdom until that time in the history of humankind. A classical example of storage of wisdom was the library of Alexandria, in ancient Egypt. Centuries later, Francis Bacon in view of the accumulation of data (experimental or observations) started to formulate and defend the need for hypothesis (Hannam, 2011). He stressed besides the transcendence of statistics for the progress of sciences. Galileo and Newton were responsible for giving birth to the modern sense of science thanks to the rational and empiric aspect that they added to it. Later on, humankind went through a period of great discoveries and inventions (Basalla, 1988). An outstanding place is taken by the print and simultaneously the circulation of books and ideas. In the 16th century a union took place that endures down to our days: science and technique. Science leaves the theoretical aspect behind little by little to start to become more practical. The techniques or instruments start to be used in a more dynamic way in the scientific process. In the context of graphic computing, for instance, we have this with the commercial software to make computer animations, compared with the programming of systems for scientific visualization. However, in the early 90s computer art based on dynamic and static images was turned into a show of new technologies in the Iberian Peninsula. The goal was to generate a new avant-garde whose mission consisted in the aesthetic homologation of the achievements of futurist science, especially in the fields of computer science, telecommunications, robotics, genetics, biology, etc. Not for nothing a myriad publications appeared where the 21st century was presented as the century of nanotechnology, biocomputering, etc. (Peterson, 2000; Cantrill, 2010). A way to reach that goal were certain international events both in Europe and America where the computer art was presented as synonymous of future and research, when in fact these events were organized with merely mercantilist purposes. Such statement stems from a diachronic analysis applying the CASTE technique, where it has been detected online a virtual but real complex social system into computer art and ICT (Information and Communication Technology) that combines some or all elements of social class, hierarchy, exclusion, endogamy, power and hereditary transmission of occupation. The difference of these events lies in the recipients of the main and secondary topics of the contents. That is, whether they are aimed at the public in general as in the Spanish case or rather at an audience of ICT professionals, computer graphics, computer animation, multimedia, etc., as is the Austrian case of Ars Electronica (www.aec.at), in its origins, or the Siggraph (www.siggraph.org) in USA. Theoretically all these events have R&D as the cornerstone of their contents, however the mercantilist factor prevails over R&D as it happens in the university educational sector in Southern Europe in the last two decades, for instance.

COMPUTER ART AND USERS OF NEW TECHNOLOGIES

In computer art, the exact accuracy is not required which is emulated in the screens of the computers such as the case of scientific visualization. As a rule, these authors worked with static images and in the 80s and early 90s they were painters, graphic designers, illustrators, etc. who went from analogue to digital media, for instance, 2D, 3D, animation, video, etc. It was these unprecedented static and dynamic images which struck the attention of the professionals of the computer sector and/or new technologies in general and the inexperienced public. Now some saw in these images a way to generate a power elite to control those productions. The goal was to control that production in the whole state territory, getting the maximum economic profits, in the least possible time and disguising them as R&D activities.

In others words, a diachronic analysis of two decades and thanks to the social networks (Facebook and Linkedin) and Google, they are now presented as real commercial businesses (Figures 1, 2 and 3 –we have hidden part of the text for privacy reasons, the example is real). Evidently, in the Iberian Peninsula at that time 98% percent of R&D was carried out in the public sector, mainly the universities. Therefore, the universities had to subsidize the contents of certain festivals aimed at the show of the static dynamic images. The word "show" is the right one, since in Spain those festivals has a toastmaster, guests, live shows, contests and awards, etc. The cost for the organizers was equal to zero, and the profits were remarkable, either because of the subsidies they got from the different autonomous communities where they took place, or those coming from the EU, state-owned telecommunications firms (whose international phone service, for instance, was among the most expensive from Lisbon to Moscow), etc. (Barnes & Meyers, 2011). Besides, the contents were to be shown to the audience also at zero cost, and also the final study projects, masters or doctor thesis of the universities which constantly promoted these shows of the images aimed at computer art, artificial life, virtual reality, Internet, etc., as it can be seen in the following figures (Cipolla-Ficarra, 1993).

Images capable of drawing the attention of the young generations, first as observers and then as producers. That is, generating them through the computer in order to project them later on the big screen, specially the cinema. In contrast, the adult users with university diplomas in anthropology, telecommunications, industrial, architects, etc. saw the need to keep on studying because in those images was the future of the Spanish ICT. It was so how these festivals served to draw potential students in departments or university institutes of

Figure 1. Wikipedia for the festival description but there is not commercial information about the organization

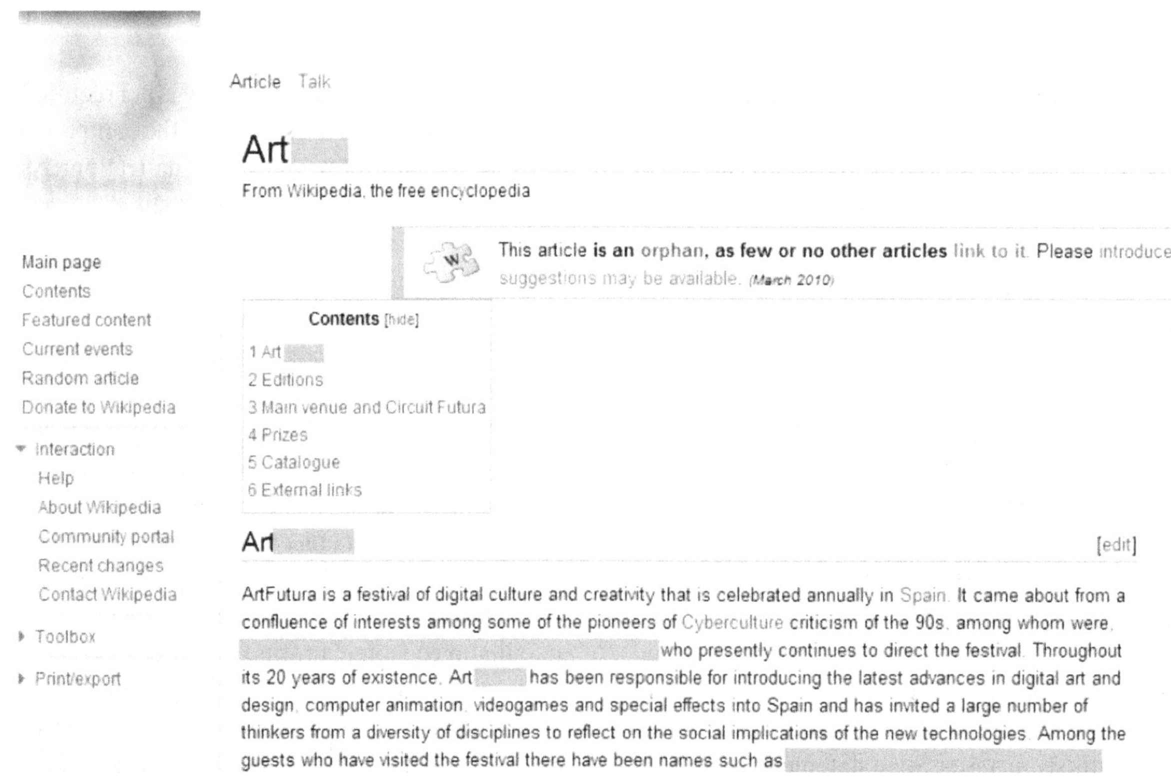

Figure 2. The festival is presented in Argentina as a non-profit organization which didn't pay taxes in Buenos Aires, for instance

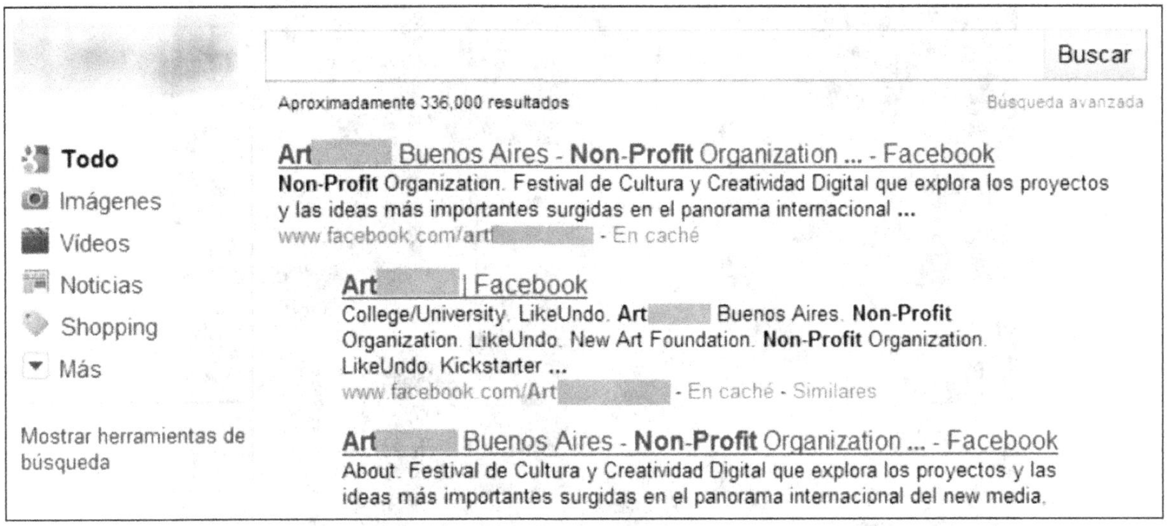

Buscar

Aproximadamente 336,000 resultados — Búsqueda avanzada

Todo
Imágenes
Videos
Noticias
Shopping
Más

Mostrar herramientas de búsqueda

Art Buenos Aires - **Non-Profit** Organization ... - Facebook
Non-Profit Organization. Festival de Cultura y Creatividad Digital que explora los proyectos y las ideas más importantes surgidas en el panorama internacional ...
www.facebook.com/art - En caché

Art | Facebook
College/University. LikeUndo. **Art** Buenos Aires. **Non-Profit** Organization. LikeUndo. New Art Foundation. **Non-Profit** Organization. LikeUndo. Kickstarter ...
www.facebook.com/Art - En caché - Similares

Art Buenos Aires - **Non-Profit** Organization ... - Facebook
About. Festival de Cultura y Creatividad Digital que explora los proyectos y las ideas más importantes surgidas en el panorama internacional del new media.

Figure 3. Lindedin shows all the information but as a transnational corporation or business enterprise in Spain: integral consulting to the businesses, business incubators, jobs, etc.

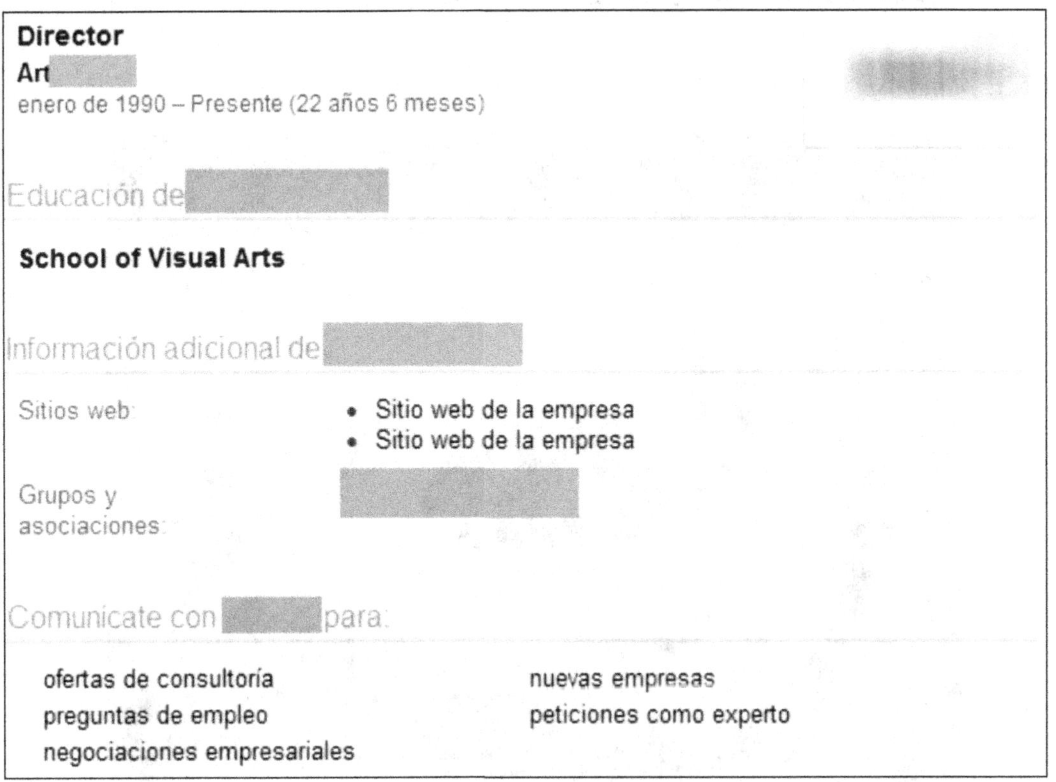

Director
Art
enero de 1990 – Presente (22 años 6 meses)

Educación de

School of Visual Arts

Información adicional de

Sitios web
- Sitio web de la empresa
- Sitio web de la empresa

Grupos y asociaciones

Comunícate con para:

ofertas de consultoría
preguntas de empleo
negociaciones empresariales
nuevas empresas
peticiones como experto

Figure 4. Generation of images using methods from artificial life – author: William Lathan

Figure 5. Evolutionism of artificial life – author: William Lathan

Figure 6. Evolutionism of artificial life – author: Yoichiro Kawaguchi (Growth)

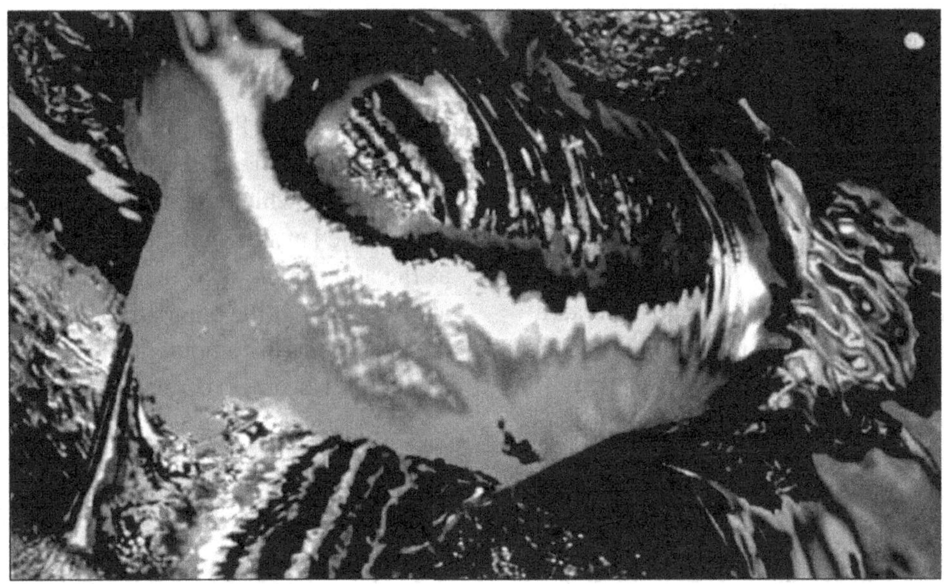

Figure 7. Moebius –Starwatcher

the audiovisual, multimedia and virtual reality, etc. Those were university institutes, audiovisual departments, computer graphics and animation, software engineering, computer and system engineering, etc., labs or usability centers, etc., who had and still have part of the administration staff in the promotion tasks of those festivals. That is, festivals which do not spend any money either in the promotion in the media, the payment to the administration staff for the sending of newsletters, generation of press releases, updating of websites, etc. because these expenses are covered by the public institutions, that is, the universities, city councils, museums, etc. That is, the promotion of festivals with profit purposes is presented internally in these public academic structures as if they were promoting a workshop, symposium or scientific conference. They presented the festival as a scientific event –Figure 1, when in reality in Figure 3 it can be seen that we are in the face of a business firm. Regrettably, with CASTE it has been seen that this university "modus operandi" hasn't changed with the passing of time, since its use has increased multifold.

In other words, the human factor still damages scientific advance in certain communities of Southern Europe. A human factor which should be controlled in the academic environments because as we can see in the following graphic there are these bidirectional interrelations between computer art and the sectors it is related to in a direct and/or indirect way: university, professional training centers, graphic and/or multimedia software/hardware manufacturers, service firms for telecommunications, mass media, ministerial institutions, city halls, provincial, regional and state governments, tourism offices, museums, banking and financing institutions, hospitals, etc.

In the Figure 8 can be seen the network of personal and financial relationships from this type of events which encompasses the avant-garde sector whether it is in the summit of power such as the authorities who finance these events, and also the basis of the population keen on knowing the latest news in computer-made images and the technological supports related to it.

THE SUMMIT VERSUS THE BASIS OF THE PYRAMID OF POTENTIAL CONSUMERS OF COMPUTER IMAGES

Today, the studies related to "digital divide" (Bauerlein, 2011) make apparent the gap that is generated because of social, economic, working reasons,

Figure 8. Private and public institutions related to the organization of pixel festivals – static and/or animated, in Spain

etc. among the potential users and the scientific environment (university and/or industrial). Obviously, these computer-generated images, shown on big screens for days, in a context of traveling show through different cities of the Spanish and Latin American geography, also foster the digital divide, especially if these festivals are aimed at the general audience. That is, a motley audience, whether it is because of the age or the educational training. These are people who do not only lack the knowledge in computer use, but they are also a pack of illiterates of the latest news in the great whole of ICT, especially inside the subsets of the mobile multimedia technology, the cloud computing, intelligent agent, etc. The members of the summit of the pyramid in Southern Europe they will keep on developing for years products and/or services subsidized with public money, for a population which will never use them or firms and industries lying outside their borders. However, these aspects are not interesting to those firms that organize those events from public institutions, such as the networks of people who promote them from the Spanish universities. That is, once the goal has been reached of having computer images of the several rungs of the pyramid of the local, national and international pyramid with a high quality, the second goal is to fill the spaces of the exhibit and cash as many entrance tickets as possible. This is the moment in which the summit and the basis of the pyramid merge into a great whole.

Now many members of the basis of the pyramid will consider taking university studies to reach the summit. However, this summit has its R&D area beyond the borders of the Iberian Peninsula, that is, in countries like the USA, Canada, UK, Japan, Germany, etc. Here is one of the reasons why these events do not only foster the digital divide phenomenon but also the so called Neet generation and the unemployed, as it can be seen in the following Figures 9 and 10:

In these figures can be seen the opposing relationships between the basis of the pyramid which intends to reach the summit, and how from the summit they try to thwart this ascending process. Now how can this reality be analyzed to elaborate a method and/or technique of analysis? The answer lies in the intersection of the formal and factual sciences (Bunge, 1981). A satisfactory study along time in that intersection has been the generation of a communicability expert for the online and offline interactive systems, for instance.

THE INTERSECTION OF THE FORMAL SCIENCES AND THE FACTUAL SCIENCES IN CASTE

The formal sciences –also known as ideal, encompass mathematics and logic among others. The main goal is the elaboration of the formal elements and the generation of guidelines that rule it or direct it. For instance, the relationships inside the Pythagorean theorem. In contrast the factual or material sciences have as their enunciation phenomena and procedures connected with facts or processes. For that reason it is said that they are interrelated with the non-scientific aspects. So far the division is related to the objective aspect. Another requisite both sciences meet is that the formal sciences demonstrate or prove their enunciations through logic, for instance, whereas factual sciences serve for the verification of the assumptions or hypothesis of a provisory character, what entails carrying out experiments and/or observations. Another two concepts which it is also necessary to link to the former ones are rationality and objectivity. This latter word requires a special transcendence in the scientific context because sometimes it is seriously challenged that scientific knowledge is objective. In our case, we have used as main techniques for the generation of CASTE direct observation and the analysis of content of the off-line and on-line information during two decades (1991-2011). Obviously these techniques have followed the principles of scien-

Figure 9. Potential users of the new technologies make up the group of digital illiterate because they neither study nor work. Digital newspaper –El Pais (www.elpais.com), 06.22.2009.

ELPAÍS.com Sociedad

Domingo, 18/12/2011, 17:29 h EL PAÍS en KIOSKO y más

Inicio Internacional Política España Deportes Economía Tecnología Cultura Gente y TV Sociedad Opinión Blogs SModa In English

Educación Salud Ciencia El Viajero El País semanal Domingo

ELPAIS.com > Sociedad

REPORTAJE: vida&artes

Generación 'ni-ni': ni estudia ni trabaja

Los jóvenes se enfrentan hoy al riesgo de un nivel de vida peor que el de sus padres - El 54% no tiene proyectos ni ilusión

JOSÉ LUIS BARBERÍA 22/06/2009

Vota Resultado 1183 votos Comentarios - 91 Twittear 36 Consiglia 1 mila

Tan preparados y satisfechos con sus vidas, y tan vulnerables y perdidos, nuestros jóvenes se sienten presa fácil de la devastación laboral, pero no aciertan a vislumbrar una salida airosa, ni a combatir este estado de cosas. El dato asomaba hace poco, sin estrépito, entre los resultados de la última encuesta de Metroscopia: el 54% de los españoles situados entre los 18 y los 34 años dice no tener proyecto alguno por el que sentirse especialmente interesado o ilusionado. ¿Ha surgido una generación apática, desvitalizada, indolente, mecida en el confort familiar? Los sociólogos detectan la aparición de un modelo de actitud adolescente y juvenil: la de los *ni-ni*, caracterizada por el simultáneo rechazo a estudiar y a trabajar. "Ese comportamiento emergente es sintomático, ya que hasta ahora se sobrentendía que si no querías estudiar te ponías a trabajar. Me pregunto qué proyecto de futuro puede haber detrás de esta postura", señala Elena Rodríguez, socióloga del Instituto de la Juventud (INJUVE).

La noticia en otros webs

- webs en español
- en otros idiomas

La crisis ha venido a acentuar la incertidumbre en el seno de una generación que creció en un ámbito familiar de mejora continuada del nivel de vida y que ha sido confrontada al deterioro de las condiciones laborales: precariedad, infraempleo,

ampliar

El virus del desánimo está minando la naturaleza vitalista y combativa de la gente joven.- JAVIER HERNÁNDEZ

tific method and have been complemented and interrelated with others belonging to the formal and factual sciences.

The word "method" stems from the Greek "meta" ("go" or "towards") and "odos" (road). The method is the way which is followed to reach a predetermined goal through a set of instruments and/or techniques in which imagination is not ruled out. In keeping with the planned objective and the sciences which are applied said instruments will change. The important thing is to set some procedures which lead to a scientifically significant research. Besides, its methodical character indicates what it is searching. In our work, we have use rhetoric questions to compile a table of heuristic evaluation. In the formulation of the questions are the primary and secondary goals of the work developed diachronically in the last two decades. The analysis of the on-line and off-line content such as interviews and formularies are some of the techniques of the social sciences which have made it possible to reach the first results of Figure 11, for instance. Questions which are accompanied by a positive or negative sign, since they can be turned into quality attributes and therefore quality metrics. In these questions are combined the formal and factual sciences, therefore there are issues related to computer graphics and their derivations related to the computer art sector: E-learning, commercial promotion, the control on the mass media, the interrelations with power inside the social structure, etc. Next the first rhetoric questions (*RQ* and *number* – alphabetical order, see Figure 11) with their matching signs

Figure 10. Many of the unemployed have a university training in audiovisual, multimedia engineering, telecommunications engineering, industrial engineering, software engineering, computer degrees, etc., that is, knowledge and/or experiences related with the ICT. Digital newspaper –El Pais (www.elpais.com), 04.27.2012.

EL PAÍS

PORTADA | INTERNACIONAL | POLÍTICA | ECONOMÍA | CULTURA | SOCIEDAD | DEPORTES

ECONOMÍA

ECONOMÍA EMPRESAS MERCADOS BOLSA FINANZAS PERSONALES VIVIENDA TECNOLOGÍA OPINIÓN/ANÁLISIS BLOGS LA CRISIS TITULARES

ESTÁ PASANDO Desempleo Paro juvenil FMI Agencias calificación Resultados bancarios Recesión económica MÁS TEMAS

El paro sube a 5,6 millones y marca un nuevo máximo en el arranque de 2012

- La tasa se eleva al 24,44% y roza el anterior récord, alcanzado en 1994
- La cifra total de parados se ha incrementado en 729.400 en un año

EL PAÍS | Madrid | 27 ABR 2012 - 09:25 CET 91

Archivado en: Paro juvenil Paro masculino Encuesta población activa Crisis económica Macroeconomía Tasa paro Recesión económica Desempleo Coyuntura económica Empleo España

Recomendar 224 Twittear 43 Enviar Compartir

La recaída en la recesión de la economía española ha provocado un fuerte aumento del paro en el arranque de este 2012. Según los datos de la Encuesta de Población Activa que ha publicado hoy el INE, el total de personas sin trabajo ha subido en 365.900 personas entre enero y marzo, lo que ha dejado el total de desempleados en 5.639.500, un nuevo máximo histórico. Del lado del empleo, en este periodo se han destruido 374.300 puestos de trabajo, con lo que el total de ocupados baja a 17.433.200.

Eskup EL PAÍS Twitter Seguir

ÚLTIMA HORA

El número de hogares con todos sus miembros en paro llega a 1.728.400. Es el dato hasta marzo, lo que supone 153.400 hogares más que en el trimestre anterior (un alza del 9,74 %) y 342.400 más que hace un año (un 24,7 % más), según la Encuesta de Población Activa.

EL PAÍS

Encuesta de Población Activa. El empleo se ha reducido en 718.500 personas en un año, de las cuales 709.700 son asalariadas y 9.900 son trabajadores por cuenta propia. La disminución anual del empleo entre los hombres (531.700 menos) es muy superior a la de las mujeres (186.800).

Figure 11. Results of the binary heuristic evaluation with regard to computer art and the future of the new technologies in the Iberian Peninsula

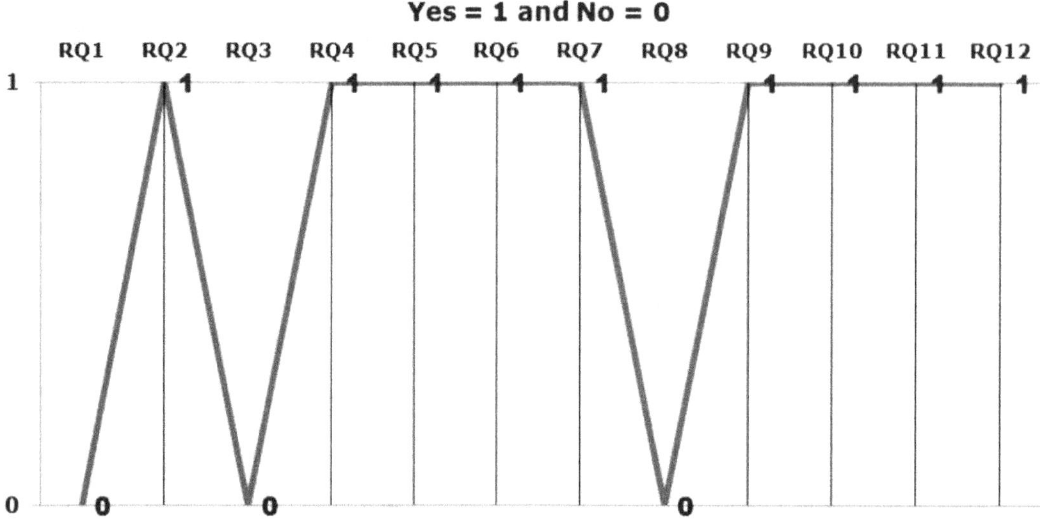

of value (in those cases in which both signs are found it means that in the universe of study they change depending on the passing of time), all of them refer to the computer art and its direct and indirect relationships with the technological sector, R&D and commercial:

1. Are the dynamic or static pixel festivals aimed at the professional public (RQ1)? (+). In this kind of events, scientific and technological quality prevails over the triviality of computer art.
2. Are the dynamic or static pixel festivals aimed to the wider audience (RQ2)? (+/-) In principle an interaction process is generated with the new technologies. However, with the passing of time, it can be seen how these festivals only strive to get the highest number of people attending the event, with the least possible cost, and strengthen the interconnections with power of the national and international institutions.
3. Are the computer art festivals organizations or cultural associations (RQ3)? (-) Theoretically, they are non-profit institutions, and related to computer art, virtual reality, scientific visualization, the architectonic reconstructions in 2D and 3D, the cinema and/or the television series in 2D and/or 3D, the videogames, etc., but the reality comes to light with the passing of time, as it can be seen in Figure 3. That is, firms with a great decision power in the future of the ICT of the local and international community. The internationalization of power takes place when they have expanded abroad, through the opening of branches which are presented to the community in situ, as cultural institutions aimed at the technological avant-gardes.
4. Are the festivals related to the new technologies, including computer art, made with public and/or private subsidies (RQ4)? (-) The management of subsidies in Southern Europe hasn't been transparent in the R&D

context and university education in the last two decades (Cipolla-Ficarra, et al., 2011; Cipolla-Ficarra & Ficarra, 2012). A myriad projects made from public institutions (universities) for private institutions but disguised as cultural organizations.

5. Are the scientific breakthroughs of a sector of computer graphics presented as a show (RQ5)? (-) The triviality of the sector of computer graphics, virtual reality, multimedia, augmented reality, etc., by a single anchorman/woman of the show along time, not only increases the number of the neet generation, but the unemployed (Figure 10). The attendees to the computer images shows do not understand the implicit complexity in generating them, although it is included in the chartered teaching centers, and get their university titles.
6. Do the presented works belong to the private sector (RQ6)? (-) The presented works have a deadline and usually they are not 100% made by the students, but by their tutors.
7. Do the presented works belong to the public sector but are managed as private companies (RQ7)? (-). Some institutes or departments of the audiovisual or computer graphics and virtual reality in the Catalan public universities, for instance, work as real corporations in the generation of image synthesis.
8. Do the presented works belong to the public sector (RQ8)? (+) As a rule, they are final project works, master or doctor thesis which must be presented in front of an evaluation committee, theoretically neutral.
9. Does the computer graphics sector, including its festivals, control the contents in the mass media with regard to the 2D, 3D, nD (RQ9)? (-) The goal of these sectors is keeping under control the contents which are published not only under the format of articles, but the publicity of those media. Consequently, power goes beyond the scientific environment and includes the set of the commercial publications.
10. Does the power wielded from the local computer graphics and all its derivations go beyond borders (RQ10)? (+/-) It is positive when the interchange of knowledge and/or experiences between the scientific sector is balanced. It will be totally negative when the goal is neocolonialism in emerging countries.
11. Is the awards phenomenon the common denominator among the different fields of graphic computing (RQ11)? (-) In the Iberian Peninsula almost all the computer animation productions, the professors and/or researchers in graphic computing, virtual reality, multimedia, audiovisual, social networks, etc., must participate in national and/or international competitions to win awards.
12. Is the promotion of events related to computer graphics and its derivations (in it computer art is included), ICT, multimedia mobile phones, video games, etc. in the mass media made through the university staff (RQ12)? (-) There are scientific environments in the Iberian Peninsula where the administration staff, professors and researchers, act as publicity or press agencies about the obtained results and promoting those institutions with which they interact economically and financially outside the campus. Activities which last decades for that staff and which have boosted their power in the social networks, generating real information bubbles which sideline in some cases the front page news of the digital versions of the papers.

In principle this set of rhetoric questions (RQ) may be presented as trite, but they are the result of the combination of several techniques and methods of the social sciences, such as: direct observation, documental compiling on-line and off-line, the analysis of content, interviews and questionnaires. Data which have been obtained along the years to analyze the described phenomenon, that is, in the Iberian Peninsula computer art is boosted with purely financial purposes and neither academic nor scientific.

LESSONS LEARNED

The utilitarian aspect is one of the intrinsic features of scientific research. The scientific results may be applied with positive or negative ends, such as can be the simulations to extirpate a malign tumor or the destructive power of a new virus –scientific visualization. Now thanks to the objectivity of science are reached planned results or not of an applicable nature. In our case, the use of techniques and/or methods of the social sciences in a diachronic way has allowed to find out that computer art is presented as a scientific field but in fact the goal is to use with mercantilist purposes, at zero cost for all those who directly or indirectly foster festivals of static and dynamic pixel in the Iberian Peninsula. Some regard the technology as an applied science. For instance, they see medicine as applied biology. But this is a limited vision, since technology is a dynamic sector of knowledge which entails a constant renovation in the explanation of the environment. Besides, it introduces knowledge and scientific methods in the resolution of practical processes. Our future work will consist in analyzing other similar European and American events to establish the network of commercial and scientific relationships which starting from interactive digital art is irradiated in a central way to each one of the sectors of the new technologies.

CONCLUSION

The link between technology and science is narrow. Scientific problems generates new problems, whose response will consist in inventing new theories or new research techniques which lead to a more perfect and deeper knowledge of the reality being considered. That is, we are in the face of a continuous cycle where diachronic vision is important to detect the deviations between knowledge and power, that is, between science and business, for instance. The results presented in the current work demonstrate the deviation of the context of computer graphics in the Iberian Peninsula. The mercantilist factor disguised in cultural non-profit institutions in the social networks can only be detected with the passing of time by a communicability expert in a fast and reliable way and with low costs.

The reality of the computer art context the future of new technologies makes apparent that many works publicly subsidized in Spain in fact have served to enrich private businesses beyond the Spanish borders. Finally CASTE has made apparent a network which theoretically is aimed at boosting the culture of the new technologies, but which does not take into account the Neet generation, nor the job market context. Where many of the unemployed in Figure 10 have made studies in engineering or degrees, masters, Ph.Ds, post-doctorates in audiovisual, multimedia, virtual reality, usability, social networks, telecommunications, etc. The future forces the societies to be more and more competitive, which entails mastering the powers which can be extracted from science and technique. However, it is also necessary to control the human factors which turn science into a simple mercantilist issue. Computer graphics, virtual reality, scientific visualization, audiovisual and all its interrelations are not exception to this reality.

REFERENCES

Barnes, M., & Meyers, N. (2011). *Mobile phones: Technology, networks and user issues*. New York: Nova Publishers.

Basalla, G. (1988). *The evolution of technology*. Cambridge, UK: Cambridge University Press.

Bauerlein, M. (2011). *The digital divide: Arguments for and against Facebook, Google, texting, and the age of social networking*. New York: Penguin Group.

Bunge, M. (1981). *The science: your method and your philosophy*. Buenos Aires, Argentina: Siglo XXI.

Cantrill, S. (2010). Computer in patient care: The promise and the challenge. *Communications of the ACM*, *53*(9), 42–47. doi:10.1145/1810891.1810907

Cipolla-Ficarra, F. (1993). Metamorfosis aplicada a la vida artificial. *Imaging*, *6*, 12–18.

Cipolla-Ficarra, F., et al. (2011). Computational informatics, social factors and new information technologies: Hypermedia perspectives and avant-garde experiences in the era of communicability expansion. Bergamo, Italy: Blue Herons Ed.s.

Cipolla-Ficarra, F., et al. (2012). New horizons in creative open software, multimedia, human factors and software engineering. Bergamo, Italy: Blue Herons Ed.s.

Cipolla-Ficarra, F., & Ficarra, V. (2012). Anti-models for universitary education: Analysis of the Catalans cases in information and communication technologies. In *Proceedings of First International on Software and Emerging Technologies for Education, Culture, Entertaiment, and Commerce: New Directions in Multimedia Mobile Computing, Social Networks, Human-Computer Interaction and Communicability (SETECEC 2012)*. Hershey, PA: IGI Global.

Hannam, J. (2011). *The genesis of science: How the Christian middle ages launched the scientific revolution*. Washington, DC: Regney Publishing.

McClellan, J., & Dorn, H. (2006). *Science and technology in world history: An introduction*. Baltimore, MD: The Johns Hopkins University Press.

Peterson, C. (2000). Taking technology to the molecular level. *IEEE Computer*, *33*(1), 46–53. doi:10.1109/2.816268

Chapter 27
Reality-Based 3D Modelling from Images and Laser Scans:
Combining Accuracy and Automation

Luigi Barazzetti
Department of Building Environmental Science and Technology, Politecnico di Milano, Italy

Marco Scaioni
Tongji University - College of Surveying and Geo-Informatics, Center for Spatial Information Science and Sustainable Development Applications, Shanghai, P.R. China

ABSTRACT

Reality-based 3D modelling is the entire process of generating a digital 3D object from a set of images or range maps. The aim of this work is to report an image- and range-based production pipeline to reconstruct complex and detailed objects with a combination of digital reconstruction techniques coupled with GPS information and maps for correct georeferencing and scaling, in order (1) to exploit the intrinsic potential and advantages of each technique, (2) to compensate for the individual weaknesses of each method, and (3) to achieve more accurate and complete surveying, modelling, interpretation, and digital results. To demonstrate the reliability, precision, and robustness of the combined use of photogrammetric and computer vision techniques for reality-based 3D modelling, several real applications are illustrated and discussed. These include cultural heritage documentation and preservation along with architectural, geological, and structural applications.

INTRODUCTION

Accurate 3D reconstructions of scenes and objects are primary goals in several fields of research. Reality-based 3D modelling is the process where an existing object is surveyed and reconstructed from different data sources and techniques. 3D models are today used by different operators in several practical applications, for example: cultural heritage documentation and preservation (Guidi, et al., 2009). cartography (Snyder, 1987), medicine (Ang & Mitchell, 2010). geology (Barazzetti,

DOI: 10.4018/978-1-4666-4490-8.ch027

Roncoroni, Scaioni & Remondino, 2011), material testing (Barazzetti & Scaioni 2010) and so on, probably they are too many to be exhaustively listed here.

Photogrammetry (Luhmann & Tecklenburg, 1992) and Computer Vision (Hartley & Zisserman, 2004) are scientific disciplines aimed at creating 3D models by exploiting data acquired with passive (mainly digital cameras) or active sensors (laser scanners or structured light systems). Different algorithms and data processing methods were developed to automate the production pipeline and reduce the manual effort of expert operators (often interactive measurements). However, in the case of complex scenes the user's interaction is still needed because fully automated approaches are prone to produce gross errors or blunders. In other words, when the survey is not only a 3D model for visualization purposes, a final check followed by manual editing seems indispensable.

At the beginning of a project, the geometric reconstruction of a scene needs a proper data acquisition plan in order to answer the following questions:

- Which instrument? do we need multiple techniques? how can we merge different data?
- Do we need a stable reference system? are measurements taken at different epochs necessary?
- Who takes the measurements?
- What about metric accuracy?
- How can we recover both position and attitude of the objects of the scene? is this always feasible?
- Which level of detail? do we need to reach a particular metric scale?
- Data acquisition time? data processing time?
- ...

and much more (probably, too many questions). This means that the goal of the survey should be absolutely clear right from the start of the project in order to satisfy the requests of the customer. Then, the expert operator has to find a good compromise between instruments and techniques, data processing algorithms and CPU time, data visualization and storage format.

Sometimes projects can be simulated beforehand, meaning that the expected theoretical accuracy is estimable through the variance-covariance matrix of a Least Squares problem (Fraser, 1996). This is the typical case of geodetic networks or photogrammetric image blocks and allows the operator to try different network geometries and understand the best one for that specific survey.

Then, different categories of data can be acquired. In general, a geodetic network can be useful to establish a common reference system for all the remaining data. The network is physically materialized by means of nails in the ground, retro-reflective targets, or prisms on top of stable nails (e.g. walls). A total station, a set of tripods, and some reflectors are the equipment for data acquisition while measurements are adjusted with standard Least Squares techniques.

If the final survey needs georeferencing (i.e. map, Cartesian or geographic coordinates) some GPS receivers allow the measurement of the geographic coordinates of some specific points with a precision better than ±1 cm (if particular techniques for data acquisition and processing are employed).

The 3D reconstruction of the whole scene is then carried out with images and laser scans. The integrated use of both methods is often a convenient choice to reduce their reciprocal disadvantages.

A laser scanning survey is made up of different scans (million points) taken from different station points. Data are registered in a common reference system (e.g. the one defined by total station data) by means of corresponding points (usually targets) or with marker-less algorithms like ICP (Besl & McKay, 1992). Then, after a preliminary noise reduction and outlier removal, a surface can be (manually or automatically) created from the registered clouds.

Images are instead processed with a mathematical formulation (Kraus, 2008; Mikhail, Bethel & McGlone, 2001) that allows the user to extract metric information from 2D projections. Today several research work demonstrated the opportunity to partially automate the data production phase, for example: (Agarwal, et al., 2009; Barazzetti, Remondino & Scaioni, 2010; Furukawa, Curless, Seitz & Szeliski, 2010; Roncella, Re & Forlani, 2011; Strecha, Pylvanainen & Fua, 2010) and the future developments are quite promising. A synthetic example of some sensors used in reality-based 3D modelling is shown in Figure 1, whereas the following sections illustrate some real surveys.

IMAGES OR LASER SCANS?

This is a very important issue. Several papers (e.g., Nex & Rinaudo, 2011; Spring, Peters Wetherelt, 2008) present a comparison and list advantages and disadvantages. In most cases, the answer depends on the object and different factors must be taken into consideration (e.g. shape, material, location, …).

The goal of this paragraph is to demonstrate how modern software for image processing can provide results similar to those achievable with laser scanners. The survey in not only an example, but an effective documentation project where an accurate reconstruction was needed. Shown in Figure 2 is the church of Santa Margherita (Casargo, Italy), that was surveyed with a set of images acquired with a Nikon D700 equipped with a 20 mm lens and some laser scans.

A geodetic network composed of 6 stations (the instrument used is a Leica TS30 and tripods were fixed during the whole survey to remove

Figure 1. Modern instruments for surveying applications

Figure 2. The church of Santa Margherita (Casargo, Italy)

repositioning errors) was employed to determine the coordinates of 24 retro-reflective targets on the church (Figure 3). This is useful to establish a stable reference system, to check the accuracy of other measurements, and to control the deformation of the image- or scan-based survey. In fact, it is important to remember that these measurements can be incorporated into adjustment processes (pseudo-observations) not only to solve for the "datum problem", but also to obtain a valid support to reduce network deformations.

In all, 136 images were automatically oriented (Figure 4), including some GCPs to obtain a georeferenced result. The overall RMSE value estimated using a set of check points was 1.1 cm, that is equivalent to the theoretical accuracy extracted from the covariance matrix. More than 15,000 3D points were found and sigma-naught was 1.07 pix. Finally, the surface was automatically extracted with the Acute3D software (www.acute3d.com) obtaining a final mesh of about 7 million triangles.

The laser survey (more than 20 scans) provided a similar geometric model that was compared with the image-based one by using the ICP algorithm of Geomagic Studio 10. The total discrepancy was about 1.5 cm and confirms the correctness of the previous reconstruction.

WHEN ARE LASER SCANS BETTER THAN IMAGES?

This paragraph illustrates a practical situation where the use of images was not feasible. The object is a big dam in Cancano (Valtellina, Italy)

Figure 3. The geodetic network around the church

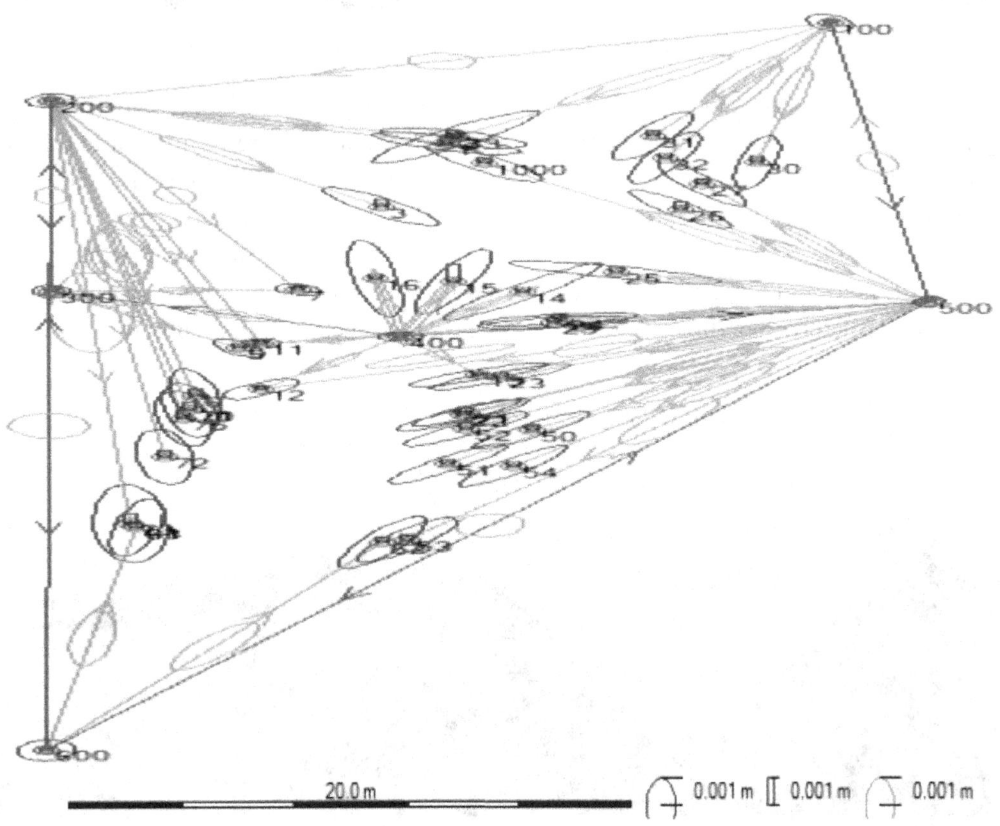

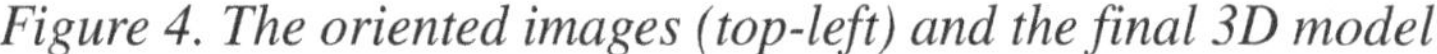

Figure 4. The oriented images (top-left) and the final 3D model

and a detailed 3D model was needed to study its static and dynamic performances (Figure 5). More details can be found in (Roncoroni, 2007).

The first limit of a project based on images concerns the texture of the object. The external wall is quite homogenous and the automatic (or manual) measurement of corresponding points in different images is extremely complicated. This problem becomes more significant in the case of automated algorithms for dense matching: it was impossible to guarantee a good distribution of 3D points for the whole structure. Another limit is the need of images with good baselines, i.e. an appropriate distribution around the object.

Figure 5. The dam of Cancano in Alta Valtellina (Italy)

Starting from these considerations, the modelling project was carried out with a laser scanner RIEGL LMS-Z420i. More than 10 scans were registered with retro-reflective targets, whose coordinates were measured with a geodetic network (Figure 6).

Some points were then measured on the dam to obtain a dense set of control points, which were used for monitoring applications. The final 3D model is a structured mesh of the dam, along with its surrounding area (Figure 7). This allowed different operators to extract other products, such as sections, orthophotos, slices, etc.

THE OPPOSITE SITUATION: AN IMAGE-BASED PROJECT

San Martino (Figure 8) is a mount close to the city of Lecco (Northern Italy). An innovative system based on MEMSs and geophones was installed to monitor the rock movement. At the beginning of this project, a 3D model was needed to find good locations for the sensors and estimate the length of connection cables. Then, these sensors were mounted by expert climbers (a radio connection between climbers and photogrammetrists allowed the correct positioning of all sensors close to the designed locations).

The final survey was carried out with a sequence of images taken with a calibrated camera (Nikon D700 mounting a Tamron 180 mm). A total of 23 images were acquired from the city. The perspective centres were measured with a GPS receiver installed on a special head (Figure 8). As can be seen, the camera-object distance is quite variable and, in some cases, superior to 1 km (Figure 9). Although a long-range laser scanner RIEGL LMS-Z420i was available, the maximum range does not exceed 800 m: a photogrammetric solution was the final choice.

The final sigma naught of bundle adjustment (Granshaw, 1980) was 0.33 pix (a priori sigma naught 1 pix, precision of image coordinates 1 pix) and the covariance matrix provided an average theoretical accuracy of the computed 3D object points of about ±8 cm (sufficient for this project). The final 3D model was extracted with dense image matching algorithms.

A COMBINED PROJECT

The previous examples demonstrated that sometimes the expert operator has to choose between images or laser scans. Other instruments (total station, GPS, ...) are instead extremely important to obtain georeferenced results, check the accuracy,

Figure 6. The geodetic network and some station points of the laser survey

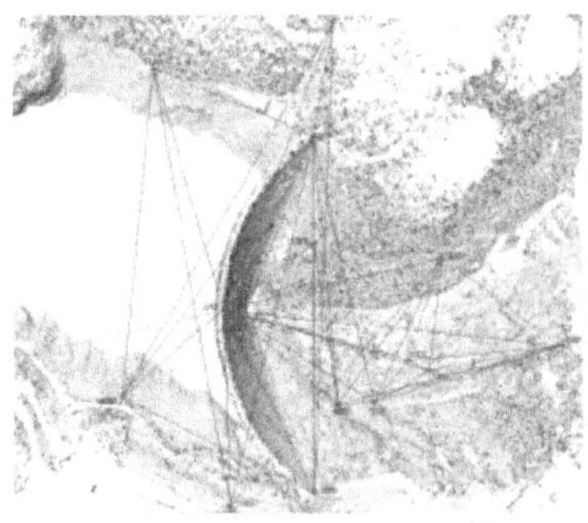
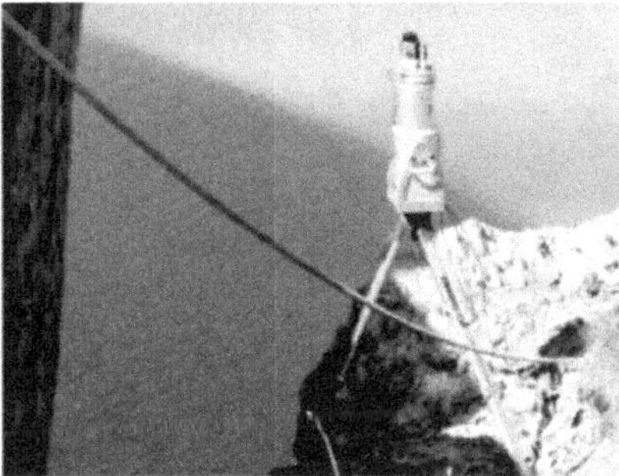

Figure 7. The multiple intersection scheme in front of the dam and the final 3D model with some drawings that were easily generated from global reconstruction

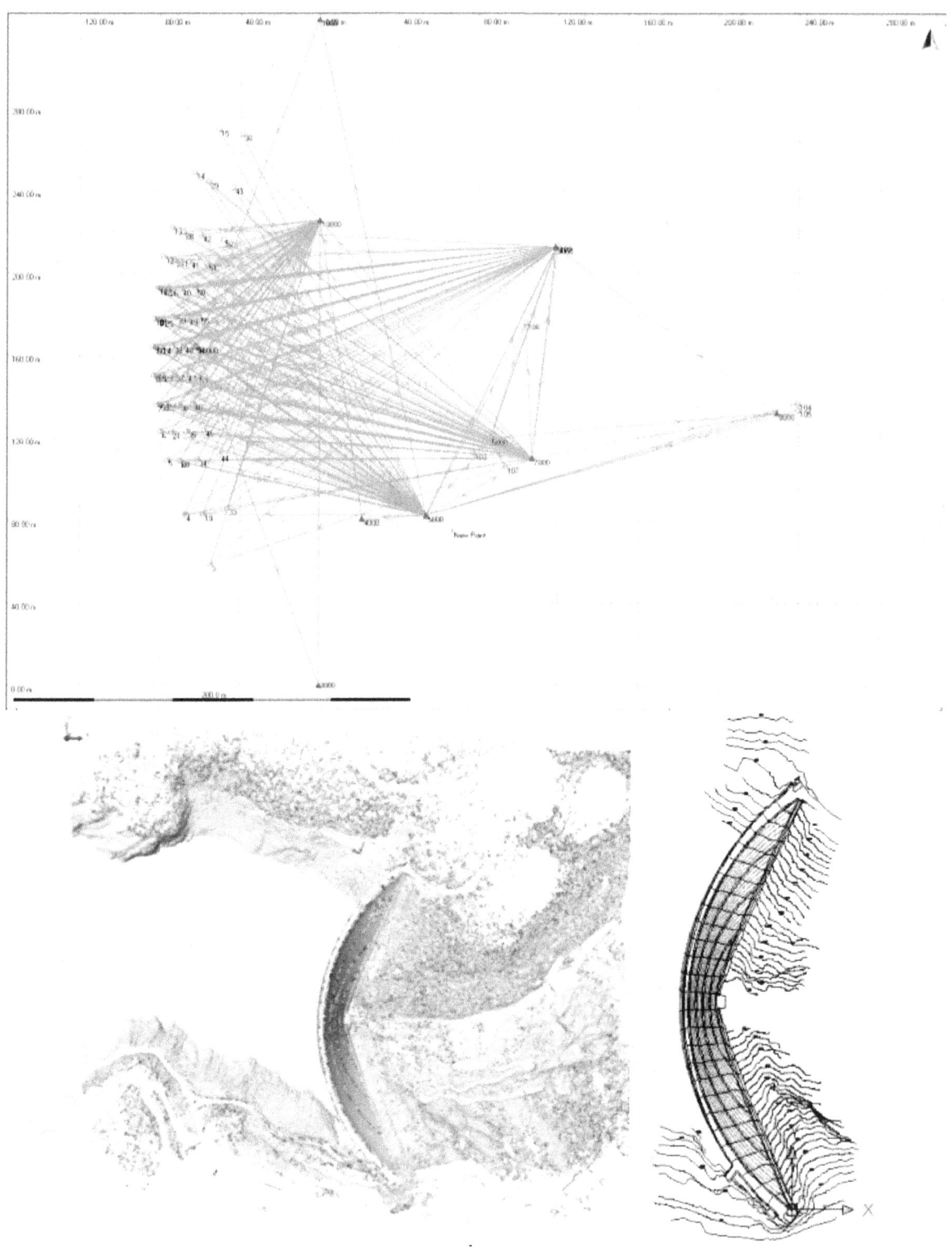

Figure 8. The mount S. Martino and the special head for image acquisition

Figure 9. The cartographic location of the images and the final 3D model

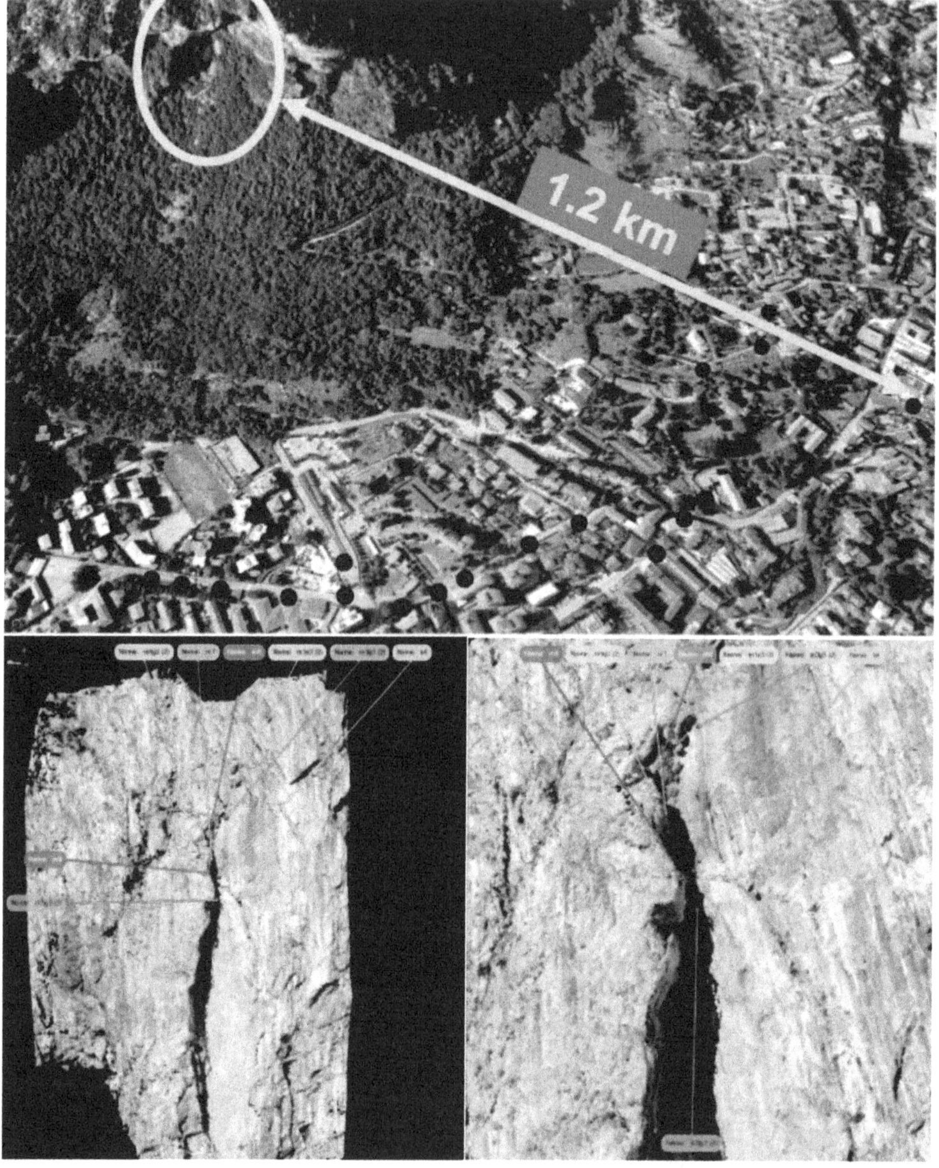

provide a stable reference system, etc. On the other hand, most real surveys need a combination of both laser scans and images because one single technique could be insufficient to complete the whole reconstruction.

Shown in Figure 10 is the lake of Cancano (Alta Valtellina, Italy). The highlighted slope (yellow circle) is periodically monitored by SAR and a 3D model was needed to simplify the visualization of this kind of data.

The survey was carried out by combining both photogrammetry and laser scanning (Figure 11). A preliminary laser scan was acquired from a point in the middle of the lake (during same days the artificial lake is partially empty and a small hill resurfaces). Then, 5 images taken from the opposite slope were included to complete the final model.

Another example is the reconstruction of the Basilica of S. Pietro al Monte (Civate, Italy - Fig-

Figure 10. The lake of Cancano and the slope to be monitored (left). Some points measured with a total station by using an intersection and then georeferenced with two GPS receivers placed on the station points (right)

Figure 11. The laser station point in the middle of the lake (left), the spatial location of 5 images taken from the opposite side of the mountain (middle), and the final 3D model (right)

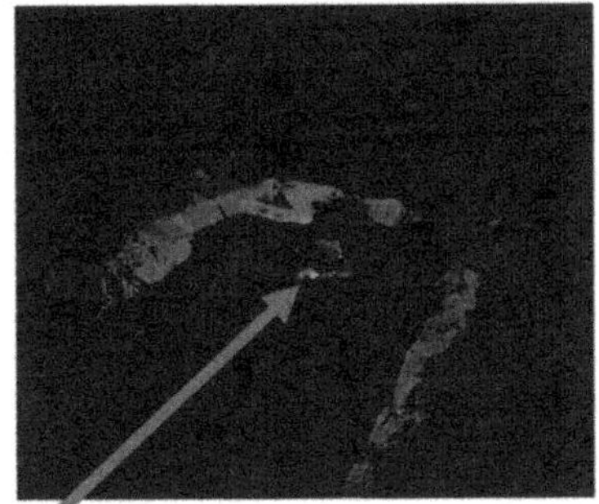

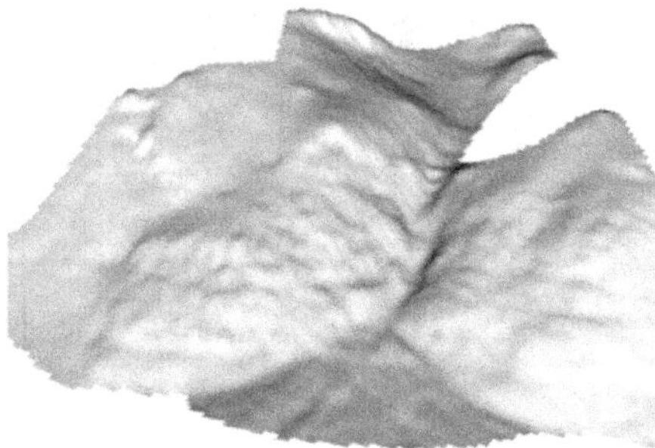

ure 12). Laser scanning technology allowed the acquisition of several scans and the production of a global model. Then, some portions were photogrammetrically modelled to obtain a better level of detail of important elements.

The last example is the metric reconstruction of the Padiglione Sud at Politecnico di Milano (Milan, Italy). A RGB orthophotos (Figure 13) was needed to offer a support for Infrared Thermography Analysis (Alba, Barazzetti, Rosina, Scaioni & Previtali, 2011) and was created with a laser survey and a set of oriented images projected onto the model.

CONCLUSION

The chapter presented some projects where images and laser scans were used to reconstruct different objects. The choice of the method depends on the

Figure 12. Top: the basilica of San Pietro al Monte (Civate, Italy) and the geodetic network (precision better than 3 mm). Middle: 5 images used to obtain a higher level of detail (needed for some specific elements). Bottom: the laser scans merged and visualized in Cinema 4D

customer's requests: sometimes images are better (and vice-versa) whereas other projects could require the integrated use of both methodologies. Other sensors, like GPS receivers and total stations, are also often necessary.

An important consideration deserve to be mentioned. According to the authors' experience, the field of surveying (or, in general, reality-based 3D modelling) comprehends an incredible number of possible practical situations. Accurate measurements are needed in a lot of scientific disciplines and have different purposes in terms of level of detail, object size, metric accuracy, etc. For this reason, it is extremely important to clarify the final aim right from the start of the project.

ACKNOWLEDGMENT

The examples discussed in this chapter were analysed by teams of expert operators. The survey of the dam was carried out by F. Roncoroni, whereas

Figure 13. Top: The laser scanning result, oriented images and final orthophoto

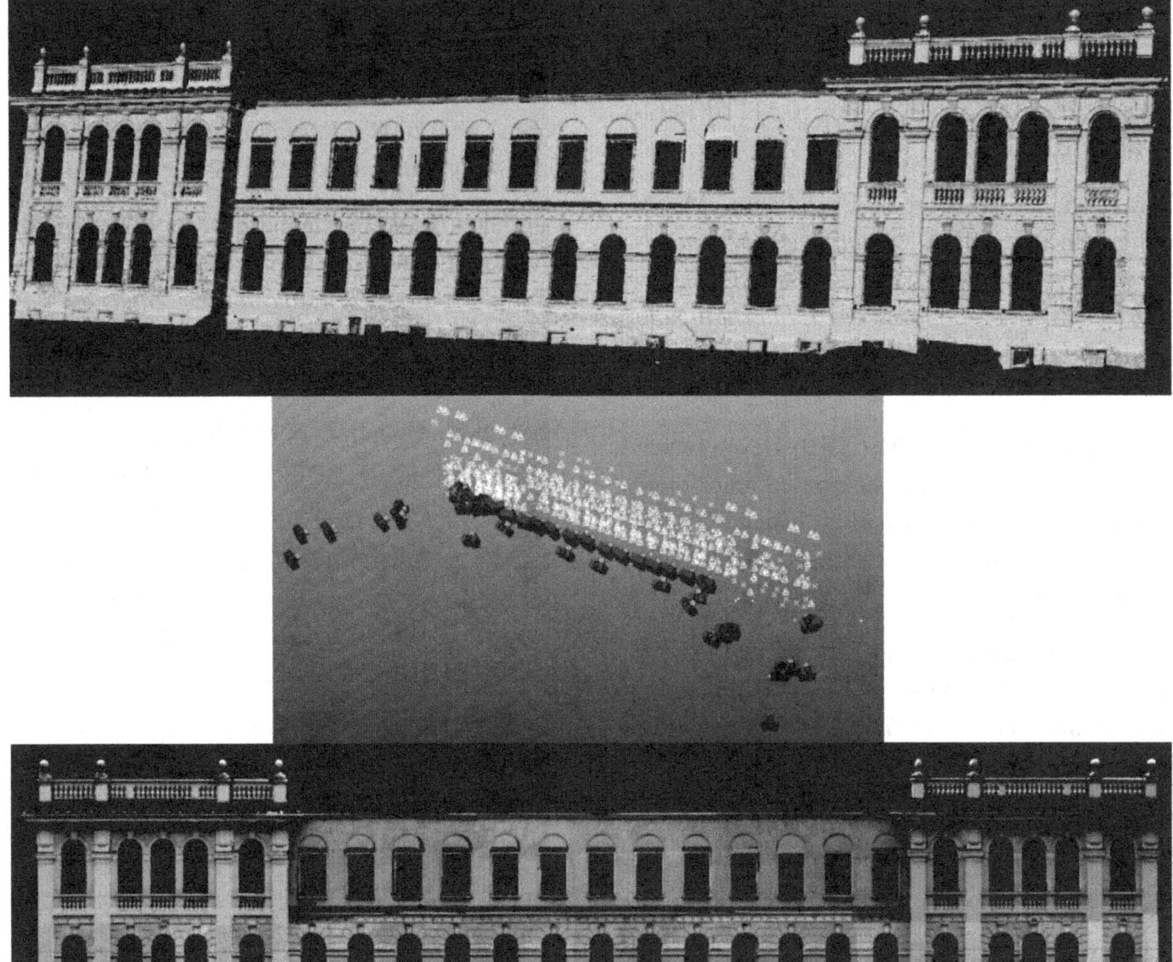

M. Alba and M. Previtali helped the authors for the churches of Santa Margherita and the basilica of S. Pietro. Acknowledgments also go to A. Giussani, F. Remondino, and J.P. Pons.

REFERENCES

Agarwal, S., et al. (2009). Building Rome in a day. In *Proceedings of International Conference on Computer Vision*. Kyoto, Japan: IEEE.

Alba, M., Barazzetti, L., Rosina, E., Scaioni, M., & Previtali, M. (2011). Mapping infrared data on terrestrial laser scanning 3D models of buildings. *Remote Sensing*, *3*(9), 1847–1870. doi:10.3390/rs3091847

Ang, K., & Mitchell, H. (2010). Non-rigid surface matching and its application to scoliosis modelling. *The Photogrammetric Record*, *25*(130), 105–118. doi:10.1111/j.1477-9730.2010.00581.x

Barazzetti, L., Remondino, F., & Scaioni, M. (2010). Orientation and 3D modelling from markerless terrestrial images: Combining accuracy with automation. *The Photogrammetric Record*, *25*(132), 356–381. doi:10.1111/j.1477-9730.2010.00599.x

Barazzetti, L., Roncoroni, F., Scaioni, M., & Remondino, F. (2011). *Automatische 3D modellierung von berghängen mit anwendung der terrestrischen photogrammetrie. 16. Internationale geodätische Woche, 13. bis 19.* Obergurgl - Ötztal / Tirol.

Barazzetti, L., & Scaioni, M. (2010). Development and implementation of image based algorithms for measurement of deformations in material testing. *Sensors (Basel, Switzerland)*, *10*, 7469–7495. doi:10.3390/s100807469 PMID:22163612

Besl, P., & McKay, N. (1992). A method for registration of 3-D shapes. *IEEE Transactions on Pattern Analysis and Machine Intelligence*, *14*(2), 239–256. doi:10.1109/34.121791

Fraser, C. (1996). Network design. In *Close Range Photogrammetry and Machine Vision*. Caithness: Whittles.

Furukawa, Y., Curless, B., Seitz, S., & Szeliski, R. (2010). Towards internet-scale multi-view stereo. In *Proceedings of IEEE Conference on Computer Vision and Pattern Recognition*. IEEE.

Granshaw, S. (1980). Bundle adjustment methods in engineering photogrammetry. *The Photogrammetric Record*, *10*(56), 181–207. doi:10.1111/j.1477-9730.1980.tb00020.x

Guidi, G. et al. (2009). A multi-resolution methodology for the 3D modeling of large and complex archeological areas. *International Journal of Architectural Computing*, *7*(1), 39–55. doi:10.1260/147807709788549439

Hartley, R., & Zisserman, A. (2004). *Multiple view geometry in computer vision*. Cambridge, UK: Cambridge University Press. doi:10.1017/CBO9780511811685

Kraus, K. (2008). *Photogrammetry: Geometry from images and laser scans*. Walter de Gruyter.

Luhmann, T., & Tecklenburg, W. (1992). Bundle orientation and 3-D object reconstruction from multiple-station panoramic imagery. *International Archives of Photogrammetry, Remote Sensing & Spatial. Information Sciences*, *34*, 181–186.

Mikhail, E., Bethel, J., & McGlone, J. (2001). *Introduction to modern photogrammetry*. Hoboken, NJ: John Wiley & Sons.

Nex, F., & Rinaudo, F. (2011). LiDAR or photogrammetry? Integration is the answer. *Italian Journal of Remote Sensing*, *43*(2), 107–121. doi:10.5721/ItJRS20114328

Roncella, R., Re, C., & Forlani, G. (2011). Performance evaluation of a structure and motion strategy in architecture and cultural heritage. *IAPRS&SIS*, *38*(5/W16).

Roncoroni, F. (2007). *Misura delle deformazioni di una diga con laser scanner terrestre*. (PhD Thesis). Politecnico di Milano, Milan, Italy.

Snyder, J. (1987). *Map projections – A working manual*. Washington, DC: United States Government Printing Office.

Spring, A., Peters, C., & Wetherelt, A. (2008). 3D laser scanning and its 2D partners. *Geoinformatics*, *11*, 50–54.

Strecha, C., Pylvanainen, T., & Fua, P. (2010). Dynamic and scalable large scale image reconstruction. In *Proceedings of CVPR'10*. CVPR.

Chapter 28
Differences between Role of Strong Ties and Weak Ties in Information Diffusion on Social Network Sites

Sanaz Kavianpour
Advanced Informatics School, Universiti Teknologi Malaysia, Kuala Lumpur, Malaysia

Zuraini Ismail
Advanced Informatics School, Universiti Teknologi Malaysia, Kuala Lumpur, Malaysia

Bharanidharan Shanmugam
Advanced Informatics School, Universiti Teknologi Malaysia, Kuala Lumpur, Malaysia

ABSTRACT

The popularity of Social Network Sites (SNSs) has increased recently. Social network sites provide platforms which operate based on exchanging information among users; therefore, information propagation is a significant topic in social networking researches. The goal of this chapter is to study the factors that have a significant role in information diffusion, then compare the role of ties in spreading information and evaluating the strength of ties. The result shows that, although strong ties have an important role, the likelihood of information diffusion by weak ties is higher.

INTRODUCTION

Nowadays many social interactions happen in online social networks; so huge amount of information is provided for social researchers on social networking sites. The number and the nature of information that are shared by social network users about different topics have a dramatic change by the growth of social networks.

People in online social networks share different information to others. Gross and Acquisiti stated that different information will be shared among

DOI: 10.4018/978-1-4666-4490-8.ch028

users based on the nature of social network sites. They argue that in most of the sites some sort of shared information is the same such as profile picture, demographic and interests. However, in match making sites the main focus is to share personal information, in business networking sites –such as LinkedIn the members tend to share professional information, and in personal publishing sites – e.g. Wordpress.com- people share their thoughts and ideas via blog posts (Gross, 2005).

Social Networking Sites (SNSs) are proficient and useful platforms which simplify the information diffusion. Once a user joins to a social network she will interconnect to other users via different types of relationships. Users share social data with other users which can be propagated to relevant users or not. Statistics from Facebook (Viswanath, et al, 2009) depicts that users have 130 friends on average. So if each friend of a user shares social data, a user will receive 130 social data that not all of them are relevant to her.

Flow of information in SNSs is huge and only a portion of this information is related to the users. Distinguishing the final audience of social data is difficult as controlling the social contexts which transfers among individuals, is not completely possible. But there are different rules which control social context in SNSs because individuals have main role in information propagation.

Propagation of information in social network sites has been addressed in recent researches due to its importance in epidemiology to understand its influence on social beliefs and extremism. Information propagation over the network depends on different elements such as users, information content, Diversity-bandwidth trade-offs, Type of the network, and the strength of ties and so on.

RELATED WORK

The communication technologies and facilities of social network sites enable users to connect to each other and to communicate more easily. These features make information propagation through social network sites one of the major subjects of the recent studies. Researchers have done study on information dissemination on social network sites from different point of view.

Brown and Reingen (1987) studied an interpersonal network with few users to evaluate the ties strength. Valente (1995, 1996) proposed critical mass models to create social systems in order to acquire rate of information diffusion. Granovetter (1973) depicted the strength of weak ties in spreading new information. Barabási (2002) stated the role of network hubs or opinion leaders in information diffusion and illustrated their relation with the scale-free properties in networks.

INFORMATION DIFFUSION

A social process in which innovation is communicated and information is rebroadcasted via channels overtime among members of a social system is a diffusion of information. Information diffusion is different from information creation. The process of information propagation varies by different factors. For example, some nodes in social networks are called as opinion leaders that mean they are the centre of information flow and they have effect on other nodes (Canright, Engø-Monsen & Weltzien, 2004). On social network sites, by capturing the users' friend list the active user can be find, and this user can be considered as opinion leader to be used in order to spread information. Some factors that have role in information diffusion are as following.

Users

Jenkins emphasizes on the role of end users in information diffusion. In information spreading end users have main role while in virus spreading users are just passive carriers without any choice to infect others or not (Magnani & Rossi, 2011). In information propagation, beside which cultural context has more chance to be spread how it is going to be spread by users in SNSs is also important and this depicts that there is difference among exposition, contagion and spreading of information. Users who expose and spread cultural context are considerably different from users who contaminate viral context.

Information Content

A rumor about an opinion or political idea can spread among any of the user of a certain node but a gossip usually spread among people who are directly connected to the certain node (Lind, et al., 2007). This correlation is not related to social influence processes. Basically it depends on the interestingness of the content among a group of friends, so as the content is more interesting it is more likely to be shared among friends. If the content is not popular, the diffusion of it depends on the friend relations. On the other hand, different contents follow various time-trends, as an example an emotional post on social media will receive huge amount of comments by users' friend but it also ends in a very short time while news post will receive less comments but it lasts longer on social network sites.

Diversity-Bandwidth Trade-offs

Bandwidth is the rate of information that broadcast per unit of time. According to Aral's theory there is the trade-off between diversity and bandwidth in dissemination of novel information (Aral & Van Alstyne, 2010). When users have close relation there is lack of diversity in the information, and when they have far relation their communication is not strong.

Type of the Network

Different kinds of online information such as news or videos frequently broaden via networks from one service to another. For example, YouTube users connect via friendship links that let them know and watch others posted videos, but once these videos posted on Facebook it will reach high visibility and as a result of that its propagation will increase.

The Strength of Ties

Relations with relatives or close friends are known as strong ties, and relations with far contacts are known as weak ties. Closeness, emotional intensity of a relation and the time spend together used to calculate strength of a tie. Normally social networks include different groups of users that are connected to each other via ties that are known as bridges. Grannoveter's stated that weak ties act as bridges while strong ties are inside groups (Granovetter, 1983). He stated that weak ties have main role in diffusion of new information. Weak ties make connection among different groups in a network so they gain information from one group and spread it to others. On the other hand, the accessibility to new information makes weak ties good targets to be referenced by other ties.

COMPARISON AMONG WEAK TIES AND STRONG TIES

In 1973, Granovetter stated that the probabilities of acquiring job through individuals who people interact with them less than their close contacts are high [8]. People frequently interact with their close friends so they form a dense cluster of strong ties, and as they connect to each other in this cluster the available information propagate among them quickly.

To discover the flow of general types of information in social network sites, besides how people are connected, the commonalities that improve the spread of information should be considered. The tendency to stay with similar people is known as homophily (A. Grabowicz, et al., 2012). This means that individuals are eager to connect with almost similar people such as same classmates, professions and other associations. According to homophily, strong ties have more interact and they are similar, so the information that they use is almost the same. In contrary, weak ties have less interaction and they are dissimilar, so they use different and new information. Weak ties are as bridges which connect strong ties from different clusters.

The probability of sharing the similar information by strong ties is more than weak ties as strong ties are close contacts that are similar to each other so the shared content by them is more interesting among them. And also strong ties are more influential, therefore they are able to convince close contacts to spread information.

The chance of sharing information among strong ties is high while the number of strong ties is low, so the likelihood of sharing information will be low. In contrary, the chance of sharing information among weak ties is low while the number of weak ties is high, so the likelihood of sharing information will be high. This result describes that although strong ties have main role in sharing similar information, the role of weak ties is much more significant in spreading novel information. In the following section, we propose a social network to evaluate the amount of information sharing via strong and weak ties.

EVALUATE THE LIKELIHOOD OF INFORMATION SHARING VIA TIES

We considered social network as a weighted graph G (N, E) in which N is the number of nodes that indicates a user and E is the number of edges which indicates the relation between nodes. We divided the graph into clusters that each cluster

Table 1. The likelihood of sharing information in two clusters

Cluster	Likelihood of Information Sharing	Amount of Information Sharing
Cluster (1)	Strong Ties: 3/10 = 0.3	0.3*10 = 3
	Weak Ties: 4/19 = 0.21	0.21*19 = 3.99
Cluster (2)	Strong Ties: 3/6 = 0.5	0.5*6 = 3
	Weak Ties: 3/15 = 0.2	0.2*15 = 3

Figure 1. Two Clusters of Social Graph with their Ties: Black Circles are Weak Ties, Green circles are active weak ties, red circles are strong ties and purple circles are active strong ties

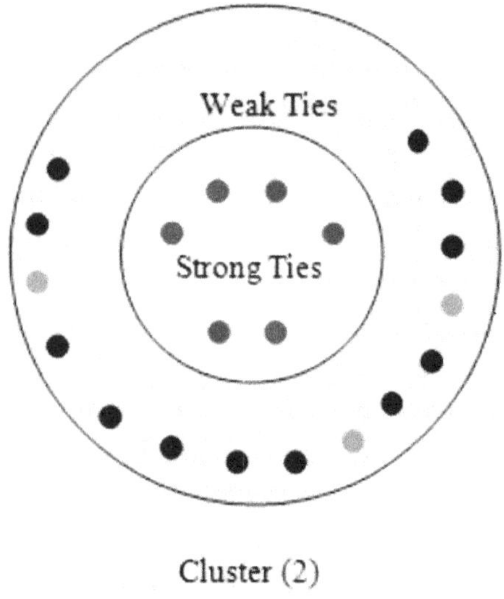

Cluster (2)

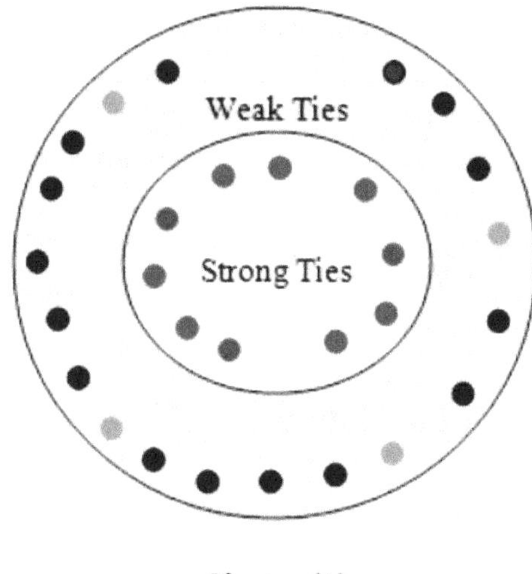

Cluster (1)

has its own strong ties and weak ties. The weights of each node is the likelihood of users' reply to another users which is depicted by [0, 1] interval.

Once user shares content, feedback from it can be used in order to obtain interaction between users and to calculate the probability of the information propagation. The information diffusion varies based on the number of strong and weak ties. And it can be calculated base on the following formula:

$$\mathrm{IS}(s) = N(S \mid A) \, / \, N(S) \quad (1)$$

$$\mathrm{IS}\ (\mathrm{w}) = N\left(W|A\right) / \, N(W) \quad (2)$$

IS(s) indicates the chance of information sharing that can be calculated by dividing the number of active strong or active weak ties by the total number of the strong or weak ties. The following table shows some results based on the Figure 1.

The results depict that the probability of sharing information via weak ties are more than strong ties and this probability has a direct relation with number of weak ties also. It means that as the number of weak ties increase the probability of spreading information will increase.

CONCLUSION AND FUTURE WORK

The popularity of Online Social Networks has increased during last decade and many people use these sites to communicate and propagate information. In this chapter we depicts that information propagation on social network sites varies by many factors, therefore studying and collecting all factors in order to cover all of them in one network is not an easy task. We depict that among all the significant factors, users play an important role in information diffusion. Users which are considered as strong and weak ties can change the amount of information sharing depend on their numbers, their strength and also depend on the information content. Therefore, controlling them from different aspects such as the number and the strength can be used in order to manage the received information to rebroadcast or block it. We observed that information spreading is changing over time. To estimate the at least time that is required for information to be propagate via different ties is subject of our future work.

REFERENCES

Aral, S., & Van Alstyne, M. (2010). The diversity-bandwidth tradeoff. *American Journal of Sociology*.

De Choudhury, M., et al. (2010). *Birds of a feather: Does user homophily impact information diffusion in social media?* Retrieved from http://cds.cern.ch/record/1270905?ln=it

Grabowicz, P. et al. (2012). Social features of online networks: The strength of intermediary ties in online social media. *PLoS ONE, 7*.

Granovetter, M. (1983). The strength of weak ties: A network theory revisited. *American Journal of Sociology*, *1*, 201–233.

Gross, R. (2005). Information revelation and privacy in online social networks. In *Proceedings of the 2005 ACM Workshop on Privacy in the Electronic Society*, (pp. 71-80). ACM.

Lind, G., et al. (2007). *Spreading gossip in social networks*. Retrieved from http://www.comphys.ethz.ch/hans/p/449.pdf

Magnani, M., & Rossi, L. (2011). The ML-model for multi-layer social networks. In *Proceedings of International Conference on Advances in Social Networks Analysis and Mining*, (pp. 5-12). IEEE.

Viswanath, B., et al. (2009). On the evolution of user interaction in Facebook. In *Proceedings of the 2nd ACM Workshop on Online Social Networks*, (pp. 37-42). New York: ACM Press.

Chapter 29
Degree of Similarity of Web Applications

Doru Anastasiu Popescu
Faculty of Mathematics and Computer Science, University of Pitesti, Romania

Dragos Nicolae
National College "Radu Greceanu" – Slatina, Romania

ABSTRACT

In this chapter, the authors present a way of measuring the similarity between two Web applications. For this, they define the degree of similarity between two Web applications, taking into account only the Webpages composed of HTML tags. The authors also introduce an algorithm used to calculate this value, its implementation being made in the Java programming language.

INTRODUCTION

Web applications have a vast usage and a fast evolution. Consequently, various models have been created in view of web applications, especially used for verification and testing, such as those presented in (Alalfi, Cordy & Dean, 2008). The extensive development of these applications requires a mechanism for measuring their quality, these aspects having been studied in many papers, such as (Cheng-ying & Yan-sheng, 2006; Sreedhar, Chari & Ramana, 2010; Popescu & Szabo, 2010; Popescu, 2011; Popescu & Danauta, 2011). This chapter aims to determine an algorithm of measuring the similarity between two web applications. Another method of measuring the similarity between web applications has been introduced in (Popescu & Danauta, 2011) and it uses a relation between the web pages of an application, relation taken from (Popescu & Szabo, 2010; Popescu, 2011; Popescu & Danauta 2012). The formula we introduce (section 2) does not use this relation. It is based on comparing the tags of two web pages, using an algorithm for determining a common subsequence for two strings of tags. The algorithm which calculates the similarity degree is presented in section 3.

DOI: 10.4018/978-1-4666-4490-8.ch029

The implementation and the results obtained with this algorithm are presented in section 4.

THE DEGREE OF SIMILARITY

Let WA1 and WA2 be two web applications. The application WA1 is considered to be composed of the web pages $p_1, p_2, \ldots, p_n$ and the application WA2 composed of the web pages $q_1, q_2, \ldots, q_m$. We will also establish a set TG of tags.

For a web page p_i we build a sequence with all its tags, excluding those which are also in TG, keeping their order and removing their attributes.

Definition 1

For two sequences of tags T_1 and T_2, associated to the web pages p_i from WA1 and q_j from WA2, we define the degree of similarity between p_i and q_j, written nr_{ij}, as being the number equal to the maximum length of a common subsequence of tags for T_1 and T_2.

Definition 2

For a web page p from WA1, we define de similarity degree of p with WA2 as being the number: *degpage*(p,WA2)=k/NT, where $k=\max\{nr_{ij} \mid 0 < j < m+1\}$, NT is the number of tags from p which are not in TG and i is an index, $0 < i < n+1$ for which $p=p_i$.

Definition 3

We define the degree of similarity between WA1 and WA2 as being the number: *deg*(WA1,WA2)=s/n, where s=*degpage*(p_1,WA2) + *degpage*(p_2,WA2) + ... + *degpage*(p_n,WA2).

Remark 1: 0< *deg*(WA1,WA2) ≤ 1.
Remark 2: If *deg*(WA1,WA2) = 1, then for any web page p_i from WA1, there is a web page q_j in WA2 so that T_1 is a subsequence of T_2, where T_1 is the sequence of tags from p_i, which are not in TG, and T_2 is the sequence of tags from q_j, which are not in TG.

Example

Let us consider the set TG={<HTML>, </HTML>, <HEAD>, </HEAD>, <TITLE>, </TITLE>, <BODY>, </BODY>}, the web application WA1 composed of the web pages p1 and p2, as well as the web application WA2 composed of the web pages q1, q2 and q3. The files P1.html, P2.html for p1, p2 and Q1.html, Q2.html, Q3.html for q1, q2 and q3 are as shown in Box 1.

We obtain the following results:

The sequences of tags, which are not in TG, for each web page:

```
Tp1=(<B>, </B>, <IMG>)
Tp2=(<I>, </I>, <BR>, <BR>, <IMG>)
Tq1=(<B>, </B>)
Tq2=(<I>, </I>)
Tq3=(<I>, </I>, <BR>, <BR>, <IMG>)
nr11=2; nr12=0; nr13=1
nr21=0; nr22=2; nr23=5
degpage(p1, WA2)=2/3=0.66
degpage(p2, WA2)=5/5=1
deg(WA1,WA2)=0.83
```

THE ALGORITHM

Using the notations from the previous sections, we will present the algorithm that calculates the degree of similarity between two web applications.

Input Data

- The path of the file containing the set of tags TG
- The path of application1
- The path of application2

Box 1.

```
P1.html
<HTML> <HEAD>
<TITLE>Web page p1</TITLE>
</HEAD>
<BODY>
<B> Picture 1 </B> <IMG SRC="pic1.
jpg">
</BODY> </HTML>
P2.html
<HTML> <HEAD>
<TITLE>Web page p2</TITLE>
</HEAD>
<BODY>
<I> Picture 1 </I>
<BR> <BR>
<IMG SRC="pic1.jpg">
</BODY> </HTML>
Q1.html
<HTML> <HEAD>
<TITLE>Web page q1</TITLE>
</HEAD>
<BODY> <B> AAAAAAAA </B>
</BODY> </HTML>
Q2.html
<HTML> <HEAD>
<TITLE>Web page q2</TITLE>
</HEAD>
<BODY> <I> BBBBBBBB </I>
</BODY> </HTML>
Q3.html
<HTML> <HEAD>
<TITLE>Web page q3</TITLE>
</HEAD>
<BODY>
<I> CCCCCCCCC </I>
<BR> <BR>
<IMG SRC="pppp.jpg">
</BODY> </HTML>
```

Used Data Structures

- **Tags:** A string vector with the tags from TG
- **files1, files2:** String vectors with the paths of each application's web pages (files1 for WA1 and files2 for WA2)
- **pages1, pages2:** String vectors with the tags from each application's web pages, which are not included in TG (pages1 for WA1 and pages2 for WA2)
- **degp:** A vector with the degree of similarity of each page from WA1 with WA2

Output Data

- The degree of similarity of WA1 with WA2
- A text file with the number of files and the number of web pages for each application

The steps of the algorithm are shown in Algorithm 1.

Remark 2: To determine the value of the variable v from the previous algorithm, we have used the dynamic programming technique (the algorithm for determining the longest common subsequence for the two data sequence (Cormen, Leiserson, Rivest & Stein, 1990).

IMPLEMENTATION

The implementation of the algorithms from section 3 builds the sequences of tags for each web page, without taking into account their attributes. Next we will present the results obtained for two web sites using the tags shown in Box 2 for the TG set:

The chart from Figure 1 presents the values obtained for the degree of similarity between the

Algorithm 1.

```
while there are unread tags in TG.txt do
     read a tag
     delete tag's attributes
     add the tag to the vector tags
end while
memorize the paths of the web pages from WA1 in files1
memorize the paths of the web pages from WA2 in files2
for i=1, n do
     while there are unread tags in files1_i do
          read a tag
          delete tag's attributes
          if the tag does not exist in tags then
               concatenate the tag to pages1_i
          end if
     end while
end for
for i=1, m do
     while there are unread tags in files2_i do
          read a tag
          delete tag's attributes
          if the tag does not exist in tags then
               concatenate the tag to pages2_i
          end if
     end while
end for
for i=1, n do
     degp_i=0
     NT=the number of tags from p_i which are not in TG
     for j=1,m do
          v=the length of the longest common subsequence
              of tags for the web pages p_i and q_j
          if v/NT > degp_i then
               degp_i=v/NT
          end if
     end for
end for
s=0
for i=1, n do
     s=s+degp_i
end for
print s/n
```

Box 2.

```
TG1=Ø
TG2={<p>, </p>, <B>, </B>}
TG3={<p>, </p>, <B>, </B>, <i>, </i>, <u>, </u>}
TG4={<p>, </p>, <B>, </B>, <i>, </i>, <u>, </u>, <meta>, <script>, </script>,
<br>, <pre>, </pre>, <center>, </center>}
TG5={<p>, </p>, <B>, </B>, <i>, </i>, <u>, </u>, <meta>, <script>, </script>,
<br>, <pre>, </pre>, <center>, </center>, <hr>, <style>, </style>}
TG6={<p>, </p>, <B>, </B>, <i>, </i>, <u>, </u>, <meta>, <script>, </script>,
<br>, <pre>, </pre>, <center>, </center>, <hr>, <style>, </style>, <img>,
<font>, </font>}
TG7={<p>, </p>, <B>, </B>, <i>, </i>, <u>, </u>, <meta>, <script>, </script>,
<br>, <pre>, </pre>, <center>, </center>, <hr>, <style>, </style>, <img>,
<font>, </font>, <strong>, </strong>, <small>, </small>}
TG8={<p>, </p>, <B>, </B>, <i>, </i>, <u>, </u>, <meta>, <script>, </script>,
<br>, <pre>, </pre>, <center>, </center>, <hr>, <style>, </style>, <img>,
<font>, </font>, <strong>, </strong>, <small>, </small>, <h1>, </h1>, <h2>, </
h2>, <h3>, </h3>}
TG9={<p>, </p>, <B>, </B>, <i>, </i>, <u>, </u>, <meta>, <script>, </script>,
<br>, <pre>, </pre>, <center>, </center>, <hr>, <style>, </style>, <img>,
<font>, </font>, <strong>, </strong>, <small>, </small>, <h1>, </h1>, <h2>, </
h2>, <h3>, </h3>, <h4>, </h4>, <h5>, </h5>}
TG10={<p>, </p>, <B>, </B>, <i>, </i>, <u>, </u>, <meta>, <script>, </script>,
<br>, <pre>, </pre>, <center>, </center>, <hr>, <style>, </style>, <img>,
<font>, </font>, <strong>, </strong>, <small>, </small>, <h1>, </h1>, <h2>, </
h2>, <h3>, </h3>, <h4>, </h4>, <h5>, </h5>, <h6>, </h6>}
```

two web applications used for testing. The one from Figure 2 presents the execution time of the program, used for the same web applications. The TG set is different from one test to another.

In order to have a relevant interpretation of the results, TG sets used for testing meet the following condition:

$TG1 \subseteq TG2 \subseteq TG3 \subseteq TG4 \subseteq TG5 \subseteq TG6 \subseteq TG7 \subseteq TG8 \subseteq TG9 \subseteq TG10$

CONCLUSION

The method of calculating the degree of similarity between two Web applications in this chapter creates a measurement mechanism for the technical novelty brought by a web application compared to other Web applications. We consider that there might also be other formulas that could reflect the facts studied in this chapter as accurately as possible.

Figure 1. The chart with the values of the degree of similarity obtained by the program

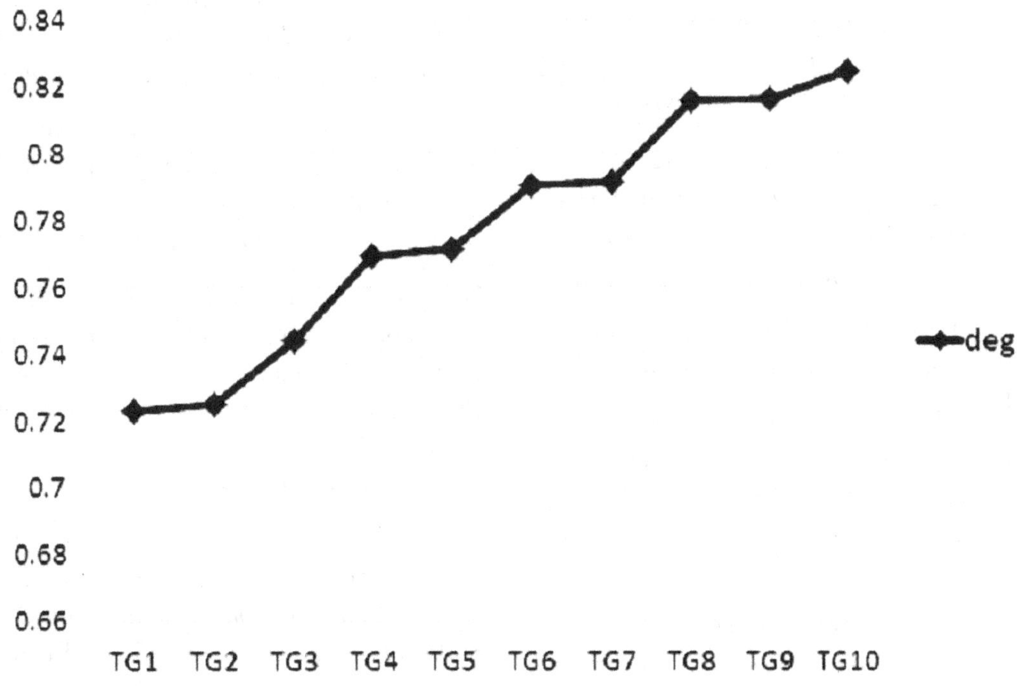

Figure 2. The chart with the execution time of the program

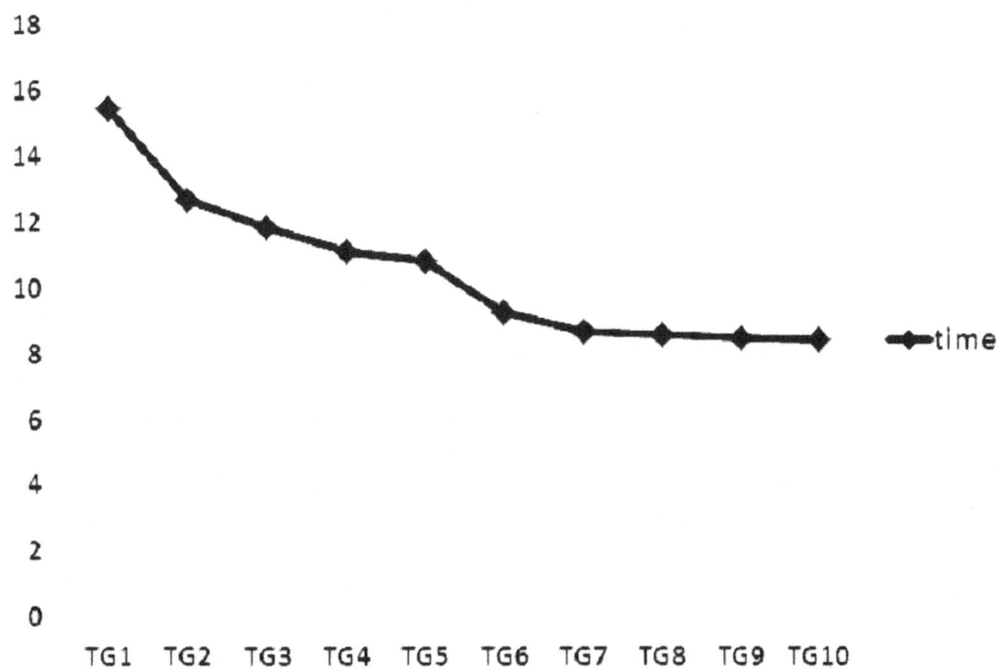

REFERENCES

Alalfi, M., Cordy, J., & Dean, T. (2008). *Modeling methods for web application verification and testing: State of art*. New York: John Wiley.

Cheng-Ying, M., & Yan-Sheng, L. (2006). A method for measuring the structure complexity of web application. *Wuhan University Journal of Natural Sciences, 11*(1).

Cormen, T., Leiserson, C., Rivest, R., & Stein, C. (1990). *Introduction to algorithms*. Cambridge, MA: MIT Press.

Popescu, D. (2011). Measuring the quality of the navigation in web sites using the cloning relation. *Analele Universitatii Spiru Haret. Seria Matematica-Informatica*, *7*(1), 5–10.

Popescu, D. (2011). Sink web pages in web application. In *Proceedings of IAPR TC3 Workshop on Partially Supervised Learning (PSL2011)* (LNCS), (vol. 7081, pp. 154-158). Berlin: Springer.

Popescu, D., & Danauta, C. (2011). Similarity measurement of web sites using sink web pages. In *Proceedings of 34th International Conference on Telecommunications and Signal Processing*. IEEE.

Popescu, D., & Danauta, C. (2012). Verification of the web applications using sink web pages. *International Journal of Computer Science Research and Application*, *2*(1), 63–68.

Popescu, D., Danauta, C., & Szabo, Z. (2010). A method of measuring the complexity of a web application from the point of view of cloning. In *Proceedings of 5th International Conference on Virtual Learning, Section Models and Methodologies*, (pp. 186-181). IEEE.

Popescu, D., & Szabo, Z. (2010). Sink web pages of web application. In *Proceedings of 5th International Conference on Virtual Learning*, Section Software Solutions, (pp. 375-380). IEEE.

Sreedhar, G., Chari, A., & Ramana, V. (2010). Measuring qualitz of web site navigation. *Journal of Theoretical and Applied Information Technology*, *14*(2), 80–86.

Chapter 30
Museum Information and Communicability Evaluation

Francisco V. Cipolla-Ficarra
ALAIPO – AINCI, Spain and Italy

Jim Carré
University of The Netherlands Antilles, Curaçao

Alejandra Quiroga
Universidad Nacional de La Pampa, Argentina

Jacqueline Alma
Electronic Arts – Vancouver, Canada

Miguel Cipolla-Ficarra
ALAIPO – AINCI, Spain and Italy

ABSTRACT

The authors present the first results of a heuristic analysis of the evolution of the commercial off-line systems related to the main European museums. The analysis is diachronic, that is, since 1990, and includes the different modalities of interactive design in the different supports for interactive information, such as floppy, CD, and DVD. The authors also present a methodology for the analysis of the presentation of the paintings and sculptures inside these systems called Museum Information and Communicability Evaluation (MICE).

INTRODUCTION

The history of the off-line multimedia systems in the 90s gave a boost to many sole proprietor companies (a single person in the ruling board) in Southern Europe devoted to the commercial production of interactive contents. Those were small businesses with fewer than five employees, including the owner of the company. In that group there were technicians and artists. This division was typical of Latin countries such as Spain, Portugal, France and Italy, just to mention a few examples. The technicians were the programmers who mainly used commercial products such as MacroMedia Director (MMDirector) or Toolbook.

There are scarce examples of that time where C++ programming was used to carry out those interactive systems. The artists, as a rule, stemming from the fine arts. Took care of the visual design, the textual content, etc. Few were the artists who hailed from the environment of the graphical arts for those multimedia systems. The commercial

DOI: 10.4018/978-1-4666-4490-8.ch030

head, who sometimes was the very owner of the single-member company, worked on grabbing the attention of the museums to publish in multimedia support the total or partial contents of their halls. Evidently, who got that authorization earned an interesting prestige in the marketing and institutional image, with regard to the competition inside his commercial productive sector. The problem lay in strengthening the human team to carry out the project within the convened schedule. The solution was to foist this commercial project on the public and/or private universities under the formula of R&D transfer. That is, part of the members of the university structures worked for small businessmen for whom the commercial factor prevailed over scientific research, in an avant-garde sector such as was off-line multimedia and later on online multimedia. This is how the students directly or indirectly related to the multimedia sector, such as can be graphic computing, systems engineering, software engineering, etc., were working for private businesses, many times disguised as final study projects or master of PhD thesis (Cipolla-Ficarra, 2010). The truth is that all this workplace chicanery from that time has not worked to lay the foundations of a great audiovisual sector, not only in those countries, but inside the European continent. Both the commercial software and the hardware used by the artists, technicians, salesmen, etc. had their patents registered at the other side of the Atlantic, that is, the American continent, although the fabrication of the computers, printers, scanners, etc., was made in Asia. The only European element was the content of the multimedia system that referred to the works of art in Europe.

FAILINGS IN SOFTWARE ENGINEERING IN EUROPE

The lack of a strong audiovisual industry aimed at the museums, the promotion of cultural and natural heritage, tourism, makes apparent the lack of vision in the future in the short, middle and long term inside the university educational sector computer-multimedia in the 90s. When we speak of computer science in the current work, we mean the engineering titles or computer science degrees as such, software and systems. In the mistaken cognitive models of the members of the formal sciences of that time, that is, mathematicians, physicists, chemists, industrial, electronic, telecommunications, etc. the contents of the European museums had to be transferred to the off-line multimedia systems by the members of the fine arts faculties, using commercial applications. The exception to that premise would be the multimedia videogames sector (Cipolla-Ficarra, 2012).

However, it was another sector which from the computer science faculties of European South which did not interest anybody at the beginning or mid 90s. Aside from this reality, this was a sector that quickly resorted to the use of programming languages. The main goal was to access the databases and manage animated and audio graphics in the least time and with the highest quality, at the moment where the users interact with the interactive systems. The speed of access to the multimedia information was influenced by the speed of the processor of the personal computers, the graphic cards, the audio cards, the memory capacity, etc. that is, the hardware component. Not for nothing many users of multimedia systems oriented to the cultural heritage constantly kept on swapping personal computers to be able to have a better interaction with the dynamic contents in the CD-ROMs –animations, videos and audio (Styliaras, G., et al., 2010). From the point of view of interactive design they resorted to a set of strategies to solve those problems, for instance, the no full screen vision of the video or the animations.

FAILINGS OF INTERACTIVE DESIGN IN THE FIRST COMMERCIAL PRODUCTS

If we take, for example, one of the first commercial multimedia systems, such as Art Gallery by

Microsoft (The Collection of the National Gallery –London) the animations were reduced and focused on the analysis of some works (Art Gallery CD-ROM, 1995). For instance, in paintings such as The Baptism of Christ, The Martyrdom of St. Sebastian, The Embarkation of the Queen of Sheba, we can see the first mistakes in the interactive design, at the moment of activating the animations, also called analysis or painting. That redundancy in the screens of inserting keys to activate the same animation generated disorientation and besides a communicability problem between the user and the multimedia system. In other words, it is not correct to resort to two options, one to activate the animation through a key called analysis or animation and another which reinitiates the animation through the painting option. The resetting of a dynamic means as in this case animation consists in leaving the animation in the first frame of the sequence it makes up. However, these two keys are not present in all the nodes of a guided link which contain animations. Next three examples of sequential nodes inside the guided link "composition and perspective".

Upon pressing on the animation option three lines of perspective are drawn on the painting as can be seen in Figure 2 (in Appendix). When the animation ends these lines disappear, and the painting goes back to the original state, that is, in the first frame of the animation. The analysis option serves to activate the animation and painting to go back to the original state, in other words, the first animation frame.

There are also failings in the reusability of static information. Inside the paintings collection there are numerous nodes that have been reused and which do not correctly adapt to the new context. There are nodes where the name of the painter appears in the first component of a collection and not in the rest, as is the case of the Martyrdom of St. Sebastian in the upper left margin of the Figures 5 and 6 (in Appendix) belong to different nodes collections. For instance, in the Figure 5 (in Appendix) of the paintings collection is the name of the painter and the date in which it was created.

All these failings of the interactive design at the time were mistakenly related with the usability of the system, especially in an era called the software quality era. One of the main goals of software engineering was to improve the quality of the products and/or systems. However, from the point of view of design, this notion is presented in a myriad occasions in an ambiguous manner. This is because as Fenton contends, both the quality and the notion of beauty are in the eyes of the beholders (Fenton, 1997).

TOWARDS MICE: MUSEUM INFORMATION AND COMMUNICABILITY EVALUATION

First of all it is necessary to consider the basic hardware elements for a multimedia system to work. In this regard we will focus on the Le Louvre museum and we will see through different examples the evolution of the hardware for the CD-Rom and DVD. In the CD-Rom Le Louvre 1995, made with MMDirector, it could work with a compatible IBM PC or a Macintosh (Le Louvre CD-ROM, 1995). The minimal configuration required in the PC environment is 386SX, 4 Mb. RAM (ideal 8 Mb), CD-Rom drive, VGA 256 screen, mouse and Windows 3.1. Any LCIII Macintosh or a more powerful device with at least 3.5 Mb RAM available for the application, CD-Rom drive, 256 screen of 13 inches or greater, operative system 7 or a later one. A couple of years later, the same product was distributed for free accompanying some newspapers in Barcelona but in two CD-ROMs. Besides, the minimal configuration of hardware had been boosted in the PC environment, for instance. DX 486 processor or higher, Windows 3.1 or Windows 95, 8 Mb RAM, 3 Mb available in the hard disk, screen 640x480, 32000 colors minimum, CD-Rom driver at double speed, blaster sound card or compatible, Microsoft mouse or compatible (this additional is striking, from the point of view of hardware, by inserting the brand of a mouse, when at that time practically nobody did it in the commercial multimedia systems). In other words, the passing of time had made apparent that one thing are the minimal requisites for the installation and another is the correct functioning of the system, where the time of response in the human computer interaction should be a few seconds. Later on, with the new millennium that very same museum would be presented in DVD support (Museo del Louvre DVD, 2012), where the technical data can be summed up in the following way: video format, 16/9, audio, stereo, DVD-PAL type, region 2. Evidently, a commercial product which can also work in the personal computer but the minimal characteristics for its connection to a DVD reader are no longer indicated. Perhaps the reason lies in the current expansion of computer systems which allow the connection to a DVD reader Tablet PC, multimedia mobile phones, note books, etc.

In the first set of products in CD-Rom support there is no commercial device which allows its correct functioning in the current computer systems, both from the point of view of the software and hardware. Consequently, they are commercial products which implicitly carried with them a sell-by date, such as has been the breakthrough of hardware towards multimedia microcomputing. Nevertheless, no producer or manufacturer had warned the user, at the moment of the purchase of the multimedia system. In the second set, that is, DVD, theoretically these problems are overcome. Nonetheless, the same as with the CD-Rom, there is a constant tendency to insert the works of art, in this case grouped in the museums in the avant-garde interactive supports, whether online or offline.

All these aspects of hardware and software make up a quality attribute which is called compatibility, inside the set of categories which make up the design of an interactive system, such as: content, presentation, navigation, structure, panchronism, etc. The reader interested in these categories of design may look up the following references (Styliaras, et al., 2010; Cipolla-Ficarra, 2010). The compatibility in the offline supports is less if they are compared with online compatibility. However, the offline supports for multimedia systems are still used in the educational processes, including the promotion and teaching of cultural and natural heritage.

ELABORATING A COMMON LANGUAGE FOR THE EVALUATION IN MICE

At the moment of the design of these hypertext, multimedia and hypermedia commercial systems of the 90s, perhaps none of their authors or producers have followed some of the following models to generate them: Garg, Tompa, Statechart, Trellis, HB1, Dexter, AHM, RMM, etc. (Cipolla-Ficarra, 2010). A short explanation of each one of them is as follows: the Garg model is oriented to the creation of multimedia documents. Besides, it allows several degrees of abstraction, therefore, it is possible to make a more detailed research of the parts that make up the document. The Tompa model used hypergraphs aimed and labeled for the design of hypertext networks. It has a finite set of nodes and edges and besides it is possible to differentiate between the content and the structure. The Statechart model is an extension of the hypergraphs. It allows to depict the structure and the navigation semantics of the hypertext systems. The Trellis model uses the Petri networks to depict the navigation semantics in the hypertext system. The Petri networks are made up by positions (nodes and content elements) and transitions (buttons) to depict a hierarchical hypertext system. The HB1 model is a management system of semantic databases. The notion of hyperbase, which in the hypermedia systems refers to the database stems from this model. The structure of the model presents primitives such as: entity, propriety, interrelations and subtypes. The Dexter Model (Dexter Hypertext Reference Model) is based on the analysis of the most relevant primitives of the following systems: Augment, Hypercard, Concordia, KMS, Intermedia and NoteCards. In this model the hypermedia system is made up of three levels: activation, storage and internal component. The AHM model (Amsterdam Hypermedia Model) is an extension of the Dexter model, which delves deeper into the temporal aspect and in the semantics of navigation. The MacWeb model is based on the concepts of the orientation towards objects, in which the types (classes) are used to understand the hypertext, and the instances to hold together the information of the hypertext (content). The RMM model (Relationship Management Methodology) resorts to the model of the RMDM data (Relationship management Data Model) for the design of the information and the links inside the hypermedia system. The RMDM is based on two dominion primitives such as "entity" and "relations" between the entities, and five primitives of access to the data: unidirectional links, bidirectional links, indexes, guided links and collection. Many of these notions stem from software engineering, especially from the quality sector. Although some of them are also used in other fields of software engineering, such as the natural languages. In other words, if a graduate in mathematics reads some of these notions he gets literally lost, because there are ambiguous concepts, since they have been extrapolated from their natural environment, without making any disambiguation process of the notions, especially those models which refer to the programming aimed at goals. Evidently, in the commercial examples that we are analyzing practically nobody has used them in Europe or the USA. Now in a heuristic evaluation method like it is described in the present work, a code or common language is needed among all the participants of the evaluation process, with the purpose of eradicating ambiguities which entail a waste of time and financial resources. After comparing several models in the context of the hypertext/hypermedia suggested by different authors (Nielsen, 1990; Horn, 1990), we have plumped for the hypertext primitives linked (Nelson, 1992) to the main notions of semiotics (Noth, 1995). The main advantage of this solution is that it responds to the possibility of evaluating each one of the components of the applications with a high accuracy degree; such as can be reached with semiotics. Next here is the listing of our first primitives and categories of the design (alphabetically ordered):

- **Element:** Content
- **Element Type:** Dynamic and Structure
- **Entity:** Content and Presentation
- **Frame:** Presentation, Content, Dynamic and Panchronic
- **Frame Principal:** Presentation, Content, Dynamic and Panchronic
- **Guided Tour:** Presentation, Structure and Dynamic
- **Hierarchical Links:** Structure and Dynamic
- **Hypertrails:** Structure and Content
- **Keyword Links:** Content
- **Link:** Structure
- **Node:** Content
- **Referential Links:** Structure and Content
- **Sememe:** Content

This set of primitives is easy to apply for the users and the designers of the system or multimedia application. This ease may foster the collaboration among the participants of the development of the interactive system, such as the programmer, the analyst, the system engineer, the usability evaluator, the communicability analysis, etc. Those charged with the implementation may discuss the application with the analyst, and have an understanding of the requirements of their work although they do not yet have available the prototype of the system or a beta version. This makes possible the division of the implementation tasks among different people, thus obtaining a greater transparency in the tasks allocated to each one of them and besides a greater consistence of the applications. This consistence is due to the fact that the heads of the implementation are guided by clear and accurate instructions, which allows to eliminate the arbitrariness of the functions of the agents who intervene in the implementation stage. An arbitrariness which is in many cases the source problems stemming from the human factors because of the failings caused, with the waste of time, and, moreover, the increase in the production costs. Finally, there are the structural alternatives. That is, the participants in the design can examine several styles of organization of the information in each area of the structure, as is the case of setting a manual guided link to an automatic collection, to observe in a quiet way an artistic content inside the hall of a museum.

DIACRONIC EVOLUTION AND EVALUATION

A communicability expert can determine through a partial analysis of a multimedia system whether a technological breakthrough has allowed to improve and increase the information an user has at his/her disposal at the moment of the interaction (Singh, 2011). We understand by partial analysis to examine a part of the system without focusing on the usability issues. In this sense, it is necessary to stress that usability is not synonymous of communicability. Usability refers to the decade of the 90s (Nielsen, 1990) and communicability has its origin in the new millennium (Cipolla-Ficarra, 2010). In the current decade we are transiting the era of communicability expansion. In this partial analysis one can resort to the notions of frame principal, guided tour, link, node and sememe. Obviously we are talking of one of the most important museums in Europe because of the great collection of works it holds. Works that have been reproduced through the digitalization of images whether they are photographs, drawings, etchings, computer made images in 2D or 3D, etc., and which are linked with explicative texts, animations or special effects, such as can be the lines drawn on a painting or the magnifying glass effect on a canvas. In our universe of study we will encompass the first evolution of an original product in 1995 (Le Louvre CD-ROM, 1995). which for reasons of costs and marketing was broken down into two offline multimedia systems (Le Louvre CD-ROM, 1997) in the late 90s until reaching the interactive DVD version of our days (Museo del Louvre DVD, 2012).

Original Version

Without any doubt we are in the face of a great multimedia project since at the time it meant opening new fields, whether from the financial point of view, the commercial market or theoretically the scientific field. Although in the latter in the practice the reasons of the failure have already been described since the start of the appearance of the commercial multimedia systems. That is, the lack of 360 degrees vision of the academic heads of the software of the time. This lack of 360 degrees vision is due to the lack of an interaction zone between the field of the formal sciences and the factual sciences as it already existed since the 80s in many places of the South American south cone. Besides, the human factor, called parochialism, impeded the integration of other professionals to those work environments. Today the consequences are not only to be seen in the millions and millions of unemployed in the Old Continent. Therefore, the millions and millions of euros of European subsidies have not served to implement or put in motion an audiovisual industry as can be found in California in the USA. An exception to this academic university reality can be found in the original system of the Louvre museum, whose dynamic and static data were limited by an average capacity of 650 Megabytes.

From the principal frame it can be seen how the presentation of the information stored in the data base has been thoroughly analyzed. There is an excellent work of infographic whose equivalent would be graphics which emulate or simulate the 2D or 3D through the use of the computer. A key element such as illumination will be present in almost every frame which make up the interactive work. An excellent example is in the frame of the work (La Liberté guidant le peuple, Eugene Delacroix, 1830). In that frame we have that three of the areas of the divine proportion enunciated by Leonardo Da Vinci, that is to say, drawing a vertical line and a horizontal one in the centre of the screen, there are four areas. Three of them are areas of great visual impact for the western user (upper right, right left, lower right). In the interface of the figure aa, upper left zone, is the image of the author. In its lower part can be found the biography, the presentation, the composition, the chronology, the hall where it is located, a small representation. In the lower horizontal part and inside the same frame we have several links to other nodes such as the dimension or scale, the zoom or nearing the canvas, the textual information and the return option to the previous node or exit of the frame. The icons which accompany the interface, although they are not mnemonic because they require a text for their explanation they turn the global design into a minimalist style and perfect with the resources of programming that a MMDirector had in the 90s. In other words, excepting some icons, the sememe of each one of the elements which make up the interface does not generate any ambiguity between the signification and the significant, in keeping with Saussure's notion of sign, for instance.

Abridged Version

The marketing of the virtual firms online of the 90s and start of the new millennium generated a kind of commercial bubble with severe consequences for electronic commerce, in view of the lack of faithfulness and trust towards the potential users of multimedia systems at the moment in which the bubble burst. The mercantilism and marketing of the 90s also led the multimedia sector off-line to a kind of bubble of the sector (Cipolla-Ficarra, et al., 2012; Styliaras, et al., 2010). After the burst of that multimedia bubble in Europe only the videogames sector would save the negative results from the commercial point of view. In that context, many original products of interactive multimedia and aimed at the cultural heritage were adapted to the new commercial demands. In the case of the Museum of the Louvre the content was divided into two abridged versions in CD-ROM but where appeared for the first time a constant component in this kind of products: the games oriented at different kinds of users, experts and non-experts since many levels of difficulty in it (the game of La Cour Carré).

The structure of the contents was lineal, and it usually ended with a guided tour or collection of links grouped under entities whose great titles are "masterpieces", "itineraries", "the building", and works (the content of this one in the second CD-ROM). The access to these four entities is grouped under the emulation of a small pyramid on the left side of the screen. However, there is another entity in the principal frame, which are the games and are not included in this emulation of pyramid. Analyzing structurally one of them such as the main itineraries, we find collections of nodes and links which refer to animals, landscapes, Bible, myths, children, portraits, love, still nature, fashion and history.

However, in these itineraries sculpture and painting are not differentiated. For instance, in domestic animals we have the painting "landscape near the buck deer". Cuyp Aelbrect (1650 approximately) and the sculpture inside the holy animals, "winged bull with human head", (713-705 B.C.). In all of them with the option of activating the textual explanation as in the original work on the right margin. The same method of presenting the information can be found in each one of the collections, such as can be the painting "La Liberté guidant le peuple" Eugene Delacroix -1830 (historic itinerary), which in contrast to the original version (Figure 7 in Appendix) here the textual information as a graphic is of lesser quality.

From the entity "masterpieces" we access La Gioconda by Leonardo Da Vinci with the traditional effect of closing-up of the image. However, in a single level of nearness or farness, that is, there were no intermediate options, as there are not either in the 2012 version in DVD support. With regard to the static images there is a tendency to emulate the reality of sculptural works, keeping the projection of shadows, which generates a three-dimensional vision of the works. This historic realism can also be seen in the use of black and white pictures.

The three-dimensional realism will be increased with the use of photography, as it can be seen in the new 2012 version, for instance. In the entity "building" a visit can be made in relation to the content of the different halls, and also in relation to the nationality of the artists. In this entity can be seen how the presence of the new computer designers with those stemming from the graphical arts, given the quality of combination of design concepts 2D and 3D, especially in the handling of the colors, typography, and the explanations in the helps for the inexperienced users, for instance.

Modern Version

The modern version based on a DVD support which increases the storage capacity of the dynamic means of an average of 650 Mb at 4.7 Gb does not present great novelties in the commercial products as the one we have in our universe of study, from the point of view of the content of the interactive design, especially in the use of the dynamic means, such as 3D animation.

On the basis of the building of the museum, the current interactive system makes a constant 360° horizontal movement along the halls, linked to the excellent quality of the color photographs. From the principal frame of the DVD we find again a common denominator or visual isotopy, in the three off-line multimedia systems, from the content or star work of the museum: The Gioconda by Leonardo Da Vinci. Once again there are four main units: guided tour, sales, masterpieces, history). Starting from them in the interaction with the system the user has several options but always following the structure of guided links or nodes collection or loop-shaped links. However, given the capacity of the support of the interactive information, in this system the use of the audio is constant. Another of the constant elements is the 360° navigation along the halls, whose picture quality is excellent, and where appear the icons where there are referential links, with dynamic or static media. Besides, the central division of the screen into two semi-frames allows to associate additional information to the comments through the use of transparencies. The transparencies are a visual resource agreeable to most users when they interact with encyclopedias, for instance. Another of the visual resources that have been kept through time are the animated red lines in 2D, to strengthen the words that the speaker is commenting. The use of the lightening also plays an important role in this vertical division of the screen, since part of it can decrease in intensity to focus the user's audiovisual attention. Another important role of that segmentation we have in the horizontal division, at the moment of generating transition effects in certain artistic works, whose details are intended to be stressed, such as can be the face of the Gioconda. There aren't here either alternatives of gradual nearing or distance to the work of Leonardo Da Vinci. However, there are more special effects (video) of the main characteristics of that work.

Finally, we present the results of the partial evaluation of the analyzed systems, in relation to quality and bearing in mind the technological resources and the limitations of the interactive design at the moment in which they were designed and produced. The analysis has been made by three communicability experts in a lab equipped with computers and the required operative systems but which surpassed the minimal conditions of the hardware, for the correct functioning of the multimedia systems. Next we present the average of the obtained results.

LESSONS LEARNED

Although there are several design models for the hypertext, multimedia and hypermedia systems, many of the commercial products in Southern Europe haven't followed them in the 90s. The reason is that the multimedia in the computer sector and/or software engineering was not considered as an area of study, but rather belonged to the set of the arts, audiovisual, information or communication sciences, etc. Only the usability engineering aspects were approached. That is, the main notions presented by Nielsen in the 90s. A decade which coincided with the quality of the software, but nobody foresaw that the learning in the use of computers would start at such an early age as some educational experts, communicators, hardware producers, etc. claimed such as McLuhan, Piaget, Gates, etc. The new millennium is synonymous with quality in interactive communication. In this sense, it is necessary to resort to simple instruments, not just to create a common language among the producers and cut production costs by using all the same notions, but also to detect failings or the positive aspects of interactive systems which even today still work in DVD or CD- Rom, in millions of homes in all the world, where the Internet broadband many times does not work very well at all, or simply there is no Internet. In the next works we will perfection the presented partial evaluation methodology until generating a kind of vademecum or style guidelines which implicitly exist in the first multimedia products related to cultural heritage. Besides, we will establish a listing of graphic design resources (2D and 3D) stemming from the programming languages and/or the current commercial applications, oriented at the off-line multimedia systems, with the purpose of increasing the motivation of the children and teenagers at the moment of interacting with that kind of contents. All of that under the high quality and low costs equation.

CONCLUSION

The passing of time demonstrates that the interactive design solutions in offline support have replicated themselves along the years, although the manufacturers have changed and the contents have always been the same. In this sense, the first multimedia systems aimed at art are still today an interesting field of study and models to be followed, even in other digital information supports which have a huge storage capacity. However, it is also necessary to underline that following a model of the 90s when the software and hardware resources in the new offline multimedia devices have considerably developed, means that the creativity in novel solutions for the contents of the museums is scarce. Evidently, the cost factor of production has its influence in the commercial products and can be appreciated in the use of photography, the video and the locution, instead of 3D computer animation, for instance. Computer graphics could considerably enrich the explanations of the works which the museums hold, bringing even closer their potential visitors. In this sense and in contrast to the myth of those who claimed in the 90s in Southern Europe that with the inclusion of the artistic heritage of a museum in a CD-Rom or in the Internet the number of visitors to those halls would decrease, reality has demonstrated that the increase of visitors has grown in an exponential way, thanks to the new technologies and especially to the online and off-line multimedia systems.

REFERENCES

Art Gallery. (1995). [CD-ROM]. Seattle, WA: Microsoft.

Cipolla-Ficarra, F. (2010). *Quality and communicability for interactive hypermedia systems: Concepts and practices for design*. Hershey, PA: IGI Global. doi:10.4018/978-1-61520-763-3

Cipolla-Ficarra, F. et al. (2010). *Advances in dynamic and static media for interactive systems: Communicability, computer science and design*. Bergamo, Italy: Blue Herons.

Cipolla-Ficarra, F. et al. (2012). *Computational informatics, social factors and new information technologies: Hypermedia perspectives and avant-garde experiences in the era of communicability expansion*. Bergamo, Italy: Blue Herons.

Fenton, N. (1997). *Software metrics: A rigorous approach*. Cambridge, UK: Chapman and Hall.

Horn, R. (1990). Mapping hypertext. Waltham, MA: Lexington.

Le Louvre. (1997). *EMME – ACTA, 1*.

Le Louvre. (1995). [CD-ROM]. Paris: Montparnasse.

Museo del Louvre. (2012). [DVD]. Roma: Gruppo Editoriale L'Espresso.

Nelson, T. (1992). *Literary machines*. Sausalito: Mindful Press.

Nielsen, J. (1990). *Multimedia and hypertext*. San Diego, CA: Academic Press.

Noth, W. (1995). *Handbook of semiotics*. Bloomington, IN: Indiana University Press.

Singh, G. (2011). The IBM PC: The silicon story. *IEEE Computer*, *44*(8), 40–45. doi:10.1109/MC.2011.194

Styliaras, G. et al. (2010). *Handbook of research on technologies and cultural heritage: Applications and environments*. Hershey, PA: IGI Global. doi:10.4018/978-1-60960-044-0

APPENDIX

Figure 1. The Baptism of Christ: initial state of the animation

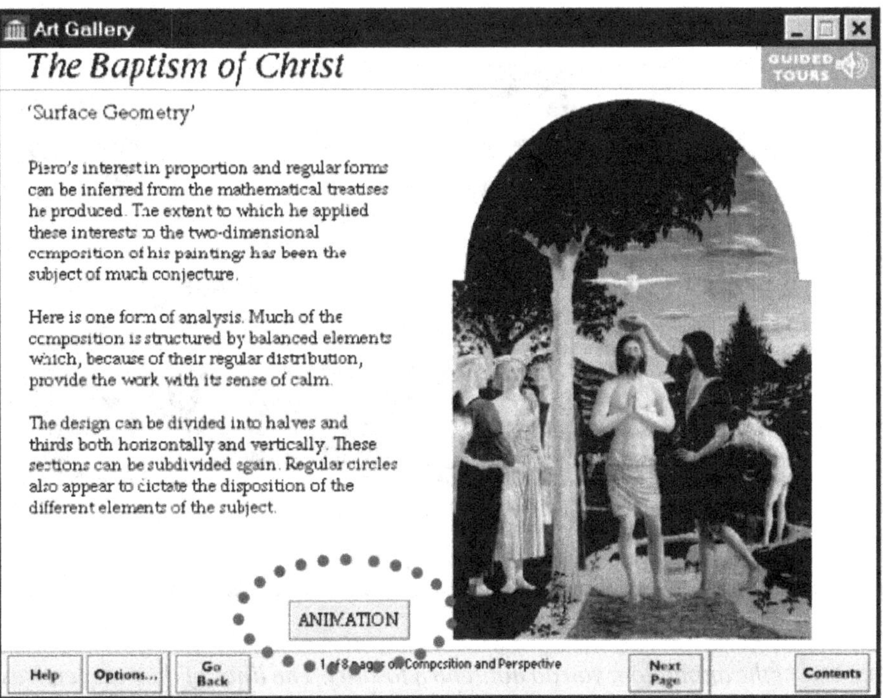

Figure 2. Two options for animation

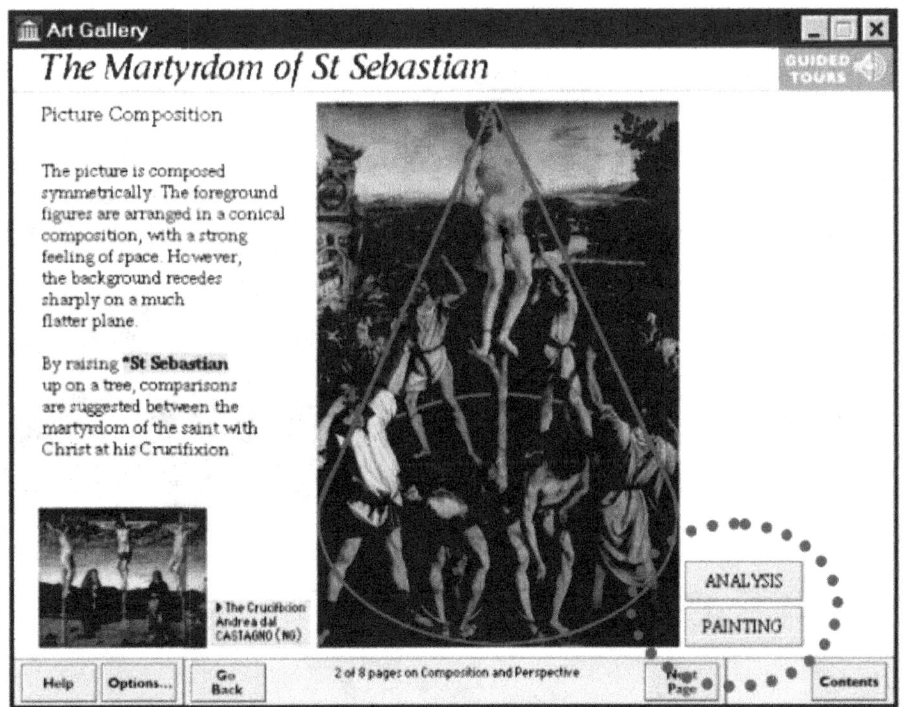

Figure 3. The animation option replaces the analysis option and painting of Figure 2

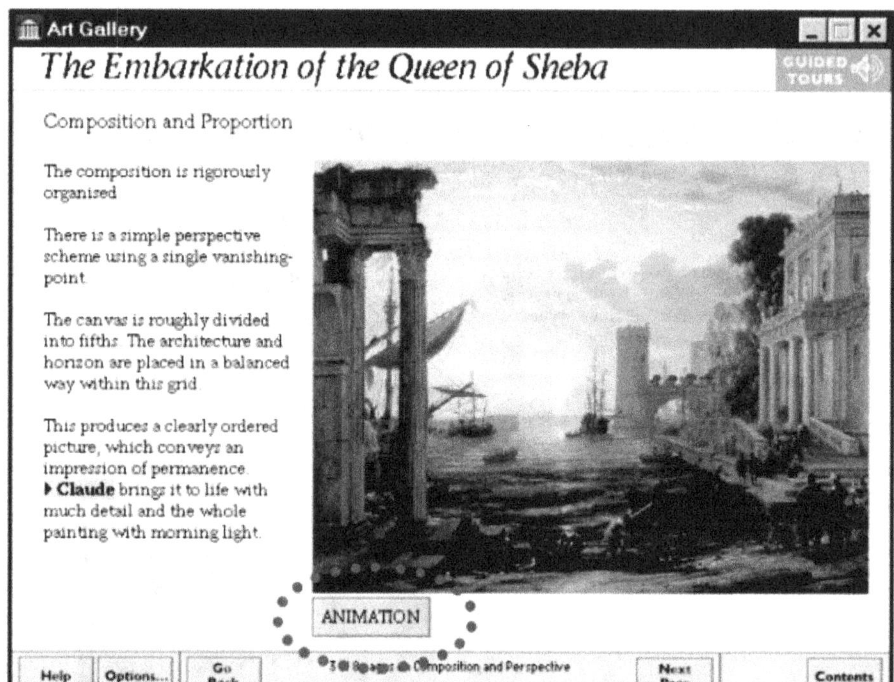

Figure 4. At the end of the animation, you do not return to start. The lines of the perspectives can be seen.

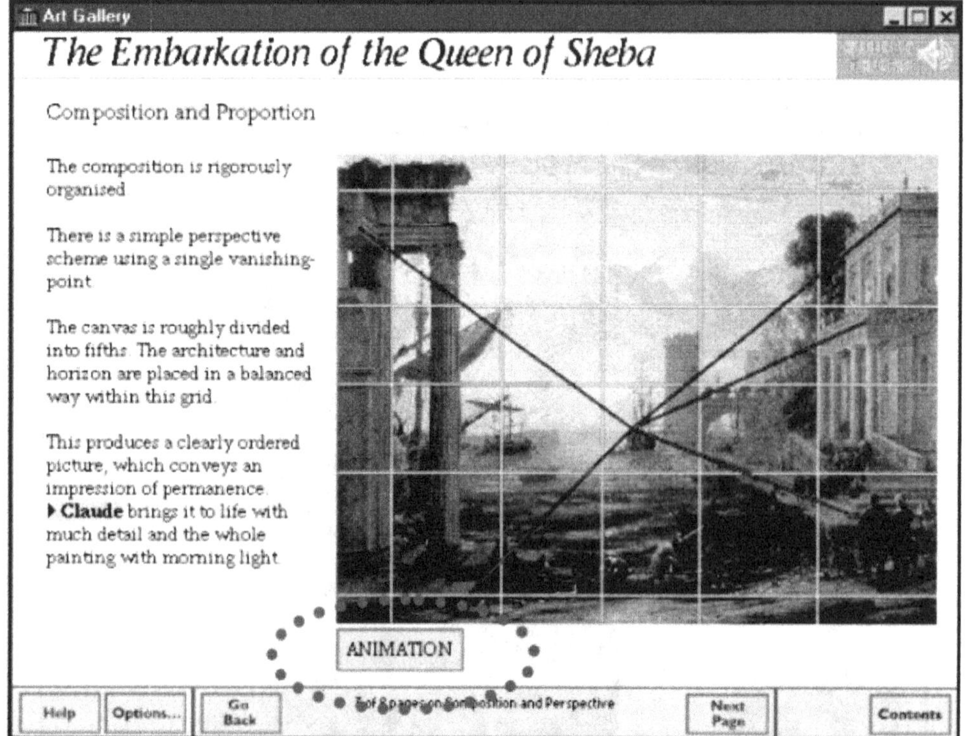

Figure 5. Elimination of the authors of the work

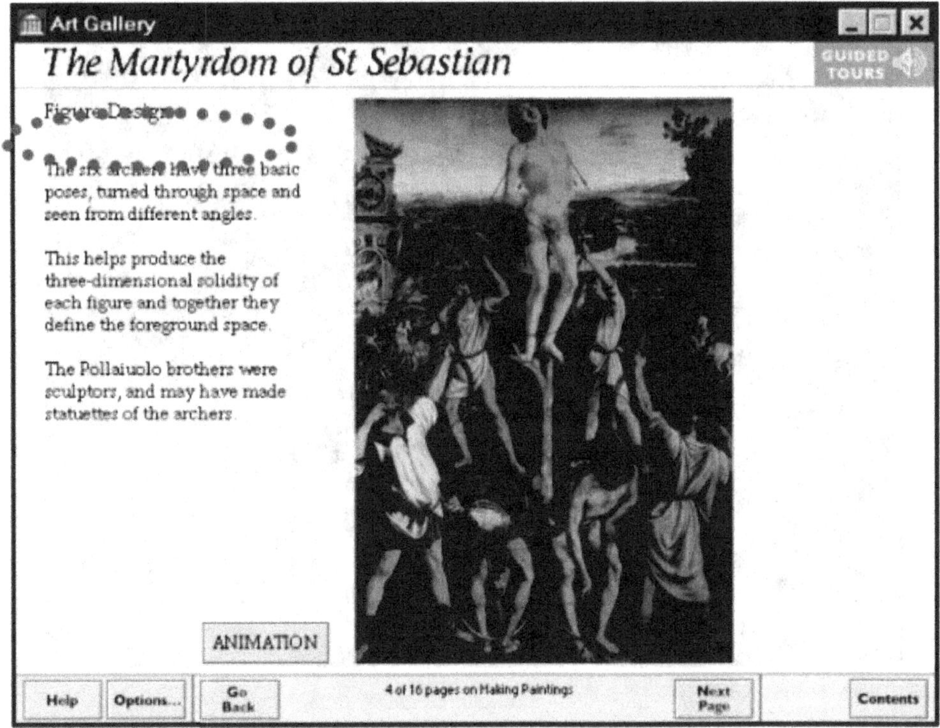

Figure 6. Below the title of the work appear their authors

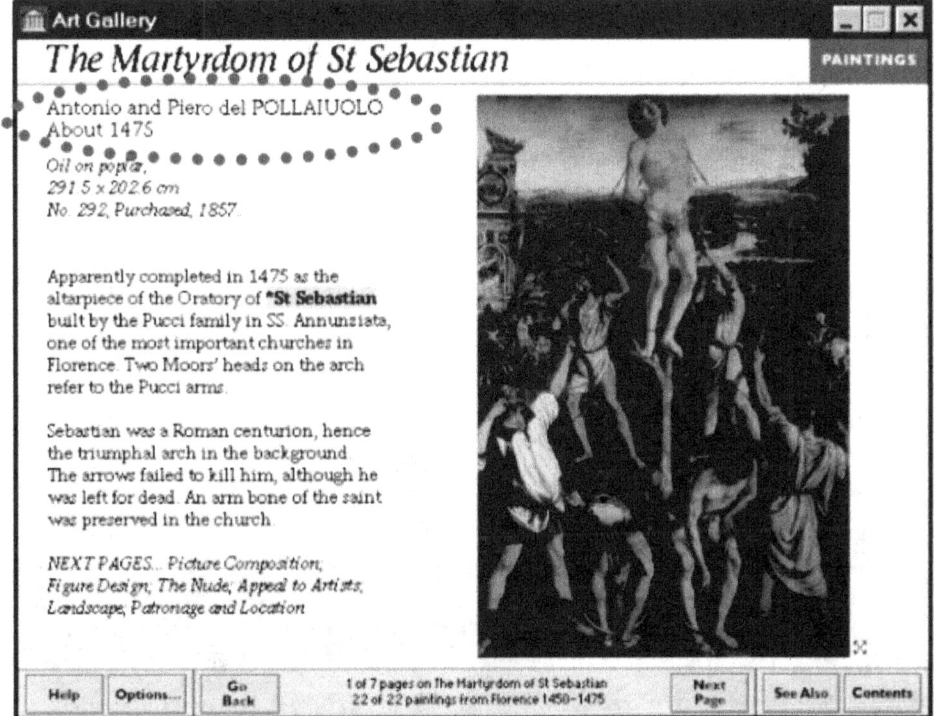

Figure 7. An excellent example of the interface of the 90s for the museums in CD-ROM support

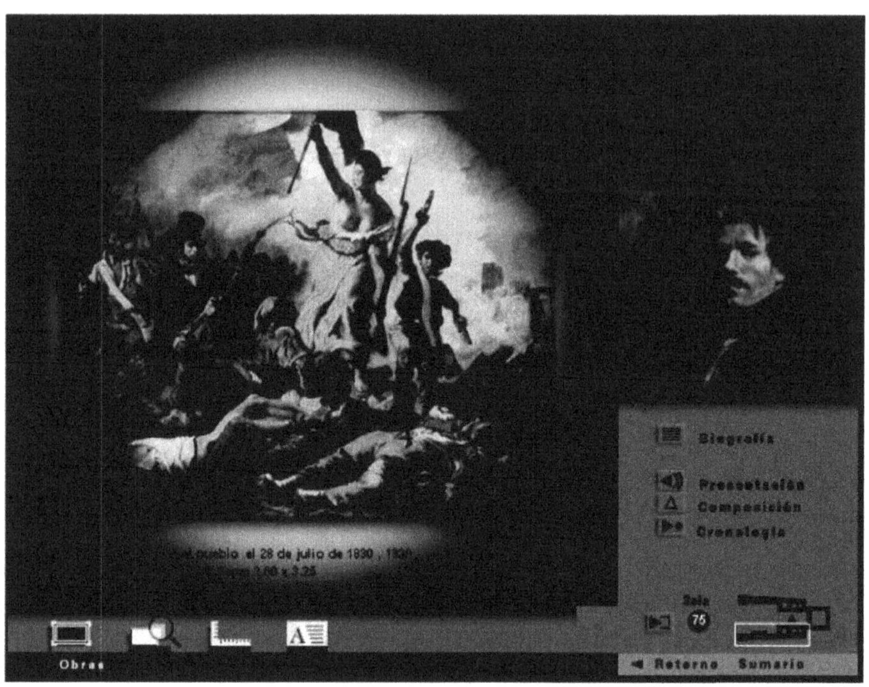

Figure 8. An interesting solution to quickly understand the dimension of a work (in the metric decimal system) inserting the figure of an adult person and making comparisons with other works of art, such as: The Beggars, Hunting Diana, etc.

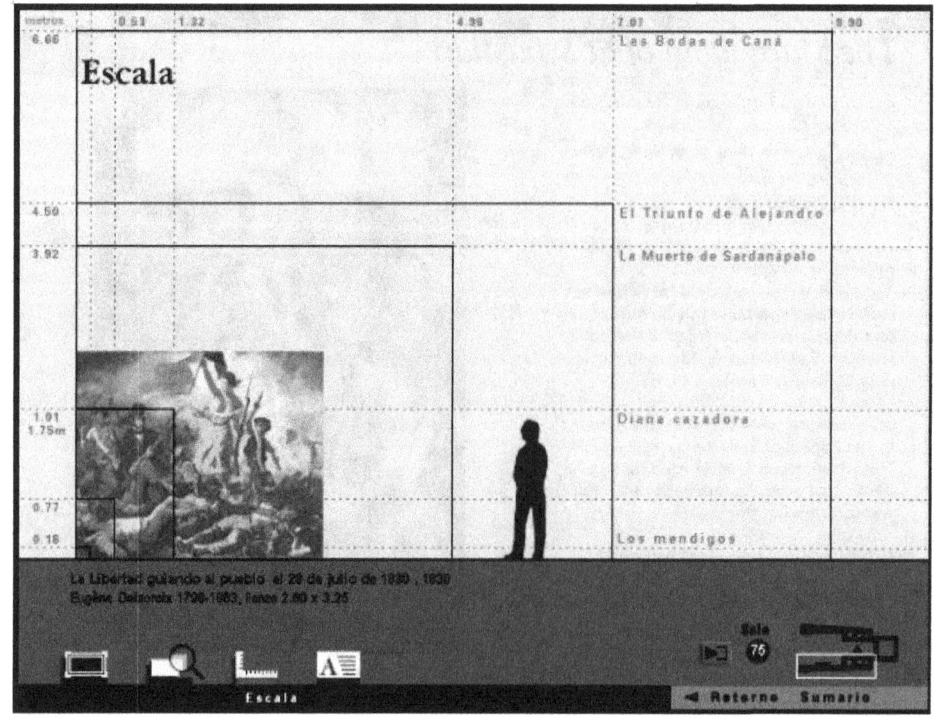

Figure 9. The classic and almost forced option of zoom to approach with the magnifying glass to the details of the artistic works

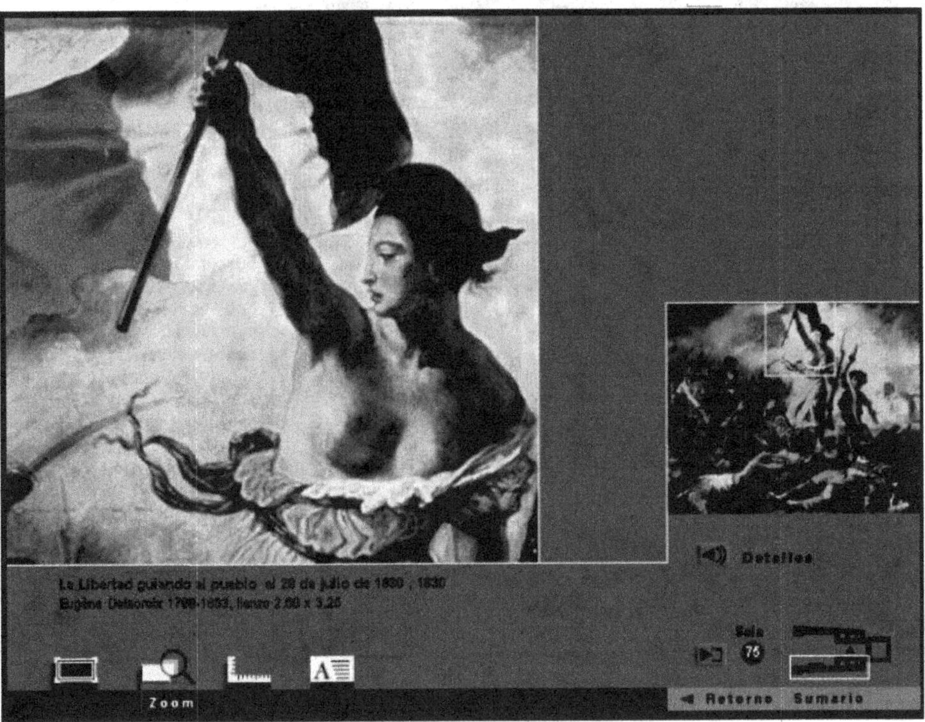

Figure 10. A succinct but precise textual information which explains the main characteristics of the work that the user is watching

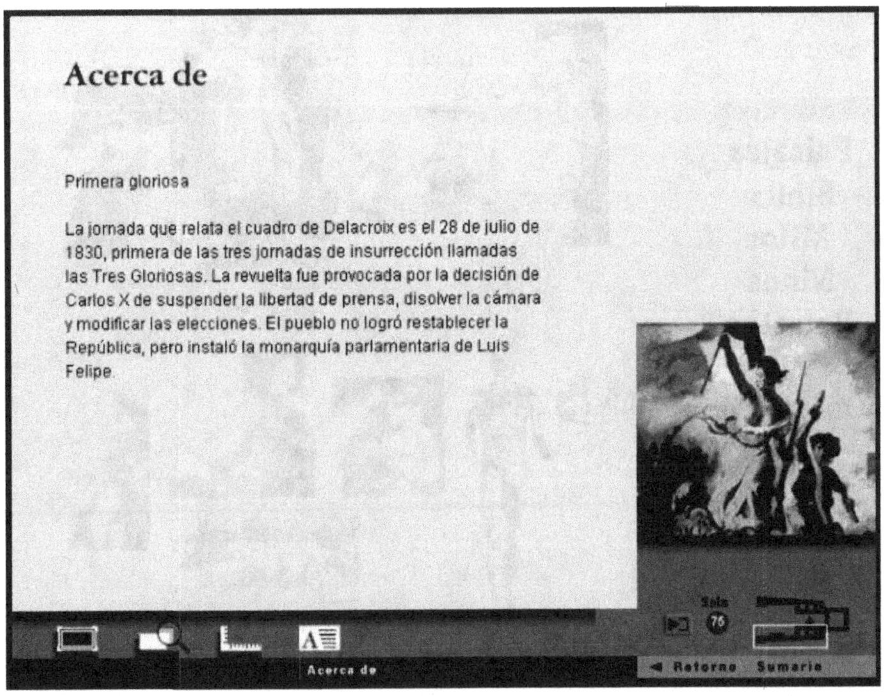

Figure 11. Museum game: La Cour Carré

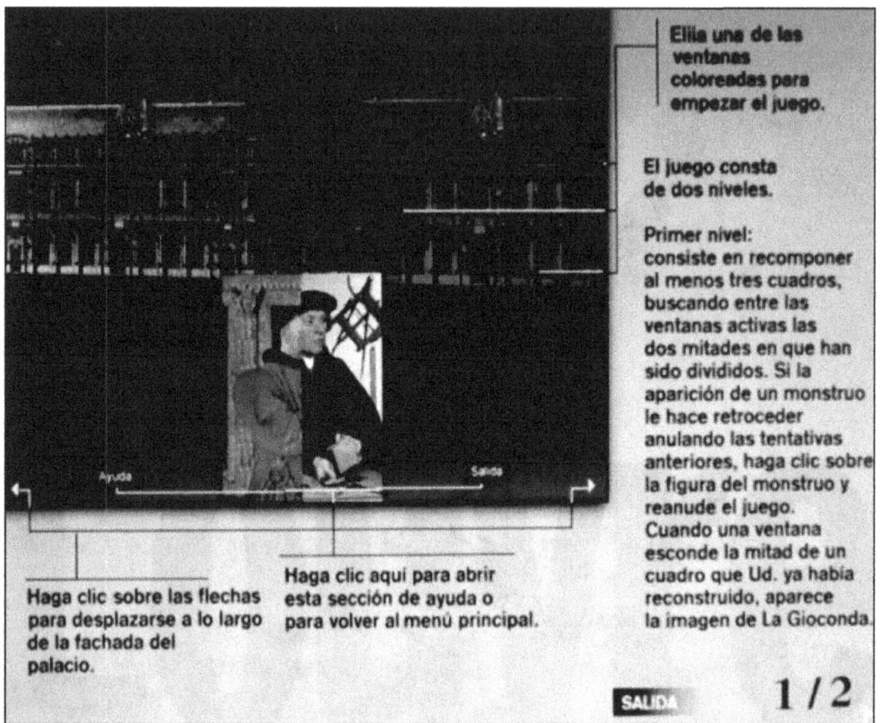

Figure 12. Itineraries – a small pyramid in the left area

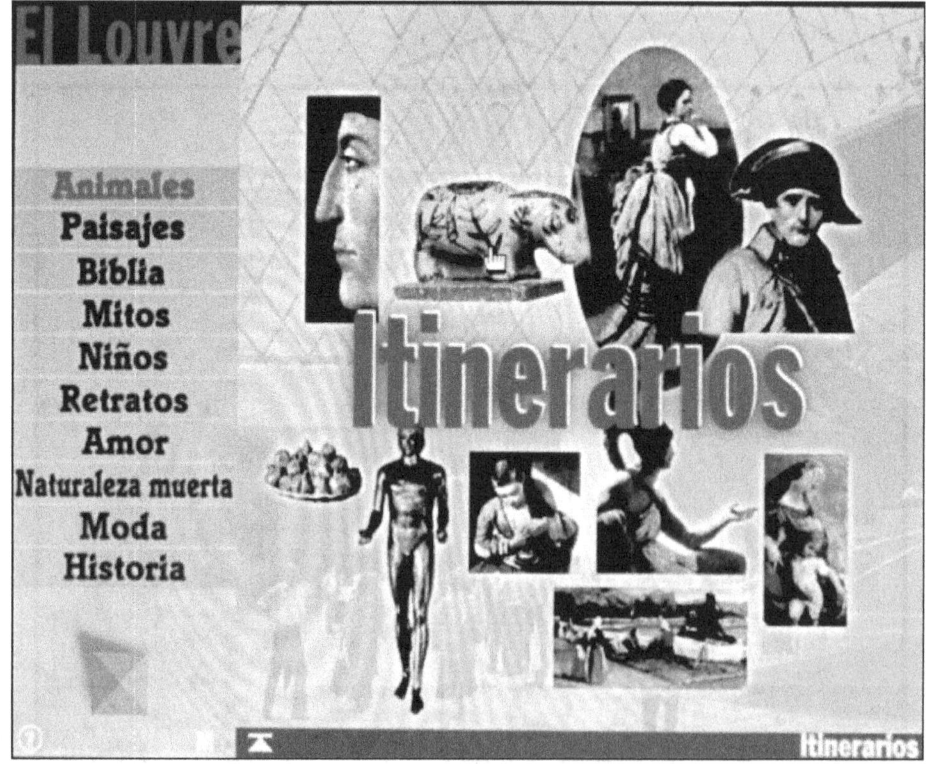

Figure 13. Illumination and realism. The shadows in the lightening of the photographs increase the notion of the real volume of the sculpture.

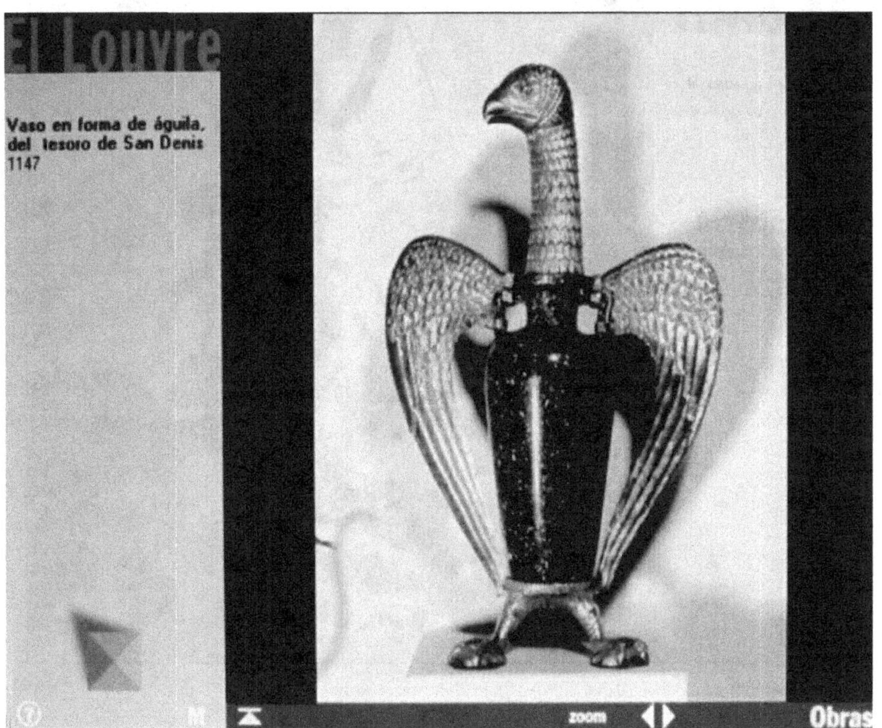

Figure 14. 3D map of the Louvre and masterpieces

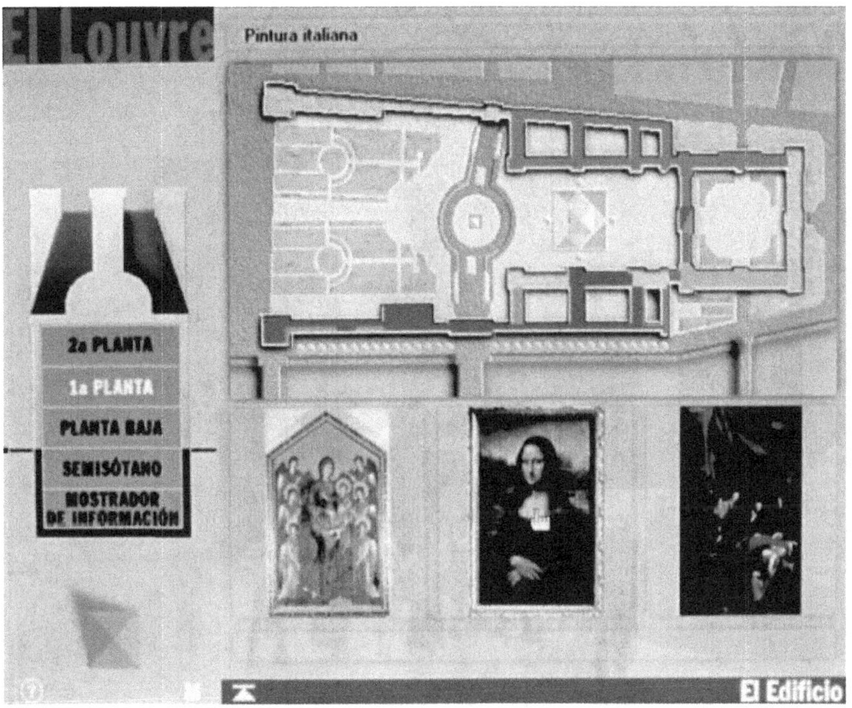

Figure 15. Full screen of the work. "La Liberté guidant le peuple".

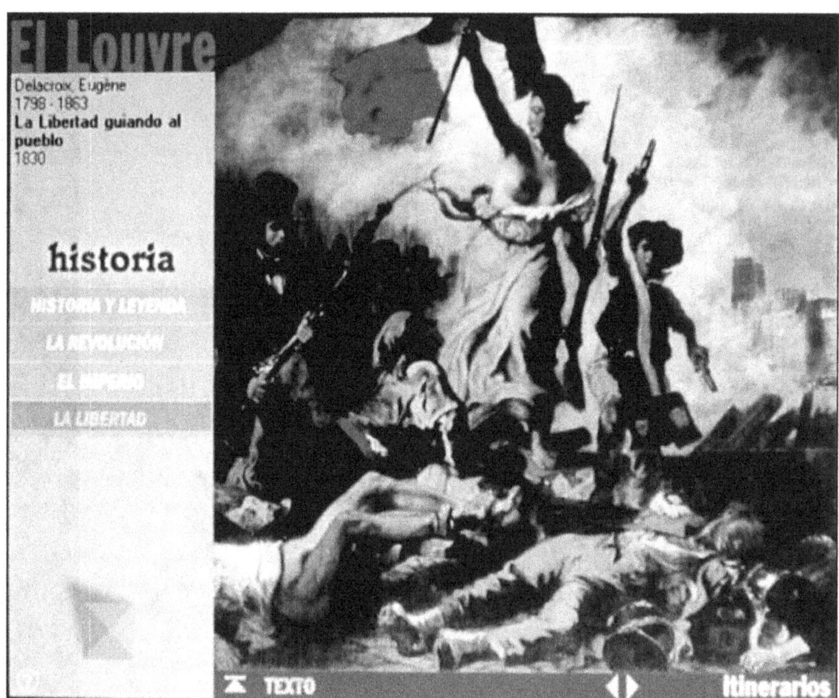

Figure 16. Correct use of the textual and visual information since the user still has a global visión of the picture at the moment of reading the text and a detailed view of the painting. The communicability is excellent due to the minimalist style and non-ambiguous of the textual or visual information.

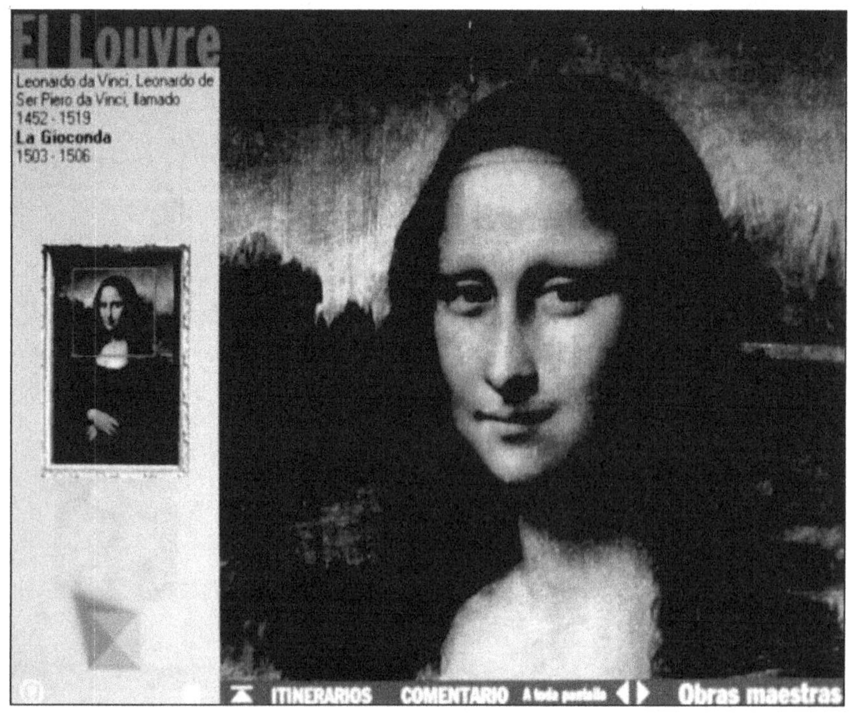

Figure 17. Louvre Museum: DVD version

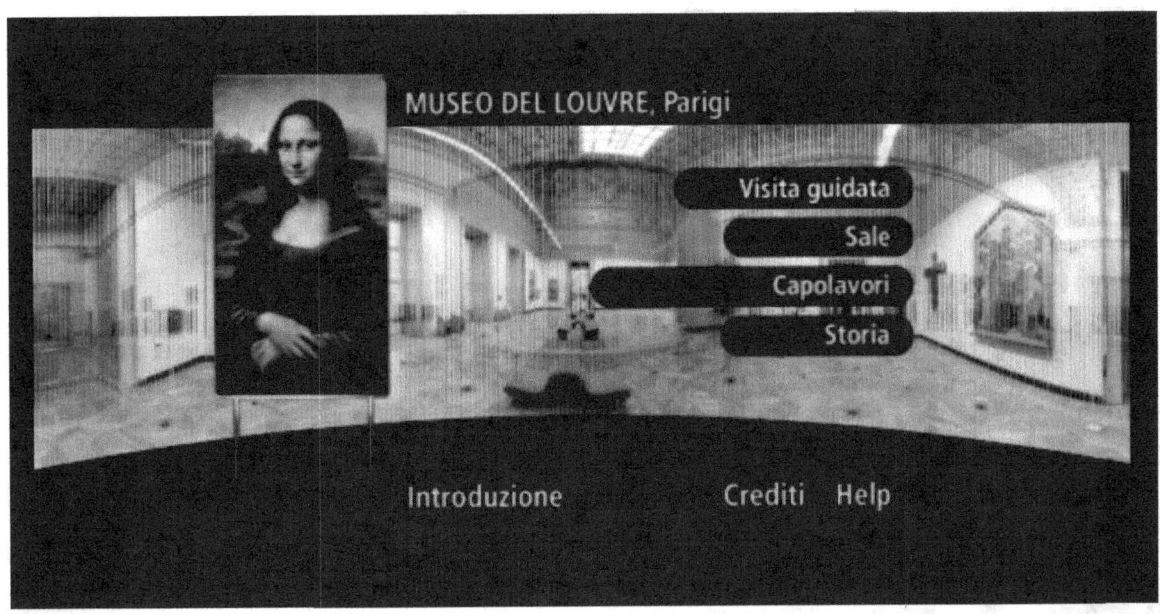

Figure 18. Global vision of two halls of the museum, including the "star" work, the Gioconda

Figure 19. Combination of the vertical and horizontal movement, in a spherical view of the halls

Figure 20. Use of read lines to boost the audio explanation

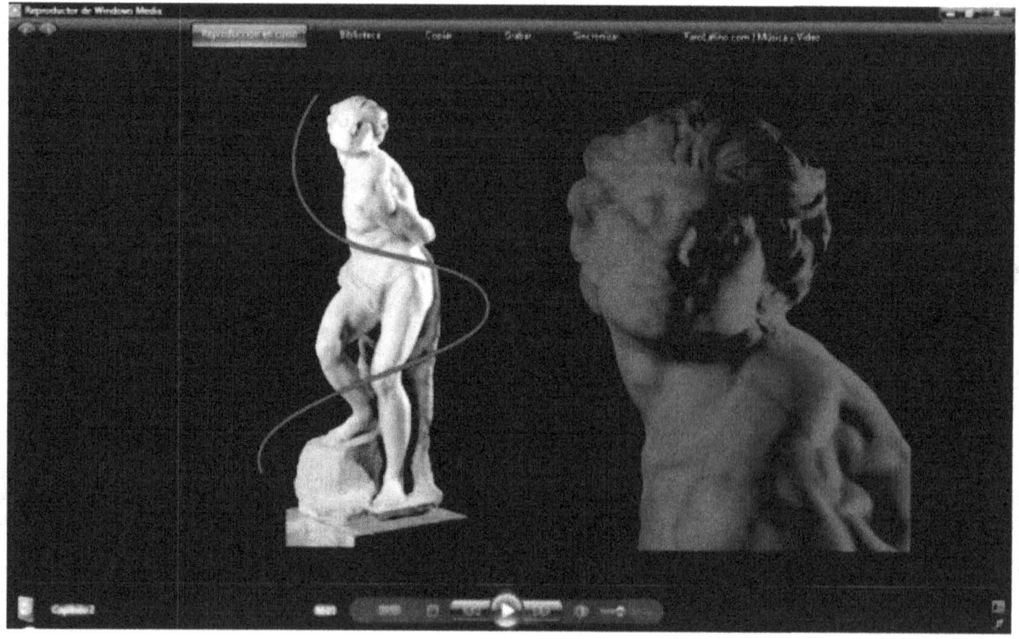

Figure 21. Different shots and details of the work which hold the centre of the frame

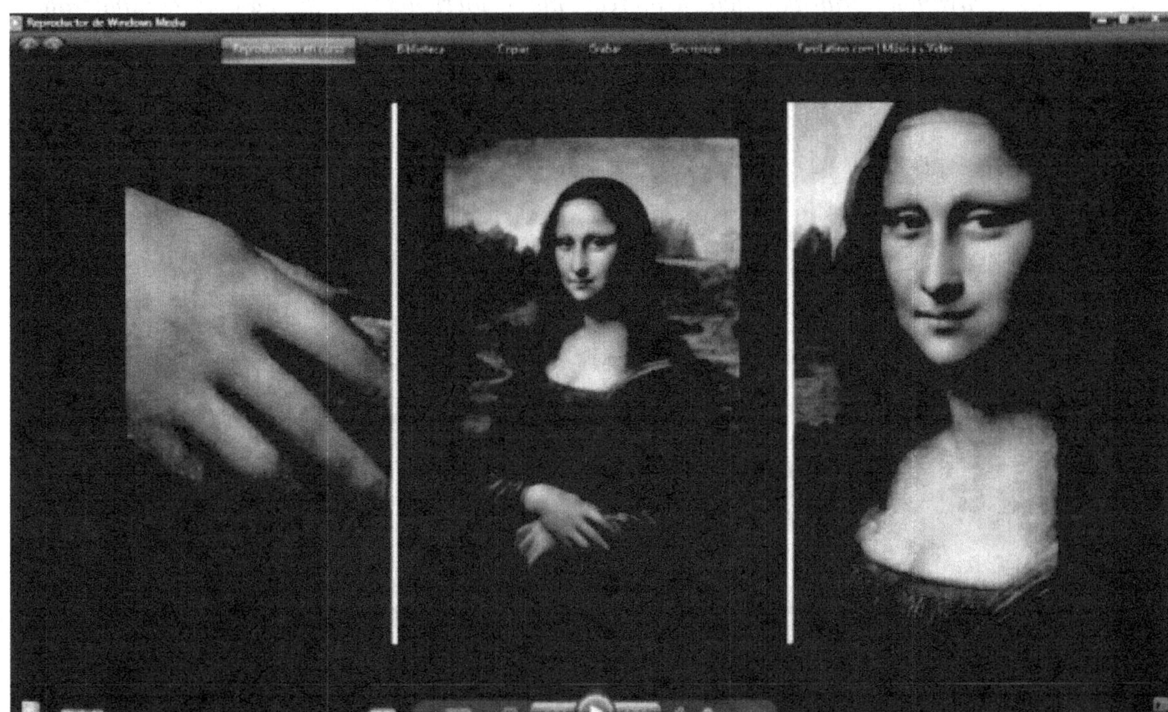

Figure 22. Horizontal rotoscoping of a sculpture in two speeds

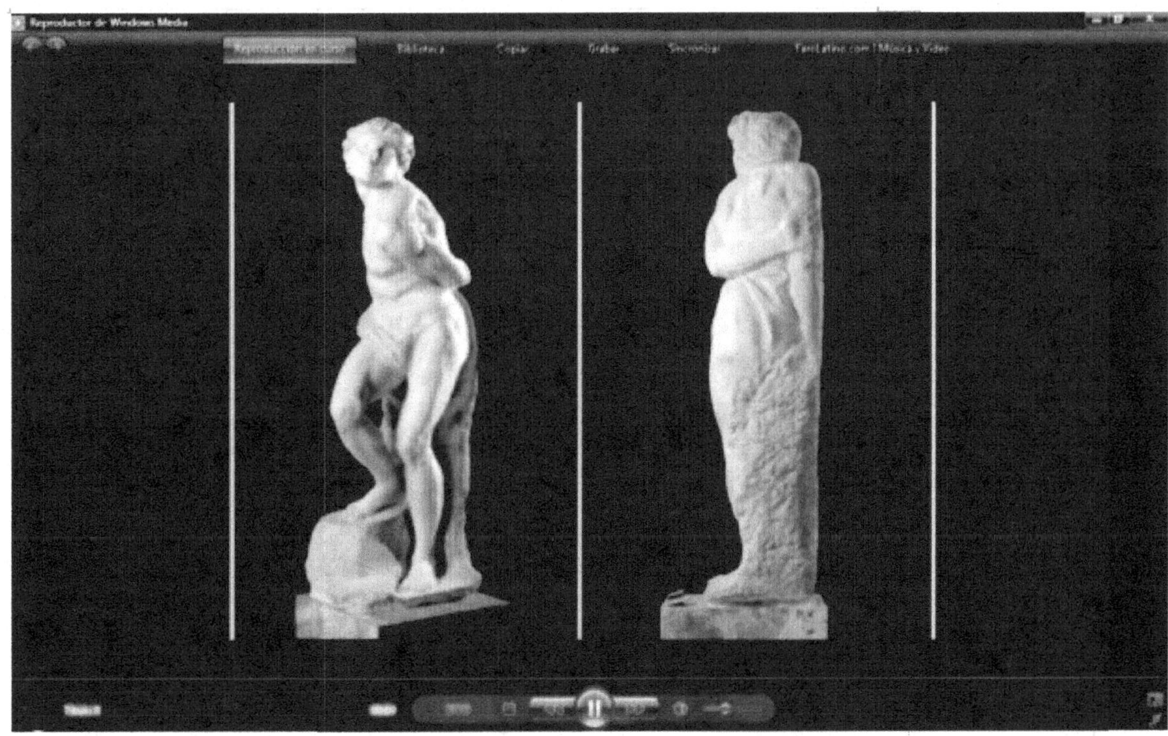

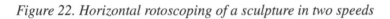

Figure 23. Minimalist iconography and non-ambiguous for the navigation and signaling of dynamic and/ or static media. Activation of transparencies to increase the visual richness of the audiovisual explanation.

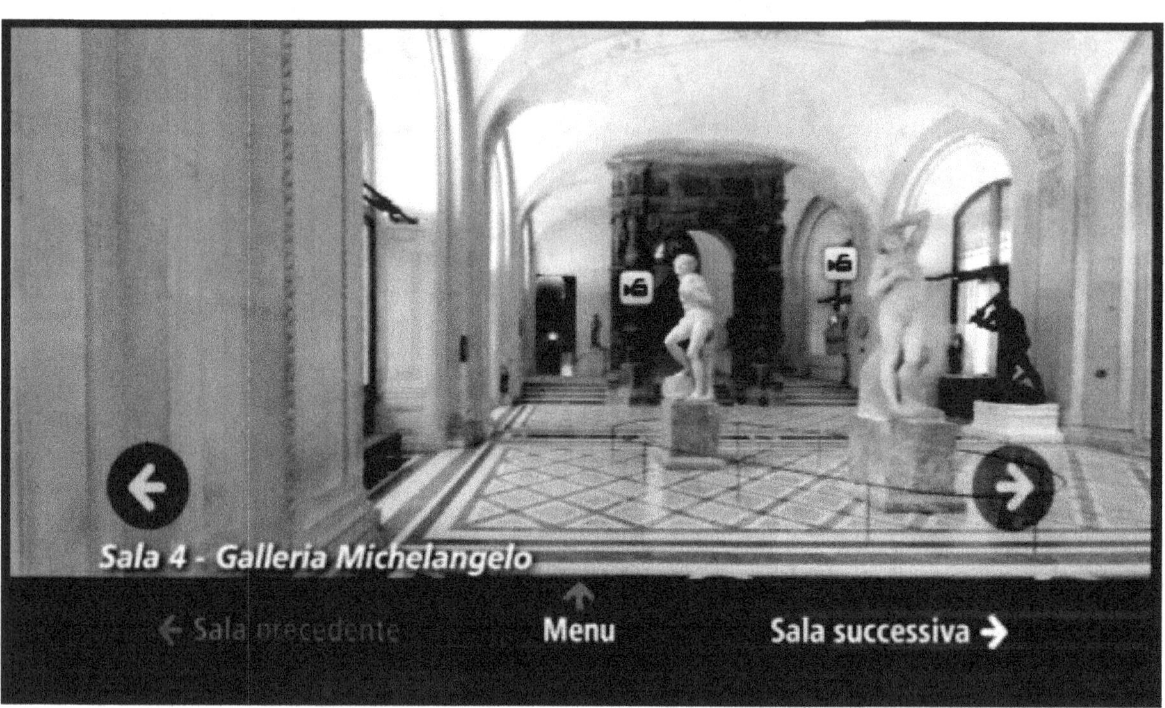

Figure 24. First quality results – partial evaluation, with MICE (the excellent quality is equal to 100%)

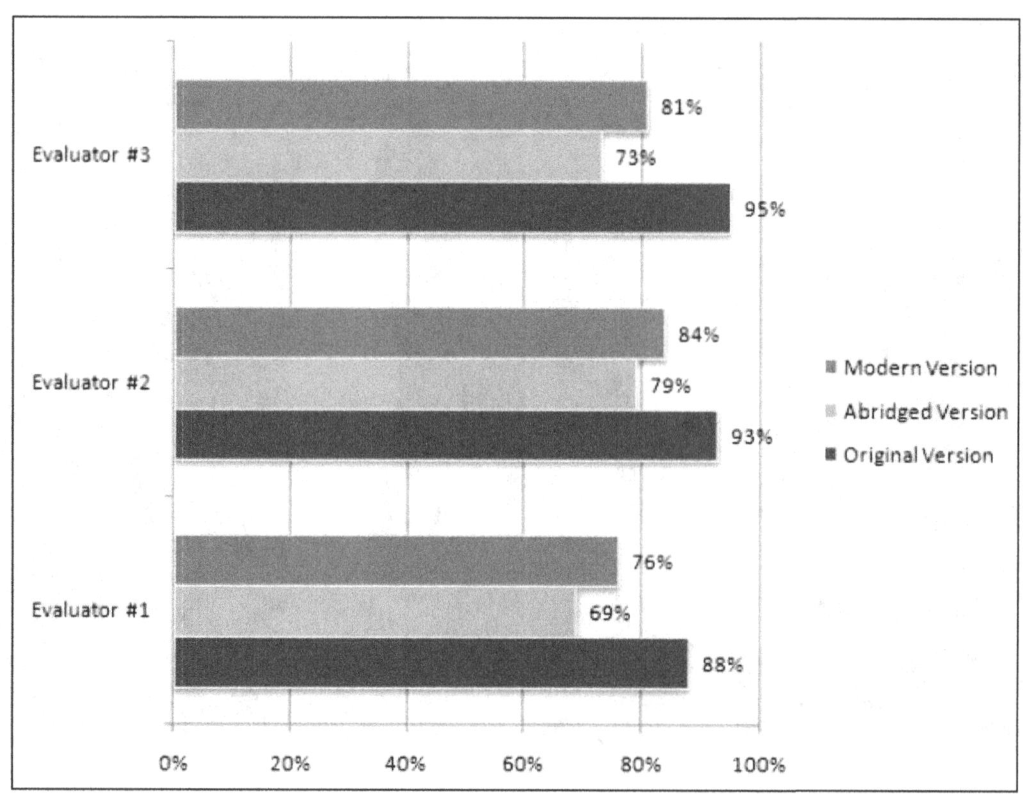

Chapter 31
Rough Set Analysis and Short-Medium Term Tourist Services Demand Forecasting

Emilio Celotto
Department of Management, Ca' Foscari University of Venice, Italy

Andrea Ellero
Department of Management, Ca' Foscari University of Venice, Italy

Paola Ferretti
Department of Economics and SSE, Ca' Foscari University of Venice, Italy

ABSTRACT

Along with a growing interest in tourism research is the effort to establish innovative methodologies that are useful to guide the tourist operators and the policy makers in selecting forecasting techniques. Nevertheless, predicting tourist demand is still lacking at a microeconomic level, while it has become a flourishing theme of research uniquely at a macroeconomic level. The main goal is to analyze Italian tourists' behaviours on the basis of statistical surveys on households, life conditions, incomes, consumptions, travels, and vacation. This research is set in the framework of Rough Sets Theory, a Data Mining technique that can easily manage categorical variables. Hence, it is suitable for the exploitation of databases collecting sample surveys data. A large selection of variables from database Sinottica, containing information on social, cultural, and behavioural trends in Italy collected by means of a psychographic survey is provided by a leading market research organization, GfK Eurisko. By defining some decision rules, some interesting relations between consumer behaviours and their corresponding tourism choices are obtained.

INTRODUCTION

Different new artificial intelligence methodologics, as effectively described in (Munakata, 2008) may be compared together with reference to the most recent tourism demand forecasting models following the frame defined in (Song & Li, 2008). As it is well-known, traditional non-causal time-series and causal econometric models are consolidated tools for macroeconomic forecasts and are able to predict tourist flows (arrivals, room nights) or turnover (expenditure, revenues, etc.) on

DOI: 10.4018/978-1-4666-4490-8.ch031

the basis of macroeconomic variables (GDP, i.e. Gross Domestic Product, CPI, i.e. Consumer Price Index, currencies exchange rates, demographic variables, oil price, lagged flows, etc.). However their informative content is limited since they are lacking for what it concerns predicting tourist demand at a microeconomic level, analyzing tourist behaviours of specific segments (cultural tourism, nature-based tourism, rural tourism, sports tourism), in particular for what concerns the segmentation of the Italian demand (domestic and outbound) and understanding consumer-tourist behaviours on the basis of statistical surveys on households, life conditions, incomes, consumptions, travels and vacation. In fact, it is generally accepted that differences in motivations, attitudes to travel and tourist behaviours depend on different factors, such as age, income, household typology (single, couple with or without children, etc.), number of incomes per household. Another very important issue is the possibility of determining and verifying the relationship between tourism behaviour and other goods and services choices in order to identify some sentry variables that are able to tell in advance to the operators the most likely evolution of specific tourist segments: in other words, the target is to identify groups of goods whose consumption is correlated to travel choices.

To address the above outlined issues we will consider Rough Sets Theory (Pawlak, 1991) an artificial intelligence technique which basically leads to discover relationships in data through a data mining process. Rough Sets Theory does not require any statistical assumptions on data distributions but only the definition of condition and decision attributes to get inductive rules (*conditions → decision*). Moreover every database table (row=objects, columns=attributes) containing both numeric and categorical data, can be translated into a set of decision rules.

Rough Sets Theory combines many important advantages: no assumptions about data are required; no need to define *a priori* functions or equations; categorical data are accepted; relationships between data are explained by simple inductive rules.

With the exception of some recent papers (see e.g. in Goh & Law, 2003; Law, Goh & Pine, 2004; Goh, Law & Mok, 2008), Rough Sets Analysis has been not intensively applied in tourism literature for predicting tourist demand, in particular at a microeconomic level.

The main objective of this paper is to produce models in terms of decision rules, which allow to discriminate between tourism choices by means of the differences in consumer behaviour. This way we can look for a set of "sentry variables", that is variables which can anticipate some trends in tourism consumption.

The paper is organized as follows. Section 2 is devoted to the introduction of the main concepts of Rough Sets Theory. In Section 3 we consider some previous tourism studies that are related to Rough Sets. Section 4 analyzes the data set and depicts the main characteristics of the used software package. Section 5 presents the main rules discovered by the methodology. Section 6 ends the paper with some conclusive observations and hints for future research.

ROUGH SETS THEORY: SOME BASIC DEFINITIONS

Rough Sets theory has been presented as *a new mathematical tool for imperfect data analysis* in (Pawlak, 1991). It concerns approximated knowledge of data that are collected in data table by means of two alternative approaches: lower/upper approximations of a data set and decision rules. In fact, Pawlak wrote: "Approximations and decision rules are two different methods to express properties of data. Approximations suit better to topological properties of data, whereas decision rules describe in a simple way patterns in data and are therefore the best means to communicate the results to the operators" (Pawlak, 2002).

Decision rules are expressed as follows:

Conditions → Decision

meaning that a decision attribute is verified when some conditions are valid. Two indicators, called *coverage* and *certainty*, give a measure of the goodness of the rule (Stefanowski, 1998). The model described in this paper is based on a set of single condition attribute rules, grouped by subject. It is therefore a modular system which can be enriched with new rules if more data will be available. The choice of single condition is aimed at identifying possible products/goods which can be interpreted as sentry variables and at obtaining more easy to understand or to communicate rules. It is not a global model explaining all the possible relationships between tourism and other sectors since the available data were a selection of the more extensive and general database held by the data provider - that is GfK Eurisko.

We recall some basic definitions in Pawlaks' Rough Sets Theory (for more details, see Pawlak, 1991). Starting from the assumption that objects characterized by the same information are *indiscernible*, on indiscernibility relation the mathematical structure of the theory is essentially set. In this way, a finite nonempty universe $\mathcal{U}$ of elements $\{x_1, x_2, \ldots, x_N\}$ is related to the finite set $\mathcal{A}$ of k attributes $\{a_1, a_2, \ldots, a_k\}$ by the domain sets V_{a_i} (for each $i = 1, \ldots, k$), i.e. the sets of all the values of each attribute a_i. The pair $S = (\mathcal{U}, \mathcal{A})$ is called an information system. For each $B \subseteq \mathcal{A}$, the universe $\mathcal{U}$ is split into a family of equivalences classes (called *elementary sets*) through the indiscernibility relation $IND(B)$ stating that two objects x_i and x_j in $\mathcal{U}$ cannot be distinguished with reference to the set of attributes in B. That is, the two objects are considered to be indiscernible or equivalent if and only if they have the same values for all attributes in the set B. When a concept X, that is a set $X \subseteq \mathcal{U}$, is composed of objects that are all in elementary sets, then all its objects can be distinguished in terms of the available attributes; otherwise, X is roughly defined. Namely, X can be approximated by the sets B*-lower* and B*-upper* approximations of X. More precisely, by denoting with $[x]_B$ the equivalence class containing x, then the B*-lower* approximation of X is

$$\underline{B}(X) = \{x \in \mathcal{U} : [x]_B \subseteq X\}$$

that is $\underline{B}(X)$ is composed of all the elementary sets that are included in X in a not ambiguous way, while the B*-upper* approximation of X

$$\bar{B}(X) = \{x \in \mathcal{U} : [x]_B \cap X \neq \varnothing\}.$$

is the set of all the elementary sets that have a nonempty intersection with X. That is, the lower approximation contains all elements that necessarily belong to the concept, while the upper approximation contains those that possibly belong to the concept. A concept X is called *exact* with respect to B if the boundary region

$$BN_B(X) = \underline{B}(X) - \bar{B}(X)$$

is empty, otherwise it is said to be *rough* with respect to B.

Any object is described by condition attributes and decision attributes, therefore the information system will be called a decision table and will be denoted by $S = (\mathcal{U}, \mathcal{C}, \mathcal{D})$ where $\mathcal{C}$ and $\mathcal{D}$ are respectively the disjoint sets of condition and decision attributes. The *decision rule induced by* x *in* S is the sequence

$$c_1(x), \ldots, c_n(x), d_1(x) \ldots, d_m(x)$$

that is

$$c_1(x),\ldots,c_n(x) \Rightarrow d_1(x)\ldots,d_m(x)$$

or in short $\mathcal{C} \rightarrow_x \mathcal{D}$, when it is supposed that there are n condition attributes and m decision attributes. The *strength* $\sigma_x(\mathcal{C},\mathcal{D})$ *of the decision rule* $\mathcal{C} \rightarrow_x \mathcal{D}$ is represented by the ratio between the support of the decision rule and the cardinality of $\mathcal{U}$, that is

$$\sigma_x(\mathcal{C},\mathcal{D}) = \frac{|\mathcal{C}(x)\cap\mathcal{D}(x)|}{|\mathcal{U}|}$$

With reference to the same decision rule $\mathcal{C} \rightarrow_x \mathcal{D}$ it is possible to set the definitions of *certainty factor,* $cer_x(\mathcal{C},\mathcal{D})$, and *coverage factor,* $cov_x(\mathcal{C},\mathcal{D})$, as

$$cer_x(\mathcal{C},\mathcal{D}) = \frac{|\mathcal{C}(x)\cap\mathcal{D}(x)|}{|\mathcal{C}(x)|}$$

$$cov_x(\mathcal{C},\mathcal{D}) = \frac{|\mathcal{C}(x)\cap\mathcal{D}(x)|}{|\mathcal{D}(x)|},$$

respectively. Clearly, the last two indexes have a probabilistic meaning: the certainty factor of the decision rule represents the conditional probability $\pi_x(\mathcal{D}\mid\mathcal{C})$ that $y \in \mathcal{D}(x)$ conditionally to the assumption that $y \in \mathcal{C}(x)$, the coverage factor of the decision rule represents the conditional probability $\pi_x(\mathcal{C}\mid\mathcal{D})$ that $y \in \mathcal{C}(x)$ conditionally to the assumption that $y \in \mathcal{D}(x)$. In other words, we can write

$$cer_x(\mathcal{C},\mathcal{D}) = \pi_x(\mathcal{D}\mid\mathcal{C})$$
$$cov_x(\mathcal{C},\mathcal{D}) = \pi_x(\mathcal{C}\mid\mathcal{D}).$$

Similarly as stated in [9] for Association Rules, given a decision rule $\mathcal{C} \rightarrow_x \mathcal{D}$ induced by x in S, it is possible to widen the set of explanatory indexes by introducing the *Conditional Probability Increment Ratio* ($CPIR_x$) index which is defined as

$$CPIR_x = \frac{\pi_x(\mathcal{D}\mid\mathcal{C}) - \pi(\mathcal{D}(x))}{1-\pi(\mathcal{D}(x))}$$

where $\pi(\mathcal{D}(x)) = \frac{|\mathcal{D}(x)|}{|\mathcal{U}|}$. $CPIR_x$ measures how much the probability of decision $\mathcal{D}$ increases when condition $\mathcal{C}$ holds. Observing that the strength of the decision rule can be rewritten as

$$\sigma_x(\mathcal{C},\mathcal{D}) = cer_x(\mathcal{C},\mathcal{D})\pi(\mathcal{C}(x)).$$

the $CPIR_x$ index can be expressed in terms of certainty, coverage and strenghts as

$$CPIR_x = \frac{cer_x(\mathcal{C},\mathcal{D}) - \sigma_x(\mathcal{C},\mathcal{D})\,/\,cov_x(\mathcal{C},\mathcal{D})}{1-\sigma_x(\mathcal{C},\mathcal{D})\,/\,cov_x(\mathcal{C},\mathcal{D})} = \frac{cer_x(\mathcal{C},\mathcal{D})cov_x(\mathcal{C},\mathcal{D}) - \sigma_x(\mathcal{C},\mathcal{D})}{cov_x(\mathcal{C},\mathcal{D}) - \sigma_x(\mathcal{C},\mathcal{D})}$$

Summarizing, the certainty factor is probably the most important index: it can be defined as the "rule probability" and measures how strong the "conclusions from the data" are (Pawlak, 2002). The coverage factor instead, gives an "explanation of the obtained results" measuring the "most probable reason" for the decision (Pawlak, 2002).

ROUGH SETS AND TOURISM

Rough sets have been applied to tourism studies since year 2000 (Au & Law, 2000; Law & Au, 2000; Au & Law, 2002) mainly dealing with classification problems. Subsequently some Authors proposed different forecasting models on the basis of traditional macroeconomic indicators and tourist arrivals. More precisely, given annual time-series (Goh & Law, 2003) analyzes the tourist flows from 10 origins to Hong Kong; in (Law, Goh & Pine, 2004) the tourist flows from Japan to Hong Kong (annual time-series) is studied; more recently, (Goh, Law & Mok, 2008) examines the tourist flows from two origins to Hong Kong working with monthly time-series. Note that all these models are built on the basis of traditional macroeconomic indicators and forecast tourist arrivals with a different concern for the discretisation procedure of the decision attribute.

Some limits of the above mentioned studies may be emphasized: the resulting rules are average rules that seem to be more suitable for classification purposes than for forecasting; the models substantially use the same independent variables (condition attributes) of the traditional econometric models; in (Goh, Law & Mok, 2008) the decision attribute (percent variation of monthly arrivals) is correctly discretised from a statistical point of view but it is not so meaningful for tourist operators (for example they claim that "the number of U.K. tourists to Hong Kong will deviate from its previous months from -2.26% to +9.54%").

There was therefore the need for a new approach to the possible synergies between tourist demand models and Rough Sets with the following characteristics:

- Decision rules generation which turns out to be really useful to the tourist operators and the policy makers;
- Measure of rules' stability or their changing in time in order to accept them as a predicting tool;
- Complementary and not competitive role towards the traditional econometric models;
- Exploitation of databases built on categorical data and therefore unsuitable for the traditional econometric models;
- Investigation about different consumption attitudes and identification of some products/services (sentry variables) whose trends may anticipate tourism dynamics.

DATA SET AND SOFTWARE PACKAGES

The research has benefited from a large selection of variables from Sinottica, a database which was made available by GfK Eurisko (GfK Eurisko, 2012), one of the world's largest market research companies and one of the leading market research organization in Italy. Sinottica provides information on social, cultural and behavioural trends in Italy by means of a psychographic survey that GfK Eurisko leads annually relying on a total of 10000 face-to-face interviews, 5000 every six months, i.e. in May/June and October/November (GfK Eurisko, 2012). The survey focuses on Italians aged 14 or more, on their features and behaviours, on their consumptions and media exposure. Data are deseasonalised. In particular we focus on the second semester of 2009 data.

The main research goal was to identify in the Sinottica database a set of attributes concerning non-tourism consumption behaviours which are strictly related to the Italian tourist demand. More precisely, we were looking for non-tourism products or services whose consumption could possibly anticipate tourists' behaviour, a sort of "sentry variables" to be used by the tourism sector stakeholders to forecast short-term to medium-term tourism demand trends. Such sentry variables should be different from the classical leading indicators used in tourism which typically are macroeconomic variables (see e.g. Kulendran & Witt, 2003). The main idea was to find such sentry variables by mining them in the database through the detection of robust ties among data. The links among data should be expressed in term of decision rules generated by means of the Rough Sets algorithms.

We paid particular attention to attributes concerning the consumption of products or services which are measured on a regular basis, e.g. by surveys provided by data collecting sources (Institutions/Companies), in order to get an independent time series of the "sentry variable"' to be used to forecast tourism demand.

We selected 155 condition attributes to obtain suitable decision rules: they are summarized by the following categories:

- Favourite subjects on newspapers (24 attributes: news, national politics, sports,...);
- Favourite subjects on magazines (28 attributes: news, gossip, travel, sports,...);
- Attending movie theatres during the last 3 months (1 attribute);
- Participation to social events during the last 3 months (14 attributes: theatres, exhibitions, fairs,...);
- Leisure (15 attributes: friends, reading, gardening,...);
- Shopping (27 attributes: price/quality and brand choices, weekly budget,...);
- Clothing (21 attributes: fashion wear, jewels, casual wear,...);
- Financial choices (12 attributes: ways to invest, risk attitudes, bank account activity,...);
- Food consumption during the last 3 months (13 attributes: frozen food, pasta, oil consumption, ...).

As decision attribute referring to vacation choices we considered the only variable "vacation of at least 7 days in the last year".

The practical application of Rough Sets Theory to real data requires a significant amount of computational effort. The results of our research, as presented in Section 5 were obtained by means of a freeware software package, ROSE2 (ROSE2, 2012), designed for Rough Sets applications by a Polish team. It requires input data in a proprietary format (ISF - Information System File) to process the information system. This software, unlike other dedicated software (see e.g., Rosetta, 2012), has no limits on the number of objects (here called examples), of condition attributes and of decision attributes.

Remark that in the following, for the sake of simplicity, conditions and decisions are always referred to the affirmative answer to the survey question. For example, we write "vacation" when the answer is "yes" to the question "Did you go on vacation in the last year?", "reader" when there is an affirmative answer to the question "Do you usually read?", and so on.

MAIN RESULTS

We describe now the main outcomes of the research represented by the rules that were identified by the Rough Sets Methodology as the most significant in terms of coverage and/or certainty factors. In particular the selection of data concerning food consumption made available by GfK Eurisko was rather poor (only few variables) and the possible choices didn't produce strong and representative rules.

Dreams Boost Tourism

Issue 1 - Reading, watching movies and trying new technology - in other words training imagination - promotes vacation.

The emerging rules corresponding to the decision "vacation " are reported in Table 1. The reading activity appears to be positively correlated with being tourists. Nearly 70% of the people who visited a bookshop and 65% of the people who

Table 1. Training imagination stimulates vacation: conditions for the decision "vacation"

Condition	Coverage	Certainty
Visited a bookstore (in the last 3 months)	48.99%	69.74%
Reader	48.95%	65.01%
Movies/DVD lover	61.79%	59.38%
Went to a cinema (in the last 3 months)	40.97%	68.95%
Technologies enthusiast	45.40%	60.06%

declared they usually read, went on vacation during the last year. Watching movies/dvd or going to a cinema, is linked to vacation planning too: nearly 60% of the people who watched films/dvd and about 70% of those who went to the cinema answered they took vacations during the last year. Finally, 60% of the people interested in new technology products, told they went on vacation during the last year.

We have therefore a first evidence of some specific aspects of personal attitudes and culture that can be considered as closely related to tourism choices. This leads to identify a first set of possible sentry variables like book sales, dvd renting and movie box office data.

The concept of new technologies as proposed by Sinottica, instead, seems to be a little bit too vague since it refers to a very composite market and we deem that a supplement of research is needed to identify a precise set of technologies whose sale data could be considered as effective sentry variables.

Richness Fosters Vacation

Issue 2 - People with high expenditure potential go on vacation.

The seeking for quality garments and the purchasing of expensive clothes look like a proxy of people's earnings and are clearly tied to tourism consumption. Consumption trend in the fashion market can therefore be used as a sentry variable for the tourism sector.

Table 2. Richness fosters vacation: conditions for the decision "vacation"

Condition	Coverage	Certainty
Haute couture clothing owner	48.08%	61.25%
Clothing accessories are important	51.92%	60.44%
High expenditure for clothing	27.70%	64.49%
Purchase of new clothes each season	74.08%	58.47%
Purchase of fashion clothes only	36.31%	57.73%
Love to spend money	52.31%	60.57%
Believe to be skilled in finance	32.36%	58.67%
Trying to get one's money worth	32.36%	59.43%
I buy what I like (regardless of the price)	29.40%	56.32%
I am willing to pay more for what makes life easier	59.07%	57.32%
Frequent impulsive buyer	32.36%	57.80%

Print Media Consumption is Related to Tourism Consumption

Issue 3 - The reading of newspapers and magazines, especially travel news, is related to tourism consumption.

Remark that newspapers and magazines readers are also considered in section 5.1 as "readers". Nearly 68% of people (see Table 3) who read travel and tourism articles on a magazine answered they went on vacation during the last year. An increase on sales of travel related magazines can be considered as a signal for an increase in tourism consumption but the low coverage suggests some caution, only 28% of people who took vacations told they read travel and tourism articles, indeed.

Cultural and Social Events

Issue 4 - cultural consumption is related to vacation.

We have to remark that many of the respondents didn't answer to questions about their social and cultural life, resulting in a large number of missing values in the related variables. Nevertheless, 66% of people who told they visited monuments

Table 3. Interest in latest news is tied to tourism consumption: conditions for the decision "vacation"

Condition	Coverage	Certainty
News reader on daily newspapers	67.01%	54.20%
Travel and vacation topics reader on magazines	28.29%	67.93%
Domestic politics news reader on daily newspapers	30.58%	61.82%

Table 4. Cultural consumption: conditions for the decision "went on vacation"

Condition	Coverage	Certainty
Visited monuments/churches (in the last 3 months)	25.76%	66.53%
Visited wine and food fairs (in the last 3 months)	27.22%	59.65%
Participated to local festivals (in the last 3 months)	39.98%	57.21%

and churches answered that they went on vacation during the last year. On the other hand, only 26% of those who took vacations told they visited monuments and churches: cultural tourism is an important market segment (high per capita expenditure) but mass tourists prefer other kinds of destinations and experiences (sun & beach).

CONCLUSION AND FUTURE RESEARCH MAIN RESULTS

This work identifies some interesting patterns within GfK Eurisko database Sinottica on Italian consumers trough a data mining process based on Rough Sets Theory. A family of decision rules is the main result of the study together with the discovery of some possible product/services whose market trends could announce variations in specific tourist segments trends. Future research is needed to improve the results so far obtained: the first task is to enlarge the available dataset introducing for example more data concerning food consumption. In fact, food consumption variables are easy to monitor (e.g. through bar codes tracing) and would be the perfect "sentry variables" if a strong relationship with tourism consumption could be detected.

In order to deal with different databases a weighted Rough Set Model could be implemented in order to obtain decision rules and the related adjusted values of the classical indicators certainty and coverage.

Currently we are dealing with the validation of the detected rules by repeating the search for emerging rules over different time windows, corresponding to different data set provided by GfK Eurisko. If the decision rules are "stable", mainly in terms of certainty factor, then "sentry variables" could be considered more reliable.

ACKNOWLEDGMENT

Special thanks to Jerzy Stefanowski, Bartlomiej Predki and Szymon Wilk of the Laboratory of Intelligent Decision Support Systems Poznan University of Technology for their kind collaboration in helping the authors to correctly use ROSE2.

REFERENCES

Au, N., & Law, R. (2000). The application of rough sets to sightseeing expenditures. *Journal of Travel Research*, *39*, 70–77. doi:10.1177/004728750003900109

Au, R., & Law, R. (2002). Categorical classification of tourism dining. *Annals of Tourism Research*, *29*, 819–833. doi:10.1016/S0160-7383(01)00078-0

GfK Eurisko. (2012). Retrieved from http://www.gfk.com/gfk-eurisko/index.en.html

Goh, C., & Law, R. (2003). Incorporating the rough sets theory into travel demand analysis. *Tourism Management*, *24*, 511–517. doi:10.1016/S0261-5177(03)00009-8

Goh, C., Law, R., & Mok, H. (2008). Analyzing and forecasting tourism demand: A rough sets approach. *Journal of Travel Research*, *46*, 327–338. doi:10.1177/0047287506304047

Kulendran, N., & Witt, S. (2003). Leading indicator tourism forecasts. *Tourism Management*, *24*, 503–510. doi:10.1016/S0261-5177(03)00010-4

Law, R., & Au, R. (2000). Relationship modeling in tourism shopping: A decision rules induction approach. *Tourism Management*, *21*, 241–249. doi:10.1016/S0261-5177(99)00056-4

Law, R., Goh, C., & Pine, R. (2004). Modeling tourism demand: A decision rules based approach. *Journal of Travel & Tourism Marketing*, *16*, 61–69. doi:10.1300/J073v16n02_05

Munakata, T. (2008). *Fundamentals of the new artificial intelligence. Neural, Evolutionary, Fuzzy and More* (2nd ed.). London: Springer.

Pawlak, Z. (1991). *Rough sets: Theoretical aspects of reasoning about data*. Boston: Kluwer.

Pawlak, Z. (2002). Rough set theory and its applications. *Journal of Telecommunications and Information Technology*, *3*, 7–10.

ROSE2. (2012). Retrieved from http://idss.cs.put.poznan.pl/site/rose.html

Rosetta. (2012). Retrieved from http://www.lcb.uu.se/tools/rosetta/index.php

Song, H., & Li, G. (2008). Tourism demand modelling and forecasting - A review of recent research. *Tourism Management*, *29*, 203–220. doi:10.1016/j.tourman.2007.07.016

Stefanowski, J. (1998). On rough set based approaches to induction of decision rules. In *Rough Sets in Knowledge Discovery* (pp. 500–529). Berlin: Physica Verlag.

Wu, X., Zhang, C., & Zhang, S. (2004). Efficient mining of both positive and negative association rules. *ACM Transactions on Information Systems*, *22*, 381–405. doi:10.1145/1010614.1010616

Chapter 32
The Promotion of European Tourism in the Emerging Countries:
Pyramidal Marketing

Francisco V. Cipolla-Ficarra
ALAIPO – AINCI, Spain and Italy

Alejandra Quiroga
Universidad Nacional de La Pampa, Argentina

Valeria M. Ficarra
ALAIPO – AINCI, Spain and Italy

ABSTRACT

The authors present the different communication strategies used for the promotion of European tourism in the emerging countries, through Power Point and pyramidal marketing. They also research the veracity and the persuasion strategies used in textual, visual, and hearing information, which go with the images in the interactive presentations. Finally, an analysis technique is presented to detect the possible potential tourists divided in relation to age, education, and knowledge of the use of computers or other interactive systems of mobile multimedia.

INTRODUCTION

While the hardware keeps on evolving faster than the software, so does the digital divide among the population of a same community. Developed or emerging, it is lengthened by the digital divide, in many places of the planet, people resort to the applications that usually accompany a commercial operative system such as Microsoft Windows for the diffusion of messages. In the traditional applications which have accompanied it since the first Windows version, for instance, the presence of

DOI: 10.4018/978-1-4666-4490-8.ch032

instruments oriented at drawing (Paint), text (Notepad and WordPad, etc.) has always been seen which would exercise millions of users for their future computer presentations, with the PowerPoint. A software which is linked to the multimedia notions since their origins, when Bob Gaskins and Dennis Austin developed it under the name of Presenter for the firm Forethought (Abela, 2008). This firm presented it as PowerPoint 1.0 in 1987 for Apple Macintosh. Obviously, with the black and white monitors, the text and the graphics were joined to generate slides. Since 1990 this application would be included in the suite Microsoft Office. With the first color monitor from Macintosh PowerPoint adapted to this novelty to use to the utmost that technological breakthrough and become an in implicit or explicit way a technological "persuasion" tool. Visually and in the audition aspect (the sound effects in the transitions of the slides) this struck powerfully the attention, using digital slides in the classrooms or conferences rooms, at the time. Now it is in the notion of union and intersection where can be found the subtle but important differences in the origins of computer multimedia. Since that moment this commercial application allows to create multimedia presentations through the making of slides which are visualized in sequence in any computer which is available with that commercial software. The presentations are subdivided into slides and each of them can contain pictures, texts, animations, sounds, links to other slides or websites. That is how the multimedia notion is linked to that commercial product, since it allows the combination between them of two or more media. If we speak of media intersection, this refers to the communicational process. In contrast, if we speak of union, we mean the technological aspect. Finally, joining the term "interactive" to the word "multimedia" makes apparent that the user in a communication process enters a feedback dynamic with the system through navigation, such as can be the links of a slide to websites online, for instance.

NAVIGATION

The concept of navigation was the cornerstone of the research works by Nicholas Negroponte and Richard Bolt (Negroponte, 1995) who developed a set of technological instruments to increase the intersection with the computer and obviously incorporated in the operative systems and/or the commercial application that we are analyzing. These instruments or tools helped to establish a link between the hypertext and the active multimedia. They bred a workspace called "Dataland" whose main resources were the cursor, the touch system (already tested in the 80s on some Hewlett Packard tactile screens), the joystick, the zooming in of the images, the use of the voice for the execution of the commands. Perhaps, when Nicholas Negroponte declares the merging of television, the print and computer science towards "a computer-based multimedia technology" (Negroponte, 1995) he was running ahead of his time towards the versions of the new PowerPoint in the second millennium. In the first decade of the 21st century that commercial application would include several novelties which can be summed up in the following way: management of the animations in an individual way and their shadows, diagrams of several types (pyramid, radials, Venn, etc.), incorporation of password, automatic generation of a picture album, integration of the CD package among several users (the CD mastering in CD of the multimedia content with a display was facilitated), implementation of the Ribbon system to improve the interface, etc. In relation to the degree of cohesion of the computer science and the different degrees of interaction in the 80s and early 90s we can make the following classification:

1. **"Sequential" Multimedia:** It is the classical multimedia technology stemming from the print and television which is characterized by the absence of informatics. For instance,

when in a class on geography are used several didactic resources at the same time, with a background music and the voice of the professor who explains what is seen.

2. **"Partially" Interactive Multimedia:** It is the case of the emulations of manual operations controlled from the computer, such as can be the forward or backwards of a song in a CD. The structuring of the information admits a partial interactivity.
3. **"Totally" Interactive Multimedia:** Each source of information is in digital format and allows a high degree of user-computer interaction. It is the example of the Figure 1, the user activates multimedia nodes (1, 2, 3) in different moments of its sequentiality which is depicted with the vertical line. As it can be seen in the figure the different elements of the nodes (animation, audio and text) do not have the same length, which damages the quality of the system by losing the synchronization among the different media. In the first node, the user sees the text, listens to the associated sound, but still does not visualize the animation; in the second node all the components start at the same time, although the end of the sequentiality will be disparate among them. In the third, while the animation and the text still go on, the audio has finished. Besides, the current access speed to the different nodes in the offline multimedia systems can be superior when examining multimedia applications online (Reisman, 1991; Cipolla-Ficarra, 2005; Meleis, 1996; Muller, 1996). In the first presentations of PowerPoint these mistakes were common due to the inexperience of the users in the use of the novel commercial application (Abela, 2008; Reisman, 1991).

These problems in the correct synchronization among the different dynamic and static means of the first presentations were disguised through the effects of the transitions between one slide and the other. The synchronization is a key element in the quality of the media which are broadcast simultaneously and which in the design category of an online and offline interactive system we call panchronism (Cipolla-Ficarra, F., 2010).

TRANSITION

The switch from one screen to another in the presentation category inside the multimedia system receives the name of transition. This notion

Figure 1. "Totally" interactive multimedia

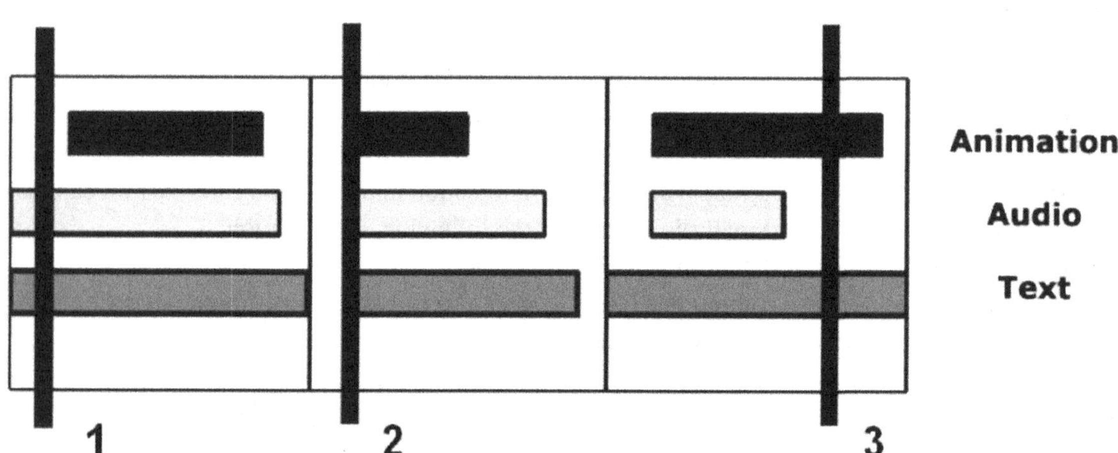

stems from the PowerPoint. In the Figure 4.45 the three stages of a transition of the puzzle type of the Argen-Visión tourism system can be seen (Argen-Visión CD-Rom, 1996). A system which had a great acceptance among the users because it added a collection of transitions which did not exist in PowerPoint. One of them was the puzzle because the same as the offline multimedia systems aimed at cultural heritage, in the mid of the 90s games were already inserted inside some systems aimed at tourism.

Emulating a puzzle between the passing of a screen to another, inside a touristic system increases the communicability of the images or pictures that are being watched, for instance. In a classical transition, we see that in the first stage there is the original screen, where the transition has already started (see screen 1). In the second stage there is the transition process (see screen 2) and in the third stage there is the target screen (see screen 3). The transitions serve to establish a coherence in the presentation of the information. The use of more than a type of transition and the speed of the switch from one screen to another in a small guided link (which does not go beyond five nodes) affects the perception of the whole by the user since he/she may consider every screen as something independent from the rest. In this case a loss of continuity takes place between the different screens which are linked among themselves. The transitions may be grouped in two ways:

1. **Irregular:** Whether it is in the shape of raindrops, puzzle, etc., as can be seen in the Figure 2. These are widely accepted by the users expert or not in the use of computers, when they interact with contents aimed at national tourism, for instance.
2. **Regular:** They have the shape of squares, rectangles, lines or dots. These classical or traditional transitions (most of them stemming from PowerPoint) are adapted internationally for the different potential groups of users. That is, they are ideal for the promotion of international tourism. The movement may have the origin in an angle, a side or the centre. Next are enumerated several types of geometrical transitions with their matching graphics. (Figure 3) and later on there are some examples of the system Argen-Visión (Figure 4 –1, 2, 3, and 4). Dissolve by pixels; Blind: Hiding or discovery from the angles; Hiding or vertical discovery from the middle of the screen; Pictures or incoming or outgoing screens; Hiding or discovery from the sides; Turns or spirals of hiding and discovery; Horizontal or vertical shifts, etc.

The transitions are also related to the cultural factors of the design of an interface. According to Leonardo Da Vinci, when he defines the "Divine Proportion" he establishes areas which draw the attention on a screen. In a rectangle there is a greater level of attention in the inner area of its surface. Besides, if two cross-shaped lines are drawn one find that the upper superior half attracts a higher level of attention than the lower left in the Latin peoples. In the following rectangles of the Figure 4.51 are shown the areas which draw the greater and the lesser attention of the Latin users, zones 1 and 4 respectively. However, not all the components of the screen can hold zone 1.

This is the reason why other dynamic and static media must be used to draw the user's attention, such as transparencies, blurring, lightening effects, etc. Besides it is necessary to consider the direction of the transitions, that is, what is the origin and the destination of the movement on the screen. A transition in diagonal shape which has its origin in the upper left angle and goes down towards the lower right angle of the of the screen is more correct for a Western than for an Eastern user. This is due to the visual direction at the moment of reading. To solve these differences, a way which has been tested with success

Figure 2. Irregular transition

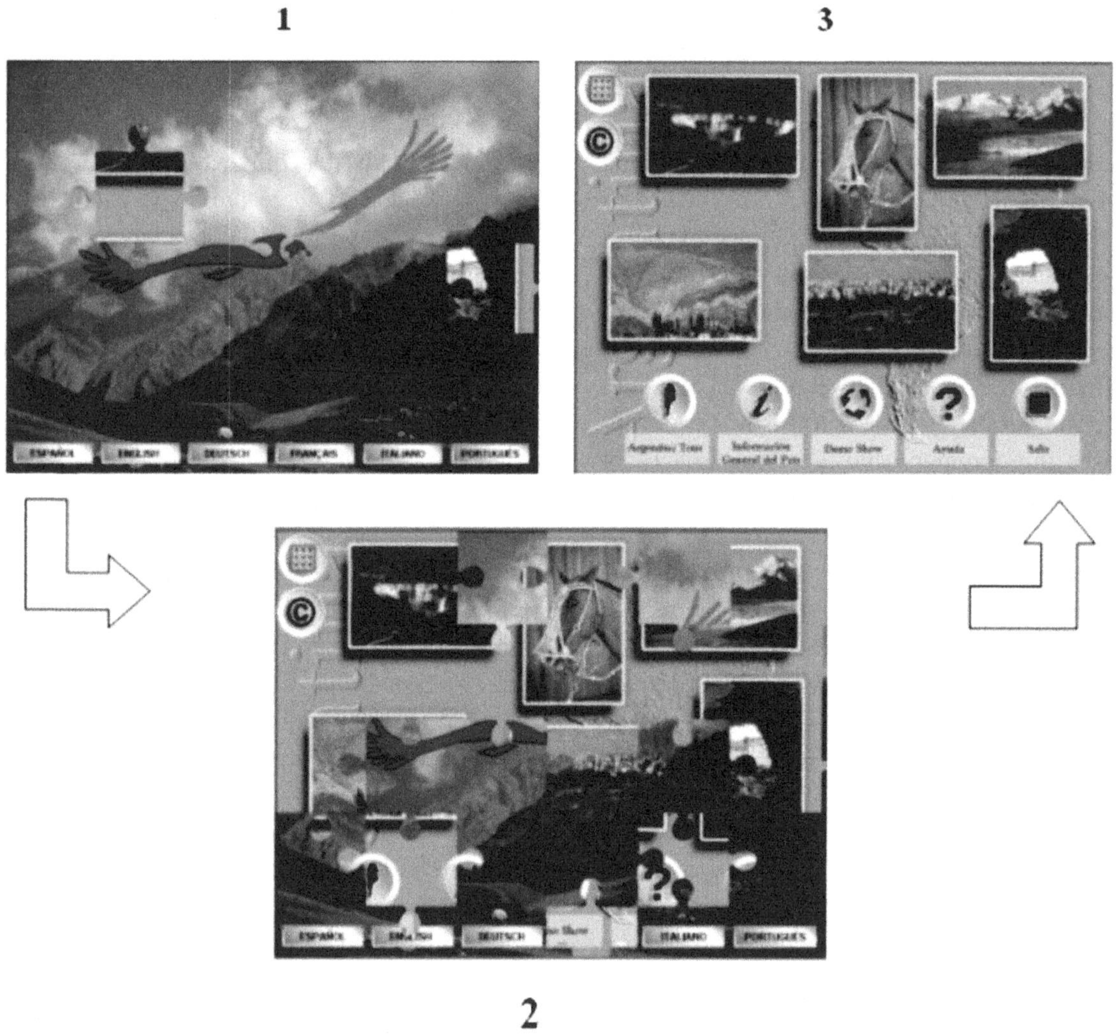

1

3

2

Figure 3. Regular transition

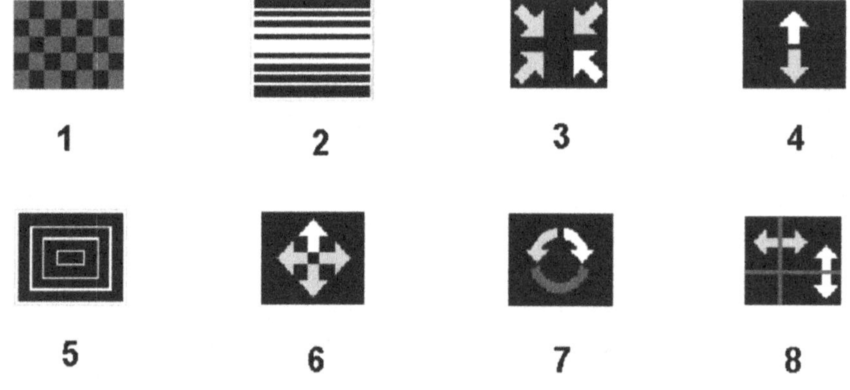

Figure 4. Geometrical transitions

Figure 5. Divine Proportion

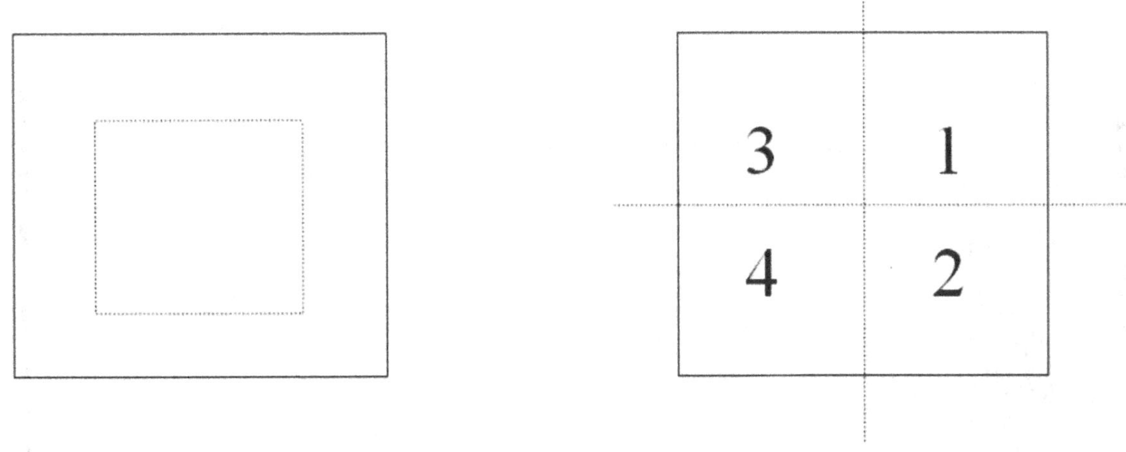

in the first multimedia systems in floppy support, developed for the subject "Mulltimedia and Communication" at the UOC (Open University of Catalonia) was the use of transitions of the dissolution type by pixels (Cipolla-Ficarra, 1996). The floppy support means that not every user had a CD-Rom reader in their PC and the remote access to the virtual campus was made through the modem, wired to the landline.

STRATEGY IN THE DIFFUSION OF CONTENTS AND CONFORMATION OF THE UNIVERSE OF STUDY

Whereas in the virtual campus the educational process takes place through an Internet connection (this entails being connected for a longer time to the landline service) the sending of messages enclosing files of the PowerPoint presentations is fast and the visualization of the content does not require being wired online to Internet. Consequently this diffusion of contents in enclosed file format turns out to be more economical than interactive online education.. The files for IBM PC or compatible are three: ppt (PowerPoint presentation), pps (only PowerPoint presentation) or pot (PowerPoint model). In the Mac-OS-X (2008) the Open Office XML format was introduced, with a better understanding of the data in the files. Its three extensions are pptx, ppsx, and potx.

Now the rhetorical question is: How to get that a message is spread the most widely possible among the potential tourists? We could answer

Figure 6. Multimedia systems in floppy support for Open University of Catalonia

that we have detected in the universe of study the pyramidal system or Saint Anthony chain. A typical chain of messages consists in a message which tries to induce the receptor to make copies of the message to later pass them on to one or more new receptors. A chain message can be regarded as a kind of meme. A meme –or mem (Cipolla-Ficarra, 2010) is, in the theories on cultural diffusion, the theoretical unit of cultural information (transmissible from an individual to another, or from a generation to the next: The commonly used methods in the chain messages include emotionally manipulating stories, pyramidal schemes or pyramidal marketing. In economics it is known as pyramid or pyramidal scheme a pattern of business that is based on the participants sending more clients with the purpose that the new participants bring profits to the original participants. The name of pyramid is given because it is required that the number of new participants is higher than the existing ones. These pyramids are considered as swindles or fraud schemes. Besides, the chains of digital messages are liable to evolve in their content, as a rule to improve their capacity of replicating along time. This happens sometimes through deliberate modifications of the chain by an expert user or through mistakes in the copy, when the user is inexpert in the use of computers (Nielsen & Mack, 1994). In the case of the expert user, in a ppt file, the text may change, eliminate or add photographs, include a background music for each one of the slides, etc. That is, in our case of study, the touristic files circulate without changes protection or password, although the PowerPoint application has the option of protecting the documents through DMR (Digital Management Rights). In other words, the password avoids that these documents can be opened to modify them. Or their contents can be read, whether for the Mac OS PowerPoint versions of PowerPoint nor with other applications of commercial software capable of opening those files, such as OpenOffice.org or Apple keynote.

With the development of the email and the Internet, the chains have become much more common and fast in spreading than when they were transmitted through a physical media, although the RFC 1855 (Netiquette Guidelines –hhtp://toolsietf.org/htlm/rfc1855) explicitly advises against them as a breach of netiquette. Although some email suppliers forbid the users the sending of e-mail messages in chain in their usage conditions. In our study, we have detected that the profile of the users, whose ages oscillate between 45 – 55 years generally does not introduce changes in the PowerPoint touristic profiles received, but they are fosterers of those pyramidal systems since they have had financial experiences in the past. We have focused on the messages received for the fostering of tourism by 10 adult professors, in schools or primary and secondary institutes in the city of Buenos Aires (Argentina). The temporal space of the study encompasses June 2011 – June 2012. As soon as the messages were received, the professors stored them in an individual file non-accessible to other users of the network. In Appendix 1 we have a random sample of some of the messages they received.

A FIRST ANALYSIS TECHNIQUE TO DETECT THE POSSIBLE POTENTIAL TOURISTS SEIZED WITH THE PYRAMIDAL SYSTEM

After the indication by many professors associations of the constant reception of messages stemming from pyramidal systems with offers of touristic trips, the presence of ppt. files was detected. Those have been accumulating along 12 months for the set of common denominators which existed in those files. Later on, a sample of said files was drawn through the assignation of a number and using a lottery drum, the numbers were randomly extracted, to make up the set of our study. That is, the PowerPoint presentations, whose files are to be found in the following link for their visualization (www.pirateando.net/work-in-progress-ra-16.html), titles of the presentations translated into English and total of slides are:

1. "A love affair with Paris", 40 slides.
2. "Amatciens, the unknown paradise in Latvia", 44 slides.
3. "Beautiful little streets from France (somewhere in France)", 30 slides.
4. "Florence" (without title), 52 slides.
5. "Greece", 83 slides.
6. "Holy Family, history-chronology", 70 slides.
7. "Hungary", 35 slides.
8. "Oneglia and the Belgranian roots", 15 slides.
9. "Opera of Paris", 35 slides.
10. "Rome, eternal city", 49 slides.
11. "The Bohemia from Paris", 29 slides.
12. "The Canary Islands", 49 slides.
13. "The other Spain, which smells of cane", 42 slides.
14. "The routes of the Tsars and Bolsheviks", 56 slides.
15. "The Transcantabric: a railway cruise", 70 slides.

The prevailing language is Spanish (97% of the presentations), but there also files with slides in English, French, Italian and Portuguese). Our first technique that we use is direct observation and visualization of each one of the slides that make up the presentation. Once the content has been visualized we proceed to the binary compilation of a table of heuristic evaluation (www.pirateando.net/work-in-progress-ra-00.html), where are allocated the categories of design that we have used in this work, through letters (P = Presentation, C = Content, etc.). There are also some open options in that table, that is, that the communicability evaluator must write, such as the total of slides, or the author of the music that usually accompanies the presentation. Total of slides, color or black & white, regular and/or irregular transition effects, commercial information (costs of services and products), biographical information (of the author of the presentation or an artist, for instance), historical information, touristic information (maps, guided visits schedules, etc.), updated information, secular or religious information, quoting of the sources of the dynamic and/or static media (music, photos, paintings, etc.) helps and/or information for the interaction (for instance, what button it is necessary to press on the mouse for the passing of the slides or whether it is an automatic presentation), synchronism between the audio and the image.

Once the binary data have been obtained, we proceed to compile an open formulary where the evaluator describes for each category of design the eventual communicability failings, and also the persuasive resources from the textual perspective, visual and audio which accompany the images, that is, respecting the categories of interactive design.

The binary data with the data of the open formulary converge on a scoring system, where o is the minimal value and 10 is the highest value. The use of direct observation, the filling of tablets and personalized comments of the evaluators allow to test the obtained data to reach a greater objectivity in the final result. A summary of the personalized comments are in Appendix 2.

LESSONS LEARNED

In the samples that has been analyzed the use of sets of pictures has been made clear, apparently with touristic purposes. In fact there are other purposes in the message which is spread in the pyramidal systems thanks to the commercial applications of great worldwide circulation such as PowerPoint. On the one hand we have the commercial aspect which with a few exceptions are related to the touristic aspect and on the other hand the religious aspect. Aprioristically a high percentage of the source of these pyramids is to be found in religious institutions of the Iberian Peninsula.

The use of the PowerPoint through messages spread in cascades from the summit of the pyramid (allegedly with a touristic or cultural purpose) towards adult people of a certain educational level (professors in our universe of study), cultural and with access to the Internet, makes apparent an international persuasive campaign to attract tourists, with a middle-high purchasing power from other countries towards religious environments of the Old World, for instance. An example is the use of classical music or that which has been known since a young age by adult people or the elderly in their youth. That is, messages aimed at the feelings and not towards reason or logic. Although the artistic-cultural heritage is very high in Europe, there are contradictions as to content and the connotations stemming from the sequential reading of those images, accompanied or not with text or music. In the last month we have detected the use of Youtube for the circulation of similar contents and we will aim our investigations towards the social networks. In the next works we will perfect the heuristic techniques used in the current work. These are our future lines of research.

CONCLUSION

These first results have allowed to detect the presence of organizations to attract constantly tourism from remote places of our planet, resorting to the persuasion and manipulation of the contents, allegedly touristic and/or neutered from the point of view of informative objectivity. Obviously, from the point of view of the communicability of the interactive design the quality of these analyzed works is small. However, this continuous sending of messages to the personal accounts of the adult users of computers serves to seize the attention of the public to which they are aimed. In other words, to motivate them, directly or indirectly, to make trips beyond their national borders. The proposed techniques have allowed to get reliable results, in a fast and economic way, since the communicability expert does not require a special lab for this kind of analysis. Besides, we have worked with two models of information, more or less objective. The objective is in the binary table, with that which can be regarded as less objective by some professionals of the formal sciences, especially in the use of some techniques of heuristic evaluation, such as the writing of comments. By inserting in both cases the need to write the total of analyzed slides, it has allowed us to quickly verify if the evaluator has really interacted with the whole system. The verification of the reached results is essential to increase the reliability in the partial evaluations, at low costs and excellent quality in the interactive multimedia systems off-line or online.

Finally, the pyramidal system of message sending is a way to increase the possibility that the emails become gathering centres of spam messages. In our case we have analyzed the tourism field, through the natural and cultural heritage which can also be found in contents with persuasive purposes, far from this kind of promotion. Now we have also detected other contents such as health and especially using the PowerPoint and the Saint Anthony chains, to present the problems of the Bellvitge Hospital, for instance, thousands of kilometers away from Catalonia (Spain). We think that little or nothing may interest to the inhabitants of Buenos Aires (Argentina) the problems of that hospital and its director which appear in the PowerPoint presentation.

REFERENCES

Abela, A. (2008). *Advanced presentations by design: Creating communications that drives action*. San Francisco, CA: Pfeiffer.

Argen-Visión. (1996). [CD-ROM]. Barcelona: Cotoinsa.

Cipolla-Ficarra, F. (1996). Evaluation and communication techniques in multimedia product design for on the net university education. In *Proceedings of Multimedia '95*. Vienna, Austria: Springer. doi:10.1007/978-3-7091-9472-0_14

Cipolla-Ficarra, F. (2005). Synchronism and diachronism into evolution of the interfaces for quality communication in multimedia systems. In *Proceedings of HCI International 2005*. Las Vegas, NV: HCI.

Cipolla-Ficarra, F. (2010). *Quality and communicability for interactive hypermedia systems: Concepts and practices for design*. Hershey, PA: IGI Global. doi:10.4018/978-1-61520-763-3

Meleis, H. (1996). Toward the information network. *IEEE Computer*, *29*(10), 69–78. doi:10.1109/2.539723

Muller, N. (1996). Multimedia over the network. *Byte*, 73-83.

Negroponte, N. (1995). *Being digital*. New York: Knopf.

Nielsen, J., & Mack, R. (1994). *Usability inspection methods*. New York: Willey.

Reisman, S. (1991). Developing multimedia applications. *IEEE Computer Graphics and Applications*, *11*(4), 52–57. doi:10.1109/38.126881

APPENDIX 1: RANDOM SAMPLE – MESSAGES

Figure 7. Tour Eiffel: Tourism promotion from Brazil or Portugal

FW: Do alto da Torre Eiffel Posta in arrivo

Rispondi | Rispondi a tutti | Inoltra | Stampa | Elimina | Mostra originale

Espetacular. **É muito bonito!!!**

No alto da Torre Eiffel (*demora um pouquinho pra carregar, mas é legal*)

Clique na foto !

Figure 8. Video online about natural heritage (Youtube)

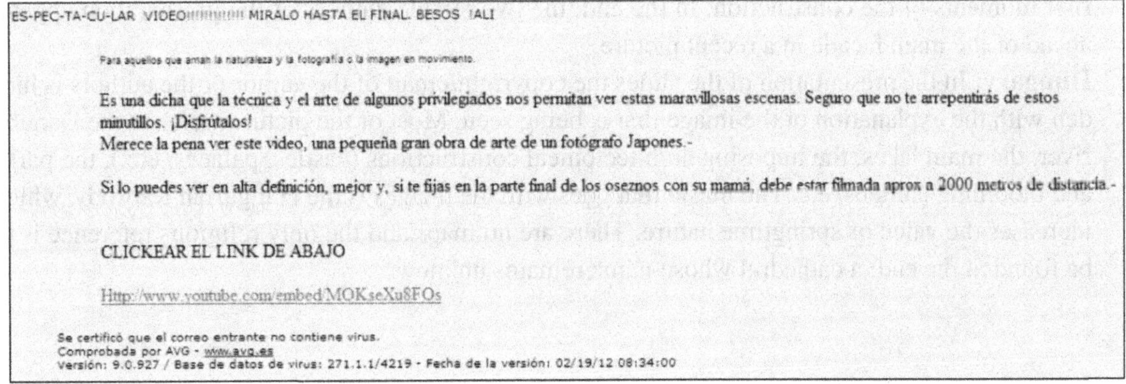

ES-PEC-TA-CU-LAR VIDEO!!!!!!!!!!!! MIRALO HASTA EL FINAL. BESOS !ALI

Para aquellos que aman la naturaleza y la fotografía o la imagen en movimiento.

Es una dicha que la técnica y el arte de algunos privilegiados nos permitan ver estas maravillosas escenas. Seguro que no te arrepentirás de estos minutillos. ¡Disfrútalos!
Merece la pena ver este video, una pequeña gran obra de arte de un fotógrafo Japones.-

Si lo puedes ver en alta definición, mejor y, si te fijas en la parte final de los oseznos con su mamá, debe estar filmada aprox a 2000 metros de distancia.-

CLICKEAR EL LINK DE ABAJO

Http://www.youtube.com/embed/MOKseXu8FOs

Se certificó que el correo entrante no contiene virus.
Comprobada por AVG - www.avg.es
Versión: 9.0.927 / Base de datos de virus: 271.1.1/4219 - Fecha de la versión: 02/19/12 08:34:00

APPENDIX 2: COMMENTS

1. **A Love Affair with Paris:** Current pictures which show some of the architectonical emblems of Paris, such as the Tour Eiffel, the Louvre Museum, the Arc of Triumph, but there are plenty of pictures about Notre Dame, with relation to the rest. Springtime pictures prevail, although there are others of the same places in other stations of the year and the day. In some cases the pictures are duplicated in vertical format, that is, two identical in the same slide.
2. **Amatciens, the Unknown Paradise in Latvia:** It starts by placing the region on a map and with the ecology issue, but in fact it is about the sale of wood houses for € 200,000. Progressively are shown the advantages of the place and the architectonical details of those constructions. The international character of the place is also stressed from the point of view of its inhabitants. There are slides of a single text, interposed with others of a single picture. In the end there is the picture of the architect or real estate agent of those houses, regarded as an "ecological genius".
3. **Beautiful Little Streets from France (Somewhere in France):** It is a set of pictures of a village in a mountain area, which have no texts, and whose background music belongs to George Moustaki: "Passe les temps".
4. **Florence (Without Title):** The presentation starts with the classical roofs of the red-tiled city, which make up a kind of toboggan towards the city. Little by little the sequence of photographs introduces the daily life of the inhabitants such as the bars, the people in the street, etc. Simultaneously are shown the typical monuments, making stress on the churches. Two slides about the humanized signalization of the traffic are striking, the curiosities of some graffiti and the lightening effects on the night pictures There are no texts.
5. **Greece (Whose Slogan is an Invitation to Know Greece Following Saint Paul's Steps, in the Gospel Route):** Summer walk through the main archeological sites of the country, where most of the pictures have references from the Bible. Some of the pictures have been pulled or widened to occupy the whole space of the slide. There are maps in English, with explanatory texts in the middle of the presentation and even the titles of the slides are written in Greek. At the end it bears the signature of the Barefooted Carmelites from Huelva (Spain), with a Yahoo.es address.
6. **Holy Family, History-Chronology:** It starts with a wide textual information and progressively are seen the historic images (black and white) with the allegedly current ones (in fact, they are from several decades ago). As background is kept an image of the façade in black and white, mainly and above it are presented explanatory texts (use of transparences) of the overlaying photographs of the different historical characters. Characters who have participated directly or indirectly since the first moments of the construction. In the end, the two female authors of the presentation appear, ahead of the main façade in a recent picture.
7. **Hungary:** In the presentation of the slides the copyright/email of the author or the authors is hidden with the explanation of the image that is being seen. Most of the pictures refer to the Danube river, the main lakes, the imposing architectonical constructions (castles, palaces, etc.), the parks and blooming gardens, etc. The music that goes with the images is the Hungarian Rapsody, which increases the value of springtime nature. There are no maps and the only religious reference is to be found at the end: a cathedral whose name remains unknown.

8. **Oneglia and the Belgranian Roots:** Combination of texts and current photographs of the town hall and main sites of the city. There is a stress on some religious frescos. The data of the author are available, who prepared the presentation as if it was a multimedia product, indicating the source of the photographs (web) and incorporating an email address. The music that goes with the images is a military march.
9. **Opera of Paris:** It starts and ends with an animated bitmap of a curtain that opens and closes. There are no texts and transitions in oval shape present recent pictures, whether it is in a general shot or detailed of the building. It has as background the music of the opera Nabuco by Giuseppe Verdi (the slaves chorus). In some of them it is feasible to recognize the photographers.
10. **Rome, Eternal City:** It is an excellent presentation where the current and springtime pictures are coupled with the copyrights of their authors. There are also pictures from the Vatican included. There are slides with the main fashionable Italian brands, design, automobiles, etc. The handling of the transition effects is correct. The chosen music is Arrivederci Roma. In the end, the author will appear who has translated the texts of the Portuguese presentation.
11. **The Bohemia from Paris:** It is a very good presentation about Parisian bohemia. A term which generates an isotopy in each one of the texts and images (photographs or paintings from Montmartre: "la boheme", for instance. There is a richness of warm colors (primary and secondary) in the pictures. Besides, there is a visit to the main sites related to that word (inclusion of bars or typical Parisian businesses). The background music is by Charles Aznavour.
12. **The Canary Islands:** Combinations of photographs with a strong commercial connotation of hotels, beaches and churches. All of them in summer time. Prevalence of the touristic commercial offer over the nature of the Islands. There is no text.
13. **The Other Spain, which Smells of Cane:** It has a starting slide where there are animated icons to signal the music and where the use of the mouse is not necessary since they are automatic. Old pictures, where first is presented a picture in black and white, then, through the animated effects of the PowerPoint appears the same but in color. Each one of the pictures has an explanatory text and the religious topics are mixed with panoramic images of natural landscapes and/or Spanish cities. In one of the pictures of the façade of the Holy Family in Barcelona the author has introduced a rainbow.
14. **The Routes of Tsars and Bolsheviks:** Oddly enough, in the first place, appears the explanatory text and later the images, some of them not so current. These are related to the orthodox churches, the Moscow subway, the Peterhof Palace, the Kazan cathedral, the churches and wood belfries in Kizhi, churches in Kolomenskoe, monastery of Valaam, etc. In the end there is a reference to the touristic website of Russia.
15. **The Transcantabric: A Railway Cruise:** It consists in the touristic promotion of a seven-days trip in a train, whose information about the prices of 2009 (written in Portuguese) already indicate us the potential users of the content, since a single cabin has a cost of € 3500 and a double € 5200. In the presentation are mixed the gastronomy of the train with that of the different cities of the north of Spain (Galicia – The Basque Country) where the train stops over in the week the trip lasts, combining train and bus to visit the national park of the Peaks of Europe. The copyright apparently belongs to a hotel (California).

Note: For the interested readers, they can check the commented files in the following website: http://www.pirateando.net/work-in-progress-ra-16.html

Chapter 33
"Cozinha da Madeira": A Sustainable Tourism Service Concept for Madeira Island

Valentina Nisi
Madeira-ITI, University of Madeira – Funchal, Portugal

Nuno Nunes
Carnegie Mellon University, USA

Kanarak Isarankura
Carnegie Mellon University, USA

Jodi Forlizzi
Madeira-ITI, University of Madeira – Funchal, Portugal

ABSTRACT

Sustainability is an outstanding global issue. Our present vision of wellbeing requires resource consumption that cannot be reproduced in a sustainable way. In this chapter, the authors present a case study of "Cozinha da Madeira" (CdM), a service design concept. CdM is a design concept that highlights how one can leverage tourism in order to promote sustainable services and experiences. Through the design of the CdM transformational experience, one invites customers to appreciate local products, resources, and traditions of the island, and in general orient themselves towards more sustainable practices in their further travels abroad as well as in their own home countries. The authors are currently developing a Web-based mobile application based on the premises and research presented in this chapter in order to deliver the service to potential users and evaluate the hypothesis.

INTRODUCTION

Sustainability is an increasingly important global issue. Quite simply, human beings, and particularly those in the western world, use resources far faster than they can be reproduced. The most popular definition of sustainability can be traced back to 1987 UN conference. Back then sustainable developments were defined as those that "meet present needs without compromising the ability of future generations to meet their needs" (WECD, 1987). Today, human beings, and particularly those in the

DOI: 10.4018/978-1-4666-4490-8.ch033

western world, use resources far faster than they can be reproduced (Manzini, Walker & Wylant, 2007; Manzini, 2005). This behavior is arguably a consequence of the seductive vision of "wellbeing" afforded, enabled and encouraged by industrialization – a vision based on personal ownership and mass consumption (Manzini, Walker & Wylant, 2007). These well-established definitions set an ideal premise, but do not clarify specific human and environmental parameters for modeling and measuring sustainable developments. For instance that sustainability requires an attitude in development that looks at natural resources (water, land and energy) and natural cycles in a way that celebrates continuity, uniqueness and placemaking. In review of the plurality of these definitions, the site or the environmental context is an important variable in most working definitions of sustainability. This plurality is address in our attempt to design a service that takes into considerations multiple issues related to sustainability and create and experience that reflects on this plurality.

Sustainability has long been a core concern in the design community, from architecture to product/service design (Blevis, 2007; Gupta & Vajic, 1999). More recently that interest grew in the HCI and interaction design communities (e.g. Blevis, 2007). From a design point of view, a sustainable system is one which maintains or enables a high "context quality" without depleting resources, highlighting that a sustainable solution must be combined with an improved quality of both social and physical life. A sustainable solution is therefore defined as the process by which products, services and know-how compose a system enabling people to achieve a result coherent with the principles of sustainability: low energy, material intensity, and a high regenerative potential (Clandinin & Connelly, 2000; Gupta & Vajic, 1999).

Furthermore, our approach builds on Manzini's concept of enabling services, where enabling means emphasizing users activity versus a disabling service, where services seem to bring comfort to its users by helping them to do less. For example services such as dry cleaning, day care for kids, elder care, not to mention holiday packages or supermarket, precooked meals are all examples of disabling services, as they seem to bring comfort to its users by helping them to do less. The idea behind disabling services to spare time and energy (Clandinin & Connelly, 2000). But, on the other hand, as humans, we are fundamentally receive pleasure from action. An enabling service can foster engagement with the service itself by promoting the pleasure derived from action, increasing the probability that these initiatives spread and develop. Through changes in the way individuals or communities act to achieve a result, social innovation is also fostered and promoted. For example, by observing creative communities where individuals initiate their own sustainable solutions, such as communal rooftop gardening in urban space or car sharing, emphasizes the value of enabling services as opportunities in co-creation and innovation (Manzini, 2005).

Designing solutions for sustainability no longer lies only on the conventional concept of re-use or re-cycle materials. It means in the first place to understand the reasons that drive the existence of specific objects and services and the experiences that those products and services enable. In order to look at such a diverse range of outcomes, we engaged with service design and an interdisciplinary team who were part of a sustainability research project. Our goal within the service design effort reported here is to observe and extract the essence of existing and traditional services that could inspire us in designing new sustainable ones.

Customers as well as companies are concerned with sustainable solutions for different motives. Companies are interested because issues related to sustainability have reached policy levels and need to be followed by companies when producing their outputs. Corporations increasingly gain in image and marketing promoting sustainability related concerns, branding themselves as sustainable can even increase their profits. On the other hand, for consumers being sustainable is a desirable attitude but is often coupled with more effort and less results. This is due to the fact that today the idea of wellbeing is still coupled with very high rate of energy consumption (transportation, electricity, printing etc.) and a series of disabling services (Manzini, 2005) where the users are disconnected from the pleasure of doing and rather connected with the idea that doing less is the desirable thing. Keeping these issues in mind, we took on the challenge of designing a sustainable service tailored to the island of Madeira.

Designing a Sustainable Service

The designers' possibility of promoting successful sustainable solutions is based on their ability to present to their possible users some alternatives that they can recognize as better solutions (for their needs and desires) and that, at the same time, may be considered as more sustainable solutions (from a social and environmental point of view). When this happens, designers, and the companies that produce and deliver the solutions, enable the users/ clients to shift from an un-sustainable system and un-sustainable behaviors to more sustainable ones.

What users demand is not a given system of products or services, but the results that these products and services enable them to achieve. The same demand for results may change in time, when new results substitute the old ones. Given a result, it can be achieved thanks to different solutions: i.e. different combinations of products, services, knowledge and user's participation (in terms of energy, time, attention and knowledge). Each one of these combinations presents different social, economic and environmental characteristics.

However, to suggest a sustainable behavior by merely adding another product or service on the market would conflict with its propose. One of the goals of the "Cozinha da Madeira" (CdM) Service Design concept is to enhance and support sustainable behavior while delivering an entertaining and culturally rich experience, by taking into consideration existing infrastructures and businesses as well as leveraging the existing values of the locality. In the case of Madera, its beautiful landscapes and fresh food and culinary tradition. CdM aims at building a model in the customer's mind so that their direct physical and mental experience of the Cdm service stored in their memories, will later guide them towards intuitively sustainable choices, such as looking at local products when shopping, interacting with the produces of the goods, or valuing traditional recipes and cooking tips. Our approach investigates a holistic view of the Madeira culture, rituals, influence, products, and services contemporary as well as past. Traditions that have been practiced for a long time in the island and have disappeared over time. This project leverages existing social and individual needs, practices and processes that can contribute to a sustainable way of living. The aim is to generate a service that motivates people by supporting them to think, act, reflect and consume sustainably. The CDM service stages for its costumers a unique experience that not only introduces them to the local culture of the place they are visiting, but motivates them to seek similar experiences also elsewhere, even in their countries of residence, by visiting local farms and picking up regional products and learning traditional recipes.

Background Research

In order to test our service design proposition, and to understand the local community, we devised a research plan based on the contextual inquiry (Beyer & Holtzblatt, 1997) and cultural probes (Gaver, Dunne & Pacenti, 1999) research techniques. Cultural probes are a popular indirect way to gather information about people and their activities. We used probes to learn about how what is to be "a Madeiran" (see Figure 1). Contextual inquiry was the other research method we used to interview users about Madeira. The practical as well as theoretical insights from this investigation, summarized below, inspired us in defining our approach and service design concept. Madeirans appear to be aware about sustainable issues. As islanders, they have always dealt with finite resources, and sustainable practices are still present in local society. This is particularly true in older generations and agricultural communities. They care more about food issues, land preservation, and traditional recipes, and prefer regional food to imported. Family gatherings and socialization happen around meals and traditional events, which are kept very much alive by the local community. Madeirans also tend to take care of their own older and younger ones through family members. The above are all examples of sustainable practices, which have many overlaps with Manzini's principles of sustainability. Hence we tried to weave them as much as possible into our service design.

These values coupled with the major source of income for the island, which is tourism, motivated the design of a service that revolves around entertaining tourists while exposing them to local traditional food and landscapes, seen as agricultural ground as well as patrimony of natural beauty.

CASE STUDY: "COZINHA DA MADEIRA"

Madeira is a luxurious subtropical island, with roughly 270,000 inhabitants. Madeira is visited by hundreds of thousands of tourists every year, due to its mild climate, breathtaking landscapes, clean waters and genuine and fresh food. As a recently modernized agricultural society, Madeira holds a lot of living knowledge and traditions regarding land, food and agriculture. The steep land and lack of transportation meant that historically, Madeira's agriculture was a family matter. Now, thanks to the rapid changes in lifestyle of the Madeira population, agriculture is not such a sought after profession as before, but the pride for the fresh and tasty products of the island and the traditional recipes that use them. The change in Madeira was rapid, with an evident overgrowing of physical infrastructures, which brought dramatic changes in lifestyle. In this fast growing process, we noticed a disruption between the way older generations were living and the way the younger generations perceive the Island. Here we want to re-apply some past knowledge into a new service. With CdM the whole island of Madeira becomes our restaurant, food supply shop and educational playground. The service envisioned allows locals and tourists to travel along determined paths around the whole island in order to collect the ingredients that will finally be prepared into a meal in the actual service provider headquarter and kitchen facility. The project invites people to experience a new way of consuming food ingredients from the field to the table. The CdM service embraces the natural beauty of the island and connects deeply with its traditions and local population. CdM brings food to life by combining people, products and experience together in a single journey. Seasonal recipes are proposed as an opportunity for visitors to tour the island and meet is local inhabitants in a meaningful and rich context: their land and food. The CdM experience targets mainly local young as well as tourists from the mainland and abroad. Both young and old are welcomed and supported by customization of the service to adapt to their needs and skills.

As Pine and Gilmore predicted, Theater provides a valid framework in order to stage experiences. CdM is a representational performance in the form of service (Gupta & Vajic, 1999). It is based on collaborative service model that welcomes participants to be part of the operational team according to their profession and interest. It emphasizes on co-creation principle where all the key players are like jigsaw pieces needed in order to deliver the service. Using the CdM website, (see Figure 2), each customer can cast him/herself in the specific role very much as an actor would be casted in a specific role in a play. CdM roles include: participant, driver, and chef. The customers cast themselves in the service

Figure 1. Cultural probes used in the research plan

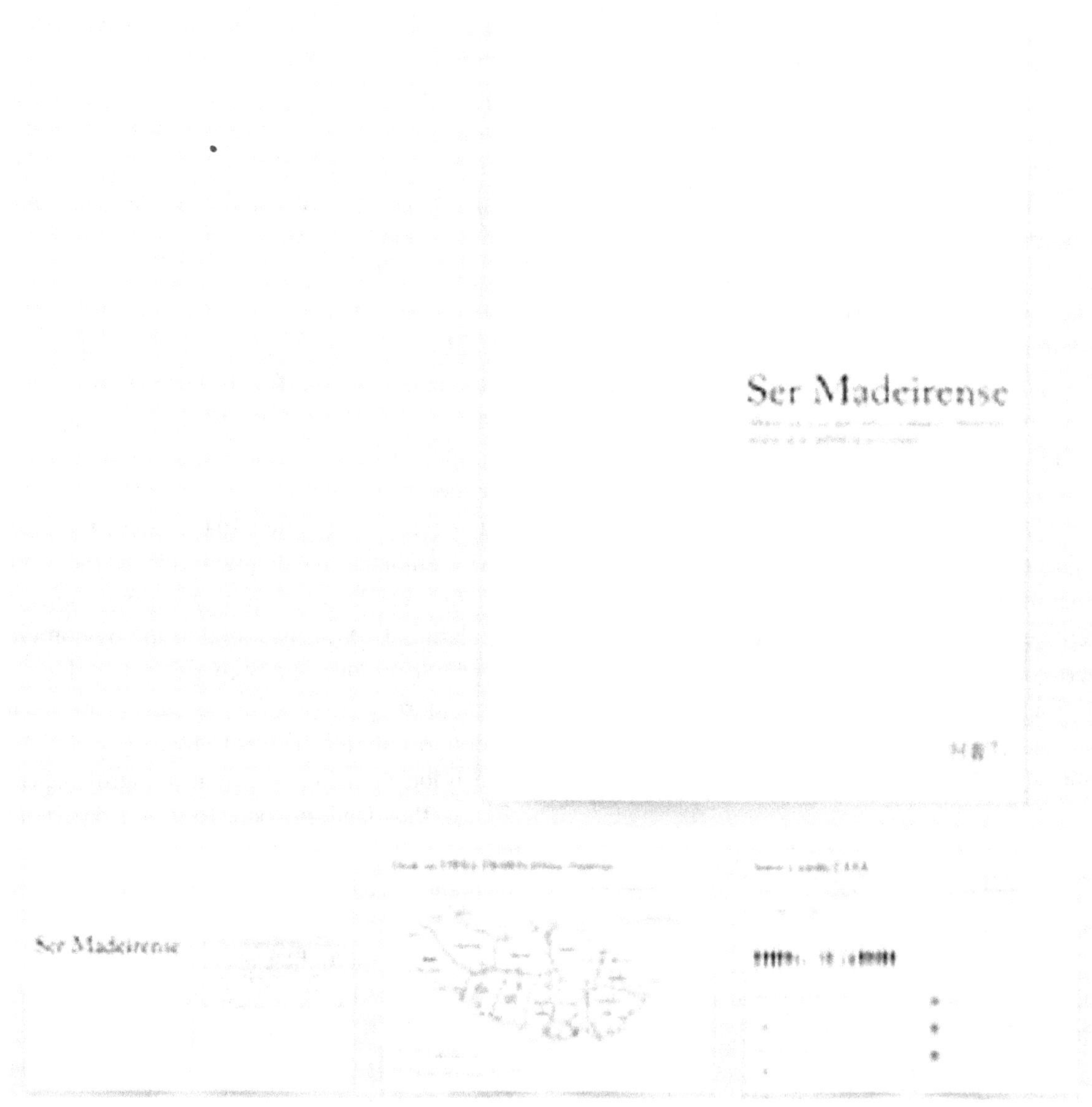

experience by signing up for their role on the website, depending on their interest. CdM is divided into three service stages, which are: Supplier Searching, Chef Searching and Participants Experience. In the Supplier Searching stage CdM staff will look for suppliers that want to engage with participants and sell their products directly to them during their food journey. The driver and chef search employees CdM staff in ensuring a competent driver and chef to be engaged with the experience and test their itinerary through the island and recipe. The Participant Experience stage involves planning and execution of the food journey in the CdM van, smooth tour of the island while purchasing ingredients and meeting local people, as well as arrangement of the dinner stage, cooking, serving and voting over the food.

Customer Journey and Service Touchpoints

The service design approach suggests the identification of the service "customer journey" as a sequence of activities that define a process in which all the dimension of the service experience can be explored (Gupta & Vajic, 1999). The definition of the customer journey enables a better identification of the service touchpoints, which is the place where customers and service come together and interact. The identification and definition of the customer journey and service touchpoints guided the ongoing research and served as the basis for generating, refining, and improving the evolving service design.

Activities in the customer's journey are broken down into "moments". Designers innovate by creating novel concepts and interactions for the moments that occur at each touchpoint. Each moment is composed of a set of resources. In complex service system design we imagine that this top-down approach is followed by a bottom-up description and negotiation of resources into a service design language that can be used across the variety of touchpoints in the service experience. As a grouping of resources in the customer journey, a touchpoint can make or break the service experience. Touchpoint identification and analysis is critical step improving the overall service process, they are the place were designers look for opportunities for innovation. In order to understand and promote sustainable practices

Figure 2. "Cozinha da Madeira" prototype website

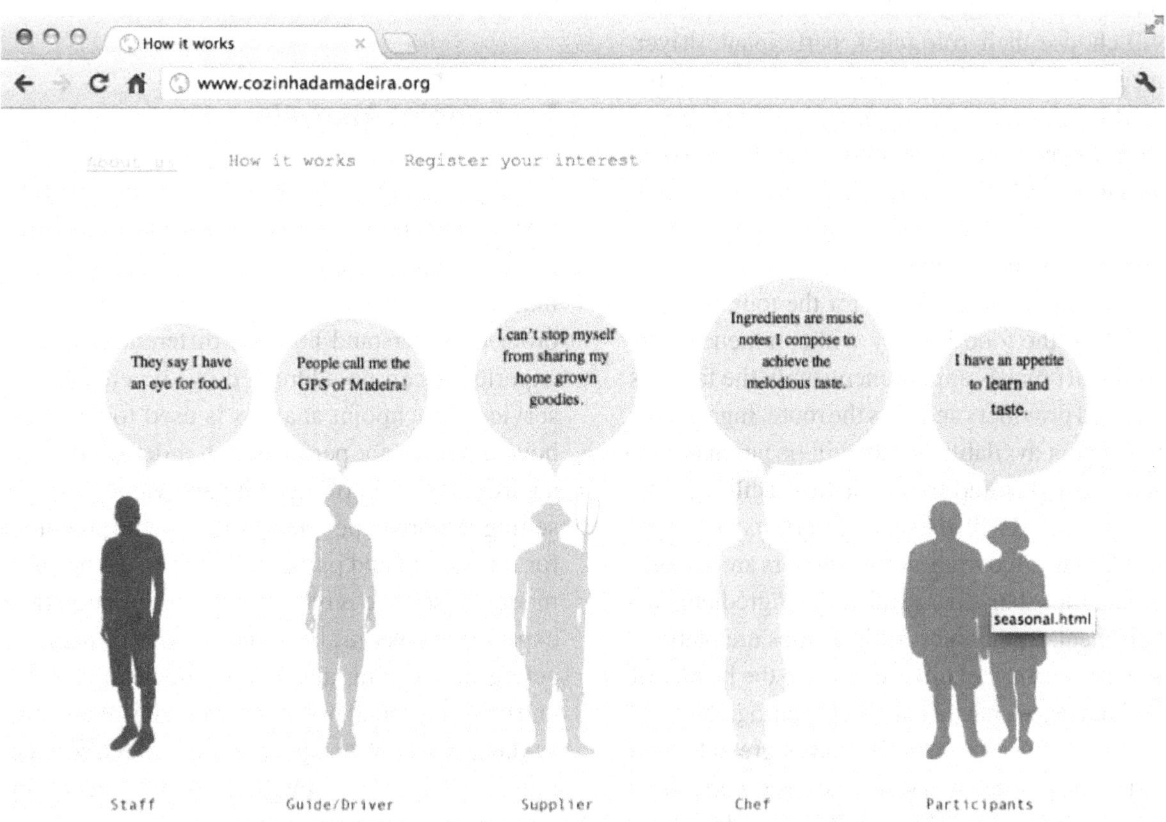

the CdM costumer journey provides a series of touchpoints opportunities based or enhanced by social context and technological aids. We create design concepts for the moments that occur at each touchpoint. Next, we outline the customer journey and touchpoint identification for the CdM service with an emphasis on the resulting experience.

"Cozinha da Madeira" Customer and Food Journey

People outside Madeira will find evidence of the CdM service through the Internet and the publicity that travel agents will display in their agencies: eye catching posters and gadgets, designed to bring out the colors, fun and the adventure of engaging with such an experience. Customers attracted by the service will orient themselves through the publicity leaflets, visiting the website and talking to the staff in the CdM headquarters office in Funchal. Once engaged with the service, customer will choose their role (chef, participant, driver, or supplier/farmer), through the website or at the CdM headquarters. A set of recipes is proposed every month, which complies with the seasonal products available on the island and the participants choice over the internet (see Figure 3). Once the recipe is chosen, participants have filled roles and enough people sign up for the tour, the date is set and the food journey will commence. The CdM staff makes appointments with the farmers and food providers and tests the route. Ingredients that are not available on site will be purchased in advance and stored in the kitchen facilities. The van associated with the service starts its journey at the CdM headquarters and customers are brought around the island to assemble the ingredients for their meal. Some intermediate stops are planned into the journey, in order to admire the beauty of the landscape, particular forest settings and agricultural sites. Farmers that have agreed to be a part of the journey will welcome customers, show them their land and share their knowledge about food and agricultural products. In the afternoon the van returns to the starting point. Customers are free to learn with the chefs how to prepare the food, go home or to the hotel, and rest before dinner is ready.

At dinnertime, everyone is seated in the kitchen/restaurant facility. The customers are served the food and hear a short introduction about its preparation and tradition. At the end of the dinner a mini questionnaire is distributed to understand the enjoyment of the journey and vote for the quality of food and overall experience. The winning dish is published on the website, and its chef gains a webpage of fame together with its recipe to be stored in the website archives. Before leaving, customers can acquire a small gift or a memorabilia form the CdM store. T- shirts, aprons and table mats will be printed for each recipe journey. Participants who take multiple journeys can collect different maps reflecting their different food journeys through the island and its recipes.

Experience Cycle and Touchpoint Analysis

An important element of the service design process is touchpoint analysis. Here we follow the cycle of experience that highlights the different facets of an activity, journey or performance in order to understand how the different stages of experience can be addressed by the envisioned service. Touchpoint analysis is used to describe how activities are performed in order to achieve a particular result of meaning and value through setting resources, people and places with potential for interaction and participation. The experience model for service is based on the assumption that experience emerges from the activity of persons acting in a setting and is embedded in context and ongoing social practices (Manzini, Walker & Wylant, 2007). When people encounter a service interface they move through stages in the process or performance over time and the experience emerges from context and social practice. According to

Figure 3. Recipe ingredients leading to customer journey

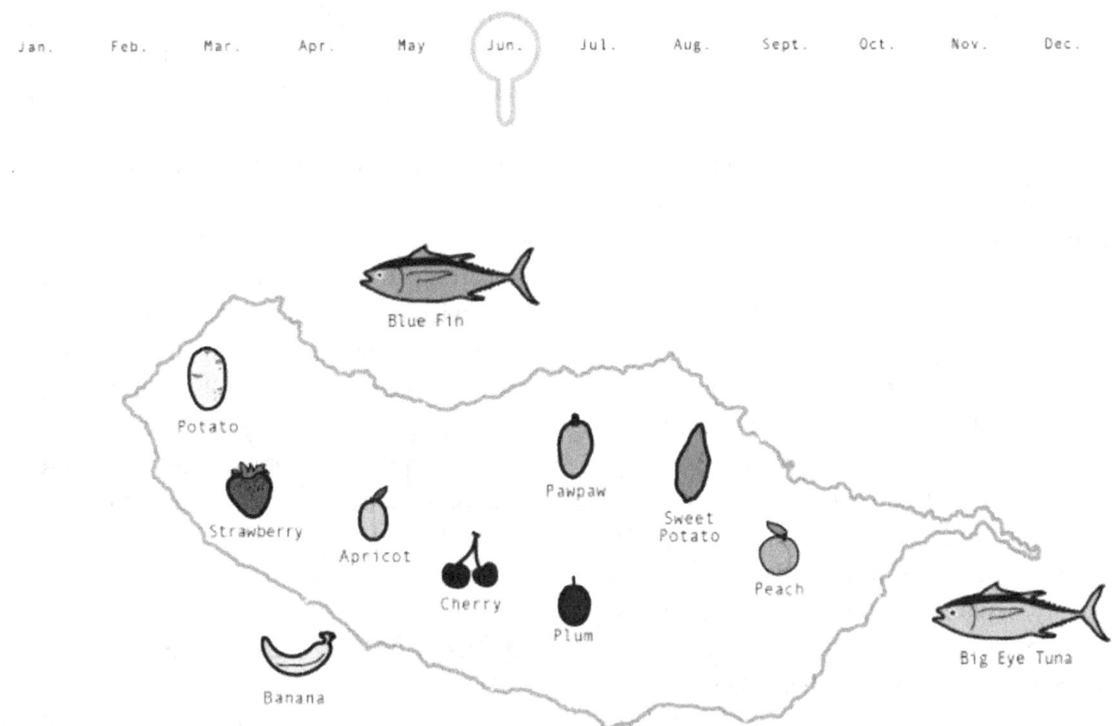

Evenson the stages of the experience cycle are (Evenson, 2006): i) connect & attract - the initial connection with the person and using that contact to make an effective and affective impression. In the CdM case study this is accomplished through online and offline Publicity and marketing material as well as the CdM website; ii) orient - the overview or preview of what's available or possible, matching expectations and allowing exploration and supporting the early stages of learning. In our service this is accomplished through online touchpoints: the website, providing a means to sign up and participate; iii) interact - the completion of valuable or valued activities while delighting the senses, skilling, and establishing expectations about the overall content of encounters. For CdM this is the CdM headquarters where staff will be available to explain the service to the customers. It also includes the transportation that takes participants around the island in search of the ingredients, the destinations to local farms where ingredients are found, explained and the encounter with local culture and the land happens. Finally where food is prepared, this touchpoint comprises the kitchen facilities and also the restaurant where the food is consumed and the voting happens; iv) extend & retain - the person comes back for more as their expectations are raised, creating loyalty and leveraging existing experiences. CdM is designed so that participants can return to the service in different roles or different seasons, and a shop where they can purchase memorabilia; v) advocate - the person actively communicates their satisfaction to others. This happens through the website and voting schema where people share their experience with others and also with the previously described memorabilia.

Service Blueprinting

Service blueprint is the systematic layout of how the service runs. This technique decomposes the service delivery process down into logical steps and sequences to facilitate and guide service design. The blueprint involves the physical evidence of the service encounter in each touchpoint, but also the frontstage service and customer actions as well as onstage actions. These actions are said to be "visible" to the customer and hence above the line of visibility. Below this conceptual line we have the backstage actions and the supporting processes. The placement of the "line of visibility" is an important design element. For example some restaurants are now re drawing their visibility line to include the kitchen in the costumer space. CdM is a representational performance in a form of a sustainable service. In order to illustrate and better understand the complex performance of the CdM experience, a service blueprint has been developed to visually explain how to co-create and stage the experience. The blueprint has been divided into three service stages, which are depicted in a separate blueprint section: the Supplier Searching stage, Chef Searching stage and Participants Experience stage (see Figure 4).

In the Participant Experience stage, each participant signs up for his/her role based on interest. For instance, the chef and the ingredient suppliers are engaged in actions both at the frontstage and the backstage of the service. We argue that this interchanging element of actor participation in the CdM is a key element in the engaging nature of transformational experiences. The enabling character of a service like CdM emerges from different actors crossing the "line of visibility".

Figure 4 illustrates a section of the blueprint for the chef as well as the Participant Experience for the CdM service. The participant co-creates the service through pushing through what would be the line of visibility of a traditional restaurant experience by engaging into many actions that traditionally would be part of the backstage (e.g. buying ingredients from the local farmers and getting involved in cooking the recipes together with the chef). In this way CdM enables tourism to be combined with learning about food, local agriculture and traditional recipes therefore promoting sustainability under a three fold aspect of respecting, learning and promoting local traditional practices and culture. This examples highlight how the different frontstage customer actions achieved from the evidence of the service touchpoints are sustained by the backstage supporting processes. This example reinforces the participation of the customer in co-creating the service through the explicit pushback of the line of visibility. By engaging the customer into many actions that traditionally would be part of the backstage (e.g. buying ingredients and cooking the recipes) we enable people to explore the island, its nature and culture and therefore promote sustainability.

EXPERIENCE PROTOTYPING

Experience is a very dynamic, complex and subjective phenomenon – as Clandinin and colleagues put "to do research into an experience is to experience it" (Clandinin & Connelly, 2000). Experiences depend upon the perception of multiple sensory qualities of a design. "Experience Prototyping" as a form of prototyping enables design team members, users and clients to gain first-hand appreciation of existing or future conditions through active engagement with prototypes (Buchenau & Suri, 2000). Buchenau and Suri identified three different places within the design and development process where Experience Prototyping is valuable: i) understanding existing user experiences and context; ii) exploring and evaluating design ideas; and iii) communicating ideas to an audience (Buchenau & Suri, 2000). In order to understand and explore (first and second activities in the Buchenau model) the concept of CdM we staged an experience prototype of the service. Through the experience prototype we were able to refine CdM processes and roles.

Our initial steps were to cast volunteers as participants in the roles of CDM staff, driver, chef,

Figure 4. Excerpts from the Service Blueprint

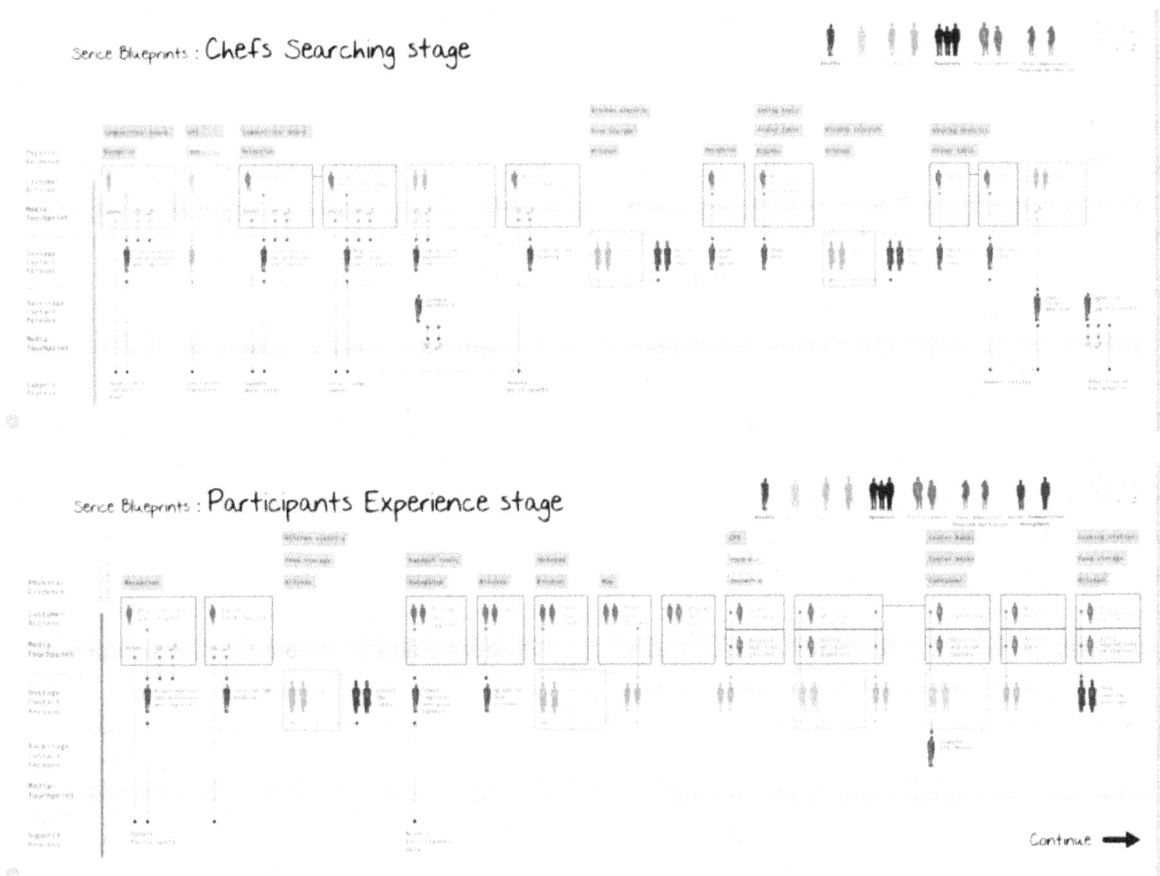

and customers. A seasonal recipe was chosen on the basis of the local chef's advice and available products. The food journey was then sketched on the map and loosely timed to last around four to five hours. The trip started with a few cars instead of a single vehicle, since we didn't have a van or minibus at our disposal. It lasted more than six hours and ended at a designated house where the CDM chef cooked the chosen recipe in the hosting kitchen, with all starting participants still engaged with the CDM experience.

The experience prototype emphasized the importance of rehearsing the food journey, timing distances between places, checking availability of products and intermediate stops. Here we summary some of the findings. It is of fundamental importance to plan the itinerary and its duration, in order to make the trip of an enjoyable duration, to reduce stress and increase spontaneity. Customers get tired during the food journey. Depending on the complexity of the recipe, the age of the participants, weather conditions, and other factors, people are likely to experience fatigue. The risk is that customers could end up too tired to want to participate in the cooking or even too tired to eat. Keeping this in mind, the food journey should be confined to half a day or plan for a resting time, before dinner. The participants cast in the roles of chef and driver should be briefed and prepared a few days before the food journey takes place. They should have a close working relationship so they can improvise detours or changes in the recipes as unexpected events take place, such as sudden changes of weather, or variation in food supplies. Not all ingredients of any recipe can be purchased during the food journey. Participants need to be informed about which ingredients will be purchased during the food journey and which ones at the supermarket, so they do not feel that something did not work in the food journey experience. Consideration needs made about how many people one chef can handle at the cooking stage and how many people can the chef actually cook for. The relationship of the chef with participant is important. Customizing the kitchen context for the chef beforehand is also desirable. The food evaluation phase of the service needs careful design. For example, what is the best way to assess the food, questionnaire, interviews, and voting? If so which groups, are expected to vote, locals or foreigners? Different participants groups will have different taste and standards. Finally, our prototype indicated that should we consider collecting comments and feedback on the overall service experience. It could be wise to collect comments before people get too engaged with food experience, in particular if alcohol will be involved. This might suggest staff part filling a questionnaire or just having an informal chat with each participant before the end of the evening.

DISCUSSION

CdM is a service that leverages local tourism, promoting a sustainable experience through the island by reconnecting people with their basic needs and Madeira natural resources. We draw on Manzini's concept of enabling service (Manzini, Walker & Wylant, 2007) to promote social innovation through changes in the way individuals or communities act in order to achieve a meaningful result. CdM uses food as a means to enhance the basic relationship between farmers and customers. We suggest a service as an opportunity to learn about how to treat food ingredients and improve the general knowledge about this leitmotif as well as making close contact with the local populations and its land and its traditions. By tackling tourism, food and farming we believe our case study could be explored in a variety of countries and culture as well as functioning as a one off experience, encouraging its participants to look at land, food and local culture and traditions in a different way. These areas of design have potential for both customization and standardization. Since experiences are co-created between service providers and customers they are highly customized elements of a service. However, since they also have a transformational design element they can be standardized, adapted, and repeated for different customers, context and service providers. In order to create and carefully design a meaningful costumer journey, the opportunity lies in a careful and innovative analysis and design of each single touchpoint, where the customers get in touch with the service and co create their own experience. In the following section we will reflect on these observations through the CdM case study.

Pine and Gilmour describe the progression of economic values from basic standardized commodities to more customized experiences all the way to transformations (Pine II & Gilmore, 1998). This concept inspired our service proposition. In order to cast our service as a transformation, we designed CdM so the transformation of the individual customers takes the form of an incentivized awareness towards sustainable issues and practice. Since experiences are co-created between service providers and customers, they are highly customized elements of a service. However, since they also have a transformational design element they can standardized and repeated for different customers, context and service providers.

While the difference between products and services is now a well-articulated argument in service designs and in general design practices, what is still in need of some clarifications is the difference between services, experiences and transformations: i) Commodities are fungible materials extracted from the natural world corresponding to the ingredient purchased and used by CdM actors; ii) Raw materials are the offering; iii) Goods are tangible products that companies standardize and then inventory. Related to our case study, sugarcane honey or passion fruit juice are the products emerging from the agricultural commodity. Here the products are the offering; iv) Services are intangible activities that are delivered for a particular client. A bar serving typical food and drinks like the local passion cocktail called poncha (a typical drink from sugarcane liquor) provides a service. In this example the operation of making and serving the Poncha Cocktail is the offering; v) Experiences are memorable events that are staged for individuals. Several tourism related companies are currently exploring this concept, for instance the staging of traditional music in several typical restaurants or the combination of restaurants and unique natural conditions such as conditions Madeirans Fajas, are isolated strips of land under 300 or more meters cliffs, picturesque locations for swimming or trekking. Here the event is the offering; and finally vi) Transformations are custom experiences designed to guide individuals through a process of change. Here the individual is the offering and in our service proposition the client will be transformed from the CdM experience into a more attentive person towards sustainable and environmental issues.

In this framework, services, experiences and transformations are distinct economic offerings, each incorporating the previous levels of the hierarchy, just as services depend on products as key components (touchpoints) for their execution. Through our case study we argue that in order for people to transition from unsustainable to sustainable ways of living, we need to design services as transformations. This should be the fundamental step in the strategic activity of design for sustainability. With CdM we conceived and designed a transformational, sensory, and memorable experience. At the end of this experience we envisage participants feeling closer to the local culture and its traditions, the people, and the beauty and wilderness of the territory. This experience should elicit respect as well as motivate change in behavior, such as respecting a beautiful land, honoring long lasting and wise traditions, connecting with the local authentic people. The transformation should take place after the experience, once reflecting ad remembering each carefully designed touch point and be recalled every time a product or a similar setting is proposed or challenged in the participant life. If the experience has touched and transformed the individual, the resulting awareness towards sustainability and its values should remain with the costumer even when retuned home and or visiting other countries. These hypothesis still remain to be tested, but helped considerably in the conception, design and experience prototyping of the service.

CONCLUSION

After researching, design and experience prototyping CdM as a transformational service experience, we concluded that the design and co-creation of memorable experiences and transformations is a key design activity in the transition towards a more sustainable set of services and solutions. Our CdM service proposition motivates costumers to adopt an enabling and sustainable stand through their actions. We envision that costumer loyalty to these services will bring increased revenues to the companies that are willing to participate as stakeholders in their delivery.

We have framed these ideas in the context of a case study for a service design concept specifically conceived to the island of Madeira, but extendable to any other country through localization of the concept. By doing this, we aim to creating local yet exportable z, valuable for tourist during their travel experience, as well as an inspiration and incentive to keep paying attention to certain sustainable issues, even once their journey is over. We believe that the CDM case study contributes to a better understanding of the research questions required to holistically address the challenge of designing innovative services for sustainability. It also promotes a clearer identification of the touchpoints and potential concepts that drive our design approach. Future work on CdM project is currently ongoing, in designing and developing a web interface to manage and deliver the service to the public. We envisage a mobile interface also supporting and enhancing the service. Evaluations of the users behavior and attitude change towards sustainable touristic experience will be possible at completion of the prototypes.

ACKNOWLEDGMENT

The authors would like to thank the SINAIS research team, in particular Jihyun Ryou, Mary Barreto and Tiago Camacho and all the participants who volunteered to the experience prototyping session of the service and that provided help and feedback conducting and defining the contextual inquiries and cultural probes.

REFERENCES

Beyer, H., & Holtzblatt, K. (1997). *Contextual design: Defining customer-centered systems*. San Francisco, CA: Morgan Kaufmann Publishers.

Blevis, E. (2007). Sustainable interaction design: Invention & disposal, renewal & reuse. In *Proceedings of CHI'2007*. New York: ACM Press.

Buchenau, M., & Suri, J. (2000). Experience prototyping. In *Proceedings of 3rd Conference on Designing Interactive Systems: Processes, Practices, Methods, and Techniques*. New York: ACM Press.

Clandinin, D., & Connelly, F. (2000). *Narrative inquiry: Experience and story in qualitative research*. San Francisco, CA: Jossey-Bass Publishers.

Evenson, S. (2006). Designing for service: A hands on introduction. In *Proceedings of CMU's Emergence Conference*. Pittsburgh, PA: Carnegie Mellon University.

Gaver, B., Dunne, T., & Pacenti, E. (1999). Design: Cultural probes. *Interaction*, *6*(1), 21–29. doi:10.1145/291224.291235

Gupta, S., & Vajic, M. (1999). The contextual and dialectical nature of experiences. In *New Service Development*. Thousand Oaks, CA: Sage.

Manzini, E. (2005). *Design for sustainability – How to design sustainable solutions*. Milano, Itlay: INDACO, Politecnico di Milano.

Manzini, E., Walker, S., & Wylant, B. (2007). *Enabling solutions for sustainable living: A workshop*. Academic Press.

Pine, B. II, & Gilmore, J. (1998). Welcome to the experience economy. *Harvard Business Review*, 97–105. PMID:10181589

Chapter 34
Story Objects:
An Interactive Installation to Excavate Immigrant History and Identity through Evocative Everyday Objects

Andreas Kratky
Institute for Multimedia Literacy, University of Southern California, USA

Daphne Ho
School of Cinematic Arts, University of Southern California, USA

ABSTRACT

Most modern globalized societies are characterized by large immigrant communities. While previously the assimilation of immigrants was often connected to "unlearning" the original cultural background, today's acculturation processes are marked by digital media, which support identity-forming by empowering communication. On the other hand, digital media often strengthen difficulties in inter-generational communication. The authors explore the use of digital interactive media to foster inter-generational communication and the transfer of cultural and historic knowledge. Story Objects is an installation that presents aspects of immigrant history alongside an individual family history leveraging food traditions and memories as a starting point to stimulate the viewers on multiple levels to engage in communication about the larger topic of immigrant identity.

INTRODUCTION

A rapidly increasing part of the population of the United States is consisting of immigrants from all parts of the world. Since the nineteenth century the United States have been the prime destination among immigrants and an important topic of American sociological research was to examine and understand the changes of the society brought about by immigration. Between 1880 and 1920 about 24 million immigrants mostly from Europe came to the United States forming a rather

DOI: 10.4018/978-1-4666-4490-8.ch034

coherent group of cultural backgrounds that these immigrants came from (Waters & Jiménes, 2005). The composition of the immigrant community of the beginning of the twenty-first century is more heterogeneous and varied. The large majority of current immigrants come from Latin America and Asia and their backgrounds are vastly different. While a high percentage of Latin American immigrants are low-skill laborers, the range among the Asian immigrants reaches from highly educated scientists, engineers and healthcare professionals on one end to uneducated peasants on the other end (Zhou & Xiong, 2005). Despite this heterogeneity the group of Asian immigrants has generally not been considered as having difficulties to assimilate to the dominant culture. The level of achievement of the 1.5 (immigrants who were born abroad and arrived in the United States as children) and second-generation immigrants (U.S. Born children of immigrant parents) of Asian descent has been strong. As Zou and Xiong report based on numbers from the 2000 U.S. census, Asian Americans aged 25 to 34 are more likely to hold a college degree than whites and equally their earnings ratio was higher compared to white families; at the same time the poverty ratio is higher.

Historically there has been a great pressure on the immigrant population to assimilate to the majority culture and the generational shifts are marked by assimilatory changes. The most important markers of these shifts are the language usage patterns in respect to the dominant and minority languages (Alba, Logan, Lutz & Stults, 2002). Immigrants who speak their host society's dominant language have better socioeconomic opportunities than those who do not. Proficiency in the dominant language is a key factor for upwards assimilation, as it is directly correlated with access and better results in education and employment. At the same time language proficiency must also be understood as social capital providing respect and reducing vulnerability and linguistic isolation (Nawyn, et al., 2012). As the second generation of immigrants from the past decades forms, patterns of assimilation and intergenerational shifts become apparent. Asian second generation immigrants have an exceptional success rate in education and in particular in the attainment of advanced degrees (25 percent of Asian men had advanced degrees such as professional, masters or doctoral degrees, compared to 8 percent of whites, 3 percent of blacks and 2 percent of Hispanics) and a similar tendency is recognizable in terms of the employment situation (Rumbaut, 2008). Along with these successes in education and employment goes a high rate of language assimilation (for example, while in the 1.5 generation Chinese immigrants only 11.5 percent claim to speak English "very well", this number grows in the second generation to 42.8, which is besides the Cambodian and Laotian group the highest increase among all immigrants. Rumbaut, 2008). The flipside of this fast adoption of English is a quick decline in the proficiency of the minority language. More than half of the foreign born members of the 1.5 generation prefer speaking English at home and three quarters of the second generation speak English at home. Among the 1.5 generation only 47 percent could speak the non-English language well and only 34 percent could read it well. Among the 2.5 generation members these abilities went down to 16 and 13 percent, and the third generation had become largely monolingual English-speaking. Compared to Spanish-speakers Asian origin groups are more likely to loose their bilingual skills by the second generation (Rumbaut, 2008).

The loss of language skills is only one salient indicator of the assimilation process and in conjunction with this loss several other aspects of preserving a relationship to the culture of the parent generation are at stake, which influence inter-generational communication and the identity forming of the 1.5 and higher generation. As Rothe, Pumariega and Sabagh state, "the process of immigration and acculturation often involves the separation and loss of attachment associated with the person's culture of origin and a transformation and re-editing of identity" (Rothe, Pumariega

& Sabagh, 2011). Besides linguistic skills, the process of acculturation encompasses a complex set of socio-economic, historical, political and psychodynamic aspects. This complex is important in the formation of identity and the "organization of self-understandings that define one's 'place in the world'" (Schwartz, Montgomery & Briones, 2006). The family setting is an important factor in the development of the children's identity and in families suffering from the pressures of immigration it can often fulfill its functions only to a limited extent. Often the first generation immigrant parents are suffering more severely from language barriers than their children and are thus more likely to be disempowered in the host society. This situation can undermine their authority and their role of providing parental leadership and guidance. In particular in settings where the children are not perfectly proficient in the language of their parents and the parents are not well versed in the dominant language the inter-generational communication can be severely reduced and "interests and shared experiences decrease and the parents and children may feel a sense of distancing that makes them feel that they are 'living in different worlds'" (Rothe, Pumariega & Sabagh, 2011).

FOSTERING INTER-GENERATIONAL COMMUNICATION

As immigration, globalization and the growth of cities are increasingly linked they lead to extremely diverse urban centers marked by the dynamics of immigration and acculturation. While historically this was a phenomenon limited to the major centers of immigration such as the United States and cities like New York and Los Angeles (Nawyn, et al., 2012). similar migration patterns start to appear even in previously homogenous cities. For example Japan, which historically had a restricted immigration policy to preserve cultural homogeneity, has changed these policies due to an aging population and increasing labor shortages, and since the 1990s an increasing number of foreign born has significantly changed the societal fabric (Schwartz, Montgomery & Briones, 2006). Similar patterns of aging societies and the need to recruit skilled and unskilled labor forces many countries to foster immigration. These growing and newly emerging gateway cities are less characterized by the opposition of one dominant culture in opposition to a set of minority cultures and the corresponding acculturation patterns are more complex and heterogeneous. They do not consist in assimilation to a dominant culture but in a more and more dynamic interaction between different cultures that extends beyond large cities to smaller suburban or rural neighborhoods (Schwartz, Montgomery & Briones, 2006). In this situation the preservation of bilingualism and the contact with the parent culture can have significant benefits. As Alba, Logan, Lutz and Stults write, "bilingualism is associated with cognitive advantages, especially when it is an educated, as opposed to 'folk,' bilingualism and can lead to educational outcomes superior to those found among English monolinguals." (Zhou & Xiong, 2005). Studies have shown that in specific settings bilinguality can be linked directly to better educational and employment successes rates (Price & Benton-Short, 2007). In this sense it is an important task to foster inter-generational communication in immigrant communities and to improve the understanding and awareness of their respective situation and history. Numerous studies have identified reasons why ruptures in the inter-generational communication occur and why bilinguality is quickly disappearing among the children of immigrants – but what are constructive measures that can prevent these ruptures or at least smooth them? As de Houwer writes, intergenerational language transmission and the education of bilingual children is independent from the socioeconomic status and depends strongly on parental input. It is to a great extent a question of engagement, the more engagement with a language a child has, the more likely it is to use this language (Lutz & Crist, 2009). If parents use their original language and expect their children to use it as well, this means avoiding bilingual discourse strategies, where the parents speak their original language and the child responds in the dominant language, the chances that the children become bilingual are higher. The traditional suggestion of 'one-person-one-language' does not guarantee bilinguality, it is a question of frequency of exposure and depth of engagement with the minority language.

Our question was thus to find a way to facilitate inter-generational communication and provide a framework for the transmission of linguistic as well as general cultural values of the parental culture. Among many second and third generation immigrant children exists a curiosity about their parents original culture and a general awareness of their immigrant status, due to societal feedback that many of them receive. This awareness, though, often does not link to a contextualization within the family history nor within the immigrant history in general. A related question was thus how we can use this curiosity to establish a better communication flow between the generations and realize a situated learning experience. Our aim was to create a framework that can work on an individual level but also scale and be applicable to other individuals and groups.

In our current society digital media and in particular the internet play an important role in the shaping of the identity of immigrant children and adolescents and often replace the role that mass media used to play (Lutz & Crist, 2009; de Houwer, 2007). While digital media allow for more freedom in the formation of identity and provide better channels to communicate among immigrant groups that used to be excluded from mass media (Lutz & Crist, 2009) they also often introduce an additional barrier in the inter-generational communication. In general media-usage is depending on the social setting, but in particular inter-generational communication between parents and children does not normally use this channel. So while we were aiming to create a digital media based solution for its scalability and the possibility to use rich media such as interviews, historic documents etc. it was clear that our solution had to address the parent-child communication in particular and thus create a framework that takes direct interaction and co-location into account.

Talking About Food

Our approach for the *Story Objects* project was to create an interactive installation that can be placed for example in community centers, local museums or other places of social encounter and serve as a stimulating and entertaining experience to foster the engagement with aspects of minority culture and immigrant history. The experience is supposed to evoke questions and personal associations among its users (who in result of the location of the installation most likely themselves have an immigrant background), which stimulate conversations between them and their relatives. The aim is to extend the experience from the installation into the respective family settings of the users and foster ongoing communication. Our choice to create a physically located installation as opposed to a web-based experience was on one hand to avoid the inter-generational media disparities as mentioned and on the other hand to create a 'special' place and occasion placed outside of the normal everyday routines that stimulate conversations that normally do not take place. The installation works in two ways: It gives an opportunity for co-presence of the different generations, e.g. during a family visit to the facility where it is exhibited, and trigger communication in the moment of exploration; in a deferred communication the person who experiences the installation brings his questions and associations to the other family members after the visit and engages into a conversation at this point.

We decided to use food as a way to connect the generations and establish a platform to exchange stories and cultural values. Food has since a long time been a topic of interest and conversation and in particular in the recent years the general interest in food has become even more important as we can conclude from numerous cooking shows on television, the popularity of cooking classes etc. Also anthropologists have since a long time studied food as it encodes important aspects of culture such as rituals and believe systems that are bound to certain ritualistic meals and ceremonies, it also contributes to the formation of identity and the maintenance of social relationships. Being part of a group with certain eating habits allows to identify with this group and to set other groups apart (Davis, 2012). Despite being a medium conducive for learning about cultural details, food also is a strong means to encode memories. Not only in Proust's description of the Madeleine we find a testimony of the qualities of food to evoke memories, in "Remembrance of Repasts" David Sutton develops an anthropological perspective based on certain food ingredients that are perceived as triggers of memories and cultural identity in specific cultures (Davis, 2012)., which is further elaborated in (Sutton, 2001). For many later generation immigrants food is the main access to their parent culture and even though recipes have been altered and adapted to local tastes they still provide a powerful connection to childhood memories of both parents and children and establish a platform to address and share these memories. Chinese cuisine, the example case in this project, has been since centuries exposed to multi-national influences and cross adaptations, which makes it a particularly suited example to trace aspects of migration and globalization (Holtzman, 2006).

The use of food as a conversational framework was intended to initiate and situate conversations between parents and children of immigrant families. In the specific example we implemented for the "Story Objects" project we focused on a family of Chinese origin who immigrated to the United States now in the second generation. This choice motivated the focus on Chinese cuisine as a starting point for inter-generational conversations. With the focus on one family we aimed to provide a concrete and realistic example case of an immigrant family history, which gives the opportunity to use real world testimonies and relate them to the bigger picture of immigrant history.

Evocative Objects

Most of the general food-inspired conversations are about specific recipes or restaurants, comparing preparation methods, quality, taste etc. While recipes can up to a certain extent be aligned with the purpose of our project, as traditional recipes and preparation methods can encode detailed cultural knowledge and relate to memories, the discussion about restaurants are inappropriate for our purposes. In our observations we have seen, though, that this kind of conversation rarely branches out into ore general aspects of family history or more general immigrant history aspects. To get away from this kind of highly specific food-talk we decided to focus on raw food-ingredients rather than specific recipes. The focus on ingredients directs the conversation more towards topics such as the preparation methods, acquisition of ingredients or their production in farming or other activities related to general procedures and occupations. This kind of conversation uses food items to access their topic but do not tend to stick too narrowly around food and cuisine. Further the use of raw ingredients has a more universal applicability and can without being limited to specific recipes trigger wider ranging associations.

The use of food items makes use of a particular capacity of objects to evoke stories and trigger thought-connections and memories. The use of objects in this function has a long tradition and – similar to food – connects to myths and rituals for example in the form of relics, talismans or lucky charms; they also relate to personal stories, experiences and memories. The term *evocative object* has served Sherry Turkle to frame an investigation into the quality and roles of objects as "companions to our emotional lives or as provocations of thought" (Turkle, 2007). This investigation collects a series of individual stories that reveal very idiosyncratic relationships of people with specific personal objects, which do not focus on the object's instrumental powers, but "on the object as a companion in life experience" (Holtzman, 2006) revealing the unique suitability of object-inspired story-telling. While the associative power of the objects in Turkle's study stems from their highly individual character, they therefore have only limited suitability to relate stories and associations to a larger audience. In comparison the choice of everyday-life food ingredients such as rice, soy-sauce or ginger realizes a useful balance between nondescriptness and universality and specific evocative power. This kind of object, due to its commonality in the food culture, is encountered by a large amount of people and is likely to connect to at least some associations and memories and at the same time, as a lot of people encounter these objects, they probably have some more personal relationship with them. In a similar way Lorraine Daston describes the role of objects in scientific study as inspiration and provocation for thoughts and findings in which "things knit together matter and meaning." (Daston, 2004).

Besides their emotional and cognitive aspects food items have the benefit that they present the tangible basis for conversation and shared experience: While recipes and restaurants remain abstract as descriptions, the food items are material instances to run into, to pick up and manipulate and thus provide the friction of reality, a tangible feeling and contour of past moments and stories. In this way the food items are recast as signifying objects that evoke complex relationships rather than being mere food items. They link stories and accounts of cultural or personal moments – recipes included – and thus extend the experience with the installation into the every-day-life of people. Encountering a similar food object in everyday-life has the chance to trigger some elements of the conversation of experiences stemming from the context of the installation – or to initiate the deferred communication with relatives who did not have the experience of the installation but share experiences with those items.

Stages of Implementation

In a first phase of the implementation of the project we tested our food-item hypothesis and conducted a series of interviews with various members of the family that is the focus of the project, which loosely circled around aspects of food and cuisine. These interview served at the same time as a test and refinement for our conversation strategy and as research to collect and produce the content for the installation. The interviews were mostly done on video and transcribed for purposes of analysis. During this phase it became clear that the conversation strategy was able to elicit several stories and events that were so far unknown and not talked about among the family members. The material from the interviews was integrated with documents from the family history, photos and home movies in order to trace a media-rich account of salient moments of the family history. The family history is part of a two-section timeline that establishes connections between events in the family history and the general history of Chinese immigration to the United States. The two sections of the timeline are forming two layers of story telling which make the immigration history relatable with the example of a specific family and draw examples of how events of the larger history can have repercussions on the smaller scale of a family. For the visitor the more personal telling of the family story provides the possibility to identify and connect potential own associations.

In a first version of the installation the timeline was realized as an interactively navigable representation, which could be explored by the viewers through scrolling and zooming. The timeline was presented on one central monitor and on several smaller monitors arranged around the central screen more detailed information such as the interviews and home-movies were presented.

In this first stage the food items were used as illustrative materials that were set up on a table together with the navigation device. The items did not have any connection beyond their contextual relationship with the content presented and were intended as a point of attraction augmenting the interactive experience with tangible objects. The objects gave an illustration of the conversational strategy centered around food.

In a second installation we wanted to strengthen the role of the food items as a central part of the installation and tie them more strongly to the experience. For this purpose we changed the navigation pattern of the installation such that the objects are now technically tied into the navigation. By placing an object on top of a central platform, which is designed to hold the various objects, the viewer can highlight elements of the timeline that relate to the chosen object. The timeline is still freely navigable but a direct correspondence between the objects and related events and stories are established. Different objects highlight different parts of the timeline and thus provide an alternative way of navigating the experience. The object-based navigation puts a non-chronological exploration in the foreground and thus provides a considerably more intuitive access to the content of the installation. The specific capability of evoking associations through the tactile properties of tangible object interaction (Tannenbaum, et al., 2011) and making the narrative potential of objects part of the interaction design was the main motivation to introduce a tangible user interface. Another motivation to explore interactions with tangible objects is their ability to foster and shape social interaction (Hornecker & Buur, 2006).

The technological implementation of the new interface structure was realized by tagging the objects with unique radio frequency identification (RFID) tags, which allow to identify which objects

Figure 1. View of the installation (second stage of installation)

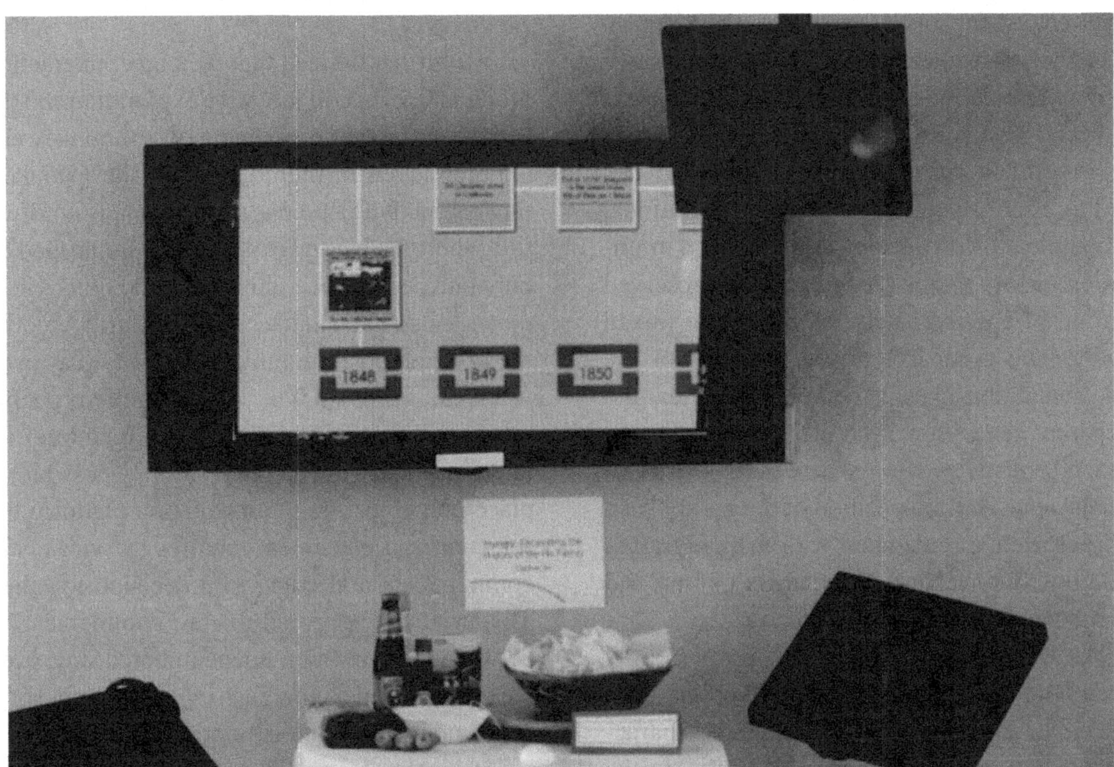

are placed on the central platform. The central platform contains the navigation device (trackball) and an RFID reader. Once an object is recognized on the platform the highlighting is applied and the timeline scrolls to the corresponding position. In order to make it easy to identify the objects as elements that can be interacted with and to suggest their specific functions the arrangement and presentation of the objects had to be restructured. The platform was shaped in such a way that it was obviously empty and ready to receive objects. The objects, as the only items available in proximity of the platform, offer themselves to be placed on the platform. Instead of a cluster arrangement the objects were lined up and placed on small platforms resembling the central platform to suggest the relationship between the different elements o the interface.

Observations

In the different stages of the implementation of the project the sample size and composition of observed participants was significantly different. In the first stage, the interview and research stage the communication was limited to the members of the larger family. The purpose of this stage was to test and refine the topics and approaches used to establish and develop inter-generational communication on the topic of family and immigration history. In the second stage we observed a group of approximately 30 viewers of mixed gender. The group comprised members of the child generation, aged in their early twenties, and the parent generation, aged in the mid-forties up to ca. 60 with a few viewers in between these two age clusters. The composition of the group had a high percentage of members with an immigration background consisting of members of first and second generation.

The third stage of the installation was only tested with a small group and more observation will be necessary to reliably assess the characteristics and responses of a larger public. In the observations of our current test group we found that the explorative aspect of the installation was much stronger and viewers spent significantly more time to explore the different items and their correspondences in the timeline (the time spent exploring approximately tripled). Once certain events were located through item interaction, the trackball interface was then used in order to explore the context of the event more in detail. The time spent in the installation was noticeably longer than in the mouse-only navigation, where viewers spent some time exploring the chronological navigation but after a while lost interest. In the object-based navigation the incentive was obviously to try most of the objects and then explore the proximity of several of the highlighted events. Our assumption is that the aspect of easy countability of the objects allowing for an extrapolation of the possible positions to visit in the installation makes the time assessment easier and fosters the engagement. The increased activity of selecting, picking and placing of objects seems to result in more active engagement and a more pleasurable experience.

We further noticed that the object interaction is conducive for collaborative exploration and the active co-present engagement of several viewers. Co-presence is further fostered by the spatial arrangement of the screens so that there is no situation where the central experience is controlled by only one person. The interviews and other video materials on the side-screens were triggered by the timeline position but continued to play even when the main timeline moves on. Two people interacting in the installation are therefore not inhibiting each other. As it is only possible to place one object on the navigation platform the selection and placement requires the viewers to communicate and come to a decision together. This principle appeared to start communication between viewers in an unencumbered way, even when they did not know each other. In comparison in the mouse-navigation based installation, which was using the objects only as illustrative additions, we observed that mostly one person was operating the mouse and controlling the experience, while others were waiting for their turn.

We found mostly groups of two people interacting while entertaining a conversation between them. The groups did not always form in a cross-generational composition as was intended at the outset of our project but it can be assumed that the overall setting is more conducive for inter-generational communication as well. Another observation was that the addition of food items (shrimp chips) intended for the viewers to eat as a snack increased the communication and time-spent in the installation. This observation was equally true for the mouse-only as well as for the object-based navigation.

CONCLUSION AND FURTHER RESEARCH

Chinese food has a particularly long and extensive tradition of multi-national influences. In nearly every larger city in the world one can find Chinese restaurants which allows even visitors of non-Chinese background to relate to the ingredients and find with them an access to the more specific information on Chinese immigrant history and the personal example of the larger setting of a Chinese family. The scenario of the first implementation was successful in this respect.

In our observations we found that the interaction with tangible objects and the explorative behavior associated with this form of interaction changed markedly how viewers engaged into conversation and how deeply they explored the offered content. It appears that the generic character of the objects made it easy for a wide range of the viewers to relate to them, and despite the nondescript nature of the objects they were able for example to make connections to specific brands they encountered in the past or in the country of origin. The time and engagement dedicated to the objects, though, suggests that the narrative potential of this kind of generic objects is limited and they only serve to stimulate the exploration and negotiate the course

Figure 2. Two people interacting with the installation (second stage of installation)

of exploration with potential other viewers present at the same time. The story-telling power that more specific objects have proven to possess (Turkle, 2007; Hegedüs, 1998; Legrady, 2001) does not get activated in this context. Continued work in this direction should re-examine the degree of specificity of the objects, balancing nondescriptness with narrative potential.

We found that the spatial arrangement of components is important to foster communication and accommodate more than one user at a time. Through the way the objects were set up and through the distribution of several screens in the installation that had a somewhat independent behavior it was possible to increase the usability of the installation for co-present usage of more than one viewer at a time.

The current installation and the observations we were able to realize with it constitute a first approach and further observations with different and larger groups should be undertaken. We assume that the context within which the installation is set up will also impact its efficiency as a communication tool. In the current situation we were only able to work in two different settings for the first and the second stage of implementation. In particular the second stage demands more observation, as we only were able to work with a small number of participants, who spent more time in the installation than in the first stage. In particular to evaluate the efficiency of deferred communication in which the encounter of similar food items in everyday live reminds people who have explored the installation of their experience and leads them to engage into communication about the topic at a later time will need more and longer term study. In the current stage we were only able to interview four people about their experience after visiting the installation.

Future work will have to investigate the qualities of places where the installation works best and in another line of research it should be explored how easily the concept can be scaled to address other immigrant backgrounds, other cultures and immigrant histories.

REFERENCES

Alba, R., Logan, J., Lutz, A., & Stults, B. (2002). Only English by the third generation: Loss and preservation of the mother tongue among the grandchildren of contemporary immigrants. *Demography*, *39*(3), 467–484. doi:10.1353/dem.2002.0023 PMID:12205753

Daston, L. (2004). *Things that talk – Object lessons from art and science*. New York: Zone Books.

Davis, K. (2012). Tensions of identity in a networked era: Young people's perspectives on the risks and rewards of online self-expression. *New Media & Society*, (14): 634–651. doi:10.1177/1461444811422430

de Houwer, A. (2007). Parental language input patterns and children's bilingual use. *Applied Psycholoinguistics,* (28), 411-424.

Elias, N., & Lemish, D. (2009). Spinning the web of identity: The roles of the internet in the lives of immigrant adolescents. *New Media & Society*, (11): 533–551. doi:10.1177/1461444809102959

Hegedüs, A. (1998). *Things spoken*. Interactive installation.

Holtzman, J. (2006). Food and memory. *Annual Review of Anthropology*, *35*, 361–378. doi:10.1146/annurev.anthro.35.081705.123220

Hornecker, E., & Buur, J. (2006). Getting a grip on tangible interaction: A framework on physical space and social interaction. In *Proceedings of the SIGCHI Conference on Human Factors in Computing systems: CHI '06*. New York: ACM Press.

Legrady, G. (2001). *Pockets full of memories.* Interactive installation.

Lutz, A., & Crist, S. (2009). Why do bilingual boys get better grades in English-only America? The impacts of gender, language and family interaction on academic achievement of Latino/a children of immigrants. *Ethnic and Racial Studies, 32*(2), 346–368. doi:10.1080/01419870801943647

Mintz, S., & Du-Bois, C. (2002). The anthropology of food and eating. *Annual Review of Anthropology, 31*, 99–119. doi:10.1146/annurev.anthro.32.032702.131011

Nawyn, S. et al. (2012). Linguistic isolation, social capital, and immigrant belonging. *Journal of Contemporary Ethnography, 41*(3), 255–282. doi:10.1177/0891241611433623

Price, M., & Benton-Short, L. (2007). Immigrants and world cities: From the hyper-diverse to the bypassed. *GeoJournal, 68*(2–3), 103–117. doi:10.1007/s10708-007-9076-x

Rothe, E., Pumariega, A., & Sabagh, D. (2011). Identity and acculturation in immigrant and second generation adolescents. *Adolescent Psychiatry,* (1): 72–81. doi:10.2174/2210676611101010072

Rumbaut, R. (2008). The coming of the second generation: Immigration and ethnic mobility in southern California. *The Annals of the American Academy of Political and Social Science,* (620): 196–236. doi:10.1177/0002716208322957

Schwartz, S., Montgomery, M., & Briones, E. (2006). The role of identity in acculturation among immigrant people: Theoretical propositions, empirical questions, and applied recommendations. *Human Development,* (49): 1–30. doi:10.1159/000090300

Sutton, D. (2001). *Remembrance of repasts.* London: Berg Publishers.

Tannenbaum, K., et al. (2011). Experiencing the reading glove. In *Proceedings of the Fifth International Conference on Tangible, Embedded, and Embodied Interaction: TEI '11.* New York: ACM Press.

Turkle, S. (2007). *Evocative objects.* Cambridge, MA: MIT Press.

Waters, M., & Jiménes, T. (2005). Assessing immigrant assimilation: New empirical and theoretical challenges. *Annual Review of Sociology, 31*, 105–125. doi:10.1146/annurev.soc.29.010202.100026

Wu, D., & Cheung, S. (2002). *The globalization of Chinese food.* Honolulu, HI: University of Hawaii Press.

Zhou, M., & Xiong, Y. (2005). The multifaceted American experiences of the children of Asian immigrants: Lessons for segemented assimilation. *Ethnic and Racial Studies, 28*(6), 1119–1152. doi:10.1080/01419870500224455

Chapter 35
Teaching Human-Computer Interaction in the Capital of Culture

Damjan Obal
Institute of Informatics (FERI), University of Maribor, Slovenia

Domen Verber
Institute of Informatics (FERI), University of Maribor, Slovenia

ABSTRACT

Human-Computer Interaction (HCI) is an essential field, yet so hard to describe. It encompasses so many disciplines from design to software engineering. Teaching HCI is an even bigger challenge, especially when it is only part of another course. Therefore, in this chapter a framework is proposed for teaching HCI based on the "double diamond" design methodology, coupled with a paradigm for experiential learning. This methodology is illustrated within a case study by students of Media Communication who participated in a course entitled Ubiquitous Systems for Media.

INTRODUCTION

The city of Maribor, Slovenia (together with Guimaraes, Portugal) officially became a European Capital of Culture (ECOC) at the beginning of 2012. The project dubbed "Maribor 2012" had begun some years before the official ceremony, with a multidisciplinary team crafting an ambitious plan on how to revive cultural ecology within the region. Maribor, along with five other partner cities (Murska Sobota, Velenje, Ptuj, Novo Mesto, and Slovenj Gradec) was to become the temporal and cultural epicenter of Europe. Whilst a team of artists and producers worked on the outlines of the cultural program, others were busy tinkering with ways to disseminate information, promote the

DOI: 10.4018/978-1-4666-4490-8.ch035

participation of visitors and the local community, and establish an acceptable bridge between events and the local environment. They foresaw this bridge as being in the form of a highly interactive web-platform accompanied by other interactive contact-points (mobile applications, interactive information kiosk, etc.) as well as with conventional techniques (information-points, brochures, advertising, etc.).

Meanwhile a different discourse was taking place at the University of Maribor within a group of MA students from the Media Communication Department. Ubiquitous Computing is a class originally meant for computer science and informatics students with basic to moderate knowledge of programming. Therefore, the original emphasis was on development, high-fidelity prototypes, and practical work. On the other hand, media-communication students often lack programming skills and are instead better equipped regarding social science, media, and design skills. The challenge was how to redesign the course to fit these students. This challenge was thus transformed into an opportunity for restructuring the course and placing more emphasis on high-level informatics, namely human-computer interaction (HCI), with the focus on user-centered design approaches.

Two sets of challenges emerged within the same city. On the one hand, we had the ECOC wanting to a) design and disseminate attractive interactive content and b) actively engage with the local community. On the other hand, the University believed that students a) needed to practice and gain knowledge of HCI and b) work on actual, real-life problems to gain real-life experience. The ECOC with its diverse and rich program was hence an ideal theme for presenting to students as an assignment. When completed properly students would learn how to design with the user in mind, learn the basics of HCI whilst working on real-life challenges within the ECOC. At the same time, Maribor and its ECOC team would establish collaboration with the local youth.

This paper illustrates the chosen approach and the interaction between students and the ECOC. It tends to answer the question of student motivation for work as well as their engagement in the local community. And more than anything it illustrates our methodology for teaching HCI to students, one that is based on experiential learning human-centered design. We start with brief introductions of both the ECOC and the Ubicomp for the Media studies. It also looks at the state and practice of HCI teaching, and concludes with a departmental case-study that covers two years of teaching a Ubicomp course to MA students. Throughout these two years the course, and especially the practical part, was redesigned with a focus-shift from implementation to ideation and problem-solving, and from prototyping and technical implementation towards understanding.

ECOC: An Invitation to Participate

The ECOC project was born out of an idea by the Greek and French Culture Ministers back in 1985. Since then, every year a city has been chosen by the Commission of the European Union and given this title for the period of one year. The Commission soon discovered that being selected as the Capital of Culture significantly impacts a city itself, and boosts its development and transformation (European Commission, 2012). The benefits are multifaceted as the cultural events usually result in further development of the city itself and its recognition throughout the region. The obvious benefits are the flow of tourists and the funding of cultural and structural projects. The city of Maribor was given the ECOC title because it needed a boost to transform itself from a former industrial city to a university city with a vibrant culture. The Commission obviously saw the potential of the city and region, which could then benefit from international exposure.

The city of Maribor with its 95,000 citizens is the second city of Slovenia, situated in the north-east of the country close to the Austrian border, whilst also being close to both Croatia and Hungary. Maribor is a city with a rich industrial history, once housing the bigger and more important factories, such as automotive and textile. During the economic transition and after separation from the rest of Yugoslavia, Maribor went through tough times with most of the big factories closing their gates. As Suzana Žilič-Fišer, the director-general of the Maribor 2012 project stated; ECOC is a possibility for not just cultural but social development of the city, its partner cities, and the region (Maribor 2012). Garcia writes extensively about how being the ECOC changes whole economies, as well as the cultural environment. He especially points out the tourism, sport, and event economies (Garcia, 2010a; Garcia, 2010b).

Even two years prior to Maribor becoming the ECOC, artists and other groups or individuals were already being invited to submit projects that could contribute to the cultural and social development of the region. The University of Maribor also embraced the project, including the Faculty of Electrical Engineering and Computer Science where the authors of this paper teach subjects such as the ubiquitous computing and designing of embedded systems. Namely, while art may be within the domains of artists (though debatable with the emergence of post-modern art), culture is a far broader term and, as Williams in (Guins & Zaragoza-Cruz, 2005) argues, one of the more complicated. With the emergence of new media channels, especially with the development of information communication technologies (ICT), there is a shift in the perception of culture that Henry Jenkins describes as 'convergence culture' (Jenkins, 2008) where old and new media collide. So what is culture then? There are numerous lenses through which it can perhaps be interpreted, may be as art, media, history or sociology. What they all have in common is that they see culture as a process of defining an environment (e.g., place, region or nation) and its people, within a certain timespan (Guins & Zaragoza-Cruz, 2005).

None of the takes on defining culture talks solely about art as the defining element of culture, yet many still feel incompetent when asked to declare themselves as contributors to culture. The presented study asked how this gap could be bridged, how to encourage at least the students to actively participate in the ECOC project, and to contribute to it. The students of Media Communication were especially approached in this regard.

Ubiquitous Systems for All

The Media Communication study-program comes under the umbrella of the Institute of Media Communication, Faculty of Electrical Engineering and Computer Sciences, at the University of Maribor, Slovenia. The mission of the Media Communication study-program is the educating of future media professionals and arming them with broad interdisciplinary skills involving certain aspects of social studies, multimedia production, computer science, web-systems and services, and visual communication. This study-program is taught according to the Bologna study system at both graduate and postgraduate levels (Institute of Media Communication, 2012).

One of the courses included in the first year of Master's degree studies is 'Ubiquitous systems in media' conducted by the Institute of Informatics. The main goal of this course is to introduce students to the roles of ubiquitous systems, teach them the basics of technological infrastructure, and conduct typical case-studies into media. After completing the course, the student should be able to understand how a ubiquitous application for use in media is implemented, to decide which technology should be applied, and to implement a simple ubiquitous application. However, the latter has proved to be a problem, which will be returned to later in the paper.

Similar courses are also conducted for students doing Computer Science and Informatics study programs. The students of these programs have enough skill and theoretical background to employ relatively complex application development on modern mobile devices. On the other hand, the students of the Media communication study program have only basic programming skills. Furthermore, the time allocated for practical work is very limited.

This problem was identified from the beginning and was looked at as a challenge. The courses for Master's degree studies were started in 2010. During the first year, instead of low-level programming, an attempt was made to introduce some sort of visual programming tools. App Inventor for Android was chosen –then Google, now under the license of MIT (MIT App Inventor, 2012). It allows those students, unfamiliar with computer programming, to create software applications for the Android operating system. App Inventor uses a graphical user interface. Users can use the dragging and dropping of different programming blocks to create an application. However, even at this level of abstraction, the results were disappointing. The students were spending a lot of time studying the tools instead of focusing on the ideation phase and the creation of creative and innovative solutions. Whilst an attempt was tried to employ user-centered design (UCD) as the default design approach, too much was still focused on the implementation.

During the second year, it was decided to use a different approach. The plan was to include the students of the faculty within the events connected to the ECOC, and to prepare solutions based on the real-life challenges thrown-up by the Maribor 2012 project. The goal remained the same: teach the students about the high-level design of ubicomp for the media channels. However, a slightly different approach was adopted (described further on), whilst also modifying the definition of ubicomp itself. We moved closer to what Resmini & Rosati described as pervasive information architecture or a cross-channel user experience' (Resmini & Rosati, 2012; Resmini & Rosati, 2009). Again, the core-definition remained but it just brought it closer to the students of Media Communication. The students needed to combine their existing knowledge and gain, in particular, those skills connected to the field of human-computer interaction (HCI). Namely, there is a gap here. Students are armed with good and practical skills ranging from visual communication to ICT, yet they are not listening to any core HCI classes. Hence, the goal was to move a level higher and cover some of the important HCI aspects whilst designing ubicomp solutions.

Rethinking HCI Education

Studies of HCI are well-established in most universities, usually presented to students of informatics or media studies. HCI topics cover a broad range from cognitive and behavioral science to user-interface design. Cynthia Y. Lester in her paper explains other disciplines of HCI as well as the rationale behind choosing certain fields of study (Lester, 2009). As it is a highly interdisciplinary field, there are numerous definitions of HCI and the concept they all have in common is the idea of the technological system interacting with users in a seamless manner to meet users' needs (Lester, 2009). Newly defined fields such as user-experience (UX) and interaction-design (IxD), as well as design approaches such as the aforementioned UCD all, in a way, fall within the domain of HCI. Yet, in Slovenia HCI is not yet embedded within the study curriculum, hence students lack the high-level knowledge. They are taught about design tools and techniques, yet they lack education regarding interactions between machines and humans, and empathy towards users. The primary goal of the Ubicomp for the Media class is not to teach them both HCI and coding and implementation skills. However, both of them are necessary when designing converged media channels like ubicomp systems, especially for non-programmers.

Hence, authors and professors working with non-programmers like Obrenović urge academia to rethink HCI education (Obrenović, 2012).

Obrenović suggested using experiential learning as a guided process of questioning, investigating, reflecting, and conceptualizing, based on direct experiences (Obrenović, 2012). Together with colleagues, they developed a framework based on an experiential learning paradigm, in order to teach advanced computing concepts to industrial-design students. Their goal was to encourage students to explore technologies without extensive programming and thus increase their awareness of the possibilities, limitations, and complexities of computer systems (Obrenović, 2012).

HCI as a discipline lying at the intersection between engineering, design, and social sciences is also a challenging topic to teach to software engineering (SE) students, and not just design students. Whilst media and design students have problems grasping the technical side (Obrenović, 2012) the SE and informatics students face challenges when designing with those future users in mind who demand designers' empathy. Designers need to be aware of the needs and goals of their users, especially when developing user-interfaces (UI). It is important to note that to the user the interface is the system (Hix & Hartson, 1993). As a solution Pyla et al. suggested integrating SE with other integral courses such as UI design, usability-engineering (UE), and system-architectures within a project environment that would mimic real-life problems (Pyla, Perez-Quinones, Arthur & Hartson, 2004). They also suggested broader collaboration amongst professors that would cover the fields from HCI to SE. On the other hand, students should learn how to collaborate with other life-cycle subgroups (Pyla, Perez-Quinones, Arthur & Hartson, 2004).

The latter was also pointed out by Polack-Wahl who argued that students must familiarize themselves with the process of understanding real-users before starting to code or design (Polack-Wahl, 2004). The students should work on real-world projects, meeting clients, and testing their solutions on real-users. The work of Polack-Wahl was close to that presented in this paper as she faced similar time-constraints as with Ubicomp for the Media class. Her solution was hands-on fast prototyping of solutions as a response to real problems/challenges. In her paper, she also pointed out the importance of students understanding the process of interaction-design (IxD), which is again in common with the presented teaching methodology (Polack-Wahl, 2004).

PROPOSED METHODOLOGY FOR TEACHING HCI

As mentioned above, Ubicomp for the Media class has been going for two years. The class is divided into two parts, the theoretical and the practical. This paper focuses more on the practical work. The methodology developed for the first year had to be revamped because of dissatisfaction with the end results. The decision was to move more towards HCI and shift focus away from technical implementation to product or service innovation. As well as other authors (Obrenović, 2012; Lester, 2009; Polack-Wahl, 2004) the idea was to encourage the students to explore and ideate more, and furthermore to work with real users. The goal was for the students to embrace user-centered design (UCD) as the default design method. UCD as a discipline has been pioneered by the likes of Don Norman and it focuses heavily on the users' goals. Cooper, Reimann, and Cronin later defined their own version of UCD; (Cooper, Reimann & Cronin, 2007). which they framed as 'goal-directed design'. The latter is a design process that spreads throughout the fields of user-experience (UX) and interaction-design (IxD). As the students were not fluent in either UX or IxD, they were familiarized briefly with the UCD process, and various approaches. Because the time-frame of the class was limited the students got hands-on experience from the beginning. The idea was for students to design a product/service prototype for the ECOC project. Similar to Polack-Wahl and Obrenović, a framework was developed containing those topics that were necessary to cover (Polack-Wahl, 2004; Obrenović, 2012).

- User-centered design
- Interaction design with the focus on interative design
- Field research with future users
- Evaluation

The goal was to:

- Encourage students to explore (Obrenovi, 2012). and ideate whilst solving real challenges
- Integrate students within the ECOC, and stimulate their engagement
- Teach students how to design user-centered ubicomp systems

Real People, Real Problems: Perfect Challenges

Before meeting with the students for the first time, we met the local representatives of the Maribor 2012 project, as well as certain other stakeholders, in order to discuss the possibilities for collaboration. They helped us identify some key challenges and gaps like the need for interactive content or the stimulation of youth engagement within the local environment.

Our goal was to encourage real UCD to happen and we did not intend to limit the students with concrete challenges. Instead, our framework consisted of four phases:

- Discover
- Define
- Develop
- Deliver

Our framework was a variation of the 'double diamond' design process developed by the Design Council, and used mainly by service designers (Design Council, 2012). We used the 'double diamond' model mostly because of its interplay between divergent and convergent thinking. Our framework also resembled others like the one based on the paradigm of experiential learning (Obrenović, 2012). As Obrenović wrote: "The challenge is to create learning environments that are complex enough to lead to unexpected experiences, but not too complex to be inaccessible to students" (Obrenović, 2012). Meaning that the students should explore and collaborate with users as well as amongst themselves, whilst they also need some direction to maintain focus on the actual challenges. This is why we argued that the goals and a broad structure needed to be set in advance, especially when working on a tight schedule. In order to describe our methodology it is best to move through all four phases of the framework and illustrate the teaching process during the autumn/winter 2011 semester.

Discover

Twenty students were enrolled in the class, and half of them were foreign students which made the course more interesting. Instead of telling the students what to do for the practical part of the course, we only presented them with the brief from the Maribor 2012 project, together with some other regional challenges. The goal was for them to explore the ecology of the challenges and discover the possibilities for improvement. The only constraint was the focus on ubiquitous media. The students had to embrace the UCD process and design and develop a prototype of an ubicomp solution.

The discovery phase was heavy on divergent thinking and unbiased ideation. We encouraged students to dive straight into it and familiarize themselves with the ecology. The deliverable of it was a shared experience with users that led to a deeper understanding (Obal & Stojmenova, 2011) and empathy. More tangible deliverables were the user-journey maps, which illustrated the problem/challenge as a whole. The focus here was not on

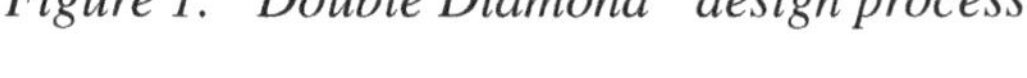

Figure 1. "Double Diamond" design process

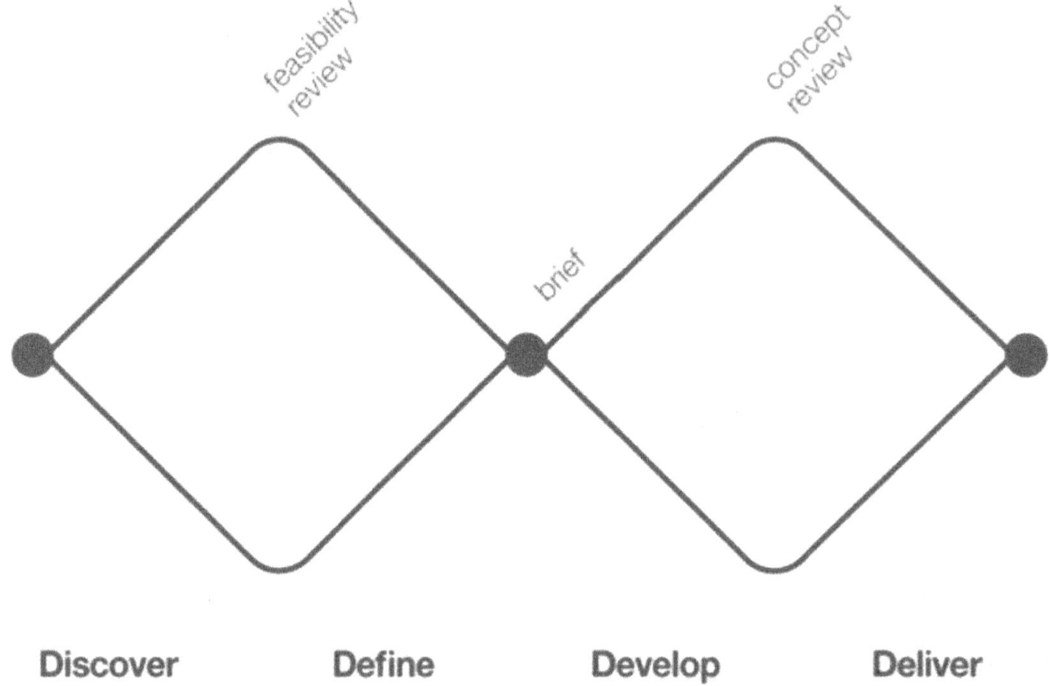

the solutions but on understanding the concept of usage or experience. Therefore, the students were urged to go out, explore the city, observe, and interact with its citizens. We did not have time to familiarize them with the research methodology such as ethnography or teach them any special techniques. However, we had a short introduction to field research with future users, especially about how to start with observation (e.g. shadowing), then on to collaboration with users, and finally to their integration within the design process (Obal & Stojmenova, 2011).

The tools used here were as simple as pen and paper, a simple camera (e.g. smart-phone) or a voice-recording device. The time dedicated for the discovery phase was limited to one week.

Define

The discovery phase yielded a collection of data in the forms of field observations, interviews, photos or impressions. Now it was time to make sense of this data and define the problems, and later on transform them into design opportunities. If the discovery phase was divergent, the defining phase was all about synthesis and convergence. From here on the students were divided into small groups and the existing user journey-maps functioned as a thinking tool whilst defining the challenges. An additionally important task was to define those users who would use their solutions. As instructors the biggest issue was limiting the students' focuses solely on the problem and not on the solution. Even if the students had envisaged the solution already, to go from A-C you have to do B as well.

The deliverable from the students was a problem-statement and the definition of a context regarding product/service usage. They had to test their problem-statement again with the users to see if the synthesis had been done correctly. The synthesis was also presented to other students, as it was desirable to foster fruitful collaboration amongst them. Some of the problems students

Figure 2. Students using shadowing and field diaries as research methods

identified were: traffic monitoring, public transport, local food spotting, personal fitness or mobile CRM. It was interesting to note that students were addressing the needs of various user groups and not only tourists, as we anticipated.

The students had almost two weeks to define the problem and come up with plan on how to design a solution.

Develop

In HCI 'develop' mostly translates into design and this was also the aim here. Design fast and iterate often were the instructions. Some students were familiar with agile and rapid development but were not used to iterating based on user-feedback. Again, the goal was to think divergence, to go for quantity at the beginning, and only fine-tune solutions towards the end. The students started designing top to bottom, looking at the bigger picture at first. Most of them decided to create a mobile or web-app prototype, but were urged to consider other touch-points and channels whilst designing.

The first deliverables were product/service blueprints glued onto the existing user journey-map to confirm it met the users' needs. Wireframe models and paper prototypes followed together with the visual language definitions, and the designs of user interfaces. As the course guided instead of led, each group decided on the design and feedback-gathering techniques. They were not armed with research skills and so were told to at least test things out on their friends and relatives. Again all groups presented their findings and low-fidelity prototypes amongst themselves, in order to obtain some constructive feedback.

Figures 3. Low fidelity paper prototypes and user journey map

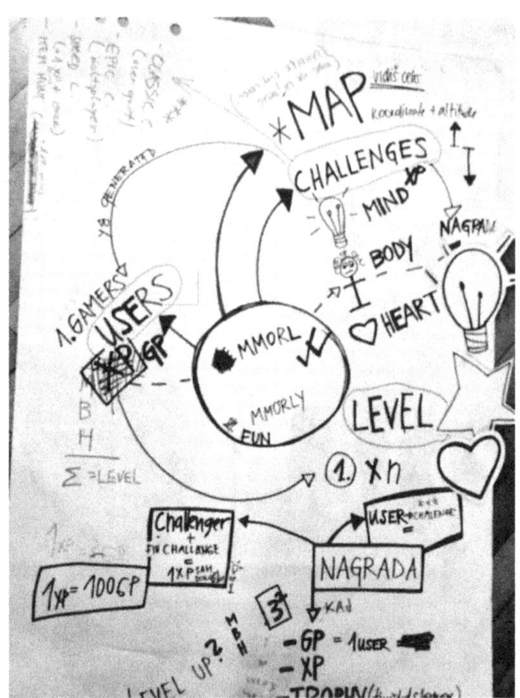

Not wanting to limit the students' creativities, certain tools were only suggested to help them prototype, like Balsamiq Mockups for low-fi prototyping. However, the students were shown how to prepare clickable mock-ups in PowerPoint or Keynote. The goal was to iterate at least three times, hence the minimum time allocated for the development phase was 4 weeks.

Deliver

As already stated, the goal of the course was not technical implementation but a proof of concept, a well-designed prototype rooted in user-goals. In the case of mobile services, the end result was a high-fidelity prototype and, in the case of novel service, the students prototyped the user experience in detail. The final challenge for the

Figures 4. Low fidelity paper prototypes and user journey map

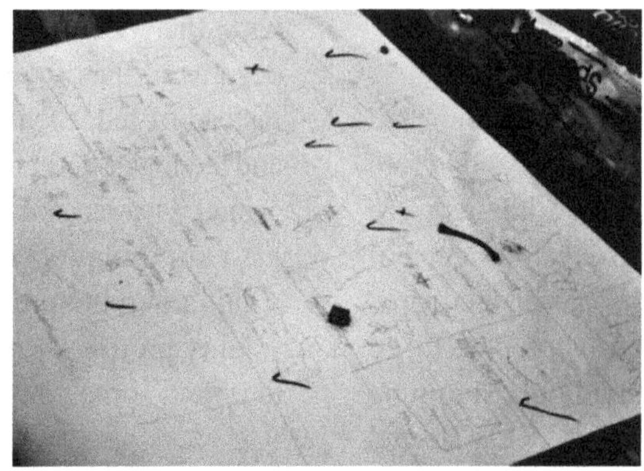

Figures 5. Low fidelity paper prototypes and user journey map

Figures 6. High fidelity clickable prototype

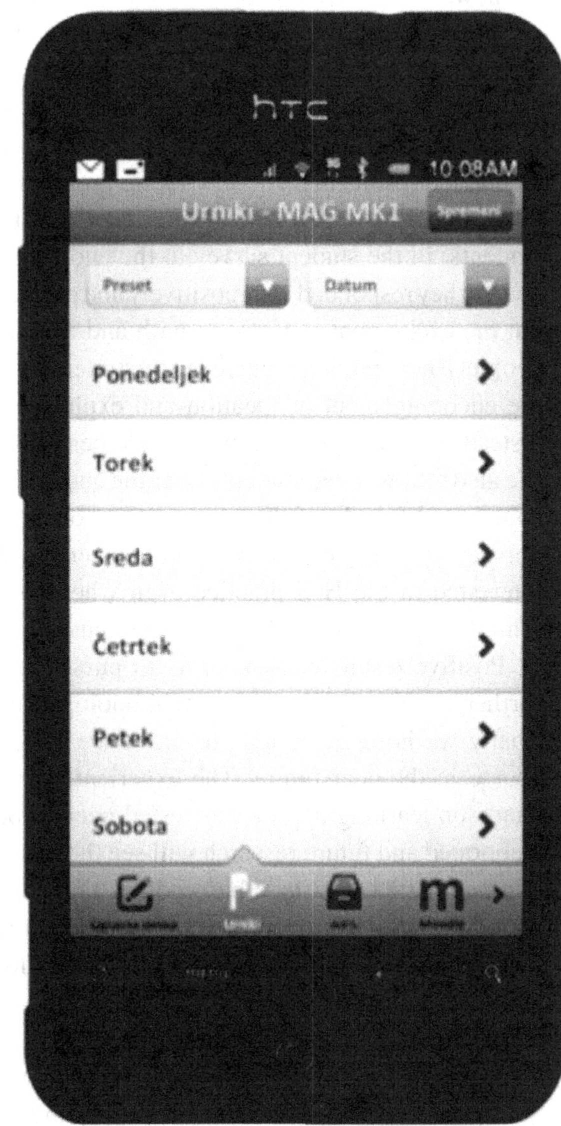

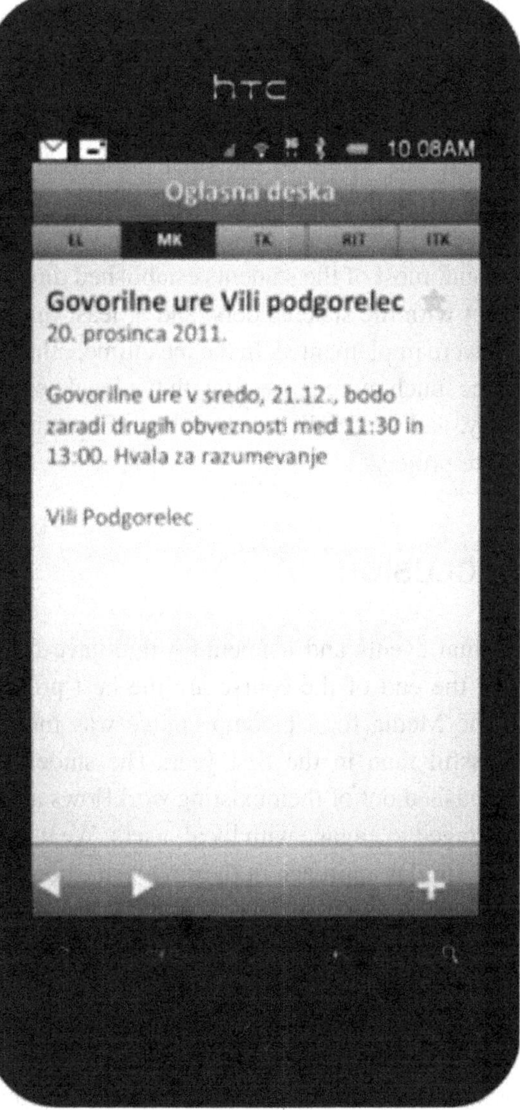

students was the last synthesis, the final pitch of their solution. Normally students present their work to teachers and get a grade for it, but such a system is unsuitable when working in the field of HCI, especially when using experiential learning, a design studio, and UCD in general. Teachers and instructors should guide the students, but final grading should also consider evaluation by the users and stakeholders. This was why an event was organized where the students would present their final ideas in front of the stakeholders and guests.

Representatives of the ECOC project in Maribor, as well as representatives of IT companies, young entrepreneurs, even investors were invited to this final event. The students condensed their ideas into a short format (max. 10 minutes) and then collated feedback from 'real' stakeholders instead of their teachers. In comparison to the first year, the levels of the final presentations were much higher, mainly because students had to present them to an outside audience. After the event, most of the students established direct contact with the stakeholders, and at least three ideas were implemented. In the meantime, others became much more engaged with the local community, and especially the European Capital of Culture projects.

CONCLUSION

The final events and happenings that have followed the end of the course are the best proof that the Media for Ubicomp course was more successful than in the first year. The students were pushed out of their existing workflows and encouraged to engage with local- users. We used a very similar approach in the first year, though there was no concrete project behind it. In addition, the students were perhaps under pressure to deliver a sophisticated product. We risked a lot with the decision to give students even more freedom regarding the final solution. However, the developed framework with clearer goals and its connection with the ECOC project provided key elements for change. The students learned about HCI, and designing with the user in mind, mainly because they were working with real problems, real people. Through the experiential learning, they were able to grasp complicated topics such as user-research, usability-engineering, and even participatory-design. The discovery phase was crucial for the students, as they became involved with the local community. Moreover, when they defined the problems they were able to adopt them as their 'own'. Further communication and collaboration with users only led to further engagement, which then led to ultimately better designs. All the students' solutions were applicative and user-centered, hence interesting for both the users and the stakeholders/investors.

The proposed methodology not only yielded elaborated results in form of working prototypes but resulted also in a better experience for the students. In the student survey at the end of the course they responded very positively and pointed out the excitement of working with and for real people. Another thing pointed out by students was the encouragement of ideation and exploration instead of push towards technical implementation. We also followed the students after the end of the course and found out that the majority of them pursued their projects further on and remained interested in the HCI practice even when their school project was finished or implemented.

Positive results encourage us to pursue and further develop our teaching methodology and finally we hope to be able to introduce a HCI course in the near future. The experiential and hands-on learning approaches tested need to be elaborated and future research will see the methodology tested also in other courses taught at the university. Future research should also study more concretely the benefits for students – for now the sample of students involved is not yet representative.

Maybe we are being overly confident, but we have come to the conclusion that if the student (designer/developer) is user-oriented and engaged, the implementation will follow, regardless of whether it will be a program code or just a visual design. Of course, this may result in biased ideas but HCI, in general, is a field dealing with complex and often subjective relations. This is just another argument for HCI education being crucial if we want our students to create good, user-friendly yet economically-viable products and services. Our case has proven that HCI could be taught, even when it is not officially within the course curriculum. It has also proved how collaboration with the local community can be a win-win situation for all involved--- a win for the city that gained access to creative and innovative youth and a win for those of us who managed to develop a working framework for teaching HCI. As for the students, the winning for them was working on real-world projects, with non-fictional stakeholders, and thus being within a constant feedback loop with future users. Of course, they were often discontent with the amount of effort needed, but in the end they stood on that stage, and pitched their ideas with almost childlike pride. Something you rarely see at most schools.

REFERENCES

Cooper, A., Reimann, R., & Cronin, D. (2007). *About face 3: The essentials of interaction design*. Indianapolis, IN: Wiley.

Design Council. (2012). Retrieved from http://www.designcouncil.org.uk/

European Commission. (2012). *Study on the European cities and capitals of culture and the European cultural months*. Retrieved from http://ec.europa.eu/culture/key-documents/european-capitals-of-culture_en.htm

Garcia, B. (2010a). Creating an impact: Liverpool's experience as European capital of culture. *Culture (Canadian Ethnology Society)*.

Garcia, B. (2010b). A cultural mega event's impact on innovative capabilities in art production: The results of Stavanger being the European capital of culture in 2008. *Innovation (Abingdon)*, *2*(4), 353–371.

Guins, R., & Zaragoza-Cruz, O. (2005). *Popular culture: A reader*. New York: Sage Publishing.

Hix, D., & Hartson, H. (1993). *Developing user interfaces: Ensuring usability through product & process*. Hoboken, NJ: John Wiley & Sons.

Institute of Media Communication. (2012). *University of Maribor*. Retrieved from http://medijske.uni-mb.si/index.php?jezik=en

Jenkins, H. (2008). *Convergence culture: Where old and new media collide*. New York: NYU Press.

Lester, C. (2009). Training and educating undergraduate students in the discipline of HCI. In *Proceedings of Second International Conferences on Advances in Computer Human Interactions 2009*. New York: IEEE Press.

Maribor. (2012). *Introduction to the ECOC project*. Retrieved from http://www.maribor2012.eu/en/ecoc/

MIT App. Inventor. (2012). Retrieved from http://www.appinventor.mit.edu/

Obal, D., & Stojmenova, E. (2011). Experience to understand: Designing a methodology for understanding kitchen interactions. In *Proceedings of the 4th Semantic Ambient Media Experience (SAME) Workshop in Conjunction with the 5th International Convergence on Communities and Technologies*. Tampere, Finland: Tampere University of Technology.

Obrenović, Ž. (2012). Rethinking HCI education: teaching interactive computing concepts based on the experiential learning paradigm. *Interaction*, *19*(3), 66–70. doi:10.1145/2168931.2168945

Polack-Wahl, J. (2004). Teaching HCI in software engineering. In *Proceedings of 34th Annual Frontiers in Education 2004 FIE 2004*. New York: IEEE Press. doi:10.1109/FIE.2004.1408564

Pyla, P., Perez-Quinones, M., Arthur, J., & Hartson, H. (2004). What we should teach, but don't: Proposal for cross pollinated HCI-SE curriculum. In *Proceedings of 34th Annual Frontiers in Education 2004 FIE 2004*. New York: IEEE Press. doi:10.1109/FIE.2004.1408713

Resmini, A., & Rosati, L. (2009). Information architecture for ubiquitous ecologies. In *Proceedings of ACM MEDES '09*. New York: ACM Press.

Resmini, A., & Rosati, L. (2012). *Pervasive information architecture: Designing cross-channel user experiences*. Burlington, MA: Morgan Kaufmann.

Chapter 36
Design and Behaviour Computer Animation for Children

Francisco V. Cipolla-Ficarra
ALAIPO – AINCI, Spain and Italy

Jim Carré
University of The Netherlands Antilles, Curaçao

Jacqueline Alma
Electronic Arts – Vancouver, Canada

Miguel Cipolla-Ficarra
ALAIPO – AINCI, Spain and Italy

ABSTRACT

A study of the three-dimensional design strategies through color, shape, and the audiovisual script for the child audience is presented in this chapter. The authors show the key elements that allow for a balanced combination between 3D design, communicability, and pedagogy. The triadic interrelations are analyzed and evaluated by communicability experts, whose results are presented graphically. Finally, there are the results of the behaviour computer animation of the main characters in the analyzed chapters from a perspective of communicability for 3D computer animation.

INTRODUCTION

The design of three-dimensional characters for a children audience is not an easy task (Cipolla-Ficarra, Quiroga & Carré, 2012) if the copyrights in analogical support material are respected, and also digital of everything that exists down to our days. Besides, it is necessary to point out the differences among characters that are presented for the first time to the potential users of interactive systems or classical audiovisual (Cipolla-Ficarra, 2012) from those which have as a previous support a literary text, for instance. In this work we will focus on a computer animation collection, with an excellent communicability such as the TV series Chuggintown (www.chuggington.com). The series tells the adventures of three student trains: Koko (green color), Wilson (it is red) and Brewster (yellow). It has integrally been developed in computer, for the Lodurum company (www.

DOI: 10.4018/978-1-4666-4490-8.ch036

Lodurum.com). The first collection of episodes contains 52 animations, with an 11 minutes duration (the whole listing in the Appendix and those which have enclosed a star-shaped character (*), means that they make up our universe of study. In each episodes the three learn new things to reach their main goal, that is, becoming expert trains. Their deeds take place in the town of Chuggintown.

COMPUTER GRAPHICS AND COMPUTER-AIDED DESIGN: 3D EVOLUTION

From the architectonic point of view it is a city that looks like the graphic evolution of Simcity (www.simcity.com) of the new millennium. Since the interactive entertainment systems, architecture has always played an important role. For centuries architecture was at the service of those people who held earthly power and spiritual power (Cipolla-Ficarra, 1994). This reality turned architecture into a profession with a solid authority with regard to other similar professions. However, with the French Revolution, the reduction of that authority takes place and new professions are seen to appear in the domain of architecture: draftsmen, projectors, builders, etc. The constant and progressive improvement of graphic software, commercial or not, in 2D and 3D, for instance, linked to the diversification in the performance, boosts the context of advance of

Figure 1. Main and secondary characters of the computer-animated series

the CAD in the most variegated sectors of building. Those professionals who have worked with AutoCAD from Autodesk (www.autodesk.com), for instance, have verified how the work group dynamic has transformed itself, cutting down the realization times, improving the storage spaces of the information and remarkably intensifying the accuracy and the quality of the results. The possibility of making 3D presentations or introducing modifications in real time in the 90s already meant a (r)evolution in all the working sectors of computer graphics, including computer animation. This evolution in the way of working was specially generated in the audiovisual productions and the interactive videogames. In the commercial market of computer pastimes, since the mid 20th century, it has been rich in historic landmarks. We briefly outline some of them: In 1962 Steve Russell created the videogame Spaceware, in the PDP-1 computer. Since that time, nobody could predict what would be the exact boundary of this kind of software products (Cipolla-Ficarra, 1999). A decade later, Notan Bushnell, with the Pong videogame, founded the company Atari. From the 70s onwards the computer games have become a kind of technological innovation, particularly in the field of computer science, television and the multimedia systems online and offline. Actually, with microcomputing, telecommunications, the multimedia systems in mobile phone sets, etc., there are millions of users of computers who play daily in the whole planet with the latest breakthroughs in software and hardware. The PCs have laid the cornerstones of constructive pastime. The Californian company Maxis (www.maxis.com), with its product SimCity and later on the Sims has known how to handle the convergence of entertainment among the users in a masterful way, with a set of components and positive values which from the point of view of communicability between the user and an interactive system which does not exist in other analogue systems. The possibility that the user of the system feels like the creator or maker of that he/she has in front is something to be valued positively. This possibility of feeling the architect of a city, in the case of Sim City, is something that the user has been grateful for along its different versions. In the case of the city of Chuggintown several parallelisms can be drawn between that city and some examples from the latest versions of SimCity 2000, SimCity 3000 or SimCity 4. Therefore, architecture is one of the sectors that has benefited the most from the CAD application and therefore where their different versions have become more generalized. The computer images in architecture have a wide set of applications, from the promotion of new constructions to increase the possibilities of the economic approval of the project to being used as the stage of audiovisual series as an educational media, as it happens in each one of the episodes of the Chuggintown series. Therefore, since the 90s there is a narrower relationship between the computer-generated architectonical images and the world of entertainment, especially with off-line and online multimedia applications, such as SimCity. A system that has been spread all around the world, without age or sex distinction. In this sense, the Chuggintown series follows that trajectory of worldwide diffusion as a result of the high quality in the communicability of its contents.

Colors: Technology, Design and Visual Communicability

The selection of the colors is another key element of the visual communicability of the episodes. The three main characters have been given a color from the set of the primary colors in the light (that is, RGB, red, green and blue) since with it a very wide range of visible colors can be depicted: the mixture of the three in equal intensities (addition) results in light greys, which ideally tend to white (Cipolla & Pentland, 1998; Eiseman & Recker, 1984). Now that which starts as a sign sent through the optical nerve turns quickly into an emotional, social phenomenon, etc. (Murch, 1984) which has in turn a subset of multiple and complex meanings. That is how wavelength of approximately 650 nm (nanometer) approximately, the light is perceived as red but it is experienced as heat or danger, romanticism or revolution, heroism or wickedness, in keeping with the cultural and personal parameters of the potential users of interactive systems or cinemagoers, TV watchers, etc. (Eiseman & Recker, 1984). The colors used in the Chuggintown animation perfectly adjust to the colors used in the last decade of the 20th century and start of the new millennium. That is, the wealth of colors stemming from other cultures in the environment of globalization, including the flowery and luminous tones. The context inside which every color unfolds the rainbow of symbols and emotions is the historical one. The design historians look to the past to decipher the human and social mystery. Next a short explanation of the three main colors of the characters: Koko (green), Wilson (red) and Brewster (yellow). Conceptual evolution of colours in relation to the field of study (psychology, art, etc.) use (industrial design, fashion, publicity communication, etc.) and transformation of meanings with the passing of time, for instance, Lüscher and Jung reflections and conclusions (Cipolla-Ficarra, 2008).

- **Green:** A green fabric conveys a sense of freshness and cheerfulness and seems to be of medium weight. Being a colour constituted by yellow and blue, it changes its appearance according to the supremacy of a shade above the others and according to the quality of its nuances: the yellow-green is gay and light; the brown-green is autumnal and mimetic; the blue-green is heavy and deep. People believe that surrounding themselves with this colour can induce to emotional stability, calm the nervous system, help reducing insomnia and irritability. Action: Possession, preserve. Purpose: Safety. Temporality: a precise moment. Sensation: Power. Historicity: barbaric, imperial, bourgeois, proletarian, freedom, radicals and conservatives.
- **Red:** A red fabric conveys heat, brilliance, sensuality, and has a strong and important presence. "This colour has always been associated to sexual desire [...] and is ——in tattoos, make-up and clothing—— a signal of appeal. As red is a boasting colour, the person who wears it shows a passionate and young image of himself, energetic and exuberant, often willing to be the protagonist and have power. In the past it represented the colour of luxury and richness, of power and sovereignty, of hierarchical status and social dignity for long: today a memory of this symbolism persists in the use of purple for cardinal's garments, for magistracy, for royal or Masonic ceremonies of investiture, besides theatre that, taking possession of these historical references, made it the colour of false-luxury". Action: to provoke an effect, to buy. Purpose: conquest. Temporality. Present. Sensation: Success. Historicity: sacrifice, royalty, corruption, popular and socialist, playful consumerism.
- **Yellow:** A yellow fabric is bright, light, joyful, warm, cheerful and lively, it conveys extroversion and youth. "People who love yellow, desire it and wear it, they want to transmit the solar aspect that is inside them, the most external and extrovert, open towards others and to novelties. People who prefer this colour thirst for life and experience [...] they express the desire to feel cheerful and expand into social life". Action: instability, change. Purpose: freedom. Temporality: future. Sensation: hope.

The reader interested in the rest of colors may look up the following references (Apple, 1992; Fernandes, T., 1995; Alison, F. et al., 1995).

New Technologies and New Colours

The 20th century has been a time of great importance for the history of color. Literally, each one of the visual disciplines has been (r)evolutionized. Each time that the rules were broken, new rules emerged to replace them. All of this is due to the appearance of new materials, new technologies which have been the basis of new plastics, paints, etc. generating important daily changes of the visual art and the productive processes. Along the decades of the 20th century technology had restrained itself to assimilating the new materials for the advance of the creative disciplines. However, by the end of the last century technology had amalgamated strongly with the art that the same computers, peripherals, etc. have become design objects until creating a new chromatic range. The range of iMac computers from Apple Computers in 1998 with a transparent plastic carcass in lively colors, joins technology and color. The same happens with the CAD applied to architecture, such is the case of the Guggenheim Museum by Frank Gehery in Bilbao, that is, through the software life was given to projects almost impossible to be carried out without the democratization of CAD (Cipolla-Ficarra, F., 2008).

The primary and secondary colors which prevail in Chuggintown are related to the technological momentum of the 90s, especially with the colors Apple Computer would use to stem the advance of Microsoft. The iMac was presented in the August of 98 leaving aside the beige color, through a motley range of primary and secondary colors whose Pantone codes can be summed up in the following way: 1505, 1935, 361, 285, etc. (Eiseman & Recker, 1984; Cipolla-Ficarra, 2008). In some way the secondary message which was sent to the computer users from the point of view of design was that the new Macintosh was for the adventurers, and not for the geeks (people fascinated by technology and computer science but with pejorative connotations in the 90s). Hence from the point of view of the technological marketing the potential users were invited to be more "chic than geek". With the momentum of the new computers in colors, the users demonstrated that style and design could influence in the purchase of a certain type of hardware and software, consequently, in the consumption of interactive contents which worked in certain computers. The style linked to color already had a market thanks to Lawrence Herberg who in 1963 suggested to the paints manufacturers the Pantone Matching System (PMS) or what means the same the Pantone relational system. This was about giving to the graphic arts sector a reliable catalogue so that the customers and designers could choose the colors freely but that at the moment of printing they did not sustain any distortion. The lively tones of the set of animated episodes which we analyze in the current work are focused on the early Pantone catalogues of the 60s. Obviously in the computer animations are also present the cultural contributions from Latin America with a novel color set which would influence the design of the late 20th century. Some of its Pantone codes are 136, 370, 184, 1795, etc. (Eiseman & Recker, 1984; Cipolla-Ficarra, 2008). Another key element was not to imitate 100% the Japanese animation, especially Pokemon. Although the influence on millions of male teenagers and Preadolescence has been high in the 90s, joined to the aesthetics of those animations which has gone beyond the visual aspect, reaching fashion and product design, in Chuggintown creativity and imagination have been used in the behaviour computer animation of each one of the animated elements of the series. In few words, the Japanese animated cartoons with strange and motley creatures destined to become massive consumption products or videogames for the latest consoles find a aesthetic vision, diametrically inverse in the trains and their city. An example in the evolution of the design for children is to be found in "Hello Kitty" (www.madhouse.co,jp). From the chromatic point of view is striking the combination of strong pinks, blues and greens which derive from red, yellow or purple colors. Some examples in the Pantone code are 230, 231, 318, 293, 361, 382, 107, 528, etc. (Eiseman & Recker, 1984; Cipolla-Ficarra, 2008). In other words, the rules of chromatic use were dismounted to give freedom to the imagination of the graphic designers and animators in the global village.

Global Illumination and Local Illumination

The illumination in Chuggintown is perfect since it keeps a high degree of realism with the natural effects and the computer-created special effects, such as rain, fog, etc. When talking of illumination can be established the following categories: the local illumination, the global illumination and the so-called hybrid techniques. All of them very well applied in each one of the episodes we have evaluated. Historically, in the context of computer graphics, were developed empirical model for the application of the "Cosenius Law" by Lambert. These make up a type called local illumination and were developed to be applied to the scan-line algorithms of the elimination of the hidden parts of the objects which make up the scenes which then would be processed to get a final image or rendering. These illumination models evaluate the geometry of the object according to their perspectives (image-space) and calculate the visible parts in an incremental way. The main authors who worked in these simple models are Warnok (1969), Bouknight (1970), Gouraud (1971), Phong (1975), etc. (Cipolla-Ficarra, 1999).

However, global lightening is restrictive since it does not take into account the influence of the transmitted illumination among the different objects which make up a scene. For instance, the reflex of the metallic parts when these are brilliant such as can be the wheels. Consequently, other models are necessary to mitigate that lack. They are those which are called "global illumination" which improve the aspect of the scene in comparison with the local illumination. The global illumination considers the "Euclidian Geometry" of the scene (object-space). Therefore, pursuing the same finality two different techniques have been developed with equally different starting points: ray tracing models and radiosity models. Briefly, ray tracing is a technique of "dependent view", That is, it calculates the visibility of the different surfaces of the objects considering the position of the point of view of who is observing as a starting point. The surfaces are supposed to be diffuse and only enlightened by the light background, without taking into account the diffusion defects of the environment. These models were developed by Catmull (1975), Bilm and Newell (1976), Whitted (1980), etc. (Cipolla-Ficarra, 1999). Radiosity is a technique of "independent sight" since as a starting point takes into account the position of the light point and considers its influence on the objects of the scene. And also the intensity of the diffuse reflection among blurry surfaces. Specular effects of the environment are not considered in virtue of the law of conservation of energy. In their origins Cook and Torrance have worked in radiosity (1982), Goral (1984), Cohen and Greenberg (1985), etc. (Cipolla-Ficarra, 1999). Now these techniques did not represent a total solution for global illumination, since the first does not consider the influence of blurry shapes and the second of specular shapes. In other words, to describe the problems on the shortcomings have been developed, in each one of the cases, some new models called hybrid techniques, having as main researchers of the late 80s Wallace (1987) and Sillion (1989). They have developed an illumination model in two stages, using the advantages of the ray tracing and the radiosity to include in the solution of the global lightening, the blurry effects and specular in any environment. In this regard, in the "Koko on call" episode (number: 19 –see Appendix) we have an excellent example, when the illumination of the scene disappears (the light that Koko has in its nose fades and is the moment in which she and the rest of objects acquire a special night vision).

MODELLING AND COMPUTER BEHAVIOUR ANIMATION

The modeling of the characters and the personality that each one of them has along the episodes make apparent the excellent quality of the final animation. The morphopsychology (knowledge related to the study of the psiche through the shape–morfo) of the characters is perfect. The modeling of each one of the components of the face of the locomotives and other animated anthropomorphic objects, are one of the greatest achievements which linked to behaviour animation give a special personality to each one of them. Without any doubt it is in the face where the greatest level of communicability is focused on these animated objects. Already in the times of Aristotle use was made of the observations deriving from researching the human face and which is called physiognomy (from the Greek physis) meaning "nature" and gnomon (meaning "judge" or "interpreter") is the assessment of a person's character or personality from his outer appearance, especially the face. Inside the face, the movement of the eyes, the brows and the mouth where the attention of the potential users of the interactive systems focuses in the first place, and also that of the spectators in front of the big cinema screen, or the "little screen", as the TV is called in many places of the European south. The most important thing is that a character is well designed and entails personality (Cipolla-Ficarra & Cipolla-Ficarra, 2009). Obviously, this has been admirably achieved in each one of the episodes where the main characters of the series interact with other friends or colleagues. The character must also be well proportioned and attractive to sight. In this sense the spherical eyes of the trains play an important role, joined to the movement of the brows, which in the case of the trains are the windscreen wipers. The designer, at the moment of creating these characters must take into account the external appearance, besides, the animation. In other words, he/she must have a full knowledge of the available software and the basic requisites to carry out a successful animation. Sometimes some of the limitations in the movement or the design of the characters and/or environment where they will move are restricted by the graphic commercial software which is usually available. For instance, the special effects related to nature such as can be fire, rain, snow, etc. However, in the studied series each one of the special effects are accurate, whether from the graphic point of view or the duration of said special effects inside the script. In other words, it is necessary that the designer used to the utmost the strong points of the available software and excludes the weak ones, since the final character, if attractive and if he has personality, does not interest the user of a videogame or a television watcher, as it has been created. Not for nothing the simplicity of the characters of the series has allowed to have a set of trains which do not only communicate among themselves, but also with the human beings and the animals along each one of the episodes. The key has been in modeling simple and succinct objects. The advantage of all of this also has a repercussion in the budget since they are faster to animate, besides, the final production costs are cut. In Chuggintown there is an ideal balance because the locomotives have been rid to the utmost of the superfluous components and keeping among themselves common elements such as lights, the whistles in the steam trains, the bells in the trams, etc. The international children audience accepts 100% these characters because they are stylized and the anthropomorphic animation has no failings.

LEARNING AND COGNITIVE COMPANIONSHIP

Another of the cardinal points of the international diffusion and acceptance by the children audience is the learning process in which are immersed the main characters of the series. In this sense can be seen the use of the notion of cognitive comradeship

(Delacôte, 1996) which is inspired in the old practice of the companionship relationship between the teacher and the apprentice, practices which the old locomotives in their different models and activities transmit the knowledge and the dexterity of the expert in domains such as taking passengers in the wagons, circulating in the middle of the fog, get their bearings in the darkness of the night, etc. These transference methods do not entail a didactic teaching, here the workmate observes the way to behave of the expert and trains trying to imitate him. This is therefore a learning process through successive approximations, obtained in the course of the realization of a multiplicity of tasks.

The skills and the knowledge thus acquired are naturally inside the social and functional context of their use (Vicente, 2003) the apprentice trains, for instance, see the use of what they are learning. In the case of conceptual learning, conceptual knowledge might be built explaining its use in a diversity of contexts to ensure a deeper comprehension of the concept and the understanding of a rich set of associations between the important concepts and the problems resolution contexts. For instance, when the trains enter the mechanic train to repair their breakdowns or learn the functioning of special wagons, such as can be those mounted on a tow truck. In some way there is a parallelism with the traditional relationship of trades mates, the procedure used by the teacher is visible and observable, it keeps a narrow relationship with the obtained product. In the classrooms, the classical pedagogical practices do not render visible to the pupils the key aspects of the procedure of the experts. The teacher transmits knowledge, but does not explicitly behave like an expert who can be seen as such by the pupil (Delacôte, 1996).

In the computer animation series we are analyzing, this didactic approach has been widely surpassed with the excellent examples that the tutors, human or not, give to the student trains. This is due to the fact that one of the characteristics of cognitive companionship is the realization of a set of activities aimed at making explicit the ways of behavior which are implicit in the experts, in such a way that the student may observe them, compare them with his own way of thinking and then, little by little, put them into practice with the help of the master and the other students. A scheme or model which is repeated constantly in each one of the episodes of the Chuggintown series.

This cognitive approach uses self-correction which entails a generation task and a criticism task. So that the cognitive learning leans in a first stage on the development of an exteriorized dialogue in which are given a solution and a critique to that solution (as a rule, there is always some train among the three main characters who tries to find alternative solutions, sometimes with positive success, but many more times with negative results). This may be reached through discussion, the alternation in the roles of teacher and pupil (reciprocal teaching), and the group resolution of problems (Delacôte, 1996). A good organization of the successive tasks allows the progressive increase of the complexity and the diversity of the tasks that have to be accomplished or the problems to be solved. Evidently, this is one of the advantages in relation to the classical companionship of the professor and apprentice and which the succession is determined by the goal of production. An approach of these characteristics is always present in each adventure of the main and secondary characters of the computer animation TV series.

EVALUATION AND RESULTS

The episodes of the TV series have been chosen in a random manner and there have been two communicability evaluators (red and blue colors in Figure 2) who have viewed the analyzed series. In this first work we have focused on the aspect of traditional design, through the color issue and the architecture of the constructions that appear in the episodes. The quality of 3D has also been

Figure 2. The results obtained in the evaluation make apparent the high quality of the computer animation series aimed at a children audience (number 0 is the minimal mark and 10 the highest or best)

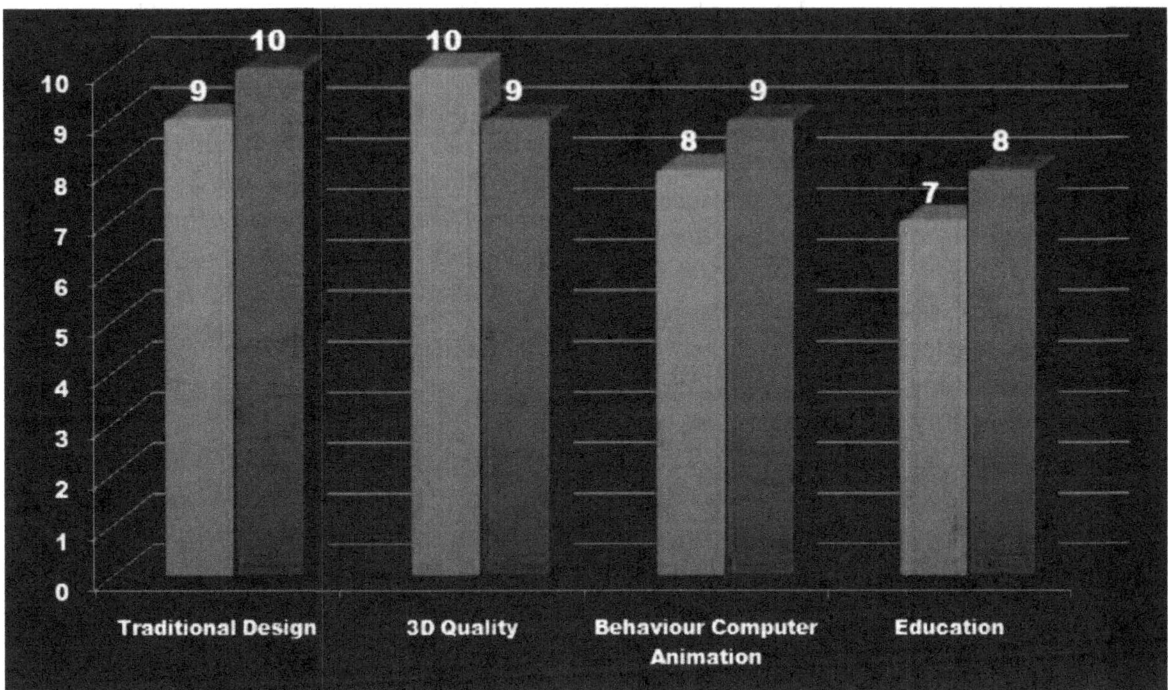

included, in particular the aspects of global illumination and the special effects related to nature, mainly. Finally there is the aspect of behaviour computer animation and education.

LESSONS LEARNED AND FUTURE WORKS

The high quality of each one of the analyzed episodes and which in later works we will enlarge to all the episodes of the series demonstrate how the 3D characters can be stylized to draw the attention of the children audience in the global village. Besides, the anthropomorphic animation of these main characters and also the secondary has no failings. We find some limitations in the modeling of the real characters such as can be the branching or symmetry effect which takes place in the arms of the human beings, which have a parallelism to the Sims. This parallelism or isotopy can also be found in the buildings which keep an interrelation with the latest versions of SimCity. A positive factor since millions of users chose this game and they see today on TV an animated series with similar constructions to those they could build. Evidently, there was a very important didactic element in that videogame which today also exists in the animated series, through the teaching and learning method based on cognitive companionship. In the future works we will try to establish links or isotopies from the pedagogical point of view, 3D design and the interactive games between this computer animation TV series and others of great communicative quality such as "The Little Prince", and the architectonic construction systems for young and adult users.

CONCLUSION

In this work, we showcase the creative capacity of the computer animation designers in 3D aimed at a children audience. These animations have an exemplary graphic quality and also the storyboard, where the behaviour computer animation acquires excellent levels of communicability. Also the didactic value of the series boosts the communicability. A communicability which can be seen in each one of the main and secondary characters, not only among them, but also in the environment which surrounds them, such as flora and fauna. In these works, we can see how the videogame has influenced the design of 3D products for television, since isotopies have been detected from the interactive design category named layout between Chuggintown and SimCity. Once again CAD applied to architecture may serve as link across time among the different multimedia supports. This is another of the positive factors in the diachronic evolution of digital design, whether interactive or not aimed at the traditional hypermedia systems or to mobile multimedia stemming from microcomputing and telecommunications, for instance. Finally, when the triadic interrelations among the main components of three-dimensional design, communicability and pedagogy have a high quality, the international circulation of these contents is usually guaranteed.

REFERENCES

Alison, F. et al. (1995). *Colours of life*. Torino, Italy: La Stampa.

Apple. (1992). *Macintosh human interface guidelines*. Cupertino, CA: Addison-Wesley.

Cipolla, R., & Pentland, A. (1998). *Computer vision for human-machine interaction*. Cambridge, UK: Cambridge University Press. doi:10.1017/CBO9780511569937

Cipolla-Ficarra, F. (1994). The three-dimensional. *Autocad Magazine*, *31*, 58–61.

Cipolla-Ficarra, F. (1999). Viz en los sistemas interactivos de entretenimiento constructivo. *Autocad Magazine*, *62*, 26–29.

Cipolla-Ficarra, F. (2008). HECHE: Heuristic evaluation of colours in homepage. In *Proceedings of Applied Human Factors and Ergonomics*. Las Vegas, NV: IEEE.

Cipolla-Ficarra, F. (2012). Software and emerging technologies for education, culture, entertaiment and commerce. In *Advanced Research and Trends in New Technologies, Software, Human-Computer Interaction and Communicability*. Hershey, PA: IGI Global. doi:10.1007/978-3-642-34010-9

Cipolla-Ficarra, F., & Cipolla-Ficarra, M. (2009). Computer animation and communicability in multimedia system and services: A trichotomy evaluation. In *Proceedings of New Directions in Intelligent Interactive Multimedia*. Heidelberg, Germany: Springer. doi:10.1007/978-3-642-02937-0_10

Cipolla-Ficarra, F., Quiroga, A., & Carré, J. (2012). Storyboard and computer animation for children: Communicability evaluation. In *Advanced Research and Trends in New Technologies, Software, Human-Computer Interaction and Communicability*. Hershey, PA: IGI Global. doi:10.1007/978-3-642-34010-9

Delacôte, G. (1996). *Savoir apprendre: Les nouvelles méthodes*. Paris: Odile Jacob.

Eiseman, L., & Recker, K. (1984). *Pantone: Storia del XX secolo a colori*. Milano, Italy: Rizzoli.

Fernandes, T. (1995). *Global interface design: A guide to designing international user interfaces*. Boston: Academic Press.

Murch, G. (1984). Physiological principles for the effective use of color. *IEEE Computer Graphics and Applications*, *4*, 49–54. doi:10.1109/MCG.1984.6429356

Vicente, K. (2003). *The human factor*. New York: Routledge.

APPENDIX: LIST OF THE EPISODES OF CHUGGINTOWN

1. Can't Catch Koko (*)
2. Wilson and the Elephant (*)
3. Clunky Wilson
4. Koko and the Tunnel (*)
5. Braking Brewster
6. Hodge and the Magnet
7. Koko and the Squirrels (*)
8. Wilson Gets a Wash
9. Brewster Goes Bananas (*)
10. Bang Klang Wilson (*)
11. Old Puffer Pete's Tour (*)
12. Late Again Eddie
13. Wilson's Smooth Moves (*)
14. Cool Wilson (*)
15. The Chugger Championship
16. Action Brewster
17. Koko's Puppy Training
18. Zephie's Zoomaround (*)
19. Koko on Call (*)
20. Outward Bound Olwin
21. Brewster and the Dragon (*)
22. Wake Up Wilson (*)
23. Brewster Knows Best
24. Koko Pulls It Off
25. Wilson and the Ice Cream (*)
26. Wilson's Wacky Tour
27. Hodge's Secret
28. Frostini's Fruit Fandango (*)
29. Zephie Ace Reporter (*)
30. Famous Emery (*)
31. Watch Out Wilson
32. Brewster's Hobby (*)
33. Zephie's Monkey Business (*)
34. Poor Old Puffer Pete (*)
35. Inspector Emery (*)
36. Nurse Wilson (*)
37. Mtambos Amazing Adventure! (*)
38. Rock-A-Bye Chatsworth (*)
39. Helpful Hodge
40. Brewster to the Rescue (*)
41. Wilson and the Paint Wagon (*)
42. Eddie Finds Time

43. M'Tumbo's Royal Tour (*)
44. Wilson and the Wild Wind
45. Old Puffer Pete's Firebox (*)
46. Jet Pack Wilson
47. Brewster's Little Helper (*)
48. Bubbly Olwin
49. Koko Takes Charge (*)
50. Wilson's Paper Trial
51. Old Puffer Pete's Big Show (*)
52. Training Time, Harrison (*)

Chapter 37
Generic Textile Structure Editor

Georges Győry
Birkbeck, University of London, UK

ABSTRACT

Non-rectilinear structures dominate traditional Andean weaving patterns. A systematic description is essential for enabling weavers to document and secure intellectual property rights and for preserving their rich cultural heritage. The author presents a system for modelling non-rectilinear as well as rectilinear weaving patterns; it is the first of its kind. The authors have implemented an editor demonstrating the capabilities of the approach and show its application.

INTRODUCTION

Rectangular weavings (like the output of common mechanical looms) exhibit a very regular structure based on warp threads running away from the weaver and one or more weft threads woven crosswise. These structures are represented in rectangular grids in existing editors.

Non-rectilinear constructions include netting, braiding, twining, knotting, interknotting, linking, interlinking, and interlacing. Sprang (interlacing warps with no wefts), is common in very old textile samples found in the Middle East, Peru, and Scandinavia. These cannot be represented in regular grids.

Editors developed for topological modelling offer functionality for domains unrelated to textile production (Barth 1986; Fleischer et al., 2003) and are unsuitable for weaving structures.

There is work concerned with modelling and simulating physical properties of textiles realistically (Hearle 1978a, 1978b; Smith & Chen, 2009) and rendering the textiles accurately in three dimensions, including, for example, draping the fabric over other objects (Adabala et al. 2003; Okabe et al., 1992). All the publications we know of in this area describe the pattern using a regular grid.

Grishanov et al. describe textile structures for classification using unit cells and topological methods (Grishanov et al., 2009) but they developed no editor.

Our objective was to develop an editor to model complex weavings and visualize the un-

DOI: 10.4018/978-1-4666-4490-8.ch037

derlying structure of the textiles (as opposed to photographs). The editor must give help to arrange the structure and the thread curves so that a user can visually identify textiles and structures. We demonstrate the editor on complex weaving patterns found in Andean textiles.

This work was done in the project "Weaving Communities of Practice" supported by the AHRC Grant AH/G012180/1.

DATA STRUCTURE

The textile is viewed from the top like knot diagrams. The basic object is the crossing of two threads. A crossing identifies the thread above the other, has a position in the plane and is numbered. In addition, it has and four links (named N(orth), W, E and S) to connect it to links of other crossings, following the segments of threads between them. At the destination of each link another link points back to its origin. A thread entering a crossing at a link either exits at the opposite link or ends there (and the opposite link will be unused). Threads can be assigned a colour at a link.

This representation implies that instead of modifying the contents of a fixed grid we have three separate problems to handle. First the user has to define the topological structure of the weaving, then the crossings have to be arranged in the plane and finally the thread passing on top of the other has to be identified at each crossing.

The editor maintains two structures: the numbered list of crossings (Figure 1) and the list of the coloured links with the colours. Threads are, in consequence, represented implicitly and changing a link will change the course of the thread.

Given the knowledge representation model, different users will wish for different interfaces to edit the same structure, for instance a non-weaver would use different operators to create a structure than the weaver who knows how it was woven.

THE EDITOR

The editor has three display modes for the structure: full structure (Figures 5 and 6), structure and coloured threads (Figure 1), coloured threads only (Figure 2, 1 – 4 from left, Figure 7 right, Figure 8). It also has a rendering mode (Figure 2 right, Figure 3). Rendering mode became necessary as commercial CAD programs refused to render tens of thousands of thread segments (determining all the occlusions being the likely problem).

As we show all the crossings and segments in the structure by default, to identify techniques and substructures, the display will be different from a photographic reproduction which shows only

Figure 1. Left: • Simple structure. Right: • Internal representation of its crossings with crossing numbers.

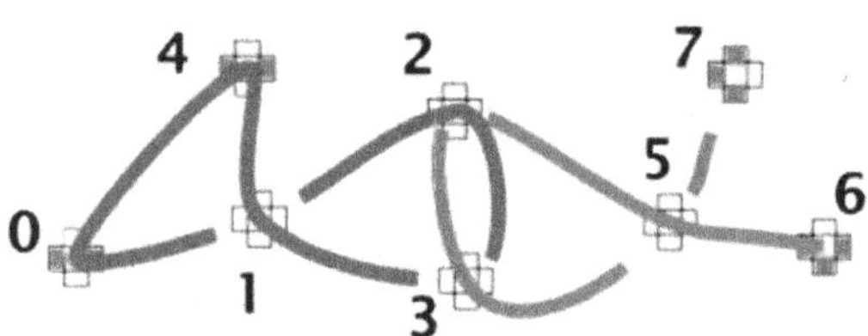

Num	Top	x	y	N	W	E	S
0	N-S	40.00	102.00	1 W	- S	- S	4 N
1	N-S	101.00	115.00	4 S	0 N	2 W	3 W
2	E-W	166.00	150.00	5 W	1 E	3 E	3 N
3	N-S	170.00	95.00	2 S	1 S	2 E	5 S
4	N-S	97.00	164.00	0 S	- S	- S	1 N
5	E-W	239.00	114.00	7 E	2 N	6 N	3 S
6	N-S	291.00	106.00	5 E	- S	- S	- S
7	N-S	261.00	162.00	- S	- S	5 N	- S

Figure 2. Display options. From left to right: • Front • Top • Back • Back + Top • Rendering • Detail of rendering.

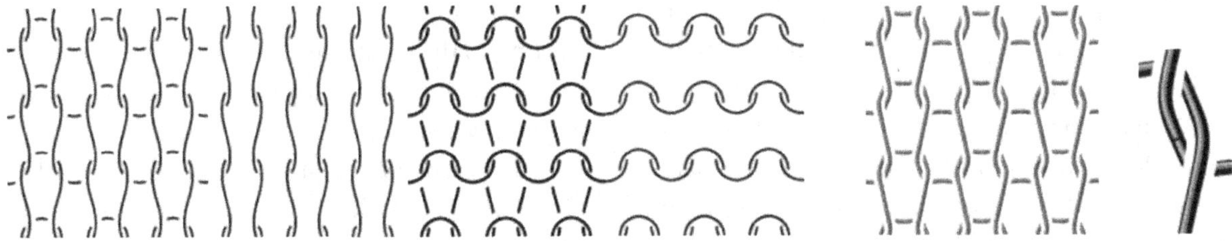

Figure 3. Modelling thread tension Left to right: • Normal • Horizontal thread tense • Both threads tense • Loose and thick threads.

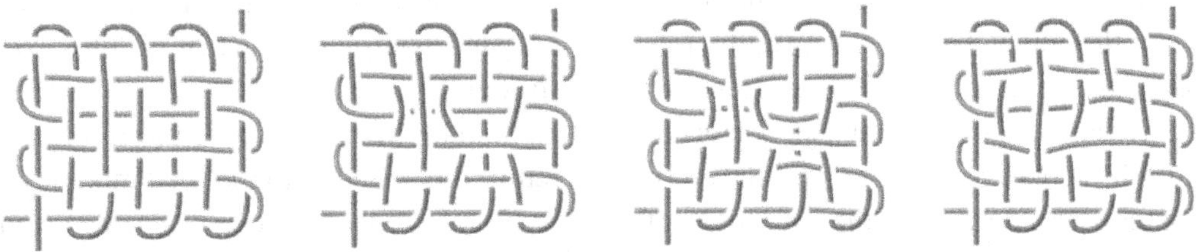

the top face of the textile (with the bottom face in another image, to be aligned with the first). In the editor we have options to not display segments with both ends at the bottom in the respective crossings (called Top) and the other side of the weaving (called Back).

Displaying structures presents two problems: to define the thread curves to display and to arrange the crossings.

Thread curves in the structure displays are Bézier curves, generated by the editor in function of the position of the neighbouring crossings (in most cases the tangent at a crossing is parallel to the secant through its two neighbours) and two parameters. One determines the "loopiness" of the curve and the other the fraction not displayed where a thread segment passes below at a crossing.

In rendering mode new curve pieces are generated, based on the midpoints of the previous ones (and having a crossing at their centre). This slightly displaces the displayed crossings but gives smoother curves. Curves are drawn with a white border and shifted lighter curves on them, to imitate light. First all the thread pieces passing below are drawn, then those passing above. In rendering mode there is no Top layer option. Another difference is that a thread with no colour will make a visible cut in other threads below in the display modes but will be invisible in rendering mode, allowing to illustrate only part of a pattern or the course of a particular thread.

Arranging the crossings models "springy" thread segments which attract two crossings in function[1] of their distance. This is done by iterations when the user clicks and drags in the background.

To avoid the structure being contracted to one point, some crossings either must be anchored manually or no force must act on them. As forces without a counterforce (attracting the end of a thread) are discarded as well as forces at a returning crossing of a thread (like at the border of a rectangular weave where ex. a N link connects to another N link), a rectangular weave will be arranged into a rectangular shape. As an option, we can discard non-opposed forces at turning crossings (ex. a N link connecting to a W, E or S link, as opposed to returning segments). Without this option a braid would contract to a string at the middle. Another option is to arrange horizontally or vertically only.

We have one parameter for arranging the crossings. This modifies the distance used to calculate the attraction (and so the attraction itself) between the two endpoints of a segment if the thread is above at one end and below at the other. The effect of tense threads or loose and thick threads can be modelled this way (Figure 3).

In the following we shall describe the main operators of the editor. These are the result of its use for documenting woven and other structures (knitting, tricot, chain mail, sprang etc.), considerations for its economy of use and for the ergonomics of the user interface. As the philosophy of the editor differs considerably from a grid editor, some use cases will also be given.

Undo / redo operations are available.

CREATING STRUCTURES

Clicking in the background will create crossings one by one. Clicking at the middle of a crossing swaps its top and bottom threads. Dragging from one link to another creates a thread segment, deleting existing segments from these links at the same time. Clicking on a link is used to colour the thread.

Bigger structures need to be created more economically. The editor has operations for creating rectangular weaves, braids and tiled (repeating) structures.

Rectilinear structures can be created with a given number of crossings in the x and y direction and individual or connected warp and weft threads (one or several of each). The top thread pattern at the crossings (like plain weave, 2 / 2 twill, satin) can be chosen and shifted.

Braids are created given a length and the threads starting to the right and/or left at each horizontal position at the top. The top thread pattern is similar to plain weave.

Tiled structures can be constructed in tiled mode. In this mode a rectilinear grid of tiles is defined, one tile is highlighted and each crossing created in the highlighted tile is repeated in all the tiles. Links created anywhere are repeated horizontally and vertically as long as both ends stay in the grid. Changing the top thread in any crossing is also repeated in all tiles. When the structure is ready, the user can exit the tiled mode and modify the structure as usual (but he cannot return the structure to the tiled mode).

Another operation to be made more economical was creating segments in quantity (as to connect structures created separately). We call this stitching and there are two ways to do it.

The first (number-based) method takes a first and a second segment. It then uses the serial numbers of the crossings to calculate increments for the starting and ending links for the next thread segment to create. The user will confirm the creation of the segments as long as he wishes to continue. This method should be used with caution after deleting and cutting crossings or pulling out a thread because the crossings left may be renumbered.

The second (link-based) method takes a first segment and the links from its starting and ending crossings that point to the next starting and ending crossings. Again, the user confirms the creation of the segments.[2]

In practice both methods are necessary. The first cannot be used to follow a thread in a complex structure and the second, to link together a series of unconnected pieces.

Cut, Copy and Paste

These operations have a limited usefulness because the new pieces created must still be stitched to the rest of the structure. Cutting can also trigger a renumbering of the crossings with side effects that may surprise the user. One use of cutting and pasting part of a structure is to separate it from the rest.

Selection

Crossings can be selected using the uppercase key. A new selection deselects already selected crossings. Uppercase-clicking in the background deselects everything.

Selection can be done individually, in a rectangle or along a thread by selecting one of its links. All the crossings on the thread are selected whether the thread intersects itself or not. A parameter can limit this selection to a given number of crossings, on the side of the crossing opposite to the link selected. This choice makes it easier to select a given length of thread from the end, as in the case of counting a given number of crossings.

Selected crossings can be deleted (causing the crossings to be renumbered) and they are displaced together. They are stretched and rotated together (or, if the selection is empty, the whole structure is stretched and rotated).

The selection can be inverted (selecting the complementary set of crossings), extended to the connected part of the structure or turned into a barrier to this extension. The extension is also useful when handling big structures that overlap, to select and displace one of them.

Top Threads at the Crossings

Top and bottom threads can be swapped in a selection.

Copying and pasting their pattern is another problem. The first difficulty is that if we use the numbering of the crossings to identify them, there is no guarantee that the topological structure is the same at the place of the copying and pasting. The second difficulty is to define the two places in the structure.

Two operations are available for reproducing a top thread pattern. The first is based on the numbering of the crossings (and the same caveats apply as to the numbering-based stitching). After the selection the user chooses to copy the pattern and then clicks on a reference crossing. Then he selects paste (or paste the inversed pattern) and another reference point. The pattern is reproduced shifted by the difference in the serial numbers of the two reference crossings. (The pattern is buffered, so immune to pasting to some of the same crossings.)

The second operation is based on the links in the structure but limited to a single thread. Its pattern (to the length limit) can be copied and after choosing to paste it the user selects another thread section where it will be reproduced. If the parameter limiting the length of the selection is bigger when pasting then the pattern will be repeated. Limiting the link-based operation to a single thread makes it non-dependent on the topological structure.

This operation replaces creating a mirror image of a pattern as far as possible. On a horizontal thread a pattern can be copied using the E link of a crossing and then pasted using the W link (on the same crossing if the symmetry is on an odd number of crossings, or on its neighbour if it is even). As the axis of symmetry may skip from one thread to another in a hand-woven textile, the loss in productiveness is not large.

Thread Duplication

A selected thread (to the given length) can be duplicated. The duplication creates new crossings linked by a new thread. On parts of the old thread running through the N and S links the new crossings are between the old ones and their E neighbours. Depending on the user's choice (called

NE or SE), on parts of the old thread running through the E and W links the new crossings can be either to the N or to the S of the old ones. For a SW choice the old and new threads (with a SE choice) can be exchanged. Another user option is to make the crossings of the new thread have the same top thread pattern as the old one or the inverted pattern. For duplicating threads in a braid the NE option avoids creating a new thread that crosses the old one.

A selected thread (or part of it) can also be "pulled out", its crossings being deleted and their past neighbours linked up. This operation triggers the renumbering of the crossings.

These two operations are quite powerful if the user can identify them as possible tools for a given problem.

Example #1

Problem: Basket weave (Figure 4) is not available as a pattern while generating rectangular weaving. How to make basket weave?

The first solution would be to generate plain weave, modify the top threads on a 4 x 4 rectangle, copy this top thread pattern ad paste it along a row, then copy the row and paste it along a column.

Figure 4. Tiled patterns. left: • basket weave, middle: • gauze, right: • tricot with open loops.

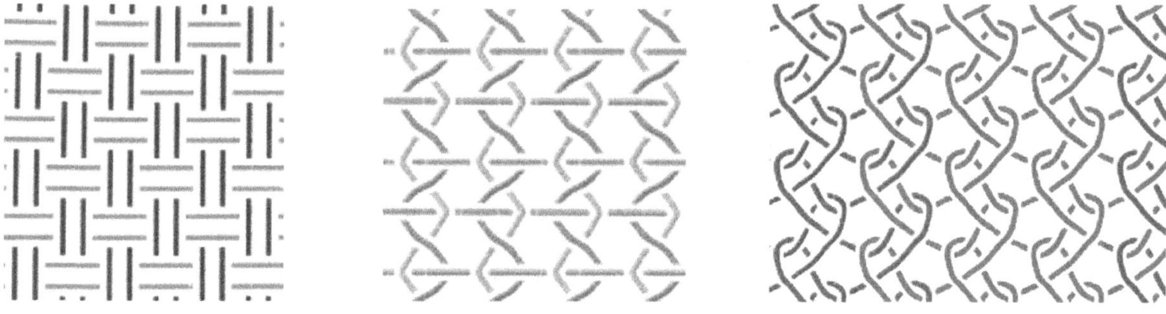

Figure 5. Insertion of several threads into a braid. Left to right: • Original braid. • One thread selected and transformed into a barrier to the extension of a selection. • The selected thread is duplicated to the NE. • The selection (the last duplicated thread) is extended and shifted to the right. • The original thread is selected again and duplicated a few more times.

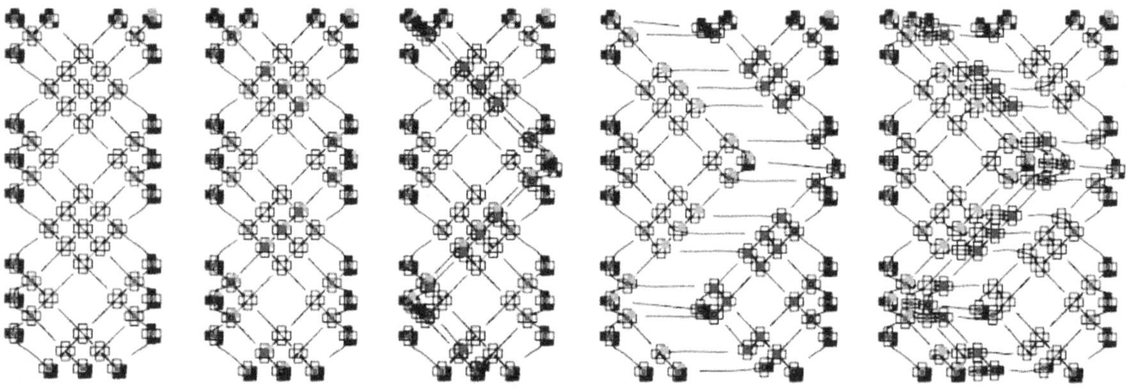

Figure 6. Arranging the crossings. Left to right: • The crossings are arranged vertically only, anchoring only the returning crossings. Notice that the crossings on the side are not marked at their bottom right corner as they are not anchored. • Crossings are arranged horizontally, anchoring all the turning crossings. Notice that all the turning crossings are marked as anchored again. • The two turning points on the duplicated thread (on the left and right side) have created their own thread during the duplication. This thread is now pulled out. Notice that the barrier to the extension of the selection is now disorganized due to the renumbering of the crossings. • The braid is arranged once more for esthetical reasons, with only the returning crossings anchored and for just a few iterations, otherwise it would lose much of its width in the middle.

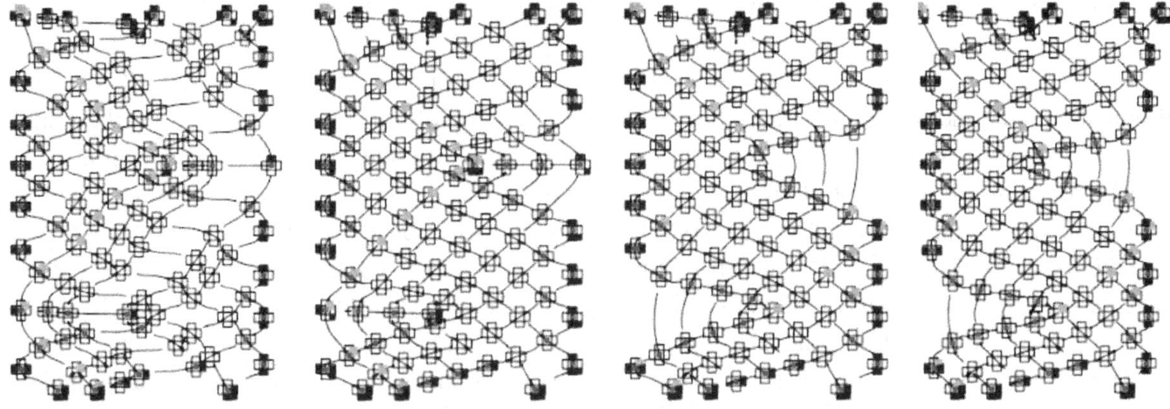

Figure 7. Left: • Weaving, detail (Victoria and Albert Museum, London, register T.60-1965. Notice the missing threads as marked). middle: • Its view in the editor, detail. right: • Detail of the previous view from the middle.

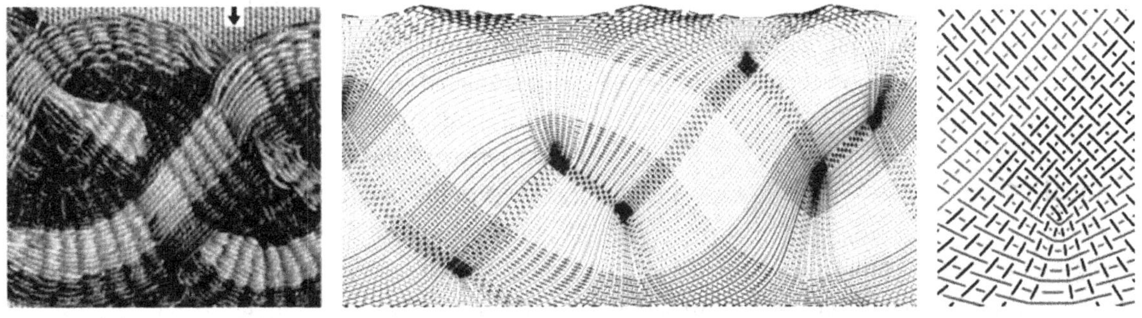

Figure 8. Creating the pattern from pieces. left: • The pieces used. middle: • New links are created. right: • Crossings are arranged.

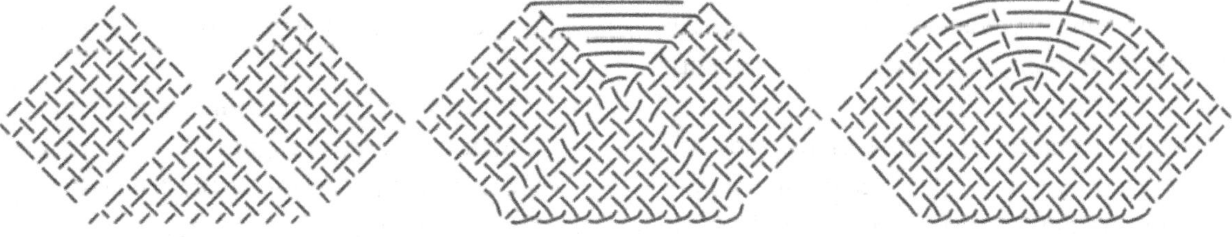

A second solution is to make a horizontally even-sized plain weave with two wefts, modify the top threads on a length 4 on one thread, copy the pattern on the thread and then paste it to unlimited length to both the wefts. Then, if needed, separate and pull out the extra thread and stitch the segments at the right and left borders to have one weft, using number-based stitching.

The third solution is to make a plain weave pattern of half the size needed with one warp and one weft and duplicate both threads (having the same top thread pattern in the duplicate), then diminish the size and finish the borders as above. Finally, stretch the weaving to double size.

The fourth solution is to start with a double-sized plain weave with individual warps and wefts and pull out half of them (2, 4, 5 and 7 from the first 8), leaving a basket weave. Redo the edges, stretch to half size and arrange the crossings.

The fifth solution is to use a tiled pattern.

In all the five cases number-based stitching still works as expected (but this has to be verified before relying on its planned use). In many other cases it can be used in several rounds (ex. first for the even- and then for the odd-numbered segments) on each edge.

Colouring a thread first and watching the colour propagate helps to avoid creating loops of threads without end.

Example #2

Arranging the crossings may take long in a large structure (we modelled structures with up to 23000 crossings). How to accelerate the process?

First solution: displace and anchor a few crossings manually. Choose these crossings so as to minimize the maximum distance (in segments) of the crossings from an anchored crossing. The idea here is to reduce the distance (in segments) that the arranging has to propagate.

Second solution: shift part of the structure before inserting new elements. In Figures 5 and 6 we do this for duplicating one thread of a braid on its whole length. In doing this, the main task is the selection of the crossings to be shifted, especially if the structure is not well organized due to the ongoing edition. We shall show a method to do the selection in Figure 5 and a way to arrange the crossings in Figure 6.

EVALUATION

The editor, called Inasawu, has been programmed in Objective C and runs under MacOS 10.4 or above. Printing structures to .pdf files results in zoom-able images. We have used the editor to model around 40 Andean and a number of other weavings to date. Some of the documented specimens consist of over 20000 crossings and all exceed the possibilities of an editor using a rectangular grid. In Figure 7 a sample from the Victoria and Albert Museum in London is shown with its structure as displayed by InaSawu. The structure is non-rectilinear and the crossings are positioned as arranged by the editor, in an informative and aesthetically pleasing way.

Nevertheless, we need to point out that modelling a complex textile like that in Figure 7 with the editor is not trivial. In order to make good use of the operations the user needs some experience to plan ahead and make an appropriate choice among different approaches. These are not equivalent in terms of the number of things the user must keep in his own memory during work, the extra crossings needed (which is a concern if the resulting model uses close to the maximum) and the resulting structures may not behave in the same way when the crossings are arranged.

Example #3

To create the model shown in Figure 7 the user can

- Stitch together rectangular pieces with triangular ones (cf. Figure 8). This approach can run into trouble if the triangular and rectangular pieces were not all rotated in the same direction. As a triangular stitching (like where the three pieces join) implies turning links, it is important to plan where these will be or the structure will behave in unexpected ways when arranged. In addition to being uneconomical, this method looks completely unnatural to a weaver.

- Create a braid, then using the second stitching method create a series of new links (cutting out a triangular piece at the side) and arrange the crossings. In this case numerous extra crossings were used and the cutouts still had to be created one by one.
- Create a braid and duplicate threads in it using the method described in more detail in *Example 2*. This is the best solution in this specific case and it was used to create the structure of Figure 7. In addition to being faster and reducing the counting to do in the editor, it avoids numerous possibilities of user error.

CONCLUSION

The existing editor is a powerful tool to model weaving structures but requires experience and thinking ahead to use its possibilities fully. It was designed with efficiency of use in mind and it allows the user to produce unweaveable structures as well.

Once the editor was operational we found that it appears contorted to weavers who would prefer using the same set of operations as in weaving, ie. to work with threads. As the operations on the threads are different in warp-faced weaving and in weft-faced weaving (and the two techniques are not combined by the same native weavers, let alone in the same textile), this would suppose different editors for the two classes of textiles.

As weavers know one technique to create one pattern and they are used to proceeding thread by thread, they do not have the habit of thinking

Figure 9. Creating the pattern using cutout. left: • New links are created in a braid. middle: • The separated crossings are deleted. right: • Crossings are arranged.

Figure 10. Creating the pattern using thread duplication. Left: • First new thread (darker colour) is created, this and the crossings above are displaced using the Extension of the selection and the Barrier to the extension operations. Notice the new threads created between the turning points (marked). Middle: • Further 3 new threads created. Right: • Crossings arranged, two threads between the turning points pulled out, one (marked) shown.

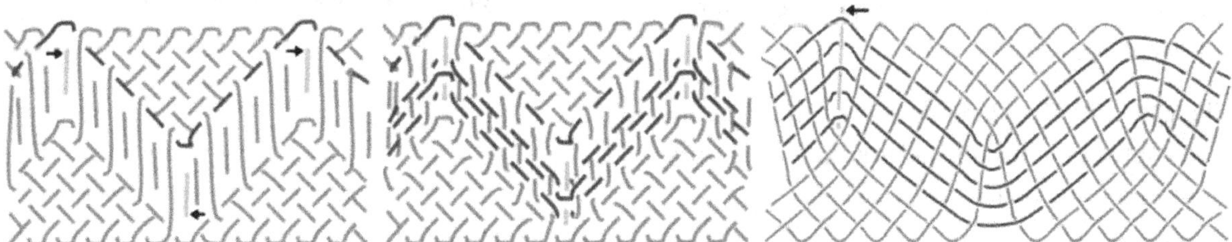

about the "most efficient" way to produce it. Restricting the set of operators to the "natural" ones in an editor for weavers has the additional advantage that no impossible structures can be created by error.

Having established that the data structure and the present operation set are useable to model elaborate weaving patterns, the next phase of work should be the development of different user interfaces with different operation sets suitable to practitioners of different trades (weavers, textile designers and museum curators having been identified so far as a minimal set).

REFERENCES

Adabala, N. Magnenat-Thalmann, N., & Fei, G. (2003). Visualization of woven cloth. In *Proceedings of the 14th Eurographics Workshop on Rendering (EGRW'03)*. EGRW.

Arnold, D., & Espejo, E. (2012a). *El textil tridimensional: La naturaleza del tejido como objeto y sujeto*. La Paz, Bolivia: Fundación Albó, Interamerican Foundation and Instituto de Lengua y Cultura Aymara.

Arnold, D., & Espejo, E. (2012b). *Ciencia de tejer en los Andes: Estructuras y tecnicas de faz de urdimbre*. La Paz, Bolivia: Fundación Cultural del Banco Central de Bolivia, Fundación Albó, Interamerican Foundation and Instituto de Lengua y Cultura Aymara.

Barth, P. (1986). An object-oriented approach to graphical interfaces. *ACM Transactions on Graphics*, *5*, 142–172. doi:10.1145/22949.22951

Brezine, C. (2009). *The Oxford handbook of the history of mathematics*. Oxford, UK: Oxford University Press.

Chen, X. (2010). Modelling of textile structure for advanced applications. *Journal of Information and Computing Science*, *5*(1), 71–80.

Collingwood, P. (1999). *The techniques of sprang: Plaiting on stretched threads*. New York: Design Books.

Fleischer, J., Tentyukov, M., & Tarasov, O. (2003). Diana and selected applications. *Nuclear Physics B - Proceedings Supplements*, *116*, 348–352. doi:10.1016/S0920-5632(03)80197-4

Glassner, A. (2002). Digital weaving, part 1. *IEEE Computer Graphics and Applications*, *22*, 108–118. doi:10.1109/MCG.2002.1046635

Glassner, A. (2003a). Digital weaving, part 2. *IEEE Computer Graphics and Applications*, *23*, 77–90. doi:10.1109/MCG.2003.1159616

Glassner, A. (2003b). Digital weaving, part 3. *IEEE Computer Graphics and Applications*, *23*, 80–89. doi:10.1109/MCG.2003.1185583

Grishanov, S., Meshkov, V., & Omelchenko, A. (2009). A topological study of textile structures: Part I: An introduction to topological methods. *Textile Research Journal*, *79*, 702–713. doi:10.1177/0040517508095600

Hearle, J. (1978a). An energy method for calculations in fabric mechanics, part L: Principles of the method. *Journal Textile Inst.*, *69*, 81–91. doi:10.1080/00405007808631425

ENDNOTES

1. This function is convex, assuring that a crossing between two fixed ones will be attracted to the midpoint.
2. All the segments (as long as they stay inside the structure) cannot be created in a single operation because the operation may not terminate.

Chapter 38
Bi-Manual 3D Painting:
An Interaction Paradigm for Augmented Reality Live Performance

Alexis Clay
ESTIA, Bidart, France

Nadine Couture
LaBRI/ESTIA, Bidart, France

Jean-Christophe Lombardo
INRIA, Sophia Antipolis, France

Julien Conan
ESTIA, Bidart, France

ABSTRACT

The rise of gestural interaction led artists to produce shows or installations based on this paradigm. The authors present the first stages of the "Sculpture Numérique" (Virtual Sculpture) project. This project was born from a collaboration with dancers. Its goal is to propose bi-manual interactions in a large augmented space, giving dancers the possibility to generate and manipulate virtual elements on stage using their hands. The first set of interactions presented in this chapter is 3D painting, where the user can generate 3D virtual matter from his hands. The movement of the hand defines a stroke, and shape is controlled by the shape of the hand. Changing the shape and orientation of the hand allows switching between three interaction modes to produce volumes, surfaces, or curves in space. The authors explore the applicative case of dance, with the goal of producing a plastic creation from choreography.

INTRODUCTION

The CARE project (Cultural Experience: Augmented Reality and Emotions), which ended in march 2011, aimed at setting up several design tools, interaction techniques and devices to augment a cultural event with emotions. With augmented ballet as one application case, our goal was to augment a ballet performance and to make a dancer interact with virtual elements on stage. This project ended in a staged demonstration that took the form of an augmented show, entitled "CARE: staging of a research project".

The Virtual Sculpture project is in the continuity of the CARE project. Our goal is to give the dancer the ability to create 3D objects and shapes

DOI: 10.4018/978-1-4666-4490-8.ch038

on stage. Those 3D elements should be visible by the audience. Our goal was hence twofold. First, we designed interactions to create 3D objects. As dance is our applicative case, we focused on body interaction and especially hand-based interaction. Natural interactions is much more understood by the audience and let a vast and free field of investigation for choreographers and dancers; enabling a technology better integration in the artistic proposal. As such, we focused on very direct interaction techniques. Second, we developed two prototypes, one in an immersive environment for training purposes and another one for a live show context.

In this chapter we describe the work achieved during the first interaction set up, part of the Virtual Sculpture project: 3D Painting, which provides matter creation from hands in a large space. That is how the user is capable of generating surfaces or volumes in a 3D space, which section is defined by his hand conformation, and which longitudinal draw is defined by his hand movement. Metaphor is direct: virtual matter seems to be generated right under the artist hand and stay fixed in space. Starting from there, space becomes a blank support where you can paint. Although we designed this interaction keeping our applicative case in mind, the metaphor uses natural aspects which makes this interaction extensible to other fields.

After a short state of the art, we describe the three interactions we suggest. Then we describe two prototypes creating 3D Painting, applying different technologies. Finally, we will discuss about future works before concluding.

STATE OF THE ART

The goal of our system is to allow the user to draw directly in a 3D space. We do not seek, however, to provide with some kind of modeling tool (like 3dsMax). Rather, we seek to give the user the ability to sketch in space. Several techniques already exist to draw directly in a 3D immersive environment. Deisinger *et al.* led a CAVE experimentation (Cave Automatic Virtual Environment) on several modeling systems calling three different techniques (Deisinger, Blach, Wesche, Breining & Simon, 2000). The first one is matter creation by "substance" injection on a given point. In this approach, the artist adds volume to matter, and his movement creates the shape. In the same manner, the *BLUISculpt* system (Keefe, Feliz, Moscovich, Laidlaw & LaViola, 2001) divides space into voxels, which the artist can paint. The second approach is surface generation. In the system being tested in (Deisinger, Blach, Wesche, Breining & Simon, 2000) the artist defines a flat polygon by points in space, and successively attaches created polygons to his sketch. Finally, the third technique, used by the third system in (Deisinger, Blach, Wesche, Breining & Simon, 2000) uses automatic surfaces generation from directives curves being drawn by the artist. This principle has been taken back from the *FreeDrawer* (Wesche & Seidel, 2001) system where the user traces B-splines in 3D space; lines defining a closed loop can be fulfilled with surfaces. Deisinger *et al.* noticed several recommendations for designing an immersive sketching tool from their experimentations. An ideal sketching tool should:

1. Be a conceptual phase tool towards a certain elaboration degree,
2. Hide its mathematical complexity,
3. Provides a real time and direct interaction,
4. Allow large scale and volume modeling, and
5. Be intuitive.

In this work we took a more artistic approach that led us to focus on the three last points. In particular, we inspired ourselves from two systems from the literature. Schkolne *et al.'s SurfaceDrawing* (Schkolne, Pruett & Schröder, 2001) allows the user to generate 3D surfaces directly from his hands, using data gloves. 3D display of the generated surfaces is performed by the *responsive workbench*, a horizontal screen able to track the user's head and therefore display stereoscopic 3D from the corresponding point of view (Figure 1.a). The user wears glasses provided with position trackers, allowing the *responsive workbench* to modify the display according to the user position. Keefe *et al.*'s *CavePainting* (Keefe, Feliz, Moscovich, Laidlaw & LaViola, 2001) provides several tangible interfaces (brush and paint bucket for example) to allow painting in the volume defined by CAVE device. The painter can trace paint strokes in the 3D space where he can stand and move (Figure 1.b). Our Virtual Sculpture prototype merges the both approaches, associating freehand Schkolne *et al.'s* interaction and Keefe *et al.'s* CAVE visualization.

SurfaceDrawing and *CavePainting* both suggest a group of interactions relative to the task to be carried out: drawing on the responsive workbench for the first one, and 3D painting for the other one. With the exception of *SurfaceDrawing* shapes generation by hand, those interactions make intervened tangible interfaces. With the aim of providing 3D Painting to dance, we want to limit interactions to hands at first.

The prototypes that we present in this chapter aim at combining the approaches from Surface Drawing and Cave Painting, bringing together hand-based interaction with painting in a large space, in which the user can move.

3D PAINTING MANUAL INTERACTIONS

The experience we acquired in the CARE project on interaction design for augmenting dance shows lead us to promote simple and direct interactions. It is also the second guideline from (Deisinger, Blach, Wesche, Breining & Simon, 2000). We imagined three interaction techniques to set the bases for 3D Painting. Independently of the devices used, we rely on the capacity to measure the position/orientation of several points on both hands given an absolute frame of reference.

The first interaction directly comes from (Schkolne, Pruett & Schröder, 2001) and allows hand surface generation. The hand conformation at a given moment defines the shape of the generated surface. At a time *t*, we consider the wrists' positions, and the articulations an tip positions of the middle finger. The curve traced by those points at *t* instant defines surface section at *t*. This section

Figure 1. (a) Surface Drawing (Schkolne, Pruett & Schröder, 2001); (b) CavePainting (Keefe, Feliz., Moscovich, Laidlaw & LaViola, 2001)

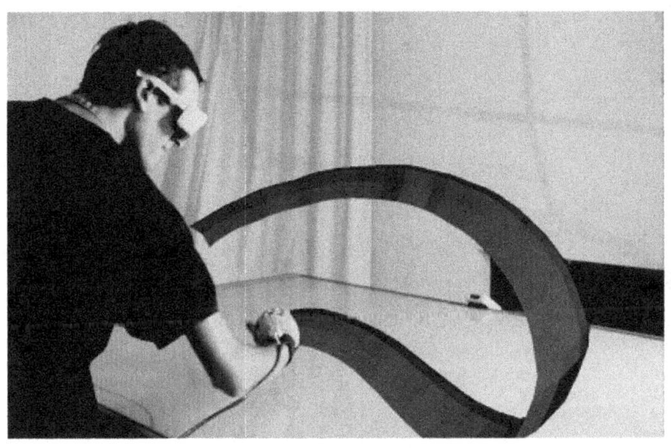

(a)

(b)

curve is periodically sampled (typically between 2 and 10 times per second). For each new curve record, surface between *t* and *t-1* sections is being generated (see Figure 2). Surface generation is achieved by performing a movement parallel to the palm's surface.

The second interaction allows volumes creation by moving the hand perpendicularly to the palm's surface (like a slap gesture). To preserve the "matter generation by hand" metaphor, the volume section being generated is equal to the visual surface occupied by the user's hand: a flat hand will generate a larger volume than a closed one.

Finally, the third interaction features curves or points creation in space. To activate this mode, the user keeps his hand closed deploying only his index and middle fingers. Matter is being generated at the end of those two points; allowing generation accuracy improvement compared to entire hand (like a tinier brush). We chose this conformation where index and middle fingers are both tights for this interaction, in order to let conformation like only tight index for pointing tasks. We currently consider this interaction only for a direct and localized matter generation, another possibility could remains on a curve generation which makes automatic closed surfaces fulfillment possible (like, Wesche & Seidel, 2001)

The main interest coming from those three interactions relies in their simplicity, based on a

Figure 2. Bézier surface drawn by hand movement

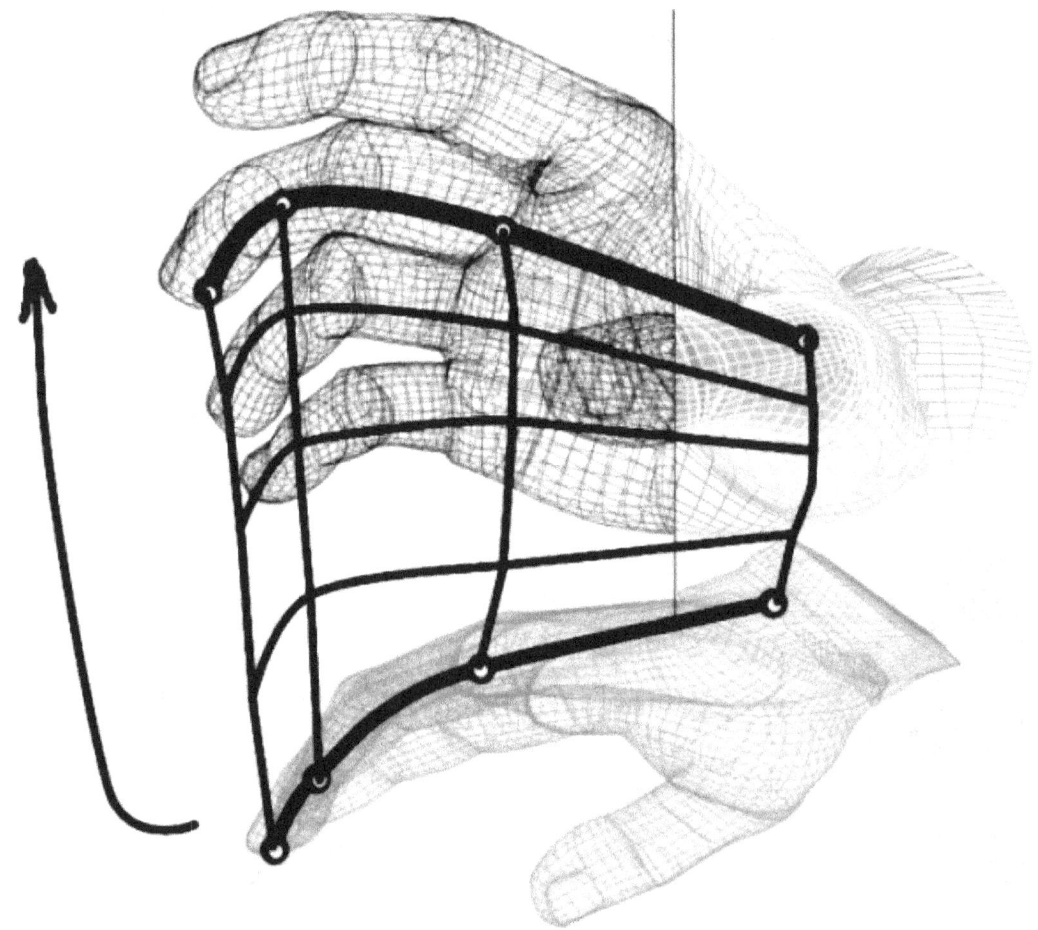

Figure 3. (a) Shapes. (b) Volumes. (c) Curves.

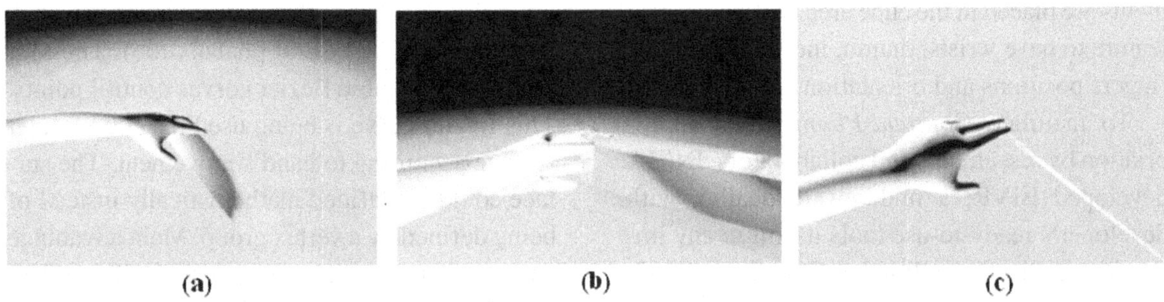

(a) (b) (c)

direct metaphor: virtual matter generated by hand (or fingers tips). Moreover, changing the active mode is being done naturally. To go from one interaction to another, we just need to change hand orientation or to tuck fingers during the movement.

We drew one last modal interaction from (Schkolne, Pruett & Schröder, 2001). Complementing the three suggested interactions above, thumb position allows going from a "draw" to a "free to move" mode. This is equivalent to a drawer moving up his pen to draw a new line. When the thumb and the palm are stuck, surface or volume is being generated. In lax position (thumb unstuck), nothing is being generated, the user is free to move is hand and replace it in the 3D space.

All those interactions can be performed with only one hand. Conformation and movement define the drawing mode, while the thumb's position triggers or deactivates the virtual matter generation. In the frame of our applicative case, this allows using both hands simultaneously, preventing an asymmetric limitation during choreography execution.

ACHIEVED PROTOTYPES

We built two prototypes which explore 3D Painting in a large space. Those two prototypes are limited to hand surface generation by now. The first one has been developed for a CAVE immersive usage. This device has got the advantage to offer a large space where action and perception spaces are superposed from the user's point of view. This kind of setting, however, is not adapted to audience presence, as a CAVE system projects 3D for a single person only. This prototype was developed with the aim of familiarizing the artists with 3D Painting. In the CAVE environment, artists can see what they are creating. Once familiar with the system, they can begin to explore the interaction techniques we propose and to suggest new ones themselves. The second prototype, in progress, is being developed towards a stage environment use, where augmentations are projected and perceptible by audience (but the artist is blind from his creations).

CAVE 3D PAINTING WITH ISIVR

The developed prototype uses immersive cube (CAVE) from INRIA Sophia-Antipolis-Méditerrannée Research Centre *Gouraud-Phong* immersive room. This environment is composed of four projection surfaces (one on the ground, three on the walls), forming a 3mx3mx3m cube approximation. It is provided with an infra-red position follower optical device (AR-DTrack). The user wears glasses equipped with infra-red reflectors; the system calculates a stereoscopic display corresponding to the current point of view for each faces, giving the illusion that virtual elements are placed in the cube area. Reflectors also feature to have wrists, thumb, index, and middle fingers positions and orientations.

To facilitate *Gouraud-Phong* room appropriation by researchers and collaborators, INRIA developed isiVR, a middleware dealing with developer's ready-to-use tools useful in any immersive applications. Based on OpenSceneGraph openSource render engine, isiVR makes management available for peripheral inputs, display devices, head-tracked stereoscopic render, and synchronized cluster utilization. This allows fellow researchers to focus on their specific issues. The developed application can be run without modifications on a standard work station as well as a high-performance immersive device (multi-display + cluster + position tracking). isiVR provides separation between physical inputs or outputs (*Devices*) and peripheral actions onto virtual scene (*Behaviors*). Its object design and plug-ins ability make behavior modifications (or additions) easy to implement. isiVR will be released under openSource license soon. Those functionalities allow us to use infra-red sensors in the immersive cube, but also to add a hand model template (*Behavior*), and finally 5DT data gloves management –*Device* (Site Web 5DT, 2012).

In this prototype, we use cube infrared sensors to follow wrists and fingers. To generate surfaces, we consider that two points defining the middle finger are directly obtained from isiVR (wrist and middle finger end). Intermediates coordinates are being obtained by a calculation composed by: wrist orientation (from distal phalanx), back hand length (from distal phalanx too). The four points define cubic Bézier curves control points. This Bézier curve is being used to set up Bézier surface according to hand's movement. The surface could be defined mathematically instead of being defined by a vertex group. Main advantage coming from this technique is to facilitate data sampling and potentially manipulate generated surfaces level of detail (LOD); avoiding too many points number. Results are available with a video at (Vidéo Peinture 3D en cube immersif, 2012).

3D PAINTING ON STAGE FOR AN AUDIENCE

As being told before, the second prototype is still in progress. The aim this time is to take back the work done during CARE project to augment a ballet scene (see video –Vidéo du projet CARE, 2012). For that purpose, we use rear projected screen on which generated surfaces will be display. Indeed, retro projection handles the problem of dancer shadow on projection surface. To record dancer movements we use MVN motion capture suit (Site web Xsens, 2012) associated with 5DT14U data gloves (Site Web 5DT, 2012). Those data gloves only give a torsion ratio (between 0 and 1) for each 14 degree of freedom of the hand (2 phalanxes per finger and 4 inter-fingers). We developed a system taking hand's measures to

Figure 4. Tesselation (1) Initial mesh. (2) First iteration. (3) Second iteration.

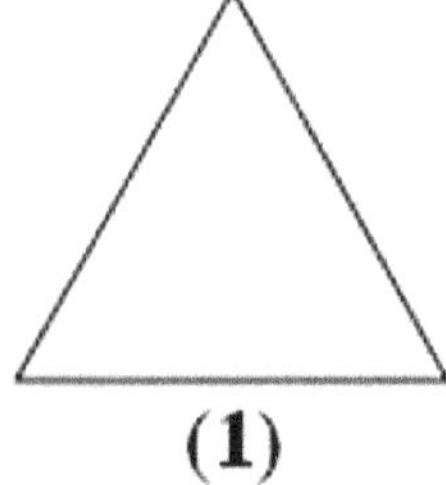

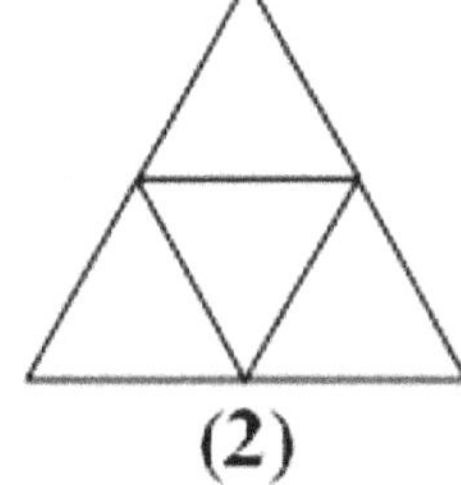

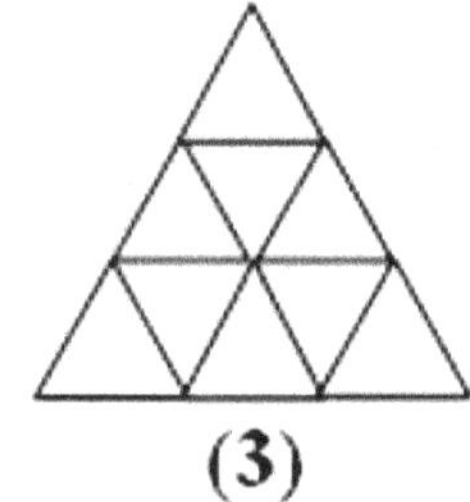

calculate each phalanx position according to the data from the gloves. The system manages data fusion between MVN and data gloves for both left and right hands (*Hand-Over*), delivering user body rigid kinematic chain segments coordinates in an absolute basis on stage.

We use Virtools software to handle graphical aspects of this second prototype. As isiVR, Virtools allows to define *Behaviors* and *Devices* to manage peripherals inputs and outputs. Virtools is based on visual programming (procedural approach like flowcharts), where behaviors are generated by logic bricks assemblies (*Building Blocks*). Coordinates flow has been implemented into Virtools to drive shapes generation. Virtools generic functions provide the two curves draws we need with that purpose. We developed a custom *Building-Block* to get back curves nodes (vertices), implement the mesh, then add the desired texture keeping in mind aesthetic strong requirements (UV-mapping).

The current issue we are tackling is the ability to modify shapes during a post processing step. With computational tessellation we will be able to add more points between those given by the motion capture. It will give a higher level of control on the shapes, dealing with multipoint modifications, smooth and textures placement for example. A maximum level of details is important to improve our generators/modifiers.

CONCLUSION AND PERSPECTIVES

We have presented in this chapter our beginning work in 3D Painting, an interaction set allowing artist to draw in a large space making virtual matter emerging under his hands. 3D Painting takes place within the Virtual Sculpture project, which goal is to deliver 3D object modeling in a large space, itself part of the Augmented Ballet project, which goal is to provide original interactions and augmentations on stage.

We propose three interaction techniques generating shapes, volumes, or curves in space. Change interaction is being intuitively done changing hand's conformation or orientation. We have developed two prototypes for surface generation. The first prototype uses an immersive cube and allows artists to familiarize themselves with suggested techniques and to explore them. The second prototype has been built up under stage visualization requirements. The artist is blind from his creations but thanks to stereoscopic display, the audience has got the illusion that 3D shapes are part of the scenic space and emerge directly from the artist hands.

Those prototypes open numerous perspectives. Our first goal is to invite choreographers and dancers to use our prototype in immersive cube to explore tools and to suggest new interactions, promoting this way a user-centered design for newer interactions. In addition, this tool has got industrial applications too. This project particularly arouse interests in domains like mechanic interactive design (fast sketches or idea illustration), or in fiber orientation specification during composite pieces design.

ACKNOWLEDGMENT

This project was partially funded by Conseil Régional d'Aquitaine (France), under the project "Sculpture Numérique".

REFERENCES

Brody, B., Chappell, G., & Hartman, C. (2002). BLUIsculpt™. In *Proceedings of ACM SIGGRAPH 2002 Conference* (SIGGRAPH '02). New York: ACM Press.

Deisinger, J., Blach, R., Wesche, G., Breining, R., & Simon, A. (2000). Towards immersive modeling – Challenges and recommendations: A workshop analyzing the needs of designers. In *Proceedings of Eurographics Workshop on Virtual Environments*, (pp. 145-156). IEEE.

Keefe, D., Feliz, D., Moscovich, T., Laidlaw, D., & LaViola, J. (2001). CavePainting: A fully immersive 3D artistic medium and interactive experience. In *Proceedings of the 2001 Symposium on Interactive 3D Graphics*. New York: ACM Press.

Schkolne, S., Pruett, M., & Schröder, P. (2001). Surface drawing: Creating organic 3D shapes with the hand and tangible tools. In *Proceedings of the SIGCHI Conference on Human Factors in Computing Systems, CHI '01*. New York: ACM Press.

Site Web 5DT. (2012). Retrieved from http://www.5dt.com/

Site Web Xsens. (2012). Retrieved from http://www.xsens.com/

Vidéo du Projet CARE. (2012). Retrieved from http://www.youtube.com/watch?v=Bbl0CxFcUZw

Vidéo Peinture 3D en Cube Immersif. (2012). Retrieved from http://www.youtube.com/watch?v=5JR3A5KQ-dg

Wesche, G., & Seidel, H. (2001). FreeDrawer: A free-form sketching system on the responsive workbench. In *Proceedings of the ACM Symposium on Virtual Reality Software and Technology* (VRST '01). New York: ACM Press.

Chapter 39
Towards a Cyber-Destructors Assessment Method

Francisco V. Cipolla-Ficarra
ALAIPO – AINCI, Spain and Italy

Alejandra Quiroga
Universidad Nacional de La Pampa, Argentina

Jacqueline Alma
Electronic Arts – Vancouver, Canada

ABSTRACT

This chapter shows the first results of a technique based on the information from Web 2.0 that can speedily and economically detect the networks or people who play, anonymously or not, the role of cyberdestroyers. The group of presented examples is useful to probe the modus operandi of the cyberdestroyers of the online information systems and the democratic promotion of scientific knowledge in the future generations of users of interactive systems both online and offline. Finally, the chapter reveals the main patterns of behaviour of a cyberdestroyer in the context of social networks.

INTRODUCTION

The momentum of the Internet would bring in its wake a series of problems related not only to the safety of the digital information, but also the appearance of pressure groups who take advantage of the anonymity of the net to attack everything which does not play by their rules, credos or other formulas who attempt against the freedom of people and democracy in the digital information society. The origin of these destructive behavior can be related to a legend of the European middle ages when in 1412 three Spanish knights from Toledo belonging to a brotherhood or fraternity called Garduña (Garduña, 2012), reached a small island of the Mediterranean (Favignana) and after setting down a series of rules for their members they headed for the current territories of Calabria, Naples and Sicily setting in motion illegal and destructive organizations. From there they would extend to the whole of Europe and the rest of the world.

DOI: 10.4018/978-1-4666-4490-8.ch039

Actually, these rules are still in force for these brotherhoods. Obviously the Internet is another tool at the disposal of these or other international criminal brotherhoods or associations with limited costs and with an almost worldwide scope of their operations. The main goal is always the same: smearing people, attack institutions, breeding conflicts, etc. Now from the technological point of view there is a wide set of applications and mechanisms stemming from the software and the hardware to prevent unauthorized access to the personalized information with the purpose of tutoring the privacy of the information, such as: firewalls, antivirus, software applications or specialized electronic devices, for instance. Besides, the legislation to tutor the computer users or other devices to receive and send digital information, it is very varied, lax and sometimes ineffective. The inefficacy is mirrored in an aspect which is not currently taken into account in the legislation for these issues, that is, the speed in detecting, stopping and repairing the damages caused in the face of unfair and unworthy attacks stemming from those who directly or indirectly receive orders from the brotherhood of their belonging. In this sense we understand by "brotherhood of belonging or medieval" to those members who use the informatics media and the Internet to spread false information with destructive purposes. This factor in the current work will also be known under the notion of "medieval brotherhood". One of the features that characterize that medieval brotherhood is that all its members behave in the same way because their acts are ruled following a set of norms or rules, which are established and maintained along the centuries and which not have changed with the new technologies. In the era of the expansion of communicability it is easy to observe how the behavior of the medieval brotherhood stays identical, in all the geography of our planet. These first conclusions are obtained thanks to the analysis of the contents and the communicability in the social networks.

In this sense we have already detected the behavior of the young members (Cipolla-Ficarra & Kratky, 2011) who devoted themselves to modifying the counter of visitors in a website which works with Linux, thanks to open source software applications stemming from Russia. Whereas the administrators of the system, webmaster, designers, etc. must follow a whole procedure to access the website (two passwords, timetable to which wants to have access, captcha (Completely Automated Public Turing test to tell Computers and Humans Apart) system to have access to the server where the website is to be found.

The destructive behavior consisted in altering the numeration or directly eliminating it as if it was a reset. In this regard this behavior temporally disappeared when other attacks were in motion allegedly from servers located in Russia, for instance, insertion of an organization in the spam distributors list or in listings to continuously receive publicity from alleged servers located in Russia and which constantly change the sending addresses, leaving unusable the options to eliminate spam the users have at their disposal. These patterns of behavior which may seem trivial cause not only a loss of time but also international disrepute, as in the case of being inserted unfairly in the listings of those people who distribute spam. A priori they can be made by young computer users, who do not necessarily must have a great knowledge of computer science but rather contacts (Cipolla-Ficarra & Ficarra, 2012). An example is the case described in the Figure 2 and Figures 9 and 10 in the Appendix. That's to say, from the social networks they may contact other people who know how to carry out these attacks, fostering the phenomenon of medieval brotherhood. Regrettably in the countries of Southern Europe the informatics legal mechanisms do not have enough resources to prevent these patterns of behavior.

SOCIAL NETWORKS: TOWARDS A FIRST ANALYSIS OF THE FUNCTIONING OF THE MEDIEVAL BROTHERHOOD

At work can be seen the behavior of the basis of these pyramids. The difference between basis and pyramid lies in the age of those who practice those attacks. The same as in a population pyramid the youngest constitute the basis and as the age grows we get closer to the summit. The advantage of the passing of time is linked to the social networks and the applications such as Linkedin, Facebook, etc. which allow to establish the links among the group of people who have contact among themselves, whether it is in the present or the past. As a rule, the systematic attacks towards people may have their origins in the professional past (Cipolla-Ficarra, et al., 2012). For instance, environments where prevail the notions of superiority of the human beings for reasons of place of birth, sex, religion, etc do not accept that other colleagues may be self-sufficient in their activities. This is not only the reason for an immediate exclusion of the group but can also become the target of continuous attacks which may last decades. The method is the same, maintain the eternal anonymity of the computer attacks. In other words and following an old Spanish saying, throwing the stone and hiding the hand. There is hardly a computer legislation in the world that allows to make a diachronic following of all those attacks along time. Here we have a first group of individuals of that medieval brotherhood which is generally related to the basis of the population pyramid. The attacks may be gradual, with highs and lows in their intensity through time. Now from the medium zone of the pyramid some go beyond that anonymity and present themselves in public, causing in a single attack of great magnitude doing the most possible harm, such as can be the post-its in specialized websites. The goal is to gain the maximum notoriety, in the least time, in a virtual community. In both cases, the reparations to the physical damage, moral, economic, etc., whether to persons or institutions is equal to zero, because although there are reply mechanisms at the disposal of those affected automatically these messages will stay recorded in the databases of those websites. Moreover, the attack to the credibility and the reliability of the people, activities, products, services, etc., take several days in being found out, until the search engines online establish the links of relations between the attacks and the websites to which they refer. Although the complaints are filed to the proper authorities, the passing of time generates the rest of the damage, such as the plummeting in the respect to towards people or the loss of value of the institutional value, if they are entities. One of the characteristics of these non-anonymous attackers are arrogance and the threats they fling at the moment in which they are announced the application of justice for the damage caused. Obviously in these cases it is not a problem of a technical failing of the firewall, or in the system of identification of the users to have access to a database, but rather patterns of behavior akin to the medieval brotherhood. The examples that are presented in the Appendix are real and for reasons of decorum towards the sciences we have hidden the surnames of those who attempt against it, anonymously or not.

SOCIAL SCIENCES AND FORMAL SCIENCES FOR THE ANALYSIS

Now, in the same way as in the legend of the three medieval knights they met in a small island of the Mediterranean, the attackers usually rally in a same place and usually repeat this encounter over and over. Therefore, a communicability analysis of the contents of the messages, linked to a semiotic study of the information in the social networks and the heuristic evaluation of the online digital information supports (Cipolla-Ficarra, et al., 2012). can easily determine the group of the medieval brotherhood that is attacking, and which surely will attack through time. The examples presented in the Appendix, the meeting place of the representatives located in cities of the American and European continent such as Asuncion (Paraguay), Barcelona (Spain), Bergamo (Italy), Bogota (Colombia), Bolzano (Italy), Cremona (Italy), Darmstadt (Germany), Girona (Spain), Lisboa (Portugal), La Plata (Argentina), Lleida (Spain), Mallorca (Spain), Mexico D.F. (Mexico), Milano (Italy), Popayán (Colombia), Trento (Italy), Valencia (Spain), Zaragoza (Spain), etc. for a systematic attack are Lisboa, Barcelona, Milano, Valencia and Trento.

The localization has been possible through the links discovered among the people, common projects, European subsidies for their productions and researches, etc. In this specific case, the material published in the databases related to computer science in Germany (see Figure 3 –Appendix). In future works we will perfect the evaluation technique until generating a systematic methodology, which starting from a diachronic and synchronic analysis of the available information online is capable of anticipating these attacks. The medieval brotherhoods have a great power of massive and international destruction through their cyberdestroyers.

Actually there is no technological mechanism to detect them and prevent their attacks. One can only act after the damage has been done. The harmful behavior is observed with the same intensity although using diverse strategies such as anonymity, in the basis as in the summit of the pyramids of those fraternities. The continuity and immunity of such behavior with the passing of time is due to their abiding by the notion "nobody can ever do anything to us". That is, they are above the judicial and legislative power. In a certain way this is true given the slowness of justice and the lack of legislation to this regard. The only way to stop them is to identify them and establish the geographical coordinates from which they act. Simultaneously, it is necessary to filter the information before their publication in specific websites which can not be erased, nor with national judicial rulings because these are sheltered by international law. From the analysis of some Web 2.0 portals related to the professional profile, it is striking the degree of persuasion that some cyberdestroyers exert to occupy places of power in structures theoretically fostering science and its derivations, without having a training or experience in keeping with that position. Aside from the contradictions between the online curriculum, between the work and the studies, given the early age of these cyberdestroyers. Obviously we are in the face of situations of great influence of the medieval brotherhood which avail themselves of the democratization of the Internet to generate irreparable damages, both in the reputation of people and institutions. Finally, the first patterns of behavior and negative values detected among the cyberdestroyers can be summed up in the following way:

- **Arrogance:** Once the attack has been carried out, they will not apologize in public for the damage they have caused.
- **Bipolar Disorder:** While they attack they may present themselves as loyal partners of their victims.
- **Bullying:** Threats towards those who prompt them to a right behavior, after having carried out the attack.
- **Envy:** One of the main sources of the attacks, typically fostered in the non-secular environments of education.
- **Incompetence:** The exaggerated length of a curriculum shows not only the untruthfulness of the presented data and the belonging to a fraternity, but also the appro-

priation of activities carried out by other people and, above all, the scarce professionalism of the attacker to carry out activities in an autonomous way.

- **Narcissism:** They use the pathway of attack (the Internet) for self-promotion and become star persuaders and superdynamic, that is, being the focus of attention in the least possible time.
- **Non-Communication:** They have serious communication problems with their colleagues (autistic), and they never give away they are preparing the attack. They will rather attack than sending a message requesting their demands previously.
- **Provocation:** They develop several strategies: copying and gluing from the same activities or contents their victims generate, or the appropriation of personality of the victim/s to enroll them in the applications of the social networks (Linkedin, Facebook, etc.), That is to say, a series of mini-attacks to probe the reactions.
- **Sadism:** They constantly mock the professional achievements of their victims.

This first listing will be widened in future works, including detailed aspects of the social psychology and behavior psychiatry. In parallel models will be built of the potential cyberdestroyers, through sociology, psychiatry and education.

LESSONS LEARNED AND FUTURE WORKS

The development of software and hardware is always ahead of the legislative advance of the new technologies, especially to shelter the honest and modest work of millions of anonymous workers, who seek the common good and raise the quality of life through the democratization of digital information. The pressure groups, organized in myriad ways, will try to boycott in a direct and indirect way those goals which many visionaries of the informatics context or communication, Marshall McLuhan, Jean Piaget, Noam Chomsky, etc., had forecast for the human beings of the new millennium. The free access to certain websites to merrily and unfairly smear those honest workers should be tutored in some way and prevent the access in the future to those who have cyberdestroyer behavior patterns from the entrepreneurial or academic environment. These cyberdestroyers are hard to change in their behavior since they belong to non-transparent organizations and which along time have proven to be more destructive than constructive for humankind. In view of the international legal void and the limits imposed from technology, and also of the rules related to the use of these technologies, there is only the alternative of pointing out the geographical point from which they carry out their attacks, although their real IP (Internet Protocol Ardes) are disguised, in the case of anonymous attackers. Those who do it publicly the very same academic, entrepreneurial or industrial bodies should exclude them automatically while the legal ruling arrives that is applicable to them for the caused damages. Ethically and aesthetically, for those institutions and their members, it is not a good outside image to have a staff that daily moves by these negative behavior patterns. In the current work we have established the first mechanisms from the information gathered in the social networks. These mechanisms will be widened with examples until establishing a methodology of analysis and generate a preventive vademecum of the potential cyberdestroyers and their modus operandi in the Internet.

CONCLUSION

The medieval brotherhoods have a great power of massive and international destruction through their cyberdestroyers. Currently there is no technological mechanism to detect them and prevent their attacks. One can only act after the damage has been done. The harmful behavior is observed with the same intensity although using diverse strategies such as anonymity, in the basis as in the summit of the pyramids of those fraternities. The continuity and immunity of such behavior with the passing of time is due to their abiding by the notion "nobody can ever do anything to us". That is, they are above the judicial and legislative power. In a certain way this is true given the slowness of justice and the lack of legislation to this regard. The only way to stop them is to identify them and establish the geographical coordinates from which they act. Simultaneously, it is necessary to filter the information before their publication in specific websites which can't be erased, nor with national judicial rulings because these are sheltered by international law. From the analysis of some Web 2.0 portals related to the professional profile, it is striking the degree of persuasion that some cyberdestroyers expert to occupy places of power in structures theoretically fostering science and its derivations, without having a training or experience in keeping with that position. Aside from the contradictions between the online curriculum, between the work and the studies, given the early age of these cyberdestroyers. Obviously we are in the face of situations of great influence of the medieval brotherhood which avail themselves of the democratization of the Internet to generate irreparable damages, both in the reputation of people and institutions.

REFERENCES

Cipolla-Ficarra, F. et al. (2012). *New horizons in creative open software, multimedia, human factors and software engineering*. Bergamo, Italy: Blue Herons.

Cipolla-Ficarra, F., & Ficarra, V. (2012). Motivation for next generation of users versus parochialism in software engineering. In *Proceedings of 2nd International Conference on Advances in New Technologies, Interactive Interfaces and Communicability (ADNTIIC 2011)*. Heidelberg, Germany: Springer.

Cipolla-Ficarra, F., & Kratky, A. (2011). Security of the automatic information on-line: A study of the controls forbid. In *Proceedings of 2nd International Conference on Advances in New Technologies, Interactive Interfaces and Communicability (ADNTIIC 2011)*. Heidelberg, Germany: Springer.

Garduña. (2012). Retrieved from http://en.wikipedia.org/wiki/Gardu%C3%B1a

APPENDIX: EXAMPLES

In the following figures (we can see how a member of the medieval priesthood who is placed in the middle part of the population pyramid sends a destructive international message. Analyzing the links of the Web 2.0 we find the relation of said message to a Portuguese professor in a European project. She from Portugal not only promotes the rent of apartments from her curriculum online in Portuguese municipalities, but also participates directly and indirectly in an international congresses organization. These are congresses organizations that devote themselves to constantly sabotaging other events, constantly postponing the deadline dates to submit the works and even publishing them in the website itself. In the figure a we can see how in less than 48 hours from a website theoretically run in a professional way by a pioneering US association and of great international prestige are observed two simultaneous attacks to a same entity. The control of these situations is equal to zero and the cyberdestroyers enjoy eternal immunity in the Internet.

Figure 1. Users protection system to access the server where the website is to be found (www.aruba.it)

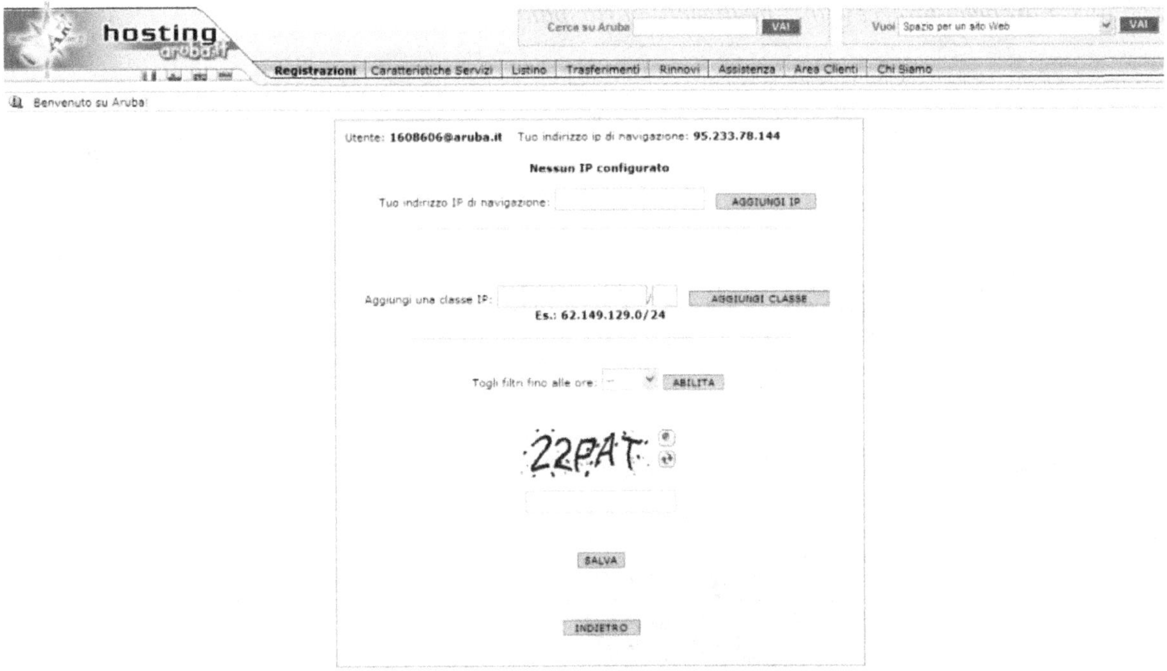

Figure 2. Total visits (www.mondoguareschi.com): Altering or eliminating the number

Figure 3. European project with "intelligent" participants

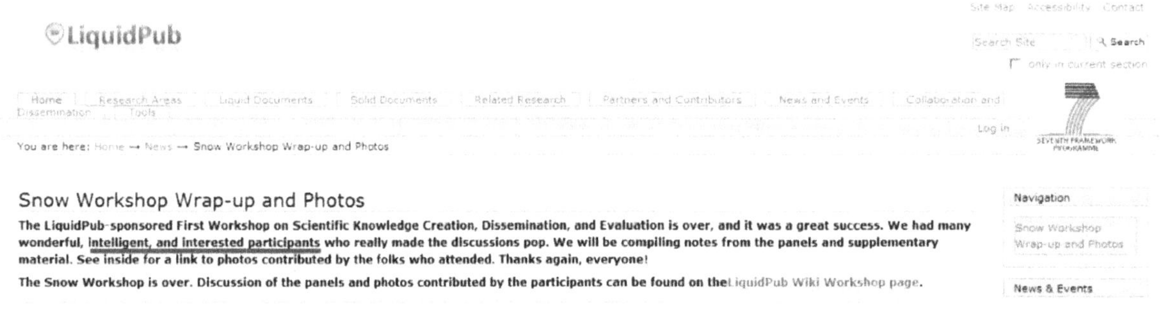

Figure 4. Curriculum vitae with villa for rent in Algarve, Portugal

- RoboCup'01, Seattle, USA, August 2-10, 2001.
- IJCAI-99 Workshop: The Third International Workshop on RoboCup, Stockholm, July 31 - August 1, 1999.
- RoboCup'98, La Villette, Paris, July 4-9, 1998.
- AIPS-98, The Fourth International Conference on AI Planning Systems, June 7-10, 1998, Carnegie Mellon University, Pittsburgh, USA.
- NSF-CNPq sponsored workshop on "Intelligent Robotic Agents," Porto Alegre, Brazil, March 17-19, 1997.
- **ICML/COLT 1997 Tutorial on "Learning in Planning".**
- Immigration Course Fall 1996.

A special site:

- **Villa for rent in Algarve, Portugal.** 

Figure 5. ACM Sigmod: A portal for scientific information online (DBWorld – http://research.cs.wisc.edu/dbworld)

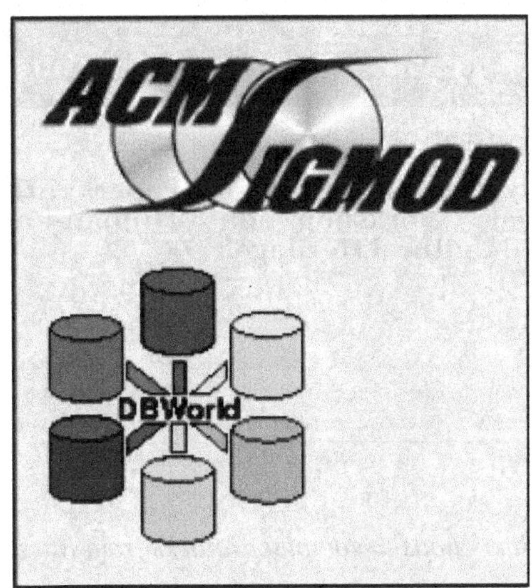

Figure 6. Iadis in DBWorld (red circle –09.11.2012): International events in Seville, Spain. Deadline September 22th, 2012. The light blue international event in Argentina has the deadline October 1st.

12-Sep-2012	conf. ann.	Doris Edison	Call for Papers: 3rd International Conference on ADNTIIC 2012 :: Cordoba, Argentina	1-Oct-2012	web page
11-Sep-2012	conf. ann.	Sherif Sakr	The 4th International Workshop on Graph Data Management: Techniques and Applications (GDM 2013)	7-Oct-2012	web page
11-Sep-2012	conf. ann.	Jaime Lloret	Deadline Extension: WEB 2013 || January 27 - February 1, 2013 - Seville, Spain	22-Sep-2012	web page
11-Sep-2012	job ann.	Rahul Singh	Postdoctoral Fellow in BioComputing	1-Apr-2013	
11-Sep-2012	conf. ann.	Alexandros Labrinidis	ICDE 2013 Call for Advanced Seminars -- ONE WEEK LEFT	17-Sep-2012	web page
11-Sep-2012	conf. ann.	Vanessa Murdock	Call for Papers: Workshop on Search and Exploration of X-Rated Information (SEXI 2013) at WSDM	30-Nov-2012	web page
11-Sep-2012	book CFC	Abdullah Rashed	Call for Chapters	30-Sep-2012	
11-Sep-2012	conf. ann.	Cristina Pascual	Deadline Extension: ICONS 2013 || January 27 - February 1, 2013 - Seville, Spain	22-Sep-2012	web page

Figure 7. Iadis in DBWorld (red circle –09.23.2012): International events in Seville, Spain. New deadline October 1st, 2012. The light blue international event in Argentina has the deadline October 1st. In other words, the same date.

24-Sep-2012	conf. ann.	Doris Edison	Call for Papers --> 3rd International Conference on ADNTIIC 2012 :: Cordoba, Argentina	1-Oct-2012	web page
24-Sep-2012	book ann.	Matt Duckham	New book on Decentralized Spatial Computing		web page
23-Sep-2012	conf. ann.	Yongrui Qin	IUPT 2013: Call for Papers	15-Jan-2013	web page
23-Sep-2012	conf. ann.	Yongrui Qin	IUPT 2013: Call for Papers	15-Jan-2013	web page
23-Sep-2012	conf. ann.	Kokou Yétongnon	CFP WEBDIS2012 (Deadline Approaching): Web based and Distributed Information Systems	30-Sep-2000	
23-Sep-2012	conf. ann.	Cristina Pascual	Last Mile submission, October 1st || DBKDA 2013 || January 27 - February 1, 2013 - Seville, Spain	1-Oct-2012	web page

Figure 8. International attack from Baglandesh: 06.19.2012

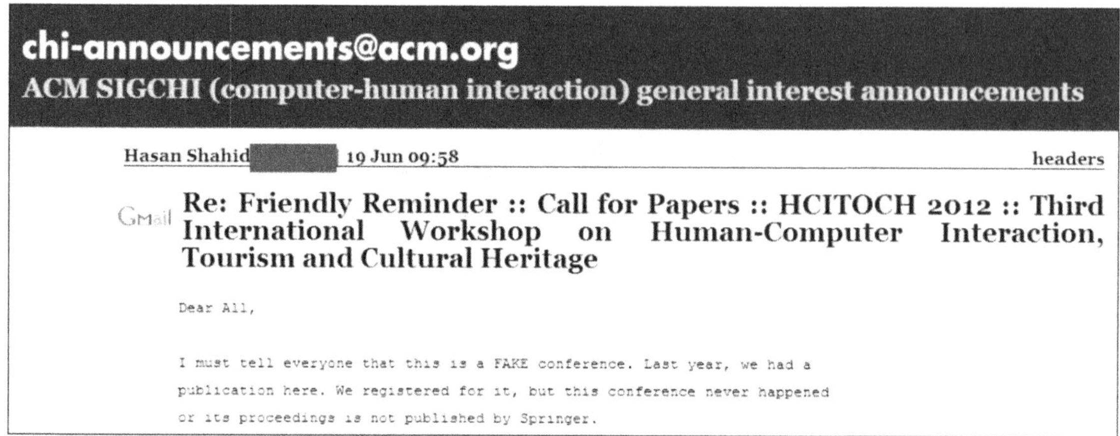

chi-announcements@acm.org

ACM SIGCHI (computer-human interaction) general interest announcements

Hasan Shahid 19 Jun 09:58 headers

GMail

Re: Friendly Reminder :: Call for Papers :: HCITOCH 2012 :: Third International Workshop on Human-Computer Interaction, Tourism and Cultural Heritage

Dear All,

I must tell everyone that this is a FAKE conference. Last year, we had a publication here. We registered for it, but this conference never happened or its proceedings is not published by Springer.

Figure 9. A portal, apparently innocuous to computer attacks from Russia

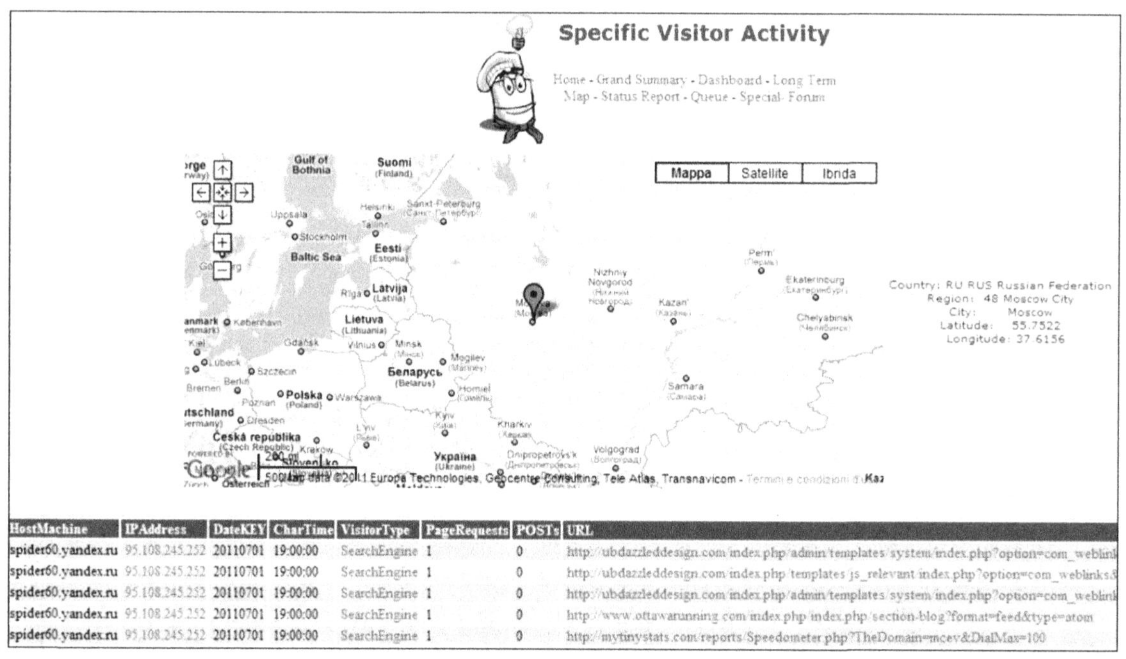

HostMachine	IPAddress	DateKEY	CharTime	VisitorType	PageRequests	POSTs	URL
spider60.yandex.ru	95.108.245.252	20110701	19:00:00	SearchEngine	1	0	http://ubdazzleddesign.com/index.php/admin/templates/system/index.php?option=com_weblin
spider60.yandex.ru	95.108.245.252	20110701	19:00:00	SearchEngine	1	0	http://ubdazzleddesign.com/index.php/templates/js_relevant/index.php?option=com_weblinks&
spider60.yandex.ru	95.108.245.252	20110701	19:00:00	SearchEngine	1	0	http://ubdazzleddesign.com/index.php/admin/templates/system/index.php?option=com_weblin
spider60.yandex.ru	95.108.245.252	20110701	19:00:00	SearchEngine	1	0	http://www.ottawarunning.com/index.php/index.php/section-blog?format=feed&type=atom
spider60.yandex.ru	95.108.245.252	20110701	19:00:00	SearchEngine	1	0	http://mytinystats.com/reports/Speedometer.php?TheDomain=mcev&DialMax=100

Figure 10. The reading of the log files is important to detect the intromission or attack to the computer system

analizo stats - Blocco note

File Modifica Formato Visualizza ?

```
05.42|23|6|2011|Direct Hit|Mozilla/5.0 (compatible; YandexBot/3.0; +http://yandex.com/bots)|95.108.245.252||spider60.yandex.ru|1
05.49|23|6|2011|http://www.google.com/search?client=safari&rls=en&q=don+camillo+museum&ie=UTF-8&oe=UTF-8|Mozilla/5.0 (Macintosh;
en-us) AppleWebKit/533.21.1 (KHTML, like Gecko) Version/5.0.5 Safari/533.21.1|99.110.44.82|http://www.google.com/search?
client=safari&rls=en&q=don+camillo+museum&ie=UTF-8&oe=UTF-8|99-110-44-82.lightspeed.lbcktx.sbcglobal.net|1
05.50|23|6|2011|http://www.facebook.com/l.php?u=http%3A%2F%2Fwww.mondoguareschi.com%2Fbrescello.php%3Flang%3Den%26page%3Dbre_mu_
(Windows NT 6.1; WOW64) AppleWebKit/534.30 (KHTML, like Gecko) Chrome/12.0.742.100 Safari/534.30|74.196.216.99|http://www.facebo
2Fwww.mondoguareschi.com%2Fbrescello.php%3Flang%3Den%26page%3Dbre_mu_001&h=5a791|c74-196-216-99.dh.suddenlink.net|1
05.50|23|6|2011|Direct Hit|facebookexternalhit/1.1 (+http://www.facebook.com/externalhit_uatext.php)|69.63.181.246||69.63.181.24
```

Chapter 40
(Re)Engineering Cultural Heritage Contexts using Creative Human Computer Interaction Techniques and Mixed Reality Methodologies

Carl Smith
Learning Technology Research Institute, London Metropolitan University, UK

ABSTRACT

The contribution of this research is to argue that truly creative patterns for interaction within cultural heritage contexts must create situations and concepts that could not have been realised without the intervention of those interaction patterns. New forms of human-computer interaction and therefore new tools for navigation must be designed that unite the strengths, features, and possibilities of both the physical and the virtual space. The human-computer interaction techniques and mixed reality methodologies formulated during this research are intended to enhance spatial cognition while implicitly improving pattern recognition. This research reports on the current state of location-based technology including Mobile Augmented Reality (MAR) and GPS. The focus is on its application for use within cultural heritage as an educational and outreach tool. The key questions and areas to be investigated include: What are the requirements for effective digital intervention within the cultural heritage sector? What are the affordances of mixed and augmented reality? What mobile technology is currently being utilised to explore cultural heritage? What are the key projects? Finally, through a series of case studies designed and implemented by the author, some broad design guidelines are outlined. The chapter concludes with an overview of the main issues to consider when (re)engineering cultural heritage contexts.

DOI: 10.4018/978-1-4666-4490-8.ch040

INTRODUCTION

Traditionally museums and site specific learning environments offer static experiences to their visitors which leave less opportunity for alternative interpretation of those exhibits. According to Cheok (2012), advances in mobile technology are moving us from an era of 'information communication' to 'experience communication'. As a result the role of cultural heritage and cultural institutions is no longer just to exhibit significant objects but to create augmented contexts which consist of rich, interactive and engaging experiences for visitors. Traditional Virtual Reality (VR) creates a world of its own which is usually totally indifferent to the physical context; in contrast MAR (Mobile Augmented Reality) is intrinsically tied to the local environment. One of the unique affordances of well designed MAR is that it should enable the creation of situations and concepts that could not have been realised with just the physical or just the virtual elements of the context because it unites the strengths, features and possibilities of both. This research is concerned with highlighting best practise in how to formulate these situations and concepts.

WHAT ARE THE REQUIREMENTS FOR EFFECTIVE DIGITAL INTERVENTION WITHIN THE CULTURAL HERITAGE SECTOR?

The central challenge for curators and educational designers is to create contexts that promote effective and engaging learning. With the generation and increasing adoption of mobile augmented reality (MAR) and mixed reality methodologies and techniques we now have the potential to explode the form and complexity of these learning contexts. The core question of this research is can we develop augmented heritage contexts that are more effective because they take advantage of the affordances of these mixed reality methods and techniques. The majority of mobile learning research and mobile app development creates experiences which tie all the requirements of the user's attention down to and onto a four inch screen. This includes the majority of MAR applications. To avoid this, new interfaces must be created that take advantage of the physical and digital affordances of each learning situation.

Gallagher (2010) defines cultural heritage as being concerned with collections of physical structures and the intangible values that they project about the culture in which they are situated. He believes MAR has the potential to augment these heritage contexts bi-directionally: "Traditionally, cultural heritage studies has explored physical structures as stable entities and the intangible values as contextually fluid; augmented reality attacks this traditional structure and demonstrates that the physical structures themselves, along with the values that they accompany, are in states of constant flux. This flux is interpreted, mediated, and reconstructed in the individual learner."

New forms of contextual representation and engineering can now do real-time interactive justice to the complexity of both the form and function of cultural heritage. However, there are some key issues to consider when deciding on a technological solution. Boyer and Marcus (2011) state that an unfortunate fact of most augmented reality applications is that screenshots of an application give a better impression of the functionality than the actual use. In addition, without thoughtful design, digital interventions risk distracting visitors from meaningful engagement with the cultural objects that they are actually designed to augment.

WHAT ARE THE AFFORDANCES OF MIXED AND AUGMENTED REALITY?

In order to achieve the aim of designing and supporting learning across physical and virtual heritage space we need to combine the affordances of the physical with the affordances of the digital.

This gives us an opportunity to reinvest value back into the full thick description of physical site specific space and at the same time ensure we are using embodied experience (and not just vision as is common in most AR) to interact with these spaces. In Kevin Slavins mobile Monday presentation 'Reality is plenty thanks' (2010) he discusses the importance of peripheral vision in learning situations by illustrating how reality is not actually communicated via a single focus. 'Reality is the whole world around us and not just what is in front of us. As a result MAR can often make things seem *less* real. Reality is only augmented when it feels different and not just when it looks different.'

Those areas which can benefit from the affordances of mixed reality are those that require greater interactivity in the learning process. A well designed augmented environment should allow the users to regularly ask their own questions while analysing the associations between pieces of information, rather than just isolated facts. Therefore the issues of what information should be presented, in what way, and in what order are essential. Arguably any application of this technology can only be justified if the user is able to interact with the object in ways which would not previously have been possible. This alternative form of interaction should significantly alter the user's relationship with the object.

In order to realise the potential of MAR or mixed reality it is necessary to appreciate the power it provides over traditional methods:

- The mixed reality environment promotes opportunities for the exploration, alteration and manipulation of complex data sets.
- Mixed reality allows the user to compare and contrast objects from a variety of disparate sources within a unified environment by creating a representation of the original context for objects and structures which have been removed from their context.
- The augmented model and environment implies an association of information with space. Mixed reality can recreate and reanimate culturally determined points of view which are essential for a more complete understanding of any structure's meaning.
- Mixed reality can provide a multiple point of view of the same object at different times or at different levels of conceptual analysis. The augmented reconstruction can also provide answers to questions of the relevancy of data and highlight discrepancies or inconsistencies in existing data.
- Mixed reality offers layers of information that otherwise could not be displayed due to the aesthetic and spatial concerns (Thian, 2012)

WHAT MOBILE AND LOCATION BASED TECHNOLOGY IS CURRENTLY BEING UTILISED WITHIN CULTURAL HERITAGE APPLICATIONS?

Marcus (2011) notes that the majority of location based AR applications fall into two categories: GPS-based and computer vision-based. Oomen, J. et al (2011) expand on these categories by creating clusters of location-based applications used by GLAMs (Galleries, Libraries, Archives, Museums), as shown in Table 1.

For the purposes of this review a number of projects from each of these categories and clusters will be discussed. An overview of the advantages and disadvantages of the GPS-based and computer vision-based solutions are summarised here:

Table 1. Clusters of location-based applications used by GLAMs

Cluster	Feature
Location-aware display of content.	Mobile applications that use the GPS function to determine the place of the device and display content connected to that location.
Contributing content by end-users.	Applications that allow users to contribute content that is linked to a certain place. This can include texts, photos, video, audio.
QR codes	Using QR codes to connect the physical space and related online content.
Browsing using an augmented reality application.	The use of a third party augmented reality browser (Layar, Wikitude or Junaio) to display content linked to a geographical location.
Location-based games and Geocaching.	The gameplay of a location-based game somehow evolves and progresses with a player's location. Geocaching is the most prominent example with a large community. Typical is a single-player kind of treasure hunt which is usually played using hand-held GPS receivers with user-hidden boxes.

GPS Based Solutions

- **Advantages:**
  - Cheap and easy to produce (GPS is free and does not require 3G or wireless connectivity).
  - Processor friendly and can make additional use of a phone's accelerometer, gyroscope, and other technology to determine the location, heading, and direction of the phone.
  - Can be used to identify zones which when entered trigger locally stored media (reducing cost and download times.
  - The content can be easily updateable with minimal technical skill.
  - Commonly available on many phones.
- **Disadvantages:**
  - Not reliable indoors - imprecise location data, difficulty discerning the heading of the phone - a serious drawback when hoping to create photo overlays.
  - Does not easily supply true context sensitivity although there are workarounds for this.

Computer Vision: 2D Marker and 3D Object Based Solutions

Computer vision based applications use powerful computer vision libraries to help the computer identify what it is seeing through a digital camera (Marcus, 2011). In many cases, this is done through the creation of a unique 2D symbol that the computer identifies and then uses to launch different forms of interactive media.

However as cultural heritage sites often do not allow obtrusive physical markers to be placed in situ it is important to include the full range of computer vision solutions within this review.

It is now becoming possible to use 2d photographs and 3d objects (of content at the actual site) as markers. A good example of this is 'The Augmented City' from metaio: (http://www.youtube.com/watch?v=ACu6rehFXBM&feature=player_embedded

To achieve the aim of triggering both 2D and 3D content via the actual physical context the following methodology can be adopted: SLAM (simultaneous location and mapping) (http://en.wikipedia.org/wiki/Simultaneous_localization_and_mapping) can be used to find feature points in the scene via the video stream and detect the ones that are consistent from frame-to-frame in order to create a 3D map of points. This map of points will then be used as a tracking model for inserting the content. The most common engine is PTAM (parallel tracking and mapping).

There are a number of natural feature tracking or 3D object tracking libraries which have been made available via the Qualcomm AR SDK (http://developer.qualcomm.com/dev/augmented-reality) and the Metaio Unifeye SDK (http://www.metaio.com/software/sdk/). Also Metaio Junaio Glue (http://www.augmentedplanet.com/2010/07/metaio-change-the-game-with-junaio-glue) and Layar vision (http://devsupport.layar.com/

entries/20331366-get-started-with-layar-vision) both allow you to register and track an image on mobile devices.

- **Advantages:**
  - Greater opportunity for context sensitivity.
- **Disadvantages:**
  - More expensive.
  - Large amounts of processing power are required meaning only the newest smartphones are capable of using this method.
  - Displaying high-quality AR content requires high frame rates and extremely responsive tracking in varying light levels.
  - AR Markers + QR codes can distract attention away from the actual heritage objects under investigation.

KEY PROJECTS

The ARCHEOGUIDE project (http://archeoguide.intranet.gr/project.htm) provides alternative approaches for accessing information at cultural heritage sites using augmented reality, 3D-visualization, mobile computing, and multi-modal interaction techniques. Particular emphasis in existing case studies is given to the virtual reconstruction of heritage sites.

Streetmuseum is an app that has been released by the Museum of London (www.museumoflondon.org.uk/streetmuseum.htm) which is an augmented reality application that provides access to hundreds of historic images of London as both 2D and 3D overlays. This system also allows users to create their own trails around London.

The British Museum have also released a project called 'the passport to the afterlife' (http://bit.ly/dLSwtH) which has successfully introduced marker based AR into museum galleries. The trail runs in the permanent Egyptian galleries. It reveals insights about the appropriate use of AR for children, the potential of mobile AR for kinesthetic learning and the importance of blending AR interaction with analog techniques to ensure a rewarding learning experience (Mannion, 2012).

The PhillyHistory.org (http://phillyhistory.org/PhotoArchive) project has an augmented reality application which allows users to point their phone at nearby buildings or streets in order to discover historic photos of that location. The application can pull information into the local environment from over 93,000 images in the growing database. All archive photos may be searched by proximity to an Address, Intersection, Place Name, or Neighbourhood. The project team have considered how their research findings and technology experiments can be applied to the larger community of cultural institutions and as a result they plan to release the PhillyHistory.org augmented reality application to the public.

A recent mobile app called 'Kew' (http://www.kew.org/visit-kew-gardens/visit-information/garden-guides/mobile-app/index.htm) released by Kew gardens aims to provide a seamless experience through a combination of a GPS enabled customizable map, a QR code reader and an augmented reality browser. Each of these technologies was used for different purposes at different locations, for instance the GPS detection technology was used for general orientation, the QR code reader was used to allow visitors to scan certain pre determined plants and the augmented reality browser was used to prompt discovery and encourage meandering exploration. Another core intention behind this technologically seamless approach was to ensure that visitors were not wedded to the phone visually but that the app would act on the periphery, as a catalyst for serendipitous learning (Mann, 2012). When evaluating the impact of the app the project team found that the GPS and QR code were more widely used by the visitors than the AR browser which was due to a lack of familiarity.

ClayVision (http://www.youtube.com/watch?v=bUL171EfEG4) reengineers the design conventions of Augmented Reality. ClayVision uses computer vision and image processing techniques to dynamically transform the appearance of building structures in real time. The digital data is not overlaid in the usual 'bubble metaphor' of traditional AR but actually becomes 'fused together with the urban environment'. This is achieved through the use of two techniques referred to as 'default texture' and 'diminished background'. This project is an example of computer vision based localisation for mobile devices which does not require the use of markers. The basic idea of their localization technique is simple: each frame of the real-time video feed is compared to a collection of photos, shot from the same location using the same device beforehand (Takeuchi & Perlin, 2012).

CASE STUDY ONE

The first MAR environment to be examined in order to extract the underlying interaction patterns used in its production involves one of the work packages from a previously funded European project. The CONTSENS project focused on the development of appropriate training and learning materials for mobile learning enhanced by context sensitive and location based delivery. For a summary of the project please visit:

(http://www.ericsson.com/ericsson/corpinfo/programs/using_wireless_technologies_for_context_sensitive_education_and_training/index.shtml)

The first work package involved creating an archaeological learning environment consisting of the digital reconstruction of 5 Cistercian abbeys in Yorkshire (including fountains abbey http://www.fountainsabbey.org.uk).

The environment (which was accessible via mobile devices) was designed to allow the visitor to explore, apply and interact with the processes of architectural construction at various levels of complexity. The MAR solution allowed the physical location to remain an essential part of the context. A comprehensive database of visualisations which contained (but did not prescribe) the entire set of reasoning that led from the design of the 2D plans to the 3D reconstructions was at the core of the MAR system (Figure 1). This declarative design was essential as the total range of knowledge contained within the application could then be utilised, allowing many diverse and wide-ranging opinions to be tested and unified for further analysis (see video: http://learning.londonmet.ac.uk/TLTC/carl/cistercians_in_yorkshire.mov)

One of the core elements of the MAR system (and an underlying skill involved in its production) is the production of the 'technology narrative' (Willis, 2010). Technology narrative essentially allows learners to shape their interaction with technology in order to build their context of learning. They are not changing the story being told but rather the form of interaction around that story. This ensures that the visitors remain active 'users' rather than passive 'readers'. This was also achieved by negating the usual push mechanism and emphasising the necessity to pull information from the system. Users could manipulate the 3D models on their mobile devices according to their own understanding of how the reconstructions should be configured (if their opinions differed from the supplied versions) ensuring the successful augmentation of context (see Cook, 2010).

Users can also drill down through the final presentation of the models (the front end to the whole data set) into all the component objects and any architectural elements within the models to gather any linked information which that element may have attached. These objects can then be extracted from their hierarchical structures, manipulated, measured and reconfigured according to the users individual research query. For a more detailed analysis of the results of the first iteration of the project please visit:

http://www.ericsson.com/ericsson/corpinfo/programs/using_wireless_technologies_for_context_sensitive_education_and_training/products/london_wp5_evaluation_report.pdf

Figure 1. A video for a brief synopsis of the project

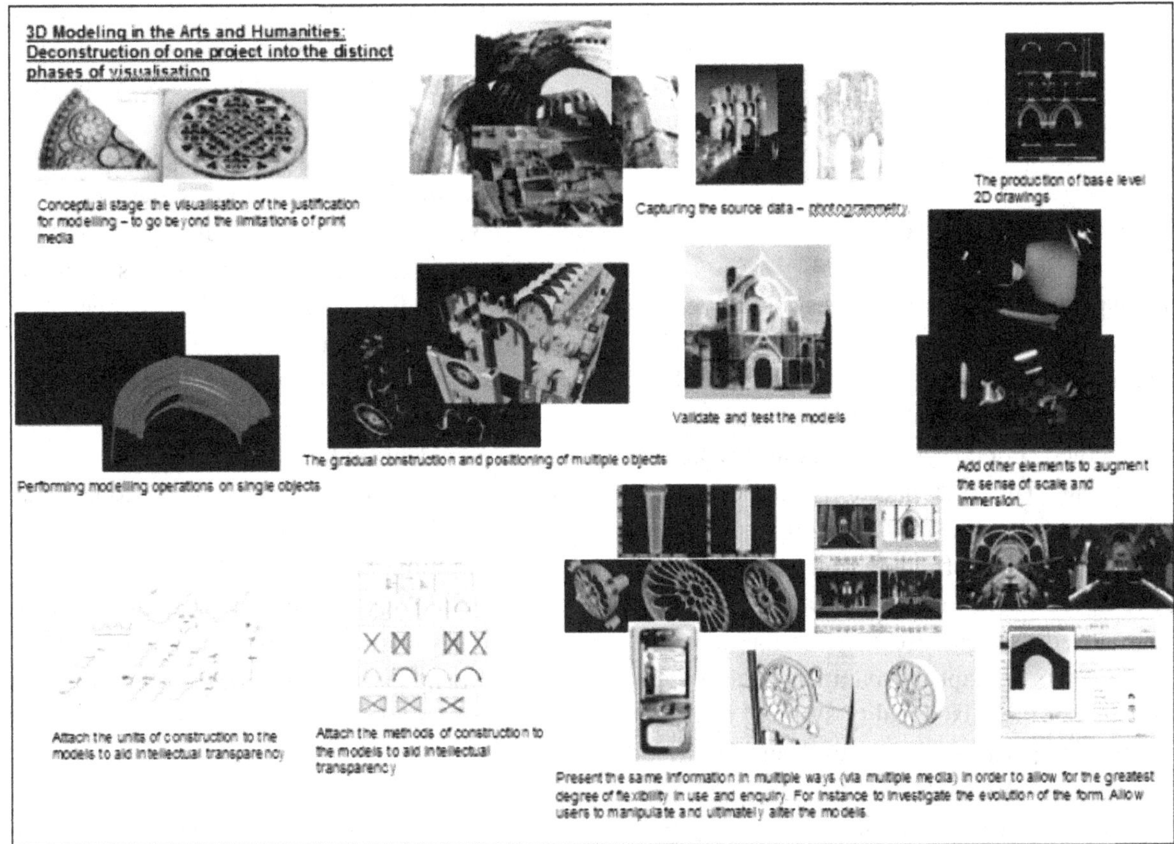

CASE STUDY TWO

This case study involved another work package of the CONTSENS project which created a MAR system to support the understanding of urban design within a heritage context. The project enabled urban designers to examine past and present representations of school architecture (Edwardian and Victorian schools) in situ to see how its organisation and restructuring related to educational discourse. The intention was for learners to examine the community from the past, in order to engage, understand, and inform the present, as urban space and society is made and remade. See a video summary of this case study here:

`http://learning.londonmet.ac.uk/TLTC/carl/urban_planning_and_education.mov`

A core mechanism of the project was to use participatory design to allow these urban designers to understand that the physical design of any educational institution has a direct impact on the delivery of the education that takes place and that learning space design shapes our behavior and influences our thinking. A database of architectural designs and 3D models of pedagogically effective schools was available to be used and adapted within the MAR system.

Another core element in this MAR environment was to incorporate the dynamic use of real time social data. The MAR designer was aware of the power of the wider social network. As a result the urban designers were able to share and critique their own work both in situ and in reflection. For a more detailed analysis of the results of the first iteration of the project please visit:

http://www.ericsson.com/ericsson/corpinfo/programs/using_wireless_technologies_for_context_sensitive_education_and_training/products/london_wp4_evaluation_report.pdf

DESIGN GUIDELINES

Some potential design guidelines could offer advice on the following: What is the most suitable digital content for this context? How should it displayed? What is the most appropriate interaction method? For how long will the augmentation be present? This final question is important for learning because most instances of visualisation are used to act as scaffolding which is designed to be removed to ensure that the learning has been internalised. Is there also scope in the intervention for users to adapt and manipulate the content elements of the mixed reality system? Have the essential properties of the context been identified, analysed and utilized?

The manipulation of context is a core function of any mixed reality system. Designing these systems extends the scope of the context to involve the use of physical space and other objects and people in the user's physical surroundings, not necessarily relevant for design previously. The following are general design guidelines that may be referenced whilst designing the digital intervention:

1. **The Digital Intervention Must Justify it's Existence:** Has the designer provided evidence that the intervention allows the user to engage with the situation on many levels that were not previously possible? Is there perhaps another method which does not require MAR that could achieve the same result?
2. **Take Advantage of Real World Interaction:** In order for users to be engaged usability needs to be intuitive. It should be easy for the user to learn how to use a system without prior training. Users should be able to accomplish a task with a minimum of interaction steps. In addition the system should provide direct and immediate feedback so that the user can adjust their actions accordingly.
3. **Context Modelling:** Designing MAR systems extends the scope of the context to involve the use of physical space and other objects and persons in the user's physical surroundings, not necessarily relevant for design previously. The manipulation of context is therefore a core function of MAR. Have the essential properties of the context been identified, analysed and utilized?
4. **Participatory Design:** Is there scope in the digital intervention for users to adapt the content elements of the MAR system?
5. **Technology Narrative:** What is the ratio of push vs pull within the system in regard to content acquisition? Does the digital intervention allow the user to remain active in their learning process?
6. **Effective Choice of Media:** Does the choice of media within the MAR system work well for the chosen target audience?
7. **Multiple Ways of Seeing:** Has the MAR environment incorporated multiple ways of seeing? Whether utilising microscopic, xray or macroscopic all these augmented ways of seeing are available within MAR systems and should be taken advantage of if appropriate.
8. **Design for Social Interaction:** Has the designer incorporated the use of real time social data into the system?
9. **Build in Adaptability:** Has the MAR designer created an appropriate level of challenge neither too easy nor too difficult which will keep the learner stimulated and motivated? Can the user themselves decide on the level of difficulty involved within the system?
10. **Interdisciplinary Media Production:** Creating MAR experiences draws on skills

from a broad range of creative disciplines including scriptwriting, sound design, interaction design, location sourcing, production management, software development and testing. Although some of these disciplines may not always be called upon it is important for the design team to be aware of them.

CONCLUSION

Site specific experience is always going to reign over the mediation or representation of that experience. MAR crucially provides both in the same space, the direct primary experience (the real world scene) and the mediated representation (the digital augmentation). Practise and theory can now feed off each other in the same space. For instance each architectural element outlined in the first case study can be tagged in both virtual and physical space. Eventually the learner will be able to: "follow the tradition of each architectural element, be it a portal, a niche or a vault; to witness its interplay with corresponding forms as spatial motifs in paintings and treatises; and in some cases see how this interplay leads to an evolution in the complexity of a form" (Veltman, 1988).

In this world of smart objects it will be possible to approach any object (using photography in this instance) and unlock everything you could ever want to know about that object (its meaning, history, content, context, close relations). Information will be folded into the space of the object and the organisation of that information will be structured by the space.

Bell (2010) asks whether learning designers of location based and mixed reality experiences are following old museum models rather than exploring augmented reality as a unique new form of interpretation. MAR (especially vision-based MAR) however is still in its infancy but has the potential to supply the kinds of interactions that initiate sense-making, construction of personal and social meaning, dialogue, and emotional responses (Thian, 2012). The impact of MAR technology is still under researched and as a result visitor experiences, or the social and educational interaction that is shaped by its characteristics and objects involved are not well documented.

The main utopian power of MAR is that we are becoming capable of creating a new immersive reality completely beyond our known limits, and that it can be embedded not in a blog, a device or a computer, but in the world (Baraona, 2012). A good example of this new immersive reality is being developed in Japan by Professor Michitaka Hirose and goes by the name of ''diet goggles'' (http://www.youtube.com/watch?v=spk-2EuZ3hk). The goggles are designed to trick dieters into eating less by digitally enlarging food whilst they are actually eating it. This is an example of context engineering and highlights the extent to which MAR can subvert our perception of the physical world. The context becomes available for the learner to 'get to everything, add to everything, keep track of everything, and tie everything together (Waltham, 1989).

The inception app uses MAR (http://inceptiontheapp.com) with sound by synchronizing an augmented layer of music and ambient noise with the world around you. The app manages to augment context by forcing the user to get into a real world context that is producing a certain sound. Unless that sound is present then the content is not released by the 'listening' app. The app actually acts as a trigger or catalyst for real world activity. This allows the inception 'environment' to become a world where a lot of other stories can take place. This is in stark contrast to the usual predefined and prescribed content of traditional non context dependent apps (which also, invariably do not tap into existing analogue skill sets).

The path to creativity is paved with open access to the process: "The way to creativity is the path of the not yet and its reality can be very important even if there is no physical product.... The world of design is not just about doing and making "things". The majority of designs and plans are never built....The challenge is not just to see what we (can) know today, but to see how our ways of knowing have changed, grown and evolved over the centuries" (Veltman, 2007).

This research is not centred on the technology but the navigational shift that results when the world itself becomes the interface. The majority of design coming out of the MAR paradigm tends to replace imagination with computer animation but imagination should itself augment the values of reality (Bachelard, 1964; Miller, 1957) sums it up with the phrase 'One's destination should never be a place but a new way of seeing things'.

REFERENCES

Bachelard, G. (1964). *The poetics of space* (M. Jolas, Trans.). New York: Academic Press.

Baraona, E. (2012). *From line to hyperreality*. Retrieved from http://www.domusweb.it/en/architecture/from-line-to-hyperreality

Bell, T. (2010). *Literature review of technology used in interpretation of sensitive cultural heritage sites*. Eugene, OR: University of Oregon.

Boyer, D., & Marcus, J. (2012). Implementing mobile augmented reality applications for cultural institutions. In J. Trant, & D. Bearman (Eds.), *Proceedings of Museums and the Web 2011*. Toronto, Canada: Archives & Museum Informatics.

Cheok, A. (2012). *Keynote multi modal sensory human*. Retrieved from http://www.adriancheok.info/post/26135544227/icalt2012-keynote-talk-multi-modal-sensory-human

Cook, J. (2010). Mobile phones as mediating tools within augmented contexts for development. *International Journal of Mobile and Blended Learning*. doi:10.4018/jmbl.2010070101

Gallagher, S. M. (2010). *The Flaneur was here: Mobile augmented reality and urban cultural heritage learning in lower Manhattan*. Edinburgh, UK: University of Edinburgh.

Hirose, M. (2012). *Future of weight loss diet goggles*. Retrieved from http://www.youtube.com/watch?v=spk-2EuZ3hk

Mann, C. (2012). A study of the iPhone app. at Kew Gardens: Improving the visitor experience. In *Proceedings of the Susie Fisher Group*. Retrieved from http://ewic.bcs.org/category/17061#1

Mannion, S. (2012). *Beyond cool: Making mobile augmented reality work for museum education*. Retrieved from http://www.museumsandtheweb.com/mw2012/programs/beyond_cool_making_mobile_augmented_reality_

Miller, H. (1957). *Big Sur and the oranges of Hieronymus Bosch*. New York: New Directions Publishing.

Oomen, J. et al. (2011). Picture war monuments: Creating an open source location-based mobile platform. In J. Trant, & D. Bearman (Eds.), *Proceedings of Museums and the Web 2011*. Toronto, Canada: Archives & Museum Informatics.

Slavin, K. (2010). *Mobile Monday presentation*. Retrieved from http://www.slideshare.net/momoams/kevin-slavin-reality-is-plenty-thanks

Smith. (2009). *WP5 art gallery and museum education: Evaluation report.* Retrieved from http://www.ericsson.com/ericsson/corpinfo/programs/using_wireless_technologies_for_context_sensitive_education_and_training/products/london_wp5_evaluation_report.pdf

Takeuchi, Y., & Perlin, K. (2012). ClayVision: The (elastic) image of the city. In *Proceedings of CHI 2012*. ACM.

Thian, C. (2012). Augmented reality—What reality can we learn from it? In *Proceedings of Asian Civilisations Museum*. Toronto, Canada: Archives & Museum Informatics.

Veltman, K. (1988). *A databank on perspective: The concept of knowledge packages*. Retrieved from http://www.sumscorp.com/articles/art9.htm

Veltman, K. (2007). Opening keynote: The new book of nature. In *Proceedings of eARCOM 07. Sistemi informativi per l'Architettura Convegno Internazionale, Con il Patrocinio di UNESCO. Ministero dei Beni Culturali*. CIPA, Regione Marche.

Willis, K. et al. (2010). Sharing knowledge about places as community building. In *Shared Encounters*. London: Springer. doi:10.1007/978-1-84882-727-1

Chapter 41
Knowledge and Background of the Multimedia Culture: A Study of the Spatio-Temporal Context in Claymation and Computer Animation for Children and Adults

Francisco V. Cipolla-Ficarra
ALAIPO – AINCI, Spain and Italy

Miguel Cipolla-Ficarra
ALAIPO – AINCI, Spain and Italy

Jacqueline Alma
Electronic Arts – Vancouver, Canada

ABSTRACT

The chapter compares three digital and analogical animation series from the referential and contextual space-temporal point of view, which are mainly aimed at the infantile audience. The study detects the key elements that make these series acceptable by the adult audience. The results of the experiments with children, teenagers, young, and adults establish trends in the contents of interactive systems for new supports such as multimedia in mobile phones.

INTRODUCTION

Currently there is a trend of commercial marketing of not differentiating digital animations from the analogical ones. That is, 2D, 3D animations, etc. computer-made, from those analogical based on stop motion animation. In the current work and inside analogical animation –stop motion (we focus on claymation – Murphy, 2008). That is, that carried out with modeling clay or any other malleable material. Now the advantage of working with malleable materials like modeling clay is that

DOI: 10.4018/978-1-4666-4490-8.ch041

not only can be applied the principles of sculpture, at the moment of creating the main characters, the scenery and its components, etc., but it also admits a free style. In other words, the characters undergo a transformation during the animation process as in the series Pingu (www.pingu.net) or rather use structures, skeletons or articulated armories like all those used in the Shaun the Sheep series (one of the series analyzed in the current work), where these articulated structures are coated with clay.

Although there are many procedures of stop motion animation, this is due to the fact that this animation technique is an animation procedure, where imagination and creativity are literally in the hands of every author who suits this technique for that he/she wants to express. That's why the stop motion possesses a great richness of methods and variations. Briefly, the origins of this technique blend with the history of cinematography itself. One of its pioneers was Segundo de Chomón, who resorted to this technique in pictures of the early 20th century (Tharrats, 2009), such as "The Haunted House" (1906) and "The Electric Hotel" (1908). In Eastern Europe it was and still remains very used to tell stories to the infantile and adult audiences. In the late 70s and early 80s it comes back to the US great screen thanks to a Californian firm specialized in special effects such as "Industrial Light & Magic" (Glintenkam, 2011). In this company it was applied for the first time a variant to the stop motion inventing the go motion for the film Star Wars Episode V- The Empire Strikes Back –1980 (Glintenkam, 2011).

In the stop motion the objects or models are photographed while they are motionless. In contrast, in the go motion a movement is applied to the

Figure 1. Shaun the Sheep: Characters and context

Figure 2. Articulated structures

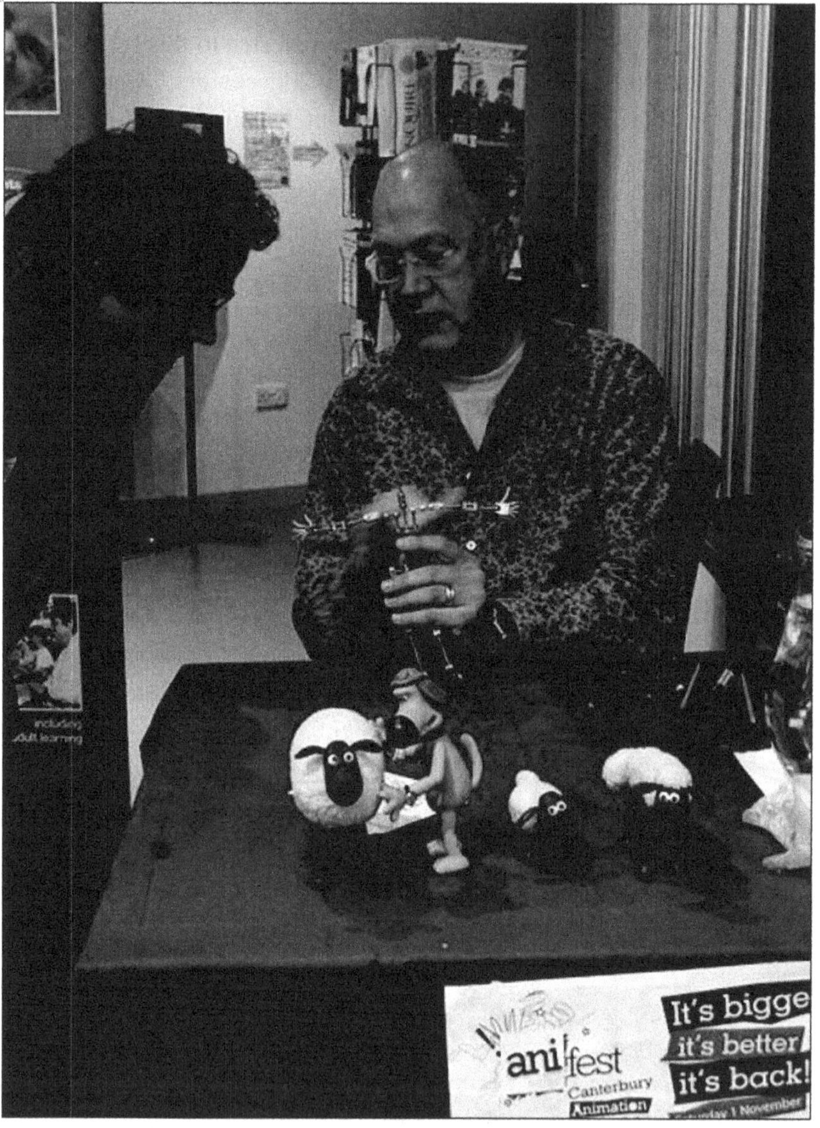

model or object which is being animated while it is being photographed. In this way a distortion is obtained in the photogram by motion blur which is present in the conventional animations of objects in movement.

The illusion of movement of the object or animated model through go motion, once the scene is projected on the screen, gains in visual realism. Since the 80s some US productions kept on using it and perfection it for the movies such as "The Nightmare Before Christmas". In Europe, the British company Aardman Animations has also made important films since the start of the new millennium, such as "Chicken Run" (2000), Wallace & Gromit. The Curse of the Were-Rabbbit (2005), the short-length Wallace & Gromit. A Grand Day Out (1989), The Wrong Trousers (1993), A Close Shave (1995) and A Matter of Loaf and Death (2008), Shaun the Sheep (2007) among others.

Figure 3. Official website with the main and secondary characters of the television series "Shaun the Sheep" (www.shaunthesheep.com) made in Aardman Animations (www.aardman.com)

THE IMPORTANCE OF THE MULTIMEDIA INTERACTIVE SYSTEMS IN THE EVOLUTION OF THE STOP MOTION ANIMATIONS

The early off-line multimedia systems have served in the 90s to generate new reading habits in the resolution of arithmetic problems. Skills for the interaction with mobile phones, etc. of the so-called digital generation, for instance: "Pingu and Friends" (www.pingu.net). Pingu, his family and friends (Figure 4) are characters created in clay for the stop motion animation and broadcast for the first time in Switzerland in 1986. In the 90s it is incorporated in the multimedia supports (Figure 5) and starting from those the new episodes of the series increase the quality of stop motion animation, especially in the modeling of characters, objects, special effects, etc. In other words, the digital media boosted the analogical animation productions.

In parallel the breakthrough of the digital generation or digital natives would take place in contrast to the digital illiterates (Bauerlein, 2011). For instance, many of the children watched on TV the stop motion animated series and they have later on interacted with the computer. Users that with the passing of time have become teenagers and they constantly interact with the computer and the cell phone, especially in the period encompassing the late 90s and start of the new millennium. In the mid-90s and late 20th century also takes place the democratization of the Internet (Cipolla-Ficarra, et al., 2010; Cipolla-Ficarra, et al., 2011). and those youngsters start to communicate with chats and social networks because

Figure 4. Spanish version of the CD-Rom

Figure 5. Multimedia Play

they have been born with the Internet, and they have a cell phone since their pre-adolescence, which allows them to handle much better than other people the new technologies. As a rule they were massive consumers of iPods and MP3, almost the only things they read are online, and they have put aside face to face communication with other people of practically similar age. Consequently, the digital generation or "digital natives" can be defined as the teenagers or youth between 12-25 years old. Those who have grown up surrounded with the new technologies. Another way to define them is by exclusion. That is, in the digital generation would be included all those who do not belong to the "digital illiterate" group –all those who have not overcome the digital divide (Bauerlein, 2011; Compainge, 2001).

Therefore, they are not a generation split by age. Nor are those born in the late 90s who lived the birth of the Internet at publicity and communicational level but all those who haven't been able to adapt after the inception of the Internet. The digital generation is made up by those people who are concerned and interested intellectually to keep a daily contact with the last computer and technological breakthroughs in multimedia telecommunications.

Users who channel their professional and personal praxis through the new technologies and with that they expect to achieve a greater efficiency in their daily activities. In our case a study of the digital generation which is practically indifferent if the animations they consume are 100% computer-made or rather with clay in the stop motion animation or motion blur, just to mention two examples.

The constant passing of the characters of childhood, after the adolescence between digital and analogical systems has generated users with a great demand in the quality of the digital images (computer animation) and high creativity, humor, etc. in the analogical images (stop motion animation). In this sense, the experience of the creators of Pingu has been very positive and the interested reader can widen these notions, in the following bibliographical references Cipolla-Ficarra, Alma & Cipolla-Ficarra, 2011; Cipolla-Ficarra, 2011; Cipolla-Ficarra, 2007) whether it is from usability and the communicability of the interactive service for children, like other details of the characteristics of that metamorphosis of the cognitive model for children, in the motivational process of learning as entertainment.

Besides, the digital animation of Pingu has allowed to have a generation of videogames users, for instance, who can distinguish between simulation and emulation of reality. That is, when the computer graphics and computer animation is used with scientific or entertainment purposes. In the former no mistakes of any kind are accepted (modeling, color, texture, lightening, movement, etc.), because the representation of the real world on the computer screen, tablet PC, TV, cinema, etc., must tend 100% to be some kind of photocopy of what is depicted. The image of a landing strip in a flight simulator must be true to reality to avoid catastrophic situations in extreme climate conditions, for instance. In contrast, in the second case, that is, the emulation for videogames, the entertainment component allows a certain gap between the real world and that depicted for artistic or entertainment reasons.

It is in this interaction between the simulation and emulation of reality in which the created characters with clay may win realism. If the main characters of the Pingu series from the 20th century are compared with the current ones, it can be seen how the passing through the off-line multimedia support such as can be a CD or a DVD has allowed to gain in realism, starting by the colors of the characters, the expression of the facial components, the elements that make up the scenery, etc. In this regard, it is possible to indicate how an additional element in the cultural reality of the South Pole penguins has been inserted in an incorrect way and kept along the decades: the igloo (the home of Pingu and his family). The igloos refer to the North Pole, and not to the South Pole.

Figure 6. Cultural factors (post-office)

This element of distortion of reality is not due to emulation or simulation, but to cultural or creative factors, such as the need of giving an enclosure to the main character and the secondary ones, along the episodes of the TV series (gift shops, bakery, post-office, etc.), although it contradicts the real world of those birds.

THE CONTEXT

Context is another of the key elements in the communicability of the content of the computer animations or with malleable material. From a narrative point of view or from the storyboard the context is the space that surrounds the character, and which fills up with specific data of the story and the characters. Among the most influential characteristics to the characters are included: the culture, the historical period, the geographical situation and the profession. Some of these essential characteristics are already listed in the description of the television series and their respective official websites: Pingu (www.pingu.net) and Shaun (www.shaunthesheep.com) for the readers interested in them.

The context or scenery, with its elements or effects (natural, the fog for instance, or artificial, like the light play and the shadow of a street lamp) may boost or not the actions that the main and secondary characters develop in the storyboard. There are simple contexts, such as the case of Pingu's South Pole, more realistic-simple like the farm of "Shaun the Sheep", of the different 3D scenarios where "The Little Prince" moves (www.thelittleprince.com), until reaching the realistic-complex because of the high quality of the 3D scenarios in "Chuggington" (www.chuggington.com). In the current work we analyze the four examples.

With regard to the characteristics of the characters and the first heuristic analysis made of the series "The Little Prince" and "Chuggington" can be looked up the following bibliographical references (Cipolla-Ficarra, 2013). The simplicity of the scenes of the Pingu series highlights a minimalist style which helps the children to focus on the static and/or dynamic objects of the scenes, and also on the deeds that Pingu carries out with his family, friends, etc. The call to attention and strengthening of motivation is achieved through constant transformations or metamorphoses of

Figure 7. The Little Prince: Computer Animation in 3D (www.thelittleprince.com)

Figure 8. Chuggington: Computer Animation in 3D (www.chuggington.com)

the main character and those who accompany him in his adventures. There is a longer description in this regard in the following reference (Cipolla-Ficarra, 2013). In contrast, in the series: "Shaun and the Sheep", the richness of the elements forces to resort to the audio, through sound effects, music, etc., to draw the attention of the children.

Culture determines the rhythm of discourse, grammar and the vocabulary. Obviously in the examples of clay animation most of the characters are not human. Consequently, special sounds are used, exclamations, very few legible words, even in the human characters such as the farmer in Shaun the Sheep, etc. Besides, there is a facial mimic which increases with the appearance of new episodes, as in the case of Pingu or Bitzer (Shaun's shepherd dog). Now if one tends to work under a component of the fundamental quartet of successful animation (simplicity, originality, universality and humor), such as universality, it is important that in the stories that make up an animation series characters from different cultures are to be found, an even from other worlds (e.g. alien scientists when they abduct Shaun and the cat Pidsley in the episode "Cat got your brain"). When characters from other cultures are in play it is necessary to carry out a more comprehensive research to make them look real (for instance, the mistake of the igloo in Pingu) and make sure that individual characters have been created and not simply a set of characters with different names who look alike and they all act in the same way.

The time or historic period is another of the key components of the context, bearing in mind that it is difficult to locate a story in a period different from the present. Now the claymation stories for children generally refer to the present. However, there are elements aimed art the adults which are underlying in these stories and which may take us towards the past or towards the future. Some examples are: a black and white television set (past) or the UFO that the aliens use (present-future) in the Shaun series or the music, whether it is from a barrel organ in Pingu (past) or a record player in Shaun (past). In contrast, in the computer animations there is always a greater presence of futuristic elements. Some examples are the sceneries or the collaborating characters or antagonists that the Little Prince encounters in each one of the planets where he lands with his plane, the flying locomotive (Action Chugger) in Chuggington, the intelligent traffic lights for the control of railway traffic, the robots in the workshop to repair the trains, etc. Evidently, in the computer animations and after having carried out many historic investigations, it will often be needed to create components which couldn't be located. In this sense, the whole material gathered in the research should be used so that the timeline seems real.

The author or authors of the storyboard usually situate the story in the places that are familiar to them and many times starting from them the characters are originated, their activities, etc. The greater is the knowledge of the place where the story is located, the lesser the need of the author or authors to make research. Consequently, time is gained in the production of the work and the costs of the digital or analogical animation are reduced. Now when certain time has passed it is necessary to return to those places to have a diachronic vision of the changes. Undeniably, the geographical situation will affect the diverse aspects of the character. That is, the distinctive features of the idiosyncrasy of a place contribute later on to shape the personality of the characters. A priori, the frenetic bustle of a city is not the same as a farm.

However, the possibility of inserting this frenzied rhythm in allegedly quiet places such as the Shaun animation, leads us to another element of our quartet, and key in the globalization of the animations, whether they are on the computer or not, such as the sense of humor. Humor considerably increases communicability not only among the different ages of the viewers, but also among the different cultures and without resorting to words.

The profession may become the context of a story. In those cases, resorting to the characters of the activities on which a script is intended to be developed, may help to delineate the profile. To such a task making an interview with open questions suffices. That is, that the interviewee may broaden with details the information that is intended to be compiled. Without any doubt once this information is processed allows to define well the context and make the characters more real. This in turn may boost the creative process and help the story become more natural and veridical.

THE WEALTH OF THE BACKGROUND IN MULTIMEDIA CULTURE

The contextual references in our case of study go beyond the visual or static aspects because other variables of the audiovisual are included: music, films, books, hypertexts, hypermedia, etc. The dynamic and the static means of the 20th century and early 21st in digital and analogical support have allowed to generate in half a century a trove of multimedial and audiovisual culture without precedent in the history of humankind and aside from the problems stemming from the generation of digital illiterates and native digitals, for instance. Although they are knowledge in the shape of a mosaic, as Abraham Moles claims (Moles, 1973), the interrelations of that knowledge from a diachronic point of view, allow that an animation work aimed in principle at the children may also be accepted by the adult audience, in the most remote places of our planet. This is due to the wealth accumulated during the passing of time of the audiovisual contents by a large share of the population with the traditional social communication media: press, cinema, TV, etc. and then with the Internet. For instance, the simplicity (another of the fundamental elements of the quartet for the success of any animated story) of Pingu which was quickly accepted by the great majority of the infant audience considering that it has been created without literary references as may be the case of the work by Antoine de Saint-Exupery "The Little Prince". In Pingu, the audiovisual imagination in the animations plays a main role because the author has understood the context of the character. Inside the context of claymotion, Pingu would be more aimed at the children of an early age, whereas in contrast we have Shaun. Which does not only entertain the youngest, but also the continuous references to "gags" from other television or cinema productions from the early 20th century in the USA may activate in the memory of the adults situations they lived, with real comedians and of worldwide circulation such as were Chaplin, Laurel and Hardy, etc. An excellent example of international popular culture is in the episode where the sheep start with different means the persecution of Timmy (the baby sheep of the series) who has climbed on her own on the 4x4 motobike. In said episode can be seen clear references to the silent comic cinema of the early 20th century. One also has to add the audition component such as the music and/or the songs of the episode "Strictly no dancing". The music and the sound effects in each one of the episodes of this series are excellent, since they accomplish the function of holding the attention of the viewers and foster the motivation to keep on watching the animation to the end. Without any doubt this is one of the main elements in what we have called in the current work "background of the multimedia culture".

RESULTS

A group of four communicability experts watched each one of the commercial episodes of the animation series: Pingu, Shaun the Sheep, The Little Prince and Chuggington. The referential components of the universe of study, whether from the point of view of the context, and also temporal, have been gathered in the following attributes of qualitative: background of multimedia culture, children communicability, adult communicability, space-time-profession orientation, localization and cultural globalization, quartet of successful animation.

Later on a random selection was made through a draw of ten chapters of each one of the television series. In this sample of study it was screened in a room by a group of 4 (C)hildren (4-11 years), 4 (J)uniors (12-17 years), and 4 (A)dults (18-64 years of age), all of them separately. Other heuristic techniques used for the compiling of the final results were the videotaped sessions, that is, the recording of reactions in front of the broadcast of the animated series and the verbalized judgments of value (think-aloud). These data were grouped in relation to the different ages, which are presented in Figure 9.

Finally, it was resorted to the use of questionnaires (detection of the subjective preferences of the viewers) with the purpose of researching what kinds of qualitative components of the computer animation and the claymation they wanted in the mobile multimedia systems. In our case were used indirect questionnaires. That is, without the presence of the communicability evaluator and they worked with the same groups of juniors and adults. The score is from 0 to 100, being the highest qualitative value 100 and the lowest 0.

The results show a trend to the short duration contents, with the most referential jokes for the

Figure 9. Results between the computer animations and the claymation. The score is from 0 to 100, with the highest qualitative value being 100 and the minimal 0.

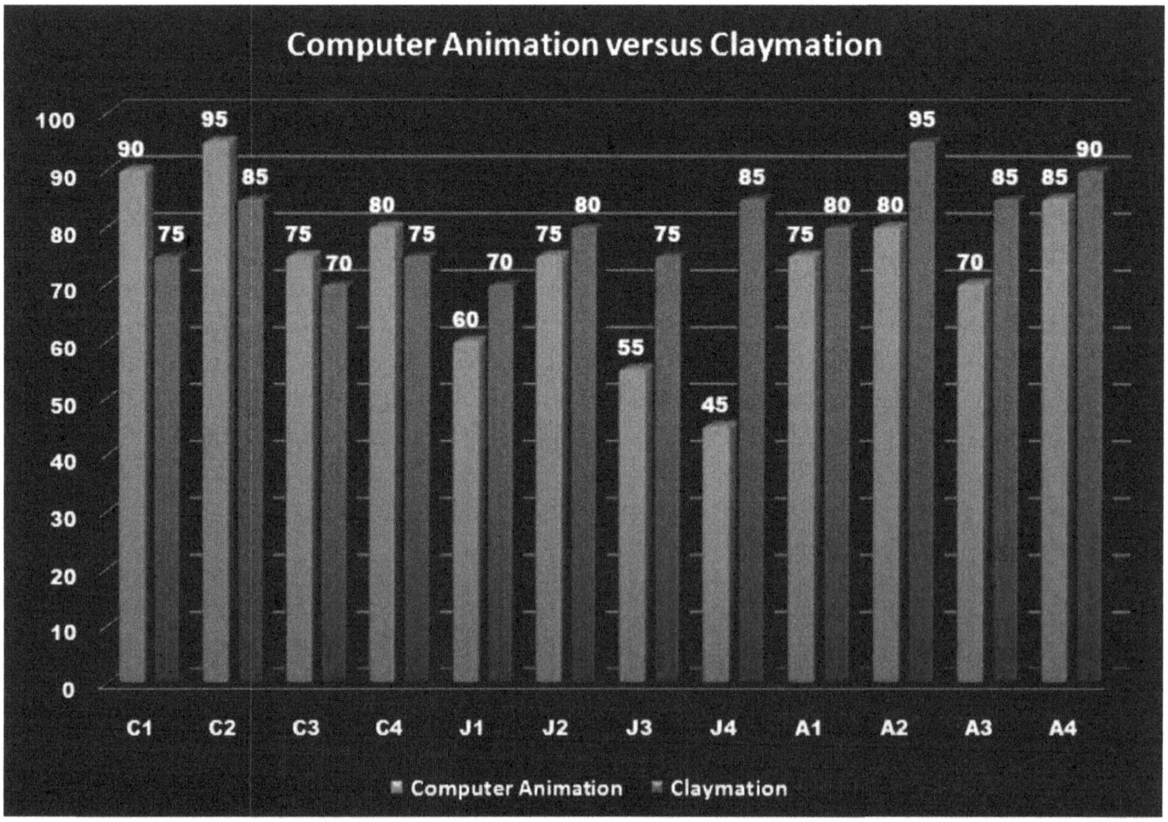

Figure 10. The series "Shaun the Sheep and Chugginton are those that have obtained the highest score

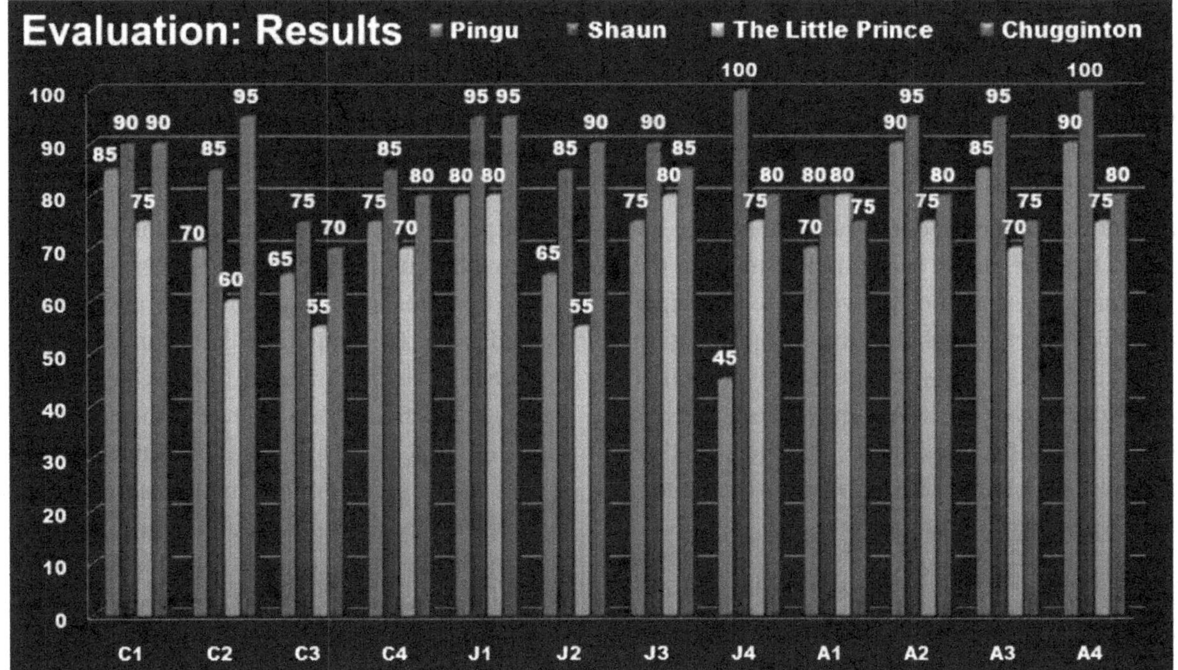

adult audience in the clay animations, especially in the series Shaun the Sheep. The young show severe difficulty to understand the animation The Little Prince, since 80% of our study haven't read the book. In all the analyzed episodes the communicability for children, teenagers, youth and adults is very positive. Two are the preferred series by the teenagers: Chugginton and Shaun: the Sheep. The adults prefer Shaun: the Sheep because of the background of multimedia culture component, because they remember certain gags, although they indicate that the originality component decreases in the quartet of fundamental components of the successful animation. However, the space-time-profession orientation, localization and cultural globalization and the fundamental quartet of successful animation are positively accepted since the 7-10 years.

LESSONS LEARNED

The current study of the space-temporal context highlights that the adult public also enjoys the digital and analogical animations such as those carried out with the stop-motion techniques. Although that context has a great importance because it makes that the characters, the actions, the passing of time, etc., increase or decrease the realism of the story. A realism which makes that the new generations and daily users of mobile multimedia phones have the ability to differentiate between a simulation and an emulation of reality, accepting analogical animations in the interactive contents of the multimedia mobile phones. However, in the "born digital" generation the lack of reading of the classics of world literature such as the work "The Little Prince" makes harder for them the understanding of the main character and his animated allies in 3D, if they do not check the Internet. In other words, there has been a shift from a mosaic culture to a culture of scarce fragmented knowledge and which are in a digital support online. That is, there is a loss of the autonomous, global knowledge interrelated with other disciplines and an increase of the need to locate that knowledge in the Internet, in the least possible time. In the incoming investigations we will try to go deeper into this aspect in the interactive communication systems. Besides, we will keep on analyzing other multimedia systems, where the dynamic means of the animation aimed at the infantile and adult audience has bidirectional relations in the humoristic components of the storyboard.

CONCLUSION

The results obtained from the evaluations from the qualitative components of a digital or analogical animation make apparent that the analyzed commercial products have an excellent level of communicability. The combination of techniques in the animations is always positive, from a diachronic and synchronic point of view, since it allows to discover new possibilities in the emulation of the reality that surrounds the human being. Now, if the animations lag behind some audiovisual parameters, that is, that they haven't been able to generate their own language, is simply due to the fact that the professionals of the animation sector haven't made any kind of theoretical research in Europe. The R&D equation in computer animations still increases the divide between the USA and the EU. To such a degree that the software for commercial graphic computing, the same as in the 20th century and early 21st century is still being made essentially in America. It is not a problem of financial resources, but rather a spate of human and social factors which have damaged the progress of the animations industry in computers or analogical media. A devastating example in the last quarter of the century is in the south of Europe. Fortunately, the classical animation techniques, such as the malleable, still boost the motivation and draw the attention of the youngest generations, especially at the moment of interacting with last generation interactive systems. That is, like their parents did (digital natives), or their grandparents, with a wide background of the multimedia culture. Most important is the quality of the contents, and the use of those animations, regardless of the support or the techniques used to generate them. An educational goal of said techniques is to keep the interest of those generations in the reading of textual contents, starting by the investigations or consultations in the new hypermedia systems offline and online, drawing always the attention towards the consultation or reading of the whole works, whether in paper support or interactive digital.

ACKNOWLEDGMENT

The authors would like to thank to Maria Ficarra, Mary Brie, Luisa Varela and Carlos for helpful comments.

REFERENCES

Bauerlein, M. (2011). *The digital divide: Arguments for and against Facebook, Google, texting, and the age of social networking*. New York: Penguin Group.

Cipolla-Ficarra, et al. (2010). *Quality and communicability for interactive hypermedia systems: Concepts and practices for design*. Hershey, PA: IGI Global. doi:10.4018/978-1-61520-763-3

Cipolla-Ficarra., et al. (2011). Computational informatics, social factors and new information technologies: Hypermedia perspectives and avant-garde experiences in the era of communicability expansion. Bergamo, Italy: Blue Herons Ed.s.

Cipolla-Ficarra, F. (2007). A study of acteme on users unexpert of videogames. In *Proceedings of HCI International*. Heidelberg, Germany: Springer.

Cipolla-Ficarra, F. (2011). Behaviour computer animation, communicability and education for all. In *Proceedings of HCI International 2011*. Heidelberg, Germany: Springer.

Cipolla-Ficarra, F. (2013). *Advanced research and trends in new technologies, software, human-computer interaction and communicability*. Hershey, PA: IGI Global.

Cipolla-Ficarra, F., Alma, J., & Cipolla-Ficarra, M. (2011). Prolepsis in computer animation for children. In *Proceedings of First International Symposium on Communicability, Computer Graphics and Innovative Design for Interactive Systems*. Heidelberg, Germany: Springer.

Compainge, B. (2001). *The digital divide: Facing a crisis or creating a myth?* Cambridge, MA: MIT Press.

Glintenkam, P. (2011). *Industrial light & magic: The art of innovation*. San Francisco, CA: Abrams.

Moles, A. (1973). *La communication*. Paris: Marabout.

Murphy, M. (2008). *Beginner's guide to animation: Everything you need to know to get started*. New York: Watson-Guptill.

Tharrats, J. (2009). *Segundo de chomon*. Paris: Harmattan.

Chapter 42
"E-Culture System": A New Infonomic and Symbionomic Technical Resource to Serve the Intercultural Communication

María Mercedes Clusella
Galileo Galilei, Argentine Foundation for Talent and Ingenuity, Argentina

María Gabriela Mitre
Galileo Galilei, Argentine Foundation for Talent and Ingenuity, Argentina

ABSTRACT

This chapter presents the results obtained by the International Institute Galileo Galilei (IIGG), a research unit of Fundaringenio, within the framework of the research project developed in 2009 that consists of the design of a basic model of "e-culture system" that can promote and disseminate world cultures, including Santiago del Esteros`s culture (the culture of a northwestern region of Argentina). Culture as a complex phenomenon is studied from the Systemic Paradigm, which is optimized by the transdisciplinary features that allow the concurrence of other complementary perspectives. The methodic process consists of the systemic modelling process and the retroprospective methodology. This process begins with the conception of the Meta Model to be achieved; the Existed Model is built in relation to its past and history. After that, the Existing Model is developed in relation to its present. Each one corresponding to the different scenarios of the events, and they are the basis of the features of "santiagueñidad." From these, an Operative Model is designed and adapted. The authors present the validation of an operative model, through analogy simulation using the technique of syntegration for the processing of empirical evidence, collected from a statistical sample selected for this purpose. The results confirm the selected features of "santiagueña" culture and the generation of a more general and comprehensive model that could be of value to other cultures and instrumental applications such as in large organizations or companies.

DOI: 10.4018/978-1-4666-4490-8.ch042

INTRODUCTION

The Argentinean Foundation for Talent and Ingenuity (FundArIngenio) is a non-formal higher-education research unit in permanent connection with universities and other educational institutions in the world. Composed of a group of academic people sharing the aim of looking beyond the horizon, this autonomous foundation with legal status was set up in 2005. Our main objective is to discuss and propound new paradigms and trans-paradigmatic processes. We also focus on studies about Cybernetics, Systemic, Complexity, Informatics, as well as their various derivations and impacts.

We are interested in communicating our achievements regarding a very complex issue: the culture of Santiago del Estero, a community under way. This challenge was taken on in 2005 and now we are in the position to report how and how much we have moved forward.

We have inherited a civilizing message that distinguishes and differentiates our community from the communities in the world. We are academic and universal, and as such we need to witness such inheritance in order to increase, refresh and launch it into the future with creativity, innovation, excellence, efficiency, effectiveness, and on an ethical as well as aesthetical basis. Our goal is not only to promote research, knowledge transmission and testimonial teaching in order to foster original and creative thinking in our province, Santiago del Estero, Argentina, but also to be a link with global thinking, in other words, to think globally and act locally. It is a two-way bridge with different tracks towards a trans-generational change.

THE SELECTED PROBLEM AND VIEWPOINT OF DEALING WITH IT

From the twentieth century humanity went through different fields of knowledge. Understanding the current complex and hyper complex reality necessarily implies to replace the classical reductionist strategy to other more holistic approaches and methodologies. The simplification of the complex reality generate difficulties, i.e. to see the items separately can create an illusion of order and control, but fails to understand reality as a whole, and still less to capture the dynamics of interactions and apparent disorder (Le Moigne, 2012; Llamazares, 2011; Morin, 1998; Mulej, 2009). This way of observing requires certain transition between paradigms which are just theoretical statements but mainly ways of thinking that generate a better attitude to comprehend and eventually understand complexity. Systemic, as the science that studies concrete and abstract systems, provides dimensions of thought, reflection, meditation and action. It allows in general recognizing and understanding objects in their context more clearly. We taken into account Mulej´s ideas that state that in a globalised and innovative society, human survival and the success of their organizations rely on *holistic observation, understanding, thinking, decision-making and action*. Thus, System Theory is not applied for a better and deeper description of its components and relationships seen from a unique point of view *but from a creative and innovative interdisciplinary creation* (Mulej, 2012).

The future lies in the symbiosis between human beings and the artifacts- conceptual or concrete- that they produce. During this process Symbiosis means articulation of the natural with the artificial, of arts with technology, of culture and civilization in a coherent whole. A new human being of the future implies new political, ecological, economic and cultural approaches (De Rosnay, 1996; De Rosnay, 2007). We directed our studies towards issues that may happen beyond the present.

Having so many examples we choose to study the complexity of human organization and the dynamic of social organization (Herrera, et al., 2011). Culture is our subject matter as an extremely complex and highly dynamic object which means understanding and comprehending changing realities in which various physical and social elements, aspects and characterization coexist and are in permanent evolution. But due to globalization and technological advances a new phenomenon occurs: the loss of cultural identity, the distinguishing features of each culture tend to fade. So that is the reason why we are interested in our culture, Santiago's Culture, which is being built every day since it comes from the past, and it is developing and projected into the future. Currently, applications of e-culture contribute to solve this problem and try to preserve and promote cultural heritage according to future challenges by disseminating it on a massive scale through Internet.

Regarding the methodology, we use retroprospectivation as a macro-process that allows us not only to know different complex phenomena but also to make decisions about how to act on them. Retroprospectivation is a methodology used by Systemics that involves the use of models and scenarios. Our aim is to build, by ideation and abstraction, a meta model represented by the ontic diagram of topics of cultures features - e-culture system. The present Meta model is subjected to evaluation and revision by the Existing model (systemic actual model of "santiagueñidad"), which is oriented by the Existed model (systemic model that represents our cultural heritage) for the systemic design and construction of the Operating model (epistemic-cognitive systemic model for the study of Santiago del Estero`s culture). The latter model is the one that best records and reports cognitive and decision-making procedures. Thus, as a multidimensional and circular sequence it could be repeated recursively. Such sequence is identified as from a part to a whole and from a whole to a part until it becomes an acceptable and satisfactory scenario. To sum up, it is a process of synergy and recursion.

Therefore we inform our achievements regarding an e-culture system which was obtained by using the retroprospectivation methodology in the study of Santiagueñidad. This challenge started in 2005 and now we report the way we have been moving forward with the methodological process that allowed the construction of the different systemic models.

BACKGROUND AND MODELS DEVELOPMENT

FundArIngenio, has been working and researching on culture as an hiper complex phenomenon since 2005 where we proposed as an hypothetical statement that the best way to study such a complex phenomenon was from Systemic perspective. During the years 2005 and 2006 some works showed our efforts to advance in the study of Santiago del Estero`s culture. The first steps corroborated that, as a scientific activity, Systemic allows to study the object in its complexity, integrating partial views- either sociological, or anthropological or others. The design of the project continued in 2008 when the Culture was studied from two different and complementary approaches: Cultural Studies (constitutes a theoretical-conceptual tool for the study of contemporary cultural phenomena which attempts to understand culture in its complexity through the generation of knowledge and the inclusion of interdisciplinarity) and Systemics Paradigm. In 2009 we proposed the analysis and design of a web interactive information system in order to promote and spread worldwide the cultural heritage of a northwestern region of Argentina for future generations. The research hypothesis is based on a new design of Symbionomic System. The methodical process consists of the systemic modelling process and the retroprospective methodology is used to design the e-culture system (Herrera, et al., 2011). The Method/technique of Syntegration by recursion allowed the generation of distinctive cultural features. The selection and application of this interactive processing technique have fostered the integration, cohesion and synergy of multiple topics and perspectives of cultural contents (Clusella, et al., 2011).

On December 2011 Fundaringenio has published an academic work with transmedia designs entitled: *santiagueñidad 21st Century. Systemic Retroprospectivation of Santiago del Estero's Culture -Argentina* (Herrera, et al., 2011; Luna, Palavecino & Leguizamón, 2011; Mulej, 2012).

The book is organized in two parts: The First Part is a traditional printed book introducing the projection of our ideas in the study of the culture of Santiago del Estero. Regarding the title of the book, it refers to the name of people from Santiago del Estero (santiagueños); and XXI Century refers not only to a period of time but mainly to a particular location where the generations experience a new way of reading the local and global reality. Also the title includes one of the keywords, Systemics, the science that studies concrete and abstract systems. This way of observing requires certain transition between paradigms which are just theoretical statements but mainly ways of thinking that generate a better attitude to comprehend and eventually understand complexity.

This communication mainly is addressed to seeking the attention of the young "digital natives", and to those colleagues who are interested in sharing these systematized intellectual contents. Our academic achievement was presented, based on our academic tradition and perspectives that have defined a prospective stance which updated a systemically-supported retroprospective procedure. This allows us to design activities by means of future scenarios from where we can imagine present performances rooted in our own tradition. Thus, our leading views are desirable futures, and among them are the possible futures. Three challenges were taken while carrying out this work: doing science; collecting art to think and feel; and formulating an ethical project

We consider that a sensitive approach based on epistemic thinking is required in order to guide our works on sciences, humanities, arts and technologies. These approaches allow us to distinguish between theory, method and technique. Therefore, we developed a strong systemic epistemology which gives sense to every plan, program and project being developed by IIGG. Otherwise in order to research, teach and provide testimonies of our own motivations and vocations for the future generations. We assume as a generational compromise the elaboration of "The Systemic Retama Doctrine" a system of ideas, epistemic-based and supported by a cosmovision that guides us towards interpreting theories and improving praxis. It is a hinge between philosophy and epistemology that allows us to have an intellective critical vision. In this way, we use the systemic paradigm as an axis of our perspective.

To sum up, the study of Santiago del Estero culture is based on FundArIngenio´s own approach, and is supported by its epistemology, philosophy, doctrine, paradigm and methodology described in more details in chapter one of the book. The book is a retroprospective description that introduces the four models for 'santiagueñidad': the existed model, the existing model, the operative model and the meta model.

In Chapter 2 we focused on the description of the existing model. This challenge led us to the essential stage of choosing the available techniques applying the generic Team Syntegrity Model® technique through the process of synergy and recursion using electronic platform (with parameters according to CHI ACM).

The culture of Santiago del Estero is strongly symbolic which allows unique perceptions, representations and ways of thinking and acting since Santiago del Estero culture is the product of an uninterrupted cultural construction along the centuries and during its historical evolution it received other cultural heritages. In the modelling process, this description corresponds to the Existing model of Santiago del Estero´s culture are functional and structural components which are identified in the defined context, and represent the characteristics in which people identify themselves with that culture. All these concepts also contributed to the design of a imaginary Meta Model of culture, achieved from the survey carried out by means of references, evidences and exploration of the existing model. Thus, is a systemic model that involves twelve elements or cultural features identifying the people of the province of Santiago del Estero. These features are described using 12 "nouns derived from verbs" or "nominalized verbs".

The IIGG research group has worked with the Team Syntegrity Model (TSM) systemic techniques created by Stafford Beer, an effective and scientifically developed method to address complex issues. It is based on an icosahedrons arquitecture, a structure that allows synergic communication. Hence, it was adapted to the Meta model and the 12 icosahedrons' vertices represent the distinctive cultural features of santiagueñidad. This process allowed the gathering of information from synergetic objects consisting of interacting topics discussed, and given a whole overview. As we see in Figure 1 they are: {1}believing (beliefs), {2}speaking, {3}singing, {4}dancings (dances), {5}story-telling, {6}ways of thinking (patterns of thought), {7}practical knowledge (alternative popular medicine), {8}doings (traditional craftwork), {9}feelings (popular religiosity), {10} living (ways of living), {11}fighting (heroic epics), {12}perceiving (perception patterns and its infuence in the construction of reality).

The procedure allowed different aspects of the culture being examined in parallel, a consensus was achieved and with the knowledge obtained the modelling of the system behavior was acceptable. The process of syntegration and recursion started with an initial matter and the participants chose the topics from which they built different approaches of the problem and then by exercising different roles they generate a circular process of dissemination of the information which results in a global vision shared by all. In this way they achieved an integrated synergy. A team member, who in this research is referred as qualified informants–disciplinary specialists (Le Moigne, 2012)

Figure 1. Meta Cultural Model of Santiagueñidad based on syntegration

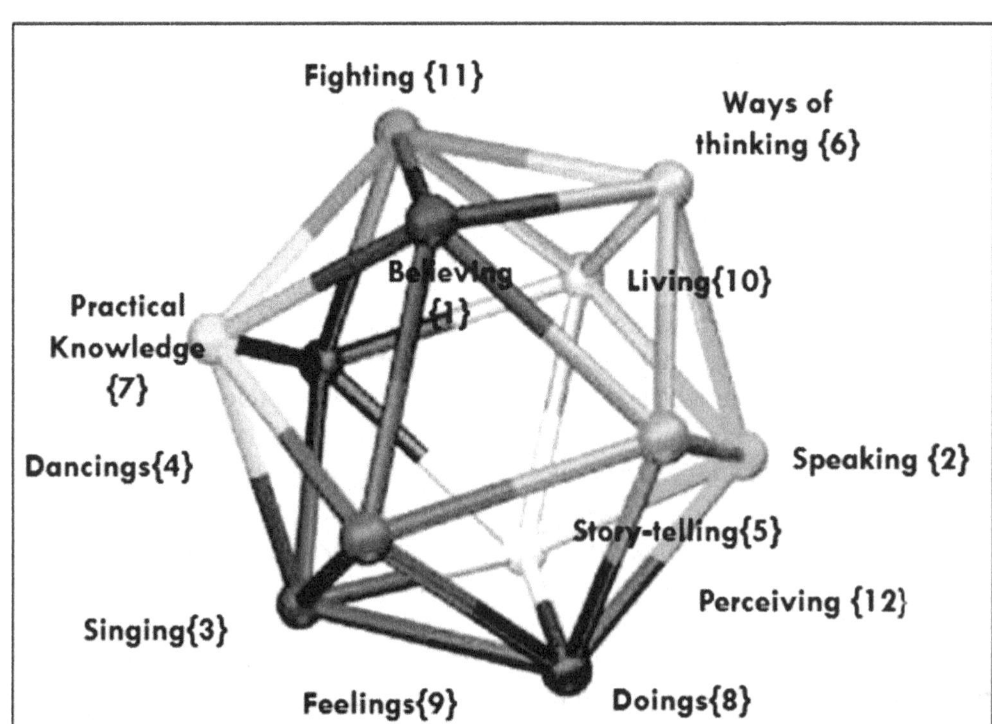

is represented in the edges (30) which adopt a position in this structure and influence one another on the 12 topics. The simulation process carried out methodically responds to a hypothetical deductive premise which through the process of integrated synergy was possible to obtain empirical evidence and allow adjustments by recursion in the systemic modelling process.

Therefore, the simulation process consisted in an electronic syntegration exercise that was designed to foster optimal communication and achieve a synergetic integration among topics and participants that allow the generation of cultural contents. Four "topics" formulated as cultural features in the Existing model were chosen in order to improve the definition of the topics selected during the process of synergy / recursion and of distillation and decanting of the minimum conceptual contents. The results obtained in this first simulation served to design a new material and adjust the procedure according to selection criteria of the qualified informants.

In chapter 3 of the book we presented a case study of local culture by designing the existed model -a historical approach (past scenario) - that provides the main characteristics or marks of cultural heritage. This approach takes into account some aspects of the big cultural processes developed by the human societies that settled down in what is nowadays Santiago del Estero province. It is a general framework of the genesis of 'santiagueña' culture carried out from the contribution of archeology, etnohistory, anthropology, history, cultural studies and art. Many authors have revealed valuable inheritance and identity traits through their works that offer a valuable description of 'santiagueñidad'. We adopt the main marks, signs and other meanings inherited from our ancestors in a global vision and deal with culture as a dynamic system. This model feeds the existing model embodied it and allows us to use at least a revision criterion of these antecedents.

Santiago del Estero's culture is the product of an uninterrupted cultural construction over the centuries. It started approximately 1700 years ago from the first American ethnic groups' experiences in relation to their habitat1. As time went by, they received the cultural heritage from other ethnic groups: the Spaniards in the 16th century as they settled and colonized the territory, the Africans in the 17th and 18th centuries who arrived as slaves and freedmen, and the Syrian-Lebaneses and Italians between the 19th and 20th centuries as immigrants. This culture is strongly symbolic with a special artistic wealth (which succeeded in reaching out to other places in the world), that possesses material, procedural, and spiritual diacritical2 elements which confer it an identity of differentiating power. To sum up, the culture of Santiago del Estero allows unique perceptions, representations and ways of thinking and acting based on an ethic ecologist and highly religious appraisal underlying the American-Hispanic biocultural mythic background

In this existed model, the legacy is immense and the characteristics are being polished up from one generation to the next. These shades, from their existence in the cultural construction of the younger generations, have to make a whole that can be decanted by recursion in order to start a new cycle. The achieved synergy and the found recursions could be expressed and presented in meaningful codes. This challenge leads us to the essential stage of choosing the available techniques in order to advance in the communication through practical reasoning of common and new technologies. The operative model will serve as the bearer of the message for the new generations, the digital natives of this new 21st Century.

In Chapter 4 (Herrera, et al., 2011) is presented the design of the operative model and the optimizing in the interaction and communicability of e-culture web applications. As the digital media has changed the regular way of approaching culture and as E-culture tries to preserve and promote cultural heritage according to future challenges using the latest technology the problematic issues to be solved in relation to the design and usability of such applications were taking into account.

The design of the Operative Model was built on the basis of emotional design and the aspects while designing user interfaces that convey emotion in e-culture applications were considered and fundamental topics optimization of language communicability were addressed. Thus, a set of guidelines for the optimization of the Operative Model were proposed.

An operative model was designed, which can be used to develop a website about santiagueñidad. It contains an interaction model based on functional and estructural components. Functional characteristics are ontogenetical, typological and offert-demand components, taking into account biosystem-tecnosystem-sociosystem relationship (Bs-Ts-Ss). These three ones, plas "sense-direction", are the estructural components. Here we give further details of this model.

The functional component is expressed through three features that characterize the structural components:

- Ontogenical, features that generate the core values of the constituent entity.
- Typological, describes the logic of typing process using creative activities that defines relevant-pertinent classes and stereotypes.
- Social requirements to meet demand - mainly specified by the Bs- and supply. This offer could not respond to real needs (technological consumerism frequently generated by the Ts).

The four structural components are:

- The central core is the Bs. People or organized groups of people who have infonomic, symbiotic, symbionomic and systemic capabilities. The Bs takes its own DIKIW values, that can be described by dual, dialectic and 4th Order-cybernetic components.
- The container is the Ts. The Ts systematically grows and varies as technologies do. Bs is connected to a universal network (Internet). Variable time dominates this component, in relation to the physical and virtual distance. Considering these variables (time and distance), the Ts can be: Proximal (equipment, techniques that are of immediate reach as TV, radio, microwave), Medial (equipment and techniques used to increase user extent, as a phone), Distal (multimedia communications networks, computers connected to social networks, home automation).
- The habitat is the Ss. Interaction between Bs and Ts is developed inside it. It allows and facilitates the eco-evolutionary movement (general and global movement) being modified by the Bs::Ts interaction. It has the following characteristics:
    - **Bio (Life):** Features defined from ethnic, heritage, fixed o chosen spatial areas, lineages, dynasties, strain.
    - **Psychosocial:** Social manners selected by emotion or belonging or commitment dimensions; customs associated with abilities, skills and competences. E.g. respect for technology, arts and sciences.
    - **Cultural:** Requirements defined by religious, racial, geographic and professional groups.
- The meaning and direction are components that determine the quantum speed about perception, intuition, prediction, insight and advance design of desirable futures (Fd), possible futures (Fp) and preferred futures (Fr) that serve the broad Bs satisfiability. The Ts:: Bs:: Ss relationship is constantly moving in that direction and meaning.

It is considered that the whole development of an e-culture web application should be carried out following the previous considerations, using agile methods based in prototyping.

Intercultural communication -mediated by ICTs and related to a systemic object culture- involves a real communicational challenge. This is due to the following aspects:

- Since it deals with the promotion of culture, a socially constructed object, the language used in intercultural communication should be suitable for transmitting emotions. Therefore, an emotional design is proposed for the web system of santiagueñidad.
- As it is an e-culture object, its modelling and implementation require electronic computing devices, which may lead to the loss of the warmth and richness of face-to-face spoken language. This paper proposes the use of an operating system to optimize interaction as a way of making up for such drawback.
- As it is an intercultural communication, it implies the use of English as an international language.

Consequently, the recommendation should be taken into account. Although there are several factors involved in the optimization of web-page usability, this project gives priority to the interaction based on language emotion and communicability. Following the present irreversible trends, the promotion and mass-spreading of a culture should be carried out using mainly web applications. In this way the message will reach a greater deal of recipients simultaneously, regardless where they are.

Such applications should fulfill the following basic requirements:

- They should follow the premise established for the emotional design: the generation of user interfaces with objects that will become thought-provoking and will cause long-lasting and memorable experiences for the subject.
- The interfaces should mainly use audiovisual language showing cultural characteristics through images, sounds and movements.
- Audiovisual objects should keep the mother tongue of the culture displayed, conserving the accent, rhythm and sensitivity characteristic of such language and taking advantage of the facial and gestural expressions of the spoken language.
- These audiovisual objects embedded in the interfaces should be supported by a written version in English as the international language par excellence.
- User interfaces should be produced, in general, in English.

The whole development of an e-culture web application should be carried out following the previous considerations, using agile methods based in prototyping. Prototyping allows, among other possibilities, a quick test and evaluation of the various alternatives of the design, thus having an impact in the quality of the final product. On the other hand, such agility makes the introduction of rapid changes possible, and prioritizes the final product rather than the documentation and early and draft deliveries. In this respect, -about new aspects to be considered in Engineering Software- we suggest that to obtain software products (which is not just a physical thing but rather abstract as system data / information / knowledge, collectively referred as information systems or SI) has become increasingly complex. As a result of these new needs have emerged new areas of knowledge, such as computer systems, informatic systems, and lately infonomic systems and simbionómic systems. These ones understood as unified conceptualizations between autopsieis and evolutionary complexity theory, according to

Joel de Rosnay. These and other issues were and are being investigated, since 2002, in FundArIngenio.

The Operative Model is obtained using the retroprospectivation process in the study of Santiagueñidad and we sustain that the validation may allow the refinement of the original Meta Model. Thus, a new retroprospectivation cycle of Santiago e-culture will emerge. This iteration cycle will improve the knowledge of this culture by identifying new characterizations. In this way, tans-generational communication will enable and facilitate the review of this unique identity.

The Second Part introduces 'Santiagueñidad, XXI Century' by means of the most relevant artistic expressions. It is a narrative ideoaudiovisual in DVD format to be seen on a PC and includes a description and a historical report of the genesis of our present culture, the 'santiagueñidad'. It aims at opening a window to the knowledge and enjoyment of Santiago del Estero's artistic and cultural heritage through three basic features: aesthetic, artistic and topic. Our aim is to make visible what is implicit in our culture, to assume our own identity. Popular artistic expression involves a new way of looking at a peculiar representation of everyday life where we can find different signs that reveal the aesthetic culture of the people from Santiago del Estero.

RESULTS OBTAINED IN THE SYSTEMIC RETROPROSPECTIVATION PROCESS IN ORDER OF ACHIEVING THE GENERAL/BASIC MODEL OF "E-CULTURE SYSTEM"

The experience has provided with significant results:

1. Regarding to the use of syntegration as dynamic support for systemic retroprospectivacion:
    a. Through this process regulated distribution of information among all the subjects was acquired in a self-regulated way.
    b. From the point of view of the interconnection and information exchange it is the most effective way of managing complexity through a group process.
    c. The electronic syntegration fostered optimal communication and the subsequent achievement of a synergistic integration among topics and participants.
    d. The flow of information allowed a maximum distribution of intelligence and Know-how of the participants in a short period.
    e. The results obtained in this first simulation served to adjust the procedure
    f. The participants showed efforts to break through the boundaries of their own disciplinary differences
2. Regarding to the 12 topics / main features which basically correspond to any culture as a system:

Based on an exercise designed for four topics given in the existing model, it is possible to widen this treatment to the twelve topics defined in the Meta model with 30 qualified informants (defined by the syntegration technique) to allow the generation of cultural contents. Dimensions, Classes and Types of 12 topics were identified and will allow their universality for other cultures. They are classified in a rank of 1 to 5 for each QI according to:

- Cognitive classes/ types: magic, wisdom, erudite, chosen
- Affective class/ sentimental, emotional, voluntary, festive
- Productive class; manual, interactive, folklore, cultural; ranks1-5

3. Regarding to the use of Qualified Informant using a purposive sample designed ad-hoc:

The criteria for selecting the Qualified Informants were defined (Le Moigne, 2012; Vargas-Llosa, 2012). Selective criteria of "eligibility" of Qualified Informants are: criteria of accessibility, sustainability, immediacy, specificity (referential), meta-conscience, capable of being prosumer (produce and consume culture according to Marina's concept, with a minimum/immediate interactive capacity; belonging to a philosophical, conceptual, epistemic field (Marina, 2003).

In the delivery of each copy of the work it was inserted an 'invitation' to the reader-navigator where they were asked to participate via web with their opinion / input / and it was given some instructions on how to link (with the drawbacks of privacy and manageable only by the investigator).

Once the population was defined it was established a purposeful selection (for 7 classes from higher participation up to lower one) of 50 'qualified' Informants (Clusella & Mitre, 2012; Vargas-Llosa, 2012). This procedure took place during the months of January to October 2012 and received effective participation of 76 percent of participants.

This made it possible to validate what was missing in this instance: that is assessing the effects and responses of people who showed an interest in this production of modelling culture system process that could be refined successively by infonomics resources based on the future application. That is why we believe that we are in a position to formalize a more general model for any practical interests, which could be suitable to different organizations, societies, and cultures or sub-cultures.

4. Regarding the validation and formulation of a General Model of "e-culture system":

The results of the inquiry process are the "empiricism" (data / information / knowledge / interpretation) of the meanings related to the 'evidence-hypothetical' search taking into account the sampling distribution of the qualified informants, by scale conceptual classes, frequencies and percentage values. The protocol report of the test evaluated (type Wilcoxon or Mann-Whitney) is summarized below.

The "*sampling distribution*" (ad-hoc selection prior intentional) Class of qualified informants was corroborated (high correspondence) according to the collection of reader response / navigator of the book. Compared distributions of design and post-survey were compared.

The general criteria were integrated as *evidence* of contrasting hypothetical-deductive. Scores are clearly marked from higher to low – taking into account an epistemic value and a predictive significance of the "knowing discipline" (Morin, 1998) according to the prior information. It can also be expressed functionally:

$F(\#class;\Delta\%) = \{(1;+2), (2;+2), (3;-4), (4;-4), (5;-2), (6;-8), (7;-10)\}$

Where the resulting set of ordered pairs are rated such that:

#Class (i= 1,...,7) = #1: High Expert's; #2: Only Expert; #3: Knowing; #4 Student's; #5: Co-autors; #6: Readers; #7: Concerned; and $\Delta\%$ = *the difference in* absolute values *between sampling frequency, with f'* evidential frequency response achieved in %.

The study of two-dimensional graph indicates the similarity and possible significant correspondence between the two phases: sampling design and post-facto processing as definitive and acceptable results in the order of 76% effective response to the consultation. According to the various options offered for the return of opinion / contribution / trial.

In summary satisfactorily observed that 'best disciplinary knowledge' opinions are communicatively more acceptable, at the same time, to 'lower vocational training' the views are simplified. This would be expected for a first approach in "trans-media" design (Seminario Trans-media, 2012).

FINDINGS

It was dealt the approaches to an "e-culture system" towards a general model, to be presented as "case study" of "santiagueñidad" as Santiago del Estero`s Culture and from there try to reach a Model suitable to other cultures. So, we conclude in the following way:

1. 12 basic features were proposed and accepted in the consultation and we considered that they may be universalized to other cultures or sub-cultures, and aimed at finding practical uses with their applications;
2. It is possible to test a dynamic articulation involving qualified informants previously selected according to the defined criteria and with the practical procedure to work for TSM;
3. Through the systemic retroprospective action it reached an acceptable approximation of contents according to hypothetical-deductive principles;
4. Concerning the methodical procedure (case of 'prototyping') according to the guidelines of the international movement CHI (Computer Human interaction) is hypothetically acceptable;
5. It is feasible the study of culture as a ultra complex phenomenon, taking as an example the case study of the culture of Santiago del Estero. The responses obtained from the perspective of current scientific knowledge, is considered an acceptable idea whit 'trans-media' format;
6. Were obtained tangible progress in re-establishing connections with the readers surfers of the book, who were selected in seven 'classes' in this first approximation related to the most remarkable features of the initial model (Model Meta) for an "e-culture system";
7. Members of the process showed a "broad interest" in learning and participating. Two thirds of the guests expressed their views. Thus it is possible to achieved a linkage participant as trans-media component;
8. Operability was achieved and it was followed a steering elemental empirical "e " design to support the argument / justification of the advances.

Finally, this work is built on three central pillars Thinking, Walking and Looking. These first three central pillars of the building account for some of the issues originated during the research group's reflection on its own reality.

1. Changing the approach: to have critical awareness, to change the way of thinking, to improve oneself.

With a well-oriented approach, that is, a certain and intelligent 'look' to understand reality, we could understand beyond the obvious, build up new scenarios and be personally and politically happy as an eternal aspiration. Prospectivating and thinking systemically are useful and efficient.

It is necessary to differentiate between viewpoint and approach. The way we look, our approach, changes during our life, according to our history, our dreams, our knowledge and thinking. It also changes because we are always different and sometimes walking together. It changes with our happiness, sadness or experiences. We can change it according to our own will (if we know how and why), but a question remains: when, how and why to change an approach. The answer could be: because it is a natural requirement of the human being to seek ethical perfection, to aspire to and look for happiness, to attempt to be communally honorable.Thus, focusing, thinking and acting systemically make us useful as well as efficient and effective.

The main challenge when doing this work was to use two dimensions: one clearly scientific, the other academic. The essay includes the mythic as an extra-scientific power, but it sometimes plays an important role in the deep reality of the intellectual creative, artist, leader, technologist, and even of the ordinary man. That is why we attempt at a conceptual account and a narration of events and facts that give rise to our surprise and sometimes satisfaction. Today, our most solid and standing search is: To look far, to look clear and to look well.

2. Critically assume a way of being and acting: an university style and spirit.

FundArIngenio has among its members people from four or five different generations who are being prepared to become leaders in humanities, sciences, culture, arts and technology. They belong to different disciplines and graduated from various higher-educational institutions. Some of them are undergraduates in their twenties, other in their thirties. The third generation is made up of those professionals over forty. Finally, those with a wide experience in systemic and a long career in teaching and researching make up the fourth generation. We are all academic people from different and various disciplines, with different ethnic backgrounds, but with the same cultural characteristics and identity, that of being 'santiagueños'. And we certainly know that we will remain university people for the rest of our life. We constantly update what we have learned and thus we exercise the skills of lifelong learning.

Everything the individual is due to their concrete existence within the social and historical process of which they are both support and product. It is the very role of intelligence to assume experience and the current historical conscience, and from that point develop critical thinking.

3. The necessary and essential context of the Chaco-Santiagueña civilization-culture.

Our group of systemists in Santiago del Estero shares common origins, trajectories and achievements. Even in the scientific field, the language and the way of thinking can not be completely neutral. In more traditional formal sciences such as Mathematics and Logics, the way of thinking are independent of the culture that serve as a meaningful area for authors, scientific communities and cognitive approaches. A culture entails a vision of the world, a way of perceiving and understanding reality. The way of apprehending the object depends on the culture, but culture, in turn, has become dependent of the way science understands reality. Only by taking into account the conditions, possibilities and restrictions that organize knowledge, can the world be understood, and this is under the concern of the science of science. As Edgar Morin emphasizes, "As long as scientific knowledge is still blind regarding its role and place in society, it will continue contributing to provide ways of death and oppression to the leading power. Although insufficient, the conscience of this role is necessary for its advantages and possibilities of liberation to be fruitful." A strategy that aims not only at conformity but also at fulfillment and feasibility.

We are aware of the need of a philosophical view of life: a practical philosophy to survive and reach happiness. Using J A Marina's thoughts and testimony, we assume the thesis on the 'flight of the creative intelligence'. We aim at building 'active communities' which are capable of reaching and achieving the flight of creative intelligence, following Marina's view.

To transfigure through art, to know through science and to transform through ethics. Shared intelligence is and will be the ideal that FundAr-Ingenio, the institution that has taken us in and stimulates us, claims. The adopted stance has a dynamism which corresponds with the following "directions":

- Flight towards ART, that transfigures the appearance of things.
- Flight towards SCIENCE, that knows better what is happening.
- Flight towards ETHICS, which transform human reality.

So the question and the determination is: Not to abandon intelectual creativity [ingenious talented people], shared goodness [fraternity] and beauty [full aesthetics]; all these using a systemic approach of a synergetised contextualised whole following certain scientific, technical and ethic principles.

These keys were arranged according to the usual scientific procedure of 'cognitive contextualization':

- To look (perceive, understand), "epistemological".
- To think (judge, justify, elaborate, invent, assess, validate), "methodological".
- To act (apply, value, spread/teach/learn/research the impact on cultures), "praxeological".

Our aim of completing the hypothetical deductive contexts is oriented towards broadening the empirical basis. Once enough evidenced is collected, when technical and technological application realities allows it, we will proceed to the systematic spreading and teaching, following the academic purposes of knowing, applying and teaching. Our long-term goal is educational, that is, shaping the university style and spirit, and our strategy is still being designed.

At last, we can state that our native people THINK and FEEL systemically; at least that is the way our people in Santiago del Estero live, but at the same time we dare say that is the way most people in Latin America do. This fact would prove our thesis that Systemic is basically transdisciplinary, and that the way of behaving in science and culture is in accordance with the renewable and transparadigmatic demands. In that direction we are heading in the twofold search for 'science' and 'culture'.

CONCLUSION

The topics of interest of FundArIngenio to look to the future toward the XXI Century are: refer and list the evolution of Computer / Informatic / Infonomic / Symbionomic and the techniques valued from scientific parameters. It also seeks to "Look away, look clear and look good" in Science, Humanities, Arts and techniques in terms of technological variants.

Consequently, from the academic a new order is held today: the symbionomic (De Rosnay, 1996). which is basically dependent on the design. Similarly, for the NTIC's of the 21 Century proposes symbionomics systems to respond to the design of components related with SystemicWare + CyberneticWare + OrganizationWare as guides to building updated HardWare + SoftWare + HumanWare. Those are hypothesis to be corroborated in research and development programs towards CHAT (Science + Arts + Humanities + Techniques) in the International Institute Galileo Galilei. Institute Federated to the International Federation for Systems Research.

REFERENCES

Clusella, M., & Mitre, M. (2012). Modelo e-culture system, en refinamiento sistémico. In *Proceedings of 8º Congresso Brasileiro de Sistemas*. Retrieved from www.pucpcaldas.br/graduacao/administracao/8voCbS/index.html

Clusella, M., Mitre, M., Santillán, A., Generoso, A., & Budán, P. (2011). Integrated synergy for cultural contents recursivity in e-culture system. In *Proceeedings of Second International Conference ADNTIIC 2011*. Heidelberg, Germany: Springer.

De Rosnay, J. (1996). *El hombre simbiótico: Miradas sobre el tercer milenio*. Madrid: Ediciones Cátedra.

De Rosnay, J. (2007). *Les scénarios du futur: Comprendre le monde qui vient*. Paris: Véronique Anger.

Herrera, I., Clusella, M., Luna Pablo, P., Mitre, M., & Santillàn M. (2011). *Santiagueñidad siglo XXI retroprospectivación sistémica de la cultura de Santiago del Estero*. Santiago del Estero: Editorial Lucrecia.

Herrera, S., Clusella, M., Mitre, M., Santillán, M., & García, C. (2011). An interactive information system for e–culture. In *Proceedings of First International Conference on ADNTIIC 2010* (LNCS), (Vol. 6616, pp. 30-43). Heidelberg, Germany: Springer.

Herrera, S., Zuain, S., Gallo, F., & Avila, H. (2012). Emotion and communicability in e-culture applications. In *Proceedings of Second International Workshop HCITOCH 2011* (LNCS), (Vol. 7546, pp. 15-24). Heidelberg, Germany: Springer.

Le Moigne, J. (2012). Sur les sciences et patiques d´ingenierie des systems complex: Sciences appliqué es (ancillaies) ou sciences (fondamentales) de conception? Interlettre chemin faisant. *Réseau Intelligence de la complexité*, (62).

Llamazares, A. (2011). *Del reloj a la flor de loto: Crisis contemporánea y cambio de paradigmas*. Buenos Aires: Editorial del Nuevo Extremo.

Luna, P., Palavecino, M., & Leguizamón, H. (2011). Enmarque en inteligencia audiovisual por sistemas infonómicos e-culture. In *Proceedings of XV Jornadas Nacionales de Investigadores en Comunicación*. Cordoba: Universidad Nacional Río Cuarto.

Marina, J. (2003). *La creación económica*. Barcelona: Deusto Ediciones.

Marina, J. (2011). *Las culturas fracasadas: El talento y la estupidez de las sociedades*. Barcelona: Anagrama.

Morin, E. (1998). *Introducción al pensamiento complejo*. Barcelona: Gedisa.

Mulej, M. (2009). *A new 4th order cybernetics and the sustainable future*. University of Maribor.

Seminario Trans-Media. (2012). *Cómo crear historias por guionado*. Buenos Aires: Segura-Galtez.

Vargas-Llosa, M. (2012). *La civilización del espectáculo*. Buenos Aires: Alfaguara.

ENDNOTES

1. It is characterized by a plain forest situated in the Chaco region of Argentina.
2. These are elements chosen by groups to represent themselves and others.

Chapter 43
Human Factors in Computer Science, New Technologies, and Scientific Information

Francisco V. Cipolla-Ficarra
ALAIPO – AINCI, Spain and Italy

Jacqueline Alma
Electronic Arts – Vancouver, Canada

Jim Carré
University of The Netherlands Antilles, Curaçao

ABSTRACT

The research work presents a set of rhetorical questions with regard to the new profile that an expert or an editor of scientific information must have regarding computer science and other interactive systems online and offline. The main interrelations between the communicator of the new technologies and those who generate or present themselves as authors of those breakthroughs are also presented, that is, the marketing of sciences. Finally, real examples that show how the economic factor prevails over the neutrality of science are inserted.

INTRODUCTION

The advance of the formal and factual sciences require a correct scientific communication so that its circulation is horizontal in all fields of society, avoiding the digital divide, which in some cases due to human or social factors imposes a vertical structure because of a few scientists, or rather, pseudo scientists. This last term refers to the appearance of the dynamic persuaders (Cipolla-Ficarra, 2010) or the cyber destroyers of scientific knowledge, for instance. The evolutional or revolutionary progress of the new technologies and the theories constantly interrupts a subtle balance, which is the result of converging and diverging forces among the

DOI: 10.4018/978-1-4666-4490-8.ch043

different environments of a community. Without any doubt the breakthroughs in the sciences and the technologies are one of the main cornerstones for the welfare of the population pyramid. However, if we analyze the structure of education and health the prospects of common good for all humanity when it comes to technological progress, the digital divide has widened in the developed countries in the last decade. In the next decade in the emerging countries that pyramid tends to become a diamond as is the case of India (Bijapurkar, 2006; Bijapurkar, 1979). Schematically, these statements can be depicted in the following way:

In few words, there is in the surface of those changes a constant destabilizing element and which stems from the world economy. Although everything changes, in the 19th century these changes occurred in a gradual way and it took decades for their consequences to be seen. Now the progress spiral is practically unlimited and its limit is in imagination or creativity. That is, the transformations go ahead of imagination. In this context, there is a need to explain and spread the reasons and the methodologies of the changes deriving from scientific and technological research, using specialized communication.

TOWARDS A NEW LANGUAGES FOR HUMAN FACTORS IN ICT

Currently the amount of information online generated and open to the general public makes it impossible to have a 360 degrees vision of the whole evolution in the ICT (Information and Communications Technology) sector, for instance. Besides, it is necessary to know how to locate and choose from the great volume of technological information, that which is 100% truthful information, with which we can be updated not only in the discoveries, but also in the inventions inside the field of the new technologies. For these actions it is necessary a first analysis of the scientific language.

Every scientific specialty has its codes and rules. Inside scientific communication it is possible to find a linguistic isotopy as to terminology and ready-made sentences (Eco, 1979; Holdcroft,

Figure 1. From the pyramid to the diamond: forecast of the change of dimension of the different social classes in India (high, medium high, medium low, low)

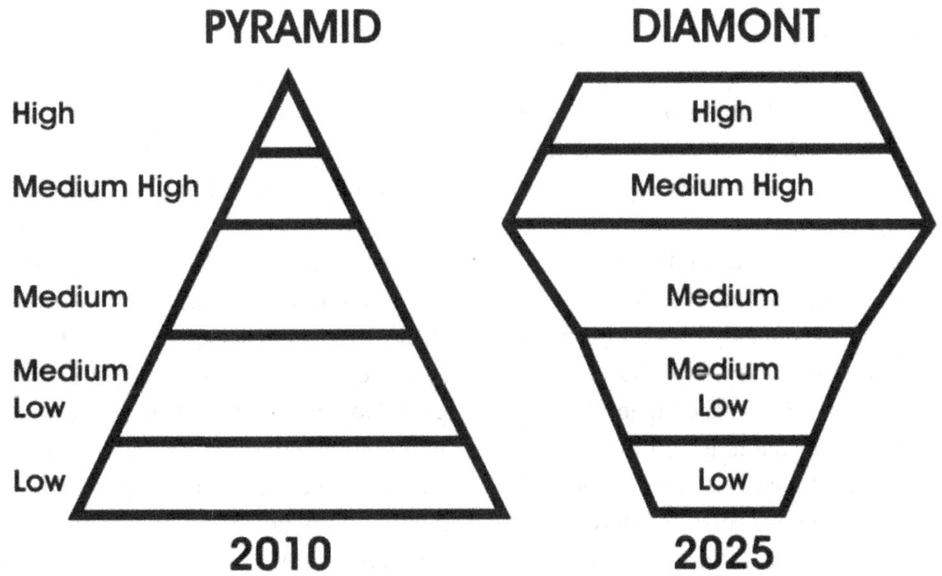

1991). Then a vocabulary of the incredible emerges which sometimes is related to the religious and confidential, such as the terms miracle, secret knowledge, reaching the ultimate truth, temptations of knowledge, etc. Consequently scientists are usually presented through the mass media, especially television of the 20th century and early 21st century as wizards, creators of miracles immersed in a context of continuous struggle against ignorance. Hence the use of terms like revolution, last frontier, avant-garde, etc., in the texts of scientific popular knowledge. The problem with these terms is that they increase the subjective factor of the information and scientific information must be presented in an objective way. At the same type it generates stereotypes which steer away from reality or scientific truth.

In the second decade of the new millennium, the labor competitiveness of the scientific sector inside the formal and factual sciences requires scientists who are far away from the ordinary working environments, such as can be a lab or a classroom. Nowadays they are placed in front of sketches or growth graphics of the firm sales. Consequently, the star scientist appears, that is, a kind of movie actor, TV, theater, etc. interrelated with the sciences. To reach a fleeting popularity, the scientist is capable of carrying out a series of research projects, constantly participating in the congresses of the five continents of the planet simultaneously, writing articles for magazines, chapters for books, etc., being a public servant and business advisor and an endless list of activities which turn him into a human creature beyond normalcy.

Although there are some of those, behind the mirage lies a gigantic work of his team of collaborators, who from anonymity do not have a moment of rest. Sometimes, with the view set on turning the scientist into a showman, the real structure of science is contaminated, which lies in the culturally developed countries in the real professionals and the future professionals (college students, engineering degrees, masters, PhD) without transcending like the real brains of scientific knowledge. Therefore to the extent to which the gap between society and science is big, the situations of injustice will prevail. An aspect which is currently analyzed in a partial manner under the title of digital divide, for instance.

Another topic for analysis is the constant pressure of the communities to consider the quantitative factor of the scientific results and to set new records, with the view of increasing the international prestige of the inhabitants of a nation. However, in the new millennium, with the global village and in the era of the expansion of communicability (Cipolla-Ficarra, et al., 2010) the qualitative factor prevails over the quantitative, whether it is in goods or services related directly or indirectly to ICT.

SCIENTIFIC MARKETING

The firms of the ICT sector are regarded as a "great lab" taking care of the qualitative aspect of the products and services, trying besides to meet the needs of the users (Cipolla-Ficarra, et al., 2011). In contrast there are those who foster "research and then transfer those results" (Potts, 1993; Pressman, 2005). However, this line has had serious problems in keeping itself through time due to the speed with which the changes in the ICTs sector took place. What is also being sidelined are those simply theoretical investigations, fostering or promoting the practical part, especially in those universities where manufacturing industries prevail. Now the first research centre of great international prestige in carrying out experiments and validation of new technologies in real projects was NASA (National Aeronautics and Space Administration). If the first line prevailed, that is, the firm or industry as a great lab, scientists would make their experiments with commercial purposes. Science acquires in this way a productive profile which can be reduced to a simple product. A product or a service require marketing for their success. The traditional mass media and the new interactive media are nowadays their best allies since they allow them to sell their achievements in a competitive global market of knowledge.

The institutions devoted to the fostering of ICTs should count with the art and the science of the public relations to create and uphold a truthful image towards the rest of society. Public relations are a science because they entail the true knowledge of things, because of their origins and consequences. The term "art" applies because they constantly require creativity to implement it and originality along time. A good image has a fundamental weight in the success of every institution and its members. However, that institutional image must respond to a reality.

For instance, it is not acceptable that a university claims to be a centre of excellence of a community or a country in computer science, and even fosters conferences of human factors, HCI (Human-Computer Interaction), software quality, etc. when in the press of national and international circulation their readers are told that they use interactive digital contents, without the corresponding payment of licenses or copyright to the authors.

As a rule, it is necessary to count with a department or head of public relations, where one of his/her functions is to contact the press to minimize the negative fallout of the institutional image as in the example of the Figure 2. Besides, as a science, the public relations keep a bidirectional relationship with sociology, the communication sciences, human relations, among others (Cipolla-Ficarra, et al., 2011). Other functions inside a great firm or lab are to plan activities expecting results in the middle and long term (it is a mistake to believe that results are obtained in the institutional image in a short term), control the information and strategies through specialized techniques, including those internal issues which may damage the institutional image. Finally, a scientific communicator must know how to select thoroughly all the information stemming from the public relations to counteract the publicity effect. In this sense, scientific communication has made great progress since its origins.

ORIGINS AND EVOLUTION OF THE INTERRELATION BETWEEN COMMUNICATORS AND SCIENTISTS

The factual and formal sciences have a period of strong growth during the periods of world war conflicts. Telecommunications, computer science, the digitalized information networks, etc. are some good examples. Since the early 20th century some US newspapers like "The New York Times" (www.nytimes.com) were worried in their editorials by the misunderstanding of the readers towards the breakthroughs inside physics and the negative aspect for democracy when the scientific achievements are not grasped by the community.

The origin of the modern scientific communication lies in the writing of editorials in paper support social communication media. Writing editorials allows a series of stylistic liberties which do not have other sections of a newspaper, where the objectivity of information should prevail. With the 1921 Science Service directed by the chemist Edwin Slosson it could be seen that he drew the attention of his readers by using short paragraphs and the use of superlatives, for instance, biggest, smallest, less, etc. (Recker, J., 2012). Besides, he resorted to the human factor turning this news into an environment where science, adventure and even human drama converged. However, this continuous interaction of the scientific context with the public context was not considered positively by the scientific sector in a great part of the 20th century. Just in the decade of the 80s, for international political reasons, which might have a negative repercussion in the financing of research, the scientific sector rediscovers in the specialized press an element to earn the trust of the general public, and therefore achieving the maintenance or even the increase of financial

Figure 2. In the Carlos III University (Madrid, Spain), theoretically an excellence centre of university teaching for the new technologies, the computer labs use in their classes interactive digital contents in an illegal way. In other words, a violation of copyright. Digital version of the Spanish newspaper "El País" (03.22.2012)

EL PAÍS

PORTADA | INTERNACIONAL | POLÍTICA | ECONOMÍA | CULTURA | SOCIEDAD | DEPORTES

CULTURA

LIBROS CINE MÚSICA TEATRO/DANZA ARTE ARQUITECTURA MODA GASTRONOMÍA EL ESPAÑOL BLOGS TENTACIONES TV TITULARES »

Demanda por 'piratería' contra la Universidad Carlos III

- Cedro (la entidad de gestión derechos del libro) abre así una batería de medidas judiciales
- El objetivo es sentar a negociar a las universidades
- El demandante asegura que la mayoría distribuye sin permiso contenidos protegidos

ANTONIO FRAGUAS | Madrid | 22 MAR 2012 - 18:16 CET 110

Archivado en: Derechos autor CRUE Universidad Carlos III Universidad Propiedad intelectual Educación superior Propiedad Legislación cultural Sistema educativo Derecho Política cultural

Antonio Fraguas Garrido
Periodista

Eskup
Twitter
Seguir

resources for their research projects. Now some of the possible causes of the break of the inter-relation between scientists and communicators can be summed up in the following way:

- The fact that the scientific community regards its results as provisory until their peers confirm their results in conferences, workshops, symposiums, etc. Evidently all this entails the passing of time, and in view of the constant evolution of the ICTs sector, it may be counterproductive for the scientific communicator.
- Internal human factors in the work team, at the moment of releasing news on the obtained results.
- Complex issues and of difficult understanding for the scientific communicator who may decide to publish it trusting the neutrality of the science with regard to the economic aspect or self-promotion of the scientific showmen.
- The oversimplified writing style of the texts for the sake of the inexperienced readers in certain matters or subjects usually prompts the criticisms in the scientific environment

because of the paucity of documentation, the elimination of the bibliographical references, the extensive comments on some definitions, etc. However, the scientists use a language for the experts in the issue, and there are several terms and/or concepts which may have another connotation or turn out to be incomprehensible for a wide majority.

Achieving a balance in the collaboration of the circulation of the scientific breakthroughs, among those who generate it, communicate their results and grasp the final message is not easy, even in the era of communicability expansion.

The scientific news, just like any other news, must respond to the six basic questions and a special one for the eventual science showmen: "What?", "Who?", "Where?", "Why?", "When?", "To what purpose?", This latte rhetoric question highlights the underlying motivations out of which the scientific sector or a representative thereof issues a news at a given moment. Now inside science it is necessary to find out how the problems are approached, what is the process, and why the researchers are studying and working, why they are wrong, why they reach the preset goals in the established deadlines, etc.

RHETORICAL QUESTIONS AND EXAMPLES

Theoretically in the 20th century the scientific news served to decrease the digital divide among the population, but the global financial factors of the new millennium make the digital divide between technology and society increase, even in the traditional geographical areas known as economically developed. The indicated distance is the consequence of a lack of scientific culture by most of the inhabitants of a community. The role of the local educational system is basic to reduce the ignorance of people, however, there are other goals. One of the goals of the new interactive mass media and the interactive online and offline systems does not only consist in informing, but also in presenting the information in a simple and likeable way, so that it strikes the attention of the audience of the contents and prompts them to stay in front of the computer screen or the television, to mention two examples. In other words, reaching a circulation of the interactive messages or not in a clear and comprehensible way. The simple circulation of knowledge is not positive. It is necessary to shape a 360º enriching view through the new interactive communication systems so that the user inside the global society can participate in the correction of the eventual errors stemming from scientific knowledge and which influences, directly or indirectly, in the information society. All of this leads us to consider a first set of rhetorical questions that we will answer in future research works:

- Does neutral science still exist not depending on economical factors?
- Are the professionals and scientists of the ICT who do not get subsidies recognized in the academic context and/or in the community for the effort they make for the common good through their research?
- Are there mechanisms to identify and group the showmen of the sciences in the new millennium, for instance, a database with free access from any place in our planet?
- How are detected and sidelined the destroyers of the scientific factor from the public or private firms?
- Is there an international deontological code to avoid that from the scientific labs false results are issued and spread?
- Do the organizations related to the scientific journalism professions have rules for those who practice their profession in an independent way, for instance the collaborators?

- What controls are there for those multinationals that use the European social funds or similar for R&D pseudo projects whose disguised purpose is to recruit future employees in their work structure, with the role of scientific destroyers inside and outside the EU borders?
- What is the ideal profile, in training and/or experience for the scientific communicator of the 21st century?
- What are the current limitations inside the interrelation between communicators and scientists?
- How can the digital divide be solved in view of the population divide between rich, poor and beggars of the societies of the European south in the second and third decade of the new millennium?
- Why does the private or religious scientific sector increase gradually its influence in the interactive communication media which show results of the formal and factual sciences which contradict their dogmas or directive rules?
- Is the transparence or objectivity feasible to a 100% between research and the transfer of scientific knowledge to the community?

Next it can be seen with a series of real examples how the European subsidies serve to power the destruction of the neutrality of science through the notion of the editor of computer science publications. One of the goals of the hypertextual systems was to make out of every computer user an editor of interactive contents. In the environment of digital information and of the social communication sciences, for instance, we can state that in many places this phrase has already been a reality for several years, with the momentum of the Internet and currently the mobile multimedia phones and microcomputing. However, it is striking how the economic subsidies inside the EU that should help to bridge the digital divide or boost the small and medium-size businesses go to great editorial groups that invoice millions of euros per year, thanks to the scientific breakthroughs inside and outside the EU borders. The problem is bigger when from those institutions are generated pseudo professionals under the title of editors, when in reality they have neither experience, nor academic training in the field of journalism or the sciences of social communication or other analogous discipline. Just having inserted as partner in EU subsidized products a multinational of scientific editions is reason enough so that once said projects are finished he is incorporated as an expert in edition. Obviously these are illogical reasons, and which obey to other commercial factors such as can be the destruction of small scientific realities, autonomous, which work without European subsidies and even with a small extension in the editorial field, that is, a potential competitor to that great multinational. The consequences for the inhabitants of the EU are negative because the neutral scientific environment will look for transparent solutions to their publications outside the European borders, that is, the economic competition of the EU. Just by making some searches with Google we can establish an interrelations map which unveil these statements (some areas of the images have been hidden for privacy reasons of the authors of the deviations or destruction of European science).

These examples make apparent that the control of the European products aimed at the databases, online trade, marketing, etc., do not have a proper follow-up. The normal thing in situations like these is that the multinational companies that invoice millions of euros yearly thanks to the work of thousands of scientists give the money they received to the European coffers. Besides, both the employee and the employer should be included in a database under the title of fraudulent projects. Reality shows that there has been an attempt to include an employee to destroy the neutral science inside and outside the EU, from

Figure 3. European projects (2009 - 2011) where already appears the future employer of the author of the research

an editorial environment related to the ICTs without having neither the academic title or the professional training at the moment of holding the workplace.

LESSONS LEARNED AND FUTURE WORKS

Many of the rules that should govern the diffusion of scientific knowledge are more an utopia than a reality, especially in front of editors of information media related to the new technologies and all their derivations. The mercantilist factor in these environments should be eradicated, and also the mechanisms of circulation of scientific ads in international specialized websites of associations of great international prestige related to the ICTs, such as ACM (Association for Computing Machinery), IEEE (Institute of Electrical and Electronic Engineers), etc. with profit purposes through the constant publicity of disguised com-

Figure 4. Curriculum Vitae of a pseudo editor in computer science (there isn't a minimal experience in press, radio, television, etc., as editor of textual, audiovisual publications, etc.)

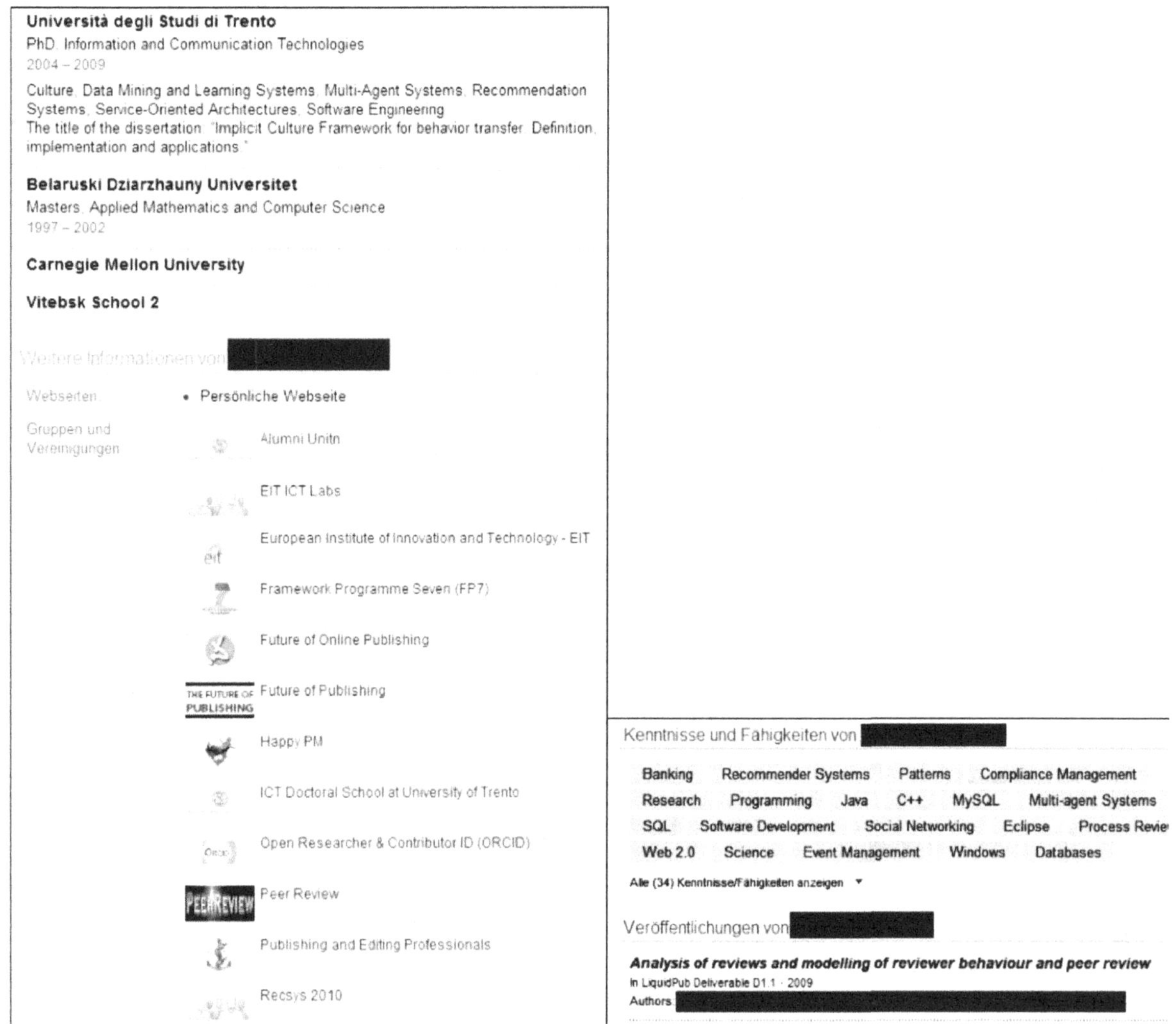

Università degli Studi di Trento
PhD, Information and Communication Technologies
2004 – 2009
Culture, Data Mining and Learning Systems, Multi-Agent Systems, Recommendation Systems, Service-Oriented Architectures, Software Engineering
The title of the dissertation: "Implicit Culture Framework for behavior transfer. Definition, implementation and applications."

Belaruski Dziarzhauny Universitet
Masters, Applied Mathematics and Computer Science
1997 – 2002

Carnegie Mellon University

Vitebsk School 2

Weitere Informationen von

Webseiten: • Persönliche Webseite

Gruppen und Vereinigungen:
Alumni Unitn
EIT ICT Labs
European Institute of Innovation and Technology - EIT
Framework Programme Seven (FP7)
Future of Online Publishing
Future of Publishing
Happy PM
ICT Doctoral School at University of Trento
Open Researcher & Contributor ID (ORCID)
Peer Review
Publishing and Editing Professionals
Recsys 2010

Kenntnisse und Fähigkeiten von

Banking, Recommender Systems, Patterns, Compliance Management, Research, Programming, Java, C++, MySQL, Multi-agent Systems, SQL, Software Development, Social Networking, Eclipse, Process Revie[w], Web 2.0, Science, Event Management, Windows, Databases

Alle (34) Kenntnisse/Fähigkeiten anzeigen

Veröffentlichungen von

Analysis of reviews and modelling of reviewer behaviour and peer review
In LiquidPub Deliverable D1.1 · 2009
Authors:

mercial activities, such as can be the appearance of books, magazines, etc. from multinationals of the scientific editorial sector, which invoice millions of euros in the Old Continent. This mercantilist factor joined to marketing destroys the advance of the formal and factual sciences. Now since their beginnings scientific communication has tried to eliminate the ignorance of the general public. Some of its goals can be summed up in the following way: being at the service of science, foster the democracy of knowledge, boost the development of the community, and raise the standard of living of the population. In few words, scientifically train the people of their community. However, this main goal must respond to a series of rhetorical questions such as those considered in the current work to avoid contradictions both in the immediate future and in the long run inside the scientific sector.

CONCLUSION

Currently the diffusion of scientific results is to be found inside organizations or pressure groups non-transparent to the rest of society. As a rule,

Figure 5. Scientific communication website (research.cs.wisc.edu/dbworld)

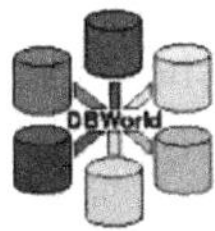

Post a Message to DBWorld

To post a message to DBWorld, you must register with DBWorld if you have not already done so, and obtain a password. When posting a message, you will be asked for your email address and password. **All messages should be directly related to database research.** Please do not post person-specific information such as resume. If you do so, you will be permanently banned from posting to DBWorld. **The following categories indicate virtually all appropriate message types; please do NOT use the News category as a generic "catch all". In particular, changes of address, surveys, "looking for jobs/people/papers/etc." msgs, and requests for information should NOT be posted to DBWorld.**

Also, please do NOT post multiple versions of the same announcement (e.g., in different formats) simultaneously. And speaking of formats, plain ascii is the best for most people to receive by mail.

Finally, since the volume of traffic is already too high, we limit each user to a total of 2 messages in any 24-hour period and 3 messages in any 7-day period. If you violate these limits, you may lose posting privileges. Also, please do not circumvent this rule by creating different email accounts then using them to post multiple messages in a short amount of time. If you do so, you will be permanently banned from posting to DBWorld. Please co-operate to keep the traffic under control. Thank you.

Please choose a message type:

- Conference announcement
- Journal
  - New journal or special issue announcement
  - Call for papers
- Book
  - New book announcement
  - Call for chapters
- Free Software
- Job announcement
- Grants
- News

Figure 6. An exaggerate use of the scientific communication channels to carry out publicity and disguised marketing campaigns against lectures, workshops, publications, etc, or to attack non-profit international associations related to the ICTs from a German publishing house (***)

17-Nov-2012	conf. ann.	Jong Hyuk Park	GPC-13/MUE-13 :Submission due exension [Dec. 5, 2012] (Springer-LNCS/LNEE Proceedings) ***
17-Nov-2012	conf. ann.	Martina Maggio	Call for Papers: ICAC2013, International Conference on Autonomic Computing
17-Nov-2012	conf. ann.	Adrian Paschke	Call for Participation: Semantic Web Applications and Tools for Life Sciences (SWAT4LS 2012)
17-Nov-2012	conf. ann.	Manolis Terrovitis	CFP: 1st International Workshop on Privacy and Security for Moving Objects, Milan, Italy
17-Nov-2012	book CFC	Amélie Bordeaux	Handbook Strategies for a Creative Future with Computer Science, Quality Design and Comunicability
17-Nov-	journal CFP	Abdelkader Hameurlain	TLKDS: Call for Journal Papers (LNCS Journal Subline) - Regular Papers ***

although they are professionals non-expert or with no knowledge in the topics at hand who stem mainly from the scientific sector of the formal sciences. It is striking that a chemist, nuclear physician, mathematician, etc., can be editors of multimedia scientific magazines, for instance. That is, publications where we find a logo in their covers of prestigious publishers of the ICT sector, for instance, but whose editors are neither experts in scientific communication and much less in social communication. In other words, it can be seen in the professional environment of scientific editing of the software, hardware, multimedia, computer graphics, e-commerce, telecommunications, etc, an absolute disadvantage of the factual sciences with relation to the formal sciences, at the moment of establishing the team of professionals who direct and/or coordinate these publications. The rhetorical questions like the brief state of the art presented in this work show that we are in front of an initial research work to unveil unions and interactions between two sectors such as science and its divulgation, with the purpose of finding a balance among the different components of these unions and interrelations which allow to define the profile of a new professional for the diffusion of scientific knowledge in the era of expansion of communicability. Finally, in the search of balance one should try to exclude all those negative components for the neutrality of sciences. That is, thoroughly investigate the human and financial factors that contradict the main principles of the universal diffusion of the scientific results, for the common good of all human beings.

ACKNOWLEDGMENT

The authors would like to thank to Maria Ficarra, Sonia Flores, and Carlos for helpful comments.

REFERENCES

Bijapurkar, R. (1979). *We are like that only understand the logic of consumer India*. Portfolio Penguin.

Bijapurkar, R. (2006). *Winning in the Indian market: Understanding the transformation of consumer India*. New York: Wiley.

Cipolla-Ficarra, et al. (2010). *Quality and communicability for interactive hypermedia systems: Concepts and practices for design*. Hershey, PA: IGI Global. doi:10.4018/978-1-61520-763-3

Cipolla-Ficarra., et al. (2011). Computational informatics, social factors and new information technologies: Hypermedia perspectives and avant-garde experiences in the era of communicability expansion. Bergamo, Italy: Blue Herons Ed.s.

Cipolla-Ficarra, F. (2010). *Persuasion on-line and communicability: The destruction of credibility in the virtual community and cognitive models*. New York: Nova Science Publishers.

Eco, U. (1979). *A theory of semiotics*. Bloomington, IN: Indiana University Press.

Holdcroft, D. (1991). *Saussure –Signs, system & arbitrariness*. Cambridge, UK: Cambridge University Press. doi:10.1017/CBO9780511624599

Potts, C. (1993). Software engineering research revisited. *IEEE Software*, *10*(5), 19–28. doi:10.1109/52.232392

Pressman, R. (2005). *Software engineering –A practitioner's approach*. New York: McGraw-Hill.

Recker, J. (2012). *Scientific research in information systems*. Berlin: Springer.

Chapter 44
Communication Technologies for Older Adults in Retirement Communities

Lauren Bowers
Georgia Institute of Technology, USA

Claudia B. Rebola
Georgia Institute of Technology, USA

Patricio Vela
Georgia Institute of Technology, USA

ABSTRACT

This chapter presents the research, development, and findings of a communication technology developed to enable older adults living in retirement communities to share public events. The project draws reference from the fields of industrial design, universal design, and computer science to design a technology for residents at a retirement community. Residents were included in the design process by evaluating designed technologies. This study demonstrates the relevance of designing simple yet innovative technologies that meet the needs of older adults.

INTRODUCTION

With technological capabilities shifting towards smart, connected, and multifunctional products, event-sharing systems are now built directly into products that we use everyday like mobile devices and personal computers (Lohr, 2012; Moore, 1965). While most people are familiar with this type of technology, the older adult population is less likely to have such experience. Furthermore, such lack of access may prevent older adults from successfully participating in events.

Retirement communities offer a unique setting for older adults to become part of a community. Through the communities, older adults have access to a number of events such as social, physical, and

DOI: 10.4018/978-1-4666-4490-8.ch044

educational activities to mention a few (Calvin, 2012) To date, aging Americans spend 27% of their time in leisure activities, in which approximately half of that time is spent watching TV and 10% socializing (Federal Interagency Forum on Aging-Related Statistics, Older Americans, 2012). Socializing is a necessary step towards avoiding depression. Lack of interaction and social support has been found to not only negatively affect the quality of life but also have negative effects on health, leading to a higher mortality rate amongst older adults (Blazer, 1982; Golden et al., 2009). Even though retirement communities afford social exposure, isolation and depression are still present.

A number of studies exist on the effects of socializing in older adults populations (Fokkema & Knipscheer, 2007; Hirsch, et al., 2000). Studies show that older adults who participate in social and group activities are healthier and happier (Fokkema & Knipscheer, 2007; Hirsch, et al., 2000). Carr reports that residents in retirement communities are likely to want more choices for lifestyle enhancements and socializing opportunities (Carr, 2010). Furthermore, Nehmer et al. propose that older adults can benefit from technologies that increase participation in social life. (Nehmer, Lindenberger & Steinhagen-Thiessen, 2010). This has led to several studies that attempt to address these issues by looking at the development of products to better enable socialization of older adults (Apted, Kay & Quigley, 2006; Iglesias, Segura & Iturburu, 2009). Descheneux et al. and Fudickar et al. both illustrate appointment management tools that address the special demands of elderly and cognitively impaired patients (Descheneaux & Pigot, 2009; Fudickar, Faerber & Schnor, 2011). Iglesias et al. presented a system, which allows users to manage their personal agendas without the use of a keyboard (Iglesias, Segura & Iturburu, 2009). This design is particularly useful for those adults suffering from movement impairment.

Following this line of work, the purpose of this project is to develop a communication technology that enables older adults to be informed about on-going events. More specifically, the goal is to develop an Event Planner (EP) that is a user-driven technology that is capable of handling event information while maintaining a simple and intuitive interface. The significance of this project is to design implementable technologies for retirement community's facilities. Moreover, the goal is to impact these communities by reducing social isolation and improve the quality of life of aging older adults.

PROJECT OVERVIEW

This project seeks to design a user-driven EP that would allow older adults at communities to easily share events. Instead of having specialized staff deciding, setting-up, and advertising on-going events, residents can share events in the community through the use of the communication technology. The communication technology could be used both by members of the community and newcomers planning for special one-time events.

Central to this project is the design of intuitive and simple technologies. In addition, the design must be a technologically simple implementation. As such, this project made use of a *sympathetic design* framework tailored to the design of communication technologies for older adults. The framework is based on the following criteria: 1- product functionality, 2- product physical interface, 3- older adults co-design, 4- universal design principles implementation; 5- product experience; and 6- off-the-shelf technology use.

First, functionality of the products should be simple to use by addressing simple and specific older adults' needs. Second, product interfaces should use physical hardware for interaction, which is an exercise in tangible computing. Physical, tangible computing can afford more accessible interfaces for older adults.

Older adults should be involved as experts in the product design process. There are a number of design research methodologies that can facilitate the user involvement as co-authors in the design process (Martin & Hanington, 2012; Massimi, Baecker. & Wu, 2007). Universal design principles must be exercised in the product design to address a wide range of older adult's abilities (Lidwell, Holden & Butler, 2003; The Center for Universal Design, 1997). There are seven principles for designing accessible products and environments to be usable by all people, to the greatest extent possible, without the need for adaptation or specialized design. These include: 1- Equitable Use; 2-Flexibility in Use; 3- Simple and Intuitive Use; 4-Perceptible Information; 5- Tolerance for Error; 6- Low Physical Effort; and 7- Size and Space for Approach and Use (The Center for Universal Design, 1997). Even though it is not a principle, enjoyment of the product should outweigh effort of use. Lastly, all of the aforementioned should be developed with off-the-shelf technologies. Emphasis should be given to those technologies that have become established so as to avoid becoming obsolete in a short term.

Design Criteria

Following the aforementioned framework, a set of criteria was developed for the EP project. The criteria include:

- The EP should be easy to understand. Actions and methods should be able to be inferred based on their labeling and positioning. There should be no confusion over the purpose of each input. Furthermore, the interaction should be simple enough that the residents can teach each other, or learn within a reasonable amount of time, should the person forget.
- The EP should be easy to use. Any element that the user interacts with should require minimal physical effort. This includes not only the manual effort required to manipulate the input, but also visual effort to see or read the elements.
- The EP interface should make use of tangible components—mechanically operated input elements for digital actions.
- The EP should utilize familiar interfaces in order to aid in accurate recognition by the user.
- The EP should be designed following the seven principles of universal design.
- The EP should be tested with older adults and incorporate their feedback in design iterations.
- The EP should be a stand-alone product. The device should be able to be set-up independently of other systems within the community and should be placed wherever is most convenient to the residents.
- The EP interface should make use of off-the-shelf technologies. This will increase the likelihood of implementation as well as the lifespan of the product. It will also make the interface more familiar and less intimidating to the older adult population.

DESIGN OVERVIEW

The EP is designed to resemble a desk and has embedded technologies that are not visible to the user. Using the EP, users can easily share event information with the community either by using a hand-written or printed flyer. It utilizes the familiarity of a photocopier by requiring users to place the printed event information under a hinged lid embedded in the desk.

After opening the lid to expose the interface, the user selects event information, such as day and time, using sliders. Once the user has properly selected the event information, the cover is lowered and a 'submit' button is pressed. This

Figure 1. Event Planner (EP)

triggers a camera embedded in the desk to take a picture of the event flyer and settings. A camera with a 170° viewing angle is the most suitable for this project (Shenzhen, 2012). as it minimizes the required distance between the camera and the photographed surface (see Figure 2). The camera is connected to a computer that can run image-processing algorithms to identify the user's event information input in real-time.

By following the aforementioned framework the EP was designed to be simple not only for the older adults but also for the image-processing algorithm. The simple graphics of the interface enable the algorithm to quickly and accurately process the information. Because the user is only allowed to configure the interface a set number of ways, the algorithm that identifies the slider locations has an easier task. The location of each option of the date and time can be given a priori, so the only image processing that needs to take place is the identification of the slider coordinates. Pre-built software libraries that are configured on an embedded computer can easily accomplish this task in real-time.

Once processed, the information is displayed by a projector onto a wall in a public area of the retirement community. The event information is organized into a grid system chronologically ordered to let the community residents see all of the upcoming events. This method allows events to be easily integrated into the system and shared with the fellow members of the community.

DESIGN DEVELOPMENT

Following the design criteria, a series of concepts were developed. After initial concept ideation, two full-scale paper prototypes were created. Paper prototypes refer to simple full-scale models that can be made of paper or other available materials to rapidly test an idea (Snyder, C., 2003). A

Figure 2. 170-degree view camera is able to capture the entire screen at a 4.5" distance

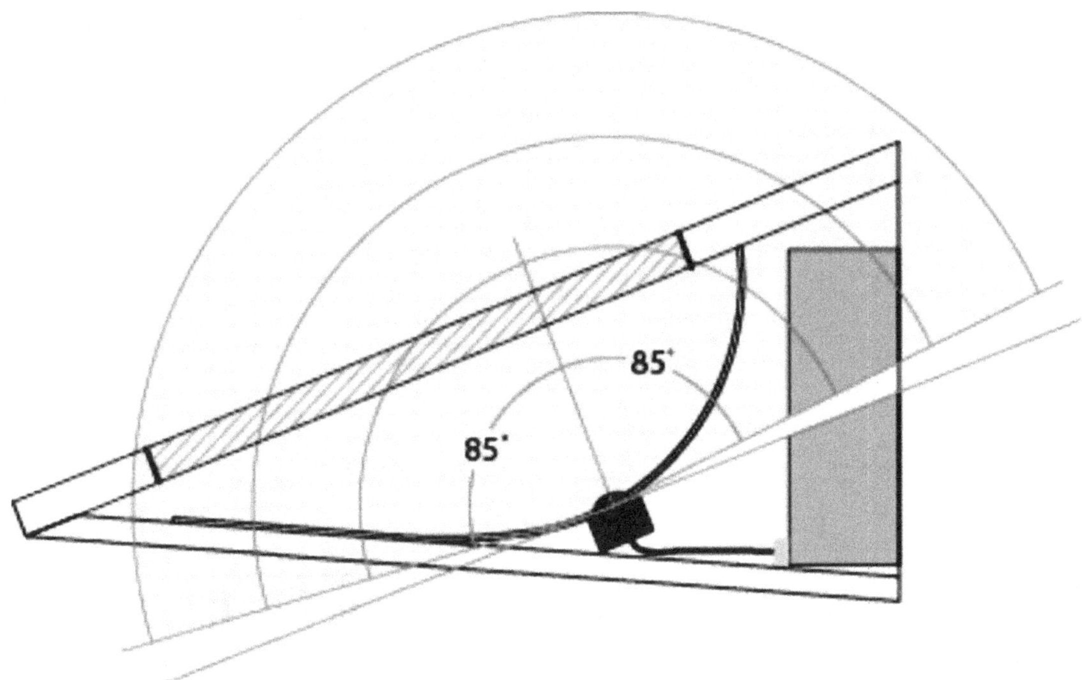

refined version was also prototyped for testing. The prototype was taken to a retirement community in order to conduct a usability testing. The goal of the user study was to test the interface and interaction design including: layout, information inclusion, text size, text location, overall text readability, ease of use, ease of learning, ease of transferring learned knowledge to another individual, and overall feelings. This information was then used to develop a second-round prototype.

Testing Prototype

The design was prototyped using foam core and printed-paper. Only the elements related to the interfaced design were prototyped. The interface of the prototype required the selection of a day and month using sliders and for the selection of time via a clock with moveable arms. The prototype was made to be full-scale in order to accurately assess font size and text spacing (see Figure 3).

The bold, high-contrast black and white colors were used in order to make the device interface more legible and easier to understand. The submit button was only accessible once the lid is closed. A large 11"x11" space allows for a flyer to be placed in either a vertical or horizontal orientation. Prototyped sliders allowed movement for the purpose of selecting a date. Day selection numbers are in 18-point font; other text elements were in 24-point font. Similarly, a functional and movable interactive clock was used for the selection of time.

Design Testing

The prototype was taken to a retirement community in order to conduct a usability testing. The testing group consisted of three volunteers, two of whom were residents at the retirement community, and the third participant was an employee that regularly plans events for the residents. Acronyms were used

Figure 3. Interface considerations during prototyping

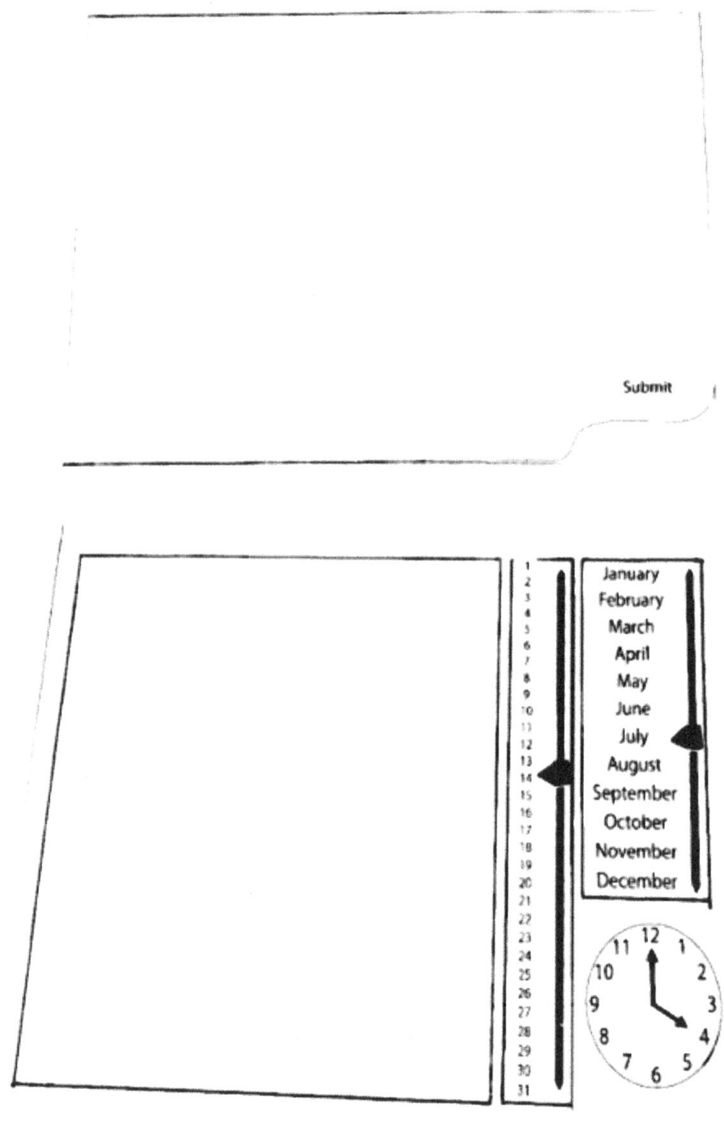

for the participants as follows: residents (P1 and P2) and employee (P3). The usability testing was performed with each participant as a group and lasted approximately one hour each.

The usability testing with participants consisted of four phases. Phase 1 was an exploratory phase where the participant was free to make her own assumptions about the functionality of the device based purely on the design elements. Phase 2 consisted of a guided learning exercise where the purpose of the device was revealed and the steps to accomplish submitting an event to the calendar were demonstrated. Phase 3 consisted of a question and answer session that focused on the specifics regarding the design and functionality. These phases were utilized for P1. The researchers moderated the usability testing with P1. However, P2 usability testing was moderated by P1. This method allowed the researchers to gain insight on validating the usability of the device from passing-knowledge sessions.

At the end of the P2 usability testing, P2 was asked to create a new self-designed event and also answered the same series of questions as P1. P3 usability testing consisted of watching P1 and P2 usability testing as well as creating a new self-designed event. P3 then answered the same series of questions as P1 and P2.

Phase 1: Exploration

As the first phase was an exploratory phase, the researchers presented P1 with the prototype and asked the participant to handle it while talking aloud to decipher its purpose. P1 was encouraged to touch and move anything that could be interacted with and was given a piece of paper with the name of an event, a date, and time written on it in order to aid her in the exploration. However, by putting the date and time inputs on the device itself as the only necessary pieces of information for use, we eliminate the need for guidelines describing what information must be on the paper. This is because the necessary items have already been extracted.

P1 determined that the device was intended for some sort of data entry involving a date and time. The submit button confirmed this interpretation in her mind. P1 also rightly concluded that the large square box was about the same size as a piece of paper. P1 initially placed the piece of paper facing right side up, but then decided that the lid made her think of a scanner and so maybe the paper was supposed to go face down. P1 adjusted the date and time selections to match those written on the paper. P1 then closed the lid and touched the submit label.

Once P1 had concluded her interpretation of the device the researchers explained that the design was intended for event planning. P1 was correct in assuming that the large blank square was intended for a paper and that the paper was expected to have some sort details about the event. P1 was also correct in assuming that the paper must go face down. What's interesting in this case is that P1's assumption was based purely on the presence of the lid.

The results of this phase helped determine the level of intuitiveness of the design. An intuitive design enables more people to participate by limiting the amount of learning that must be accomplished by the user, which is one of the design criteria. However, if learning is required, there should be minimal trial and error as the user moves through the various input options and discovers the nature of the product.

Phase 2: Guided Learning

During Phase 2, the researchers described the meaning and properties of the design. The overall properties of the design, including those components that were not prototyped, such as the desk and use of the projector, were also explained.

Once the mental map had been created, P1 was asked to create and input a new event with no guidance from the researchers. P1 was given a piece of paper and a marker to create her event. P1 talked aloud through the steps of submitting it to the calendar. After selecting the time and date preferences P1 promptly closed the lid and again touched the submit label. These results indicate that P1 was able to successfully create an event.

Phase 3: Question and Answer

While Phases 1 and 2 focused on how the elements of the design related to functionality and meaning, Phase 3 focused on the specific features and design details. Phase 3 consisted of a series of questions asked by the researchers regarding the design. Participants were asked about their opinions regarding the font size, text readability, layout, and how the provided features enabled the user to successfully submit an event. Participants were also asked questions related to their feelings about the device, specifically if they thought that it would be useful, if it was easy to use and understand, and if tasked, how well they thought that they could teach another member of the community how to use it.

While P1 did not have difficulty with the text size, it was recommended that a larger font size might be helpful for other community members. P1 also discussed the possibility of adding a 'repeat' function for those events that occur regularly. When asked about the ease-of-use and learnability P1 claimed that *"it is so easy, anyone could use it."* P1 also felt very confident in teaching other residents how to use the device.

Overall, the results of this phase indicate that participants are enthusiastic at the prospect of actually having a device such as this installed for use in the retirement community.

Phase 4: Passing Knowledge

During Phase 4, P2 and P3 joined the testing session. The goal of this phase was to validate if P1's new knowledge about the device would be properly transferred to another resident. Results of this phase indicate that P1 was able to explain the operation to P2. While P2 expressed less confidence than P1 did after being taught, P2 still agreed to and successfully completed the task of creating and inputting a new event into the system.

Unlike P1, P2 did not regularly plan events for the community. P2 also agreed that the participant could teach another community member how to use the device and had no problems with the font and text size. When asked about the ease-of-use and learnability, P2 responded with high reviews that correlated with her ability to pick up the knowledge from P1.

During the testing, P3 was observing when P1 taught P2 how to use the device. As such, P3 also learned from the residents and was given the opportunity to create and submit an event. P3 routinely plans events for the community and actually used a real upcoming event as the basis for her event. With no further instruction from the researchers, P3 was able to successfully use the device.

When asked about the design details, P3 also expressed a desire to have a 'repeat' option. P3 also had no problem reading the text, but again expressed concerns that others might.

Overall Results

Overall, all participants expressed a desire to have the design at the retirement community. P3 believed it would have a positive impact on the level of happiness and social activity for the residents. P3 commented that aside from resident-sponsored events, such as card games, book readings, or movie screenings, there were also community-sponsored events that were important for the residents to attend. Since few residents had access to or actively used e-mail or other electronic communication devices, the primary method of distributing information was by flyer or word-of-mouth. As such, by having a centralized collection and an organized information display, P3 believed that the implementation of the design would make it easier for both the residents and staff to stay informed and up-to-date on the community's events.

All three participants were happy with the use of sliders as a selection method because it allowed for every option to be visible and was easy to understand. The clock-based time feature was also deemed successful, as the participants were all familiar with viewing time in that manner. When asked about color, the participants thought it best to leave the device in black and white for high-contrast readability.

Design Refinement

Usability testing results were incorporated in the development of a second prototype. New features include larger fonts and additional sliders for year, am/pm, and repeat options. The refined design is approximately 12" in height and 21" in width. All typography was refined to be 27-point font, except the date selection numbers, which are 23-point font size. All typography utilizes a bold sans-serif with high contrast (black and white) to maximize the readability.

Special considerations were given to the overall design features and accessibility of the device. The overall desk size is 46" long and 18" deep. Materials include natural wood finishes and white contrasted by black details. The desk features a built-in container for pens and markers on the surface and a built-in compartment in the side holds blank paper for writing events. A large blank surface yields itself as a workspace for writing out events. The bottom of the desk is angled to accommodate the embedded camera. Because the camera has a 170-degree view angle, the bottom of the desk can be almost flat with a high-point of 30" and a low-point of 28.5". The design sticks out from the wall 18.5" at a height of 30" off the ground. These measurements respond to the need for the design to be wheelchair accessible (see Figure 4). Total overall height reaches 38". Highest point of items is 36.4". Lastly, the design is connected to a projector, which is mounted overhead and displays the calendar.

CONCLUSION

Designing communication technologies for older adults in retirement communities still remains a challenge. On one hand, using digital technologies can significantly contribute to improved interactions in a community. On the other hand, adoption of such technologies can be challenging for the older adult population due to the nature of the technology. This chapter presented the research, development, and findings of a communication technology, the EP, developed to enable older adults living in retirement communities to share public events. This project utilized a *sympathetic*

Figure 4. Accessible design considerations for implementation

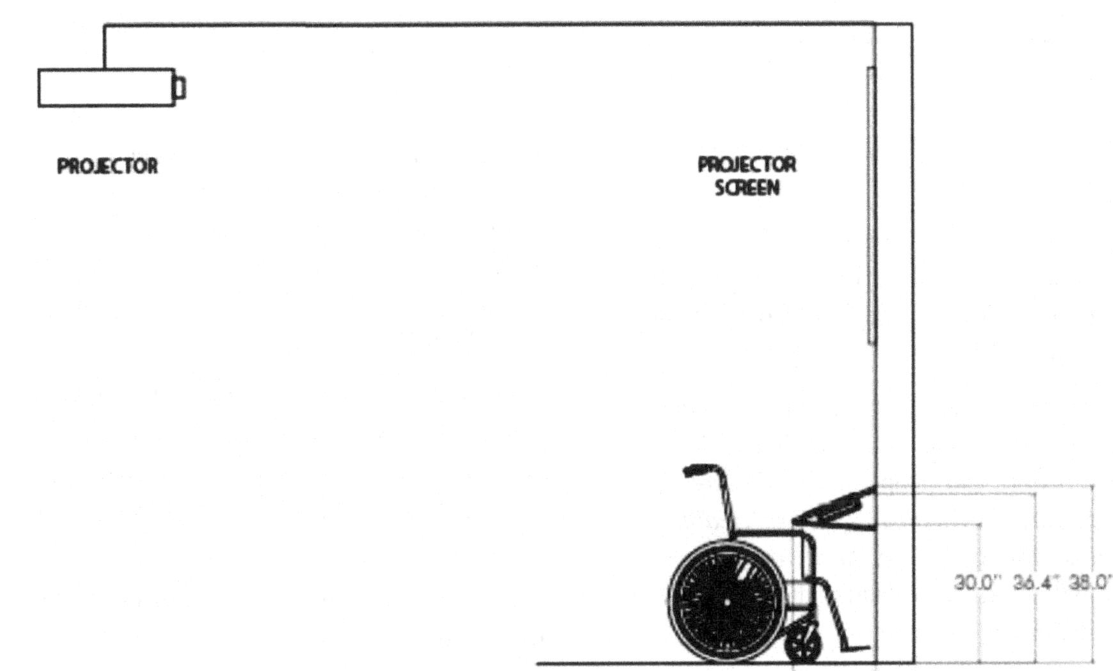

design framework that guided the design process. This project showcases that event planning technologies are possible and adoptable for older adults if properly designed. In future work, tests with larger groups should be performed to further refine the design. Future studies should also emphasize the use of auditory feedback during the use of such a device.

REFERENCES

Apted, T., Kay, J., & Quigley, A. (2006). Tabletop sharing of digital photographs for the elderly. In *Proceedings of SIGCHI Conference on Human Factors in Computing Systems*. Montréal, Canada: ACM.

Blazer, D. (1982). Social support and mortality in an elderly community population. *American Journal of Epidemiology*, *115*(5), 684–694. PMID:7081200

Calvin, C. (2012). *Welcome to Presbyterian homes of Georgia*. Retrieved from http://www.calvincourt.org

Carr, A. (2010). *What does the future hold for the senior living industry?* Retrieved from http://progressiveretirement.wordpress.com/2010/06/29/what-does-the-future-hold-for-the-senior-living-industry/

Center for Universal Design. (1997). *The principles of universal design*. Retrieved from http://www.ncsu.edu/ncsu/design/cud/about_ud/udprinciplestext.htm

Descheneaux, C., & Pigot, H. (2009). Interactive calendar to help maintain social interactions for elderly people and people with mild cognitive impairments. In *Ambient Assistive Health and Wellness Management in the Heart of the City*. Heidelberg, Germany: Springer. doi:10.1007/978-3-642-02868-7_15

Federal Interagency Forum on Aging-Related Statistics. Older Americans (2012). Key indicators of well-being. Washington, DC: Author.

Fokkema, C., & Knipscheer, K. (2007). Escape loneliness by going digital: A Quantitative and qualitative evaluation of a dutch experiment using ECT to overcome loneliness among older adults. *Aging & Mental Health*, *11*(5), 8. doi:10.1080/13607860701366129 PMID:17882587

Fudickar, S., Faerber, S., & Schnor, B. (2011). KopAL appointment user-interface: An evaluation with elderly. In *Proceedings of 4th International Conference on Pervasive Technologies Related to Assistive Environments*. IEEE.

Golden, J. et al. (2009). Loneliness, social support networks, mood and cellbeing in community-dwelling elderly. *International Journal of Geriatric Psychiatry*, *24*(7), 694–700. doi:10.1002/gps.2181 PMID:19274642

Hirsch, T., et al. (2000). The ELDer project: Social, emotional, and environmental factors in the design of eldercare technologies. In *Proceedings of the 2000 Conference on Universal Usability*. New York: ACM Press.

Iglesias, R., Segura, N., & Iturburu, M. (2009). The elderly interacting with a digital agenda through an RFID pen and a touch screen. In *Proceedings of the 1st ACM SIGMM International Workshop on Media Studies and Implementations that Help Improving Access to Disabled Users*. New York: ACM Press.

Lidwell, W., Holden, K., & Butler, J. (2003). *Universal principles of design: 100 ways to enhance usability, influence perception, increase appeal, make better design decisions, and teach through design*. Rockport.

Lohr, S. (2012). The age of big data. *The New York Times*.

Martin, B., & Hanington, B. (2012). *Universal methods of design: 100 ways to research complex problems, develop innovative ideas, and design effective solutions*. Beverly Hills, CA: Rockport Publishers.

Massimi, M., Baecker, R., & Wu, M. (2007). Using participatory activities with seniors to critique, build, and evaluate mobile phones. In *Proceedings of the 9th International ACM SIGACCESS Conference on Computers and Accessibility*. New York: ACM Press.

Moore, G. (1965). Cramming more components onto integrated circuits. *Electronics Magazine*, *38*(8), 4.

Nehmer, J., Lindenberger, & Steinhagen-Thiessen, E. (2010). Aging and technology—Friends, not foes. *The Journal of Gerontopsychology and Geriatric Psychiatry*, *23*(2), 55–57. doi:10.1024/1662-9647/a000016

Shenzhen. (2012). *3rd eye electronics co., L. 170 degree view 12V mini security camera*. Retrieved from http://www.alibaba.com/product-gs/524362888/170_degree_view_12V_mini_security.html

Snyder, C. (2003). *Paper prototyping: The fast and easy way to design and refine user interfaces*. San Francisco, CA: Morgan Kaufmann.

Chapter 45
Home Automation by Brain-Computer Interface

Eduardo G. Nieva
Facultad de Ciencias Exactas, Físicas y Naturales, Universidad Nacional de Córdoba, Argentina

María F. Peralta
Facultad de Ciencias Exactas, Físicas y Naturales, Universidad Nacional de Córdoba, Argentina

Diego A. Beltramone
Facultad de Ciencias Exactas, Físicas y Naturales, Universidad Nacional de Córdoba, Argentina

ABSTRACT

In the present work, the authors use the Brain Computer Interface technology to allow the dependent persons the utilization of the basic elements of their house, such as turning on and turning off lamps, rolling up and down a roller shutter, or switching on the heating system. For doing this, it is necessary to automate these devices and to centralize its managing in a platform, which constitutes a domotics system. In order to achieve this, the authors have used the MindWave NeuroSky ® commercial device. It is affordable, portable, and wireless, and senses and delivers the computer the electroencephalographic signals produced in the frontal lobe and the levels of attention, relaxation, and blinking to the computer. In order to determine the efficiency of the obtained signals a test software was designed, which verified the operation´s device with different persons. The authors conclude that the easiest way to control the attention levels is concentrating on a certain point, and the way to control the relaxation levels is by closing the eyes. As a second step, the authors develop a software that takes the signal from the EEG (Electro Encephalo Graphy) sensor, processes it, and sends signals via USB to an Arduino board, which is associated with electronics that complies the different tasks. The user chooses the action by managing the attention levels. When they are higher than a particular threshold value, the action is executed. In order to disable this action, the user must lower the threshold level and overcome it again. This is the simplest and fastest way to handle, but it brings several problems: if the user concentrates for any other reason and this signal exceeds the threshold, it causes the activation of an involuntary action. To solve this problem, the authors use a three variables combination that can become independent of each other thru training properly. These variables are attention, meditation, and blink. When you comply with the three simultaneous previously established conditions, the action is executed, and when they return to fulfill the conditions, the action is deactivated. The software also has the feature of personalizing its conditions, so it can be best for any user, even a novice one.

DOI: 10.4018/978-1-4666-4490-8.ch045

Figure 1. Connection between two types of technologies: BCI and Domotics

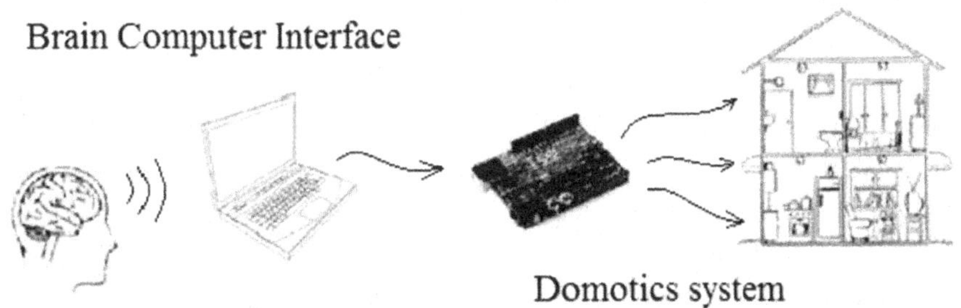

INTRODUCTION

In Argentina there are a significant number of people with any type of motoric disability, leaving them unable to act autonomously in their daily lives. Considering this problem, we use the Brain Computer Interface (BCI) technology to allow these persons control the basic elements of theirs home. In order to do this, it is necessary to make an adaptation of those elements or devices – what it si called an automation of them – and a centralized management by the user on a single platform. Usually this is called a Domotics System. Therefore, we can say that there is a connection between kind of technologies: BCI and Domotics.

OBJECTIVES

Overall Objective

Allow an independent performance of people with difficulties or motor disabilities (but with an intact intellectual activity) into their home, and to improve their keepers services helping the tasks accomplishment by an automation an access of the house´s present devices through a Brain Computer Interface.

Specific Objectives

1. To study the operation of the Acquisition Signals' device, MindWave.
2. To design the implementation system.
3. To make a software application, including:
    a. Acquisition of the sensed values.
    b. Based on these values, to execute the choice of a particular action (such as turn on a lamp).
    c. Send to an Arduino board a value representing the selected action.
4. To program an Arduino:
    a. To get the value that represents the action selected from the previous software.
    b. To set the corresponding state (1 or 0) in every pin of the Arduino board according to the action to perform. Each pin will have a device housing associated.
    c. To modify the operation of various devices located in a conventional home so they can be handled by the Arduino.

Target Users

Although the system can be used by anyone for fun, leisure or systems optimization, potential users and for whom this project is oriented are dependent persons, who have lost their autonomy because of a disability acquired secondary accidents, injuries or illnesses involving serious motoric problems and impeding their natural communication with the outside world.

According with Roberto Hornero these people can be classified according to their pathology, lesion or functional impairment in two groups (Sánchez, 2011):

1. Those with degenerative diseases, where the muscle function decreases over time, reaching complete movement loss. As an example we can find neuromuscular diseases, such as amyotrophic lateral sclerosis (ALS) and neuromuscular dystrophy.
2. Those without degenerative diseases, where there is not a muscular paralysis progression. This happens in apoplexies (better known stroke), brain injury, spinal cord injury or myelopathies and amputations.

In all of these cases, the individual cognitive activity is usually not affected, but their peripheral nerve routes, neuromusculars plates and muscles. As Roberto Hornero Sánchez says, in more complex diseases, such as high quadriplegia, the person loses almost completely the ability to perform voluntary movements and stays completely trapped in his body (Sánchez, 2011): unable to perform any physical interaction, in the conventional way, with his environment. Thus, as today therapies that can completely cure the damage physiology doesn't exist, it is necessary to implement a new form of communication with the environment that does not depend on the functioning of the nervous and muscular pathways. This interaction between the brain and the environment constitutes the technology called Brain Computer Interface, where once the subject is able to interact with the machine, already it can handle any device that is available to it.

To become aware of the incidence of these disorders in society and the need to obtain a solution, we will present some information on its presence in Argentina:

Table 1. Pathologies that generate motor disability

Pathology	Incidence in Argentina	Reference
Multiple sclerosis	18-20 cases every 100.000 habitantes inhabitants.	Kollmann & Simeoni (2012)
ELA	About 2000 inhabitants.	Rodriguez, et al. (2011)
Muscular dystrophy	1 every 3500 born alive per year.	Kollmann & Simeoni (2012)
Muscular dystrophy	34,4% of Major of 18 years - 1 ACV every 4 minutes.	Kollmann & Simeoni (2012)

MATERIALS AND METHODS

Brain Computer Interface

This technology constitutes a method of interaction of the persons with the computer, which implies an alternative communication for individuals with significant motor disabilities, because it does not depend on the operation of normal output pathways of the brain to the peripheral nerves and muscles (Gentiletti, Taberning, & Acevedo, 2007). This human-machine interaction is able to translate the user's intentions in a real interaction with a physical or virtual world (Minguez, 2012).

The fundament of a BCI is the measurement of the cerebral activity, his processing to get hold of the characteristics of interest and according to these, the realization of a user desired action.

Software

In order to process the signals a software in language Java using the IDE Netbeans 7.2 was developed. This software consists of three blocks: Acquisition, Storage and Processing.

Signal Acquisition

To take the electrical signals that occur in the brain with every thought we use the commercial device MindWave ® from NeuroSky's company, for being an inexpensive, portable device, of easy use for the entire population (without special knowledge), wireless, open source which is provided as a development kit.

Figure 2. Brain Computer Interface

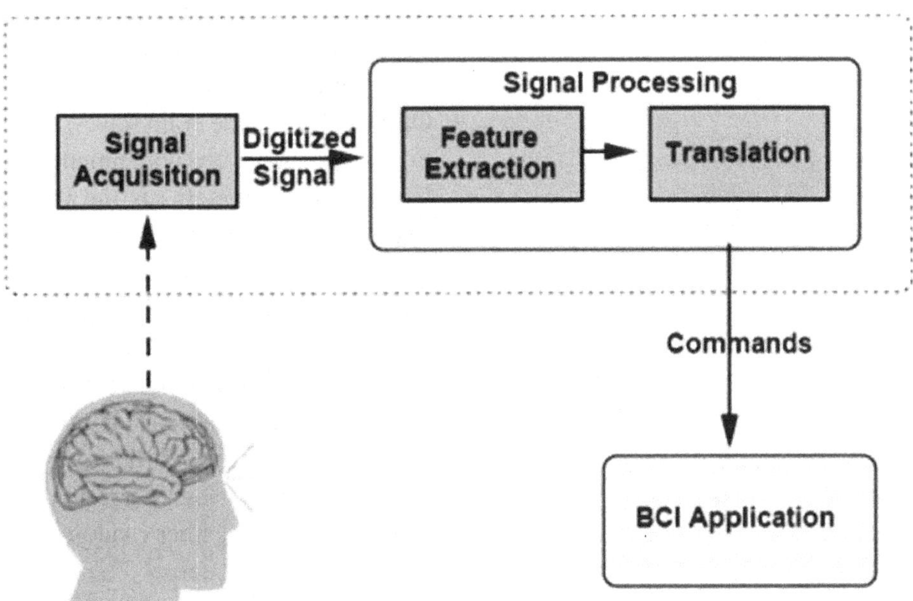

Figure 3. Block diagram of the developed software

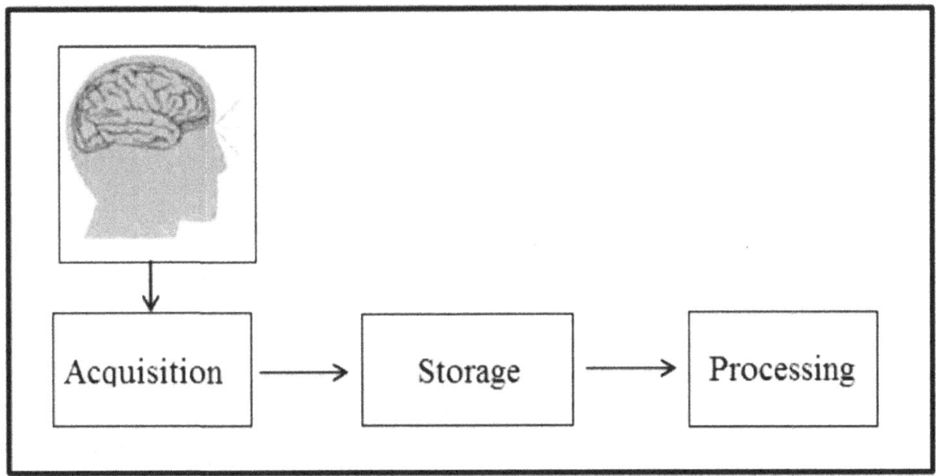

The values that we use in our work, which are among those returned by the device, are the levels of *concentration, relaxation* and *blink detection*.

The prefrontal cortex, in the front of the brain, is where the high thought takes place. The emotions, states of mind, of concentration, etc. are all dominant in this area. This is the reason for placing the main sensor of the MindWave in a position known in the neurosciences as FP1, specifically in the"10-20" distribution.

Different brain states are the result of different neuronal interaction patterns. These patterns lead to the formation of waves which are characterized by specific amplitudes and frequencies. For ex-

Figure 4. Mindwave

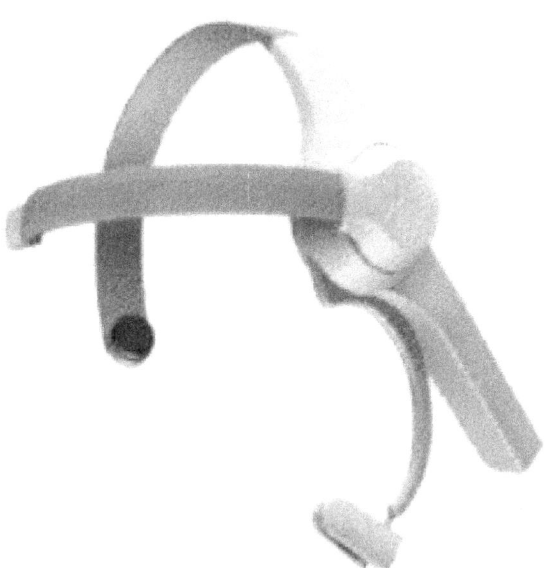

ample, brain waves between 12 and 30 Hz, are called beta waves, they are associated with concentration, while waves from 8 to 12 Hz, alpha waves, are associated with calm and relaxation. Often, eclipsing the brain waves, muscle contraction is also associated with unique wave patterns. Isolating these patterns is the way NeuroSky's devices detect blinks.

The only sensor in FP1 provides a high degree of freedom. MindWave can simultaneously measure multiple brain states. All the electrical devices, including computers, lamps, sockets, etc. generate a certain level of "electrical noise" in the environment. This noise is often sufficiently strong to hide the brainwaves. As a result, EEG's laboratory devices will gather random readings when

Figure 5. Constitutive elements of the Mindwave device

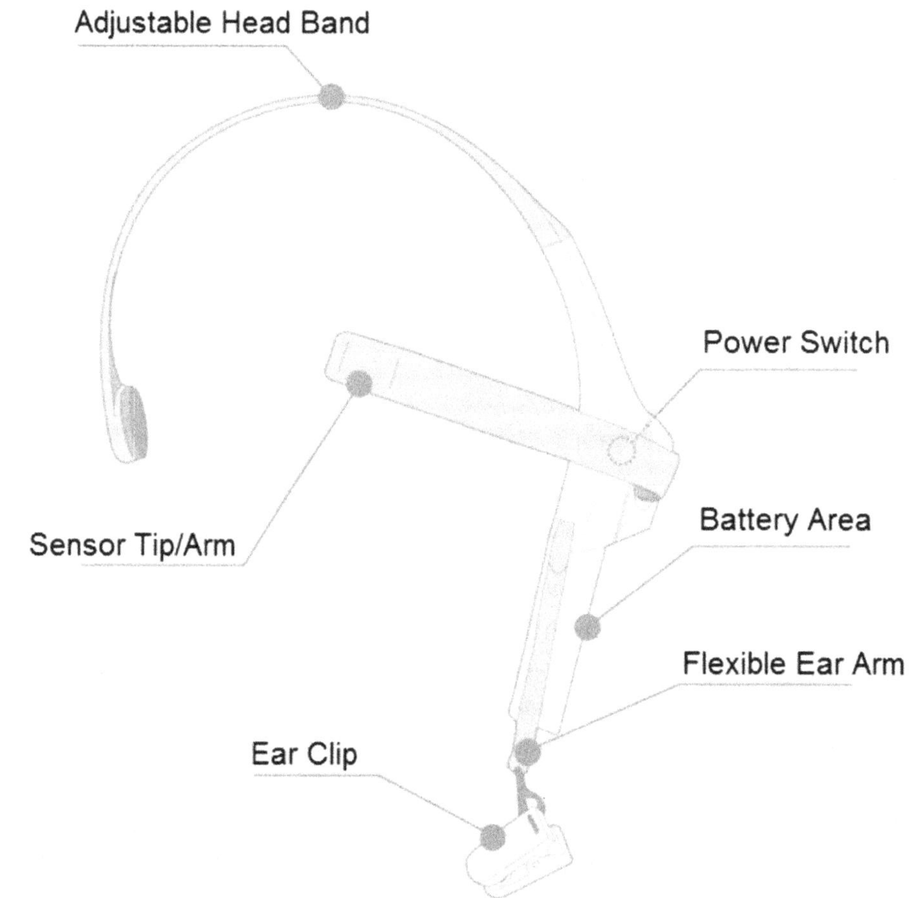

both the electrode of reference and the primary electrode are connected to an object which is not emitting brainwaves. The traditional clinical EEG has avoided this problem by measuring the brainwaves in strictly controlled environments, where there are no lights, devices, etc. those interfere with the EEG signal. Furthermore, in order to increase the brain wave signal they a thick gel that increases the conductivity is used. Given that EEG devices have migrated from the laboratory to the homes, where the majority of the people not have rooms devoid of electronic interference, nor want to apply a conductive liquid each time they use the device, the company has focused theirs efforts to make devices with sensors free of gels and in noisy environments without mitigate these challenges.

This innovative technology uses dry electrodes (without gel) bathed in gold, unlike the traditional electrodes with gel that they are of silver - silver chloride. In the next image we can appreciate that the differences between the signals obtained with one and another sensor are negligible. It is demonstrated that is obtained 96% accuracy with respect to the configuration of a conventional EEG (NeuroSky ®, Inc., 2009).

Part of NeuroSky's development includes the cancellation of the noise cancellation. For this it uses signal amplification; filters to eliminate sound frequencies known as muscles, pulse and electrical devices; Notch filters to remove noise from the power supply, which varies from 50 to 60 Hz depending on the geography of the world geography.

Another sector of NeuroSky's development consists of the electrical engineering. The extrapolation of the brain wave signals from the noise requires both a reference point as a grounding circuit. Grounding makes the tension body was the same as that of the handset. The reference is in use for reducing the environmental noise across the process known as common mode rejection. The earlobe is a location that experiences the same ambient noise that the main sensor located in the

Figure 6. In blue we see the signal obtained by the sensor MindWave. In red we see the same signal obtained with a conventional gel sensor.

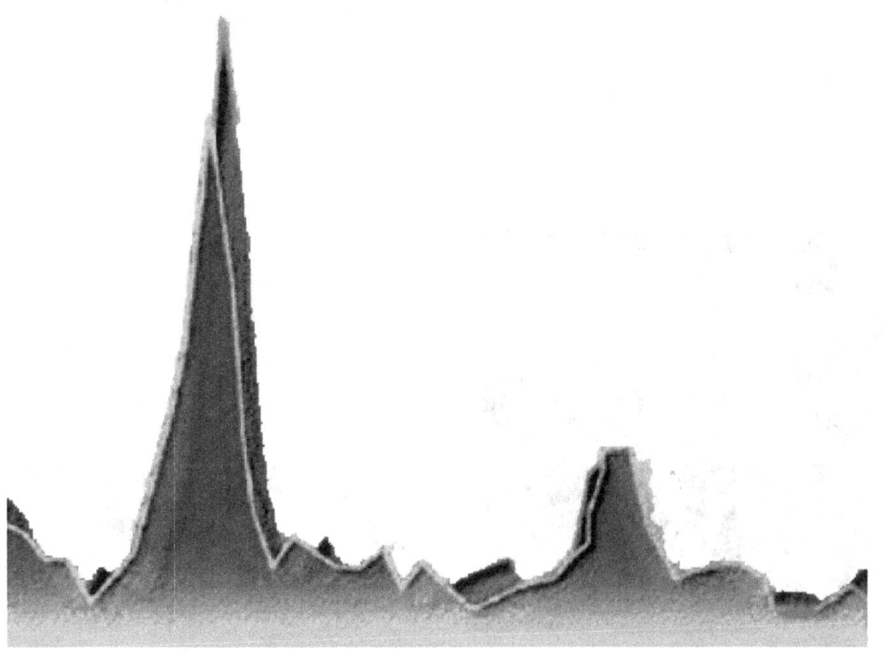

front, but with a minimum of neuronal activity. Therefore, it is crucial that the connection of the ear was firmly tight.

Storage

This stage is only a control way for further processing. It is very useful because in a future it is possible to evaluate the managing and growth of the users at the moment of using the program.

The advantage of storing the information takes root in that in a future, with the quantity sufficient of samples, the program can be optimized, or in handling otherwise the algorithms used for the accused of the signs.

The statistics provided by the program help to build interfaces friendlier, more intuitive and accessible, chasing the beginning of the universal design (Universal-Design, 2012).

Signal Processing

Once the signal arrives to the computer wireless, next thing to do receive the data packet, delivered by NeuroSky ®, which selects the levels of attention, meditation and blink. Once inside the system, it is possible to proceed in two ways, chosen by the user: the first is to only use a signal provided by the Mindwave, such Attention, and when a value exceeds certain threshold an action is executed, for example to turn on a lamp. To generate the opposite effect it is only necessary to have signals below the threshold level. This is the simplest and fastest way to handle the software, but this facility has the consequence that any interaction with the media increasing the level of concentration beyond the threshold will enable or disenable the action, but not necessarily by the the user´s will.

To solve this disadvantage that appears it was decided to incorporate a combinations structure based on three principal signals that the Mindwave delivers. We began analyzing what kind of signal is easier to control and we conclude that the blinking was a very controllable variable. And using a combination of the variables Attention and Meditation in different proportions we achieve to create a "key" in order that the action is activated or deactivates by major difficulty, but that it is not impossible to perform.

In summary, when it generates a combination of the three signals Attention, Meditation and blinking simultaneously, it is executed or is disabled the action. For this to be accessible, the Attention and Meditation values are fully configurable to any user who is starting to use the application, for most novice he was, he can use the program.

Figure 7. Arduino UNO. Left: upper front. Right: Base Plate.

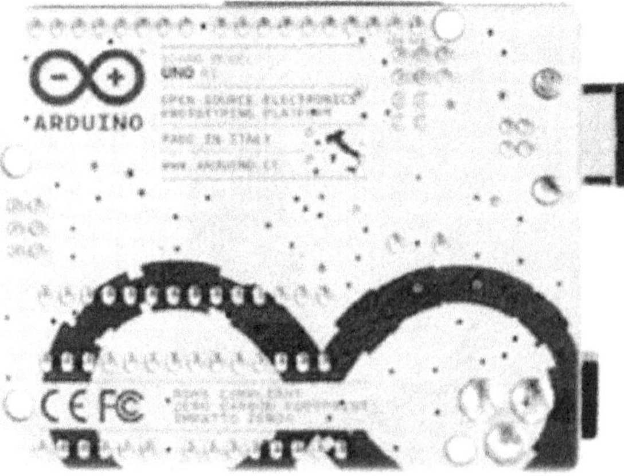

Home Automation

To achieve the ultimate objective-devices management in the home-through Concentration, Meditation and Blinking levels, atually we are progressing in the software development. It consists of a series of actions that can be selected according to a particular combination of thresholds of Attention, Meditation and Blinking, which it can be personalized for each user, according to their ability to achieve those values. Once the action was selected, the program sends a specific signal to an Arduino UNO board.

Arduino board is a prototype of an open-source electronics platform, based on a flexible hardware and software and easy to use. It has 13 digital and 6 analog pins that can be configured as input (the platform checks the values and according to them performs the function for which it has been programmed) or output (the platform deliver from 0 to 5V, according to their programming). This allows you to connect it to a lot of devices, handle them.

In our application, the board receives signals from the home management software according to the action selected by the user, and across the output pins turns on or off the selected device. The input pins are used to obtain several sensors values, as a feedback that allows the verification if the correct devices operation and user-selected actions.

Until now we have tested the performance of the following actions, by connecting simultaneously with Arduino:

1. Turn on and turn off a lamp.
2. Going up and down a curtain.
3. Switch on and switch off a fan.

It is planned to implement a temperature sensor, a light sensor, handling various illumination intensities and the management of a television remote control to complete the prototype system.

CONCLUSION

Considering the objectives, we can say that we have a good comprehension not only about the Mindwave functioning but also the ways of managing to pay Attention and Relaxation modes, which are keys to handle the actions inside the program. The advantage is that our software is highly configurable, making it more versatile and accessible, thus putting it to a lot of users who need it.

The electronics used for the automatic are simple and easy to obtain and all codes are open by GLPv3 license, so you can get to any developer who is interested in the topic, both to improve the software or user requirements.

Finally, the software is being developed, so clinical test in patients with motor disabilities were not done yet. In the near future it will incorporate a training system that will be more flexible, for that the learning curve was such that the user performs actions in less time.

REFERENCES

Arduino. (2012). Retrieved from http://arduino.cc/en/Main/ArduinoBoardUno

Gentiletti, G., Taberning, C., & Acevedo, R. (2007). *Interfaces cerebro computadora: Definición, tipos y estado actual*. Paraná: Universidad Nacional de Entre Ríos.

Imserso. (2012). Retrieved from http://www.imserso.es/InterPresent1/groups/imserso/documents/binario/08_18idi.pdf

Kollmann, A., & Simeoni, E. (2012). *Exoesqueleto de miembro superior con detección de intención*. Córdoba: Universidad Nacional de Córdoba.

Minguez, J. (2012). *Tecnología de interfaz cerebro-computador. Università di Saragozza. NeuroSky®. (2009). Brain wave signal (EEG)*. NeuroSky.

NeuroSky. (2012). Retrieved from http://www.NeuroSky.com/

Rodriguez, G., Fulgenzi, E., & Milstein, C. (2011). *Día mundial de la esclerosis lateral amiotrófica (ELA)*. Academic Press.

Sánchez, R. (2011). *Brain computer interface (BCI) aplicado al control de dispositivos demóticos para incrementar la accesibilidad de las personas dependientes en el hogar digital y su entorno habitual Domo-BCI*. Valladolid: Universidad de Valladolid.

Universal-Design. (2012). Retrieved from http://www.universaldesign.com/

Chapter 46
The Excellence of the Video Games:
Past and Present

Francisco V. Cipolla-Ficarra
ALAIPO – AINCI, Spain and Italy

ABSTRACT

This chapter presents a diachronic vision of the evolution of the main classical games in the computer followed by a look at computer-assisted teaching until the mid-nineties. Later, systems aimed at education in off-line and online support are analyzed simultaneously. Through this diachronic study, how many design features have endured until the present day can be seen.

INTRODUCTION

Playing is one of the most important activities of the human being, it is an experience of freedom and at the same time it teaches to manoeuvre inside the framework of some given rules. The human being plays because he/she is amused by it, it entertains us, it encourages us to tackle new challenges, such as daily learning.

The interactive systems and the communicability in the design open up many chances of research from the pedagogical point of view such as the human-computer interaction. In the communicability lies implicit the cognitive principle (textuality), with the perception (images and sounds). Both converge towards a biunivocal relationship named "edutainment". That is, a term that derives from education + entertainment.

Edutainment is a way in which education from the point of view of the understanding of the information and the educational contents joins entertainment, under a prospect of collaboration. The cognitive sciences are also interested in learning and emotions (Beverly, 2000; Cipolla-Ficarra& Cipolla-Ficarra, 2009), especially such as the entertainment and surprise, which play an important role.

It is not in vain that the multimedia interactive systems aimed at entertainment must include in their dynamical and static means contents to foster

DOI: 10.4018/978-1-4666-4490-8.ch046

the knowledge of the different sciences. That is why since the early multimedia interactive systems in off-line support in the 90s it has been intended to fulfil a set of secondary and main goals for the smallest users, such as:

- Activities related to reading ability: language understanding and assimilation of the main language difficulties.
- Stimuli for creativity: listen or composing music sounds, reading of tales, drawing, attention to the science world, etc.
- To boost the notions of mathematics: measure, count, calculate, recognition of the sets, etc.
- Develop the coordination of the hand and the eye.

In other terms, it is considered as edutainment that software that is used with didactic purposes but which contains elements from the cognitive model in the design belonging to the videogames. Through a series of strategies are developed cognitive skills which stimulate attention and motivation in environments recreated by the computer. In order for an educational game to fulfil the function of educating by entertaining it must respond to some of the main features which are next listed:

- The structure and the access to the information must stimulate the player, better if the goals to be reached are established.
- Keep the maximum of known elements by the potential users, especially in the construction of the interface metaphor.
- Variety of non-repetitive contents. That is, to foster the quality attribute of usability of information in the interactive systems, by resorting to the notion of perspective, for instance. There is also a reference to the attribute of richness in the dynamic and static means to foster the learning process in regard to the potential users. For instance, at the moment of looking up an interactive encyclopaedia a child can appreciate the animation and sound effects, whereas an adult, because of time reasons regards them as a kind of waste of time at the moment of accessing what he is searching.
- Use of world-renowned characters such as those stemming from literature, animation cinema in the computers, comic, etc. In the case of virtual characters created for a given interactive system, all of them should be extremely well-made, that is, with an elegant style and in agreement with the content.
- Include several games and didactic activities in relation to the potential user's skills, without causing any frustration in the user.

Currently in many education centres in Southern Europe the reigning educational culture regards computer playing as harmful to the young users, especially in the first years in which they attend schools. Contrary to this, the studies made by Piaget, for instance, have demonstrated that the processes that guide the game and those which foster learning are similar (Piaget, 1993). In the behaviourist conception of people, reality is not a discovery, but rather a continuous construction of people. That is, it is based on the development of an asymmetrical model instead of a single model of a magisterial nature. Under this perspective playing is not a kind of escape of the materiality of the present, but rather a specific dimension (neither spatial nor temporal) of the behaviour that allows to rebuild reality. It is a space where to exercise for the pupils to live in society. That is why it is necessary that there is an intersection between the real world of the child and his activities outside school.

TOWARDS A CLASSIFICATION OF THE VIDEO GAMES

In the last years of the 20th century the commercial factor also had a negative influence on the classification of the interactive systems in Southern Europe, because they ignored the content and the potential users. The correct thing is to talk of content. This, linked to the other design categories: presentation or layout, content, navigation, structure, compatibility or conectibility and panchronic (Cipolla-Ficarra & Cipolla-Ficarra, 2008; Cipolla-Ficarra, et al., 2011) has for instance allowed firms such as Microsoft to be pioneers in this field. They, since the early 90s and until the first years of the new millennium established the first non-commercial classification criteria through their off-line multimedia encyclopaedias, that is, guided by the contents and the goals they pursued, in the interaction of the potential users: consultation, entertainment, study, etc. Next we present some sets and subsets of contents for videogames that take into account some variables related to human-centered design, such as the age of the potential users, the storage support of the programs and the databases used for the interactive system such as their diachronic factor.

Role and Adventure Games

This is one of the groups of videogames that has undergone a greater transformation in the last 25 years, especially with the dynamic means and the support of the interactive systems. Before the floppy files were downloaded in the hard disk of the computer, then there was a transition to the CD-ROM and DVD with the possibility of copying them in the hard disk for a greater speed in the interaction. Obviously the amount of 2D and 3D animations and special effects, such as the quality of audio have increased with the passing of time. From one interaction with the computer keyboard there has been a switch to the mouse and the joystick. Currently there is a tendency towards other interaction systems, such as the voice, the eye movement, touch, etc. although this last way of interaction was developed decades ago, especially in the tourist information standpoints or in the cash dispensers of the banking institutions, and which currently is being proposed in the entertainment systems of the immersive multimedia, for instance. These videogames belong to several genres of content: police, magical, historical, literary, artistic, etc. In them, the user is transported to a virtual world where reality tends to be more by simulation than by emulation. Some examples of videogames which have been historic are: Blade Runner, Final Fantasy, Monkey Island, Tomb Raider among others.

Action Games

In this set of games we can establish several subsets:

- **Run and Jump:** Is about those videogames where the user has the mission of fleeing risk situations. A couple of classical examples are Rayman or Supermario. Their origins are in the tridimensional screens of the computers of the 80s and many of them have been taken to tridimensional environments for the interaction in the Net or in multimedia phones, for instance, Asterix and Cleopatra (Gameloft), a videogame with 11 different levels.
- **Shooters:** Here lies the origin of the controversy among educators, parents and young users of the video games, since they are considered in many cases the epicentre of the violence in high school institutions. Here the user must almost always shoot at everything that comes into sight. Although the tridimensional graphics are not of high quality to gain speed in the movements, they have been increasing the final rendering of the scenes, and of some objects that make it up, creating the optical illusion

in the user that they are moving in a 3D space. The weaponry is multifarious as the enemies who range from people to robots, immersed in real landscapes, semi-real or science-fiction. Some of these videogames that are inserted in the current subset are: Quake, Doom and Half Life.

- **Sports:** These are the ones that have allowed to give a quality breakthrough in the interaction of the videogames since they have put an end to passivity of the movement in the users whereas they are interacting, such as is the case of many Wii products of the Nintendo enterprise. However, already in their origins these videogames required a great interaction in the early 90s through the keyboard or joystick for soccer, basketball, golf, motorcycling, car racing, etc. Later on the graphic quality has been perfected, until reaching the quality of a television image, and the great breakthrough were the Nintendo interactive systems, for instance. Some good examples are the following videogames: NBA, FIFA, Personal Trainer and Dakar Rally.
- **Classical:** Usually they have their origin in the real world. Inside them it is feasible to establish the following three subsets:
    - **Game Rooms Emulators:** They had their origins in the real gambling slot machines rooms. Tetris, labyrinths and wall breaker.
    - **Table Games:** This is about existing games such as cards, checkers, chess, monopoly, etc. They allow group playing but also to measure the ability of each player against the computer.
    - **Logical Games:** In this subset are the memory games, puzzles, didactical quizzes, sudoku, mainly. Currently we see how some of them have been transferred to the videoconsoles to exercise language, logic memory and intelligence, especially among the elderly.
    - **Simulation Games:** Although a videogame is a simulation of something else, the players and also the designers and the videogames programmers know very well which of are those that are included in this set. Many of them derive from flight simulators such as the Microsoft Flight Simulator 2004 or Racer Free Car Simulation (Berens & Howard, 2002; Eberly, 2001). That is, these are games that reproduce as faithfully as possible those situations that must be faced in real life, from driving a car to flying a plane to managing a city as a mayor, etc. In regard to the city and its inhabitants, there are games which have evolved jointly with graphic computer science, and have used to the utmost the latest news in software and hardware, such as in the case of Simcity. Without any doubt an excellent example of what a videogame for teenagers and adults should be like, in the simulators category. Its author Will Wright has allowed the development of other similar products such as Simearth and SimAnt (Eberly, 2001).

SIMCITY AND THE SIMS: A NEW ERA FOR VIDEO GAMES

In the decade of the 90s the users started to leave the keyboards, mice and joysticks plugged to the PCs to interact with the videogames to switch to the new support of the videoconsoles by two international manufacturers such as Sony and Nintendo. It was the time of the launching of the videogames and which increased exponentially the multimedia industrial sector in Europe, for instance. Some tridimensional interactive games such as: Tomb Raider, Monkey Island, Dune, Doom, SimCity, etc. with a low quality in rendering the animated images in the first versions served as the access to Internet of millions of users. These are especially the games belonging to the simulators category, which are called in the USA "Godgame", that is, the games where a god is personified. Almost all of them have had in their origins the CD-ROM support (Civilization, Afterlife, etc.) and some of them have evolved in the later versions in DVD and Internet. One of the more widespread videogames at that time was the SimCity, programmed in 1985, whose programmes and videogames files were stored on a floppy. Its mentor was Will Wright. He is regarded as a pioneer in the simulation games (Eberly, 2001).

In 1989 international commercialization started through the software house Maxis. Will Wright and Jeff Braun founded that enterprise in '87. Between 1990 and 1991 other multimedia interactive systems appeared which were aimed at entertainment and which belonged to the category of the simulators: SimEarth and SimAnt. The latter is an interesting good example of the life of the ants in their anthill. In the meantime, the versions of SimCity kept on being updated, using the new novelties of hardware and graphic computer science, animated or static, such as were SimCity 2000 and 3000. At the same time there were other novelties inside the current videogames category and by the same software company, such as SimTower and SimLife. In 1997 it was sold to the Electronic Arts company (www.ea.com) and Will Wright was the chief designer of the videogames.

The secret of SimCity consisted partly in the fact of building cities whose inhabitants were pleased with the services provided by the authorities of the community to which they belonged (in this sense it can be said that it has been a

Figure 1. First SimCity –floppy version (1989)

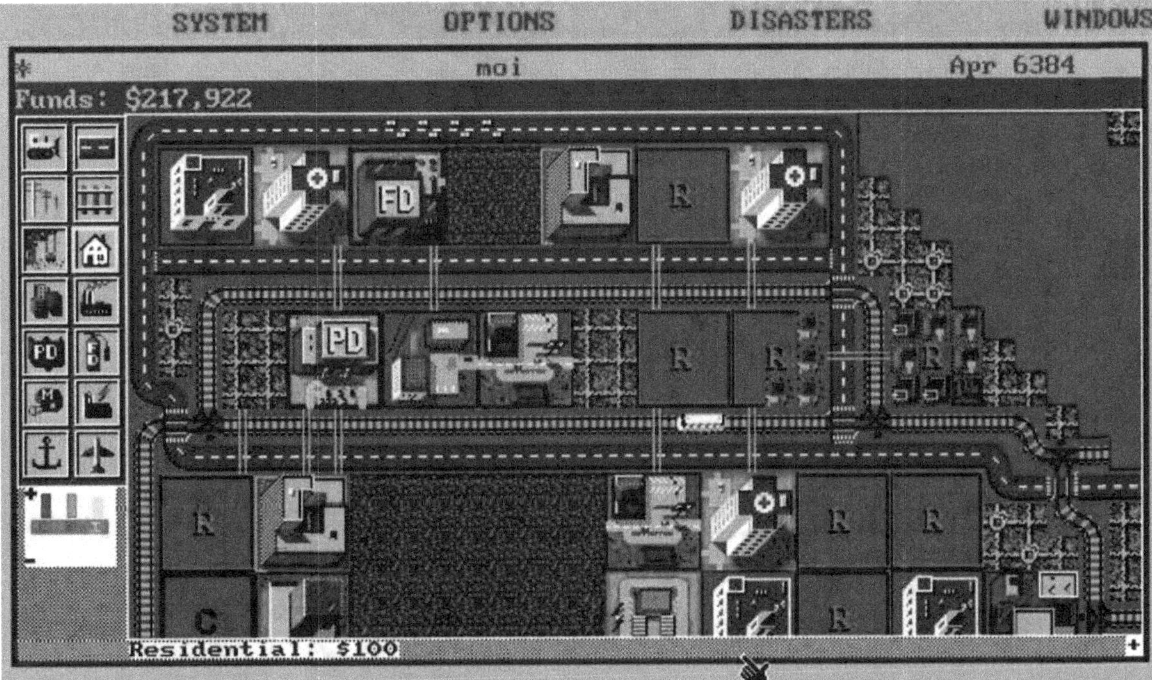

Figure 2. SimCity 2000 –flopys (1993)

Figure 3. SimCity 3000. First CD-ROM version (1997)

harbinger of e-government) and see the growth of the population with the passing of time and the improvement of the city. It is not in vain that the small tents became supermarkets, the houses mansions, and the same with the other buildings. In other words, the qualitative progress of the community, that is, to improve the life quality of its citizens. Along this line of work and following these cognitive models in the design, the new developments of the software would converge in the social aspect of the inhabitants.

In 1999 appeared The Sims (Figure 6). Here the main goal focused on the happiness of the people, because the game simulated the life of a group of people from different age groups and to whom different physical, professional, and personality profiles are given (Berens & Howard, 2002; Eberly, 2001). With the passing of time, these characters evolve in each one of the aspects of training and working life, etc. Without any doubt this was a videogame which simulated the social life of millions of inhabitants in Western culture. The commercial success of the videogame led the designers and programmers to generate additional modules as if it were a commercial operative system, such as: House Party, Hot Date and Vacation. Later on this was adapted to the videoconsoles such as Play Station and the online version.

LESSONS LEARNED

The success of the design in the SimCity videogame and later on The Sims, lies in some principles presented by Papert, Minsky and Piaget, that is,

Figure 4. SimCity 4 –CD-ROM's (2003)

Figure 5. SimCity Societies –DVD (2007)

Figure 6. Characters 3D and the simulation of the life

the possibility of a fun learning building whatever the user wishes, as it happens in the traditional Lego. Mitchel Resnick experimented with children in the construction of robots (Maragliano, 2004). The experiments were carried out with his programming language Starlogo. In it, multiple instructions were executed simultaneously by the robots, simulating the way in which certain processes take place in nature. For instance, a rudimentary version of what would be the SimAnt which simulates the life of an ant in the anthill, it allows us to see the mechanism of its general functioning, since the behaviour of each ant is determined by its situation, by the perception it has towards the other aunts which are close to it, and by a set of rules. Like the objects of StarLogo by Resnick the ants change their situation in relation to the role they are playing in that moment, and where they are located. Interacting with SimAnt you learn of the existence of the ants pheromones, that is, their chemical element, virtual in this case, through which the ants, just like the objects from StarLogo communicate among themselves. In another video game related to nature such as SimLife, different species of plants and animals can be obtained due to the mutations. In these games underlies the factor of creativity and planning. In this regard Wright has included in the cognitive model of his videogames the possibility that each user has of redefining the game's rules in relation to his/her manifest or latent wishes, as Freud contended in his work "The Interpretation of Dreams" (Sigmund, 2005). This is the reason why there are natural disasters in SimCity and in the Sims the characters may die. The user interacts with a very wide virtual reality given the options that these simulators implicitly have and this user needs time to analyze them and experiment with them. Little by little the user gets acquainted with them until attaining a high interaction level with the multimedia system.

Obviously the communicability factor underlies the design of each one of the video games, and it is in the video games of the simulator type where each one of the components of the metaphor of the interface must be studied down to the latest detail (Cipolla-Ficarra, Cipolla-Ficarra, & Harder, 2008) so that the potential users can fulfil the satisfaction requisite in the interaction process, just as Nielsen enunciated (Nielsen, 1992). Although he was opposed at the beginning to measuring the quality of the interactive systems (Nielsen, 1996) with our quality attributes, methodology and heuristic techniques, decomposing the elements that make up the design of these systems and establishing relationships between them, through the concepts and experiences of the formal and factual sciences it has been possible to establish some metrics for quality.

CONCLUSION

The multimedia products in off-line support overcome by far the quality of the portals dedicated to pastime and on-line training of languages, mathematics, classical games, etc. of numerous websites whose content is edutainment. The hardware factor or technological novelty surpasses the software or the content with communicability. The main problem is the lack of professionalism of the agents who take part in the design of the interactive systems. Many of them stem from the formal sciences and they devote themselves to the computer videogames because they have children who like to play with computers. That is, their family environment is the lab. However, they lack training in the context of the factual sciences. In the literature we find an endless series of works where the technological factor makes apparent the presence of young multimedia users and monomedia researchers. We find the exception in great commercial companies which in the last few decades have known how to use to the utmost the studies of Papert, Minsky, etc., such as the simulation games in Marshall Mc Luhan's global village. In the 90s the CD-ROM support allowed a bridge to be built among professionals with great experience in the context of graphic arts, cinematography (for instance, tracking animation), television, radio, the specialized magazines, etc. and the era of digital and interactive communication. That is, those contents were more oriented at edutainment than to the current interactive systems. The positive factor of the current videogames is the possibility of inserting physical movements while there is an interaction with them. However, an endless number of variables remains in the local and global context of the users to be analyzed in the future, and all of them tend to increase the communicability and usability of the interactive applications.

ACKNOWLEDGMENT

The author would like to thank Maria Ficarra, Daniela and Carlos their helps and contributions.

REFERENCES

Berens, K., & Howard, G. (2002). *Videogaming*. London: Rough Guides.

Beverly, A. (2000). *Instructional and cognitive impacts of web-based education*. Hershey, PA: Idea Group Publishing.

Cipolla-Ficarra, F., et al. (2011). Computational informatics, social factors and new information technologies: Hypermedia perspectives and avant-garde experiences in the era of communicability expansion. Bergamo, Italy: Blue Herons Ed.s.

Cipolla-Ficarra, F., & Cipolla-Ficarra, M. (2008). Interactive systems, design and heuristic evaluation: The importance of the diachronic vision. In *Proceedings of New Directions in Intelligent Interactive Multimedia*. Heidelberg, Germany: Springer. doi:10.1007/978-3-540-68127-4_64

Cipolla-Ficarra, F., & Cipolla-Ficarra, M. (2009). Computer animation and communicability in multimedia system and services: A trichotomy evaluation. In *Proceedings of New Directions in Intelligent Interactive Multimedia*. Heidelberg, Germany: Springer-Verlag. doi:10.1007/978-3-642-02937-0_10

Cipolla-Ficarra, F., Cipolla-Ficarra, M., & Harder, T. (2008). Realism and cultural layout in tourism and video games multimedia systems. In *Proceedings of 1st Workshop Communicability MS08*. New York: ACM Press.

Eberly, D. (2001). *3D game engine design*. San Francisco, CA: Morgan Kaufmann Publishers.

Maragliano, R. (2004). *Nuovo manuale di didattica multimediale*. Rome: Laterza.

Nielsen, J. (1992). The usability engineering life cycle. *IEEE Computer*, *25*(3), 12–22. doi:10.1109/2.121503

Nielsen, J. (1996). Usability metrics: Tracking interface improvements. *IEEE Software*, *6*(13), 12–13.

Piaget, S. (1993). *Children's machine: Rethinking school in the age of computer*. New York: Basic Books.

Sigmund, F. (2005). *The interpretation of dreams*. New York: Barnes & Noble.

Chapter 47
Using Genetic Algorithm for Scheduling Tasks of Computational Grids in the Gridsim Simulator

João Phellipe
Universidade do Estado do Rio Grande do Norte (UERN), Brazil

Carla Katarina
Universidade do Estado do Rio Grande do Norte (UERN), Brazil

Francisco das Chagas
Universidade Federal Rural do Semi-Árido (UFERSA), Brazil

Dario Aloise
Universidade Federal Rural do Semi-Árido (UFERSA), Brazil

ABSTRACT

Computer processing power has evolved considerably in recent years. However, there are problems that still require many machines to perform a large amount of processing in a parallel and distributed way. In this context, the task scheduling in a distributed system present many algorithms. In this chapter, the authors present a scheduler based on genetic algorithms in order to distribute tasks more efficiently in a computational grid; it has been implemented in GRIDSIM, a computational grid simulator with the features and attributes of a real grid.

INTRODUCTION

Since the computing outset, one the most interesting issue in this research area has been the increase of computer power processing (Distefano, et al., 2010). As time passes, new software technologies require hardware increasingly powerful (Bahi, Contassot-Vivier & Couturier, 2007). This technology trend has demanded from processors distributors a fast technological development. However, many times, the technology used in a processor cannot alone satisfy the cases which the

DOI: 10.4018/978-1-4666-4490-8.ch047

resources processing demand is huge, emerging as well, the parallel machines with a larger number of processors (Davis & Petrini, 2004).

For some applications, a large number of processors makes an inappropriate solution, due to the project economic viability in the construction or acquisition of suitable parallel machines (Baduel, L., et al., 2006). The grid computing has become a viable solution for those cases which present a great processing demand (Baduel, et al., 2006; Foster, 2002; Foster, Kesselman & Tuecke, 2001).

According to (Foster, 2002; Foster, Kesselman & Tuecke, 2001; Hey & Trefethen, 2003; Taurion, 2010) the grid computing is a distributed computing model that uses geographically and administratively the available resources. Individual users may access the computers and the data in a transparent way, without considering geographical position, operating system, accounts administration and other details (Buckley, 2010).

In grids computing, the details are abstracted and the resources are virtualized (Gentzsch, Grandinetti & Joubert, 2010) i.e., the whole computational grid is showed to user as a unique resource. The grid used can be done in many areas that require large amount of processing such as: image processing, optimizing calculation, pharmaceutical industry, natural disaster simulations, etc. A huge problem faced in grid computing is the tasks scheduling, although it is known as an allocation problem (Foster, 2002). it differs from allocation problems in the conventional distributed systems. This problem is much more complex, given the dynamic nature (in which come in and out of the grid, use restrictions, etc.) and the high degree of resources heterogeneity (architectures, operating systems, different location) and tasks that must be monitored. According to (Garey & Johnson, 1990) the tasks scheduling is a NP-complete problem, and according to (Luke, 2009). using heuristics is in fact, the most used approach in practice in order to deal with the difficulty in problems with these features. In (Linden, 2012). the genetic algorithms usually present a better performance than the specific heuristics. In optimization problems, if one wishes to achieve a goal or a value, even if it is in an interval, this is called objective or objective function (Abraham, Buyya & Nath, 2000). The objective can be maximized or minimized, seeking the maximum values or minimum for the problems' functions, complying with restrictions presented for the model.

The scheduling problem presents many goals to be achieved in a general way, for instance, reduce the total time for the tasks execution, reduce the total time of idle processors, increase the processing efficiency. In this paper, we have considered two goals: time execution of each task and the total time of the system execution. In Figure 1 is shown an example of a computational grid, which a user sends a task block for the scheduler, and it divides the tasks among the available computers for processing, receiving the tasks processed and sending back to the user.

The simulation presents a fast way of algorithms analysis on large scale for distributed systems and heterogeneous resources, since the material cost would be prohibitive for the work conclusion. Another advantage is that reduces the complexity and the extra work that would be necessary to manage real machines, add or remove new machines, network setup, communication and security (Xhafa, Kolodziej & Bogdaski, 2010). Simulation also becomes effective when working with big hypothetical problems, but in another way, it would require a large amount of active users and resources, which is very difficult to coordinate and build a large scale environment for research purposes.

The GridSim tool (Buyya, 2012) allows to model and simulate entities in parallel with distributed computing, users, applications, resources and schedulers, for development and algorithms evaluation for scheduling. It makes easier to create different classes of heterogeneous resources that can be aggregated using schedulers to solve computing applications and intensive data. A resource may be a single processor or multiprocessor

Figure 1. Example of computational grid operation

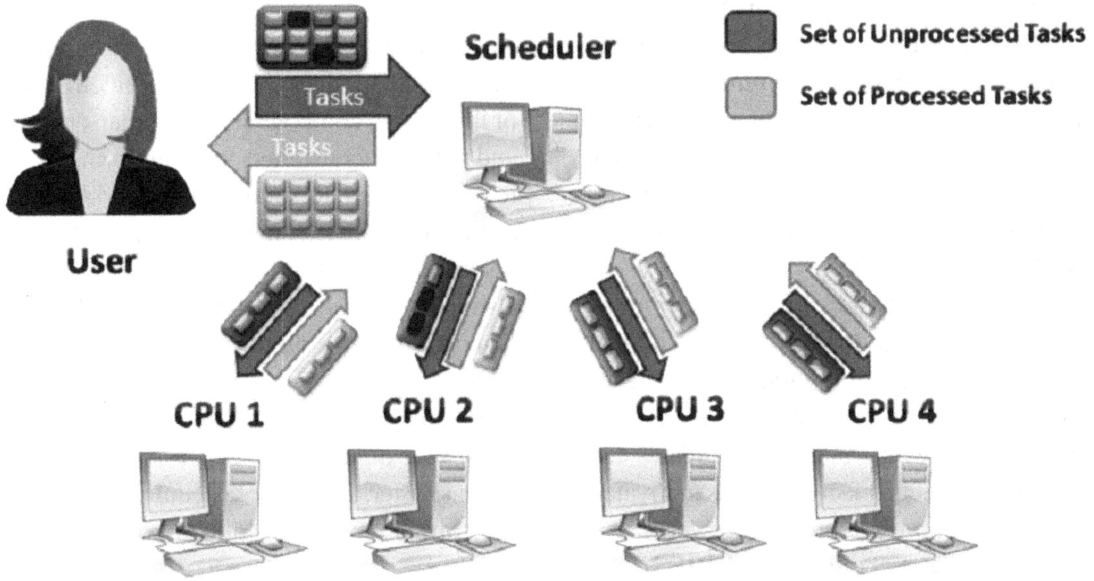

with shared or distributed memory and managed by time schedulers and shared space.

This paper is structured as follows. First, we present a literature review and the related work (Section 2). Next, we approach the grid scheduling and the scheduling problem (Section3). Then, we present a new scheduling policy, the algorithm used and the algorithm performance equations (Section 4). Following, simulation results and discussions (Section 5). Finally, we draw some conclusions (Section 6).

In this paper, a task scheduling policy based on genetic algorithm has been implemented in the GRIDSIM simulator, in order to obtain a shorter time of tasks execution.

RELATED WORK

In related work, we present heuristic approaches. In (Xhafa & Abraham, 2008). is showing how heuristics and meta-heuristics may be addressed to the scheduling problem presenting, also a detailed review of it.

Simulated Annealing is found in (Abraham, Buyya & Nath, 2000; Braun, et al., 2001). in these works are presented probabilistic local search techniques, which is based on an analogy with thermodynamics for the tasks scheduling.

Tabu Search is explored in (Abraham, Buyya & Nath, 2000; Braun, et al., 2001) it was done as a local search for interactively, move a solution to a better solution using as a stop criterion, a limit number of attempts.

In (Abraham, Buyya & Nath, 2000) are shown how the approaches could be made using hybrid meta-heuristics for tasks scheduling.

In (Xhafa & Abraham, 2008) were used hybrids of ants colony and Tabu search. Other approaches to AI problem are in (Xhafa & Abraham, 2008)

Schedulers based on GA are mentioned in (Abraham, Buyya & Nath, 2000; Braun, et al., 2001; Xhafa, Kolodziej & Bogdaski, 2010). The main limitation of these studies is that they do not perform a comparison with a large number of machines in order to find a cost benefit between machines and tasks, as well as they do not perform a comparative with an amount of tasks variable in order to find the scheduler efficiency based on GA regarding to scheduling conventional algorithms.

Another limitation is that they present results specifically focused on the optimization and combination areas. The best results acquired from the variables are used in order to algorithms may converge to a result in which was considered acceptable by them, but without showing the benefits obtained for the distributed systems.

The solution presented in this paper aims to perform a task scheduling in computational grids using GA reducing the total time of tasks executions, intending specifically to reduce the processing time, which therefore increases the grid efficiency. Another factor that has motivated this study was because there are no works that mention metaheuristics creation in GRIDSIM.

Grid Scheduling

Due to complexity of network systems and distributed applications on large scale, different versions and programming modes may be considered (Xhafa & Abraham, 2008). Taking into account the problem version in Subsection 3.1 that does not consider any restrictions on the tasks transfer, interdependent of data, and also the economic and cost policies concerning resources.

Our concern is about the programming, which is necessary to achieve high performance applications and from the users grids perspective, to offer Quality of Service (QoS) in the grid system. This programming appears in applications that can be solved by dividing them into many independent works, submitting them to grid and combining the partial results in order to obtain the final solution.

In addition, there is a need to allocate applications user-independent for grid resources. It is considered the scenario in which the works sent to the grid are independents and not preemptive, i.e., they cannot change the resource in which the task has been assigned since its execution is started, unless it has been removed from the grid.

Formulation of the Problem

According to (Foster, 2002; Foster, Kesselman & Tuecke, 2001) the scheduling problem consists of three main components: consumers, resources and policies. Consumers are users with programs to be processed. Resources are the grid machines available for processing. Policy may specify the goals that a scheduling system can satisfy. It can also specify in the implementation level, the tasks mapping method to the resources. The policy chosen to implement a scheduler may affect users and resource providers. The policy used in this paper uses a model based on GA.

In (Foster, 2002) the scheduler is designed to meet one or more of the following common goals:

- Maximize the output flow of data system,
- Using resources in order to obtain the best possible performance,
- Expansion of energy saving, processing and time,
- Decrease the processing time of an application.

In (Abraham, Buyya & Nath, 2000) studies, they reinforce that the tasks scheduling is important in the sense that, the more efficient is the scheduler, more economic is the processing, since we have idle processors, so that the tasks will be less time in the processors. In this work, we improve the scheduler efficiency reducing the total time of tasks execution, making a better use of idle processors.

To capture the main features in computational grids, it has to be processed a model of such features. To formulate the problem, we need an computational estimate of processing load in each task and the computational capacity of each resource. In this work, we used the Standard Workload Format (SWF) (Chapin, et al., 1999). It is possible to undertake that this formulation is in practice applicable, since it is easy to know the computing capability of each resource and the computational needs requirements of tasks can be known from specifications defined by user, from historical data or forecasts.

Therefore, it is made an usual assumption which is known by computing capacity of each resource, an estimate or forecast of computational needs (load) of each work, and the previous workload of each resource. SWF model allows the insertion of possible inconsistencies between tasks and grid resources. In addition, it is still possible to capture different features of heterogeneous distributed systems as the computing coherence, resources heterogeneity and the tasks heterogeneity. A formal definition about instance of the problem inside a SWF matrix is given by its data fields.

Since the goal of this work is reducing the total time of the execution and consequently the idle processors time. Thus, the fields taken into consideration in the simulations were 1,2,3,4 and 5.

It is shown in Figure 2, an example of the tasks set abstraction, where each line represented by different colors, improves the view corresponding to a task and the numbers of each line represent a data field of each task.

These data fields are:

1. **Task Number:** Count field starting from 1, works in this paper as a task identifier;
2. **Delivery Time:** In seconds. The earlier time in which the log refers is zero and is the time delivery of the first task. The lines in the log are sorted in increasing order of delivery time. The tasks are also listed in this order, this is used so that to know when the task arrives in the scheduler in order to be distributed among resources;
3. **Waiting Time:** In seconds. The difference between the task delivery time and the moment in which the task really started to run. While exists a task with a time higher than the presence time of free computational node, the scheduler will try to decrease this value;
4. **Execution Time:** In seconds. Time in which the work was executed (end time - start time). This is the main field used in the scheduling policy, reducing this value, it is reduced the sum of the total execution time;
5. **Number of Processors Allocated:** Entire. In most cases this is also the number of processors that the task uses.

The algorithm aims to reduce the value of the total execution time by relocating tasks to idle processors, reducing the waiting time and increase the number of processors allocated.

There are a total out of 18 data fields. In future work, we intend to use more data fields in order to make the scheduler policy more reactive.

THE NEW SCHEDULER BASED ON GENETIC ALGORITHM

This section presents the design and implementation of the scheduling policy using the genetic

Figure 2. Example of a set of tasks

algorithm. Each grid scheduler is designed to be part of a specific architecture for the resources management. The scheduler presented here was designed to be compatible with other tools which make part of a resource allocation system.

The Algorithm

Algorithm 1 pseudo-code expresses the approaching ideas of the genetic algorithm regarding to the scheduler.

To a better understanding of the genetic algorithm used in this paper, a flowchart with the algorithm is shown in Figure 3. In Figure 4 is shown the simulator execution flow, which the arrows indicate the flow. The tasks selected by the user entering the simulator and are scheduled according to policy chosen, then submit the simulation data.

The Scheduling Policy Based on Genetic Algorithm

The scheduling algorithms performance was assessed by means of simulations graphs in tasks allocation, modeled from real applications. The tasks set used in this work are available for researching in (Feitelson, 2012).

Therefore, the algorithms performance comparisons using the same tasks set is possible. In order to allow researchers to assess their algorithms, it is proposed a tasks set and graphics

Algorithm 1.

```
Input: Initial Population
Output: Best solution found until the algorithm STOP
Begin Genetic Algorithm
While all individuals values of the initial population is not obtained Do
        Foreach individual Do
        Assign a task to each processor so that the earlier processing time of
tasks with the least time of idle processors can be acquired();
        endForeach
Calculate the evaluation function();
endWhile
Select the best individuals of initial population using Roulette method ();
repeat
        Create a new population();
         Perform a crossover operation ();
         Perform a mutation operation ();
         List the remaining individuals of the previous population, through
elitism();
         Assess individuals according to the evaluation function();
until the stop criterion is no longer reachable;
End
```

Figure 3. Flowchart for the genetic algorithm operation

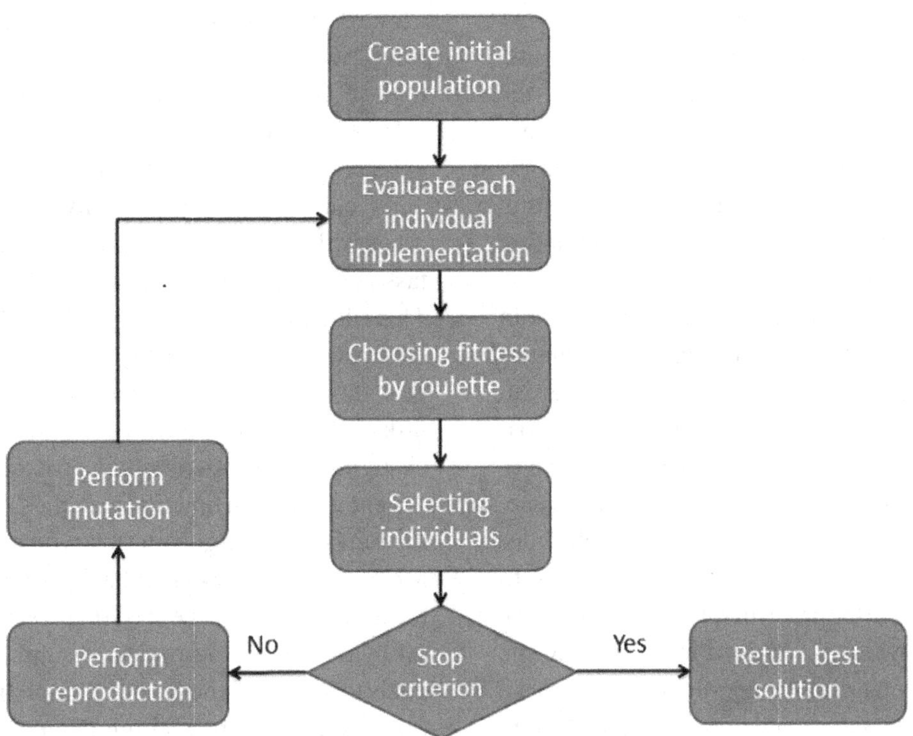

Figure 4. Flowchart of tasks scheduling in GRIDSIM using genetic algorithm

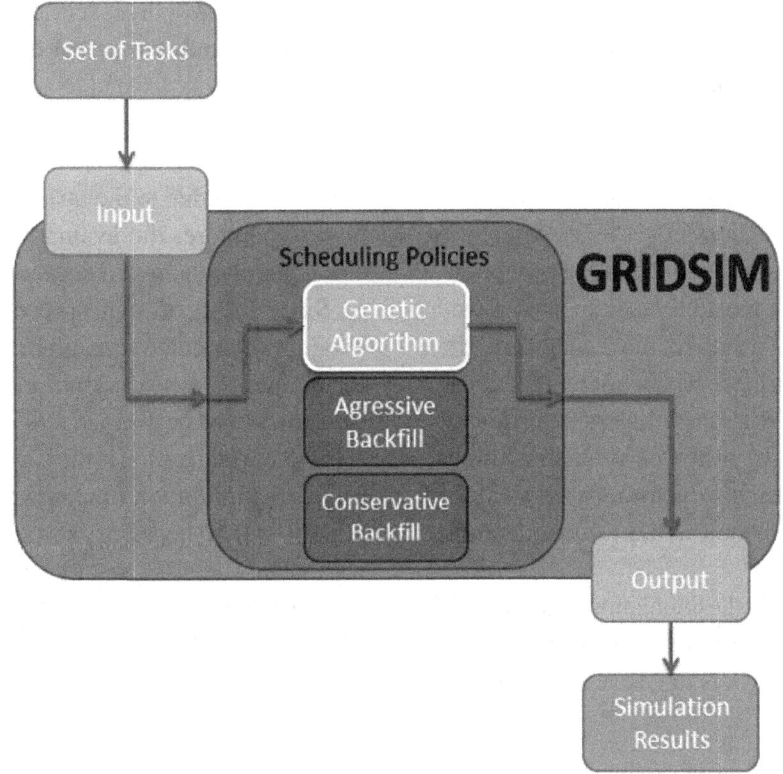

generation methods. For this, each tasks set is represented by a single SWF file.

In a grid environment, the goals of users and resources providers can be conflicting, i.e., the goals are such that, when trying to improve a performance criterion, other criterion can be degraded. A search based on genetic algorithm can reconcile the conflicting goals by attempting to satisfy all involved.

A search based on genetic algorithm can obtain a value nearly optimal in a reasonable amount of time, even when the room for solution is great. Grid scheduling is an optimization problem (Foster, 2002). Weights can be used with each goal to change the scheduling behavior in execution time, allowing prioritize multiple goals. A scheduler based on genetic algorithm can adapt easily to small changes in the problem space (Linden, 2012). In this paper, this is obtained by measuring the weight of each attribute measured, as long these weights are variables which multiply the factors that we want to improve. We can increase these variables when we want to achieve a higher value in the evaluation function or decrease when the demand is the opposite. Thus, a scheduler based on genetic algorithm for the grid tasks distribution was chosen for the problem proposed in resources allocation.

The selection function in the algorithm is choosing the population elements that will participate the reproduction process, i.e., select the individuals parents who will be in the new population. This choice must be made in such a way that the population members more adapted to the environment have a higher chance of reproduction, which in this case is a scheduling more efficient, i.e., those that have a higher evaluation function value. The way in which was used to make the individuals selection is the roulette method (Linden, 2012).

Each individual of the population will occupy a roulette portion, proportional to the fitness index. With this, the individuals that have a high fitness will occupy a greater portion than the ones that have a lower fitness. This roulette wheel is rotated many times, where the rotate amount varies according to the population size. In each roulette rotation is selected an individual that will participate in the generation process of the new population.

A chromosome or an individual represents a task scheduling submitted to resources. Each tasks set represents a population and is a SWF file. This file format can contain many tasks that may have restrictions with many precedence levels. A new chromosome is generated by permuting the tasks in a scheduling but keeping the resource and changing the task that will be processed.

The evaluation function is a scheduling quality measure defined in goals terms, which is desired to achieve. Thus, the user may have goals to minimize the execution total time and still meet the deadline set by user, while a provider resources can have goals to minimize the session completion time, or execution total time and minimize the idle time of compute nodes. By simply assigning weights shown in Equation 9, which are the restrictions to achieve.

Allocation resources service attempts to schedule a tasks number together during a processing session. Many tasks lead to a better use of nodes, because the scheduler may be able to allocate tasks in the idle time spaces in computational nodes left out due to the task precedence restrictions. Therefore, the evaluation function is the cumulatively goals of a users number.

Since the tasks can have different sizes for obtaining a cumulative result from many tasks and for obtaining a metric of multiple goals measured, the values must be normalized. A task feature that helps in normalization is the task critical moment. This is the minimum time in which a task can be processed if all necessary resources are available without any delay. A session can have p independent tasks. Be $t_{tarefafinal}(i)$ the total execution time of i-th task and be T_{je} the accumulated value of execution time in tasks p. Be t_{st} is the endtime of the last task for a given scheduling. In Equation 1, it is shown how to calculate the execution total time of all tasks and this formula is used to measure the scheduler policy performance.

$$T_{je} = \sum_{i=1}^{p} t_{tarefafinal}(i) \quad (1)$$

To calculate normalized value of the execution cumulated time in each task is used the Equation 2.

$$T_{jnormalizado} = \frac{T_{je}}{T_{st} * p} \quad (2)$$

Be $t_{deadlineTarefa}(i)$ the endtime of the i-th task, and be $T_{dt}(i)$ the delay in the encounter of requirement endtime for the i-th task, i.e.; the endtime of task is used to indicate the maximum period of the task time. Its calculation is in Equation 3.

$$T_{dt}(i) = \left(t_{tarefafinal}(i) - t_{deadlinetarefafinal}(i)\right) \quad (3)$$

For ($t_{tarefafinal}(i) > t_{deadlinetarefafinal}(i)$) (else receives 0). The cumulative delay of the final deadline is defined by Equation 4.

$$T_{dt} = \sum_{i=1}^{p} (T_{dt}(i)) \quad (4)$$

Denoting t_{st} as the endtime of final task for a given schedule. We set the delay of the cumulative final delay time normalized in Equation 5.

$$T_{dn} = \frac{T_{dt}}{t_{st} * p} \quad (5)$$

Be $t_c(i)$ the critical time of i-th task, T_c is being the largest value $t_c(i)$ on all tasks being scheduled, and t_{st} being the endtime for the final task for a given scheduling. And denoting ω as the session total time. we can calculate its value in Equation 6.

$$\omega = \left(1 - \frac{T_c}{T_{st}}\right) \quad (6)$$

Node idleness appears due to processing times not used, which need to be left in order to meet the previous restrictions of tasks.

Be m the spaces number in the j-th node and be let n compute nodes number. Be $t_{gs}(j; k)$ the initial time of k-th idle time of the j-th node, and be $t_{gs}(j; k)$ the endtime of the k-th idle time of j-th node. In Equation 7 is shown how to perform this calculation.

$$T_{ge} = \sum_{p=1}^{n} \left(\sum_{k=1}^{m} (t_{ge}(j,k) - t_{gs}(j,k)) \right) \quad (7)$$

Be T_{gen} the idle accumulated time of all n nodes. In Equation 8 is shown how to calculate this value.

$$T_{gen} = \frac{T_{ge}}{(t_{st} * p)} \quad (8)$$

Thus, the four components α, β, θ and λ could be weights for obtaining the function evaluation F:

$$F = 1 - \left(\frac{(\pm * \acute{E} + {}^{2} * T_{jen} + {,} * T_{dn} + » * T_{gen})}{(\pm *^{2} * {,} * »)} \right) \quad (9)$$

The four weights (α, β, θ and λ) are used to prioritize any special component according to tasks needs or users, or the resources provider. By simply assigning a greater value for any weights associated to the performance equations and the evaluation function will tend to select the chromosome which promotes the search scenario desired, converging to the solution that is wanted to achieve.

Right after the fitness function for each chromosome of initial population is calculated, the average value of the fitness functions and the standard deviation will be calculated. If standard deviation reaches a threshold low enough, then an acceptable solution is available and it is said that the genetic algorithm has converged. Once the algorithm converges to a solution, the generation of a new population is not necessary. However, once the initial population was generated randomly, without any consideration of the solution quality, the standard deviation is not likely to be lower than the acceptable limit of the solution, and the available chromosomes at this stage are not susceptible to provide an acceptable solution. Then, in order to avoid great places, the scheduler is designed to immediately move to the generation of the first new population, based on the initial population.

To generate a new population, the elitism method is used. First, a fitness functions set is built. Random numbers are generated to select the candidates from the existing population in order to generate the new population. Methods (selection, crossover, mutation and elitism) are used together to generate a new population.

The rate crossover r_c is chosen to promote the algorithm fast convergence. This rate was chosen to be use in grid schedulers through a large experiments number. If the existing population size is P, then the parents r_c * P are chosen through the selection process in order to create an equal number of descendants for the new population. For selection method, we used the "Roulette Diagram" due to its simplicity. Also, the scheduler performs very well with this diagram.

The crossing process may produce illegal chromosomes which can duplicate the same task. We used the uniform crossover method for permuting (Luke, 2009) when is generated two chromosomes descendants of two parents chromosomes having two main steps. In the first step, be P1 the first individual selected for reproduction, P2 the second individual selected, D1 the first descending resulting from the crossing of P1 and P2, and D2 the second resulting.

Randomly, is generated a binary mask (M) of length l and a random integer j receiving 0 or 1. Then, in each position (i) of M such that M[i] = j (respectively for the second individual M [i] = 1-j) we have copied P1 [i] for D1 [i] (respectively P2 [i] for C2 [i]). In Figure 5 is shown an example of crossing process.

The rate mutation rm is experimentally chosen, also to promote the fast convergence. If the existing population size is P, rm * P, chromosomes are chosen through the selection process in order to create an equal number of chromosomes for the new population.

The mutation process is used to guide the new population from a ideal local value. For a mutation process, it is randomly generated an integer j for each position (i) and then swap the elements in the positions i and j of the chromosome. A high rm value can reverse the progress toward convergence. Therefore, this value should be selected in each case, by means of a careful study, in order to let the new population size equal to the existing population size. After the crossing and mutation processes have been used, the remaining chromosomes are selected from the ones among the existing population, making them identical to the best existing chromosomes chosen through the selection process and this refers to elitism. The algorithm 3.1 expresses the basic ideas of the GA approach.

Figure 5. Crossover process example

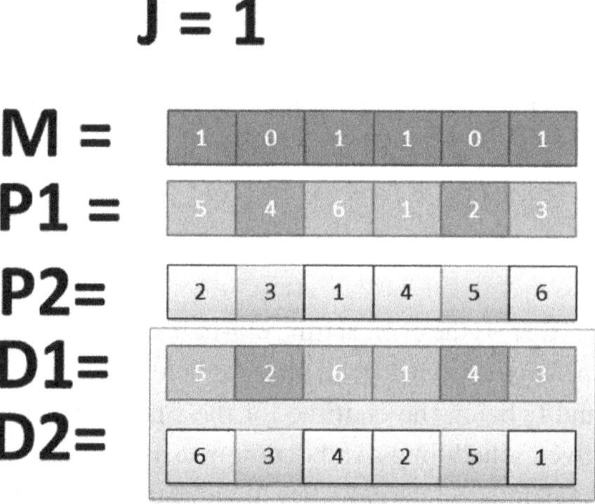

RESULTS AND DISCUSSION

The simulated machines have the following features:

1. 2 Processors per machine.
2. 100 Mbits of baud rate in the network.
3. 377 Mips of processing power per processor.

The scheduler based on genetic algorithm in this study was designed to schedule multiple tasks. Each task can contain many other tasks, each one with arbitrary precedence restrictions and arbitrary execution times. The algorithm tries the multipurpose optimization (decreasing the execution total time, to increase the scheduler efficiency, etc.) for the competition criterion.

The first tests set to obtain the tasks scheduling results contained nearly from 1.950 to more than 3.000 tasks with arbitrary precedence restrictions and execution times. The simulations values of the scheduling algorithms that go along with GRIDSIM are the same of machines and tasks. By solving the same problem using the same simulator features, it was possible to compare the solutions obtained via the best simulations results with the scheduler results based on genetic algorithm. Simulations were made to perform tasks of different SWF files. The files used in the experiments were:

- SDSC_BLUE_01.txt –included in the simulator.
- SDSC_BLUE_02.txt – included the simulator.
- NASA-under-1993 -3.1-nbl – obtained from (Feitelson, D., 2012).
- OSC-Clust-2000 -3.1-nbl – obtained from (Feitelson, D., 2012).
- LLNL-Atlas-2006 -2.1-nbl – obtained from (Feitelson, D., 2012).
- SDSC-pair - 1995 -3.1-nbl – obtained from (Feitelson, D., 2012).

From these experiences were obtained the best values of crossing rate, mutation rate and the convergence criterion.

After three validations with 100 simulations each, were scheduled the SWF files listed previously in a nodes variable number. The results showed that the scheduler is able to meet multiple goals and converges to the solution in a reasonable number of generations. The values obtained through our algorithm were compared with great values given (Buyya, 2012) for the tasks, which are included the simulator and with the values provided in (Feitelson, 2012) for the tasks, which are not included and validating the algorithm implemented in this work.

Six SWF files containing from 1.950 to more than 50.000 tasks were selected for the test. The tasks in each file has different precedence limitations. Overall, many parents and multiple descendants. The tasks has many fields and each field has an arbitrary size. In addition, the execution time of each task is variable. The experiments with schedulers were performed from 64 to 1.024 nodes with the sdsc_blue_02.txt file. And a test including all files with just 64 compute nodes. Great values were obtained from files in some scheduler simulations using the genetic algorithm policy and in most cases the acceptable approximate values.

The values are shown in Figure 6, demonstrate the values obtained with the variability of the machines amount. In this table, although the gains shown regarding to the machines amount is not large, the scheduler performance using genetic algorithm policy is higher, except when the machine number exceeds the tasks amount to be scheduling.

For a smaller compute nodes number, the effort required in the optimization is quite high. Usually, a heuristic algorithm will work best for a larger nodes number than for a smaller. A two nodes case could be considered as a degenerate case. When the choice is limited to only two nodes,

Figure 6. Table of total time values of the GRIDSIM simulation comparing

	Número de máquinas - Timespan em segundos					
1950 tarefas	64 Maquinas	128 Máquinas	256 Máquinas	512 Máquinas	764 Máquinas	1024 Máquinas
Agressive backfilling	4193086	4377605	2829396	1616401	1356503	1354434
Conservative backfiling	4201438	4370754	2829517	1631777	1356503	1354434
AggressiveMultiPartitions	4193086	4377605	2829396	1616401	1356503	1354434
ARConservative	4201438	4370754	2829517	1631777	1356503	1354434
SelectiveBackfill	4379843	4543232	2911274	1681533	1357309	1354434
Algorítmo Genético	4022707	4293508	2770043	1602618	1356503	1354434

the optimization process may not do much better than the heuristic algorithm that is included in the simulator. The simulation results is graphically shown in Figure 7.

In Figure 8 is shown the simulation time total of 64 machines changing the tasks amount.

There are two crucial parameters to be selected: The crossover and mutation rates. Experiments were performed to select the suitable values. Ten simulations with the blue_sdsc_01. txt file with 50 tasks were implemented. The initial population of 100 chromosomes was generated. A large values set for the crossover and mutation rates was used. In each case, the new generations of population were created, and even the convergence was achieved with a standard deviation of 9.8 x 10-7.

For mutation rate, experiments showed that the value 0.01 will lead to convergence. With any larger value, even with a very large crossover rate, the convergence may not be obtained. Therefore, the mutation rate ended up at 0.01. With this value in the mutation rate, experiments for crossover rate between 0.70 to 0.80 were performed. We found out that with a crossover rate between 0.72 and 0.78, the same value for evaluation function was obtained. In order to select a generations number and the required population size for obtaining the

Figure 7. Graphic of total time values of the GRIDSIM simulation comparing

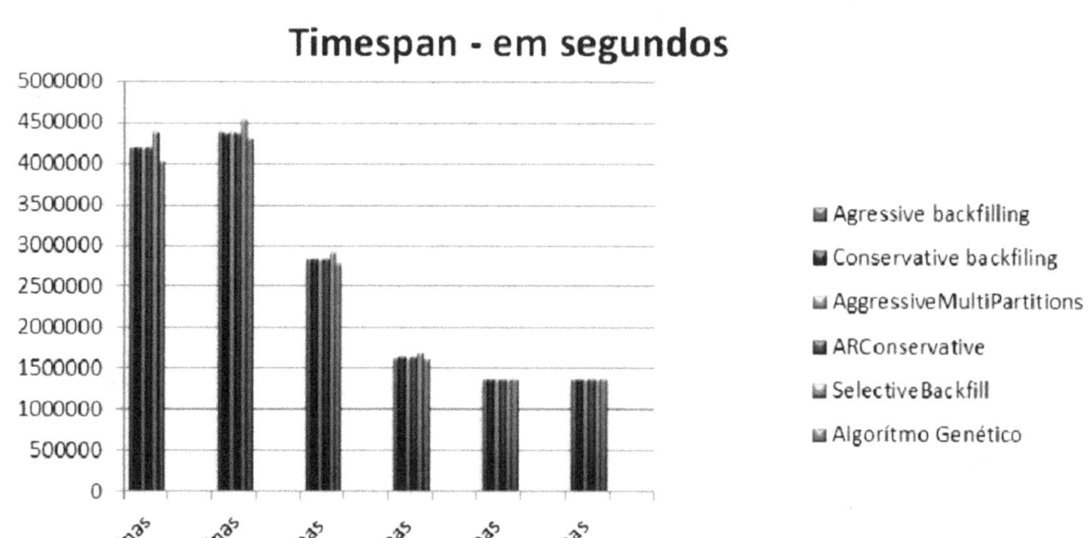

Figure 8. Graphic of total time values of the GRIDSIM simulation changing

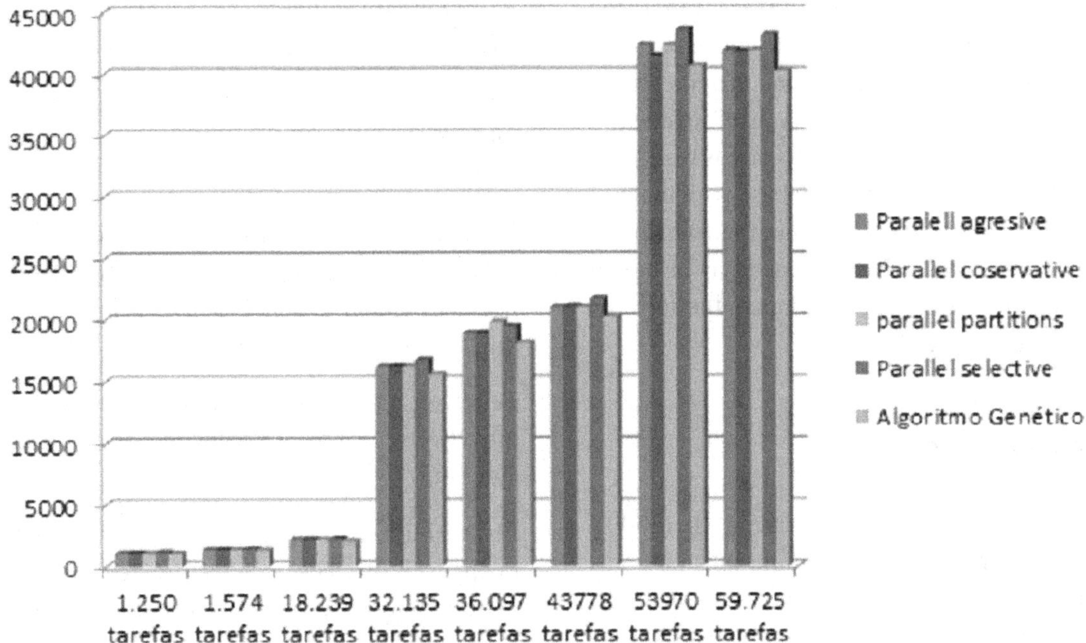

scheduling, experiments were conducted with a change in the population size from 10 to 200.

Now, it is possible two conclusions from this experiment. First, the parameters chosen for crossover and mutation rates appear to be suitable for the problem resolution. Second, the population size of 100 seems to work well for the model. In this paper, experiments using genetic algorithms had good results using two points in the crossover and mutation operators with a selection probability of 1.0 .

Finally, 8 different files set were considered. The tasks were mapped into a system of 64 machines. The results shown in Figure 8 reveal that in all cases, the scheduler based on GA is able to obtain better results than the conventional algorithms of the GRIDSIM simulator. This happens because of FCFS policy of the conventional algorithms. The scheduler based on GA considers all tasks that are being scheduled as a single set and tries to find a configuration in which satisfies the goals, while the conventional algorithms first schedule the tasks that came first, without taking anything into account and scheduling other tasks at the same time. This leads to a lower performance regarding to the scheduler based on genetic algorithm.

CONCLUSION

In this paper, we presented a scheduler based on genetic algorithm for the GRIDSIM simulator. The scheduler had a higher performance compared to the conventional algorithms in a reasonable time. It is an interesting initiative, which serves as basis for creating more detailed applications that will use the new resources available on the grid, such as: larger processing power, memory and energy savings.

Also, it is able for scheduling multiple tasks with arbitrary restrictions and different execution times, satisfying multiple goals. It was checked its functionality with more than 10.000 tasks, which is much more than a scheduler may be required to perform this at once. The crossover rate, the mutation index and the population size that might be suitable to the scheduler, all these were taken into account in this work. The multiple tasks simulation with realistic features has presented good results with the suitable evaluation function for grids scheduling. The results of this work may be used to develop a large database with the best completion times and the minimum and maximum times of idle nodes. This database may be useful for researchers in order to compare the features of new scheduling algorithms.

REFERENCES

Abraham, A., Buyya, R., & Nath, B. (2000). Nature's heuristics for scheduling jobs on computational grids. In *Proceedings of 8th IEEE International Conference on Advanced Computing and Communications (ADCOM 2000),* (pp. 45-52). IEEE.

Baduel, L. et al. (2006). *Grid computing: Software environments and tools*. Berlin: Springer-Verlag.

Bahi, J., Contassot-Vivier, S., & Couturier, R. (2007). *Parallel iterative algorithms: From sequential to grid computing*. London: Chapman & Hall/CRC.

Braun, T. et al. (2001). *A comparison of eleven static heuristics for mapping a class of independent tasks onto heterogeneous distributed computing systems*. Academic Press. doi:10.1006/jpdc.2000.1714

Buckley, P. (2010). *The rough guide to cloud computing: 100 websites that will change your life*. Rough Guides.

Buyya, R. (2012). *Gridsim*. Retrieved from http://www.buyya.com/gridsim

Chapin, S. et al. (1999). *Benchmarks and standards for the evaluation of parallel job schedulers*. Academic Press. doi:10.1007/3-540-47954-6_4

Davis, K., & Petrini, F. (2004). *Achieving usability and efficiency in large-scale parallel computing systems*. Academic Press.

Distefano, S. et al. (2010). Cloud@Home: A new enhanced computing paradigm. In *Handbook of Cloud Computing* (pp. 75–594). Boston: Springer. doi:10.1007/978-1-4419-6524-0_25

Feitelson, D. (2012). *Workload.* Retrieved from http://www.cs.huji.ac.il/labs/parallel/workload/swf.html

Foster, I. (2002). The physiology of the grid: An open grid services architecture for distributed systems integration. In *The physiology of the grid*. Academic Press.

Foster, I., Kesselman, C., & Tuecke, S. (2001). The anatomy of the grid –Enabling scalable virtual organizations. *The International Journal of Supercomputer Applications*, 15.

Garey, M., & Johnson, D. (1990). *Computers and intractability: A guide to the theory of NP-completeness*. New York: W. H. Freeman.

Gentzsch, W., Grandinetti, L., & Joubert, G. (2010). *High speed and large scale scientific computing: Advances in parallel computing*. London: IOS Press.

Hey, A., & Trefethen, A. (2003). The data deluge: An e-science perspective. In *Grid Computing - Making the Global Infrastructure a Reality* (pp. 809–824). New York: Wiley.

Linden, R. (2012). *Algoritmos geneticos*. BRASPORT.

Luke, S. (2009). *Essentials of metaheuristics*. Lulu.

Taurion, C. (2010). *Grid computing - Um novo paradigma computacional*. BRASPORT.

Xhafa, F., & Abraham, A. (2008). *Meta-heuristics for grid scheduling problems*. Academic Press.

Xhafa, F., Kolodziej, J., & Bogdaski, M. (2010). A web interface for meta-heuristics based grid schedulers. In *Proceedings of the 2010 International Conference on P2P, Parallel, Grid, Cloud and Internet Computing,* (pp. 405-410). Washington, DC: IEEE Computer Society.

Chapter 48
Web Divide and Paper Unite: Towards a Model of the Local Tourist Information for All

Francisco V. Cipolla-Ficarra
ALAIPO – AINCI, Spain and Italy

Jacqueline Alma
Electronic Arts – Vancouver, Canada

Miguel Cipolla-Ficarra
ALAIPO – AINCI, Spain and Italy

Alejandra Quiroga
Universidad Nacional de La Pampa, Argentina

ABSTRACT

The authors present the first results of a study intending to unify the quality criteria of the local touristic information in digital support (Internet) and analog (paper). An analysis is made of the reading preferences of touristic information on last generation digital screens (tablet PC and multimedia mobile phones), traditional (desktop computers), and analog (brochures, magazines, and newspapers).

INTRODUCTION

Although the information in multimedia phones support is starting to be the common denominator among the teenager and young population, among the adults and the elderly the use of the computer is still essential. Between both technological devices we have the PC tablets which may serve as a kind of bridge. It is these bridges among generations which allow to establish the communication strategies with neutral information purposes or commercial marketing. In both cases communicability must always be present, regardless of whether the message is analogous or digital. In the field of the new devices it is necessary to add the usability of those devices.

Usability and communicability are not synonymous between themselves (Cipolla-Ficarra, et al., 2010; Nielsen, 1993). One of the main problems in the mobile devices is the amount of information which can be included on a single screen, without any need to carry out additional operations such as the pressure on the keys of the mobile device, the use of the pencil on the screens or the fingers on the keyboard, whether it is to move the sheet or activate links with additional information. These

DOI: 10.4018/978-1-4666-4490-8.ch048

operations which may be trivial for a teenager are not so for an older person. An example are the information dots on structures related to tourism, such as can be the bus terminal, the train station, the ports or the airports, to mention a few examples.

In the case of the ports, an excellent example has been an information point in the Industrial Polygon of the Zona Franca (1991-1992), where the trucker arrived and in a very simple interface he had the map to load or download the goods (Cipolla-Ficarra, et al., 1993). From the point of view of interactive design, the user was the focus of the design, that is, the ergonomics had to have two levels: the first, where the direct interface element was installed (button, keyboard, etc.) and the second the communicability of the screen. An information point stand in the 90s and beginnings of usability engineering had to be quick, provide possible solutions to the mistakes of the users, visually likeable and with movements simulating reality. By working with a tactile screen, the user can see that as soon as he/she puts the finger on the screen (Shneiderman, et al., 2010), the selected button stirs up (sinking, change of color, dimension, etc.).

Without any doubt, this movement may be trivial from the point of view of interaction but it is very important that it is present. Other variables should be added, such as the eventual interaction mistakes of the users with the computer devices and always try to take care of the connection between the eye and the finger. The main beneficiary of an information point is not so much the user but that who sends the message. It is a communication of quality or prestige, since it offers an improvement of service. Certainly in this the user is considered, by knowing the services that will be offered, whether it is information on the geographical position on a map, the services or places to be visited, etc. in digital interactive support or not.

Finally in the evolution of the obtainment of that information in the early nineties and practically half the second decade of the 21 century is that said information is got nowadays in microcomputing devices which can be held in a single hand. Whereas the cabins containing the computers of the port in Barcelona were six meters tall and eight tons of concrete were used. This example makes highlights in itself the importance of interactive information over use of paper, such as the maps in different languages which are handed out to the tourists or users of services.

TOURIST INFORMATION: ORIENTATION AND ACCESIBILITY

One of the problems to be solved in tourism is the orientation of those people who find themselves for the first time in a place they do not know. In the case of physical places such as train stations, airports, etc., the signals system plays a very important role. However, even if a place is well signaled, the cultural factor inherent to it may keep the visitors in a state of disorientation (Fernandes, 1995). If to this factor we add the accessibility to the physical places, many of the potential passengers of an international airport, for instance, may decide to change their airport terminal in the future due to the orientation problems. An excellent example of signalization and accessibility in a European international airport is to be found in Amsterdam.

Orientation and accessibility are two quality attributes which are to be found in the earliest offline interactive systems and which have served as a model for the online systems, in the touristic context, for instance. Traditionally these quality attributes have been considered at the moment of the interactive design and the evaluation of usability. Those attributes were turned into metrics in such methodologies and quality criteria such as MECEM: Metrics for the Communications Evaluation in Multimedia (Cipolla-Ficarra, 2000). and MEHEM: A Methodology for Heuristic Evaluation in Multimedia (Cipolla-Ficarra, 1999). Next there are a few examples and the interested reader may widen these issues in the following bibliographical references (Cipolla-Ficarra, 1996; Cipolla-Ficarra, 1997).

The accessibility to the information in the last generation interactive users for those users who have difficulties in the use or the purchase of devices (digital divide for financial reasons, for instance), among other variables, forces the tourism information stands to resort to the use of paper (Cipolla-Ficarra, 2010). Paper still remains a useful tool to solve matters as important as: Where am I? and Where can I go? In less than a minute, with just indicating two spots on the paper map. Obviously a multimedia phone device or a PC tablet wired to the Internet can give us a myriad information in real time, on a digital map.

The problem is that not all the users have economic access to these technologies or know how to use them, profiting 100% of their potentialities. Consequently, in the 21st century paper may unite synergies in the quality of the information services for tourists and those devices wired to the Internet in order to offer a better information thanks to the augmented reality, for instance. Although the trend is to digitalize the maps in the great cities of touristic destinations that have WiFi, the tourism information offices still print their maps and handing them out in a non-free way (the tourist has to pay them), in paper support, as it happens in many Scandinavian cities or in Venice (Italy).

The advantage of the use of maps in small communities is the thematic information related to their economic and cultural activities such as parks and gardens, craftsmanship fairs, local folklore, gastronomy, the small museums, etc. Although this information may be duplicated in an exact way or approximate in the area reserved for touristic information, on the poaper every town will leave its personal footprint from the point of view of design, the format of the map, the kind of paper and system of printing used, etc. In other words, tending to achieve their own identity to differentiate it from their neighboring localities. Now this local information must gather a series of common denominators among the localities that make up a same geographical area (Cipolla-Ficarra, 2010).

Through these common denominators it is necessary to generate an identifying local corporative image, to differentiate among the globalization of the contents of the tourism sector, especially in the context of the interactive design of microcomputing multimedia systems, static or mobile. Starting from this main goal we have been collecting European touristic information, of free distribution and in paper format in the last 5 years. This material makes up a part of the corpus of analysis of the current work. In the corpus of analysis we have from brochures, magazines, etc. down to maps and interactive systems in offline support, that is, CD-ROM and DVD.

CORPUS OF ANALYSIS, EVALUATION AND RESULTS

In the early interactive systems in CD-Rom support of the mid-nineties the graphic paper arts went into the digital support and the quality of many products aimed at international tourism were excellent, bearing in mind the relation synchronism-technological available for the production of those systems. Then because of reasons of the widening of the capacity of information in the offline supports such as the DVD and the reduction of the cost of the videos it was aimed at the use and circulation of these interactive systems where the dynamic audiovisual information would surpass the textual.

In the first CD-ROMs the static means prevailed over the dynamic means. The reason was the space that the dynamic means took (audio, animations and video). However, in the mid-nineties and inside the field of interactive design of Southern Europe there was a trend to use and/or experiment with all the software and hardware resources at the disposal of the producers of interactive systems. In our corpus of analysis we also count with a wide range of CD-ROMs and videos from America and Europe.

In other words, the corpus is made up by 1254 components (those to be found in the Internet are not included) in the different analogical and digital supports (a small set of examples: Figures 1, 2, and 3), in several languages and formats gathered since 1990 down to the present. When we refer to the results of the current corpus we are talking of a sample which has been randomly chosen in a draw (a barrel is used where each number refers to a single component of the corpus).

We also resort to this procedure when the Internet websites are analyzed. In our case we have aimed at a geographical region known as "Sierras de Córdoba", is a mountain range in central Argentina. We have focused on two categories of design such as content and presentation, since we are also working with analogical means. The users who have participated in the experiments are adults (ages comprising between 35 and 40 years) with knowledge in the use of computers and last generation devices in microcomputing and multimedia mobile phones and none of them has a technical or technological diploma in tourism.

A total of 40 people have been evaluated, divided into four groups. Each group had the same number of components of the random sample of the corpus, that is, 24 components: 4 DVDs, 4 CDs, 4 magazines, 4 brochures and 4 tourism guides). Each group has been assigned a set of tasks to be carried out through the information available in analogical support and another in digital support offline and online. The tasks have been grouped in the following way:

- Locate the first post office through the main square of the city (T1).
- Select at least one or two of the points of touristic interest excluding the museums (T2).
- Situate the areas where the markets or craftsmanship fairs take place, with their matching dates or timetables (T3).

Figure 1. Thematic and touristic map (brochure) in "Sierras de Córdoba", Argentina

Figure 2. Roads and local information (leaflet) in "Huerta Grande, Sierras de Córdoba", Argentina

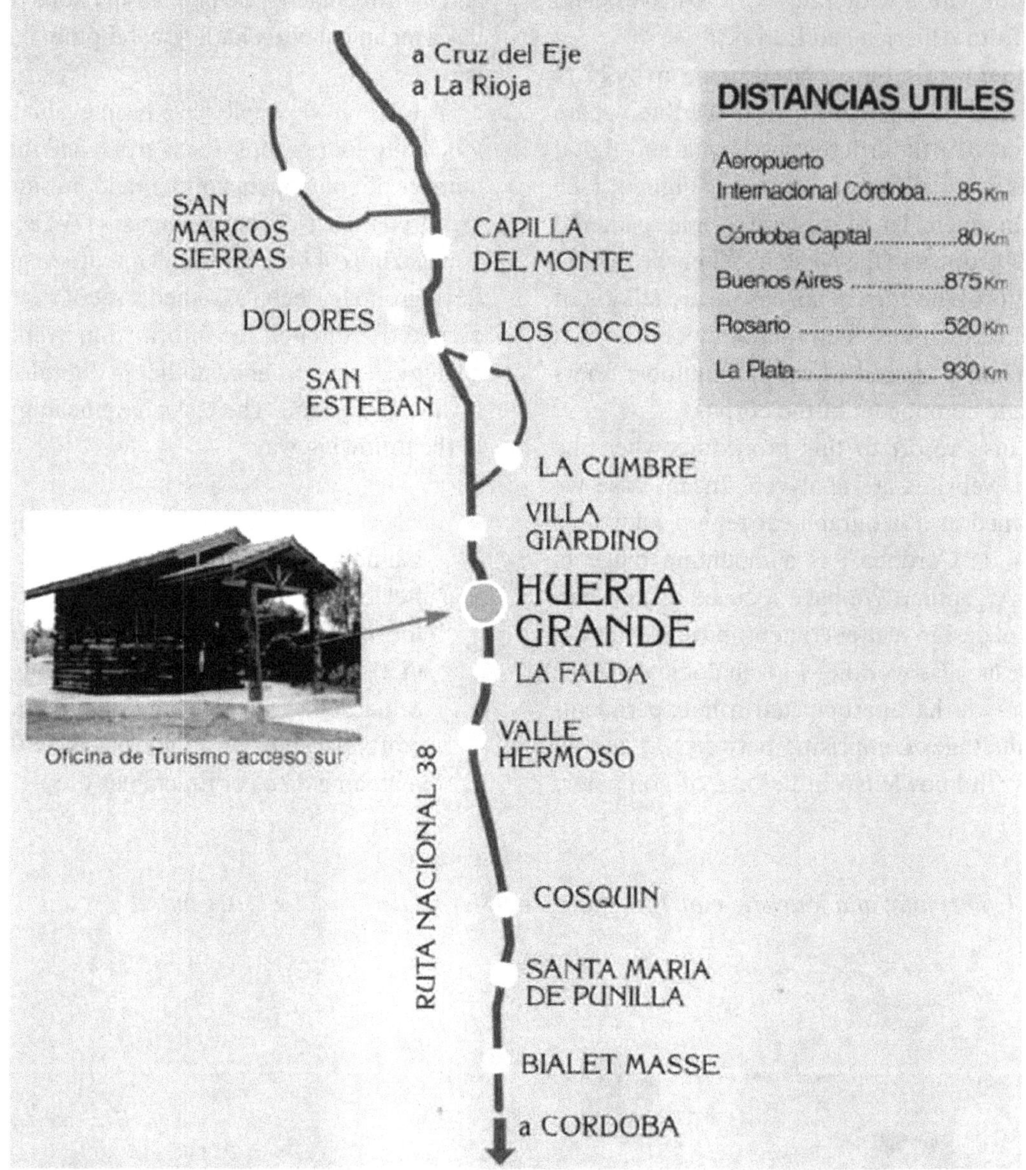

- Determine the cost of the entrance to the museums (T4).
- Establish whether the town which is visited has WiFi zones (T5).

For each task, the users wrote down the time spent (less than a minute, between 1 and 2 minutes, between 2 and 4 minutes, over 4 minutes). In their turn the communicability experts through the direct observation technique also wrote down the times to verify the accuracy of the obtained results. The obtained results (figure 4) were grouped in time averages first for each one of the groups and finally through the group of analogical means and digital means.

As means of interactive digital communication the users have used: computers, PC tablets and multimedia mobile phones. Whereas the ana-

Figure 3. UNESCO cultural heritage (DVD) in Cerro Colorado "Sierras de Córdoba", Argentina)

Figure 4. Results obtained in carrying out (T)asks related to tourism, using (A)nalogical and (D)igital media into four (G)roups

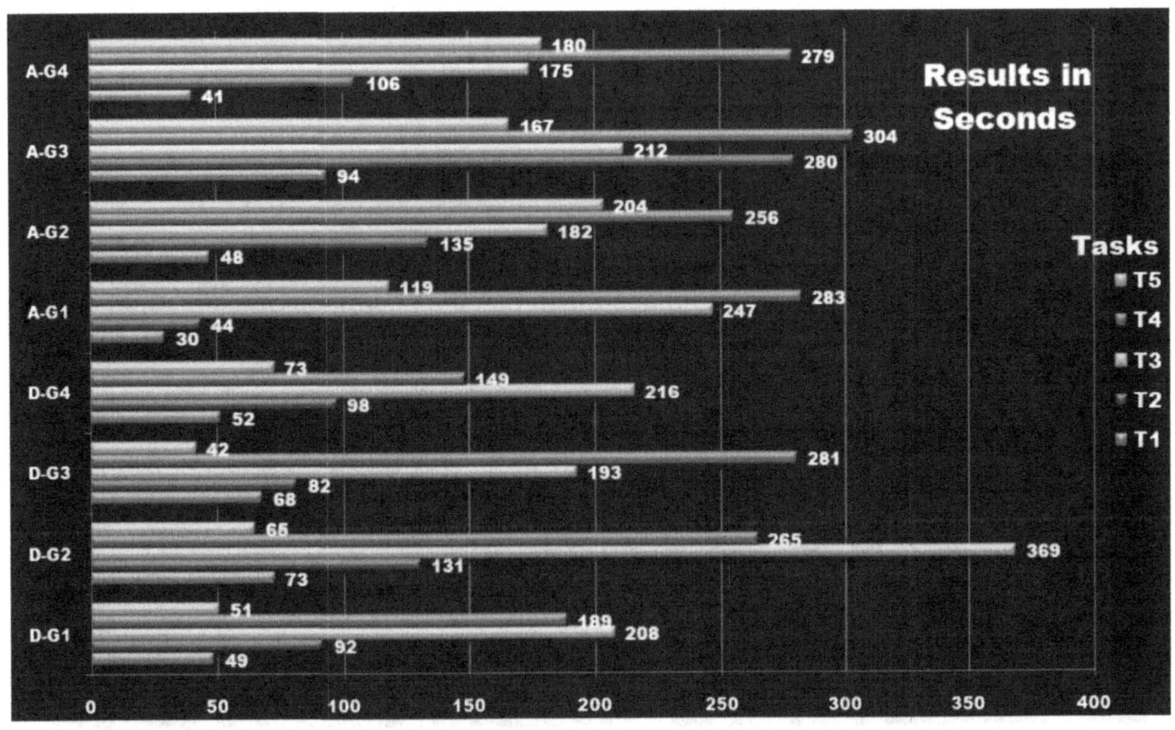

logical media (paper support) were: magazines, catalogues, tourism guides and maps. In both media and from the point of view of visual design were also analyzed the ambiguity or not of the icons related to the touristic information on the maps. To such an end files were created with each one of the icons that appeared in the maps of our universe of study. The difference between analogical media and digital media is in Figure 5:

The experiments carried out have allowed to verify the validity and compatibility of the analogical and digital information, although there is a trend to the preference of paper for the maps with the points of touristic interest.

LEARNED LESSONS AND FUTURE WORKS

The results make apparent that from the point of view of communicability the paper support still remains an adequate media for touristic promotion in small towns, in the face of users of the new technologies. For instance, the users who have participated in the evaluation and who seek the real and non-virtual information offices still prefer the signals in analogical maps, seeking the opening timetables of a museum on a brochure, study the touristic itineraries in a guidebook, etc. In contrast, they prefer to know down to the tiniest detail of what they could find in the main streets of those densely populated cities and crammed with souvenirs shops, for instance.

In future works we will insert new groups of users, such as the students of technical computer science institutes and those belonging to the early courses of university computer science. Besides, we will generate a wide listing of touristic activities to be carried out but in groups. Finally, we will generate a prototype of touristic information for the different digital screens in last generation computer science or microcomputing.

CONCLUSION

Regardless of the support that is used in offering touristic information, as time passes the users of interactive systems gradually acquire a set of elements which allow them to orient themselves

Figura 5. The minimum value of ambiguity is 0 and the maximum is 100

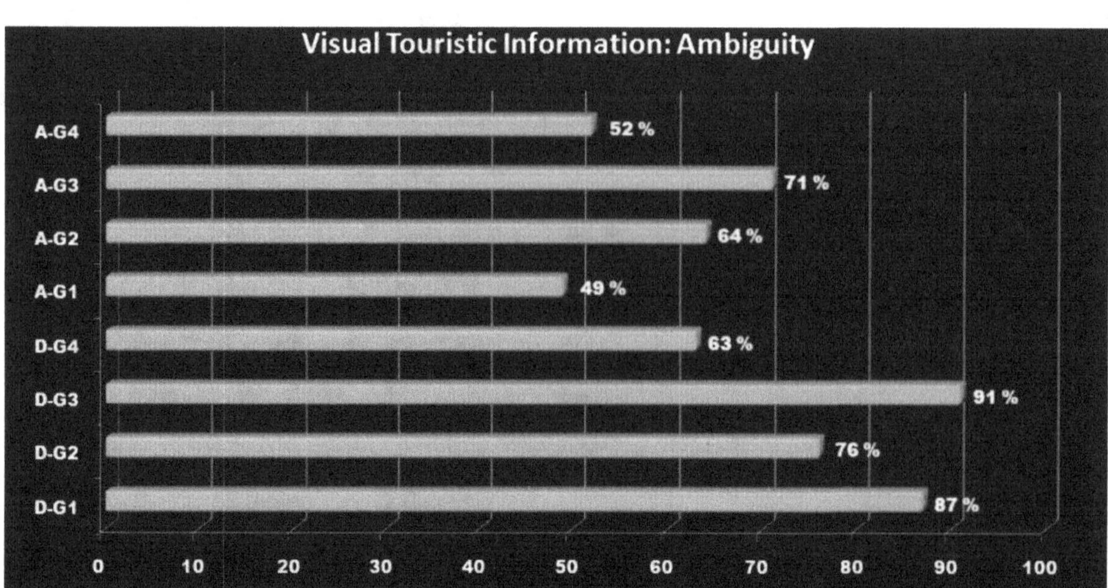

and predict the behavior of the computer system they are using. When this production is natural and the empathy of the communicability has high level qualities, it is feasible to obtain a minimalist design in the interfaces of the different interactive systems. To the extent to which the interactive design distances itself from these principles, paper will still play a main role. This is a reality of the analysis of the reading preferences of the touristic information on last generation digital screens, with users who were born under the digital era, such as those who have collaborated in the current work.

Now from the touristic point of view the small towns may get interesting results when the information faithfully reflects the reality the visitors will find when they arrive at those places. Besides, if every town generates its own identity, including common denominators inside the same geographical area, with the rest of municipalities which make up a region, then it is possible to compete internationally with other touristic destinations. This statement is feasible, as long as the quality rules are respected in both digital and analogical information, as it has been seen in this study.

ACKNOWLEDGMENT

The authors would like to thank to Maria Ficarra, Mary Brie, Luisa Varela, Valeria Villarreal, Doris Edison, Pamela Fulton, Marie Bordeaux, Donald Nilson, Jim Carré, and Carlos for helpful comments.

REFERENCES

Cipolla-Ficarra, et al. (1993). Barcelona media: Del comic infográfico a los interactivos. *Imaging –. Press Graph*, *3*, 46–52.

Cipolla-Ficarra, et al. (2010). *Quality and communicability for interactive hypermedia systems: Concepts and practices for design*. Hershey, PA: IGI Global. doi:10.4018/978-1-61520-763-3

Cipolla-Ficarra, F. (1996). Evaluation and communication techniques in multimedia product design for on the net university education. In *Multimedia on the Net*. Vienna, Austria: Springer-Verlag. doi:10.1007/978-3-7091-9472-0_14

Cipolla-Ficarra, F. (1997). Evaluation of multimedia components. In *Proceedings of International Conference on Multimedia Computing and Systems*. New York: IEEE Computer Society.

Cipolla-Ficarra, F. (1999). MEHEM: A methodology for heuristic evaluation in multimedia. In *Proceedings of Sixth International Conference on Distributed Multimedia Systems (DMS'99)*. Elsevier.

Cipolla-Ficarra, F. (2000). MECEM: Metrics for the communications evaluation in mutimedia. In *Proceedings of International Conference on Information Systems Analysis and Synthesis – ISAS 2000*. Orlando, FL: ISAS.

Cipolla-Ficarra, F. (2010). Human-computer interaction, tourism and cultural heritage. In *Proceedings of HCITOCH 2010*. Berlin: Springer.

Fernandes, T. (1995). *Global interface design: A guide to designing international user interfaces*. Boston: Academic Press.

Nielsen, J. (1993). *Usability engineering*. London: Academic Press.

Shneiderman, B. et al. (2010). *Designing the user interface: Strategies for effective human-computer interaction*. New York: Addison Wesley.

Chapter 49
Generic Model of a Multi-Agent System to Assist Ubiquitous Learning

Elena B. Durán
Departamento de Informática, Facultad de Ciencias Exactas y Tecnologías, Universidad Nacional de Santiago del Estero, Argentina

Margarita M. Álvarez
Departamento de Informática, Facultad de Ciencias Exactas y Tecnologías, Universidad Nacional de Santiago del Estero, Argentina

Silvina I. Únzaga
Departamento de Informática, Facultad de Ciencias Exactas y Tecnologías, Universidad Nacional de Santiago del Estero, Argentina

ABSTRACT

Ubiquitous learning (u-learning) is a new educational paradigm that takes place in a ubiquitous computing environment and allows proper content for learning at convenient place and time, thus matching the student features and needs. The development of u-learning applications requires considering the user characteristics and necessities and the complex set with multiple ways of mobility, diverse mobile technology, diversity of carriers, and also the diversity of learning situations that might happen. The agent technology and the Semantic Web with ontologies offer efficient tools to manage this problem. On the other hand, the complexity inherent in this kind of application requires adequate strategies to manage the multiple components and interrelations. In this chapter, a model-based development approach is proposed to obtain a generic model of the system, and the architecture of it as a set of software agents.

DOI: 10.4018/978-1-4666-4490-8.ch049

INTRODUCTION

Nowadays the huge development in wireless communication technology has made an impressive progress, introducing the creation of a new field in computer science, namely, ubiquitous or pervasive computing. This new area in computer science tries to add to the everyday objects such things as the capacity of computing, wireless communication, and the interaction between both, creating a new model of the reality where these objects operate, in order to facilitate the tasks for people. The main purpose of ubiquitous computing is to identify the user, find out the location, deduce intentions and necessities and act according to them. Ubiquitous computing tries to dramatically change the present paradigm for human-computer interaction, offering an aid to anyone who is the focus of the attention.

Particularly, in the field of education, ubiquitous computing has fostered the rise of a new way of learning: the ubiquitous learning (u-learning), which encloses a set of educational activities, supported by technology, that is available anywhere and at anytime, from a great variety of devices. In a ubiquitous learning environment students learn with a PDA (Personal Digital Assistant), a WebP, a Tablet or a PC, indoors or outdoors, individually or in groups. The main characteristics of computer assisted ubiquitous learning are: persistence, accessibility, immediacy, interaction and situated learning activities (Chen, Kao, Sheu, & Chiang, 2004; Curtis, Luchini, Bobrowsky, Quintana, & Soloway, 2002). This set of characteristics explains why the generation of systems developed to assist the ubiquitous learning is a complicated task.

To tackle this problem, Semantic Web, software agent technology and personalization techniques show up as valid alternatives to enhance the development of the ubiquitous assisted learning systems.

The semantic Web or Web 3.0 is the new generation Web that makes it possible to express the information in an accurate way, understandable by the computer, to share and reuse information, and to understand which terms describe the meaning of data. One of the key components of the semantic Web is ontologies, which are an exhaustive and precise conceptual schema, within one or several given domains. They are built to enhance communication and for information exchange between different systems and entities, thus solving persistence and accessibility problems for the systems, which support ubiquitous learning

Agents use the needed technologies to extract information from the Web, to assist the search for information based on metadata, to interpret the retrieved information obtained by the ontology, and to process information (Antoniou & Harmelen, 2004).

Personalization, in particular, is considered to be a powerful methodology to improve the efficiency in the search for information and decision making. It enables us to design systems able to suggest relevant and personalized information for users, according to their characteristics and preferences, based on a User Model. Therefore, the application of personalization techniques offers the student situated learning activities, that is to say, adjusted to the context in which they operate.

The architecture of a Web system is introduced in this paper, consisting of a set of software agents responsible for the maintenance of the required ontologies to personalize the various services of the ubiquitous learning environment.

THEORETICAL FRAMEWORKS

Ubiquitous Learning

Thanks to the rapid development of wireless communication and mobile devices technologies there is a trend for u-learning to become a promising solution to educational problems in which the situation of students is detected and proportional assistance to each student is delivered (Chen,

Li, & Chen, 2007; Hwang, Tsai, & Yang, 2008; Kuo, Hwang, Chen, & Wang, 2007; Si, Weng, & Tseng, 2006).

U-learning is the result of merging e-learning and ubiquitous computing.

Moreover, ubiquitous computing is defined as a computing environment weaved into the fabric of everyday life and it becomes invisible (Weiser, 2003). Invisibility is the most important feature in ubiquitous computing. The user is exposed to a few sets of available services and is unaware of the implementation of complex systems that support the services (Satyanarayanan, 2001).

This brings the human-computer interaction to a different dimension, where the user is surrounded by a complete and intelligent environment, consisting of devices or sensors which communicate to each other, and functions which deliver a set of consolidated services. Therefore, in the field of ubiquitous computing, software agents, services and devices should perfectly articulate and cooperate in order to assist human goals such as to prefigure necessities, negotiate for a service, act on behalf of the user, and deliver services anywhere and at anytime.

Ubiquitous computing environment devices, services and agents should be aware of their contexts and automatically adapt to the changing contexts, what is known as context of conscience. Any information that could be used to describe the situation of an entity is referred by context, anytime an entity is a physical informatics person, place or object.

In a learning process, context consists of two fundamental environments, namely, the learning context and the mobile/ubiquitous context. In the learning context environment, many authors have presented different interpretations of the term "context", and they seem to concur that a learning context refers to the environment, situations, tools, materials, persons (in terms of social networks), and learning activities. To be more accurate, learning context is characterized by students, learning objects and the learning pathway, where the set of learning activities is achieved under the light of a specific pedagogic approach.

Context, in mobile and ubiquitous environments is mostly summarized in the space and temporal aspects of the user situation. Based on changes and proprieties of these two attributes, users of these systems will be informed on the different personalized services which are available to them (Siadaty, Torniai, Gašević, Jovanovic, & Marek-Hatala, 2008).

Ontologies

The term ontology originated in philosophy, a discipline that intends to offer a systematic explanation of existence, by means of the study of the nature of being, its basic categories and its relations. Although it is a robust area for research in this field, ontology is now an object of research, development and application in other disciplines now related to computer science, artificial intelligence, Semantic Web, and knowledge, among others. From a technological point of view, many definitions have been produced, but the most frequent to be found is that from (Gruber, 1993) who defines it as "an explicit explanation of a conceptualization".

Ontologies try to formulate a conceptual, exhaustive and accurate framework about a specific domain, with the aim of facilitating the communication, reuse and share information between organizations, computers and humans (Ramos & Nuñez, 2007).

Ontology is a hierarchy of concepts with attributes and relations that define a harmonized terminology to indicate semantic networks of interrelated units of information. It defines a common vocabulary to share information within a specific domain, and such vocabulary consists of classes or concepts, class properties or attributes, and relations between classes (Fermoso-García, Sánchez-Alonso, & Sicilia, 2008). Then, the components for ontology are classes, attributes, and the information about its meaning and limitations.

Software Agents

In general, an agent is anything that can be considered perceiving the environment by means of sensors, and responds or acts in the environment by means of effectors [16].

Thus, it is possible to find different kind of agents, among them human agents, robotic agents, and software agents, the latter consisting in a computer program to be run in an environment, and that performs actions to attain the goals for which it was designed, and its perceptions and actions are controlled by means of instructions given in a particular language (Franklin & Graesser, 1996).

Intelligent agents can be thought of as a part of the software which successfully completes a task using environmentally gathered information and acting in an appropriate manner until the task is fulfilled. Intelligent agent is define as "a software entity that, based on its own knowledge, performs a set of operations to fulfill the needs of a user or another program, whether by taking the initiative or because any of the users has required to do it" (Wooldridge & Jennings, 1995).

A program must have the following features to be considered an intelligent agent (Russell & Norvig, 1996).

- **Autonomy:** Agents operate without the direct intervention of humans or any other one, and have some kind of control over their actions and internal state. They must be able to produce actions independently of the user.
- **Social Ability:** Agents are able to interact with other Agents or a human user.
- **Reactivity:** Agents perceive their environment, and respond in a timely fashion to changes that occur in it.
- **Pro-Activeness:** Agents do not simply act in response to their environment; they are able to react by taking the initiative without the intervention of any user to activate it.
- **Object Oriented to Final Goal:** Divides a complex task into several smaller activities in order to attain a complex goal.
- **Rationality:** Always acts to achieve specific goals and never in the opposite direction.
- **Adaptability:** Agents should be able to adjust to user habits, ways of work and necessities based on previous experiences.
- **Collaboration:** Agents should be able to indicate important information even when a user had delivered ambiguous information.

Other characteristics of intelligent agents found in most of the literature in this area are: dynamic action (agent actions should be independent from space and time), temporal continuity (agents should not stop and resume certain tasks, they rather act in a continuous process), and mobility (agents could be transferred from a machine to another one and be supported even by different architectures and platforms).

Besides, a multi-agent system is defined as a software system, a flexible connected network consisting of multiple agents contending, cooperating, and working together with the aim of finding answers, solving problems or delivering services which surpass the capacity or knowledge of any other agent acting individually (Durfee, Lesser, & Corkill, 1989).

In a multi-agent system, agents have knowledge different from the domain, diverse responsibilities, and apply different intern agent architectures.

RELATED WORK

Much related work can be found which is concerned with the research done in the core of the present article. Main contributions of other authors are summarized in this section that is related to:

educational ontologies, and in particular ontologies for ubiquitous learning systems, Personalization in ubiquitous learning systems, and Agent Technologies applied to learning systems.

Background of Applied Ontology to Ubiquitous Learning

In the last decade, a lot of research has been done on the use of ontologies as a possible approach to explain the implicit knowledge of certain domains, to overcome the problem of semantic heterogeneity and to integrate information that comes from different data sources. In educational informatics, ontologies play an important and always increasing role, driven by many research works. Specific ontologies have been developed to support personalized learning in Semantic Web, such as: domain, user, observation and presentation ontologies.

Regarding ontology application to ubiquitous learning systems the following works can be mentioned:

In (Tao, Xiao, Hang, Hung, & Da-Qing, 2004) is proposed an ontology-based formal context model using OWL dealing with issues such as semantic context representation, reasoning, knowledge sharing and context classification. Based on this context model, Service-Oriented Context-Aware Middleware (SOCAM) architecture is introduced for the production of context sensitive services.

An ontology-based framework, m-LOCO, is based on ontologies such as: learning design ontology, user domain ontology, and learning objects ontology, and its main purpose is to capture context information in learning mobile environments (Siadaty, Torniai, Gašević, Jovanovic, & Marek-Hatala, 2008). A work introduced by Yang et al. presents a context model that formally defines context description for student services. In this work, student and content ontologies are defined (Yang, Angus Chen, Tseng, & Shen, 2006).

CALA-ONT, ontology based context model and a conceptual architecture to supply context sensitive learning services in ubiquitous learning environments are introduced in (Myoung-Woo & Dae-Jea, 2008). The proposed model is focused on a context sensitive manager to supply learning services according to context changes in student environments. Ontology expresses the school environment. The research also suggests the possibility of producing reasoning about context and learning services by means of the use of architecture and ontology.

Background for the Application of Agents in Ubiquitous Learning Systems

A work introduced by da Silva et al. (Da-Silva, Mendes-Neto, & Muniz, 2011). describes the implementation of an agent-based approach for recommending learning objects in ubiquitous learning environments. The use of learning objects in standard ways enable, among other benefits, the possibility of reusing contents and the interoperability between different systems of learning management.

Multi-agent architecture, MMA, for learning support systems in a ubiquitous or pervasive environment is presented in (Maiga, Qing, Tzu-Chien, & Lin., 2008). The project prefigures the construction of a MMA-based learning environment with many agents with different abilities. For instance, one agent is able to detect the location of a student, another agent plans the user learning path, and a third agent is able to guide the user in a journey through the real world, and then another one can look for and access a map on behalf of the user. All the agents can communicate and cooperate with each other. The project expects the agents to automatically determine the physical location of the users, find the adequate learning path, make plan for distributed learning and guide the users that are learning in the real world (Maiga, Qing, Tzu-Chien, & Lin., 2008).

Vladoiu and Constantinescu (Vladoiu& Constantinescu, 2011) introduce a multi-agent architecture for context sensitive systems and the learning scenario for a ubiquitous learning environment. A variety of agents is described, such as: device agents, Spatial Information Grid (SIG) agents, reasoning agents, knowledge mining agents, information retrieving agents, etc.

GENERIC MODEL APPLICATIONS TO SUPPORT UBIQUITOUS LEARNING

In order to deal with the complexity attached to informatics applications able to support ubiquitous learning, it is proposed to approach the task considering a model-based design, since these applications are provided with the following characteristics: they allow emphasizing certain aspects of a problem while hiding others; they are comprehensible for users and developers, they are accurate in the sense that they allow precise representation of the modeling object, they are predictive since they can be used to infer correct conclusions, and they are easier to construct and study than is the system itself. Therefore, and considering that a model is apt at: specifying the system (structure and behavior); understanding the system (if there is one already); reasoning and validating the system (detect design errors and omissions; execute the model, infer and demonstrate attributes), and guiding the implementation, then it is decided to approach the support application design for ubiquitous learning basing the design on a set of models representing the more relevant characteristics of the problem. In Figure 1 the generic model for ubiquitous learning applications is shown. These applications can be represented through the following models:

Figure 1. Generic Model Applications to Support Ubiquitous Learning

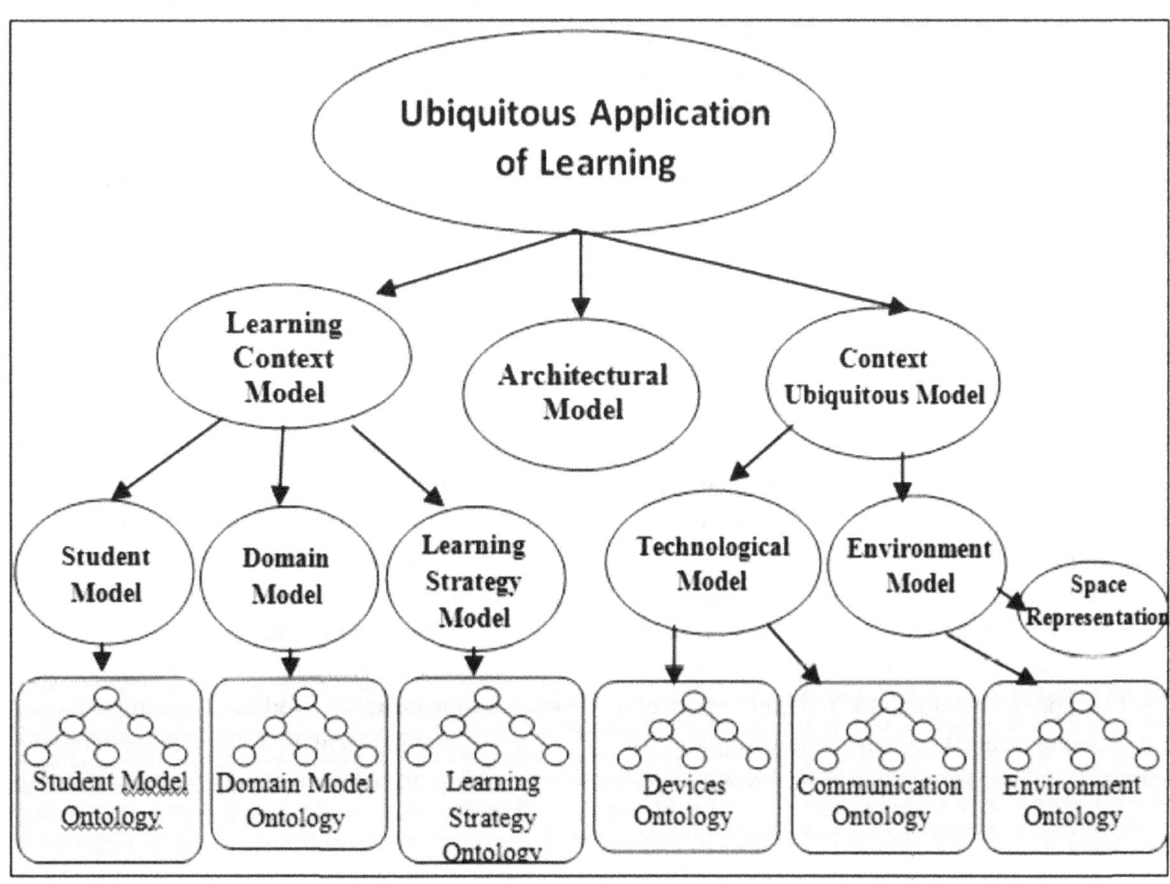

- **Architectural Model:** Represents the software architectural type to be used for the implementation of each particular application. Following architectures are considered: *Client* when the application is developed to be installed and executed in a mobile device, and is able to access external resources; *Client-Server:* when the application is developed in two parts, one of them is installed and executed in mobile devices and the other one is installed and remain accessible in the server; *Web Server,* when the application is developed to be installed and remain accessible in a server. From the browser of a mobile device the application -installed in a server- can be accessed.

In order to represent the contextual information on learning situations, and to supply the students with personalized and context sensitive contents and activities, concise and comprehensible representation methods are required. For this purpose, we consider ontologies as the pertinent candidate for ubiquitous context representation in open environments because of their flexibility, expressibility and extensibility. Also, they are provided with reasoning mechanisms on available context data, and it is possible to deduce knowledge from implicit established situations.

Ubiquitous and context sensitive applications were widely discussed by researches in several areas of this domain. Based on the requirements and characteristics of each of these domains, the term "context" has been interpreted in different ways and diverse approaches have been applied to capture contextual information. One of these domains is the ubiquitous learning environment. In particular, the ubiquitous learning environment comprises two fundamental areas, namely, the learning context and the mobile/ubiquitous context (Siadaty, Torniai, Gašević, Jovanovic, & Marek-Hatala, 2008). Therefore, in this work two generic models are proposed to represent the ubiquitous learning environment: the learning context model, with which students, contents, activities and a pedagogic approach can be represented, and ubiquitous context model, with which spatial and temporal aspects of the student user can be represented.

Learning context model is composed of three models:

- **Student Model:** Consists of one ontology that describes the more relevant characteristics of the student for personalization (student identification, academic data, learning style, capacities, knowledge, personality, group behavior, namely: roles, collaboration capacity, etc., information preferences and her/his ubiquity information).
- **Domain Model:** Is composed of an ontology that describes the organization, representation and structure of learning objects.
- **Learning Strategy Model:** Is composed of an ontology that describes actions that can be offered the student to achieve the most meaningful learning in a ubiquitous context.

The ubiquitous context model consists then of two models:

- **Technological Model:** Is composed of an Ontology for Devices that describes the different devices a student is able to use (PDA, sensors, mobile phones, tablets, etc.) and the software they support, and then an Ontology for communication that describes the different communication systems between system and user.
- **Environment Model:** Is composed of an Environment Ontology describing the different environments where learning

can be achieved (home, work site, learning resource center) related to a Space Representation.

All the indicated ontologies are comprised in a more general ontology referred to as ONTO-AU, which is described in (Alvarez, Duran, & Unzaga, 2012).

Multi-Agent System Architecture

In order to manage all the above mentioned models it is proposed to implement a set of software agents. So, the multi-agent system, personalized for ubiquitous learning support (Figure 2), consists of ten software agents. Three of them are interface agents that enable the system to interact with users (students), with mobile computing devices and with communication systems (wired and wireless networks). Six agents are responsible for maintaining the system ontologies, and the remaining one is responsible for coordinating the system personalization services (interface, content offering, pedagogical activities –individually or collaboratively- learning strategies, recommendations, navigation, etc.).

- **User Interface Agent:** Is responsible for presenting the different personalized services and information to students, offering ubiquitous learning a support application; and capturing the requests the student introduces into the system, as well as the answers obtained by the system.
- **Device Interface Agent:** Is responsible for identifying the type of device used by

Figure 2. Multi-agent system architecture

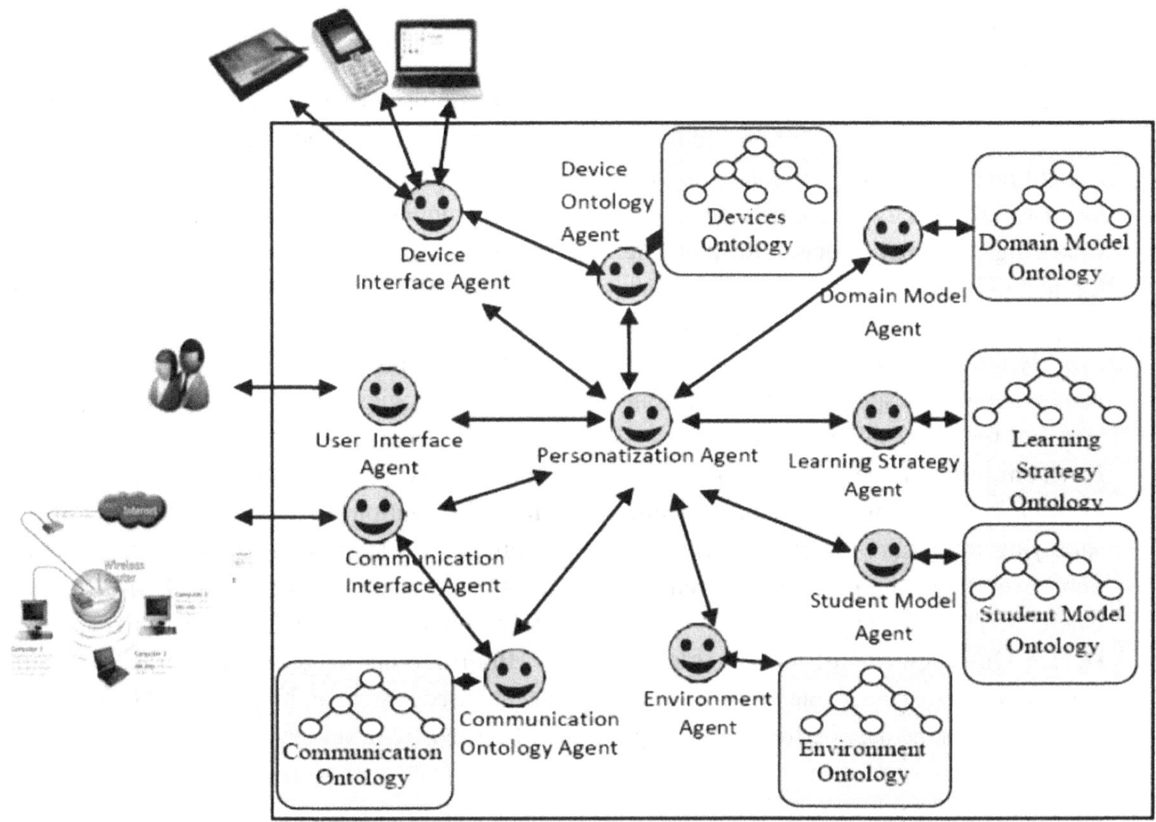

a specific user in a certain moment and communicating it to the personalization agent in order to personalize the services and information offered to the user, in accordance with the type of the device used.

- **Communication Interface Agent:** Responsible for identifying the type of communication system (Internet, intranet, etc.) that a specific user utilizes in a certain moment, and communicating it to the personalization agent in order to be able to personalize services and information offered to the user, in accordance with the used communication system.
- **Domain Model Agent:** Responsible for maintaining the domain ontology and offering information about the learning objects that the personalization agent will offer to students according to their profile, educational scenario and educational strategy, and according to the device and the communication net used by the specific user, in a certain place and time.
- **Student Model Agent:** Responsible for maintaining the student model ontology and offering the personalization agent the needed information to personalize the services according to the student profile.
- **Learning Strategy Agent:** Responsible for maintaining the learning strategy ontology and supplying the most appropriate strategy for a specific user to the personalization agent, in a specific ubiquitous context, and for a determined domain.
- **Environment Agent:** Responsible for maintaining the environment ontology and supplying information to the personalization agent about the educational scenario where the learning is applied.
- **Device Ontology Agent:** Responsible for maintaining the device ontology according to changes the user performs, and supplying information on such devices to the personalization agent in order to be able to personalize the services and information offered to the user according to the type of device that is used in a determined moment.
- **Communication Ontology Agent:** Responsible for maintaining the communication ontology according to the changes informed by the Communication Interface agent in function of the communication system that the student uses for connecting to the ubiquitous learning application.
- **Personalization Agent:** Responsible for personalizing the different services offered to the user according to the available information brought by other agents, and communicating it to the User Interface Agent in order to interact with the student.

CONCLUSION AND FUTURE WORK

The main advantage of the proposed model is the possibility of managing a set of sub-models which helps to approach, in the simplest way, the principal problems inherent to Web applications for the ubiquitous learning support. The proposed generic model could be instantiated for particular applications, adapting each sub-model to the specific case.

Also, the proposed agent architecture and the use of ontologies offer the system an important flexibility, since each agent will be able to independently decide what is needed to fulfill the targets and offer solutions to a user or to another agent. Then, they are appropriate for acting in changing and unpredictable environments as it is in the case of ubiquitous environment for learning.

Both the proposed generic model and the multi-agent based system architecture will be available to be used by developers of ubiquitous mobile learning environment applications, to enhance the possibility of assisting students in their learning tasks, anywhere and at anytime.

We are currently working on the detailed design of the proposed ontologies. In the short term, the instantiation of the proposed generic model for a ubiquitous learning scenario to assist students when they are doing the supervised professional practice (PPS) is anticipated.

REFERENCES

Alvarez, M., Duran, E., & Unzaga, S. (2012). *ONTO-AU: Una ontología para sistemas de apoyo al aprendizaje ubicuo*. Tucumán: VIII Jornadas de Ciencias y Tecnologías de Facultades de Ingeniería del NOA.

Antoniou, G., & Harmelen, F. (2004). *A semantic web primer*. Cambridge, MA: The MIT Press.

Chen, C., Li, Y., & Chen, M. (2007). Personalized context-aware ubiquitous learning system for supporting effectively English vocabulary learning. In *Proceedings of Seventh IEEE International Conference on Advanced Learning Technologies*. IEEE.

Chen, Y., Kao, T., Sheu, J., & Chiang, C. (2004). A mobile scaffolding-aid-based bird –watching learning system. In *Proceedings of International Workshop on Wireless and Mobile Technologies in Education*. New York: IEEE Press.

Curtis, M., Luchini, K., Bobrowsky, W., Quintana, C., & Soloway, E. (2002). Handheld use in K-12: A descriptive account. In *Proceedings of the International Workshop on Wireless and Mobile Technologies in Education*. IEEE Computer Society.

Da-Silva, L., Mendes-Neto, F., & Muniz, R. (2011). An agent-based approach for supporting ubiquitous learning. *International Journal of Scientific & Engineering Research*, *2*(9).

Durfee, E., Lesser, V., & Corkill, D. (1989). Trends in cooperative distributed problem solving. *IEEE Transactions on Knowledge and Data Engineering*, *1*(1), 63–83. doi:10.1109/69.43404

Fermoso-García, A., Sánchez-Alonso, S., & Sicilia, M. (2008). Una ontología en OWL para la representación semántica de objetos de aprendizaje. *V Simposio Pluridisciplinar sobre Diseño y Evaluación de Contenidos Educativos Reutilizables*. Salamanca. Retrieved from http://www.web.upsa.es/spdece08/contribuciones/176_Fermoso_ Sanchez_Sicilia_LOMOWL.pdf

Franklin, S., & Graesser, A. (1996). Is it an agent, or just a program? A taxonomy for autonomous agents. In *Proceedings of Third International Workshop on Agent Theories, Architectures, and Languages, Budapest*. Heidelberg, Germany: Springer.

Gruber, T. (1993). *Toward principles for the design of ontologies used for knowledge sharing*. Retrieved from http://citeseer.ist.psu.edu/gruber93toward.html

Hwang, G., Tsai, C., & Yang, S. (2008). Criteria, strategies and research issues of context-aware ubiquitous learning. *Journal of Educational Technology & Society*, *11*(2), 81–91.

Kuo, F., Hwang, G., Chen, Y., & Wang, S. (2007). Standards and tools for context-aware ubiquitous learning. In *Proceedings of Seventh IEEE International Conference on Advanced Learning Technologies*. IEEE.

Maiga, C., Qing, T., Tzu-Chien, L., & Lin, O. (2008). Multi-agent architecture-based location-aware service project for ubiquitous learning. In *Proceedings of 16th International Conference on Computers in Education*. IEEE.

Myoung-Woo, H., & Dae-Jea, C. (2008). Ontology context model for context-aware learning service in ubiquitous learning environments. *International Journal of Computers*, *2*(83), 193–200.

Ramos, E., & Nuñez, H. (2007). *Ontologías: Componentes, metodologías, lenguajes, herramientas y aplicaciones*. Universidad Central de Venezuela.

Russell, S., & Norvig, P. (1996). *Inteligencia artificial, un enfoque moderno*. Prentice Hall.

Satyanarayanan, M. (2001). Pervasive computing: Vision and challenges. *IEEE Personal Communications*, *8*, 10–17.

Si, N., Weng, J., & Tseng, S. (2006). Building a frame-based interaction and learning model for u-learning. In *Proceedings of 3rd International Conference on Ubiquitous Intelligence and Computing*. IEEE.

Siadaty, M., Torniai, C., Gašević, D., Jovanovic, J., & Marek-Hatala, M. (2008). m-LOCO: An ontology-based framework for context-aware mobile learning. In *Proceedings of Sixth International Workshop on Ontologies and Semantic Web for E-Learning in Conjunction with ITS*. ITS.

Tao, G., Xiao, Hang, W., Hung, K., & Da-Qing, Z. (2004). An ontology-based context model in intelligent environments. *Computer and Information Science,* (6), 270–275.

Vladoiu, M., & Constantinescu, Z. (2011). U-learning within a context-aware multiagent environment. *International Journal of Computer Networks & Communications*, *3*(1). doi:10.5121/ijcnc.2011.3101

Weiser, M. (2003). The computer for the 21st century. *IEEE Pervasive Computing / IEEE Computer Society [and] IEEE Communications Society*, 19–25.

Wen-Chung, S., & Shian-Shyong, T. (2009). A knowledge-based approach to retrieving teaching materials for contextaware learning. *Journal of Educational Technology & Society*, *12*(1), 82–106.

Wooldridge, M., & Jennings, N. (1995). Intelligent agents: Theory and practice. *The Knowledge Engineering Review*, *10*(2), 115–152. doi:10.1017/S0269888900008122

Yang, J., Angus, F., Chen, R., Tseng, S., & Shen, Y. (2006). Context model and context acquisition for ubiquitous content access in u-learning environments. In *Proceedings of the IEEE International Conference on Sensor Networks, Ubiquitous, and Trustworthy Computing*, (Vol. 2, pp. 78–83). IEEE.

Chapter 50
MLW and Bilingualism: Case Study and Critical Evaluation

Daniela López De Luise
CIIS Lab – Buenos Aires, Argentina

Débora Hisgen
CIIS Lab – Buenos Aires, Argentina

ABSTRACT

The language acquisition and generation process is complex and non-linear. The child goes through a series of progressive stages with distinct characteristics. The statistic study of production by age or linguistic groups can be complemented with linguistic models based on morphosyntactic wavelet technology to improve the understanding of concurrent phenomena, which underlie linguistic reasoning.

INTRODUCTION

Psycholinguistics is cross-discipline area of knowledge between linguistics and psychology. Its main subject of study is the relation that can be established between linguistic knowledge and the mental processes implied by it (Dictionary ELE, 2012).

As an example of the first contributions that work across linguistics, neuropsychology and psychology, we can mention: Leonard Bloomfield, Hans Furth, Ivar Loovas, Alfred Strauss, Paula Menyuk (Bloomfield, 2009; Furth, 1966; Lovaas, 1977; Strauss& Werner, 1942; Menyuk, 1969) and among the most recent ones, Bertrand Russel, Karl Pribram, Juan Azcoaga, etc. (Russell, 1905; Pribram, 1971; Azcoaga, 1986).

Even with their differences (behaviorist, innatist and constructivist theories) they share the common element of an interest in studying the impact of the acquisition of languages that are alternative to the mother tongue in the process of reasoning.

The aim of this work is to present a model of language manipulation and automated extraction of essential information from a set of given expressions from natural language. This model was implemented in a prototype, and expects to

DOI: 10.4018/978-1-4666-4490-8.ch050

become a tool for the evaluation and simulation of the psycholinguistic processes that take place during comprehension and speech. The different aspects of the model as applied in the prototype have been already evaluated before (López De Luise & Soffer, 2008a, 2008b; López De Luise, 2010a, 2010b, 2010c, 2010d). The main focus here is the evaluation of the model in the context of bilingualism. For this, we shall first lay out the current accepted theories about bilingualism, and analyze the formal and technical aspects that have been left uninterpreted or given a biased interpretation (Section I). The use of linguistic computation can cover these problems or at least contribute to a better understanding of certain aspects. Later we shall describe the main aspects of the linguistic reasoning model, which consists of Morphosyntactic wavelets (Section II). In Section III we present cases from real texts and the result of applying the model to them. We shall also undertake comparative statistics to gain a deeper understanding of the influence of second language acquisition at an early age in the reasoning process. Section IV details some of the implications, derivations and applications of the model to the field.

EARLY BILINGUALISM AND ITS CONSEQUENCES

The first researches in the field suggest that learning two languages in childhood was detrimental for the child's cognitive capacity (Darcy, 1963) and that bilingualism was a source of mental confusion and brought about linguistic disadvantages.

Today all of these statements are challenged by other authors who consider them to be unfounded (Cummins, 1978). From the results obtained in the application of the model we can infer that both perspectives can be thought as being right and wrong in some respect.

When the child speaks two languages fluidly, he knows more than a word for the same object or concept. Some researches consider this as an element in favor of the child's cognitive flexibility.

In relation to the model and the evaluations of the statistics section, this multiplicity appears as an element that might in some respect significantly focus the reasoning process, not as a weakening factor but as a mere adaptation to the requirements of the environment.

Many works in the field of psychopedagogy point out certain cognitive advantages that bilingualism may generate in the development of reasoning. Technically they are based in works by Ellen Bialystok, who has published several works which at the same time are extensions of ideas presented by her during the 80s.

According to a study by Ellen Bialystok on children of 4 to 8 years of age (Bialystok, Michelle, & Martin, 2008), bilingual children appear to be more efficient at solving problems with deceptive information than monolingual ones. This tendency can be observed both in verbal and non-verbal tasks. It suggests that the development of the executive function[1] in general terms, and of the inhibitory function in particular, is influenced by bilingualism. Although this has not been proved conclusively, statistic evidence allows us to establish some kind of relation between bilingualism and the reasoning process. The problem on which this work is focused is learning the true nature and features of this relation, something that might not be as simple and direct as the author implies. The evaluation of the construction of the model will allow us to analyze these nontrivial aspects.

On *In Other Words* (Hakuta & Bialystok, 1994) Ellen Bialystok and Kenji Hakuta suggest that bilingualism forces the child to think in a more complex manner and increases metalinguistic awareness, that is, it brings about a greater language sensitivity in general and a greater awareness of meaning and structure in the language

(Bialystok, 1988). However, in Bialystok's own works, her statistics show significant deficiencies in vocabulary management (Bialystok, 2001).

On this matter, Cummings found that if a second language (L2) is acquired when the first language (L1) or mother tongue still has not reached a certain competence threshold, the child might develop "semi-lingualism" or "limited bilingualism", a state of low linguistic competence in every acquired language, which represents a serious expressive and communicative disadvantage compared to monolingual children (Cummins, 1979).

Since the statements in E. Bialystok work are so convincing and had such a profound impact in the activities of the field, we shall begin with an evaluation of some aspects of the statements and conclusions of one of her more referenced works.

Observations on Early Bilingualism

As a starting point for a reevaluation of commonly accepted observations and assessments, we shall analyze some aspects of the work published by Bialystok and Martin(2004). This text was selected as one of the most frequently cited works in the community analyzing the relation between bilingualism and cognitive development. The analysis consists of two parts: A general discussion (where general statements and hypotheses are evaluated), a statistical analysis (where statistics and their applicability to the chosen samples are analyzed), and other remarks (more related to the content and conclusions of the Results section).

General Discussion

Bialystock's analysis is mainly based in the following working hypotheses:

1. Bilingual children are better at concept representation.
2. Bilingual children are more efficient at solving problems of moderate difficulty.
3. Bilingual children are not more efficient with problems of high difficulty.
4. Bilingual children are more efficient at tasks with a predominance of perceptual information.
5. Bilingual and non-bilingual children are equally efficient at tasks with a semantic predominance.

We shall now evaluate these hypotheses and analyze the resulting inferences from a critical standpoint that allows us to view aspects and particularities based on the original work.

Hypothesis 1: Bilingual children are better at concept representation.

There are two observations to make to this statement:

Observation 1a: The concept of "the opposition of perceptual tasks vs. predominantly semantic tasks" are ideas taken from the interpretation of the findings of Kirkham et al. obtained from a modification of the DCCS test that was modified and administered to monolingual children of 3 and 4 years old (Kirkham, Cruess, & Diamond, 2003). That paper states that the success the four year olds achieved over the three year olds is based on the non-perseverance when facing the perceptual stimulus.

In her work Bialystok formulates thus the following correlation: If the child succeeds at the test, it means he does not persevere in paying attention to the perceptual stimulus, and therefore has a better cognitive performance. This way, the objective of the test that was originally cited loses focus, since it does not analyze bilingualism nor elaborates these aspects. The Kirkham test shows the evolutionary development of a function or skill that takes place in a span of several months. On the other hand, the Bialystock test is applied to children who are in the midst of this process and does not take into consideration the normality variables (age range in which children acquire the skill).

This explanation is in itself a reductionist approach which states that "it is only efficient (in cognitive terms) if it ignores perception", and this is in relation to a single four-card test. It is analogous to the affirmation that a development in the walking skill of a child four months before another child will have a better performance in the tracks when he runs a race.

The simulations made with the prototype will show the relations between concepts with monolingual and bilingual/non-monolingual children, where the organization of information would be indicative of the way the definitive organization of the concept is related to the way the child is stimulated at these stages. This way, what is being tested with these statements is that for the child to be an early bilingual, he is receiving stimulation and being introduced to bilingualism through perception, which is logical, given he still has not mastered reading and writing.

In this regard, intensive learning of any other subject through perception would yield similar results, since the child has simply adapted to communicate with these techniques.

Observation 1b: The work states that "Constant experience in attending to one of the languages and ignoring the other might enhance the ability of bilinguals to selectively attend to appropriate cues and inhibit attending to others".

There are no evidences in the paper that show that this statement can be applied to generic reasoning. It is possible to assert that this practice is a logical consequence of stimulation and training in this kind of inhibition, and for the inhibitory case alone when it is applied to the language coding/ decoding, which in general terms does not imply any real impact on the reasoning process. This problem is related to what is mentioned in 1a.

Hypothesis 2: Bilingual children are more efficient at solving problems of moderate difficulty.

Observation 2a: According to Bialystok, "The need to encode, interpret and associate words from two languages with a common concept of the world requires more advanced representation because the connections between the words exist at a higher or more abstract level".

This is a reasoning that stems from interpretation, but on the other hand, with the model we can see that what is needed is an "additional connection" between both representations of the same word, which "hinders" the functioning of one or both languages (depending on how advanced bilingualism is). There are never clear signs of a more complex structure, but of more lengthy ones, which require greater relative effort. All the evidence found is eventually compatible with the concept of an "additional connection". Of course this does not imply an inhibition of the child's abilities, but of adaptation to processing the more likely stimuli in a more efficient manner, and the less likely ones in a less efficient manner. This is the reason why the efficiency of bilingual children in vocabulary management is greater than it is for non-bilingual ones.

Hypothesis 3: Bilingual children are not more efficient with problems of high difficulty.

This hypothesis can be tested with the same observations as **2a**.

Hypothesis 4: Bilingual children are more efficient at tasks with a predominance of perceptual information.

Observation 4a: Bialystok's work mentions: "Tasks across various cognitive domains have shown that bilingual children develop control over attention more efficiently than monolinguals but that there is no difference between the two groups in progress with analysis of representations".

As we mentioned earlier, the bilingual child's "advantages" are not in reasoning, but in the immediate coding/decoding process, due to factors of mere adaptation to perceptual stimuli. The paper does not prove either that this differentiation applies to any type of representation (e.g., numeric or symbolic)

Hypothesis 5: Bilingual and non-bilingual children are equally efficient at tasks with a semantic predominance.

Observation 5a: This hypothesis can be evaluated with the same observations as **4a**.

Statistical Analysis

From following statistical procedures, some matters have arisen that deserve an explicit analysis. We will look into some of those matters below.

Statistical Test for the First Study

In the first experiment conducted (referred to as Study 1) of the abovementioned paper, in reference to the method used and particularly in the description of the two samples: They consist of a total of 67 children, distributed as shown below.

Sample 1: 36 monolingual children, English speakers (18 boys and 18 girls), with an average age of 59.1 months. Mother tongue: English.

We should note that there has been no analysis or evaluation of neither the standard deviation nor the mode for the ages. Without the deviation we cannot take into consideration the representativeness of the sample, since among children of this age a difference of a month can prove significant for the assessment of maturity. (For example, the difference between being able to walk or not, or for the construction and/or interpretation of 2 or 3-word sentences).

In this regard, another important observation to make is that if a difference between means as a result from the sample's size is expressed, the standard deviation used in the calculation of ANOVA must be the square root of the mean (Root Mean Square Error, RMSE). ANOVA is based on the hypothesis that the standard deviation is the same for every used group/sample, and the RMSE represents an estimator for the standard deviation (Hopkins, 2000). RMSE can be though as the mean of the standard deviation of every group. These non-trivial matters are not specified anywhere in the document.

Sample 2: 31 bilingual children, Chinese/English speakers (21 boys and 10 girls). The average age of this group is 58.9 months. Mother tongue: Chinese.

There is an imbalance between boys and girls, which means that it cannot be measured statistically. (See Montilla, 2010). It should be noted that in this case no analysis was made on the impact of the standard deviation in age, either.

These samples cannot be compared either; the comparison should have been between native

English speakers and native English speakers who are learning a second language.

The variation in results could be due to the different mother tongue and, consequently, the way of building reasoning from it. Chinese language is analytical (it shows a tendency towards monosyllabic words and the lack of derivative or inflective procedures, so that complex words are almost always a result of compounding) and tonal –for the way in which a syllable can have different meanings according to the tone(E.o.d.i.d.M.h., 2012). In general terms, the syntactic sequence of the sentence is similar to the structure of: theme-comment, modifying element-modified element, a structure found in many languages, like Spanish or English, though a careful study reveals greater differences among those showing this structure.

This means that is normal to expect the conceptual construction of a native Chinese speaker to be different to that of a native English speaker, as it depends on his exposition to the language.

It is also important to note the great bias of this sample, since Chinese writing is ideographic (Glass, Peckham, & Sanders, 1972) or logographic[2], therefore it is expected that children are used to encoding visual stimuli in a more efficient manner.

Additional observations can be made:

- Both populations are geographically close: this holds no significance. What would have been interesting is an evaluation of samples in which every individual attended the same school and the same extra-curricular organizations.
- It is stated that both samples include children of the same socioeconomic status. There is no information in the paper that shows this (income level of the family, level of education, housing conditions, health, etc.). So how is this aspect evaluated?
- It is stated that children in this sample are undergoing a program for bilingual children: this calls for an evaluation of the teaching methods of those centers, which, as they are usually based on visual stimuli, would create an alternative explanation to the relative better ability regarding visual stimuli: it is simply a matter of training.

As regards the selection of candidates, the author determined it by administering three placement tests, Raven Test, Forward Digit Span, and Peabody Test, also known as PPVT.

While scientific reasons exist that rule out considering these tests as applicable for this age group, we shall nevertheless analyze some observations in Bialystok's criteria for the selection of the sample.

Quote 1: "In previous research, children with a weak knowledge of one of their languages, more appropriately called second-language learners, did not exhibit the same cognitive advantages as did children who were more balanced bilinguals".

If this was the case, there should be an evaluation of equivalent performance in the alternative language (in this case, with Chinese). The paper completely lacks this study, as it does and evaluation of the degree of effective use of the alternative language of the analyzed individuals.

On the other hand, in the conclusion section, the author herself states that "Despite a rigid selection criterion, the monolingual children (M = 112.2, SD = 15.2) outperformed bilingual children (M = 87.8, SD = 10.6), on the PPVT t(65) = 7.09, p<.01". This is a logical conclusion when considering that these are two different populations that are being compared (Chinese-speaking children against English-speaking children). Their command of English vocabulary is different, simply because the children are not English speakers.

Quote 2: "The PPVT test was given first, so children who failed to meet this criterion did not proceed with the other tests".

Here there is a statement about how the selection was biased:

- The comparison involves different populations (an English native one and a Chinese native one), which means the author could be verifying Wittgenstein's old theory about the incidence of mother tongue on the world reasoning process, or perhaps the adaptation of the test subjects to the special teaching method in bilingual centers for children.
- Children are only selected by the ability they show in only one type of test about language (without the oral evaluation of questions nor other kind of evaluation)
- Bilingual children are selected by the ability they show in only one of the languages: English. Their skill in the mother tongue is never evaluated.

  Quote 3: "The additional constraint for the present study was that 3-year-olds rarely have enough proficiency in two languages to be classifiable as bilingual".

The paper argues that bilingualism is essential for that kind of management of visual stimuli and reasoning, but it also declares that it won't work on bilingual subjects. This is either a contradiction or shows that what is being analyzed are not the effects of bilingualism, as the samples do not actually belong to the study universe (i.e., bilinguals).

Statistical Analysis of the Second Study

The second experiment is referred to as Study 2 in the abovementioned paper. There, Bialystok states that: "...by comparing a new group of monolingual and bilingual children on two conditions that differed in this manner..."

What this means is that the sample shown above is not used again for this study. There is no reason supporting this change in the sample.

In reference to the method used, and particularly to the description of both samples: They consist of a total of 67 children, distributed as shown below.

Sample 2: 15 monolingual children, English speakers and 15 bilingual speakers of French and English. It is quite complex to validate the sample and its results in this case:

- ◦ In contrast with the previous sample, the second language is now French. It must be understood that the variable is different, as it is no longer the case of a Germanic language (English) being compared with one from the Sino-Tibetan family (Chinese), which is an analytical, tonal and ideographic language. This set of tests has a distinctly different bias, as native speakers of French speak a Romance language (with its five diacritics and two types of ligatures), as opposed to those of the Germanic language.
- ◦ It is not stated whether the bilingual children are all native to another French-speaking country. Taking dialects into consideration, this is an important distinction to be made.
- ◦ Even when it is mentioned that they typically speak French at home, it is not established whether their proficiency level is equivalent, and due to the nature of the study, this is an important point to be made.
- ◦ Average ages are different to the previous sample, and between both samples; it is not stated whether the difference is a significant one.
- ◦ Just like in the previous test, neither the incidence of the age dispersion nor the sample distribution is analyzed.

Other Remarks

From a statistical standpoint, measuring and results should be reevaluated, for the following reasons:

- Conditions of applicability of ANOVA and CHI-SQUARED tests do not appear to have been respected, or at least no information was presented on that matter.
- Conditions of applicability of ANOVA and CHI-SQUARED tests leave many unresolved questions, for example, with gender considerations and for a lack of a complete description of the samples and tests.
- The sample is biased for being composed of two populations of different kinds of language families.

It would also be convenient to review the statistical methodology proposed by the author, since it applies Student's t-test but without proving the conditions for its applicability:

Student's t-test is also applied, but its conditions are also doubtful:

1. If the sample sizes of both groups being compared are equal, the original Student's t-test is highly tolerant to the presence of unequal variances, otherwise the results can be biased. In these samples the sample sizes are different.
2. The samples are mismatched (from independent samples, they are used when two random sample groups, which are independent and have an identical distribution from the two populations that are being compared), as it should have been done with an equal number of samples in both groups.
3. If the original definition by Student about his t-test is being used, the two populations being compared need to have the same variances. This evaluation was not performed on the samples in none of the cases.
4. Parameters for the t-test are unspecified: the value for the null hypothesis (μ_0, if it's one or two-tailed). A parameter of n=67 is assumed, according to the paper's data.

Which of Student's conditions must not be violated? Variances are assumed to be homogeneous ($\sigma_1^2=\sigma_2^2$) for both samples. This can be tested using an F-test for equality of variances, Levene's test, Bartlett's test, or Brown-Forsythe's test, or making an estimation using a Q-Q plot graphic. No results are shown for any of these alternatives. Glass, Peckham and Sanders (1972) pointed out that for practical purposes (Glass, Peckham, & Sanders, 1972), proving variance homogeneity is not necessary when the sample sizes are equal, which is not the case for the current work.

Moreover, the use of Student's test assumes a regular distribution in population. This assumption can only be violated with large samples, a fact that is not tested in the paper.

On the other hand, Boneau, Scheffé (Boneau, 1960; Eisenhart, 1959) and others have proved that when sample sizes are different ($n1 \neq n2$) and the larger sample is selected from the population with the greatest variance (called "positive condition"), the t statician in Student's test is conservative. Therefore: 1) increments the value of the weighted variance, 2) increments the t denominator, 3) decreases the calculated value for t, and 4) decreases the usefulness of Student's test for finding a difference between means, which could explain the reason for the conclusion that both populations are similar in the Digits Span and Raven's tests.

Note: the opposite happens when the larger sample is obtained from the population with the smaller variance, called negative condition, the t statician in Student's test.

Below we shall analyze some observations on Bialystock's criteria for the application of the tests.

Quote 1: "These scores were examined in three-way repeated measures ANOVA for game (4), phase (2) and language group (2)".

It is logical to think of ANOVA as a suitable test for these analyses, which for their characteristics are subjected to Cumulative Type I Errors (Hopkins, 2000). In the results shown it is remarkable to observe the variation for coefficient p. In this regard, the following is noted:

1. Improvement in the pre-switch (but doesn't clarify whether it is for both) for the game type and phase, which is explained as a manifestation of the game's difficulty with a p level in 10 E-3 or 10E-4.
2. It shows a level of significance visibly smaller for a p type sample being 2 or 3 orders of magnitude smaller than with cases indicated in a) for this study alone.
3. In the interactions between parameters: games - p phase is at E-4, while for p group games it is at E-2. Again, p values seem to be changing.

This seems to imply that some kind of correction was made to p's value to obtain some signification (for example Tukey, Duncan, Bonferroni, etc.), but unfortunately it is not mentioned whether there was any post-hoc test.

On the other hand, it is worth noting that the use of ANOVA is safer against Type I Error than t-student.

It must be mentioned that results are not validated at any point of the paper. The statistic used to talk about how well the ANOVA model fits the data (It's not used that frequently), but you can extract an R2 just like you do for a straight line. The R^2 represents how well all the levels of the grouping (nominal) variable fit the data.

Quote 2: "The mean scores used in the ANOVA analyses are summary scores of all the children. Since some of the scores in the post-switch phase were approximately 50%, they might reflect chance responding as opposed to perseveration".

In this regard, it can be inferred that results are due to the fact that "This would indicate that the children had not encoded the stimuli in any particular way", which does not have to be that way.

For example, it could be that the considered variables are not providing enough information to show whether there is a coding of the stimulus. From this point, assuming that the children are guessing, begins a deduction based on a classification of the children groups without any basis, separating those among them with 0-3 correct answers from group 4-6 and the rest (7-10).

Having split the population (already a biased and reduced one at that) in three parts, a CHI-SQUARED test is applied to see whether populations can be compared or not. The results are dubious at best.

As a general rule, it shall be demanded that 80% of the cells in a contingency table must have expected values larger than 5. Thus, in a 2x2 table it will be required that all of the cells fulfill this condition, even if in practice it can be allowed for one of them to show expected frequencies slightly below this value.

Therefore, it can be said that the condition of applicability for CHI-SQUARED is not respected.

This is due to the fact that in this case there are between 1 and 28 instances (individuals) in the cells, with an approximate average of 22, and from the significant differences between guessers and non-guessers, it can be inferred that children are not guessing.

The number of individuals in each sample is as follows (taken from Table 1, pp. 332):

- Average of individuals in each population (12, 10, 12, 10, 12, 10, 12, 10)
- Minimum number of individuals for each subpopulation (4, 4, 6, 2, 2, 1, 5, 8)
- Maximum number of individuals for each subpopulation (28, 21, 16, 21, 21, 18, 17, 13)

These samples are not significant enough, due to their low number of individuals, but even so they are taken as valid and it is concluded that bilingual children have a better performance in the color-shape game. On the other hand, pp. 336 inadequately shows CHI-SQUARED results for color-shape and color-object, since no degrees of freedom are defined.

THE LINGUISTIC REASONING MODEL USED

In the previous sections we introduced Bialystok's concept of the possibility that bilingualism improves executive functions (the ability to perform at certain types of task in an efficient manner), but we have also pointed out some weaknesses in the work.

In order to make a correct assessment of the effects it has on reasoning, it is necessary to gain a better understanding of the abstraction process, what it is and how it manifests in the diverse production and situations of everyday life, and also about some consequences that have not been closely analyzed: lexical impoverishment.

Wittgenstein said: "The limits of my language are the limits of my world" (Wittgenstein, 1987). An exponent of logical atomism, he states that the world is comprised of simple elements (facts), and through analysis we can reach those elements, but also stresses the importance of the way in which signs are combined. It therefore focuses its interest in this back and forth relationship between the world and language, as in the combinatory logic of these elements.

The model, by simulating the reasoning process in relation to language, allows for a plausible explanation for this: internally developed structures are less complex and are significantly altered in the acquisition of alternative structures for internal representations of the same information. This makes it simpler for the model to elicit from a certain type of false options. But it also implies it has less capacity for the evaluation of concurrent causes or complex information.

Table 1. Sentence distribution for dialogs

Spanish			English		
Dialog ID	**Number of Sentences**	**Accumulated Sentences**	**Dialog ID**	**Number of Sentences**	**Accumulated Sentences**
1	25	25	7	25	25
2	20	45	8	18	43
3	8	53	9	8	51
4	30	83	10	30	81
5	14	97	11	14	95
6	15	112	12	16	111

Therefore, the bilingual child might tend to have a decreased ability for the definition of abstract concepts related to the information they contain (this is further explained in the statistics section).

As a result, it is possible to state that bilingualism cannot be considered exclusively as a cognitive benefit, since it can also have negative effects on the cognitive and academic progress, and these deserve a careful analysis. The present work is focused on the assessment of the possible consequences and limitations that could be brought about by early bilingualism (acquired in the stages where L1 is not yet consolidated), and analyzes its causes and effects with help from the linguistic model).

Internal Organization

The prototype is flexible, created from the need to represent the use of Spanish language in a computer, and the automatic handling of sentences in natural language. Its principal aim is to be able to maintain a conversation in natural language with a native Spanish speaker, making use of the features of the interlocutor's own dialect. To this end, it has been provided with the ability of learning to handle sentences as it uses the language.

It is comprised of a series of memories and organized structures according to the Morphosyntactic Linguistic Wavelet (MLW) model (López De Luise, 2010d) which proves useful for developing a series of internal functionalities: information organization, automated summarizing, content indexing, automated dialogs, etc. (López De Luise, 2008).

The MLW concept is essential for the proper functioning of the prototype, as it defines the criteria for content hierarchy and accessibility. Its basic features are:

- Flexibility.
- Great deal of automatism.
- Applicability for different needs: as a content indexer, for summarizing content, as support for a more natural man-machine interface, in content analysis, etc.

The following is a summary of the internal organization of the prototype and further below, and with some degree of detail, we shall explain the working mechanism of MLW.

Architecture

Due to the complexity needed for its functioning, the prototype assumes a global division in layers for linguistic information processing (Hisgen & López De Luise, 2010).

- **Internal Structure:** Is a language-dependent layer. For the current implementation of the prototype, sentences are taken from Spanish. The greatest task of this layer is transforming these sentences in the native language into a series of structures that are independent of language, called HBS (Homogeneous Basic Structures), which consist of a series of parameters and values that describe each syntagm (word, punctu-

Figure 1. Layered structure of the prototype

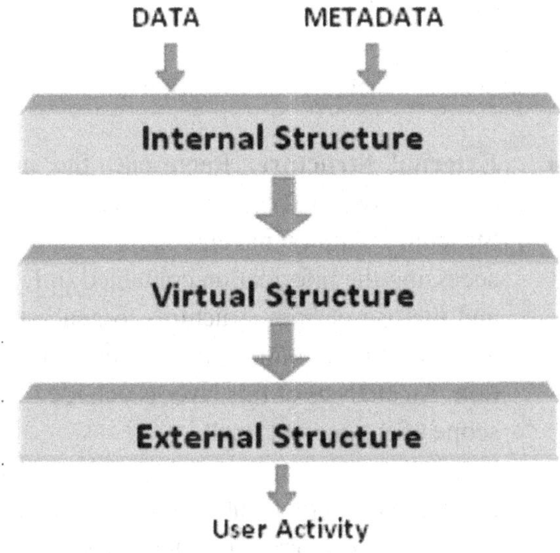

ation mark, number, symbol, etc.) and their morphosyntactic features. These structures will be the information units to be fed to the MLW found in the Virtual Structure.

- **Virtual_Structure:** Once built, HBS are organized in structures called E_{ci} (Inner Structure Arrangement, from "Estructura de Composición Interna" in Spanish). Then, by means of a filtering process through Morphosyntactic Wavelets (MLW) these structures are organized and broken down into certain types of metadata which will largely depend on the filtering parameters used in the MLW process. The result is an E_{ci} (Inner Structure Arrangement, "Estructura de Composición Interna" in Spanish) E_{ci}s can be described as structures that relate words. These are inserted in a global memory which is organized according to the results of the MLW filtering of the E_{ci}s that result from processing each sentence.

Subsequent filtering will configure a network of E_{ci}s with different levels of grouping by "affinity" or similarity. Each grouping is called an E_{ce}, which are logical structures that model the relationship between words. The network that they form after their final arrangement is an oriented graph representing the content extracted from learned sentences. The process of insertion of an E_{ci} into an E_{ce} is called "assimilation".

- **External Structure:** Represents the interface between the user and the Virtual Structure. Allows navigation of E_{ce}s for accessing the information contained in E_{ci}, and the use of both structures to generate an appropriate output during conversation. An analysis of this layer is outside the scope of the present work.

The prototype implements a series of internally organized memories designed to support the functioning of these three layers. Some of the most important memories are:

- **TCM Memory (Transient Composition Memory):** Holds recent sentences. E.g.: The morning is hot.
- **PS Memory (Parsed Structure Memory):** Contains the HBS arranged into sequences of syntactic categories. It is used in the construction of E_{ci}s. E.g.: ARTICLE +NOUN + VERB+ ADJECTIVE
- **RS Memory (Response Structure Memory):** Holds the sequence of usable structures in the practice of the language, in the context of a dialog. In other words, it informs which is the possible PS to provide an answer to the current sentence in the dialog stored in the TCM. E.g.: TCM.sentence$_1$:-The morning is hot → PS$_1$:- ARTICLE + NOUN + VERB + ADJECTIVE TCM.sentence$_2$:-It's true, it's hot. → PS$_2$:- VERB + NOUN +, + VERB + ADJECTIVE RS$_1$: PS$_1$:- PS$_2$
- **E_{ci} Memory (Inner Structure Arrangement):** Is a record of all the E_{ci} structures that have been processed up to that point. They are built using MLW in the manner describer in Appendix A. Figure 2 exemplifies the result obtained with the TCM.sentence$_2$ sentence. In this case, several rules were applied: Rule 99 was applied to HBS^2_1 (derived from the "It's" stream) and HBS^2_2 (derived from the "true" stream), Rules 4 and 5 to HBS^2_3 (derived from the "," stream), Rule 5 to HBS^2_4 (derived from the "it's" stream) and Rule 99 to HBS^2_5 (derived from the "hot" stream). A detailed description of the proposed rules can be found in (López De Luise, 2008).
- **E_{ce} Memory (Outer Structure Arrangement):** Is the record of all the E_{ce} structures that have been generated as a consequence of the successive assimilation of E_{ci}s. They are constructed by using

MLW in the manner described in Appendix B. E.g.: With a preexisting E_{ce} network as in Figure 3, E_{ci}^{1} and E_{ci}^{2} are assimilated.

The process of assimilation will result in the network of Figure 4, where $E_{ce}^{1,3}$ and E_{ci}^{2} are included in E_{ce}^{1}.

Morphosyntactic Linguistic Wavelets (MLW)

Morphosyntactic wavelets owe their name to traditional wavelets, which are mathematical functions used for decomposition and filtering of numerical data as in Fourier's analysis They are useful for processing signals of different types that can be somehow translated into numeric sequences. By using them, data can be compressed and decomposed into a set of components and parameters. In the case of MLW, data is not numeric, so the conversion process (construction of HBS) is not a trivial one. Additionally, the filtering process itself must consider some aspects related to linguistics, this is why filtering is performed with heuristics instead of mathematical functions.

Nonetheless, both types of wavelets share the same basic features, which include:

Figure 2. Example of an E_{ci} derived from a sentence

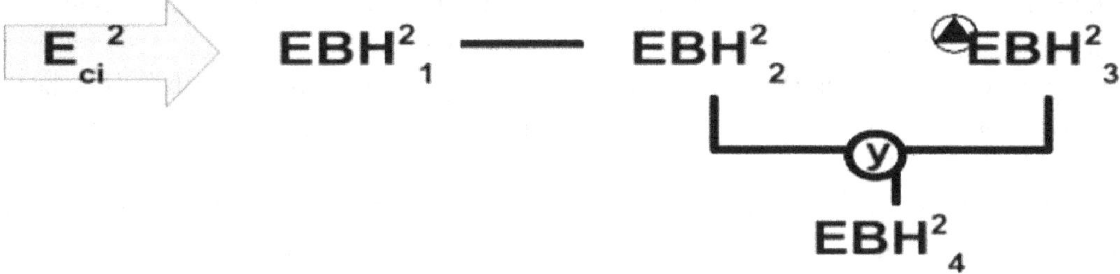

Figure 3. Initial E_{ce} network

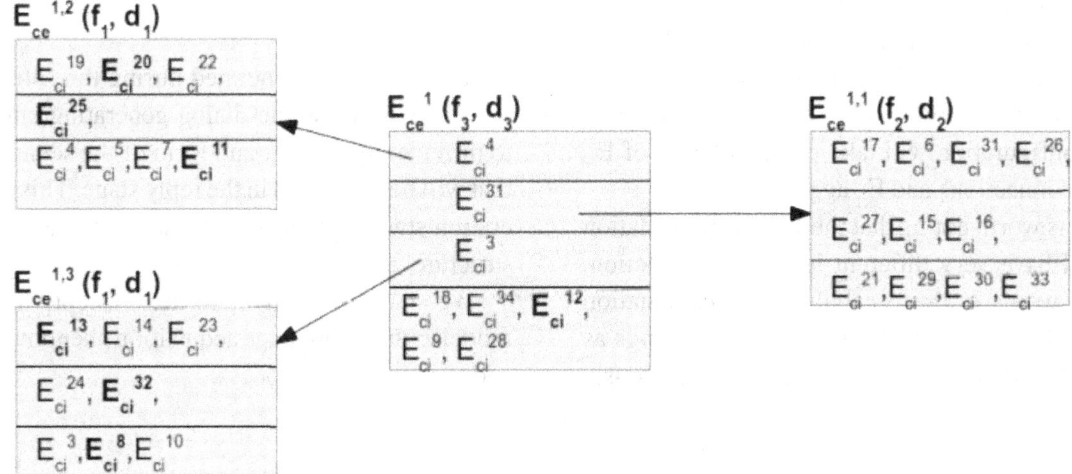

Figure 4. E_{ce} network after the assimilation of E_{ci}^{1} and E_{ci}^{2}

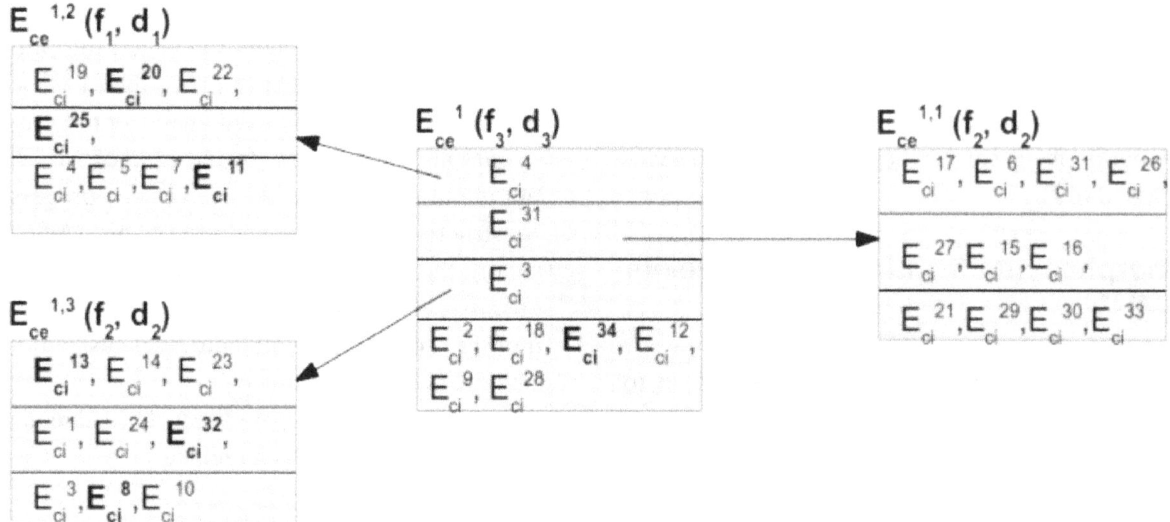

- Information decomposition,
- Adjustable granularity in the decomposition process,
- Automatic detection of relevant information as part of the filtering process, and
- Possibility of reconstructing the information in a more compact manner.

These features determine the MLW heuristics that are applied to sentences. The metadata obtained through decomposition (that is, the output from morphosyntactic filtering) and filtering parameters constitute the information learned by the prototype through the input sentences. Each sentence has some information that can be learned. Learning will be achieved according to the type of information contained in each sentence, and its configuration will take place in terms of E_{ce} interconnections and E_{ci} agglutinations.

It is worth noting that the learned information could have very different levels of abstraction, from words in the vocabulary and punctuation (low abstraction level), more complex things as formal sentence structures according to previously learned types of expressions or the context of use for certain words (medium abstraction level), and up to automatic topic detection, related information detection[3], etc., which constitute more of a discursive level.

The use of MLW allows the prototype to automatically extract certain information that lets it:

- Distinguish relevant from irrelevant data.
- Define the main topic in terms of words contained in the sentences themselves.
- Define levels of detail.
- Hierarchically organize the information contained in the sentences.

The memories generated during the filtering process will allow the dialog generating engine to provide the content and form of the sentences that will be generated in the reply stage. This generation stage, which is contained in the external structure, is still undergoing analysis.

We shall now articulate the concepts in the model with the language acquisition phenomenon and the reasoning process.

Semantic Memory

Linguists acknowledge the existence of a mental lexicon and a semantic memory. The first is a lexicographic dictionary, while the second one does not belong so strictly to linguistics and could hold mental representations of the world knowledge of the individual –concepts and relations between concepts (Linsday & Norman, 1977). There are several studies about the development of both structures. Kolers (Kolers, 1963) among others, maintains the existence of parallel storage for L1 and L2, while Ehri and Ryan (Ehri & Ryan, 1980) argue the opposite.

In the case of the existence of a unified storage, an impossibility would arise of deactivating L1 in favor of L2 (or vice versa), which would imply that the language practice would be permanently affected due to the early simultaneity of both.

Paradis (1981) states that bilingual individuals "have an exclusive group of mental representations but they organize them differently, depending on whether they verbalize a thought in L1 or L2, and it is in that respect that they function in a different way cognitively when talking or decoding in L1 or L2". This way, the linguistic process would be forced to manage a single conceptual system (semantic memory) while having two lexical storages from which to alternately choose. Sadly, these statements have yet to be proven conclusively (López, 2008).

From the perspective of the model implemented, it can be noted that content is effectively organized in parallel, one for each language, decreasing the depth capacity of the storage levels and degrading the performance for language use. This is why the vocabulary that the model tends to use lacks the depth and richness of the monolingual model.

Reflexivity

For Dewey (1989) reflective thought is an achievement for the individual. "...implies that something is believed in (or disbelieved in), not on its own direct account, but through something else which stands as witness, evidence, proof, voucher, warrant; that is, as ground of belief". Every reflective thought is a process of detecting relations, though not any relations, as it searches until it finds the most accurate relation that the conditions allow. (p. 81)

With young children (approximately between 5 and 6 ages), a marked difference between linguistic and cognitive levels can be noted. Three categories for reflexiveness are established: implicit (E_0), semi-explicit (E_1) and complex explicit ($E_{2/3}$).

They can be evaluated in relation to levels of awareness (Dorcasberro, 2011) –that is, levels of knowledge. This agrees with the findings of Barriga, who states that (Barriga-Villanueva, 2002): "The evolution of language, more than a mere linear progression from primitive or early structures to more complex or later ones, it is a series of changes, arrangements and rearrangements by means of which, the child, after using certain forms and structures, begins to distinguish new and previously undiscovered relations and regularities among them".

It is notable that in the model, structures also reorganize themselves through several stages, first homogeneously (Hisgen & López De Luise, 2010) then in classes and finally hierarchically. After some time in which learning is consolidated, they tend to constitute themselves as something immutable or almost immutable, as part of the same system that is permanently marked in its functioning.

In (Dorcasberro, 2011) we can see that these hypotheses that are focused on pre-school children, become affected by two considerable factors:

- Animistic and magical thought coexist with nominal realism.
- Pre-operative and concrete thought, which is characteristic of such age.

Finally, they conclude that evolution of thought is merely a hierarchical process, slow and gradual, that is not linear but includes phases of different mental logics.

In this respect, the model agrees in certain aspects about the organization of hierarchies (Hisgen & López De Luise, 2010) and the existence of stages prior to such an organization.

Abstraction

In *The Psychology of Intelligence* (Piaget, 1999) Piaget compiles the lectures for the course he offered at the Collège de France in 1942, summarizing his research on the psychogenetics of intelligence. There he posits that logic is the basis for thought, and that consequently intelligence is a generic term to describe the set of logical operations that human beings are capable of, ranging from perception, classification, substitution, and abstraction operations among others, and (at least) up to proportional calculus.

In respect to his relation with the production and practice of language, vocabulary holds an intricate relationship with the abstraction process, as ontologies are considered in some way or another according to it.

Lexical impoverishment (which was mentioned earlier) can also be evaluated as a reflex mechanism of a certain kind of alteration in the abstraction process.

The Reasoning Model

It is interesting to notice how with respect to the origin of language, the three schools of thought agree with the approach presented here:

- The fact that language acquisition is subconscious or human-exclusive is compatible with the existence of structures within the model that are manifested automatically and are not dependent on the specific language being used. In fact, if non verbal languages (i.e., an iconographic or sign language) were to be translated to accurate structures, with a certain content-structure association, the concept structuring model would work in a similar way to the one presented here, generating organized knowledge structures and weighting frequently used structures and conditioning their organization to the type of content at hand.
- If we consider that thought precedes language, internal structures developed as part of the model will also precede any practice of language, and they could well be considered to be a representation of this ability of the human brain, as long as their effects can be statistically compatible in both cases (this fact shall be evaluated in the statistics section).
- If we consider the existence of a language of thought that is different from the practiced language, this is also compatible with the existence and development of structures with their own format, one that is internal to the model, and which results curiously independent from the type of language.
- Therefore, it could be thought that if structures adapt in a Darwinian way to the needs of the speaker, there would be some kind of deterioration of the process in favor of an improvement in alternation. Some of these alterations are mainly analyzed in the statistics section.

CASE STUDIES

In order to study how the model reacts to bilingualism, a dataset containing 112 sentences in Spanish and 111 sentences in English. Dialogs display the sentence distribution shown in Table 1.

Learning Dialogs in Spanish

In order understand the evolution of knowledge inside the model, the prototype was taught only dialogs in Spanish. The evaluation was performed from the perspective of relative growth of the memories involved in linguistic reasoning. It is important to remark that the statistics in this paper are just a demonstration of the behavior of the reasoning model. The corresponding statistics can be found in the bibliography.

These memories were already mentioned in the section which describes the architecture of the prototype. For the purposes of this work, the only relevant memories to evaluate are PS (which determines how language structures are learnt), RS (which determines how contextualization is learnt) and TCM (which determines short term memory). Table 2 shows the evolution of these 3 memories as the system learns.

Table 2. Evolution of memories with Spanish dialogs

ID	PS	RS	TCM
1	1620	1630	1722
2	1230	1327	1487
3	623	654	722
4	1871	1890	1915
5	931	974	1002
6	1004	1039	1086

It can be observed that the information of each memory increases proportionally with each dialog. Increase of bytes is an objective measurement of the content's quantity growth in each memory, since it is directly proportional to the quantity of the information represented. Notice that the content of the dialog makes growth different in each case. The graphic shows the learning process dialog by dialog, that is, after each dialog the memories are cleaned (the contents acquired during the learning process are erased). Notice that the richness of the dialog has a significant influence on the learning process. Dialog with few sentences provide few examples of how language is constructed, and therefore less information is acquired about this language. This is shown in the slow growth of the memories related to structures and contextualization.

It has already been shown in (Hisgen & López De Luise, 2010) that the growth of memories tends to decrease when they keep receiving expressions which are similar to those already learnt and ultimately growth can be almost zero. To detect

Figure 5. Evolution of memories as learning of Spanish sentences progresses (Table 2)

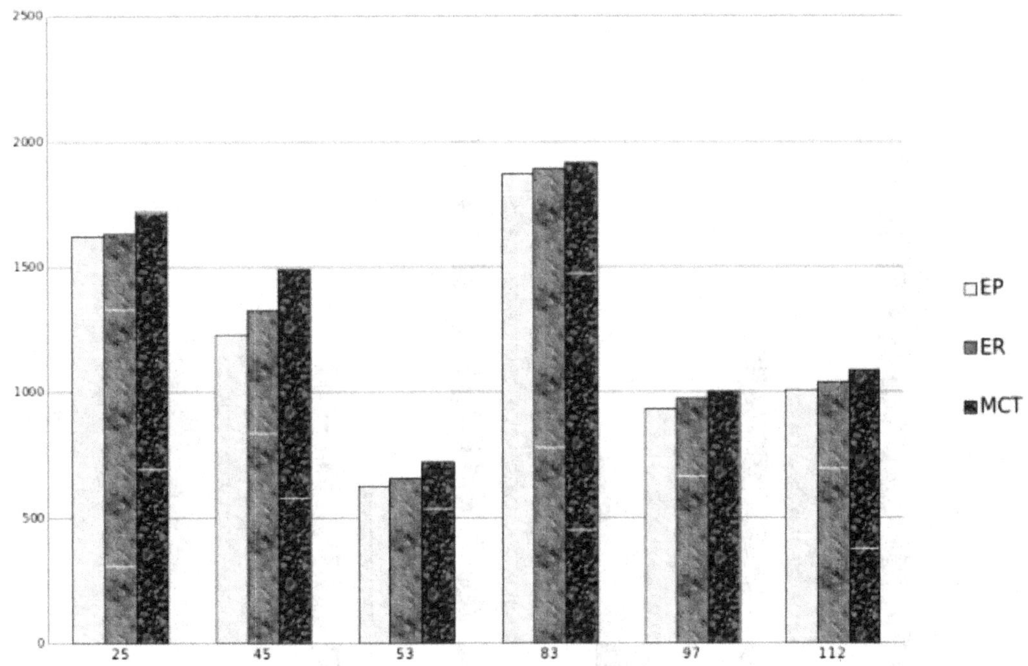

this, it was only necessary to preserve the content of the memories during the whole learning process. For the context of this article, memories were cleaned in order to study the initial language construction process.

Learning Dialogues in English

The process was repeated, but this time the dialogs were in English. Table 3 shows the respective growths.

Table 3. Evolution of memories with English dialogs

ID	PS	RS	TCM
1	1950	2122	2310
2	1503	1634	1710
3	85	923	988
4	2168	2234	2387
5	1224	1374	1425
6	1365	1437	1510

As can be seen, growth is again proportional to the richness of the language that is being learnt. There is an evident systematic difference between the growth of PS and RS, as compared with Spanish sentences: By observing the numbers, it can be seen that in every case growth ratio is lower in PS than in RS. As regards this ratio, PS/RS_{spa} are within the range [.93, .99], which is systematically lower than PS/RS_{eng} values [.89, .97]. This would indicate that sentence structure is more varied in Spanish dialogs than in English ones. Therefore, memories have expanded at a different rate, clearly showing that the level of effort needed to learn the structures of these languages is different. Therefore, it could be concluded that producing a sentence (generating natural language) in one language would demand different strategies than producing it in another language, since PS use requires more optimization for Spanish than for English. From this point of view, it's clear than the model will have visible reasoning differences depending on the language it is working on.

Figure 6. Evolution of memories as learning of English sentences progresses

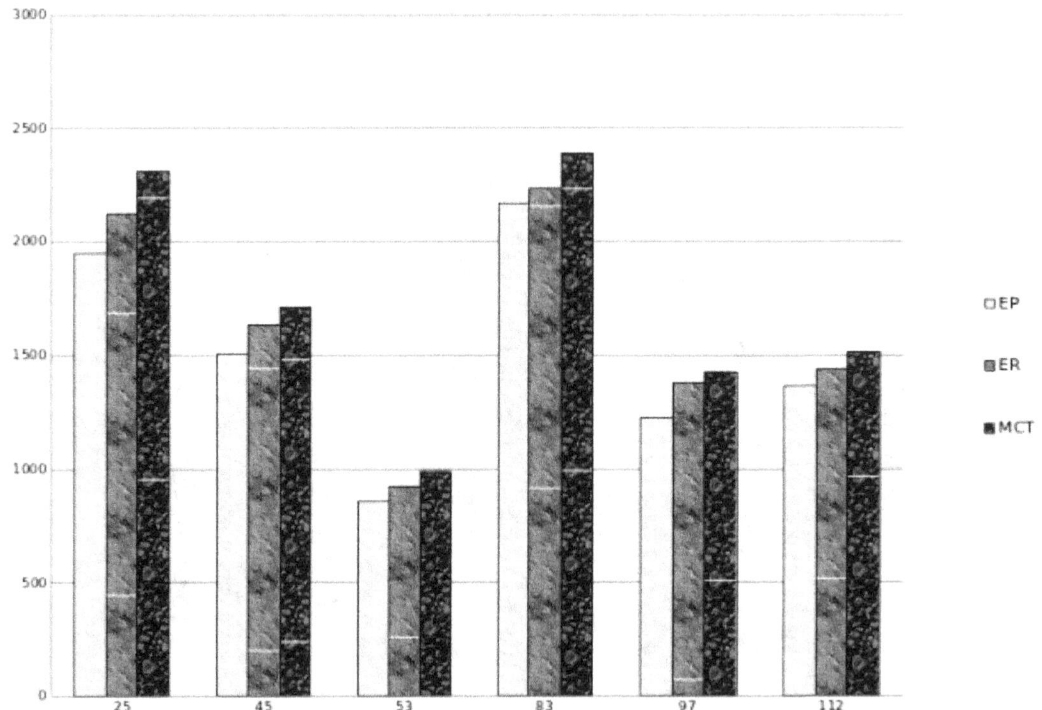

Admitting that the model is certainly a representation of human linguistic behavior, such behavior supports the theory that organization of content is related to the initial stimuli received when learning.

Simultaneous Learning of Dialogs in Both Languages

In order to analyze the behavior of memories faced with learning content in two different languages, the Spanish dialogs were learnt first and then the English dialogs, keeping memory content. This would simulate the case of learning a second language alter having acquired structures of a previous language. Table 4 shows the evolution of studied memories.

As we can see, memories follow result trends presented in previous tests. An optimization is observed, which means that memories expand more slowly after acquiring the first dialogs, since they are reusing previous knowledge. On previous tests, this reuse was not possible since memories were cleaned before learning a new dialog. TCM memory is eliminated; therefore, it does not expand since it is only used to contextualize sentences within the same dialog when interacting with the interlocutor. Results of this first analysis are interesting.

Numbers obtained clearly point to the reuse of structures just from the beginning, with an insignificant reduction regarding the PS and RS. This confirms that advantages of early learning actually lie in the organization of memories and not in the amount of content learnt.

IMPLICATIONS, DERIVATIONS AND APPLICATIONS

This paper has shown how the prototype's reasoning can be used to analyze statistic evidence to explain how bilingualism would shape linguistic reasoning, generating a language manipulation modality which stabilizes and consolidates over time. The model's behavior allows concluding that the type of language appears to actually affect the

Table 4. Evolution of memories first with Spanish dialogs and then with English dialogs

ID	PS	RS	TCM
	Spanish		
1	1620	1630	1722
2	280	930	1487
3	3	36	722
4	63	88	1915
5	39	54	1002
6	12	35	1086
	English		
1	1899	2101	2310
2	1270	600	1710
3	800	302	988
4	529	34	2387
5	104	73	1425
6	107	15	1510

Table 5. Evolution of bilingual memories in Spanish and English

ID	(S)panish/(E) nglish	PS	RS	TCM
1	S	1620	1630	1722
1	E	1899	2101	2310
2	S	274	924	1487
2	E	1264	593	1710
3	S	3	21	722
3	E	798	293	988
4	S	59	77	1915
4	E	523	23	2387
5	S	39	54	1002
5	E	91	65	1425
6	S	10	23	1086
6	E	86	14	1510

internal acquisition and construction process of structures related to language production.

As shown throughout this presentation, there is also a relationship between the richness of the dialog and consolidation of information in the structures closely related with linguistic production. This correlates perfectly with data shown by other authors, whose papers have shown that learning starts with a certain initial organization which changes with knowledge consolidation, showing what could be called a progressive "stratified" growth.

As regards comments by Juan Azcoaga, organization of information, study of the model seems to support the concept of language regionalization, compatible with the concept of "neuro-seme".

As further work, additional Studies are expected to assess other aspects of reasoning such as emotionality, capability in other areas such as pure creativity and artistic creativity. Additionally, it would be interesting to extend the model to use a native language other than Spanish.

REFERENCES

Azcoaga, J. (1986). Aprendizaje fisiologico y aprendizaje pedagógico. Buenos Aires: El ateneo.

Barriga-Villanueva, R. (2002). *Estudios sobre habla infantil en los años escolares*. México: El Colegio de México.

Bialystok, E. (1988). Levels of bilingualism and levels of linguistic awareness. *Developmental Psychology*, (24): 560–567. doi:10.1037/0012-1649.24.4.560

Bialystok, E. (2001). *Bilingualism in development: Language, literacy, and cognition.* New York: Cambridge University Press. doi:10.1017/CBO9780511605963

Bialystok, E., & Michelle, M. (2004). Attention and inhibition in bilingual children: Evidence from the dimensional change card sort task. *Developmental Science*, *7*(3), 325–339. doi:10.1111/j.1467-7687.2004.00351.x PMID:15595373

Bialystok, E., Michelle, M., & Martin, R. (2008). The development of two types of inhibitory control in monolingual and bilingual children. *Bilingualism: Language and Cognition*, *11*, 81–93.

Bloomfield, L. (2009). *Introduction to the study of language*. New York: Henry Holt.

Bonneau, C. (1960). The effects of violationof assumptions underlying the test. *Psychological Bulletin*, *57*, 49–64. doi:10.1037/h0041412 PMID:13802482

Bruner, J. (2012). Constructivist theory. Retrieved from http://www.instructionaldesign.org

Chomsky, N. (1974). *Estructuras sintácticas*. Mexico: Siglo XXI.

Cummins, J. (1978). Educational implications of mother tongue maintenance in minority-language children. *Canadian Modern Language Review*, 34.

Cummins, J. (1979). Cognitive/academic language proficiency, linguistic interdependence, the optimum age question and some other matters. Working Papers on Bilingualism, (19), 121-129.

Darcy, N. (1963). Bilingualism and the measure of intelligence: Review of a decade of research. *The Journal of Genetic Psychology*, (82): 259–282. doi:10.1080/00221325.1963.10532521 PMID:14085429

Delval, J. (1998). *El desarrollo humano*. Buenos Aires: Siglo XXI.

Dewey, J. (1989). *Cómo pensamos: Nueva exposición de la relación entre pensamiento reflexivo y proceso educativo*. Barcelona: Paidós.

Dictionary, E. L. E. (2012). Centro virtual Cervantes. Retrieved from http://cvc.cervantes.es/ensenanza/biblioteca_ele/diccio_ele/indice.htm

Dorcasberro, A. (2011). El niño, la lengua y el bilingüismo: La reflexividad del niño bilingüe acerca de la noción de lengua y de bilingüismo, Multidisciplina. Acatlan Magazine, (8), 89-109.

Downing, A. (1983). Aspectos del bilingüismo. Transactions of Ier. Congreso Nacional de Lingüística Aplicada. AESLA, Murcia.

Ehri, L., & Ryan, E. (1980). Performance of bilinguals in a picture-word interference task. *Journal of Psycholinguistic Research*, (9): 285–302. doi:10.1007/BF01067243 PMID:7391998

Eisenhart, C. (1959). *The assumptions underlying the analysis of variance*. New York: Wiley.

Furth, H. (1966). *Thinking without language: Psychological implications of deafness*. New York: The Free Press.

Garon, N., Bryson, S., & Smith, I. (2008). Executive function in preschoolers: A review using an integrative framework. *Psychological Bulletin*, (134): 31–60. doi:10.1037/0033-2909.134.1.31 PMID:18193994

Glass, G., Peckham, P., & Sanders, J. (1972). Consequences of failure to meet assumptions underlying fixed effects analyses of variance and covariance. *Review of Educational Research*, *42*, 237–288. doi:10.3102/00346543042003237

Hakuta, K., & Bialystok, E. (1994). *In other words: The science and psychology of second-language acquisition*. New York: BasicBooks.

Hisgen, D., & López De Luise, D. (2010). Dialog structure automatic modeling. In Proceedings of MICAI'10. Heidelberg, Germany: Springer-Verlag.

Hopkins, W. (2000). *A new view of statistics*. Academic Press.

Hopkins, W. (2000). A new view of statistics. In *Generalizing to a Population: Confidence Limits*. Academic Press.

Kirkham, N., Cruess, L., & Diamond, A. (2003). Helping children apply their knowledge to their behavior on a dimension-switching task. *Developmental Science*, *6*(5), 449–476. doi:10.1111/1467-7687.00300

Kolers, P. (1963). Interlingual word associations. *Journal of Verbal Learning and Verbal Behavior*, (2): 291–300. doi:10.1016/S0022-5371(63)80097-3

Leopold, W. (2010). *Speech development of a bilingual child*. Evanston, IL: Northwestern University Press.

Linsday, P., & Norman, D. (1977). *Human information processing: An introduction to psychology*. New York: Academic.

López, M. (2008). Efectos de la segunda lengua en la escritura de sujetos bilingües. Transactions of XXXVII Simposio Internacional de la Sociedad Española de Lingüística (SEL). Publication services of Universidad de Navarra.

López De Luise, D. (2008). Mejoras en la usabilidad de la web a través de una estructura complementaria. (PhD Thesis). Universidad Nacional de La Plata, La Plata, Argentina.

López De Luise, D. (2010a). *An autonomous robot prototype using Concept Learning model*. ICSCA.

López De Luise, D. (2010b). *Automatic content extraction on the web with intelligent algorithms*. ICAART.

López De Luise, D. (2010c). *Automatic extraction of content on the web with intelligent algorithm*. ICMLDA.

López De Luise, D. (2010d). *Morphosyntactic linguistic wavelets for knowledge management. Tech Open book: Intelligent Systems*. Project WIH.

López De Luise, D., & Soffer, M. (2008a). *Modelización automática de textos en castellano*. ANDESCON.

López De Luise, D., & Soffer, M. (2008b). *Automatic text processing for spanish texts*. CERMA.

Lovaas, O. (1977). *The autistic child: Language development through behavior modification*. New York: John Wiley.

Macnamara, J. (1966). *Bilingualism and primary education: A study of Irish experience*. Edinburgh, UK: Edinburgh University Press.

Menyuk, P. (1969). *Sentences children use*. Cambridge, MA: MIT Press.

Montilla, J. (2010). Relevance of statistical tests: T and F, to compare means for independent samples. Academia, 9(18), 4-14. Escuela Oficial de Idiomas de Málaga. (2012). Retrieved from http://www.eoimalaga.net/

Paradis, M. (1981). *Neurolinguistic organization of a bilingual's two languages*. Columbia, SC: Hornbeam.

Piaget, J. (1999). *La psicologia de la inteligencia*. Barcelona: Critica.

Porter, M. (1980). An algorithm for suffix stripping. *Program*, *14*(3), 130–137. doi:10.1108/eb046814

Pribram, K. (1971). *Languages of the brain: Experimental paradoxes and principles in neuropsychology*. Englewood Cliffs, NJ: Prentice-Hall.

Russell, B. (1905). On denoting. Mind Magazine, 14.

Skinner, B. (1957). *Verbal behavior: Acton*. Copley Publishing Group. doi:10.1037/11256-000

Strauss, A., & Werner, H. (1942). Disorders of conceptual thinking in the brain-injured child. *The Journal of Nervous and Mental Disease*, *96*(2), 153–172. doi:10.1097/00005053-194208000-00004

Wittgenstein, L. (1987). *Tractatus logico-philosophicus*. Madrid: Alianza.

Wittgenstein, L. (1988). *Investigaciones filosoficas*. México: Instituto de Investigaciones Filosóficas UNAM.

ENDNOTES

1 According to Garon, Bryson and Smith in an extended revision about research on the development of the executive function (Garon, Bryson, & Smith, 2008), it is between the ages of 3 and 5 years that children begin showing goal-directed behaviors which are controlled voluntarily, by inhibiting automated behaviors and focusing their attention in the key aspects of the problem's resolution. This set of emerging capacities has been called "executive function".

2 An ideogram is an icon, conventional image or symbol, that represents an entity, an abstract relation or ideas, but no words or phrases that signify it, even though in the writing for certain languages it is used to mean a given word, morpheme or phrase, without representing each one of its syllables or phonemes.

3 Given that enough related information has been fed to the prototype.

APPENDIX A: CONSTRUCTION OF E_{CI}

The first step to build an Internal Composition Structure (**E**$_{ci}$ in Spanish) is to take the HBS derived from the original sentence. Given the example in Section II.1.1, sentences are:

- **TCM.sentence$_1$:**-The morning is hot
  - **PS$_1$:**- ARTICLE + NOUN + VERB + ADJECTIVE
- **TCM.sentence$_2$:**-It's true, it's hot.
  - **PS$_2$:**- VERB + NOUN +, + VERB + ADJECTIVE
  - **RS$_1$:** PS$_1$:- PS$_2$

In order to derive the HBSs of TCM.sentence$_1$, it must be translated to the universal internal format, taking Table 6 as a reference, each descriptor field is calculated for each of the s_i character chain, from left to right.

Table 6. Descriptor calculation for s_i

Descriptor	Detail	Possible values
tipo-pal (type of s_i)	This descriptor takes the concept that basic statements within s are combinations of noun + verbs.	{sustantivo, verbo, otro} (noun, verb, other)
pal-ant-tipo(type of s_{i-1})	The value is *other* if there is a stream s_{i-1}, otherwise it is none. It is used to infer the most likely type for s_i. It describes the fact that s_i is the first stream in s.	{ninguna, otro} (none, other)
long-palabra (stream length)	It is the number of characters in s_i. Takes s_i as a syntagm. It is relevant for inferring pal-ant-tipo (López De Luise, 2008).	[0..N+]
cant-vocales-fuertes (number of strong vowels)	The number of occurrences of "a", "e", "o" in s_i. As with *long-palabra*, its relevance is shown statistically (López De Luise, 2008).	[0..N+]
cant-vocales-debiles (number of strong vowels)	It is the number of occurrences of "i", "u" in s_i. It has the same relevance as *long-palabra*.	[0..N+]
empieza-mayuscula (does s_i start with uppercase?)	Denotes whether s_i starts with uppercase. It has the same relevance as *long-palabra*.	{si, no} (yes, no)
Stem	It is the invariant root of s_i, when it is detected as a known word in the current vocabulary (that is, the vocabulary learned up to that moment). It follows the algorithm designed by Porter applied to the current lenguage (Porter, 1980).	{a..z,A..Z,0..9}
id-palabra (s_i identification)	It is a unique identifier that represents s_i . For practical reasons it is currently s_i, because it is used to generate sentences during a dialog and to feed vocabulary.	s_i
p_o (evaluation of s_i as part of s)	Strength of s_i as part of the sentence. The calculation of this field is described below.	[-2..+2]

As a result of applying these indications, a series of descriptors is obtained, as shown in Table 7.

Table 7. Descriptors for s_1 and s_2

	Descriptor {*tipo-pal, pal-ant-tipo, long-palabra, cant-vocales-fuertes, cant-vocales-debiles, empieza-mayuscula, stem, id-palabra, p_o*}
EBH^1_1	{otro, ninguna, 2, 1, 0, si, la, la, *0*}
EBH^1_2	*{sustantivo, otro, 6, 3, 0, no, manan, mañana, 0 }*
EBH^1_3	{verbo, otro, 4, 2, 0, no, est, está, *0* }
EBH^1_4	{otro, otro, 8, 3, 1, no, calur, calurosa, 0}
EBH^2_1	{verbo, ninguna, 2, 1, 0, si, es, es, *0* }
EBH^2_2	{sustantivo, otro, 6, 2, 0, no, verdad, verdad, 0}
EBH^2_3	{verbo, otro, 4, 2, 0, no, est, está, 0}
EBH^2_4	{otro, otro, 8, 3, 1, no, calur, calurosa, 0}

The value of p_0 is obtained based on Table 8, which shows a series of character chains pointing to oppositions and/or graduations related to the same word or another word in its context.

Table 8. Opposition and ambiguity in EBH

Opposition Pattern (v_i)	**Ambiguity Pattern (v_i)**	**Ambiguity Pattern (v_i)**
no X (-1) [no] sin X (-1) [without] des X (-1) inh X (-1) anti X (-1) dis X (-1)	muy X (0.7) [very] algo X (0.24) [somewhat] mucho/a(s) X (1.9) [a lot of] escaso/a(s) X (-0.33) [little/few] excesivamente X (-1.99) [excessively] abundantemente X (1.2) [abundantly] demasiado/a(s) X (-1.5) [too much/many]	tan X (0.9) [so] poco/a(s) X (0.12) [little/few] bastante(s) X (0.8) [enough] escasamente X (-0.33) [barely] excesiva/o X (-1.8) [too much] abundante(s) X (1.3) [abundant] exageradamente X (-1.99) [exaggeratedly] exagerada/o(s) X (-1.90) [exaggerated]

These particles are identified in the chain extracted from the sentence (usually corresponds to a word or symbol), which generates the current EBH^i_j and when they exist, a defined value is determined in brackets, as a value of p_0. If there are none of these patters in the chain that originates the HBS (EBH), the value is $p_0 = 0$.

Then, obtained EBH^i_js will be inserted to build an E_{ci} structure. In order to identify the interconnection pattern of each HBS (EBH), assembly tables must be used. These tables are also based in certain special components. In general, these rules are based in the identification of prepositions, connection particles and simple symbols or words with little semantics, which are often used specifically in the global context of sentence construction. Each rule has its identification. Table 9 shows some examples for illustrative purposes.

Table 9. E_{ci} construction rules as a composition of $EBH^{i}_{1...n}$

ID	Rule	Symbol
1	A de B [y | o C[y |o ...]] (A of B [and | or C[and |or ...]])	A ... C B
4	A y|e B [XXX] (A and|or B [XXX])	A B y XXX
7	A o B [XXX] (A or B [XXX])	A B o XXX
31	A se B (A then B)	A→B

These numbers (rule ID) are used for assembling the E_{ci}, identifying the type of relation of the HBS components within the structure.

In the rule table, A, B and C are character chains that often belong in the vocabulary. Characters in bold indicate special symbols or special chains. The square brackets indicate optionality –e.g., in rule 7, the sentence can contain "A or B" or "A or B XXX", where XXX can be a character chain contained in one of the rules or else a simple character chain. In some rules, the pattern can be interpreted in many ways –e.g., in rule 4, the pattern can be either "A or B" or "A or B XXX". The ellipsis indicate recursiveness in the definition –e.g., in rule 1, the pattern can be interpreted as "A of B [and] or C]", or as "A of B", or "A of B or C", "A of B and C and D", etc. For more information, refer to (López De Luise, 2008).

After applying the rules, a graph such as the one shown in figure A.i results. This is a valid representation of the text, page or original sentence within dialog (López De Luise, 2008).

Figure 7. (A.i.) E_{ci} graphs derived from TCM.sentence$_1$ and TCM.sentence$_2$

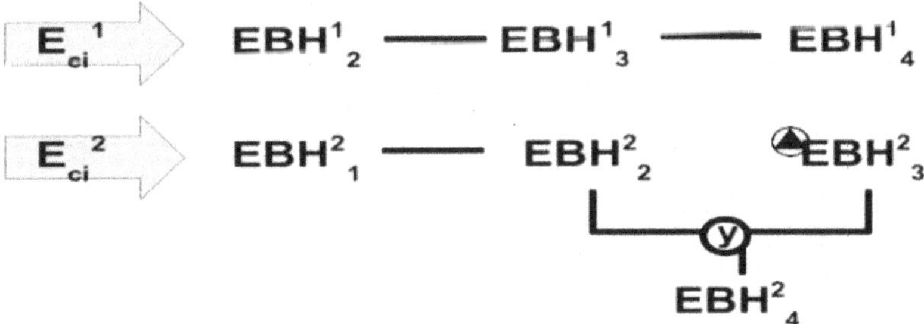

These graphs are translated in practice as a sequence of “plain” entries, similar to those presented in Table 10, where the most relevant elements are highlighted from a practical standpoint to accelerate access times and recovery of the information contained in E_{ci}.

Table 10. Plain version of E_{ci}^{1} and E_{ci}^{2}

E_{ci}	Graphic Version	(p_o^{ECI} (rule, indicator-flag, EBH)...)
E_{ci}^{1}	EBH^1_2 — EBH^1_3 — EBH^1_4	(0.0 (99,0,EBH^1_2) (99,0,EBH^1_3) (99,0,EBH^1_4))
E_{ci}^{2}	EBH^2_1 — EBH^2_2 EBH^2_3 (y) EBH^2_4	(0.0 (99,0,EBH^2_1) (99,0,EBH^2_2) (5,0,EBH^2_3) (4,1,EBH^2_4) (99,0,EBH^2_5))

This format allows for direct filtering through the MLW and easier handling in terms of files and relational databases within the prototype. The case presented in the table has been somewhat simplified to avoid showing aspects related to the deployment of the prototype, but basically they are tuples with a value called p_o^{ECI}, the applied rule, and indicator (1 or 0) in case the HBS derives in an indicator word, and the specific HBS. *Indicator words* are marks for special cases in which table heuristics used during conversion detect that the specific HBS or any of the immediately subsequent HBS has a close relationship with the topic being discussed. These indicator words will be then used in combination with the $_{po}$ for higher abstraction processes, such as automatic summary, keywords, etc.

The field p_o^{ECI} is calculated based on the po values of each of the HBS components of the E_{ci}. This combination is performed according to the following formula:

$p_o^{ECI}= (p_o^{EBH(i)}+p_o^{EBH(i-1)})/2$ for $EBH_i...EBH_n$ derived from $s=\{s_1...s_n\}$

For E_{ci}^{1}, it results from the combination of $EBH_2...EBH_4$:

$p_o^{ECI}=(((p_o^{EBH(1)}+p_o^{EBH(2)})/2+p_o^{EBH(3))}/2)+p_o^{EBH(4)})/2$ with $EBH_1...EBH_4$ derived from TCM.sentence$_1$ (1)(1)

APPENDIX B: MLW AND CONSTRUCTION OF E_{CE}

From the E_{ci}, MLW filtering can be applied. Basically, the specific heuristics to be applied to the general filtering metaheuristics needs to be defined. Then, the new E_{ci}, is inserted in the existing E_{ce} read, using the decomposition parameters of the previous decomposition. These stops are described in detail below.

MLW Filtering

The steps below consist in deriving the MLW metaheuristic into a heuristic applicable to the prototype. This requires the following steps:

Step 1: define a data tuple to be filtered. Regardless of data origin, they must be organized according to the following construction requirements:

Task 1a: it must be generated with a weight p_0 which defines its weighting as information generator. This weight must occupy the first position.

Task 1b: the rest of the tuple must be composed by morphosyntactic descriptors (see Table A.i).

Task 1c: Each tuple must represent a character chain with a unique meaning.

Step 2: Define the filter sequence. The heuristic is expressed through a specific selection of algorithms. All the algorithms used so far are clustering algorithms, with various characteristics. Algorithms included: simple k-means, Expectation Maximization, db-scan, etc.

Each algorithm will use at leas a type of distance (in this context, these shall be of the type specified in (2)). In the match filter-distance, the pair *(f,d)*, is called filter. These are given this name because they will represent a certain aspect of the E_{ci}, which is actually implicit in its content.

$$\text{dist}_f(E_{ci}^{new},E_{ci}^{old})=\text{Ó}_{d=\{\text{numeric descriptor}\}}\ \text{á}_d \times [E_{ci}^{new}(d)-E_{ci}^{old}(d)] + \text{Ó}_{a=\{\text{non-numeric descriptor}\}}\ \text{á}_a \times \text{ä}_a$$

with $\text{ä}_a = 1$ *if* $E_{ci}^{new}(a) = E_{ci}^{old}(a)$, *and* $\text{ä}_a = 0$ *in other case.*(2)

There can be several *(f, d)* filters, and each of them expresses a certain heuristic, a new E_{ci} criterion assessment, as members of a possible cluster.

These filters are organized a top-down access table. Thus, the first filter is the first clustering criterion, which should represent the quickest and broadest method of classifying E_{ci} content.

Table 11. Filter table

ID	Description
(f_1,d_1)	k-means with k=5, d_1 as defined in (2)
(f_2, d_2)	k-means with k=5, $d_2 \neq d_1$
...	...
(f_n,d_n)	Expectation Maximization, $d_n=d_1$

On each application of the MLW, correct distances must be specified. For the current experiment, the distance can be any one that adapts to nominal data combination: Binary (count the number of discrepancies in each character's ACII code), hamming (1 for different values, 0 for equal values), special nominal (a distance usually defined using tables or more sophisticated algorithms), etc.

To sum up, the tasks for this step are:

Task 2a: Define a clustering algorithm sequence.
Task 2b: For each algorithm, define one or more distances to be applied based on descriptors.
Step 3: Define operation thresholds (these are the true heuristic parameters). These control the operation mechanics and sensitivity of the filter to content differences within structures. The tasks are:
Task 3a: Define the LQ threshold. This threshold is used to change the filter f_i to f_{i+1} or, if the end of the filter table has been reached, to split E_{ce} en two or more E_{ce} nodes (to be described in detailed below).
Task 3b: Define the $\mathbf{P_0T}$ threshold. This threshold defines if a filter specified in the *Filter table* needs to be removed or changed.

On of the properties of the MLW is that they determine combinations (f_i,d_i). Selection of these combinations is analogue to selection of parent functions in traditional wavelets, since it governs the way in which information is organized in the graph. The cohesion of each E_{ce} node throughout the various learning stages will be higher or lower based on the heuristics selected to build the E_{ci} clusters. There is a cohesion metrics which defines quality cohesion:

$$C(E_{ce}) = \mathbf{Ó\ dist(E^*{}_{ci}{}^{i}, E^*{}_{ci}{}^{j})}(3)$$

In (3), $E^*{}_{ci}{}^{i}$ is considered the centroid *j* within the E_{ce} node and besides, its $i \neq j$. This means that this cohesion is the accumulation of the various distances between the centroids defined by the filter being used.

As the amount of assimilated information grows, the content of the node starts to diverge and needs to be reorganized based in a more sophisticated criterion. This is done when $C(E_{ce}) > LQ$. In these cases, the current filter (f_i,d_i) is replaced for a better one (f_{i+1},d_{i+1}).

When this process has been repeated several times, the last filter is reached and the filter can no longer be replaced. In this case, content divergence requires splitting the node in at least two more cohesive nodes. This process can lead to the transference of many or all the E_{ci} from the parent node to one or more child nodes, which are more cohesive.

When the restructuring is generated, new eigenvalues are defined –typically, the representative E_{ci} within the cluster. If child nodes are generated, the parent node will only retain an eigenvalue which represents the whole child node. At the same time, the child node will start organizing based on the first filter that appears on the *Filter table*, as did the parent node when it was originated. The change in the parent node will no longer replace its filter, which will continue to be the pair (f_k, d_k), being *k* the last filter.

Locus Definition

Each E_{ci} is processed, filtered as shown above, to obtain a series of parameters which enable locus definition. The locus is the point of insertion. During the filtering process, one or more existing nodes are traversed until the highest similarity is reached –i.e., the shortest distance according to the node filtering criteria (minimum $d_n(E^{*j}_{ci}, E_{ci}(m))$ being E^{*j}_{ci} the eigenvalue E_{ci} of cluster *j* in the current E_{ce} and $E_{ci}(m)$, the E_{ci} being assimilated).

An E_{ce} is an organized set of E_{ci}s. An E_{ci} is in turn an organized element which belongs to a single cluster within the E_{ce}. Some of these will be the centroids which share certain typical characteristics of the elements which compose their respective clusters.

In order to define the locus, a comparison between these representative elements and the new elements is required to determine whether the content must be assimilated at this point or in another node. Similarities among the elements which were not compared the search for the locus are ensured by the MLW filtering process itself, which was used to build the nodes.

Previous Works have shown that there is a correlation between the relative position of nodes and the concept stored in them (López De Luise D., 2010d). This is mainly due to the fact the E_{ce} obtained by the MLW filtering process at the initial stages –probably at the highest levels– are the result of the promotion of child centroids. Child nodes will at the same time be depurated based on the same criterion, resulting in a top-down organization where top nodes represent the dominant characteristics in the set and the following lower detail levels, to a certain extent guided by their centroids.

The figure A.ii shows an assumed existing "E_{ce} node network". The last two E_{ci} obtained will be inserted in this network.

This figure assumes various E_{ci} which are already inserted and a set of E_{ce}. Nodes $E_{ce}^{1,2}$, $E_{ce}^{1,3}$ and $E_{ce}^{1,1}$ are children of E_{ce}^{1}. Below is a description of the steps required to find the locus and the specifications of these steps for E_{ci}^{1} and E_{ci}^{2}.

Figure 8. (A.ii.). E_{ce}. Nodes

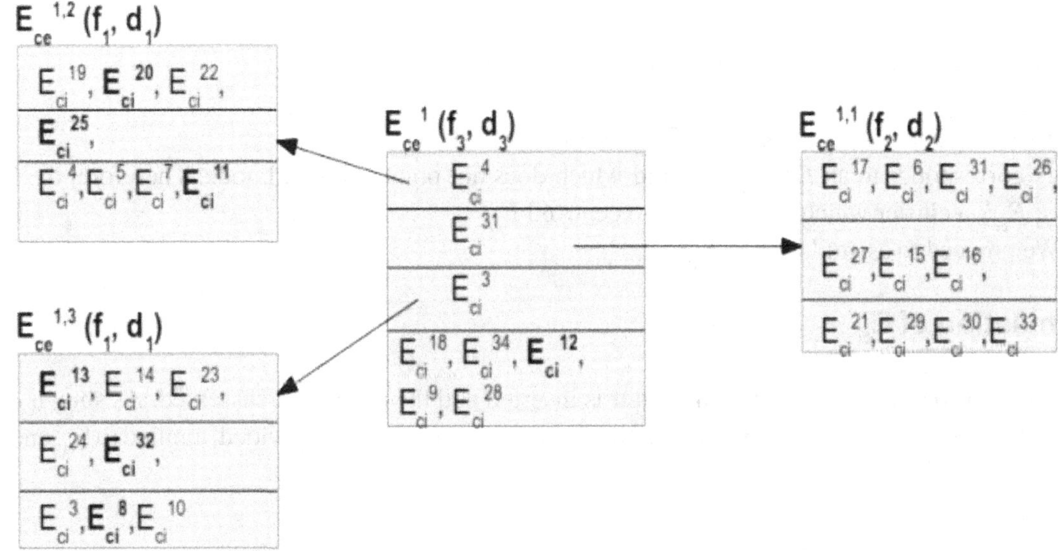

General Description of the Steps Applied to Find the Locus

First access E_{ce}^{1} and apply d_3 to find a d* which complies with the formula:

$$d^*=min\ \{d_1(E^{*4}_{ci},E_{ci}(1)),\ d_1(E^{*3}_{ci},E_{ci}(1)),\ d_2(E^{*31}_{ci},E_{ci}(1)),\ d_3(E^{*12}_{ci},E_{ci}(1))\} \quad (4)$$

That is, the minimum gap between E_{ci}^{1} and the eigenvalues E_{ce}^{3}, E_{ce}^{4}, E_{ce}^{31}, E_{ce}^{12}. This search can give several results:

Step 1: $d^* \geq d_3(E^{*i}_{ci},E^{*j}_{ci})$, with i, j centroids in E_{ce}^{1}: In this case f_3 is again applied to all the elements of the node and then we proceed to step 2; otherwise, we skip to step 3.
Step 2: $d^* \geq d_3(E^{*i}_{ci},E^{*j}_{ci})$ again with i, j centroids in E_{ce}^{1}: Applied to an instance similar to $C(E_{ce}) > LQ$. This instance is described in the next section.
Step 3: d* corresponds to an E^{*m}_{ci} centroid which points to a child node: We skip to child node and review the instance from step 1.
Step 4: d* corresponds to an E^{*m}_{ci} centroid which does not point to a child node: We proceed to assimilation. The locus found is cluster m represented by centroid E^{*m}_{ci}.

Specific Steps for E_{ci}^{1} and E_{ci}^{2}

Steps for $\mathbf{E_{ci}^{1}}$, with figure A.ii: as reference:

1. ***d**** is calculated and $d^* < d_1(E^{*i}_{ci},E^{*j}_{ci})$ results for node E_{ce}^{1}.
2. ***d**** corresponds to an E^{*m}_{ci} centroid which points to a child node. If $d^*=d_1(E^{*3}_{ci},E_{ci}(1))$, we move forward to $E_{ce}^{1,3}$.
3. ***d**** is calculated and $d^* < d_3(E^{*i}_{ci},E^{*j}_{ci})$, results for node $E_{ce}^{1,3}$.
4. ***d**** corresponds to an $E^{*m=32}_{ci}$ centroid which does not point to a child node. Therefore, the locus is: $E_{ce}^{1,3}$, a cluster which corresponds to centroid E_{ci}^{32}.
5. Once the locus is defined, the next step is assimilation of E_{ci}^{1}, as described in the next section.

Location of the locus of $\mathbf{E_{ci}^{2}}$, using figure A.ii as reference:

1. ***d**** is calculated and $d^* < d_1(E^{*i}_{ci},E^{*j}_{ci})$ results for node E_{ce}^{1}.
2. ***d**** corresponds to an $E^{*m=12}_{ci}$ centroid which does not point to a child node. Therefore, the locus is: E_{ce}^{1}, a cluster which corresponds to centroid E_{ci}^{12}.
3. We proceed to assimilation of $\mathbf{E_{ci}^{2}}$.

Assimilation of E_{ci}

As the locus is defined for each E_{ci}, this latter is inserted and the centroids reassessed. As shown in the section above, first the general steps are described and then an example is provided, applied to E_{ci}^{1} and E_{ci}^{2}.

General Description of the Steps Applied Assimilate E_{ci}

Step 1: Insert the E_{ci} in the locus defined.
Step 2: Apply the active filter (f_i,d_i).
Step 3: Calculate applying the filter which is currently valid in that node. Being said filter (f_i,d_i).
Step 4: If $C(E_{ce}) > LQ$, then proceed to ***Step 5***, otherwise skip to ***Step 9***.
Step 5: Aggregate $C(E_{ce}^{m})$ for filter ***i*** within the filter table associated to E_{ce}^{m}. This aggregated $AcumCE_{ce}$ is compared against threshold P_0T: If it is exceeded, the filter specified in the *Filter table* needs to be removed or changed.
Step 6: If ***i=k***, being ***k*** the last filter in the Filter table, then proceed to ***Step 8***, otherwise skip to ***Step 7***.
Step 7: Migrate the active filter (f_i,d_i) associated to E_{ce}^{m} at (f_{i+1},d_{i+1}).. Proceed to ***Step 2***.
Step 8: Split the parent node E_{ce}^{m} as shown below:

For each cluster ***c=1..N,*** being ***N*** the clusters of node:

Step 8a: If $C(E_{ce}^{m})/N > dist(E^{*c}_{ci}, E_{ci}^{j})$, then do not remove the E_{ci}^{j} from the cluster. Ir al *Paso* 8f.
Step 8b: Being $C(E_{ce}^{m})/N > dist(E^{*c}_{ci}, E_{ci}^{j})$, do not remove E^{*c}_{ci} from E_{ce}^{m}.
Step 8c: Create and point to a child node $E_{ce}^{m,c}$ from node E_{ce}^{m}.
Step 8d: Populate child node $E_{ce}^{m,c}$ with the E_{ci}^{j} of the cluster ***c***, removing them from node E_{ce}^{m}.
Step 8e: Apply filter (f_1,d_1), identify the centroids and associate the filter to $E_{ce}^{m,c}$.
Step 8f: If ***c<N*** proceed to Step 8a, otherwise, skip to Step 9.
Step 9: The assimilation has been completed.

Specific Steps for E_{ci}^{1} and E_{ci}^{2}

Now E_{ci}^{1} and E_{ci}^{1} will be assimilated, taking figure A.ii as reference, the locus defined in B.2.ii and steps specified in B.3.i.

Assimilation of E_{ci}^{1}:

1. Insert E_{ci}^{1} in $E_{ce}^{1,3}$, a cluster which corresponds to centroid E_{ci}^{32}.
2. Apply the active filter (f_1,d_1)
3. Calculate $C(E_{ce}^{1,3})$ using Equation 3 with d_1.
4. *Given* $C(E_{ce})=7.5 > LQ=3.0$
5. Aggregate $C(E_{ce}^{1,3})$ for filter 1 in the filter table associated to the node.
6. ***i=1<k***, then there is no need to split the node in child nodes and we can proceed to migrate the filter to a better one.
7. Migrate the active filter (f_1,d_1) associated to $E_{ce}^{1,3}$ a (f_2,d_2).
8. Apply the active filter (f_2,d_2)
9. Calculate $C(E_{ce}^{1,3})$ using the Equation 3 with d_2.
10. *Given* $C(E_{ce})=0.5 \leq LQ=3.0$
11. The assimilation has been completed. The network E_{ce} is now as shown in figure A.iii. For this figure, it was assumed that eigenvalues do not vary after insertion of E_{ci}^{1}.

Similarly, steps for inserting E_{ci}^{2} are as follows:

Figure 9. (A.iii.). E_{ce}. Node network after insertion of E_{ci}^{1}

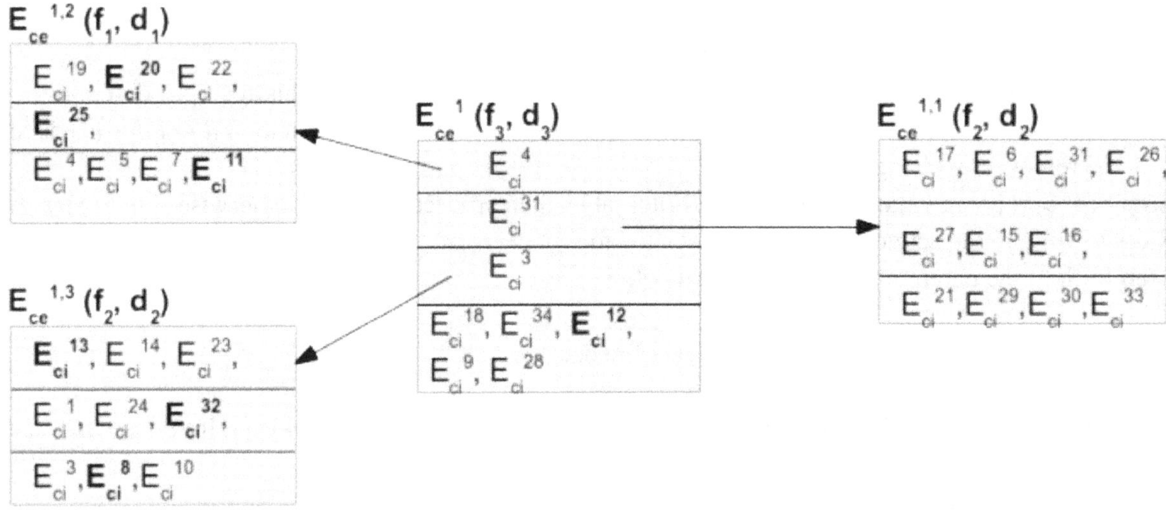

1. Insert $\mathbf{E_{ci}^{2}}$ in E_{ce}^{1}, a cluster which corresponds to centroid $\boldsymbol{E_{ci}^{12}}$.
2. Apply the active filter $\boldsymbol{(f_3,d_3)}$
3. Calculate $\boldsymbol{C(E_{ce}^{1})}$ using the Equation 3 with d_3.
4. *Given* $\boldsymbol{C(E_{ce})=1.5 \leq LQ=3.0}$
5. The assimilation has been completed. The network E_{ce} is now as shown in figure A.iv. For this figure, it was assumed that eigenvalues migrate from $\mathbf{E_{ci}^{12}}$ to $\mathbf{E_{ci}^{34}}$ after insertion of $\mathbf{E_{ci}^{2}}$.

Figure 10. (A.iv.). E_{ce}. Node E_{ce} node network after insertion of E_{ci}^{2}

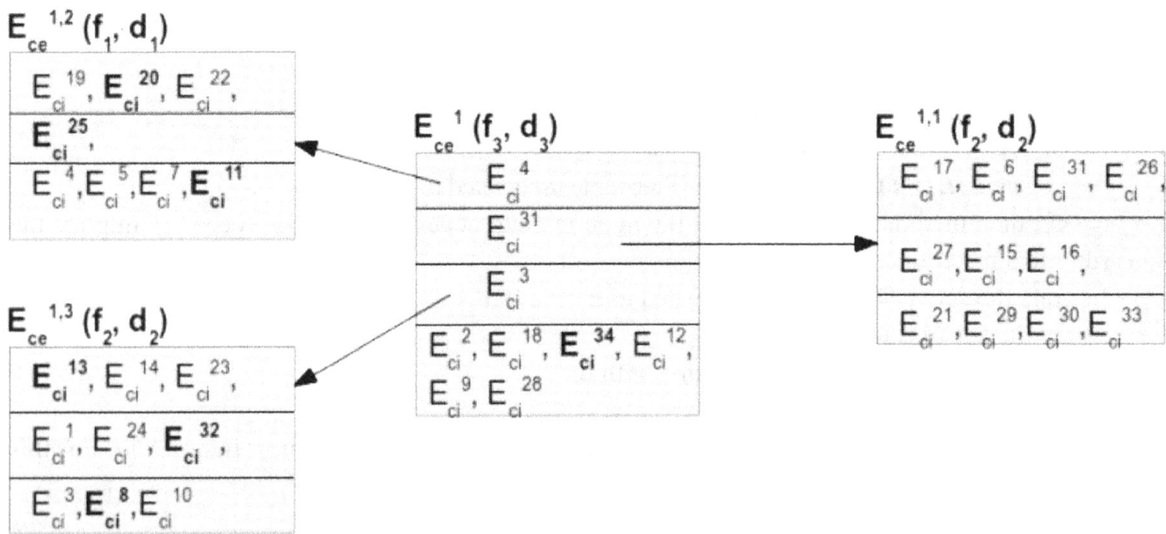

Chapter 51
Revision of the Groupware Users Interface Development Methods

Mabel del V. Sosa
Departamento de Informática, Facultad de Ciencias Exactas y Tecnologías, Universidad Nacional de Santiago del Estero, Argentina

ABSTRACT

Complexity inherent to groupware systems implies a considerable effort in design and development because of the need of multi-discipline collaboration work and the technical difficulty involved in the task (shared data, complicated collaborative activities, task distribution, group awareness, feedthrough, etc.). A key element for usability is the groupware user interface disposed to the enhancement of the group work quality in such aspects as coordination, communication, collaboration, etc. Different fields of computer science, HCI (Human Computer Interaction), CSCW (Computer Supported Cooperative Work), UCD (User Centered Design), and SE (Software Engineering), have contributed with the methodology, process, and tools model, which facilitates and improves different aspects of user interface development for collaborative environments. Still, the analyzed proposals do not completely cover the development process of a complete groupware system where interactive aspects are integrated with collaborative issues, not only in the interface but also in the application itself. Methodological proposals are analyzed in this chapter to detect how far they go in covering the development issues and trying to detect the strong and feeble points of every one, identifying the relevant aspects not yet covered in the fields dedicated to user interface development in this kind of system.

INTRODUCTION

Currently, in organizations, people commonly work in groups or teams, constantly interacting to achieve more productivity and better performance. On the one hand, the development of technology has prompted the creation of systems with the capability of providing the organizations with better work environments, to improve and facilitate the interaction, communication and group work, and in such a way to attain the proposed goals. Group-work-oriented systems are more and more

DOI: 10.4018/978-1-4666-4490-8.ch051

common and necessary, due to the increasing user demand of this modality and to the development of a solid network technology and infrastructure.

This kind of system is developed in the CSCW (Computer Supported Cooperative Work) field and is known under the term of groupware.

Complexity inherent to groupware systems implies a considerable effort in the design and development, because of the need of multi-discipline collaboration work and the technical difficulty that is involved in the task (shared data, complicated collaborative activities, task distribution, group awareness, feedthrough, etc.). A key element for usability is the groupware user interface which helps the enhancement of group work quality in such aspects as coordination, communication, collaboration, etc.

In this field different methodologies and process models have been proposed, allowing it to develop the user interface. Some of them have united the interactive with the collaborative aspects, but not totally covering the whole groupware system development process in an integrated way. This chapter is oriented to the exploration and analysis of the existing methodologies for the interface development in collaborative applications, also called groupware.

Methodological proposals have been analyzed according to the way the development is approached, the field from which they emerge, and the language and notations for their own specification, for the purpose of detecting the strong and feeble points of each proposal.

GROUPWARE

The software for CSCW systems is called groupware (Ellis, Gibbs, & Rein, 1991). Groupware is defined as 'a computing-based system, able to support groups of users implicated in common tasks or goals, which supplies an interface to a shared environment'. It is also known as collaborative system because it allows multiple users to concurrently work on the same project (Bannon & Schmidt, 1991). The term CSCW is used to define the research educational area, while groupware defines the technology of this educational area.

CSCW, as a discipline, describes how to develop groupware applications, aiming at studying, practically and in theory, how people work in cooperation, and how groupware application affects the group behavior. The purpose is to understand the way in which people interact and collaborate with each other in order to propose a technological development able to assist the communication, collaboration and group coordination process. A group is defined as a 'complex social system which develops multiple and interdependent functions in multiple concurrent projects.' The specific features of a group process, which contribute to the groupware application development, are versatile: they are related to the individual work patterns (skills, knowledge styles, modes, behavior restrictions), which contribute to the group work and to the human communication characteristics (way of speech to take commitments and actions); they are related to the group, including issues related to the design of the group work (environment, participant commitment, group awareness, distributed cognition) and also items related to the group dynamics (collaborative processes, group performance and behavior); and lastly, they are related to the organization including the knowledge representation areas (organization structure and role of each participant), the organization design (capacity to develop support tools for the group work, integrating specified goals) and issues related to the management (activities, persons and resources).

In order for the groupware to fulfill the goal of increasing the efficacy of the group work, three basic activities will be brought up:

1. **Coordination:** Oriented to manage the dependency links of the group activities to attain a defined goal (Larson, 1992). In general, an organization operates using

coordination mechanisms such as mutual adjustment, direct supervision, work procedure, result and method standardization, etc. In order to model the group coordination, regulations and standards should be defined which rule the organization operations, and technological tools should be identified to support the distributed work.

2. **Communication:** Allows information exchange among human beings. The purpose is to achieve high quality communication so that the transmitter and the receiver perceive the same concept. Also, the communication should be efficient, in relation to the minimal intake of resources. Several elements are pinpointed in communication: participants, information to be transmitted and the environment. Equally, in an informatics system it is possible to recognize each element: information stored in documents, devices and interaction protocols that make possible the exchange, and modes and types of communication, for instance, face to face communication, synchronous communication, etc.
3. **Collaboration:** Demands a higher degree of participation to attain a specified goal. In other words, collaboration assumes intended and coordinated participation of group members. The system should allow users to work collaboratively. Functionally, it should offer the user groups with a common goal, the possibility of performing any task in a collaborative way.

GROUPWARE USER INTERFACE

User interface is defined as "a set of protocols and techniques for the exchange of explicit information between applications and users" (Larson, 1992). It is the medium through which the user can communicate with a machine or a computer, and includes every contact point existing between users and machines.

Interface is a key issue for system usability, particularly, in groupware type applications, where requirements related to the actual group work dynamics are imposed, such as communication, coordination, collaboration and resources sharing. Besides, it facilitates the individual activity of the work group participants. Therefore, interfaces in this type of systems should be able to support the interaction between users and the system, so that individual and common tasks in the group may be performed, and social interaction of the group members attained (Penechicot, et al., 2001).

Group awareness and feedthrough are aspects to be considered while building a groupware user application interface. Group awareness indicates the knowledge of the activities the group performs and it means the understanding of the full state of systems, including past and present activities, and also possible future activities. An important aspect of the collaboration activity is to sustain the awareness about other people. The usability feature is enhanced if this awareness is taken into account while designing groupware interfaces. When the design supports group awareness it would be possible to know who is collaborating and where (information about other users in relation to the shared environment, indicating at least the identity and presence of users), and what is going on (activity being developed, position in the system, state, changes that are introduced, objects that are used). It is also important that the user actions are shown to other collaborating users who work on the same task (feedthrough). If it is possible to answer these questions, then users would be able to simplify their verbal communication, coordinate actions with one another, and give a helping hand to each other.

No less important are the interface *shared objects* created by users, which can be handled in a collaborative way. So, a user would be able to utilize elements created by others and also the shared workspace of group members to promote ideas and works. Such a way of collaboration is achieved in the space. In this place, the collaboration style is partly defined and the collaboration is in its own context. Usually, a workspace is defined within a greater environment which encompasses it, known as collaborative scenario. Finally, the shared information space is mentioned, to avoid unnecessary duplication of the effort and ensure that all members are using the same information. The group needs facilities to integrate the intake, storage, navigation and browsing of multimedia information available for all group members.

Finally, there are other elements integrating the collaborative system which are only mentioned but not developed in this chapter, for instance, work load, cooperative tasks, multi-user interface, concurrency control, etc.

GROUPWARE USER INTERFACE CONSTRUCTION METHODOLOGY

Several fields of informatics like IHC, CSCW, DCU, and IS have proposed methodologies, process models, and tools oriented to guide the user interface development for collaborative systems. Nevertheless, the analyzed proposals have not covered the whole groupware system development process where interactive and collaborative aspects merge together, not only in the interface but also in the application itself. Besides, during the last years, the focus has shifted from tool centered programs to a user centered development and, at the present, to a group centered development. The user and the environment centered system design is an aspect of the IHC area.

Some of the more representative antecedents of the user interface design for collaborative environments are listed below.

In the CSCW field, one of the more renowned methodologies which systematically deals with analysis and design of collaborative systems is AMENITIES (Penechicot, et al., 2001). This methodology is based on a behavioral and a tasks model for the application analysis and design. It allows the performance of collaborative system conceptual modeling, focused to the group and dealing with behavioral (dynamism, evolution, etc.) and structural aspects (organization, rules, etc.). The specification obtained by means of an exclusive notation called Como-UML, includes relevant information (components, user tasks, domain elements, person-to-machine dialogues and person-to-person dialogues, presentations, etc.) in order to create a user interface. Nevertheless, at present, there is not a proposal for obtaining and implementing the user interface. For the verification of the formal model colored Petri Nets are used, which allows it to simulate the system and validate consistency, completeness, etc. requirements, and evaluate the usability at the level of tasks. Amenities implement a mechanism which fortify the group awareness to improve the collaboration process and allows alternate interactions between participants in asynchronous operations and in real time operations.

Furthermore, considering Amenities as a starting point, cooperative patterns were incorporated, reusable during the construction of the system conceptual model (Isla-Montes, 2007). Other modifications on Amenities prompted the capture, representation and documentation of situations that are usually common at the early stages of modeling. They can be used again in applications of other projects. The obtained advantage is twofold: from the point of view of the process it accelerates the modeling, and considering the specification, it enhances the generated model and the attached documentation.

TOUCHE (Penechicot, 2007) can be mentioned for user interface design in collaborative environments. It is a process model and a methodology which deals with everything from the elicitation of requirements to the final implementation. It applies a user-centered and a task-directed approach. During the analysis stage, mechanisms are delivered to specify the organization of system participants, their functions, and the person-to-computer-to-person interaction. The products or devices of the whole process are strongly connected, and helps the interrelation and traceability within the stage. This model, even though it helps the user interface design in CSCW environments, it is not centered in the functionality of this type of applications, as it is shown in the work of (Penechicot, 2007) since the user interface design is exclusively considered in this stage.

Like Amenities, the Touche model has been extended and in further stages defeasible argumentation techniques (González, et al., 2009) have been incorporated. The goal is to improve the capacity of the CSCW development process model by means of the inclusion of a rule-based approach for efficient reasoning which deals with incomplete and inconsistent information. However, most of these models are unproductive when the matter is about formalizing the user common sense. In the last years, argumentation systems have become more and more important in various areas of Artificial Intelligence, mainly as a vehicle to facilitate rational decision making when dealing with incomplete and inconsistent information. In this way, the development capacity for CSCW applications is enhanced.

The CIAM proposal (Molina, et al., 2008) considers collaboration and cooperation aspects, and their relation with user interface development, in a differentiate way. This approach guides the designer at the moment of modeling the system. It starts with specifications of higher level of abstraction, and as the process is in progress, it becomes more concrete and get near to the user interface final design. Notations in this stage support the differentiated modeling in cooperative and collaborative tasks. CIAM supports more efficiently this approach and has more semantic capacity in this representation than the rest of the proposals dealing with the design in the presentation layer of the CSCW system. However, less attention is centered to the usability aspects.

CIAM has been extended by means of the automatic interface generation, trying to generate final user interfaces which better satisfy and support the requirements of interaction and collaboration between users (Paredes-Velasco, et al., 2010).

Most of the proposals based on the use of a model -among which are the collaborative type- are prone to the Model-Oriented Software Development. Among the more recent proposals which apply this methodology, the following are listed: Giraldo, W. J.et al. propose an approach based on the use of different techniques and notations. System functionality is specified with UML, User Interface description is performed with usiXML, and to describe collaboration and interaction aspects CIAN (Collaborative Interactive Applications Notation) is applied (Giraldo, et al., 2008). Model integration is performed with the Software Engineering process and uses CIAT (Collaborative Interactive Applications Tool). This chapter is specifically centered on the user interaction models and has a light introduction to the usability aspects. Gallego F et al. took as a base the CIAF (Collaborative Interactive Application Framework). It is an extension which considers the user interface functional and interactive aspects (Gallego, Molina, Bravo, & Giraldo, 2010). In this framework different models and notations are utilized which represent relevant issues, such as the collaborative systems collaboration and interaction, patterns identification, and software components to generate collaborative, interactive and functional applications.

Finally, there are some approaches to the interface design which combine and integrate frameworks, models and notations in the IS and CSCW fields, like those introduced by (Rodriguez,-María, Garrido, Hurtado, & Noguera, 2007) and (Vellis, 2009).

METHODOLOGICAL PROPOSAL ANALYSIS FOR CSCW

Even when many documents show that it is possible to integrate different tools, actual proposals do not cover the whole process of a groupware system, and still are gaps between the system functionality development processes and the user interface development which supports them.

A great number of difficulties of the groupware application development that are still present have already been noticed by Grundin and mentioned again by (Jiménez, 2011). They deal with the dependency between development of critical aspects such as the ratio of contribution and profit of participants, the possibility of modifying preset social processes, the improvisation degree that stands in collaborative activity, etc. To these difficulties others have been added by Wang et al., referring the user characterization, considering the homogeneity degree of users, the collaborative work role distribution, the identification of the dependency of decision makers, etc. (Jiménez, 2011). In the development process of collaborative application, a key stage is the identification of the user necessity and the specification of its real requirements. Later on, these requirements should be integrated into flexible and generic architectures, so that every goal of the group and the individual would be correctly and efficiently fulfilled. Therefore, according to what was mentioned by Endsley et al., the collaborative work requirements are the principal source of complexity in the collaborative application development. In this way communications, collaboration, task coordination and interpretation and the follow up of the common work construction process are improved.

Up to this moment, specification languages which exist for the SI have a lack of expressiveness to represent the characteristics related to the user collaboration, awareness and quality factors. For instance, non functional requirement specification, like the awareness, is not a bare triviality, due to the quantity and diversity of requirements with which it is related, and for the high importance it has in terms of the final system architecture. Besides, the technique of the Requisite Engineering field which better fits the collaborative system specification is not clearly identified (Rodriguez-María, Garrido, Hurtado, & Noguera, 2007).

The lack of notations to support the modeling of the collaborative and interactive aspects is evident. Theoretical and computing models are required to specify the computer supported group activities in a more convenient way. There is a lack of notations to accurately model the cooperative and collaborative activities, and they are not focused on interactive aspects and group work. Such limitations make incomplete the semantics of collaborative application specifications (Molina, et al., 2008).

So, the main problem in the collaborative application user interface is the interaction design to support group work. At present, there are different approaches and tools which deal with system interaction modeling. These methods introduce conceptual models to capture the structural, navigational and presentational aspects in an abstract way. However, the user interaction is not considered at the same level as the rest of the applications. Their presentation models are mainly centered in a presentation model, where components are determined which might appear in the user interface, their design characteristics and the feeling and visual dependency existing between them and the information disposition of the application (Jiménez, 2011).

In Table 1 the most known methodologies in the CSCW for groupware development are represented and the central aspects considered in them. They are referred as much to the application functionality as to the user interface (UI). In Table 2 the main characteristics of collaborative group work are represented which are considered in this chapter. On both tables, "+" and "-" indicate the more or less degree of attention with which the studied methodologies are focused to each aspect:

Summarizing, a necessity of counting on techniques which facilitate the creation of readable

Table 1. Main aspects resulting from CSCW methodologies

	Methodologic Aspects of the Groupware System						
	Analysis and Design System Functionality					User Interface Implementation	
Methodologies Framework	**Requirements**	**Organiza-tion**	**Roles**	**Tasks**	**Group Knowledge**	**Presentation**	**Interaction**
Amenities	+	+	+	+	-	-	-
Touche	+	+	+	+	+	+	-
Ciam	+	+	+	+	+	+	-
Other	-	+	+	+	-	+	-

Table 2. Group work aspects considered by CSCW methodologies

Aspects/Methodologies	Amenities	Ciam	Touche
Coordination	+	+	+
Collaboration	-	+	+
Cooperation	+	+	+
Usability	+	-	-
Group Awareness	+	+	+
Feedthrough	-	+	-
Distributed Cognition	-	+	-

and extendible models, able to clearly represent not only the functional requirements (collaboration, coordination and communication) but also the non functional requirements, which appear from the user need of being aware of the presence or absence of other users, knowing what actions are they applying and on what devices or resources they operate, being aware of the errors produced by others and the management of shared resources, etc.

It is also required to count on methodologies which deal with the development process as a whole, (from the requirements elicitation to the user interface implementation), integrated, with an important level of traceability between the obtained models in each of the stages, including notations or languages with semantics capacity within the integral methodological framework.

Lastly, a clear identification of quality requirements related to group work, able to support evaluation tasks and the collaborative application maintenance.

CONCLUSION

Notwithstanding the fact that there are several proposals which come from IHC, CSCW, and IS fields which apply to the collaborative systems modeling, it is still detected that there is not a proposal which considers interaction and collaboration aspects in an articulated and integrated way.

Based on approaches and methods that were found in the antecedents and on their own analysis, two main problems are considered: first, the problem related to the collaborative application development, and second, the problem directly related to the user interface of those applications. There are many works that indicate the possibility of integrating different approaches and tools, but the concrete proposals do not attain to cover the whole groupware system development process. There is still a gap between the development processes of the functional system and the user interface development which provides the support.

REFERENCES

Bannon, L., & Schmidt, K. (1991). CSCW: Four characters in search of a context. In J. Bowers, & S. Benford (Eds.), *Studies in Computer Supported Cooperative Work: Theory, Practice and Design*. Amsterdam: North-Holland.

Ellis, C., Gibbs, S., & Rein, G. (1991). Groupware: Some issues and experiences. *Communications of the ACM, 34*(1), 38–58. doi:10.1145/99977.99987

Gallego, F., Molina, A., Bravo, C., & Giraldo, W. (2010). A proposal for model-based design and development of group work tasks in a shared context. In *Proceedings of the 7th International Conference on Cooperative Design, Visualization, and Engineering*. Heidelberg, Germany: Springer.

Garrido, J., Gea, M., & Rodríguez, M. (2005). Requirements enginnering in cooperative systems. In *Requirements Enginnering for Sociotechnical Systems*. Hershey, PA: Idea Group, Inc.

Giraldo, W., et al. (2008). A model based approach for GUI development in groupware systems. In *Proceedings of 14th International Workshop*. Omaha, NE: CRIWG.

González, M. et al. (2009). Development of CSCW interfaces from a user-centered viewpoint: Extending the TOUCHE process model through defeasible argumentation. In M. Kurosu (Ed.), *Human Centered Design*. Heidelberg, Germany: Springer. doi:10.1007/978-3-642-02806-9_109

Isla-Montes, J. (2007). *Modelado conceptual de sistemas cooperativos en base a patrones en amenities. (Tesis Doctoral)*. Granada: Editorial Universidad de Granada.

Jiménez, R. (2011). *Metodología de generación automática de aplicaciones colaborativas. (Tesis de Máster)*. Madrid, Spain: Universidad Autónoma de Madrid.

Larson, J. (1992). *Interactive software*. Englewood Cliffs, NJ: Yourdon Press.

Molina, A. I. et al. (2008). CIAM: A methodology for the development of groupware user interfaces. *Journal of Universal Computer Science, 14*(9). PMID:20390048

Paredes-Velasco, M., et al. (2010). *CIAM extendido con generación automática de IU frente a metodologías no guiadas: Evaluación de una experiencia con COFARCIR*. Retrieved from http://eciencia.urjc.es/dspace/bitstream/10115/4206/1/interaccion2010b.pdf

Penechicot, V. (2007). *Task-oriented and user-centred process model for developing interfaces for human-computer-human environments*. (PhD Dissertation). Universidad de Castilla-La Mancha.

Penechicot, V., et al. (2001). *Una aproximación al proceso de diseño e implementación de interfaces de usuario para aplicaciones groupware*. Actas del Noveno Congreso Internacional Interacción.

Rodriguez,-María, L., Garrido, J., Hurtado, M., & Noguera, M. (2007). An approach to the model-based design of groupware multi-user interfaces. *Lectures Notes in Computer Science, 4715*, 157-164.

Teruel, M., Navarro, E., López Jaquero, V., Montero, F., & González, P. (2011). An empirical evaluation of requirement engineering techniques for collaborative systems. In *Proceedings of 15th International Conference on Evaluation and Assessment in Software Engineering*. Durham, UK: IEEE.

Vellis, G. (2009). Model-based development of synchronous collaborative user interfaces. In *Proceedings of EICS'09*. New York: ACM Press.

Chapter 52
Web Attacks and the ASCII Files

Francisco V. Cipolla-Ficarra
ALAIPO – AINCI, Spain and Italy

Alejandra Quiroga
Universidad Nacional de La Pampa, Argentina

Jim Carré
University of The Netherlands Antilles, Curaçao

ABSTRACT

The chapter analyzes the destructive human factors exercised from the environment of the university training directly or indirectly related to the ICTs (Information and Communication Technologies). Through a first set of examples, the authors lay bare the early patterns of behavior of those professors from southern Europe belonging to departments or faculties of university training, languages and computer systems, software engineering, computer science and systems engineering, architecture and telecommunications, audiovisual, and fine arts. Finally, they present the results of a strategy to disguise attacks through a Website to advertise international events.

INTRODUCTION

One of the fields of the new technologies where a myriad disciplines converge is multimedia, whether from the technological point of view "union of media" and from the communicational point of view "intersection of media" (Cipolla-Ficarra, et al., 2010). The other one is the human-computer intersection. In both cases the focus is the user, who through a computer or another last generation interactive communication media such as can be a Tablet PC, a multimedia mobile phone, etc., gets wired to the net to come into play with other users. In the generation of those products and/or services we can see several well differentiated groups, for instance, those who design new products and/or services (a small elite), users who buy those goods and services (including the small elite who designs them), and also those users who are excluded from that consumption by the digital divide. This constant inclusion and exclusion of people or users from

DOI: 10.4018/978-1-4666-4490-8.ch052

the latest breakthroughs of the new technologies generate conflicts, from the design stage to the access to the online information.

Now part of those conflicts stem from the scarce professionalism of the members of the former elitist group, belonging to the university teaching, software engineering, computer science and systems engineering, architecture and telecommunications, audiovisual and the fine arts, etc. They have joined the ranks of an exponential marketing which runs contrary to the principles that rule the sciences. Directly or indirectly, they have destroyed the multimedia term, in Spain, since the democratization of the internet in the 90s, for instance. In that same country, in the first decade of the new millennium, they have also underrated or trivialized the term human-computer interaction, out of simple commercial reasons. An analogous reality not only in other countries of Southern Europe, but also in many other places in the north of Europe, where currently it is impossible to draw the boundaries between private business and public university research, for instance, when it comes to transfer of knowledge and technologies.

The scarce professionalism of the members of the ICT (Information and Communications Technology) who constantly devote themselves to the attack inside the scientific environment can be glimpsed in certain negative patterns of behavior, such as (alphabetical order):

- Cloning of alien experiences and trainings, especially of those ICTs professionals who are the target of the attacks.
- Copy and glue the syllabuses from other universities.
- Establishing access control mechanisms to the websites, in a explicit or implicit way, where they publicize continuous training courses, masters, workshops, conferences, etc. with high costs but low quality and work prospects practically equal to zero. For instance, the mechanism where are controlled the seconds of connection to a website.
- Making up destruction fraternities against all those who stand for the fundamental principles which rule the formal and factual sciences.
- Persecuting the real ICT professionals for decades, copying their activities, research results, meddling and destroying their work team, slandering and smearing them privately and publicly.
- Underrating or trivializing the knowledge and/or experience of those scientists who are daily attacked.

These are some of the negative patterns of behavior that have been detected in Southern Europe, for a quarter of a century and which the interested reader can widen in the following bibliographical references (Cipolla-Ficarra, et al., 2011; Cipolla-Ficarra, & Kratky, 2011; Cipolla-Ficarra, Ficarra, & Cipolla-Ficarra, 2011).

FAILURE OF THE UNIVERSITY EDUCATION SYSTEM AND ACTIVATION OF THE DESTROYING MECHANISMS OF THE SCIENCES

Now the current problem of that behavior that disown not only the normal functioning of the sciences, but also have negative consequences for the rest of the community since which they act, such as can be the millions of unemployed or the NEET generation (Not in Employment, Education or Training), is the perpetuity and immunity of those negative behavior patterns from the inside of the classrooms in Southern Europe. In other words, it is contradictory to find quality or educative excellence courses, creativity, culture, etc., when those who direct them, although they are professors or emeritus professors show a negative behavior towards the progress of the sciences through the constant attack to other colleagues inside or outside their country of origin. It is not logical to speak of educative excellence, exportable educational models, creative solutions, etc., in places where the unemployed reach the millions of youth. Besides, those many numbers show a system and a misguided educational structure which has been taking shape for a long time.

The local organizing group of the event of Figure 1 has exercised its influence for decades in the context of graphic computing, with all its derivations: multimedia, hypermedia, virtual reality, augmented reality, etc. whose results for the community where they are located are practically nil or are submerged under the current reality of unemployed among the professionals of that field of computer science they have shaped themselves. One of the greatest problems that exist in order to unveil these patterns of destructive behavior to the national and international science is the use of accurate language, with which these phenomena can be described. In general terms we are talking about scientific context of the Computer and Information Science and/or Information and Communication Technologies since which this destructive behavior takes place, using the old trick of "throwing the stone and hiding the hand".

Figure 1. Organization of international events of doubtful transparency since the access to the primary information such as the topics list is missing

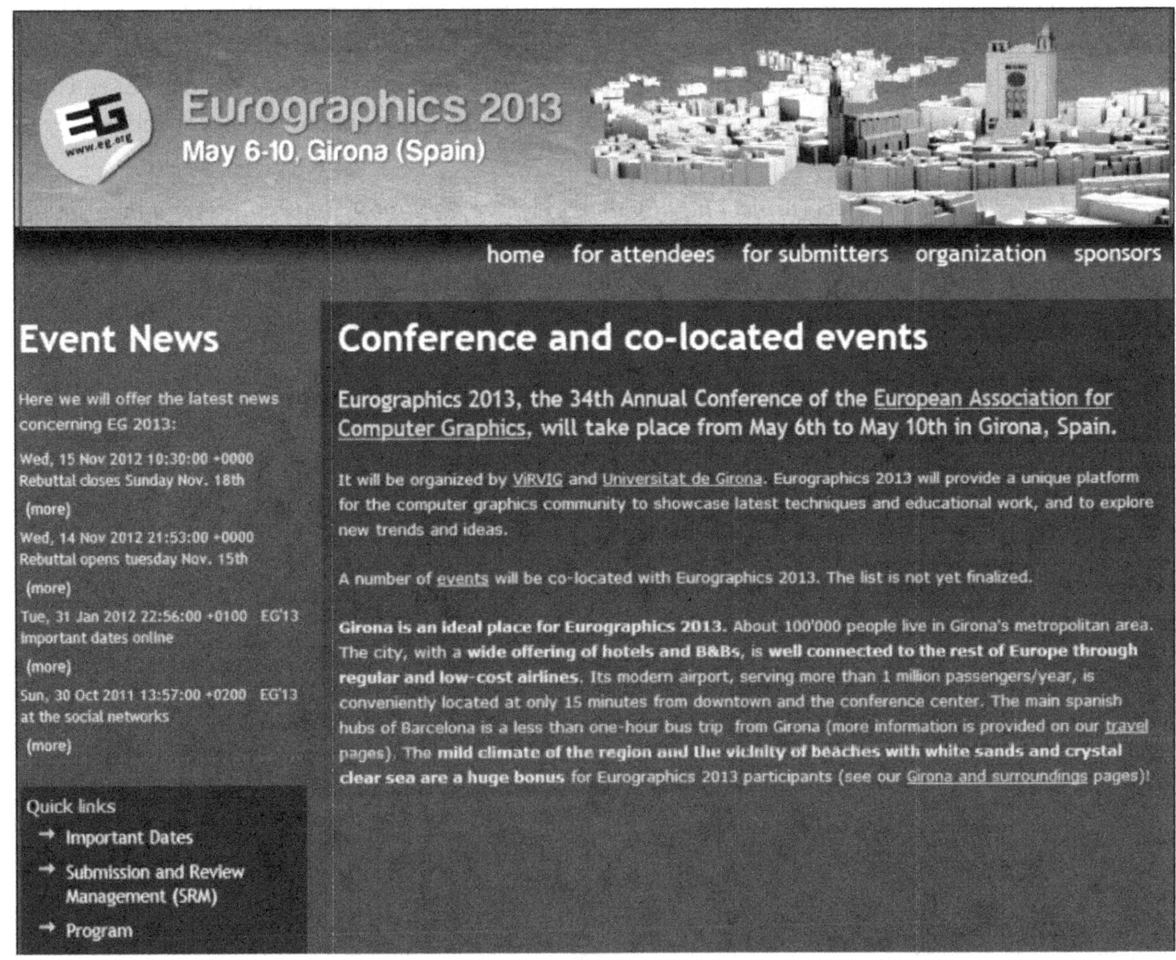

This is a typical behavior of those who emulate the medieval fraternities in the 21st century (called in the current work "Medieval Brotherhood Phenomenon", e.g., bullying, stalking, sadism, racism, etc.) and in which the parochialism to which they belong is governed by the essential rule "nobody can ever do anything to us". In other words, we are in the need of using a language akin to the social sciences in a context of Computer and Information Science and/or Information and Communication Technologies. In that sense, we are working to create the style guidelines which meet the principles of the formal and factual sciences.

However here it is necessary here it is necessary to differentiate the term information since it has a different meaning among several European languages. This word in Spain is associated to the information sciences, that is, journalism, whereas in Italy it is related to computer science. However, a graduate in computer science in Italy can direct even the PhDs thesis. Whereas in Latin America that reality is unworkable. The problem lies in the fact that from the university environment the computer science graduates or other formal sciences use the strategies of journalism to foster parochialism. The direct and indirect purpose is the destruction of the sciences, through information duality. An example of informative duality may be the partners who appear in a European project allegedly with R&D purposes but in reality all is about seizing potential employees, using the financial funds of the EU. At the same time the ultimate purpose of that who has fostered or signed that R&D European project are not the results of the project in itself, but rather to get a job in some of those companies they have as partners. In few words, these are ghosts projects, since they have no continuity in time, in the mid and long term. That is, the future lines of research of those projects will never be carried out by those who have signed them and the partners who have supported them.

In the example from Figure 2 can be seen how the private firms not only do not spend money in

Figure 2. Understanding project (project.liquidpub.org) where the Italian universities lend their facilities and the Spanish or German partners support them because it is a way to travel and select staff for free from the ICTs with working purposes in Europe

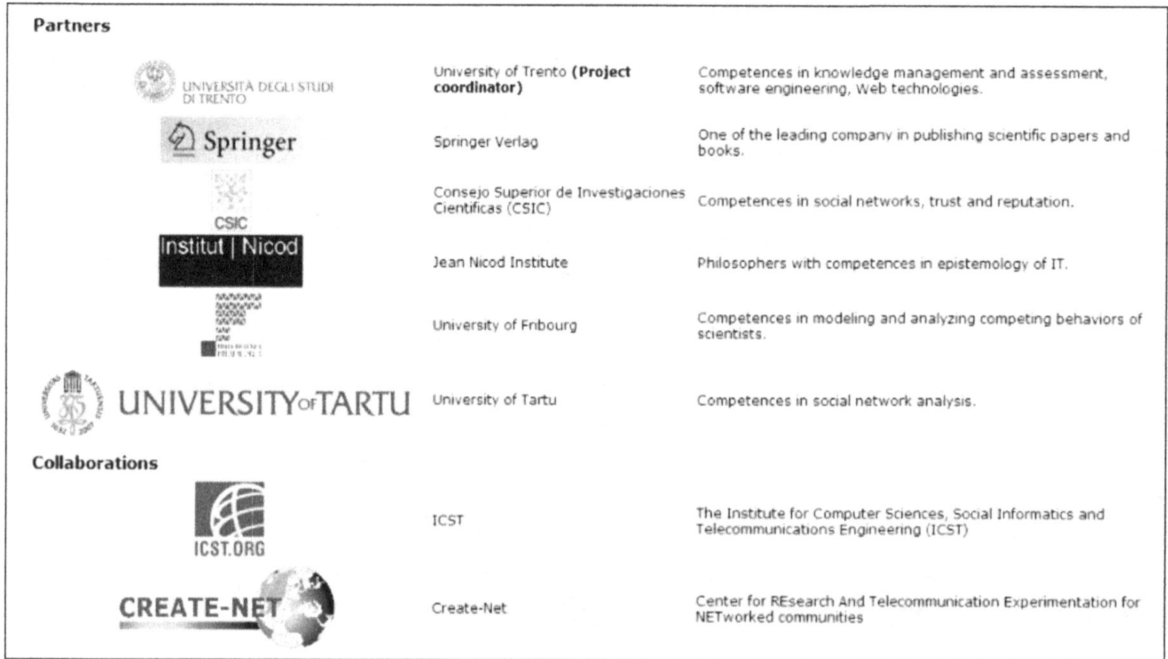

the staff selection, but also their potential candidates can use the university structures before finishing their training cycle in keeping with the mercantilist purposes of the future jobs they will occupy in those firms. In few words, make their practices, final projects in engineering or graduates (industrial, computer science, systems, etc.), master thesis, PhD thesis, etc. according to the needs of the future employer.

Now the financial resources in this kind of projects have clustered for decades the destructor ghosts of the sciences in Southern Europe, intensifying in the last decades the phenomenon of parochialism of the medieval brotherhood. It is very easy to detect them through their constant participation in high level conferences, workshops, and which take place randomly in the most paradisiacal places of our planet (Hawaiian islands, Caribbean islands, Côte d'Azur in France, etc.). The goal is not to widen their knowledge, but rather international tourism, paid by the public universities or the research centres, for instance. As a rule, those who submit the research works are not even responsible for that research, but rather the heads of the departments or labs, whose ages may be above 70 or 80 years of age in Southern Europe. Those heads of department, belonging to the medieval brotherhood, are charged with activating a sort of persecution or academic stalking, of all those professionals who may make interesting advances variegated and original, with financial budgets equal to zero euros. It is those chiefs who will give the order of "throwing the stones and hide the hand", resorting to a myriad destructive strategies. We can also find those patterns of behavior among the young who integrate parochialism. In all those cases, there is one or many personality disorders, such as: Asperger Syndrome, Autism, Bipolar Disorder, etc. These disorders are uncovered through an analysis of the text, especially in the messages they issue, whether in the private correspondence or the posts online. With the destructive purpose, those destructive messages are released, gaining a quick visibility online and the European law is still lax, slow or inexistent to solve those problems.

STRATEGIES OF THE CYBER DESTRUCTORS: THE ASCII FILES

The destroyers of the medieval brotherhoods have a set of strategies for their modus operandi immune to the Internet international legislation. One of them goes back to the origins of the hypertext, the ASCII messages. To such extent that in the 21st century a simple message generated in ASCII code (text) is distributed in ad websites, such as a and b without previous controls and without any responsibility for that who issues them like the one that habilitates its distribution.

Contents which can be included in a simple way by anybody, without previous verification of the credibility and/or veracity of the information it contains. Once published, in less than a minute those messages are internationally distributed. Since it is a file in ASCII format, that is, few bytes or kilobytes, automatically it is placed in the first places of the search engines such as Google, Yahoo, etc. As a rule, the first page. A reality which can be seen in the Figure 2, at the moment of seeking information about an international event such as can be its initials, it appears in the first page of the search results. The problem is that in the face of defamation, slanders, disguised or open attacks, etc., there is no legal mechanism in Europe so that they are erased in an automatic way by the people who manage those websites, in view of the complaints filed to the competent authorities by the victims of those infamies. They only have the reply right. That is, to issue another message counteracting the first, thus generating a kind of infinite semiosis (Colapietro, 1993). This semiosis is activated through the personality disorders of the attackers. They do not only issue constant unjustified responses or disorienting about their manifest or disguised attacks, but they also threaten their victims with other retaliations (Richards, 1999). That is, that the victims must shut up to the destructors.

These are criminal actions which should be gathered urgently in the international penal codes of digital information (McQuade, et al., 2009; Cole, 2009). However, an immunity can be seen which goes beyond the local, provincial, regional and state borders. The legal problem is that some countries not only do not adhere to it or to the international agreements in the matter of the rights and duties of digital information (Cole, 2009), but they make of the free use of the internet not only an abuse or libertinage, but also a constant source of conflicts in the science environment.

Another of the problems of the ACM, IEEE, etc., is that the victims of the attacks do not learn about them until after a few weeks. That is, when they see in the first pages of the online searchers a simple ASCII file with the attack message, which is immune to the European legal framework, and also indelible for a quick elimination.

In the Appendix can be seen different examples of that home page with the passing of time, through Google. The consequences of the harm to the credibility, morale, finances, etc. can't be quantified because we are in the face of a value

Figure 3. Threats received from Bangladesh from a cyber destructor (August 2012), through a ASCII message in the portal ACM (www.listserv.acm.org/archives/chi-announcements.html)

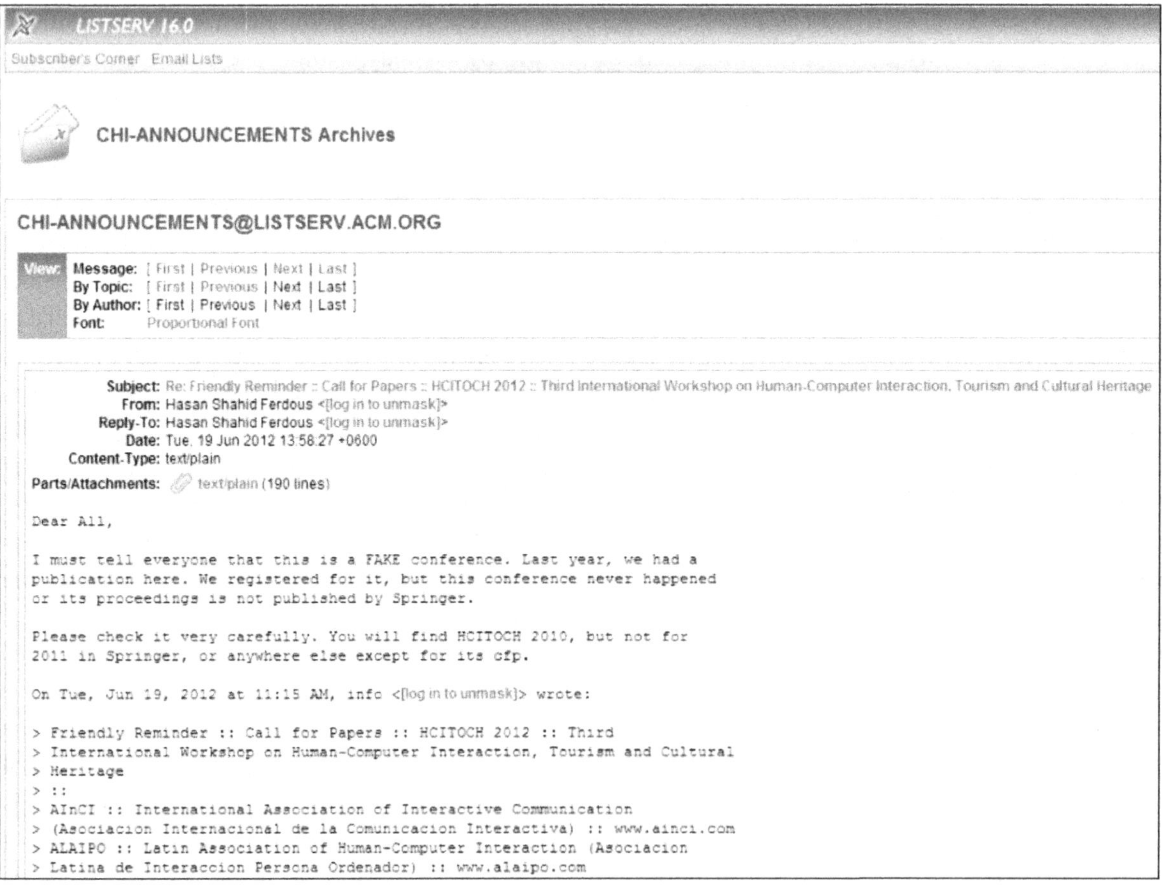

LISTSERV 16.0

Subscriber's Corner Email Lists

CHI-ANNOUNCEMENTS Archives

CHI-ANNOUNCEMENTS@LISTSERV.ACM.ORG

View: Message: [First | Previous | Next | Last]
By Topic: [First | Previous | Next | Last]
By Author: [First | Previous | Next | Last]
Font: Proportional Font

Subject: Re: Friendly Reminder :: Call for Papers :: HCITOCH 2012 :: Third International Workshop on Human-Computer Interaction, Tourism and Cultural Heritage
From: Hasan Shahid Ferdous <[log in to unmask]>
Reply-To: Hasan Shahid Ferdous <[log in to unmask]>
Date: Tue, 19 Jun 2012 13:58:27 +0600
Content-Type: text/plain
Parts/Attachments: text/plain (190 lines)

Dear All,

I must tell everyone that this is a FAKE conference. Last year, we had a publication here. We registered for it, but this conference never happened or its proceedings is not published by Springer.

Please check it very carefully. You will find HCITOCH 2010, but not for 2011 in Springer, or anywhere else except for its cfp.

On Tue, Jun 19, 2012 at 11:15 AM, info <[log in to unmask]> wrote:

> Friendly Reminder :: Call for Papers :: HCITOCH 2012 :: Third
> International Workshop on Human-Computer Interaction, Tourism and Cultural
> Heritage
> ::
> AInCI :: International Association of Interactive Communication
> (Asociacion Internacional de la Comunicacion Interactiva) :: www.ainci.com
> ALAIPO :: Latin Association of Human-Computer Interaction (Asociacion
> Latina de Interaccion Persona Ordenador) :: www.alaipo.com

or attribute of human quality such as the reputation or prestige. This is forged during decades by honest, modest professionals and who have never got a cent of a euro in financial subsidies for the works they have developed.

THE ANALYSIS AND THE RESULTS OF THE MESSAGES ALLEGEDLY NEUTRAL IN A SCIENTIFIC WEBSITE

The analyzed website ACM SIGMOD – DB-WORLD (research.cs.wisc.edu/dbworld) is a tablet in Html made up by the columns in Table 1.

The analysis of the website is activated since the first "normal" message from a Danish publisher, in the European summer period. We point out that that website had never been used before to attack organizers of international events, related to the ICTs and who allegedly had a partner in that publishing house for scientific publications (in fact it was a kind of Trojan horse).

Starting from that message, others have been activated for the manifest attacks (similar topics lists, coincidental deadlines, parochialism of the members of the scientific committees, etc.) or latent (to enclose immediately the posted message, another from the publisher that smears its partners, the use of the same name of the people who enclose new messages to breed confusion, cacophony between the name and the surname (Kathrin Kirchner), KK, whose sound of the two initial letters "ca-ca" means human excrement, such as can be seen in Figure 4 (! and ?), etc.

In our first analysis we focused on these two great sets of strategies for the manifest or latent attacks, every time an online message was posted. A trimester has been analyzed. The period encompassing between 08.20.2012 and 11.22.2012. These results may be summed up in the Table 2.

Table 1. ACM SIGMOD – DBWORLD (research.cs.wisc.edu/dbworld)

Sent	Message Type	From	Subject	Deadline	Web Page
(Date on which the advert is inserted)	(call for papers, call for chapters, job announcements, etc.)	(name and surname of the person who inserts the advert)	(the reason, that is, the call to submit works in a magazine, congress, workshop, the appearance of a new book, etc.) It is in this section where a filein ASCII format can be enclosed	For the submission of the works, proposals for magazines, presentation of jobs requests, etc.	Link to a website

Figure 4. Example of the modalities of attacks (http://research.cs.wisc.edu/dbworld/browse.html). Once extended the deadline to submit works, automatically a cacophony appears with the surname of the Argentine President (Kirchner) who posts the message (see second ?) and the reference to the German publisher.

15-Nov-2012	job ann.	Jan Mendling	Pre-Doc and Post-Doc Position in Business Process Management and Logistics (WU Vienna)
15-Nov-2012	news	Sonia Flores	CFP :: Deadline >> STILL OPEN << Third International Conference ADNTIIC 2012 :: Cordoba, ARGENTINA
15-Nov-2012	book CFC	Kathrin Kirchner ! ?	INNOVATIONS IN KNOWLEDGE MANAGEMENT Call for Chapters
15-Nov-2012	conf. ann.	Doris Edison	CFP :: Deadline >> Still Open << Third International Conference ADNTIIC 2012 - Cordoba, Argentina
15-Nov-2012	book ann.	Horst Eidenberger	New Book on Content-Based Analysis and Classification of Multimedia Data

Table 2. Results of manifest and latent attacks between 08.20.2012 and 11.22.2012, Website ACM Sigmod–DBWORLD (http://research.cs.wisc.edu/dbworld/browse.html)

Data	Attacks
08.20.2012:: 08.26.2012	1
08.27.2012:: 09.02.2012	14
09.03.2012:: 09.09.2012	6
09.10.2012:: 09.16.2012	12
09.17.2012:: 09.23.2012	11
09.24.2012:: 09.30.2012	18
10.01.2012:: 10.07.2012	23
10.08.2012:: 10.14.2012	9
10.15.2012:: 10.21.2012	7
10.22.2012:: 10.28.2012	18
10.29.2012:: 11.04.2012	12
11.12.2012:: 11.18.2012	14
11.19.2012:: 11.22.2012	19
Total	154

The obtained results show the existence of a group of people interrelated among themselves who in a systematic and coordinated way devote themselves to a manifest and latent attack from scientific websites. That is, we are in the presence of the medieval brotherhood phenomenon. A traceable phenomenon inside and outside the European borders. Besides, it has been detected that those websites are used by multinationals of the software, hardware, publishing, etc., to disguise campaigns with financial or marketing purposes. This is a topic of study stemming from the current work which will serve for future research.

LESSONS LEARNED AND FUTURE RESEARCH

It is not easy to present topics like those approached in the current work due to the use that is made of language in non-social contexts. However, they are human and social factors which have to be treated in some way since they cause severe damage not only in the computer sector, educational, productive, etc. but also in the future of the new generations of a community who will spend goods and services stemming from the ICTs. This statement can be checked with the information stemming from the statistics in relation to the Neet phenomenon or the high rates of unemployed youth in the EU. To find the linguistic balance between the language of the formal sciences and the factual sciences is one of our main goals for future research. What is obvious is that once more the analysis of the text, in this case in files in ASCII format and Html websites is essential to detect deviations in the use of information systems and theoretically scientific, due to the human factors. Human factors which tend to a convergence of said factors inside pressure groups in the Internet until generating a kind of brotherhood. Inside it, it is easy to observe personal behavior disorders which turn into social in the moment they join forces and strategies, with a single purpose: destroy the fundamental principles which govern universal scientific knowledge in the era of expansion of communicability. The legal void or the slowness in applying justice in front of the cyber destructors is generating the origin of a kind of infinite semiosis between cyber destroyers and their cyber victims. The first results obtained make apparent unbalanced behaviors by the cyber destructors, when they go from anonymity to popularity with their attacks in the internet. A popularity which is increased in the Internet thanks to the collaboration of the members of parochialism. For instance, when they make links to ASCII destructive messages or the provocation through ads, in the same virtual places where they attack daily. Although the legislation tutors the privacy of the cyber destructors, we will establish some outlines including the maps of the public and/or private institutions where the parochialism for cyber destruction is present.

CONCLUSION

In the current work it has been showed that the scientific websites are used with purposes alien to the sciences. Besides, there is no mechanism to filter the diffusion of news detrimental to the normal functioning of ads of interest to the scientific community, in websites generated directly or indirectly by associations of great international prestige such as ACM or IEEE. Even those websites are used by international multinational companies of the scientific publishing sector, for instance, not only to carry out smearing campaigns of professionals, associations, educational institutions, etc. of the new technologies sector, but rather to freely promote their products: CD, DVD, etc. Evidently one of the main problems in this kind of research work is to generate a neutered language, between formal sciences and factual sciences to denounce or describe qualitatively and quantitatively the human and social factors, which are affecting the normal development of the ICTs. Finally and going back to the origins of the hypertext and the Internet the textual messages in ASCII format still have a great power of influence and in relation to the human purposes they can be constructive or destructive.

ACKNOWLEDGMENT

The authors would like to thank to Maria Ficarra, Sonia Flores, Pamela Fulton, Mary Brie, Doris Edison, Luisa Varela, Marie Bordeaux, Valeria Villarreal, Aida Marinesko, Donald Nilson, Winston Havilland and Carlos for the help.

REFERENCES

Cipolla-Ficarra, et al. (2010). *Quality and communicability for interactive hypermedia systems: Concepts and practices for design*. Hershey, PA: IGI Global.

Cipolla-Ficarra., et al. (2011). Computational informatics, social factors and new information technologies: Hypermedia perspectives and avant-garde experiences in the era of communicability expansion. Bergamo, Italy: Blue Herons Ed.s.

Cipolla-Ficarra, F., Ficarra, V., & Cipolla-Ficarra, M. (2011). New technologies of the information and communication: Analysis of the constructors and destructors of the European educational system. In *Proceedings of ADNTIIC 2011*. Heidelberg, Germany: Springer.

Cipolla-Ficarra, F., & Kratky, A. (2011). Security of the automatic information on-line: A study of the controls forbid. In *Proceedings of ADNTIIC 2011*. Heidelberg, Germany: Springer.

Colapietro, V. (1993). *Semiotics*. New York: Paragon House.

Cole, E. (2009). *Network security*. Indianapolis, IN: Willey.

McQuade, S. et al. (2009). *Cyber bullying: Protecting kids and adults from online bullies*. Westport, CT: Praeger.

Richards, J. (1999). *Transnational criminal organizations, cybercrime, and money laundering: A Handbook for law enforcement officers, auditors, and financial investigators*. Boca Raton, FL: CRC Press.

APPENDIX

Figure 5. Google: search results on the day: 11.08.2012 (page #1)

adntiic 2012

Búsqueda   Aproximadamente 19 600 resultados

Web
Imágenes
Vídeos
Noticias
Shopping
Más

Mostrar herramientas de búsqueda

ADNTIIC 2012 - AInCI
www.ainci.com/ADNTIIC-2012/conference_ADNTIIC_2012.html - En caché
Advances in New Technologies, Interactive Interfaces and Communicability (**ADNTIIC 2012**): Design, E-commerce, E-learning, E-health, E-tourism, Web 2.0 and ...

no becarios - ALAIPO
www.alaipo.com/ADNTIIC-2012/conference_ADNTIIC_2012_news.html - En caché
Advances in New Technologies, Interactive Interfaces and Communicability (**ADNTIIC 2012**): Design, E-commerce, E-learning, E-health, E-tourism, Web 2.0 and ...

ADNTIIC 2012 : Third International Conference on Advances in New ...
www.wikicfp.com/cfp/servlet/event.showcfp?eventid=23402... - En caché
ADNTIIC 2012 : Third International Conference on Advances in New ...
3 dic - 5 dic   Córdoba – Argentina

DBWorld: Recent Messages
research.cs.wisc.edu/dbworld/browse.html - En caché
Doris Edison, **ADNTIIC 2012** :: Cordoba, Argentina :: Deadline Approaching :: Call .... 27-Oct-2012, news, Pamela Fulton, **ADNTIIC 2012** :: Cordoba, Argentina ...

DBWorld Message - Computer Sciences Department
research.cs.wisc.edu/dbworld/messages/2012.../1348048967.html - En caché
"Advances" in "New Technologies", Interactive Interfaces and Communicability (**ADNTIIC 2012**) :: "Software" and Emerging Technologies for Education, Culture, ...

Imágenes de **adntiic 2012**

[Dbworld] HCITOCH 2012 / **ADNTIIC 2012** / SETECEC ... - Old Nabble
old.nabble.com/-Dbworld--HCITOCH-2012---ADNTIIC-2012---SETECEC-2012-proceedings-are-NOT-published-by-Springer-td34324884.h... - En caché
***
[Dbworld] HCITOCH 2012 / **ADNTIIC 2012** / SETECEC 2012 proceedings are NOT published by Springer. Dear DBWorld members, Recently, several CFPs of ...

[Dbworld] HCITOCH 2012 / **ADNTIIC 2012** / SETECEC ... - Old Nabble
old.nabble.com/-Dbworld--HCITOCH-2012---ADNTIIC-2012---SETECEC-2012-proceedings-are-NOT-published-by-Springer-td3432488... - Copia cache
***
[Dbworld] HCITOCH 2012 / **ADNTIIC 2012** / SETECEC 2012 proceedings are NOT published by Springer. Dear DBWorld members, Recently, several CFPs of ...

Figure 6. Google: search results on the day: 11.16.2012 (page #1)

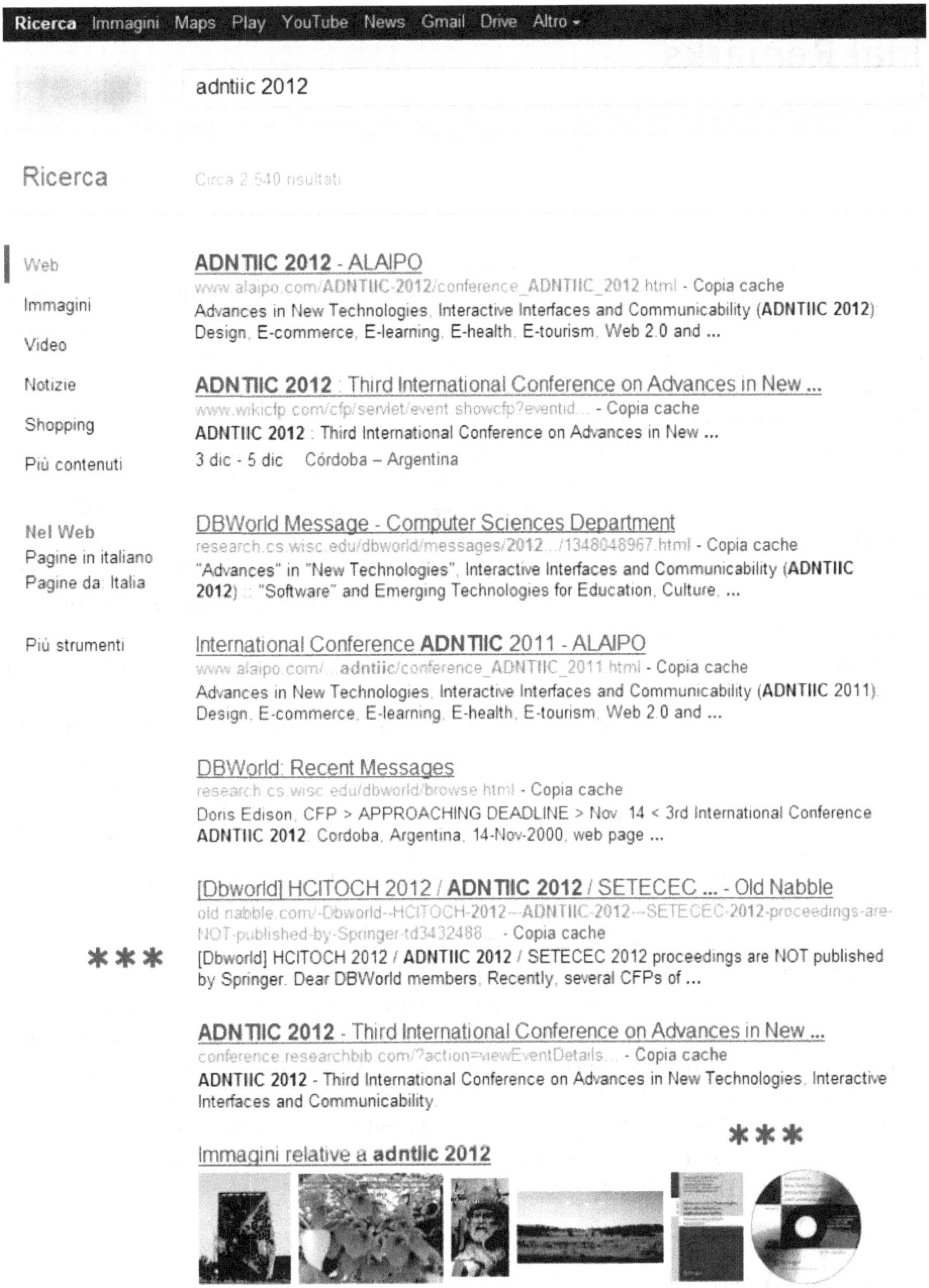

Ricerca Immagini Maps Play YouTube News Gmail Drive Altro

adntiic 2012

Ricerca

Circa 2.540 risultati

Web
Immagini
Video
Notizie
Shopping
Più contenuti

Nel Web
Pagine in italiano
Pagine da: Italia

Più strumenti

ADNTIIC 2012 - ALAIPO
www.alaipo.com/ADNTIIC-2012/conference_ADNTIIC_2012.html - Copia cache
Advances in New Technologies, Interactive Interfaces and Communicability (**ADNTIIC 2012**): Design, E-commerce, E-learning, E-health, E-tourism, Web 2.0 and ...

ADNTIIC 2012 : Third International Conference on Advances in New ...
www.wikicfp.com/cfp/servlet/event.showcfp?eventid... - Copia cache
ADNTIIC 2012 : Third International Conference on Advances in New ...
3 dic - 5 dic Córdoba – Argentina

DBWorld Message - Computer Sciences Department
research.cs.wisc.edu/dbworld/messages/2012.../1348048967.html - Copia cache
"Advances" in "New Technologies", Interactive Interfaces and Communicability (**ADNTIIC 2012**) :: "Software" and Emerging Technologies for Education, Culture, ...

International Conference **ADNTIIC** 2011 - ALAIPO
www.alaipo.com/...adntiic/conference_ADNTIIC_2011.html - Copia cache
Advances in New Technologies, Interactive Interfaces and Communicability (**ADNTIIC** 2011): Design, E-commerce, E-learning, E-health, E-tourism, Web 2.0 and ...

DBWorld: Recent Messages
research.cs.wisc.edu/dbworld/browse.html - Copia cache
Doris Edison, CFP > APPROACHING DEADLINE > Nov. 14 < 3rd International Conference **ADNTIIC 2012**. Cordoba, Argentina, 14-Nov-2000, web page ...

[Dbworld] HCITOCH 2012 / **ADNTIIC 2012** / SETECEC ... - Old Nabble
old.nabble.com/-Dbworld--HCITOCH-2012--ADNTIIC-2012--SETECEC-2012-proceedings-are-NOT-published-by-Springer-td34332488... - Copia cache
*** [Dbworld] HCITOCH 2012 / **ADNTIIC 2012** / SETECEC 2012 proceedings are NOT published by Springer. Dear DBWorld members, Recently, several CFPs of ...

ADNTIIC 2012 - Third International Conference on Advances in New ...
conference.researchbib.com/?action=viewEventDetails... - Copia cache
ADNTIIC 2012 - Third International Conference on Advances in New Technologies, Interactive Interfaces and Communicability.

Immagini relative a **adntiic 2012** ***

Final Remarks

Throughout these pages, it has been possible to verify some of the technological breakthroughs and high quality solutions that open new horizons and challenges in the scientific community and within the framework of the formal and factual sciences, especially in the intersection area that they generate. It is a 360° vision in the new technologies of interactive communication in this peculiar era that we are going through as humankind as a whole, which is called the era of the expansion of communicability. This era of the quality of communication requires new professionals. The academic profile of those professionals was already presented at the end of the 20th century and redefined at the start of the current decade.

However, because of mercantilist factors, stemming from the Garduña factor, belonging to the public, private, or hybrid sector, there is the constant danger to denaturalize it inside the scientific context, particularly in the Old World. Evidently, one must not lose hope in the new generations of scientists, nor the patience with those who constantly practice the sport of boycotting the freedom of scientific knowledge, keeping in mind that in life one can fight even against a malign tumor—non-Hodgkin's lymphoma stage 4—but not against evil and ignorance.

To all the authors of the submitted works, a very deep gratitude. This acknowledgement is not only due to their open lines for future research, but also for having trusted us in a very special period, like that lived in 2012, that is, the attacks to stop the current project from carrying forward the circulation of all these works, in international conferences, workshops, and symposia format, guided by key words: dignity, freedom, equlity, fraternity, and solidarity. However, from that dysfunction we have achieved the divulgation function of scientific knowledge.

We once again repeat our deepest gratitude to all the members of the publishing house for having helped us at a very difficult crossroads in a very timely manner. All of them have collaborated to find a solution for us in record time, always showing kindness, earnestness, and very high professionalism. A particular acknowledgement is due to all those who devote themselves to evaluating the works quickly and also to the keynote speakers of 2012 in the different international events.

Lastly, the following is set of thoughts to meditate and ponder in the face of adverse situations: "When a country is well governed, poverty and a mean condition are things to be ashamed of. When a country is ill governed, riches and honors are things to be ashamed of" (Confucius, n.d.); "It is easy in the world to live after the world's opinion; it is easy in solitude to live after our own; but the great man is he who in the midst of the crowd keeps with perfect sweetness the independence of solitude" (Emerson, n.d.); and "Be a Columbus to whole new continents and worlds within you, opening new channels, not of trade, but of thought" (Thoreau, 1854).

Francisco V. Cipolla-Ficarra
ALAIPO – AINCI, Spain and Italy

REFERENCES

Confucius. (n.d.). *Analects.* Retrieved from classics.mit.edu/Confucius/analects.2.2.html

Emerson, R. W. (n.d.). *Self reliance.* Retrieved from http://www.bartleby.com/5/104.html

Thoreau, H. D. (1854). *Walden; or, life in the woods*. Boston: Academic Press.

Compilation of References

Abela, A. (2008). *Advanced presentations by design: Creating communications that drives action*. San Francisco, CA: Pfeiffer.

Abowd, G. et al. (1999). Towards a better understanding of context and context-awareness. In *Handheld and Ubiquitous Computing* (pp. 304–307). Heidelberg, Germany: Springer. doi:10.1007/3-540-48157-5_29

Abraham, A., Buyya, R., & Nath, B. (2000). Nature's heuristics for scheduling jobs on computational grids. In *Proceedings of 8th IEEE International Conference on Advanced Computing and Communications (ADCOM 2000)*, (pp. 45-52). IEEE.

Adabala, N. Magnenat-Thalmann, N., & Fei, G. (2003). Visualization of woven cloth. In *Proceedings of the 14th Eurographics Workshop on Rendering (EGRW'03)*. EGRW.

Adelstein, F., Gupta, S., Richard, G., & Schwiebert, L. (2004). *Fundamentals of mobile and pervasive computing*. New York: McGraw Hill.

Agarwal, S., et al. (2009). Building Rome in a day. In *Proceedings of International Conference on Computer Vision*. Kyoto, Japan: IEEE.

Agathos, A., & Fisher, R. (2003). Colour texture fusion of multiple range images. In *Proceedings of Fourth International Conference on 3-D Digital Imaging and Modeling (3DIM'03)*, (pp. 139-146). 3DIM.

Aggarwal, K., Singh, Y., Kaur, A., & Malhotra, R. (2009). Empirical analysis for investigating the effect of object-oriented metrics on fault proneness: A replicated case study. *Software Process Improvement and Practice*, *16*(1), 39–62. doi:10.1002/spip.389

Aittala, M. (2010). Inverse lighting and photorealistic rendering for augmented reality. *The Visual Computer*, *26*(6), 669–678. doi:10.1007/s00371-010-0501-7

Akca, D., et al. (2007). Performance evaluation of a coded structured light system for cultural heritage applications. In *Proceedings of Society of Photo-Optical Instrumentation Engineers (SPIE) Conference*. SPIE.

Akkiraju, R. (2006). Semantic web services. In *Semantic web services – Theory, tools, and applications* (pp. 191–216). Hershey, PA: Idea Group.

Alalfi, M., Cordy, J., & Dean, T. (2008). *Modeling methods for web application verification and testing: State of art*. New York: John Wiley.

Alba, M., Barazzetti, L., Rosina, E., Scaioni, M., & Previtali, M. (2011). Mapping infrared data on terrestrial laser scanning 3D models of buildings. *Remote Sensing*, *3*(9), 1847–1870. doi:10.3390/rs3091847

Alba, R., Logan, J., Lutz, A., & Stults, B. (2002). Only English by the third generation: Loss and preservation of the mother tongue among the grandchildren of contemporary immigrants. *Demography*, *39*(3), 467–484. doi:10.1353/dem.2002.0023 PMID:12205753

Alison, F. et al. (1995). *Colours of life*. Torino, Italy: La Stampa.

Almeida, A., et al. (2008). SOUND=SPACE opera. In *Proceedings of 7th International Conference on Disability Virtual Reality and Associated Technologies with ArtAbilitation*, (pp. 347-354). IEEE.

Alvarez, M., Duran, E., & Unzaga, S. (2012). *ONTO-AU: Una ontología para sistemas de apoyo al aprendizaje ubicuo*. Tucumán: VIII Jornadas de Ciencias y Tecnologías de Facultades de Ingeniería del NOA.

Amagasa, T., Kitagawa, H., & Komano, T. (2007). Constructing a web service system for large-scale meteorological grid data. In *Proceedings of 3rd IEEE International Conf. on e-Science and Grid Computing*, (pp. 118-124). IEEE.

Amazon. (2012). Retrieved from aws.amazon.com/ec2

Ander-Egg, E. (1986). *Techniques of social investigation* (21st ed.). Buenos Aires, Argentina: Hvmanitas.

Anderson, R. (2001). *Security engineering – A guide to building dependable distributed systems*. Indianapolis, IN: Wiley.

Anderson, R., & Brackney, R. (2005). *Understanding the insider threat*. Santa Monica, CA: RAND Corporation.

Ang, K., & Mitchell, H. (2010). Non-rigid surface matching and its application to scoliosis modelling. *The Photogrammetric Record*, *25*(130), 105–118. doi:10.1111/j.1477-9730.2010.00581.x

Anicic, D. et al. (2007). *A semantically enabled service oriented architecture*. Heidelberg, Germany: Springer.

Antoniou, G., & Harmelen, F. (2004). *A semantic web primer*. Cambridge, MA: The MIT Press.

Apple. (1992). *Macintosh human interface guidelines*. Cupertino, CA: Addison-Wesley.

Apple. (2012). Retrieved from www.apple.com/iphone/features/siri.html

Apted, T., Kay, J., & Quigley, A. (2006). Tabletop sharing of digital photographs for the elderly. In *Proceedings of SIGCHI Conference on Human Factors in Computing Systems*. Montréal, Canada: ACM.

Aral, S., & Van Alstyne, M. (2010). The diversity-bandwidth tradeoff. *American Journal of Sociology*.

Arduino. (2012). Retrieved from http://arduino.cc/en/Main/ArduinoBoardUno

Argen-Visión. (1996). [CD-ROM]. Barcelona: Cotoinsa.

Argyrous, G. (2005). *Statistics for research with guide to SPSS*. Thousand Oaks, CA: SAGE Publications Ltd.

Aristotle,. (2004). *Rethoric*. New York: Dover Publications.

Arnold, D., & Espejo, E. (2012). *El textil tridimensional: La naturaleza del tejido como objeto y sujeto*. La Paz, Bolivia: Fundación Albó, Interamerican Foundation and Instituto de Lengua y Cultura Aymara.

Arnold, D., & Espejo, E. (2012). *Ciencia de tejer en los Andes: Estructuras y tecnicas de faz de urdimbre*. La Paz, Bolivia: Fundación Cultural del Banco Central de Bolivia, Fundación Albó, Interamerican Foundation and Instituto de Lengua y Cultura Aymara.

Art Gallery. (1995). [CD-ROM]. Seattle, WA: Microsoft.

Arya, S., Mount, D., Netenyahu, N., Silverman, R., & Wu, A. (1998). An optimal algorithm for approximate nearest neighbour searching fixed dimensions. *Journal of the ACM*, *45*(6), 891–923. doi:10.1145/293347.293348

Ashar, H., & Skenes, R. (1993). Can Tinto's student departure model be applied to non-traditional students? *Adult Education Quarterly*, *43*(2), 90–100. doi:10.1177/0741713693043002003

Auer, S., Bizer, C., Kobilarov, G., & Lehmann, J. (2007). *Dbpedia: A nucleus for a web of open data*. The Semantic Web. doi:10.1007/978-3-540-76298-0_52

Au, N., & Law, R. (2000). The application of rough sets to sightseeing expenditures. *Journal of Travel Research*, *39*, 70–77. doi:10.1177/004728750003900109

Au, R., & Law, R. (2002). Categorical classification of tourism dining. *Annals of Tourism Research*, *29*, 819–833. doi:10.1016/S0160-7383(01)00078-0

AWS-Amazon. (2012). Retrieved from aws.amazon.com/sdkforandroid

Azcoaga, J. (1986). Aprendizaje fisiologico y aprendizaje pedagógico. Buenos Aires: El ateneo.

Azuma, R., Baillot, Y., Behringer, R., Feiner, S., Julier, S., & MacIntyre, B. (2001). Recent advances in augmented reality. *IEEE Computer Graphics and Applications*, *21*(6), 34–47. doi:10.1109/38.963459

Bachelard, G. (1964). *The poetics of space* (M. Jolas, Trans.). New York: Academic Press.

Baduel, L. et al. (2006). *Grid computing: Software environments and tools*. Berlin: Springer-Verlag.

Bahi, J., Contassot-Vivier, S., & Couturier, R. (2007). *Parallel iterative algorithms: From sequential to grid computing*. London: Chapman & Hall/CRC.

Ball, P., & Ruben, M. (2004). Mario Ruben color theory in science and art: Ostwald and the Bauhaus. *Angewandte Chemie*, *43*(37), 4842–4847. doi:10.1002/anie.200430086 PMID:15317016

Bannai, N., Agathos, A., & Fisher, R. (2004). Fusing multiple color images for texturing models. In *Proceedings of 2nd International Symposium on 3D Data Processing, Visualization and Transmission (3DPVT'04)*, (pp. 558-565). 3DPVT.

Bannon, L., & Schmidt, K. (1991). CSCW: Four characters in search of a context. In J. Bowers, & S. Benford (Eds.), *Studies in Computer Supported Cooperative Work: Theory, Practice and Design*. Amsterdam: North-Holland.

Baraona, E. (2012). *From line to hyperreality*. Retrieved from http://www.domusweb.it/en/architecture/from-line-to-hyperreality

Barazzetti, L. (2011). Metric rectification via parallelograms. In *Proceedings of SPIE Optics+Photonics*, (Vol. 8085, pp. 23-26). Munich, Germany: SPIE.

Barazzetti, L., Remondino, F., & Scaioni, M. (2010). Orientation and 3D modelling from markerless terrestrial images: Combining accuracy with automation. *The Photogrammetric Record*, *25*(132), 356–381. doi:10.1111/j.1477-9730.2010.00599.x

Barazzetti, L., Roncoroni, F., Scaioni, M., & Remondino, F. (2011). *Automatische 3D modellierung von berghängen mit anwendung der terrestrischen photogrammetrie. 16. Internationale geodätische Woche, 13. bis 19*. Obergurgl - Ötztal / Tirol.

Barazzetti, L., & Scaioni, M. (2010). Development and implementation of image based algorithms for measurement of deformations in material testing. *Sensors (Basel, Switzerland)*, *10*, 7469–7495. doi:10.3390/s100807469 PMID:22163612

Barnes, M., & Meyers, N. (2011). *Mobile phones: Technology, networks and user issues*. New York: Nova Publishers.

Barrantes, D. et al. (2011). *Nuevos formatos para la función universitaria*. San José: Editorial de la Universidad de Costa Rica.

Barrier, M. (2003). *Hollywood cartoons: American animation in its golden age*. Oxford, UK: Oxford University Press.

Barriga-Villanueva, R. (2002). *Estudios sobre habla infantil en los años escolares*. México: El Colegio de México.

Barth, P. (1986). An object-oriented approach to graphical interfaces. *ACM Transactions on Graphics*, *5*, 142–172. doi:10.1145/22949.22951

Basalla, G. (1988). *The evolution of technology*. Cambridge, UK: Cambridge University Press.

Basili, V., Briand, L., & Melo, W. (1996). A validation of object-oriented design metrics as quality indicators. *IEEE Transactions on Software Engineering*, *22*(10), 751–761. doi:10.1109/32.544352

Baskinger, M. (2008). Pencils before pixels: A primer in hand-generated skectiching. *Interaction*, *15*(2), 28–36. doi:10.1145/1340961.1340969

Bauerlein, M. (2011). *The digital divide: Arguments for and against Facebook, Google, texting, and the age of social networking*. New York: Penguin Group.

BBC. (1997). *Pingu and friends*. [CD-ROM]. London: BBC.

Bebis, G., Egbert, D., & Shah, M. (2003). Review of computer vision education. *IEEE Transactions on Education*, *46*(1), 2–21. doi:10.1109/TE.2002.808280

Bell, T. (2010). *Literature review of technology used in interpretation of sensitive cultural heritage sites*. Eugene, OR: University of Oregon.

Bendazzi, G. (1999). *Cartoons: One hundred years of cinema animation*. Bloomington, IN: Indiana University Press.

Berens, K., & Howard, G. (2002). *Videogaming*. London: Rough Guides.

Bergamasco, F., Albarelli, A., & Torsello, A. (2011). Image-space marker detection and recognition using projective invariants. In *Proceedings of International Conference on 3D Imaging, Modeling, Processing, Visualization and Transmission*. Hangzhou, China: IEEE.

Bergeron, B. (2003). *Essentials of knowledge management*. Hoboken, NJ: John Wiley & Sons.

Berners-Lee, T., Hendler, J., & Lassila, O. (2001). The semantic web. *Scientific American*, 29–37.

Besl, P., & McKay, N. (1992). A method for registration of 3-D shapes. *IEEE Transactions on Pattern Analysis and Machine Intelligence*, *14*(2), 239–256. doi:10.1109/34.121791

Besser, H., & Donahue, S. (1996). Introduction and overview: Perspectives on distance independent education. *Journal of the American Society for Information Science American Society for Information Science*, *47*(11), 801–804. doi:10.1002/(SICI)1097-4571(199611)47:11<801::AID-ASI1>3.0.CO;2-6

Beverly, A. (2000). *Instructional and cognitive impacts of web-based education*. Hershey, PA: Idea Group Publishing.

Beyer, H., & Holtzblatt, K. (1997). *Contextual design: Defining customer-centered systems*. San Francisco, CA: Morgan Kaufmann Publishers.

Bialystok, E. (1988). Levels of bilingualism and levels of linguistic awareness. *Developmental Psychology*, (24): 560–567. doi:10.1037/0012-1649.24.4.560

Bialystok, E. (2001). *Bilingualism in development: Language, literacy, and cognition*. New York: Cambridge University Press. doi:10.1017/CBO9780511605963

Bialystok, E., & Michelle, M. (2004). Attention and inhibition in bilingual children: Evidence from the dimensional change card sort task. *Developmental Science*, *7*(3), 325–339. doi:10.1111/j.1467-7687.2004.00351.x PMID:15595373

Bialystok, E., Michelle, M., & Martin, R. (2008). The development of two types of inhibitory control in monolingual and bilingual children. *Bilingualism: Language and Cognition*, *11*, 81–93.

Bichlmeier, C., Heining, S. M., Feuerstein, M., & Navab, N. (2009). The virtual mirror: A new interaction paradigm for augmented reality environments. *IEEE Transactions on Medical Imaging*, *28*(9), 1498–1510. doi:10.1109/TMI.2009.2018622 PMID:19336291

Bieman, J., Andrews, A., & Yang, H. (2003). Understanding change-proneness in OO software through visualization. In *Proceedings of 11th IEEE IWPC*. IEEE.

Bijapurkar, R. (1979). *We are like that only understand the logic of consumer India*. Portfolio Penguin.

Bijapurkar, R. (2006). *Winning in the Indian market: Understanding the transformation of consumer India*. New York: Wiley.

Bishop, M. (2005). The insider problem revisited. In *Proceedings of New Security Paradigms Workshop 2005*. New York: ACM Press.

Bishop, M. (2009). *Introduction to computer security*. Boston: Addison Wesley.

Blazer, D. (1982). Social support and mortality in an elderly community population. *American Journal of Epidemiology*, *115*(5), 684–694. PMID:7081200

Blevis, E. (2007). Sustainable interaction design: Invention & disposal, renewal & reuse. In *Proceedings of CHI'2007*. New York: ACM Press.

Bloomfield, L. (2009). *Introduction to the study of language*. New York: Henry Holt.

Bobba, R., Muggli, J., & Pant, M. (2009). Usable secure mailing lists with untrusted servers. In *Proceedings of the 8th Symposium on Identity and Trust on the Internet*, (pp. 103-116). IEEE.

Bobick, A. et al. (1999). The KidsRoom: A perceptually-based interactive and immersive story environment. *Presence (Cambridge, Mass.)*, *8*(4), 367–391. doi:10.1162/105474699566297

Bobrich, J., & Otto, S. (2002). Augmented maps. *Geospatial Theory. Processing and Applications*, *34*(4), 891–923.

Bolter, J. (2004). Theory and practice in new media studies. In *Digital Media revisited: theoretical and conceptual innovations in digital domains*. Cambridge, MA: MIT Press.

Bonneau, C. (1960). The effects of violationof assumptions underlying the test. *Psychological Bulletin*, *57*, 49–64. doi:10.1037/h0041412 PMID:13802482

Boorsch, S. (1993). *Six centuries of master prints*. New York: Cincinnati Art Museum.

Borst, W. (1997). *Construction of engineering ontologies for knowledge sharing and reuse*. (PhD thesis). University of Twente, Enschede, The Netherlands.

Bowe, R. (1992). *Interactive music systems: Machine listening and composing*. Cambridge, MA: MIT Press.

Boyer, D., & Marcus, J. (2012). Implementing mobile augmented reality applications for cultural institutions. In J. Trant, & D. Bearman (Eds.), *Proceedings of Museums and the Web 2011*. Toronto, Canada: Archives & Museum Informatics.

Bradski, A., & Kaehler, A. (2008). *Learning OpenCV: Computer vision with the OpenCV library*. Sebastopol, CA: O'Reilly Media Inc.

Braun, T. et al. (2001). *A comparison of eleven static heuristics for mapping a class of independent tasks onto heterogeneous distributed computing systems*. Academic Press. doi:10.1006/jpdc.2000.1714

Brezine, C. (2009). *The Oxford handbook of the history of mathematics*. Oxford, UK: Oxford University Press.

Briand, L., Wust, J., & Lounis, H. (2001). Replicated case studies for investigating quality factors in object oriented designs. *Empirical Software Engineering: An International Journal*, *6*, 11–58. doi:10.1023/A:1009815306478

Bride, E. (2011). The IBM personal computer: A software-driven market. *IEEE Computer*, *44*(8), 34–39. doi:10.1109/MC.2011.193

Brody, B., Chappell, G., & Hartman, C. (2002). BLUIsculpt™. In *Proceedings of ACM SIGGRAPH 2002 Conference* (SIGGRAPH '02). New York: ACM Press.

Brown, M., & Lowe, D. (2003). Recognizing panoramas. In *Proceedings of International Conference on Computer Vision,* (Vol. 2, pp. 1218-1225). IEEE.

Brown, D. et al. (2002). Evaluating web page color and layout adaptations. *IEEE MultiMedia*, *9*(1), 86–89. doi:10.1109/93.978356

Brown, M., & Lowe, D. (2007). Automatic panoramic image stitching using invariant features. *International Journal of Computer Vision*, *74*(1), 59–73. doi:10.1007/s11263-006-0002-3

Brownworth, A. (2012). *How location services work on mobile devices*. Retrieved from http://anders.com/cms/389

Bruner, J. (2012). Constructivist theory. Retrieved from http://www.instructionaldesign.org

Bruner, J. (1966). *Toward a theory of instruction*. Cambridge, MA: Belknap Press of Harvard University Press.

Bruner, J. (1968). *Processes of cognitive growth: Infancy*. Worcester, MA: Clark University Press.

Buchenau, M., & Suri, J. (2000). Experience prototyping. In *Proceedings of 3rd Conference on Designing Interactive Systems: Processes, Practices, Methods, and Techniques*. New York: ACM Press.

Buckley, P. (2010). *The rough guide to cloud computing: 100 websites that will change your life*. Rough Guides.

Bundesamt fuer Sicherheit in der Informationsgesellschaft (BSI). (2005). *Common criteria for information technology security evaluation, part 3*. Retrieved from http://www.bsi.de/cc/ccpart3v2_3.pdf

Bunge, M. (1981). *The science: your method and your philosophy*. Buenos Aires, Argentina: Siglo XXI.

Bunge, M. (2001). Systems and emergence, rationality and imprecision, free-wheeling and evidence, science and ideology: Social science and its philosophy according to van den Berg. *Philosophy of the Social Sciences*, *31*(3), 404–423. doi:10.1177/004839310103100307

Burrows, M., Abadi, M., & Needham, R. (1990). A logic of authentication. *ACM Transactions on Computer Systems*, *8*, 18–36. doi:10.1145/77648.77649

Burt, P., & Adelson, E. (1983). A multi-resolution spline with application to image mosaics. *ACM Transactions on Graphics*, *2*(4), 217–236. doi:10.1145/245.247

Buxton, W. (2007). *Sketching user experiences: Getting the design right and the right design*. San Francisco, CA: Morgan Kaufmann.

Buyya, R. (2012). *Gridsim*. Retrieved from http://www.buyya.com/gridsim

Buzzi, M., Gennai, F., Petrucci, C., & Vinciarelli, A. (2011). Italian standard certified electronic mail: Posta elettronica certificata (PEC). In *Proceed. 5th International Conference on Methodologies, Technologies and Tools enabling e-Government,* (pp. 13-29). IEEE.

Calvert, G., Spence, C., & Stein, B. (2004). *The handbook of multisensory processes*. Cambridge, MA: MIT Press.

Calvin, C. (2012). *Welcome to Presbyterian homes of Georgia*. Retrieved from http://www.calvincourt.org

Campbel, D., & Stanley, J. (1963). *Experimental and quasi-experimental designs for research*. Chicago: Rand McNally and Co.

Campell-Kelly, M., & Aspray, W. (2004). *Computer: A history of information machine*. New York: Basic Books.

Camurri, A., et al. (2010). The stanza logo-motoria: An interactive environment for learning and communication. *Proceedings of SMC Conference, 51*(8).

Camurri, A., Mazzarino, B., & Volpe, G. (2004). Analysis of expressive gestures: The eyesweb expressive gesture processing library. [LNAI]. *Proceedings of Gesture-Based Communication in Human-Computer Interaction, 2915*, 460–467. doi:10.1007/978-3-540-24598-8_42

Cantrill, S. (2010). Computer in patient care: The promise and the challenge. *Communications of the ACM, 53*(9), 42–47. doi:10.1145/1810891.1810907

Carr, A. (2010). *What does the future hold for the senior living industry?* Retrieved from http://progressiveretirement.wordpress.com/2010/06/29/what-does-the-future-hold-for-the-senior-living-industry/

Carr, N. (2010). *The shallows: What the internet is doing to our brains*. New York: W.W. Norton & Company.

Carroll, J. (2009). *Making use: Scenario-based design of human-computer interactions*. Cambridge, MA: MIT Press.

Carr, S. (2000). As distance education comes of age, the challenge is keeping the students. *The Chronicle of Higher Education, 46*(23), A39–A41.

Cassim, J., & Dong, H. (2003). Critical users in design innovation. In *Inclusive Design: Design for the Whole Population*. London: Springer-Verlag. doi:10.1007/978-1-4471-0001-0_32

Center for Universal Design. (1997). *The principles of universal design*. Retrieved from http://www.ncsu.edu/ncsu/design/cud/about_ud/udprinciplestext.htm

Chang, S., Hsu, G., & Huang, S. (2005). Location-aware mobile transportation information service. In *Proceedings of 2nd International Conference on Mobile Technology, Applications and Systems*. IEEE.

Chapin, S. et al. (1999). *Benchmarks and standards for the evaluation of parallel job schedulers*. Academic Press. doi:10.1007/3-540-47954-6_4

Chen, C., Li, Y., & Chen, M. (2007). Personalized context-aware ubiquitous learning system for supporting effectively English vocabulary learning. In *Proceedings of Seventh IEEE International Conference on Advanced Learning Technologies*. IEEE.

Chen, Y., Kao, T., Sheu, J., & Chiang, C. (2004). A mobile scaffolding-aid-based bird –watching learning system. In *Proceedings of International Workshop on Wireless and Mobile Technologies in Education*. New York: IEEE Press.

Chen, C. (1996). *Early Chinese work in natural science: A re-examination of the physics of motion, acoustics, astronomy and scientific thoughts*. Hong Kong: University Press.

Cheng-Ying, M., & Yan-Sheng, L. (2006). A method for measuring the structure complexity of web application. *Wuhan University Journal of Natural Sciences, 11*(1).

Chen, H. (2011). Social intelligence and cultural awareness. *IEEE Intelligent Systems, 26*(4), 80–91. doi:10.1109/MIS.2011.21

Chen, X. (2010). Modelling of textile structure for advanced applications. *Journal of Information and Computing Science, 5*(1), 71–80.

Cheok, A. (2012). *Keynote multi modal sensory human*. Retrieved from http://www.adriancheok.info/post/26135544227/icalt2012-keynote-talk-multi-modal-sensory-human

Chidamber, S., & Kemerer, C. (1994). A metrics suite for object oriented design. *IEEE Transactions on Software Engineering*, *20*(6), 476–493. doi:10.1109/32.295895

Cho, Y., Lee, J., & Neumann, U. (1998). A multi-ring color fiducial system and a rule-based detection method for scalable fiducial-tracking augmented reality. In *Proceedings of International Workshop on Augmented Reality*. IEEE.

Chomsky, N. (1974). *Estructuras sintácticas*. Mexico: Siglo XXI.

Chow, S. (2007). *PHP web 2.0 mashup projects*. Birmingham, AL: Packt Publishing.

Cipolla-Ficarra, et al. (1993). Barcelona media: Del comic infográfico a los interactivos. *Imaging –. Press Graph*, *3*, 46–52.

Cipolla-Ficarra, F. (1997). Evaluation of multimedia components. In *Proceedings of IEEE Multimedia Systems*. IEEE.

Cipolla-Ficarra, F. (1998). MEHEM: A methodology for heuristic evaluation in multimedia. In *Proceedings of 7th Symposium on Analysis, Design and Evaluation of Man-Machine Systems – Human Interface*. Kyoto, Japan: Elsevier.

Cipolla-Ficarra, F. (1999). MEHEM: A methodology for heuristic evaluation in multimedia. In *Proceedings of Sixth International Conference on Distributed Multimedia Systems (DMS'99)*. Elsevier.

Cipolla-Ficarra, F. (2000). MECEM: Metrics for the communications evaluation in mutimedia. In *Proceedings of International Conference on Information Systems Analysis and Synthesis – ISAS 2000*. Orlando, FL: ISAS.

Cipolla-Ficarra, F. (2005). Synchronism and diachronism into evolution of the interfaces for quality communication in multimedia systems. In *Proceedings of HCI International 2005*. Las Vegas, NV: HCI.

Cipolla-Ficarra, F. (2007). A study of acteme on users unexpert of videogames. In *Proceedings of HCI International*. Heidelberg, Germany: Springer.

Cipolla-Ficarra, F. (2008). Communicability design and evaluation in cultural and ecological multimedia systems. In *Proceedings of ACM Multimedia '08*. New York: ACM Press.

Cipolla-Ficarra, F. (2008). Eyes: A virtual assistant for analysis of the transparency and accessibility in university portal. In *Proceedings of International Conference on Applied Human Factors and Ergonomics*. Las Vegas, NV: AEI.

Cipolla-Ficarra, F. (2010). Human-computer interaction, tourism and cultural heritage. In *Proceedings of HCITOCH 2010*. Berlin: Springer.

Cipolla-Ficarra, F. (2011). Behaviour computer animation, communicability and education for all. In *Proceedings of HCI International 2011*. Heidelberg, Germany: Springer.

Cipolla-Ficarra, F. (2011). Usability engineering versus social sciences: An analysis of the main mistakes. In Advances in Dynamic and Static Media for Interactive Systems: Communicability, Computer Science and Design. Bergamo, Italy: Blue Herons Ed.s.

Cipolla-Ficarra, F. (2012). New horizons in creative open software, multimedia, human factors and software engineering. Bergamo, Italy: Blue Herons Ed.s.

Cipolla-Ficarra, F. (2012). The argentinization of the user centered design. In *Proceedings of 2nd International Conference on Advances in New Technologies, Interactive Interfaces and Communicability*. Heidelberg, Germany: Springer.

Cipolla-Ficarra, F., & Ficarra, V. (2012). Anti-models for universitary education: Analysis of the Catalans cases in information and communication technologies. In *Proceedings of First International on Software and Emerging Technologies for Education, Culture, Entertaiment, and Commerce: New Directions in Multimedia Mobile Computing, Social Networks, Human-Computer Interaction and Communicability (SETECEC 2012)*. Hershey, PA: IGI Global.

Cipolla-Ficarra, F., & Ficarra, V. (2012). Motivation for next generation of users versus parochialism in software engineering. In *Proceedings of 2nd International Conference on Advances in New Technologies, Interactive Interfaces and Communicability (ADNTIIC 2011)*. Heidelberg, Germany: Springer.

Cipolla-Ficarra, F., & Kratky, A. (2011). Security of the automatic information on-line: A study of the controls forbid. In *Proceedings of 2nd International Conference on Advances in New Technologies, Interactive Interfaces and Communicability (ADNTIIC 2011)*. Heidelberg, Germany: Springer.

Cipolla-Ficarra, F., Alma, J., & Cipolla-Ficarra, M. (2011). Prolepsis in computer animation for children. In *Proceedings of First International Symposium on Communicability, Computer Graphics and Innovative Design for Interactive Systems*. Heidelberg, Germany: Springer.

Cipolla-Ficarra, F., Cipolla-Ficarra, M., & Harder, T. (2008). Realism and cultural layout in tourism and video games multimedia systems. In *Proceedings of 1st ACM International Workshop on Communicability, Design and Evaluation in Cultural and Ecological Multimedia System*. New York: ACM Press.

Cipolla-Ficarra, F., et al. (2011). Computational informatics, social factors and new information technologies: Hypermedia perspectives and avant-garde experiences in the era of communicability expansion. Bergamo, Italy: Blue Herons Ed.s.

Cipolla-Ficarra, F., et al. (2011). Handbook of advance in dynamic and static media for interactive systems: Communicability, computer science and design. Bergamo, Italy: Blue Herons Ed.s.

Cipolla-Ficarra, F., et al. (2011). Handbook of computational informatics, social factors and new information technologies: Hypermedia perspectives and avant-garde experiencies in the era of communicability expansion. Bergamo, Italy: Blue Herons Ed.s.

Cipolla-Ficarra, F., et al. (2011). Handbook of advance in dynamic and static media for interactive systems: Communicability, computer science and design. Bergamo, Italy: Blue Herons Ed.s.

Cipolla-Ficarra, F., et al. (2012). New horizons in creative open software, multimedia, human factors and software engineering. Bergamo, Italy: Blue Herons Ed.s.

Cipolla-Ficarra, F., Ficarra, V., & Cipolla-Ficarra, M. (2011). New technologies of the information and communication: Analysis of the constructors and destructors of the European educational system. In *Proceedings of ADNTIIC 2011*. Heidelberg, Germany: Springer.

Cipolla-Ficarra, F., Nicol, E., & Cipolla-Ficarra, M. (2010). Research and development: Business into transfer information and communication technology. In *Proceedings of First International Conference on Advances in New Technologies, Interactive Interfaces and Communicability-ADNTIIC 2010* (LNCS), (Vol. 6616, pp. 44-61). Berlin: Springer.

Cipolla-Ficarra, F., Nicol, E., & Cipolla-Ficarra, M. (2010). Vademecum for innovation through knowledge transfer: Continuous training in universities, enterprises and industries. In *Proceedings of International Conference on Innovation through Knowledge Transfer, Innovation KT 2010*. Heidelberg, Germany: Springer.

Cipolla-Ficarra., et al. (2011). Computational informatics, social factors and new information technologies: Hypermedia perspectives and avant-garde experiences in the era of communicability expansion. Bergamo, Italy: Blue Herons Ed.s.

Cipolla-Ficarra, F. (1993). Metamorfosis aplicada a la vida artificial. *Imaging*, *6*, 12–18.

Cipolla-Ficarra, F. (1994). The three-dimensional. *Autocad Magazine*, *31*, 58–61.

Cipolla-Ficarra, F. (1996). Evaluation and communication techniques in multimedia product design for on the net university education. In *Proceedings of Multimedia '95*. Vienna, Austria: Springer. doi:10.1007/978-3-7091-9472-0_14

Cipolla-Ficarra, F. (1999). Viz en los sistemas interactivos de entretenimiento constructivo. *Autocad Magazine*, *62*, 26–29.

Cipolla-Ficarra, F. (2001). *Communication evaluation in multimedia–Metrics and methodoloty*. Mahwah, NJ: LEA.

Cipolla-Ficarra, F. (2008). Dyadic for quality in hypermedia systems. In *Proceedings of Applied Human Factors and Ergonomics*. Las Vegas, NV: AEI.

Cipolla-Ficarra, F. et al. (2010). *Advances in dynamic and static media for interactive systems: Communicability, computer science and design*. Bergamo, Italy: Blue Herons.

Cipolla-Ficarra, F. (2010). *Persuasion on-line and communicability: The destruction of credibility in the virtual community and cognitive models*. New York: Nova Science Publishers.

Cipolla-Ficarra, F. (2010). *Quality and communicability for interactive hypermedia systems: Concepts and practices for design*. Hershey, PA: IGI Global. doi:10.4018/978-1-61520-763-3

Cipolla-Ficarra, F. (2010). *Persuasion on-line and communicability: The destruction of credibiltiy in the virtual community and cognitive models*. New York: Nova Publishers.

Cipolla-Ficarra, F. et al. (2010). *Advances in new technologies interactive interfaces and communicability*. Heidelberg, Germany: Springer.

Cipolla-Ficarra, F. et al. (2011). *Human-computer interaction, tourism and cultural heritage*. Heidelberg, Germany: Springer. doi:10.1007/978-3-642-18348-5

Cipolla-Ficarra, F. et al. (2012). *Computational informatics, social factors and new information technologies: Hypermedia perspectives and avant-garde experiences in the era of communicability expansion*. Bergamo, Italy: Blue Herons.

Cipolla-Ficarra, F. et al. (2012). *New horizons in creative open software, multimedia, human factors and software engineering*. Bergamo, Italy: Blue Herons.

Cipolla-Ficarra, F. (2012). Software and emerging technologies for education, culture, entertaiment and commerce. In *Advanced Research and Trends in New Technologies, Software, Human-Computer Interaction and Communicability*. Hershey, PA: IGI Global. doi:10.1007/978-3-642-34010-9

Cipolla-Ficarra, F. (2013). *Advanced research and trends in new technologies, software, human-computer interaction and communicability*. Hershey, PA: IGI Global.

Cipolla-Ficarra, F., & Cipolla-Ficarra, M. (2008). HECHE: Heuristic evaluation of colours in homepage. In *Proceedings of Applied Human Factors and Ergonomics*. Las Vegas, NV: AIE.

Cipolla-Ficarra, F., & Cipolla-Ficarra, M. (2008). Interactive systems, design and heuristic evaluation: The importance of the diachronic vision. In *Proceedings of New Directions in Intelligent Interactive Multimedia*. Heidelberg, Germany: Springer. doi:10.1007/978-3-540-68127-4_64

Cipolla-Ficarra, F., & Cipolla-Ficarra, M. (2009). Computer animation and communicability in multimedia system and services: A trichotomy evaluation. In *Proceedings of New Directions in Intelligent Interactive Multimedia*. Heidelberg, Germany: Springer. doi:10.1007/978-3-642-02937-0_10

Cipolla-Ficarra, F., Nicol, E., & Cipolla-Ficarra, M. (2010). Computer graphics and mass media: Communicability analysis. In *Proceedings of Advances in New Technologies, Interactive Interfaces and Communicability*. Heidelberg, Germany: Springer.

Cipolla, R., & Pentland, A. (1998). *Computer vision for human-machine interaction*. Cambridge, UK: Cambridge University Press. doi:10.1017/CBO9780511569937

Clandinin, D., & Connelly, F. (2000). *Narrative inquiry: Experience and story in qualitative research*. San Francisco, CA: Jossey-Bass Publishers.

Clarke, E., Grumberg, O., & Peled, D. (1999). *Model checking*. Cambridge, MA: The MIT Press.

Claus, D., & Fitzgibbon, A. (2005). Reliable automatic calibration of a marker-based position tracking system. In *Proceedings of IEEE Workshop on Applications of Computer Vision*, (pp. 300-305). IEEE.

Clusella, M., & Mitre, M. (2012). Modelo e-culture system, en refinamiento sistémico. In *Proceedings of 8° Congresso Brasileiro de Sistemas*. Retrieved from www.pucpcaldas.br/graduacao/administracao/8voCbS/index.html

Clusella, M., Mitre, M., Santillán, A., Generoso, A., & Budán, P. (2011). Integrated synergy for cultural contents recursivity in e-culture system. In *Proceeedings of Second International Conference ADNTIIC 2011*. Heidelberg, Germany: Springer.

Colapietro, V. (1993). *Semiotics.* New York: Paragon House.

Cole, E. (2009). *Network security.* Indianapolis, IN: Willey.

Collingwood, P. (1999). *The techniques of sprang: Plaiting on stretched threads.* New York: Design Books.

Collins, K. (2008). *Game sound: An introduction to the history, theory, and practice of video game music and sound design.* Cambridge, MA: MIT Press.

Compainge, B. (2001). *The digital divide: Facing a crisis or creating a myth?* Cambridge, MA: MIT Press.

Confucius. (n.d.). *Analects.* Retrieved from classics.mit.edu/Confucius/analects.2.2.html

Consejo Universitario. (2001). *Reglamento de régimen académico estudiantil. San Pedro, Ciudad Universitaria Rodrigo Facio: Unidad de Información. Centro de Información y Servicios Técnicos.* San José: Universidad de Costa Rica.

Consejo Universitario. (2004). *Acta de la sesión no. 4919.* San José: Universidad de Costa Rica. Retrieved from http://cu.ucr.ac.cr/actas/2004/4919.pdf

Cook, J. (2010). Mobile phones as mediating tools within augmented contexts for development. *International Journal of Mobile and Blended Learning.* doi:10.4018/jmbl.2010070101

Cooper, A., Reimann, R., & Cronin, D. (2007). *About face 3: The essentials of interaction design.* Indianapolis, IN: Wiley.

Cope, D. (1992). Computer modeling of musical intelligence in experiments in musical intelligence. *Computer Music Journal, 16*(2), 69–83. doi:10.2307/3680717

Cope, D. (2004). *Virtual music: Computer synthesis of musical style.* Cambridge, MA: MIT Press.

Corel. (1995). *The interactive alphabet CD-ROM.* Ottawa, Canada: Corel.

Corel. (1995). *Nikolai's trains CD-ROM.* Ottawa, Canada: Corel.

Cormen, T., Leiserson, C., Rivest, R., & Stein, C. (1990). *Introduction to algorithms.* Cambridge, MA: MIT Press.

Cottini, L. (2002). *Fare ricerca nella scuola dell'autonomia.* Milano, Italy: Mursia.

Cressie, N. (1991). *Statistics for spatial data.* New York: John Wiley and Sons, Inc.

Cummins, J. (1979). Cognitive/academic language proficiency, linguistic interdependence, the optimum age question and some other matters. Working Papers on Bilingualism, (19), 121-129.

Cummins, J. (1978). Educational implications of mother tongue maintenance in minority-language children. *Canadian Modern Language Review*, 34.

Curtis, M., Luchini, K., Bobrowsky, W., Quintana, C., & Soloway, E. (2002). Handheld use in K-12: A descriptive account. In *Proceedings of the International Workshop on Wireless and Mobile Technologies in Education.* IEEE Computer Society.

Darcy, N. (1963). Bilingualism and the measure of intelligence: Review of a decade of research. *The Journal of Genetic Psychology*, (82): 259–282. doi:10.1080/00221325.1963.10532521 PMID:14085429

Da-Silva, L., Mendes-Neto, F., & Muniz, R. (2011). An agent-based approach for supporting ubiquitous learning. *International Journal of Scientific & Engineering Research, 2*(9).

Daston, L. (2004). *Things that talk – Object lessons from art and science.* New York: Zone Books.

Davenport, G., & Friedlander, G. (1995). Interactive transformational environments: Wheel of life. In E. Barrett, & M. Redmond (Eds.), *Contextual media: Multimedia and interpretation* (pp. 1–25). Cambridge, MA: MIT Press.

Davis, K. (2012). Tensions of identity in a networked era: Young people's perspectives on the risks and rewards of online self-expression. *New Media & Society*, (14): 634–651. doi:10.1177/1461444811422430

Davis, K., & Petrini, F. (2004). *Achieving usability and efficiency in large-scale parallel computing systems.* Academic Press.

Davis, L., & DeMenthon, D. (1995). Model-based object pose in 25 lines of code. *International Journal of Computer Vision, 15*, 123–141. doi:10.1007/BF01450852

Davis, R., Shrobe, H., & Szolovits, P. (1993). Whait is a knowledge representation? *AI Magazine, 14*, 17–33.

Dbworld. (n.d.). Retrieved from http://research.cs.wise.edu/dbworld

De Choudhury, M., et al. (2010). *Birds of a feather: Does user homophily impact information diffusion in social media?* Retrieved from http://cds.cern.ch/record/1270905?ln=it

de Houwer, A. (2007). Parental language input patterns and children's bilingual use. *Applied Psycholoinguistics,* (28), 411-424.

De Rosnay, J. (1996). *El hombre simbiótico: Miradas sobre el tercer milenio.* Madrid: Ediciones Cátedra.

De Rosnay, J. (2007). *Les scénarios du futur: Comprendre le monde qui vient.* Paris: Véronique Anger.

Dean, D., Berson, T., Franklin, M., Smetters, D., & Spreitzer, M. (2001). Cryptography as a network service' in NDSS '01. In *Proceedings of Eighth Annual Network and distributed System Security Symposium.* San Diego, CA: IEEE.

Debevec, P., & Malik, J. (1997). Recovering high dynamic range radiance maps from photographs. In *Proceedings of Siggraph.* New York: ACM Press. doi:10.1145/258734.258884

Deisinger, J., Blach, R., Wesche, G., Breining, R., & Simon, A. (2000). Towards immersive modeling – Challenges and recommendations: A workshop analyzing the needs of designers. In *Proceedings of Eurographics Workshop on Virtual Environments,* (pp. 145-156). IEEE.

Delacôte, G. (1996). *Savoir apprendre: Les nouvelles méthodes.* Paris: Odile Jacob.

Delval, J. (1998). *El desarrollo humano.* Buenos Aires: Siglo XXI.

Descartes, R. (2010). *The geometry of Rene Descartes.* Whitefish, WI: Kessinger Publishing.

Descheneaux, C., & Pigot, H. (2009). Interactive calendar to help maintain social interactions for elderly people and people with mild cognitive impairments. In *Ambient Assistive Health and Wellness Management in the Heart of the City.* Heidelberg, Germany: Springer. doi:10.1007/978-3-642-02868-7_15

Design Council. (2012). Retrieved from http://www.designcouncil.org.uk/

Dewey, J. (1989). *Cómo pensamos: Nueva exposición de la relación entre pensamiento reflexivo y proceso educativo.* Barcelona: Paidós.

Dictionary, E. L. E. (2012). Centro virtual Cervantes. Retrieved from http://cvc.cervantes.es/ensenanza/biblioteca_ele/diccio_ele/indice.htm

Distefano, S. et al. (2010). Cloud@Home: A new enhanced computing paradigm. In *Handbook of Cloud Computing* (pp. 75–594). Boston: Springer. doi:10.1007/978-1-4419-6524-0_25

Dorcasberro, A. (2011). El niño, la lengua y el bilingüismo: La reflexividad del niño bilingüe acerca de la noción de lengua y de bilingüismo, Multidisciplina. Acatlan Magazine, (8), 89-109.

Downing, A. (1983). Aspectos del bilingüismo. Transactions of Ier. Congreso Nacional de Lingüística Aplicada. AESLA, Murcia.

Dubberly, H. (2011). Extending negroponte's model of convergence. *Interaction, 18*(5), 74–79. doi:10.1145/2008176.2008193

Duda, R., & Hart, P. (1972). Use of the Hough transformation to detect lines and curves in pictures. *Communications of the ACM, 15*(1), 11–15. doi:10.1145/361237.361242

Durfee, E., Lesser, V., & Corkill, D. (1989). Trends in cooperative distributed problem solving. *IEEE Transactions on Knowledge and Data Engineering, 1*(1), 63–83. doi:10.1109/69.43404

Eberly, D. (2001). *3D game engine design.* San Francisco, CA: Morgan Kaufmann Publishers.

Eco, U. (1996). *A theory of semiotics.* Bloomington, IN: Indiana University Press.

Egbert, D., Bebis, G., McIntosh, M., LaTouttette, N., & Mitra, A. (2003). Computer vision research as a teaching tool in CS1. In *Proceedings of Frontiers in Education* (pp. 17–22). IEEE.

Ehri, L., & Ryan, E. (1980). Performance of bilinguals in a picture-word interference task. *Journal of Psycholinguistic Research,* (9): 285–302. doi:10.1007/BF01067243 PMID:7391998

Eiseman, L., & Recker, K. (1984). *Pantone: Storia del XX secolo a colori*. Milano, Italy: Rizzoli.

Eisenhart, C. (1959). *The assumptions underlying the analysis of variance*. New York: Wiley.

El Examen de la Selva. (2011). Retrieved from http://docenciauniversitaria.ucr.ac.cr/juego/juego.html

El-Hakim, S., Gonzo, L., Picard, M., Girardi, S., & Simoni, A. (2003). Visualisation of frescoed sur-face: Buonconsiglio castle, aquila tower, cycle of months. In *Proceedings of International Workshop on Visualisation and Animation of Reality-Based 3D Models*. IEEE.

Elias, N., & Lemish, D. (2009). Spinning the web of identity: The roles of the internet in the lives of immigrant adolescents. *New Media & Society*, (11): 533–551. doi:10.1177/1461444809102959

Ellis, C., Gibbs, S., & Rein, G. (1991). Groupware: Some issues and experiences. *Communications of the ACM*, *34*(1), 38–58. doi:10.1145/99977.99987

Ellison, N., Steinfield, C., & Lampe, C. (2007). The benefits of facebook friends: Social capital and college students' use of online social network sites. *Journal of Computer-Mediated Communication*, *12*, 1143–1168. doi:10.1111/j.1083-6101.2007.00367.x

Elqursh, A., & Egammal, A. (2011). Line-based relative pose estimation. In *Proceedings of IEEE Conference on Computer Vision and Pattern Recognition (CVPR 2011)*. Providence, RI: IEEE.

Emam, K, & Melo, W. (1999). The prediction of faulty classes using object-oriented design metrics. *Technical report: NRC 43609*.

Emerson, R. W. (n.d.). *Self reliance*. Retrieved from http://www.bartleby.com/5/104.html

Enos, T. (2010). *Encyclopedia of rhetoric and composition: Communication from ancient times to the information age*. New York: Routledge.

Erl, T. (2005). *Service-oriented architecture: concepts, technology, and design*. Upper Saddle River, NJ: Prentice Hall/Pearson PTR.

European Commission. (2012). *Study on the European cities and capitals of culture and the European cultural months*. Retrieved from http://ec.europa.eu/culture/key-documents/european-capitals-of-culture_en.htm

Evenson, S. (2006). Designing for service: A hands on introduction. In *Proceedings of CMU's Emergence Conference*. Pittsburgh, PA: Carnegie Mellon University.

Facebook Authentication. (2012). Retrieved from http://developers.facebook.com/docs/authentication/

Facebook Statistics. (2012). Retrieved from http://www.facebook.com/press/info.php?statistics

Fails, J. A., et al. (2005). Child's play: A comparison of desktop and physical interactive environments. In *Proceedings of the 2005 Conference on Interaction Design and Children (IDC '05)*. New York: ACM Press.

Fairchild, D. (2005). Color appearance models. In *Imaging Science and Technology* (Vol. 3). Hoboken, NJ: John Wiley and Sons.

Federal Interagency Forum on Aging-Related Statistics. Older Americans (2012). Key indicators of well-being. Washington, DC: Author.

Feitelson, D. (2012). *Workload*. Retrieved from http://www.cs.huji.ac.il/labs/parallel/workload/swf.html

Feng, Z., Been-Lirn Duh, H., & Billinghurst, M. (2008). Trends in augmented reality tracking, interaction and display: A review of ten years of ISMAR. In *Proceedings of the 7th IEEE/ACM International Symposium on Mixed and Augmented Reality*. Washington, DC: IEEE/ACM.

Fenton, N. (1997). *Software metrics: A rigorous approach*. Cambridge, UK: Chapman and Hall.

Fermoso-García, A., Sánchez-Alonso, S., & Sicilia, M. (2008). Una ontología en OWL para la representación semántica de objetos de aprendizaje. *V Simposio Pluridisciplinar sobre Diseño y Evaluación de Contenidos Educativos Reutilizables*. Salamanca. Retrieved from http://www.web.upsa.es/spdece08/contribuciones/176_Fermoso_ Sanchez_Sicilia_LOMOWL.pdf

Fernandes, T. (1996). *Global interface design: A guide to designing international user interfaces*. Boston: Academic Press.

Fiala, M. (2010). Designing highly reliable fiducial markers. *IEEE Transactions on Pattern Analysis and Machine Intelligence*, *22*, 1066–1077. PMID:20489233

Ficarra, F. (1993). Eurographics. *PressGraph-Imaging*, *3*, 22–30.

Fischer, K., & Müller, J. (2011). Inter-organizational Interoperability through integration of multiagent, web service, and semantic web technologies. In *Proceedings of Agent-Based Technologies and Application for Enterprise Interoperability* (pp. 55–75). Toronto, Canada: IEEE.

Fleischer, J., Tentyukov, M., & Tarasov, O. (2003). Diana and selected applications. *Nuclear Physics B - Proceedings Supplements*, *116*, 348–352. doi:10.1016/S0920-5632(03)80197-4

Fokkema, C., & Knipscheer, K. (2007). Escape loneliness by going digital: A Quantitative and qualitative evaluation of a dutch experiment using ECT to overcome loneliness among older adults. *Aging & Mental Health*, *11*(5), 8. doi:10.1080/13607860701366129 PMID:17882587

Foster, I. (2002). The grid: A new infrastructure for 21st century. *Science Physics Today*, *55*(2), 42–47. doi:10.1063/1.1461327

Foster, I. (2002). The physiology of the grid: An open grid services architecture for distributed systems integration. In *The physiology of the grid*. Academic Press.

Foster, I., Kesselman, C., & Tuecke, S. (2001). The anatomy of the grid –Enabling scalable virtual organizations. *The International Journal of Supercomputer Applications*, 15.

Franklin, S., & Graesser, A. (1996). Is it an agent, or just a program? A taxonomy for autonomous agents. In *Proceedings of Third International Workshop on Agent Theories, Architectures, and Languages, Budapest*. Heidelberg, Germany: Springer.

Fraser, C. (1996). Network design. In *Close Range Photogrammetry and Machine Vision*. Caithness: Whittles.

Freebase Data. (2012). Retrieved from http://wiki.freebase.com/wiki/Freebase_data/

Freebase Terms of Service. (2012). Retrieved from http://wiki.freebase.com/wiki/Terms_of_Service/

Freebase Wiki. (2012). Retrieved from http://wiki.freebase.com/wiki/

Frei, C., & Schar, C. (1998). A precipitation climatology of the Alps from high-resolution raingauge observations. *International Journal of Climatology*, *18*, 873–900. doi:10.1002/(SICI)1097-0088(19980630)18:8<873::AID-JOC255>3.0.CO;2-9

Freund, Y., & Schapire, R. (1999). A short introduction to boosting. *Journal of Japanese Society for Artificial Intelligence*, *14*(5), 771–780.

Fudickar, S., Faerber, S., & Schnor, B. (2011). KopAL appointment user-interface: An evaluation with elderly. In *Proceedings of 4th International Conference on Pervasive Technologies Related to Assistive Environments*. IEEE.

Fung, Y. (1983). *A history of Chinese philosophy* (Vol. 2). (D. Bodde, Trans.). Princeton, NJ: Princeton University Press.

Furtado, A. et al. (2011). Improving digital game development with software product lines. *IEEE Software*, *28*(5), 30–37. doi:10.1109/MS.2011.101

Furth, H. (1966). *Thinking without language: Psychological implications of deafness*. New York: The Free Press.

Furukawa, Y., Curless, B., Seitz, S., & Szeliski, R. (2010). Towards internet-scale multi-view stereo. In *Proceedings of IEEE Conference on Computer Vision and Pattern Recognition*. IEEE.

Gabrielsson, A. (2001). Emotions in strong experiences with music. In *Music and emotion: Theory and research*. Oxford, UK: Oxford University Press.

Gabrielsson, A., & Lindstrom, E. (2001). The influence of musical structure on emotional expression. In *Music and Emotion: Theory and Research*. Oxford, UK: Oxford University Press.

Gage, J. (2000). *Color and meaning: Art, science, and symbolism*. Berkeley, CA: University of California Press.

Galeyev, B., & Vanechkina, I. (2001). Was scriabin a synesthete? *Leonardo*, *34*(4), 357–362. doi:10.1162/00240940152549357

Gallagher, S. M. (2010). *The Flaneur was here: Mobile augmented reality and urban cultural heritage learning in lower Manhattan.* Edinburgh, UK: University of Edinburgh.

Gallego, F., Molina, A., Bravo, C., & Giraldo, W. (2010). A proposal for model-based design and development of group work tasks in a shared context. In *Proceedings of the 7th International Conference on Cooperative Design, Visualization, and Engineering.* Heidelberg, Germany: Springer.

Garcia, B. (2010). Creating an impact: Liverpool's experience as European capital of culture. *Culture (Canadian Ethnology Society).*

Garcia, B. (2010). A cultural mega event's impact on innovative capabilities in art production: The results of Stavanger being the European capital of culture in 2008. *Innovation (Abingdon), 2*(4), 353–371.

Garcia-Sanchez, F. et al. (2006). An ontology-based intelligent system for recruitment. *Expert Systems with Applications, 31*, 236–248. doi:10.1016/j.eswa.2005.09.023

Garden, M., & Dudek, G. (2005). Semantic feedback for hybrid recommendations in Recommendz. In *Proceedings of International Conference on e-Technology, e-Commerce and e-Service (EEE'05).* New York: IEEE Press.

Gardner, H. (1983). *Frames of mind: The theory of multiple intelligences.* New York: Basic Books.

Garduña. (2012). Retrieved from http://en.wikipedia.org/wiki/Gardu%C3%B1a

Garduña. (n.d.). *Wikipedia.* Retrieved from http://en.wikipedia.org/wiki/Garduña

Garey, M., & Johnson, D. (1990). *Computers and intractability: A guide to the theory of NP-completeness.* New York: W. H. Freeman.

Garfinkel, S., Margrave, D., Schiller, J., Nordlander, E., & Miller, R. (2005). How to make secure email easier to use. In *Proceedings of the SIGCHI Conference on Human Factors in Computing Systems,* (pp. 701 710). ACM.

Garon, N., Bryson, S., & Smith, I. (2008). Executive function in preschoolers: A review using an integrative framework. *Psychological Bulletin,* (134): 31–60. doi:10.1037/0033-2909.134.1.31 PMID:18193994

Garrant, T. (2006). *Writing for multimedia and the web: A practical guide to content development for interactive media.* Boston: Focal Press.

Garrido, J., Gea, M., & Rodríguez, M. (2005). Requirements enginnering in cooperative systems. In *Requirements Enginnering for Sociotechnical Systems.* Hershey, PA: Idea Group, Inc.

Gartell, L., Hoff, E., & Sklair, C. (1991). Robust image features: Concentric contrasting circles and their image extraction. In *Proceedings of Cooperative Intelligent Robotics in Space.* Washington, DC: IEEE.

Gartner Inc. (2011). *Gartner says sales of mobile devices grew 5.6 percent in third quarter of 2011, smartphone sales increased 42 percent.* Retrieved from http://www.gartner.com/it/page.jsp?id=1848514

Gaver, B., Dunne, T., & Pacenti, E. (1999). Design: Cultural probes. *Interaction, 6*(1), 21–29. doi:10.1145/291224.291235

Gellersen, H., Schmidt, A., & Beigl, M. (2002). Multi-sensor context-awareness in mobile devices and smart artifacts. In *Multi-Sensor Context-Awareness in Mobile Devices and Smart Artifacts* (pp. 341–351). Dordrecht, The Netherlands: Kluwer Academic Publishers.

Gentiletti, G., Taberning, C., & Acevedo, R. (2007). *Interfaces cerebro computadora: Definición, tipos y estado actual.* Paraná: Universidad Nacional de Entre Ríos.

Gentzsch, W., Grandinetti, L., & Joubert, G. (2010). *High speed and large scale scientific computing: Advances in parallel computing.* London: IOS Press.

Gere, C. (2008). *Digital culture.* London: Reaktion Books.

GfK Eurisko. (2012). Retrieved from http://www.gfk.com/gfk-eurisko/index.en.html

Giraldo, W., et al. (2008). A model based approach for GUI development in groupware systems. In *Proceedings of 14th International Workshop.* Omaha, NE: CRIWG.

Glass, G., Peckham, P., & Sanders, J. (1972). Consequences of failure to meet assumptions underlying fixed effects analyses of variance and covariance. *Review of Educational Research, 42,* 237–288. doi:10.3102/00346543042003237

Glassner, A. (2002). Digital weaving, part 1. *IEEE Computer Graphics and Applications, 22,* 108–118. doi:10.1109/MCG.2002.1046635

Glassner, A. (2003). Digital weaving, part 2. *IEEE Computer Graphics and Applications, 23,* 77–90. doi:10.1109/MCG.2003.1159616

Glassner, A. (2003). Digital weaving, part 3. *IEEE Computer Graphics and Applications, 23,* 80–89. doi:10.1109/MCG.2003.1185583

Glintenkam, P. (2011). *Industrial light & magic: The art of innovation.* San Francisco, CA: Abrams.

Global and China Digital Still Camera (DSC). (2011). *Industry report.* Retrieved from http://www.reportlinker.com

Goh, C., & Law, R. (2003). Incorporating the rough sets theory into travel demand analysis. *Tourism Management, 24,* 511–517. doi:10.1016/S0261-5177(03)00009-8

Goh, C., Law, R., & Mok, H. (2008). Analyzing and forecasting tourism demand: A rough sets approach. *Journal of Travel Research, 46,* 327–338. doi:10.1177/0047287506304047

Golbeck, J., & Hendler, J. (2006). Filmtrust: Movie recommendations using trust in web-based social networks. In *Proceedings of IEEE Consumer Communications and Networking,* (pp. 282-286). IEEE.

Golden, J. et al. (2009). Loneliness, social support networks, mood and cellbeing in community-dwelling elderly. *International Journal of Geriatric Psychiatry, 24*(7), 694–700. doi:10.1002/gps.2181 PMID:19274642

Gollmann, D. (1999). Insider fraud. In *Security Protocols (LNCS)* (Vol. 1550, pp. 213–219). Heidelberg, Germany: Springer. doi:10.1007/3-540-49135-X_29

Gollmann, D. (2008). *Computer security.* New York: McGraw Hill.

González, A. (2003). Una pedagogía de la diversidad y de la equidad: propuestas para una nueva relación profesor– alumno. *Ethos Educativo, 27,* 55–65.

González, M. et al. (2009). Development of CSCW interfaces from a user-centered viewpoint: Extending the TOUCHE process model through defeasible argumentation. In M. Kurosu (Ed.), *Human Centered Design.* Heidelberg, Germany: Springer. doi:10.1007/978-3-642-02806-9_109

Google. (2012). Retrieved from www.google.com/apps

Grabowicz, P. et al. (2012). Social features of online networks: The strength of intermediary ties in online social media. *PLoS ONE, 7.*

Granovetter, M. (1983). The strength of weak ties: A network theory revisited. *American Journal of Sociology, 1,* 201–233.

Granshaw, S. (1980). Bundle adjustment methods in engineering photogrammetry. *The Photogrammetric Record, 10*(56), 181–207. doi:10.1111/j.1477-9730.1980.tb00020.x

Grasic, B., & Podgorelec, V. (2008). Customer relationship management system architecture based on semantic web technologies. In *Proceedings of the 31st International Convention MIPRO 2008,* (pp. 204-209). MIPRO.

Greenbaum, J., & Kyng, M. (1991). *Design at work: Cooperative design of computer systems.* Hoboken, NJ: Lawrence Erlbaum Associates.

Greenberg, R. (1998). Image processing for teaching: Transforming a scientific research tool into an educational technology. *Journal of Computers in Mathematics and Science Teaching, 17*(2), 149–160.

Greenberg, R., Raphael, J., Keller, J., & Tobias, S. (1998). Teaching high school science using image processing: A case study of implementation of computer technology. *Journal of Research in Science Teaching*, *35*(3), 297–327. doi:10.1002/(SICI)1098-2736(199803)35:3<297::AID-TEA4>3.0.CO;2-M

Grishanov, S., Meshkov, V., & Omelchenko, A. (2009). A topological study of textile structures: Part I: An introduction to topological methods. *Textile Research Journal*, *79*, 702–713. doi:10.1177/0040517508095600

Grosof, B. (2003). Semantic web services: Obstacles and attractions, introduction to panel. In *Proceedings of 12th International Conference on the World Wide Web*. Retrieved from http://ebusiness.mit.edu/bgrosof/paps/talk-sws-panel-intro-www2003.pdf

Gross, R. (2005). Information revelation and privacy in online social networks. In *Proceedings of the 2005 ACM Workshop on Privacy in the Electronic Society*, (pp. 71-80). ACM.

Gruber, T. (1993). *Toward principles for the design of ontologies used for knowledge sharing*. Retrieved from http://citeseer.ist.psu.edu/ gruber93toward.html

Guidi, G. et al. (2009). A multi-resolution methodology for the 3D modeling of large and complex archeological areas. *International Journal of Architectural Computing*, *7*(1), 39–55. doi:10.1260/147807709788549439

Guins, R., & Zaragoza-Cruz, O. (2005). *Popular culture: A reader*. New York: Sage Publishing.

Gupta, S., & Vajic, M. (1999). The contextual and dialectical nature of experiences. In *New Service Development*. Thousand Oaks, CA: Sage.

Gyimothy, T., Ferenc, R., & Siket, I. (2005). Empirical validation of object-oriented metrics on open source software for fault prediction. *IEEE Transactions on Software Engineering*, *31*(10), 897–910. doi:10.1109/TSE.2005.112

Haag, A., Goronzy, S., Schaich, P., & Williams, J. (2004). *Emotion recognition using bio-sensors: First step towards an automatic system, affective dialogue systems*. Tutorial and Research Workshop, Kloster Irsee.

Haeberli, P. (1994). *A multifocus method for controlling depth of field*. GRAFICA Obscura.

Hakuta, K., & Bialystok, E. (1994). *In other words: The science and psychology of second-language acquisition*. New York: BasicBooks.

Hall, M. (2000). Correlation-based feature selection for discrete and numeric class machine learning. In *Proceedings of the 17th International Conference on Machine Learning*, (pp. 359-366). IEEE.

Han, A., Jeon, S., Bae, D., & Hong, J. (2008). Behavioural dependency measurement for change proneness prediction in UML 2.0 design models. In *Proceedings of Computer Software and Applications 32nd Annual IEEE International*. IEEE. doi:10.1109/COMPSAC.2008.80

Hannam, J. (2011). *The genesis of science: How the Christian middle ages launched the scientific revolution*. Washington, DC: Regney Publishing.

Hansen, T. (2004). *RFC 3888: Message tracking model and requirements*. Retrieved from http://tools.ietf.org/html/rfc3888

Hanush, T. (2010). *Texture mapping and true orthophoto generation of 3D objects*. (PhD thesis). Swiss Federal Institute of Technology (ETH), Zurich, Switzerland.

Hartl, A., Gruber, L., Arth, C., Hauswiesner, S., & Schmalstieg, D. (2011). Rapid reconstruction of small objects on mobile phones. In *Proceedings of IEEE Computer Society Conference*, (pp. 20-27). IEEE.

Hartley, R., & Zisserman, A. (2004). *Multiple view geometry in computer vision*. Cambridge, UK: Cambridge University Press. doi:10.1017/CBO9780511811685

Healey, J. (2000). *Wearable and automotive systems for affect recognition from physiology*. (PhD thesis). MIT, Cambridge, MA.

Hearle, J. (1978). An energy method for calculations in fabric mechanics, part L: Principles of the method. *Journal Textile Inst.*, *69*, 81–91. doi:10.1080/00405007808631425

Hegedüs, A. (1998). *Things spoken*. Interactive installation.

Henderson-Sellers, B. (1996). *Object oriented metrics: Measures of complexity*. Englewood Cliffs, NJ: Prentice Hall.

Henrio, L., Kammüller, F., & Lutz, B. (2011). Aspfun: A typed functional active object calculus. *Science of Computer Programming*.

Herlocker, J., Konstan, J., & Riedl, J. (2000). Explaining collaborative filtering recommendations. In *Proceedings of the 2000 ACM Conference on Computer Supported Cooperative Work*, (pp. 241-250). ACM.

Herrera, I., Clusella, M., Luna Pablo, P., Mitre, M., & Santillàn M. (2011). *Santiagueñidad siglo XXI retro-prospectivación sistémica de la cultura de Santiago del Estero*. Santiago del Estero: Editorial Lucrecia.

Herrera, S., Clusella, M., Mitre, M., Santillán, M., & García, C. (2011). An interactive information system for e–culture. In *Proceedings of First International Conference on ADNTIIC 2010* (LNCS), (Vol. 6616, pp. 30-43). Heidelberg, Germany: Springer.

Herrera, S., Zuain, S., Gallo, F., & Avila, H. (2012). Emotion and communicability in e-culture applications. In *Proceedings of Second International Workshop HCI-TOCH 2011* (LNCS), (Vol. 7546, pp. 15-24). Heidelberg, Germany: Springer.

Hevner, K. (1936). Experimental studies of the elements of expression in music. *The American Journal of Psychology*, *48*, 246–268. doi:10.2307/1415746

Hey, A., & Trefethen, A. (2003). The data deluge: An e-science perspective. In *Grid Computing - Making the Global Infrastructure a Reality* (pp. 809–824). New York: Wiley.

Higbee, J. (2003). *Curriculum transformation and disability: Implementing universal design in higher education*. Minneapolis, MN: University of Minnesota.

Hirose, M. (2012). *Future of weight loss diet goggles*. Retrieved from http://www.youtube.com/watch?v=spk-2EuZ3hk

Hirsch, T., et al. (2000). The ELDer project: Social, emotional, and environmental factors in the design of eldercare technologies. In *Proceedings of the 2000 Conference on Universal Usability*. New York: ACM Press.

Hisgen, D., & López De Luise, D. (2010). Dialog structure automatic modeling. In Proceedings of MICAI'10. Heidelberg, Germany: Springer-Verlag.

Hix, D., & Hartson, H. (1993). *Developing user interfaces: Ensuring usability through product & process*. Hoboken, NJ: John Wiley & Sons.

Hoffman, P. (1999). *Enhanced security services for S/MIME: Request for comments: 2634*. Retrieved from http://www.ietf.org/rfc/rfc2634.txt

Hofstein, A., & Lunetta, V. (2004). The laboratory in science education: Foundations for the twenty-first century. *Science Education*, *88*(1), 28–54. doi:10.1002/sce.10106

Holdcroft, D. (1991). *Saussure –Signs, system & arbitrariness*. Cambridge, UK: Cambridge University Press. doi:10.1017/CBO9780511624599

Holton, D. (2010). Constructivism + embodied cognition = enactivism: Theoretical and practical implications for conceptual change. In *Proceedings of AERA 2010 Conference*. AERA.

Holtzman, J. (2006). Food and memory. *Annual Review of Anthropology*, *35*, 361–378. doi:10.1146/annurev.anthro.35.081705.123220

Hoober, S., & Berkman, E. (2011). *Designing mobile interfaces*. Sebastopol, CA: O'Reilly.

Hoover, A. (2003). Computer vision in undergraduate education: modern embedded computing. *IEEE Transactions on Education*, *46*(2), 235–240. doi:10.1109/TE.2002.808264

Hopkins, W. (2000). A new view of statistics. In *Generalizing to a Population: Confidence Limits*. Academic Press.

Horn, R. (1990). Mapping hypertext. Waltham, MA: Lexington.

Hornecker, E., & Buur, J. (2006). Getting a grip on tangible interaction: A framework on physical space and social interaction. In *Proceedings of the SIGCHI Conference on Human Factors in Computing systems: CHI '06*. New York: ACM Press.

Hosmer, D., & Lemeshow, S. (1989). *Applied logistic regression*. New York: Wiley.

Huang, C. (2009). The study of the automated music composition for games. In *Proceedings of Conference on Digital Game-Based Learning*. Hong Kong: IEEE.

Huang, C., Lu, H., & Chou, Y. (2008). The study of the automated composition for the music in Taiwanese Hakka Mountain song style. In *Proceedings of the International Conference on Computer and Network Technologies in Education*. Hsinchu, Taiwan: IEEE.

Huang, C. (2011). A novel automated way to generate content-based background music using algorithmic composition. *International Journal of Sound. Music and Technology*, *1*(1), 11–16.

Huang, N., & Diao, S. (2008). Ontology-based enterprise knowledge integration. *Robotics and Computer-integrated Manufacturing*, *24*(4), 562–571. doi:10.1016/j.rcim.2007.07.007

Hull, R., & King, R. (1987). Semantic database modeling: survey, applications, and research issues. *ACM Computing Surveys*, *19*, 201–260. doi:10.1145/45072.45073

Hwang, G., Tsai, C., & Yang, S. (2008). Criteria, strategies and research issues of context-aware ubiquitous learning. *Journal of Educational Technology & Society*, *11*(2), 81–91.

Iglesias, R., Segura, N., & Iturburu, M. (2009). The elderly interacting with a digital agenda through an RFID pen and a touch screen. In *Proceedings of the 1st ACM SIGMM International Workshop on Media Studies and Implementations that Help Improving Access to Disabled Users*. New York: ACM Press.

Illich, I. (1973). *Tools for conviviality*. London: Calder & Boyars.

Imserso. (2012). Retrieved from http://www.imserso.es/InterPresent1/groups/imserso/documents/binario/08_18idi.pdf

Institute of Media Communication. (2012). *University of Maribor.* Retrieved from http://medijske.uni-mb.si/index.php?jezik=en

Isla-Montes, J. (2007). *Modelado conceptual de sistemas cooperativos en base a patrones en amenities. (Tesis Doctoral)*. Granada: Editorial Universidad de Granada.

Jboss. (2012). Retrieved from www.jboss.org

Jenkins, H. (2008). *Convergence culture: Where old and new media collide*. New York: NYU Press.

Jennings, S. (2003). *Artist's color manual: The complete guide to working with color*. New York: Chronicle Books.

Jiménez, R. (2011). *Metodología de generación automática de aplicaciones colaborativas. (Tesis de Máster)*. Madrid, Spain: Universidad Autónoma de Madrid.

Jnasen, W., & Grance, T. (2011). *NIST SP 800-144 guidelines on security and privacy in public cloud computing*. Washington, DC: NIST.

Joannis, H. (1965). *De l'étude de motivation à la création publicitaire et à la promotion des ventes*. Paris: Dunod.

Kahn, R., & Kellner, D. (2007). Technology, politics and the reconstruction of education. *Policy Futures in Education*, *5*(4), 439. doi:10.2304/pfie.2007.5.4.431

Kammüller, F., & Preibusch, S. (2007). An industrial application of symbolic model checking – The TWIN-elevator case study. *Computer Science Research and Development*, *22*(2), 95–108.

Karat, C., Brodie, C., & Karat, J. (2006). Usable privacy and security for personal information management. *Communications of the ACM*, *49*(1), 56–57. doi:10.1145/1107458.1107491

KC Class. (2012). Retrieved from www.kc-class.eu

Keefe, D., Feliz, D., Moscovich, T., Laidlaw, D., & LaViola, J. (2001). CavePainting: A fully immersive 3D artistic medium and interactive experience. In *Proceedings of the 2001 Symposium on Interactive 3D Graphics*. New York: ACM Press.

Keiichirou, U., Toshiyuki, A., & Hiroyuki, K. (2008). A FUSE-based tool for accessing meteorological data in remote servers, scientific and statistical database management. *Lecture Notes in Computer Science*, 592–597.

Kelley, T., & Littman, J. (2001). *The art of innovation: Lessons in creativity from ideo*. New York: Doubleday.

Kennedy, G. (1994). *A new history of classical rethoric*. Princeton, NJ: Princeton University Press.

Kerka, S. (1996). *Distance learning, the internet, and the world wide web*. ERIC Digest.

Kerlow, I. (2000). *The art of 3D computer animation and imaging*. New York: John Wiley.

Kerlow, I. (2009). *The art of 3D computer animation and effects*. New York: John Wiley.

Khomh, F., Penta, M., & Gueheneue, Y. (2009). An exploratory study of the impact of code smells on software change-proneness. In *Proceedings of 16th Working Conference on Reverse Engineering*. IEEE.

Kirkham, N., Cruess, L., & Diamond, A. (2003). Helping children apply their knowledge to their behavior on a dimension-switching task. *Developmental Science*, *6*(5), 449–476. doi:10.1111/1467-7687.00300

Kleinberg, J. (2007). Challenges in mining social network data: Processes, privacy, and paradoxes. In *Proceedings of Conference on Knowledge Discovery and Data Mining*. IEEE.

Koh, J., & Kim, Y. (2003). Sense of virtual community: a conceptual framework and empirical validation. *International Journal of Electronic Commerce*, *8*(2), 76.

Kolers, P. (1963). Interlingual word associations. *Journal of Verbal Learning and Verbal Behavior*, (2): 291–300. doi:10.1016/S0022-5371(63)80097-3

Kollmann, A., & Simeoni, E. (2012). *Exoesqueleto de miembro superior con detección de intención*. Córdoba: Universidad Nacional de Córdoba.

Kraus, K. (2007). *Photogrammetry: Geometry from images and laser scans*. Walter de Gruyter. doi:10.1515/9783110892871

Krueger, M., Gionfriddo, T., & Hinrichsen, K. (1985). Videoplace –An artificial reality. In *Human factors in computing systems*. New York: ACM Press.

Kulendran, N., & Witt, S. (2003). Leading indicator tourism forecasts. *Tourism Management*, *24*, 503–510. doi:10.1016/S0261-5177(03)00010-4

Kuo, F., Hwang, G., Chen, Y., & Wang, S. (2007). Standards and tools for context-aware ubiquitous learning. In *Proceedings of Seventh IEEE International Conference on Advanced Learning Technologies*. IEEE.

Lane, N. et al. (2010). A survey of mobile phone sensing. *IEEE Communications*, *48*, 140–150. doi:10.1109/MCOM.2010.5560598

Lan, L., & Zhong-Dan. (1999). Linear n-point camera pose determination. *IEEE Transactions on Pattern Analysis and Machine Intelligence*, *21*(8), 774–780. doi:10.1109/34.784291

Larson, J. (1992). *Interactive software*. Englewood Cliffs, NJ: Yourdon Press.

Laurel, B. (2004). Narrative construction as play. *Interaction*, *11*(5), 75–76. doi:10.1145/1015530.1015568

Law, R., & Au, R. (2000). Relationship modeling in tourism shopping: A decision rules induction approach. *Tourism Management*, *21*, 241–249. doi:10.1016/S0261-5177(99)00056-4

Law, R., Goh, C., & Pine, R. (2004). Modeling tourism demand: A decision rules based approach. *Journal of Travel & Tourism Marketing*, *16*, 61–69. doi:10.1300/J073v16n02_05

Le Louvre. (1995). [CD-ROM]. Paris: Montparnasse.

Le Louvre. (1997). *EMME – ACTA, 1*.

Le Moigne, J. (2012). Sur les sciences et patiques d´ingenierie des systems complex: Sciences appliqué es (ancillaies) ou sciences (fondamentales) de conception? Interlettre chemin faisant. *Réseau Intelligence de la complexité*, (62).

Le Phuoc, D., Parreira, J. X., Hausenblas, M., Han, Y., & Hauswirth, M. (2010). Live linked open sensor database. In *Proceedings of 6th International Conference on SemanticSystems*. I-SEMANTICS.

Lee, T., & Höllerer, T. (2009). Multithreaded hybrid feature tracking for markerless augmented reality. *IEEE Transactions on Visualization and Computer Graphics*, *15*(3), 355–368. doi:10.1109/TVCG.2008.190 PMID:19282544

Legrady, G. (2001). *Pockets full of memories*. Interactive installation.

Lensch, H., Heidrich, W., & Seidel, H. (2000). Automated texture registration and stitching for real world models. In *Proceedings of 8th Pacific Conference on Computer Graphics and Applications*, (pp. 317-326). IEEE.

Leopold, W. (2010). *Speech development of a bilingual child*. Evanston, IL: Northwestern University Press.

Lester, C. (2009). Training and educating undergraduate students in the discipline of HCI. In *Proceedings of Second International Conferences on Advances in Computer Human Interactions 2009*. New York: IEEE Press.

Lidwell, W., Holden, K., & Butler, J. (2003). *Universal principles of design: 100 ways to enhance usability, influence perception, increase appeal, make better design decisions, and teach through design*. Rockport.

Liebowitz, D., & Zisserman, A. (1998). Metric rectification for perspective images of planes. In *Proceedings of the IEEE Computer Society Conference on Computer Vision and Pattern Recognition*. IEEE.

Light, A. (2004). Audience design: Interacting with networked media. *Interaction*, *11*(2), 60–63. doi:10.1145/971258.971279

Li, H., Manjunath, B., & Mitra, S. (1995). Multisensor image fusion using the wavelet transform. *Graphical Models Image Processing*, *57*(3), 235–245. doi:10.1006/gmip.1995.1022

Lind, G., et al. (2007). *Spreading gossip in social networks*. Retrieved from http://www.comphys.ethz.ch/hans/p/449.pdf

Linden, R. (2012). *Algoritmos geneticos*. BRASPORT.

Linsday, P., & Norman, D. (1977). *Human information processing: An introduction to psychology*. New York: Academic.

Li, S., Kwok, J., & Wang, Y. (2002). Multifocus image fusion using artificial neural networks. *Pattern Recognition Letters*, *23*, 985–997. doi:10.1016/S0167-8655(02)00029-6

Liu, J., Wong, C., & Hui, K. (2003). An adaptive user interface based on personalized learning. *IEEE Intelligent Systems*, *18*, 52–57. doi:10.1109/MIS.2003.1193657

Livingstone, S., & Brown, A. (2005). Dynamic response: Real-time adaptation for music emotion. In *Proceedings of the Second Australasian Conference on Interactive Entertainment*. Sydney, Australia: Australasia.

Li, W., & Henry, S. (1993). Object oriented metrics that predict maintainability. *Journal of Systems and Software*, *23*, 111–122. doi:10.1016/0164-1212(93)90077-B

Li, W., Henry, S., Kafura, D., & Schulman, R. (1995). Measuring object –oriented design. *Journal of Object Oriented Programming*, *8*(4), 48–55.

Llamazares, A. (2011). *Del reloj a la flor de loto: Crisis contemporánea y cambio de paradigmas*. Buenos Aires: Editorial del Nuevo Extremo.

Lohr, S. (2012). The age of big data. *The New York Times*.

Lok, B. (2004). Toward the merging of real and virtual spaces. *Communications of the ACM*, *47*(8), 49–53. doi:10.1145/1012037.1012061

Lomuscio, A., Qu, H., & Raimondi, F. (2009). *MCMAS: A model checker for the verification of multi-agent systems. Computer Aided Verification, (LNCS)*. Heidelberg, Germany: Springer.

López De Luise, D. (2008). Mejoras en la usabilidad de la web a través de una estructura complementaria. (PhD Thesis). Universidad Nacional de La Plata, La Plata, Argentina.

López De Luise, D. (2010). *An autonomous robot prototype using Concept Learning model*. ICSCA.

López De Luise, D. (2010). *Automatic content extraction on the web with intelligent algorithms*. ICAART.

López De Luise, D. (2010). *Automatic extraction of content on the web with intelligent algorithm*. ICMLDA.

López De Luise, D. (2010). *Morphosyntactic linguistic wavelets for knowledge management. Tech Open book: Intelligent Systems*. Project WIH.

López De Luise, D., & Soffer, M. (2008). *Modelización automática de textos en castellano*. ANDESCON.

López De Luise, D., & Soffer, M. (2008). *Automatic text processing for spanish texts*. CERMA.

López, M. (2008). Efectos de la segunda lengua en la escritura de sujetos bilingües. Transactions of XXXVII Simposio Internacional de la Sociedad Española de Lingüística (SEL). Publication services of Universidad de Navarra.

Lorenz, M., & Kidd, J. (1994). *Object-oriented software metrics*. Englewood Cliffs, NJ: Prentice Hall Object-Oriented Series.

Lourakis, M. (2009). Plane metric rectification from a single view of multiple coplanar circles. In *Proceedings of 16th IEEE International Conference on Image Processing (ICIP)*. IEEE.

Lovaas, O. (1977). *The autistic child: Language development through behavior modification*. New York: John Wiley.

Lo, W., & Choobineh, J. (1999). Knowledge-based systems as database design tools: A comparative study. *Journal of Database Management*, *10*, 26–40. doi:10.4018/jdm.1999070103

Lowe, D. (1999). Object recognition from local scale-invariant features. In *Proceedings of International Conference on Computer Vision*. IEEE.

Lowe, D. (1991). Fitting parameterized three-dimensional models to images. *IEEE Transactions on Pattern Analysis and Machine Intelligence*, *13*(5), 441–450. doi:10.1109/34.134043

Lowe, D. (2004). Distinctive image features from scale-invariant keypoints. *International Journal of Computer Vision*, *10*(56), 181–207.

Lubar, K. (2004). Color music. *Leonardo Journal*, *37*(2), 127–132. doi:10.1162/0024094041139283

Lucaites, J. (1998). *Contemporary rhetorical theory: A reader*. New York: The Guilford Press.

Luhmann, T., & Tecklenburg, W. (2002). Bundle orientation and 3-D object reconstruction from multiple-station panoramic imagery. *International Archives of Photogrammetry, Remote Sensing & Spatial. Information Sciences*, *34*, 181–186.

Luke, S. (2009). *Essentials of metaheuristics*. Lulu.

Luna, P., Palavecino, M., & Leguizamón, H. (2011). Enmarque en inteligencia audiovisual por sistemas infonómicos e-culture. In *Proceedings of XV Jornadas Nacionales de Investigadores en Comunicación*. Cordoba: Universidad Nacional Río Cuarto.

Lu, R., & Zhang, S. (1998). *Automatic generation of computer animation*. Berlin: Springer-Verlag.

Lutz, A., & Crist, S. (2009). Why do bilingual boys get better grades in English-only America? The impacts of gender, language and family interaction on academic achievement of Latino/a children of immigrants. *Ethnic and Racial Studies*, *32*(2), 346–368. doi:10.1080/01419870801943647

Macnamara, J. (1966). *Bilingualism and primary education: A study of Irish experience*. Edinburgh, UK: Edinburgh University Press.

Magnani, M., & Rossi, L. (2011). The ML-model for multi-layer social networks. In *Proceedings of International Conference on Advances in Social Networks Analysis and Mining*, (pp. 5-12). IEEE.

Maiga, C., Qing, T., Tzu-Chien, L., & Lin, O. (2008). Multi-agent architecture-based location-aware service project for ubiquitous learning. In *Proceedings of 16th International Conference on Computers in Education*. IEEE.

Maldonado, T. (1992). *Lo real y lo virtual*. Barcelona: Gedisa.

Malhotra, R., & Jain, A. (2011). Software effort prediction using statistical and machine learning methods. *IJACSA*, *2*(1).

Malhotra, R., Kaur, A., & Singh, Y. (2010). Application of machine learning methods for software effort prediction. *ACM SIGSOFT Software Engineering Notes*, *35*.

Mann, C. (2012). A study of the iPhone app. at Kew Gardens: Improving the visitor experience. In *Proceedings of the Susie Fisher Group*. Retrieved from http://ewic.bcs.org/category/17061#1

Mannion, S. (2012). *Beyond cool: Making mobile augmented reality work for museum education*. Retrieved from http://www.museumsandtheweb.com/mw2012/programs/beyond_cool_making_mobile_augmented_reality_

Mann, S. (2002). Mediated reality with implementations for everyday life. *Presence (Cambridge, Mass.)*.

Manzini, E. (2005). *Design for sustainability – How to design sustainable solutions*. Milano, Itlay: INDACO, Politecnico di Milano.

Manzini, E., Walker, S., & Wylant, B. (2007). *Enabling solutions for sustainable living: A workshop*. Academic Press.

Maragliano, R. (2004). *Nuovo manuale di didattica multimediale*. Rome: Laterza.

Maribor. (2012). *Introduction to the ECOC project*. Retrieved from http://www.maribor2012.eu/en/ecoc/

Marina, J. (2003). *La creación económica*. Barcelona: Deusto Ediciones.

Marina, J. (2011). *Las culturas fracasadas: El talento y la estupidez de las sociedades*. Barcelona: Anagrama.

Martin, B., & Hanington, B. (2012). *Universal methods of design: 100 ways to research complex problems, develop innovative ideas, and design effective solutions*. Beverly Hills, CA: Rockport Publishers.

Marturana, H., & Varela, F. (1980). *Autopoiesis and cognition: The realization of the living*. Boston: Kluwer. doi:10.1007/978-94-009-8947-4

Marty, C., & Marty, R. (1992). 99 *réponses sur la sémiotique*. Montpellier, France: Réseau académique de Montpellier, CRDP/CDDP.

Mashup. (2012). *Wikipedia*. Retrieved from http://en.wikipedia.org/wiki/Mashup_(web_application_hybrid)

Massimi, M., Baecker, R., & Wu, M. (2007). Using participatory activities with seniors to critique, build, and evaluate mobile phones. In *Proceedings of the 9th International ACM SIGACCESS Conference on Computers and Accessibility*. New York: ACM Press.

Matsen, P. (1990). *Readings from classical rhetoric*. Carbondale, IL: Southern Illinois University Press.

Maxwell, B. (2001). A survey of computer vision education and text resources. *International Journal of Pattern Recognition and Artificial Intelligence*, *15*(5), 757–773. doi:10.1142/S0218001401001131

Mayo, M. (2007). Games for science and engineering education. *Communications of the ACM*, *50*(7), 30–35. doi:10.1145/1272516.1272536

McClellan, J., & Dorn, H. (2006). *Science and technology in world history: An introduction*. Baltimore, MD: The Johns Hopkins University Press.

McMillan, K. (1992). *Symbolic model checking –An approach to the state explosion problem*. (PhD Dissertation). School of Computer Science, Carnegie Mellon University, Pittsburgh, PA.

McMillan, K. (1995). *Symbolic model checking*. Boston: Kluwer Academic Publishers.

McQuade, S. et al. (2009). *Cyber bullying: Protecting kids and adults from online bullies*. Westport, CT: Praeger.

Mediación Virtual. (2011). Retrieved from http://mediacionvirtual.ucr.ac.cr

Meleis, H. (1996). Toward the information network. *IEEE Computer*, *29*(10), 69–78. doi:10.1109/2.539723

Menyuk, P. (1969). *Sentences children use*. Cambridge, MA: MIT Press.

Microsoft. (2012). Retrieved from www.microsoft.com/windowsazure

Mikhail, E., Bethel, J., & McGlone, J. (2001). *Introduction to modern photogrammetry*. Hoboken, NJ: John Wiley & Sons.

Mikkonen, T., & Taivalsaari, A. (2011). Reports of the web's death are greatly exaggerated. *IEEE Computer*, *44*(5), 30–36. doi:10.1109/MC.2011.127

Milgram, P., Takemura, H., Utsumi, A., & Kishino, F. (1994). Augmented reality: A class of displays on the reality-virtuality continuum. In *Proceedings of the SPIE Conference on Telemanipulator and Telepresence Technologies*, (pp. 282-292). SPIE.

Miller, H. (1957). *Big Sur and the oranges of Hieronymus Bosch*. New York: New Directions Publishing.

Millington, I., & Funge, J. (2009). *Artificial intelligence for games*. Burlington, VT: Morgan Kaufmann.

Minguez, J. (2012). *Tecnología de interfaz cerebro-computador. Università di Saragozza. NeuroSky®. (2009). Brain wave signal (EEG)*. NeuroSky.

Minnery, B., & Fine, M. (2009). Neuroscience and the future of human-computer interaction. *Interaction*, *14*(2), 70–75. doi:10.1145/1487632.1487649

Mintz, S., & Du-Bois, C. (2002). The anthropology of food and eating. *Annual Review of Anthropology*, *31*, 99–119. doi:10.1146/annurev.anthro.32.032702.131011

Mistry, P., Maes, P., & Chang, L. (2009). WUW - Wear ur world: A wearable gestural interface. In *Proceedings of the 27th International Conference on Human Factors in Computing Systems*. Boston: IEEE.

MIT App. Inventor. (2012). Retrieved from http://www.appinventor.mit.edu/

Mitrovic, A., Martin, B., & Suraweera, P. (2007). Intelligent tutors for all: The constraint based approach. *IEEE Intelligent Systems*, *22*(4), 38–45. doi:10.1109/MIS.2007.74

Moles, A. (1971). *Art et ordinateur*. Paris: Casterman.

Moles, A. (1973). *La communication*. Paris: Marabout.

Molina, A. I. et al. (2008). CIAM: A methodology for the development of groupware user interfaces. *Journal of Universal Computer Science*, *14*(9). PMID:20390048

Montilla, J. (2010). Relevance of statistical tests: T and F, to compare means for independent samples. Academia, 9(18), 4-14. Escuela Oficial de Idiomas de Málaga. (2012). Retrieved from http://www.eoimalaga.net/

Moore, G. (1965). Cramming more components onto integrated circuits. *Electronics Magazine*, *38*(8), 4.

Moreno, R., & Mayer, R. (2007). Interactive multimodal learning environments. *Educational Psychology Review*, 309–326. doi:10.1007/s10648-007-9047-2

Morgan, D. (1998). *The focus group guidebook*. Thousand Oaks, CA: Sage Publications.

Morin, E. (1998). *Introducción al pensamiento complejo*. Barcelona: Gedisa.

Moscariello, S., Kasturi, R., & Camps, O. (1997). Image processing and computer vision instruction using Java. In *Proceedings of IEEE Workshop on Undergraduate Education and Image Computation*. IEEE.

MSDN. (2012). *MSDN: Chapter 2 - Designing applications for Windows phone 7*. Retrieved from http://msdn.microsoft.com/en-us/library/gg490770.aspx

MSDN. (2012). *Networking and web services*. Retrieved from http://msdn.microsoft.com/en-us/library/cc645029(v=VS.95).aspx

MSDN. (2012). *Designing service contracts*. Retrieved from http://msdn.microsoft.com/en-us/library/ms733070.aspx

MSDN. (2012). *Stored procedure basics*. Retrieved from http://msdn.microsoft.com/en-us/library/ms191436.aspx

MSDN. (2012). *User-defined function basics*. Retrieved from http://msdn.microsoft.com/en-us/library/ms191007.aspx

Mulej, M. (2009). *A new 4th order cybernetics and the sustainable future*. University of Maribor.

Muller, N. (1996). Multimedia over the network. *Byte*, 73-83.

Munakata, T. (2008). *Fundamentals of the new artificial intelligence. Neural, Evolutionary, Fuzzy and More* (2nd ed.). London: Springer.

Murch, G. (1984). Physiological principles for the effective use of color. *IEEE Computer Graphics and Applications*, *4*, 49–54. doi:10.1109/MCG.1984.6429356

Murphy, M. (2008). *Beginner's guide to animation: Everything you need to know to get started*. New York: Watson-Guptill.

Museo del Louvre. (2012). [DVD]. Roma: Gruppo Editoriale L'Espresso.

Myoung-Woo, H., & Dae-Jea, C. (2008). Ontology context model for context-aware learning service in ubiquitous learning environments. *International Journal of Computers*, *2*(83), 193–200.

Nasoz, F., Alvarez, K., Lisetti, C., & Finkelstein, N. (2003). Emotion recognition from physiological signals for presence technologies. *International Journal of Cognition, Technology and Work*, *6*(10).

Nawyn, S. et al. (2012). Linguistic isolation, social capital, and immigrant belonging. *Journal of Contemporary Ethnography*, *41*(3), 255–282. doi:10.1177/0891241611433623

Negroponte, N. (1995). *Being digital*. New York: Knopf.

Nehmer, J., Lindenberger, & Steinhagen-Thiessen, E. (2010). Aging and technology—Friends, not foes. *The Journal of Gerontopsychology and Geriatric Psychiatry*, *23*(2), 55–57. doi:10.1024/1662-9647/a000016

Nelson, T. (1992). *Literary machines*. Sausalito: Mindful Press.

NeuroSky. (2012). Retrieved from http://www.NeuroSky.com/

Nex, F., & Rinaudo, F. (2011). LiDAR or photogrammetry? Integration is the answer. *Italian Journal of Remote Sensing*, *43*(2), 107–121. doi:10.5721/ItJRS20114328

Nielsen, J. (1990). *Multimedia and hypertext*. San Diego, CA: Academic Press.

Nielsen, J. (1992). The usability engineering life cycle. *IEEE Computer*, *25*(3), 12–22. doi:10.1109/2.121503

Nielsen, J. (1993). *Usability engineering*. London: Academic Press.

Nielsen, J. (1996). Usability metrics: Tracking interface improvements. *IEEE Software*, *6*(13), 12–13.

Nielsen, J., & Mack, R. (1994). *Usabilty inspection methods*. New York: John Wiley.

Niem, W., & Broszio, H. (1995). Mapping texture from multiple camera views onto 3D-object models for computer animation. In *Proceedings of International Workshop on Stereoscopic and Three Dimensional Imaging*, (pp. 99-105). IEEE.

Niu, Y., Li, X., Meng, X., Sun, J., & Dong, H. (2006). A constraint-based user interface design method for mobile computing devices. In *Proceedings of 1st International Sympsium on Pervasive Computing and Applications*. IEEE. doi:10.1109/SPCA.2006.297595

NOAA's National Weather Service. (2012). Retrieved from http://www.nws.noaa.gov/observations.php

Nöth, W. (1995). *Handbook of semiotics*. Bloomington, IN: Indiana University Press.

Obal, D., & Stojmenova, E. (2011). Experience to understand: Designing a methodology for understanding kitchen interactions. In *Proceedings of the 4th Semantic Ambient Media Experience (SAME) Workshop in Conjunction with the 5th International Convergence on Communities and Technologies*. Tampere, Finland: Tampere University of Technology.

Obrenović, Ž. (2012). Rethinking HCI education: teaching interactive computing concepts based on the experiential learning paradigm. *Interaction*, *19*(3), 66–70. doi:10.1145/2168931.2168945

Oomen, J. et al. (2011). Picture war monuments: Creating an open source location-based mobile platform. In J. Trant, & D. Bearman (Eds.), *Proceedings of Museums and the Web 2011*. Toronto, Canada: Archives & Museum Informatics.

Paradis, M. (1981). *Neurolinguistic organization of a bilingual's two languages*. Columbia, SC: Hornbeam.

Paredes-Velasco, M., et al. (2010). *CIAM extendido con generación automática de IU frente a metodologías no guiadas: Evaluación de una experiencia con CO-FARCIR*. Retrieved from http://eciencia.urjc.es/dspace/bitstream/10115/4206/1/interaccion2010b.pdf

Parodi, A., et al. (2011). *DRIHMS: The white paper*. Retrieved from http://www.drihms.eu/publications/material/White%20Papers%20Drihms_final.pdf

Patzakis, J. (2003). *New incident response best practices: Patch and proceed is no longer acceptable incident response procedure* (White Paper). Pasadena, CA: Guidance Software.

Paul, H. (2007). *Music for new media: Composing music for video games, web sites, presentations, and other interactive media*. Boston: Berklee Press.

Pawlak, Z. (1991). *Rough sets: Theoretical aspects of reasoning about data*. Boston: Kluwer.

Pawlak, Z. (2002). Rough set theory and its applications. *Journal of Telecommunications and Information Technology*, *3*, 7–10.

Penechicot, V. (2007). *Task-oriented and user-centred process model for developing interfaces for human-computer-human environments*. (PhD Dissertation). Universidad de Castilla-La Mancha.

Penechicot, V., et al. (2001). *Una aproximación al proceso de diseño e implementación de interfaces de usuario para aplicaciones groupware*. Actas del Noveno Congreso Internacional Interacción.

Péninou, G. (1972). *Intelligence de la publicité*. Paris: Robert Laffont.

Perny, P., & Zucker, J. (2001). Preference-based search and machine learning for collaborative filtering: The film-conseil movie recommender system. *Revue I*, *1*, 1–40.

Pesci, A., Bonali, E., Galli, C., & Boschi, E. (2011). Laser scanning and digital imaging for the investigation of an ancient building: Palazzo d'Accursio study case (Bologna, Italy). *Journal of Cultural Heritage*.

Peterson, C. (2000). Taking technology to the molecular level. *IEEE Computer*, *33*(1), 46–53. doi:10.1109/2.816268

Petrucci, C., Gennai, F., Shahin, A., & Vinciarelli, A. (2011). *La posta elettronica certificata*. Retrieved from http://datatracker.ietf.org/doc/rfc6109/

Piaget, J. (1999). *La psicologia de la inteligencia*. Barcelona: Critica.

Piaget, S. (1993). *Children's machine: Rethinking school in the age of computer*. New York: Basic Books.

Picard, R., Vyzas, E., & Healey, J. (2001). Toward machine emotional intelligence: Analysis of affective physiological state. *IEEE Transactions on Pattern Analysis and Machine Intelligence*, *23*(10), 1175–1191. doi:10.1109/34.954607

Pine, B. II, & Gilmore, J. (1998). Welcome to the experience economy. *Harvard Business Review*, 97–105. PMID:10181589

Pittarello, F., & Stecca, R. (2011). Mapping physical objects to digital functions: A tangible interface for querying and navigating a multimedia database. In *Proceedings of 22nd International Workshop on Database and Expert Systems Applications*. Washington, DC: IEEE.

Polack-Wahl, J. (2004). Teaching HCI in software engineering. In *Proceedings of 34th Annual Frontiers in Education 2004 FIE 2004*. New York: IEEE Press. doi:10.1109/FIE.2004.1408564

Popescu, D. (2011). Sink web pages in web application. In *Proceedings of IAPR TC3 Workshop on Partially Supervised Learning (PSL2011)* (LNCS), (vol. 7081, pp. 154-158). Berlin: Springer.

Popescu, D., & Danauta, C. (2011). Similarity measurement of web sites using sink web pages. In *Proceedings of 34th International Conference on Telecommunications and Signal Processing*. IEEE.

Popescu, D., & Szabo, Z. (2010). Sink web pages of web application. In *Proceedings of 5th International Conference on Virtual Learning*, Section Software Solutions, (pp. 375-380). IEEE.

Popescu, D., Danauta, C., & Szabo, Z. (2010). A method of measuring the complexity of a web application from the point of view of cloning. In *Proceedings of 5th International Conference on Virtual Learning, Section Models and Methodologies*, (pp. 186-181). IEEE.

Popescu, D. (2011). Measuring the quality of the navigation in web sites using the cloning relation. *Analele Universitatii Spiru Haret. Seria Matematica-Informatica*, *7*(1), 5–10.

Popescu, D., & Danauta, C. (2012). Verification of the web applications using sink web pages. *International Journal of Computer Science Research and Application*, *2*(1), 63–68.

Porter, M. (1980). An algorithm for suffix stripping. *Program*, *14*(3), 130–137. doi:10.1108/eb046814

Posnett, D., Bird, C., & Devanbu, P. (2009). An empirical study on the influence of pattern roles on change –proneness. *Empirical Software Engineering*, *16*, 396–423. doi:10.1007/s10664-010-9148-2

Potts, C. (1993). Software engineering research revisited. *IEEE Software*, *10*(5), 19–28. doi:10.1109/52.232392

Power, D. (2002). *A brief history of spreadsheets*. Retrieved from http://dssresources.com/history/sshistory.html, version 3.6

Pressman, R. (2005). *Software engineering –A practitioner's approach*. New York: McGraw-Hill.

Previtali, M., Barazzetti, L., Scaioni, M., & Yixiang, T. (2011). An automatic multi-image procedure for accurate 3D object reconstruction. In *Proceedings of 4th International Congress on Image and Signal Processing*. IEEE.

Pribram, K. (1971). *Languages of the brain: Experimental paradoxes and principles in neuropsychology*. Englewood Cliffs, NJ: Prentice-Hall.

Price, M., & Benton-Short, L. (2007). Immigrants and world cities: From the hyper-diverse to the bypassed. *GeoJournal*, *68*(2–3), 103–117. doi:10.1007/s10708-007-9076-x

Pridmore, T., & Hales, W. (1995). Understanding images: An approach to the university teaching of computer vision. *Engineering Science and Education Journal*, *4*(4), 161–166. doi:10.1049/esej:19950406

Probst, C., Hansen, R., & Nielson, F. (2006). Where can an insider attack? In *Proceedings of Formal Aspects of Security and Trust (LNCS)* (Vol. 4691). Heidelberg, Germany: Springer.

Prusinkiewicz, P. (2000). Simulation modeling of plants and plant ecosystems. *Communications of the ACM*, *43*(7), 84–93. doi:10.1145/341852.341867

Pyla, P., Perez-Quinones, M., Arthur, J., & Hartson, H. (2004). What we should teach, but don't: Proposal for cross pollinated HCI-SE curriculum. In *Proceedings of 34th Annual Frontiers in Education 2004 FIE 2004*. New York: IEEE Press. doi:10.1109/FIE.2004.1408713

Qian, C., Haiyuan, W., & Toshikazu, W. (2004). Camera calibration with two arbitrary coplanar circles. In *Proceedings of European Conference on Computer Vision (ECCV 2004)*. ECCV.

Qiu, G., Guan, J., Duan, J., & Chen, M. (2006). Tone mapping for HDR image using optimization – A new closed form solution. In *Proceedings of ICPR 2006*. ICPR.

Rajasekaran, P., Millcr, J., Verma, K., & Sheth, A. (2005). *Enhancing web services description and discovery to facilitate composition*. Heidelberg, Germany: Springer. doi:10.1007/978-3-540-30581-1_6

Ramos, E., & Nuñez, H. (2007). *Ontologías: Componentes, metodologías, lenguajes, herramientas y aplicaciones*. Universidad Central de Venezuela.

Recker, J. (2012). *Scientific research in information systems*. Berlin: Springer.

Reddy, R. (1996). The challenge of artificial intelligence. *IEEE Computer*, *29*(10), 86–98. doi:10.1109/2.539726

Reed, D., Gannon, D., & Larus, J. (2012). Imagining the future: Thoughts on computing. *IEEE Computer*, *45*(1), 25–30. doi:10.1109/MC.2011.327

Reeves, B., & Nass, C. (1996). *The media equation: How people treat computers, television, and new media like real people and places*. Cambridge, UK: Cambridge University Press.

Reisman, S. (1991). Developing multimedia applications. *IEEE Computer Graphics and Applications*, *11*(4), 52–57. doi:10.1109/38.126881

Reitmayr, G., Eade, E., & Drummond, T. (2005). Localisation and interaction for augmented maps. In *Proceedings of IEEE International Symposium on Mixed and Augmented Reality*. Vienna, Austria: IEEE.

Remondino, F., & Fraser, C. (2006). Digital camera calibration methods: Considerations and comparisons. *International Archives of Photogrammetry. Remote Sensing and Spatial Information Sciences*, *36*(5), 266–272.

Resmini, A., & Rosati, L. (2009). Information architecture for ubiquitous ecologies. In *Proceedings of ACM MEDES '09*. New York: ACM Press.

Resmini, A., & Rosati, L. (2012). *Pervasive information architecture: Designing cross-channel user experiences*. Burlington, MA: Morgan Kaufmann.

Richards, J. (1999). *Transnational criminal organizations, cybercrime, and money laundering: A Handbook for law enforcement officers, auditors, and financial investigators*. Boca Raton, FL: CRC Press.

Roble, D., & Zafar, N. (2009). Don't trust your eyes: Cutting-edge visual effects. *IEEE Computer*, *42*(7), 35–41. doi:10.1109/MC.2009.222

Rocchini, C., Cignoni, P., & Montani, C. (1999). Multiple texture stitching and blending on 3D objects. In *Proceedings of Eurographics Rendering Workshop*. IEEE.

Rodriguez,-María, L., Garrido, J., Hurtado, M., & Noguera, M. (2007). An approach to the model-based design of groupware multi-user interfaces. *Lectures Notes in Computer Science, 4715*, 157-164.

Rodriguez, G., Fulgenzi, E., & Milstein, C. (2011). *Día mundial de la esclerosis lateral amiotrófica (ELA)*. Academic Press.

Roman, D., Fisher, M., & Cubillo, J. (1998). Digital image processing-an object-oriented approach. *IEEE Transactions on Education, 41*(4), 331–333. doi:10.1109/13.728270

Roncella, R., Re, C., & Forlani, G. (2011). Performance evaluation of a structure and motion strategy in architecture and cultural heritage. *IAPRS&SIS, 38*(5/W16).

Roncoroni, F. (2007). *Misura delle deformazioni di una diga con laser scanner terrestre*. (PhD Thesis). Politecnico di Milano, Milan, Italy.

Rørmark, R. (2009). *Thanatos – A learning RTS game AI*. (Master Thesis). University of Oslo, Oslo, Norway.

ROSE2. (2012). Retrieved from http://idss.cs.put.poznan.pl/site/rose.html

Rosebush, J. (1992). *Historical computer animation*. New York: ACM.

Rosenbloom, A. (1999). Toward an image indistiguishable from reality. *Communications of the ACM, 42*(8), 28–30. doi:10.1145/310930.310960

Rosetta. (2012). Retrieved from http://www.lcb.uu.se/tools/rosetta/index.php

Rossi, E., Caretto, L., & Scheid, V. (2007). *Shen: Psycho-emotional aspects of Chinese medicine*. Church Livingstone.

Rothe, E., Pumariega, A., & Sabagh, D. (2011). Identity and acculturation in immigrant and second generation adolescents. *Adolescent Psychiatry*, (1): 72–81. doi:10.2174/2210676611101010072

Roth, W., & Lawless, D. (2001). Computer modeling and biological learning. *Journal of Educational Technology & Society, 4*(1), 13–25.

Rousseeuw, P., & Leroy, A. (1987). *Robust regression and outlier detection*. New York: John Wiley. doi:10.1002/0471725382

Rovai, A. (2002). Building sense of community at a distance. *International Review of Research in Open and Distance Learning, 3*(1).

Rumbaut, R. (2008). The coming of the second generation: Immigration and ethnic mobility in southern California. *The Annals of the American Academy of Political and Social Science*, (620): 196–236. doi:10.1177/0002716208322957

Russell, B. (1905). On denoting. Mind Magazine, 14.

Russell, S., & Norvig, P. (1996). *Inteligencia artificial, un enfoque moderno*. Prentice Hall. Satyanarayanan, M. (2001). Pervasive computing: Vision and challenges. *IEEE Personal Communications, 8*, 10–17.

Sánchez, R. (2011). *Brain computer interface (BCI) aplicado al control de dispositivos demóticos para incrementar la accesibilidad de las personas dependientes en el hogar digital y su entorno habitual Domo-BCI*. Valladolid: Universidad de Valladolid.

Sarkar, S., & Goldgof, D. (1998). Integrating image computation in undergraduate level data structures education. *International Journal of Pattern Recognition and Artificial Intelligence, 12*, 1071–1080. doi:10.1142/S0218001498000609

Saussure, F. (1983). *Course in general lingistics*. New York: McGraw-Hill.

Scharver, C. et al. (2004). Designing cranial implants in a haptic augmented reality environment. *Communications of the ACM, 47*(8), 32–39. doi:10.1145/1012037.1012059

Schilit, B., & Theimer, M. (1994). Disseminating active map information to mobile hosts. *IEEE Network, 8*, 22–32. doi:10.1109/65.313011

Schkolne, S., Pruett, M., & Schröder, P. (2001). Surface drawing: Creating organic 3D shapes with the hand and tangible tools. In *Proceedings of the SIGCHI Conference on Human Factors in Computing Systems, CHI '01*. New York: ACM Press.

Schubart, C. (1983). Ideen zu einer Aesthetik der Tonkunst (1806). In *A History of Key Characteristics in the 18th and Early 19th Centuries*. UMI Research Press.

Schuler, D., & Namioka, A. (1993). *Participatory design: Principles and practices*. Hillsdale, NJ: Lawrence Erlbaum Associates.

Schwartz, S., Montgomery, M., & Briones, E. (2006). The role of identity in acculturation among immigrant people: Theoretical propositions, empirical questions, and applied recommendations. *Human Development*, (49): 1–30. doi:10.1159/000090300

Schweppe, M. et al. (2011). Adapting a virtual world for theatrical performance. *IEEE Computer*, *44*(12), 33–38. doi:10.1109/MC.2011.354

Segeberg, R. (2009). *EaseMail: Easy accessible secure email.* (Master Thesis). Brigham Young University, Provo, UT. Revtrieved from http://contentdm.lib.byu.edu/ETD/image/etd2925.pdf

Seidl, T., & Kriegel, H. (1998). Optimal multi-step k-nearest neighbor search. *SIGMOD Record*, 154–165. doi:10.1145/276305.276319

Seminario Trans-Media. (2012). *Cómo crear historias por guionado*. Buenos Aires: Segura-Galtez.

Shalaik, B., & Winstanley, A. (2011). Delivering real-time bus tracking information on mobile devices. In *Future Information Technology* (pp. 139–147). Heidelberg, Germany: Springer. doi:10.1007/978-3-642-22309-9_17

Sharafat, A., & Tavildari, L. (2007). A probabilistic approach to predict changes in object-oriented software systems. In *Proceedings of 11th European Conference on Software Maintenance and Reengineering*. IEEE.

Shaw, E., Ruby, K., & Post, J. (1998). The insider threat to information systems. *Security Awareness Bulletin, 2*(98).

Shenzhen. (2012). *3rd eye electronics co., L. 170 degree view 12V mini security camera*. Retrieved from http://www.alibaba.com/product-gs/524362888/170_degree_view_12V_mini_security.html

Shevell, S. (2003). *The science of color*. Amsterdam: Elsevier.

Shneiderman, B. et al. (2010). *Designing the user interface: Strategies for effective human-computer interaction.* New York: Addison Wesley.

Si, N., Weng, J., & Tseng, S. (2006). Building a frame-based interaction and learning model for u-learning. In *Proceedings of 3rd International Conference on Ubiquitous Intelligence and Computing*. IEEE.

Siadaty, M., Torniai, C., Gašević, D., Jovanovic, J., & Marek-Hatala, M. (2008). m-LOCO: An ontology-based framework for context-aware mobile learning. In *Proceedings of Sixth International Workshop on Ontologies and Semantic Web for E-Learning in Conjunction with ITS*. ITS.

Sigmund, F. (2005). *The interpretation of dreams*. New York: Barnes & Noble.

Siltanen, S. (2012). Theory and applications of marker-based augmented reality. *VTT Science, 3*.

Siltanen, S., & Woodward, C. (2006). Augmented Interiors with digital camera images. In *Proceedings of Seventh Australasian User Interface Conference (AUIC2006)*. ACS.

Simon, G., Fitzgibbon, A., & Zisserman, A. (2000). Markerless tracking using planar structures in the scene. In *Proceedings of International Symposium on Augmented Reality*, (pp. 120-128). IEEE.

Singh, G. (2011). The IBM PC: The silicon story. *IEEE Computer*, *44*(8), 40–45. doi:10.1109/MC.2011.194

Singh, Y., Kaur, A., & Malhotra, R. (2010). Empirical validation of object-oriented metrics for predicting fault proneness models. *Software Quality Journal*, *18*(1), 3–35. doi:10.1007/s11219-009-9079-6

Site Web 5DT. (2012). Retrieved from http://www.5dt.com/

Site Web Xsens. (2012). Retrieved from http://www.xsens.com/

Skinner, B. (1957). *Verbal behavior: Acton.* Copley Publishing Group. doi:10.1037/11256-000

Slavin, K. (2010). *Mobile Monday presentation.* Retrieved from http://www.slideshare.net/momoams/kevin-slavin-reality-is-plenty-thanks

Smith. (2009). *WP5 art gallery and museum education: Evaluation report.* Retrieved from http://www.ericsson.com/ericsson/corpinfo/programs/using_wireless_technologies_for_context_sensitive_education_and_training/products/london_wp5_evaluation_report.pdf

Snyder, C. (2003). *Paper prototyping: The fast and easy way to design and refine user interfaces.* San Francisco, CA: Morgan Kaufmann.

Snyder, J. (1987). *Map projections – A working manual.* Washington, DC: United States Government Printing Office.

Song, H., & Li, G. (2008). Tourism demand modelling and forecasting - A review of recent research. *Tourism Management, 29*, 203–220. doi:10.1016/j.tourman.2007.07.016

Sosinsky, B. (2011). *Cloud computing bible.* Hoboken, NJ: Wiley.

Sousa-Santos, B. et al. (2009). Head-mounted display versus desktop for 3D navigation in virtual reality: A user study. *Multimedia Tools and Applications, 41*(1), 161–181. doi:10.1007/s11042-008-0223-2

Spence, C., Senkowski, D., & Röder, B. (2009). Crossmodal processing. *Experimental Brain Research, 198*(2-3), 107–111. doi:10.1007/s00221-009-1973-4 PMID:19690844

Spring, A., Peters, C., & Wetherelt, A. (2008). 3D laser scanning and its 2D partners. *Geoinformatics, 11*, 50–54.

Sreedhar, G., Chari, A., & Ramana, V. (2010). Measuring qualitz of web site navigation. *Journal of Theoretical and Applied Information Technology, 14*(2), 80–86.

Stefanowski, J. (1998). On rough set based approaches to induction of decision rules. In *Rough Sets in Knowledge Discovery* (pp. 500–529). Berlin: Physica Verlag.

Stone, M. (1974). Cross-validatory choice and assessment of statistical predictions. *Journal of the Royal Statistical Society. Series A (General), 36*, 111–147.

Strauss, A., & Werner, H. (1942). Disorders of conceptual thinking in the brain-injured child. *The Journal of Nervous and Mental Disease, 96*(2), 153–172. doi:10.1097/00005053-194208000-00004

Strecha, C., Pylvanainen, T., & Fua, P. (2010). Dynamic and scalable large scale image reconstruction. In *Proceedings of CVPR'10.* CVPR.

Styliaras, G., Koukopoulos, D., & Lazarinis, F. (2011). *Handbook of research on technologies and cultural heritage: Applications and environments.* Hershey, PA: IGI Global.

Sugimoto, A. (2000). A linear algorithm for computing the homography from conics in correspondence. *Journal of Mathematical Imaging and Vision, 13*, 115–130. doi:10.1023/A:1026571913893

Sutton, D. (2001). *Remembrance of repasts.* London: Berg Publishers.

Takeuchi, Y., & Perlin, K. (2012). ClayVision: The (elastic) image of the city. In *Proceedings of CHI 2012.* ACM.

Tannenbaum, K., et al. (2011). Experiencing the reading glove. In *Proceedings of the Fifth International Conference on Tangible, Embedded, and Embodied Interaction: TEI '11.* New York: ACM Press.

Tao, G., Xiao, Hang, W., Hung, K., & Da-Qing, Z. (2004). An ontology-based context model in intelligent environments. *Computer and Information Science,* (6), 270–275.

Tauber, A., & Rössler, T. (2010). A scalable interoperability architecture for certified mail systems. In *Proceedings of IEEE 12th Conference on Commerce and Enterprise Computing,* (pp. 9-16). IEEE.

Taurion, C. (2010). *Grid computing - Um novo paradigma computacional.* BRASPORT.

Teruel, M., Navarro, E., López Jaquero, V., Montero, F., & González, P. (2011). An empirical evaluation of requirement engineering techniques for collaborative systems. In *Proceedings of 15th International Conference on Evaluation and Assessment in Software Engineering.* Durham, UK: IEEE.

Terzopoulos, D. (1999). Artificial life for computer graphics. *Communications of the ACM, 42*(8), 32–43. doi:10.1145/310930.310966

Tharrats, J. (2009). *Segundo de chomon*. Paris: Harmattan.

Thayer, E. (1989). *The biopsychology of mood and arousal*. New York: Oxford University Press.

Thian, C. (2012). Augmented reality—What reality can we learn from it? In *Proceedings of Asian Civilisations Museum*. Toronto, Canada: Archives & Museum Informatics.

Thoreau, H. D. (1854). *Walden; or, life in the woods*. Boston: Academic Press.

Tinto, V. (1993). *Leaving college: Rethinking the causes and cures of student attrition*. Chicago: University of Chicago Press.

Tosone, A., & Frost, C. (2006). Leonardo da Vinci: The complete works. Cincinnati, OH: Davis & Charlie F+W Publications.

Trastour, D., Bartolini, C., & Preist, C. (2003). Semantic web support for the B2B e-commerce pre-contractual lifecycle. *Computer Networks, 42*, 661–673. doi:10.1016/S1389-1286(03)00229-9

Tsantalis, N., Chatzigeorgiou, A., & Stephanides, G. (2005). Predicting the probability of change in object oriented systems. *IEEE Transactions on Software Engineering, 31*(7), 601–614. doi:10.1109/TSE.2005.83

Turkle, S. (2007). *Evocative objects*. Cambridge, MA: MIT Press.

Ubisoft. (1994). *Peter and the numbers*. [CD-ROM]. Paris: Ubisoft.

Ubisoft. (1995). *Kiyeko and the lost night CD-ROM*. Paris: Ubisoft.

Universal-Design. (2012). Retrieved from http://www.universaldesign.com/

Valentine, D., & Zaslavsky, I. (2009). *CUAHSI universities allied for water research, CUAHSI WaterML 1.0 specification, WaterML 1.0 schema description*. San Diego, CA: University of California at San Diego.

van Sinderen, et al. (2006). Supporting context-aware mobile applications: An infrastructure approach. *IEEE Communications, 44*, 96-104.

Vann, B., & Hinton, B. (1994). Workplace social networks and their relationship to student retention in on-site GED programs. *Human Resource Development Quarterly, 5*(2), 141–151. doi:10.1002/hrdq.3920050205

Vargas-Llosa, M. (2012). *La civilización del espectáculo*. Buenos Aires: Alfaguara.

Vellis, G. (2009). Model-based development of synchronous collaborative user interfaces. In *Proceedings of EICS'09*. New York: ACM Press.

Veltman, K. (1988). *A databank on perspective: The concept of knowledge packages*. Retrieved from http://www.sumscorp.com/articles/art9.htm

Veltman, K. (2006). *Undestanding new media: Augmented knowledge and culture*. Alberta, Canada: University of Calgary Press.

Veltman, K. (2007). Opening keynote: The new book of nature. In *Proceedings of eARCOM 07. Sistemi informativi per l'Architettura Convegno Internazionale, Con il Patrocinio di UNESCO. Ministero dei Beni Culturali*. CIPA, Regione Marche.

Veron, E. (2004). *La semiosis social: Fragmentos de una teoría de la discursividad*. Barcelona, Spain: Gedisa.

Vicente, K. (2003). *The human factor*. New York: Routledge.

Vidéo du Projet CARE. (2012). Retrieved from http://www.youtube.com/watch?v=Bbl0CxFcUZw

Vidéo Peinture 3D en Cube Immersif. (2012). Retrieved from http://www.youtube.com/watch?v=5JR3A5KQ-dg

Viswanath, B., et al. (2009). On the evolution of user interaction in Facebook. In *Proceedings of the 2nd ACM Workshop on Online Social Networks*, (pp. 37-42). New York: ACM Press.

Vladoiu, M., & Constantinescu, Z. (2011). U-learning within a context-aware multiagent environment. *International Journal of Computer Networks & Communications, 3*(1). doi:10.5121/ijcnc.2011.3101

Vygotsky, L. (1986). *Thought and language*. Cambridge, MA: MIT Press.

W3. (2012). Retrieved from www.w3.org/TR/html5

Wagner, J., Kim, J., & André. (2005). From physiological signals to emotions: Implementing and comparing selected methods for feature extraction and classification. In *Proceedings of IEEE International Conference on Multimedia & Expo*. IEEE.

Wagner, D., Reitmayr, G., Mulloni, A., Drummond, T., & Schmalstieg, D. (2010). Real time detection and tracking for augmented reality on mobile phones. *IEEE Transactions on Visualization and Computer Graphics*, *16*(3), 355–368. doi:10.1109/TVCG.2009.99 PMID:20224132

Wang, P., Bishop, I. D., & Stock, C. (2009). Real-time data visualization in collaborative virtual environments for emergency response. In *Proceedings of the Surveying & Spatial Sciences Institute Biennial International Conference*. Adelaide, Australia: Surveying & Spatial Sciences Institute.

Waters, M., & Jiménes, T. (2005). Assessing immigrant assimilation: New empirical and theoretical challenges. *Annual Review of Sociology*, *31*, 105–125. doi:10.1146/annurev.soc.29.010202.100026

WeatherBug. (2012). Retrieved from http://en.wikipedia.org/wiki/ Surface_weather_observation

Weather Underground. (2012). Retrieved from http://www.wunderground.com/

Wehlage, G., Rutter, R., & Smith, G. (1989). *Reducing the risk: Schools as communities of support*. New York: The Falmer Press.

Weiser, M. (2003). The computer for the 21st century. *IEEE Pervasive Computing / IEEE Computer Society [and] IEEE Communications Society*, 19–25.

Weka. (2013). Retrieved from http://www.cs.waikato.ac.nz/ml/weka/

Wen-Chung, S., & Shian-Shyong, T. (2009). A knowledge-based approach to retrieving teaching materials for contextaware learning. *Journal of Educational Technology & Society*, *12*(1), 82–106.

Wesche, G., & Seidel, H. (2001). FreeDrawer: A free-form sketching system on the responsive workbench. In *Proceedings of the ACM Symposium on Virtual Reality Software and Technology* (VRST '01). New York: ACM Press.

Wharton, W., & Howorth, D. (1971). *Principles of television reception*. London: Pitman Publishing.

Williams, M., Cornford, D., Bastin, L., Jones, R., & Parker, C. (2011). Automatic processing, quality assurance and serving of real-time weather data. *Computers & Geosciences*, *37*, 353–362. doi:10.1016/j.cageo.2010.05.010

Willis, K. et al. (2010). Sharing knowledge about places as community building. In *Shared Encounters*. London: Springer. doi:10.1007/978-1-84882-727-1

Windows Azure. (2012). Retrieved from watoolkitwp7.codeplex.com

Winkler, V. (2011). *Securing the cloud: Cloud computer security techniques and tactics*. Amsterdam: Elsevier.

Winsor, P. (1992). *Automated music composition*. University of North Texas Press.

Wittgenstein, L. (1987). *Tractatus logico-philosophicus*. Madrid: Alianza.

Wittgenstein, L. (1988). *Investigaciones filosoficas*. México: Instituto de Investigaciones Filosóficas UNAM.

Wolfram, E. (1965). Chinese regional stereotypes. *Asian Survey*, *5*(12), 596–608. doi:10.2307/2642652

Wooldridge, M., & Jennings, N. (1995). Intelligent agents: Theory and practice. *The Knowledge Engineering Review*, *10*(2), 115–152. doi:10.1017/S0269888900008122

Wu, D., & Cheung, S. (2002). *The globalization of Chinese food*. Honolulu, HI: University of Hawaii Press.

Wu, X., Zhang, C., & Zhang, S. (2004). Efficient mining of both positive and negative association rules. *ACM Transactions on Information Systems*, *22*, 381–405. doi:10.1145/1010614.1010616

Xhafa, F., Kolodziej, J., & Bogdaski, M. (2010). A web interface for meta-heuristics based grid schedulers. In *Proceedings of the 2010 International Conference on P2P, Parallel, Grid, Cloud and Internet Computing*, (pp. 405-410). Washington, DC: IEEE Computer Society.

Xhafa, F., & Abraham, A. (2008). *Meta-heuristics for grid scheduling problems*. Academic Press.

Yahoo Weather. (2012). Retrieved from http://weather.yahoo.com/

Yang, J., Angus, F., Chen, R., Tseng, S., & Shen, Y. (2006). Context model and context acquisition for ubiquitous content access in u-learning environments. In *Proceedings of the IEEE International Conference on Sensor Networks, Ubiquitous, and Trustworthy Computing*, (Vol. 2, pp. 78–83). IEEE.

Zack, M., McKeen, J., & Singh, S. (2009). Knowledge management and organizational performance: An exploratory analysis. *Journal of Knowledge Management*, *13*(6), 392–409. doi:10.1108/13673270910997088

Zalta, E. et al. (2006). *Stanford encyclopedia of philosophy: Epistemic logic*. Stanford, CA: Stanford University.

Zanolla, S., et al. (2011). When sound teaches. In *Proceedings of 8th Sound and Music Computing Conference*, (pp. 64-69). IEEE.

Zanolla, S., et al. (2011). Teaching by means of a technologically augmented environment: The stanza logomotoria. In *Proceedings of of INTETAIN 2011 Conference*. Genova, Italy: INTETAIN.

Zhou, M., & Xiong, Y. (2005). The multifaceted American experiences of the children of Asian immigrants: Lessons for segemented assimilation. *Ethnic and Racial Studies*, *28*(6), 1119–1152. doi:10.1080/01419870500224455

Zhou, Y., Leung, H., & Xu, B. (2009). Examining the potentially confounding effect of class size on the associations between object oriented metrics and change proneness. *IEEE Transactions on Software Engineering*, *35*(5), 607–623. doi:10.1109/TSE.2009.32

About the Contributors

Francisco V. Cipolla-Ficarra is a professor, researcher, and writer. He has a PhD in Multimedia (1999), B.A. in Social Communication (1988), B.A. in Computer Programming and Systems Analysis (1983). He was the manager and coordinator of the first human-computer interaction lab in Barcelona, Spain (1997 – 1999) and is a professor in American and European universities, technical and professional colleges (1981 – present) in the subjects of computer science, computer graphics and animation, human-computer interaction, design, and multimedia. He is the CEO of Blue Herons Editions, coordinator of AInCI (International Association of Interactive Communication – www.ainci.com) and ALAIPO (Latin Association International of Human-Computer Interaction – www.alaipo.com). His main research interests are HCI, communicability, quality, auditory evaluation of interactive systems, computer graphics and animation, social communication, semiotics, e-learning, video games, and ecological and cultural heritage, and he is a member of ACM and IEEE.

* * *

Andrea Albarelli worked in the industry for 10 years before receiving his Ph.D. in Computer Science from the University Ca'Foscari Venice in 2010. He has taught Computer Architecture, Information Theory, and Computer Vision. He co-authored more than 40 peer-reviewer technical papers, mainly in the field of Computer Vision, with particular attention to issues of representation and processing of 3D data and the adoption of Game Theory in the context of Pattern Recognition problems, ranging from point-pattern matching to surface registration. He has participated in several research and technology transfer projects funded by both public and private partners. Since 2010, he is a founding member of an academic spin-off acting as a bridge between industry and Computer Vision research. In 2010, he was the winner of the tender "IMPRESA," sponsored by the Ministry of Economic Development, the prize "Working Capital" for innovative young researchers, and the "NVIDIA Best Paper Award." In 2011, he won the "Award for Research" established by Venice University to reward young researchers exhibiting the highest scientific impact.

Jaqueline Alma lives and works in Vancouver (BC), Canada. She was a professor at the HEC Montréal École de Gestion, British Columbia Institute of Technology, and Vancouver Film School. She received her B.A., Masters, and Doctorate degree in Computing and IT from the Simon Fraser University and University of British Columbia. The main areas of the interest are computer science, database, interactive design, video games, computer animation, cinema digital, and business technology management.

Dario Aloise holds a degree in mathematics from the Federal University of Rio Grande do Norte (1975), MSc in Engineering Systems and Computing at the Federal University of Paraíba / C. Grande (1983), and Ph.D. in Systems Engineering and Computer Science from COPPE / UFRJ (1992). Currently, he is a professor at the State University of Rio Grande do Norte (UERN), packed in the Department of Computer, and a retired teacher (category III Associate) from Federal University of Rio Grande do Norte (UFRN). He operates in the Graduate Program in Computer Science at UERN / UFERSA and Graduate Program in Production Engineering (PEP) / UFRN. He has experience in the areas of Computer and Systems and Production Engineering, with emphasis on analysis of Algorithms, Complexity of Computer and Operations Research. He operates on the following topics: heuristics and metaheuristics, graph theory, combinatorial optimization, operations research applications in the oil sector, and NP-hard problems in general.

Margarita Alvarez has a Masters in Software Engineering and is a Specialist in Teaching Higher Education. She is a computer engineer, informatics department professor, and researcher at the Institute for Research in Informatics and Information Systems in the Exact Science and Technology Faculty, National University of Santiago del Estero, Argentina, and the Chaco Austral National University Professor, Argentina.

Ankita Jain Bansal is a research scholar with Delhi Technological University (formerly Delhi College of Engineering), Delhi, India. She received her Masters degree in Computer Technology and Applications (CTA) from Delhi Technological University. Her research interests are software quality, software metrics, and statistical and machine learning models. She has published several papers in international journals and conferences.

Danny Barrantes is a graphic designer, digital media artist, and lecturer at University of Costa Rica. His contributions and current work deal with fields such as aesthetics, digital environments, and learning processes. He has been researching and teaching since 2007 and today he conducts his doctoral studies about Perspectives of University Teaching in Times of Digital Media at the University of Bremen, Germany. He has a Licentiate degree in Graphic Design from the University of Costa Rica and a Master of Science in Digital Media from the University of Bremen. His artistic work has been shown at different venues in Costa Rica and Germany, and his current projects are situated in computer art. Danny Barrantes lives in Bremen, Germany.

Luigi Barazzetti received a bachelors degree in Civil Engineering in July 2004 and a Masters degree in Civil Engineering (Surveying and Monitoring) in December 2006. In February 2011, he received a PhD cum laude in Geomatics and Infrastructures at Politecnico di Milano. Since 2008, he has been directly concerned with the work of the IC&T Laboratory at the Politecnico di Milano. His research activities are based around matching, registration, and adjustment of satellite, aerial and close-range images. He has had numerous papers published (more than 80) in both national and international levels. He has held, or taken an active part in, more than 30 conferences on the topic of photogrammetry and laser scanning.

Tatiana Bedrina is Ph.D. student of the University of Genoa, Course of Computer Science and Information Technologies for Systems Monitoring and Management of Environmental Risk. The Ph.D. research consists from Hydro-Meteorological component, led by the International Center on Environmental Monitoring Research Foundation, Savona, and ICT component, led by CNR IMATI, Genoa. The research topic is harvesting, aggregation, and integration of weather information from Web Weather Networks.

Diego Antonio Beltramone is an electrical / electronic engineer, founder and former president of the foundation Inclubyte, general coordinator of Ebano Team, and in charge of electronics and interface area. He is a professor of "Rehabilitation Engineering" at the Faculty of Exact, Physical, and Natural Sciences (FCEFyN) of the Universidad Nacional de Córdoba (UNC), director of the respective laboratory, director of the Bioengineering Department FCEFyN-UNC, former member of the Office of Educational Inclusion of People with Disabilities-UNC, provincial council accessibility member (Cordoba, Argentina) of the technical aids commission in particular. He is a board member at SABI (Argentina Bioengineering Society) and of the SABI rehabilitation engineering chapter. He is the current chapter president rehabilitation engineering at SABI, member of the Institute of Electrical And Electronics Engineers (IEEE), a speaker at national and international conferences, director of several integration projects (pregraduate theses) of Electrical Engineering and Biomedical Engineering, postgraduate theses and research, and extension projects on the subject of technology applied to improve the quality of life for people with disabilities.

Filippo Bergamasco received a MSc degree (with honors) in Computer Science from Ca'Foscari University of Venice, Venice, Italy, in 2011, and is currently a PhD candidate at the University of Venice. His research interests are in the area of computer vision, spreading from 3D reconstruction, game-theoretical approaches for matching and clustering, structure from motion, augmented reality, and photogrammetry. He has been involved in many commercial computer vision projects for industry and entertainment, including structured light scanner solutions, pipes measurement system for automotive, interactive vision-based museum exhibitions, and AR applications for embedded devices.

Lauren A. E. Bowers is currently Interaction Designer at General Electric's Global Research Center. She has also worked at Siemens in the product development area. She holds a BS in Industrial Design from the Georgia Institute of Technology. While at Georgia Tech, she has been associated with internationally recognized laboratories and grant projects including CATEA and the Mobility RERC. Her career demonstrates excellence in the design discipline showcasing numerous recognitions and awards, including her work featured in student exhibitions at the Museum of Design Atlanta.

Raffaella Brumana has a Masters degree in Architecture at the Politecnico di Milano (110/110 with honours), Ph.D. in Geodetic and Topographic Sciences. Since 2002, she is Associate Professor at Politecnico di Milano (ABC Department – Architecture, Built Environment, and Construction Engineering), member of the faculty council of the School of Doctoral Studies in "Geodesy and Geomatics" at Politecnico di Milano and of "Architecture, Built Environment, and Construction Engineering." She has authored more than 100 scientific publications in peer-reviewed scientific journals, and an IT book on *Technical Specification on Georeferencing Cultural Heritage for the Risk Map of RL*. Her main research activities are geoinformation data management and WEB GIS in the cultural and environmental heritage survey, SDI, geoclustering, 3DOpen source information platform (geo-portal), tools and Web services implementation INSPIRE compliant, UAV data collection and on site data integration of satellite data, 4D BIM modelling, Object Recognition-Reconstruction (ORR), laser scanner, and photogrammetry.

Marina Buzzi is a technologist at the "Istituto di Informatica e Telematica" of the Italian National Research Council in Pisa, where she leads the group "Web Accessibility and Usability." She has more than 15 years' experience in networking and Internet Services design. Her current research topics include accessibility, usability, eGovernment services, and RFID systems. She is a member of the technical group for Italian Certified Electronic Mail she follows the activities of the technical groups of W3C (World Wide Web Consortium) and IETF (Internet Engineering Task Force). She has been a professional member of ACM since 2004, and she follows the activities of the Accessibility and Computing group (SIGACCESS).

Sergio Canazza received a Degree in Electronic Engineering from the University of Padova, Italy. He is Director of Centro Multimediale e di E-Learning di Ateneo (CMELA) and Assistant Research Professor ("Professore Aggregato") at the Department of Information Engineering, University of Padova, where he is responsible for the course of "Fundamental of Informatics," and lecturer for the course of "Sound and Music Computing." His main research interests involve 1) expressive information processing, 2) auditory displays, and 3) audio documents preservation and restoration. He is author or co-author of more than 140 publications in international journals and refereed international conferences. He has been 1) general chairman and member of technical committees at several conferences and 2) project manager in European projects.

Jim Carré is a teacher in Curaçao Island. He received his Masters degree in Psychology in Florida (USA). He has a B.A. in Computer Science (Brazil). Furthermore, he studied in Faculty of Societal and Behavioral (Curaçao) and Informatics (Venezuela). His recent topics of interest are psychology, psychiatry, cognitive models, marketing and commerce, e-learning models, learning systems, artificial intelligence, systems security, and augmented reality.

Emilio Celotto is Researcher at CISET – Ca' Foscari University. He has a Msc Mathematics (1987, University of Padova), Executive Master in Tourism Economics and Management (1994, Ca' Foscari University). His expertise focuses on the development and application of mathematical and statistical models and techniques, forecasting methodologies, and database creation.

Miguel Cipolla-Ficarra is a professor and research. He has a PhD. in Power Electronic Engineering (1996), B.A. in Electronic Engineering – Telecommunications (1990), B.A. in Electric Engineering (1999). He is a professor in European universities, technical and professional colleges (1987 – present), a software project manager: design, development, and implementation of algorithms, a product manager, application engineer, and technical sales engineer in international projects, director of laboratory in F&F Multimedia Communic@tions Corp., technical manager in AInCI (International Association of Interactive Communication – www.ainci.com) and ALAIPO (Latin Association International of Human-Computer Interaction – www.alaipo.com). His main research interests are interfaces, usability engineering, interactive systems, telecommunication, computer sciences, networks, industrial design, programmation, automation, motors on microprocessor, ecological energy, e-commerce, and computer-aided education.

Alexis Clay is an assistant professor in Computer Science at ESTIA, the Institute of Advanced Industrial Technologies, Southwest of France. He received his PhD in Computer Science from the University of Bordeaux in 2009. His research focuses on movement interaction and multimodality. Alexis Clay uses augmented dance as an application case and has developed a long-term collaboration with performing arts.

Andrea Clematis is a Research Director at CNR – IMATI since 2001. He graduated in Mathematics at the University of Genoa in March 1982. His research interests include the following topics: parallel computing, parallel algorithms for spatial data processing, parallel algorithms for image processing, grid and cloud, software fault tolerance, compiler design, embedded systems. In his research activity, he applied parallel and distributed processing in different fields including: geographic information systems, bioinformatics, infomobility and transportation systems, research infrastructures for meteorological and hydrological science, cloud services for small medium enterprises, grid computing in industrial applications, cooperative environments and future internet.

Maria Mercedes Clusella is a computer engineer graduated from Catholic University of Santiago del Estero, Argentine. She is the author or co-author of academic papers, books, and studies related with systems sciences, director in charge of the International Institute Galileo Galieli, member of the International Federation on Systems Research, technical assistant of the Department of Science and Technology of the Catholic University, and in charge of graduates of the Faculty of Applied Mathematics at the same university.

Julien Conan is a Research Engineer at ESTIA, the Institute of Advanced Industrial Technologies, Southwest of France. He obtained his engineering degree at ESTIA in 2012. He now participates in the development of the PEPSS platform, which is focused on prototypes evaluation and usage testing.

Nadine Couture is Professor at ESTIA, the Institute of Advanced Industrial Technologies, Southwest of France, and member of the research center LaBRI (UMR CNRS 5800). She is in charge deputy of ESTIA-RECHERCHE. She received her PhD in Computer Science from University Bordeaux 1 in 1994. Her current research focuses on tangible and gestural interaction.

Maurizia D'Antoni is a specialist in Educational Psychology, with a Doctorate in Social Communication. She is a teacher and a researcher at University of Costa Rica and National University, in Costa Rica, departments of Psychology and College Education. Research interests in critical pedagogy, cultural-historical psychology and its present applications in Latin America; this has included community critical psychology. She is involved in university community work with communities living in social exclusion.

Francisco das Chagas graduated in Sciences with specialization in Mathematics from the State University of Rio Grande do Norte (1994), Masters in Computer and Systems from Federal University of Rio Grande do Norte (2002), and Ph.D. in Electrical and Computer Engineering from the Federal University of Rio Grande do Norte (2009). He is an Assistant Professor IV at the State University of Rio Grande do Norte and has experience in the area of computer science, with an emphasis on algorithm analysis and computational complexity, acting on the following topics: combinatorial optimization, geographic information systems, logistics in petroleum industry, reinforcement learning, and numerical computational methods. He currently collaborates with the Ministry of Education as an evaluator of undergraduate courses.

Maša Dobrina graduated from social sciences at the University of Ljubljana, Slovenia, and is a PhD student of media communication at the Faculty of Electrical Engineering and Computer Science, University of Maribor, Slovenia. Her main research interests include user oriented optimization, creative multimedia, innovative media technologie, and systems evaluation. She has been active in preparing various e-learning materials for students of technical sciences.

Elena Durán has a PhD in Computer Science, Masters in Software Engineering, is a Specialist in Teaching Higher Education, a Computer Engineer, and an Informatics School Director. She is an Informatics Department professor and researcher at the Institute for Research in Informatics and Information Systems in the Exact Science and Technology Faculty, National University of Santiago del Estero, Argentina. She is also a professor of Applied Mathematics Faculty in Catholic University of Santiago del Estero, Argentina.

Andrea Ellero is Associate professor at the Dept. of Management, Ca' Foscari University of Venice. He has a Msc. in Mathematics (University of Padova, 1987) and a Ph.D. in Mathematics for Economic Decisions (University of Trieste, 1993). His research interests include optimization, revenue management, multicriteria decision methods, agent-based modeling, tourism, and marketing.

Paola Ferretti is currently an associate professor at the Dept. of Economics, Ca' Foscari University of Venice. She has a Msc. in Mathematics (University of Padova, 1987) and a Ph.D. in Mathematics for Economic Decisions (University of Trieste, 1991). Her present research interests include analysis of risk and uncertainty attitude, optimal prevention and time dependence, rough sets theory, tourist behavior, and insurance.

Maria Valeria Ficarra is a lawyer, has a B.A. in Union Law (2003), Masters in International Legal Practice (2008). She is a member of AInCI (International Association of Interactive Communication) and ALAIPO (Latin Association International of Human-Computer Interaction), Barcelona, Spain. Her main research interests are labour and international law, legal and business strategies, problem-solving techniques, leadership, psychology, sociology, communication, cultural understanding, and cooperation.

Gian Luca Foresti is Full Professor of Computer Science at Univ. of Udine, where he is the Vice-Director of the Department of Mathematics and Computer Science and Director of the AVIRES Lab. His main interests involve (a) multi sensor data and information fusion, (b) computer vision and image processing, (c) artificial neural networks and pattern recognition. Prof. Foresti is author or co-author of more than 250 papers published in international journals and refereed international conferences, and he was responsible for several international research projects. He was general chairman and member of technical committees at several conferences where he has been co-organizer of several special sessions on data fusion, image processing, and pattern recognition, and serves as a reviewer for several international journals and for the European Union in different research programs.

Jodi Forlizzi holds interdisciplinary appointments as associate professor both in Carnegie Mellon's School of Design and its Human-Computer Interaction Institute. She is also the A. Nico Habermannn Chair in the School of Computer Science. She teaches graduate level courses in advanced interface and interaction design. She is interested in how people experience products, in order to develop a theory of experience as it relates to interaction design.

Francesco Gennai has worked for the Italian National Research Council (CNR) since 1984. He is responsible for network systems and Internet services at the CNR Institute of Information Science and Technologies "A. Faedo" (ISTI, http://www.isti.cnr.it/). An expert network designer, over the years he has been involved in national and international computer network projects including developing countries such as Albania, Algeria, Nigeria, and Egypt. He is a member of the Italian Research Network (GARR) security group and is a consultant for academic, public, and private institutions throughout Italy. He is a co-author of RFC 6109 and responsible for the interoperability tests of Italian Certified Electronic Mail systems.

Boštjan Grašič received his PhD degree in Computer Science from the University of Maribor, Slovenia. His main research interests include semantic technologies, service-oriented architecture, and knowledge management in organizations. He has authored some journal papers and presented his research results at several international conferences.

Georges Győsry is a mathematician from the University of Debrecen, Hungary. He went to France in 1982 and got a DEA of Computer Science from the University of Paris XI (Orsay) in Artificial Intelligence, then a DESS in Information Systems from the IAE (Sorbonne). In 2003, he wrote and defended a Doctoral thesis in Computer Vision. As he could not be given a research job at a (state) university over 50, he moved to England and has been doing research there since at University College London, Imperial College, University of Sheffield and Birkbeck College. His main areas of interest are artificial intelligence, knowledge representation problems, and computer vision.

Marjan Heričko received his PhD in Computer Science and Informatics from the University of Maribor in 1998. He is a full professor at the University of Maribor, as well as the deputy head of the Institute of Informatics and the head of the Laboratory of Information Systems. His main research interests include all aspects of information systems development with an emphasis on software and service engineering, agile methods, mobile solutions, advanced software architectures and patterns, knowledge management and semantic technologies, and distributed object models performance and efficiency. He has published more than 300 research papers and participated in numerous research and applied projects.

Débora Hisgen is an IS Engineer (Universidad de Palermo: Buenos Aires, Argentina). She is a NLP researcher since August 2009. Her courses and seminars include UP – CIS IEEE, Repositories Processing: Linguistics Strategies (August 2010) at the Universidad de Palermo (Buenos Aires), Argentina.

Daphne Ho completed her undergraduate studies in English and Creative Writing at the University of Southern California (USC). She was also an honors student at the Institute for Multimedia Literacy of the School of Cinematic Arts at USC, where she realized her honors thesis project, *Hungry*.

Chih-Fang Huang, Assistant Professor at the Department of Information Communications at Kainan University, was born in Taipei city. He is the chairman of Taiwan Computer Music Association. He acquired both a PhD in mechanical engineering and a Masters degree in music composition, respectively. His research includes automated music composition and the intermedia integration.

Kamarak Isarankura has a MSc and is a research assistant in the project "SINAIS" in Madeira Interactive Technologies Institute, Portugal.

Zuraini Ismail is an Associate Professor at UTM Advanced Informatics School, Universiti Teknologi Malaysia International Campus, Kuala Lumpur. Her research interest lies in information security management systems, information security policy, information security – awareness and ethics, information system management security, cyber security, knowledge management, e-Government and IT outsourcing.

Nuno Jardim holds a Ph.D in Software Engineering and is Associate Professor in Computer Science at the University of Madeira, Portugal. Nuno's research interests lie in the application of models to software and system design; currently, he's applying that to the domains of sustainability, service design, and tools.

Florian Kammueller is a professor in Middlesex University London and Privatdozent, Technische Universität Berlin. His research interests are security, verification, and formal methods. He is a member of the Foundations of Computing group at Middlesex University London.

Sašo Karakatič is a PhD student and is working as a teaching assistant and a researcher at the Faculty of Electrical Engineering and Computer Science at the University of Maribor. His main research interest is in the field of Machine Learning and Data Mining, with the focus on the evolutionary algorithms. He is the author of journal and conference papers where he combines his passion of machine learning with Semantic Web, social networks, and electronics. During his PhD studies, he has also been working with the Faculty of Mathematics and Informatics at the University of Plovdiv, where he collaborated as an exchange student.

Sanaz Kavianpour studied Masters of Computer Science (Information Security) at the Advanced Informatics School, Universiti Teknologi of Malaysia International Campus, Kuala Lumpur. She has published eight papers in local and international conferences, journals, and books in the fields of social networking, information diffusion, anonymity, and algorithms.

Mitja Krajnc received his B. Sc. Degree in Computer Science from University of Maribor, Slovenia, in 2010. He joined the Faculty of Electrical Engineering and Computer Science at University of Maribor as an assistant for field of informatics in 2010. His areas of interests include context-aware systems and mobile systems. As of late, he has also been interested in interoperability between mobile systems and mobile cloud computing. He has participated in several national research and applied projects. He was also on the organizing committees of several national conferences.

Andreas Kratky is assistant professor in the Interactive Media and Games Division and the Media Arts and Practice Division of the School for Cinematic Arts of the University of Southern California. Kratky's work is broadly interdisciplinary and comprises research in human-computer interaction and in digital humanities as well as numerous award-winning media art projects. His research is widely published and several of his art works are published as interactive media on DVD and in art catalogues.

Tiina Kymäläinen is research scientist at VTT Technical Research Centre of Finland in the Digital Service Design Department. At VTT, she has been studying and designing future user interfaces and intelligent environments for over a decade. Tiina Kymäläinen is also a Doctoral candidate and researcher at AALTO University: School of Arts, Design, and Architecture, in Department of Design. Her Doctoral thesis relates to the co-design process of do-it-yourself smart services.

Chih-Hsiang Liang, a graduate student at Department of Information Communication, Yuan Ze University, Taiwan, is focused on the research of synesthesia between color and music using algorithmic composition.

En-Ju Lin is currently a PhD student at Institute of Music Informatics, University of Music Karlsruhe, Germany. She graduated from Ethnomusicology Institute, National Taiwan Normal University, in 2005. Her research is focused on music and emotion.

Jean-Christophe Lombardo is a research engineer at INRIA in Nice, France, in Information Technology and Services. Previously, he worked in CSTB and in Sanofi. He received his PhD in Computer Sciences at Université Joseph Fourier, Grenoble, in 1996, on physically based computer animation, deformable object-oriented particle system. His current work focuses on Immersive Space conception and VR software development.

María Daniela López De Luise has a degree in System Analysis from the School of Engineering, Buenos Aires University (1989), Engineering degree in Computer Science (2004), degree in Expert System Engineering (1997), and did her Doctoral Studies in Informatics Engineering, degree granted by UNLP (National University at La Plata), July 8, 2008. She is the director of CI2S Lab (Computational Intelligence & Information Systems Lab), since June 2013, professor in Universidad Autónoma de Entre Ríos (Entre Ríos, Argentina) and in Universidad AUSTRAL (Buenos Aires, Argentina). She received the national Sadosky 2012 Award and is the president and founder of IEEE CIS Argentina chapter and is currently IEEE CIS Argentina chapter treasurer.

Ruchika Malhotra is an assistant professor at the Department of Software Engineering, Delhi Technological University (formerly as Delhi College of Engineering), Delhi, India. She was an assistant professor at the University School of Information Technology, Guru Gobind Singh Indraprastha University, Delhi, India. She received her Masters and Doctorate degree in Software Engineering from the University School of Information Technology, Guru Gobind Singh Indraprastha University, Delhi, India. She has received the IBM Best Faculty Award 2013. She is executive editor of *Software Engineering: An International Journal*. She is coauthor of a book *on Object Oriented Software Engineering* published by PHI Learning. Her research interests are in software testing, improving software quality, statistical and adaptive prediction models, software metrics and the definition, and validation of software metrics. She has published 70 research papers in international journals and conferences.

Carla Katarina de Monteiro Marques is an associate professor at the Computer Science Department of the University do Estado do Rio Grande do Norte, where she teaches Computer Networks. She has a Doctor degree in Computer Science, works in grid computing, performance analysis, reconfiguration system, agent-based simulation, and coloured petri nets.

Maria Gabriela Mitre has a bachelors in Information Systems from National University of Santiago del Estero, Argentine, is the author or co-author of academic scientific papers, chairman of the executive committee, board secretary, and CMU director of the Argentine Foundation for Talent and Ingenuity. She is a professor in educational organizations and in charge of the Technical Secretary of the Qualifications and standings board of local high schools levels and is co-responsible of the Design and Development of Software Engineering in the area of Medical Informatics belonging to the Italian Hospital of Buenos Aires.

Dragos Nicolae is absolvent of the "Radu Greceanu" National College, Slatina, Romania, and now he continues his studies at the Polytechnic University of Bucharest, Faculty of Automation and Computer Science. He had excellent results in a number of contests programming, using C/C++ and Java languages.

Eduardo Gabriel Nieva, a native of the City of Salta, Argentina, Eduardo moved to the City of Córdoba to start his studies as biomedical engineer. After five years, he submitted his final project in the National University of Cordoba. Along the way, he studied English, French, and Portuguese and became a Java developer that gave some skills to perform his project. He submitted to severals congresses and national and internationals papers about his project. The cources he has taken were on telemedicine, energy and sustainnability, biocompatibility, medical equipment installation. Currently, he is a teaching assistant chief of the Department of Medical Informatics in the Faculty of Medicine.

Valentina Nisi is currently Assistant Professor at the University of Madeira, Portugal, where she teaches and researches in the areas of Digital Interactive Design, Art, and Media. Her most recent efforts are investigating how to integrate sustainability concerns with digital art and interactive media.

Damijan Novak graduated in 2011 in Computer Science at the Faculty of the Electrical Engineering and Computer Science on the University of Maribor. He is currently a teaching assistant and postgraduate student at the faculty where he received his academic degree. His current research subjects are data mining algorithms and artificial intelligence in computer games. His special focus is in artificial intelligence research in real-time strategy games where players affect recognition, player strategy model, and player behaviour methods are being developed. Other fields of interest are mobile applications and cloud computing.

Damjan Obal is a PhD researcher and teaching assistant in the field of Informatics at the University of Maribor. His research focus is in the intersection of human-computer interaction, interaction design, participatory design, human-centered design, and ubiquitous computing. He is an interdisciplinary researcher collaborating with designers, developers, and key stakeholders in his research projects. Results of his work are scientific publications as well as product and service prototypes. During his research, he also developed a research/design methodology for involving users in the design process called EPUI and a methodology for gathering meaning called Play in/out. At the university, Damjan works with students and teaches User Experience Design, Ubiquitous Systems in the Media, and Technologies of Collaboration. Damjan is an active member of the user experience community both locally and internationally, and a member of organizations: IxDA (Slovenia Chapter president), SIGCHI, and UXPA (former UPA).

Daniela Oreni, architect, obtained a Ph.D. in Conservation of Architectural Heritage and a postgraduate degree at the School of Conservation of Architectural and Landscape Heritage of Politecnico di Milano (Polimi); she is an adjunct professor in the course of Innovative Surveying Technologies, Urban and Environmental Survey at Polimi, and of History of Restoration of the Architecture at University of Parma. Since 2003, she is collaborating with Sithec – Gicarus Laboratory at Polimi by actively participating in architectonic and archaeological international campaign of survey. Since 2008, she is temporary researcher at Best-ABC Department (Polimi). She is expert in heritage survey and documentation, archival research focused on the study of historical maps, cataloguing, and digital technologies applied to cultural heritage.

Antonio Parodi has a Ph.D. in Fluodynamics and Modelling of Environmental Systems from the University of Padova, is an expert in atmospheric modelling and statistical analysis of extreme events in the development of simplified models of dry and moist convection and the study of the main sources of uncertainty in the high resolution numerical modelling of deep moist convective processes. Since 2003, he has developed teaching activities at the University of Genova in the following fields: hydraulics, fluid mechanics, dynamics of atmosphere, and computational methods in environmental engineering.

María Florencia Peralta is a Biomedical Engineer from the National University of Cordoba, works as a pasant in the Material's Lab in the Faculty of Exacts, Physics, and Nature Sciencs, as a pasant on investigation in the Department of Physiology on the same faculty, and as pasant in the operating room in the Allende's clinic to RAOMED S.A. She has attended and submitted to different congresses and took courses in between Seminary in energy and sustainability (Nuclear Reactor RA0), health care in biomedical engineering, English course in University of Cambridge, French course, etc.

Claudio Petrucci was born in Rome and graduated in electronic Engineering at the University "La Sapienza." He worked for 20 years in a major Italian IT group, with special emphasis on the implementation and management of large software projects for both private clients and public administration. He then moved on to work for a public organization that is responsible for defining strategies, guidelines, and control over projects of the Italian public administration. In this context, he contributed to the design and implementation of Certified Electronic Mail (PEC) from the beginning. He is one of the authors of RFC 6109; he maintains relations with both the IETF and with ETSI.

João Phellipe graduated in Computer Science from the Federal Rural University of the Semi-Arid (2010). Has a Master's degree in computer systems by the Graduate Program in Computer Science – UERN / UFERSA. He has experience in the area of Computer Science, with an emphasis on evolutionary algorithms and intelligence, acting on the following subjects: artificial intelligence, distributed systems.

Vili Podgorelec is a professor of Computer Science at the University of Maribor, Slovenia. His main research interests include intelligent systems, semantic technologies, software engineering, medical informatics, and computational intelligence. He has been participating in many national and international research projects and is author of several journal papers on computational intelligence, software engineering, and medical informatics. Dr. Podgorelec has worked as a visiting professor or researcher at several universities around the world, including University of Osaka, Japan, University of Nantes, France, University of La Laguna, Spain, University of Madeira, Portugal, and University of Applied Sciences Seinäjoko, Finland. He received several international awards and grants for his research activities.

Doru Anastasiu Popescu is lecturer at the Faculty of Mathematics and Computer Science, University of Pitesti, Romania. He has a PhD in Computer Science, 2011, and has published over 35 papers in scientific journals and international conferences in the fields of algorithms, Web programming, Web applications, and programming languages. He has participated in numerous research programs working with various institutions and is a member of national and international committees in the field of computer science.

Mattia Previtali received a bachelors degree in September 2008 and a Masters degree in Civil Engineering in December 2010 at Politecnico di Milano, Italy. Currently, he is PhD student in Geomatics and Infrastructures at Politecnico di Milano since January 2011. Since 2011, his research activities take place at the IC&T Laboratory at the Politecnico di Milano. His research fields are image matching, close-range photogrammetry, and terrestrial laser scanning.

Christian W. Probst is an associate professor in the Language-Based Technology section of the Department of Applied Mathematics and Computer Science at the Technical University of Denmark. His main research interests are in the areas of programming languages, optimizing compilers, and abstract machines, as well as modelling and analysis of systems.

Alfonso Quarati has been a Researcher at the Institute for Applied Mathematics and Information Technology (IMATI) of the Italian National Research Council (CNR) in Genoa since 1997. His current research interests cover models and tools for grid and cloud computing, QoS assessment and performance evaluation methodologies, mashup and Web-services design, and collaborative working technologies.

Alejandra Quiroga received a bachelors degree in Computer Sciences in 1983 (Bahia Blanca, Argentina). She has an educational bachelor in 1988 (Buenos Aires, Argentina) and a Masters degree in Computer Engineering in 2004 (Sweden). She is currently a teaching assistant (La Pampa, Argentina) and PhD student. Her current research subjects are education, user-centered design, open source software, software engineering, and robotics. New fields of interest are computer graphics, computer-aided design, computer vision, Semantic Web, and cloud computing.

Franco Raimonid is a professor in Middlesex University, London. His research interests include model checking for extensions of temporal logics, formal methods, multi-agent systems, and modal logics.

Claudia B. Rebola is a tenure track Assistant Professor in the School Industrial Design at Georgia Institute of Technology. She is co-founder and organizer of the Design and Technologies for Healthy Aging (DATHA) coalition initiative and head of the D-Matters Studio Lab housed at the Center for Assistive Technologies and Environmental Access (CATEA). A native of Argentina, she holds a Ph.D. in Information Design and a Master of Industrial Design from North Carolina State, and a Bachelor of Industrial Design from Universidad Nacional de Cordoba. Her focus is on design for aging and her interests are in application areas tailored to healthy aging with an emphasis on humanizing technology, empowering users and celebrating the value of simplicity and tangibility in user-product interactions. Her focus is on communication/socialization technologies, intergenerational design and health with special emphasis on exercising universal design, tangible interfaces, and participatory design methods.

Antonio Rodà is assistant research professor in Department of Information Engineering from University of Padova, Italy.

Marco Scaioni graduated and achieved a PhD in Geodetic and Mapping Sciences at Politecnico di Milano, Italy. Currently, he is Professor at Tongji University, College of Surveying and Geo-Informatics, Shanghai (P.R. China), since December 2011. He is affiliated with the Center for Spatial Information Science and Sustainable Development Applications. His research fields are mainly close-range photogrammetry, terrestrial laser scanning, satellite and terrestrial remote sensing, geo-hazards, and polar research. His major current projects are focusing on spatial sensor networks for landslide monitoring/ forecasting and application of remote-sensing data to evaluate ice mass-balance in Antarctica. He is chairman of the ISPRS Working Group V/3 on Terrestrial Laser Scanning in 2012-2016. He is member of the Editorial board of *Applied Geomatics* (Springer) and the *European Journal of Remote Sensing*.

Bharanidharan Shanmugam is a Researcher/Senior Lecturer/Consultant at Advanced Informatics School, Department of Information Security, Universiti Teknologi Malaysia (UTM). He holds Doctorate degree in computer science specializing in network security from UTM. He has vast experience in mentoring and his research area is focusing more into ethical hacking and its countermeasures.

Sanni Siltanen (Lic.Sc.–Tech) is senior scientist in 3D tracking team at VTT Technical Research Centre of Finland. She has been working in augmented reality related projects over ten years. Besides algorithm and application development, she has been considering human factors in augmented reality. Sanni Siltanen has co-authored over 20 research papers in this field and contributed to various customer projects as well. Her special interests are augmented and diminished reality, computer vision, indoor visualizations, and user experience.

Carl Smith is Director of the Learning Technology Research Institute (LTRI), where he also works as a Senior Research Fellow in Creativity and Learning Technologies. His background is in Computer Science and Architecture.

Mabel del V. Sosa has a Master in Software Engineering (Polytechnic University of Madrid – National University of Santiago del Estero, Argentina) and a Computer in Engineering (Universidad Católica de Santiago del Estero, Argentina). She is an assistant professor at the National University of Santiago del Estero, Argentina. Her research collaborations include demarcation of educational computing discipline to guide the development, use, and evaluation of learning resources that support people and machines, accredited project research for CICyT – National University of Santiago del Estero (2012-2013). Currently, she guides the Research Project Códe 23/C110 acreditado por el Consejo de Instigaciones Científicas y Tecnológicas (CICyT) de la UNSE, 2012 – 2015. Her areas of interest include software engineering, computer-supported collaborative work, and knowledge and information management education.

Andrea Torsello received his PhD in Computer Science at the University of York, UK, and is currently working as Assistant Professor at University Ca Foscari Venice, Italy. His research interests are in the areas of computer vision and pattern recognition, in particular, the interplay between stochastic and structural approaches as well as game-theoretic models with applications in 3D reconstruction and recognition. Dr. Torsello has published more than 80 technical papers in refereed journals and conference proceedings and has been in the program committees of numerous international conferences and workshops. In 2011, he was recognized as "distinguished alumnus" by the University of York, UK. He held the position of chair and is currently the vice-chair of the Technical Committee 15 of the International Association for Pattern Recognition, a technical committee devoted to the promotion of research on graph-based representations in pattern recognition.

Silvina Únzaga has a Masters in Software Engineering and is a specialist in teaching higher education, computer engineer, Informatics Department professor, and researcher at the Institute for Research in Informatics and Information Systems in the Exact Science and Technology Faculty, National University of Santiago del Estero, Argentina.

Patricio A. Vela received the BS and PhD degrees from the California Institute of Technology in 1998 and 2003, respectively, where he worked on geometric nonlinear control. After working as a postdoctoral researcher in computer vision at the Georgia Institute of Technology, he joined the School of Electrical and Computer Engineering, Georgia Institute of Technology in 2005, where he is now an associate professor. His research interests lie in computer vision and geometric nonlinear control and are focused on improving the algorithms underlying decision and control processes in automated systems.

Domen Verber is assistant professor on the Faculty of the Electrical Engineering and Computer Science at the University of Maribor. His main research subjects are ubiquitous computing, high performance computing, and computer games. Other topics of interest include evolutionary algorithms, cloud computing, and integrated systems.

Alessandro Vinciarelli was born in Rome and graduated in Computer Science Engineering at "Roma Tor Vergata" University. He has more than 8 years of ICT experience and in particular in information security. He worked several years for an Italian Public Administration as a Certified Electronic Mail (PEC) expert, where he has contributed to the design, implementation, and audit of PEC itself. He is one of the authors of RFC 6109. Now, he works for the Italy's Greater Information and Communication Technology Provider and System Integration Company as a security specialist with a strong know how about privacy and identity and access management. He is certified ISO 27001 lead auditor, ITIL v3 foundation, ISIPM with OSSTTMM, CISSP, and privacy skills.

Serena Zanolla is a PhD in Multimedia Communication (University of Udine) and special educational needs teacher in a primary school. She has the task of supporting primary school children with learning difficulties and/or disabilities in order to optimize their potential within a variety of educational settings. Her main interest is to develop teaching methods that respond to individual differences and benefit all children. In particular, she is interested in implementing innovative instructional paths exploiting the motor component of learning. Since technology can help achieve this goal, the Stanza Logo-Motoria, an example of interactive and multimodal environments, may prove to be a good place to start.

Index

L

M

O

P

Q

R

S

T

U

V

W